Warman's
ANTIQUES
& COLLECTIBLES
PRICE GUIDE

31st Edition

The Essential Field Guide to the Antiques and Collectibles Marketplace

Edited by
ELLEN T. SCHROY

**Completely Illustrated
and Authenticated**

**krause
publications**

700 E. State Street • Iola, WI 54990-0001
Telephone: 715/445-2214

Volumes in the Encyclopedia of Antiques and Collectibles

Published by

 **krause publications**

700 E. State Street • Iola, WI 54990-0001
Telephone: 715/445-2214

Please call or write for our free catalog of publications.
Our toll-free number to place an order or obtain a free catalog is 800-258-0929 or
please use our regular business telephone 715-445-2214 for editorial comment and
further information.

ISBN 0-87069-750-1
ISSN 0196-2272

Library of Congress Catalog Card No. 82-643542

Manufactured in the United States of America

1 2 3 4 5 6 7 8 9 0   6 5 4 3 2 1 0 9 8 7

EDITORIAL STAFF

ELLEN T. SCHROY
Editor

HARRIET GOLDNER
Editorial Assistant

BOARD OF ADVISORS

INTRODUCTION

WARMAN'S—SERVING THE TRADE FOR 49 YEARS

In 1994 **Warman's Antiques and Their Prices** became **Warman's Antiques and Collectibles Price Guide** in order to address the growing popularity of post-war collectibles. The last edition saw an increase in the size of the book, both physically and editorially. This allowed us to increase the size of the type and photos, and to add several new features. Now this 31st edition has a new editor. As always, you can expect more, never less, from **Warman's**.

Individuals in the trade refer to this book simply as **Warman's**, a fitting tribute to E. G. Warman and the product that he created. **Warman's** has been around for 49 years, 25 years longer than its closest rival. We are proud as peacocks that **Warman's** continues to establish the standards for general antiques and collectibles price guides in 1997, just as it did in 1972 when its first rival appeared on the scene.

Warman's, the antiques and collectibles "bible," covers objects made between 1700 and the present. It always has. Because it reflects market trends, **Warman's** has added more and more 20th-century material to each edition. Remember, 1900 was 97 years ago—the distant past to the new generation of twentysomething and thirtysomething collectors.

The general "antiques" market consists of antiques (for the purposes of this book, objects made before 1945), collectibles (objects of the post-World War II era that enjoy an established secondary market), and desirables (contemporary objects that are collected, but speculative in price). Although **Warman's** contains information on all three market segments, its greatest emphasis is on antiques and collectibles.

Also note the book's subtitle: *The Essential Field Guide to the Antiques and Collectibles Marketplace*, first introduced in the 27th Edition. This indicates that **Warman's** is much more than a list of object descriptions and prices. It is a basic guide to the field as a whole, providing you with the key information you need every time you encounter a new object or collecting category.

"WARMAN'S IS THE KEY"

Warman's provides the keys needed by auctioneers, collectors, dealers, and others to understand and deal with the complexities of the antiques and collectibles market. A price list is only one of many keys needed today. *Warman's 31st Edition* contains many additional keys including: histories, marks, reference books, periodicals, collectors'

clubs, museums, reproductions, videotapes, and special auctions. Useful buying and collecting hints also are provided. Used properly, there are few doors these keys will not open.

Warman's is designed to be your first key to the exciting world of antiques and collectibles. As you use the keys this book provides to advance further in your specialized collecting areas, **Warman's** hopes you will remember with fondness where you received your start. When you encounter items outside your area of specialty, remember **Warman's** remains your key to unlocking the information you need, just as it has for over 49 years.

ORGANIZATION

Listings: Objects are listed alphabetically by category, beginning with ABC Plates and ending with Zsolnay Pottery. If you have trouble identifying the category to which your object belongs, use the extensive index in the back of the book. It will guide you to the proper category.

We have made the listings descriptive enough so that specific objects can be identified. We also emphasize items that are actively being sold in the marketplace. Some harder-to-find objects are included to demonstrate market spread—useful information worth considering when you have not traded actively in a category recently.

Each year as the market changes, we carefully review our categories—adding, dropping, and combining to provide the most comprehensive coverage possible. **Warman's** quick response to developing trends in the marketplace is one of the prime reasons for its continued leadership in the field.

Krause Publications also publishes other Warman's titles. Each utilizes the Warman's format and concentrates on a specific collecting group, e.g., American pottery and porcelain, Americana and collectibles, coins and currency, country, English and continental pottery and porcelain, glass, jewelry, and paper. Several are in second or subsequent editions. Their expanded coverage compliments the information found in **Warman's Antiques and Collectibles Price Guide**.

History: Collectors and dealers enhance their appreciation of objects by knowing something about their history. We present a capsule history for each category. In many cases this history contains collecting hints or other useful information.

References: Books are listed in most categories to help you learn more about the objects. Included are author, title, publisher, and date of publication or most recent edition. If a book has been published by a small firm or individual, we have indicated "published by author." Beginning with this edition, the address from which to obtain these hard-to-locate sources is included when possible.

Many of the books included in the lists are hard to find. The antiques and collectibles field is blessed with a dedicated core of book dealers who stock these specialized publications. You will find them at flea markets and antiques shows and through their advertisements in trade publications. Books go out of print quickly, yet many books printed over 25 years ago remain the standard work in a category. Used book dealers often can locate many of these valuable reference sources. Many dealers publish annual or semi-annual catalogs. Ask to be put on their mailing lists.

If you would like a complete address and phone number for any of the book publishers listed in the references, send a SASE to Ellen Schroy, 135 S Main St, Quakertown, PA 18951. Often the publisher can direct you to a source for their hard-to-find, currently in-print books, and may even provide copies directly.

Periodicals: The newsletter or bulletin of a collectors' club usually provides the concentrated focus sought by specialty collectors and dealers. However, there are publications, not associated with collectors' clubs, about which collectors and dealers should be aware. These are listed in their appropriate category introductions.

In addition, there are several general interest newspapers and magazines which deserve to be brought to our users' attention. These are:

Antique & The Arts Weekly, Bee Publishing Company, 5 Church Hill Road, Newton, CT 06470, http://www.the-bee.com/aweb

Antique Review, PO Box 538, Worthington, OH 43085

Antique Trader Weekly, PO Box 1050, Dubuque, IA 52001, http://www.csmonline.com

AntiqueWeek, PO Box 90, Knightstown, IN 46148, http://www.antiqueweek.com

Antiques (The Magazine Antiques), 551 Fifth Avenue, New York, NY 10017

Antiques & Collecting, 1006 South Michigan Avenue, Chicago, IL 60605

Collector News & Antique Reporter, Box 156, Grundy Center, IA 50638

Collectors Journal, PO Box 601, Vinton, IA 52349

Inside Collector, 225 Main Street, Suite 300, Northport, NY 11768

Maine Antique Digest, PO Box 358, Waldoboro, ME 04572, http://www.maineantiquedigest.com

MidAtlantic Monthly Antiques Magazine, PO Box 908, Henderson, NC 27536

New England Antiques Journal, 4 Church Street, Ware, MA 01082

New York-Pennsylvania Collector, Drawer C, Fishers, NY 14453

Today's Collector, 700 E State St, Iola, WI 54990, http://www.Krause

Yesteryear, PO Box 2, Princeton, WI 54968

Space does not permit listing all the national and regional publications in the antiques and collectibles field. The above is a sampling. See David J. Maloney, Jr.'s *Maloney's Antiques & Collectibles Resource Directory*, 3rd Edition (Antique Trader Books, 1995) or Harry L. Rinker's *Price Guide To Flea Market Treasures*, 4th Edition (Krause Publications, 1997) for a more detailed list.

Collectors' Clubs: Collectors' clubs add vitality to the antiques and collectibles field. Their publications and conventions produce knowledge which often cannot be found elsewhere. Many of these clubs are short-lived; others are so strong that they have regional and local chapters.

Museums: The best way to study a specific field is to see as many documented examples as possible. For this reason, we have listed museums where significant collections in that category are on display. Special attention must be directed to the complex of museums which make up the Smithsonian Institution in Washington, D.C.

Reproductions: Reproductions are a major concern to all collectors and dealers. Throughout this edition, boxes will alert you to known reproductions and keys to recognizing them. Most reproductions are unmarked; the newness of their appearance is often the best clue to uncovering them. Specific objects known to be reproduced are marked within the listings with an asterisk (*). The information is designed to serve as a reminder of past reproductions and to prevent you from mistaking them for period items.

We strongly recommend subscribing to *Antique & Collectors Reproduction News*, a monthly newsletter that reports on past and present reproductions, copycats, fantasies, and fakes. Send $32 for twelve issues to: ACRN, Box 71174, Des Moines, IA 50325. This newsletter completed its fourth year of publication at the end of 1995. Consider buying all available back issues. The information they contain will be of service long into the future.

Special Auctions: In the 31st Edition, we have chosen to feature boxes highlighting auction houses. To qualify for placement in one of these boxes, auction houses had to meet several specific requirements. First, they must actively hold auctions solely devoted to that specialty. Second, they must provide a catalog and prices realized. Often the catalogs become an important part of a collection, serving as reference and identification guides. Many of the auction companies featured hold more than one auction annually. Some work with a particular collectors' club or society. It is our hope that these boxes will give collectors and those searching for specific objects a better idea of who to contact. Warman's is designed to give collectors and dealers a lot of clues to find out what they have, what it is worth, and where to sell it!

These special auction boxes are not intended, however, to diminish the outstanding work done by the generalists,

REPRODUCTION ALERT

SIX BOOKS ABOUT REPRODUCTIONS AND FAKES YOU NEED TO READ

Knowledge is power. Although all but two of the following books are out of print, you are well advised to make the effort to locate and read a copy.

Hammond, Dorothy. *Confusing Collectibles: A Guide to the Identification of Contemporary Objects.* Wallace-Homestead, 1969, revised edition 1970.

Kaye, Myrna. *Fake, Fraud or Genuine? Identifying Authentic American Antique Furniture.* Little, Brown and Company, 1987, available in paperback from Bullfinch Press.

Lee, Ruth Webb. *Antique Fakes and Reproductions, Enlarged and Revised.* Published by author, first printed in 1938, eighth edition issued in 1966. Read fourth edition or higher.

Mills, John Fitz Maurice and John M. Mansfield. *The Genuine Article: The Making and Unmasking of Fakes and Forgeries.* London: British Broadcasting Company, 1979.

Peterson, Harold L. *How Do You Know It's Old? A Practical Handbook on the Detection of Fakes for the Antique Collector and Curator.* Charles Scribner's Sons, 1975.

Young, Norman S. *Fabulous but Fake: The Professional's Guide to Fake Antiques, Vol. I.* Published by author, 1993.

REPRODUCTION ALERT

UNDERSTANDING THE TERMINOLOGY

"Reproduction" has become a generic term used to describe a wide range of contemporary objects. Collectors use a much more sophisticated vocabulary.

A reproduction is an exact copy of a period piece. The only allowable exception is interior construction that is not visible. A reproduction made from a period model is a restrike.

A copycat is a stylistic reproduction, similar in shape, form, and/or decorative motif to a period piece but not an exact copy. Most so-called reproductions are actually copycats. Copycats can be very deceptive.

A fantasy piece is a shape or form that did not exist during the initial period of manufacture or licensing. A coffee table in the Chippendale design motif or a contemporary limited edition plate with a picture of Marilyn Monroe are examples. While fantasy pieces are collected, their value is usually less than period pieces.

A fake is an object deliberately made to deceive. It is often a one-of-a-kind item. Reproductions, copycats, and fantasy items usually are mass produced and far easier to spot as a result.

those auctioneers who handle all types of material. The fine auctions like Garth's, Skinner's, and Sloan's, provide us with excellent catalogs all through the year covering many aspects of the antiques and collectibles marketplace. Several categories had too many auction houses to list. For example, most auctioneers sell furniture, clocks, and fine arts. We just couldn't list them all. In addition to these auction house boxes, we hope you will consult the master list of auction houses included in this edition. We are sure that any one of them will be eager to assist in consigning or selling antiques and collectibles.

Index: A great deal of effort has been expended to make our index useful. Always begin by looking for the most specific reference. For example, if you have a piece of china, look first for the maker's name and second for the type. Remember, many objects can be classified in three or more categories. If at first you don't succeed, try, try again.

Photographs: You may encounter a piece you cannot identify well enough to use the index. Consult the photographs and marks. If you own several editions of **Warman's**, you have available a valuable photographic reference to the antiques and collectibles field. Learn to use it.

PRICE NOTES

In assigning prices we assume the object is in very good condition. If otherwise, we note this in our description. It would be ideal to suggest that mint, or unused, examples of all objects exist. The reality is that objects from the past were used, whether they be glass, china, dolls, or toys. Because of this, some normal wear must be expected. In fact, if an object such as a piece of furniture does not show wear, its origins may be more suspect than if it does show wear.

Whenever possible, we have tried to provide a broad listing of prices within a category so you have a "feel" for the market. We emphasize the middle range of prices within a category, while also listing some objects of high and low value to show market spread.

We do not use ranges because they tend to confuse rather than help the collector and dealer. How do you determine if your object is at the high or low end of the range? There is a high degree of flexibility in pricing in the antiques field. If you want to set ranges, add or subtract 10 percent from our prices.

One of the hardest variants with which to deal is the regional fluctuations of prices. Victorian furniture brings widely differing prices in New York, Chicago, New Orleans, or San Francisco. We have tried to strike a balance. Know your region and subject before investing heavily. If the best buys for cameo glass are in Montreal or Toronto, then be prepared to go there if you want to save money or add choice pieces to your collection. Research and patience are key factors to building a collection of merit.

Another factor that affects prices is a sale by a leading dealer or private collector. We temper both dealer and auction house figures.

PRICE RESEARCH

Everyone asks, "Where do you get your prices?"
They come from many sources.

First, we rely on auctions. Auction houses and auctioneers do not always command the highest prices. If they did, why would so many dealers buy from them? The key to understanding auction prices is to know when a price is high or low in the range. We think we do this and do it well. The 31st edition represents a concentrated effort to contact more regional auction houses, both large and small. The cooperation has been outstanding and has resulted in an ever growing pool of auction prices and trends to help us determine the most up-to-date auction prices.

Second, we work closely with dealers. We screen our contacts to make certain they have full knowledge of the market. Dealers make their living from selling antiques; they cannot afford to have a price guide which is not in touch with the market.

Over 50 antiques and collectibles magazines, newspapers, and journals come into our office regularly. They are excellent barometers of what is moving and what is not. We don't hesitate to call an advertiser and ask if his listed merchandise sold.

When the editorial staff is doing field work, we identify ourselves. Our conversations with dealers and collectors around the country have enhanced this book. Teams from **Warman's** are in the field at antiques shows, malls, flea markets, and auctions recording prices and taking photographs.

Collectors work closely with us. They are specialists whose devotion to research and accurate information is inspiring. Generally, they are not dealers. Whenever we have asked them for help, they have responded willingly and admirably.

BOARD OF ADVISORS

Our Board of Advisors is made up of specialists, both dealers and collectors, who feel a commitment to accurate information. You'll find their names listed in the front of the book. Several have authored a major reference work on their subject.

Our esteemed Board of Advisors has increased in number and scope. Participants have all provided detailed information regarding the history and reference section of their particular area of expertise as well as preparing price listings. Many furnished excellent photographs and even shared with us their thoughts on the state of the market.

We are delighted to include those who are valuable members, officers, and founders of collectors' clubs. They are authors of books and articles, and many frequently lecture to groups about their specialties. Most of our Advisors have been involved with antiques and collectibles for over 20 years. Several are retired, and the antiques and collectibles business is a hobby which encompasses most of their free time. Others are a bit younger and either work full time or part time in the antiques and collectibles profession. We asked them about their favorite publications, and most responded with the names of specialized trade papers. Many told us they are regular readers of *AntiqueWeek* and the *Maine Antique Digest*.

One thing they all have in common is their enthusiasm for the antiques and collectibles marketplace. They are eager to share their knowledge with collectors. Many have developed wonderful friendships through their efforts and are enriched by them. If you wish to buy or sell an object in the field of expertise of any of our Advisors, drop them a note along with an SASE. If time permits, they will respond.

BUYER'S GUIDE, NOT SELLER'S GUIDE

Warman's is designed to be a buyer's guide suggesting what you would have to pay to purchase an object on the open market from a dealer or collector. **It is not a seller's guide to prices**. People frequently make this mistake. In doing so, they deceive themselves. If you have an object listed in this book and wish to sell it to a dealer, you should expect to receive approximately 50 percent of the listed value. If the object will not resell quickly, expect to receive even less.

Private collectors may pay more, perhaps 70 to 80 percent of our listed price, if your object is something needed for their collection. If you have an extremely rare object or an object of exceptionally high value, these guidelines do not apply.

Examine your piece as objectively as possible. As an appraiser of antiques and collectibles, I spend a great deal of time telling people their "treasures" are not rare at all, but readily available in the marketplace.

In respect to buying and selling, a simple philosophy is that a good purchase occurs when the buyer and seller are happy with the price. Don't look back. Hindsight has little value in the antiques and collectibles field. Given time, things tend to balance out.

ACKNOWLEDGMENTS

Do wah diddy...time for a new tune on the jukebox, time to put on the oldies that we Baby Boomers enjoy! Time to shake up this old Warman's and bring it up to date, move some categories around as we keep the beat with our tapping toes! Let's add some new voices to the band and sing some new lyrics! That's just what we have done: taken the energy of a new editor and staff and added to that some new categories and advisors.

We have started with this bright red cover and, hopefully, we have continued the energy right through these pages with some new features. You will find up-to-date information and pricing for your favorite antiques and collectibles. Our standard clues to assist you in finding more information are supplemented by more fax numbers, e-mail addresses, and web sites. One new feature is the auction house boxes which you will find scattered throughout the book. These new auction boxes guide you to some of the best special auctions in America. Hopefully, this will take your collecting to another level of fun and enjoyment. Our Board of Advisors has grown to include more wonderful dealers and collectors who have shared their expertise with us. We have shortened the State of the Market to give us room to bring you more prices and other pertinent information.

It's never easy to fill someone else's shoes, especially when they are size 12's. However, sometimes you must just put on another pair of socks, or two, and see how they fit. Happily, there is plenty of room to grow, and as the new editor of **Warman's Antiques and Collectibles Price Guide**, that's just what I'm intending to do. By now you have probably noticed a new name on the cover, mine! If you are a dedicated Warman's reader, you may recognize my name. I have been training for this position for the past fourteen years. That training has been extensive and, at many times, fun, as I learned how to gather information, analyze data, prepare the manuscript, sort the photographs, and take into account all the little things that go into writing an antiques price guide. My teacher was, yes, the great Harry L. Rinker. Even though we do not see each other daily anymore, we are still friends and have many common interests. Harry met his goal with Warman's and then passed his baton to me. I sincerely hope that old E. G. Warman is smiling on me and will approve of the changes to his price guide.

The transition from employee to editor was a very smooth one thanks to the help of the following people: Christopher Kuppig, Edna Jones, Mary Green, Troy Vozzella, Tony Jacobson, and Nancy Ellis. Their support has been terrific. I am also blessed with the continued support of members of the former Warman's family with constant encouragement from Stanley and Katherine Greene and Jocelyn Mousely. Even though the former Rinker Enterprises, Inc., family has changed, we keep in touch and share in each others' joys and accomplishments. While rereading the acknowledgments from the 30th edition of **Warman's Antiques and Collectibles Price Guide**, the phrase "1995 is the year it happens at Rinker Enterprises" must be extended to include the early part of 1996 when major changes occurred. We endured blizzards, floods, and personal growth and tragedies until April, when several of us said good-bye and went off in different directions.

The support of Harriet Goldner, my trusted assistant and friend, has been invaluable. Her experience is similar to mine in that she has had excellent teachers and a background well versed in antiques and collectibles. She fluently speaks this strange language of compotes vs. comports, repoussé, églomisé, etc. Add to that excellent proofreading skills and attention to detail and I am sure you will see some real improvements in this edition of **Warman's Antiques and Collectibles Price Guide**.

While this has been a year of personal and professional growth for me, I hope you will agree that there have been major improvements to Warman's in our expanded Board of Advisors. I am the first one to admit that my education is on-going and I have looked to our Board of Advisors for their assistance in many fields, from architectural elements to mechanical banks to flow blue to jewelry to world's fair to yard-long prints. This group of willing volunteers has not only given assistance in their own particular areas, but often offered suggestions and advice in other areas. These kind folks will always have a special thanks from me.

As always, let me know how you like the improvements by writing to me at 135 S Main St, Quakertown, PA 18951-1119, or e-mail at schroy@voicenet.com. Now have a wonderful time reading the new and improved **Warman's**!

Ellen T. Schroy
November 1996

STATE OF THE MARKET

The state of the antiques and collectibles marketplace is great! Let's not get all bogged down with what is selling where, let's just enjoy the excitement of the crowd!

Throughout the past year and through travels around the country, visits to antique shops, shows, flea markets, and malls, one thing was constantly observed: people were buying—perhaps not the most expensive item in the booth, but objects and money were changing hands and keeping the economy moving. Some dealers may not have done as well as others, but is not that the way it goes with free enterprise?

The antiques and collectibles marketplace seemed to have more energy than in past years. Auctions were king. Major auctions of items belonging to many celebrities, and even sales of the possessions of ordinary folks, made head-lines. Nightly news accounts of the Jackie Onassis auction delighted us as prices went higher and higher. Few of us stopped to analyze why, but simply enjoyed the enthusi-asm for the last of the Camelot era. Other major auctions were held all through the year as fantastic collections and many households came to the market. Eager new owners found many items to include in their ever-growing collec-tions. The cycle of resale is working just fine. According to the *Wall Street Journal*, Christie's and Sotheby's have grossed over $1.5 billion in 1995 through their worldwide auctions. Yes, worldwide—the antiques and collectibles marketplace is very international. Live auctions are well-attended in person as well as being attended by telephone bidders—even those consulting over cellular phones.

Smaller auction houses are not being left in the dark; they are becoming more aggressive with their advertising, offering more catalogs, videos, and telephone-bidding opportunities. Gone are the days when you could only attend an auction within driving distance. Now with well-written and beautifully illustrated catalogs, someone in California can admire and eagerly bid on a Rookwood vase being sold in Ohio.

Many high-end antiques and even expensive col-lectibles changed hands. The infamous Honus Wagner (T206) baseball card was sold again for $28,600. This par-ticular baseball card, c1910, was actually cracked, and failed to meet the high of $115,000 that another card, in slightly better condition, reached in the late 1980s. The all-time auction high for a mint-condition Honus Wagner card, however, is the staggering $640,000 achieved by Christie's in September 1996 for the same card that had been sold by Sotheby's for $451,000 in 1991.

A small country auctioneer in Pennsylvania sold a paint-decorated schrank for a record price of $170,000, and other records were shattered throughout the year.

Does this mean that the market is spiraling out of reach for the average buyer? Probably not. Many fine examples sold below their auction-house estimates. There are still many wonderful antiques and collectibles to be found and sold to new owners.

Auctioneers learned the value of the press as well as the benefits of returning to the area of origin with some major auctions. News of major auctions and high prices travels fast, and even faster today with the Internet and major press coverage. Dealers are also becoming more techno-logically savvy and are learning to use high-tech tools to help boost sales. Unfortunately, those who do not are falling behind.

Those of us with a little less disposable income tend to seek out the middle-range antiques and collectibles. As always, antiques and collectibles are important to our dec-orating schemes, and we search and search for just the right piece, often at just the right price. Condition is criti-cal, and damaged pieces are left for another day.

New collectors are finding many enticements in the lower tier of the marketplace. Many delightful pieces can be found with some searching—perhaps the venue is somewhat less glamorous than a big auction house, but just as much fun can be had while searching through an open-air flea market or a garage sale. Everyone is looking for that special piece in these arenas, searching for that one-in-a-million object that can result in a jump to the top of the market in one leap. Realistically, these treasures are few and far between, but they do exist and can be discov-ered by those who enjoy the hunt as much as they enjoy the object.

Probably the biggest change in the antiques and col-lectibles marketplace is the use of the computer and World Wide Web. One only has to explore the thousands of sites to find his heart's desire, strike a deal with e-mail or fax, and then it's back to surfing the Net for more fun. In a field where a price guide or new reference book can immedi-ately affect prices, the computer will someday also do that. To date, most dealers are sticking to the published refer-ence books when pricing and then listing their objects for sale in cyberspace. If the piece fails to find a buyer in cyberspace, the dealer still has the option of including the same piece in his shop or show, finding a buyer the old-fashioned way.

Internet Web sites, or addresses, exist for every part of the antiques and collectibles marketplace. You can go online and chat for hours about your favorite pieces, ask questions of experts, and research all kinds of information. Everyone—from auctioneers, dealers, and collectors' clubs—has home pages. Some of these home pages are more exciting than others, and, like everything else, you must decide which ones suit your particular needs. The Alderfer Auction Company has an interesting site at http://www.alderfercompany.com. They list information pertaining to their upcoming auctions and other information of interest to collectors and dealers. One sparkling site is http://www.facets.net/facets. Here dealers list their wares for sale and include beautiful color images, as well as detailed descriptions, references to standard books, etc. A collectors' club with a very informative home page is the Tea Leaf Collectors Club at http://ourworld.compuserve.com/homepage/da. Many of these Web sites are growing, changing, and constantly improving. They are fun to visit and probably will become an integral part of the antiques and collectibles marketplace as we look forward to the next century!

Part of what makes the Internet work so well is the fast exchange of ideas between participants. Antiques collectors and dealers have always been a very loosely bonded network. Ideas and information are passed on every day. *Warman's* is very fortunate to have the guidance of a Board of Advisors who eagerly share their information. They not only submit information on the background of their categories and offer current price listings, but they also offer their opinions on the state of the market. Mechanical Banks Advisor James Maxwell was realistic when he reported that some bank prices have declined in the last year. He feels that the quantity and quality of the banks coming into the marketplace over the last few months have given buyers many opportunities to add to their collections while paying less. He predicts that "this downward swing will continue for many years to come and that banks will arrive at a more realistic and much lower price level." He further predicts that "the lower prices will stabilize in seven years and not begin to climb again for at least 10–12 years." This conclusion is based on James's careful study of the fluctuations in the mechanical bank market over the last 60 years. He is optimistic that this downward swing will bring new collectors into the market and help keep the allure of these appealingly designed banks alive for us all.

In response to advisor Michael Ivankovich's suggestion, we've added a new section—Wallace Nutting-Like Photographers. Michael reported growing collector interest in these types of photographers and is planning several specialized auctions relating to them as well as to Wallace Nutting items. Evalene Pulati, our Valentines advisor, states that "there has been an abundance of valentines on the market these past few years due to all the publicity we get each year, plus several old-time collectors have passed on and their holdings have gone to the big auction houses, both here and in England, giving collectors many pieces at affordable prices." She sees more and more machine-made types of valentines coming into the marketplace and finds collectors eagerly make room for them.

One of the most exciting new ways to explore the antiques and collectibles marketplace was introduced by Sotheby's this past November. They offered a CD-ROM of the Joseph H. Hazen art collection. This venue may possibly change the way antiques and collectibles are marketed in the future. The Hazen CD-ROM is impressive in that it includes a narrative tour by Sotheby's Senior Vice President John Tancock, as well as artist biographies, a timeline, and a zoom device to view the artwork. A biography of Joseph H. Hazen, a philanthropist, attorney, and film producer, gives the viewer insight into the collector. An in-depth analysis of the major paintings in the collection provides further information. The CD-ROM was offered before the auction, along with an illustrated catalog. Surely, this combination will become valuable as a reference tool and, perhaps, will even become a collectible in its own right.

Antiquing is a fun pastime for many folks. Some like to just look, while others are eager to find something for their ever-growing collections. **Warman's Antiques and Collectibles Price Guide** should be one of the many tools used to add to this enjoyment.

AUCTION HOUSES

The following auction houses cooperate with **Warman's** by providing catalogs of their auctions and price lists. This information is used to prepare **Warman's Antiques and Collectibles Price Guide,** and volumes in the Warman's Encyclopedia of Antiques and Collectibles. This support is truly appreciated.

Albrecht & Cooper Auction Services
3884 Saginaw Rd
Vassar, MI 48768
(517) 823-8835

Sanford Alderfer Auction Company
501 Fairgrounds Rd
Hatfield, PA 19440
(610) 368-5477
web site:
http://www.alderfercompany.com
e-mail:
auction@alderfercompany.com

Andre Ammelounx
The Stein Auction Company
PO Box 136
Palantine, IL 60078
(847) 991-5927

The Armans Collector's Sales and
Services
PO Box 4037
Middletown, RI 02842
(401) 849-5012

Arthur Auctioneering
RD 2, PO Box 155
Hughesville, PA 17737
(717) 584-3697

Aston Professional Auctioneers &
Appraisers
2825 Country Club Rd
Endwell, NY 13760-3349
(607) 785-6598

Bailey's Antiques
102 E Main St
Homer, MI 49245
(517) 568-4014

Noel Barrett Antiques & Auctions,
Ltd.
PO Box 1001
Carversville, PA 18913
(610) 297-5109

Robert F. Batchelder
1 W Butler Ave
Ambler, PA 19002
(610) 643-1430

Bill Bertoia Auctions
1881 Spring Rd
Vineland, NJ 08360
(609) 692-1881

Biders Antiques Inc.
241 S Union St
Lawrence, MA 01843
(508) 688-4347

Brown Auction & Real Estate
900 East Kansas
Greensburg, KS 67054
(316) 723-2111

Butterfield & Butterfield
7601 Sunset Blvd
Los Angeles, CA 90046
(213) 850-7500

Butterfield & Butterfield
220 San Bruno Ave
San Francisco, CA 94103
(415) 861-7500

C. C. Auction Gallery
416 Court
Clay Center, KS 67432
(913) 632-6021

W. E. Channing & Co., Inc.
53 Old Santa Fe Trail
Santa Fe, NM 87501
(505) 988-1078

Chicago Art Galleries
5039 Oakton St
Skokie, IL 60077
(847) 677-6080

Christie's
502 Park Ave
New York, NY 10022
(212) 546-1000
web site:
http://www.sirius.com/~christie/

Christie's East
219 E 67th St
New York, NY 10021
(212) 606-0400

Cincinnati Art Galleries
635 Main St
Cincinnati, OH 45202
(513) 381-2128

Mike Clum, Inc.
PO Box 2
Rushville, OH 43150
(614) 536-9220

Cohasco Inc.
Postal 821
Yonkers, NY 10702
(914) 476-8500

Dargate Auction Galleries
5607 Baum Blvd
Pittsburgh, PA 15206
(412) 362-3558
web site: http://www.dargate.com
e-mail: awkshun@aol.com

Marlin G. Denlinger
RR3, Box 3775
Morrisville, VT 05661
(802) 888-2775

Dorothy Dous
1261 University Drive
Yardley, PA 19067-2857
(215) 321-7367

William Doyle Galleries, Inc.
175 E 87th St
New York, NY 10128
(212) 427-2730
web site:
http://www.doylegalleries.com

Dunbar Gallery
76 Haven St
Milford, MA 01757
(508) 634-8697

Dunning's Auction Service
755 Church Road
Elgin, IL 60123
(847) 741-3483

Early Auction Co.
123 Main St
Milford, OH 45150
(513) 831-4833

Ken Farmer Realty & Auction Co.
105A Harrison St
Radford, VA 24141
(703) 639-0939
web site: http://kenfarmer.com
e-mail: info@kenfarmer.com

Fine Tool Journal
27 Fickett Rd
Pownal, ME 04069
(207) 688-4962
web site:
    http://www.wowpages.com/FTJ/

Steve Finer Rare Books
PO Box 758
Greenfield, MA 01302
(413) 773-5811

William A. Fox Auctions Inc.
676 Morris Ave
Springfield, NJ 07081
(201) 467-2366

Freeman/Fine Arts Co. of
  Philadelphia, Inc.
1808 Chestnut St
Philadelphia, PA 19103
(610) 563-9275

Garth's Auction, Inc.
2690 Stratford Rd
PO Box 369
Delaware, OH 43015
(614) 362-4771

Green Valley Auctions, Inc
Route 2, Box 434
Mt Crawford, VA 22841
(540) 434-4260

Greenberg Auctions
7566 Main St
Sykesville, MD 21784
(410) 795-7447

Guernsey's
136 E 73rd St
New York, NY 10021
(212) 794-2280

Hake's Americana & Collectibles
PO Box 1444
York, PA 17405
(717) 848-1333

Gene Harris Antique Auction
  Center, Inc.
203 South 18th Ave
PO Box 476
Marshalltown, IA 50158
(515) 752-0600

Norman C. Heckler & Company
Bradford Corner Rd
Woodstock Valley, CT 06282
(203) 974-1634

Leslie Hindman, Inc.
215 W Ohio St
Chicago, IL 60610
(312) 670-0010

Michael Ivankovich Auction Co.
PO Box 2458
Doylestown, PA 18901
(215) 345-6094

Jackson's Auctioneers & Appraisers
2229 Lincoln St
Cedar Falls, IA 50613
(319) 277-2256
e-mail: jacksons @corenet.net

James D. Julia Inc.
Rt 201 Skowhegan Rd
PO Box 830
Fairfield, ME 04937
(207) 453-7125

Lang's
30 Hamlin Rd
Falmouth, ME 04105
(207) 797-2311

Leonard's Auction Company
1631 State Rd
Duncannon, PA 17020
(717) 957-3324

Howard Lowery
3818 W Magnolia Blvd
Burbank, CA 91505
(818) 972-9080

Joy Luke
The Gallery
300 E Grove St
Bloomington, IL 61701
(309) 828-5533

Martin Auctioneers Inc.
PO Box 477
Intercourse, PA 17534
(717) 768-8108

McMasters Doll Auctions
PO Box 1755
Cambridge, OH 43725
(614) 432-4419

Wm. Frost Mobley
PO Box 10
Schoharie, NY 12157
(518) 295-7978

Wm. Morford
RD #2
Cazenovia, NY 13035
(315) 662-7625

New England Auction Gallery
PO Box 2273
W Peabody, MA 01960
(508) 535-3140

New Hampshire Book Auctions
PO Box 460
92 Woodbury Rd
Weare, NH 03281
(603) 529-7432

Richard Opfer Auctioneering Inc.
1919 Greenspring Dr
Timonium, MD 21093
(410) 252-5035

Pacific Book Auction Galleries
133 Kerney St, 4th Floor
San Francisco, CA 94108
(415) 989-2665
web site:
    http://www.pomo.nbn.com/pba

Pettigrew Auction Company
1645 S Tejon St
Colorado Springs, CO 80906
(719) 633-7963

Phillips Fine Art Auctions
406 E 79th St
New York, NY 10021
(212) 570-4830

Postcards International
PO Box 5398
Hamden, CT 06518
(203) 248-6621
e-mail: PostcrdInt@aol.com

Poster Auctions International
601 W 26th Street
New York, NY 10001
(212) 787-4000

David Rago Auctions, Inc.
333 S Main St
Lambertville, NJ 08530
(609) 397-9374

Lloyd Ralston Toys
173 Post Rd
Fairfield, CT 06432
(203) 255-1233

L. H. Selman Ltd
761 Chestnut St
Santa Cruz, CA 95060
(408) 427-1177
web site: http://www.selman.com
e-mail: lselman@got.net

Skinner, Inc.
Bolton Gallery
357 Main St
Bolton, MA 01740
(508) 779-6241

Skinner, Inc.
The Heritage on the Garden
63 Park Plaza
Boston MA 02116
(617) 350-5429

C. G. Sloan & Company Inc.
4920 Wyaconda Rd
North Bethesda, MD 20852
(301) 468-4911
web site: http://www.cgsloan.com

Smith House Toy Sales
26 Adlington Rd
Eliot, ME 03903
(207) 439-4614

R. M. Smythe & Co.
26 Broadway
New York, NY 10004-1710

Sotheby's
1334 York Ave
New York, NY 10021
(212) 606-7000
web site: http://www.sothebys.com

Michael G. Strawser
200 N Main St, PO Box 332
Wolcottville, IN 46795
(219) 854-2859

Swann Galleries, Inc.
104 E 25th St
New York, NY 10010
(212) 254-4710

Theriault's
PO Box 151
Annapolis, MD 21401
(301) 224-3655

Toy Scouts
137 Casterton Ave
Akron, OH 44303
(216) 836-0668
e-mail: toyscout@salamander.net

Treadway Gallery, Inc.
2029 Madison Rd
Cincinnati, OH 45208
(513) 321-6742
web site:
    http://www.a3c2net.com/tread-
    waygallery

Victorian Images
PO Box 284
Marlton, NJ 08053
(609) 985-7711

Vintage Cover Story
PO Box 975
Burlington, NC 27215
(919) 584-6900

Web Wilson Antiques
PO Box 506
Portsmouth, RI 02871
800-508-0022

Winter Associates
21 Cooke St Box 823
Plainville, CT 06062
(203) 793-0288

Wolf's Auctioneers
1239 W 6th St
Cleveland, OH 44113
(614) 362-4711

Woody Auction
Douglass, KS 67039
(316) 746-2694

ABBREVIATIONS

The following are standard abbreviations which we have used throughout this edition of **Warman's**.

4to = 8 x 10"
8vo = 5 x 7"
12mo = 3 x 5"
ADS = Autograph Document Signed
adv = advertising
ah = applied handle
ALS = Autograph Letter Signed
AQS = Autograph Quotation Signed
C = century
c = circa
circ = circular
cov = cover
CS = Card Signed
d = diameter or depth
dec = decorated
dj = dust jacket
DQ = Diamond Quilted
DS = Document Signed
ed = edition
emb = embossed
ext. = exterior
Folio = 12 × 16"
ftd = footed
gal = gallon
ground = background
h = height
hp = hand painted
hs = high standard
illus = illustrated, illustration
imp = impressed
int. = interior
irid = iridescent
IVT = inverted thumbprint
j = jewels

K = karat
l = length
lb = pound
litho = lithograph
ls = low standard
LS = Letter Signed
mfg = manufactured
MIB = mint in box
MOP = mother-of-pearl
NE = New England
No. = number
opal = opalescent
orig = original
os = orig stopper
oz = ounce
pat = patent
pcs = pieces
pgs = pages
pr = pair
PS = Photograph Signed
pt = pint
qt = quart
rect = rectangular
sgd = signed
sngl = single
SP = silver plated
SS = Sterling silver
sq = square
TLS = Typed Letter Signed
unp = unpaged
vol = volume
w = width
yg = yellow gold
# = numbered

ABC PLATES

History: The majority of early ABC plates were manufactured in England and imported into the United States. They achieved their greatest popularity from 1780 to 1860. Since a formal education was uncommon in the early 19th century, the ABC plate was a method of educating the poor for a few pennies.

ABC plates were made of glass, pewter, porcelain, pottery, or tin. Porcelain plates range in diameter from 4³⁄₈ to slightly over 9½ inches. The rim usually contains the alphabet and/or numbers; the center features animals, great men, maxims, or nursery rhymes.

References: Susan and Al Bagdade, *Warman's English & Continental Pottery & Porcelain,* Second Edition, Wallace-Homestead, 1991; Mildred L. and Joseph P. Chalala, *A Collector's Guide to ABC Plates, Mugs and Things,* Pridemark Press, 1980; Noel Riley, *Gifts for Good Children,* Richard Dennis Publications, 1991.

Collectors' Club: ABC Plate/Mug Collectors, 67 Stevens Ave, Old Bridge, NJ 08857.

Glass

6" d
Cane pattern, alphabet on stippled rim, clear	45.00
Dog's-head center	45.00
Jumbo, emb alphabet border	95.00
President Garfield, profile bust center, clear, frosted alphabet border	50.00
Starburst pattern, alphabet border, scalloped rim, clear, New Martinsville	35.00
7" d, milk glass, plain center, emb alphabet border, beaded rim	50.00
8" d, Stork pattern, clear	85.00

China, plate, "Marine Railway Station, Manhattan Beach Hotel," brown transfer, 7" d, $165.00.

Porcelain or Pottery

5½" d, children, dog, parrot, and verse, multicolored transfer scene, emb alphabet border	45.00
5¾" d, little girls in flower garden, black transfer center, emb alphabet border, marked "J & G Meakin," 1851	65.00
6" d	
Fox and Grapes, black transfer, red trim, marked "J Meir & Son, Tunstall, England"	55.00

Dr Franklin Maxim Proverb, two men in office scene, "If You Would Know The Value Of Money Try To Borrow Some—Creditors Have Better Memories Than Debtors"	145.00
6¼" d, zebra, black transfer, polychrome enamel dec, Staffordshire	90.00
6½" h, Noah and the Ark, religious transfer center, emb alphabet border	75.00
7" d, colored transfer, boy in period attire carrying basket, imp "Meakin"	110.00
7¼" d, Nations of the World, green transfer center, brown transfer alphabet, white ground, marked "Tunstall, England"	75.00
7½" d, cricket game, multicolored transfer center, Staffordshire	135.00

Tin

3" d, girl and boy rolling hoop	110.00
5½" d, Liberty	65.00
6" d, two kittens playing with yarn	50.00
7⅛" d, Who Killed Cock Robin	115.00
8" d	
Mary Had A Little Lamb	140.00
Monkey on Barrel, litho dec	65.00
9" d, Hey Diddle Diddle	55.00

ADAMS ROSE

History: Adams Rose, made about 1820 to 1840 by Adams and Son in the Staffordshire district of England, is decorated with brilliant red roses and green leaves on a white ground.

G. Jones and Son, England, made a variant known as "Late Adams Rose," which has a dirty-white ground. The colors in this pattern are not as brilliant and pieces sell for less than the original Adams Rose.

Bowl, 9" d, early, rare size, mint condition	500.00
Creamer, 5¾" h, early	325.00
Cup and Saucer, handleless	
Early	215.00
Late, rose dec on saucer, blue spatter	115.00

Cup and Saucer, 6" d saucer, handleless, $215.00.

Plate

    6⅞" d, two purple luster bands on border **65.00**

    7½" d, single rose, rust and green florals, raised basketweave border, two purple luster bands on border **125.00**

    8½" d, red, blue, green, and black flowers, imp "Adams," wear, minor pinpoints, stains, price for pr **250.00**

    9" d, red, green, and black design **75.00**

    10½" d, red, green, and black design **150.00**

Platter, 17⅝" d, early, emb scalloped rim **450.00**

Soup Plate, 10¼" d **175.00**

Sugar Bowl, cov, early **345.00**

Teapot, cov, late **265.00**

Vegetable Dish, cov, 12⅝" d, early **500.00**

ADVERTISING

History: Before the days of mass media, advertisers relied on colorful product labels and advertising giveaways to promote their products. Containers were made to appeal to the buyer through the use of stylish lithographs and bright colors. Many of the illustrations used the product in the advertisement so that even an illiterate buyer could identify a product.

Advertisements were put on almost every household object imaginable and were constant reminders to use the product or visit a certain establishment.

References: *Advertising & Figural Tape Measures,* L-W Book Sales, 1995; Al Bergevin, *Drugstore Tins and Their Prices,* Wallace-Homestead, 1990; A. Walker Bingham, *The Snake-Oil Syndrome,* Christopher Publishing House, 1994; Michael Bruner, *Advertising Clocks,* Schiffer Publishing, 1995; ———, *Encyclopedia of Porcelain Enamel Advertising,* Schiffer Publishing, 1994; Doug Collins, *America's Favorite Food: The Story of Campbell Soup Company,* Harry N Abrams, 1994; Douglas Congdon-Martin, *America for Sale,* Schiffer Publishing, 1991; ———, *Tobacco Tins,* Schiffer Publishing, 1992; Douglas Congdon-Martin and Robert Biondi, *Country Store Antiques,* Schiffer Publishing, 1991; ———, *Country Store Collectibles,* Schiffer Publishing, 1990; Fred Dodge, *Antique Tins,* Collector Books, 1995; Warren Dotz, *Advertising Character Collectibles,* Collector Books, 1993; ———, *What a Character! 20th Century American Advertising Icons,* Chronicle Books, 1996; James L. Dundas, *Collecting Whistles,* Schiffer Publishing, 1995; Tony Fusco, *Posters Identification and Price Guide,* Second Edition, Avon Books, 1994.

Ted Hake, *Hake's Guide to Advertising Collectibles,* Wallace-Homestead, 1992; Bill and Pauline Hogan, *The Charlton Standard Catalogue of Canadian Country Store Collectables,* Charlton Press, 1996; Bob and Sharon Huxford, *Huxford's Collectible Advertising,* Third Edition, Collector Books, 1996; Thomas Patrick Jacobsen, *Pat Jacobsen's First International Price Guide to Fruit Crate Labels,* Patco Enterprise (437 Minton Ct, Pleasant Hill, CA 94523), 1994; Ray Klug, *Antique Advertising Encyclopedia,* Vol. 1 (1978, 1993 value update) and Vol. 2 (1985), L-W Promotions; Mary Jane Lamphier, *Zany Characters of the Ad World,* Collector Books, 1995; Norman E. Martinus and Harry L. Rinker, *Warman's Paper,* Wallace-Homestead, 1994; Patricia McDaniel, *Drugstore Collectibles,* Wallace-Homestead, 1994; Gerald S. Petrone, *Tobacco Advertising,* Schiffer Publishing, 1996; Don and Carol Raycraft, *American Country Store,* Wallace-Homestead, 1994; Bob Sloan and Steve Guarnaccia, *A Stiff Drink and a Close Shave,* Chronicle

Books, 1995; Louis Storino, *Chewing Tobacco Tin Tags,* Schiffer Publishing, 1995; Neil Wood, *Smoking Collectibles,* L-W Book Sales, 1994.

Periodicals: *Creamers,* PO Box 11, Lake Villa, IL 60046; *Paper Collectors' Marketplace,* PO Box 128, Scandinavia, WI 54917; *The Advertising Collectors Express,* PO Box 221, Mayview, MO 64071.

Collectors' Clubs: Antique Advertising Assoc of America, PO Box 1121, Morton Grove, IL 60053; Button Pusher, PO Box 4, Coopersburg, PA 18036; Inner Seal Collectors Club, 6609 Billtown Rd, Louisville, KY 40299; National Assoc of Paper and Advertising Collectibles, PO Box 500, Mount Joy, PA 17552; Porcelain Advertising Collectors Club, PO Box 381, Marshfield Hills, MA 02051; The Ephemera Society of America, PO Box 95, Cazenovia, NY 13035; Tin Container Collectors Association, PO Box 440101, Aurora, CO 80014.

Museums: American Advertising Museum, Portland, OR; Museum of Transportation, Brookline, MA; National Museum of American History, Archives Center, Smithsonian Institution, Washington, DC.

Additional Listings: See *Warman's Americana & Collectibles* for more examples.

Almanac, Bradley's Fertilizer C, 1888 .... **20.00**

Ash Shovel, Treasure Line Stoves and Ranges, The Adams Furniture Co, tin litho, distributed by D Moore Co, Hamilton, Ontario, name on handle, illus on shovel **325.00**

Ashtray, Taittinger Champagne, France **75.00**

Bank, Pittsburgh Paints, glass **45.00**

Banner, 48 × 23", Kellogg's Corn Flakes, c1920 ...... **265.00**

Bath Tub, "Hot Bath, Big D Hotel, 1895, 25 cents" red, yellow, and green lettering, galvanized, coffin shape **95.00**

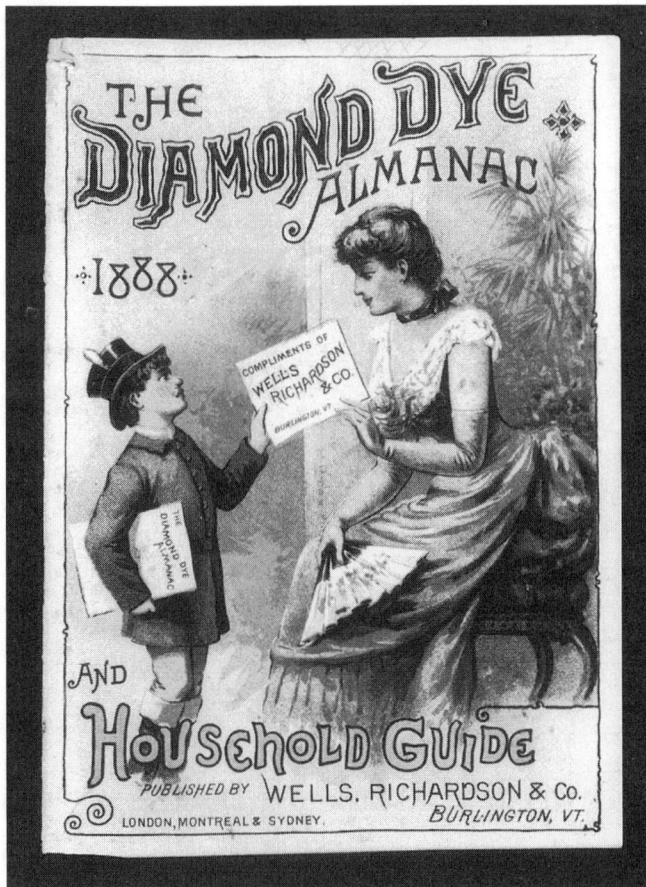

Almanac, 1888, Diamond Dye Almanac and Household Guide, Wells, Richardson & Co, Burlington, VT, 84 pgs, $25.00.

Booklet
    Compliments of the Shaker Inn, Latham, NY **15.00**
    Honest Scrap Tobacco, dog and cat illus, 1910 .... **30.00**
    McCormick Farm Equipment, 3½ × 6″ folder opens to 18 × 19″, printed on both sides, farm machinery illus, descriptive text, c1911 .... **20.00**
    60th Anniversary of Woolworth's, 1939, multicolored, merchandise photos **22.00**
Bookmark, diecut ivory grained sheet celluloid
    Bair & Lane Real Estate, Greensburg, PA, printed by Mee Co, Coshocton, OH, red and yellow rose motif **15.00**

Blotter, Shields Lumber and Coal Co, candlestick telephone, red and black, 6½ × 3½″, $5.00.

Totem Pole Route, multicolored dec, Pacific Coast Steamship logo flag, text for cruises from various West Coast cities to Alaska, c1920 .... **85.00**
Bottle Rack, wooden, marked "Benjamin's 10-cent High Grade Soft Drink, Property of Hazelton Bottle Co." **250.00**
Bowl, Geneva, Iowa, General Store, spongeware, blue, rust, and orange **150.00**
Box, Bachelor's Friend Socks, "A He-Man Gift!", 1940s **35.00**
Bridge Card, Lucky Strikes, Loretta Young **15.00**
Broadside, 18¾″ w, 24¾″ h, black and white, Public Sale, Wayne County, OH, 1873, printed by Crescent Print Orrville, framed **440.00**
Button Hook, Miller's Cocoa, multicolored windmill image with "M" flag on spire, celluloid, wire button hook, early 1900s **50.00**

Button, The Sharples Co/The Tubular Cream Separator, white ground, blue dress, red separator, 1¼″, $22.00.

Cabinet, counter top
    Davol Baby Nipples **75.00**
    Dexter Braids, spool type, 2 drawers **170.00**
    Diamond Dye, black metal **135.00**
    Dy-O-La Dyes, wood, tin insert **95.00**
    Munyons Homeopathic Remedies **225.00**
    Springs, eight compartmented drawers, oak, black lettering **480.00**
Calendar
    26″ l, Grand Union Tea Company, 1908, little girl having a tea party with doll and kitten, framed .. **280.00**
    26½″ l, Mass & Steffen Fur Co, 1944 .... **115.00**
Candy Dish, cov, Schrafft's Chocolates, 6″ sq, Massachusetts pattern **30.00**
Chair, folding, wooden
    Cross Cut Cigarettes, oil portrait of young lady on front, painting of cigarette package on back **275.00**
    Red Goose Shoes **75.00**
Cigarette Lighter
    French Steak Co, chrome steel, red and gold enameled metal wrapper, back with text for meat products, marked "Direct," c1920 .... **35.00**
    White Sewing Machines, figural sewing machine shape **25.00**
Clicker, Page's Creamery Butter, "Kleen-Maid," multi-

Box, Grandpa's Wonder Soap, Beaver Soap Co, Dayton, OH, 2½ × 4⅓ × 1½″, $360.00.

colored tin litho, youngster carrying yellow sign board over shoulders, 1930s 50.00

Clock

    McCord Motor Gaskets, metal and glass 95.00

    Sauers Extract 1,650.00

Counter Plate, El Producto, glass 25.00

Dexterity Puzzle, Forbes Quality Coffee, silvered tin frame holding glass, full-color paper playing service of coffee canister, four balls fit into canister lid rim, German, c1900 .... 80.00

Display

    Clarkes Thread, diecut, paper soldier, complete set of 12 .... 225.00

    Moline Plow Co, US Standardized Wagon Door, wood, orig paint 800.00

Coffee Can, Our Jewel Roasted Coffee, Ericsson's Mills, Brooklyn, NY, dark blue ground, lighter blue, cream, silver, red, young girl's face, blue knob, $325.00.

Display Stand, Teabury Gum, vaseline glass, pedestal . 135.00

Doll, Cream of Wheat, uncut 45.00

Doorstop, figural, black cat, Black Cat Whiskey, Ullman Einstein Co, Cleveland 2,750.00

Game, Welch's Grape Juice Indian Woo Woo Game, orig bottles 70.00

Ink Blotter, Keller Mfg Co, Allentown, PA, Christmas, 1929, 2½ × 6″ rect booklet of blotters, dec celluloid cover with Christmas manger scene, printed by Whitehead and Hoag Co 20.00

Flyer, Georges Ice Cream, black-and-white newsprint, 4″ w, 9¾″ h, $10.00.

Jar, cov

    Buffalo Peanuts, glass, emb, orig top 120.00

    Candy Bros Manufacturing Co, St Louis, 4 lb 75.00

    Dr Stevens Cough Drops, paper label 65.00

Lapel Pin, Pabst Breweries, multicolored enamel dec . 15.00

Lunch Box

    Gillies Co Coffee, 4¾″ h, tin litho pail, boys playing football on one side, girls at seashore on other, bail handle, minor scratches 330.00

    Pedro Tobacco, tin 150.00

Match Holder, Havana Cigars, emb knight on horseback 45.00

Match Safe, Hercules Powder Co, Pittsburg, Kansas, metal, celluloid wrap, pocket size 150.00

Menu

    Hotel Astor, New York City watercolor scene, 1945 7.00

    Mickey Mantel's Holiday Inn Menu, c1930 .... 75.00

    RH Macy's, large, 1937 .... 25.00

Notepad, Southern New England Telephone Co, simulated red good luck stamp on cov, black inscription, blue Bell System logo on back 20.00

Pail

    Beaver Brand Peanut Butter, 3½″ h, slat sided, narrower at top, gold enamel, beaver and foliage on front and reverse 1,100.00

    Big Sister Peanut Butter, 3½″ h, slant sided, Halloween images, Suffolk, VA, slight dent and wear on lid 315.00

    Coogan, Jackie, 3¾″ h, blue, straight sided, full color

image of Jackie eating slab of peanut butter bread on front, emb directions on lid 1,155.00

Fairyland Peanut Butter, 3¼" h, straight sided, teacher and children in classroom, New Castle, PA, pry-off lid, minor rim wear 550.00

Friends Tobacco, bail handle 50.00

Jumbo Peanut Butter, 3½" h, slant sided, Jumbo head on front, diagonal stripes, plain back, nursery rhyme lid 2,420.00

Sweet Girl Peanut Butter, 4¾" h, straight sided, tin litho, portrait of girl on front, children building sand castles on reverse, bright tin 1,210.00

Uncle Wiggily Peanut Butter, 3½" h, slant sided, tin litho, multicolored seaside image, Uncle Wiggily and animal children, 1923 ....2,750.00

Wilson's Peanut Butter, 3" h, straight sided, tin litho, Mother Goose and girl on front, Old Woman and Shoe on reverse, pry-off lid, minor edge scratches 550.00

Painting, oil on canvas, McElwain Barton Shoe Co, Kansas City, MO, Eskimo Brand Rubbers, R Atkinson Fox, 1916 ....5,500.00

Paperweight

    Bell Telephone, bell shape, cobalt blue glass 45.00

    Golden Pheasant Gunpowder, multicolored 35.00

    Puritan Coke, brass, figural, pilgrim 195.00

Pin

    ¾" l, Heinz pickle 15.00

    ⅞" d, celluloid, diecut, black and white, "Local and Long Distance Telephone" logo symbol on front, Bell System, c1905 .... 40.00

    1 × 1" diecut, celluloid hanger, small stickpin, blue and white, reverse inscribed "When In Doubt Telephone and Find Out/Use The Bell," Bell System, c1905 .... 42.00

Pinback Button

    ⅞" d

        Blue and white rotary telephone dial, center inscribed "I'm For Automatic," issued by Auto Elec Co, early 1900s 18.00

        Red and white, "Soldiers and Sailors' Comfort Club," candlestick telephone with crossed military rifles, issued by Hawthorne Works of Western Electric, c1920 .... 20.00

        Red, white, and blue independent telephone logo on light blue ground, "Central Telephone & Electric Co, The Up-to-Date Telephone Company," early 1900s 15.00

        Swift's Premium Ham, multicolored image, brown smoked ham, white ground, black letters, c1896 .... 20.00

    1" d

        Blue and white, "Have You Called Home To-Day?" c1920 .... 10.00

        Bond Bread, yellow sunburst, white letters, green ground, 1930s 12.00

        Red, white, and blue "Federal Telephone," shield logo, early 1900s 18.00

    1¼" d, Master Bread, blue-tone portrait of youngster wearing derby, orange rim, black and white letters, 1930s 20.00

    1½" d, The Citizens Ice Company, gold letters and rim, turquoise ground 15.00

Mirror, Beautyskin, Chichester Chemical Co, Phila, girl in pink dress, yellow flowers, green ground, 2½ × 1½", $35.00.

    1¾" d, Old Reliable Coffee, multicolored graphic .. 45.00

    2 × 5½" white fabric ribbon with pinback, John Dough, multicolored baker figure made of bread loaf and biscuit body parts, apron inscribed "John Dough Raised On Fleischmann's Yeast," ribbon inscribed in blue "15th Annual Excursion/Binghamton Retail Grocers Association to Watkins, N.Y./July 23, 1914" 150.00

Pitcher, 4¾" h, Crawford Cooking Ranges, flow blue dec, adv on both sides, marked "Hanley Co" 235.00

Plate, Quick Service Laundry Co, tin, early 1900s 35.00

Pocket Mirror

    1¾", Wholesale Lumber, Columbus, OH, red design and inscription, white ground 45.00

    1¾ × 2¾", New King Snuff, multicolored illus of tobacco snuff jar, inscribed "Scotch-King," bright white ground 65.00

    2⅛" l

        Angelus Marshmallows, multicolored, blond-haired cherub holding gold trumpet, sash inscribed "A Message of Purity," cherub standing on product crate, dark green ground, rim curl inscription includes name of sponsor Rueckheim Bros & Eckstein, Chicago, early 1900s . 100.00

        Franklin Mills Co, multicolored illus of Lockport, NY, factory, "Home of Wheatlet & Franklin Flour," inscribed "All The Wheat That's Fit To Eat," early 1900s 85.00

        The Great Majestic, The Modern Range, multicolored illus of 1900s housewife using cast iron stove 80.00

    2¼" l, Victor Artists, black and white photo portraits of eight recording stars, c1920, minor wear to mirror silvering 65.00

    2½" l, blue and white, celluloid, issued for Missouri and Kansas Telephone Co of Bell System and American Telephone & Telegraph, early 1900s . 65.00

2¾" l

Foot-Schulze-Glove, oval, multicolored illus of rural scene, large center billboard of rubbers and arctic footwear, early 1900s **60.00**

Lodge Convention, full color illus of modern lodge building titled "Jerusalem," another building titled "Damascus," inscribed "To Rochester 1911," route passes through pyramids, tiny individuals on camels in foreground **75.00**

3½" l, Pacific Coast Lumber, Seattle **17.50**

Poster

Arm & Hammer, birds **35.00**

Cetacolor, "Prevents Wash Goods from Fading 10¢ Package," pretty girl illus **165.00**

Levi's Round-Up, Cowboy Lore, by Joe Mora, 1950 **395.00**

Ragged Edge Cigars, cigar box illus **550.00**

Pot Scraper, Sharples Cream, 1909 .... **295.00**

Record Brush, 2½" d, RCA, red, green, and blue, white Christmas theme celluloid, green holly wreath, red RCA and "His Master's Voice", black and white center inscription of Philadelphia record shop, dark green velveteen underside,1930s **35.00**

Salesman's Sample

Barber's Chair, Koch, fully operational, porcelainized and nickel-plated cast iron, leather and brass, orig carrying case **18,700.00**

Calendar, blond Vargas girl seated on blue chair, black fan, shaded rose ground, c1937 .... **125.00**

Furnace, Lennox, 1930s **330.00**

Sample Book, Johns & Co. cigar labels, 27 labels **350.00**

Sewing Kit, 1" d, 2¼" h, glossy white thin wooden replica of milk bottle, red inscription "Ryder's Dairy Inc," thin removable lid, segmented into spool for black and white thread, thread holder with removable brass cap over needle storage, base inscribed "Made in Germany," 1930s **60.00**

Sign

Anheuser-Busch Budweiser Girl, self-framed tin **3,300.00**

Blackwell's Durham Tuchfarber, tin litho, restoration.**4,400.00**

Bull Frog Shoe Polish, double-sided tin litho **4,400.00**

Butte Brewery, tin litho, 1897, crease at top, dents. **7,250.00**

DuPont, Generations Have Used DuPont Powders, hunters and bird dogs, self framed **1,750.00**

Sign, White House Shoes, The H. D. Beach Co, Coshocton, OH, 19⅜ x 9¼", $145.00.

Enterprise Stoves and Ranges, flange **150.00**

Fairbanks Gold Dust Washing Powder, Cleans Everything, self-framed tin, frame rusted, some restoration **4,400.00**

Falstaff and Happiness, self-framed tin, 1914, lower right scratches **2,200.00**

Grape-Nuts, self-framed tin, 20 × 30" **5,500.00**

International Harvester Gasoline Engines, diecut tin, double sided, repaired hole **1,800.00**

Jesse Moore's Whiskey, Kaufmann & Strauss, emb tin litho, tack hole, wear, red letters **11,000.00**

Keil Key, diecut metal flange **150.00**

Kibbs Salted Jumbo Peanuts, Springfield, MA, tin .. **125.00**

Iroquois, tin **35.00**

Mail Pouch Tobacco, Bloch Bros, diecut, reglued broken arm **4,300.00**

Miller Brewing, Madame Calve as Carmen, Wolf & Co, 1901 ....**4,250.00**

Mission of California, tin **35.00**

Munsing Wear, seated woman with two cherubs ...**3,300.00**

New Jersey Contracting and Supply Co., Suppliers of Everything Electrical, wood, oval, black, yellow, and red **100.00**

N. Shepard's Inn, double sided, painted wood, pewter gray paint, black letters, central Indian figure, other side with same lettering, New England, 1819 ....**4,312.00**

Power Lube Motor Oil, double sided, porcelain, chipped, some fading **770.00**

Ramleh Turkish Cigarettes, framed litho, minor stain **1,800.00**

Red Dot Cigars, cigar shape, folding cardboard **30.00**

Rexall, 70 × 46", porcelain **225.00**

Westminster Whiskey, Settled Out of Court, Ritter & Co, self-framed tin, 26 × 38" **5,500.00**

String Holder, Dutch Boy Paints, Atlantic White Lead, some restoration to eyes **2,250.00**

Stud, Ride Ruby Rims/Vesper Cycles, white letters, maroon ground, sponsor H B Shatluck & Son, Boston. **20.00**

Thermometer

Doans Kidney Pills, diecut wood **165.00**

Kerns Bread **55.00**

Mail Pouch, metal **110.00**

Sign, Campbell Kids, metal, 23¼ × 14½", $75.00.

RC Cola, blue and white 35.00
Salem Cigarettes 35.00

Tin

Bagleys Wild Fruit Tobacco 35.00
Blue Parrot Coffee, 6″ h, cylindrical, yellow ground, red stripe at top and bottom, blue parrot on branch, descriptive reverse, very minor damage and scratches 5,500.00
Central Union 35.00
Dairy Maid Crackers 25.00
Dixie Queen Tobacco 250.00
Elephant Java Coffee, 7¾″ l. rect, tin litho, elephant on front, boat and train on side panels, descriptive verse, minor flaking and wear 715.00
Foltz Maid Coffee, 6″ h, cylindrical, tin litho, child seated at table drinking cup of coffee on front and back, minor spotting 625.00
King Cole Coffee, 5¾″ h, cylindrical, tin litho, servant offering coffee to King Cole 245.00
Mayo's Tobacco 100.00
Mi-Lady Coffee, 6″ h, cylindrical, tin litho, woman admiring her image in mirror 1,100.00
Molasses Crunch 30.00
Nic Nac Store Tobacco 350.00
Ojibwa Store Tobacco 750.00
Old Soldier Tobacco, paper label 300.00
Peter Pan Peanut Butter 20.00
Planters Peanuts, black, red, and blue 30.00
Possum Cigar, red and black 65.00
Seal of North Carolina Tobacco, canister 250.00
Sterling Store Made Tobacco 275.00
Swell Blend Coffee, 6″ h, cylindrical, tin litho, sailing steamer on front, guarantee medallion on reverse, minor dents 235.00
Sweet Burley Store Tobacco 450.00
Sweet Cuba Tobacco, green, round 40.00
Sweet Mist Chewing Tobacco, canister 200.00
Tiger Chewing Tobacco, cylinder shaped, 5-lb size 75.00
Turkey Coffee, 10½″ h, cylindrical, tin litho, wild turkey image on front and reverse, red lettering, minor scratches 660.00
Webster's Coffee, 6″ h, cylindrical, tin litho, woman pouring coffee on front and reverse, minor dents and damage 385.00
Wright, J, Co., Winner Cut Plug Tobacco 100.00
Yum Yum 250.00

Tip Tray

Cohen Bros, Somerset, multicolored outdoor scene, hunting dog, 1907 clothing adv 250.00
Evervess Sparkling Water, parrot 50.00
Rockford High Grade Watches, pretty girl, some damage 118.00

Tobacco Cutter, Thos C Jenkins 200.00

Toy

Endicott Johnson Shoes, green and white tin litho spinner top, name in red, 1930s 30.00
Haller Baking Co, Fortune Top, red, white, and blue tin litho spinner top, ten fortune readings, c1930 35.00
Howell's Root Beer, wooden acrobat 145.00

Tray, Myersdale Brewing Co, "Makers of Pure Beer & Porter, Auld Lang Syne #107," 1910, two St Bernard dogs smoking cigars, colorful steins 230.00

Tray, Anheuser-Busch, oval, tin litho, Standard Adv Co, Coshocton, OH, 1909, 16½ × 13½″, $1,200.00.

Tumbler, etched "Christmas Greetings, 1901, Olsen's Big New Store" 45.00
Wagon, Good Will Soap, wooden box-type seat, wooden wheels, painted yellow, red trim, black lettering 800.00
Watch Fob, 1925 AMA Gypsy Tours, silvered brass, center yellow, dark green, red, and black enameled American Motorcycle Assoc symbol, reverse inscribed "Perfect Score/National Motorcycle Gypsy Tour/1925" 85.00
Whistle, Texaco, aluminum thimble-style whistle, red enamel band inscribed "Shell's Texaco Service," c1940 .... 25.00

ADVERTISING TRADE CARDS

History: Advertising trade cards are small, thin cardboard cards made to advertise the merits of a product. They usually bear the name and address of a merchant.

With the invention of lithography, colorful trade cards became a popular way to advertise in the late 19th and early 20th centuries. They were made to appeal especially to children. Young and old alike collected and treasured them in albums and scrapbooks. Very few are dated; the prime years for trade card production were 1880 to 1893; cards made between 1810 and 1850 can be found, but rarely. By 1900 trade cards were rapidly losing their popularity, and by 1910 they had all but vanished.

References: Kit Barry, *The Advertising Trade Card,* Book 1, published by author, 1981; Robert Jay, *The Trade Card in Nineteenth-Century America,* University of Missouri Press, 1987; Norman E. Martinus and Harry L. Rinker, *Warman's Paper,* Wallace-Homestead, 1994; Jim and Cathy McQuary, *Collectors Guide to Advertising Cards,* L-W Promotions, 1975, out-of-print; Murray Cards (International) Ltd. (comp.), *Cigarette Card Values,* Murray Cards (International) Ltd., 1994.

Periodicals: *Card Times,* 70 Winified Lane, Aughton, Ormskirk, Lancashire L38 5DL England; *Trade Card Journal,* 109 Main St, Brattleboro, VT 05301.

Collectors' Club: Trade Card Collector's Assoc, PO Box 284, Marlton, NJ 08053.

Additional Listings: See *Warman's Americana & Collectibles* for more examples.

Beauty

Buckingham's Dye for The Whiskers, metamorphic, gentleman with chest-length white beard changes to black beard, adv on back **12.00**
Campbell's Hair Cutting & Shaving Saloon, black and blue **45.00**
Colaine Headache Powders, puzzle reverse **40.00**
Compliments of Seely Manuf Co Perfumer's, Detroit, MI   **10.00**
Hoyt, E W, & Co, perfumed calendar, 1893 ....   **10.00**
Jap Rose Toilet Talcum Powder, diecut, talcum can, Oriental woman illus **12.00**
Radway's Ready Relief, Stops Pain, two girls **40.00**
Thorne's Hair Bazaar, 1881 ....   **12.00**

Beverages

Arbuckle Coffee, pictorial US history with maps **5.00**
Great Atlantic & Pacific Tea Co, Dinah praises A & P teas and coffees, black landlord and renter's conversation on bottom, adv on back, 1884, 8 × 9" **25.00**
Hires Root Beer, An Uninvited Guest **20.00**
Lion Coffee, Mrs President Cleveland **10.00**
Royal Garden Teas, September with birthstone **5.00**
Victor Coffee, four horses pulling chariot **7.50**

Clothing & Accessories

AST Co, black-tipped shoes, school teacher illus, 1880   **7.50**
Automatic Shoe Heel Co, diecut, black shoe, brown sole   **45.00**
Ball's Health Preserving Corsets, multicolored **10.00**
Beals, Torrey & Co, Boots and Shoes, Palmer Cox Brownies **10.00**
Broadhead Dress Goods, litho illus **12.00**
Buster Brown Shoes, children and dog, 1909 ....   **12.00**
Cherry, Robt, Germantown, Phila, shoes, woman looking at shoe box **12.00**
Draper & Maynard Co Gloves & Mittens, plant vignette on reverse **12.00**
Fisk, Clark & Flaggs Gloves, two gentlemen, gold ground   **10.00**
Libby & Spier, clothing, New Year greeting, steel engraving **15.00**

A. Wurtenberg Dry Goods, diecut drum shape, 3³⁄₈ × 3⁵⁄₁₆", $5.00.

McCormick Harvesting Machine Co, 6¹⁄₄ × 4¹⁄₁₆", $12.00.

Marshall & Ball Clothiers, horse, adv on back **5.00**
New Globe Patented Shirts, caricature illus, sepia and black **18.00**
Prevost, M.V., Fine Millinery, diecut, fan shape, comical animals **55.00**
Reed's, Joseph, Finest Clothing, Philadelphia **12.00**
Solar Tip Shoes, wise/foolish man story **155.00**
Spun Glass Rusil Finish Dress Linings, litho illus **17.50**
Strawbridge & Clothier, man carrying packages **10.00**
Taylor & Rogers Clothing, black and green, vignette ..   **25.00**

Farm Machinery & Supplies

Bickford & Huffman, Macedon, NY, farm tools, 1886 .   **25.00**
Bucker & Gibbs Plow Co, Canton, OH **20.00**
Clinton Plow Co, Clinton, MI, children illus **25.00**
Deering Implements, mower on reverse **15.00**
Dietericks Harness Oil, horse and elves **35.00**
McCormick, diecut, hand shape **12.00**
Princess Plow Co, Canton, OH, The Princess of Wales Plow, full color, four pages, Princess on cov **17.50**
Russell & Co, Massillon, OH, threshers, engines, sawmills, litho illus **17.50**
Sharples Bros, Philadelphia, cream separator, chromolitho of girl and bunny **15.00**

Food

American Breakfast Cereals, 1883 ....   **15.00**
Baltimore Oyster Co, 1884 calendar on reverse **40.00**
Bordens Eagle Brand Condensed Milk, child and cat illus   **7.50**
Compliments of Clark Bell, The Cash Grocers, adv on reverse **15.00**
Deep Sea Mess Mackerel, litho illus **7.50**
Dixon's Ice Cream, Keamy statue in military park **7.50**
Emmerson's Albumenoid Food, 1886 ....   **5.00**

G. W. Fairchild Diamonds, Watches, and Jewelry,
Bridgeport, CT, blank back, 2⅝″ × 4¹/₁₆″, $5.00.

Fleischmann & Co Yeast, litho illus 10.00
Greenfield's Chocolate Sponge, child carrying box, po-
    liceman directs traffic, 1915 .... 12.00
Hecker's Buckwheat, hold to light type 20.00
Kenton Baking Powder, owl and moon 10.00
Libbey's Extracts of Beef, calendar on reverse 20.00
Mellins Food, litho illus 10.00
Niox de Coco, For Puddings, Pies, Pastries, woman
    served by blacks 12.00
Quaker Oats, mechanical 40.00
Ridges Food For Infants & Invalids, litho illus 10.00
Shaker Oven Baked Beans, 2 × 3½″ 35.00
Syrup of Figs, Fig Syrup Co, CA, folder 12.00
Thurber's Canned Vegetables 7.50
Tip Top Baking Powder, litho dog illus 15.00
Van Houtens Cocoa, litho trains illus 12.00
Wilsons Cooked Meats, sailor illus 15.00

Laundry and Soaps

Bon-Ton Polish, two girls playing with dolls and dog .. 5.00
Empire Wringer, fox wedding 15.00
Fairbanks Gold Dust Twins 50.00
Lifebuoy Soap, woman holding life preserver with boy
    holding product 24.00
New Process Starch, double view, Chinese man and
    woman 12.00
Niagara Starch, well-dresseded long-haired lady holding
    product, full color 5.00
Packer's Tar Soap, mother washing baby, full color ... 4.00
Sapillo, diecut, watermelon shape, black face 20.00
Sweet Home Family Soap, Larkin & Co, Palmer Cox
    Brownies riding bicycle 15.00
Viola Cream Skin Soap, folder, skin-care information . 17.50

Williams' Yankee Soap, red, white, and blue flag, beige
    ground 100.00

Medical

Ayer's Hair Vigor 15.00
Carter's Little Nerve Pills, boy and girl hugging large dog 7.50
German Corn Remover, metamorphic 20.00
Jayne's Expectorant, children begging, 1890 .... 7.50
Loose's Red Clover, As a Cure for Cancer, men fighting
    bear 7.50
Krauter Bitters, elaborate center panel, three folds 5.00
Peckhams Croup Remedy, woman and girl 5.00
Schenk's Pulmonic Syrup, hold to light type, sleeping
    children and kitten 12.00
Tarrants Seltzer Aperient, metamorphic 15.00

Miscellaneous

Detroit Evening News Excursion from Detroit to the Sea,
    1881 .... 255.00
Dutch Boy Paints, mechanical, diecut, blue, white, yel-
    low, and red 15.00
Entertainment and Shaker Sale, 2½ × 3¾″ 35.00
Hotel & Cafe Butler, Seattle, Halloween card, 1907, Tiny
    Tads Co, NY, artist sgd 235.00
Knaust Bros & Co, Cincinnati, OH, toy bazaar, Santa
    illus 17.50
McAuslan & Wahelin Co, Toyland, Holyoke, MA, me-
    chanical, Santa writes on blackboard, black, white,
    and red, adv on reverse 35.00
Metropolitan Life, diecut, chromolitho, three little girls
    having tea party, boy wearing baker's hat 30.00
Rochester Lamps, Bridal Chamber, hotel int. view 10.00
Youth's Companion, A National Family Paper, litho illus,
    1889, folder 20.00
Weathersbury, Eliza, Froliques, Petite Opera, litho illus 10.00

Nautical

Boston and Hingham Steamboat Co, folder, Hotel Nan-
    tasket, back with ship map from Boston, timetable
    inside 80.00
Citizens Evening Line, stock-type image, red adv on re-
    verse, 1883 timetable, prices, slight filled-in chip .. 95.00

Wilson & McCallay Tobacco Co, Middletown, OH, color litho factory
and product illus, black-and-white text on back, 5¾″ × 3½″, $7.50.

Gregg Co Philadelphia Line for San Francisco, blue and red letters, light blue ground, adv on reverse for Coleman & Co, New York, Pickering, Boston 315.00

Lund's Pioneer Line, Florida steamer line, red and black lettering, adv on reverse 80.00

Norddeustcher Lloyd Bremen, colorful graphic design and printing 125.00

Peoples Line, cats image, red and yellow, reversed white lettering on black ground, New York to Albany route adv on reverse 80.00

Stonington Night Line, black and white schematic, timetable from Stonington to Boston on reverse 125.00

Pianos and Organs

Claredon Pianos, little girl holding tennis racket and ball   35.00
Gardner, R D, Organs, black illus, light green ground .   15.00
Weaver Organ Factory, multicolored 27.50
Wheellock Piano, litho illus 10.00

Stoves and Ranges

Dixon's Stove Polish, child listening to watch 7.50
Florence Oil Stoves, restaurant kitchen scene 40.00
Glenwood Ranges & Heaters, pretty girl in hat 7.50
Gold Coin & Gold Medal Stoves & Ranges, litho illus .   15.00
Happy Thought Range, diecut, jelly-roll shape 7.50
Jewel Stoves, litho illus 17.50
Monarch Vapor Ranges, diecut, loaf of bread shape ...   45.00
Rising Sun Stove Polish, folder 20.00

Thread and Sewing

Clarks ONT Thread, boy fishing 10.00
De Long Hook and Eye, Eclipses Everything, Columbus showing Indians eclipse 32.00
Domestic Sewing Machine, father playing with children   15.00
Eureka Silk, girl having tea party 10.00
Merrick's Thread, hot-air balloon, In Search of the North Pole 10.00
New Home Sewing Machine, dogs chasing man 15.00
Packards Sewing Machine Needles, case photo pasted on card 17.50
Singer Sewing Machines, women seated at sewing machine, children having tea party, 1889, folder 25.00
Standard Sewing Machine, woman playing croquet ...   15.00
Wheeler & Wilson, delivery of sewing machine by horse and buggy, full color, black and white illus on back with adv, horizontal 15.00
Williamatic Thread, The People's Favorite Hobby 17.50

Tobacco

Capadura Cigar, comical jockey illus 10.00
Clinton, Harry, Tobacco Dealer, children holding king cigar, man smoking 12.00
Horsehead Tobacco, horse's head, plug in mouth 10.00
Keisey's Cigars, soldiers 7.50
King Bull 3¢ Cigar, risqué metamorphic, diecut opening, adv on back 35.00
Liggett & Meyers 35.00
Newspaper Plug, Where is Mother, five puppies 7.50

Old Judge Cigarettes 12.00
Target Plug Tobacco, multicolored 35.00

AGATA GLASS

History: Agata glass was invented in 1887 by Joseph Locke of the New England Glass Company, Cambridge, Massachusetts.

Agata glass was produced by coating a piece of peachblow glass with metallic stain, spattering the surface with alcohol, and firing. The resulting high-gloss, mottled finish looked like oil droplets floating on a watery surface. Shading usually ranged from opaque pink to dark rose, although pieces in a pastel opaque green also exist. A few pieces have been found in a satin finish.

Bowl
   5" d, 2½" h, ruffled, peachblow, uniform oil spot dec   770.00
   5¼" d, 3" h, ruffled, deep peachblow, allover bright blue oil spots staining 750.00
   8" w, 4" h, green opaque, agata staining, gold etching, minor wear to staining 1,150.00
Celery Vase, 6½" h, crimped top, peachblow, agata staining, gold trim 1,750.00
Creamer, 3¾" h, 5" w, green opaque, deep blue staining, gold trim 1,450.00
Finger Bowl, 5¼" d, 2⅝" h, deep raspberry shading to creamy pink, allover gold mottling, blue accents ...   995.00
Lemonade Tumbler, 5⅛" h, 2½" d top, 1⅜" d base, peachblow, pronounced mottling, gold tracery 1,250.00
Mug, 2¼" h, green opaque, agata stain, applied handle   300.00
Pitcher, 7½" h, 6½" w, deep wild rose shading to white, gold staining, blue spots, applied reeded shell handle with staining 2,750.00
Plate, 6⅝" d, ribbon candy fluted rim, peachblow, agata staining, gold trim 850.00
Spooner, 4½" h, 2½" w, sq top, wild rose shading, agata staining, small areas of wear 850.00
Toothpick Holder, 2½" h, peachblow coloration, dark mottling, gold tracery, New England 685.00
Tumbler, 3¾" h, good pattern of spots 625.00

Juice Tumbler, 3¾" h, $625.00.

Vase, 7¾" h, lily, deep tricorn fold top, glossy peachblow, blue-gold ext. spotted dec extending to applied pedestal foot 1,265.00

AMBERINA GLASS

History: Joseph Locke developed Amberina glass in 1883 for the New England Glass Works. "Amberina," a trade name, describes a transparent glass which shades from deep ruby to amber. It was made by adding powdered gold to the ingredients for an amber-glass batch. A portion of the glass was reheated later to produce the shading effect. Usually it was the bottom which was reheated to form the deep red; however, reverse examples have been found.

Most early Amberina is flint-quality glass, blown or pattern molded. Patterns include Diamond Quilted, Daisy and Button, Venetian Diamond, Diamond and Star, and Thumbprint.

In addition to the New England Glass Works, the Mount. Washington Glass Company of New Bedford, Massachusetts, copied the glass in the 1880s and sold it at first under the Amberina trade name and later as "Rose Amber." It is difficult to distinguish pieces from these two New England factories. Boston and Sandwich Glass Works never produced the glass.

Amberina glass also was made in the 1890s by several Midwest factories, among which was Hobbs, Brockunier & Co. Trade names included "Ruby Amber Ware" and "Watermelon." The Midwest glass shaded from cranberry to amber, and the color resulted from the application of a thin flashing of cranberry to the reheated portion. This created a sharp demarcation between the two colors. This less-expensive version was the death knell for the New England variety.

In 1884 Edward D. Libbey was given the use of the trade name "Amberina" by the New England Glass Works. Production took place during 1900, but ceased shortly thereafter. In the 1920s Edward Libbey renewed production at his Toledo, Ohio, plant for a short period. The glass was of high quality.

Marks: Amberina made by Edward Libbey in the 1920s is marked "Libbey" in script on the pontil.

References: Gary Baker et al., *Wheeling Glass 1829–1939,* Oglebay Institute, 1994, distributed by Antique Publications; Kenneth Wilson, *American Glass 1760–1930,* 2 vols., Hudson Hill Press and The Toledo Museum of Art, 1994.

Reproduction Alert: Reproductions abound.

Additional Listings: Mount Washington.

Berry Set, 9" sq master bowl, ten 4⅞" sq individual bowls, Daisy and Button pattern, minor edge roughness, small flakes, some color variation, price for assembled 11-piece set **110.00**
Bowl
  4½" d, 2¼" h, tricorn, Venetian Diamond pattern .. **325.00**
  4½" d, 2¾" h, Swirl pattern, blue swirl bands, bell-tone flint, Mt Washington **295.00**
  4⅜" d, 2¾" h, Diamond Quilted pattern, rim chip, wear on base **90.00**
  5" l, 4½" w, 1½" h, oblong, slight ribs, Mt Washington **425.00**
Carafe, 9" h, 5" d, Venetian Diamond pattern, applied amber rigaree around neck, New England **750.00**
Celery Vase
  6½" h
    Diamond Quilted pattern **375.00**
    Optic Expanded Diamond pattern, New England **400.00**
  6¾" h, corset shape, flattened hobnail dec, Mt Washington **850.00**

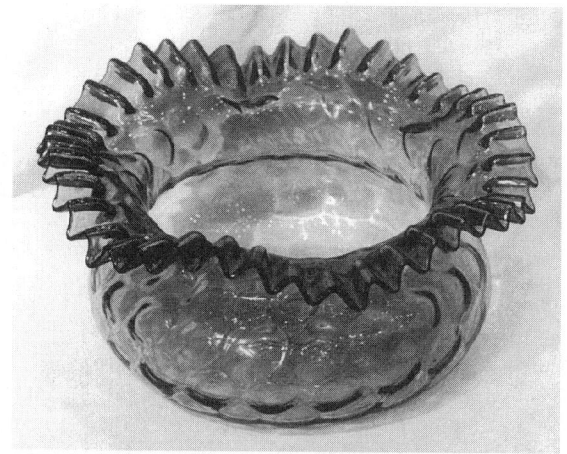

Bowl, Coin Spot pattern, flared hexagonal ruffled rim, 9" d, 4½" h, $600.00.

Centerpiece, 14" l, boat shape, Daisy and Button pattern, Hobbs Brockunier **950.00**
Cologne Bottle, 8½" h, honey amber color, nine optic panels, deep fuchsia neck and quatraform opening, color blushed on orig stopper, Libbey, #3041 .....**1,750.00**
Cracker Jar, 5" h, 5½" w, Joseph Locke, New England, cover missing **550.00**
Cream Pitcher, 4⅞" h, 3⅜" d, bulbous, evenly shaded, applied amber handle **145.00**
Cruet, deep colors, Inverted Thumbprint pattern, orig stopper, Mt Washington **425.00**
Dish, leaf shape, ftd, pressed, Gillander **1155.00**
Hair Receiver, 4½" d, 2" h, two piece, deep fuchsia shading to amber, partial Libbey label **1,750.00**
Jack-in-the-Pulpit Vase, 5" h, 5¾" d, shape #3014, 1917 Libbey signature on ground pontil **1,200.00**
Lamp Shade, gas type, 4" d, threaded **200.00**
Marmalade, cov, 5¼" h, Inverted Thumbprint pattern, white metal cov, Mt Washington **200.00**
Pickle Castor, Inverted Thumbprint pattern, silver plated frame marked "James Tufts," matching cov **395.00**
Pitcher
  4½" h, Coinspot pattern, enameled painted dec, reeded handle **250.00**
  5" h, Daisy and Button pattern, deep color, amber handle, Hobbs, Brockunier **425.00**
  6½" h, 6½" w, Inverted Thumbprint pattern, sq top, deep amber applied reeded handle, bell-tone flint, New England **475.00**
Posy Pot, 3" d, applied wishbone feet, berry pontil **300.00**
Punch Cup, 2½" h, 18 optic panels, New Enlgand **135.00**
Spooner
  4" h, Diamond Thumbprint pattern, petticoat shape, scalloped top, Mt Washington **850.00**
  4½" h, Optic Diamond Quilted pattern, New England **235.00**
Sugar Bowl, cov, 4¼" h, Inverted Thumbprint pattern, New England **375.00**
Toothpick Holder
  2¼" h, 1½" w, Baby Inverted Thumbprint pattern, sq top, New England **295.00**
  2⅜" h
    Diamond Quilted pattern, tricorn lip **220.00**

Optic Diamond Quilted pattern, squared top,
   New England 295.00

Tumbler

   3¾" h, Honeycomb pattern 75.00

   4" h, bell-tone flint, New England

      Herringbone pattern 145.00

      Venetian Diamond pattern 135.00

Vase

   6¾" h, fuchsia roll-down lip, Optic Diamond pattern,

      pale amber body 485.00

   7½" h, cylindrical, elongated Thumbprint pattern .. 175.00

   8½" h, corset shape, 1" wide turned down brim,

      twelve optic panels, Libbey, shape #3010, 1917,

      sgd in pontil 1,475.00

   11½" h, Thumbprint pattern, applied colorless rigaree

      and flower, minor chips and damage to rigaree . 275.00

   15" h, lily shape, sgd "Libbey" 850.00

AMBERINA GLASS, PLATED

History: The New England Glass Company, Cambridge, Massachusetts, first made Plated Amberina in 1886; Edward Libbey patented the process for the company in 1889.

Plated Amberina was made by taking a gather of chartreuse or cream opalescent glass, dipping it in Amberina, and working the two, often utilizing a mold. The finished product had a deep amber to deep ruby red shading, a fiery opalescent lining, and often vertical ribbing for enhancement. Designs ranged from simple forms to complex pieces with collars, feet, gilding, and etching.

A cased Wheeling glass of similar appearance had an opaque white lining but is not opalescent and does not have a ribbed body.

Bowl, 8" d, 3½" d, excellent coloration, dark mahogany
   top border, 12 dark mahogany vertical stripes alternating with 12 vertical opalescent fuchsia clear
   stripes, off-white casing 7,500.00

Creamer, squatty, applied clear amber handle 3,300.00

Cruet, 6¼" h, deeply ribbed, trefoil top, amber handle,
   amber faceted stopper 3,950.00

Pitcher, 7½" h, 6½" w, deep ruby shading to amber,
   oyster white lining, blue highlights, 12 vertical ribs,
   applied amber handle 7,200.00

Tumbler, 3¾", $1,900.00.

Salt Shaker, ribbed 900.00

Spooner, 4" h, paneled, ground pontil 2,000.00

Tumbler, 4" h, deep fuchsia shading to ruby to amber,
   opal white lining 950.00

Vase, 3¼" h, bulbous 2,550.00

AMPHORA

History: The Amphora Porcelain Works was one of several pottery companies located in the Teplitz-Turn region of Bohemia in the late 19th and early 20th centuries. It is best known for art pottery, especially Art Nouveau and Art Deco pieces.

Marks: Several markings were used, including the name and location of the pottery and the Imperial mark, which included a crown. Prior to World War I, Bohemia was part of the Austro-Hungarian Empire, so the word "Austria" may appear as part of the mark. After World War I the word "Czechoslovakia" may be part of the mark.

Additional Listings: Teplitz.

Basket, 9½" w, 5½" h, oval, roses dec 225.00

Bust, 12" h, 7" h, woman, 18th C garb, brown, gold, rust,
   and pink, sgd "Turn Wien Ew Depose" and "made
   in Austria," some roughage 350.00

Ewer, 13" h, matte gold sponged ground, matte mauve
   molded water lily handle and top 1,500.00

Figure, 17½" h, peasant woman carrying baskets, tan and
   brown, marked "Amphora, Austria" 595.00

Pitcher, 6¼" h, four brown figural chicks on base, pink
   and green jewels, matte ground, figural rooster's head
   spout, tan, green, and dark green enamels 165.00

Planter, 12½" l, 11" h, boy wearing short pants, coral
   cap, basket on ground 600.00

Plaque, 12½" h, figural, maiden with flowing hair, peering through cabbage head, cream, green, and purple
   glaze, gilt highlights, imp "Amphora, 1720/9," red
   printed mark "Turn-Teplitz-Bohemia," inscribed "Ed.
   Stellmacher," chips to leaf ledges, c1900 ....1,500.00

Vase

   5½" h, stork, green, blue, and orange enamels, mottled tan ground, back bands at top and base, two
      small handles 145.00

   6½" h, multicolored raised parrot, cobalt blue top and
      base bands, blue dot and flower border, mottled
      beige satin ground, two small rim handles, marked
      "Capina," imp "Austria, Amphora" 200.00

   7" h, brown incised dec, light tan ground, eight blue,
      red, and green circular jewels on neck band, four
      large oval jewels below, enameled red and green
      ovals, cobalt blue foot and neck, marked "Amphora Made in Czechoslovakia" 100.00

   10" h, rose, green, and blue jeweled matte shell design 95.00

   10¼" h , brick red irises, green leaves, gold outlines,
      turquoise beading, cream shaded to beige ground,
      serpent handles, fluted rim 220.00

   12" h, woman holding seeds in apron, leaning on

Vase, pink roses, green shaded ground, imp crown and Amphora marks, minor chips on roses, 11" h, $320.00.

tree-trunk vase, man holding firewood and lantern, pastel colors, 1903, price for facing pr **750.00**

17½" h, baluster, blue green, applied foliage **165.00**

20" h, bulbous ovoid body, incised dec, large condor fronting band of intertwining vines, pendent grape cluster, geometric borders, dark blue, medium blue, green, brown, tan, purple, and pink, printed mark ''Czechoslovakia, Amphora, 813,'' c1925 .**1,725.00**

Wall Pocket, 9" h, blue band with flowers, basketweave ground **120.00**

ANIMAL COLLECTIBLES

History: The representation of animals in fine arts, decorative arts, and on utilitarian products dates back to antiquity. Some religions endowed certain animals with mystical properties. Authors throughout written history used human characteristics when portraying animals.

Glass has been a popular material in making animal-related collectibles. Dishes with an animal-theme cover were fashionable in the early 19th century. In the years between World Wars I and II, glass manufacturers such as Fostoria Glass Company and A. H. Heisey & Company created a number of glass animal figures for the novelty and decorative-accessory markets. In the 1950s and early 1960s, a second glass-animal craze swept America led by companies such as Duncan & Miller and New Martinsville-Viking Glass Company. A third craze struck in the early 1980s when companies such as Boyd Crystal Art Glass, Guernsey Glass, Pisello Art Glass, and Summit Art Glass began offering the same animal figure in a wide variety of collectible glass colors, with some colors in limited production.

The formation of collectors' clubs and marketing crazes, e.g., flamingo, pig, and penguin, during the 1970s increased the popularity of this collecting field.

References: Elaine Butler, *Poodle Collectibles of the 50's & 60's*, L-W Book Sales, 1995; Diana Callow et al., *The Charlton Price Guide to Beswick Animals*, The Charlton Press, 1994; Jean Dale, *The Charlton Standard Catalogue of Royal Doulton Animals*, The Charlton Press, 1994; ———, *The Charlton Standard Catalogue*

of Royal Doulton Beswick Storybook Figurines, The Charlton Press, 1994; Marbena Jean Fyke, *Collectible Cats*, Book I (1993, 1995 value update), Book II (1996), Collector Books; Lee Garmon and Dick Spencer, *Glass Animals of the Depression Era*, Collector Books, 1993; Everett Grist, *Covered Animal Dishes*, Collector Books, 1988, 1993 value update; Frank L. Hahn and Paul Kikeli, *Collector's Guide to Heisey and Heisey By Imperial Glass Animals*, Golden Era Publications, 1991; Todd Holmes, *Boyd Glass Workbook*, published by author, 1992; Jan Lindenberger, *501 Collectible Horses*, Schiffer Publishing, 1996.

Periodicals: *Boyd Crystal Art Glass Newsletter*, PO Box 127, 1203 Morton Ave, Cambridge, OH 43725; *Canine Collector's Companion*, PO Box 2948, Portland, OR 97208; *Collieactively Speaking*, 428 Philadelphia Rd, Joppa, MD 21085 *Collie Courier*, 428 Philadelphia Rd, Joppa, MD 21085; *Hobby Horse News*, 5492 Tallapoosa Rd, Tallahassee, FL 32303; *Jody & Darrell's Glass Collectibles Newsletter*, PO Box 180833, Arlington, TX 76096; *Jumbo Jargon*, 1002 West 25th St, Erie, PA 16502; *MOOsletter*, 240 Wahl Ave, Evans City, PA 16033; *TRR Pony Express*, 71 Aloha Circle, Little Rock, AR 72120.

Collectors' Clubs: Boyd Art Glass Collectors Guild, PO Box 52, Hatboro, PA 19040; Canine Collectibles Club of America, Suite 314, 736 N Western Ave, Lake Forest, IL 60045; Cat Collectors, 33161 Wendy Dr, Sterling Heights, MI 48310; Folk Art Society of America, PO Box 17041, Richmond, VA 23226; Frog Pond, PO Box 193, Beech Grove, IN 46107; National Elephant Collector's Society, 380 Medford St, Somerville, MA 02145; Wee Scots, Inc., PO Box 1512, Columbus, IN 47202.

Museums: American Kennel Club, New York, NY; American Saddle Horse Museum Assoc, Lexington, KY; Dog Museum, St Louis, MO; Frog Fantasies Museum, Eureka Springs, AR; International Museum of the Horse, Lexington, KY; Stradling Museum of the Horse, Patagonia, AZ.

Additional Listings: See specific animal collectible categories in *Warman's Americana & Collectibles*.

Advisor: Jocelyn C. Mousley.

Note: Prices for glass animal figures are for the colorless variety unless otherwise noted.

Barnyard

Animal Covered Dish, hen on nest, 4¾" l, pottery, brown and white **135.00**

Ashtray, two pigs with sheet music, heart shape, marked ''Germany'' **65.00**

Bank, pig, pottery

Brown and white sponging, cream ground, 6" l **135.00**

Corky Pig, pink, Hull **70.00**

Calendar, 15 × 29", Squire's Arlington Pork, pig in center with cornstalks, 1932, matted and framed, some months missing **175.00**

Candy Container, papier-mâché

Hen, gray, chick on each side, bottom closure **85.00**

Rooster **225.00**

Clicker, pig, blue and white, marked ''O.I.C.'' **17.50**

Cookie Jar, gray donkey with cart **425.00**

Diecut, figural, cow, various colors and sizes, DeLaval Cream Separator adv on reverse of each, price for 8 pc set **660.00**

Display, 24" h, figural, rooster, Weatherbird Shoes, plaster of paris, multicolored, breast reads "weatherized, leather Bird Shoes," top feather cracking **495.00**

Doorstop, cast iron, ram, flat sided, worn polychrome repair, 7¼" h **300.00**

Figure
    Bull, frosted glass, Lalique **250.00**
    Chickens, hen and rooster, carved wood, old patina, red painted detail, bead eyes, 6½" h, pr **440.00**
    Pig, Staffordshire, 3" h, 1950 .... **45.00**
    Rabbit, sewer pipe, seated, 10" l, initialed "R.L." .. **445.00**

Figure, Battersea enamel, blue speckled head, rose breast, green, purple, red, black, yellow, and green wings, dec on base with bird, dandelion, marked, 2½ × 1½ × 2½", $3,650.00.

Inkwell, pink pig sitting on top, green well **85.00**

Painting, oil on canvas
    4 × 5½", Ducks and Ducklings at the Water's Edge, and Hens and Chicks by the Barn Door, Carl Jutz, both sgd "C Jutz," large period frames, price for pr **25,300.00**
    18¼ x 24", Shepherd with Flock, Anton Mauve (1838–1888), sgd lower left **3,000.00**
    20 × 24", Girl with Sheep in a Landscape, Levi Wells Prentice (1851–1935), sgd lower left **2,900.00**
    32 × 44", barn scene, sgd "Bahguant" **715.00**

Pin, rooster, large green painted tail, Bakelite **400.00**

Pinback Button, 1¾" d, Aberdeen Angus, black and white center photo of bull, rim inscribed for Denison, IA breeder, c1900 .... **20.00**

Poster, 17 × 26", Kellogg & Bulkeley Co. Egg Food, Hartford, CT, workers at egg farm loading cartons onto train, others packing, framed **715.00**

Salt and Pepper Shakers, pr
    Pigs, pink, Kreiss **20.00**
    Roosters, Watt Pottery **450.00**

Salt, master, two pigs alongside bucket, stamped "Made in Germany" **50.00**

Shooting Gallery Figure, 6½" h, donkey, cast steel **195.00**

Tape Measure, celluloid, hen and chicks **40.00**

Toothpick Holder, chick with wishbone and egg, SP .. **65.00**

Toy
    Donkey, pull, stuffed, amber velvet body, glass eyes, black mohair tail and mane, tin wheels, wooden base, 13" l **300.00**

Sheep, wood and papier-mâché, white wool coat, ribbon collar, 6" h, marked "Germany" **165.00**

Wall Pocket, rooster, white ground, red, blue, green, and yellow spray glaze, Morton Pottery **20.00**

Weather Vane
    13¼" h, rooster, sheet steel cutout, old white repaint, wooden base **140.00**
    21" h, rooster, copper, gilt, and verdigris surface, trace of old dark red paint, c19th C **1,955.00**

Windmill Weight, bull, cast iron
    13" h, 14¼" w, Hanchett Bull, full bodied, two-part casting, rough finished edges, repainted, one horn replaced, made by Simpson Company Fairbury, Nebraska **495.00**
    18" h, old red and white repaint, raised letters "Fairbury, Nebr" **990.00**

Birds

Andirons, 14" h, cast iron, copper wash, owls perched on branch, yellow glass eyes, c1920 .... **145.00**

Ashtray, 8" l, brass and steel, figural bird shape, cigar cutter and match holder **140.00**

Bank, cast iron, 5" h
    Goose, standing, traces of old gold paint **85.00**
    Owl, "Be Wise Save Money," worn gold paint **95.00**

Bookends, pr
    5¼" h, pelicans, brass, stylized, marked "Hagenauer" **45.00**
    5½" h, rook, lavender, marked "Rookwood Pottery," shape 2275, c1920 .... **435.00**

Calendar Plate, owl on open book, Berlin, NE, 1912 .. **35.00**

Cane Handle, 5½" l, wood, carved bird's head, ivory beak, glass eyes **55.00**

Doorstop, cast iron
    Duck **150.00**
    Parrot on perch in ring **155.00**

Chocolate Mold, duck, clamp and hinge, marked "Germany" **70.00**

Figure
    Blue Jay, porcelain, Kaiser **95.00**
    Cardinal, Pennsbury Pottery, #120 .... **225.00**
    Ducks, incised Steuben signature, price for pr **385.00**
    Goose, glass
        Duncan Miller, fat, crystal **180.00**
        Heisey, wings down **225.00**
    Owl, Howard Pierce **35.00**
    Scarlet Tanager, Pennsbury Pottery, #104R **245.00**
    Swan, New Martinsville, glass, large **40.00**

Lamp, table, 14¾" h, figural, wrought iron and glass, egret poised on one leg, reticulated body, blue and white translucent glass with metallic inclusions, pyramid base, black/gray marble plinth, iron sgd "Chapelle Nancy," glass inscribed "Muller Freres Luneville" **9,000.00**

Music Box, bird in cage, wind-up, marked "Gesch" .. **325.00**

Mustard Jar, cov, owl, milk glass, screw top, glass insert, Atterbury **165.00**

Napkin Ring, owl sitting on stump, Nippon China **225.00**

Pitcher, 14" h, duck, glass and pewter, hinged mouth, scroll work wings **450.00**

Sculpture, 26" h, blown glass, exotic bird on platform perch, gold-flecked blue and white **230.00**

Stein, Bibite on shield held between claws, Mettlach
#2036 .... **950.00**
Toy, pull, duck, colorful felt, cast iron wheels, button
eyes, Steiff, button on foot, minor wear and moth
repair **330.00**
Vase, 9″ h, molded macaws among berried branches,
ovoid, amber frosted glass, molded ''R Lalique,
France,'' inscribed ''France'' **8,500.00**
Wall Pocket, mallard duck in flight, naturalistic colors,
Morton Pottery **12.00**
Watch Fob, figural brass owl, braided human hair chain **125.00**

Cats

Advertising Mirror, White Cat Union Suits, oval **35.00**
Bank, Goebel **25.00**
Bench, 25″ l, poplar, old worn white and black paint,
ends cut out as cat silhouettes with arched backs, cat
faces applied to front edge, some edge damage **330.00**
Candy Container, papier-mâché **60.00**
Doorstop, bisque, Siamese **40.00**
Figure
4 × 6″, Siamese, Brad Keeler **50.00**
5¾″ h, sewer pipe, seated, hand tooling **770.00**
7″ l, sewer pipe, sleeping, hand tooling **340.00**
Letter Holder, Holt Howard **70.00**
Netsuke, 1¼″ h, Japanese, Good Luck cat, painted black
spots, red ribbon **150.00**
Painting, 10½ × 9½″, oil on board, unidentified artist,
kittens and puppies in tub, framed **330.00**
Plate, 6″ d, blue border, Siamese kitten in center **35.00**
Print, 15½ × 19½″, My Little White Kittens Taking the
Cake, Currier and Ives, C4338, stains and tears in
margins, framed **225.00**
String Holder, figural
Marked ''Holt Howard'' **50.00**
Marked ''Made in England'' **45.00**
Tape Measure, brass, circular, emb cat's head, glass
eyes, c1910 .... **85.00**
Toothpick Holder, winking type, Enesco **20.00**
Toy, 12″ l, rag type, dark brown velvet, glass eyes, em-
broidered features **70.00**
Vase, cat's head, Lefton China **50.00**

Dogs

Cookie Jar, Dalmatian, McCoy **50.00**
Doorstop, cast iron
Bulldog, full bodied, orig polychrome paint, marked
''LAGS,'' some wear **220.00**
French Bull Terrier, full bodied, old black and white
paint, normal wear **190.00**
German Shepherd, facing forward, Hubley **125.00**
Setter, Hubley **150.00**
Engraving, 12 × 17″, wolfhound, engraved ''Columbian
Expo'' seal, George Barrier **200.00**
Figure
Ceramic
Airedale, Erphila **45.00**
Dachshund, Royal Doulton **100.00**
German Shepherd, Royal Dux **45.00**
Pekinese, Royal Doulton **55.00**

**Pipe Rack, terrier, painted plaster, rock-
style base, wood standard and pipe holder,
metal label ''King, NY,'' 7⅞″ h, $40.00.**

Spaniel, 13″ h, seated, red and white polychrome,
Staffordshire, price for pr **495.00**
Chalk
Nipper, 4″ h, marked ''Victor,'' c1930 .... **125.00**
Spaniel, 5¼″ h, seated, oval yellow base, black
and white, red collar, price for pr **220.00**
Spaniel Type, 7½″ h, worn orig yellow, red, and
black paint **220.00**
Plaster, German Shepherd, 12″ h, Rin-Tin-Tin, mul-
ticolored **75.00**
Humidor, glass panels, raised dogs on leather cov **80.00**
Napkin Ring, figural, SP **35.00**
Nutcracker, 12″ l, cast iron, Harper Co, Chicago, base
reads ''Dog Tray Nutcracker,'' some paint loss **85.00**
Painting, watercolor on paper, matted and framed
14½ × 17½″, English Setter on Point, sgd ''Edm. H.
Osthaus,'' and ''Vivian Nov. 21st, '97'' **605.00**
29¾″ × 25¾″, Irish Setter, sgd ''Will Rannells,'' mat-
ted and framed **300.00**
Paperweight, Hubley
French Bulldog **50.00**
Sealyham **40.00**
Pin, figural, Scotties, Bakelite **75.00**
Pin Box, 3¼″ d, porcelain, greyhound on pillow, flowers,
polychrome enamel dec, gilt trim, Staffordshire **110.00**
Place-Card Holder, Pekinese, Hubley **125.00**
Plaque, 5″ sq, bronze, Dachshund Club of America, sgd
''K. Lane'' **95.00**
Rug, 40 × 49″, hooked yarn, landscape with two dogs,
stream, blue, green, brown, white, some wear and
fading, light stains **550.00**
Peanut Butter Pail, 3½″ h, W Clark, multicolored tin
litho, dog sled and Canadian snow scene, minor
scratches and dents **245.00**
Sign, 11½ × 5″, Segars Bulldog, John Merriam's Bulldog
painting, pressed cardboard, brass plate on gold
frame **470.00**
Sprinkling Bottle, Poodle **120.00**
Stuffed Toy, 24″ h, gray and white, glass eyes, ride or

Teapot, marked "Made in China," 9¾" l, 6¾" h, $45.00.

push type, tubular steel frame, red paint, rubber wheels, wood footrests, marked "Northern Ireland"   **165.00**
Teapot, Dachshund, Erphila **98.00**
Toy, wood and papier-mâché, white woolly coat, fur tail, glass eyes, ribbon collar, basket in mouth, marked "Germany" **330.00**

Horses

Bank, 4¼" h, cast iron, horse, horseshoe, Buster Brown, and Tige, marked "Buster Brown Good Luck" worn gold and bronze paint **150.00**
Catalog, Smith Sons Harness Co, Buffalo, NY, c1915, 95 pages, 9 × 12¼", high-grade horse collars, harness, whips, bells, blankets, etc **56.00**
Cigarette Lighter, 7" h, table type, figural, horse's head, ceramic, marked "Japan" **30.00**
Figure, glass, amber, Heisey type, unmarked, 5" h **165.00**
Match Safe, figural
   Horse's Head **295.00**
   Horse's Hoof **295.00**
Painting, 16 × 20", oil on canvas, Crickmore/Portrait of a Race Horse and Jockey, Henry Stull, sgd lower left, titled on reverse with horse's pedigree, craquelure, framed **4,025.00**
Poster
   12 × 20", Donaldson Fair, Newport, KY, sulkies racing down stretch, matted and framed **175.00**
   18 × 24", Golden Tonic, black and white, text and horse illus **75.00**
Print, 12" w, 16¼" h, Our Pony, Kellogg & Bulkeley, hand-colored litho, curly-maple beveled frame, old alligatored varnish finish **110.00**
Sign, 19 × 22", Vacuum Oil Co, Jay Eye See, sulky with rider, paper, matted and framed, c1884 ....   **55.00**
Weather Vane, 9¼" h, tin, full bodied, traces of old paint   **45.00**
Windmill Weight, 17½" h, cast iron, emb "Dempster"   **330.00**

Wild Animals

Bank
   Brass, bear with pig, 5¼" h **110.00**
   Cast Iron
      Bear with honey pot, Hubley **240.00**
      Lion, standing, worn gold paint, 5¼" h **70.00**

Bottle Opener, figural, elephant **85.00**
Bucket, advertising, Schepp's Cocoanut, yellow and black monkeys, emb tin lid, 3¾" h **140.00**
Chocolate Mold, tin, two-piece type
   Bear, tin clips, 9" h **220.00**
   Elephant, 8" l **275.00**
Creamer, elephant, Shawnee **35.00**
Figure
   Bisque, elephant, Royal Dux **45.00**
   Brass, giraffe, 18" h, pr **85.00**
   Ceramic
      Elephant, trunk up, Royal Dux **145.00**
      Hippo, lavender, three mushrooms dec **120.00**
   Porcelain
      Lion, 3½" h, amber, green, and brown **45.00**
      Polar Bear, mother and cub, Bing & Grondahl ..   **95.00**
      Zebra, Staffordshire **275.00**
   Pottery, lion, 9½" l, clay, old pale green paint, rect base **250.00**
Napkin Ring, figural, fox, SP **35.00**
Nodder, monkey, papier-mâché, Victorian dress, 11" h   **295.00**
Pitcher, monkey, 10" h, figural, majolica **495.00**
Planter, bear, 8" d, Kay Finch **165.00**
Shoehorn, 14" l, lion's head, brass **85.00**
Sprinkler Bottle, elephant, pink and gray **95.00**
Tape Measure, kangaroo, baby's head on pull tab **95.00**
Toy, monkey, 17" h, Yes-No, Schuco **450.00**
Vase, 2½" h, spherical cameo glass, waisted flared neck, burnt orange frosted ground, enameled black cougar, foliate neck dec, engraved "Daum Nancy" **2,500.00**

ARCHITECTURAL ELEMENTS

History: Architectural elements, many of which are handcrafted, are those items which have been removed or salvaged from buildings, ships, or gardens. Part of their desirability is due to the fact that it would be extremely costly to duplicate the items today.

Beginning about 1840 decorative building styles began to feature carved wood and stone, stained glass, and ornate ironwork. At the same time, builders and manufacturers also began to use fancy doorknobs, doorplates, hinges, bells, window locks, shutter pulls, and other decorative hardware as finishing touches to elaborate new homes and commercial buildings.

Hardware was primarily produced from bronze, brass, and iron, and doorknobs also were made from clear, colored, and cut glass. Highly ornate hardware began appearing in the late 1860s and remained popular through the early 1900s. Figural pieces that featured animals, birds, and heroic and mythological images were very popular, as were ornate and very graphic designs that complimented the many architectural styles that emerged in the late 19th century.

Fraternal groups, government and educational institutions, and individual businesses all ordered special hardware for their buildings. Catalogs from the era show hundreds of patterns, often with a dozen different pieces available in each design.

The current trends of preservation and recycling of architectural elements has led to the establishment and growth of organized salvage operations that specialize in removal and resale of elements. Special auctions are now held to sell architectural elements from churches, mansions, office buildings, etc. Today's decorators often design an entire room around one architectural element, such as a Victorian marble bar or mural, or use several as key accent pieces.

References: Ronald S. Barlow (comp.), *Victorian Houseware, Hardware and Kitchenware,* Windmill Publishing, 1991; Margarete Baur-Heinhold, *Decorative Ironwork,* Schiffer Publishing, 1996; Len Blumin, *Victorian Decorative Art,* available from ADCA (PO Box 126, Eola, IL 60519), n.d.; Michael Breza and Craig R. Olson (eds.), *Identification and Dating of Round Oak Heating Stoves,* Southwestern Michigan College Museum (58900 Cherry Grove Rd, Dowagiac, MI 49047), 1995; Maude Eastwood wrote several books about doorknobs which are available from PO Box 126, Eola, IL 60519; Constance M Greiff, *Early Victorian,* Abbeville Press, 1995; J. L. Mott Iron Works, *Mott's Illustrated Catalog of Victorian Plumbing Fixtures for Bathrooms and Kitchens,* Dover Publications, 1987; J. P. White's Pyghtle Works, Bedford, England, *Garden Furniture and Ornament,* Apollo Books, 1987; Philip G. Knobloch, *A Treasure of Fine Construction Design,* Astragal Press, 1995; Henrie Martinie, *Art Deco Ornamental Ironwork,* Dover Publications, 1996; James Massey and Shirley Maxwell, *Arts & Crafts,* Abbeville Press, 1995; Ted Menten (comp.), *Art Nouveau Decorative Ironwork,* Dover Publications, n.d.; *Ornamental French Hardware Designs,* Dover Publications, 1995; Alan Robertson, *Architectural Antiques,* Chronicle Books, 1987; Edward Shaw, *The Modern Architect* (reprint), Dover Publications, 1996; *Turn of the Century Doors, Windows and Decorative Millwork,* Dover Publications, 1995 reprint.

Periodical: *American Bungalow,* PO Box 756, Sierra Madre, CA 91204.

Collectors' Club: Antique Doorknob Collectors of America, Inc, PO Box 126, Eola, IL 60519.

Additional Listings: Stained Glass.

Advisor: Web Wilson.

SPECIAL AUCTION

Web Wilson Antique Hardware Auction
PO Box 506
Portsmouth, RI 02871
(800) 508-0022

Arch, 96 × 206″, Eastlake, cornice, dentils, anthemion-leaf brackets, incised panels, fluted columns, paneled base 475.00
Architectural Ornament
    35¼ × 38¾″, Art Deco, cast aluminum scene of farmer sharpening scythe, plate-glass mirror backing 900.00
    68″ l, eagle, cast iron, orig finish, spread wings, perched on half-globe base, cemetery gate type, American, c1870 .... 4,000.00
Barber Pole, 64″ h, turned wood, half round, layers of old polychrome paint, wear and age cracks 250.00
Barn Door, 39½ × 71″, pine, three boards, two wide battens, orig wrought-iron strap hinges, midsection with seven slots cut with curved scallop, traces of old red paint, PA 10.00

Catalog
    American Carving & Mfg Co, Grand Rapids, MI, 1906, 129 pgs, 9¼″ × 12″, Catalog No. 14, fancy carvings and moldings 110.00
    Berger Bros Co, Philadelphia, PA, 1919, 192 pgs, 6 × 9″, Catalog No. 7, tinners and roofers supplies 55.00
    Hyde-Murphy Co, Ridgway, PA, 1911, 22 pgs, 4 × 8″, The Acme of Beauty In Design & Finish, half-tones, tinted door styles, millwork 20.00
    Iroquois Door Co, Buffalo, NY, 1915, 44 pgs, 6¼ × 9¼″, Catalog No. 414, front doors, vestibule doors, French doors 35.00
    Sears, Roebuck & Co, Chicago, IL, 1929, 120 pgs, 8½ × 11″, printed wrapper, Honor Built Modern Homes, sepia perspective and int., floor plans .. 50.00
Ceiling Medallion, 31″ d, plaster, acanthus leaf dec ... 100.00
Doorbell Pull, cut glass, tapered shank, 1¾″ d 55.00
Doorknob
    Board of Education, City of Chicago, 2¼″ d 65.00
    Brocade pattern, Corbin, fine knurling on edges, 2½″ d, c1884 .... 35.00
    Glass
        Mercury, well-turned pewter base, rosette dated 1872, 2¼″ d 70.00
        Root Beer colored, European-sized shank, 2¾″ d 65.00
    Knight's head, reeded rim dec, attributed to Mallory Wheeler, minor oxidation, c1880, 2½″ d 180.00
    Statue of Liberty, c1910, 2¼″ d 225.00
    Treasury Seal, large, straight shank 120.00
    YMCA, c1910 .... 25.00

Doorknob, bronze, plumed knight, marked "Mfd By Metal Comp Cast Co.– R. E. Mfg Co. Sole Agt's" on reverse, $660.00. Photograph courtesy of Web Wilson Antique Hardware Auction.

Doorknob and Matching Plate, Christensen pattern, Russell & Erwin, 1899, 10 × 2¼″ plate, 2¼″ d knob, price for set 700.00
Door Peephole, 6½ × 3¼″ plate, 3½″ peep hole, Art Deco style, c1920 .... 65.00
Doorplate, Aesthetic Movement style, emb bluebirds, butterflies, and bamboo, 8½ × 2″, price for pr 95.00
Floor Screen, 69¾″ w, 53″ h, handblocked, three panels, figural putti holding floral vine and urn on each panel, classical portrait bust medallion dec plinth, Defossee & Karth, Paris, c1860 .... 650.00

Garden Furniture, suite, c1850, settee 47½" l, $935.00. Photograph courtesy of Neal Auction Company.

Fountain Ornament, 18" l, bronze, figural Art Nouveau winged nymph standing over spigot opening, back cast with single tulip framed by morning glories, cast from model by G Obiois, sgd in bronze, tag inscribed "E Biot Paris Vrai Bronze" 675.00

Garden Furniture, cast iron
   Bench
      41" l, vintage design, geometric grill seat, worn and weathered white repaint, rusted bottom cross brace 110.00
      58" l, fern design, seat labeled "Mfg by the Kramer Bros Fdy Co Dayton, O," worn, weathered white repaint 880.00
   Chair, 29" h, vintage design, geometric grill seat, worn and weathered white repaint 85.00
   Table, 21" d, vintage design, worn and weathered white repaint 110.00

Garden Urn, cast iron
   17 × 34", rect base, open grill work panels, florentine handles 425.00
   28 × 20", scrolling branches, central face, Baltimore area, 19th C 700.00

Mantel, Renaissance, carved walnut, hidden panels and niches with carved conquistador surrounds, relief fascia, overmantel carved battle scenes depicting Norman Conquest 45,100.00

Paving Brick, 4⅞" w, hexagonal, star dec 25.00

Plaque, 24" d, brass, emb relief portraits of Rubens and Holbein, battered, minor repairs, dark patina 120.00

Sculpture Column, 40¼" h, alabaster, white, 11" sq top over ring-turned supports, circular graduated step-molded octagonal base, Victorian 425.00

Sun Dial, 13½" d, bronze, greenish black patina, Alexander S Calder 3,250.00

Staircase, Victorian, 21 steps, curved, newel post, 52 spindles 1,000.00

Towel Bar, jadite, pr 65.00

Traffic Light, 96½" h, cast-iron base, green metallic paint, some damage, wired as lamp 385.00

Wall Sconce, 13½" h, 5" d, gilt bronze, three sides with central panel of pierced rect devices, linear framework supporting rect green irid glass panels, cast cubes at each corner, stepped, rect wall bracket, Frank Lloyd Wright for Francis W Little House, Peoria, IL, c1902 .... 7,700.00

ART DECO

History: The Art Deco period was named after an exhibition, "l'Exposition Internationale des Arts Décorative et Industriels Modernes," held in Paris in 1927. Its beginnings succeed those of the Art Nouveau period, but the two overlap in time as well as in style.

Art Deco designs are angular with simple lines. This was the period of skyscrapers, movie idols, and the Cubist works of Picasso and Legras. Art Deco motifs were used for every conceivable object being produced in the 1920s and 1930s (ceramics, furniture, glass, and metals) not only in Europe but in America as well.

References: Victor Arwas, *Glass: Art Nouveau to Art Deco,* Rizzoli, 1977; Lillian Baker, *Art Nouveau & Art Deco Jewelry,* Collector Books, 1981, 1994 value update; Bryan Catley, *Art Deco and Other Figures,* Antique Collectors' Club, 1978; Alfred W. Edward, *Art Deco Sculpture and Metalware,* Schiffer Publishing, 1996; Tony Fusco, *Art Deco Identification and Price Guide,* Avon Books, 1993; Mary Gaston, *Collector's Guide to Art Deco,* Collector Books, 1989, 1994 value update; Steven Heller and Louise Fili, *Italian Art Deco: Graphic Design between the Wars,* Chronicle Books, 1993; ———, *Streamline: American Art Deco Graphic Design,* Chronicle Books, 1995; Francis Joseph, *Collecting Carlton Ware,* Francis Joseph Publications, 1994; Henrie Martinie, *Art Deco Ornamental Ironwork,* Dover Publications, 1996; Theodore Menten, *The Art Deco Style,* Dover Publications, n.d.; Francis Salmon, *Collecting Susie Cooper,* Francis Joseph Books, 1995; Wolf Uecker, *Art Nouveau and Art Deco Lamps and Candlesticks,* Abbeville Press, 1986; Howard and Pat Watson, *Collecting Art Deco Ceramics,* Kevin Francis, 1993.

Periodical: *The Echoes Report,* PO Box 2321, Mashpee, MA 02649.

Collectors' Clubs: Canadian Art Deco Society, #302-884 Bute St, Vancouver, British Columbia V6E 1YA Canada; Carlton Ware International, PO Box 161, Sevenoaks, Kent TN15 6GA England; Chase Collectors Society, 2149 W Jibsail Loop, Mesa, AZ 85202; International Coalition of Art Deco Societies, One Murdock Terrace, Brighton, MA 02135; Miami Design Preservation League, PO Bin L, Miami Beach, FL 33119; Twentieth Century Society, 70 Cowcross St, London EC1M 6DR England.

Museums: Art Institute of Chicago, Chicago, IL; Copper-Hewitt Museum, National Museum of Design, Smithsonian Institution, New York, NY; Corning Museum of Glass, Corning, NY; Jones

Museum of Glass and Ceramics, Sebago, ME; Virginia Museum of Fine Arts, Richmond, VA.

Additional Listings: Furniture and Jewelry. Also check glass, pottery, and metal categories.

Bookends, pr, dancing flappers, colorful, cold-painted
bronze **150.00**
Bowl, blue, silver rim, lotus flower shape, 1914, marked
"Bavaria" **55.00**
Box, 9½" l, steel, flowers, butterflies shaded gilt inlay,
hand-wrought feet, butterfly hinges, and clasp, inlay
partially covered with dark varnish **635.00**
Cake Server, silver, shaded blade, birds, scrolls, and festoons
dec, BR Hempel, Polish, 20th C **90.00**
Chandelier, 26" l, 15" d, six radiating chrome ribs with
gilded accents, base of six angular peach frosted glass
shield-shaped wing forms, trumpet-form ceiling cap
with stepped cone and ball at base, shades sgd in
cameo "Maynadier," French, c1930 ....**3,000.00**
Cigarette Case, 4¼" h, enameled and silver gilt, rect,
black ground, two red bands, white metal geometric
inlay, gilt int., inscribed, French **250.00**

Cigarette Box, two compartments, painted brass, red ground, black highlights, int. cigarette holder, ashtray insert, 7¼" l, 3½" w, 3" h, $65.00.

Clock, mantel
10½" h, rect case, gilt clock face, black painted Arabic
chapters, polished onyx steps, triangular gilt-edged
reserves, enameled red and black geometric
formation, French, c1925 ....**2,000.00**
14½" h, rect base, white and veined marble, diamond-shaped
face, Arabic chapters, mounted
bronze fox on haunches and crow perched in tree,
light brown patina, sgd "P Sega," French title
plaque **750.00**
Cocktail Set, chrome cocktail shaker, four matching
glasses with ruby bowls, chrome stems, price for set **50.00**
Cup
Danish silver, 2¾" h, cylindrical, waisted body,
slightly flaring everted lip, flat base, monogrammed,
Georg Jensen, c1925 .... **395.00**
Sterling silver, cov urn form, ribbed body and foot,
ivory finial, attributed to Erik Magnussen for Gorham,
10 oz, c1925, finial chipped **215.00**
Decanter, 13⅝" h, 4¼" d, amethyst, three sided, enam-

eled gold, brown, and red Art Deco designs, three-sided
spear-point stopper **110.00**
Dress, flapper style, heavily beaded, rosy beige, minor
damage **65.00**
Figure
12¼" h, nude dancer, bronze, cast from model by D
Charol, sgd **300.00**
29½" l, muscular male moving marble block with
pole, marble and black onyx base, sgd "Bezin" .**1,350.00**
Furniture
Armoire, 82½" h, rosewood veneer, silvered-bronze
mounts, mirrored, French **1,600.00**
Chair
Armchair, fireside type, embroidered cornucopia
with flowers, rose colored velvet upholstery,
36" h, price for pr **1,495.00**
Side, carved walnut, arched back, reeded fans,
bowed seat rail, reeded tapering cylindrical
legs, c1925, French, price for pr **750.00**
Suite, silvered bronze, 32" w, 19" d, 78" h domed-top
vitrine, conforming etched frosted glass panel,
single door opening to shelves, mirrored back; 35"
w, 14" d, 16" h coffee table, inset black glass top,
scroll feet; 35" w, 14" d, 85" h, domed mirrored
console, divided into beveled sections, floral and
scroll work¾ frame, half-round table, black glass
top, 2 scroll supports; framed mirror; 22" w, 12"
d, 46" h black plinth, rect top, sq standard continuing
to stair-step base **24,150.00**
Table, dining, 54" l, 22" d, 31" h, burled walnut,
double rect top, pedestal base, open geometric
design, American, c1930 ....**13,520.00**
Inkwell, 2¾" h, 14 k gold, glass inkwell with gold hinged
lid, sq gold platform, engine-turned parallel striated
lines, monogrammed, marked "William B Kerr, Newark,
NJ," retailed by Brand Chatilion Co, c1925 ... **375.00**
Lamp, 10½" h, 6½" d, woman standing by brass pole
topped by brass leaf, hanging brass mesh basket holds
orig clear glass candle cup, red glass jewels, bronzed
finish, round base, French **315.00**
Jug, pottery, marked "Charlotte Rhead"
5¾" h, multicolored leaf dec, gray ground, green trim **360.00**
9" h, 4¾" d, pottery, green bands, green and gold
leaves, mottled light gray ground **185.00**
Perfume Bottle, yellow, black triangles, deep rose, gold
lines blue base, clear neck **95.00**
Smoker's Set, SS, rect cigarette box, match box holder,
reed bar dec 9.5 troy oz **200.00**
Tea Caddy, 3¾" h, Danish silver, ovoid, waisted tapering
neck, Georg Jensen, c1925 .... **450.00**
Tea Service, SP, 6¾" h teapot, creamer, cov sugar, 17" l
rect tray with raised border, upright disc form, ebony
C–scroll handles, half-moon ebony finial, D-shaped
cov sugar, designed by Fjerdinngstad for Christofle,
price for 6-pc set **2,500.00**
Vanity Bag, mesh, goldtone, attached top with Art Deco
design **135.00**
Vase
5⅞" h, opalescent glass, ovoid, everted rim, molded
spike artichoke leaves from shoulder molded
"Muller" signature **175.00**
8¾" h, 5½" d, pottery, green bands, pink, blue, and

Vase, Longwy, yellow florals, blue ground, dark blue vertical stripes, 5½″ h, $250.00.

lavender spring flowers, green leaves, mottled
    light beige ground, marked "Charlotte Rhead" .. **200.00**
Wall Hanging, 34″ l, 12″ d, 36″ h, sheet bronze, Spanish
    galleon, wrought-iron frame and chair **4,600.00**

ART NOUVEAU

History: Art Nouveau is the French term for the "new art" which had its beginning in the early 1890s and continued for the next 40 years. The flowing and sensuous female forms used in this period were popular in Europe and America. Among the most recognized artists of this period were Gallé, Lalique, and Tiffany.

The Art Nouveau style can be identified by flowing, sensuous lines, florals, insects, and the feminine form. These designs were incorporated into almost everything produced during the period, from art glass to furniture, silver, and personal objects. Later wares demonstrate some of the characteristics of the evolving Art Deco style.

References: Victor Arwas, *Glass: Art Nouveau to Art Deco,* Rizzoli, 1977; Lillian Baker, *Art Nouveau & Art Deco Jewelry,* Collector Books, 1981, 1994 value update; Constance M Greiff, *Art Nouveau,* Abbeville Press, 1995; Ted Menten (comp.), *Art Nouveau Decorative Ironwork,* Dover Publications, n.d.; Bengt Nystrom, *Rorstrand Porcelain,* Abbeville Press, 1995; Albert Christian Revi, *American Art Nouveau Glass,* reprint, Schiffer Publishing, 1981; Wolf Uecker, *Art Nouveau and Art Deco Lamps and Candlesticks,* Abbeville Press, 1986; Roberta Waddell, *The Art Nouveau Style,* Dover Publications, n.d.; Kenneth Wilson, *American Glass 1760–1930,* 2 vols., Hudson Hill Press and The Toledo Museum of Art, 1994.

Museum: Virginia Museum of Fine Arts, Richmond, VA.

Additional Listings: Furniture and Jewelry. Also check glass, pottery, and metal categories.

Andirons, pr, gilt brass, scroll dec, bust of woman **750.00**
Basket, 11″, Kayserzinn pewter **195.00**
Bowl, SP rim and handles **85.00**
Bust, 9½″ h, bronze, style of Emmanuel Villanis, brown
    patina **300.00**

Candlesticks, pr
    5¾″ h, silver, Georg Jensen **4,600.00**
    12″ h, bronze, bobeche suspended on baluster tripod
        standard, leaf-form legs **750.00**
Carpet, 18′ 7″ × 14′, wool, beige field strewn with olive
    and tan scrolling designs, sgd "Victor Horta,"
    c1900 ....**19,550.00**
Chamberstick, Kayserzinn pewter, floral dec **85.00**
Clock
    14″ h, brass finish, girl with flowing hair, lotus blossom on front, sunburst, scrolls and leaf cutouts on
        each side, Warner, 1898–1904 ....**245.00**
    23¾″ h, bronze, figural, dark brown patina, inscribed
        "Marcel Debut 98," Siot foundry stamp, dated
        1898 ....**3,500.00**
Creamer and Sugar, gilt SS, floral and lead dec, vermeil
    int., 16 troy oz **295.00**
Dish, bronze, figural, maiden seated on edge of water
    lily blossom, sgd "Cahuzac" **325.00**
Dresser Set
    SP, 10½″ l hand mirror, hair brush, and comb, chased
        repousse, maiden in backless gown, long flowing
        tresses, wave scrolls and flowers border, Britannia
        Artistic Silver Co, Chicago, c1905, 3 pcs **195.00**
    SS, elaborate floral repousse, putti bearing fruit baskets, 9″ l handled brush, 7½″ comb, 7″ l hand
        brush, 11″ hand mirror, 4¼″ d powder jar, Gorham **900.00**
Figure
    8¾″ h, ivory, young nude woman, poised on right
        foot, drapery, ebony base, inscribed "R Middegaels," c1925 ....**2,950.00**
    22″ h, parcel gilt, silvered, and patinated bronze,
        partly draped figure seated on crescent moon, star
        on forehead, arms raised above head holding
        flowing robes, plinth base, inscribed "H Levasseur," plaque inscribed "Etoile du Berger Par Levasseur," c1900 ....**5,500.00**
Frame, 11½″ h, SS, arched crest, chased pendant husks,
    clusters of fruit, velvet cov back with easel support
    back, marked "Walker & Hall, Birmingham," 1911 **1,125.00**

Bookends, pr, cast metal, bronze, green finish, seated maidens, 7½″ h, $220.00.

Clock, white metal case, bronze finish, 1890 and 1894 patent dates, 8½", $85.00.

Fruit Stand, 12½" l, SS, wide floral and open-work re-
pousse sides, low foot, 22 troy oz 625.00
Furniture
  Bedroom Suite, 74" w × 56" h double-bed head-
    board and footboard inlaid with trumpet creeper,
    floral carved crest rails, carved whiplash borders,
    marble-topped dresser with carved mirror, pr of
    night tables, price for 5 pc set 7,900.00
  Cabinet, 30" w, 14" d, 54½" h, inlaid mahogany and
    various woods, brass, ornate galleried back,
    leaded door with inverted hearts, c1900 .... 875.00
  Chair, arm, Karpen Bros, mahogany, reed and tendril
    carved frame, undulating crest rail, high-relief
    carving of female heads and poppy blossoms,
    poppy carved scrolled armrests, conforming seat
    rail, cabriole legs, upholstered, c1900 ....1,250.00
  Desk, 51" l, 30" w, 32½" h, Majorelle, fruitwood,
    lobed rect top, stylized Queen Anne's lace on
    scalloping apron, three desk drawers, hardware
    cast with matching foliate motif, four carved legs,
    replaced leather top 8,900.00
  Suite, 42¾" l settee and armchair, cherry, Karpen
    Bros, Liberty & Co upholstered seat cushions,
    metal labels, c1900, price for pr 1,265.00
Glove Box, SP, 15½" l, 6" w, 6½" h, rect, hinged domed
  lid, chased sides, repeating band of dragonflies 450.00
Goblet, 6⅝" h , Russian silver, gilt int., maker's mark
  "NC," Moscow hallmarks, c1890 .... 125.00
Jardiniere, 18" h, terra-cotta, rect, figural, nymph in flow-
  ing gown holding blossom, standing against vine cov
  wall, sgd "J Causse," orig liner 595.00
Lamp, 23" h, table, 18" d domed six panel caramel glass
  shade, patinated metal overlay, patinated metal base 460.00
Mirror, hand, 10¼" l, 6" w, Christmas Angel, holly and
  star dec, marked "Quadruple Plate" 115.00
Mug, 5⅜" h, Seattle Expo, three colorful women, Adams 365.00
Perfume Lamp, 9¼" h, opal white vase, Art Nouveau
  style replication heat cap, single socket fittings 815.00
Powder Box, cov, 4" d, SS lid, repousse design of maiden
  and roses, cut glass base 250.00
Sculpture, 11" h, The Intruder, graceful woman in flow-

ing robes standing on edge of circular dish while
  small turtle on opposite side watches, sgd "Bessie
  Potter Vonnoh II–XII," inscribed "Roman Bronze
  Works NY" along base edge, bronze, golden patina **8,625.00**
Tea Set, porcelain, 10½" h teapot, creamer, sugar, four
  cups and saucers, painted pink and green thistle
  leaves, acorns, and dragonflies, white ground, printed
  "J & C Kopenhagen" mark **300.00**
Torchere, 84" h, Louis XVI, gilt bronze, marble, five-light
  candelabra, c1880, electrified, price for 4 pc set ..**28,750.00**
Tray, 11¼" l, bronze, shaped oval, nude long-haired
  woman and mermaid, two bodies form sides of rippled pool, medium green patina, c1900 .... **900.00**
Vase
  12" h, stoneware, brown matte finish, sculptured
    woman's face surrounded by flowing hair, sculp-
    tured flowers at base, two handles, sgd "A.
    Stuchly" on reverse, minor damage, price for pr   **200.00**
  13½" h, 7½" d, pottery, Boch Freres, egg-shell finish,
    wide band of pelicans, blue and turquoise striped
    ground, yellow line borders, stamped "Made in
    Belgium Bausch Firieze LaLouviere," further
    stamped "D984CH Catteau," **1,035.00**
  14" h, molded lacy rims, stylized green, mottled blue
    and brown flowers and leaves, designed by Eliza
    Simmace, Jane Rombol, Jr Assistant, imp Doulton
    Lambeth marks, price for pr **900.00**
  24" h, silver, trumpet, wavy mouth, pierced border,
    weighted pierced circular foot, applied chrysan-
    themum blossoms, applied blossoms and leaves,
    engraved sinuous stems, monogrammed, Shreve
    & Co San Francisco, c1900, 72 ozs **4,125.00**
Vide Poche, 10" l, Woman with Owls, woman's head,
  arms extended on edge overlapping figural two owl's
  wings, sgd and inscribed "copyright 1911 Harriet W
  Frishmuth #6" on reverse, stamped "Gorham Co
  Founders QIL" on reverse, bronze, rich brown patina**3,335.00**

ART POTTERY (GENERAL)

History: The zenith of the art pottery movement occurred in the late 19th and early 20th centuries. Over a hundred companies produced individually designed and decorated wares which served utilitarian as well as aesthetic purposes. Artists moved about from company to company, some forming their own firms.

References: Susan and Al Bagdade, *Warman's Americana Pottery and Porcelain,* Wallace-Homestead, 1994; Carol and Jim Carlton, *Colorado Pottery,* Collector Books, 1994; Paul Evans, *Art Pottery of the United States,* Second Edition, Feingold & Lewis Publishing, 1987; Lucile Henzke, *Art Pottery of America,* Revised Edition, Schiffer Publishing, 1996; Ralph and Terry Kovel, *Kovels' American Art Pottery,* Crown Publishers, 1993.

Periodical: *Arts & Crafts Quarterly,* 9 Main St, Lambertville, NJ 08530.

Collectors' Clubs: American Art Pottery Assoc, PO Box 525, Cedar Hill, MO 63016; Pottery Lovers Reunion, 4969 Hudson Dr, Stow, OH 44224.

Videotapes: Ralph and Terry Kovel, *Collecting with the Kovels: American Art Pottery,* 2 tapes, Antiques, Inc., 1995.

Museums: Cincinnati Art Museum, Cincinnati, OH; Everson Museum of Art of Syracuse and Onondaga County, Syracuse, NY; Newcomb College Art Gallery, New Orleans, LA; Zanesville Art Center, Zanesville, OH.

Additional Listings: See Clewell, Clifton, Cowan, Dedham, Fulper, Grueby, Jugtown, Marblehead, Moorcroft, Newcomb, North Dakota School of Mines, Ohr, Owens, Paul Revere, Peters and Reed, Rookwood, Roseville, Van Briggle, Weller, and Zanesville.

Notes: Condition, design, and glaze quality are the key considerations when buying art pottery. This category includes only companies not found elsewhere in this book.

SPECIAL AUCTIONS

Cincinnati Art Galleries
635 Main St
Cincinnati, OH 45202
(513) 381-2128

Jackson's Auctioneers & Appraisers
2229 Lincoln St
Cedar Falls, IA 50613
(319) 277-2256

David Rago Auctions, Inc.
333 North Main St
Lambertville, NJ 08530
(609) 397-9374

Treadway Gallery, Inc.
2029 Madison Rd.
Cincinnati, OH 45208
(513) 321-6742

AETCO, vase, 12⅜" h, blue micro-crystalline matte glaze, unmarked **200.00**
American Encaustic Tile, inkwell, 1⅞" h, 5" l, 6" l, double, lids, blue ground, white clouds, emb emblem . **95.00**
Arequipa
   Bowl, 9" d, 4¾" h, light blue glossy glaze, molded flower and leaf dec, rolled rim, marked **45.00**
   Vase
      3½ × 3", squat bulbous, squeeze-bag dec, gold and blue stylized flowers, deep green ground, dec by Frederick Rhead, c1912, blue-ink period mark **2,000.00**
      8 × 5", eight sided, tapering rim, emb leaves, matte red-brown glaze, imp mark, small base bruise, minute glaze flakes inside rim **950.00**
Beaver Falls, tile, 6" sq, landscape, Viennese style, gold lustered trees and farm scene, dec by L Hooton, emb "BFATCO," wormy chestnut frame **425.00**
Bennett, John
   Jar, cov, 3⅞" h, Limoges-style glaze, chrysanthemum dec, incised artist's monogram on side, base incised "J. Benn N.Y.," c1880 .... **225.00**
   Vase
      7½ × 5¼", bulbous, crisply painted allover red

roses, green leaves, olive ground, "J Bennett/ New York" painted in green, several glaze nicks at base **1,300.00**
      9 × 4", bottle shape, flaring rim, finely painted white and yellow apple blossoms, green leaves, cobalt blue ground, painted "J Bennett/ 101 Lex Ave/NY/1077/CR" **1,200.00**
Bybee, Seldon, vase, 5⅞" h, three handles, strong crystalline green over brown glaze, marked with outline of Kentucky enclosing name, early 1930s **75.00**
California Faience
   Bowl, 4½" d, medium blue, glossy glaze **125.00**
   Flower Frog, sailboat shape **35.00**
   Vase, 5" h, 2¾" d, bottle shape, flared rim, feathered blue matte finish, incised mark **500.00**
Cambridge Pottery
   Bowl, 6½ × 3", Acorn, green glossy glaze, marked **60.00**
   Ewer, 7½" h, Oakwood, cream, yellow, and green blended glaze, numbered **120.00**
   Tile, 6" sq, floral, high relief, majolica type **30.00**
   Vase, 9" h, dog portrait, brown glaze, sgd "AV Lewis" **675.00**
Catalina Pottery
   Pot, 4 × 5", oxblood **200.00**
   Vase, 6" h, 6½" d, lavender glaze, flaring rim, ink-stamp mark **400.00**
Cincinnati Faience, c1890, umbrella stand, 20" h, applied sea life, blue glaze, gold accents, sgd **990.00**
Jervis Oyster Bay, vase, 4¾" h, 2¾" d, flaring, excised and enameled mistletoe dec, light blue and brown, textured ground, incised vertical OB mark, ¼" tight line at rim, glaze neck on side near top **850.00**
Martin Brothers
   Fern Vase, 10¾ × 5¾", incised and sculpted dec, olive green, royal blue, and oatmeal, two handles, incised "R. W. Martin/London/1-1876" rim chip professionally repaired **550.00**
   Statue, 3½ × 3", furry monster grappling with writhing snake, oatmeal, gunmetal, and light green, incised "RW Martin/London/Southall/3-1890" **1,800.00**
Morgan, Matt, jardiniere, 8¾ × 8¾", bulbous, two angular handles, slip-relief white flowers, textured blue and brown ground, gold leaf, dec by NJ Hirshfield, imp oval mark "N.J.J./9." **400.00**
Norse Pottery
   Bowl, 6⅛" h, incised bird dec on body and shoulder, three small human heads as feet, imp logo and shape number 61 .... **450.00**
   Vase
      3⅞" h, salamander handles, three small animal heads as feet, snugly fitted metal insert, imp logo and shape number 70 .... **500.00**
      9¼" h, cylindrical, incised ducks encircling body, imp logo and shape number 99, professionally repaired base chips **600.00**
Pewabic
   Bowl, 2⅛" h, hand thrown, volcanic brown over yellow over cream glaze, base sgd with large "P" painted in white slip **200.00**
   Vase
      3½" h, hand thrown, organic turquoise over luster red glaze, maple leaf Pewabic logo, notation "S-2," c1906 .... **475.00**

5¼" h, flared body, irid turquoise and gray, imp circular "Pewabic Detroit" logo, pinhead size flakes **500.00**
Pilkinton, vase, 4½ × 5", squatty, Sonstone, pinched neck, flaring rims, hare's-fur crystalline copper and amber flambes, price for pr **550.00**
Pisgah Forest
  Cream Pitcher, 4½" h, 5¼" d, white cameo relief of pioneering scene, blue marbled ground, dec by Walter Stephen, raised potter's mark, marked "1951/Stephen" **175.00**
  Mug, 3⅜" h, cameo dec of finely detailed clog dancers, dec by Walter Stephen, raised logo on base **100.00**
  Pitcher, 6" h, 6¼" d, white cameo relief of pioneering scene, blue matte ground, blue flambe base, dec by Walter Stephen, marked "1953/Cameo/Stephen/Long Pine/Ardennes" **375.00**
  Teapot, 5¼" h, white cameo relief of pioneering scene, light blue ground, dec by Walter Stephen, raised potter's mark "1951/Stephen" **200.00**
  Vase
    5½" h, 3½" d, baluster, white and blue crystalline, golden ground, emb potter's mark **350.00**
    9" h, 6½" d, bulbous, collar rim, white and blue crystalline flambe over creamy white and olive flambe ground, raised potter's mark, 1940 ... **700.00**
Rushmore Pottery, bowl, peppered blue matte glaze, incised "Rushmore Pottery, Black Hills" **75.50**
Shearwater
  Figure, 5" h, prancing horse, gunmetal green **120.00**
  Vase, 5½" h, hand thrown **90.00**
Stockton, vase, 10¾" h, crescent shape, naturalistic flowers, green, brown, and yellow, Rekston glaze, unmarked **425.00**
Teco
  Bowl, 6¾" d, variegated green matte glaze, marked twice on base **325.00**
  Lamp, 28" h, 20" d shade, four-handled organic base, veined matte green glaze, orig green and pink slag glass shade, orig fittings **7,500.00**
  Vase
    7⅛" h, four buttressed handles, rose colored matte glaze, marked twice on base, repaired rim chips **500.00**
    13" h, 6¾" h, tapering, four buttressed handles, even medium-dark-green finish, #286, die stamped "Teco/286," two small rim nicks ...**3,800.00**
Valentien, Albert, vase, 15" h, 5½" d, painted matte, bulbous base, bulging neck, golden CA poppies, green foliage, golden brown to yellow ground, imp lozenge mark and artist's initials **23,000.00**
Vance-Avon
  Pitcher, 9⅛" h, slip trailed trefoil yellow flowers with purple centers, green leaves and stems, base marked "Avon W. Pts. Co" ink-stamp logo, minor scratches to some flowers **700.00**
  Shaving Mug, 4" h, slip-trailed trefoil yellow flowers with purple centers, green leaves and stems, base marked "R, 531" painted in green slip, incised "L" **300.00**
  Soap Dish, cov, orig drain, 4", slip-trailed trefoil yellow flowers with purple centers, green leaves and

Walrath, figure, nude woman laying on stomach, face supported by hands, foot raised at ankles and locked, mustard color, greenish base, impressed "Walrath/1912," 4¾" l, $450.00.

stems, base marked "Avon W. Pts. Co" ink-stamp logo **400.00**
  Wash Pitcher and Bowl, 12" h pitcher, 16⅜" d unglazed unmarked bowl, slip-trailed trefoil yellow flowers with purple centers, green leaves and stems, pitcher imp "Avon W. Pts. Co" ink-stamp logo, minor stains in bowl, professionally repaired chip to pitcher lip **1,500.00**
Volkmar, Charles, planter, 7½ × 18½ × 12½", four ftd, slip painted polychrome fox-hunting scene, Barbotine style for Emile Galle, sgd "Chas. Volkmar" on side, "EG" under base, some minor chipping **375.00**
Walley Pottery, vase
  5¾" h, bud, elongated cylindrical neck flaring to bulbous base, matte green glaze, brown glaze at neck, imp mark "W. J. W." **275.00**
  12¼" h, tapering cylinder, short neck, angled shoulder, two applied loop handles, two molded trout designs, imp mark "W. J. W.," orig paper label .**2,300.00**

ARTS AND CRAFTS MOVEMENT

History: The Arts and Crafts Movement in American decorative arts took place between 1895 and 1920. Leading proponents of the movement were Elbert Hubbard and his Roycrofters, the brothers Stickley, Frank Lloyd Wright, Charles and Henry Greene, George Niedecken, and Lucia and Arthur Mathews.

The movement was marked by individualistic design (although the movement was national in scope) and re-emphasis on handcraftsmanship and appearance. A reform of industrial society was part of the long-range goal. Most pieces of furniture favored a rectilinear approach and were made of oak.

References: Steven Adams, *The Arts & Crafts Movement,* Chartwell Books, 1987; *Arts and Crafts Furniture: The Complete Brooks Catalog of 1912,* Dover Publications, 1996; Michael E. Clark and Jill Thomas-Clark (eds.), *J. M. Young Arts and Crafts Furniture,* Dover Publications, 1994; Paul Evans, *Art Pottery of the United States,* Second Edition, Feingold & Lewis Publishing, 1987; *Furniture of the Arts & Crafts Period With Prices,* L-W Book Sales,

1992, 1995 value update; Bruce Johnson, *The Official Identification and Price Guide to Arts and Crafts,* Second Edition, House of Collectibles, 1992; ———, *The Pegged Joint,* Knock on Wood Publications, 1995; Elyse Zorn Karlin, *Jewelry and Metalwork in the Arts and Crafts Tradition,* Schiffer Publishing, 1993; *Limbert Arts and Crafts Furniture: The Complete 1903 Catalog,* Dover Publications, n.d.; James Massey and Shirley Maxwell, *Arts & Crafts,* Abbeville Press, 1995; Kevin McConnell, *More Roycroft Art Metal,* Schiffer Publishing, 1995; Roycrofters, *Roycroft Furniture Catalog, 1906,* Dover Publications, 1994; Joanna Wissinger, *Arts and Crafts: Metalwork and Silver* and *Pottery and Ceramics,* Chronicle Books, 1994.

Periodicals: *American Bungalow,* PO Box 756, Sierra Madre, CA 91204; *Style 1900,* 17 S Main St, Lambertville, NJ 08530.

Collectors' Clubs: Foundation for the Study of the Arts & Crafts Movement, Roycroft Campus, 31 S Grove St, East Aurora, NY 14052; Roycrofters-At-Large Assoc, PO Box 417, East Aurora, NY 14052; William Morris Society of Canada, 1942 Delaney Dr, Mississaugua, Ontario, L5J 3L1, Canada.

Museums: Elbert Hubbard Library-Museum, East Aurora, NY; Museum of Modern Art, New York, NY.

Additional Listings: Roycroft, Stickleys, and art pottery categories.

SPECIAL AUCTIONS

David Rago Auctions, Inc.
333 North Main St
Lambertville, NJ 08530
(609) 397-9374

Treadway Gallery, Inc.
2029 Madison Rd
Cincinnati, OH 45208
(513) 321-6742

Bowl
  2 × 4½", flaring hand-wrought circular copper, red patina, imp sq Harry Dixon mark **425.00**
  5" d, 1¾" h, hammered silver, stamped "Sterling, Hand Beaten at The Kalo Shops, Park Ridge, Illinois," 4 troy oz **375.00**
Candlesticks, pr
  14½ x 7", brass, flat bobeches, flaring stems, wide circular base, orig inserts, attributed to Jessie Preston **600.00**
  15" h, hammered silver, tulip shape, stamped "Sterling, Hand Wrought at The Kalo Shops, G152H," 42 troy oz **3,450.00**
Catalog, Orinoka Mills, New York, NY, 1928, 24 pgs, 9 × 12", printed stiff paper, "The Secret of Beautiful Homes," E. Davis Seal, ten color studies featuring window and upholstery treatments with Orinoka fabrics **32.00**
Chandelier, 20" sq, flaring four-sided green slag glass, wooden chain **500.00**
Cigarette Box, cov, 3½" sq, 2" h, hammered pewter,

enameled top with polychrome seascape with sailboat, cedar lined, sgd "Made in England/Tudric/Pewter/01021/Made by Liberty and Co." **750.00**
Clock, 4 × 2¾ x 1¾", SS, MOP inlay, turquoise cabochons, enameled face, Archibold Knox, sgd "L & Co/Anchor/Lion/G/5217" **7,500.00**
Curtain Panels, jute, printed stylized pattern of red fruit and green foliage, neutral ground, eight 72 × 15" vertical panels, four 14 × 34" fringed valances, price for 12 pc set **1,200.00**
Door Knocker, 7" l, copper, handmade **220.00**
Frame, 16" sq, quartered oak, raised oak trim, circular Art Nouveau print, some loss to beading **350.00**
Furniture
  Chair, arm, 38 × 28½ × 24", Harden, straight crest rail, five vertical back slats, four slats under rounded arms, drop in spring seat, through tenons, orig medium color **950.00**
  Morris Chair, Shop of the Crafters, #333, inlaid design **7,700.00**
  Settee, 38 × 54 × 24", Hardee, straight crest rail, eleven vertical slats, four slats under lower wavy arms, drop in spring seat, orig dark finish **2,300.00**
  Table
    Center, 28" d, 30" h, hexagon top, four slab legs, four-spindled construction, two keyed tenon stretchers **550.00**
    Trestle, 84" l, unsigned **15,000.00**
Hat Rack, 20 × 29", three-rail gate form, cross bars dec with lettered motto "May the Hinges of Friendship Never Grow Rusty," five hat pegs **220.00**
Humidor, 5 × 10 × 7", wrought copper, enameled red, green, and black, peacock feathers, cedar lined, orig dark brown patina, Art Crafts Shop, stamped mark .**1,200.00**
Jardiniere, 8½ × 11, hammered copper, rolled rim, orig dark brown patina, attributed to Dirk Van Erp **400.00**
Lamp, table
  18" h, 17" d, Dirk Van Erp, hammered copper and mica, conical shade with four orig mica panels, tapering base, orig reddish brown patina, two orig sockets **14,000.00**
  26" h, 27" d, Limbert, octagonal faceted shade, reticulated panels showing Dutch scenes, backed with gold and dense green-colored slag glass, octagonal hammered copper base with cutout windows backed with deep green glass, orig acorn pulls, orig dark patina, four sockets **8,000.00**
Motto, Taber, Prang Art Co, oak frame
  20 × 14", int. cottage scene, English peasant couple, 1904 .... **195.00**
  21 × 14", A Drop Of Ink May Make A Million Think, 17th C philosophers in period library, 1907 .... **190.00**
Planter, 33" l, 9½" d, 31½" h, rect oak box, four sq spindle legs joined by shaped stretcher **385.00**
Print
  8½ × 6¾", color woodblock print, dock scene of boats and houses, mauve, black, and golden yellow, sgd "H.T.G.," titled and pencil signed on border, matted and framed under glass **350.00**
  20 × 28", Karl Otto Matthei, color litho, beach scene, boats, seagulls, soft blue and taupe, sgd lower left, framed under glass **350.00**

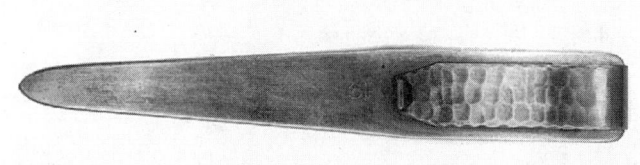

Roycroft, letter opener, hammered copper, impressed "Roycroft," 7½", $75.00.

Tea Set, hammered pewter, cov teapot with bamboo handle, creamer, sugar, two-handled tray, imp "H Tudric/English Pewter/Liberty and Co." **650.00**

Tray, 14¼" d, hammered silver, circular floral form, engraved Arts and Crafts style monogram, stamped "Sterling and Wrought, Kalo Shop, Chicago, USA, #H958l," dated 1929 by inscription on back **1,150.00**

Vase
- 5¾" h, artist sgd "CWB," Philadelphia Guild **650.00**
- 8¼ × 6½", hammered copper, bulbous, tapered rim, dark brown orig patina, Dirk Van Erp open box mark **1,300.00**
- 9¾ × 4½", SS on bronze, ftd base, silver weeds, dark brown ground, fine orig patina, Heintz, stamped "HAMS" **425.00**

Waste Basket, 13" sq, 15½" h, flaring, four sided, four faceted posts **350.00**

AUSTRIAN WARE

History: Over 100 potteries were located in the Austro-Hungarian Empire in the late 19th and early 20th centuries. Although Carlsbad was the center of the industry, the factories spread as far as the modern-day Czech Republic.

Many of the factories were either owned or supported by Americans; hence, their wares were produced mainly for export to the United States.

Marks: Many wares do not have a factory mark but only the word "Austrian" in response to the 1891 law specifying that the country of origin had to be marked on imported products.

Additional Listings: Amphora, Carlsbad, Royal Dux, and Royal Vienna.

Bowl, 9¾" h, light green irid rim, allover hexagon pattern, patinated metal fluted cylindrical standard, circular base with pierced rim, two applied arching lotus-leaf cast handles, c1900 .... **275.00**

Chocolate Pot, cov, hp grapes dec, gold mark **75.00**

Creamer, 7⅛" h, blue glaze, floral panel **50.00**

Dresser Set, tray, two cov boxes, pin tray, multicolored floral dec, price for 6 pc set **125.00**

Figure, 4½" h, 6" l, bronze, three frogs playing leap frog, cold painted in shades of green, early 20th C **1,725.00**

Jewel Box, 7" l, 3¼" h, gilt bronze, piano shape, small cylinder music box, stamped "Austria" **345.00**

Lamp Base, 13½" h, porcelain, two putti with blue drape, foliate base, late 19th C **60.00**

Lamp, table, 26½" h, bronze, desert oasis, warrior on camel, slave girl, cold painted, sgd "Bergman" **4,315.00**

Mirror, 6" d, hand, silver and mauve guillouche enamel,

fitted powder compartment, lid dec with miniature portrait of lovers in garden, stamped "Made in Austria," control marks "Sterling #0112312" **690.00**

Model, 12" l, 13" h, 17th C galleon, gilt silver and enamel, studded with half pearls and cabochon cut amethysts, 48 troy oz **1,725.00**

Palace Urn, 45" h, 11" d, porcelain, baluster, cobalt blue ground, central portion with two scenic panels, one of Christopher Columbus presenting treasures from new world to King Ferdinand, reverse side with scene of Spanish nobleman dispensing justice, both sgd "E Latter," base and lid dec with fine gilt floral filigree, two portrait panels, one with cavalier with maid, other with scholar with maiden, back neck dec with two portrait panels of muses, base stamped "Vienna, FD Austria" **17,250.00**

Pitcher, 4¼" h, 4¼" d, hp china, red and yellow roses, pastel ground, marked "Vienna Austria" **50.00**

Plate, 10¼" d, still life of fruit and vegetables, sgd "F Lilsner," wide cobalt blue border with gilt floral filigree, marked with blue shield mark "FD Vienna Austria," price for pr **1,380.00**

Portrait Plaque, 19½" d, artist sgd "F Dorfl," titled on reverse
- Dievier Weltthule, maroon and gold border with emb floral dec, marked with blue shield "FD Vienna Austria" **5,750.00**
- Raub der Lubinerinnen, antique green and gold border with emb floral dec, marked with blue shield "Vienna, F & D Austria" **6,050.00**

Sculpture, 19½" h, bronze, dancers, Bruno Zach, sgd and imp "BK," price for pr **3,740.00**

Tray, 15" l, pierced handles, beaded rim, ornate gold, green, and purple grape clusters, artist sgd "Koch" . **120.00**

Bowl, white porcelain, scalloped edge, swirl and shell relief, two rose floral motifs, gilded, 11" d, 2⅞" h, $70.00.

Tureen, cov, pink and blue flowers **30.00**

Vase
- 8⅛" h, pottery, cylindrical, wide mouth, band of raised circular gold flowers with blue centers, gold stems, blue ground, imp marker's mark "Paul Dachset," early 20th C **495.00**
- 9¾" h, conical, deep red, purple irid shaded to amber and blue, relief thistle plant dec, tripod stand, patinated metal ring with three applied dragonflies, c1900 .... **400.00**

25¾" h, porcelain, enameled classical subjects within panels, gilt borders, deep red ground, 19th C, repairs, hairline **2,415.00**

Sizes (approximate):

Folio	12 × 16 inches
4to	8 × 10 inches
8vo	7 × 7 inches
12mo	3 × 5 inches

AUTOGRAPHS

History: Autographs appear on a wide variety of formats—letters, documents, photographs, books, cards, etc. Most collectors focus on a particular person, country, or category, e.g., signers of the Declaration of Independence.

References: Mark Allen Baker, *All-Sport Autographs*, Krause Publications, 1994; ———, *Collector's Guide to Celebrity Autographs*, Krause Publications, 1996; George S. Lowry, *Autographs: Identification and Price Guide*, Avon Books, 1994; Norman E. Martinus and Harry L. Rinker, *Warman's Paper*, Wallace-Homestead, 1994; J. B. Muns, *Musical Autographs*, Second Supplement, published by author, 1994; Susan and Steve Raab, *Movie Star Autographs of the Golden Era*, published by authors, 1994; Kenneth W. Rendell, *Forging History: The Detection of Fake Letters & Documents*, University of Oklahoma Press, 1994; ———, *History Comes to Life*, University of Oklahoma Press, 1996; George Sanders, Helen Sanders and Ralph Roberts, *Sanders Price Guide to Sports Autographs*, 1994 Edition, Scott Publishing, 1993; ———, *The 1994 Sanders Price Guide to Autographs*, Number 3, Alexander Books, 1994.

Periodicals: *Autograph Collector*, 510-A S Corona Mall, Corona, CA 91720; *Autograph Review*, 305 Carlton Rd, Syracuse, NY 13207; *Autograph Times*, 2303 N 44th St, No. 225, Phoenix, AZ 85008; *Autographs & Memorabilia*, PO Box 224, Coffeyville, KS 67337; *The Collector*, PO Box 255, Hunter, NY 12442.

Collectors' Clubs: Manuscript Society, 350 N Niagara Street, Burbank, CA 95105; Universal Autograph Collectors Club, PO Box 6181, Washington, DC 20044.

Addition Listings: See *Warman's Americana & Collectibles* for more examples.

Notes: The condition and content of letters and documents bear significantly on value. Collectors should know their source since forgeries abound and copy machines compound the problem. Further, some signatures of recent presidents and movie stars were done by machine rather than by the persons themselves. A good dealer or advanced collector can help spot the differences.

Abbreviations: The following are used to describe autograph materials and their sizes.

Materials:

ADS	Autograph Document Signed
ALS	Autograph Letter Signed
AQS	Autograph Quotation Signed
CS	Card Signed
DS	Document Signed
FDC	First Day Cover
LS	Letter Signed
PS	Photograph Signed
TLS	Typed Letter Signed

SPECIAL AUCTION

Swann Galleries, Inc.
104 E 25th St
New York, NY 10010
(212) 254-4710

Colonial America

Hopkins, Stephen, Declaration of Independence signer, partially printed document, sgd as Colonial Governor and Captain General of Rhode Island, 1-page small oblong folio, May 12, 1760, commission to Josiah King as Justice of the Peace, Providence Co, dark printed coat of arms at top, wax seal at upper left, countersigned by Thomas Ward as Secretary, large signature **875.00**

Hopkinson, Francis, Declaration of Independence signer, Treasurer of Loans, DS, 1-page oblong 8vo, July 8, 1780, ornately engraved 6 months sight draft, countersigned by Nath. Appleton, Commissioner of the Continental Loan Office of Massachusetts Bay . **575.00**

Rittenhouse, David, inventor, astronomer, statesman, ADS, sgd as Treasurer of Pennsylvania, 1-page oblong 8 vo, June 5, 1787, to Henry Wynkoop, Treasurer of Bucks County, Pa. ordering him to pay surveyor Andrew Ellicott **1,100.00**

Williams, William, Declaration of Independence signer, autograph note, sgd "Wm Williams," 2⅜ × 2" sheet, May 25, 1773, note regarding Lebanon Records, dark writing and signature **185.00**

Wooster, David, Revolutionary War General, French and Indian War officer, ALS, 1-page 4to, Greenwich, June 24, 1775, regarding orders received from Governor Trumball to march 7 companies of regiment and whole of Col. Waterbery's to New York **3,600.00**

Wythe, George, Declaration of Independence signer, ADS, sgd as Clerk of the House of Burgesses, 1 1/2-page small folio, Williamsburg, VA, giving John Randolph title to 10-acre tract of land adjoining southern boundary of Williamsburg, entire document in Wythe's hand, large dark signature **1,900.00**

Foreign

Frederik VII, King of Denmark, partially printed document sgd as King, in French, 2-page small folio, Oct 20, 1862, boldly signed, wax and paper seal, small portrait of the King **225.00**

Henry IV, King of Castile, half-brother of Queen Isabella, LS, in Spanish, 1-page oblong 8 vo, Salamanca, May 13, 1465, to Count of Arcos, thanking Count for letter and expressing pleasure over recent actions, docketed on verso **1,750.00**

Marconi, Guglielmo, Italian physicist, wireless telegraph inventor, TLS, 1-page 8vo, letter of Marconi House, London, June 3, 1926, agreeing to sit for cartoon by Robert L. Ripley for publication in *Radio-Transmission* **650.00**

Rodin, Auguste, French sculptor, ALS, in French, 1-page 12mo, regrets and comments about beautiful watercolor **850.00**

Tennyson, Alfred, English poet, passport, orig dark red morocco leather case, partially printed document sgd, 1-page folio, August 15, 1860, sgd by Tennyson at lower left, vignettes of coats of arms, French consular stamp, name stamped in gold on flap **1,800.00**

General

Edison, Thomas A., American inventor, ALS, 1-page 8vo lined paper, in pencil, sgd "Edis," early 1920s, to Wolnitzky, Edison Service Record Club, re marketing of phonograph records **1,100.00**

Einstein, Albert, physicist, TLS, in German, 1-page 4to, orig envelope, Princeton, May 11, 1951, to Dr Dorothea Koening, Vanderbilt University, Nashville, re sister's health, with complete translation **2,300.00**

Kennedy, Jacqueline, printed document, sgd "Mrs John F Kennedy" as First Lady, in pencil, 3¼ × 9¼", c1961, Eastern Air Lines form allowing bill to be charged to her account **350.00**

Madison, Dolley, First Lady, 2-page 4to letter, Feb 23, 1816, to her from Phoebe Morris, regarding personal matters, events in Washington **275.00**

Peale, Rembrandt, American artist, ALS, 1-page 4to, NY, Nov 29, 1835, to Prosper M Wetmore, Regent of the University of NY, asking Wetmore to consider 2nd edition of Peale's book, *Graphics...,* as manual on drawing **1,900.00**

Saint-Gaudens, Augustus, American sculptor, designer of $20 gold piece, ALS, 1-page, 8vo with integral leaf, June 18, 1897, New York, to James Grant Wilson, author of *Appleton's Cyclopedia of American Biography,* regarding photograph to be sent to Wilson, accompanied by two later portraits of Saint-Gaudens **650.00**

Whitman, Walt, American poet, ALS, 1-page 2¾ × 5" oblong, Camden, NJ, Dec 16, 1884, thank you note for book sent by European admirer, double matted and framed with 3 × 5" photograph of elderly Whitman **1,900.00**

Wright, Wilbur, aviation pioneer, ALS, 1-page 4to, Dayton, OH, Oct 28, 1911, Wright Co. stationery, to Mr. W. H. Sheehan re inquiry, offers personal attention, and will consult with brother when he returns from Kitty Hawk **12,000.00**

Literature

Aldrich, Thomas Bailey, American poet and novelist, cabinet photography by J Notman of Boston, inscribed and signed at bottom as "Miss Sally Fairchild's friend, T B. Aldrich" **250.00**

Carroll, Lewis (Charles L. Dodgson), English author, ALS, 1 1/2-page oblong 8vo, Christ Church, Oxford, Oct 23, 1890, to Mrs. Dyer, regarding financial matter .**1,500.00**

Field, Eugene, American poet, manuscript sgd, 1-page small 8vo, orig envelope, unpublished 10 line untitled poem, printed text in facsimile of his handwriting, penned signature **550.00**

Hemingway, Ernest, American, sgd and inscribed book, A Farewell to Arms, 355-page 8 vo, emb royal blue cloth, front flyleaf inscribed, slight wear to spine ...**2,400.00**

O. Henry, William Syndey Porter, American author, ALS, 3-page 8vo, New York, July 9, 1905, thank you note **1,750.00**

Stowe, Harriet Beecher, American author, autograph quotation signed, 1-page 8vo, 1894 .... **750.00**

Twain, Mark (Samuel L. Clemens), American author, ALS, 1-page small 12mo, mourning stationery, orig envelope, Riverdale on the Hudson, Jan 29, 1902, to lawyer regarding upcoming court case regarding publishers using works without permission, accompanied by ALS from E C Stedman, Jan 22, 1902, offering to take the stand in same case **2,200.00**

Wilder, Thornton, American playwright and novelist, typescript sgd, 26-page 4to, one-act play titled *The Happy Journey,* personal inscription, signed, and dated May 13, 1962, on final page **250.00**

Wolfe, Thomas, American author, TLS, 1-page 4to, New York, July 13, 1935, thank you note **1,200.00**

Military

Eisenhower, Dwight D., TLS, 1-page 4to, official letterhead as Supreme Commander to the Allied Expeditionary Force, Sept 25, 1944, to Col TA Roberts, San Antonio, TX, orig envelope, candid lengthy letter with condolences over loss of son, importance of communication between current and retired members of the armed forces and superiors **1,450.00**

Hitler, Adolph, Nazi Fuhrer, TDS, 1-page large 4to, Fuhrer's Headquarters, June 14, 1941, wartime military appointment for promotion of Kaempfe, Commander of the 31st Division and Dader, Commander of the 2nd Division, to Generals in the Artillery, sgd by Hitler and Walter von Brauchitsch, Commander in Chief of the Army, large emb Nazi eagle and swastika seal to side **2,400.00**

Jodl, Alfred, pro-Hitler general, Chief of Operations Staff of the Armed Forces, sgd surrender to the Allies, card sgd "A. Jodl, generaloberst, 20/6/1946," Spandau cell number written on back, laminated **150.00**

Mussolini, Benito, Italian Fascist dictator, partially printed DS, 1-page 8vo, c1929, subscription document from Smithsonian Institution, Washington, DC, tan Smithsonian seal, large dark signature, accompanied by c1932 photographic postcard of full-figured uniformed Mussolini, mounted **675.00**

Ruggles, Daniel, Confederate General, ADS, sgd as Brigadier General, 1-page 8vo, Vicksburg, July 15, 1862, to Gen Van Dorn, reports hostile enemy activities and requests more troops **1,275.00**

St Clair, Arthur, ALS, Revolutionary War General, 1 3/4-page 4to, integral address leaf in his hand, Pittsburgh, Oct 1, 1808, to Daniel St Clair, at Penn Square, Montgomery County, PA, regarding early iron industry and its effects on war and domestic production **850.00**

Music

Bartok, Bela, Hungarian composer, pianist, and folklorist, PS, 7 × 9½", sepia, early 1940s, profile portrait, bold black ink signature, photographer Ernest Nash, NY, stamp on back **985.00**

Caruso, Enrico, operatic tenor, sgd drawing, in ink, 6¾ × 7¼" image on 7½ × 10¼" sheet, verso Hotel Knickerbocker stationery, bold geometric bust-length caricature identified as Enrico Scognamiglio in 1923 auction of Enrico Caruso items, sgd "Enrico Caruso NY 1913" beneath lower right corner of drawing .. **950.00**

Key, Francis Scott, partial ADS, 2 × 8" oblong sheet, Washington, DC, April 5, 1928, legal document ... **350.00**

Porter, Cole, composer and lyricist, sgd and inscribed black and white photo, 2¾ × 3¾", middle-age studio portrait, black ink inscription **600.00**

Rimsky-Korsakov, Nikolai, Russian composer, musical quotation sgd, 3½ × 5½" Russian postcard, three bars of music and lyrics from opera *Sadko,* name sgd in full, reverse of card with view of St Petersburg, "May 20, 1904" penned at bottom **6,500.00**

Smith, Samuel Francis, American clergyman, composer of *America,* autograph manuscript sgd, 1-page 8vo, entire first verse of *America,* noted song was written in 1832 .... **775.00**

Sousa, John Philip, American composer and bandmaster, ALS, 1-page 8vo, Oct 18, 1923, letterhead of Huntingdon Valley (PA) Country Club to friend's wife re audition **275.00**

Strauss, Richard, German composer, ALS, in German, 1 full-page large 4to, Gotha, April 14, 1927, to Ernst Lert in Milan, regarding costumes for Strauss' ballet *The Legend of Joseph* and better opera sets for his *Der Rosenkavalier* **1,250.00**

Stravinsky, Igor, Russian composer, TLS, 1-page 4to, letterhead, Hollywood, August 25, 1954, to attorney Arnold Weissberger, NY, regarding relationship with Columbia Records, boldly signed in black ink, accompanying carbon copy of Aug 23 letter to David Oppenheim at CBS Records **450.00**

Wagner, Richard, German composer, ALS, in French, 2-page 8vo, Zurich, Dec 12, 1857, regarding score for performance at Royal Court in London **3,500.00**

Presidents

Harrison, William Henry, ALS, 1-page 4to, Washington, Dec 26, 1825, letter to veteran concerning pension and benefits **3,600.00**

Jackson, Andrew, ALS, sgd as President, 1-page folio, Feb 9, 1830, to Samuel D Ingham, Secretary of Treasurer, asking how to handle political pressure caused by request made by Governor of Maryland, verso penned by Jackson "The Secretary of the Treasurer" **7,500.00**

Madison, James, ALS, 1-page 4to, Washington, April 20, 1808, sgd as Secretary of State, to Attorney General Caesar Augustus Rodney, re Daniel Clark, Representative to Congress from Orleans Territory of Louisana **7,500.00**

Roosevelt, Franklin D, TLS, 1-page 4to, White House letterhead, April 23, 1935, to Kenneth Condit, Editor of *American Machinist* magazine, thanking him for date regarding aging of American metalworking equipment **850.00**

Eisenhower, D. D., framed and matted picture, separate autograph, $90.00.

Taft, William Howard, DS, 1-page large folio on vellum, April 26, 1911, appointing Emil Theiss as Captain in Navy, with vignettes of eagle at top, Neptune taming sea horses on lower portion, also flags, canon, swords, and other war accouterments, emb seal, countersigned by G L Meyer as Secretary of the Navy **650.00**

Truman, Harry S., ALS, 1-page 4to, orig envelope, Kansas City, July 27, 1955, to J Frank Rope, regarding card printed by United Pacific Railroad Co which illustrated poker hands which he hoped to use in future poker games **2,500.00**

Show Business

Burke, Billie, autograph note sgd, 1-page 8vo, April 30, 1923 .... **175.00**

Fitzgerald, Ella, sgd "Best Wishes - Ella Fitzgerald," blue ballpoint ink, small piece of blue paper, affixed to black and white photograph **245.00**

Hendrix, Jimi, receipt, 3½ × 5½", sgd and inscribed in back in pencil "Love to you Jimi Hendrix" **920.00**

Laurel, Stan, British born stage and screen actor, TLS, 1-page 8vo, hotel stationery, May 17, 1961, thanks for recent honorary Academy Award and reference to late partner Oliver Hardy **550.00**

Madonna, baseball glove, brown leather Wilson glove, used by Madonna in "A League of Their Own," sgd in black felt pen, "Madonna - Penny Marshall - Tom Hanks - Geena Davis" **1,380.00**

McCartney, Paul, handwritten orig lyrics for "When I'm 64" from Sgt Pepper album, lyrics in variant sequence, revisions, c1967 ....**40,250.00**

Ringling, John, American circus owner, performer, philanthropist, partially printed DS, 2-page legal folio, Nov 4, 1916, artist's contract and release, between Barnum & Bailey circus and the Four Melillo sisters, an acrobatic contortionist's act, $175 per week for 1917 season **600.00**

White, George, founder of revue series "George White's Scandals," ALS, 2-page 8 vo, Seattle, Oct 1, 1914, to theatrical manager Charles Dillingham, Globe Theater, asking for job in musical **575.00**

Sports

Clemente, Roberto, baseball player, PS, 4 × 6", black and white, wearing Pirates uniform, bold signature . **215.00**

Johnson, Jack, heavyweight boxing champion, postcard, sgd "Jack Johnson/Former Heavyweight/Champion of the World/Good Luck" in black ink, Oct 14, 1937, postmark **250.00**

Mack, Connie, baseball, official National League baseball, 1932, seven other signatures including Eddie Collins and Lefty Gomez **675.00**

Tunney, Gene, boxing, TLS, 8 × 10" personal stationery, 1932, to Commander James J Lee regarding lectures for Veterans of Foreign Wars, large black ink signature **195.00**

Statesmen

Austin, Stephen F, Texas colonizer, manuscript document sgd, 1-page oblong 8 vo, Jan 23, 1811, promissory note sgd by Daniel Phelps, sgd by Austin and Timothy Phelps as witnesses **1,850.00**

Clay, Henry, American, complete 4to address leaf, free franked "Free H. Clay" as US Senator at upper right, addressed to George Getz, Reading, PA, red stamped "Free," circular red "Washington D. C. Apr 21" postmark, intact red wax seal **150.00**

Henry, Patrick, American, partially printed DS, 1-page small 4to, May 9, 1875, as Governor of Virginia, commission of Thomas Winn Lieutenant of the 4th Company, paper seal, ornate borders, double matted with engraving of him, maple and black wood frame ...**4,200.00**

Peale, Charles Wilson, American patriot and artist, autograph note sgd, 3½ lines on 3 × 7" oblong sheet, Philadelphia, Jan 29, 1780, sgd as member of the Pennsylvania General Assembly, requesting State Treasurer David Rittenhouse pay for nails used in renovation and repairs to Independence Hall in 1780 due to damage by British Occupation in Philadelphia in 1777 and 1778, countersigned by William Hollinshead and Jacob Schreiner of the "Committee of Assembly," very dark bold Peale signature **8,900.00**

Webster, Daniel, ALS, signed as Secretary of State, 2-page 4to, Washington, Sept 24, 1841, to Joshua A Spencer, US Attorney for the Northern District of New York, at Utica, regarding incident of hostilities along Canadian border **1,750.00**

AUTOMOBILES

History: Automobiles can be classified into several categories. In 1947 the Antique Automobile Club of America devised a system whereby any motor vehicle (car, bus, motorcycle, etc.) made prior to 1930 is considered an "antique". The Classic Car Club of America expanded the list focusing on luxury models from 1925 to 1948. The Milestone Car Society developed a list for cars for the years 1948 to 1964.

Some states, such as Pennsylvania, have devised a dual registration system for older cars—antique and classic. Models from the 1960s and 1970s, especially convertibles and limited-production models, fall into the "classic" designation, if they are used accordingly.

References: Dennis A. Adler, *Corvettes*, Krause Publications, 1996; Quentin Craft, *Classic Old Car Value Guide*, 23rd Edition, published by author, 1989; James M. Flammang, *Standard Catalog of American Cars, 1976–1986*, Second Edition, Krause Publications, 1989; ——, *Standard Catalog of Imported Cars, 1946–1990*, Krause Publications, 1992; ——, *Volkswagen Beetles, Buses and Beyond*, Krause Publications, 1996; Patrick R. Foster, *The Metropolitan Story*, Krause Publications, 1996; John Gunnell, *Marques of America*, Krause Publications, 1994; —— (ed.), *100 Years of American Cars*, Krause Publications, 1993; ——, *Standard Catalog of American Cars, 1946–1975*, Third Edition, Krause Publications, 1992; Beverly Kimes and Henry Austin Clark, Jr., *Standard Catalog of American Cars, 1805–1942*, Third Edition, Krause Publications, 1996; Ron Kowalke, *Standard Guide to American Muscle Cars*, Second Edition, Krause Publications, 1996; Jim Lenzke and Ken Buttolph, *Standard Guide to Cars & Prices*, Ninth Edition, Krause Publications, 1996; Robert Murfin (ed.), *Miller's Collectors Cars Price Guide 1994–1995*, Reed International Books, 1994, distributed by Antique Collectors' Club; Gerald Perschbacher, *Wheels in Motion*, Krause Publications, 1996.

Periodicals: *Auto Trader Old Car Book*, 14549 62nd St. North, Clearwater, FL 34620; *Automobile Quarterly*, 15040 Kutztown Rd, PO Box 348, Kutztown, PA 19530; *Car Collector & Car Classics*, 1241 Canton St, Roswell, GA 30076; *Cars & Parts*, PO Box 482, Sidney, OH 45365; *DuPont Registry*, 2502 N Rocky Point Dr #1095, Tampa, FL 33607; *Hemmings Motor News*, PO Box 256, Bennington, VT 05201; *Old Cars Price Guide*, 700 E State St, Iola, WI 54990.

Collectors' Clubs: Antique Automobile Club of America, 501 West Governor Rd, PO Box 417, Hershey, PA 17033; Classic Car Club of America, 1645 Des Plaines River Rd, Suite 7, Des Plaines, IL 60018; Milestone Car Society, PO Box 24612, Indianapolis, IN 46224; Veteran Motor Car Club of America, PO Box 360788, Strongsville, OH 44136; Willys/Kaiser/AMC Jeep Club, 1511 19th Ave W, Bradenton, FL 34205.

Notes: The prices below are for cars in running condition, with a high proportion of original parts and somewhere between 60 and 80 percent restoration. *Prices can vary by as much as 30 percent in either direction.*

Many older cars, especially if restored, are now worth more than $15,000. Their limited availability makes them difficult to price. Auctions, more than any other source, are the true determinant of value at this level.

Alfa Romeo
   1938, Spyder, red and black **225,000.00**
   1961, Spyder Veloce, small taillights, orig int., rebuilt
      engine **15,000.00**
   1964, Giulia Sprint Speciale, red and black leather,
      one owner **36,000.00**
AMC
   1965, Rambler Ambassador 990, new int. and paint **2,875.00**
   1987, Renault GTA, convertible, 5 speed, needs top **1,650.00**
Aston Martin
   1978, V8 coupe, gray and black int., 5 speed **28,500.00**
   1984, Lagonda, dark blue, tan int. **49,500.00**
Auburn, 1936, 852 all weather phaeton, tan, brown trim,
   orange striping and wheels, dark brown leather, tan
   top and boot **115,000.00**
Austin
   1962, A60 Cambridge Wagon **3,800.00**
   1967, Mini 850 Countryman Van Deluxe, beige and
      red **3,000.00**
BMW
   1959 Isetta, ground-up restoration, blue and gray .**10,500.00**
   1973, 2002TH, gold brown Recaro int., ground-up
      restoration **10,000.00**
   1977, 320I, orig paperwork, manuals **3,950.00**
Buick
   1924, Model 51A Brougham, 4-door sedan, re-
      stored **12,000.00**
   1937, Special Model 46C, rumble seat convertible
      coupe, old high-line restoration **17,500.00**
   1940, 585 Coupe, green **14,500.00**
   1941, coupe, convertible, all orig, one owner **14,500.00**
   1946, Straight Eight, all orig **11,900.00**
   1951, Deluxe, 4 door, all orig **9,500.00**
   1954, Century, convertible, automatic, burnt orange
      and white **18,500.00**
   1961, LeSabre, 4 door, bubble-top sedan, white, sec-
      ond owner **19,500.00**
   1966, Riviera, turquoise, new motor **3,200.00**
Cadillac
   1930, V16 4335, convertible, four tones of red,
      sweep cowl panel **295,000.00**
   1934, 35D, biplane bumpers, needs restoration **7,900.00**
   1939, Imperial sedan, jump seats, restored gray int.,
      black lacquer paint **20,000.00**
   1942, 75 Series, limousine, needs restoration **3,900.00**
   1948, Fleetwood Series 75, bar behind seat, new
      chrome and paint **20,995.00**
   1949, sedan, 4 door, orig int., silver gray **7,000.00**
   1953, deVille, green, needs restoration **3,900.00**
   1955, Eldorado, convertible, black, red int., sabre
      wheels **25,000.00**
   1959, 4-door hardtop, light blue, orig owner **15,500.00**
   1978, Eldorado Barritz, white, leather seats **10,000.00**
Chevrolet
   1918, touring, low mileage **15,000.00**
   1931, coupe, 5 window, olive and medium brown,
      pale yellow pinstriping, brown mohair int. **8,500.00**
   1933, coupe, 3 window, rumble seat, runs, needs
      work **8,500.00**
   1939, Master Deluxe, sedan, 2 door, Granville gray **9,500.00**
   1958, Corvette, 327, 2 tops, needs paint **20,000.00**
   1959, El Camino, 350 V8 ....**3,950.00**

Truck, Chevrolet, 1932 Huckster, $6,000.00.

   1966, Corvette, 327, Nassau blue, teak, all orig ...**27,000.00**
   1968, Nova, sedan, 2 door, 6 cylinder **3,000.00**
Chrysler
   1929, Roadster, convertible, 6 cylinder, green and
      black **19,500.00**
   1930, coupe, rumble seat, blue and black wood
      spoke wheels **8,900.00**
   1949, Town & Country convertible, woody, brown,
      tan top **40,000.00**
   1956, New Yorker, St Regis, 2 door, hardtop, red,
      white, and black, wire wheels **7,500.00**
Daimler, 1979, DS420 limousine, claret and black, fawn
   leather **12,500.00**
Datsun, 1965, SPL-310 Fairlady, convertible, red, older
   amateur restoration **3,200.00**
DeSoto, 1959, Sportsman, 2-door hardtop, heather blue
   and white, restored **11,950.00**
Dodge
   1929, sedan, 4 door **5,000.00**
   1934, fire truck **7,995.00**
   1973, Charger, 340 Magnum, yellow, side stripes,
      orig tires, black bucket seats **13,500.00**
Ferrari, 1956, 250 GT Boano, low roof coupe, dark
   bronze metallic, tan leather **75,000.00**
Ford
   1926, Model T, roadster, folding "fat man" steering
      wheel **5,750.00**
   1936, coupe, 3 window, orig int. **18,000.00**
   1946, business coupe **12,995.00**
   1953, pick-up, F-100 ....**5,500.00**
   1956, Sunliner, convertible, blue and white, new top
      and int. **10,000.00**
   1964, XL, convertible, red, red int., white top **5,900.00**
   1965, Mustang, hard top, ivy, gold vinyl top, rebuilt
      engine and transmission **7,500.00**
Jaguar, 1954, XK 120, roadster, red and black **29,500.00**
Lamborghini, 1970, Espada, silver, black leather, full
   mechanical restoration **28,500.00**
Mercedes, 1959, Model 219, 4 door **4,900.00**
MG
   1957, MGA, roadster, mineral blue, gray int., ground-
      up restoration **12,000.00**
   1967, MBG roaster, red, black leather, wire wheels **4,500.00**
Oldsmobile
   1949, 88, fastback, rust, needs restoration **3,000.00**
   1956, 98 Starfire, convertible, white, green leather **19,500.00**
   1968, Supreme, 2 door, hardtop **2,500.00**

Packard, 1937, Twelve, coupe roadster **195,000.00**
Pontiac
    1941, Streamliner Torpedo, 2 door, new int., re-
      painted **8,400.00**
    1955, Starchief Custom, 2 door, new turquoise and
      cream paint, new int. **9,300.00**
    1962, Grand Prix, new paint and top **13,500.00**
    1967, Firebird, black **5,900.00**
    1980, Trans Am, Indy pace car **4,300.00**
Plymouth
    1941, Special Deluxe, 2 door **2,500.00**
    1946, wagon, woody, needs restoration **5,000.00**
    1963, Belvedere, hardtop **1,800.00**
Porsche, 1958, Speedster, black and red, restored **49,500.00**
Rolls-Royce, 1951, Silver Dawn, burgundy and silver **28,500.00**
Saab, 1968, Sonett **4,000.00**
Studebaker, 1962, GT Hawk, 3 speed, bucket seats ...**2,000.00**
Toyota, 1977, Land Cruiser FJ40, 2 door, factory yellow,
    removable hardtop **10,500.00**
Triumph, 1967, Mk III, two tops, needs paint **2,750.00**
VW
    1959, Rometsch Coupe, restored, Okrasa motor. ..**35,000.00**
    1966, convertible, custom int., restored **4,500.00**
    1971, Super Beetle, convertible, yellow, needs work**2,995.00**
Willys, 1949, Jeepster, convertible, yellow, black top
    and int. **6,900.00**

AUTOMOBILIA

History: The number of items related to the automobile is endless. Collectors seem to fit into three groups—those collecting parts to restore a car, those collecting information about a company or certain model for research purposes, and those trying to use automobile items for decorative purposes. Most material changes hands at the hundreds of swap meets and auto shows around the country.

References: Mark Anderton and Sherry Mullen, *Gas Station Collectibles,* Wallace-Homestead, 1994; Scott Benjamin and Wayne Henderson, *Gas Pump Globes,* Motorbooks International, 1993; Bob Crisler, *License Plate Values,* King Publishing, 1994; Leila Dunbar, *Motorcycle Collectibles,* Schiffer Publishing, 1996; Gordon Gardiner and Alistair Morris, *The Price Guide and Identification of Automobilia,* Antique Collectors' Club, n.d.; John A. Gunnell, *Car Memorabilia Price Guide,* Krause Publications, 1995; Todd P. Helms, *The Conoco Collector's Bible,* Schiffer Publishing, 1995; Ron Kowalke and Ken Buttolph, *Car Memorabilia Price Guide,* Krause Publications, 1996; Rick Pease, *Filling Station Collectibles,* Schiffer Publishing, 1994; Jim and Nancy Schaut, *American Automobilia,* Wallace-Homestead, 1994; Don Stewart, *Antique Classic Marque Car Keys,* Second Edition, Key Collectors International, 1993; B. J. Summers and Wayne Priddy, *Value Guide to Gas Station Memorabilia,* Collector Books, 1995; Michael Karl Witzel, *Gas Station Memories,* Motorbooks International, 1994.

Periodicals: *Automobilia News,* PO Box 3528, Glendale, AZ 85311; *Car Toys,* 14347 Albers St #102, Sherman Oaks, CA 91401; *Hemmings Motor News,* PO Box 256, Bennington, VT 05201; *Mobilia,* PO Box 575, Middlebury, VT 05753; *Petroleum Collectibles Monthly,* 411 Forest St, LaGrange, OH 44050; *WOCCO,* 36100 Chardon Rd, Willoughby, OH 44094.

Collectors' Clubs: Automobile Objects D'Art Club, 252 N 7th St, Allentown, PA 18102; Classic Gauge & Oiler Hounds, Rte 1, Box 9, Farview, SD 57027; Hubcap Collectors Club, PO Box 54, Buckley, MI 49620; International Petroliana Collectors Assoc, PO Box 937, Powell, OH 43065; Spark Plug Collectors of America, 14018 NE 85th St, Elk River, MN 55330.

Advertising Display, 12¼ × 24½″, Kwickwork Auto Enamels, half of spoked auto tire, available colors featured on spokes **650.00**
Ashtray, United States Tires, spoke wheel, plated, marked "Handel," clear glass base, 6″ l **100.00**
Bank, Flying A, Veedol Oil **25.00**
Book, How To Open A Tire Repair Shop, C. A. Shaler, Waupun, WI, 24 pgs, 5¾″ × 9″, c1924 .... **26.00**
Calendar, 20½″ h, Habit's Fast Freight Line, 1930, stake truck illus **15.00**
Catalog
    Auto Parts Co, Chicago, IL, 1915, 128 pgs, 6½ × 9½″, Catalog No. 8, automobile, cyclecar, motorcycle and marine supplies **25.00**
    Ford Motor Co, Detroit, MI, Ford Times, 1917, 48 pgs, 6 × 8¾″, No. 6, Volume 10 .... **25.00**
    General Motors Corp, Detroit, MI, 1949, 32 pgs, 5½ × 7½″, titled "The Search That Never Ends," illus of Chevrolet, Pontiac, Buick, Cadillac **15.00**
    Kingham Trailer Co, Louisville, KY, 1940, 8 pgs, 8½ × 11″, self wrappers, Universal heavy-duty trailers, halftones of commercial trailer trucks **40.00**
    Meeker Mfg Co, Dayton, OH, 1921, 32 pgs, 4 × 9″, Catalog of Rims and Wheels, Firestone and Goodyear **32.00**
    Troy Carriage Sun Shade, Troy, OH, 1909, 24 pgs, 8 × 9¼″, line of automobile fronts, braided lace holds binding **118.00**
Clock
    Elgin, dashboard type, 1920s **80.00**
    Oldsmobile, 1900s **145.00**
Decanter, Mack Trucks, 75th Anniversary, Wild Turkey, gold bulldog top **50.00**
Flag Attachment, California Auto club **45.00**
Horn Button, Diamond T, custom **45.00**
License Plate, Arizona, copper, 1934 .... **75.00**
Oil Can, Autocraft Motor Oil, Pierce Lubricating Oil Co, NY, 2-gallon size, 24″ h **30.00**
Postcard, aerial view, Ford Motor Co, c1930 .... **50.00**
Poster, chromolitho, framed
    G Holley & Co, French automobile dealer, woman in red suit, gentleman in duster, early 1900s **1,045.00**
    Minerva Motors, Belgium, cars outside opera, 30 × 20″ **525.00**
    Morgan and Wright Tires, boy in driving outfit. 25 × 17½″ **400.00**
Print, color litho, abduction of young lady while companion complains, early auto, riders on horseback, sgd "Meunier 92/100," 21 × 14″ **40.00**
Radiator Cap, 5¾″ h, cast metal, woman **45.00**
Sign, porcelain enamel, double sided
    De Sota, Plymouth, Approved Service, round, extended center band, bright red, yellow, and blue, checkerboard center, 42″ d, large chips to borders **300.00**
    International Trucks, round, red, large white letters,

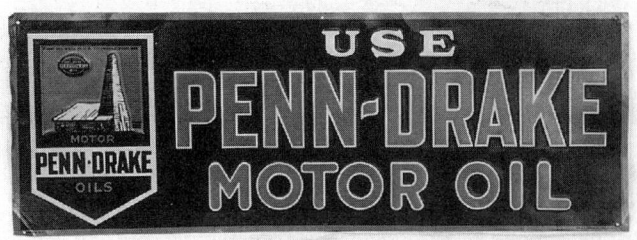

Sign, Penn-Drake Motor Oil, embossed tin litho, black ground, orange letters, The H. L. Moore Co, Cochranton, PA, 27⁷⁄₈ × 9⁵⁄₈″, $55.00.

center diamond logo, 42″ d, surface and border chips **495.00**

Oldsmobile General Motors, marquee shape, brown, large white letters, multicolored center crest, white border stripe, 28 × 60″, overall chip spots and surface wear **605.00**

Willy's "Jeep" Service, round, red, white and blue, large white lettering, 42″ d, minor wear **440.00**

Thermometer, Indy Motor Speedway, tire and flags logo **60.00**

Vase, bud

7¼″ h, marigold carnival glass, Tree of Life pattern, replacement brackets, price for pr **55.00**

7½″ h, dark amethyst pressed glass, replacement brackets, price for pr **30.00**

7¾″ h, mercury glass, one orig bracket, price for pr **30.00**

Watch Holder, 6½″ h, figural chrome boat-tail car, watch grille, ashtray, rubber wheels **750.00**

BACCARAT GLASS

History: The Sainte-Anne glassworks at Baccarat in Voges, France, was founded in 1764 and produced utilitarian soda glass. In 1816 Aime-Gabriel d'Artiques purchased the glassworks, and a Royal Warrant was issued in 1817 for the opening of Verrerie de Vonôche á Baccarat. The firm concentrated on lead-crystal glass products. In 1824 a limited company was created.

From 1823 to 1857 Baccarat and Saint-Louis glassworks had a commercial agreement and used the same outlets. No merger occurred. Baccarat began the production of paperweights in 1846. In the late 19th century the firm achieved an international reputation for cut glass table services, chandeliers, display vases, centerpieces, and sculptures. Products eventually included all forms of glassware. The firm still is active today.

Reference: Jean-Louis Curtis, *Baccarat,* Harry N. Abrams, 1992; Paul Jokelson and Dena Tarshis, *Baccarat Paperweights and Related Glass,* Paperweight Press, 1990 (distributed by Charles E. Tuttle Co.).

Additional Listings: Paperweights.

Animal

Bear, large **2,800.00**

Horse, Japanese type **80.00**

Owl, 4″ h **70.00**

Porcupine, sgd **130.00**

Starfish, sgd **100.00**

Turtle, sgd **90.00**

Atomizer, 5″ h, 3½″ l, oval, etched crystal body, chrome top, marked **85.00**

Biscuit Jar, cov, 6″ h, etched ground, cranberry flowers, leaves, and vines, lid marked **400.00**

Bowl, 5½″ d, cameo, clear etched leaf ground, chartreuse floral dec **100.00**

Candelabra, pr, 22½″ h, amberina socket and bobeche, clear cut base, cut prisms **450.00**

Candlestick, Odilon, 6″ h, twisted **40.00**

Cologne Bottle, 6¼″ h, 2½″ d, Rose Tiente Swirl, cylindrical, deep shoulder, short cylindrical neck, flat flaring rim, matching stopper **75.00**

Decanter, 14″ h, amphora shape, lightly ribbed, collared stem, slightly domed foot, conforming stopper, factory acid stamp mark **265.00**

Dish, 10″ l, oblong, crystal **230.00**

Dresser Set, Art Deco, amberina, swirl, brass rack with beveled mirror, marked, price for 5 pc set **650.00**

Fairy Lamp, blue **150.00**

Goblet, 6½″ h, cranberry over green, cameo floral cutting, double teardrop stem, gold trim **300.00**

Lamp, 19½″ h, oil, candlestick form, swirled molded receptacle and base, early 20th C, price for pr **420.00**

Lamp Base, 8½″ h, 3⅝″ d, Rose Tiente, amberina coloring, emb swirl and scroll pattern, orig burner **150.00**

Perfume Bottle, clear, orig stopper, marked, price for pr **140.00**

Water Bottle, light red shading to amber, 7″ h, $50.00.

Powder Jar, cov, Rose Tiente Swirl, cylindrical, clear knob **95.00**

Rose Bowl, 3″ d, cranberry, lace enamel dec **155.00**

Scent Bottle, 3½″ h, Toujours Fidele, Art Deco, c1930 **500.00**

Tray, leaf, price for pr **80.00**

Tumbler, 3½″ h, Rose Tiente, marked **65.00**

Vase

6¼″ h, 3¾″ d, ftd, flaring rim, overall floral and vine etching, sgd **85.00**

10¼″ h, inverted bell form, five etched urns with tall scrolling branches, printed factory mark, 20th C **800.00**

12″ h, 4½″ d, cameo, cylindrical, cut beige to frost, jousting medieval knights, gilt highlights **690.00**

BANKS, MECHANICAL

History: Banks which display some form of action while accepting a coin are considered mechanical banks. Mechanical banks date back to ancient Greece and Rome, but the majority of collectors are interested in those made between 1867 and 1928 in Germany, England, and the United States. Recently, there has been an upsurge of interest in later types, some of which date into the 1970s.

Initial research suggested that approximately 250 to 300 different or variant designs of banks were made in the early period. Today that number has been revised to 2,000–3,000 types and varieties. The field remains ripe for discovery and research.

Over 80 percent of all cast-iron mechanical banks produced between 1869 and 1928 were made by J. E. Stevens Co., Cromwell, Connecticut. Tin banks are usually of German origin.

References: *Collectors Encyclopedia of Toys and Banks,* L-W Book Sales, 1986, 1993 value update; Al Davidson, *Penny Lane, A History of Antique Mechanical Toy Banks,* Long's Americana, 1987; Don Duer, *A Penny Saved: Still and Mechanical Banks,* Schiffer Publishing, 1993; Bill Norman, *The Bank Book: The Encyclopedia of Mechanical Bank Collecting,* Collectors' Showcase, 1984.

Collectors' Club: Mechanical Bank Collectors of America, PO Box 128, Allegan, MI 49010.

REPRODUCTION ALERT

Reproductions, fakes, and forgeries exist for many banks. Forgeries of some mechanical banks were made as early as 1937, so age alone is not a guarantee of authenticity. In the following price listing, two asterisks indicate banks for which serious forgeries exist, and one asterisk indicates banks for which casual reproductions have been made.

Notes: While rarity is a factor in value, appeal of design, action, quality of manufacture, country of origin, and history of collector interest also are important. Radical price fluctuations may occur when there is an imbalance in these factors. Rare banks may sell for a few hundred dollars while one of more common design with greater appeal will sell in the thousands.

The values in the list below accurately represent the selling prices of banks in the specialized collectors' market. Some banks are hard to find, and establishing a price outside auction is difficult.

The prices listed are for original old mechanical banks with minor repairs, in sound operating condition, and with a majority of the original paint intact.

Advisor: James S. Maxwell, Jr.

SPECIAL AUCTION

**Bill Bertoia Auctions
1881 Spring Rd
Vineland, NJ 08360
(609) 692-1881**

Acrobats, blue base, minor wear to polychrome, 7¼" l, N1010-A **2,400.00**
Aunt Dinah and the Good Fairy **14,000.00**
Baby Elephant, lead and wood **3,700.00**
Bank Teller, iron, tall man behind three-sided lattice-work grill **5,000.00**
**Bear and Tree Stump, iron 450.00
**Bill E. Grin, iron 400.00
**Bird on Roof, iron 575.00
Bowling Alley, wood and iron, ball knocks down wooden pins and rings bell **12,500.00**
**Boy and Bulldog, brass 500.00
Boy Robbing Bird's Nest, iron 1,050.00**
Boy Scout with Tray, tin 550.00
**Bucking Mule, iron 575.00
Bull and Bear, brass 20,000.00**
Bureau, wood, Serrill patent 300.00
**Butting Goat, tree stump 475.00
*Cabin, iron 600.00
Camera, iron 1,250.00**
**Cat & Mouse, iron, cat stands on hands 720.00
Chinaman with Queue, tin 400.00
Circus, iron **3,200.00**
Clever Dick, tin 250.00
Clown Bust, acorn-shaped hat, iron 850.00
Clown on Lattice Base, tin clown with tray on iron base, does flip **2,800.00**
*Creedmore, worn polychrome, iron, 10" l 250.00
Cupola, iron, man in circular building 950.00
Darky Fisherman, lead **5,200.00**
Dinah, iron 575.00
Ding Dong Bell, tin, windup **3,000.00**
Dog Standing, tin, nods head 350.00
**Eagle and Eaglets, wear to polychrome, trap and glass eyes missing, 8¼" l, N2230-B 450.00
**Elephant, iron, tusks on wheels 700.00
*Elephant and Three Clowns 700.00
**Elephant with Howdah, iron, pull tail 220.00
Feed the Kitty, pot metal **5,000.00**

Monkey and Organ Grinder, Hubley Mfg Co, Lancaster, PA, $500.00.

**Ferris Wheel, iron and tin, no markings (smaller than Bowen's Pat. model) 3,500.00
Five-Cent Adding Machine, iron 450.00
**Football, iron, boy and shed 1,400.00
Fortune Wheel, tin 400.00
Giant in Tower, iron 3,000.00
**Girl Skipping Rope, iron 4,500.00
**Glutton, iron, lifts turkey 3,000.00
**Goat, Frog, and Old Man, iron 2,000.00
Grenadier, iron 1,400.00
Guessing, lead and iron, woman's figure 2,500.00
Hall's Yankee Notion, iron 1,400.00
Hen and Chick, iron 875.00
**Hindu, iron 320.00
**Hold the Fort, iron, seven holes 900.00
Home, tin 875.00
Horse Race Savings Bank, tin, Pat. Oct. 5, 1897 ...1,700.00
Huntley and Palmers Biscuit Tin, pullout drawer ...1,800.00
Indian Chief, aluminum, bust, black face with headdress 2,000.00
Japanese Ball Tosser, tin, windup 2,500.00
John Bull's Money Box, iron 4,500.00
**Jolly Nigger
   Aluminum, bar and screw side 400.00
   Iron, butterfly tie 300.00
Lighthouse, pot metal 1,500.00
Lion, tin 500.00
Little Jack Horner, tin, windup 2,000.00
Little Joe, iron 450.00
Magician Bank, orig paint 325.00
**Magic Man, iron 450.00
Magic Slate, tin 1,500.00
**Mama Katzenjammer, iron, dark blue dress painted to neck, 1905–08 ....2,350.00
Mammy and Child, red dress, minor wear to polychrome, 7⅝" h, N3790-A 2,200.00
Memorial Liberty Bell, iron 350.00
**Merry-Go-Round, iron, semi-mechanical version ...1,500.00
**Milking Cow, broken replaced fence, tail replaced, 9⅞" l, N3870 ....1,275.00
Model Railroad Drink Dispenser, tin 3,300.00
Model Railroad Ticket Dispenser, tin 3,300.00
**Monkey , iron, drop coin in stomach 550.00
Motor, iron, trolley car 2,200.00
Musical Savings, wood and tin, Regina music box ...2,800.00
National, iron 500.00
North Pole, iron 3,200.00
Old Woman in Shoe, iron 20,000.00
Organ Grinder and Bear, windup, bell, very minor wear to polychrome, trap missing, 5¼" h, N4350-A 2,800.00
Paddy and Pig, black coat, minor wear to polychrome, 8" h, N4400 ....1,200.00
Panorama, iron 1,100.00
Patronize the Blind Man, iron 1,150.00
**Pelican with Arab, iron 700.00
**Pelican with Man Thumbing Nose, iron 750.00
**Perfection Registering, iron, girl at blackboard ...1,200.00
**Piano, iron, modern conversion to musical 5,500.00
Picture Gallery 1,200.00
Popeye Knockout, tin 950.00
Preacher in Pulpit, iron 5,500.00
Professor Pug Frog, iron 1,600.00
Puss and Boots, iron 7,000.00

Queen Victoria, brass, bust 3,000.00
Rabbit, iron, small 350.00
Registering Dime Savings 375.00
Robot, aluminum 5,000.00
**Rooster, iron 250.00
Sailor Face, tin 325.00
Sambo, iron 1,000.00
**Santa Claus, iron 500.00
Savo, tin, rect with soldiers 100.00
Seek Him Frisk, iron, dog chases cat up tree 7,000.00
Sentry, tin, raises bugle 300.00
Shoot That Hat, iron 5,000.00
**Smith X-Ray, iron 7,500.00
**Snap It, iron 1,000.00
Springing Cat, lead 2,500.00
Squirrel, lead 2,200.00
Starkies Aeroplane 15,000.00
Stollwerk, tin, vending 1,000.00
*Stump Speaker 750.00
**Tabby, iron 400.00
Tank and Cannon, iron 1,450.00
Target Building, iron 400.00
*Teddy and the Bear 450.00
Thrifty Animal, tin 200.00
Tid-Bits Automatic Money Box, tin 4,000.00
Toad on Stump, iron 375.00
Tommy, iron 1,200.00
**Trick Donkey, iron 1,400.00
**Tricky Pig, iron, risque 4,500.00
**Turtle, iron 2,000.00
Twentieth Century Savings Bank 750.00
Uncle Tom, iron, no lapels 200.00
**Uncle Tom, iron, no star 250.00
Village Schoolmaster, tin, windup 2,000.00
Watch, tin, dime disappears, several varieties ...350.00
Watch Dog Savings, wood 450.00
Winner Savings, tin and glass horse race 1,500.00
Wishbone, iron 5,000.00
Woodchopper, iron 450.00
Woodpecker, tin, 1940s 325.00

BANKS, STILL

History: Banks with no mechanical action are known as still banks. The first still banks were made of wood or pottery or from gourds. Redware and stoneware banks, made by America's early potters, are prized possessions of today's collectors.

Still banks reached a golden age with the arrival of the cast-iron bank. Leading manufacturing companies include Arcade Mfg. Co., J. Chein & Co., Hubley, J. & E. Stevens, and A. C. Williams. The banks often were ornately painted to enhance their appeal. During the cast-iron era, banks and other businesses used the still bank as a form of advertising.

The tin lithograph bank, again frequently a tool for advertising, reach its zenith during the years 1930 to 1955. The tin bank was an important premium, whether a Pabst Blue Ribbon beer can bank or a Gerber's Orange Juice bank. Most tin advertising banks resembled the packaging of the product.

Almost every substance has been used to make a still bank—die-cast white metal, aluminum, brass, plastic, glass, etc. Many of the early glass candy containers also converted to a bank after the candy was eaten. Thousands of varieties of still banks were made, and hundreds of new varieties appear on the market each year.

References: Savi Arbola and Marco Onesti, *Piggy Banks,* Chronicle Books, 1992; *Collector's Encyclopedia of Toys and Banks,* L-W Book Sales, 1986, 1993 value update; Don Duer, *A Penny Saved: Still and Mechanical Banks,* Schiffer Publishing, 1993; Earnest Ida and Jane Pitman, *Dictionary of Still Banks,* Long's Americana, 1980; Andy and Susan Moore, *Penny Bank Book, Collecting Still Banks,* Schiffer Publishing, 1984, 1994 value update.

Periodical: *Glass Bank Collector,* PO Box 155, Poland, NY 13431.

Collectors' Club: Still Bank Collectors Club of America, 4175 Millersville Rd, Indianapolis, IN 46205.

Museum: Margaret Woodbury Strong Museum, Rochester, NY.

Cast Iron

Aunt Jemima, painted blue, silver spoon, red bandanna, AC Williams, 5⅞" h 235.00
Baseball Player, painted gold, red hat, AC Williams, 5¾" h 245.00
Battleship
   Maine, japanned, gold highlights, Grey Casting Co, 4⅝" l 220.00
   Oregon, painted olive brown, gold guns, red-trimmed stacks, J & E Stevens Co, 4⅞ × 6" 415.00
Bear, painted brown, blue and yellow honey coin pot, Hubley, 6½" h 440.00
Be Wise, owl, painted gold, Arcade, 4⅞" h 250.00
Boy Scout, painted gold, red brim, marked "Made in Canada," 5⅞" h 300.00
Boy with Football, boy painted red, large silver painted football, AC Williams, 5⅛" h 2,310.00
Bulldog, seated, painted green, marked "Made in Canada," 3⅞" h 90.00
Captain Kidd, multicolored, 5⅝ × 4⅛", repainted 145.00
Dolphin, painted gold, young sailor in small dinghy marked "Dolphin," Grey Iron Casting Co, 4½" l ... 580.00
Domed, painted silver, gold dome and highlights, AC Williams, 5" h, repainted 35.00
Furnace, polished chrome finish, marked "Fonderie de Lislet," French, slot on top, 8½" h, 5½" d 145.00
Golliwog, painted red, white, and blue, John Harper, England, 5½" h 495.00
Good Luck Horseshoe, Buster Brown, Tige, and horse, painted black and gold, Arcade, 4⅛ × 4¾" 275.00
Gunboat, painted blue, white upper deck, blue-trimmed masts, 2¾" h, 8½" l 880.00
Horse, prancing, painted black, marked "Made in Canada," 4⅛ × 4¾" 200.00
Independence Hall, side marked "Birthplace of American Independence," Enterprise Mfg, slot in tower, 8⅞ × 6¼" 525.00
Indian, with tomahawk, Hubley 110.00
Kitty, painted white chest, bow around neck, Hubley, 4¾" h 145.00
Majestic Radio, bronze plated, steel back, Arcade, 4½" h 145.00
Mammy, hands on hips, orig colorful paint, Hubley, 5¼" h 580.00
Mutt & Jeff, comical pose, AC Williams, 4¼ × 3½" ... 220.00

"Give Me a Penny," black, red hat, and coat, gold letters, turn pin, 5¾", $150.00.

Old 2nd National Bank, 1871, Aurora, IL 35.00
Pershing, General, patent 1917 .... 75.00
Red Goose Shoes, painted red, emb slot in back, Arcade, c1910, 3¾" h 275.00
Roosevelt, Teddy, bust 250.00
Safe
   3⅛" h, 2½" w, painted black, emb gold painted animals, dial on front, slot on top, patented 1881 .. 275.00
   4¾" h, painted green and black, gold stenciling, two panel hinged door, coin slot in top 175.00
   5½" h, nickel plated, cast angels, recessed door, pull out carry handle on top, Kenton, 5½" h 135.00
Sailor, painted, silver uniform, blue scarf and hat, Hubley, 5⅝" h 135.00
Santa, painted red and white, green tree, Hubley, 5⅞" h, replaced screw 385.00
Sharecropper, "Give Me A Penny," polychrome, light rust 85.00
Shell Out, painted white, JE Stevens Co, 2½ × 4¾" ... 440.00
State Bank
   4⅛" h, japanned, gold-bronze highlights 195.00
   5" h, japanned, roof gables, traces of gold highlights, finial missing 50.00
   6¾" h, painted silver, c1900, repainted 50.00
Steamship, painted silver, paddle wheel emb "Arcade," orig Arcade sticker, 7½" l 495.00
Tower Bank, scale-size casting, base "Tower Bank," John Harper, Ltd, USA, 8⅞ × 6¼" 305.00
Traders Bank, detained street names emb at sides, scale casting, Canada, 8½" h, 9½" w, finials missing 990.00
Transvaal Money Box, beaded figure wearing suit and tall hat, pipe in mouth, England, 6" h 210.00
US Treasury, painted white, red roof, sheet metal base, Grey Iron Casting Co, 3¼ × 3¾" 135.00
Woolworth Building, tall skyscraper, Kenton, c1915, 8⅛" h 135.00

Glass

Bank of Independence Hall, clear, tin base, 7¼" h, chips 60.00
Clock, mantle type, painted, tin closure, 3¾" h 25.00
Log Cabin, milk glass, orig paper label, worn gold 40.00
Pig, painted, old, 4¼" l 25.00
Radio, clear, emb details 25.00

Papier-Mâché

James Bank, taffy ad on tin top, 7″ h **12.00**
Kewpie, worn polychrome, trap missing, 5″ h **35.00**
Pig, Hitler's face, emb "Save For Victory, Make Him
    Squeal" **130.00**

Pottery

Acorn, redware, brown-flecked glaze, 4″ h, chips **25.00**
Beehive, stoneware, incised "A penny saved is a penny
    earned," two-tone gray bisque and brown metallic
    Albany slip, 3¼″ h, 4¾″ d **190.00**
Cat, head, white clay, green glaze, 3⅜″ h **95.00**
Dutch Girl, worn polychrome, 4¾″ h, chips **50.00**
Elephant, white clay, green glaze, 5¼″ h **45.00**
Face, smiling, Roseville **170.00**
Indian, bust, china, hp, full headdress, coin slot in back,
    4″ h **40.00**
Owl, Rockingham brown glaze, 6¼″ h **125.00**
Pig, yellowware, blue and brown sponging, 6″ l, chips **245.00**
Possum, Rockingham brown glaze, 5½″ h, professional
    repairs **95.00**
Safe, Marvel, brown glaze, marked "Austria," 3½″ h .. **35.00**

Tin

Calumet Baking Powder, red cylindrical cardboard
    body, tin lid, tin litho face of child, 6″ h **150.00**
Church
    3½″ h, 2½″ w, litho, steeple tower, stained windows
      graphics, coin slot on root, Stollwerck, Germany,
      c1908 .... **275.00**
    15¼″ h, tin and wood, old gold paint **250.00**
Clown, tin litho, clown playing mandolin, ball shape,
    mounted on three posts, 2½″ d **135.00**
Doghouse, tin litho, simulated wood finish, dog standing
    in doorway, Saxony, 2″ h, 2½″ l **300.00**
Grandpa Dukes, tin litho bust, comical expression, coin
    slot in simulated straw hat, 2¼″ h, 2½″ w **235.00**
Hansel and Gretel, litho, children and old lady at old
    brick house, Stollwerck, Germany, 2¼″ × 2½″ **210.00**

BARBER BOTTLES

History: Barber bottles, colorful glass bottles found on shelves and counters in barber shops, held the liquids barbers used daily. A specific liquid was kept in a specific bottle, which the barber knew by color, design, or lettering. The bulk liquids were kept in utilitarian containers under the counter or in a storage room.

Barber bottles are found in many types of glass—art glass with various decorations, pattern glass, and commercially prepared and labeled bottles.

References: Keith E. Estep, *The Shaving Mug & Barber Bottle Book,* Schiffer Publishing, 1995; Richard Holiner, *Collecting Barber Bottles,* Collector Books, 1986; Ralph & Terry Kovel, *The Kovels' Bottles Price List,* Tenth Edition, Crown Publishers, 1996; John Odell, *Digger Odell's Official Antique Bottle and Glass Collector Magazine Price Guide Series,* Vol. 1, published by author (1910 Shawhan Rd, Morrow, OH 45152), 1995.

Note: Prices are for bottles without original stoppers unless otherwise noted.

Amber, Hobbs Hobnail **225.00**
Amethyst, enameled white daisies **200.00**
Canary, Hobnail, three pouring rings, round top, smooth
    base **50.00**
Cobalt Blue, enameled white daisies **200.00**

Blue Opal Swirl, 6⅞″ h, $125.00.

Cranberry, Inverted Thumbprint **270.00**
Mary Gregory, white enameled young boy, amethyst
    ground **250.00**
Loetz, cobalt blue ground, purple streaks, seared mouth,
    smooth base, c1870 .... **190.00**
Opalescent
    Coin Spot, cranberry **150.00**
    Stars and Stripes, blue **170.00**
    Spanish Lace, cranberry **165.00**
    Waffle, light blue, rolled lip **95.00**
Spatter Glass, light blue and white, polished mouth and
    base **210.00**
Violet Blue, applied Art Nouveau enamel dec **275.00**

BAROMETERS

History: A barometer is an instrument which measures atmospheric pressure, which, in turn, aids weather forecasting. Low pressure indicates the coming of rain, snow, or storm; high pressure signifies fair weather.

Most barometers use an evacuated and graduated glass tube which contains a column of mercury. These are classified by the shape of the case. An aneroid barometer has no liquid and works by a needle connected to the top of a metal box in which a partial vacuum is maintained. The movement of the top moves the needle.

Brass, 5½″ d, Aneroid, Holosteric, ring hanging mount,
    marked "France, USLH Establishment" from New
    London Lighthouse **295.00**
Mahogany
    George III, 39″ d, wheel, broken arch pediment, baluster body, silvered dial thermometer, convex mirror and level, inscribed "J Hood Watchmaker Cupar Fife," early 19th C, restoration **475.00**

Hepplewhite

37¾" h, figured mahogany veneer, inlay, silvered engraved faces with "P. Guarnerio, Peterborough," ivory knob, finial missing, mercury tube empty **580.00**

39" h, veneer, inlay, silvered engraved faces with "Lionel...Co., London," broken thermometer bulb, mercury tube intact, replaced finial, veneer and edge damage **320.00**

42" h, engraved silver dials for temperature, barometric change, largest dial engraved with eagle carrying olive branch above buildings, Leoni, NY, early 19th C **1,840.00**

Neoclassical, inlaid, barometer and thermometer, Dutch **3,450.00**

Victorian, 35¾" h, stick, allover carved case, DE Lent, Rochester, NY **300.00**

Ormolu, 34" h, 13" d, banjo, Louis XVI style, rect molded cornice, foliate wreath crest over thermometer, flanked by disengaged colonettes, circular barometric dial sgd "Colin a Paris," conforming cove-molded case flanked by putti, urn crest flanked by fruiting branches **950.00**

Polychrome, wooden, Italian, German mechanism, tan, green, and brick red painted case, gilt tassels and swags, loss to paint and crack in wood bezel, 20th C **475.00**

Banjo, English, mahogany case, hygrometer, thermometer, barometer, balancing level, A & V Cattania of York, 38½", $375.00.

Rosewood

28" h, stick type, orig label on back, Timby, Model #4, c1860 . . . . **400.00**

37" h, stick type, William IV, waisted case, ivory scale, brass border, sgd "S A Caile, Newcastle," c1835 . . . .**1,650.00**

38¼" h, engraved brass, silvered brass dials, Charles Wilder, Peterborough, NH, Woodruff's Patent June 5, 1860, minor veneer damage **990.00**

41½" h, banjo case, Victorian, T Palmer and Green, Clerkenwell, English **250.00**

BASKETS

History: Baskets were invented when man first required containers to gather, store, and transport goods. Today's collectors, influenced by the country look, focus on baskets made of splint, rye straw, or willow. Emphasis is placed on handmade examples. Nails or staples, wide splints which are thin and evenly cut, or a wire bail handle denote factory construction which can date back to the mid-19th century. Decorated painted or woven baskets rarely are handmade, unless they are American Indian in origin.

Baskets are collected by (a) type—berry, egg, or field, (b) region—Nantucket or Shaker, and (c) composition—splint, rye, or willow.

Reference: Don and Carol Raycraft, *Collector's Guide to Country Baskets,* Collector Books, 1985, 1994 value update.

Museums: Heard Museum, Phoenix, AZ; Old Salem, Inc., Winston-Salem, NC.

REPRODUCTION ALERT

Modern reproductions abound, made by diverse groups ranging from craft revivalists to foreign manufacturers.

Note: Limit purchases to baskets in very good condition; damaged ones are a poor investment even at a low price.

3½ × 4", cup style, woven multicolored splint, curved handle on side **55.00**

3½ × 13½", very finely woven rye straw **150.00**

5½ × 6" x 3½" h plus bentwood handle, woven splint, buttocks, varnished, some damage **115.00**

5¾" d, 4¼" h, Nantucket, work, pivoting cov, Nantucket Island, MA, early 20th C **2,990.00**

7 × 7½ × 4¼" h, woven splint, 20 ribs, bentwood handle, good color, rim wrap damage **85.00**

8" d, 3¼" h, woven splint, round, bentwood handle, 33 ribs, good age and color, minor break in rim **115.00**

8½ × 9 × 8" h, woven splint, buttocks, dark patina, cut downs in handle, Crossville, TN type **150.00**

9" l, 6" h, swing handle, raised bottom, New York state, c1860 . . . . **170.00**

9 × 10", woven splint, hanging half, brown highlights, brown patina, 5 percent loss **55.00**

9½" d, 8" h, Nantucket, work, hinged cov, turned finial, Nantucket Island, MA, 20th C, some warping **1,035.00**

9½ × 10", woven splint, herb drying, old dark surface **40.00**

10 × 7½ × 8½" h, woven splint, melon type, old green paint, rim wear **145.00**

10 × 9", woven birch splints, loom, wrap dec **85.00**

11" d, Nantucket, int. stenciled "R Folger maker Nan-

tucket, Mass," base branded "W Clovering," repaired swing handle, splint breaks 575.00
11 × 9", woven splint, wrapped handle, scalloped rim, old brown patina, Caswell County, NC 525.00
11 × 11½ x 6½" h, woven splint, buttocks, bentwood handle, minor wear, good color, old dark stain in bottom 90.00
11 × 13 × 11" h, woven oak splint, buttocks, traces of polychrome paint, washed surface, rim wear 150.00
11 × 14½", woven oak splint, rect, double lid 400.00
11½ × 12" x 4½" h, woven splint, round, bentwood rim handles 115.00

Easter, red and green, straw handle, red woven straw trim, multicolor woven basket, 12¼" l, 8½" w, 5¼" d, 11½" h, $65.00.

12 × 9¾ × 11½" h, woven splint, rect, blue highlights, wrapped rim, dark patina 120.00
12 × 10", woven splint, hanging half, buttocks, dark highlights, cloth-wrapped rim and handle, shaped back section over rim 110.00
12 × 10 × 9", woven splint, buttocks, patina, unusual tall double-wrapped rim, minor bottom wear 100.00
12 × 13" x 7½" h plus bentwood handle, woven splint, buttocks, eighty rib weave, over varnish, wear, some damage and holes 235.00
12¼" d, Nantucket, hinged bail handle, SP Boyer, "Boyer" stamped on base, minor losses 1,150.00
12½" d, Nantucket, oval, labeled "Made on board... shoal lightship Issac Hamblen," splint loss to wrapped rim 1,610.00
13 × 12", woven multicolored splints, herb drying, edge wear 40.00
14 × 12", woven splint, tall ovoid storage, old green paint, handles missing 75.00
14 × 13½" d, woven splint, round storage style, brown surface 65.00
14½ × 15½ x 10" h plus bentwood handle, woven splint, buttocks, sixty rib weave, traces of old green, over varnish, some damage and holes 245.00
15 × 10" h, woven splint, swivel handle, round, 33 ribs, some damage and repair 140.00

15 × 13½ x 13" h, woven splint, unusual wide splints at rim, breakage at handle on one side 85.00
16½ × 12½ × 13" h, woven splint, flower, rect, wrapped handle, dark highlights dyed in splints 285.00
17 × 8 × 14½" h, woven splint, boat shape, unusual curved handle, red and green highlights, edge wear 85.00
18 × 10 × 14½" h, woven splint, wool drying, wire nails 250.00
18 × 14 × 10", woven splint, kindling, alternating red splints, wire nails 55.00
19 × 15", woven splint, round storage style, sturdy construction, dry weathered surface 110.00
20 × 20", woven rye straw, cov, tapered sides, early 19th C 330.00
24 × 16 × 10" h, woven splint, gathering style, bottom and edge wear, gray patina, unusual carved handle found on firkins 150.00
28 × 15 × 12", woven rye straw, oval, storage, Piedmont, NC, origin 345.00
30 × 20½ × 17½" h, woven birch splints, rect storage 80.00
31 × 16", woven splint, feather storage, wrapped handles, brown patina 110.00
36 × 26 × 18", woven splint, cotton gathering, Roevan County, NC 310.00
40 × 30 × 28", woven rye straw, cov, NC origin, 18th or 19th C 575.00

BATTERSEA ENAMELS

History: Battersea enamel is a generic term for English enamel-on-copper objects of the 18th century.

In 1753 Stephen Theodore Janssen established a factory to produce "Trinkets and Curiosities Enamelled on Copper" at York House, Battersea, London. Here the new invention of transfer printing developed to a high degree of excellence, and the resulting trifles delighted fashionable Georgian society.

Recent research has shown that enamels actually were being produced in London and the Midlands several years before York House was established. However, most enamel trinkets still are referred to as "Battersea Enamels," even though they were probably made in other workshops in London, Birmingham, Bilston, Wednesbury, or Liverpool.

All manner of charming items were made, including snuff and patch boxes bearing mottos and memory gems. (By adding a mirror inside the lid, a snuff box became a patch box). Many figural whimsies, called "toys," were created to amuse a gay and fashionable world. Many other elaborate articles, e.g., candlesticks, salts, tea caddies, and bonbonnières, were made for the tables of the newly rich middle class.

Reference: Susan Benjamin, *English Enamel Boxes,* Merrimack Publishers Circle, 1978.

Advisors: Barbara and Melvin Alpren.

Bonbonnière, King Charles Spaniel, oval, black and white, yellow ground, pastoral scene lid, c1770, Bliston 2,950.00
Candlestick, 10½" h, white ground, landscape vignettes, pink ground, gold scroll borders, c1770, Bliston ...4,200.00
Counter Box, 1½" d, ivory, fanned playing cards top, center inscribed "Lady Luck," tortoiseshell lined, c1770 .... 995.00

Box, St Ann's Well, Buxton, scenic, black letters and scene, gold trim, white, blue base, 1¾" × 1½" × 1", $395.00.

Mirror Holder, 2" d, enameled copper, "Sacred to Friendship," polychromed mourning scene, tomb and classically attired woman, slight damage, price for pr 230.00

Patch Box

    3/4" d, round, "Keep this for my Sake," slip lid, c1775, Bliston 325.00

    1½" d, oval, "A Trifle from Abroad," white, blue ship, red wavy border, c1775, Bliston 575.00

    2" l, elongated oval, "May we join hands in Hymens bands," pink base, hinged top, painted pastoral church and motto 225.00

Scent Bottle Holder,½ × 1¼ × 2¼", pink florals with trellis, leafy green, c1775, Bliston 325.00

BAVARIAN CHINA

History: Bavaria, Germany, was an important porcelain production center, similar to the Staffordshire district in England. The phrase "Bavarian China" refers to the products of companies operating in Bavaria, among which were Hutschenreuther, Thomas, and Zeh, Scherzer & Co. (Z. S. & Co.). Very little of the production from this area was imported into the United States prior to 1870.

Bowl

    8½" w, octagon, reticulated rim, polychrome garden setting center scene of youth and maiden, blue and gilt rim, marked "Bavaria" 22.00

    10" d, 2¼" h, deeply scalloped and scrolled rim, brushed gold trim, large pink roses and buds, green leaves, castle mark and "RC Monbijou" .. 35.00

Celery Tray, hp, multicolored parrots, white ground ... 40.00

Chocolate Set, roses and floral bouquets, gold trim, cov chocolate pot, six cups and saucers, price for 13-pc set 225.00

Coffee Set, 9¼" h cov coffeepot, creamer, cov sugar, scrolled and melon-ribbed blank, multicolored floral dec, gold rim and trim, crown mark with "Bavaria, Creidlitz, Germany", price for 5-pc set 125.00

Compote, 8¼" d, openwork edge, fruit dec 35.00

Demitasse Set, porcelain, white ground, polychrome birds transfer dec, gilt trim, teapot, creamer, sugar,

five cups, six saucers, Schwarzenhammer, 20th C, price for 16-pc set 45.00

Dish, 7¾" × 11¼", fluted and scalloped rim, two sections, center scrolled handle, medallions of Venus, Mars, Neptune, blue ground, gold tracery and trim, crown mark with "Royal Bavarian, Germany" 75.00

Dresser Set, hand mirror and brush, hp portrait of lady, long flowing hair entwined with gold streamers and flowers, ornate handles, marked "R.C. Bavaria," price for 2-pc set 155.00

Fish Set, fish in underwater setting, different scene on each of ten plates and serving platter, marked "Mignon, Bavaria," price for 11-pc set 1,800.00

Marmalade Jar, cov, matching underplate, two handles, hp pink roses, cream ground, black and gold trim .. 115.00

Oyster Plate, 9" w, crescent shape, shaded blue ground, five shell-shaped depressions, one round shell 115.00

Plate

    7¾" d, Arbutus pattern, pink and green draped flowers border, gold trim 12.00

    8½" d, cat and roses 35.00

    10¾" d, white center, wide gold-encrusted rim band, delicate floral design, marked "Bavaria," price for 12-pc set 430.00

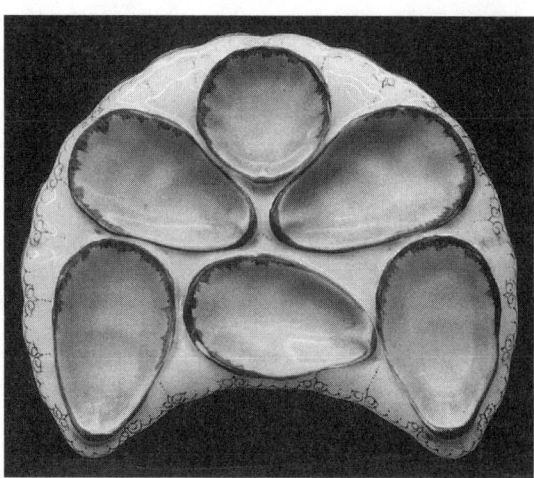

Oyster Plate, half-moon shape, six oyster openings, shaded blue, gold border, 9" d, $55.00.

Portrait Plate, 10½" d, Edwardian woman, crown mark and "Bayreuth" 100.00

Table Set, hp roses and gold trim, artist sgd, marked "J & C", creamer, cov sugar, salt and pepper shakers, toothpick holder, price for 5-pc set 150.00

Toothpick Holder, pink flowers, green leaves, shaded ground, gold rim, marked "Versailles/R C Bavaria" 45.00

BELLEEK

History: Belleek, a thin, ivory-colored, almost-iridescent porcelain, was first made in 1857 in county Fermanagh, Ireland. Production continued until World War I, was discontinued for a period of time, and then resumed. The Shamrock pattern is most familiar, but many patterns were made, including Limpet, Tridacna, and Grasses.

There is an Irish saying: If a newly married couple receives a gift of Belleek, their marriage will be blessed with lasting happiness.

Several American firms made a Belleek-type porcelain. The first was Ott and Brewer Co. of Trenton, New Jersey, in 1884, followed by Willets. Other firms producing this ware included The Ceramic Art Co. (1889), American Art China Works (1892), Columbian Art Co. (1893), and Lenox, Inc. (1904).

Marks: The European Belleek Company used specific marks during given time periods, which makes it relatively easy to date a piece of Irish Belleek. Variations in mark color are important, as well as the symbols and words.

First mark	Black	Harp, Hound, and Castle	1863–1890
Second mark	Black	Harp, Hound, and Castle and the words "Co. Fermanagh, Ireland"	1891–1826
Third mark	Black	"Deanta in Eirinn" added	1926–1946
Fourth mark	Green	same as third mark except for color	1946–1955
Fifth mark	Green	"R" inside a circle added	1955–1965
Sixth mark	Green	"Co. Fermanagh" omitted	1965–March 1980
Seventh mark	Gold	"Deanta in Eirinn" omitted	April 1980–December 1992
Eighth mark	Blue	Blue version of the second mark with "R" inside a circle added	January 1993–present

References: Susan and Al Bagdade, *Warman's English & Continental Pottery & Porcelain,* Second Edition, Wallace-Homestead, 1991; Richard K. Degenhardt, *Belleek,* Second Edition, Wallace-Homestead, 1993; Mary Frank Gaston, *Collector's Encyclopedia of Knowles, Taylor & Knowles China,* Collector Books, 1996; Timothy J. Kearns, *Knowles, Taylor & Knowles,* Schiffer Publishing, 1994.

Collectors' Club: The Belleek Collectors' Society, 144 W Britannia St, Taunton, MA 02780.

Museum: Museum of Ceramics at East Liverpool, East Liverpool, OH.

Additional Listings: Lenox.

American

Bowl, 4½" d, 2" h, ruffled edge, heavy raised gold florals and stems, pastel sponge dec base, CAC **135.00**
Cider Pitcher, 9" h, apples, artist sgd "CKB," Lenox ... **125.00**
Coffee Set, 3 pc, turquoise, gold garlands, pink roses, Lenox, price for 3 pc set **325.00**
Creamer and Sugar, 6" h, floral dec, gilt trim, pedestal, CAC **185.00**
Cup and Sugar, Coxon **40.00**
Demitasse Cup, cream int., gilt rim, SS holder, Willets, brown mark **45.00**
Pitcher, 6" h, 8" handle to spout, strawberries and leaves, gold trim, artist sgd "Leroy," CAC **340.00**

Salt, 2" d, 1⅛" h, master, three ftd, hp green and tan leaves, gold trim, CAC **65.00**
Stein, 7¼" h, hp dec, monk drinking from bottle, Lenox, green palette mark **135.00**
Tea Set, 6" h teapot, Oriental subjects, silver overlay, Lenox, early 20th C, price for 3-pc set **290.00**
Teapot, mauve, floral border, Willets **95.00**
Urn, 7" h, ftd, rose dec, swan handles, Lenox, green wreath mark **175.00**
Vase
    Pastels, artist sgd, Lenox **295.00**
    Yellow glaze, 7¼" h **90.00**

Irish

Basket
    10¾" l, Syndeham, two handles, four-strand plaiting, allover pearl glaze, painted floral dec, imp pads marked "Belleek R Ireland," mid 20th C **690.00**
    11¼" l, cov, oval, three-strand plaiting, applied floral dec, 1st black mark, chips to relief **1,995.00**
    12¼" l, cov, oval, three strand plaiting, applied floral dec, 1st black mark, small chips to relief **2,185.00**
Cake Tray
    Pink and yellow glazed handles, price for pr **90.00**
    Pretzel handles, openwork sides, basketweave center **115.00**
Condiment Jar, cov, 2½" w, 5" h, white ground, gold trim, SS holder marked "RW & S" **125.00**
Cornucopia Vase, Shamrock, 6th green mark **60.00**
Creamer
    Echunis, tinted, 1st black mark **185.00**
    Neptune, pink trim, 2nd black mark **65.00**
Creamer and Sugar, Shamrock, 3rd black mark **120.00**
Cup and Saucer
    Neptune, pink trim, 3rd black mark **55.00**
    Tridacna, pink trim, 1st black mark **55.00**
Dish
    Heart shape
        4⅛ x 4½ x 1¾", basketweave, four-strand plaiting **335.00**
        6" d, 3rd black mark **85.00**
    Leaf, 3rd black mark **40.00**
Flowerpot, 11" w, 6⅜" h, Finner, harp-form handles, ribbed lower body, applied floral designs, 2nd black mark, chips to relief **1,265.00**
Pitcher, 9¼" h, pear shape, C-form handle, pale floral applied dec **120.00**
Plate
    7¼" d, Institute, deep pink and gold trim, monogram center, 1st black mark, shallow chip under rim . **85.00**
    8" d, Tridacna Tea Ware, #D467, 2nd black mark . **90.00**
Sauce Boat, shell form **60.00**
Sugar, open, Institute, pink trim, 2nd black mark **85.00**
Tea Set
    Limpet, teapot, two cups and saucers, six 8" d plates, price for 12-pc set **225.00**
    Shamrock, 3rd black mark, price for 15-pc set **595.00**
    Shell form, teapot, creamer, and sugar, price for 5-pc set **150.00**
Teapot
    Grass Ware, 5¾" h, printed brewing instructions beneath cov, printed mark, c1880, slight chips to spout lip **520.00**

Cup and Saucer, white, gold dec, Willetts, $95.00.

Doorbell, brass and iron, Aesthetic pattern, lever action, 4″ d, $60.00. Photograph courtesy of Web Wilson Antique Hardware Auction.

Shell form, fixed branch-shaped handle 270.00
Toast Stand, cov, green-roofed house, rect tray 80.00
Tobacco Box, 6½ × 3¾″, Mask Tea Ware, cobalt blue
   luster, 3rd black mark 295.00
Vase
   Aberdeen, 7¼″ h, applied floral dec, pearl luster, 2nd
     black mark 550.00
   Sea Horse, #D130, 1st black mark 579.00
   Spherical, floral top, allover floral applique, three
     squat feet 110.00

BELLS

History: Bells have been used for centuries for many different purposes. They have been traced as far back as 2697 B.C., though at that time they did not have any true tone. One of the oldest bells is the "crotal," a tiny sphere with small holes, a ball, and a stone or metal interior. This type now appears as sleigh bells.

True bell making began when bronze, a mixture of tin and copper, was invented. Bells are now made out of many types of materials—almost as many materials as there are uses for them.

Bells of the late 19th century show a high degree of workmanship and artistic style. Glass bells from this period are examples of the glassblower's talent and the glass manufacturer's product.

Collectors' Clubs: American Bell Association, Alter Rd, Box 386, Natrona Heights, PA 15065; American Bell Association International, Inc, 7210 Bellbrook Dr, San Antonio, TX 78227.

Museum: Bell Haven, Tarentum, PA.

Catalog, Meneely Bell Co, Troy NY, 1920, 47 pgs, half-
   tones of bells and chimes, 6¼ × 9¼″ 65.00
Cigar Counter, brass, cast-iron base, marked "Russel &
   Erwin Mfg Co, New Britain, CT, USA, Pat'd Aug 1,
   96, Rd No. 269895" 275.00
Church
   20″ d, steeple, molded signature "Made by Meneely
     Bell Co. at Troy, N.Y., 1911," orig mounting
     bracket, wooden base 325.00
   27″ h, triple, graduated stand, domed cross finial .. 95.00
Desk
   Side tap, bronze, white marble base, c1875 .... 45.00
   Twister type, double chime, c1850 .... 75.00
Door, round
   3½″ d, Corbin's, crank activated 55.00
   4″ d, Connell's Patent, dated 1874 on reverse 65.00
   4¾″ d, undecorated, patented 1879 and 1882 ..... 40.00

Fire, 11½″ l, hand, metal, iron spring-loaded clapper,
   turned wooden handle 225.00
Hand
   Brass, figural
     Napoleon, raised Battle of Waterloo scene 75.00
     Victorian Lady, plumed hat 70.00
   Bronze, figural, windmill, turning blades, emb stone-
     work 90.00
   China, hp roses, Limoges 50.00
   Glass, 5″ h, Bohemian, pink ext. overlay, cream int.,
     amber glass handle, rigaree, and clapper, applied
     pink and cream flower, green glass leaves 195.00
   Pot Metal, police-helmet shape, Queen Elizabeth II
     coronation 38.00
   Pottery, 5¼″ h, Southern Belle, Ceramic Arts Studio 75.00
   Silver, 4⅝″ h, SS, cupid blowing horn, figural handle,
     frosted finish, foliate strapwork border, Gorham
     Mfg Co, c1870 .... 725.00
School
   Desk type 25.00
   Hand held, brass, No. 7, wooden handle 45.00
Sleigh
   28 brass graduated bells from 1⅛ to 3¾″ d, 105″ l
     leather strap 300.00
   34 bells, leather strap 75.00
   42 bells, straight throats, leather strap 70.00

Sleigh Bells, orig leather strap, $75.00.

Souvenir, 5¾" h, glass, 1893 World's Fair, clear, circular logo surrounded by acid-etched florals and banners, int. shoulder emb "1893 WORLD'S COLUMBIAN XPOSITION (sic)", frosted finish twisted handle with star at top, metal clapper, attributed to Libbey Glass ... 285.00

Temple, 13½" h, 16½" d, Japanese, attributed to Tenryuji Temple, Japan, September, the 9th year of Eisho, 1504 A.D., wooden striker 520.00

BENNINGTON AND BENNINGTON-TYPE POTTERY

History: In 1845 Christopher Webber Fenton joined Julius Norton, his brother-in-law, in the manufacturing of stoneware pottery in Bennington, Vermont. Fenton sought to expand the company's products and glazes; Norton wanted to concentrate solely on stoneware. In 1847 Fenton broke away and established his own factory.

Fenton introduced to America the famous Rockingham glaze, developed in England and named after the Marquis of Rockingham. In 1849 he patented a flint enamel glaze, "Fenton's Enamel," which added flecks, spots, or streaks of color (usually blues, greens, yellows, and oranges) to the brown Rockingham glaze. Forms included candlesticks, coachman bottles, cow creamers, poodles, sugar bowls, and toby pitchers.

Fenton produced the little-known scroddled ware, commonly called lava or agate ware. Scroddled ware is composed of differently colored clays which are mixed with cream-colored clay, molded, turned on a potter's wheel, coated with feldspar and flint, and fired. It was not produced in quantity as there was little demand for it.

Fenton also introduced Parian ware to America. Parian was developed in England in 1842 and known as "Statuary ware." Parian is a translucent porcelain which has no glaze and resembles marble. Bennington made the blue and white variety in the form of vases, cologne bottles, and trinkets.

The hound-handled pitcher is probably the best-known Bennington piece. Hound-handled pitchers were made by about 30 different potteries in over 55 variations. Rockingham glaze was used by over 150 potteries in 11 states, mainly in the Midwest, between 1830 and 1900.

Marks: Five different marks were used, with many variations. Only about twenty percent of the pieces carried any mark; some forms were almost always marked, others never. Marks include:

1849 mark (4 variations) for flint enamel and Rockingham
E. Fenton's Works, 1845–1847, on Parian and occasionally on scroddled ware
U. S. Pottery Co., ribbon mark, 1852–1858, on Parian and blue and white porcelain
U. S. Pottery Co., lozenge mark, 1852–1858, on Parian
U. S. Pottery, oval mark, 1853–1858, mainly on scroddled ware.

References: Richard Carter Barret, *How to Identify Bennington Pottery*, Stephen Greene Press, 1964; William C. Ketchum, Jr., *American Pottery and Porcelain*, Avon Books, 1994.

Museums: Bennington Museum, Bennington, VT; East Liverpool Museum of Ceramics, East Liverpool, OH.

Additional Listings: Stoneware.

Bennington Pottery

Book Flask, 11" h, 8¼" h, 4 qt, flint enamel, titled "Ladies Companion," pale cream underglaze, flowing tan, brown, and ochre, overall green coloring, spotted and flowing coloration, Barret Plate 411, professional repair and reglazing 3,850.00
Bottle, 9⅜" h, figural, coachman, brown and tan Rockingham glaze, c1850 .... 225.00
Bowl, 11⅞" d, flint enamel, imp 1849 mark 145.00
Bust, 5" h, parian, girl with bird on shoulder 75.00
Candlestick
  6⅝" h, flint enamel glaze, Barret Plate 198 .... 465.00
  6⅞" h, flint enamel glaze, Barret Plate 198 .... 715.00
  7¾" h, Rockingham glaze, Barret Plate 197 .... 360.00
  8" h, Rockingham glaze with black flecks, Barret Plate 198 .... 470.00
  8⅜" h, mottled olive glaze, Barret Plate 196, lip has old professional repair 360.00

Candlesticks, flint enamel, brown and olive, trumpet stand, 8¼" h, price for pr, $1,200.00.

Coffeepot, 12¾" h, flint enamel, paneled sides, helmet-shaped cov, pale cream underglaze, flowing tan, deep blue, and orange glaze, Barret Plate 136, professional restoration to tip of spout and edges 1,980.00
Curtain Tiebacks, 4½" h, 4½" d, flint enamel, pale cream underglaze, flowing medium brown to dark brown, semi-flowing green, Barret Plate 200, price for pr .. 440.00

Cuspidor, 10″ d, scroddleware, white body, fine dark striations, Barret Plate 186, small flakes and hairlines in base 300.00
Ewer, 7″ h, parian, raised grapevine dec 185.00
Nameplate
7⅜″ l, Rockingham glaze, one white letter "F," scrolling-type shape, Barret Plate 203 .... 250.00
8¼″ l, Rockingham glaze, rect shape, Barret Plate 203, chip on one end 250.00
Pie Plate, 8¼″ d, imp 1849 mark 175.00
Pitcher
8″ h, Alternate Rib pattern, yellow, black, and brown flint enamel, Mark IX-A, Barret Plate 24, very minor wear, pinpoint flake 990.00
9½″ h, hound handle, molded vintage dec, hounds, and stag, Rockingham glaze, Barret Plate 34 .... 615.00
12½″ h, flint enamel, scalloped ribs, Barret Plate 167 770.00
Relish Dish, 10″ l, Rockingham glaze 350.00
Toby Jug, 6⅜″ h, Benjamin Franklin, seated, pipe and wine goblet, mottled brown Rockingham glaze, 1849–58 .... 550.00

Jug, J. Norton & Co, 1859–61, double bird on flower, 17½″, 4 gal, $750.00.

Toothbrush Holder, cov, flint enamel, Alternate Rib pattern 500.00
Vase, 10″ h, tulip shape, black olive flint enamel, Barret Plate 213, pinpoint flakes 910.00
Wash Bowl and Pitcher, 4½″ h, 13½″ d bowl, 12½″ h pitcher, flint enamel, Alternate Rib pattern, scrolled handle, emb scrolls on bowl, pale cream underglaze with yellow and brown bowl, additional blue on pitcher, imp "United States Pottery Company/Bennington, VT" on bowl, Barret Plate 169, minor glaze rubs on bowl 4,200.00

Bennington-Type Pottery

Cake Mold, 9½ × 4″, Rockingham glaze 150.00
Frame, 8 × 7″, oval, Rockingham glaze 325.00
Pitcher, 9¼″ h, hound handle, emb hunt scenes, base hairlines, wear and chip on table ring 330.00
Plate, 9 sq, emb design, Rockingham glaze 290.00
Soap Dish, round, Rockingham glaze 85.00
Trinket Box, 5″ l, natural colors, flowers and grapes dec 65.00

BISCUIT JARS

History: The biscuit or cracker jar was the forerunner of the cookie jar. Biscuit jars were made of various materials by leading glassworks and potteries of the late 19th and early 20th centuries.

Note: All items listed have silver-plated mountings unless otherwise noted.

5½″ d, Wedgwood, light green jasper dipped body, applied yellow trellis, white floral dec, SP rim, handle, and cov, imp mark, restored hairline 825.00
6″ h, 5½″ d, Crown Milano, barrel shape, pale yellow ground shades to cream white, deep pink apple blossoms, green leaves, gray-green branches, SP Pairpoint lid and collar, "P" in diamond logo emb in floral motif 685.00
6½″ h, 5¼″ d, Bristol glass, satin finish, opaque beige ground, pink roses, gold leaves, gray foliage, SP top, rim, and handle 195.00
7″ h, Royal Bonn, sq, floral design, SP top and handle . 120.00
7½″, Wedgwood, Britannia Ware, cylindrical, white on blue, classical figure and tree dec, swing handle, ball feet, late 19th or early 20th C 220.00
7¾″ h, William and Mary pattern, English opalescent glass 875.00
8½″ h, Mt Washington, clear ground, tapering body, molded in scrolls, gold highlights, gold single-petal blossoms each framed by elaborate gold feather scrolls, small side cartouches of clear glass framed by fancy gold scrolls, lid sgd "MM 4425," collar, flame finial, and bail with worn gilt finish 1,500.00
9½″ h, Carlton Ware, multicolored floral dec, cobalt blue trim, SP handle, Staffordshire 120.00
9½″ h, 5½″ d, Wave Crest, shaded yellow to opal, morning glories dec, pewter lid and bail 230.00
10″ h, 8″ d, opal ware, pale purple ground, red and purple lilacs, resilvered fittings 300.00
10½″ h, 5½″ w, Pomona glass, 1st ground, acanthus-leaf design, excellent staining, applied wishbone base, crack in base 200.00

Wave Crest, square, ball corners, two horizontal wavy lines across body, green to white, transfer and painted floral design, SP top, $230.00.

BISQUE

History: Bisque or biscuit china is the name given to wares that have been fired once and have not been glazed.

Bisque figurines and busts, which were popular during the Victorian era, were used on fireplace mantels, dining room buffets, and end tables. Manufacturing was centered in the United States and Europe. By the mid-20th century, Japan was the principal source of bisque items, especially character-related items.

References: Susan and Al Bagdade, *Warman's English & Continental Pottery & Porcelain,* Second Edition, Wallace-Homestead, 1991; Elyse Karlin, *Children Figurines of Bisque and Chinawares,* Schiffer Publishing, 1990; Sharon Weintraub, *Naughties, Nudies and Bathing Beauties,* Hobby House Press, 1993.

Bank, 3″ h, fox's head, wearing eyeglasses 375.00
Bust, 11″ h, 6½″ d, young man, blond hair, blue eyes, gray hat, colored flowers, tan vest with pink and blue, allover dainty pink florals on shirt, blue base, imp ''M. B.'' 325.00
Candleholder, 8″ h, double, figural, girl leaning against bridge in woods, Germany, late 19th C 50.00
Cigar Holder, 4¼″ h, tree stump, bird chasing insect, Germany, 19th C 45.00

Mantel Clock, French, Louis XVI, figural, Perseus freeing Andromeda, enamel dial sgd ''Ridel a Paris,'' oval plinth base, late 18th C, 19″ h, $3,500.00.

Figure
6¾″ h, seated Oriental lady, fan behind nodding head, Continental 200.00
7½″ h, elegantly dressed couple, French, late 19th C, price for pr 230.00
12¼″ h, 3¾″ d, French-style blond couple, girl carrying tambourine, boy with horn, fancy pink hats and baskets, raised gold dot dec, German, price for pr 325.00
13″ h, The Engagement, price for pr 400.00
18″ h, 18th C French maiden, green anchor mark, stamped ''Exposition 1878 Medaille Do'or, Paris'' 145.00
18½″ h, medieval courting couple, stamped ''M.F. #122'' 290.00

19″ h, 18th C French bride and groom, applied blue seal marked ''P.B.,'' minor imperfections 145.00
23″ h, classic maiden, standing beside low wall 120.00
Half Doll, 5″ h, 3″ d, gray hair, band in hair, both hands and arms away from body, nude bust, marked ''5275 Germany'' 130.00
Match Holder, 8″ h, figural, hunter with pipe, dog with bird in mouth, marked ''Made in Germany,'' c1900 105.00
Nodder, 4¾″ h, poodle and bulldog, oval base 165.00
Piano Baby, 8″ l, 5½″ h, crawling infant, white gown, chubby legs, Heubach mark 425.00
Planter, 7¼ × 5¼ × 3½″, figural, cupids with shell, marked ''Japan'' 50.00
Snow Baby, 1″ h, sitting, arms outstretched, marked ''Germany'' 50.00
Toothpick Holder, 4½″ h, figural, dwarf, blue pants, green hat 30.00
Vase, 6¼″ h, 3½″ d, figural, Indian Chief head, feather headdress, braids, blue crown and ''NP'' mark, c1900 155.00

BITTERS BOTTLES

History: Bitters, a ''remedy'' made from natural herbs and other mixtures with an alcohol base, often was viewed as the universal cure-all. The names given to various bitter mixtures were imaginative, though the bitters seldom cured what their makers claimed.

The manufacturers of bitters needed a way to sell and advertise their products. They designed bottles in many shapes, sizes, and colors to attract the buyer. Many forms of advertising, including trade cards, billboards, signs, almanacs, and novelties, proclaimed the virtues of a specific bitter.

During the Civil War a tax was levied on alcoholic beverages. Since bitters were identified as medicines, they were exempt from this tax. The alcoholic content was never mentioned. In 1907, when the Pure Foods Regulations went into effect, ''an honest statement of content on every label'' put most of the manufacturers out of business.

References: Ralph and Terry Kovel, *The Kovels' Bottles Price List,* Tenth Edition, Crown Publishers, 1996; John Odell, *Digger Odell's Official Antique Bottle and Glass Collector Magazine Price Guide Series,* Vol. 2, published by author (1910 Shawhan Rd, Morrow, OH 45152), 1995; Carlyn Ring, *For Bitters Only,* published by author, 1980; J. H. Thompson, *Bitters Bottles,* Century House, 1947; Richard Watson, *Bitters Bottles,* Thomas Nelson and Sons, 1965.

Periodicals: *Antique Bottle and Glass Collector,* PO Box 187, East Greenville, PA 18041; *The Bitters Report,* PO Box 1253, Bunnell, FL 32110.

Atwood's Jaundice Bitters, twelve sided, aqua, applied sq collar lip, open pontil base, 6⅜″ h, c1850 ...... 295.00
Begg Dandelion Bitters, Chicago, IL, sq, amber 150.00
Brown's Celebrated Indian Herb Bitters, figural, Indian queen, gold amber, rolled lip, smooth base, 12¼″ h, c1870 .... 450.00
Dr C D Warner, honey amber, tooled lip, smooth base, emb ''Dr C. D. Warner, Reading, Mich/German Hop Bitters/Warner 1880,'' 9⅞″ h, c1880 .... 375.00
Dr J Hostetter's Stomach Bitters, olive green, applied tapered lip, smooth base, 8½″ h, c1870 .... 150.00

Augauer Bitters, green, label front and back, $75.00.

BLACK MEMORABILIA

History: The term "Black memorabilia" refers to a broad range of collectibles that often overlap other collecting fields, e.g., toys and postcards. It also encompasses African artifacts, items created by slaves or related to the slavery era, modern Black cultural contributions to literature, art, etc., and material associated with the Civil Rights Movement and the Black experience throughout history.

The earliest known examples of Black memorabilia include primitive African designs and tribal artifacts. Black Americana dates back to the arrival of African natives upon American shores.

The advent of the 1900s saw an incredible amount and variety of material depicting Blacks, most often in a derogatory and dehumanizing manner that clearly reflected the stereotypical attitude held toward the Black race during this period. The popularity of Black portrayals in this unflattering fashion flourished as the century wore on.

As the growth of the Civil Rights Movement escalated and aroused public awareness to the Black plight, attitudes changed. Public outrage and pressure during the early 1950s eventually put a halt to these offensive stereotypes.

Black representations are still being produced in many forms, but no longer in the demoralizing designs of the past. These modern objects, while not as historically significant as earlier examples, will become the Black memorabilia of tomorrow.

References: Patiki Gibbs, *Black Collectibles Sold in America,* Collector Books, 1987, 1996 value update; Kenneth Goings, *Mammy and Uncle Mose,* Indiana University Press, 1994; Dee Hockenberry, *Enchanting Friends: Collectible Poohs, Raggedies, Golliwoggs & Roosevelt Bears,* Schiffer Publishing, 1995; Jan Lindenberger, *More Black Memorabilia,* Schiffer Publishing, 1995; J. L. Mashburn, *Black Americana: A Century of History Preserved on Postcards,* Colonial House, 1996; Myla Perkins, *Black Dolls 1820–1991* (1993, 1995 value update), *Book II* (1995), Collector Books; Dawn Reno, *Encyclopedia of Black Collectibles,* Wallace-Homestead, 1996; Jean Williams Turner, *Collectible Aunt Jemima,* Schiffer Publishing, 1994.

Periodical: *Blackin,* 559 22nd Ave, Rock Island, IL 61201.

Collectors' Club: Black Memorabilia Collector's Assoc, 2482 Devoe Ter, Bronx, NY 10468.

Museums: Great Plains Black Museum, Omaha, NE 68110; Museum of African American History, Detroit, MI.

REPRODUCTION ALERT

Reproductions are becoming an increasing problem, from advertising signs (Bull Durham tobacco) to mechanical banks (Jolly Nigger). If the object looks new to you, chances are that it is new.

Dr John Bull's Compound Cedron Bitters, Louisville, KY, sq, olive green, applied tapered lip, smooth base, 9¾" h, c1870 ....**1,000.00**

Dr Petzoid's Genuine German Bitters, amber, 10⅜" h . **110.00**

Dr Stephen Jewetts' Celebrated Health Restoring Bitters, rect, beveled corners, honey amber, sq collar lip, iron pontil base, orig label, 7⅛" h, c1840 ....**1,500.00**

East India Root Bitters, Geo P Clapp, sq, tapered, golden amber, applied tapered lip, smooth base, emb, 9½" h, c1870 ....**450.00**

E E Hall's Bitters, amber, broken blister on base, 9" h . **75.00**

Electric Brand Bitters, H E Bucklen & Co, Chicago, IL, sq, amber **50.00**

McKeevers' Army Bitters, stylized drum with cannonballs on top, golden amber, applied tapered lip, smooth base, 10¾" h, c1875 ....**1,800.00**

National Bitters patent 1867, figural, ear of corn, amber **250.00**

Phoenix Bitters, J N Moffat, New York, Price $1, olive, pontil, applied lip, 5½" h **180.00**

Old Homestead Wild Cherry Bitters, cabin shape, golden amber, applied tapered lip, smooth base, 9¾" h, c1870 ....**225.00**

Old Sachem, amber, flake on lip, 9⅜" h **85.00**

Pond's Bitters, Unexcelled Laxative, sq, amber, paper label **30.00**

Simons Centennial Bitters, figural, bust of George Washington, golden amber, applied ring lip, smooth base, 10" h, c1876 ....**1,500.00**

Star Kidney and Liver Bitters, sq, amber, 8⅞" **50.00**

S T Drake's Plantation Bitters, amber, six logs, 9¾" h .. **115.00**

Suffolk Bitters, Philbrook & Tucker, Boston, figural, pig, yellowish amber, ground lip, emb, 10" l, c1870 ....**225.00**

Tonola Bitters, J T Higby, Milford, CT, sq, amber **165.00**

Walker's Cocktail Bitters, round, lady's-leg neck, amber **650.00**

Ware Patented 1866/The Fish Bitters, clear, tooled lip, smooth base, emb, 11½" h **475.00**

Advertising
Box, Solidhead, Eyelets, black boy illus **35.00**
Shipping Box, Gold Dust Twins, cardboard **175.00**
Sign, Treasure Steel Ranges, 35½" w, 49" h, canvas, Acme Sign Co, Ohio, Mammy standing proudly next to ornate stove, two young children eating

cookies, two adv signs hanging in background, framed, some professional restoration 1,320.00

Store Display, Log Cabin Smoking Tobacco, 8 × 15 × 9″, wooden chest, hinged lid, black man outside cabin smoking pipe **450.00**

Tray, serving, Calumet Baking Powder, Dixie Biscuit Baker, Mammy illus **50.00**

Advertising Trade Card, Sanford's Ginger, Potter Drug and Chemical Co, Boston, black girl with child in watermelon cradle, multicolor, Forbes, Boston, $15.00.

Autograph
Carver, George Washington, signed typed letter, botanist, inventor, educator, 1-page 4to, Tuskegee Institute letterhead, orig envelope, Oct 18, 1932, to young poet friend **575.00**

Ellington, "Duke," Edward Kennedy, first-day cover honoring Edward MacDowell, American composer, postmarked May 13, 1940, small printed photograph of Ellington attached **250.00**

Bank, mechanical
Bad Accident, boy jumps into road, donkey rears and cart and driver thrown backward, letters upside down, J & E Stevens Co, designed by Charles A Bailey, c1891 ....**1,155.00**

I Always Did 'Spise A Mule, mule and boy, mule turns around, kicking boy over, throws coin from bench into bank below, J & E Stevens Co, designed by James H Browne, patented 4/27/1897 ....**1,045.00**

Mammy and Child, when coin is placed in slot in mammy's apron, she lowers spoon to feed baby on her lap, her head lowers, baby's legs rise, Kyser & Rex Co, designed by Alfred C Rex, patented 10/21/1884, repainted kerchief **4,510.00**

Book
Blacks in the Marine Corps **20.00**

History of Slavery, J & H Miller, 1858, leather bound, wood cuts, 800 pages **125.00**

Through Missouri on a Mule, Thomas Jackson, 1904 **55.00**

Bottle Opener, black boy wearing bow tie, cast iron .. **100.00**

Bust, carved and painted amber, tribesman, rope-type dec around neck, black-painted base, late 19th C ..**3,740.00**

Candy Jar, Mammy, laughing **550.00**

Children's Books
A Story of Our Gang, Whitman, 1929, 20 pgs, hardcover **70.00**

Beloved Belindy, Johnny Gruelle, 1926, 90 pgs, 2nd edition **50.00**

The Story of Little Black Sambo, McLoughlin Brothers, Springfield, MA, 1931, 16 pgs **20.00**

Clock, black girl, eyes move, windup **250.00**

Clothespin Holder, ceramic, Mammy **495.00**

Cookbook, *Aunt Jemima's Magical Recipes,* 1952, 26 pgs **35.00**

Cookie Jar
Mammy, Pearl China **900.00**
Mandy, OCI **350.00**

Creamer, 3¼″ h, 5″ w, Mammy, Cameo China, name sgd in gold "cCc. Co", c1940 .... **185.00**

Diorama, 10″ w, 7″ h, beeswax, finely detailed seated Black man, arm extended towards seated Black woman, detailed facial gestures, human hair, American, c1890 .... **320.00**

Doll, 10″ h, Topsy Turvey, black composition head and body, three pigtails **95.00**

Dresser Jar, Butler **365.00**

Figure
11″ h, 3½″ d, bisque, African princess, blue tunic, red and gold belt, pink scarf draped over shoulders, multicolored striped turban with upright feathers, cornucopia of flowers in one hand, bird perched on other, white circular base with gold scrolls and trim, French, c1860 .... **515.00**

19″ h, carved and painted, African colonial soldier, separately carved red-dyed fez with tassel, carved cylindrical head resting on flat body form with intricately carved uniform detail, applied carved wooden cartridge box and bayonet, aluminum buttons, shorts carved with side satchel, two tubular legs mounted in separately carved and attached bare feet, c1900 .... **495.00**

Flour Sack, Aunt Jemima, 25 lbs, c1940 .... **65.00**

Game, knock-down type, cloth and wood, five Mammy figures, painted cloth faces, printed skirts and scarves, attached by large hinge to 4½″ plank, early 20th C, price for pr **660.00**

Hitching Post, 47″ h, cast iron, jockey, painted, 20th C, minor imperfections **690.00**

Hose Caddy, 35½″ h, figural, boy wearing coveralls, striped shirt, straw hat, one arm extended to hold hose, orig polychrome paint, orig hose fittings, early 20th C, unused condition **145.00**

Humidor, 8½″ h, majolica, bust of dark brown skinned man, bisque finish, high glazed hat, hair, and collar **425.00**

Incense Burner, black boy **250.00**

Lunch Box, tin, Dixie Kid, worn top **450.00**

Manuscript Document Signed, Bill of Sale
1776, 1½ pgs, 8 × 10″, Frederick Co, Maryland, Jan

29, 1776, for "two Negroes the one a Boy Named Harry about fourteen years of age the other a Girl Named Margery about eleven years old..." being sold by Thomas Alldridge to William Murdoch Beall for £140 .... 775.00

1821, 1 pg, 8 × 10", Washington, DC, Sept 12, 1821, for four slaves, "...a Negro woman named Milley with her three children—Charity, Henry and Annette..." sold by Brooke Williams to Margaret Dashiell for $400 .... 225.00

1843, 2 pages, small folio, Washington, DC, Nov 28, 1843, combined bill of sale and manumission for "...negro slave Catharine Murry, aged now about twenty one years...," sold by James Dodds to John Smith for term of five years after which she is to be "...entirely free from bondage or slavery" ... 225.00

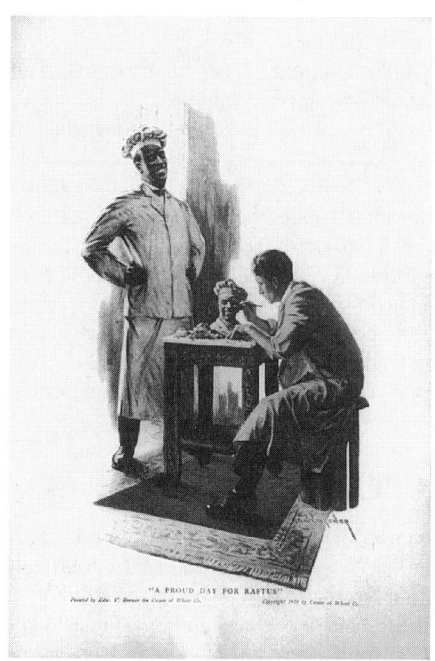

Magazine Tear Sheet, *People's Home Journal,* **printed color, sgd E. V. Brewer, March 1914, 11 × 16", $25.00.**

Milliner's Model, 15" h, painted gesso, black woman, paper label "Wadleigh's Fashionable Millinery and aprons...474 Washington St, Boston," late 19th C, repairs, gesso and paint loss 460.00

Painting, 45½ × 33", *The Negro and the Alligator,* Thomas Hart Benson, oil on canvas, c1927 ....198,000.00

Pancake Shaker, Aunt Jemima 65.00

Paper Dolls, Forbes Co, minstrel show, standup type, uncut, framed, 1896 .... 120.00

Peanut Butter Pail, 3½" h, Pickaninny, tin litho, slant sided, black baby on front, mirror image on reverse, FM Hoyt & Co, slight damage 310.00

Peg Board, 11 × 7", "We Needs," wooden shopping list, Mammy, c1930 .... 90.00

Pencil, celluloid alligator eating boy 50.00

Perfume Bottle, 2½" h, Golliwog, orig box 450.00

Plate, 9" d, Famous and Dandy, white ground, multicolored center, 1930s 95.00

Poster, 20 × 28", Jack "Smoke" Gray Comedian, Neil O'Brien Super Minstrels, graphic image of black minstrel holding bag of chickens, large rooster in background, bust cameo of comedian 525.00

Print

Benton, Thomas Hart, Aaron, lithograph on wove paper, 1941, edition of 250, published by American Associated Artists, NY, sgd in pencil and in matrix, framed 1,150.00

Currier & Ives, The Coon Hunt, matted 255.00

Salt and Pepper Shakers, pr

Bald boy, girl in straw hat 225.00

Butler and maid, 6" h 150.00

Children in basket 95.00

Elderly Couple, valentine dec 195.00

Jonah and the Whale 65.00

Mammy and Chef, Pearl China 95.00

Sultan Kids 50.00

Sheet Music

Aunt Jemima's Picnic Day, 1914 .... 255.00

Little Alabama Coon, 1893 .... 30.00

Three Little Words, 1930 .... 20.00

Sign

Fern Glen Rye, self-framed tin

"Honey Tip" Schroeder's Whiskey, painted frame 1,300.00

"I'se in perdickermont," scratches 2,250.00

Paul Jones Whiskey, wood, "Temptation of St Anthony" 650.00

Rochelle Club Beverages, multicolored, young boy, soda in one hand, hot dog in other, saying "Aint dat Sumtin," 14½ × 22", overall staining 165.00

Slave Shackles, wrought iron, small size 750.00

Spoon Rest, Mammy, face 95.00

String Holder, Mammy, big face 450.00

Sugar Bowl, cov, Chef, Cameo China 285.00

Syrup, Mammy, Weller 875.00

Table, 30½" d, 24½" h, carved and ebonized wood, kneeling Blackamoor figure supporting glass table top, Venetian 2,800.00

Tablecloth, 52 × 48", cotton, Mammy serving pie 85.00

Teapot, black boy and elephant 65.00

Toy

Alabama Coon Jigger, tin litho clockwork dancer, dance-floor base, Strauss Mfg, USA, 10" h, new arms 275.00

Black Boy on Velocipede, hp tin figure, clockwork, fully cloth dressed, three cast-iron spoked-wheeled velocipede, Stevens & Brown, 1870 patent 2,310.00

Butler, carved and painted wood, uniformed, 19th C, 14" h, imperfections 435.00

Jubilee Platform Waltzers, three jointed wood and cloth-dressed dancers, rect dovetailed base, Ives, 1876 patent, orig box 9,570.00

Preacher, clockwork figure, cloth dressed, standing, tin book in hand, raised painted red wooden pulpit with gold stenciling, Ives, missing bible 2,310.00

Spic & Span, The Hams What Am, tin litho clockwork, drummer and violinist, Louis Marx, 1924, 10½" h 1,430.00

Wall Plate, Mammy, Rockingham 155.00

BLOWN THREE MOLD

History: The Jamestown colony in Virginia introduced glassmaking into America. The artisans used a "free-blown" method.

Blowing molten glass into molds was not introduced into America until the early 1800s. Blown three-mold glass used a predesigned mold that consisted of two, three, or more hinged parts. The glassmaker placed a quantity of molten glass on the tip of a rod or tube, inserted it into the mold, blew air into the tube, waited until the glass cooled, and removed the finished product. The three-part mold is the most common and lends its name to this entire category.

The impressed decorations on blown-mold glass usually are reversed, i.e., what is raised or convex on the outside will be concave on the inside. This is useful in identifying the blown form.

By 1850 American-made glassware was relatively common. Increased demand led to large factories and the creation of a technology which eliminated the smaller companies.

Reference: George S. and Helen McKearin, *American Glass,* reprint, Crown Publishers, 1941, 1948.

Collectors' Club: National Early American Glass Club, PO Box 8489, Silver Spring, MD 20907.

Museum: Sandwich Glass Museum, Sandwich, MA.

Basket, 4" d, 4½" h, colorless, rayed base, solid applied
    handle, pontil scar **295.00**
Bowl, colorless
    5" d, rounded sides, outward folded rim, rayed base,
        pontil scar **195.00**
    6¼" d, folded rim, twelve-diamond base, pontil scar **200.00**

Bowl, clear, rayed base, McKearin GIII-21, 1⅞" deep, 5" d, $225.00.

Carafe, 9½" h, dark yellow-amber, rayed base, deep pontil scar **2,400.00**
Cordial, 3" h, colorless, stemmed **750.00**
Creamer
    4⅜" h, brilliant sapphire blue, GI-29, ftd, applied
        round base, applied solid handle, fine curled end-
        ing, flared mouth, tooled rim, ringed base with
        pontil, Boston & Sandwich, c1820 ....**2,200.00**
    7½" h, colorless, applied handle, small rim chip,
        check at base of handle **115.00**
    Geometric, canary, strap handle **225.00**
Cruet, sapphire blue, molded neck rings, rayed base,
    pontil scar, orig solid tam o'shanter stopper **475.00**
Cup Plate, 3⅞" d, folded rim, rayed base, pontil scar,
    three McKearin labels, ex-collection George Mc-
    Kearin and TMR Culbertson, McKearin GII-1 ...... **600.00**

Decanter, qt, colorless, flaring lip, three pairs of quilled
    neck rings, pontil scar, type two stopper, New Eng-
    land, McKearin GII-18 .... **195.00**
Dish, 5⅜" w, 1¾" l, colorless, leaded glass, folded-over
    lip, pontil scar, New England, c1825, McKearin GIII-
    25 .... **150.00**
Flip Glass, 5¾" h, colorless, pontil scar, New England,
    c1825, McKearin GII-18 .... **175.00**
Hat, 2⅝" h, 2¼" d, sapphire blue, folded rim, ringed and
    pontil base **850.00**
Inkwell, 1⅞" h, 2¾" d, amber, drum shape, faint ringed
    base, pontil scar **125.00**
Lamp, peg, 4" h, 3" d, clear, GII-18, heavy applied solid
    pegs, period tin matching double burners, short fac-
    tory ground neck, price for pr **1,450.00**
Mustard Jar, cov, 5¼" h, colorless, plain base, orig
    pressed finial, hollow blown cov, pontil scar, Mc-
    Kearin GI-24 .... **125.00**
Pan, 1½" h, 5" d, McKearin GI-6 .... **175.00**
Pitcher, 7" h, colorless, rayed base, manipulated mouth,
    pontil scar, hollow applied handle **275.00**
Salt, master, 2¼" h, purple-blue, rayed and ringed base,
    pontil scar **750.00**
Sugar, 2½" h, 5" d, brilliant sapphire blue, GI-29, rolled
    flanged lip, solid applied base with pontil, attributed
    to Boston & Sandwich, c1820 ....**3,250.00**
Toilet Water Bottle, 5¾" h, violet blue, flake on top, orig
    damaged tam o'shanter lid **200.00**
Tumbler, 3⅛" h, colorless, leaded glass, blue rim, pontil
    scar, New England, c1825, McKearin GI-24 ....**1,800.00**
Whiskey Taster, 1⅝" h, colorless, ringed base, pontil .. **195.00**

BOEHM PORCELAINS

History: Edward Marshall Boehm was born on August 21, 1913. Boehm's childhood was spent at the McConogh School, a rural Baltimore County, Maryland, school. He studied animal husbandry at the University of Maryland, serving as manager of Longacre Farms on the Eastern Shore of Maryland upon graduation. After serving in the air force during World War II, Boehm moved to Great Neck, Long Island, and worked as an assistant veterinarian.

In 1949 Boehm opened a pottery studio in Trenton, New Jersey. His initial hard-paste porcelain sculptures consisted of Herefords, Percherons, and dogs. The first five to six years were a struggle, with several partnerships beginning and ending during the period. In the early 1950s Boehm's art porcelain sculptures began appearing in major department stores. When Eisenhower presented a Boehm sculpture to Queen Elizabeth and Prince Philip during their visit to the United States in 1957, Boehm's career accelerated.

Boehm contributed the ideas for the images and the techniques used to produce the sculptures. Thousands of prototype sculptures were made, with over 400 put into production. The actual work was done by skilled artisans. Boehm died on January 29, 1969.

In the early 1970s a second production site, called Boehm Studios, was opened in Malvern, England. The tradition begun by Boehm continues today.

Many collectors specialize in Boehm porcelain birds or flowers. Like all of Boehm's sculptures, pieces in these series are highly detailed, signed, and numbered.

Reference: Reese Palley, *The Porcelain Art of Edward Marshall Boehm,* Harrison House,1988.

Collectors' Club: Boehm Porcelain Society, PO Box 5051, Trenton, NJ 08638.

Birds

American Eagle, #498	**950.00**
American Redstarts, #40138	**750.00**
Baby Blue Jay, #436	**180.00**
Baby Crested Flycatcher, 7″ h, #458R	**120.00**
Baby Goldfinch, #448	**120.00**
Baby Wood Thrush, #444D	**125.00**
Black-Capped Chickadee, 8½″ h, #438	**130.00**
Blue Heron, #200-19	**275.00**
Brown Thrasher, black feather mark, #400-26R	**850.00**
Cardinal, female, #415	**625.00**
Catbird and two hyancinths	**1,320.00**
Cedar Waxwing and cherries, painted bisque, #40017	**350.00**
Cygnet	**175.00**
Downy Woodpecker, #427	**1,000.00**
Eastern Bluebird. #442	**145.00**
Fledgling Blackburnian Warbler, #478	**180.00**
Fledgling Kingfisher, 6½″ h, #449	**130.00**
Fledging Magpie	**110.00**
Horned Lark, grapes, #400-25	**2,500.00**
Hummingbird, cactus base, #440	**900.00**
Indigo Bunting, #429	**750.00**
Nuthatch, ivy and moneywort base, #469	**500.00**
Oven Bird, 10″ h	**725.00**
Ring-Neck Pheasants, #409	**800.00**
Robin, daffodils base, #472	**1,900.00**
Tree Sparrow, 8″ h, #468	**130.00**
Warbler	**1,320.00**
Western Bluebirds, pr, #494	**375.00**
Yellow-Shafted Flicker, with chipmunk, #400-16	**950.00**

Other

Daisies, #3002	**750.00**
Polo Player, 1964 replica of piece commissioned in 1957 by President Eisenhower for Queen Elizabeth	**1,210.00**
Pussy Willows, pr, #200-28	**195.00**
Queen Elizabeth Rose, #300-91	**1,200.00**
Royal Blessings Rose, #300-99	**1,200.00**

BOHEMIAN GLASS

History: The once independent country of Bohemia, now a part of the Czech Republic, produced a variety of fine glassware: etched, cut, overlay, and colored. Their glassware, which first appeared in America in the early 1820s, continues to be exported to the U.S. today.

Bohemia is known for its "flashed" glass that was produced in the familiar ruby color, as well as in amber, green, blue, and black. Common patterns include Deer and Castle, Deer and Pine Tree, and Vintage.

Most of the Bohemian glass encountered in today's market is from 1875 to 1900. Bohemian-type glass also was made in England, Switzerland, and Germany.

References: Sylvia Petrova and Jean-Luc Olivie (eds.), *Bohemian Glass,* Abrams, 1990; Robert and Deborah Truitt, *Collectible Bohemian Glass,* R & D Glass, 1995.

Reproduction Alert.

Beaker	
4½″ h, blue and white overlay, arched panels with gilt ivy and stylized foliage on oval white overlay, flaring base, mid 19th C	**225.00**
4¾″ h, green flashed, circular and oval cut windows, multicolored enameled flowers, gilt lines	**215.00**
5″ h, pink flashed opaque, cut stylized leaves and drapery, enamel and gilt flowering branches, flaring base, late 19th C	**475.00**
5¼″ h, white on amethyst overlay, quatrefoil and circular cut windows, painted trailing roses	**250.00**
Bottle, 12¼″ h, blue cut to clear, frosted-leaf dec	**450.00**
Center Bowl, 9″ d, 11½″ h, ribbed and ruffled green irid glass bowl, elaborate metal base with three cherubs playing flutes	**520.00**

Bowl, ftd, ten panels, shaped top, leaf and grape design, 3⅛″ top diameter, 2″ h, $45.00.

Cruet, amber cut to clear, carved floral arrangement intaglio, three oval panels with ruby flashing, carved floral swags, five cut-to-clear neck panels with gold scrollwork, sixteen dec cut panels on amber cut to clear stopper, gold edges, base sgd "4," stopper base sgd "4"	**750.00**
Decanter	
15½″ h, ruby cut to clear, geese dec, cut stopper ..	**140.00**
15¾″ h, ruby cut to clear, floral dec, orig stopper ..	**120.00**
Goblet	
5″ h, amber overlay, cut and frosted forest scenes, early 20th C	**85.00**
5¾″ h, ruby overlay, raised panels, faceted body, gilt scrolled ground, late 19th/early 20th C, wear, chips, price for 12-pc set	**1,840.00**
8½″ h, amethyst cut to clear, early 20th C	**25.00**
Lamp, 25″ h, candlestick type, amber overlay, cut and frosted foliate panels, price for pr	**500.00**
Tumbler, 4¼″ h, clear, leaded glass, pontil scar, enameled German inscription, florals, heart, two hands shaking, dated 1727	**550.00**

Vase
  9" h, amber, enameled flowers, gold trim 495.00
  10" h, pinched oval, flared rim, green-cased amber-
    mottled body, silver resist vertical foliate motif .. 230.00
  11¾" h, mold blown quatraform lobed body, lustered
    purple and yellow-amber swirled striations, pol-
    ished at rim, attributed to Kralik 435.00
  13¾" h, enamel and gilt dec, ruby-flashed trim 600.00
Wine Ewer, 10¼" h, amber flashed, cut and etched
  grapevines and clusters dec 400.00
Wine Glass, 7¾" h, ruby overlay, raised blue, amethyst,
  and ruby panels, faceted body, gilt scrolled ground,
  late 19th/early 20th C, wear, chips, price for 12-pc
  set 1,840.00

BOOKS, AMERICANA

History: America's fascination with local, regional, state, and national history owes its origin to the nation's centennial in 1876. The next 30 years witnessed a proliferation of histories, atlases, genealogies, and photographic studies. Historical groups organized and published pamphlets or annual studies. An ongoing renewal of interest in local history occurred with the historic preservation movement of the 1950s. As communities and states celebrated the milestone anniversaries of their establishment—50th, 75th, 100th, etc.—committees organized celebrations, one by-product of which was a local-history publication. The number of these types of books and pamphlets ranges in the hundreds of thousands.

References: *American Book Prices Current*, Bancroft-Parkman, published annually; Ron Barlow and Ray Reynolds, *The Insider's Guide to Old Books, Magazines, Newspapers, Trade Catalogs*, Windmill Publishing (2147 Windmill View Rd, Cajon, CA 92020), 1995; Ian C. Ellis, *How to Find, Buy, and Sell Used and Rare Books*, Perigree Books, 1996; *Huxford's Old Book Value Guide*, Seventh Edition, Collector Books, 1995; Marie Tedford and Pat Goudey, *The Official Price Guide to Old Books*, House of Collectibles, 1994; John Wade, *Tomart's Price Guide to 20th Century Books*, Tomart Publications, 1994; Nancy Wright, *Books*, Avon Books, 1993.

Periodicals: *A B Bookman's Weekly*, PO Box AB, Clifton, NJ 07015; *Bookseller*, PO Box 8183, Ann Arbor, MI 48107; *Book Source Monthly*, 2007 Syossett Dr, PO Box 567, Cazenovia, NY 13035; *Rare Book Bulletin*, PO Box 201, Peoria, IL 61650.

Additional Listings: See Miniature Books, Paperback Books, and Western Americana in *Warman's Americana & Collectibles*.

Notes: The prices listed below serve as a model for local-history publications. Compare similar items to this listing—prices are approximately the same nationwide for the identical type of material. More recent publications, i.e., within the last 25 years, rarely are valued above their initial selling price.

  Remember, condition is perhaps the greatest factor in correctly pricing a book. Local and regional books will bring slightly higher prices in the areas about which they are written.

American Guide Service, WPA, Federal Writer's Project
  Maine, A Guide, Down East, 1939, 1st ed, 1st print-
    ing, map 32.00

South Dakota—A Guide, Pierre, SC, 1938, 1st ed,
  438 pgs 75.00
Armstrong, Sperry, *Great River, Wide Land: Rio Grande
  Through History,* Macmillan, 1967, 1st ed 12.00
Banta, R E, *Hoosier Caravan—A Treasury of Indiana Life
  and Lore,* Indiana University Press, 1975, 2nd ed, dj 22.00
Barber, John W and Howe, Henry, *Historical Collections
  of the State of New York...Its History and Antiquities,
  with Geographical Descriptions of Every Township in
  the State,* NY, 1846, modern cloth, folding map, 13
  wood engraved plates, missing several pgs 50.00
Beverly, Robert, *History & Present State of Virginia,* 1st
  ed, University of North Carolina, 366 pgs, index, dj 22.00
Boucher & Hedley, *Old and New Westmoreland, PA,* 4
  vol, over 2,500 pgs, illus, portraits, 8 × 11" 165.00
Bowles, Samuel, *Across the Continent, A Summer's Journey to the Rocky Mountains,* 1865, 452 pages 63.00
Brown, Henry Collins, *Valentine's Manual of Old New
  York,* Valentine's Manual, Inc, 1927, 392 pgs, color
  and black and white illus 30.00
Burley's U S Centennial Gazetteer & Guide 1876, 892
  pgs, adv and Centennial info 30.00
Calvert, Mary, *Dawn Over the Kennebec,* Twin City
  Printery, Lewiston, 1983, 1st ed, 452 pages, color and
  black and white illus, folded map 13.00
Carr, Clark, *The Illini: A Story of the Prairies,* McClurg,
  1904, 468 pgs, worn, frayed edges 16.00
Cawley, James and Margaret, *Tables of Old Grafton,* A
  S Barnes, 1974, Vermont village folklore 9.50
Condt, Uzal W, *The History of Easton, Pennsylvania,
  1739–1885,* Easton, 1889, 500 pgs, illus 150.00
Day, Sherman, *Historical Collections of the State of
  Pennsylvania,* Philadelphia, 1848, 708 pgs, 165
  wood engravings 75.00
Donovan, F, *Mile-Posts on the Prairie, Minneapolis and
  St Louis Railroad,* 1950, 2nd ed, indexed, worn dj . 25.00
Edgell, Scott, *Sketches of Lake Wawasee,* IN Historical
  Society, Indianapolis, 1967, companion to *Early Wa-
  wasee Days* by Eli Lilly, blue-green cloth cov 15.00
Everts, Louis H, *History of the Connecticut Valley in*

Massachusetts, Philadelphia, 1879, 2 volumes, 1,111 pgs, illus and portraits,½ leather, edge wear **110.00**

Fielder, Mildred, *Lawrence County (South Dakota) Dakota Territory Centennial 1861–1961,* 1960, 186 pages, photographs, Centennial Committee **18.00**

French, J H, *Gazette of the State of New York...A Complete History and Description of Every County, City, Town, Village and Locality,* Syracuse, R P Smith, 1860, 8th ed, 8 × 10", leather-backed cloth, slightly worn, rear inner hinge broken, engraved title page, 12 steel engraved plates, map missing **65.00**

Gibson, John, *History of York County, Pennsylvania,* Chicago, 1886, 979 pgs, litho plates,½ leather, 8 × 10" **175.00**

Greater Greenburg Profile, Westmoreland County, PA, 1962, 440 pgs, 8 × 11", heavy paper covers **20.00**

Harvey, C B, *Genealogical History of Hudson and Bergen Counties, New Jersey,* 1900, 627 pgs, index, illus, maps, faded leather cover **55.00**

Huntley, Elizabeth Valentine, *Peninsula Pilgrimage, An Off Beat Journey through Stately Historic Virginia,* Princeton, NJ, 1974, reprint of 1941 ed, 398 pgs, 150 illus, dj **12.00**

In the Maine Woods, Bangor & Aroostook Railroad, Bangor, 1911, wraps, 168 pgs, illus **10.00**

Ingalls, F, *The Valley Road, the Story of Virginia Hot Springs,* 1949 .... **11.00**

Jenkins, Howard M, *Historical Collections Relating to Gwynedd, A Township of Montgomery County, Pennsylvania,* Philadelphia, 1884, 400 pgs, illus, rebound **90.00**

Lake's Atlas Columbiana County, OH, 1870, 1st ed, 69 pages, black and white maps, landowner's names, business directory, 13 × 16", rebound leather **230.00**

Leslie's Official Pictorial History of the Spanish-American War, Washington, DC, 1899, 614 pages, photographs, 12 × 17½", worn cover **95.00**

Ligonier Bicentennial 1758–1958, Westmoreland County, PA, 70 pgs, 8 × 11" **35.00**

Marotta, E, *Washington County, PA, The Second 100 Years,* 1985, 172 pages, 8 × 11" **35.00**

McKinney, Wm W, *Early Pittsburgh Presbyterianism...1758–1839,* Pittsburgh, 1938, 345 pgs, map .. **20.00**

Nicewarner, Gladys Bull, *Michigan City, Indiana—The Life of a Town,* 1980, 365 pgs, history, illus, photographs, blue cloth cover, sgd by author **55.00**

Nicklin, Phillip, *A Pleasant Peregrination Through The Prettiest Parts Of Pennsylvania Performed by Peregrine Prolix,* Philadelphia, 1836, 148 pgs, orig publisher's cloth **95.00**

Polk, R L, *Fort Wayne, Indiana City Directory,* Detroit, MI, 1,098 pgs, business adv, names, and addresses **25.00**

Quaife, Milo, *History of the Ordinance of 1787 and the Old Northwest Territory,* 1937, NW Territory Celebration Commission, 95 pgs, illus, maps, stiff covers **27.00**

Rich, Louise, *The Coast of Maine: An Informal History and Guide,* Crowell, NY, 1975, 385 pgs, illus **7.00**

Shank, Wesley L, *The Iowa Catalog: History American Buildings Survey,* University of Iowa Press, 1979, 158 pgs, hard cover **15.00**

Stocker, Rhamanthus, *Centennial History of Susquehanna Co, PA,* 1887, 851 pgs, detached cov, worn **75.00**

Trumball, H Hammon, *The Memorial History of Hartford County Connecticut 1633–1884,* Boston, 1886, 2 vol, 1,278 pgs, 8 × 10", illus, wear **100.00**

Watrous, Jerome, Lt Col, *Memoirs of Milwaukee County, Including Genealogical & Biographical Records,* Madison, WI, Historical Assoc, 1909, 2 volumes,¾ leather, spine damage **70.00**

Wells, J, *Chislom Massare-Pictore of Home Rule in Mississippi,* 1878, 313 pgs, history, post Civil War crimes **29.00**

Winger, Otto, *The Photawatomi Indians,* Elgin Press, 1959, 159 pgs, 1st ed, tribe histories, photographs, orange dec cloth cov **18.00**

BOOTJACKS

History: Bootjacks are metal or wooden devices that facilitate the removal of boots. Bootjacks are used by placing the heel of the boot in the U-shaped opening, putting the other foot on the back of the bootjack, and pulling the boot off the front foot.

Advertising, Mussleman's Plug Tobacco, cast iron **125.00**
Bronze, 9½" l, Naughty Nellie **175.00**
Cast Iron
    9¼" l, beetle, worn black paint **40.00**
    10½" l, cricket, labeled "Boot Jack, the Tri State Foundry Co, Cincinnati, Ohio," worn black paint **40.00**
    13" l, open heart and circle, scalloped sides **220.00**
    19" l, two pheasants, brushes **225.00**
Wood
    11" l, folding **40.00**
    17" l, pine, primitive, hole for hanging **40.00**
    22" l, walnut, hearts and diamonds openwork **50.00**
    25" l, pine, oval ends, sq nail construction **35.00**

Wood and metal, spring mechanism, 15", $50.00.

BOTTLES, GENERAL

History: Cosmetic bottles held special creams, oils, and cosmetics designed to enhance the beauty of the user. Some also claimed, especially on their colorful labels, to cure or provide relief from common ailments.

A number of household items, e.g., cleaning fluids and polishes, required glass storage containers. Many are collected for their fine lithographed labels.

Mineral water bottles contained water from a natural spring. Spring water was favored by health-conscious people between the 1850s and 1900s.

Nursing bottles, used to feed the young and sickly, were a great help to the housewife because of their graduated measure markings, replaceable nipples, and the ease with which they could be cleaned, sterilized, and reused.

References: Ralph & Terry Kovel, *The Kovels' Bottles Price List,* Tenth Edition, Crown Publishers, 1996; Peck and Audie Markota, *Western Blob Top Soda and Mineral Bottles,* Second Edition, published by authors, 1994; John Odell, *Digger Odell's Official Antique Bottle and Glass Collector Magazine Price Guide Series,* Vols. 1 through 8, published by author (1910 Shawhan Rd, Morrow, OH 45152), 1995; Diane Ostrander, *A Guide to American Nursing Bottles,* 1984, Revised Edition by American Collectors of Infant Feeders, 1992; Michael Polak, *Bottles,* Avon Books, 1994; Dick Roller (comp.), *Indiana Glass Factories Notes,* Acorn Press, 1994.

Periodicals: *Antique Bottle And Glass Collector,* PO Box 187, East Greenville, PA 18041; *Canadian Bottle and Stoneware Collector,* 179D Woodridge Crescent, Nepean, Ontario K2B 7T2 Canada.

Collectors' Clubs: American Collectors of Infant Feeders, 5161 W 59th St, Indianapolis, IN 46254; Federation of Historical Bottle Collectors, Inc, 88 Sweetbriar Branch, Longwood, FL 32750; Midwest Antique Fruit Jar & Bottle Club, PO Box 38, Flat Rock, IN 47234; New England Antique Bottle Club, 120 Commonwealth Rd, Lynn, MA 01904; San Bernardino County Historical Bottle and Collectible Club, PO Box 6759, San Bernardino, CA 92412.

Museums: Hawaii Bottle Museum, Honolulu, HI; National Bottle Museum, Ballston Spa, NY; Old Bottle Museum, Salem, NJ.

Additional Listings: Barber Bottles, Bitter Bottles, Figural Bottles, Food Bottles, Ink Bottles, Medicine Bottles, Poison Bottles, Sarsaparilla Bottles, and Snuff Bottles. Also see the bottle categories in *Warman's Americana & Collectible*s for more examples.

Cosmetics

Boswell & Warner's Colorific, cobalt blue, rect, indented panels, tooled sq hip, c1880, 5½" h	**85.00**
Mexican Hair Renewer, cobalt blue, oval, tooled double ring lip, side strap, c1880, ⅞" h	**125.00**
Violet Dulce Vanishing Cream, eight panels, 2½" h ...	**15.00**

Food Bottles

Badger Farm Creameries, Portsmouth, NH, round, emb, quart	**10.00**
Chestnut Farms, Chevy Chase Dairy, round, emb, quart	**20.00**
Heinz, ketsup, urn shape, blob top, 7" h	**15.00**
Pepper Sauce, ERD & Co, Pat. Feb 77, green	**35.00**
Universal Store Bottle, 5¢ round, emb, pint	**8.00**
White House Vinegar, round, light green, emb bottom, 9" h, cork top	**5.00**

Household

EZ Stove Polish, aqua, 6" h	**10.00**
Jennings Bluing, aqua, blob top, 7" h	**7.50**
Sanford's Library Paste, amber, emb, label, 1 pt	**15.00**

Mineral or Spring Water

Adams Spring Mineral Water, Lake County, CA, Dr WR Prather Prop, light blue, c1895, 11½" h	**20.00**

Mineral, Adams Springs Mineral Water, Lake County, CA, Dr. W. R. Prather, Prop, light blue, c1895, 11½" h, $20.00.

Congress Spring Co, Saratoga, NY, dark green, qt, tapered top, ring	**45.00**
Empire Spring Co, E Saratoga, NY, dark green, qt	**35.00**
Gardner & Co, Hackettstown, NJ, sapphire blue, bulbous lip with flake, 6½" h	**65.00**
Oak Orchard Acid Springs, teal green, qt	**65.00**
Thompson's Premium Mineral Water, ten-pin shape, Union Soda Works, San Francisco, aqua, blob top	**40.00**

Nursing

Acme Nursing Bottle, emb monogram and star, W T & Co (Whitall, Tatum Co, Millville, NJ)	**125.00**
Empire Nursing Bottle	**50.00**
Sunny Babe, emb full-length figure of baby lying on tummy	**20.00**
Three Star Nurser, Pat June 19, 1894	**50.00**

BRASS

History: Brass is a durable, malleable, and ductile metal alloy consisting mainly of copper and zinc. The height of its popularity for utilitarian and decorative art items occurred in the 18th and 19th centuries.

References: Mary Frank Gaston, *Antique Brass & Copper,* Collector Books, 1992, 1994 value update; Rupert Gentle and Rachael

Feild, *Domestic Metalwork 1640–1820,* Revised, Antique Collectors' Club, 1994; Henry J. Kaufmann, *Early American Copper, Tin & Brass,* Astragal Press, 1995; Dana G. Morykan and Harry L. Rinker, *Warman's Country Antiques & Collectibles,* Third Edition, Wallace-Homestead, 1996.

REPRODUCTION ALERT

Many modern reproductions are being made of earlier brass forms, especially such items as buckets, fireplace equipment, and kettles.

Additional Listings: Bells, Candlesticks, Fireplace Equipment, and Scientific Instruments.

Andirons, pr
 12½" h, turned standards, urn and scroll motif, c1900 **200.00**
 12¾" h, cannonball finials, c1920 .... **50.00**
Bed Warmer
 36" l, floral tooled lid, turned wooden handle **200.00**
 40¾" l, engraved lid, turned wooden handle, traces of old graining **275.00**
Bird Cage, sq, ornate, brass and copper, 19th C **300.00**
Bookends, pr, 7¾" h, George Washington, red, white, and gold paint, 1932 .... **75.00**
Candle Lamp, 12¼" h, 5"d, heavy brass base, fancy brass scrolls and flowers at top of post, brass chains, blue opaline glass shade **315.00**
Candlestick
 Set, graduated set, baluster shaft, pr 14½" h Ace of Diamonds, pr 12¼" h King of Diamonds, pr 11¾" Queen of Diamonds, pr 11¾" h Diamond Prince, pr 10¾" h Diamond Princess, English **1,350.00**

Candlesticks, beehive, push-ups, 9" h, price for pr, $150.00.

Single
 9" h, Queen Anne, Continental, first half 18th C, very minor dents **290.00**
Candle Sconce, pr
 17¾" h, beveled mirrors, worn **90.00**
 18½" h, ornate, three candle sockets **325.00**

Carriage Lamp
 9½" h, marked ''Neverout Insulated Kerosene Safety, Rose Mfg Co, Philadelphia, USA,'' price for pr .. **250.00**
 23½" h, ball finials, two etched-glass side panels, ball ends, price for pr **160.00**
Clock Jack, 12½" l, marked ''G Salter & Co. Improved'' **100.00**
Cross, Russian, cast
 6½ × 3¾", pierced finial, pectoral type, 18th C ... **165.00**
 6½ × 4¼", wall, four-color enamel dec, 19th C ... **95.00**
Egg Cooker, Dutch, 18th C **495.00**
Electroliers, 17¾" h, three lights, suspended amethyst and cut-crystal prisms, electrified, price for pr **300.00**
Figure, 15½" l, leaping cat, black lacquered wooden base, attributed to Hagenauer **900.00**
Heater, 8¼" d, 7½" h, octagonal, pierced, four turned feet, bail handle, four lines inscribed on top in Dutch **300.00**
Icon, Russian, cast
 4 × 5½" open, triptych, St Nicholas center panel, wings display Annunciation and Feast Days, 18th C **165.00**
 7 × 15½" open, folding, Church Feasts, each leaf divided into quadrants with different feast, back panel displaying cross and outer walls of Jersualem **440.00**
Inkwell, 8¼" w, 3" h, Arts and Crafts design, hammered finish, strap-work hinges, dark patina, ceramic insert **200.00**
Kettle, 13" d, spun, iron bale handle, orig label ''American Brass Kettle'' **85.00**
Lamp
 10½" h, gimbal, saucer base **140.00**
 20" h, cranberry-flashed receptacle and shade, trefoil-shaped stem and base, faceted prisms, marked ''J & I Cox, New York,'' c1880, electrified **550.00**
 25" h, Baroque Revival, oil, molded high-relief figures and foliage, scrolled base, converted, price for pr **1,610.00**
 28" support tube, hanging, gas light, two burners, etched crystal shades, black and copper stripes . **165.00**
Noodle Maker Roller, 8½" w, marked ''F Crafts, Rochester, NY'' **60.00**
Pail, 9½" h, 6" h, spun, iron bale handle, marked ''Haydens Patent'' **75.00**
Sauce Pan, 5¾" to 8½", wrought-iron handles, price for assembled set of 5 .... **330.00**
Skimmer, 18¼" l, starflower-shaped holes, wrought-iron handle **60.00**
Taper Jack, with wick, English, early 19th C **380.00**
Tea Kettle, 8" h, gooseneck spout, turned wooden handle **60.00**
Telescope, five sections, orig lens cap **165.00**
Tool, leg calipers **60.00**
Trivet
 7¼ × 12¼ × 5½" h, reticulated, lion and unicorn, English **195.00**
 10⅝" l, punch-engraved date 1826, replaced feet .. **60.00**
Warming Pan, orig turned handle **175.00**
Wick Trimmer, 9½" l, orig tray **90.00**

BREAD PLATES

History: Beginning in the mid-1880s special trays or platters were made for serving bread and rolls. Designated ''bread plates'' by collectors, these small trays or platters can be found in porcelain, glass (especially pattern glass), and metals.

Bread plates often were part of a china or glass set. However, many glass companies made special plates which honored national heroes, commemorated historical or special events, offered a moral maxim, or supported a religious attitude. The subject matter appears either horizontally or vertically. Most of these plates are oval and ten inches in length.

Reference: Anna Maude Stuart, *Bread Plates and Platters,* published by author, 1965.

Additional Listings: Pattern Glass.

Advertising, Pioneer Flour Mill, San Antonio, clear pressed glass	**40.00**
Historical Glass	
Beecher	**65.00**
Garfield Memorial	**45.00**
Liberty and Freedom	**65.00**
Three Presidents, frosted	**75.00**
U S Grant	**50.00**
Majolica	
Etruscan, emb fern leaves and wheat sheaves	**265.00**
Pond Lily pattern	**200.00**
Pattern Glass	
Basketweave, amber	**40.00**
Beaded Loop	**30.00**
Crying Baby, frog on plate, 13″ d	**99.00**
Deer and Pine Tree	**45.00**
Finecut and Panel, amber	**48.00**
Garden of Eden, 9¼ x 12½″	**40.00**
Minerva	**60.00**
Rock of Ages, clear, milk glass center	**125.00**
Royal Lady, vaseline	**130.00**
Scroll with Flowers	**30.00**
Three Graces	**50.00**
Wheat	**30.00**
Silver	
12″ l, reticulated sides, wheat design, monogrammed, marked "Tiffany & Co., Sterling," 15 troy oz, minor dents	**440.00**
14″ l, basketweave tray partially covered by tromp l'oeil casually folded napkin with linen look, fringed hem, Pavel Ovchinnikov, Moscow, 1874	**5,520.00**

Last Supper, Frosted Grape Leaf pattern border, 10⅞ × 7″, $75.00.

BRIDE'S BASKETS

History: A ruffled-edge glass bowl in a metal holder was a popular wedding gift between 1880 and 1910, hence the name "bride's basket." These bowls can be found in most glass types of the period. The metal holder was generally silver plated with a bail handle, thus enhancing the basket image.

Over the years, bowls and bases became separated and married pieces resulted. If the base has been lost, the bowl should be sold separately.

Reference: John Mebane, *Collecting Bride's Baskets and Other Glass Fancies,* Wallace-Homestead, 1976.

Reproduction Alert: The glass bowls have been reproduced.

Note: Items listed below have a silver-plated holder unless otherwise noted.

7½″ d, 3¾″ h, rich pink ext. with opalescent stripes, gold lustered int., sq ruffled edge, Monet Stumpf, Patin ..	**115.00**
9″ d, shiny finish peachblow bowl, applied amber rim, SP Wilcox holder	**200.00**
9″ d, 12″ h, rose amber Coin Spot Mt Washington bowl, SP sgd Pairpoint stand, c1880	**875.00**
9½″ sq, Diamond Quilted MOP satin bowl, deep blue shading to pale blue int., blue shading to white ext., applied frosted crimped edge, Mt Washington	**600.00**
9¾″ d, 11″ h, off-white ext., shaded rose int., crystal ruffled edge, Rogers & Bros SP basket with two small hands, chains, fruit design on holder	**295.00**
9¾″ l, 16″ h, cased reticulated decagonal-waisted SS basket-form frame, panels of C-scrolls, flowers, cartouches with couples, amatory trophies, lacy openwork, quiver and bow motif centered on swing handle, conforming clear-glass liner, Louis XVI style, pseudo hallmarks, early 20th C	**1,210.00**

Cased, pink int. with spattered rose dec, purple rim, SP pedestal base, $125.00.

10″ d, 2½″ h, deep rose shading to pink satin bowl, ruffled, enameled floral dec	**225.00**
10½″ d, blue and white spangled glass, applied clear twist handle	**275.00**
10½″ d, 12½″ h, oval satin bowl, blue int., white ext., pleated rim, applied frosted ribbon edge, ornate ftd Forbes frame	**250.00**
11″ d, 11½″ h, tricorn Crown Milano bowl, six large pansies, pale purple and orange tracery medallions, pale yellow int., orig tricorn ftd Pairpoint stand	**3,000.00**

11¼" d, 3¼" h, 3⅝" d base, bowl only, deep shaded to
   light pink overlay, enameled yellow daises, rust centers, small blue flowers **225.00**
11½" d, 12" h, dark red satin glass shaded to cream,
   ruffled and crimped rim, SP stand **275.00**
11½" d, 13½" h, ruffled white shading to pink to raspberry bowl cased in white, plum dec, gold branches,
   hanging ferns, gold-dotted florals, ornate double-han-
   dled silver frame, figural flowers on handle and base **395.00**
13½" h, pierced and engraved SS, boat shape, Whiting,
   1916, approximately 28 troy oz **825.00**
14" l, oval yellow-green bowl cased in pink, encrusted
   gold flowers, brass flower-form stand, minor wear
   from stand **385.00**

BRISTOL GLASS

History: Bristol glass is a designation given to a semi-opaque glass,
usually decorated with enamel and cased with another color.

Initially, the term referred only to glass made in Bristol, England, in the 17th and 18th centuries. By the Victorian era, firms
on the Continent and in America were copying the glass and its
forms.

Candelabra, three arm, green and clear blown and cut
   glass, spiral-twist design standards, arms and finial set
   on round folded rim base, ormolu fittings, English,
   c1780, some damage, one drip cup and candle cup
   cracked, price for pr **1,600.00**
Cruet, 6¾" h, enameled floral dec **40.00**
Decanter, 8⅜" h, gray, encrusted floral engraving, butterflies, gilt trim, vase-like stopper **50.00**
Dresser Set, pr 9¾" h cologne bottles, cov powder jar,
   olive gray, white enameled herons, price for set ... **50.00**
Ewer, 4½" h, 2¾" d, turquoise, enameled pink flowers,
   white and green leaves, yellow scrolls, gold trim, applied turquoise handles, price for pr **180.00**
Garniture, 23" h, pink, enameled floral dec, scalloped
   rims, price for pr **100.00**
Goblet, 10¾" h, pedestal base, opaque blue ground,
   polychrome enamel floral dec, gilt trim **85.00**
Lamp, 27" h, glass globe and body molded in high-relief
   foliate and cherub's-head dec, polychrome enameled
   floral reserves, brass mounts, Victorian, electrified . **475.00**
Miniature Lamp, 10" h, 4¾" d, white shaded to soft blue,
   dainty enameled orange flowers, green leaves, sq ruffled shade, base with matching flowers, brown flying
   bird, applied opalescent shell feet, orig burner and
   chimney **885.00**
Patch Box, 1" h, 1¼" d, hinged, soft pink ground, enameled brown and white bird **100.00**
Sweetmeat Jar, 5½" h, 4½" d, floral garlands and butterflies dec, SP top and bail handle **125.00**
Urn, cov, 24" h, 9" d, chocolate brown, foliage, birds,
   and butterflies, 19th C, price for pr **1,495.00**
Vase
   2¾" h, 2¼" d, turquoise blue, glossy opaque, pink
      florals, gold scallops, gold trim **40.00**
   3⅞" h, blue, polychrome enameled flowers, ruffled
      rim **20.00**
   6⅛" h 2½" d, turquoise blue, glossy opaque, gold and

Pitcher, smoky gray, blue handle, gold
dec, 5½" h, $42.50.

white trim, small pink roses, blue opalescent handles, price for pair **135.00**
8¼" h, aqua, polychrome enameled flowers, price for
   pair **200.00**
11" h, pink and white, applied enamel flowers and
   leaves, ftd **70.00**

BRITISH ROYALTY COMMEMORATIVES

History: British commemorative china, souvenirs to commemorate coronations and other royal events, dates from the 1600s,
with the early pieces being rather crude in design and form. With
the development of transfer printing, c1780, the images on the
wares more closely resembled the monarchs.

Few commemorative pieces predating Queen Victoria's reign
are found today at popular prices. Items associated with Queen
Elizabeth II and her children, e.g., the wedding of HRH Prince
Andrew and Miss Sarah Ferguson and the subsequent birth of their
daughter HRH Princess Beatrice, are very common.

Some British Royalty commemoratives are easily recognized
by their portraits of past or present monarchs. Some may be in
silhouette profile. Royal symbols include crowns, dragons, royal
coats of arms, national flowers, swords, scepters, dates, messages,
and monograms.

References: Susan and Al Bagdade, *Warman's English & Continental Pottery & Porcelain,* Second Edition, Wallace-Homestead,
1991; Douglas H. Flynn and Alan H. Bolton, *British Royalty Commemoratives,* Schiffer Publishing, 1994; Lincoln Hallinan, *British
Commemoratives,* Antique Collectors' Club, 1993; Eric Knowles,
Miller's Royal Memorabilia, Reed Consumer Books, 1994.

Collectors' Club: Commemorative Collector's Society, The Gardens, Gainsborough Rd, Winthrope, New Newark, Nottingham
NG24 2NR England.

Additional Listings: See *Warman's Americana & Collectibles* for
more examples.

Autograph
   Edward VII, letter sgd "Albert Edward" as Prince of
      Wales, 3 pgs, 5 × 7", Marlborough House, Jan
      13, inviting Lady Cork and her husband to visit at
      Sandringham, instructions on best train to take and

that Duke and Duchess of Mecklenburg will be joining them **275.00**

Edward VIII, note sgd "Edward" in pencil, both sides of 3½ × 4½" printed Marlborough House card, dated London July 3, 1904, note regarding forgotten prayer book **850.00**

Elizabeth I, letter sgd "Elizabeth R," 1-pg small folio, Manor of Sempringham, Aug 30, 1566, to Sir Henry Sidney, in charge of an English garrison in Ireland, offering additional military assistance by appointing Edward Randolph as Colonel in charge of 1,000 foot soldiers to go to Ireland to fight Shane O'Neill, bounded in 19th C fine red hard-grained morocco, upper cover with elaborate gilt roll-tooled border, gilt lettering in center, silk front and rear fixed end papers, fine condition, bold dark signature **29,000.00**

George I, letter sgd "Mon Frere/Votre Bon Frere/George R" in French, 1 pg, 8 ×10", integral address leaf, bears two small red wax seals, some red ribbon still attached, Kensington, Sept 8, 1725, to Leopold, Duke of Lorraine, re Treaty of Hanover **1,400.00**

George III, letter sgd, 1 pg, 8 × 10", Windsor, Feb 25, 1797, to son Frederick, Duke of York, praising strategy for dealing with French invading forces on coast of Wales **2,500.00**

George V, document, 1 pg, large folio, St James, May 24, 1948, approving President Truman's commission of C. Porter Kuykendall to Consul General at Lagos, countersigned by British labor leader Ernest Beven as Foreign Secretary **375.00**

James II, manuscript document, sgd as Duke of York and Lord High Admiral, half page, small folio, April 7, 1672, to Sir Walter Vane, Commander in Chief, issuing orders to board one of His Majesty's ships, countersigned by M. Wren **900.00**

William IV, sgd letter, 1 pg, 8 × 10", St James, London, asking correspondent to meet Duke and Duchess the following day, light water stains ... **285.00**

Beaker, 3½" h

Elizabeth II, 1953 Coronation, Poole **35.00**

George V/Mary, 1911 Coronation, Bishop and Stonier **75.00**

Bell, metal, police-helmet shape, Queen Elizabeth II .. **38.00**

Bowl

Edward VIII, 1937 Coronation, Grindly, 6¼" d **45.00**

Elizabeth II, crown shape, marked "Queen Elizabeth II, 2 June 1953" to commemorate coronation, 8" d, 4" h **50.00**

Victoria, In Memorium, 1901, pressed glass, 9½" d **120.00**

Box, Elizabeth II, 1977 Jubilee, raised flowers, Crown Staffordshire, 1⅞" d **20.00**

Bust, Victoria, parian, circular plinth base, inscribed "To Commemorate the 60th Year of Her Reign 1837–1897" **750.00**

Cake Plate, Victoria, 1907 Jubilee, sepia portraits, residences, Man of War, 10¾" d **140.00**

Cup and Saucer

Andrew/Sarah, 1986 Wedding, Colclough **20.00**

Charles/Diana, 1981 Wedding, Duchess **25.00**

Edward VII/Alexandria, 1888 Silver Wedding Anniversary, coat of arms, oversized **175.00**

Tin, Queen Victoria, 1900, "I wish you a happy New Year," red ground, blue border, 6¼ × 3⅜ × 1⅛", $50.00.

Jug, George VI/Elizabeth 1937 Coronation, musical, sepia portraits, Princess Elizabeth/Margaret on reverse, Shelley **275.00**

Lithophane, crown, and cipher, 2¾" h

Alexandra, 1902, cup **200.00**

George V, 1911, mug **175.00**

Mary, 1911, cup **275.00**

Loving Cup, Elizabeth II, 1972 Silver Wedding Anniversary, Paragon, 3" h **150.00**

Mug

Charles, 1969 Investiture as Prince of Wales, gold dragon, feathers, black ground, Portmerion Pottery, 4" h **50.00**

Duke and Duchess of Windsor, In Memorium, black and white portraits, Dorincourt, 3⅜" h **60.00**

Edward VIII, Coronation **50.00**

Victoria, 1887 Jubilee, color beaded crown and ribbon, William Whiteley, 3¼" h **95.00**

Paperweight

Charles/Diana, 1981 Wedding, black and white portraits, 2¾" d **25.00**

Victoria/Albert, black and white portraits, color, glitter, 2⅞" d **45.00**

Pinback Button

Edward VII, multicolored portrait, gold trim, c1902 **25.00**

Edward VII and Alexandra, multicolored portraits, gold trim, c1902 .... **60.00**

Edward VIII

1920, Prince of Wales, black and white military portrait, blue rim, white letters **35.00**

1937, Coronation, multicolored portrait, white trim **30.00**

George VI, Elizabeth I, red, white, and blue portrait, 1939 Canadian visit **20.00**

Pin Tray, George VI, 1937 Coronation, sepia portrait, Royal Crown Derby, 3" sq **40.00**

Pitcher, Elizabeth II, 1953 Coronation, brown portrait, Royal Doulton, 6¼" h **200.00**

Plate

Edward VII/Alexandra, 1902 Coronation, color portraits, 7" d **50.00**

Elizabeth II, 60th Birthday, large color portrait, Coalport **75.00**

George VI, 1937 Coronation, clear glass **45.00**

Princess Margaret, birth, parakeets, flowers, Paragon,
6″ d **75.00**
Victoria, 150th Anniversary of Coronation, gold portrait, 10½″ d **140.00**
Shaving Mug, Edward VIII, 1937 Coronation, sepia por-
trait **75.00**
Teapot
Edward VII/Alexandra, 1902 Coronation, color por-
traits, 4¾″ h **75.00**
George V/Mary, 1911 Coronation, color portraits
with Prince of Wales, bone china **250.00**
Tea Set, Elizabeth II, 1953 Coronation, teapot, creamer,
and sugar, relief portraits, Jasperware, white on royal
blue, Wedgwood. price for set **350.00**
Tin, color portrait
Andrew/Sarah, 1986 Wedding, 8″ d **15.00**
Edward VII/Alexandra, 1902 Coronation, Ridgway
Ltd. Tea **120.00**
Elizabeth II, 1953 Coronation, hinged lid, Rowntree **25.00**
Princess Mary, 1922 Wedding **40.00**

**Tumbler, Coronation of George VI,
1937, Made in England, 4⅜″ h, $38.00.**

BRONZE

History: Bronze is an alloy of copper, tin, and traces of other
metals. It has been used since Biblical times not only for art objects, but also for utilitarian wares. After a slump in the Middle
Ages, the use of bronze was revived in the 17th century and
continued to be popular until the early 20th century.

References: Harold Berman, *Bronzes: Sculptors & Founders
1800–1930,* Vols. 1–4 and Index, distributed by Schiffer Publishing, 1996; *Catalog of the Society des Beaux Arts, Paris,* Schiffer
Publishing, 1995 reprint; *1886 Catalog of the French Bronze
Foundry of F. Barbedienne of Paris,* Schiffer Publishing, 1995 reprint; Pierre Kjellberg, *The Bronzes of the Nineteenth Century,*
Schiffer Publishing, 1994; Lynne and Fritz Weber, *Jacobsen's Thirteenth Painting and Bronze Price Guide,* January 1992 to January
1994, Weber Publications, 1994.

Notes: Do not confuse a ''bronzed'' object with a true bronze. A
bronzed item usually is made of white metal and then coated with

a reddish-brown material to give it a bronze appearance. A magnet will stick to it but not to anything made of true bronze.

A signed bronze commands a higher market price than an
unsigned one. There also are ''signed'' reproductions on the market. It is very important to know the history of the mold and the
background of the foundry.

Andirons, pr, 13¾″ h, Diego Giacometti style, stamped
''Made in France'' **1,850.00**
Blotter, rocker type, Zodiac pattern, sgd ''Tiffany Studios'' **90.00**
Bookends, pr
6¼″ h, kneeling youth, partially clothed, marked ''J
Konti, 1911'' **440.00**
7″ h, seated classical philosopher with scroll in hand,
by T Ullman, retailed by B Altman & Co, German **575.00**
7¾″ h, cranes, marked ''Oscar B Bach'' **440.00**
Bust
10″ h, jester, sgd ''Dee Frank,'' sq slate base **120.00**
14½″ h, man, sgd ''F Peleschka,'' early 20th C, Continental **210.00**
Candelabra, 36″ h, classical beauty standing on marble
and gilt-bronze plinth, supporting three-branch candelabra, artist sgd ''Boureky,'' 19th C, price for pr **27,600.00**
Candlesticks, pr, Iota pattern, Robert Jarvie, c1910 ...**13,800.00**
Cash Register, 21″ h, labeled ''Lincoln Hotel,'' National
Cash Register **625.00**
Compote, 15¼ × 12¼″ oval, cylindrical cut-crystal
bowl, four columns, circular bronze base, claw feet,
Empire style, Austrian **1,200.00**
Desk Garniture, champleve dec, calendar, two inkwells,
hand blotter, and wax seal **140.00**
Dresser Tray, 14″ l, twin-handled tray, scrolling Baroque
border, polychrome champleve enamel dec, French **500.00**
Fountain Figure, 20½ × 15″ Faun figure, 21¼ × 19½″
rusticated marble plinth, 18th C, restoration **1,100.00**
Figure
7½″ h, seated mother and child, after Raphael, European, 19th C **325.00**
9″ h, nude wrapping herself in drapery against breeze,
composition base **270.00**
9½″ h, soldier, standing, naturalistic base, rich brown
patina, inscribed ''On. Vielle,'' French **160.00**
10″ h, woman sowing, Semeuse, after Drouot,
stamped ''E.V.1, 74,'' rouge marble base **240.00**
11½″ h, peasant woman, after E Drouot, standing,
pitchfork held behind back, naturalistic base,
rouge marble plinth inscribed ''E. Drouot,'' Paris
foundry mark, label on base inscribed ''Moisse-
neuse Expon des Beaux Arts'' **500.00**
11½″ h, 8½″ d, Nude Sprite, gold patina, incised
''Austria,'' A over T, marble base **300.00**
12″ l, lion, chip-carved marble base, after Dela-
brierre, French, early 20th C **610.00**
13¼″ h, nude Egyptian dancer, green and white socle,
sgd ''A Lowenthal,'' c1906, repaired **290.00**
13½″ h, maiden and her suitor, circular base, gilt,
black variegated marble plinth, price for pr **675.00**
16″ h, Oriental figure riding elephant, thick green
patina, Chinese **300.00**
18″ h, 17″ d, soldier on horseback, rich brown patina,
incised ''E. Aahgepe,'' Russian, 20th C **520.00**

Figure, French Army Officer, Franco-Prussian War, holding paper, base inscribed "Alsace-Lorraine," Nous L'aurons, signed "L. Gregoire," mid-1870s, 13³/₈" h, $1,300.00.

22" h, cupids, rock-work base, Continental, 20th C,
　price for pr **1,955.00**
23" h, dancing Fawn, cymbals and concertina, manner of De Vries, patinated, French, late 19th C ..**2,300.00**
24" h, girl with water bucket, brown and green patina,
　sgd "Pompon," early 20th C **460.00**
32" h, David, sgd "A Katsch" on base, H Noack founder, German **1,350.00**
Incense Burner, 23" h, 20" d, elephant feet and handles, low relief of exotic birds among foliage, cov dec with pierced floral design, elephant finial, gold highlights, Chinese **1,325.00**
Inkwell, 7¹/₂" l, sparrow on branch, painted, c1910 .... **350.00**
Lamp, 22¹/₂" h, raised dragons on base, brass font, opaque white shade with gold-painted dragons, electrified, 19th C **350.00**
Plaque
　6" d, circular, Thomas Koschat and Alpen Rose, 1 Feb 1907, by Hans Schaefer, late 19th C, mounted in wooden frame, price for pr **145.00**
　12 × 17¹/₂", relief Christian subject matter, by J Urbanina, 20th C, mounted in carved-oak frame with foliage, price for pr **575.00**
Ritual Vessel, 12¹/₂" h, archaic-form, ftd, ovoid, conforming lid and handle, Taotic-mask bands, flanges on all four sides **230.00**
Sculpture
　13¹/₂" h, 18" w, spread-winged eagle on rock crag, variegated marble plinth, A Santini, Paris **100.00**
　13³/₄" h, maiden dancing with castanets, removable gown, circular marble plinth, losses to marble .. **400.00**
　15⁵/₈" h, In Grecian Dress, maiden in flowing gown, sgd and inscribed "Bessie Potter Vonnoh No. XI," base inscribed "Roman Bronze Works, NY" on side, golden patina **11,500.00**
　19" h, The Star, nude with one arm extended toward sky, sgd and dated "Harriet W Frishmuth 1918" on base, stamped "Gorham Co Foundry/G/A/C #42" on base edge, brown patina, low plinth base**6,325.00**
　25¹/₂" h, Diana with Bow, brown patina, marble plinth **900.00**
Life size, Mercury, holding caduceus over his head,

sgd by artist Nate Chote, foundry mark "Fonderia-Artistica Primo Capecho, Pistoria, Italy" **45,100.00**
Tray, 9" d, Abalone pattern, sgd "Tiffany Studios" **200.00**
Vase, 14¹/₄" h, 12" d, ftd, low-relief dragon among waves, multi patinated, brown finish, Japanese **490.00**

BUFFALO POTTERY

History: Buffalo Pottery Co., Buffalo, New York, was chartered in 1901. The first kiln was fired in October 1903. Larkin Soap Company established Buffalo Pottery to produce premiums for its extensive mail-order business. Wares also were sold to the public by better department and jewelry stores. Elbert Hubbard and Frank Lloyd Wright, who designed the Larkin Administration Building in Buffalo in 1904, were two prominent names associated with the Larkin Company.

Early Buffalo Pottery production consisted mainly of semi-vitreous china dinner sets. Buffalo was the first pottery in the United States to produce successfully the Blue Willow pattern. Buffalo also made a line of hand-decorated, multicolored willow ware, called Gaudy Willow. Other early items include a series of game, fowl, and fish sets, pitchers, jugs, and a line of commemorative, historical, and advertising plates and mugs.

From 1908 to 1909 and again from 1921 to 1923, Buffalo Pottery produced the line for which it is most famous—Deldare Ware. The earliest of this olive green, semi-vitreous china displays hand-decorated scenes from English artist Cecil Aldin's *Fallowfield Hunt*. Hunt scenes were done only from 1908 to 1909. English village scenes also were characteristic of the ware and were used during both periods. Most pieces are artist signed.

In 1911 Buffalo Pottery produced Emerald Deldare, which used scenes from Goldsmith's *The Three Tours of Dr. Syntax* and an Art Nouveau-type border. Completely decorated Art Nouveau pieces also were made.

Abino, which was introduced in 1912, had a Deldare body and displayed scenes of sailboats, windmills, or the sea. Rust was the main color used, and all pieces were signed by the artist and numbered.

In 1915 the manufacturing process was modernized, giving the company the ability to produce vitrified china. Consequently, hotel and institutional ware became the main production items, with hand-decorated ware de-emphasized. The Buffalo firm became a leader in producing and designing the most-famous railroad, hotel, and restaurant patterns. These wares, especially railroad items, are eagerly sought by collectors.

In the early 1920s, fine china was made for home use. Bluebird is one of the patterns from this era. In 1950 Buffalo made their first Christmas plate. These were given away to customers and employees primarily from 1950 to 1960. However, it is known that Hample Equipment Co. ordered some as late as 1962. The Christmas plates are very scarce in today's resale market.

The Buffalo China Company made "Buffalo Pottery" and "Buffalo China"—the difference being that one is semi-vitreous ware and the other vitrified. In 1956 the company was reorganized, and Buffalo China became the corporate name. Today Buffalo China is owned by Oneida Silver Company. The Larkin family no longer is involved.

Marks: Blue Willow pattern is marked "First Old Willow Ware Mfg. in America."

Reference: Seymour and Violet Altman, *The Book of Buffalo Pottery,* reprinted by Schiffer Publishing, 1987.

Commercial

Bowl, 9″ d, green and brick-red border, cream ground, made for Roycroft **425.00**
Cup and Saucer, George Washington **275.00**
Plate, 10½ × 8½″, green and brick-red border, cream ground, made for Roycroft **425.00**

Deldare

Calling Card Tray, 7″ d, Ye Lion Inn, sgd by artist M Gerhardt, logo and date 1909 .... **330.00**
Candlestick, 9⅛″ h, town scenes, black slip artist's initials "E.B.," logo and date 1909, minor chips **100.00**
Charger, 12″ d, The Landing, hp scene of ducks, pelican, and waterfowl, stylized Art Nouveau flowers and butterflies border, artist's name "W Foster" and title painted on front, back marked with transfer-type logo and date 1911, professionally repaired hairline **800.00**
Chop Plate, 12″ d, Ye Lion Inn, artist's initials "BS," logo and date 1908 .... **550.00**
Cup and Saucer **175.00**
Eggcup, double, Village Scene **265.00**
Mug, 4¼″ h
   Fallowfield Hunt, sgd by artist A Wade, logo and date 1908 .... **275.00**
   Ye Lion Inn, logo and date 1908 .... **220.00**
Pitcher, 8¾″ h, octagonal, Dr Syntax Setting Out of the Lakes, sgd by artist M Gerhardt, logo and date 1911 **2,475.00**
Plate
   7¼″ d, Ye Village Street, sgd by artist J Nekola, logo and date 1909 .... **110.00**
   8¼″ d, Ye Town Crier, sgd by artists J Gerhardt and L Newman, logo and date 1908 .... **100.00**

Emerald Deldare, plate, "Dr. Syntax Robbed of His Property," 7″ d, $525.00.

9½″ d, Fallowfield Hunt, The Start, sgd by artist W Folter, logo and date 1908 .... **220.00**
Platter, 13½″ l, An Evening at Ye Lion Inn, sgd by artist B Wilson, logo and date 1908 .... **550.00**
Tankard, 12¼″ h, The Fallowfield Hunt, Hunt Supper, sgd by artist W Folter, logo and date 1908 .... **2,475.00**
Vase, 8½ × 6″, bulbous, tapering, Ye Village Schoolmaster, colonial street scenes, black ink mark **375.00**

Emerald Deldare

Charger, 12½″ d, Dr Syntax Sketching the Lake, polychrome dec of man on horseback, emerald border, green ink-stamp mark **850.00**
Cup and Saucer, Dr Syntax at Liverpool **500.00**
Fern Dish, 8″ d, butterflies and flowers **850.00**
Plate, 8¼″ d, Art Nouveau dec **400.00**
Vase, 8″ h, kingfisher, dragonflies, iris, and water lilies **1,200.00**

Historical and Commemorative

Mug, 3½″ h, Beechland Farms **100.00**

Mug, green, Calumet Club, 1915, 4⅜″, $85.00.

Pitcher
   5⅛″ h, Geranium pattern, strong blues, transfer-type logo **275.00**
   6½″ h, Landing of Roger Williams, scenes include view of Betsy Williams' cottage, logo and dated 1906 and 1907 on base **400.00**
   6¾″ h, The Whirl of the Town—Fox Hunt, unique logo, obscured date, c1906 .... **500.00**
Plate
   7½″ d, Niagara Falls **65.00**
   10″ d, Capitol Building, Washington, DC, canton green, eagle and banner mark, c1905 .... **55.00**
   10¼″ d, Independence Hall, Philadelphia, PA, green transfer **70.00**

Miscellaneous

Butter Pat, Gaudy Willow **35.00**
Child's Feeding Dish, Mary Had A Little Lamb **65.00**
Cup and Saucer, Blue Willow **35.00**
Dinner Service, Maple Leaf, price for 100-pc set **400.00**
Dresser Tray, 10½ × 13¾″, Abino Ware, rect, band of sheep on village street, blue highlights, 1913 ......**1,750.00**

Hair Receiver, Abino Ware, sailing ship, blue highlights, 1913, sgd ''WE Simpson'' 650.00
Plate
   9¼'' d
      American Herring Gull **65.00**
      Ducky Goose **65.00**
      Wild Ducks **65.00**
   10½'' d, Gaudy Willow **150.00**
Platter
   11 × 14'', Buffalo Hunt, adapted from Frederick Remington's painting ''Her Calf,'' deep blue-green transfer dec, logo and date 1907 .... **250.00**
   Deer **110.00**
Tea Set, child's, Baby Bunting **275.00**
Vegetable Bowl, Blue Willow **50.00**

BURMESE GLASS

History: Burmese glass is a translucent art glass originated by Frederick Shirley and manufactured by the Mt. Washington Glass Co., New Bedford, Massachusetts, from 1885 to c1891.

Burmese glass colors shade from a soft lemon to a salmon pink. Uranium was used to attain the yellow color, and gold was added to the batch so that on reheating, one end turned pink. Upon reheating again, the edges would revert to the yellow coloring. The blending of the colors was so gradual that it is difficult to determine where one color ends and the other begins.

Although some of the glass has a glossy surface, most pieces were acid finished. The majority of the items were free blown, but some were blown molded in a ribbed, hobnail, or diamond-quilted design.

American-made Burmese is quite thin and, therefore, is fragile, and brittle. English Burmese was made by Thos. Webb & Sons. Out of deference to Queen Victoria, they called their wares ''Queen's Burmese.''

REPRODUCTION ALERT

Reproductions abound in almost every form. Since uranium can no longer be used, some of the reproductions are easy to spot. In the 1950s, Gunderson produced many pieces in imitation of Burmese.

Abbreviations:
   MW   Mount Washington
   Wb   Webb
   a.f.   acid finish
   s.f.   shiny finish

Advisors: Clarence and Betty Maier.

Bonbon bowl, 2'' h, 5¼'' l, 4½'' w, optic-ribbed sides, turned-in edges, s.f., MW **385.00**
Creamer, 2⅝'' h, enameled vintage dec, ruffled rim ... **275.00**
Cruet
   6½'' h, melon ribbed, mushroom stopper, blush to yellow shading, s.f., MW **1,085**
   6¾'' h, melon ribbed, orig mushroom stopper **1,085.00**

Fairy Lamp
   3½'' h, Cricklite base, lemon-yellow connecting wafer, pink bowl, piecrust edge, Wb **750.00**
   3¾'' h, pyramid, Burmese shade, clear base, Wb ... **245.00**
   5½'' h, 5¾'' w, cup holder signed ''Clarke's Cricklite Trademark,'' flaring crimped skirt, bowl-shaped base, Wb **950.00**
Gaslight Shades, pr, 3¾'' h, 5'' d, 2⅜'' fitter, fluted edge, MW, price for pr **750.00**
Mustard Pot, 4½'' h, barrel shape, vertical ribs, bail, metal collar, hinged lid, s.f., MW **375.00**
Rose Bowl
   3'' h, hexagonal mouth, polychrome enameled flowers **385.00**
   3¼'', prunus blossom dec, yellow ground, square top, Wb **345.00**
Salt Shaker, 4¼'' h, cylindrical, ribbed body, s.f., MW . **197.50**
Toothpick Holder
   2¾'' h
      Elongated diamond quilted design, s.f., MW **285.00**
      Prunus blossom dec, bulbous shape, Wb **750.00**
Tumbler
   Pastel salmon shading to creamy yellow, MW **285.00**
   Peaches and cream coloring, s.f., MW **375.00**
Vase
   5'', flower-shaped bowl, butter-cream to lemon-yellow blush, s.f., Wb **750.00**
   7'' h, trumpet shape, MW **335.00**

Vase, inverted bell shape, flared scalloped and pinched rim, pedestal base with scalloped rim, acid finish, 4'' h, $425.00.

   8'' h, turquoise forget-me-nots and peach-colored roses, double-gourd shape, MW **1,250.00**
   8½'' h, Pairpoint quadruple-plate holder in shape of an Oriental man, MW **385.00**
   11'' h, 6'' d, white daisies, lemon-yellow ground, No. 146, MW **1,750.00**
   12'' h, ibis in flight, pyramids, palm tree, and sand dunes, rosy-pink blush, drilled ⅜'' hole in base, MW **2,750.00**
   23½'' h, trumpet shape, c1890, MW **1,250.00**

BUSTS

History: The portrait bust has its origins in pagan and Christian traditions. Greek and Roman heroes dominate the earliest examples. Later, images of Christian saints were used. Busts of the "ordinary man" first appeared during the Renaissance.

During the 18th and 19th centuries, nobility, poets, and other notable persons were the most frequent subjects, especially on those busts designed for use in a home library. Because of the large number of these library busts, excellent examples can be found at reasonable prices, depending on artist, subject, and material.

Reference: Lynne and Fritz Weber, *Jacobsen's Thirteenth Painting and Bronze Price Guide,* January 1992 to January 1994, Weber Publications, 1994.

Additional Listings: Ivory, Parian Ware, Soapstone, and Wedgwood.

Bronze
> 9½" h, Athena, wearing helmet, defined facial features, fishscale yoke with relief Medusa head, 19th C **200.00**
> 17" h, 11½" d, young woman, medieval revival, doré bronze, marble socle, bronze incised with title and "A. Gory", c1910 .... **2,590.00**
> 17¾" h, maiden, parcel gilt, gilt and dark brown patina, socle base, inscribed "G" **1,950.00**
> 23¼" h, Benjamin Franklin, after Jean-Antoine Houdon, French, 19th C, green patina **750.00**
> 31½" h, Lincoln, George Edwin Bissell, copyright 1904, cast by Gorham Foundries, Inc **4,840.00**

Creamware, 8½" h, Reverend John Wesley, gray hair, pink-tinted flesh, black and white clerical robes, black self-socle base, inscribed "The Revd John Wesley M. Died Mar 2, 1891, Aged 88, Enoch Wood Sculp. Burslem," Staffordshire, c1791, chips to base **400.00**

Marble
> 13½" h, 7¾" d, Diana, socle base, Italian, 19th C .. **575.00**
> 19" h, maiden, drape extending over one shoulder, one breast exposed, flowing hair, flower and fruit garland in hair extending to shoulder, after Carpeaux, 19th C, price for pr **2,600.00**

Parian, John Bright (English Orator, Statesman, Quaker), 1811–89, Robinson Leadbetter, $95.00.

> 21" h, 14" d, Napoleon, incised "A. Cipriani," Italian, 19th C, losses **490.00**
> 21¼" h, Caesar Augustus, Continental, c1900 ...... **1,950.00**
> 22" h, 16" d, Sara Bernhardt, platform base, incised "Pineschi G" **1,265.00**

Parian
> 11¼" h, Charles Dickens, raised circular base, attributed to Robinson & Leadbetter, late 19th C **290.00**
> 11¾" h, Alexandra, pedestal base, imp "Crystal Palace Art Union, F M Miller Sculpt, Pub'd Feb 11, 1863, Copeland" **225.00**
> 16" h, maiden, garland of flowers in hair, black pedestal base **195.00**

Porcelain
> 4¼" h, girl, flowers in hair, Vienna **300.00**
> 10½" h, John Wesley, pink luster, enamel dec, Staffordshire, England, c1825 .... **1,035.00**

Terra-Cotta, 24" h, maiden, sgd "A Carrier-Belleuse," French, c1850 .... **6,000.00**

BUTTER PRINTS

History: There are two types of butter prints: butter molds and butter stamps. Butter molds are generally of three-piece construction—the design, the screw-in handle, and the case. Molds both shape and stamp the butter at the same time. Butter stamps are generally of one-piece construction but can be of two-piece construction if the handle is from a separate piece of wood. Stamps decorate the top of butter after it is molded.

The earliest prints are one piece and were hand carved, often heavily and deeply. Later prints were factory made with the design forced into the wood by a metal die.

Some of the most common designs are sheaves of wheat, leaves, flowers, and pineapples. Animal designs and Germanic tulips are difficult to find. Prints with designs on both sides are rare, as are those in unusual shapes, such as half-rounded or lollipop.

Reference: Paul E. Kindig, *Butter Prints and Molds,* Schiffer Publishing, 1986.

Reproduction Alert: Reproductions of butter prints were made as early as the 1940s.

Mold

Cow pattern, hinged wooden frame **360.00**
Grapes pattern, porcelain, individual size **85.00**
Klappmodel, Maltese cross, five sections, woman drawing water from pump house with pine tree, flowers, tree in bloom, radiating tulips in center pc, 6½" d .. **420.00**

Print

Cow, tree, poplar, round, one-pc turned handle, dark patina, 4½" d **195.00**
Double
> Carved intaglio star and leaves with chip-carved fluted border, floral pattern on reverse, lathe-turned from single piece of wood, c1840, 5" d, small age crack **220.00**
> Chip carved, falling leaves pattern, small leaf print on handle **75.00**

Eagle and rose, pedestal form, highly chip carved, whittle marks **600.00**

Palm held, deep gouge and chip-carved rosette designs, concentric border **220.00**

Pestle shape, chip-carved radiating leaf patterns, notched border **200.00**

Eagle, scrubbed poplar, round, one-pc turned handle, 4¼" d, minor age cracks **385.00**

Elliptical, lightly carved two-way design, primitive form   **55.00**

Floral over leaf, lollipop handle, deeply carved from one pc of wood, PA, c1830, age crack in handle **210.00**

Flower on one side, pinwheel on other, scrubbed poplar, lollipop, handle marked "Grandma's Butter Printer," 7¾" l **360.00**

Double lollipop style, acorn and floral design, $250.00.

Geometric starflower, scrubbed poplar, lollipop, 9" l .. **250.00**

Intaglio floral design, round, fluted border, c1840, 4½" d **80.00**

Maple Hill Dairy, relief carved **65.00**

Pennsylvania Crown Tulip, chip carved **85.00**

Pineapple, semicircular, pine, 3⅜ × 7", worn patina, replaced turned inserted handle **110.00**

Rosette

Chip and gouge carved, chip-carved fluted border, round, c1850, 3½" d **55.00**

Six-pointed design alternating crosshatch and striated designs, chip and gouge carved, round, c1850, 3½" d **95.00**

Striated Tulip, deeply gouge carved, border of chip and gouge-carved radiating triangles, round, PA, 1830, 4" d **270.00**

Tulip, deeply cut, scrubbed poplar, round, one-pc turned handle, 4¼" d, wear **275.00**

CALENDAR PLATES

History: Calendar plates were first made in England in the late 1880s. They became popular in the United States after 1900, the peak years being 1909 to 1915. The majority of the advertising plates were made of porcelain or pottery and the design included a calendar, the name of a store or business, and either a scene, portrait, animal, or flowers. Some also were made of glass or tin.

Periodical: *The Calendar,* 710 N Lake Shore Dr, Barrington, IL 60010.

Additional Listings: See *Warman's Americana & Collectibles* for more examples.

1908, 8" d, holly sprays, Russell Clothing House adv .. **20.00**

1909

8½" d, flower girl, souvenir Abrams, WI **40.00**

9" d, John Kemper Harness Maker, Butler, PA, Mediterranean woman in center, marked "Vorrey" .. **30.00**

9½" d, Gibson-girl-type portrait, calendar months, fruit, and floral border, WI adv **35.00**

1910

6⅞" d, compliments of Geo H Farquhasson, Cooperstown, NY, marked "Semi Porcelain" **35.00**

1910, Compliments of Geo. H. Farquharson, Cooperstown, NY, 6⅞", $35.00.

7" d, violets with ribbon banner, emb gold scalloped edge, JL McCue adv **30.00**

10" d, woman in garden center, calendar months border **30.00**

1911, 8½" d, gray fence with three rabbits and two birds, JW Morey adv **30.00**

1912, 8½" d, hot-air balloon **75.00**

1914, 9¼" d, Washington's Tomb, Milford, DE, artist sgd "A Smith" **40.00**

1916, 8¼" d, American flag, eagle with shield **35.00**

1919, 8¼" d, American flag, John J Rutgers Co, Holland, MI adv **40.00**

1921, Tabor & Pukwana, SD **60.00**

1922, game birds and hunting dog **45.00**

CALLING CARD CASES AND RECEIVERS

History: Calling cards, usually carried in specially designed cases, played an important social role in the United States from the Civil War until the end of World War I. When making formal visits, callers left their card in a receiver (card dish) in the front hall. Strict rules of etiquette developed. For example, the lady in a family was expected to make calls of congratulations and condolence and visits to the ill.

The cards themselves were small, embossed or engraved with the caller's name and often decorated with a floral design. Many handmade examples, especially in Spencerian script, can be found. The cards themselves are considered collectible and range in price from a few cents to several dollars.

Note: Don't confuse a calling card case with a match safe.

Calling Card Cases

Abalone Shell, 4¼″ h, pearl, engraved shield and flowers   **85.00**

Ivory, 4½″ h, intricate flower carving **240.00**

Nephrite, carved, 3¼″ h, upright rect form, hinged opening enameled white and translucent red, gold-mounted hinges and clasp set with diamonds, marked with initials of Workmaster August Hollming, ''Fabergè'' in Cyrillic and ''56 standard, St Petersburg,'' c1900 ....**5,175.00**

Pearl, 4″ h, engraved-silver diamond medallion **75.00**

Silver

3⅞ × 2⅜″, rounded rect case, repousse and chased as imitation pressed leather, gilt pansies, Japanese lantern dec, loops and suspension chain, marked ''Wood & Hughes,'' c1880 ....   **850.00**

Rect, one side dec with Philadelphia Water Works, other side with church, American, 19th C **425.00**

Tortoiseshell, 3⅝″ h, nacre, wire floral inlay **120.00**

Calling Card Receiver, Art Nouveau, naked lady, 10½″ w, 7¼″ l, 1½″ h at handles, $485.00.

Receivers

Brass, 3¼″ × 7″, Art Nouveau nude woman stretched across front **125.00**

Glass, 9½″ h, 6″ d top, 8″ d base plate, deep rose DQ MOP satin glass plates, tightly ruffled, applied glass edge, flowers and butterflies dec, one side of each turned up to fit into metal frame emb with leaves and flowers **975.00**

Pottery, 6³⁄₁₆ × 4½″, Art Nouveau, Hotel Astor center, buggies and horseless carriages in foreground, Germany **75.00**

Silverplated, 10½″ h, tray for calling cards, mirror, and fancy ornate stand with name of jeweler engraved on bottom, orig paper label adv on back of mirror, marked ''James W Tufts'' **620.00**

CAMBRIDGE GLASS

History: Cambridge Glass Company, Cambridge, Ohio, was incorporated in 1901. Initially, the company made clear tableware, later expanding into colored, etched, and engraved glass. Over 40 different hues were produced in blown and pressed glass.

The plant closed in 1954. Some of the molds were later sold to the Imperial Glass Company, Bellaire, Ohio.

Marks: Five different marks were employed during the production years, but not every piece was marked.

References: Gene Florence, *Elegant Glassware of the Depression Era*, Revised Sixth Edition, Collector Books, 1995; National Cambridge Collectors, Inc., *The Cambridge Glass Co., Cambridge, Ohio* (reprint of 1930 catalog and supplements through 1934), Collector Books, 1976, 1996 value update; ———, *The Cambridge Glass Co., Cambridge, Ohio, 1949 thru 1953* (catalog reprint), Collector Books, 1976, 1996 value update; ———, *Colors in Cambridge Glass*, Collector Books, 1984, 1993 value update; Naomi L. Over, *Ruby Glass of the 20th Century*, Antique Publications, 1990, 1993–94 value update.

Periodical: *The Daze,* PO Box 57, Otisville, MI 48463.

Collectors' Club: National Cambridge Collectors, Inc., PO Box 416, Cambridge, OH 43725.

Museums: Cambridge Glass Museum, Cambridge, OH; Museum of the National Cambridge Collectors, Inc., Cambridge, OH.

Ashtray, Nude, #3011 line

Cobalt Blue **400.00**

Dianthus **500.00**

Moonlight **550.00**

Pistacho **500.00**

Banana Stand, Caprice, moonlight, small **295.00**

Bonbon

Apple Blossom, topaz, handle, 5½″ d **24.00**

Wildflower, ftd, gold trim, 7″ h **35.00**

Bowl

Candlelight, 2 handles **125.00**

Caprice, large **65.00**

Rose Point, 12″ d, flared, #3400-4 ....   **60.00**

Rubina, ram's-head handles **750.00**

Shell & Dolphin, Crown Tuscan, 8″ d, ftd **75.00**

Bowl, underplate, Apple Blossom, yellow **50.00**

Butter Dish, cov, Rose Point, 5¼″, #3400-52 ....   **150.00**

Cake Plate, No. 731, Rosalie pink, sgd **185.00**

Candlesticks, pr

Azurite, 9″ h **90.00**

Daffodil, #72 ....   **140.00**

Martha, #494 ....   **38.00**

Rose Point, 2 light, #3400-647 ....   **100.00**

Candy, cov

Caprice, pink, #165 ....   **130.00**

Rose Point, cut knob **120.00**

Celery and Relish, Elaine, #3900-125, 9″ l **22.00**

Champagne

Caprice, pink **48.00**

Nude, #3011 line, smoke **450.00**

Cheese and Cracker, Rose Point, #3400 ....   **140.00**

Cheese Compote, Apple Blossom, peachblo/dianthus pink, gold trim **45.00**

Candlesticks, pr, Heliotrope, 10" h, 75.00.

Cigarette Box, cov, Dolphin and Seashell pattern, green	**65.00**
Cigarette Holder, No. 1337, round, amethyst	**20.00**
Cocktail	
Caprice, blue	**55.00**
Nude, #3011 line	
Cobalt Blue	**525.00**
Ebony stem, 3 oz	**160.00**
Compote	
Caprice, pink, #136, 7" h	**160.00**
Daffodil	**100.00**
Nude, #3011 line, smoke, short	**560.00**
Rose Point, 4 toes, #3400-13	**40.00**
Seashell, Crown Tuscan, 4½" d	**40.00**
Condiment Set, Caprice, moonlight, #109, 5 pcs	**525.00**
Cordial	
Caprice, moonlight, 1 oz	**150.00**
Rose Point, pulled stem	**95.00**
Creamer and Sugar	
Caprice, moonlight, #42	**60.00**
Diane, scrolled handles	**25.00**
Cup and Saucer, Daffodil	**48.00**
Cuspidor, Caprice, moonlight, #250, 3½" h	**360.00**
Decanter, Caprice, amethyst, #187, 35 oz, Farber holder	**435.00**
Eggcup, Nude, #3011 line, cobalt blue	**900.00**
Flower Frog	
Draped Lady, amber, 8½" h	**145.00**
Two Kid	
Amber	**180.00**
Crystal	**150.00**
Green	**195.00**
Goblet	
Caprice, moonlight	**45.00**
Crackle, No. 3797	**80.00**
Diane, 9 oz	**25.00**
King Edward	**15.00**
Nude, #3011 line, smoke	**560.00**
Rose Point, #3121, 10 oz	**27.00**
Ice Pail, Rose Point, #P672	**260.00**
Iced Tea Tumbler, King Edward	**16.00**
Ivy Bowl, Nude, #3011 line	
Amethyst	**250.00**
Smoke	**500.00**

Jug	
Caprice, moonlight, #183, ball, 80 oz	**390.00**
Rose Point	
76 oz, #3400-100	**380.00**
80 oz, #3400-141, Doulton	**400.00**
Martini Pitcher, Rose Point	**500.00**
Mayonnaise Plate, Rose Point, indent, 7" d	**20.00**
Oyster Cocktail, Candlelight	**50.00**
Pitcher, Rose Point, Doulton style, high handle	**345.00**
Plate	
Apple Blossom, yellow, 11½" d	**30.00**
Candlelight, 8" d	**25.00**
King Edward	
7½" d	**8.00**
8¼" d	**10.00**
Rose Point	
7½" d	**18.00**
9" d, SS Rose Point band	**200.00**
10½" d	**160.00**
Tally Ho, Carmen, 9½" d	**20.00**
Punch Bowl Set, Tally Ho, bowl, base, twelve cups, applied green, amethyst, or amber handles	**175.00**
Relish	
Candlelight, #3900-120	**85.00**
Caprice, moonlight, 3 part	**40.00**
Elaine, #3900/125, 9" l, 3 part	**22.00**
Gadroon, Crown Tuscan, #3500-64, 3 part, 3 ftd, handle, 10" d	**95.00**
Portia, 5 part	**125.00**
Rose Point, #3500/67, 12" d, 6 pc	**360.00**
Salad, Caprice, moonlight, #57, 10" d	**250.00**
Salad Set, Caprice, moonlight, 13" bowl, 16" platter ...	**500.00**
Sandwich Server, Rose Point, center handle, 11" d	**95.00**
Shaker, Wildflower, ftd	**20.00**
Sherbet, tall	
King Edward	**13.00**
Rose Point	**22.00**
Sherry	
Rose Point, 2 oz	**60.00**
Wheat Sheaf, 3 oz	**6.50**
Shrimp Cocktail and Liner	
Candlelight	**80.00**
Rose Point	**90.00**
Swan, 6½" h, yellow	**130.00**
Torte Plate, Rose Point, 14" d	**130.00**
Tumbler	
Apple Blossom, amber, 10 oz, ftd	**20.00**
Candlelight	**45.00**
Caprice	
Amethyst, #188, 2 oz	**70.00**
Blue, set of eight 6-oz, eight 3-oz, eight 8-oz ...	**720.00**
Rose Point, 5 oz, ftd	**20.00**
Vase	
Caprice, moonlight, 3½" h	**460.00**
Seashell, Crown Tuscan, 8½" h, ftd	**75.00**
Silver Overlay, pillow shape, ebony, flowers and leaves, #1228, 9" h	**350.00**
Rose Point, 10" h, bud, #274	**60.00**
Water, tall, Caprice, #300	
Moonlight	**42.50**
Pink	**60.00**
Whiskey, Caprice, clear	**15.00**

Wine
  Candlelight **70.00**
  Caprice, moonlight, #300 .... **85.00**
  Rose Point, 3½ oz **60.00**

CAMEO GLASS

History: Cameo glass is a form of cased glass. A shell of glass was prepared; then one or more layers of glass of a different color(s) was faced to the first. A design was then cut through the outer layer(s) leaving the inner layer(s) exposed.

This type of art glass originated in Alexandria, Egypt between 100 and 200 A.D. The oldest and most famous example of cameo glass is the Barberini or Portland vase which was found near Rome in 1582. It contained the ashes of Emperor Alexander Serverus, who was assassinated in 235 A.D.

Emile Gallé is probably one of the best-known cameo glass artists. He established a factory at Nancy, France, in 1884. Although much of the glass bears his signature, he was primarily the designer. Assistants did the actual work on many pieces, even signing Gallé's name. Other makers of French cameo glass include D'Argental, Daum Nancy, LeGras, and Delatte.

English cameo pieces do not have as many layers of glass (colors) and cuttings as do French pieces. The outer layer is usually white, and cuttings are very fine and delicate. Most pieces are not signed. The best-known makers are Thomas Webb & Sons and Stevens and Williams.

Marks: A star before the name Gallé on a piece by that company indicates that it was made after Gallé's death in 1904.

References: Victor Arwas, *Glass Art Nouveau to Art Deco,* Rizzoli International Publications, 1977; Alastair Duncan and George DeBartha, *Glass by Gallé,* Harry N. Abrams, 1984; Ray and Lee Grover, *English Cameo Glass,* Crown Publishers, 1980; Albert C. Revi, *Nineteenth Century Glass,* reprint, Schiffer Publishing, 1981; John A. Shuman, III, *The Collector's Encyclopedia of American Art Glass,* Collector Books, 1988, 1994 value update.

REPRODUCTION ALERT

Copycat and fantasy Gallé-marked cameo glass began flooding the American market in the early 1990s. Most of these newer pieces are manufactured using a sand blasting rather than an acid etching technique.

The edges of the cuttings in modern Gallé pieces are crisp and sharp in contrast to the smooth edges associated with the acid etching technique. Look for a sharp distinction between the design and ground. Period pieces will show subtle shading in color transitions, not clear distinctions. Flat ground rims are another feature of modern copycats and fantasy pieces.

American

Mount Washington
  Bride's Bowl, 8" d, 11¾" h, sq ruffled edge, deep pink shading to lighter pink at top, two griffins, floral

spray, orig Pairpoint SP holder with three loop handle and cherries dec **1,950.00**
  Bowl, 8" d, 4" h, sq, ruffled edge, blue over white, two winged griffins holding up scroll, floral spray **1,475.00**
  Lamp, parlor, 21" h, brilliant deep yellow over white, woman with basket of flowers on base, matching floral design on 10" d shade, fancy brass base and font, orig chimney **8,500.00**
  Rose Bowl, 3½" d, rose shading to white, rushes and trees dec, eight-crimp top, bottom ground flat, imprinted "Mount Washington" **695.00**
Steuben, 14½" h, 5" d, yellow jade and blue aurene, deep yellow cut in Art Deco floral and leaf pattern .**4,950.00**
Tiffany, vase, 6½" h, 6¾" w, 3" d, irid gold, deep green cameo-carved leaves, vines, bulbous form, rounded then flaring neck, sgd "2449J L.C.T. Tiffany Favrile" **4,500.00**

English

Stevens and Williams
  Perfume Bottle, 4" h, bulbous, red ground, carved white trailing fuchsias, hinged spherical silvered metal cap, c1900 .... **395.00**
  Vase
    4" h, barrel shape, bright blue ground, white overlay, cameo ferns, grasses, and wild thistle, sod border, circular "Stevens & Williams Art Glass" trademark on base **1,400.00**
    12" h, vasiform, cinnamon orange-red ground, white overlay, cameo blackberry blossoms, buds, fruits, and thorny branches above and below medial flower border, butterfly and insect in flight, marked "Stevens & Williams Stourbridge Art Glass" **4,500.00**
Unknown Maker
  Biscuit Jar, 5¾ × 5⅜", frosted deep red ground, opaque white carved flowers, SP top **2,400.00**
  Bowl, 8¼" × 4", frosted blue ground, opaque white carved flowers, leaves, and branches **2,250.00**
  Sweetmeat Jar, 4¾" d, 3" h, frosted deep cranberry ground, opaque white carved apple blossoms and leaves, SP top, rim, and handle **1,200.00**
  Vase
    5" h, baluster shape, robin's-egg blue cased in opal glass, white cameo enamel leaves and buds . **250.00**
    7" h, 5" w, corset shape, cranberry ground, white overlay, carved sweet peas, leaves, branches, and butterfly in flight **1,750.00**
    7½" h, 5¼" d, baluster shape, stippled blue ground, white neck band, carved white clematis branch with foliage **3,750.00**
    11⅞" h, 6" d, baluster shape, everted lip, dark brown ground, very deeply carved, three white dancing girls with outstretched arms, foliage carved around neck and upper section, attributed to Woodall **5,000.00**
Webb, Thomas & Son
  Bowl, 6" d, 1⅛" h, deep blue ground, white carved pale blue foxglove branch, butterfly, pale blue rim, pontil incised "1/6107" **650.00**
  Cologne Bottle, 7½" h, bulbous, pastel yellow body, white overlay hand-carved roses, buds, leaves,

thorny branches, and butterfly, leaf-spike border, matching glass stopper with rose bud and leaf dec, Webb four-sided medallion on base **4,750.00**

Cup and Saucer, 2¾″ h, 5″ d saucer, cranberry glass over clear, carved prunus blossoms, leaves, branches, large butterfly and 25 buds **550.00**

Perfume Bottle, 5½″ h, 2¾″ w, sq, citron yellow ground, white overlay, allover carving of wild roses, detailed leaves and buds, orig silver spring hinge cov **2,750.00**

Vase

7½″ h, 6½″ w, pillow shape, brilliant blue ground, white overlay, carved wild rose dec, two large roses, twelve leaves, large butterfly in flight on reverse, full authentic signature **2,750.00**

10½″ h, blue ground, white carved open cabbage rose blossom, passion flower blossom, three single-petal flowers, foliage, three bands of geometric designs **2,450.00**

French

D'Argental

Box, cov, 6⅞″ d, compressed spherical form, central knop on lid, yellow ground, mauve overlay, carved roses, lid sgd in cameo **1,250.00**

Perfume Bottle, 3¾″ h, dark brown cut to amber, expansive forest landscape, sgd, orig atomizer top detached **230.00**

Vase, 10¾″ h, fiery opalescent amber baluster body, double overlaid in red and dark maroon, cameo cut and etched two horizontal bands of thorny rose bushes with blossoms above bands, sgd "D'Argental" with cross in motif **990.00**

Daum Nancy

Bowl, 9¼″ w, 11½″ d, 4¼″ h, half round, mottled pastel blue, green, and frosted white, layered and etched inside and out with red cherries on leafy branches, raised motif highly polished, five cherries and two lustered applied handles, inscribed "Daum (cross) Nancy" **3,680.00**

Pitcher, 9½″ h, flattened oval body, transparent forest green, etched horizontal panels alternating etched and polished with five-petal blossoms, reverse carved and relief, conforming applied handle, gold enamel dec, base sgd "Daum (cross) Nancy"**2,185.00**

Vase

13½″ h, tall slender double trumpet form, deep purple shaded to colorless base, acid textured and etched tulip blossoms, butterfly in flight, gold highlights, gold mark on base "Daum (cross) Nancy," flat chip at lower edge **520.00**

15¼″ h, trumpet form, green, yellow, and brown tree and foliate designs, blue field, ground down, uneven rim, signature etched in base . **800.00**

De Vez

Bell, 8¼″ h, 6½″ d, red on amber, carved daisy flowers and leaves, metal handle, tassel-shaped clapper on chain **8,025.00**

Tumbler, 5″ h, barrel shape, amber frosted ground, red starflowers, green leaves **850.00**

Vase, yellow ground, amber dec, sgd "Richard," 12½″ h, $1,250.00.

Vase

7¾″ h, blue on yellow on white, 3″ h Heidi-type girl dressed in cape and patched dress, hand raised shielding eyes, standing on rocky crag with goat, mountains, village, and trees in background **4,050.00**

14″ h, 6¼″ d, bulbous base, long tapering cylindrical neck, cut blue to frost, flowers and leaves, sgd "De Vez" **1,035.00**

Gallé

Bowl, 7½″ d, wide squatty bulbous body, small short pedestal foot, wide flat rolled rim, milky white overlaid with deep gray-green cut swirling leafy fruiting branches, sgd in cameo, c1900 .... **825.00**

Box, cov, 5″ d, 2½″ h, squatty, cushion form, wide low-domed cov, frosted clear lined with pink and overlaid in amber and yellow, acid etched and carved nasturtium blossoms and leaves, cov sgd in cameo **1,150.00**

Decanter, 11″ h, 4¼″ d, baluster shape, cut green to mauve to shaded frost, flowers and leaves, sgd "Galle," matching stopper **1,725.00**

Lamp, table

11″ h, 10¾″ d pointed conical shade, matching spherical base, gray shaded with lemon yellow, overlaid in red and crimson, cut flowering prunus branches, buds, and leaves, simple bronze mount, shade and base sgd in cameo, c1900**23,000.00**

31″ h, 14″ d dome shade, matching slender cylindrical base, encased in elaborate scrolling foliate bronze mounts, four large scrolling bronze leaf-form feet, gray splashed with pink and olive green, overlaid in lime green, rust, and maroon, cut and unfurling fern fronds and grasses, fire polished, shade supported on bronze flower-head arms, shade and base sgd in cameo **36,800.00**

Miniature, vase, 3⅜″ h, wide baluster-form body, short rolled neck, yellow overlaid in pale blue and aubergine, cut violets and leaves, sgd in cameo, c1900 .... **690.00**

Night-Light, Veilleuse, 6½″ h, gray body mottled with orange, overlaid with dark amber, cut crocus blossoms and leaves, pierced gilt-metal mounts, sgd in cameo, electrified, c1900 ....**1,840.00**

Vase

3½″ h, flattened bell form, pastel pink and frost white overlaid in olive green, etched blossoms, buds, and leafy vines, sgd in cameo design .. **425.00**

5⅝″ h, Les Roses de France series, internal applied dec, ftd, broad squatty bulbous body, tapering to flaring neck, transparent lime green splashes with opalescence, overlaid in pale green, cut all around, impressionistic verdant summer landscape, skies above martelè, obverse applied in high relief, dusty pink rose, slender rose stems, three lime green leaves, lime green over rose and lavender over white, wheel carved, sgd in intaglio, c1902 .... **200,500.00**

8¾″ h, slightly swelled cylindrical body tapering at top to widely flaring, deeply ruffled rim, clear splashed with gray and puce, overlaid in puce, cut morning glory blossoms, buds, and leaves, fire polished, sgd in cameo, c1900 ....**2,875.00**

9¾″ h, tall slender tapering cylindrical body, flaring rim, frosted pastel yellow layered in amethyst and dark purple, acid-etched and wheel-cut large iris blossoms, spiked leaves, cameo sgd, paper label ''Emile Galle Nancy Paris'' .**3,450.00**

10½″ h, shouldered ovoid body, short lobed neck, base tapering sharply to double ring foot, pale amber overlaid in caramel at base, cut ascending leaf ends, enameled around shoulder with dahlias and leaves, shades of crimson, mint green, yellow, orange, and brown, sgd in intaglio, c1900 ....**17,250.00**

12¾″ h, wide ovoid body tapering to thick molded wide mouth, tapering sharply down-flared foot, gray shaded with pale yellow, overlaid in amber and molded in low-, medium-, and high-relief plum branches laden with fruit, sgd in cameo, c1900 ....**23,000.00**

17¼″ h, thick squatty cushion base tapering to very tall cylindrical neck, gray shading to lavender at base, overlaid with lavender and green, cut wisteria, sgd in cameo, c1900 ....**1,850.00**

19½″ h, disc foot, expanding cylinder, narrow neck, flared mouth, gray shaded with yellow, overlaid burnt sienna, cut falling maple leaves, sgd in cameo, c1900 ....**3,165.00**

20″ h, classic baluster body, short flaring neck, applied pedestal base, gray mottled with yellow, overlaid pale olive green and brown, cut tranquil river landscape, sgd in cameo, c1900, rim chips **8,400.00**

Wall Sconce, 11¼″ h, 7″ w, gray shaded with lemon yellow, overlaid in red and deep burgundy, cut flowering leafy rose branches, simple gilt bronze foliate mounts, sgd in cameo, c1900, price for pair **16,100.00**

Legras, vase, 10¼″ , modified trumpet shape, deep red

leaves and cherries, semi-martele frosted round, sgd in cameo **750.00**

Muller Freres

Bowl, 6″ d, bulbous, sloped sides, shaped oval mouth, mottled translucent white glass, cases shades of brown, eight cut finches perched on branches, etched ''Muller Freres/Luneville'' **450.00**

Lamp, table, 14¾″ h, domed cameo shade, mottled orange ground, brown overlay, carved leaves and berries on tendril vines, sgd in cameo, openwork wrought-iron four-arm base, curling vine motif ..**3,850.00**

Vase, 17¼″ h, 6″ d, river landscape, trees in foreground, sailboats and mountains in distance, cut mauve to frosted amber pink, sgd ''Muller Freres''**3,165.00**

St Louis, vase, 9¾″ h, 3¾″ d, cylindrical, cut cranberry to frost, irises, gold highlights **300.00**

CAMERAS

History: Although photography generally is considered to have had its beginning in 1839, it is very unusual to find a camera made before 1880. These cameras and others made before 1925 are considered to be antique cameras. Most cameras made after 1925 that are no longer in production are considered to be classic cameras. American, German, and Japanese cameras are found most often.

References: John S. Craig, *General Catalog of Photographica*, published by author, 1993; James and Joan McKeown (eds.), *Price Guide to Antique & Classic Cameras, 1992–1995*, Ninth Edition, Centennial Photo Service, 1994; Douglas St. Denny (ed.), *The Hove International Blue Book Guide Prices for Classic and Collectable Cameras,* Hove Foto Books, 1992.

Periodicals: *Camera Shopper*, 313 N Quaker Lane, PO Box 370279, West Hartford, CT 06137; *Shutterbug*, PO Box F, Titusville, FL 32781.

Collectors' Clubs: American Photographic Historical Society, Inc, 1150 Avenue of the Americas, New York, NY 10036; American Society of Camera Collectors, 4918 Alcove Ave, North Hollywood, CA 91607; International Kodak Historical Society, PO Box 21, Flourtown, PA 19301; Leica Historical Society of America, 7611 Dornoch Lane, Dallas, TX 75248; Movie Machine Society, 50 Old Country Rd, Hudson, MA 01749; National Stereoscopic Assoc, PO Box 14801, Columbus, OH 43214; Nikon Historical Society, PO Box 3213, Munster, IN 46321; Photographic Historical Society, PO Box 39563, Rochester, NY 14604; Zeiss Historical Society, PO Box 631, Clifton, NJ 07012.

Museums: Cameras & Images International, Boston, MA; Fleetwood Museum, North Plainfield, NJ; George Eastman Museum, Rochester, NY; International Cinema Museum, Chicago, IL; Smithsonian Institution, Washington, DC.

Additional Listings: See *Warman's Americana & Collectibles* for more examples.

Notes: Value of cameras is affected by both exterior and mechanical conditions. Particular attention must be given to the condition of the bellows, if cameras have them.

Adlake Plate, sliding knob, side door, c1898 .... **65.00**

Akeley, lightweight aluminum, hand crank, tripod, c1917 .... **600.00**

American Optical Co, Henry Clay Camera, 5 × 7 cut
film, 1896 .... **275.00**
Ansco No. 4, Model D, wooden case **75.00**
Bell's Straight Working Panorama camera, BG 100, hor-
izontal format, folding bellows, 5 panoramic expo-
sures **250.00**
Blair, No. 3, Weno Hawkeye box type, c1900 .... **25.00**
Conley Camera Co, Rochester, NY, Junior, folding plate,
1900 .... **35.00**
Eastman Kodak
Autographic Folding Cartridge 2A, Model B, 1920s **75.00**
Six-20 Camera, Kodak Anastigmat 10mm f4.5 coated
lens, No. 1 Diodak shutter, 620 roll film, c1935 **20.00**
3B Quick Focus, Meniscus Achromatic lens, rotary
shutter, 125 roll film, c1906 .... **125.00**

**Eastman Kodak, Brownie, #2A, 3¼ × 5 ×
6", #116 film, $25.00.**

Franke
Rollei 16S, subminiature, Tessar 25mm f2.8 lens,
black **75.00**
Rolleiflex New Standard 1939, Zeiss Tessar 75mm
lens, Synchro-Compur shutter, c1939 .... **50.00**
Goerz, Stereo Ango, Goerz Dagor 120 mm f6.8 lens,
film pack adapter, rising and sliding lens panel,
c1906 .... **200.00**
Jumbo Century Studio Camera, No. 4A, wood, lens,
hand-held rubber squeeze bulb, brass hardware, orig
label, made by Folmer Graphlex Corp, Rochester, NY **100.00**
Polaroid Land Camera, Model 95B, unused **50.00**
Ross Twin Lens Reflex, Ross Homocentric f6.3 lens,
Bausch & Lomb pneumatic shutter, rotating back,
c1891 .... **575.00**
Samei Sangyo, Japan, Samoca 35lli, 35mm, c1957 .... **15.00**
Scovill 4 × 5" Vertical View Camera, R Morrison, NY,
lens, rotating stops, holder, and case, c1881 .... **250.00**
Universal Camera Corp, NY, Mercury I, 35mm half
frame, Tricor 35mm f3.5 lens, rotary sector, c1947 . **35.00**
Voigtlander, Brauncschweig, Germany, Bergheil, Keilar
12cm 14.5 lens, Compur shutter, folding plate, c1930 **50.00**
Watson View Camera, bush Rapid Symmetrical lens,
Thornton Pickard behind lens shutter, mahogany
finish, brass fittings, reversible and tilting back,
c1890 .... **375.00**
Zeiss, Contraflex, Walz filter kit, wide angle and tele-
photo lens, orig instruction book and case **275.00**

CANDLESTICKS

History: The domestic use of candlesticks is traced to the 14th
century. The earliest was a picket type, named for the sharp point
used to hold the candle. The socket type was established by the
mid-1660s.

From 1700 to the present, candlestick design mirrored furniture
design. By the late 17th century, a baluster stem was introduced,
replacing the earlier Doric or clustered column stem. After 1730
candlesticks reflected rococo ornateness. Neoclassic styles followed in the 1760s. Each new era produced a new style of candlesticks; however, some styles became universal and remained
in production for centuries. Therefore, when attempting to date a
candlestick, it is important to try to determine the techniques used
to manufacture the piece.

References: Margaret and Douglas Archer, *The Collector's Encyclopedia Of Glass Candlesticks,* Collector Books, 1983; Veronika
Baur, *Metal Candlesticks,* Schiffer Publishing, 1996; Kenneth Wilson, *American Glass 1760–1930,* 2 vols., Hudson Hills Press and
The Toledo Museum of Art, 1994.

4¾" h, SS, Persian taste, scalloped circular nozzle, urn-
shaped candle cup, spreading cylindrical support,
dished circular base with pierced and scalloped border, niello inlaid mounts on handle, candle cup, and
base, marked "Tiffany & Co," 1889, 8 oz, 10 dwt .**6,400.00**
6" h, wrought iron, two-way ratchet type, hanging and
jamb hooks, American, c1790 .... **180.00**
6¾" h
Brass, saucer base, primitive **250.00**
Silver, Sterling, Japanese taste, serpentine removable
nozzle, shaped cylindrical stem, sq dished base
with shaped brim, four scroll feet, applied beetle
on base, spot-hammered surface, engraved monogram, marked "Tiffany & Co," c1885, price for
pr **6,600.00**
7½" h, brass, Queen Anne, petal base, Joseph Wood,
England, 1730–40, both sgd on base, repairs, minor
dents, price for pr **1,380.00**
8" h
Iron, spiral, wooden base, Continental, c1825 ..... **180.00**

Brass, 7⅜" h, price for pr, $65.00.

Pewter, beaded detail, pushups, one stem resoldered, price for pr 120.00

8½" h

Brass, domed base, primitive 225.00

Glass, opaque white, lacy, Gothic detail, French, small flakes 165.00

8⅞" h, porcelain, blue and white dec, Meissen 75.00

9" h, Krome Kraft, Farber Bros, Art Deco nude woman, price for pr 200.00

9½" h

Brass, octagonal, floral engraving, French, remains of silver plating under base, minor repair, polished 660.00

Bronze, Empire style, patinated putti standard, supporting ormolu nozzle, standing on ormolu hemisphere, plinth, price for pr 450.00

9¾" h, brass, Queen Anne, English, mid 18th C 1,840.00

9⅞" h, fiery opalescent glass, French, chips and one with crack in socket 165.00

10" h

Brass, Doric fluted columns, sq base, early 19th C, price for pr 90.00

Silver, sterling, Neoclassical style, monogrammed, removable bobeches, weighted, Reed and Barton, price for pr 525.00

10¼" h, bronze, 3 bladed disks on stem, circular dished drip pan, bell-shaped base, overall arabesque dec, Venetian, 15th C, price for pr 4,250.00

10⅜" h, 4½" d, brass, figural, dolphins, English, polished, price for pr 255.00

10½" h, glass, vaseline, flint, New England, c1890 .... 160.00

10⅝" h, pressed glass, clear, crosses, pewter sockets, marked "Ripley's Patent Pending," one with chips on foot, price for pr 125.00

10¾" h, pewter, removable bobeches, price for pr 250.00

11" h, brass, turned standard with star, wave, and diapering motifs, round base with scroll and rosette band, removable bobeche, French, 19th C 600.00

11⅞" h, brass, King of Diamonds, push-up, English, polished, price for pr 425.00

12" h, glass, amethyst, angular cup, optic-ribbed shaft, deeply cupped pedestal, folded-foot rim 230.00

12⅜" h, brass, King of Diamonds, push-up, English, polished, price for pr 625.00

12½" h, doré, figural, rustic lad and maiden, circular base, Continental, price for pr 280.00

18" h, hog scraper, American, c1800 .... 230.00

20" h, bronze, baluster shaft dec with dragon and phoenix, tripod feet, Japanese, price for pr 170.00

CANDY CONTAINERS

History: In 1876 Croft, Wilbur and Co. filled small glass Liberty Bells with candy and sold them at the Centennial Exposition in Philadelphia. From that date until the 1960s, glass candy containers remained popular. They reflect historical changes, particularly in transportation.

Jeannette, Pennsylvania, a center for the packaging of candy in containers, was home for J. C. Crosetti, J. H. Millstein, T. H. Stough, and Victory Glass. Other early manufacturers included: George Borgfeldt, New York, New York; Cambridge Glass, Cambridge, Ohio; Eagle Glass, Wheeling, West Virginia; L. E. Smith,

Mt. Pleasant, Pennsylvania; and West Brothers, Grapeville, Pennsylvania.

References: *Candy Containers,* L-W Book Sales, 1996; George Eikelberner and Serge Agadjanian, *The Complete American Glass Candy Containers Handbook,* revised and published by Adele L. Bowden, 1986; Jennie Long, *An Album of Candy Containers,* published by author, Volume I (1978), Volume II (1983).

Collectors' Club: Candy Container Collectors of America, PO Box 352, Cleveland, OH 01824.

Museums: Cambridge Glass Museum, Cambridge, OH; L. E. Smith Glass, Mt. Pleasant, PA.

Additional Listings: See *Warman's Americana & Collectibles* for more examples.

Notes: Candy containers with original paint, candy, and closures command a high premium, but beware of reproduced parts and repainting. The closure is a critical part of each container; if it is missing, the value of the container drops considerably.

Small figural perfumes and other miniatures often are sold as candy containers.

Airplane, glass

P-38, Play Toy Co, cardboard closure 135.00

Spirit of St Louis, West Bros, tin wings and wheels . 375.00

Airplane, T. H. Stough Co, Jeannette, PA, 5", clear glass, tin wings, $55.00.

Automobile, glass

Sedan, VG Co, tin wheels, tin closure 75.00

Station Wagon, woody, JH Millstein cardboard closure 40.00

Bank, tin, litho, glass insert 35.00

Basket, milk glass, emb grapes and vines 40.00

Bug, 8½" h, composition, sitting up, smiling, black top hat and glasses, red umbrella, Germany 125.00

Bus, glass, Victory Lines Special, gray paint, cardboard closure 50.00

Cannon, 3¾" l, glass, red tin carriage, two pierced wheels, tin screw-on cap 400.00

Cash Register, 2⅝" h, glass 300.00

Cat, black

5" h, papier-mâché, West Germany 22.00

5½" h, horn, papier-mâché, West Germany 40.00

7" h, cone shape, papier-mâché, West Germany ... 60.00

Chaplin, Charlie, glass 135.00

Chick, 6½" h, egg-shaped body 42.00

Chicken on Egg, Germany 35.00

Church, tin, litho, glass insert **35.00**
Clown and Rocking Horse, glass, blue **225.00**
Devil, 7″ h, cone shape, papier-mâché, West Germany **60.00**
Dog
    3¾″ h, glass, sitting Bulldog, open base, inside flanges **35.00**
    11″ l, papier-mâché, Dalmatian puppy **30.00**
Donkey, 5″ l, papier-mâché, glass eyes, blanket, Germany **225.00**
Duck
    6½″ h, egg-shaped body **42.00**
    7″ h, composition, lady duck in pink bonnet purple int., Germany **95.00**
Fire Engine, 5″ l, glass, emb "Fire Dept" in circle on top, JC Crosetti **35.00**
Football, tin, litho **20.00**
Frog, 4¼″ h, milk glass, sitting upright, traces of green and brown paint, tin screw-on cap **300.00**
Globe, glass, raised continents and degree lines, metal screw-on cap, spins on metal stand, marked "Pat appl'd For" **385.00**
Golf Club, 4⅝″ l, glass, plain neck, marked "DRGM" . **45.00**
Hen on Nest, 6″ h **48.00**
Iron, glass, Play Toy Co, orig closure and paper cord .. **60.00**
Kangaroo, 5¼″ h, glass, sitting, holding cricket bat, traces of black paint, metal screw-on cap **2,000.00**
Kettle, glass, TH Sough, paper handle, slotted cardboard closure **25.00**
Liberty Bell, glass, amber **50.00**
Locomotive, 4½″ l, clear glass **95.00**
Milk Bottle, glass, VG Co, emb "Dolly's Milk" **40.00**
Owl, glass, traces of paint, tin cap closure, 1920s **70.00**
Pipe, glass, ornate bowl, swirl stem **50.00**
Pistol, glass, JR 22, Whitling Jim, TH Stough **25.00**
Pumpkin
    4″ h, papier-mâché **22.00**
    7″ h, cone shape, papier-mâché, West Germany ... **60.00**
Pumpkin Man, 5½″ h, papier-mâché, West Germany .. **22.00**
Rabbit, 4½″ h, basket **38.00**
Radio, glass, VG Co, emb tune-in buttons, tin closure . **90.00**
Rolling Pin, 7″ l, glass, metal cap ends, turned wooden handles, marked "VG Co Jnet Pa ¾ oz" **175.00**
Santa
    3½″ h, hanging, face **35.00**
    7″ h, fur beard, tree **22.00**
    7¼″ h, fur beard, red cloth coat **55.00**
    9″ h, bread and tree, happy face **25.00**
    10″ h **28.00**
Schoolhouse, tin, litho, glass insert **25.00**
Snowman
    4½″ d, round **15.00**
    5″ d, round, glass eyes, marked "Germany" **38.00**
    5½″ h, cap, glass eyes **28.00**
    6¼″ h, umbrella **35.00**
    7¼″ h, top hat, tree, and carrot nose **28.00**
    9″ h, stick and bells **40.00**
Spark Plug **185.00**
Submarine, tin, glass hull **275.00**
Suitcase, 2½″ h, glass, wire handle, emb straps and patent, tin closure **40.00**
Telephone, candlestick, Victory Glass **42.00**
Turkey, papier-mâché, West Germany
    4½″ h, hen **32.00**

    5½″ h, Tom **42.00**
Wheelbarrow, glass, VG Co, red tin wheels, tin closure **50.00**
Witch, 7″ h, cone shape, papier-mâché, West Germany **60.00**

CANES

History: Canes and walking sticks were important accessories in a gentleman's wardrobe in the 18th and 19th centuries. They often served both a decorative and utilitarian function. Glass canes and walking sticks were glassmakers' whimsies, ornamental rather than practical.

References: Linda L. Beeman, *The Cane Collector's Directory*, published by author, 1993; Joyce E. Blake, *Glasshouse Whimsies*, published by author, 1984; Catherine Dike, *Cane Curiosa*, Cane Curiosa Press (250 Dielman Rd, Ladue, MO 63124), 1983; ——, *Canes in the United States*, Cane Curiosa Press (250 Dielman Rd, Ladue, MO 63124), 1994; ——, *La Canne*, Cane Curiosa Press (250 Dielman Rd, Ladue, MO 63124), 1987; Ulrich Klever, *Walkingsticks*, Schiffer Publishing, 1996; Francis H. Monek, *Canes through the Ages*, Schiffer Publishing, 1995; Jeffrey B. Snyder, *Canes from the Seventeenth to the Twentieth Century*, Schiffer Publishing, 1993.

Periodical: *Cane Collector's Chronicle*, 99 Ludlum Crescent, Lower Hutt Welling, New Zealand.

Collectors' Club: International Cane Collectors, 24 Magnolia Ave, Manchester-by-the-Sea, MA 01944.

Museums: Essex Institute, Salem, MA; Remington Gun Museum, Ilion, NY; Valley Forge Historical Society, Valley Forge, PA.

Notes: Carved wood and ivory canes are frequently considered folk art and collectors pay higher prices for them.

Canes

Ebony, 35″ l, chip-carved shaft, elephant's-head handle, ivory tusks and eyes, horn tip, India **500.00**
Equestrian Measuring, 35½″ l; wooden body covered in alligator hide, burl tip, extracting brass measuring rod calibrated to measure the height of a horse in hands, small oval silver presentation plaque attached to top handle reads "Given to W. E. Atkinson by E. A. Lund-Sept. 5, 1946" **1,050.00**
Folk Art
    Bearded Christ-like man, carved by PA Civil War surgeon, provenance attached, late 19th C **120.00**
    Dog's head, hickory, one pc, American, late 19th C, 33″ l **75.00**
    Polychromed bird on handle, one pc, carved, PA, late 19th C, 35″ l **170.00**
    Two blue birds with relief-carved and painted wing detail handle, red bead inset eyes, tapered blue painted root shaft, American, late 19th C **770.00**
Ivory, 34¾″ l, carved fist clenching coiled snake, inset red glass eyes, acanthus leaf and beaded ring base, tapered whalebone shaft, American, late 19th C ...**1,750.00**
Scrimshaw
    33″ l, rope and diamond point carved whalebone shaft, L-shaped whale ivory handle, wooden separators, 19th C **575.00**

34″ l, coconut-wood shaft, carved whale ivory clenched hand, 19th C **450.00**

Sword, 36″ l, composite wooden cane covered entirely with fine leather L-shaped handle, SS cap with engraved monogram, silver ferrule, elliptical double-edged 29″ l sword blade, ⅝″ at the ricasso and tapering to a point, floral motif etched blade sgd "G. Gabrun/Napoli/1837," Italian, 19th C, damage to silver handle cap and minor losses to leather covering, deep rust areas on blade, uncleaned **350.00**

Walking Sticks

31½″ l, scrimshaw, seven whale ivory sections, eight-sided balloon-shaped knob, 19th C **395.00**

33″ l, ivory and whalebone, 19th C, knop separated from shaft **460.00**

34″ l, burled, several knobs with carved heads or animals, horn handle **310.00**

35″ l

Bamboo, concealed gun type, L-shaped horn grip, .32-caliber brass revolver located approximately 9″ from handle with twists to open, nickel-silver end cap removes to fire, European, late 19th C, minor wear, trigger mechanism located at base of grip is broken and missing **325.00**

Cleveland, Grover, cast white metal figural head, worn ebonized shaft **90.00**

36″ l, bamboo, L-shaped staghorn grip, coin silver ferrule, concealed narrow tapering steel rapier-type 29″ blade marked "Solingen" near ricasso, wear, light rust to blade, loose ferrule **175.00**

36½″ l, curly maple, slender tapered chamfers **210.00**

37½″ l, tattoo folk art type, pony, gazelle, fish, crane, lizard, and snake, knob handle **75.00**

CANTON CHINA

History: Canton china is a type of Oriental porcelain made in the Canton region of China from the late 18th century to the present. It was produced largely for export. Canton china has a hand-decorated light- to dark-blue underglaze on white ground. Design motifs include houses, mountains, trees, boats, and bridges. A design similar to willow pattern is the most common.

Borders on early Canton feature a rain and cloud motif (a thick band of diagonal lines with a scalloped bottom). Later pieces usually have a straight-line border.

Early, c1790–1840, plates are very heavy and often have an unfinished bottom, while serving pieces have an overall "orange peel" bottom. Early covered pieces, such as tureens, vegetable dishes, and sugars, have strawberry finials and twisted handles. Later ones have round finials and a straight, single handle.

Marks: The markings "Made in China" and "China" indicate wares which date after 1891.

Bidet, 23¾″ l, 19th C, cracks, minor chips **260.00**

Bowl

8¾″ d, undertray, pierced form **550.00**

10⅛″ d, center, 19th C **260.00**

19½″ d, minor rim chips **400.00**

Candlesticks, pr, 7″ h, trumpet shape, flat bobeche **2,400.00**

REPRODUCTION ALERT

Several museum gift shops and private manufacturers are issuing reproductions of Canton china.

Charger, 24½″ d, alternating shaped medallions of figures and birds, flower-strewn ground **1,200.00**

Creamer, 5½″ h, white, rose border, gold trim **165.00**

Dish, 10⅜″ l, shaped, chips **230.00**

Fruit Basket, 11″ l, 4¾″ h, reticulated, mismatched undertray, 19th C **550.00**

Fruit Bowl, 9½″ w, sq, cut corner, 19th C, slight foot chips **475.00**

Ginger Jar, cov, 8¾″ h, 19th C, imperfections **275.00**

Milk Jug

7¾″ h, 19th C, chips **490.00**

8¼″ h, 19th C, chips, repair to handle **520.00**

Plate, 8¾″ d, 19th C, chips, price for 15-pc set **750.00**

Plate, water's edge scene, 1800–20, 10″ d, $60.00.

Platter

14½″ l, octagonal, 19th C, very minor chips **345.00**

15½″ l, octagonal, well and tree **400.00**

18⅛″ l, well and tree, 19th C, minor rim chips **635.00**

18¾″ l **690.00**

Sauce Tureen, 6¾″ l, 19th C, chips, restoration **275.00**

Serving Dish

9″ sq, blue and white **225.00**

10″ l, almond shape, blue and white **225.00**

Syllabubs, 4″ h, minor chips and cracks, price for 7-pc set **460.00**

Tank, 25½″ d, 7½″ h, 19th C, mahogany stand with imperfections **4,312.50**

Teapot, 8½″ h, dome top, 19th C, chips **550.00**

Tureen, cov, 10¾″ l, minor chips **750.00**

Vegetable Dish, cov, 19th C

8″ l, chips, restoration, one with mismatched lid, price for pr **575.00**

9⅜″ l, minor chips, restoration, price for pr **525.00**

CAPO-DI-MONTE

History: In 1743 King Charles of Naples established a soft-paste porcelain factory near Naples. The firm made figurines and dinnerware. In 1760 many of the workmen and most of the molds were moved to Buen Retiro, near Madrid, Spain. A new factory, which also made hard-paste porcelains, opened in Naples in 1771. In 1834 the Doccia factory in Florence purchased the molds and continued production with them in Italy.

Capo-Di-Monte was copied heavily by other factories in Hungary, Germany, France, and Italy.

REPRODUCTION ALERT

Many of the pieces in today's market are of recent vintage. Do not be fooled by the crown over the "N" mark; it also was copied.

Bonbonniére, oblong, scalloped corners, serpentine shaped sides, bas-relief Greek mythological dec, underglaze blue "N" surmounted by crown mark **1,500.00**

Box, cov, 4¾" l, emb, polychromed frolicking cherubs, crowned "N" mark **150.00**

Candleholders, 12½" h, blanc de chine, Classic Revival style, figural, maiden supporting flower, gold highlights, blue crown mark and "N," imperfections, price for 4-pc set **650.00**

Candlesticks, pr, double, cherubs dec **135.00**

Centerpiece, 12" h, 17" l, 11" w, blanc de chine, Classic Revival style, balustrade dec with floral garlands and scrollwork, surmounted by four dancing Greek maids, gold highlights, blue crown mark and "N," imperfections **1,265.00**

Figure

   9½" h, 8½" w, kneeling boy with camera, taking photo of young girl, on brick wall, crowned "N" and initials mark **150.00**

   10½" h, fisherman, seated man, red tassel cap, smoking pipe, holding net to be mended, sgd "G Armani" **190.00**

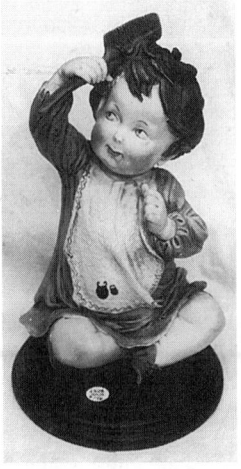

Figure, child with comb, signed "G. Armani," late, $150.00.

12" h, 13" w, frolicking couple, blue crown mark and "N," minor damage **150.00**

Jewelry Box, 9 × 6 × 3¼", oblong, bow-shaped ends, six maidens in garden on lid, fawns and flowers on sides, hinged metal frame **500.00**

Plaque, 9 × 16¾", continuous Olympian scene of drunken revelers and gods, early 20th C **480.00**

Plate, 7¼" d, raised baskets of flowers and gilding, rev printed "Fatto a Capo-di-Monte, 1818," repairs, price for 12-pc set **175.00**

Triptych, 10" h, 10" w, continuous scene of peasants and soldiers fighting before carriage, 20th C **460.00**

Urn, cov, 15" h, 7½" w, molded body, cherubs and grapes, bacchus-head handles, floral leaf cov, price for pr **395.00**

Vase, 13" h, cylindrical, pedestal base, ring and domed foot, relief molded, classical figures, polychrome dec, relief-molded putti around foot, price for pr **260.00**

CARLSBAD CHINA

History: Because of changing European boundaries during the last 100 years, German-speaking Carlsbad has found itself located first in the Austro-Hungarian Empire, then in Germany, and currently in the Czech Republic. Carlsbad was one of the leading pottery manufacturing centers in Bohemia.

Wares from the numerous Carlsbad potteries are lumped together under the term "Carlsbad China." Most pieces on the market are post-1891, although several potteries date to the early 19th century.

Bowl

   12" w, 2" h, sq, pale peach shading to pale blue, center transfer of five classical maidens, gold foliage, marked "Victoria-Carlsbad" **85.00**

   16" l, 9" w, oval, fluted top, hp, purple and blue flowers, gold trim **45.00**

Cake Plate, 12" d, violets, pierced gold handles, marked "Victoria, Carlsbad, Austria" **45.00**

Chocolate Pot, 10" h, multicolored daisies, gold trim, white ground **95.00**

Ewer, 9½" h, enameled blue an yellow poppies, blue and pink enameled ground, gold ivy figural pierced handle, marked "Carlsbad" under crown, "Made in Austria" **195.00**

Miniature Lamp, 8½" h, porcelain base, Bristol-glass shade, orange, blue, and lavender flowers, scrolling gold trim, nutmeg burner, marked "Victoria, Carlsbad, Austria" **425.00**

Pitcher, 11" h, cobalt blue bands, gold trim, pink round **100.00**

Plate, 7⅝" d, scalloped, pink and yellow roses spray, green buds and leaves, gold trim, white ground, c1905 .... **32.50**

Portrait Plate, 9" d, blond woman, heavy gold trim **50.00**

Sugar Shaker, Bluebird pattern, marked "Victoria-Carlsbad" **45.00**

Teapot, cov, hp, relief scrolls, marked "Carlsbad 1892" **50.00**

Vase, 8½" h, portrait of monk reading newspaper, pink and gold, two handles, marked "Carlsbad, Victoria" **60.00**

Gravy Pitcher and underplate, two-handled plate, yellow and pink roses, green leaves, gold trim, 3 × 9" pitcher, 5⅝ × 9¼" plate, $75.00.

CARNIVAL GLASS

History: Carnival glass, an American invention, is colored pressed glass with a fired-on iridescent finish. It was first manufactured about 1905 and was immensely popular both in America and abroad. Over 1,000 different patterns have been identified. Production of old carnival glass patterns ended in 1930.

Most of the popular patterns of carnival glass were produced by five companies—Dugan, Fenton, Imperial, Millersburg, and Northwood.

Marks: Northwood patterns frequently are found with the "N" trademark. Dugan used a diamond trademark on several patterns.

References: Gary E. Baker et al., *Wheeling Glass,* Oglebay Institute, 1994 distributed by Antique Publications; Carol O. Burns, *The Collector's Guide to Northwood Carnival Glass,* L-W Book Sales, 1994; Bill Edwards, *The Standard Encyclopedia of Carnival Glass,* Fourth Edition, Collector Books, 1994; Marion T. Hartung, *First Book of Carnival Glass to Tenth Book of Carnival Glass* (series of 10 books), published by author, 1968 to 1982; William Heacock, James Measell and Berry Wiggins, *Dugan/Diamond,* Antique Publications, 1993; ———, *Harry Northwood, The Wheeling Years, 1901–1925,* Antique Publications, 1991; Marie McGee, *Millersburg Glass,* Antique Publications, 1995; Tom and Sharon Mordini, *Carnival Glass Auction Prices, 1994,* published by authors, 1995.

Collectors' Clubs: American Carnival Glass Assoc, 9621 Springwater Ln, Miamisburg, OH 45342; Canadian Carnival Glass Assoc, 107 Montcalm Dr, Kitchner, Ontario N2B 2R4 Canada; Collectible Carnival Glass Assoc, 3103 Brentwood Circle, Grand Island, NE 68801; Heart of America Carnival Glass Assoc, 4305 W 78th St, Prairie Village, KS 66208; International Carnival Glass Assoc, RR #1, Box 14, Mentone, IN 46539; Lincoln-Land Carnival Glass Club, N951, Hwy 27, Conrath, WI 54731; New England Carnival Glass Club, 27 Wells Rd, Broad Brooks, CT 06016; Tampa Bay Carnival Glass Club, 101st Ave N, Pinellas Park, FL 34666.

Museum: Fenton Art Glass Co, Williamstown, WV.

Notes: Color is the most important factor in pricing carnival glass. The color of a piece is determined by holding it to the light and looking through it.

Acanthus, Imperial, plate, marigold **195.00**
April Showers, Fenton, vase
   11½" h, blue **70.00**

   12½" h, amethyst **55.00**
Autumn Acorn, Fenton, ice cream bowl, purple **90.00**
Basket, Northwood, bushel-basket shape, two side handles
   Amethyst **110.00**
   Blue **175.00**
   Marigold **125.00**
Beaded Cable, Northwood, rose bowl
   Aqua opalescent **325.00**
   Green **175.00**
Beaded Shell, Dugan, creamer, marigold **95.00**
Beads, Northwood, bowl, green **65.00**
Blackberry Spray, Fenton, compote, ftd, green **45.00**
Blackberry Wreath, Millersburg, bowl, 10" d, blue **1,150.00**
Brocaded Acorn, Fostoria, ice bucket, moveable handle,
   6" h, ice blue, gold trim **125.00**
Broken Arches, Imperial, punch set, marigold, 7 pcs .. **450.00**
Butterfly and Berry, Fenton
   Berry Set, marigold, 7 pcs **300.00**
   Bowl, marigold
      4¾" d **30.00**
      8¼" d, ftd **65.00**
   Pitcher
      Amethyst **375.00**
      Marigold, 9" **275.00**
   Spooner, marigold **80.00**
   Tumbler, marigold, 4¼" h **45.00**
   Vase, 9" h, blue **75.00**
Captive Rose, Fenton
   Bowl, 8" d, 3" h, ruffled, fluted, amethyst **60.00**
   Bowl, 8⅞" d, green **48.00**
Cherries, Dugan, compote, peach opalescent **85.00**
Concave Diamonds, unknown maker, tumbler, ice blue,
   price for set of six **250.00**
Corinth, Dugan, bowl, 7" d, amethyst **30.00**
Cosmos, Millersburg, bowl, marigold
   9" d, ruffled **30.00**
   10" d **65.00**
Dahlia, Dugan, pitcher, amethyst **1,100.00**
Daisy and Drape, Northwood vase, white **275.00**
Daisy and Plume, Northwood-Dugan, rose bowl, green **35.00**
Diamond Point, unknown maker, vase, 10" h, amethyst **85.00**
Dragon's Tongue, Fenton, bowl, ftd, large, marigold ..**2,200.00**
Dutch Twins, unknown maker, ashtray, marigold **45.00**
Farmyard, Dugan, plum
   Bowl **50.00**
   Chop Plate **50.00**
Fashion, Imperial, punch cup, marigold **20.00**
Feather and Heart, Millersburg, tumbler, marigold **75.00**
Finecut and Roses, Northwood, rose bowl, green **225.00**
Fisherman, Dugan, mug, amethyst **135.00**
Fish Net, Dugan, epergne, peach opalescent **550.00**

Grape and Gothic Arches, tumbler, marigold, $35.00.

Northwood's Grape, pitcher, green, $300.00.

Floral and Grape, Dugan, water set, pitcher and four tumblers, marigold	190.00
Good Luck, Northwood, bowl, piecrust edge	
Electric blue	795.00
Marigold, 8½″ d	175.00
Grape, Imperial	
Basket, marigold, 10″ d	50.00
Bowl, 9½″ d, marigold	35.00
Plate, 8½″ d, ruffled, smoke	95.00
Punch Cup, marigold	20.00
Water Carafe, amethyst	225.00

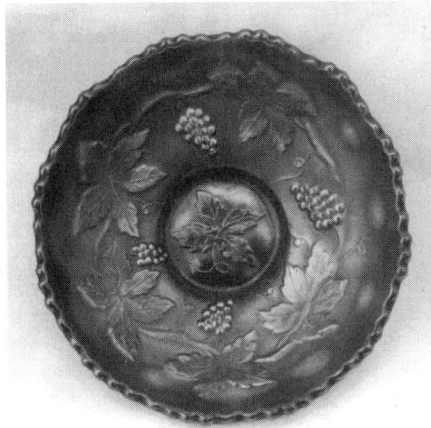

Heavy Grape, bonbon, purple, $60.00.

Grape and Cable, Northwood	
Bowl, 8½″ d, basketweave, piecrust edge, green	75.00
Creamer, purple, "N" mark	85.00
Pitcher, 8¼″ h, purple	210.00
Plate, green	295.00
Punch Bowl and Base, 12″ d, 12″ h, purple, marked "Northwood"	880.00
Punch Cup, amethyst	40.00
Salad Bowl, ftd, points straight up, white	675.00
Sugar, cov, purple, "N" mark	105.00
Tumbler, 4″ h, ftd, purple	25.00
Water Set, pitcher and six tumblers, marked "Northwood"	
Marigold	350.00
Purple	550.00

Grape and Gothic Arches, Northwood, tumbler, marigold	35.00
Greek Key, Northwood, tumbler, green	195.00
Hearts and Flowers, Northwood, bowl, ice blue	600.00
Heavy Grape, Imperial	
Bowl, marigold	
6½″ d	40.00
9″ d	35.00
Sherbet, marigold	20.00
Heavy Web, Dugan, bowl, 12″ sq, peach opalescent	2,200.00
Holly and Berry, Dugan, bowl, 6″ d, marigold	50.00
Holly, Fenton, bonbon, adv, two handles, marigold	110.00
Holly Sprig, Millersburg, Bonbon, green	95.00
Honeycomb, Dugan, rose bowl, peach opalescent	200.00
Horse's Head, Fenton, ice cream bowl, 6½″ d, marigold	155.00
Inverted Strawberry, unknown maker, tumbler, marigold	300.00
Iris, Fenton, buttermilk goblet, marigold	48.00
Jewels, Imperial, centerpiece bowl, ftd, red	595.00
Kittens, unknown maker, cup and saucer, marigold	250.00
Lattice and Daisy, Dugan, tumbler, marigold	30.00
Leaf and Beads, Northwood or Dugan	
Bowl, 7″ d, ftd, green	90.00
Rose Bowl, aqua opalescent	395.00
Leaf Chain, Fenton	
Bowl, blue	115.00
Plate, 7″ d, marigold	150.00
Tumble-Up, marigold	80.00
Leaf Rays, Dugan, nappy, handle, peach opalescent	65.00
Louisa, Westmoreland	
Candy Dish, ftd, aqua	135.00
Plate, aqua	135.00
Luster and Flute, Northwood, hat, marigold	50.00
Lustre Rose, Imperial, bowl	
5″ d, green	10.00
6½″ d, stippled, golden smoky marigold	65.00
Maple Leaf, Dugan, tumbler, marigold	30.00
Nippon, Northwood, bowl, 9″ d, marigold	40.00
Octagon, Imperial, bowl, 8½″ d, marigold	25.00
Orange Tree, Fenton	
Mug, marigold	30.00
Powder Jar, cov, marigold	60.00

Oriental Poppy, Northwood
    Tumbler, white **165.00**
        Water Set, pitcher and six tumblers, purple **1,045.00**
Peacock, Millersburg, plate, purple, multicolored irid . **795.00**
Peacock and Grape, Fenton, bowl, fluted, aqua **135.00**
Peacock and Urn, Northwood, bowl, ruffled, marigold **145.00**
Peacock Tail, Fenton, bowl, 7" d, ruffled, blue **55.00**

Peacock at the Fountain, butter dish, purple, $225.00.

Pebbles, Dugan, bowl, 8½" d, ruffled, amethyst **25.00**
Persian Medallion, Fenton, bonbon, blue **115.00**
Petal and Fan, Dugan, sauce, 6" d, peach opalescent . **40.00**
Pony, Dugan, bowl, ruffled, 8½" d, marigold **155.00**
Poppy Show, Northwood, vase, 12" h, cobalt blue **65.00**
Question Marks, Dugan, bonbon, marigold **45.00**
Rainbow, Northwood, compote, amethyst **115.00**
Raspberry, Northwood, water set, pitcher, six tumblers,
    green **550.00**
Ripple, Imperial, vase
    8½" h, green **75.00**
    12½" h, amethyst **135.00**
Rococo, Imperial, vase, 4¼" h, marigold **160.00**
Rose Show, Northwood, plate
    Cobalt Blue **2,100.00**

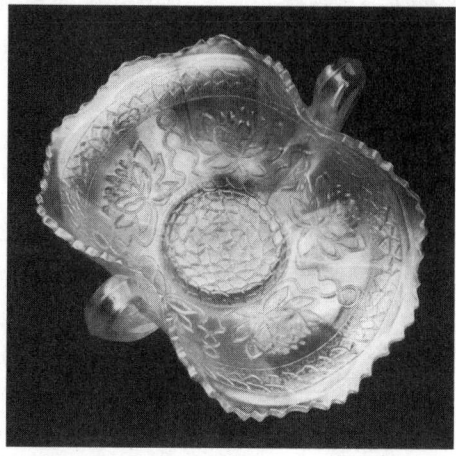

**Pond Lily, Fenton, bonbon, 2 handles, white, 7¼"
d, 3½" h, $85.00.**

Emerald Green **7,500.00**
Marigold **500.00**
White **650.00**
Rustic, Northwood, vase
    8½" h, crimped, ruffled edge, marigold **50.00**
    15" h, funeral, marigold **250.00**
Sailboats, Fenton
    Sauce, 6" d, ruffled, marigold **40.00**
    Wine, marigold **35.00**
Shell and Jewel, Westmoreland, creamer, marigold ... **35.00**
Single Flower, Dugan, bowl, tricornered, peach opales-
    cent **90.00**
Smooth Rays, Westmoreland
    Bonbon, marigold **75.00**
    Bowl, 7⅛" w, amethyst, marked "N" **115.00**
Spiralex, English, vase, marigold **45.00**
Stag and Holly, Fenton, bowl, ruffled, 7½" d, blue **225.00**
Stork in the Rushes, Dugan, vase, marigold **30.00**
Strawberry, Fenton, Millersburg, Northwood
    Bonbon, marigold **35.00**
    Bowl, piecrust edge, green **250.00**
Thistle, Fenton, bowl, 8½" d, 3-in-1 edge, amethyst ... **115.00**
Three Fruits, Northwood, bowl, 9" d
    Amethyst, satiny blue int. **265.00**
    Green **140.00**
Two Flower, Fenton, bowl, 9" d, marigold **45.00**
Two Fruits, Fenton, bonbon, divided, marigold **55.00**
Vintage, Millersburg
    Bowl, 10" d, green **150.00**
    Fernery, blue **60.00**
    Ice Cream Bowl, master, marigold **95.00**
    Mug, banded, marigold **35.00**
Wild Panel, Northwood, Fenton, Imperial, epergne, 4-
    lily, green **1,250.00**
Wild Rose, Northwood, bowl, ftd, open edge, green .. **90.00**
Windmill, Imperial, bowl, 6" d, marigold **25.00**

**Wishbone, plate, sawtooth edge, marigold, ftd,
8" d, $80.00.**

Wishbone, Northwood
    Bowl, 8¼" d, ruffled, ftd, amethyst **170.00**
    Tumbler, amethyst **150.00**
Zipper Loop, Imperial, oil lamp, 8" h, squatty, marigold **575.00**

CAROUSEL FIGURES

History: By the late 17th century, carousels were found in most capital cities of Europe. In 1867 Gustav Dentzel carved America's first carousel. Other leading American firms include Charles I. D. Looff, Allan Herschell, Charles Parker, and William F. Mangels.

References: Charlotte Dinger, *Art of the Carousel,* Carousel Art, 1983; Tobin Fraley, *The Carousel Animal,* Tobin Fraley Studios, 1983; Frederick Fried, *The Pictorial History of the Carrousel,* Vestal Press, 1964; William Manns, Peggy Shank, and Marianne Stevens, *Painted Ponies,* Zon International Publishing, 1986; Dana G. Morykan and Harry L. Rinker, *Warman's Country Antiques & Collectibles,* Third Edition, Wallace-Homestead, 1996.

Periodicals: *Carousel Collecting & Crafting,* 3755 Avocado Blvd, Suite 164, La Mesa, CA 91941; *Carousel News & Trader,* Suite 206, 87 Park Avenue West, Mansfield, OH 44902; *Carousel Shopper,* Zon International Publishing, PO Box 6459, Santa Fe, NM 87502.

Collectors' Clubs: American Carousel Society, 3845 Telegraph Rd, Elkton, MD 21921; National Amusement Park Historical Assoc, PO Box 83, Mount Prospect, IL 60056; National Carousel Assoc, PO Box 4333, Evansville, IN 47724.

Museums: Carousel Museum of America, San Francisco, CA; Heritage Plantation of Sandwich, Sandwich, MA; Herschell Carrousel Factory Museum, North Tonawanda, NY; International Museum of Carousel Art, Portland, OR; Merry-Go-Round Museum, Sandusky, OH; New England Carousel Museum, Inc., Bristol, CT.

Notes: Since carousel figures were repainted annually, original paint is not a critical factor to collectors. "Park paint" indicates layers of accumulated paint; "stripped" means paint has been removed to show carving; "restored" involves stripping and repainting in the original colors.

Catalog, Herschell-Spillman Co, N Tonawanda, NY, 1907, 33 pages, 6 × 9", Catalog E, Amusement Outfitters, steam or electric, riding galleries, merry-go-rounds, organs, well illus, foxed **190.00**
Camel
European, 75" l, running, detailed fur, layered trappings with tassels, c1910 ....**6,600.00**
Matthieu, French, 49" l, Arabian, strolling pose, two saddles, fringed blanket and tassels, c1932 .....**3,850.00**
Cat, Dentzel, American, 54" l, finely carved detailed fur, fish in mouth, c1903 ....**27,500.00**
Chicken, French, 39" l, standing, detailed feathers, expressive face, orig brass handle, c1910 ....**11,550.00**
Deer, Herschell-Spillman, American, 58" l, outside row, standing, dec trappings, deeply carved detailed fur, dog's head on saddle cantle, real antlers, c1910 ..**23,100.00**
Dog, Herschell-Spillman, American, 54" l, jumping, expressive face, c1905 ....**6,875.00**
Donkey, Bayol, French, 60" l, standing on hind legs, whimsical expression, long perky ears, neck strap with bell, carved bells on trappings, orig handles, c1895 ....**16,500.00**
Dragon, Anderson, English, 69" l, leaping, fierce expression, etched mirrored jeweled eye, hinged neck, double saddle, c1900 ....**11,000.00**

Elephant, American, 52" l, walking, expressive face, scalloped blanket, tusks, c1880 ....**11,550.00**
Giraffe, Looff, American, 50" l, crisscrossed blanket, two eagle heads on saddle cantle, c1895 ....**16,500.00**
Goat, Henri Devos, French, 36" l, jumping, expressive face, carved body, straps and blanket, c1920 ......**3,500.00**
Horse
Anderson, English, 73" l, galloping, double saddle, elaborately carved leaves, scrolls, and ribbon dec, c1895 ....**4,500.00**
Carmel, Charles, American, 43" l, stander, alert expression, windswept mane, jeweled scalloped trappings, c1905 ....**8,800.00**
Dentzel, American, prancer, old paint, orig, no restoration, stand included **8,250.00**
Looff, American
50" l, jumper, alert expression, full mane, scalloped straps, c1895 ....**5,500.00**
64" l, prancer, gentle expression, full mane, checkered blanket, two eagle's heads with glass eyes at saddle cantle, c1895 ....**7,700.00**
PTC, American
48" l, jumper, animated pose, layered trappings, raised forelock, flowing mane, c1916 ....**5,500.00**
65" l, stander, outside row, flowing mane, draped forelock, tucked head, multi-layered strap dec with star motif, bridle rosette with jewel, c1919 .... **22,000.00**
Rhode Island origin, orig gray paint, repainted white and pink, chartreuse saddle, some gilded dec, ... **27,500.00**
Spillman, American, 58" l, jumper, jeweled trappings, fringed blanket, rose on breast strap, c1924 .....**6,500.00**

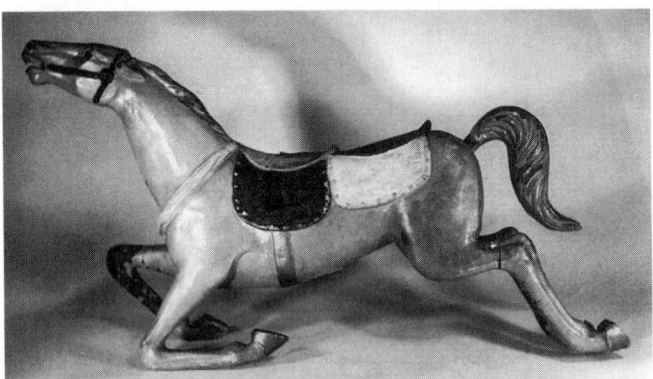

Horse, jumper-type, outer row, 28" l, $2,200.00.

Lion, German, 33" l, roaring expression, intricately carved man, c1890 ....**3,200.00**
Organ Facade, European, 81" h, carved roses, butterfly, and scroll work, early 1900s **5,500.00**
Pig, Herschell-Spillman, American, 44" l, jumper, deeply rippled blanket, ribbon and bow on neck, curly metal tail, c1914 ....**16,500.00**
Pony, American, 42" h, carved wood, polychrome dec, cream color, black saddle, light horsehair tail **350.00**
Rabbit
Devos, Henri, French, 42" l, tail with bow, breast strap, orig brass handles, c1920 ....**2,750.00**

Hubner, German, 46" l, animated racing pose, detailed fur, layered trappings with tassels, c1890   **4,950.00**
Rooster, Spooner, English, 57" l, running, detailed feathers, hinged neck, double saddle, factory nameplate, c1890 ....**4,500.00**
Seal, European, 31" l, 38" h, ball on nose, saddle, mounted on pedestal, c1925 ....**1,750.00**
Zebra, PTC/E Joy Morris, American, 56" l, proud stance, tapered blanket, fringed straps, c1903 ....**22,000.00**

CASTOR SETS

History: A castor set consists of matched condiment bottles held within a frame or holder. The bottles are for condiments such as salt, pepper, oil, vinegar, and mustard. The most commonly found castor sets consist of three, four, or five glass bottles in a silver-plated frame.

Although castor sets were made as early as the 1700s, most of the sets encountered today date from 1870 to 1915, the period when they enjoyed their greatest popularity.

3-bottle
    Cobalt blue with cut panels, SP frame, open salt, mustard pot, pepper shaker, silver mustard spoon, 7" h, 2¾" d **135.00**
    Milk glass, salt and pepper shakers, mustard container, orig matching undertray **225.00**
    Ribbed acid finish Burmese glass, salt and pepper shakers, matching mustard pot with spoon, SP holder **425.00**
    White satin glass, ribbed, SP Pairpoint holder **225.00**
4-bottle
    Acid-finished Burmese glass, ribbed, salt and pepper shakers, mustard and vinegar, SP holder marked "F. B. Rogers" **650.00**
    Clear, octagonal paneled pressed glass bottles, pewter stand, attributed to Israel Trask, 7½" h **225.00**
    Daisy and Button, amber, glass holder **125.00**
5-bottle
    China, Blue Willow pattern, matching holder **125.00**
    Clear pressed glass bottles and jars, SP frame, French. 10½" h **195.00**
    Flint glass, Bellflower pattern, two bottles with period stoppers, pewter stand, 11¼" h **300.00**
    Gothic pattern, one bottle replaced, pewter frame . **125.00**
    Heavy Paneled Finecut pattern, SP holder **100.00**
6-bottle
    Amberina, metal holder, marked "Aurora, 487" ...**2,000.00**
    English, George III, oval SP stand, center handle, pierced reticulated sides and scroll feet, four glass bottles, castor, and mustard pot with spoon, early 19th C **250.00**
7-bottle, English, George III, cut glass bottles, SS collars, and caps, silver galleried canoe shaped tray, scroll feet, marked "Peter, Ann & William Bateman, London," 1801 ....**1,500.00**
8-bottle, eight cut glass bottles and jars, George III, Classic Revival style stand dec with gadrooned edge, shell and leaf motif, made in London by Daniel Pantifex, 1810, one ring holder broken, minor chips, one replaced stopper, 10" l, 8" w, 10½" h **980.00**

5-bottle, flint glass, Gothic pattern, pewter standard, c1860, made by Sandwich, 10½" h, one stopper missing, $195.00.

CATALOGS

History: The first American mail-order catalog was issued by Benjamin Franklin in 1744. This popular advertising tool helped to spread inventions, innovations, fashions, and necessities of life to rural America. Catalogs were profusely illustrated and are studied today to date an object, identify its manufacturer, study its distribution, and determine its historical importance.

References: Ron Barlow and Ray Reynolds, *The Insider's Guide to Old Books, Magazines, Newspapers, Trade Catalogs,* Windmill Publishing (2147 Windmill View Rd, Cajon, CA 92020), 1995; Norman E. Martinus and Harry L. Rinker, *Warman's Paper,* Wallace-Homestead, 1994; Lawrence B. Romaine, *A Guide to American Trade Catalogs 1744–1900,* Dover Publications, n.d.

Museums: Grand Rapids Public Museum, Grand Rapids, MI; National Museum of Health and Medicine, Walter Reed Medical Center, Washington, DC.

Additional Listings: See *Warman's Americana & Collectibles* for more examples.

Advisor: Kenneth Schneringer.

A G Spalding & Bros, 1903, 84 pgs, Spalding's Athletic Library, How to Swim **15.00**
A Schoenhut Co, Philadelphia, PA, c1910, 46 pgs, Humpty-Dumpty Circus toys **118.00**
Adriance Platt & Co, Poughkeepsie, NY 1888, 16 pgs, mowers and reapers **63.00**
Allen, Brock & Smith, Inc, New York, NY, 1914, 56 pgs, women's clothing and shoes **23.00**
Army & Navy Supply Co, Richmond, VA, c1924, 28 pgs **9.00**
Austin, Nichols & Co, Chicago, IL, 1922, 64 pgs, groceries **23.00**
Baldwin Piano Co, Cincinnati, OH, 1921, 36 pgs **47.00**
Bausch & Lomb Optical Co, Rochester, NY, 1896, 264 pgs **162.00**

Bradley & Hubbard Mfg Co, Meriden, CT, 1918, 54 pgs **66.00**

Brazel Novelty Co, Cincinnati, OH, c1920, 64 pgs, fireworks, holiday decorations, balloons, etc. **96.00**

C L Berger & Sons, Boston, MA, 1910, 226 pgs, engineers' and surveyors' instruments **128.00**

Carriage & Harness Mfg, Elkhart, IN, 1885, 64 pgs **185.00**

Chase Brass & Copper Co, Baltimore, MD, c1931, 2 pgs **22.00**

Chemical Toilet Corp, Syracuse, NY, c1925, 18 pgs ... **18.00**

Chevrolet Motor Co, Detroit, MI 1925, 28 pgs **28.00**

Chicago Pneumatic Tool Co, Chicago, IL, c1898, 48 pgs **32.00**

Cleveland Metal Products, Cleveland, OH, 1915, 32 pgs, "Aladdin" aluminum cooking utensils **34.00**

Copeland & Thompson, Inc, New York, NY, 1940, 80 pgs, Spode dinnerware **33.00**

Creek Chub Bait Co, Garrett, IN, c1929, 16 pgs **38.00**

Diebold Safe & Lock Co, Canton, OH, 1914, 19 pgs .. **48.00**

E H Sheldon & Co, Muskegon, MI, c1920, 88 pgs, industrial school and laboratory furniture **39.00**

Edwin Cigar Co, Inc, New York, NY, 1929, 20 pgs **138.00**

Elmer Richards Co, Chicago, IL, 1913, 88 pgs, fall and winter women's fashions **26.00**

Elswick Cycles Ltd, London, England, 1939, 42 pgs ... **32.00**

Empire Harness Co, Buffalo, NY, 1915, 8 pgs **14.00**

Empire Portable Forge Co, Syracuse, NY, 1884, 16 pgs **18.00**

Enterprise Mfg Co of PA, Philadelphia, PA, 1898, 80 pgs, The Enterprising Housekeeper by Helen Louise Johnson **23.00**

F A O Schwarz, New York, NY, 1962, 102 pgs **47.00**

Fenton Label Co, Philadelphia, PA, c1920, 32 pgs, gummed labels and advertising stickers **18.00**

Galloway Terra-Cotta Co, Philadelphia, PA, c1916, 44 pgs, pottery vases, pot stands, pots, saucers, etc. ... **172.00**

Gimble Brothers, New York, NY, 1920, 280 pgs, fall and winter clothing for women and children **30.00**

Globe-Wernicke Co, Cincinnati, OH, 1923, 24 pgs, sectional bookcases **34.00**

Goldblatt Tool Co, Kansas City, MO, 1920, 88 pgs ... **34.00**

Catalog, The Larkin Plan, No 94, 50th Anniversary, Fall and Winter, 1925, 240 pgs, illus, 8 × 11", $20.00.

Goodyear Tire & Rubber Co, Akron, OH, 1919, 36 pgs **29.00**

H Channon Co, Chicago, IL, 1913, 120 pgs, tents & canvas specialities **38.00**

Henderson Desk Co, Inc, Henderson, KY, 1909, 32 pgs **47.00**

International Harvester, Chicago, IL, c1911, 24 pgs ... **43.00**

International Silver Co, Meriden, CT, 1939, 76 pgs **32.00**

J H Steward, England, c1892, 84 pgs, binoculars, field and race glasses **53.00**

J L Taylor & Co, New York, NY, c1920, 12 pgs, men's suits and overcoats **19.00**

J Wiss & Sons Co, Newark, NJ, c1920, 88 pgs, scissors, razors, nail files, etc. **72.00**

James S Barron & Co, New York, NY, 1888, 26 pgs, woodenware, willow ware and hardware **185.00**

John Danner Mfg Co, Canton, OH, 1911, 24 pgs, sectional bookcases **46.00**

John Wanamaker Co, New York, NY, 1906, 8 pgs, special white sale **21.00**

Kenneth Lynch & Son, Inc, New York, NY, 1940, 16 pgs, weather vanes **34.00**

Keramic Supply Co, Indianapolis, IN, c1928, 64 pgs, china painting materials **22.00**

Keuffel & Esser Co, New York, NY, 1913, 566 pgs, drawing materials, surveying instruments **59.00**

L B Ramsdell, Gardner, MA, c1880, 40 pgs, children's wagons, toy chairs, desks **75.00**

L Basch & Co, Chicago, IL 1918, 92 pgs, diamond importers and jewelry manufacturers **39.00**

L Templin & Sons, Calla, OH, 1896, 32 pgs, flower seeds and bulbs **20.00**

Landers, Frary & Clark, New Britain, CT, 1919, 55 pgs, "Universal" cutlery, electrical kitchen appliances, table service pieces, etc. **48.00**

Larkin Co, Buffalo, NY, 1910, 32 pgs **32.00**

Lehigh Portland Cement Co, Allentown, PA, 1927, 36 pgs **15.00**

Lionel Toy Crop, Hillside, NJ, 1958, 54 pgs **37.00**

Majestic Mfg Co, St Louis, MO, c1924, 22 pgs **21.00**

Marvin Smith Co, Chicago, IL 1896, 90 pgs, farm machinery and agricultural implements **68.00**

Milton Bradley Co, Springfield, MA, c1923, 17 pgs ... **35.00**

Morris Sklar Co, Philadelphia, PA, c1927, 8 pgs, home lighting fixtures **19.00**

Nehi Bottling Co, Ponca City, OK, c1929, 8 pgs, premium catalog **16.00**

Newark Valley Wagon Co, Newark Valley, NJ, 1883, 26 pgs **59.00**

Patterson Mfg Co, Philadelphia, PA, 1910, 41 pgs, hammocks and couches **78.00**

Remington Arms Co, Ilion, NY, 1909, 64 pgs **81.00**

Richardson Manufacturing, Worcester, MA, 1886, 16 pgs, new model "Buckeye" mower **48.00**

Sears, Roebuck & Co, Chicago, IL, 1915, 148 pgs, January/February sale **34.00**

Standard Auto & Radio Co, Chicago, IL, 1936, 34 pgs . **13.00**

Sullivan Granite Co, Westerly, RI, 1922, 47 pgs **48.00**

Three Springs Fisheries, Frederick, MD, 1932, 40 pgs, water lilies & goldfish **18.00**

W W Kimball Co, Chicago, IL, c1920, 36 pgs, organs . **38.00**

Wendell & Co, New York, NY, 1924, 112 pgs, jewelry manufacturers **49.00**

Wisconsin Refrigerator Co, Eau Claire, WI, 1893, 32 pgs **44.00**

Wm Deering & Co, Chicago, IL, 1889, 36 pgs, grain-cutting machinery **64.00**

CELADON

History: The term *celadon,* meaning a pale grayish green color, is derived from the theatrical character Celadon, who wore costumes of varying shades of grayish green, in Honore d'Urfe's 17th-century pastoral romance, *L'Astree.* French Jesuits living in China used the name to refer to a specific type of Chinese porcelain.

Celadon divides into two types. Northern celadon, made during the Sung Dynasty up to the 1120s, has a gray to brownish body, relief decoration, and monochromatic olive green glaze. Southern (Lung-ch'uan) celadon, made during the Sung Dynasty and much later, is paint-decorated with floral and other scenic designs and is found in forms which would appeal to the European and American export market. Many of the southern pieces date from 1825 to 1885. A blue square with Chinese or pseudo-Chinese characters appears on pieces after 1850. Later pieces also have a larger and sparser decorative patterning.

Reproduction Alert.

Bowl
    7" d, straight flared bowl, small foot rim, int. molded floral rim, central flower head, Korean, Choson dynasty, firing faults to glaze **290.00**
    7½" d, 3½" h, molded leaf design, Longquan, early Ming Dynasty, Chinese **900.00**
    10½" d, white raised enamel emblems and scholar's implements, everted rim, cylindrical foot, 19th C **275.00**
Dish, 9½" d, serrated edge, ftd, birds, flies, and insects among flowers dec, Chinese Export porcelain, 19th C, chips to foot **275.00**

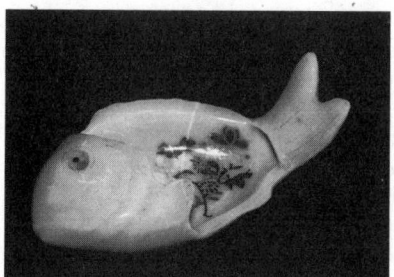

Condiment, fish shape, 5½" l, $55.00.

Ewer, 3⅝", ovoid, ribbed, plain shoulder, loop handle, upright spout, blue-green glaze, burnt orange foot rim, Southern Sung Dynasty **900.00**
Jar, 5" h, globular form, pale green glaze, Yongzheng mark, 1723–35 .... **4,950.00**
Lamp Base, converted vase, minor damage **75.00**
Platter, 18" l, birds, flies, and insects among flowers dec, Chinese Export porcelain, 19th C **300.00**
Rose Jar, cov, 5¾ × 4¼", three part, bulbous, pink, red and blue relief flowers, green foliage, gold trim **195.00**
Vase
    6" h, Mongul style, low relief-carved Indian lotus motif, exotic bloom carved handles, surmounted lotus-form knot cov **2,875.00**

    7¼" h, stick type, incised dragon, lingzhi, and scrolling clouds, flared rim, rolled foot, 19th C **375.00**
    10¾" h, high-shouldered form, sides tapering to slightly flared base, inlaid white and black slip, band of scrolling lotus, upright lotus borders above and below, Korean, Koryo dynasty, 13th C, old neck and foot repair **2,530.00**
    12¾" h, bottle form, single applied chilong crawling around neck, underglaze Qianlong seal mark ... **1,150.00**

CELLULOID ITEMS

History: In 1869 an Albany, New York, printer named John W. Hyatt successfully developed and patented the world's first semi-synthetic thermoplastic, which was made from camphor and pyroxylin, a type of nitrocellulose. Hyatt and his brother Isaiah named the material "Celluloid," a contraction of the words cellulose and colloid, and began production at the Celluloid Manufacturing Company in Newark, New Jersey.

By the mid-1870s the Hyatt brothers were successfully making pyroxylin plastic in imitation of expensive luxury materials. In the early days of its commercial development, celluloid was used for only a few utilitarian applications. However, by the 1880s fabricating companies were busy molding the plastic into a variety of fancy articles, fashion accessories, and novelty items.

As the industry grew, several other factories went into business making pyroxylin plastic identical to Hyatt's Celluloid but licensed under different trade names: Pyralin (manufactured by Arlington Co., Arlington, New Jersey), Fiberloid (Fiberloid Corp., Indian Orchard, Massachusetts), and Viscoloid (Viscoloid Co., Leominster, Massachusetts). Even though these companies branded their products with proper trade names, today the word "celluloid" is used generically and encompasses all forms of this early plastic.

The ease with which celluloid can be molded and the abundance of available man-made material helped the industry to grow tremendously. However, pyroxylin plastic did have one major drawback: extremely flammable nitrocellulose was used in the production process. Nevertheless, because celluloid products imitated expensive luxury items, the plastic copies became increasingly popular with the working and middle classes.

Used as a replacement for ivory, amber, and tortoiseshell in hundreds of different utilitarian and novelty applications, it wasn't until the development of the motion picture industry that celluloid gained an identity all its own. In addition to camera film, it was also used by animation artists who drew cartoons on transparent sheets of the material called cels. By filling such unique roles, celluloid was no longer viewed exclusively as a substitute material but became valued in its own right.

By 1930 and the advent of the modern plastics age, the use of celluloid began to decline dramatically. Development of nonflammable safety film eventually ended the use of celluloid in the movies, and by 1950 production in the United States had ceased altogether. Japan, however, continued to manufacture celluloid for many years thereafter, and small amounts are still being made for specialty items such as musical-instrument inlay and ping-pong balls.

Marks: Viscoloid Co. manufactured a large variety of small hollow animals that ranged in size from 2 to 8 inches. Most of these toys are embossed with one of three trademarks: "Made in USA," an intertwined "VCO," or an eagle with a shield.

Advisor: Julie P. Robinson.

Advertising

Clothing Brush, 3" d, circular brush, colorful picture of Parisian Novelty Co building, makers of Fiberloid Advertising Novelties, Chicago **85.00**

Ink Blotter, 2½" × 6", rect booklet of blotters, decorative celluloid cover showing a manger scene, Keller Mfg Co, Allentown, PA, Christmas 1929, printed by Whitehead and Hoag Co **20.00**

Letter Opener, 8½" l, amber and green pearlescent, "Dupont Viscoloid, February 23, 1931" **18.00**

Pocket Mirror, oval, violet motif, "Use Mennen's Violet Talcum Powder" **35.00**

Tape Measure, 1¼" d, pull-out tape, colorful picture of Colgate's Fab Soap Flakes, printed by Bastian Bros Co, Rochester, NY **25.00**

Decorative Items and Fancy Goods

Album, 8" × 11", celluloid-covered photo album, picture of pretty girl, roses **85.00**

Clock, 5" l, mantle, Greek Revival style, gray pearlescent celluloid, imitation amber columns, c1930 .... **30.00**

Collar Box, celluloid applied over wooden box, multiple compartments for collars, cuffs, and links, dark green, ivy florals, bright pink lining **55.00**

Dresser Set
    Fiberloid, "Fairfax Gold Fiberloid," variegated brown and gold, powder box, hair receiver, mirror, brush, comb, file, 2 button hooks, scissors, clothing brush **85.00**

Dresser Set, nail file box, shoe horn, two boxes, amber base, pearlized black flower and leaf, $125.00.

    Pyralin, DuBarry pattern, brush, comb, button hook, clothing brush, dresser tray, hair receiver, hand mirror, manicure implements, buffer, salve box, powder box, vase, and frame **145.00**

Dresser Tray, white celluloid tray, glass center, diecut couple over lace background **20.00**

Frame, 6" × 8", rect frame, oval ivory celluloid center, ruffled edges, wire easel back **18.00**

Handkerchief Box, sq, light green, raised white swag decoration around edge, classical woman in center, light pink lining **85.00**

Hatpin Holder, conical, fashioned from ivory-colored strips of celluloid, basketweave design, weighted base **85.00**

Jewelry Box, grand-piano shape, imitation amber, embossed floral trim, black and gold **35.00**

Manicure Set, 5" × 7", cream-colored embossed celluloid applied over wooden box, cottage scene, fitted with manicure tools, light blue lining, box **45.00**

Necktie Box, rect, embossed "Neckties" reverse painted on lid, dark green, yellow, and cream, c1900 ...... **85.00**

Vanity Set, Arch Amerith, Celluloid Co, clear and pearlescent amber, embossed floral design, original case with 9 pc, c1927 .... **45.00**

Vase, 12", imitation tortoiseshell, conical, round weighted base **25.00**

Novelties

Letter Opener, 11", figural handle of lighthouse, heavy ivory-colored celluloid, Celluloid Novelty Co, c1890 **85.00**

Pincushion, 4½" h, Lighthouse, CT, souvenir, figure of soldier standing at attention on pincushion base, "Made in Japan" **25.00**

Salt and Pepper Shakers, pr, souvenir of Washington, DC, metal with celluloid coating, pictures of Washington Monument and Capital **12.00**

Travel Sewing Kit, shaped celluloid case, SS thimble and scissors, "Germany" **65.00**

Toys

Aviator, 6", orange suit, "Made in Japan" **55.00**

Bathing Beauty, 9", green bathing suit and cap, holding umbrella, "Made in Japan" **75.00**

Boar, 3⅓", brown, Paul Hunaeus of German, "PH" trademark **65.00**

Boy with fishing pole and fish, 6", "Made in Japan" ... **75.00**

Camel, bright orange, Dupont oval trademark **25.00**

Doll
    9½", girl and boy dressed in ethnic costumes, Rheinische Gummiund Celluloid Fabrik Co, Germany, turtle in diamond trademark, price for pr **125.00**
    12", realistic baby doll, "Made in U.S.A. by Viscoloid Co." **95.00**

Duck, wearing policeman's uniform, movable arms and legs, blue or chartreuse highlights, VCO trademark **75.00**

Giraffe, yellow, brown spots, Petticolin of France, eagle's-head trademark **65.00**

Lobster, 1¾", bright red, detailed shell **35.00**

Rattle
    Shield shape, pink, blue flowers, "Baby" **12.00**
    Stork shape, 6" l, "Made in Japan" **35.00**

Roly Poly, 1½", woman with kerchief, "PH" trademark **75.00**

Utilitarian Items

Shaving Brush, imitation ivory handle, badger hair bristles, Kent of England **12.00**

Soap Container, two-pc box, rect, rounded corners, overall embossed fleur-de-lis, Celluloid trademark . **12.00**

Straight Razor

    Imitation ivory handle, figural bamboo, embossed, "Made in Germany" **14.00**

    Imitation tortoiseshell handle, "Made in Germany"

String Holder, ivory-grained twist-apart sphere, weighted pedestal base **45.00**

CHALKWARE

History: William Hutchinson, an Englishman, invented chalkware in 1848. It was a substance used by sculptors to imitate marble and also was used to harden plaster of paris, creating confusion between the two products.

Chalkware pieces, which often copied many of the popular Staffordshire items made between 1820 and 1870, was cheap, gaily decorated, and sold by vendors. The Pennsylvania German folk art pieces are from this period.

Carnivals, circuses, fairs, and amusement parks gave away chalkware prizes during the late 19th and the 20th centuries. These pieces often were poorly made and gaudy.

References: Dana G. Morykan and Harry L. Rinker, *Warman's Country Antiques & Collectibles,* Third Edition, Wallace-Homestead, 1996; Ted Soufe, *Midway Mania: A Collectors Guide to Carnival Plaster Figurines, Prizes, and Equipment 1900–1950,* L-W Books, 1985.

Additional Listings: See Carnival Chalkware in *Warman's Americana & Collectibles.*

Notes: Don't confuse the chalkware carnival giveaways with the earlier pieces. Prices for the later chalkware items range from $10 to $50.

Bank, 9½" h, dove form, repaired **100.00**

Bookends, pr, buccaneer busts, sgd "Herzel" **250.00**

Bust, 11¼" h, woman, titled "Micaela," pedestal base, painted **145.00**

Figure

    4" h, cat, laying on oval pillow base, mouse in mouth, orig polychrome paint **425.00**

    5¼" h, rooster, orig red, yellow, and black paint ... **485.00**

    5½" h, cat, red and black painted highlights, American, mid 19th C **275.00**

    6" h, dog, red and black painted highlights, American, mid 19th C **265.00**

Figure, ewe and lamb, 4" d, 7¼" h, 8⅝" l, $300.00.

    6 × 9½", stag, painted and smoked dec, PA, c1850 **420.00**

    6¼" h,. squirrel, polychrome paint **300.00**

    7½" h

        Santa Claus, very worn surface, traces of paint, mostly mottled brown **65.00**

        Spaniel, worn orig yellow, red, and black paint . **220.00**

    8¼" h, Santa, worn polychrome, slight hairline **495.00**

    8¾" l, ewe and lamp, orig red, yellow, and black paint, repaired cracks **525.00**

    9" h

        Cat holding ball, polychrome paint **120.00**

        Spaniel smoking pipe, gray-white, red and black ears, yellow collar, c1885 .... **100.00**

    10½" h, dogs, Staffordshire style, gold and black highlights, PA or OH, late 19th C, price for pr **365.00**

Vase, 9" h, squirrel holding nut, 1930s **40.00**

CHARACTER AND PERSONALITY ITEMS

History: In many cases, toys and other products using the images of fictional comic, movie, and radio characters occur simultaneously with the origin of the character. The first Dick Tracy toy was manufactured within less than a year after the strip first appeared.

The golden age of character material is the TV era of the mid-1950s through the late 1960s. Some radio premium collectors might argue this point. Today, television and movie producers often have their product licensing arranged well in advance of the initial release.

Do not overlook the characters created by advertising agencies, e.g., Tony the Tiger. They represent a major collecting subcategory.

References: Pauline Bartel, *Everything Elvis,* Taylor Publishing, 1995; Bill Blackbeard (ed.), *R. F. Outcault's The Yellow Kid,* Kitchen Sink Press, 1995; Bill Bruegman, *Cartoon Friends of the Baby Boom Era,* Cap'n Penny Productions, 1993; ———, *Superhero Collectibles,* Toy Scouts, 1996; *Cartoon & Character Toys of the 50s, 60s, & 70s,* L-W Book Sales, 1995; Roger Case and Sharon Korbeck (eds.), *Toys & Prices,* Third Edition, Krause Publications, 1995; Richard DeThuin, *The Official Identification and Price Guide to Movie Memorabilia,* House of Collectibles, 1990; Warren Dotz, *Advertising Character Collectibles,* Collector Books, 1993; ———, *What a Character! 20th Century American Advertising Icons,* Chronicle Books, 1996; Ted Hake, *Hake's Guide to Cowboy Character Collectibles,* Wallace-Homestead, 1994; ————, *Hake's Price Guide to Character Toy Premiums,* Collector Books, 1996.

Jack Koch, *Howdy Doody,* Collector Books, 1996; Mary Jane Lamphier, *Zany Characters of the Ad World,* Collector Books, 1995; David Longest, *Character Toys and Collectibles* (1984, 1992 value update), Second Series (1987, 1990 value update), Collector Books; Richard O'Brien, *Collecting Toys,* Seventh Edition, Books Americana, 1993; Jerry Osborne, *The Official Price Guide to Elvis Presley Records and Memorabilia,* House of Collectibles, 1995; Susan and Steve Raab, *Movie Star Autographs of the Golden Era,* published by authors, 1994; Harry L. Rinker, *Hopalong Cassidy,* Schiffer Publishing, 1995; Jon D. Swartz and Robert C. Reinehr, *Handbook of Old-Time Radio,* Scarecrow Press, 1993; Jon R. Warren, *Collecting Hollywood: The Movie Poster Price Guide,* Third Edition, American Collectors Exchange,

1994; Dian Zillner, *Hollywood Collectibles* (1991), *The Sequel* (1994) Schiffer Publishing.

Periodicals: *Autograph Times*, 2303 N 44th St, #225, Phoenix, AZ 85008; *Baby Boomer*, PO Box 1050, Dubuque, IA 52004; *Big Reel*, PO Box 1050, Dubuque, IA 52004; *Button Pusher*, PO Box 4, Coopersburg, PA 18036; *Celebrity Collector*, PO Box 1115, Boston, MA 02117; *Classic Images*, PO Box 809, Muscatine, IA 52761; *Collecting Hollywood,* American Collectors Exchange, 2401 Broad St, Chattanooga, TN 37408; *Cowboy Collector Newsletter*, PO Box 7486, Long Beach, CA 90807; *Frostbite Falls Far-Flung Flier*, PO Box 39, Macedonia, OH 44056; *Hollywood & Vine,* Box 717, Madison, NC 27025; *Hollywood Collectibles,* 4099 McEwen Dr, Suite 350, Dallas, TX 75224; *Movie Advertising Collector*, PO Box 28587, Philadelphia, PA 19149; *Movie Collector's World*, 17230 13 Mile Rd, Roseville, MI 48066; *Television History Magazine*, 700 E Macoupin St, Staunton, IL 62088; *The TV Collector Magazine*, PO Box 1088, Easton, MA 02334.

Collectors' Clubs: All About Marilyn, PO Box 291176, Hollywood, CA 90029; Beatles Fan Club, 397 Edgewood Ave, New Haven, CT 06511; Betty Boop Fan Club, 6025 Fullerton Ave, Apt 2, Buena Park, CA 90621; C.A.L./N-X-211 Collectors Society, 727 Youn Kin Pkwy So, Columbus, OH 43207; Camel Joe & Friends, 2205 Hess Dr, Cresthill, IL 60435; Charlie Tuna Collectors Club, 7812 NW Hampton Rd, Kansas City, MO 64152; Dagwood-Blondie Fan Club, 541 El Paso, Jacksonville, TX 75766; Dick Tracy Fan Club, PO Box 632, Manitou Springs, CO 80829; Dionne Quint Collectors, PO Box 2527, Woburn, MA 01888; Howdy Doody Memorabilia Collectors Club, 8 Hunt Ct, Flemington, NJ 08822; Official Popeye Fan Club, 1001 State St, Chester, IL 62233; R. F. Outcault Society, 103 Doubloon Dr, Slidell, LA 70461; Three Stooges Fan Club, PO Box 747, Gwynedd Valley, PA 19437.

Videotapes: *Dionne Quintuplet Dolls: 1934–1939,* Sirocco Productions, 1992; *Shirley Temple Dolls & Memorabilia,* Sirocco Productions, 1994.

Additional Listings: See *Warman's Americana & Collectibles* for expanded listings in Cartoon Characters, Cowboy Collectibles, Movie Personalities and Memorabilia, Shirley Temple, Space Adventurers, and TV Personalities and Memorabilia.

SPECIAL AUCTIONS

Hake's Americana & Collectibles
PO Box 1444
York, PA 17405
(717) 848-1333

Toy Scouts
137 Casterton Ave
Akron, OH 44303
(216) 836-0668

Character

Boop, Betty
    Animation Art, 8½ × 11", Betty in top hat, ink on
       paper, Max Fleicher Studios, c1930, unframed .. **950.00**

Carnival Chalkware, 14½" h, c1930 .... **175.00**
Perfume Bottle, 3½" h, glass, figural, painted facial
    features, dark red plastic cap, c1930 .... **50.00**
Pin, 1" h, enamel on silvered brass, Betty playing
    violin, 1930s **200.00**
String Holder, wooden, wall mounted, souvenir-type
    decal **38.00**
Bounce, Billie, pinback button, 1¼" d, "Compliments of
    Billie Bounce," red ground, blue uniform, 1904 T C
    McClure copyright, W W Denslow character **250.00**
Brown, Buster
    Blotter, unused **15.00**
    Bowl, 3½" d, Buster pouring hot milk into Tige's bowl **15.00**
    Clicker, 1¼" l, Buster Brown Shoes, multicolored,
       c1900 .... **40.00**
    Napkin Ring, celluloid **30.00**
    Pinback Button, 1¼" d, New York Herald/Young
       Folks, c1902, missing back paper **250.00**
    Receipt Book, Buster and Tige **135.00**
    Rug, Buster and Tige **275.00**
    Shoe Rack, H D Beach, Coshocton, OH, tin litho,
       Buster and Tige supporting metal rack for shoe
       display, 11⅝" h, missing tin-plate shoe holder .. **550.00**

Advertising Pinback Button, Buster Brown Bread, celluloid, multicolored, W. E. Long Co, Chicago, 1½" d, $20.00.

Campbell Kids
    Doll, cloth, straw stuffed, painted eyes, c1909 ..... **250.00**
    Feeding Dish, Buffalo Pottery **50.00**
    Spoon, 6" l, SP, boy on handle, c1920 .... **15.00**
Elsie, Borden's
    Apron, cloth **85.00**
    Book, *Funbook Cut Toys and Games*, 7 × 10",
       1940's, mint, unused **70.00**
    Buttons, 3 × 4¼" store card, full-color Elsie image as
       cut-out after buttons removed, ¾" d diecut white
       plastic Elsie in daisy-ring border, copyright 1949 **25.00**
    Canister, malted milk **95.00**
    Clapper, tin **160.00**
    Coffee Mug **125.00**
    Flashlight, tractor trailer **150.00**
    Game, hand held **150.00**
    Milk Wagon, 8" **400.00**
Felix the Cat
    Carnival Chalkware, 12½"h **75.00**
    Clicker, 1½" h, black Felix, dark reddish brown
       ground, angry expression, 1930s **50.00**

Doorstop, wood **50.00**
Pinback Button, 1⅛″ d, litho, red and black center reads "31 Comics In Color Sunday Detroit Times," Felix, Skippy, Papa Katzenjammer, Jiggs, Barney Google, the Toonerville Trolley Skipper, and two female characters peeking around center, yellow ground, 1930s **40.00**
Valentine, mechanical, German, framed **65.00**
Gangbusters, target game, P H Lord & Co, Marx, 1940, orig box **375.00**
Google, Barney, pinback button, 1⅛″ d, "Sunday Herald and Examiner 30 Comics," litho, dark blue on white, bright orange ground, 1930s **20.00**
Gump, Andy
Bank, 4⅜″ h, cast iron, worn polychrome, newspaper missing **600.00**
Sheet Music, 9¼ x 12¼″, full-color images on front cov, 1923 copyright **35.00**
Hooligan, Happy, pinback button, 1¼″ d, "Is Everybody Happy?," full Happy figure, cream ground, light red type, c1910 .... **20.00**
Howdy Doody
Bank, 4 × 7″, china, red and blue striped shirt, blue neckerchief, rubber trap, 1950s **425.00**
Mask, 8 × 9″, molded rubber, orig red, white, and blue tag with characters, Bob Smith copyright, c1950 .... **85.00**
Plaque, Howdy, Clarabelle, Mr. Bluster, multicolored **100.00**
Watch, silvered metal case, plastic crystal over Howdy dial, diecut eyes slowly move clockwise, plaid fabric band, Bob Smith copyright, 1948–51 **165.00**

Howdy Doody, mug, plastic, red, decal, $24.00.

Jiggs and Maggie
Ashtray, 38″ h, carved and painted flat wooden silhouette, metal tray, c1930 .... **150.00**
Pinback Button, 1″ d, Detroit Times Contest, black, white, and red, lucky number **25.00**
Puzzles, set of 4, 1932 .... **45.00**
Katzenjammer Kids, pinback button, 1⅛″ d, "Sunday Herald and Examiner 30 Comics," dark blue on white, bright orange ground, Papa Katzenjammer smoking cigar, 1930s **25.00**
Killowatt, Reddy
Mechanical Pencil, 5″ l, hard plastic and chrome, pocket clip, c1950 .... **20.00**
Plate, 9″ d, Syracuse China, 1940s **125.00**

Krazy Kat
Pin, 1¼″ h, brass, black enamel, white enamel bow, yellow rhinestone eyes, c1920 .... **80.00**
Pinback Button
1″ d, black on white, Ignatz, 1970s **15.00**
1⅜″ d, dark green, black image and printing, Los Angeles Evening Herald & Express, serial number **25.00**
Li'l Abner
Glass, 6¼″ h, full-color portrait of Daisy Mae **20.00**
Key-Chain Puzzle, 2″ h, white Shmoo, green and dark red, late 1940s **60.00**
Pinback Button, 1⅝″ d, Knoxville Shmoo Booster—Be a Shmoo, black and white, c1940 .... **100.00**
Tab, tin litho, 2¼″ h, Sealtest Ice Cream Shmoo Club, black and white Shmoo, orange ground, c1949 . **25.00**
Little Orphan Annie
Mug, 3″ h, plastic, Ovaltine premium **30.00**
Nodder, 4″ h, bisque, Germany **90.00**
Pinback Button, 1⅜″ d, dark green, black image and printing, Los Angeles Evening Herald & Express, serial number **25.00**
Watch, brass, compass and sundial combination, Egyptian hieroglyphics on back, Ovaltine, 1938 **65.00**
MAD
Model Kit, Alfred E Neuman, plastic pieces, orig instruction sheet, uncut sign sheet, orig box, 1965 E C Publications copyright **225.00**
Pinback Button, 1½″ d, Merry Easter, full color, Easter rabbit holding basket ready to descend down chimney on snow-covered roof, subscription premium, copyright 1987 .... **20.00**
Mr Peanut, Planters
Coloring Book, 8 × 11″, Planters Nut & Chocolate Co publication, c1920, 32 pgs, only one pg colored **50.00**
Top, 2½″ h wooden spinner, red, yellow and blue decal on large end with Mr Peanut, c1930s **80.00**
Mullins, Moon, pinback button, 1⅜″ d, dark green, black image and printing, Los Angeles Evening Herald & Express, serial number **25.00**
Mutt & Jeff
Blotter, 4 × 9″, black, white, and red, "The Musical Comedy Sensation of the Age," unused **30.00**
Movie Poster, 28 × 41″, *A Tropical Eggspedition*, 1920s **425.00**
Pinback Button, 1¼″ d, black on cream, "Join The Evening Telegraph Mutt & Jeff Club," c1920 .... **75.00**
Peanuts Gang
Commemorative Medal, 1½′ d, Snoopy Moon Landing, silver, Snoopy in space suit and helmet, inscribed "All Systems Are Go!," reverse with Snoopy in space helmet sitting on top of doghouse and slogan "First Landing on the Moon/Commemorative 1969," facsimile Schulz signature, 1969 copyright on back **30.00**
Pin, 1⅝″ h, Charlie Brown, heavy brass, enameled orange shirt, black shoes **75.00**
Popeye
Bank, dime register, 1929 .... **72.00**
Big Little Book, *Popeye*, Saalfield, 1934, Elzie Cristler Segar **35.00**

Cereal Bowl, 1935 .... **60.00**
Eggcup, china, figural **120.00**
Fountain Pen, 1930 .... **25.00**
Pinback Button
   1⅜″ d, dark green, black image and printing, Los
   Angeles Evening Herald & Express, serial num-
   ber **25.00**
   1⅝″ d, Onward Popeye, white figure, blue outline,
   light blue ground, c1960 .... **15.00**
Skippy, pinback button, 1″ d, Detroit Times contest but-
   ton, black, white, and red **20.00**
Smokey Bear
   Key Ring and Fob, 3¼″ h, bright brass luster, darker
   brass fob, c1970 .... **15.00**
   Pinback Button, 2⅛″ d, Smokey's Timbertennial,
   bright red and white, 1964 International Falls,
   MN, event, pr of small bears stand by Smokey's
   legs and slogan **85.00**
   Ring, plastic, raised brown image, yellow plastic,
   c1970 .... **15.00**
   Tab, tin litho, 2¼″ d, "I'm Helping Smokey Prevent
   Forest Fires," brown lettering, bright yellow
   ground, unbent, 1980s **5.00**
Tarzan
   Advertising Poster, 5 × 18″, "Delicious Ice Cream in
   Tarzan Cups," full-color illus, 1930s **115.00**
   Better Little Book, *The Son of Tarzan,* Whitman, Edgar
   Rice Burroughs, 1939 copyright **60.00**
Tracy, Dick
   Big Little Book, *The Super Detective,* Whitman Better
   Little Book, 1939, Chester Gould artist and author,
   432 pgs, hardcover **30.00**
   Camera, orig box **175.00**
   Children's Book, *Dick Tracy Meets the Night Crawler,*
   orig dust jacket **25.00**
   Pinback Button, Dick Tracy Secret Service Patrol,
   1940s **35.00**
   Toy, tin, ramp walker, Nurse Nora figure pushing
   Bonnie Braid in carriage, orig box **175.00**
Yellow Kid
   Movie Flip Book **125.00**
   Pinback Button
      No. 15, money and paint can, "Paint New York
      Red" **30.00**
      No. 46, Yale University pennant **65.00**
      No. 50, mailing letter to Liz, closed tin back **50.00**
   Stickpin, ¾″ h painted white metal diecut, 1¼″ l stick-
   pin, c1896 .... **75.00**

Personality

Allen, Jimmie
   Booklet, *Jimmie Allen Air Battle,* Skelly Gas premium,
   1935 .... **35.00**
   Member Certificate, 8 × 11″, parchment paper, green
   border, red seal, "Full Fledged Pilot Member,"
   Richfield Oil issue, c1934 .... **50.00**
   Whistle, secret signal **20.00**
Autry, Gene
   Pinback Button, 1¼″ d
      "Gene Autry," black and white image, dark red

shirt accents, face, kerchief, and hat band,
bright yellow ground **15.00**
"Gene Autry/Durst Bros Dairy," Gene holding six-
gun in black over yellow printing, black and
yellow rim **125.00**

Gene Autry, guitar, Emenee Musical Toys, plastic, genuine strings, orig box, 32″ l, $125.00.

Bergen, Edgar and Charlie McCarthy
   Bank, 7½″ h, white metal, polychrome dec **85.00**
   Radio-Show Ticket, 1½ × 3½″, tan and black, from
   "Edgar Bergan With Charlie McCarthy," March,
   1951 show, Columbia Broadcasting System,
   Coca-Cola sponsor **25.00**
   Sheet Music, *Love Walked In,* 1938 Goldwyn Follies
   musical **85.00**
Bogart, Humphrey, pinback button, 2½″ d, black and
   white photo, cream ground, brown and black letter-
   ing, "Humphrey Bogart Starring in the African
   Queen, Mr. Plateau Invites You to the Plateau Party,"
   c1951 .... **60.00**
Cassidy, Hopalong
   Button, ½″ d, silvered brass, black-lettered name ... **15.00**
   Compass Ring, black-metal hat missing **40.00**
   Juice Glass **100.00**
   Mechanical Pencil, 5¼″ l, Scripto, white plastic bar-
   rel, dark green and red imprint "Harmony Farms/
   Hoppy's Favorite Milk/Phone CL3-7432" **150.00**
   Pin, white metal bar pin, silver luster, crossed guns,
   suspended thin brass chain, c1950 .... **80.00**
   Pinback Button
      1⅛″ d, "Hopalong Cassidy," black and yellow
      litho, 1950 .... **25.00**
      2″ d, "Hopalong Cassidy in the Daily News,"
      black, cream, and red **60.00**
   Tab, 2″ h, tin litho, "Burry's Hopalong Cassidy Cook-
   ies," multicolored, Sheriff, unbent **45.00**
Chaplin, Charlie
   Figure, 2½″ d, lead **95.00**
   Pencil Box, tin, sgd "H. Clive" **75.00**
   Pinback Button, ⅞″ d, "Charlie Chaplin in Modern
   Times," blue, bright yellow round, string holding
   celluloid charm of Charlie with cane, red outfit,
   black derby, 1936 .... **50.00**

Premium, figure, 13" h, "Dancing Charlie Illusion," jointed, orig package and instructions **145.00**

Crabbe, Buster
Pinback Button
1¼" d, black and white photo, bright orange ground, c1950 .... **35.00**
1⅝" d, litho, black and white photo, red ground, white rim "Member Buster Crabbe Western Club," c1950 .... **80.00**
Program, Aqua Parade, 1948 .... **20.00**

Dionne Quintuplets
Bowl, five girls illus **170.00**
Cake Plate, serving knife **300.00**
Candy Box, Baby Ruth **190.00**
Magazine Adv, 31½ × 14½" h, color, 1935, girls and house adv **125.00**
Mug, one girl illus **75.00**

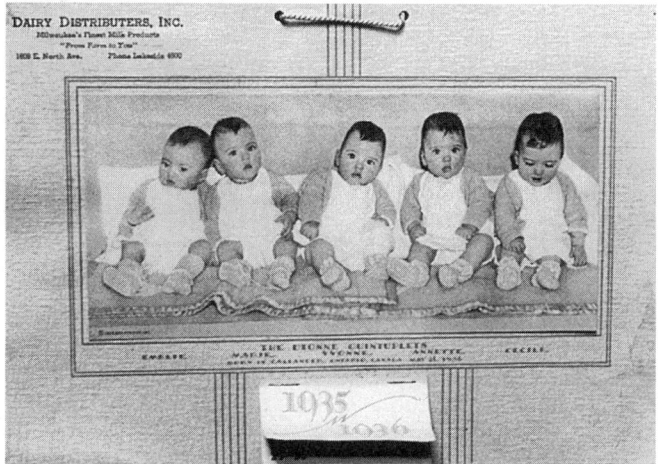

Dionne Quintuplets, calendar, 1935–36, Dairy Distributors, Inc, Milwaukee, WI, multicolored picture, 11¼ × 8", $20.00.

Durante, Jimmy, puppet, hand, Umbraigo, sidekick, composition face, mustache and hat, 1945 .... **120.00**
Fields, W C, pinback button, 2¼" d, black and white, litho, "W. C.," slogan "Be Safe—We Care," Upjohn, 1970s **12.00**
Gish, Lillian, pinback button, 13/16" d, black and white photo, Egyptian Oasis Cigarettes, c1920 .... **20.00**
Laurel & Hardy
Figure, Knickerbocker, bend-em's, rubber faces, clothed soft bodies, price for set **75.00**
Mask, 9" h, paper, printed caricature face, marked "Laurel & Hardy's Laughing 20's," c1966, price for pr **40.00**
Planter, 7½" h, porcelain, standing together, planter in back, 1940s **145.00**
Lindbergh, Charles
Game, Lucky Lindbergh, orig instructions **35.00**
Photograph, 8 × 10", brown tone, standing by plane, wearing dress suit, c1927 .... **25.00**
Lone Ranger
Badge, "The Lone Ranger—A Republic Picture," 1¼" horseshoe-shaped, brass, luster worn, Lone Ranger riding Silver **35.00**

Charm, 1" d, dark red plastic frame, inset full-color cardboard photo of Tonto, 1950s **12.00**
Game Token, 1" d, aluminum disk, portraits of Lone Ranger and Tonto, c1950 .... **15.00**
Good Luck Token, 1½" h, aluminum casing, 1948 penny, good luck symbols, "Keep Me and Never Go Broke," reverse reads "Pioneer/Belts/Braces/Wallets/Superman-Lone Ranger for Boys" **100.00**
Silver Bullet, 1¼" l, removable end cap holds compass, 1940s, scattered tarnish **20.00**

Marx Brothers
Program, 8½ × 11", Curtain Time Variety Show, 16 pgs, 1945, black, white, and maroon cov **70.00**
Sheet Music, *Alone,* 1935 MGM film, blue photo, orange, blue, and white cov **35.00**

McCoy, Tim, pinback button, 1¾" d, black and white photo, black ground, 1930s **75.00**

Mix, Tom
Pinback Button
7/8" d, dark brown and light tan litho, Tom surrounded by lasso as border, issued by Canvas Products Co, 1935 .... **75.00**
1¾" d, "Tim Mix Circus," black and white photo, black ground, 1930s **120.00**
Ring, brass, side images of six gun and longhorn steer, Ralston checkerboard logo with raised initials "TM", inscribed "Ralston/Tom Mix Straight Shooters", worn luster **90.00**

Presley, Elvis
Locket, 5/8" h, heart shape, name in black, c1956 ... **40.00**
Pinback Button, 7/8" d
"I Want You, I Need You, I Love You," Gold Record, 1956, black and white photo, gold rim .. **20.00**
"Love Me Tender," red, white, and blue litho .. **15.00**

Rogers, Roy
Bowl **80.00**
Charm, 1" h, blue plastic frame, black and white glossy paper photo, seated sideways, face turned front **25.00**
Pinback Button, 13/16" d, Post's Grape-Nut Flakes, Canadian, 1953 copyright
"Buttermilk" **55.00**
"Dale Evans" **60.00**
"Roy Rogers," yellow ground **50.00**

Temple, Shirley
Children's Book, *Birthday Book,* 6th birthday, unused **65.00**
Paper Dolls, ten outfits, cut, orig box **35.00**
Pinback Button, 1¼" d, brown-tone photo, light pink rim, Ideal Dolls, 1930s **75.00**

Wynn, Ed, figure, 10" h, cardboard, bright paper label, Fire Chief outfit, movable arms and legs, c1930 .... **65.00**

CHELSEA

History: Chelsea is a fine English porcelain which was designed to compete with Meissen. The factory began operating in the Chelsea area of London, England, in the 1740s. Chelsea products are divided into four periods: Early (1740s), 1750s, 1760s, and Derby (1770–1783). In 1924 a large number of the molds and models of figurines were found at the Spode-Copeland Works, and many items were brought back into circulation.

Marks: Different marks were used during the different Chelsea periods:

Early	incised triangle and raised anchor
1750s	red raised anchor
1760s	gold anchor.

Bowl, 7⅝" d, oval, lotus molded, rose, purple, blue, yellow, green, iron-red, and gray painted int., inset hovering beside floral bouquet, brown-edged petal-molded rim, red anchor mark 1,000.00

Clock, 10⅞" h, molded as floral bouquet, central sunflower enclosing clock, works by Fladgate, scroll-molded base, multicolored pastels, c1761, gold anchor mark, some restoration 12,000.00

Creamer, 5¼" h, gilt trim, dated 1835 .... 80.00

Cup and Saucer, striped pink tulip and columbine dec, yellow ground, gilt rim, scroll and puce foliage handle, gold anchor mark, c1760 .... 395.00

Figure, gardening peasant couple, man resting on spade, woman using watering can 200.00

Patch Box, 1" l, lady's face, black domino mask, mounted rose-cut diamond eyes, mounted pink stone mouth, faceted rock crystal cov, hinged gold-mounted rim, c1755 ....1,200.00

Plate, 8" d, striated purple, blue, and gray painted tulip, iron-red dotted center, brown-edged scalloped rim, red anchor mark 7,750.00

Teabowl and Saucer, Queen Charlotte pattern, iron red, gold, and blue, spiral fluted 200.00

Wax Seal, ¾" h, figural, red squirrel, mounted on gilt-metal ring, c1755 .... 295.00

Pastille Burner, purple ground, red, pink, blue, and yellow pastel flowers, gold outlining, gold anchor mark, 5½" h, 4⅛" w, $225.00.

"CHELSEA" GRANDMOTHER'S WARE

History: "Chelsea" Grandmother's ware identifies a group of tablewares with raised reliefs of either grapes, sprigs of flowers, or thistles on white ground. Some examples are lustered.

The ware was made in the first half of the 19th century in England's Staffordshire district by a large number of manufacturers. The "Chelsea" label is a misnomer but is commonly accepted in the antiques field.

Bowl, 6½" d, Sprig	**25.00**
Butter Pat, Thistle	**17.50**
Coffeepot, Grape	**200.00**
Cup and Saucer, handleless	
Grape	**35.00**
Sprig	**40.00**
Thistle	**40.00**

Eggcup, Grape, marked "Royal Adderley/Blue Chelsea/Ridgway Potters Ltd," $40.00.

Plate	
7¼" d, Grape	**20.00**
8" d, Sprig	**20.00**
9"d, Grape	**25.00**
Sauceboat, Grape	**35.00**
Sugar, cov, Grape	**65.00**
Teapot, cov, Sprig	**125.00**
Vegetable Bowl, cov, Thistle	**65.00**
Washbowl and Pitcher, Vintage, copper luster dec	**495.00**

CHILDREN'S BOOKS

History: Because there is a bit of the child in all of us, collectors always have been attracted to children's books. In the 19th century, books were popular gifts for children, with many of the children's classics written and published during this time. These books were treasured and often kept throughout a lifetime.

Developments in printing made it possible to include more attractive black and white illustrations and color plates. The work of artists and illustrators has added value beyond the text itself.

References: E. Lee Baumgarten, *Price Guide for Children's & Illustrated Books for the Years 1880–1960 Sorted by Artist* and *Sorted by Author,* published by author, 1996; David & Virginia Brown, *Whitman Juvenile Books,* Collector Books, 1996; Richard E. Dickerson, *A Brownie Bibliography,* Second Edition, Golden Pippin Press, 1995; Virginia Haviland, *Children's Literature, a Guide to Reference Sources* (1966), first supplement (1972), second supplement (1977), third supplement (1982), Library of Congress; Diane McClure Jones and Rosemary Jones, *Collector's Guide to Children's Books, 1850 to 1950,* Collector Books, 1996; Jack Matthews, *Toys Go to War,* Pictorial Histories Publishing, 1994; Edward S. Postal, *Price Guide & Bibliography to Children's & Illustrated Books,* M & P Press, 1995; *Price Guide to Big Little*

Books & Better Little, Jumbo Tiny Tales, A Fast Action Story, etc., L-W Book Sales, 1995; Steve Santi, *Collecting Little Golden Books,* Second Edition, Books Americana, 1994.

Periodicals: *Book Source Monthly,* 2007 Syossett Dr, PO Box 567, Cazenovia, NY 13035; *Martha's KidLit Newsletter,* PO Box 1488, Ames, IA 50010; *Mystery & Adventure Series Review,* PO Box 3488, Tucson, AZ 85722; *Yellowback Library,* PO Box 36172, Des Moines, IA 50315.

Collectors' Clubs: Horatio Alger Society, 4907 Allison Dr, Lansing, MI 48910; Society of Phanton Friends, 4100 Cornelia Way, North Highlands, CA 95660.

Libraries: American Antiquarian Society, Worcester, MA; Free Library of Philadelphia, Philadelphia, PA; Library of Congress, Washington, DC; Lucile Clark Memorial Children's Library, Central Michigan University, Mount Pleasant, MI; Pierpont Morgan Library, New York, NY; Toronto Public Library, Toronto, Ontario, Canada.

Additional Listings: See *Warman's Americana & Collectibles* for more examples and an extensive listing of collectors' clubs.

Abbreviations:

dj	dust jacket
n.d.	no date
pgs	pages
teg	top edges gilt
unp	unpaged
wraps	paper covers

Adventures of Paddy Beaver, Thornton Burgess, Toronto, McClelland & Stewart, 1943, 1st ed, drawings, dj .. **20.00**

Adventures of Ray Coon, Nancy Bryd Turner, 1934, Barnes & Bridgman, 1923 .... **15.00**

Alice for the Very Young, 1967 .... **23.00**

Alice in Wonderland with Cut Out Pictures, cover by Julia Green, 1917 .... **148.00**

Alice's Adventure in Wonderland, Lewis Carroll, M. A. Monohue & Co. 236 pgs, green cov **15.00**

Alphabet Book, Whitman, 1935, linen finish, soft cov, 10 × 13″ **10.00**

Black Beauty, Edgar Lee version, illus by H. L. Miller, Saalfield, 1905 .... **20.00**

Book of Penny Toys, illus by Mabel Dearmer, 1899 ... **375.00**

Boys and Girls of Book Lane, Nora Smith, 1923, 11 stories, Jessie Wilcox Smith plates **300.00**

Boy Scouts through the Big Timber, H Carger, A L Burt, 1912, 256 pgs, gray cloth cov, pictures on cov and spine, wear **8.00**

Camel with the Wrinkled Knees, Johnny Gruelle, Volland **75.00**

Children's Garden of Verses, R L Stevenson, Octopus Books, 1979, 1st edition, large size **15.00**

Child's Book of Famous Stories, Penrhyn Coussens, Jessie Wilcox Smith illus, Garden City, NY, 1940 ..... **20.00**

Comical Doings, Ernest Nister, dressed animals, Lewis Wain illus **175.00**

Daddy Long Legs, J Webster, Thrushwood Books, 1940 **10.00**

Danny Decoy, John Held, A S Barnes, 1942, author sgd **20.00**

Dr. Rabbit & Grumpy Bear, Thomas Clark Hinkle, illus by M Winter, Rand McNally, 1934 .... **15.00**

Thompson, Ruth Plumly, *The Hungry Tiger of Oz,* John R. Neill illus, Reilly & Lee Co, Chicago, 1926, 7 × 9½ × 1½″, 261 pgs, $100.00.

Edith and the Bear Lend a Hand, Dare Wright, dj **45.00**

Enchanted Island of Yew, Frank Baum and Fanny Y Cory, 1903, first state of 3rd ed **295.00**

Flower Children, Elizabeth Gordon, M T Ross illus, 1910, Volland, 78th ed **70.00**

Friendly Fairies, Johnny Gruelle, 1919, Volland, 27th ed **60.00**

Girl in the Woods, Grace L Hill, Lipcott, 1st ed, 1942 . **10.00**

Golden Arrow, Bill and Bernard Martin, Tell-Well Press, 1950, 1st ed, sgd by Bill Martin **25.00**

Gnome King of Oz, Plumley Thompson, 1st ed, 1927 . **295.00**

Grimm's Fairy Tales, Anderson, matched set in slip box, 1945, bright blue pictorial covers, 373 and 343 pgs, lavish color **45.00**

Holiday Time on Butternut Hill, Harrison Cady, 1929 . **95.00**

How Peter Rabbit Went to Sea, 1935 .... **90.00**

Hunting for the Hidden Gold, Hardy Boys, F W Dixon, 1928, gray cover **8.00**

Jerry Todd & The Oak Island Treasure, Leo Edwards, 1925 .... **8.00**

Jolly Jump-Ups, R L Stevenson, McLoughlin, 1941, pop-up, loose hinge **25.00**

Kantner's Illustrated Book of Objects, 1895, 2,000 engravings, explanations in English and German **95.00**

Little Black Sambo, 1919 .... **85.00**

Little Brown Koko Has Fun, 2nd edition, 1945, dj **95.00**

Little Garden People, Marion Bryson, illus by Ann Pearsal Sharp, Akron, Saalfield, 1938, 8 × 10 .... **45.00**

Little Slam Bang, Helen Vanderveer, illus by F C Ransom, Volland, 1928, 1st ed **30.00**

Lost Wagon Train, Zane Grey, 1936, binding loose ... **5.00**

Max und Mortiz, 1968 .... **60.00**

Modern Explorers, Thomas Frost, McLoughlin Bros, Arctic explorers on cov **55.00**

Nancy Drew Cookbook Clues to Good Cooking, Keene, NY, 1974, 159 pgs **15.00**

Neighborly Poems, B F Johnson (James Whitcomb Riley), Bowe Merrill, 1891, 1st ed **10.00**

Popeye and the Pirates, animated, Julian Wehs, 1943 . **125.00**

Puppy Stories, Evien Beaudry, illus by Diana Thorne, Akron, Saalfield, Pub, 1934, 8 × 10, pictorial cov . **20.00**

Raggedy Ann Stories, Johnny Gruelle, Volland **75.00**

Return of Tarzan, Edgar Burroughs, 1967, Western Pub **6.00**

Santa Claus Big Picture and Story Book, M A Donohue & Co, Dec, 1914, color picture board cov, title page loose, worn **27.00**

Seven Ages of Childhood, Jessie Wilcox Smith, 1st ed . **175.00**

Sunbonnet Babies Book, E O Grover, 1902, orig jacket **55.00**

Tale of Mr Tod, Beatrice Potter, 1939, dj **50.00**

Tarzan and the Jewels of Opar, Edgar Burroughs, 1918 **8.00**

Tasha Tudor's Bedtime Book, Tasha Tudor, 1977 ..... **45.00**

Teddy Bears in Hot Water, 1907 .... **75.00**

Three Bears, linen, 1933 .... **552.00**

Through the Looking Glass, 1960s **26.00**

Thundering Herd, Zane Grey, Harper's, 1925, 1st ed .. **24.00**

Tom Swift & His Motorboat, tan cov **8.95**

Tom Swift & His Sky Racer, Victor Appleton, 1911, 207 pgs, ads in back **9.00**

Twins in the West, D Whitehall, Barse & Hopkins, 1920, 1st ed, bright cov **10.00**

Uncle Wiggly's Happy Days, 1947, color illus by Rache **45.00**

White Elephant and Other Tales From Old India, Georgene Faulkner illus, 1929 Rainbow ed, 92 pgs **20.00**

Yellow Knight of Oz, Plumley Thompson, 1st ed, 1930 **285.00**

Young Folks Annual, 1910, Dewolf & Fisk Boston Publishers, chromolithograph, color illus, hard cov **55.00**

CHILDREN'S FEEDING DISHES

History: Unlike toy dishes meant for play, children's feeding dishes are the items actually used in the feeding of a child. Their colorful designs of animals, nursery rhymes, and children's activities are meant to appeal to the child and make mealtimes fun. Many plates have a unit to hold hot water, thus keeping the food warm.

Although glass and porcelain examples from the late 19th and early 20th centuries are most popular, collectors are beginning to seek some of the plastic examples from the 1920s to 1940s, especially those with Disney designs on them.

References: Doris Lechler, *Children's Glass Dishes, China and Furniture,* Vol. I (1983), Vol. II (1986, 1993 value update), Collector Books; Dana G. Morykan and Harry L. Rinker, *Warman's Country Antiques & Collectibles,* Third Edition, Wallace-Homestead, 1996; Noel Riley, *Gifts for Good Children: The History of Children's China, Part I, 1790–1890,* Richard Dennis Publications, 1991; Margaret and Kenn Whitmyer, *Collector's Encyclopedia of Children's Dishes: An Illustrated Value Guide,* Collector Books, 1993.

Bowl, 7½" d, two Dutch children **85.00**

Cereal Set, cereal bowl, mug, and plate

    6" d, plate, Nursery Rhyme, Jack and Jill, marked "Royal Bayreuth" **145.00**

    8" d plate, 2⅜" d bowl, 8¼" l, porringer, SS, sides divided into four scenic fairy tale panels, Art Nouveau strapwork, gilt int., marked "Tiffany & Co," c1907, 32 oz, 10 dwt **9,350.00**

Feeding Dish

    Animals, divided, Walker China **20.00**

Duck in Hat, Blue Ridge Pottery **55.00**

Girl feeding teddy, 8" d **65.00**

Jigsaw, Blue Ridge Pottery **90.00**

Scottie and girl, 7" d **65.00**

Mug

    ABC, African animals **70.00**

    Girl and sailor boy, German silver **38.00**

    Little Bo Peep, glass, 3½" h **65.00**

    Uniformed boy in automobile **38.00**

Plate, Robinson Crusoe Milking, $40.00.

Plate

    6½" d, Dr Franklin Maxim, "It Is Hard for an Empty Bag to Stand Free," pawn shop scene, black line border **95.00**

    8" d, Little Tommy Tucker, Royal Doulton **65.00**

Teapot, cov, Duck in Hat, Blue Ridge Pottery **125.00**

CHILDREN'S NURSERY ITEMS

History: The nursery is a place where children live in a miniature world. Things come in two sizes. Child scale designates items actually used for the care, housing, and feeding of the child. Toy or doll scale denotes items used by the child in play and for creating a fantasy environment which copies that of an adult or his own.

Cheap labor and building costs during the Victorian era encouraged the popularity of the nursery. Most collectors focus on items from the years 1880 to 1930.

References: Marguerite Fawdry, *An International Survey of Rocking Horse Manufacture,* New Cavendish Books, 1992; Doris Lechler, *Children's Glass Dishes, China and Furniture,* Vol. I (1983), Vol. II (1986, 1993 value update), Collector Books; Patricia Mullins, *The Rocking Horse: A History of Moving Toy Horses,* New Cavendish Books, 1992; Lorraine May Punchard, *Playtime Kitchen Items and Table Accessories,* published by author, 1993; Herbert F. Schiffer and Peter B. Schiffer, *Miniature Antique Furniture: Doll House and Children's Furniture from the United States & Europe,* Schiffer Publishing, 1995; Tony Stevenson and Eva Marsden, *Rocking Horses: The Collector's Guide to Selecting, Restoring, and Enjoying New and Vintage Rocking Horses,* Courage Books, 1993.

Museum: The Victorian Perambulator Museum of Jefferson, Jefferson, OH.

Additional Listings: Children's Books, Children's Feeding Dishes, Children's Toy Dishes, Dolls, Games, Miniatures, and Toys.

ABC Plate, pink, braille and emb letters **60.00**
Baby Carriage, 53" l, wood and bamboo, wire spoke wheels, white repaint, reupholstered head and bottom rests, some insect damage, labeled "The Gendron, Toledo, O" **220.00**
Banner, Chinaman's Party, multicolored, c1880s **195.00**
Birth Gift, SS, monogrammed dish with child's gods, toys, and symbols of wealth, deep bowl with pillowed infant surrounded by Japanese gods, monogrammed fork, knife, and spoon, satin and velvet rosewood case, Arthur J Bond, Yokohama, 1911 ....**2,200.00**
Carriage, 58" l, 36" h, black and white horse over one small wheel pulling carriage over two larger wheels, ornate scrolled handle, orig paint, metal rails and buggy wheels, molded composition horse cov with hand-stitched horsehide, horsehair tail and mane, English, c1875 ....**2,300.00**
Caudle Cup, four hallmarks in cartouche **325.00**

Chamber Pot, blue-and-white Oriental scene, 8" d, 4¾" h, $175.00.

Cut-Out Book, Pied Piper Peep Show, c1920 .... **60.00**
Desk, curly maple **3,300.00**
Flatware, silver
    Infant Feeding Spoon, emb alphabet in bowl **175.00**
    Spoon, marked "W. F. Robinson, Delaware," price for 4-pc set **825.00**
    Sugar Tongs, marked "B.S." **295.00**
    Youth Set, cherubs playing different musical instruments, patent 1878, orig box **295.00**
Furniture
    Bed, Sheraton, wooden, turned legs and posts, wooden slat railings, old green paint, 29 × 48 × 30½" **250.00**
    Chair, Adirondack, wooden lawn type, 27" h **75.00**
    Screen, folding, Victorian, 3 panels, oak and brass, sheered fabric **825.00**
    Table and chairs, ice cream type **650.00**
Instruction Kit, Soap Box Derby, c1940 .... **20.00**
Mug, 3" h, SS, presentation inscription dated 1890 .... **65.00**

Painting, oil on canvas
    24" w, 30" h, portrait of young child with *Harper's Weekly* dated 1867, good int. scene with drum, plant, carpet, cleaned and minor touchup repair, penciled inscription naming subject on back, old shadowbox frame **4,235.00**
    42" w, 60" h, double portrait of boy and girl in garden, rebacked, cleaned, restored, modern frame **1,575.00**
Potty Chair, wicker, orig finish, play tray **195.00**

Crib, pine, American, turned posts and spindles, shaped crest rail and foot rail, turned and tapered feet on casters, $357.50. Photograph courtesy of Morton M. Goldberg Auction Galleries.

Print, 10⅞" w, 15" h, The Little Drummer Boy, Rub-A-Dub-Dub, Currier and Ives, hand-colored lithograph, stains and paper creases, modern frame **130.00**
Purse, 5" l, emb tin, worn litho of blue, gold, red, and black cats **335.00**
Quilt, 67 × 52", log cabin, fan quilting, American, early 20th C, minor stains **180.00**
Rattle, SS, coral ring **375.00**
Rocking Horse, 46" l, old white and black repaint, replaced black-yarn mane and tail, red vinyl saddle, orig worn landscape painting on footrest **335.00**
Sled, 34" l, wooden construction, steel-tipped runners, orig varnish, top painted red, gold, black, maroon, and white stenciled and freehand floral dec **580.00**
Sleigh
    34" l plus tongue, dec wood frame, wrought-iron fittings, orig red and white paint, green and black trim, worn orig purple velvet upholstery **2,035.00**
    46" l, push type, red repaint, painted flowers, orig upholstery, some age cracks and damage **510.00**

Spurs, Buck 'N Bronc, orig box 80.00
Toddler Walker, 30" l, wooden, chicken heads, worn
    polychrome, marked "Rock-A-Tot" 135.00
Tray, Dogs in School, tin litho, Tea Tray Co, Newark,
    NY, rect, rows of dogs as students, red border 880.00
Wagon, wooden, Huckster, red paint, orig condition ..1,100.00
Whistle, tin, revolving cage with kangaroo, c1920 .... 60.00

CHILDREN'S TOY DISHES

History: Dishes made for children often served a dual purpose—playthings and a means of learning social graces. Dish sets came in two sizes. The first was for actual use by the child when entertaining friends. The second, a smaller size than the first, was for use with dolls.

Children's dish sets often were made as a sideline to a major manufacturing line, either as a complement to the family service or as a way to use up the last of the day's batch of materials. The artwork of famous illustrators, such as Palmer Cox, Kate Greenaway, and Rose O'Neill, can be found on porcelain children's sets.

References: Doris Lechler, *Children's Glass Dishes, China and Furniture,* Vol. I (1983), Vol. II (1986, 1993 value update), Collector Books; Lorraine May Punchard, *Playtime Kitchen Items and Table Accessories,* published by author, 1993; ———, *Playtime Pottery and Porcelain from the United Kingdom and the United States,* Schiffer Publishing, 1996; Margaret and Kenn Whitmyer, *Collector's Encyclopedia of Children's Dishes,* Collector Books, 1993.

Collectors' Club: Toy Dish Collectors, PO Box 159, Bethlehem, CT 06751.

Akro Agate
    Cup and Saucer, Interior Panel, jade 20.00
    Tea Set, Raised Daisy, orig box, price for 13-pc set 225.00
China
    Creamer and Sugar, cov, Willow Ware, blue and
        white 30.00
    Cup and Saucer, green luster, saucer with scene of
        girl and Golliwog 48.00
    Dinnerware, Willow Ware, blue and white, 20-pc set 80.00
    Tea Set
        Bavaria, tumbling Kewpies, emb scrolling and
            gold trim, cov teapot, creamer, cov sugar, five
            cups and saucers, five plates, sgd "Copyrighted
            Mrs Rose O'Neill Wilson Kewpies–Bavaria,"
            price for 20-pc set 550.00
        German
            African Animals, covered teapot, 6 plates, price
               for 8-pc set 15.00
            Cats at play, price for 16-pc set 55.00
            Girl, dog, chicken, and lambs, service for six
               plus waste bowl, price for 18-pc set 325.00
            Roosevelt Bears, some pieces professionally re-
               stored, price for 16-pc set 265.00
        Hand Painted, bluebirds, cov gooseneck tea pot,
            sugar, creamer, four cups and saucers, four
            plates, Japanese 200.00
        Nippon, hp, Indians, teepees, animals, cov teapot,
            sugar, pitcher, cup and saucer 200.00
        Occupied Japan, Willow Ware, blue and white,
            price for 18-pc set 375.00

Tea Set, tin, Dutch boy and girl, $35.00.

    Staffordshire, blue foliate border, country-town
        center reserves, white ground, teapot, cov
        sugar, creamer, waste bowl, four cups and sau-
        cers, English, late 19th C, chips, cracks, price
        for 12-pc set 495.00
Milk Glass
    Basket, cov, emb "Peepers" 185.00
    Candleholders, pr, Swirl pattern
        Green 60.00
        White 35.00
Pattern Glass
    Butter Dish, cov, Pennsylvania, dark green, gold trim 110.00
    Cake Stand, Thistle, 6½" d, 3½" h 75.00
    Creamer
        Amazon 20.00
        Liberty Bell 90.00
    Cup, Dahlia, apple green 85.00
    Cup and Saucer, Wee Branches 90.00
    Mug, Wee Branches 30.00
    Spooner, Hawaiian Lei 22.50
    Sugar, cov, Rooster, dog finial 250.00
    Table Set
        Doyle's 500, amber 325.00
        Stippled Vine and Beads 350.00
        Twin Snowshoes 250.00
Tin
    Mug, 2½" h, Little Bo Peep 20.00
    Tea Set, dogs and cats, red, blue, and white, marked
        "Germany," price for 9-pc set 95.00

CHRISTMAS ITEMS

History: The celebration of Christmas dates back to Roman times. Several customs associated with modern Christmas celebrations are traced back to early pagan rituals.

Father Christmas, believed to have evolved in Europe in the 7th century, was a combination of the pagan god Thor, who judged and punished the good and bad, and St. Nicholas, the generous Bishop of Myra. Kris Kringle originated in Germany and was brought to America by the Germans and Swiss who settled in Pennsylvania in the late 18th century.

In 1822 Clement C. Moore wrote "A Visit From St. Nicholas" and developed the character of Santa Claus into the one we know today. Thomas Nast did a series of drawings for *Harper's Weekly* from 1863 until 1886 and further solidified the character and appearance of Santa Claus.

References: Robert Brenner, *Christmas Past,* Third Edition, Schiffer Publishing, 1996; ———, *Christmas through the Decades,* Schiffer Publishing, 1993; Jill Gallina, *Christmas Pins Past and Present,* Collector Books, 1996; George Johnson, *Christmas Ornaments, Lights & Decorations* (1987, 1995 value update), Vol. II (1996), Vol. III (1996), Collector Books; Polly and Pam Judd, *Santa Dolls & Figurines Price Guide: Antique to Contemporary,* Revised Hobby House Press, 1994; Chris Kirk, *The Joy of Christmas Collecting,* L-W Book Sales, 1994; James S. Morrison, *A Vintage View of Christmas Past,* Shuman Heritage Press, 1995; Mary Morrison, *Snow Babies, Santas and Elves: Collecting Christmas Bisque Figures,* Schiffer Publishing, 1993; Dana G. Morykan and Harry L. Rinker, *Warman's Country Antiques & Collectibles,* Third Edition, Wallace-Homestead, 1996; Margaret Schiffer, *Christmas Ornaments: A Festive Study,* Schiffer Publisher, 1984, 1995 value update; Lissa and Dick Smith, *Christmas Collectibles,* Chartwell Books, 1993; Margaret and Kenn Whitmyer, *Christmas Collectibles,* Second Edition, Collector Books, 1994.

Periodicals: *I Love Christmas,* PO Box 5708, Coralville, IA 52241; *Ornament Collector,* RR #1, Canton, IL 61520.

Collectors' Club: Golden Glow of Christmas Past, 6401 Winsdale St, Golden Valley, MN 55427.

Additional Listings: See *Warman's Americana & Collectibles* for more examples.

Advisors: Lissa and Dick Smith.

Advertising
Bank, molded rubber, Santa Claus holding a coin, toys in pack, marked "Christmas Club A. Corp, N.Y. 1972" **6.00**
Booklet, "When All the World Is Kin," 5 × 4", collection of Christmas stories, Christmas giveaway, Fowler, Dick and Walker, The Boston Store, Wilkes-Barre, PA **7.00**
Calendar 3" h, 7" l, celluloid, Christmas scene with holly border and 1929 calendar, giveaway from The Penny Specialty Shop, Selingsgrove, PA **15.00**
Candy Container, 10" h, pressed cardboard, white snowman with black hat, red composition berry nose, holding a red cloth net bag, marked "Harry & David" on base **75.00**
Candy Tin, oval basket with swing handles, red and green with two snow people on lid, "Satin Finish Madison Mixed Hard Candies," Ludens Inc, Reading, PA **32.00**
Cracker Tin, 2½" h, 11" l, 8" w, Christmas scene on hinged lid, red and gold trim on sides, marked "NBC" on base **25.00**
Matches, 4 × 2", "Season's Greetings" and winter scene on cover, intact matches create Christmas scene, Boehmer's Garage, Milton, PA **14.00**
Trade Card, child holding snowballs, "THE WHITE is King of all Sewing Machines 80,000 now in use," reverse reads "J. Saltzer, Pianos, Organs and Sewing Machines, Bloomsburg, Pa." **10.00**
Bubble Light Candolier, off-white plastic candleholder, hold five candles with bubble lights **35.00**

Candy Box, cardboard
"Christmas Greetings," 4½" l, 3" h, three carolers, USA **4.00**
"Merry Christmas"
Four-Sided Cornucopia, 8" h, Santa, sleigh, and reindeer over village rooftops, string bail, USA **35.00**
Pocketbook Style, 6 × 5", tuck-in flap, Santa in store window with children outside, marked "USA" **15.00**
Candy container, 5" h, glass, red Santa climbing into chimney, metal screw-on base, Victory Co, Jeannette, PA **80.00**

Candy Container, St. Nicholas, papier-mâché, red coat, blue pants, 5³⁄₈", $50.00.

Children's Book
Denslow's Night Before Christmas, Clement C Moore, W W Denslow illustrator, M A Donohue & Co, 1902 .... **25.00**
The Night Before Christmas, Clement C Moore, Corrine Malvern illustrator, A Golden Book, Golden Press, 1975 .... **8.00**
Rudolph the Red-Nosed Reindeer, Robert L May, Maxton Publishers, Inc, 1939 .... **12.00**
Figure
Father Christmas
Composition, 7" h, pink face, red cloth coat, painted blue pants and black boots, mounted on mica-covered cardboard base marked "Japan" **90.00**
Papier-mâché, 8" h, hollow molded, plaster-covered, white coat, black boots, sprinkled with mica **300.00**
Nativity, 7" h, composition, marked "Germany" ... **12.00**
Reindeer
Celluloid, 4" h, white **7.00**
Pot Metal, 1" h, marked "Germany" **18.00**
Santa Claus
Celluloid, 3" l, molded, one-piece Santa, sleigh and reindeer **35.00**
Cloth, handmade, embroidered facial features, cotton batting stuffing, 1940s **30.00**
Cotton batting, 3" h, red, attached to cardboard house, marked "Japan" **48.00**
Hard plastic, 5" h, Santa on green plastic skis, USA **10.00**
Pressed Cardboard, 10" h red hat and jacket, black boots, 10" h **90.00**

Ornament, snowman, mercury glass, red hat, green broom, 3¾", $40.00.

Santa Claus Head, 14" h pressed cardboard, store display	95.00
Sheep, 3" h, composition body, carved wooden legs covered with cloth or wool, glass eyes	40.00
Feather Tree, 4" h, green goose-feather wrapped branches with metal candleholders, round wooden base painted white with green trim, marked "Germany"	400.00

Greeting Cards

"Christmas Greetings," booklet style, embossed die-cut cover, color litho pictures on int. pages, The Art Lithographic Publishing Co	18.00

"Merry Christmas"

Dime coin card, Whitman, 1950s	5.00
Series of six envelopes decreasing in size, small card in last envelope, American Greeting Publishers, Cleveland, USA, 1933	12.00
"Sincere Good Wishes," purple pansy with green leaves, greeting inside, Raphael Tuck & Sons, 1892	7.00

House

Cardboard

Cardboard base and fence, 4 × 5", sponge trees, marked "USA"	10.00
Mica-covered and/or glitter, 2 × 2", wire loop on top, marked "Czechoslovakia"	7.00
Street scene, 7 × 8", four houses and a church, marked "Germany, mica-covered"	30.00
Log, 3 × 4", mica-covered wooden roof, red wooden chimney, marked "Germany"	12.00
Lantern, 8" h, four sided, peaked top, wire bail, metal candleholder in base, black cardboard, colored tissue paper scenes, 1940s	25.00

Ornament

Angel

4" h, wax over composition, human hair wig, spun glass wings, cloth dress, Germany	55.00
8" h, chromolitho, tinsel and lametta trim, pr	15.00
Ball, 2" d, glass, silvered, any color	3.00
Beads, 72" l, glass, multicolored ½" beads, "Japan" on paper label	8.00
Bulldog, 3" h, Dresden, three-dimensional, marked "Germany"	250.00
Camel, 4" h, cotton batting, Germany	160.00
Cross, 4", beaded, two-sided, silvered, wire hanger, "Czechoslovakia" on paper label	18.00
Drummer Boy, 3" h, wax, hollow, metal ring hanger, USA	5.00
Father Christmas, 10" h, chromolitho, blue robe, on donkey, tinsel trim	25.00
Mandolin, 5" h, glass, unsilvered, wrapped in lametta and tinsel	45.00
Parakeet, 5" h, glass, multicolored, spun glass tail, mounted on metal clip	23.00
Pear, 3" h, cotton batting, mica highlights, paper leaf, wire hanger, Japan	12.00
Santa Claus in Chimney, 4", glass, Germany	75.00
Swan, 5 × 6", Dresden, flat, gold with silver, green, and red highlights	150.00
Tree Top, 11" h, three spheres stacked with small clear glass balls, silvered, lametta and tinsel trim, attached to blown glass hooks,	90.00

Postcard, Germany

"Happy Christmas Wishes," Santa steering a ship	10.00
"May Your Christmas Be Merry and Gay," photo card, sepia tones, Father Christmas with fur cap peeking between two large wooden doors	18.00
"Merry Christmas," children trimming candle-lit tree	3.50

Putz

Brush Tree, 6" h, green, mica-covered branches, wooden base	8.00

Christmas Tree Fence

Cast Iron, silver, ornate gold trim, fifteen 10" segments with posts, Germany	600.00
Wood, 48" l, folding red and green sections, USA	35.00
Choir Boy, 3" h, hard plastic, red and white	4.00
Scrapbook, 11½ × 9", brown leather cover, embossed Father Christmas figures and gold holly leaves, marked "PAT. MARCH 1876"	125.00

Toy

Jack-in-the-Box, 9½" h, "Santa Pops," hard plastic, red felt hat, orig box, Tigrett Industries, 1956	30.00
Merry-Go-Round, windup, celluloid, green and red base, four white reindeer heads, Santa sitting under umbrella, Santa spins around, stars hanging from umbrella bounce off bobbing deer heads, orig box, Japan	65.00
Santa, 10" h, battery operated, metal covered with red and white plush suit and hat, soft plastic face, holding metal wand with white star light, wand moves up and down and lights up while Santa turns head	90.00

CIGAR CUTTERS

History: Counter and pocket cigar cutters were used at the end of the 19th and the beginning of the 20th centuries. They were a popular form of advertising. Pocket-type cigar cutters often were a fine piece of jewelry that attached to a watch chain.

Reference: Jerry Terranova and Douglas Congdon-Martin, *Antique Cigar Cutters and Lighters,* Schiffer Publishing, 1996.

Advertising

Betsy Ross 5¢ Cigars, nickel-plated placard with paper image of Betsy surrounded by emb wording, cast-iron base, lever on base pushed to expose cigar cutter, damage to adv	310.00

Brunhoff Manufacturing Co., framed Havana Cigar adv on top, 1906, cast iron, counter type **400.00**

Country Gentleman 5¢, chrome plated, ornate counter-top plate **110.00**

Fifth Avenue Cigar, key wind pocket type **45.00**

Hotel Sherman, figural streetlight, red globe, ornate base, marked "Reed & Barton" **250.00**

Louis Bergdull Brewing Co, Philadelphia, china, patent 1904, cigar cutter and ashtray, wording around match holder on top, 5″ w, 4″ h **165.00**

Master Workman, decal, long handle **85.00**

Tutt's Liver Pills, captain's wheel, cast metal, adv on reverse, wheel spins to expose cigar cutters, 6″ w, 6″ h, some surface rust **550.00**

Figural

Arrowhead, SP, enamel dec, pocket knife type **125.00**

Boy sitting on ornate rock, metal, 7″ h **400.00**

Burro, heavy cast iron, base lever pushed to operate cigar cutter, ears and tail move, cigar snuffer on saddle with emb pots and pans, minor paint loss **525.00**

Crying Child, cast iron, painted black, gray base, cigar in mouth, 4¾″ h, 4½″ l **415.00**

Ship's Wheel, brass-plated tin, handle revolves to expose cigar cutter, 5″ h, minor surface rust **65.00**

Trumpet, brass, pocket knife type **50.00**

Silver, sterling, pocket type

Fob **25.00**

Scissors, repoussé dec **45.00**

CIGAR STORE FIGURES

History: Cigar store figures were familiar sights in front of cigar stores and tobacco shops starting about 1840. Figural themes included Sir Walter Raleigh, sailors, Punch figures, and ladies, with Indians being the most popular.

Most figures were carved in wood, although some also were made in metal and papier-mâché for a short time. Most carvings were life size or slightly smaller and were brightly painted. A coating of tar acted as a preservative against the weather. Of the few surviving figures, only a small number have their original bases. Most replacements were necessary because of years of wear and usage by dogs.

Use of figures declined when local ordinances were passed requiring shopkeepers to move the figures inside at night. This soon became too much trouble, and other forms of advertising developed.

References: Edwin O. Christensen, *Early American Wood Carvings,* Dover Publications, n.d.; A.W. Pendergast and W. Porter Ware, *Cigar Store Figures,* The Lightner Publishing Corp., 1953.

General Butler, 30½″ h, counter-top type, painted carved pine, cigar clenched in mouth, navy blue jacket with gold buttons, red and white striped trousers and bow tie, mounted on gray-painted base **1,800.00**

Indian Chief

27½″ h, counter type, pine, holding bunch of cigars in raised right hand, feathered headdress, orange costume, green cloak, leather fringed leggings, mounted on sq painted base, 19th C **8,250.00**

88″ h, pine, arm raised shielding eyes, bunch of cigars in other hand, one foot resting on rock, wearing feathered headdress, feather-trimmed costume with leggings, painted green, red, and yellow, orig base inscribed "Ed A Feltham, Cigars and Tobacco," orig bars surround top of base, c1880 .**36,500.00**

Indian Princess, 61″ h, carved wood, gold over polychrome, weathered, age cracks, loose three-feather headdress **1,575.00**

Indian Princess, yellow dress, blue feathers, 56½″ h figure, 16″ h base, replaced green base, $3,200.00.

Indian squaw, 45½″ h, carrying box quiver, applied carved and polychromed arrows, circular bosses and tomahawk, painted, mounted on metal base, left arm missing, American, c1870 ....**26,000.00**

CINNABAR

History: Cinnabar, a ware made of numerous layers of a heavy mercuric sulfide, often is referred to as vermilion because of the red hue of most pieces. It was carved into boxes, buttons, snuff bottles, and vases. The best examples were made in China.

Bowl, 8″ d, garden scene, blue enamel int. **225.00**

Box, 3¾ × 5⅜″, Chinese figures in garden setting **95.00**

Cup, 4½″ d, dragon handles, c1900 .... **225.00**

Dish, 10¾″ d, deeply carved, leafy melon vines, black lacquer base **900.00**

Incense Burner, pagoda type, Taoist mask design, c1900 **1,300.00**

Jar, 4″ h, flowering plants, carved floral scrolls, diaper ground, domed cov, gilt-metal rim and finial, price for pr **150.00**

Plate, 12¾″ d, double dragon design **375.00**

Tray, 15″ l, bird and flower scene, reddish brown **625.00**

Vase, 10½″ h, ovoid, long cylindrical neck, carved lotus flowers and leaves, high foot rim with scrolling floral band, price for pr **295.00**

Box, Cinnabar, Chinese figures in garden, 3¾ × 5⅝″, $95.00.

CLAMBROTH GLASS

History: Clambroth glass is a semi-opaque, grayish-white glass which resembles the color of the broth from clams. Pieces are found in both a smooth finish and a rough sandy finish. The Sandwich Glass Co. and other manufacturers made clambroth glass.

Barber Set, two barber bottles, powder shaker, price for
   3-pc set **135.00**

Barber bottle, witch hazel, M. A. Co, 7″ h, $65.00.

Bowl, 7⅝″ d, 2⅝″ h, folded rim **75.00**
Box, cov, 5″ l, multicolored florals, engraved SP holder **75.00**
Dresser Jar, 4½″ h, orig octagonal stopper **225.00**
Eggcup, cov, Diamond Point pattern **950.00**
Ewer, 10¼″ h, blown, applied cranberry rim, applied
   clambroth handle, heat check on foot, base of handle
   ground **140.00**
Flagon, 10½″ h, blown, applied handle, pewter lid,
   marked "Prosit" **150.00**
Toothpick Holder, basket shape, Sandwich **215.00**

CLARICE CLIFF

History: Clarice Cliff, born on January 20, 1899, in Tunstall, Staffordshire, England, was one of the major pottery designers of the 20th century. At the age of thirteen, she left school and went to Lingard, Webster & Company where she learned freehand painting. In 1916 Cliff was employed at A. J. Wilkinson's Royal Staffordshire Pottery, Burslem. She supplemented her in-house training by attending a local school of art in the evening.

In 1927 her employer sent her to study sculpture for a few months at the Royal College of Art in London. Upon returning, she was placed in charge of a small team of female painters at the Newport Pottery, taken over by Wilkinson in 1920. Cliff designed a series of decorative motifs which were marketed as "Bizarre Ware" at the 1928 British Industries Fair.

Throughout the 1930s Cliff added new shapes and designs to the line. Her inspiration came from art magazines, books on gardening, and plants and flowers. Cliff and her Bizarre Girls gave painting demonstrations in the stores of leading English retailers. The popularity of the line increased.

World War II halted production. When the war ended, the hand painting of china was not resumed. In 1964 Midwinter bought the Wilkinson and Newport firms.

The original names for some patterns have not survived. It is safe to rely on the handwritten or transfer-printed name on the base. The Newport pattern books in the Wilkinson's archives at the Hanley Library also are helpful.

Marks: In the summer of 1985 Midwinters produced a series of limited-edition reproductions to honor Clarice Cliff. They are clearly marked "1985" and contain a special amalgamated backstamp.

References: Susan and Al Bagdade, *Warman's English & Continental Pottery & Porcelain,* Second Edition, Wallace-Homestead, 1991; Richard Green and Des Jones, *The Rich Designs of Clarice Cliff,* published by authors, 1995 (available from Carole A. Berk, Ltd, 8020 Norfolk Ave, Bethesda, MD 20814); Leonard R. Griffin and Susan Pear Meisel, *Clarice Cliff,* Harry N. Abrams, 1994; Howard and Pat Watson, *Clarice Cliff Price Guide,* Francis-Joseph Books, 1995.

Collectors' Club: Clarice Cliff Collector's Club, Fantasque House, Tennis Drive, The Park, Nottingham, NG7 1AE, England.

REPRODUCTION ALERT

In 1986 fake *Lotus* vases appeared in London and quickly spread worldwide. Very poor painting and patchy, uneven toffee-colored Honeyglaze are the clues to spotting them. Collectors also must be alert to patterns being added to plain items bearing the "Clarice Cliff" backstamp.

In the summer of 1985, Midwinters produced a series of limited edition reproductions to honor Clarice Cliff. They are clearly dated 1985 and contain a special amalgamated backstamp.

Notes: Bizarre and Fantasque are not patterns. Rather they indicate the time frame of production—Bizarre being used from 1928 to 1937 and Fantasque from 1929 to 1934.

Bowl, 7⁵/₈″ d, 2⁷/₈″ h, Rhodanthe, blended orange, yellow, gray, brown, and black stylized plants, cream ground, stamp marks 375.00

Condiment Set, teepee shape, salt, pepper, and mustard, colored bands, sgd "Clarice Cliff, Wilkinson, England" 125.00

Lotus Jug
 7¹/₈″ d, 11¹/₄″ h, Aurea, green, blue, brown, gray, yellow, and rose stylized plants, cream ground, stamp marks 920.00
 7¹/₈″ d, 11³/₈″ h
  Crocus Lotus, orange, blue, purple, and green stylized flowers, yellow bands, rust and green on cream ground, stamp marks 690.00
  Gardenia, orange, blue, black, purple, rust, and green stylized floral band, orange, yellow, and rust bands, cream ground, stamp marks 1,265.00
 7¹/₄″ d, 11³/₈″ h, Secrets, yellow, rust, brown, green stylized landscape, green, yellow, rust, and brown bands, cream ground, stamp marks 1,380.00
 7¹/₄″ d, 11⁵/₈″ h
  Coral Firs, orange, red, yellow, and brown stylized scenic band, black outlining, brown, rust, and yellow bands, cream ground, stamp mark ... 800.00
  Delicia Citrus, orange, yellow, blue, and green stylized fruit, pale green, brown, yellow, and gray grip, cream ground, stamp marks 520.00

Luncheon Service, Gay Day, yellow, orange, and green, four 4″ d plates, four cups and saucers, price for 16 pc set 635.00

Marmalade Jar, Celtic Harvest, chrome lid, sgd "Celtic Harvest, Clarice Cliff, Newport Pottery, England" .. 70.00

Pitcher
 6⁵/₈″ h, 3⁵/₈″ d, Rhodanthe, blended orange, yellow, brown, and gray stylized plants, cream ground, stamp marks 435.00
 7″ h, 4″ d, Secrets, yellow, rust, brown, and green stylized landscape, cream ground, stamp marks . 520.00
 7³/₄″ h, 7″ w, Fantasque, orange and black flowers . 750.00

Pitcher, raised fruit and berries, brown and yellow leaves, twisted rope band, green int., 7³/₄″ h, $425.00.

9¹/₂″ h, Delecia, heavily carved, grapes and leaves, green, blue, lavender, yellow, and orange drip glaze, ink stamp mark "hand painted Delecia by Clarice Cliff, Wilkinson, Ltd, England," small tight hairline 300.00

Plate
 8″ d, Jonquil, marked "Bizarre by Clarice Cliff," some wear to face 60.00
 10″ d, Bizarre, yellow, green, orange, and gilt hp dec, magenta ground, magenta stamp marks, imp mark, first edition, 1934 .... 410.00

Teapot, 6¹/₂″ h, 9″ w, Harvest, fruit and florals, orange, yellow, and green 230.00

Vase
 7″ h, 3″ d, Inspiration Lily, purple lilies, blue-green ground 375.00
 7³/₄″ h, 4″ d, Delicia Citrus, black and green drips surrounding lemons and orange 575.00
 8″ h, 5¹/₂″h, orange, yellow, and black bands 230.00
 8¹/₄″ h, 6″ d, Coral Firs, trees and landscape 690.00
 9¹/₄″ h, 8″ d, corset, green, blue, yellow and brown floral sprays 800.00
 12¹/₄″ h, Budgies, green and yellow birds, concial cream ground 410.00

CLEWELL POTTERY

History: Charles Walter Clewell was first a metal worker and secondarily a potter. In the early 1900s he opened a small shop in Canton, Ohio, to produce metal overlay pottery.

Metal on pottery was not a new idea, but Clewell was perhaps the first to completely mask the ceramic body with copper, brass or "silvered" or "bronzed" metals. One result was a product whose patina added to the character of the piece over time.

Since Clewell operated on a small scale with little outside assistance, only a limited quantity of his artwork exists. He retired at the age of 79 in 1955, choosing not to reveal his technique to anyone else.

Marks: Most of the wares are marked with a simple incised "Clewell" along with a code number. Because Clewell used pottery blanks from other firms, the names "Owens" or "Weller" are sometimes found.

References: Paul Evans, *Art Pottery of the United States,* Second Edition, Feingold & Lewis Publishing Corp., 1987; Ralph and Terry Kovel, *Kovels' American Art Pottery,* Crown Publishers, 1993.

Museum: John Besser Museum, Alpena, MI.

Ashtray, 3¹/₄″ d, copper, circular imp mark "Clewell, Canton, OH," 1922 .... 185.00

Bowl, 4¹/₂″ d, riveted overlay finish, sgd, circular imp "Clewell Coppers" seal 215.00

Vase
 6⁵/₈″ h, turquoise and brown over brown copper, engraved "Clewell 441," accompanied by brochure entitled *The Bronze Production of C. W. Clewell of Canton, O,* undated, 4 pgs, price for vase and brochure 500.00
 6³/₄″ h, green-over-orange patina, stylus mark, "Clewell 441 25," minor glaze abrasions 500.00

Vase, handle, Vance Avon blank, 12½″ h, 5⅝″ w, $350.00.

7¼″ h, black and green patina, stylus mark, "Clewell 351-2-6" **550.00**

7½″ h, bud, flared rims, crusty green patina, applied copper coating, engraved "Clewell 338-2-6," price for pr **475.00**

10¾″ h, 6″ d, bulbous, collar rim, dark orange and verdigris patina, marked "Clewell 286-2-6," scuffed finish, fine hairlines in metal jacket only **475.00**

13½″ h, 5½″ d, corset shape, flat top, orange-brown and frothy green patina, etched "Clewell 258-2-9" **700.00**

CLIFTON POTTERY

CLIFTON

History: The Clifton Art Pottery, Newark, New Jersey, was established by William A. Long, once associated with Lonhuda Pottery, and Fred Tschirner, a chemist.

Production consisted of two major lines: Crystal Patina, which resembled true porcelain with a subdued crystal-like glaze, and Indian Ware or Western Influence, an adaptation of the American Indians' unglazed and decorated pottery with a high-glazed black interior. Other lines included Robin's-Egg Blue and Tirrube. Robin's-Egg Blue is a variation of the crystal patina line but in blue-green instead of straw-colored hues and with a less-prominent crushed-crystal effect in the glaze. Tirrube, which is often artist signed, features brightly colored, slip-decorated flowers on a terracotta ground.

Marks: Marks are incised or impressed. Early pieces may be dated and impressed with a shape number. Indian wares are identified by tribes.

References: Paul Evans, *Art Pottery of the United States,* Second Edition, Feingold & Lewis Publishing Corp., 1987; Ralph and Terry Kovel, *Kovels' American Art Pottery,* Crown Publishers, 1993.

Biscuit Jar, cov, 7″ h, 4¼″ d, gray-brown ground, enameled running ostrich and stork, florals, bail handle **295.00**

Cologne Bottle, 8⅞″ h, white ground, hp butterfly and flowers, Victorian **45.00**

Cruet, 5¾″ h, hp swallows, blue ground, orig stopper . **50.00**

Decanter, 11½″ h, rose shading to deep rose, purple flowers, gilt butterfly on neck, applied handle, marbleized rose and white stopper **125.00**

Goblet, 10¾″ h, opaque blue, polychrome enamel floral dec, gilt trim, pedestal base **85.00**

Ring Box, cov, 1¾″ d, turquoise, gold flowers and leaves **50.00**

Sweetmeat Jar, 4″ h, hp ducks and cranes, robin's-egg blue ground, cow finial **375.00**

Vase

3¼ × 3½″, bulbous, heavily emb fish, fine olive green crystal patina glaze, clay showing through at high points, incised "Clifton/CAP/1906/108," some minor roughness at high points **650.00**

10 × 7¼″, Crystal Patina, organic form, double handles, yellow and celadon matte crystalline flambe, incised "Clifton/1906/CAP/171," underglaze separation to top rim **375.00**

CLOCKS

History: The sundial was the first man-made device for measuring time. Its basic disadvantage is well expressed by the saying: "Do like the sundial, count only the sunny days."

Needing greater dependability, man developed the water clock, oil clock, and the sand clock, respectively. All these clocks worked on the same principle—time was measured by the amount of material passing from one container to another.

The wheel clock was the next major step. These clocks can be traced back to the 13th century. Many improvements on the basic wheel clock were made and continue to be made. In 1934 the quartz crystal movement was introduced.

The recently invented atomic clock, which measures time by radiation frequency, only varies one second in a thousand years.

References: Robert W. D. Ball, *American Shelf and Wall Clocks,* Schiffer Publishing, 1992; Philip Collins, *Pastime,* Chronicle Books, 1993; Brian Loomes, *Painted Dial Clocks,* Antique Collector's Club, 1994; Tran Duy Ly, *Seth Thomas Clocks &* Movements, Arlington Book Co., 1996; Derek Roberts, *Carriage and Other Traveling Clocks,* Schiffer Publishing, 1993; John Ware Willard, *Simon Willard and His Clocks,* Dover Publications, n.d.

Periodicals: *Clocks,* 4314 W 238th St, Torrance, CA 90505.

Collectors' Club: National Association of Watch and Clock Collectors, Inc, 514 Poplar St, Columbia, PA 17512.

Museums: American Clock & Watch Museum, Bristol, CT; Greensboro Clock Museum, Greensboro, NC; National Assoc of Watch and Clock Collectors Museum, Columbia, PA; National Museum of American History, Washington, DC; Old Clock Museum, Pharr, TX; The Time Museum, Rockford, IL; Willard House & Clock Museum, Grafton, MA.

Notes: Identifying the proper model name for a clock is critical in establishing price. Condition of the works also is a critical factor. Examine the works to see how many original parts remain. If repairs are needed, try to include this in your estimate of purchase price. Few clocks are purchased purely for decorative value.

Miscellaneous

Advertising

General Electric, shell, figural, refrigerator, white heavy metal case, electric, 5¼ × 9″ **115.00**

Jacob Lucks Clothier, Watkins, NY, figural, dog, black man holding sign above **175.00**

Lucky Strike Tobacco, 1870–80, regulator, 8-day time movement, black and gold lower glass sgd "Haskell & Adams, Boston, Mass," replaced paper dial, New Haven Clock Co, 24″ h **250.00**

Monells Teething Cordial for Children, 1875, 8-day time movement, raised gold letters, Somers Clock Co, 30½″ h **850.00**

Peter's Shoes, c1930, alarm, Art Deco, New Haven Clock Co, 4 × 4″ **65.00**

Purina Poultry Chows, electric, three dials, red, white, and blue checkerboard bag shape **50.00**

Weatherford, rooster in center, 17″ d **550.00**

Alarm

Attleboro, 36 hour, nickel plated case, owl dec, 9″ h ... **75.00**

Bradley, brass, double bells, Germany **40.00**

Champion, 30 hour, American movement, metal frame, ornamental feet, 9″ h **75.00**

New Haven, c1900, 30 hour, SP case, perfume-bottle shape, beveled glass mirror, removable cut glass scent bottle, beaded handle **185.00**

Thomas, Seth,, 1919, 1-day time and alarm movement, second bit, metal case, 10¼″ h **50.00**

Automation, George III, 3rd quarter 18th C, bracket, gilt-bronze-mounted mahogany, quarter striking, made by Thomas Gardner, triple fusee, striking nest of eight bells, elaborately engraved backplate, dial with dials for strike/silent and chime/not chime and date aperture, arch with automation of blacksmith's shop, domed case fitted with figural and foliate mounts, ogee bracket feet, 20″ h, 14½″ w, 9″ d **18,700.00**

Blinking Eye, figural, owl, unknown maker, c1920, nickel-plated white-metal front, green eyes, 30-hour level movement, hardwood case, paper dial, nickel-plated bezel, beveled glass, 6½″ h **375.00**

Boat, Seth Thomas, Thomaston, CT, 1880, nickel-plated brass case, painted dial, seconds indicator, 8-day double-wind movement with lever escapement, 6¼″ d **100.00**

Garniture, 3 pc

Louis XV/XVI, c1895, porcelain, ormolu and gilt-metal mounted, painted figures and portraits, foliate and masks mounts, pr of conforming candlesticks, 16½″ h **1,035.00**

Louis XVI Style, marble and ormolu, works stamped "L. P. Japy & Cie," dial sgd "R. Moyson," 16½″ h, pr of three-light candelabra **750.00**

Gaslight, American, 1900, cast brass bezel and feet, 30-hour lever movement, milk glass shade, 5¾″ d **175.00**

Gravity

American, c1925, brass case, powered by weight of clock movement descending along two posts, lifting movement back winds the clock for another 24 hours, marked "Patented 8/2/21," 10¼″ h ... **200.00**

French, c1940, retailed by Shreve, Crump & Low, Boston, powered by the fall of the movement along brass rails, reminding accomplished by lifting the movement back to the top of rails, mahogany case, turned columns and brass finials, 30-hour movement, porcelain dial, polished stone drum case, 17″ h **800.00**

Kitchen, New Haven Clock Co, c1930, white painted case, 8-day time movement, 11¾″ h **65.00**

Lamp, B Bradley, Boston, MA, mechanism on top ignites small brass lamp when alarm strikes, solid walnut case, carved dec, 30-hour time and alarm movement, paper-on-zinc dial, orig brass pendulum, H G Davies, NY, 1865 movement, Bradley illuminating alarm mechanism, orig paper label on back, 14½″ h **1,200.00**

Marine Lever

Pratt, D & Son, c1880, 30-hour time movement, second bit, 8″ h **75.00**

Thomas, Seth, c1890, 15-day time movement, two barrels, oak veneered case, 8½″ h **90.00**

Night-Light, Standard Novelty Co, NY, nickel-plated case, 30-hour lever Ansonia movement, revolving milk glass dome, 6″ h **225.00**

Paperweight, E N Welch, Bristol, CT, 1860, Briggs Rotary Patent, rotary escapement mounted on turned wooden base, cast feet, orig glass dome, nickel-plated pendulum ball, 8″ h **300.00**

Ship, Chelsea, 1920, 8-day time brass movement, second bit, 5¼″ d **200.00**

Table, Swiss, 8-day time only, back plate sgd "W Allemann," half-round banded onyx case, Limoges enameled dial, side panels dec with medieval figures, artist sgd "Richay", 8½″ h **2,070.00**

Water, English, oak and brass, marked "B Kindle-1651-Halifax," 30″ h **200.00**

Shelf

Acorn

Brown, JC, Bristol, CT, 8-day time and strike, driven by fusee spring, laminated light and dark wooden case, fine old finish, orig glass tablet with city scene, carriages, and buildings, maker's label on back, minor retouching on lower glass **15,000.00**

Forestville Mfg Co, Bristol, CT, 1847, laminated wood, lyre-shaped arms, 8-day time and strike lyre fusee movements, pendulum, painted zinc dial, orig upper glass, painted green trim, 24½″ h **750.00**

Beehive

Chelsea, 1900, brass, porcelain dial, 5¼″ h **50.00**

New Haven Guide, 1-day, strike, castle scene **165.00**

Thomas, Seth, inlaid mahogany case, 8-day brass time and strike movement, quarter-hour Sonora chimes, 14½″ h **400.00**

Waterbury Clock Co, c1870, rosewood veneered case, 8-day time, strike, and alarm brass movement, 18¾″ h **75.00**

Box or Cottage

Ansonia, c1870, rosewood veneered case, 8-day time and strike brass movement, 18¼″ h **75.00**

Brewster & Ingraham, 1845–50, mahogany case, 30-hour time and strike movement, 13¼″ h **150.00**

Gilbert & Co, c1890, rosewood veneered case, orig

glass and dial, 8-day time and strike movement, 13½" h **125.00**

New Haven Clock Co, c1880, rosewood veneered case, 8-day time and strike movement, 13¾" h . **125.00**

Terry, S B, c1840, mahogany case, 30-hour time and alarm ladder brass movement, 11" h **175.00**

Thomas, Seth, c1850, rosewood veneered case, 30-hour time and strike movement, half lyre movement, patent dated dial, orig glass, 14½" h **150.00**

Waterbury Clock Co, c1890, rosewood veneered case, 30-hour time and strike movement, 13½" h **95.00**

Bracket

Bigelow & Kennard, c1875, ornate oak case, brass and silver dial, fretwork, 8-day movement, Westminster chimes, 14" h **2,300.00**

Harley, William, Chelsea, mid 18th C, George III, ebonized, arched painted dial, subsidiary date hand and strike silent control, conforming arched hooded case, brass ogee bracket feet, sgd plate, 15" h **4,200.00**

Louis XIV Style, boulle, sgd "Martenot a Paris," matching 60" h bracket **4,600.00**

Roskel, Robert, London, early 19th C, Regency, ebonized, circular silvered dial with Roman numerals, molded brass bezel, arched case, surmounted bail carrying handle, brass ogee bracket feet, dial sgd, 15" h, 10" w **1,800.00**

Unknown maker, 19th C, triple fusee time and quarter-hour strike movement, coiled gong, Westminster chimes, gilt-brass face with applied scrollwork, silver chapter rings with Roman numeral markers, fancy hands, heavily carved oak case with acanthus leaves, fruit clusters, female figures, dragons, 27" h, 16" w, 12" d **3,165.00**

Calendar

Davis Clock Co, Columbus, MS, column flat top, 8-day strike, 7" dial, 25" h **450.00**

Ithaca Clock Co, 1870, cottage-style case, 8-day time, strike, and calendar movement, club escapement, orig backboard with label, 22¼" h **600.00**

Thomas, Seth, c1880, walnut veneered case, 8-day time, strike, and calendar movement, orig instruction label, 25¾" h **650.00**

Welch Spring Co, c1870, rosewood veneered case, 8-day time and strike, BB Lewis calendar movement, 19¼" h **350.00**

Candlestick, SB Terry, c1840, milk glass base, 30-hour time brass movement, 10" h **300.00**

Carriage

French, brass and glass

4¼" h, typical case, leather case and key **160.00**

4⅜" h, plain case, sold by Cecil Roy, Sussex Place, Kensington **120.00**

4½" h, plain case **130.00**

5¼" h, 3¾" w, stamped "H.N. & C," subsidiary alarm and dial, early 20th C **435.00**

5¾" h **100.00**

7" h, jeweled escapement, half-hour strike mechanism on gong, push repeat, ornate gilt brass case, engraved floral dec, beveled glass panels, champleve dec front and side panels, minor chip to front glass **4,025.00**

Shelf, E. Terry & Son, pillar and scroll, c1820, $1,700.00. Photograph courtesy of Aston Auctioneers.

9" h, brass, retailed by Camerden & Forster, NY, visible count wheel, compass and thermometer, later beige marble base, late 19th C **1,610.00**

Swiss, 5½" h, 3½" w, brass, quarter repeating, petite and grande sonnerie striking on two gongs, alarm, c1890, illegible retailer **1,150.00**

Waterbury Clock Co, Waterbury, CT, 1907, miniature, cast gilt-brass case, porcelain dial, maker's trademark, 30-hour time movement, lever escapement **175.00**

Crystal Regulator

Ansonia, c1910, visible escapement, porcelain dial, beveled plate-glass front, back, and sides, decorative brass corners, spring wing, 8-day strike, 4" dial, 12 × 7½" **475.00**

Bailey, Banks & Biddle, c1880, curved front door, 8-day time and strike brass movement, mercury pendulum, 11" h **350.00**

Kitchen, gingerbread style

Ansonia, X-O, oak case, 8-day, hour and half-hour strike, 6" dial, 22½" h **175.00**

Gilbert, Wm, Forest, oak case, 8-day strike, 7" dial, tablet with bird and butterfly in marsh setting, 24½" **200.00**

Ingraham, Mt Vernon, solid-oak relief of Mt Vernon on crest, 8-day, half-hour strike, highly emb octagonal door, 22" h **300.00**

Kroeber Clock Co, Wanderer, walnut case, 8-day gong strike, 6" d fancy dial, elaborate geometric tablet, 23"h **300.00**

New Haven Clock Co, c1915, pressed oak case, 8-day time, strike, and alarm movement, 24½" h .. **95.00**

Waterbury Clock Co, pressed-oak case, 8-day time, strike, and calendar brass movement, barometer and thermometer, 22" h **350.00**

Welch, oak case with bust portrait of Admiral Sampson on crest, ship on tablet, 8-day half-hour strike, cathedral bell, 6" dial, 24"h **300.00**

Lyre, French, Empire, mask with crown above lyre strings flanked by pr of facing swan's heads holding swag over Roman-numeral enamel dial, Baccarat crystal base, center ormolu mounted ribbon-tied swag and trumpet, works marked "Archambult, Paris," 20" h **2,250.00**

Mantel

Birge, Mallory & Co, Bristol, CT, second quarter 19th C, Empire, mahogany, enamel dial, eglomise panel with splint balusters, carved eagle **450.00**

Boston Clock Co, c1890, onyx, 8-day, half-hour cathedral strike, 7j movement, gilt-bronze ornaments, 10" h **295.00**

French

Basalt, bronze, and cloisonné, Egyptian Revival, sphinxes, mask and ring handles, rocaille feet, 16½" l, late 19th C **300.00**

Brass, bow-shaped front, floral garland, enameled circular face, mercury pendulum, 10¼" h **325.00**

Brass and glass, drum movement, half-strike on gong, mercury-filled pendulum, retailed by Bigelow, Kennard, c1900, 9¾" h **750.00**

Cloisonné and Gilt Metal, oval, works by "L. Marti, Paris," jeweled dial, mercury-filled pendulum, later wooden base, c1900, 10" h **635.00**

Gilt Bronze, third quarter 19th C, seated woman on shaped chair, elaborately molded foliage base, 14½" h, 12¼" w **1,150.00**

Gilbert Clock Co, c1903, black marbleized wooden case, 8-day time and strike movement, bell top, 18½" h **200.00**

New Haven Clock Co, c1920, mahogany tambour case, 8-day time and strike movement, Westminster chimes, 8¾" h **125.00**

Russell & Jones, marble-finished wooden case, Tennessee marble columns, 8-day time and slow strike movement, 5" d, 10" h **125.00**

Sessions, c1930, mahogany tambour case, 8-day time and strike movement, 10" h **75.00**

Thomas, Seth, glass and brass, 8-day movement, gong strike, later walnut base, 11" h **320.00**

Marble

Black, Empire Revival, gilt bronze mounts, temple form, four supporting columns, rect base, bun feet, c1840, 19" h **635.00**

Green, Empire Revival, gilt-bronze mounts, spread-wing eagle, floral urn finials, c1875, 22¼" h **1,265.00**

Red, circular face, rect case and base, c1900 ...... **345.00**

Massachusetts Shelf

Balch, Daniel, Jr., Newburyport, MA, c1790, Federal, mahogany, two sets of reeded pilasters, lower door with keystone and arch, scrolled pediment, plinth with brass urn and flame finials, brass dial, 28½" h **12,000.00**

Sherwin, William, Buckland, MA, c1830, maple, 30-hour time and strike wooden works, shaped crest, turned feet, turned columns flanking glazed door with mirror tablet, paper label, orig wooden dial and weights, stenciling removed from crest **900.00**

Metal

Brass, Ansonia, Art Deco, c1920, 8-day time and strike movement, 10¾" h **175.00**

Bronze, French, Charles X, 19th C, bronze winged maiden clasping torch, drawing back the "Veil of Night," rect base, relief chariot and putti, 20" h .**1,150.00**

Cast Iron, N Pomeroy, Bristol, CT, c1865, MOP inlay, gold dec, 30-hour level movement inscribed by maker, painted zinc dial, nickel-plated balance wheel visible through opening in dial, orig pendulum, 10¼" h **275.00**

Gilt Bronze, Poierier and Bouge, Paris, Louis Philippe, early 19th C, circular engine-turned dial, faux stone wall forms seat for figural cupid, green marble base, draped with flowers and ribbons, flower-form feet, 12 × 5 × 19" **4,500.00**

Nickel, F Kroeber Clock Co, NY, c1880, carriage type, gilt front, glass sides, 6½" h **275.00**

Ormolu, unknown French maker, Charles X, c1825, lyre form, putti supported by dolphins, rect pedestal base, half-hour strike, glass dome, 18" h ...**1,800.00**

Pot Metal, N Shure Co, c1934, figural, knight, silvered finish, 30-hour movement **95.00**

Miscellaneous

Bartholomew, EG & W, c1830, carved pineapple finials and paw feet, refinished case and splat, 30-hour wooden time and strike movement, 25½" h **250.00**

Boardman & Wells, c1830, half columns, stenciled, eagle on crest, replaced bell, 30-hour brass time and strike movement, 32" h **425.00**

Forestville Mfg Co, c1840, Empire, triple-decker, 8-day time and strike weight-driven brass movement, 36" h **300.00**

Goodman, EO, c1850, rosewood veneered case, 8-day time and strike brass movement, orig label and hands, 15⅛" h **500.00**

Hart, Orrin, c1830, mahogany veneer case, stenciled columns and splat, 30-hour time and strike wooden movement, 34½" h **275.00**

Hoadley, Silas, c1930, stenciled columns and splat, 30-hour upside-down time, strike, and alarm wooden movement, 36" h **750.00**

Ingraham Clock Co, c1870, Grecian model, rosewood veneer case, 30-hour time and strike movement, 15¼" h **200.00**

Seymour, William & Porter, c1825, mahogany case, gilded columns and eagle splat, 8-day wooden time and strike movement, 36"h **600.00**

Terry, Eli & Sons, c1825, carved columns, splat and feet, 8-day time and strike wooden movement, 37" h **900.00**

Thayer, E, c1830, carved pillars and splat, 30-hour Groaner wooden movement, 35" h **350.00**

Thomas, Seth, Plymouth, CT, c1818, Empire

Mahogany veneer, ogee panels, turned columns, reverse-painted glass with orig flower dec, brass works, paper label "Seth Thomas, Plymouth Hollow, Conn," 19" h, minor veneer damage, wear to face **440.00**

Rosewood veneer, grained and gilded columns, brass works, face labeled "Seth Thomas," weights and pendulum, 16" h, damage to veneer **220.00**

Federal, mahogany, mahogany veneer, 30-hour strap wooden movement, restoration, 30¼" h, 17" w **3,105.00**

Unknown maker, c1835, rosewood and bronze, recumbent whippet, case inlaid with stringing and carved beading, half-moon feet 865.00

Ogee

Ansonia, c1880, crotch-grain mahogany veneered case, orig lower glass, 30-hour time and strike movement, 18¾" h 150.00

Bristol Brass & Clock Co, c1880, veneered, 30-hour time and strike movement, orig label, 19" h 95.00

New Haven Clock Co, zebra-striped wooden case, Weight No. 2, 1-day strike, 26" h 200.00

Waterbury Clock Co, c1870, Empire, mahogany veneered case, 30-hour time, strike, and alarm movement, 19" h 200.00

Pillar and Scroll

Downes, Ephraim, Bristol, CT, c1830, Federal, carved mahogany, shaped crest, three brass urn finials above hinged glazed door, eglomise panel with houses and pond, tapering columns, bracket feet, 31 × 17½" 750.00

Hodges, Erastus, Torrington Hollow, CT, c1830, mahogany and mahogany veneer, 30-hour wooden weight-driven movement, restored, 29" h, 13¼" w **3,220.00**

North, Norris, Wolcottville, CT, swan's neck, three brass urn finials, painted dial with foliate spandrels, scene of cottage in woods, 30⅜" h **1,450.00**

Terry, Eli, Plymouth, CT, mahogany and mahogany veneer, paper label, early 19th c, 17¼" w, 4¾" d, 31½" h, imperfections **2,415.00**

Thomas, Seth, Plymouth, CT, c1805, Federal, swan's neck pediment, three brass urn finials, glazed door, eglomise panel with houses and floral band, white painted wooden dial, Roman chapter ring, floral spandrels, flanked by colonnettes, shaped apron, bracket feet **3,850.00**

Porcelain Case

French, painted and gilded, elaborately scrolled case, molded shells, figures, and masks, painted foliage, Jacob Petit, factory marks, wear, c1840 .... **1,495.00**

Kroeber, F, c1880, 8-day time and strike movement, 12" h 250.00

Vienna, c1890, domed top, temple-form case, painted allover with oval figural panels, peach ground, factory marks, 17½" h **4,600.00**

Portrait Pendulum, framed gilt bronze and champleve enamel, urn and enamel center finials, 2 urn finials atop enameled columns, rect beveled glass panel case, custom maroon velvet stand, 17" h **1,000.00**

Skeleton, unknown maker, Victorian, Gothic Revival, mid 19th C, Gothic style pinnacles, foliage pierced dial, fusee movement, white marble base, glass dome, 16" h **1,400.00**

Steeple

Birch & Fuller, Bristol, CT, double-decker, mahogany veneer, orig reverse painted glass door panels, fusee movement, brass works, orig label, pendulum, and key, old dark finish, 26½" h **2,250.00**

Boardman, Chauncey, c1840, 30-hour fusee time and strike movement, 20" h, refinished case, replaced glass door 100.00

Brewster & Ingraham, c1840, rosewood veneered case, frosted and cut glass door, 19¼" h 350.00

Gilbert, Wm, mahogany veneer, painted sailing ship on glass, 8-day movement, 19¾" h, restored dial 250.00

Pratt, Daniel, 1850-60, rosewood veneered case, orig glass with St Louis courthouse, 8-day time and strike movement, 19½" h 300.00

Waterbury Clock Co, Waterbury, CT, 1875, mahogany veneered case, floral transfer glass, 30-hour time and alarm movement, painted zinc dial, orig paper label and pendulum, 15" h, glass tablet background repainted, replaced minute hand ... 300.00

Tall Case

Avery, John, Preston, CT, c1770, Chippendale, cherry, hood with three flame finials, scalloped whale's-tails fretwork, arched glazed door, brass engraved dial, Roman and Arabic chapter rings, sweep seconds ring, calendar-day aperture, engraved C-scroll spandrels, engraved signature, fluted colonnettes above waisted case, arched thumb-molded cupboard door, applied scalloped banding, ogee bracket feet, 92¾" h, 17½" w, 9⅞" d, baseboard replaced **44,000.00**

Boyle, Robert, London, George III, late 18th C, mahogany, brass stop-fluted columns on hood, arched paneled door and base, 85" h **2,990.00**

Christ, Daniel, Kutztown, PA, c1785, Chippendale, carved walnut, molded swan's-neck crest hood, flower-head carved terminals, three turned finials, arched glazed door, white painted dial with moon phases, minute and date registers, inscribed ''Daniel Christ,'' fluted colonnettes, waisted case with shaped door, fluted quarter columns, molded base with styl-

Tall Case, 8 day, Berks County, PA, c1830, cherry case with flame graining, $6,150.00. Photograph courtesy of Aston Auctioneers.

ized leaf-carved panel and fluted quarter columns, ogee bracket feet, 98¾″ h **28,600.00**

Cummens, William, Roxbury, MA, c1805, mahogany, pierced fretwork crest hood, three brass phoenix and urn finials, arched glazed hinged door, white painted dial with minute register, painted harbor scene centers inscription "Warranted by Wm Cummens," brass stop-fluted colonnettes with brass Corinthian capitals, waisted case with crossbanded hinged door, quarter columns, cross banded base, 99″ h **17,600.00**

Ellicott, Joseph, Buckingham, PA, c1760, Queen Anne, mahogany, hood with stepped and molded flat top, arched and glazed door, brass dial with silvered Roman and Arabic chapter rings, inscribed day of the month indicator, C-scroll foliate spandrels, polychrome scene of Colonial man in lush landscape with Indians, hood flanked by colonnettes, waisted case, astragal bead-molded cupboard door, box base, bracket feet, 87¾″ h, 19¼″ w, side pane of hood cracked **25,000.00**

German, Elite Clock Co, oak case, moon dial face marked "Daniel Pratt's Son, Boston, MA", rope bonnet top, glazed, carved columns, keyhole opening on single door, bun feet **1,980.00**

Hassam, Stephen, Charlestown, NH, c1780, Chippendale, cherry, hood with three reeded plinths, brass finials, arched molded cornice, glazed door, inscribed engraved brass dial, 8-day brass weight-driven movement, brass-mounted reeded columns, tombstone molded door flanked by brass-mounted reeded quarter columns, scrolled ogee bracket feet, old finish **5,000.00**

Herold, Charles P, Philadelphia, cherry, brass-mounted swan neck pediment over arched brass and steel calendar dial with plate, rect pendulum door, shaped apron, straight bracket feet, 90″ h, 20¾″ w, 11″ d, works motorized, feet replaced **1,800.00**

Hoadley, S, Plymouth, CT, pine, old worn reddish brown grained finish, plain bonnet with molded cornice, beaded-edge door, cove molding, dovetailed base, wooden works, painted wooden face with Masonic dec, labeled "S. Hoadley, Plymouth," 83″ h, second hand missing, replaced weights **1,960.00**

Hoadley, Silas, Plymouth, CT, early 19th C, grain-painted case, 30-hour weight-driven wooden movement, imperfections, 77½″ h, 17″ w, 9½″ d **2,100.00**

Hopkins, Asa, Litchfield, CT, 1820-30, cherry, 30-hour wooden pull-up weight-driven movement, refinished, imperfections, 91½″ h **2,990.00**

Howard, E & Co, Boston, c1912, Adam style, carved mahogany case, broken-arched pediment over floral garland cornice, arched, glazed clockface and pendulum door over shield-carved panel, flanked by two garland-carved cabinet doors, step-molded base, 96″ h, 56″ w, 17″ d **3,500.00**

Huston, William, Philadelphia, c1780, Chippendale, carved mahogany, molded swan's-neck crest, two urn and flame finials, center ball and steeple finial, tympanum with carved acanthus leaves, arched glazed door, engraved brass dial with moon phases, minute and calendar registers, stop-fluted columns with cast-metal Corinthian capitals, waisted case with

shaped hinged door, fluted quarter columns, paneled base, ogee bracket feet **16,500.00**

Lavenworth, William, Albany, NY, c1820, red and dark brown graining to represent mahogany, wooden floral dec dial inscribed "W. Lavenworth, Albany", imperfections, 85″ h **2,530.00**

Owen & Sile, Chester, PA, 1790-1810, Chippendale, carved mahogany, 8-day, white painted dial, sgd "Owen & Sile, Chester," painted moon face, hood with scrolled pediment with dentil molding and rosettes, centering an urn and leaf finial above trailing leaves, glazed arched door and fluted colonnettes, waisted case with leaf-carved molding over a shaped door flanked by fluted quarter columns, shield-panel base, ogee bracket feet, works may not be orig to case, 97½″ h **17,500.00**

Pearsall & Embree, NY, late 18th C, Federal, mahogany, arched hood surmounted by peaked pediment, brass acorn finials, waisted case with shaped inlay, brass stop-fluted quarter columns, molded base with bracket feet, 96″ h **6,500.00**

Scale, William, London, early 18th C, George I, walnut case, silvered annular ring, Roman hours and Arabic minutes, maker's signature, day of week, moon phase, arched dial, arched and stepped hood, waisted case, 99″ h **8,000.00**

Taber, S, New England, early 19th C, country Federal, grain painted, arched glazed door flanked by freestanding columns, flat top hood, waisted case with thumb-molded door, molded base, short bracket feet, painted dial, 83″ h **1,750.00**

Unknown Maker

Boston, MA, Federal, c1790, mahogany, inlaid, old finish, brass weight-driven 8-day movement, imperfections, 95¼″ h **9,200.00**

Cherry, old worn alligatored varnish, freestanding columns on bonnet, broken arch pediment with carved sunburst rosettes, overlapping door, molding between sections, bracket feet, brass English works, second hand, calendar movement, painted metal face, worn and flaked floral dec with bird crest, weights, pendulum, key, 90½″ h, center brass finial replaced, side finials missing, age cracks in case **6,110.00**

Cherry, old dark finish, four freestanding columns on bonnet, chamfered corners, broken-arch pediment, gooseneck arches, turned rosettes, turned finials, ring-turned quarter columns on waist, beaded-edge door, chambered corners in base, scrolled apron, ball feet, brass gears in wooden plates, painted wooden face with flowers, cornucopia, and oval portrait of lady, 92½″ h, small repairs, restoration, replaced weights and pendulum **1,760.00**

Pine, Shenandoah Valley, VA, c1790, cherry, cherry veneers, yellow pine secondary wood, broken-arch pediment, urn finials over arched door flanked by full turned columns, veneered frieze over single door with line inlay, chamfered corners with lamb's tongue, scalloped skirt, bracket feet, 8-day, moon phase, enamel face, horizontal backboards, 99″ h, 18½″ w, 9½″ d **8,250.00**

Vernon, Thomas, London, 18th C, mid-Georgian, cross-banded walnut, molded borders on case, 87″ h **3,335.00**

Wagstaffe, Thomas, London, c1785, George III, mahogany, pierced fretwork crest hood, three brass ball and steeple finials, glazed hinged door, engraved silvered and brass dial with minute and calendar date registers, inscribed "Tho Wagstaffe, London," hinged shaped door below, brass stop-fluted quarter columns, paneled base with brass stop-fluted quarter columns, bracket feet, 105″ h **6,500.00**

Watson, L, Cincinnati, Hepplewhite, cherry case, old mellow finish, dovetailed bonnet, molded gooseneck and turned rosettes, applied moldings, chamfered corners, overlapping door, scalloped apron, French feet, wooden works, painted wooden face labeled "L. Watson, Cincinnati," flaking on face, poor repairs, replaced center brass eagle, side finials missing, 91¾″ h **2,970.00**

Willard, Aaron, Jr, Boston, Federal, inlaid mahogany, pierced fretwork crest on hood, three finials, arched glazed door, white painted dial, sgd "Aaron Willard Jr", waisted case with hinged molded door, fluted quarter columns, bracket feet **10,950.00**

Wall

Art Deco, cherry case, 8-day Westminster chimes movement, orig finish, 35″ h 325.00

Banjo

Chelsea, c1920, mahogany case, 8-day time and strike spring-driven movement, marine lever, 33″ h 600.00

Cummens, William, Boston, MA c1810, 8-day T-bridge movement, cross-banded mahogany frames, painted tablets, sea creatures pulling shell boat with drive, old finish, orig brass finial, 34″ h **2,400.00**

Federal, attributed to Boston, c1820, mahogany and mahogany veneer, 8-day weight drive movement, T-bridge suspension, 33½″ h, imperfections **3,105.00**

Howard & Davis, c1850, #1, grain-painted case, 8-day weight-driven time movement, second bit, orig painted and sgd dial, replaced glasses, 50″ h **2,100.00**

Howard, E. & Co., Boston, mid 19th C, grain painted to resemble rosewood, weight-driven movement, orig eglomise maroon and black tablets, minor imperfections, 28½″ h **1,725.00**

Hutchins, Levi, Concord, NH, 1820, gold front, painted iron dial, 8-day time movement with T-bridge and step train, pendulum, 42″ h 850.00

New Haven Clock Co, c1920, inlaid mahogany case, eagle finial, dec door, 12-day time movement, 17⅝″ h 175.00

Plymouth Clock Co, Thomaston, CT, c1920, mahogany, eagle finial, two glasses with Washington and Mt Vernon dec, painted dial, 8-day time and strike movement, chime rod, 29″ h 150.00

Thomas, Seth, c1920, mahogany case, 8-day time spring-driven movement, 30″ h 250.00

Unknown Maker, mahogany case

Brass works, worn painted metal base, repair to case, waisted door frame replaced, reverse-painted glass replaced, 29″ h 665.00

Regulator, wall, Seth Thomas, #2, oak case, original dial, restored and refinished, **$750.00.**

Scalloped face rim, reverse-painted glass panels, brass trim, orig weight and pendulum, found in Exeter, NH, some repaint, minor damage, 34″ h **1,265.00**

Waterbury Clock Co, c1912, Willard #3, 8-day time weight-driven movement, orig glass, 43½″ h 850.00

Whiting, Samuel, Concord, MA, 1820, gilded bracket, painted glasses, painted iron dial, 8-day time movement, step train, T-bridge, period lead weight, marked "SW", 41″ h **1,600.00**

Willard, Aaron, Boston, early 19th C, Federal, gilt-wood, eglomise panels surrounded by gilded twist frames, enamel dial and finial, 40″ h **9,550.00**

Calendar

Ansonia, drop octagon, 8-day, strike, rosewood veneer, gilt molding, 24″ h 300.00

Ingraham Clock Co, 1870-80, figure eight, rosewood case, 8-day time and strike movement, B B Lewis calendar, two labels, 30″ h 750.00

Ithaca, No. 2 Bank, oak case, 8-day, 61″ l **2,750.00**

Jerome & Co, Register, 8-day, 33¾″ l **1,500.00**

Thomas, Seth, c1875, office, rosewood veneered case, 8-day time movement, calendar on bottom, 32½″ h **1,650.00**

Cuckoo

German, Black Forest, c1881, 1-day, quarter-hour strike, carved ivy dec, 24″ l 425.00

Keebler Clock Co, Philadelphia, PA, 1920, pressed log design, leaves, flowers, nest of birds, brass spring pendulum, 5 × 4 × 1¾″ 125.00

Lux, 1942, hunting scenes, synthetic carved wooden deer's head with glass eyes, spread antlers, two rifles, quail and rabbit, half-hour strike, 4″ dial, white raised Roman numerals, 75″ chain, 16″ h, 10″ w 250.00

Gallery

Brewster & Ingraham, c1840, round, 8-day east/west time movement, sgd orig wooden dial, 13″ d ... 400.00

Howard, E, ivory painted case, 8-day time, balance-wheel movement, 13½″ d 250.00

Thomas, Seth, c1890, Arcade model, mahogany finished case, 30-day time movement, orig label, repainted dial, 23" d **350.00**

Lyre

Taber, E, Roxbury, MA, c1810, mahogany case, finial, 8-day weight-driven time movement, 41" h . **3,750.00**

Unknown Maker, 19th C, mahogany sides and face, eagle finial lyre throat glass, door glass with eagle and cornucopia dec, 40½" h **4,250.00**

Mirror

Morrill, Benjamin, New Hampshire, 1810–20, wheelbarrow 8-day time weight-driven movement, orig label, 30¼" h **4,500.00**

Unknown Maker, c1820, gilded front, crest, and bracket, painted tablet, painted wooden dial, 8-day time brass movement, lead weight and period pendulum, 42" h **675.00**

Regulator

Ansonia Clock Co, Ansonia, CT, 1900, rosewood grained poplar case, paper-on-zinc dial, black and gold tablet, 8-day time and strike movement, pendulum, paper label, 24½" h **400.00**

Boston Clock Co, 1880, painted cherry case, 8-day time movement, 34" h **800.00**

Gilbert, c1910, pressed oak case, 8-day time and strike movement, refinished, 32½" h **375.00**

Howard, c1880, #60, black walnut case, 8-day beat escapement movement, second bit, mercury pendulum, 80" h **9,000.00**

Ingraham, E, c1910, pressed-oak case, 8-day time and calendar spring-driven movement, 36" h ... **450.00**

Little & Eastman Co, Boston, MA, c1890, quarter-grain oak case, sgd 8-day time movement, 35¼" h **700.00**

Pratt, Daniel & Sons, c1870, rosewood veneered case, 8-day time movement, 21½" h **225.00**

Terry, Silas B, Plymouth, CT, 1830, mahogany veneered case, painted zinc dial, black and gold tablet, solid-plate 8-day time piece, replacements and refinished, 33½" h **600.00**

Thomas, Seth, 1860s, model #1, mahogany case, 8-day weight-driven time movement, calendar on bottom, orig dial and label, 41¼" h **1,600.00**

Waterbury Clock Co, Waterbury, CT, 1910, oak case, painted zinc dial, 8-day time and strike movement and half-hour strike, pendulum, 32" h **400.00**

Schoolhouse

Ingraham, c1900, pressed-oak case, 8-day time, strike, and calendar movement, 18¾" h **325.00**

Jerome, c1850, 8-day, 12" dial, octagon, mahogany and rosewood case **300.00**

New Haven Clock Co, c1870, mahogany veneered case, 8-day time movement, 24" h **250.00**

Sessions Clock Co, c1915, oak case, 8-day time, strike, and calendar movement, orig label, 19½" h **30.00**

Waterbury Clock Co, c1890, mahogany veneered case, short dewdrop, 8-day time and calendar movement, 24" h **250.00**

Wag on the Wall

Dutch, 18th C, 30-hour time and strike pull-up movement, painted and scroll front, pierced crest of lion

and flower vase, standing lions flank face, angel dec at top corners of face, old weights, pendulum, and wall bracket, paint touch-up, repairs, 28" h . **800.00**

Keinzle, wooden case, brass and steel works, wooden plates, painted face, mismatched weights and pendulum, crack in face, late 19th C, 8¼" h **200.00**

CLOISONNÉ

History: Cloisonné is the art of enameling on metal. The design is drawn on the metal body, then wires, which follow the design, are glued or soldered on. The cells thus created are packed with enamel and fired; this step is repeated several times until the level of enamel is higher than the wires. A buffing and polishing process brings the level of enamels flush to the surface of the wires.

This art form has been practiced in various countries since 1300 B.C. and in the Orient since the early 15th century. Most cloisonné found today is from the late Victorian era, 1870–1900, and was made in China or Japan.

Reference: Lawrence A. Cohen and Dorothy C. Ferster, *Japanese Cloisonné,* Charles E. Tuttle Co., 1990.

Collectors' Club: Cloisonne Collectors Club, PO Box 96, Rockport, MA 01966.

Museum: George Walter Vincent Smith Art Museum, Springfield, MA.

Box, cov

4¾" d, 2¾" h, rounded form, butterflies among flowering branches, turquoise ground, Chinese, 19th C **345.00**

6" l, rect, rounded corners, wisteria, pines, scrolls, and birds of paradise, Japanese, inner flange separated, slight fracture to lid **325.00**

Charger, 14¼" d, central phoenix, red ground, lotus and dragon panels on cream ground, late 19th or early 20th C **150.00**

Cup, 4" h, ftd, butterflies and flowers, lappet borders, Chinese, 19th C **100.00**

Desk Set, brush pot, pen, pen tray, blotter, and paper holder, Japanese, price for set **130.00**

Figure

7¼" h, prancing horse, left front leg raised, neck curved, mouth open, allover tightly scrolled lotus, Chinese, 18th/19th C, damage **320.00**

21" h, prancing deer carrying two-handled vase on its back, two dragons chasing flaming pearl on rect base, Chinese, 19th/20th, losses **575.00**

Garniture, 9" h, gilt-bronze urn, multicolored foliage design, two bronze putti, onyx base, French, early 20th C **865.00**

Incense Burner, 19¾" h, globular, three dragon's-head feet, high curving handles, scrolling lotus and ancient bronzes motif, openwork lid, dragon finial, raised Quinlong six character mark, damage **815.00**

Jar, cov, 6" h, ovoid, green over central band of scrolling flowers, domed lid, ovoid finial, marked "Ando Jubei," 20th C **230.00**

Planter, 11" l, quatralobe, classical symbol and scroll dec, blue ground, Chinese, price for pr **200.00**

Teakettle, 10½″ h, multicolored scrolling lotus, medium blue ground, lappets border, waisted neck with band of raised auspicious symbols between key-fret borders, floral-form finial, double handles, Chinese, 19th C **690.00**

Teapot, 4¾″ d, 3¼″ h, central band of flowering chrysanthemums on pink ground, shoulder with shaped cartouches of phoenix and dragon on floral and patterned ground, lower border with chrysanthemum blossom on swirling ground, flat base with three small raised feet, single chrysanthemum design, spout and handle with floral design, lid with two writhing dragons on peach-colored ground, Japanese, late 19th/early 20th C **4,025.00**

Urn, 23¾″ h, ovoid, slightly waisted neck, peony dec, black ground, base plaque marked ''Takeuchi Chubei,'' Japanese, late 19th C, Shichi Ho Company, Owari **690.00**

Vase

3⅝″ h, shouldered form, long slender neck flaring at rim, colored enamels, spider chrysanthemums and songbirds, midnight blue ground, Japanese, Meiji period, price for pr **550.00**

4¾″ h

High shouldered form, gray writhing dragon, black ground, fitted box, Japanese, price for pr **1,150.00**

Ovoid

Continual scene of geese on riverbank, flowering bushes and mountains in distance, Japanese **2,875.00**

Waisted neck, pink, blue, yellow, and white blooming spider chrysanthemum branch, silver wires, bright green wireless ground, silvered rims, Japanese, 20th C **460.00**

Waisted short neck, slightly flared mouth, even yellow overall glaze, small border of circles at mouth and base, unidentified stamped mark, late 19th C **690.00**

6″ h, six sided, each side with shield below floral band, alternating dragon and phoenix motif, flecked blue ground, Japanese, early 20th C **460.00**

7¼″ h, ovoid

Songbirds among multicolored fruiting branches, white ground, price for pr **1,035.00**

Waisted neck, everted rim, three songbirds among flowering branches, colored enamels, silver wire, dark blue ground, marked silver rim, wire Ando Jubei mark on base, orig box **865.00**

8⅞″ h, flattened ovoid, large cartouches of dragon with serpent and phoenix flying among vines, surrounded by flowering vines, black ground, Japanese, Meiji period **8,350.00**

9⅛″ h, angled shoulder, ovoid, waisted neck, multicolored flowering chrysanthemum, bright blue ground, Meiji period, Ota, minor crazing **1,380.00**

9⅝″ h

Angular baluster, single naturalistic scene of songbirds among flowering trees and bushes, midnight blue ground, lappet foot and rim borders, Japanese, early 20th C **1,725.00**

High angled shoulder, straight sides, short waisted neck, eagle perched on flowering cherry tree,

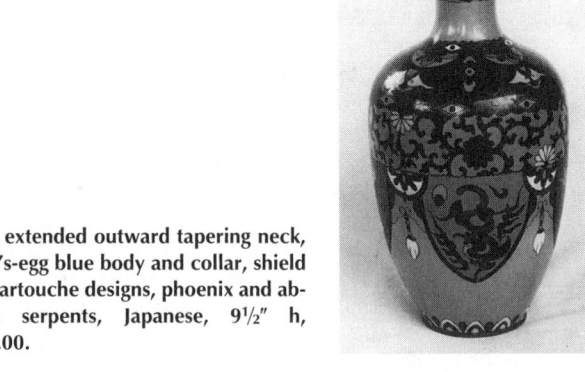

Vase, extended outward tapering neck, robin's-egg blue body and collar, shield and cartouche designs, phoenix and abstract serpents, Japanese, 9½″ h, $700.00.

wisteria and bamboo below, dark blue ground, lappet borders above and below, late 19th C, price for pr **2,300.00**

10″ h, silver wire dec, slender iris, deep blue ground, Japanese, base sgd ''Obei Tsukuru,'' scratches, fracture **375.00**

12″ h, slender ovoid, waisted neck and foot, beetle and cricket resting on flowering branches, midnight blue ground, Japanese, early 20th C **1,955.00**

12¼″ h, ovoid, waisted neck, inverted rim, two songbirds among prunus and bamboo, colored enamels with silver wire, dark blue ground, stamped silver rim, wire Ando Jubei mark on base, Meiji period, orig fitted box **4,975.00**

12½″ h, pigeon-blood glaze, cranes in flight over sea, Japanese, Meiji Period, sgd ''Matsuno,'' one with crazing, price for pr **1,000.00**

12⅞″ h, pear form, single yellow rose, green ground, Ando Jubei, 20th C **1,100.00**

14¾″ h, Iron Age form, classical symbol and scroll dec, blue ground, Chinese, price for pr **300.00**

22″ h, ovoid, long slender neck, overall pomegranate, lotus, and chrysanthemum flowers, upright-leaves neck border, white ground, 18th C, drilled base, price for pr **2,645.00**

CLOTHING

History: While museums and a few private individuals have collected clothing for decades, it is only recently that collecting clothing has achieved a widespread popularity. Clothing reflects the social attitudes of a historical period.

Christening and wedding gowns abound and, hence, are not in large demand. Among the hardest items to find are men's clothing from the 19th and early 20th centuries. The most sought after clothing is by designers, such as Fortuny, Poirret, and Vionnet.

References: *Altman's Spring and Summer Fashions Catalog, 1915,* Dover Publications, 1995 reprint; C. Willett and Phillis Cunnington, *The History of Underclothes,* Dover Publications, 1992; Maryanne Dolan, *Vintage Clothing,* Third Edition, Books Americana, 1995; ———, *Women's Fashions of the Early 1900s,* Dover Publications, 1992; Roseanne Ettinger, *'50s Popular Fashions for*

Men, Women, Boys & Girls, Schiffer Publishing, 1995; *Gimbel's Illustrated 1915 Fashion Catalog,* Gimbel Brothers, Dover Publications, 1994; Douglas Gorsline, *What People Wore,* Dover Publications, 1994; Carol Belanger Grafton, *Fashions of the Thirties,* Dover Publications, 1993; Kristina Harris, *Victorian & Edwardian Fashions for Women,* Schiffer Publishing, 1995; ———, *Vintage Fashions for Women,* Schiffer Publishing, 1996; *Home Pattern Company 1914 Fashions Catalog,* Dover Publications, 1995 reprint; Ellie Laubner, *Fashions of the Roaring '20s,* Schiffer Publishing, 1996; Jan Lindenberger, *Clothing & Accessories from the '40s, '50s, & '60s,* Schiffer Publishing, 1996; Jo Anne Olian (ed.), *Children's Fashions 1860–1912,* Dover, 1994; ——— (ed.), *Everyday Fashions of the Forties as Pictured in Sears Catalogs,* Dover Publications, 1992; Franklin Simon & Co, *Franklin Simon Fashion Catalog for 1923,* Dover Publications, 1993; Pamela Smith, *Vintage Fashion & Fabrics,* Alliance Publishers, 1995; Diane Snyder-Haug, *Antique & Vintage Clothing,* Collector Books, 1996; Sheila Steinberg and Kate E. Dooner, *Fabulous Fifties: Designs for Modern Living,* Schiffer Publishing, 1993; Meredith Wright, *Everyday Dress of Rural America,* Dover Publications, 1992.

Periodicals: *Glass Slipper,* 653 S Orange Ave, Sarasota, FL 34236; *Lady's Gallery,* PO Box 1761, Independence, MO 64055; *Lill's Vintage Clothing Newsletter,* 19 Jamestown Dr, Cincinnati, OH 45241; *Vintage Clothing Newsletter,* PO Box 88892, Seattle, WA 98138; *Vintage Connection,* 904 N 65th St, Springfield, OR 97478; *Vintage Gazette,* 194 Amity St, Amherst, MA 01002.

Collectors' Clubs: The Costume Society of America, PO Box 73, Earleville, MD 21919; Vintage Fashion and Costume Jewelry Club, PO Box 265, Glen Oaks, NY 11004.

Museums: Bata Shoe Museum, Toronto, Canada; Fashion Institute of Technology, New York, NY; Los Angeles County Museum (Costume and Textile Dept.), Los Angeles, CA; Metropolitan Museum of Art, New York, NY; Museum of Costume, Bath, England; Philadelphia Museum of Art, Philadelphia, PA; Smithsonian Institution (Inaugural Gown Collection), Washington, DC; Wadsworth Athenaeum, Hartford, CT.

Additional Listings: See *Warman's Americana & Collectibles* for more examples.

Note: Condition, size, age, and completeness are critical factors in purchasing clothing. Collectors divide into two groups: those collecting for aesthetic and historic value and those desiring to wear the garment. Prices are higher on the West coast; major auction houses focus on designer clothes and high-fashion items.

Baby Sacque, cotton, embroidered, Victorian	**45.00**
Bed jacket, rayon, pink, ruffled collar, c1940	**15.00**
Blouse, cotton, white, large collar, crochet accents, fitted at waist	**35.00**
Blouse and Skirt, lace and net, black, 1918	**70.00**
Bodice and Skirt, child's, gray striped silk, printed black flock, black velvet trim, c1876	**65.00**
Camisole, lace, c1890	**28.00**

Cape
Felt, red, black appliqued scrollwork, intricate rows of top stitching, knee length at front, gradually lengthening curve to back, size 8, 1890s	**550.00**
Fringed, child's, 1860s	**48.00**
Chemise, linen, short sleeves, lawn frill trim, monogrammed, c1820	**40.00**

Christening Dress, pin-tucked lace, 1890	**65.00**

Coat
Buckskin, black satin trim, lighter-colored leather appliqued leaves, double-sided wood and glass case with supporting stand, formerly Buffalo Bill Cody's, supporting provenance documentation	**3,680.00**
Cashmere, black, passementerie-trimmed collar and cuffs, size 8, c1900	**70.00**
Lace, Edwardian, toddler's	**62.00**
Wool, steamer-blanket type, navy and dark green plaid, red satin lining, Charles James, size 6, partially relined	**19,550.00**
Velvet, brown, brown floral ribbon-striped silk lining, labeled "A. Guerin & I. Ferrier 12 East 32nd St, New York," sleeves and front trim removed, 1890s	**145.00**
Doublet, gentleman's, velvet, emerald green, gold sequins and paste jewels, embroidered, hose, late 18th C, 17th C style, European, altered	**175.00**

Dress
Day, crepe, black, round neck, padded shoulders, crossed self tab detail at waist front, red, navy, and green gingham and plain applique at yoke, label "Adrian Original," early 1940s	**3,450.00**

Evening
Rayon Crepe, printed red, blue, yellow, green, and black flowers, ivory ground, cutout flowers on long slip dress straps and low back, slight train, label "Schiaparelli 4 rue de la Paix Paris model no. 4396," size 4, 1930s	**2,100.00**

Silk Satin, black
Slip torso, curved bands and tabs, black tulle tiered cutaway skirt, label "Tappè Inc. Modes 9 West 57th St New York," Herman Patrick Tappè, size 4, c1930, damage to tulle	**690.00**
Woven with groups of seven pinstripes, sleeveless, cutout halter neckline, draped at front hip, self bow and streamers on back, handwritten and dated Charles James label, size 6, c1945	**49,450.00**
Girl's, lace, c1890	**55.00**
Walking style, cut-velvet-style terry jacket bodice, wool gauge skirt, large faux buttons and loops, size 10, label "B. Altman Co. Paris New York," c1910, some alterations	**175.00**
Duster, lawn, white, watteau back, lace trim, handmade, c1930	**75.00**
Evening Coat, claret cut velvet, meandering flowers and floral ribbon pattern, wide shawl collar, size 6, c1910	**145.00**

Jacket
Net, ecru, vermicular pattern cord embroidery, linen bands at edges and seams, side slits, long cuffed sleeves, size 6, Edwardian	**290.00**
Paisley, edged with silk and wool fringe, size 6, late 19th C	**490.00**

Velvet
Apricot, gilt stenciled Islamic pattern, kimono style, short sleeves, hip length, round faille label "Mariano Fortuny Venise," size 6–8, 1920s	**5,465.00**
Aubergine, fitted waist, flared back, hip length, rounded patch pockets, gold metal and cut steel round buttons, raised roses, size 2, 1880s	**290.00**

Jacket, Cree, moose hide, green, blue, yellow, pink, black, and red floral beadwork, faceted brass beads, early 20th C, 33" l, $1,650.00. Photograph courtesy of W. E. Channing & Co, Inc.

Jacket and Pants, buckskin, type worn by player in wild west show 345.00
Nightie, Edwardian, lacy 45.00
Pajamas, satin, pink, ribbon rosettes, crochet trim, c1920 90.00
Peignoir, lawn, cream, hand-embroidered dots, flowering vines, inset scalloped lace bands, size 6, c1900 200.00
Petticoat, quilted down, paisley cotton, red, yellow, and green, horizontal serpentine quilting, labeled "McClintock's Patent Purified Russian Down Skirt, Philadelphia, 1876–Paris, 1878, No. 10, Length 40 inches" 230.00
Riding Habit, wool, black, lady's side-saddle type, 2 pcs 125.00
Robe, Oriental
    40" l, silk embroidered, courtesans in garden settings roundels, flowers and butterflies, medium blue ground, gold braided and embroidered borders and sleeve bands, cloud collar border around neck, red silk lining, Chinese 1,035.00
    53" l, informal, lady's, 19th C, gauze, pink, counted cross-stitch, blue, pink, turquoise, yellow, and green butterflies and prunus, white gauze borders, white gauze inner sleeves with butterfly and prunus 4,025.00
    54" l, informal, lady's, 19th C, gauze, green, counted cross-stitch, blue, red, yellow, and purple fish swimming among algae, matching black gauze borders, inner sleeves in white gauze with similar motif 4,255.00
    55½" l, lady's, gauze, red, counted cross-stitch, eight green, blue, yellow, white, and pink floral roundels, terrestrial diagrammed lishui stripe at hem, late 19th C 4,485.00
    58" h, silk embroidered, nine gold dragons surrounded by flaming pearls and bats, medium blue ground, above border of waves, neck with band of gold dragons on dark blue ground with wave,

bat, swastika designs among clouds, Chinese, 19th C, damage, fading 1,035.00
Suit, boy's, double-breasted, velvet pants, silk shirt, 1907   50.00
Teddy, silk, peach, hairpin-lace yoke 30.00
Trousers, child's, flannel, bib top, Victorian, white 95.00
Wedding Gown, satin, wax flowers, beaded hat, Victorian 225.00

CLOTHING ACCESSORIES

References: Joanne Dubbs Ball and Dorothy Hehl Torem, *The Art of Fashion Accessories,* Schiffer Publishing, 1993; Adele Campione, *Men's Hats,* Chronicle Books, 1995; ———, *Women's Hats,* Chronicle Books, 1989; Kate E. Dooner, *A Century of Handbags,* Schiffer Publishing, 1993; ———, *Plastic Handbags,* Schiffer Publishing, 1992; Rod Dyer and Ron Spark, *Fit to Be Tied: Vintage Ties of the Forties and Early Fifties,* Abbeville Press, 1987; Roselyn Gerson, *Vintage Vanity Bags and Purses,* Collector Books, 1994; Richard Holiner, *Antique Purses,* Second Edition, Collector Books, 1987, 1994 value update; Lynell K. Schwartz, *Vintage Purses at Their Best,* Schiffer Publishing, 1995; Desire Smith, *Hats with Values,* Schiffer Publishing, 1996; Mary Trasko, *Heavenly Soles,* Abbeville Press, 1989.

Museum: Whiting and Davis Handbag Museum, Attleboro Falls, MA.

Additional Listings: See *Warman's Americana & Collectibles* for more examples.

Apron, cotton, green and white checkered, hand sewn   40.00
Bonnet, spoon type, minor wear, 1860s 60.00
Booties, baby's, wool, cream, red-braid trim, c1850 ...   85.00
Chasuble, velvet, crimson, orphrey-embroidered colored silks, metal thread, roundels of Madonna and Child, four Saints within strapwork, Spanish, 16th C 2,750.00
Collar
    Leopard, 3¼" w, 1930s 85.00
    Satin, 2" w, beaded, braided 16.00
Garter's, child's, Lord Milford, orig card 15.00
Gloves, men's, beadwork, stamp marks identifying them as "W. C. Cody Show". c1900 ....   270.00
Handbag
    Beaded
        3½ × 3½", white, maroon, green, red, blue, and gold, minor bead loss and wear, sgd "A Whitemore 1832" 115.00
        8 × 8", eagle, "A.H.W. to C.D....Anna N. Whitemore '36," multicolored dec, white ground, gold trim, tattered white satin binding and drawstring, minor bead loss to fringe 460.00
    Leather, gold, box shape, pavé rhinestones, double-looped leather handles, Arnold Scacci, 5 × 3½"   60.00
    Mesh, 14 k gold, scrolling frame, three sapphires and two diamonds suspended from oval link chain and ring, 31 dwt 750.00
    Needlepoint, 5 × 6¾" red, brown, white, yellow, two-tone blue ground, green fringe, green silk ruffle trim, sgd "Anna Whitemore 1832", minor wear   240.00
    Silk File, black, reeded 14 k gold frame and link-chain handle, round diamond clasp with pavé diamond terminals, sgd "Cartier" 2,070.00

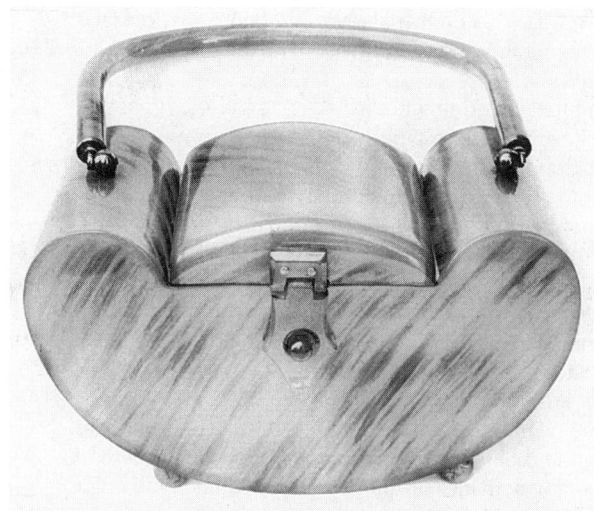

Purse, celluloid, plastic clasp, metal hinges, mfg by Llewellyn, Inc, trademark "Llewsid Jewel," 8¼" w, $70.00.

Silver, 2¾ × 2¼", Russian, hinged lid engraved in Cyrillic "In Remembrance," chain, hallmarked "84, Moscow," Nikolai Alexsev maker **145.00**

Hat

   Cloche, felt flowers, 1920s **55.00**

   Cowboy, felt, round, leather band fitted with brass mounts, documentation as to provenance from Tom Mix Wild West Riders show, 20th C **230.00**

   Derby, black felt **25.00**

   Plush, Edwardian, plumes, coral flowers **245.00**

   Straw, white, navy underbrim, white flower, Frank Olive **22.50**

Hatbox, wallpaper cov, c1820 .... **225.00**

Parasol, child's, silk and lace, bond handle, 1860s **165.00**

Shawl

   Paisley, large **225.00**

   Silk, woven lacy design, triangle, 60" w, 30" l **135.00**

Stockings, nylon, orig package **35.00**

Sweater, child's, puppies motif, red, tan, and white, c1950 .... **25.00**

Veil, ecru net and lace, full-length, 1918 .... **120.00**

COALPORT

History: In the mid-1750s Ambrose Gallimore established a pottery at Caughley in the Severn Gorge, Shropshire, England. Several other potteries, including Jackfield, developed in the area.

About 1795 John Rose and Edward Blakeway built a pottery at Coalport, a new town founded along the right-of-way of the Shropshire Canal. Other potteries located adjacent to the canal were those of Walter Bradley and Anstice, Horton, and Rose. In 1799 Rose and Blakeway bought the Royal Salopian China Manufactory at Caughley. In 1814 this operation was moved to Coalport.

A bankruptcy in 1803 led to refinancing and a new name—John Rose and Company. In 1814 Anstice, Horton, and Rose was acquired. The South Wales potteries at Swansea and Nantgarw

were added. The expanded firm made fine-quality, highly decorated ware. The plant enjoyed a renaissance from 1888 to 1900.

World War I, decline in trade, and shift of the pottery industry away from the Severn Gorge brought hard times to Coalport. In 1926 the firm, now owned by Cauldon Potteries, moved from Coalport to Shelton. Later owners included Crescent Potteries, Brain & Co., Ltd., and finally, in 1967, Wedgwood.

References: Susan and Al Bagdade, *Warman's English & Continental Pottery & Porcelain,* Second Edition, Wallace-Homestead, 1991; Michael Messenger, *Coalport 1795–1926,* Antique Collectors' Club, 1990.

Additional Listings: Indian Tree Pattern.

Box, cov, 3" l, egg shape, gilt dec, applied turquoise, red, and blue enamel jewels, c1900 .... **1,725.00**

Cup and Saucer, 4¾" d saucer, gilt dec, turquoise enamel jewels, c1900, married **260.00**

Dessert Service, partial, assembled, Rock and Tree pattern, Imari palette, gilt edges, c1805–10, price for 19-pc set **3,575.00**

Dinner Service, partial, iron-red bellflower vine intertwined with gilt scrolling foliate vine, feather-molded gilt rims, c1820, price for 132-pc set **17,600.00**

Ink Stand, 6½" l, crescent shape, yellow foliate scroll border, gilt-edged orange band, gold diamond devices border, gilt foliate dec on top, four pen holes, three larger apertures, two ink pots, pounce pot, c1805 .... **500.00**

Plate, 9" d, scalloped gold border, hp fruits, artist sgd "Gosling" **150.00**

Plate, ecru, gold dec, bellflower bands, scalloped edges, raised wreath, 1815–25, impressed "9," 9½" d, $35.00.

Platter, 10¾" l, Tobacco Leaf pattern, Chinese Export style, underglaze blue, turquoise, chartreuse, iron-red, yellow, green, salmon, rose, puce, and gold, scalloped rim with underglaze blue band, four underglaze blue flowering branches on underside, c1805, price for pr **2,500.00**

Teapot, 6" h, cobalt blue underglaze, red floral enamel, gilt trim, wear, repaired finial **360.00**

Vase

   4½" d, cobalt blue center, raised gilt foliate dec, oval portrait medallion titled "Omphale", c1900 .... **1,035.00**

8¾" d, gilt dec, turquoise enamel jewels, raised gold foliate designs, shield-shaped panels, swan handle, c1900 .... 635.00

COCA-COLA ITEMS

History: The originator of Coca-Cola was John Pemberton, a pharmacist from Atlanta, Georgia. In 1886 Dr. Pemberton introduced a patent medicine to relieve headaches, stomach disorders, and other minor maladies. Unfortunately, his failing health and meager finances forced him to sell his interest.

In 1888 Asa G. Candler became the sole owner of Coca-Cola. Candler improved the formula, increased the advertising budget, and widened the distribution. A "patient" was accidentally given a dose of the syrup mixed with carbonated water instead of still water. The result was a tastier, more refreshing drink.

As sales increased in the 1890s, Candler recognized that the product was more suitable for the soft-drink market and began advertising it as such. From these beginnings a myriad of advertising items have been issued to invite all to "Drink Coca-Cola."

References: Gael de Courtivron, *Collectible Coca-Cola Toy Trucks,* Collector Books, 1995; Shelly Goldstein, *Goldstein's Coca-Cola Collectibles,* Collector Books, 1991, 1996 value update; Allan Petretti, *Petretti's Coca-Cola Collectibles Price Guide,* Ninth Edition, Nostalgia Publications, Wallace-Homestead, 1994; Randy Schaeffer and Bill Bateman, *Coca-Cola,* Running Books, 1995; B. J. Summers, *B. J. Summers' Guide to Coca-Cola,* Collector Books, 1996; Jeff Walters, *The Complete Guide to Collectible Picnic Coolers & Ice Chests,* Memory Lane Publishing, 1994; Al Wilson, *Collectors Guide to Coca-Cola Items,* Vol. I (revised: 1987, 1993 value update), Vol. II (1987, 1993 value update), L-W Book Sales; Al and Helen Wilson, *Wilson's Coca Cola Guide,* Schiffer Publishing, 1994.

Collectors' Club: Coca-Cola Collectors Club, PO Box 49166, Atlanta, GA 30359.

Museums: Coca-Cola Memorabilia Museum of Elizabethtown, Inc, Elizabethtown, KY; World of Coca-Cola Pavilion, Atlanta, GA.

Additional Listings: See *Warman's Americana & Collectibles* for more examples.

Notes: Dates of interest: "Coke" was first used in advertising in 1941. The distinctively shaped bottle was registered as a trademark on April 12, 1960.

Ashtray, aluminum emb, 1950s 5.00
Banner, 13 × 41", "have a Coke Compliments of this Store," 1950s 30.00
Blotter, 1955, children at party scene 5.00
Bottle Opener, eagle head, 1912-20 .... 100.00
Button,¾" d, uniform type, c1910 .... 45.00
Calendar
    1917, woman holding glass 900.00
    1923, lady holding bottle 375.00
    1931, boy and dog 475.00
    1942, man, woman, and snowman 95.00
Chalkboard, tin, 1958 .... 95.00
Change Tray, 4½ × 6", oval, tin litho, 1914 version, full-color Coca-Cola girl, green-gold pattern rim, tiny Coca-Cola copyright, maker's name "Passaic Metal-

ware Co," scorch mark on one hand, two on lace shawl, minimal overall wear 250.00
Cigar Band 35.00
Cigarette Lighter, tiny bottle 25.00
Clock, schoolhouse type, octagon, Roman numbers, E Ingraham Co, Bristol, CT, 1903 .... 1,750.00
Crossing-Guard Sign, tin, double sided, diecut of policeman on one side, logo and bottle on other, two bases, c1950 .... 1,870.00
Cuff Links, pr,½" d silvered brass with red and white paper insert under celluloid, two paper adv on threaded center spindle, red ground, orig card, c1921 50.00
Display Case, watches, 1950 .... 145.00
Door Push, plastic, bottle shape, c1950 .... 145.00
Game, Game of Health, 8½ × 17¼" folded cardboard game board, 1934 Canadian copyright, youthful health activities from rising to bedtime, full-color Coke and Canadian maple leaf symbol 125.00
Glass, bell shape, 1929–40 .... 5.00
Ice Chest, metal, red and white 60.00
Ice Pick, "Drink Coca-Cola in Bottles" 6.00
Menu Board, tin, 1939 .... 75.00
Needle Case, 2 × 3" stiff paper, full-color art front and back, copyright 1924, adv text on inner panels, orig small package of needles 75.00

Blotter, "Season's Greetings...," Haddon Sunblom artist, 12½ × 10½", $5.00.

Pencil Clip, cello disk mounted on bright silver-luster tin clip, red ground, 1940–50
    "Drink Coca-Cola," yellow lettering 22.00
    "Drink Coca-Cola in Bottles," white lettering 20.00
Pencil Sharpener, 1¾" h, white metal, replica bottle, red enamel finish, inset metal sharpener blade on back, marked "Made in Bavaria," 1930s, wear to enamel 50.00
Pinback Button, Hi Fi Club, yellow and green lettering, brown Coke bottle, red 45-RPM record, 1950s 25.00
Pocket Knife, two stainless blades, marked "Remington," c1930 .... 100.00

Pocket Watch, "Time for Cold Bottle of Coca-Cola," 1920s **750.00**

Pop gun, 4½ × 8", diecut cardboard, full-color Santa on both sides, imprint of local supplier, 1954 copyright, unused **40.00**

Premium, tie, 15" l red-cord bolo tie, emb brass 1" slide clasp, frontal portrait of Kit Carson by Coca-Cola bottle, two small brass balls on ends, sponsorship premium for TV series "The Adventures of Kit Carson," c1951 .... **85.00**

Script, Coke Time TV Broadcast, 8½ × 11" mimeographed paper 16-pg typewritten script, Wed, July 22, 1953, starring Eddie Fisher, host Don Ameche, DeMarco Sisters as special guests **35.00**

Sign

   Cardboard, 14 × 30, oblong, bottle and hamburger, "Tasty together!", 1934 .... **150.00**

   Glass, 8 × 12", "Drink Coca-Cola, Please Pay when Served," 1932 .... **750.00**

   Neon, bottle in circle, 1942, lighted, metal frame .. **900.00**

   Paper, 10 × 30", man holding hot dog and bottle, "An Ice Cold with a Red Hot," metal strip top and bottom **275.00**

   Porcelain, 12 × 29", "Coca-Cola Sold Here Ice Cold," 1940s **225.00**

   Tin, 11 × 35", c1941 .... **180.00**

Syrup Bottle, paper label under glass, 1920s **300.00**

Thermometer, 5½ × 7", diecut tin, color replica of unopened bottle, recessed thermometer, 1950s **75.00**

Tray

   1905, 10½ × 13", oval **1,750.00**

   1910, 10½ × 13¼" **500.00**

   1916, 8½ × 19", oblong **250.00**

   1938, 10½ × 13¼", seated lady holding bottle **95.00**

Umbrella, 1920s **750.00**

Vending Machine, 36" h, 24" w, V-23, "Coca-Cola 10 Cents, Drink Coca-Cola in Bottles," revolving white top, orig working condition **1,895.00**

Window Display

   Bathing Beauty, water skiing, trifold, 1922 ....**6,000.00**

   Circus, big top with several smaller tents, circus wagons, animals, bands, concession stands, price for 17 pcs, c1929 ....**3,200.00**

   Revolving Door, sign over door reads "The Pleasantest Place in Town," fashionably dressed patrons, 1930s **1,500.00**

COFFEE MILLS

History: Coffee mills or grinders are utilitarian objects designed to grind fresh coffee beans. Before the advent of stay-fresh packaging, coffee mills were a necessity.

The first home-size coffee grinders were introduced about 1890. The large commercial grinders designed for use in stores, restaurants, and hotels often bear an earlier patent date.

Reference: Joseph Edward MacMillan, *The MacMillan Index of Antique Coffee Mills,* Cherokee Publishing, 1995.

Collectors' Club: Association of Coffee Mill Enthusiasts, 657 Old Mountain Rd, Marietta, GA 30064.

Commercial

Enterprise, No. 3, cast iron, two wheels, orig red paint and decals, 15" h **600.00**

Fairbanks-Morse, two wheels, brass finial, white paint, 38" h **360.00**

Golden Rule, cast iron **200.00**

John C Dell & Sons, sand-blasted and primed cast iron, brass hopper, 33" d wheels, 66" h **900.00**

Metal handle, one drawer with porcelain knob, Imperial No 1 Mill, mfg by Arcade Co, Pat June 5, 1894, 6⅞" sq, $70.00.

Domestic

A Keine, dovetailed curly-maple case, drawer with lacy-glass pull, replaced tin hopper, wrought-iron fittings, handled marked, 7 × 7" **385.00**

Brighton, cast iron, wall type, mounted on wooden board **75.00**

Charles Parker Co, cast-iron handle and crank, tip top and filter, 14¼" h **85.00**

De Ve, wood, copper-plated top and crank, drawer, 4¼" h **45.00**

Imperial, dovetailed box, 5½" sq **35.00**

Peugeot Freres Brevetes, cast iron, wood drawer, emb brass label, black paint over green, wooden base, French, c1900 .... **70.00**

Strobridge Coffee Mill, Logan & Strobridge, walnut base, cast-iron top, cast floral design and label, corner chip on drawer, 8¼" h **110.00**

Rock Hard, Garant-Sewaarborge, maple, aluminum hopper, drawer **30.00**

Unmarked, emb cast-iron top, slide-open hopper, 13" h **65.00**

COIN-OPERATED ITEMS

History: Coin-operated items include amusement games, pinball machines, jukeboxes, slot machines, vending machines, cash registers, and other items operated by coins.

The first jukebox was developed about 1934 and played 78-RPM records. Jukeboxes were important to teenagers before the advent of portable radios and television.

The first pinball machine was introduced in 1931 by Gottlieb. Pinball machines continued to be popular until the advent of solid-state games in 1977 and advanced electronic video games after that.

The first three-reel slot machine, the Liberty Bell, was invented in 1905 by Charles Fey in San Francisco. In 1910 Mills Novelty Company copyrighted the classic fruit symbols. Improvements and advancements have led to the sophisticated machines of to-day.

Vending machines for candy, gum, and peanuts were popular from 1910 until 1940 and can be found in a wide range of sizes and shapes.

References: Michael Adams, Jurgen Lukas, and Thomas Maschke, *Jukeboxes,* Schiffer Publishing, 1995 Richard M. Bueschel, *Collector's Guide to Vintage Coin Machines,* Schiffer Publishing, 1995; ———, *Lemons, Cherries and Bell-Fruit-Gum,* Royal Bell Books, 1995; ———, *Pinball 1,* Hoflin Publishing, 1988; ———, *Slots 1,* Hoflin Publishing, 1989; Richard Bueschel and Steve Gronowski, *Arcade 1,* Hoflin Publishing, 1993; Herbert Eiden and Jurgen Lukas, *Pinball Machines,* Schiffer Publishing, 1992; Bill Enes, *Silent Salesmen Too, The Encyclopedia of Collectible Vending Machines,* published by author (8520 Lewis Dr, Lenexa, KS 66227), 1995; Eric Hatchell and Dick Bueschel, *Coin-Ops on Location,* published by authors, 1993; Bill Kurtz, *Arcade Treasures,* Schiffer Publishing, 1994.

Periodicals: *Always Jukin',* 221 Yesler Way, Seattle, WA 98104; *Antique Amusements, Slot Machines & Jukebox Gazette,* 909 26th St NW, Washington, DC 20037; *Around the Vending Wheel,* 5417 Castana Ave, Lakewood, CA 90712; *Coin Drop International,* 5815 W 52nd Ave, Denver, CO 80212; *Coin Machine Trader,* 569 Kansas SE, PO Box 602, Huron, SD 57350; *Coin-Op Classics,* 17844 Toiyabe St, Fountain Valley, CA 92708; *Coin Slot,* 4401 Zephyr St, Wheat Ridge, CO 80033; *Gameroom Magazine,* 1014 Mt Tabor Rd, New Albany, IN 47150; *Jukebox Collector,* 2545 SE 60th Street, Des Moines, IA 50317; *Loose Change,* 1515 S Commerce St, Las Vegas, NV 89102; *Pin Game Journal,* 31937 Olde Franklin Dr, Farmington, MI, 48334; *Scopitone Newsletter,* 810 Courtland Dr, Ballwin, MO 63021.

Collectors' Club: Bubble-Gum Charm, 24 Seafoam St, Staten Island, NY 10306

Museum: Liberty Belle Saloon and Slot Machine Collection, Reno, NV.

Additional Listings: See *Warman's Americana & Collectibles* for separate categories for Jukeboxes, Pinball Machines, Slot Machines, and Vending Machines.

Advisor: Bob Levy.

Notes: Because of the heavy usage these coin-operated items received, many are restored or, at the very least, have been repainted by either the operator or manufacturer. Using reproduced mechanisms to restore pieces is acceptable in many cases, especially when the restored piece will then perform as originally intended.

Arcade

Fortune Teller, Princess Doraldina, Rochester, NY, c1928, 5¢, lifelike, gives fortune **11,000.00**

Penny Arcade, Grip Tester, Shake with Your Uncle Sam, Howard, 1¢, American, c1904, cast-iron relief bust of Uncle Sam, paper dial, oak stand with cast-iron base, original paint, 66″ h, $17,250.00. Photograph courtesy of Sotheby's, New York.

Grip Tester, Shake with Your Uncle Sam, Howard, c1904, 1¢, 66″h **17,250.00**
Photo Viewing Machine, American Mutoscope, NY, c1920, 1¢, metal, orig photos and paper marquee .**1,100.00**

Gum Machines

Adams, c1934, four column, tab gum vendor, chrome, decal, 22″ h **75.00**
Ford, c1950, round globe, gumballs, large, organizational use, 12″ h **60.00**
Master, c1923, 1¢, confection, 16″ h **200.00**
Penny King, c1935, four-in-one, rotates, Art Deco style, four glass compartments **500.00**
Pulver, c1930, 1¢, two column, porcelain, stick dispenser, policeman figure rotates, 21″ h **500.00**

Jukeboxes

Seeburg, Model 100R, c1954, high fidelity, classic style, plays 45s **2,000.00**
Wurlitzer, Model 1015, c1946, The Bubbler **7,500.00**

Miscellaneous

Cash Register, National Brass, Model 317, c1910, barber-shop size, orig marquee **700.00**
Pinball, Jolly Roger, c1967, four player **200.00**
Scale, American Scale, Fortune Model, c1937, 1¢, health chart **200.00**

Slot Machines

Caille, Superior, c1929, three reel, fancy design, 5¢ ...**1,400.00**
Groetchen, Columbia, c1936, three reel, high maintenance, 25¢ **500.00**
Jennings, Standard Chief, c1947, three reel, classic design, 10¢ **1,200.00**
Mills, Jewel Hightop, c1948, three reel, rugged and popular style, 5¢ **1,000.00**

Vending, Ajax, Fresh Hot Nuts, three units, aluminum, Newark, NJ, $200.00.

Pace, All Star Comet, c1936, three reel, side mint vendor, 5¢ **1,400.00**
Watling, Rolatop, c1935, three reel, gold coins on front, 25¢ **2,800.00**

Vending Machines

Card, slot dispenser, various subjects, exhibit supply, c1930, table top, 12″ h, 10″ w **175.00**
Cigarettes, Advance, c1930, 15¢, 30″ h, 14″ w **100.00**
Coke, Vendo V81, c1955, 6½, 8, or 10 oz bottles, orig condition **1,200.00**
Food, Horn and Hardart Automat Dispenser, c1902, four-item unit **1,200.00**
Matches, Edwards Mfg Co, c1930, Diamond, one to four books, 13½″ h **225.00**
Nut, Ajax, Newark, NJ, c1947, three-unit vendor, serves hot nuts, 21½″ h **200.00**
Pen, Vendorama, Victor Corp, c1962, oak case, 20″ h, 14″ w **50.00**
Perfume, Perfumatic, c1950, four fragrances, 10¢ spray, pink, 16″ h, 18″ w **125.00**
Stamp, Dillion Mfg, c1930, two selections, 12 × 12″ . **75.00**

Slot Machine, The Puritan Bell, 5¢, 9⅛″ d, 7⅜″ w, 10¼″ h, $125.00.

COMIC BOOKS

History: Shortly after comics first appeared in newspapers of the 1890s, they were reprinted in book format and often used as promotional giveaways by manufacturers, movie theaters, and candy and stationery stores. The first modern-format comic was issued in 1933.

The magic date in comic collecting is June 1938 when DC issued Action Comics No. 1, marking the first appearance of Superman. Thus began the golden age of comics, which lasted until the mid-1950s and witnessed the birth of the major comic book publishers, titles, and characters.

In 1954 Fredric Wertham authored *Seduction of the Innocent,* a book which pointed a guilt-laden finger at the comic industry for corrupting youth, causing juvenile delinquency, and undermining American values. Many publishers were forced out of business while others established a "comics code" to assure parents that their comics were compliant with morality and decency standards upheld by the code authority.

The silver age of comics, mid-1950s through the end of the 1960s, witnessed the revival of many of the characters from the golden age in new comic formats. The era began with Showcase No. 4 in October 1956, which marked the origin and first appearance of the Silver-Age Flash.

While comics survived into the 1970s, it was a low point for the genre; but in the early 1980s a revival occurred. In 1983 comic book publishers, other than Marvel and DC, issued more titles than had existed in total during the previous 40 years. The mid- and late 1980s were a boom time, a trend which appears to be continuing into the 1990s.

References: Mike Benton, *Comic Book in America,* Taylor Publishing, 1989; ———, *Crime Comics,* Taylor Publishing, 1992; ———, *Science Fiction Comics,* Taylor Publishing, 1992; ———, *Superhero Comics of the Golden Age,* Taylor Publishing, 1992; ———, *Superhero Comics of the Silver Age,* Taylor Publishing, 1992; *Comic Buyer's Guide Annual,* Krause Publications, issued annually; Duncan McAlpine (comp.), *Comic Values Annual,* 1996 Edition, Antique Trader Books, 1995; Robert M. Overstreet, *The Overstreet Comic Book Price Guide,* 26th Edition, Avon Books, 1996; Robert Overstreet and Gary M. Carter, *The Overstreet Comic Book Grading Guide,* Avon Books, 1995; Don and Maggie Thompson (eds.), *Comic Book Superstars,* Krause Publications, 1993; ——— (eds.), *Marvel Comics Checklist & Price Guide,* Krause Publications, 1993; Maggie Thompson and Brent Frankenhoff, *Comic Book Checklist & Price Guide,* Third Edition, Krause Publications, 1996.

Periodicals: *Archie Fan Magazine,* 185 Ashland St, Holliston, MA 01746; *Comic Book Market Place,* PO Box 180900, Coronado, CO 92178; *Comics Buyer's Guide,* 700 E State St, Iola, WI 54990; *Comics Interview,* 234 Fifth Ave, New York, NY 10001; *Comics Source,* 2401 Broad St, Chattanooga, TN 37408; *Duckburg Times,* 3010 Wilshire Blvd #362, Los Angeles, CA 90010; *Hogan's Alley,* PO Box 47684, Atlanta, GA 30362; *Overstreet Comic Book Marketplace,* 1996 Greenspring Dr, Suite 405, Timonium, MD 21093; *Western Comics Journal,* 1703 N Aster Place, Broken Arrow, OK 74012; *Wizard: The Guide To Comics,* 151 Wells Ave, Congers, NY 10920.

Collectors' Clubs: American Comics Exchange, 351-T Baldwin Rd, Hempstead, NY 11550; Fawcett Collectors of America & Magazine Enterprise, too!, 301 E Buena Vista Ave, North Augusta, SC 29841.

Videotape: *The Overstreet World of Comic Books,* Overstreet Productions and Tom Barker Video, 1994.

Museums: International Museum of Cartoon Art, 300 SE 5th Ave, #5150, Boca Raton, FL 33432; Museum of Cartoon Art, Rye, NY.

REPRODUCTION ALERT

Publishers frequently reprint popular stories, even complete books, so the buyer must pay strict attention to the title, not just the portion printed in oversized letters on the front cover. If there is any doubt, look inside at the fine print on the bottom of the inside cover or first page. The correct title will be printed there in capital letters.

Also pay attention to the dimensions of the comic book. Reprints often differ in size from the original.

Note: The comics listed below are in near-mint condition, meaning they have a flat, clean, shiny cover that has no wear other than tiny corner creases; no subscription creases, writing, yellowing at margins, or tape repairs; staples are straight and rust free; pages are supple and like new; generally just-off-the-shelf quality.

Pre-Golden Age

Ace Comics, No. 4, David McKay Publications	125.00
Famous Funnies, No. 3, Buck Rogers strip reprints begin	500.00
King Comics, No. 12, strip reprint, David McKay Publications	80.00
Western Picture Stories, No. 1, Comics Magazine Co .	300.00

Golden Age

Adventure Comics, No. 271, orig of Luthor, DC	40.00
All Star Western, No. 67, National Periodical Publications	30.00
Amazing Stories, Armageddon 2419, first Buck Rogers Story, April 1961	45.00
Batman, No. 140, Joker story	30.00
Cisco Kid Comics, No. 2, Dell Publishing	20.00
Dennis the Menace, No. 11, giant Christmas issue, Winter 1962	10.00
Donald Duck, No. 134, Gold Key	4.00
Flash Comics, No. 35, National Periodical Publications	150.00
Giant	
#25	90.00
#37	90.00
#51	70.00
GI Combat, No. 33	7.50
Gunsmoke, No. 17, Dell	15.00
Jungle Comics, No. 57, Fiction House Magazine	50.00
Love Romances, No. 57, Marvel	7.50
March of Comics, No. 116, Roy Rogers	20.00
Mickey Mouse, No. 68, Dell	3.50
Rawhide Kid, No. 1, Atlas	75.00

Romantic Love, No. 19	15.00
Sheena, Queen of the Jungle, No. 12, Fiction House Magazine	45.00
Space Patrol, No. 2, Ziff-Davis Publishing Co	100.00
Star Spangled War Stories, No. 22, National Periodical Publications	15.00
Tarzan, Dell	12.00
Tessie the Typist, No. 2	15.00
Uncle Scrooge, No. 55, Gold Key	10.00
Walt Disney Comics, No. 37, Donald Duck, Dell	60.00
Weird Mysteries No. 7, Gillmore Publications	75.00
Wonder Woman, No. 35, National Periodical Publications	50.00

Andy Panda, Dell, Feb-April 1958, $.60.

Silver Age

Amazing Spiderman, No. 200, Marvel	2.00
Aquaman, No. 4, DC	45.00
Captain America, No. 250, Marvel	2.00
Daredevil, No. 20, Marvel	7.50
Fantastic Four, Marvel, No. 23	50.00
House of Mystery, No. 180, DC	33.00
Marvel Team Up, No. 15	4.50
Strange Tales, No. 120, Marvel	12.00
Top Cat, No. 10, Gold Key	3.00
X-Men, No. 29, Marvel	10.00

Post-Silver Age

Airboy, No. 6, Eclipse	3.50
Battlestar Galactica,. No. 3, Marvel	1.00
Conan the Barbarian, No. 20	5.00
Dagar the Invincible, No. 2	4.00
Dragonforce, No. 5	3.00
Mighty Miles, No. 6	33.00
The Saga of the Swamp Thing, No. 20, DC	2.50
Star Trek, No. 5, DC	3.50

Sun Runners, No. 1, Pacific **2.00**
T.H.U.N.D.E.R. Agents, No. 2 .... **12.00**

COMPACTS

History: In the first quarter of the 20th century, attitudes regarding cosmetics changed drastically. The use of make-up during the day was no longer looked upon with disdain. As women became "liberated", and as more and more of them entered the business world, the use of cosmetics became a routine and necessary part of a woman's grooming. Portable containers for cosmetics became a necessity.

Compacts were made in myriad shapes, styles, combinations and motifs, all reflecting the mood of the times. Every conceivable natural or man-made material was used in the manufacture of compacts. Commemorative, premium, souvenir, patriotic, figural, Art Deco, and enamel compacts are a few examples of the types of compacts that were made in the United States and abroad. Compacts combined with other forms, such as cigarette cases, music boxes, watches, hatpins, canes, and lighters, also were very popular.

Compacts were made and used until the late 1950s when women opted for the "Au Naturel" look. The term "vintage" is used to describe the compacts from the first half of the 20th century as distinguished from contemporary examples.

References: Juliette Edwards, *Compacts,* published by author, 1994; Roselyn Gerson, *Ladies Compacts,* Collector Books, 1996; ————, *Vintage Ladies Compacts,* Collector Books, 1996; ————, *Vintage Vanity Bags and Purses: An Identification and Value Guide,* Collector Books, 1994; Frances Johnson, *Compacts, Powder and Paint,* Schiffer Publishing, 1996; Laura M. Mueller, *Collector's Encyclopedia of Compacts, Carryalls & Face Powder Boxes,* Collector Books, 1994, 1996 value update.

Collectors' Club: Compact Collectors Club, PO Box 40, Lynbrook, NY 11563.

Additional Listings: See *Warman's Americana & Collectibles* for more examples.

Advisor: Roselyn Gerson.

Amita, damascene compact, gold and silver floral motif, black matte lid, Japan **125.00**

Art Deco, chrome, blue and white, 2³⁄₄ × 2¹⁄₄", $18.00.

Arden, Elizabeth, light blue harlequin-shaped compact **150.00**
Art Deco, blue enamel geometric pattern, rose-cut diamond closure and front motifs, 14K yellow gold, orig box, sgd "Flato", minor wear to enamel **2,875.00**
Beetle Shape, novelty, compact, plastic, red **100.00**
Black enamel, painted poodle on white enamel disk on lid **50.00**
Champlevé, red and goldtone, hand-mirror shape, lipstick concealed in handle, red cabochon lipstick thumbpiece, Italy **350.00**
Coro, vanity case/watch, horseshoe shape, black enamel, snap closing, powder and rouge compartments **175.00**
Croco, compact, round, blue, zipper, decorative multicolored court inset on lid, Israel **50.00**
Coty, compact
    Hand-mirror shape, plastic, Coty trademark powder puffs dec on lid, lipstick in handle **65.00**
    Rect, Jingle Bells, goldtone **150.00**
Elgin
    Compact, goldtone, colorful enamel swirls, "G. E. Color TV" logo on top **150.00**
    Compact/Music Box, silvered, three gilt deer on lid, Anniversary Waltz, black carrying case **125.00**
Evans
    Compact, pink and yellow goldtone basketweave .. **190.00**
    Vanity Case, Tap Sift, white cloisonné, black stylized skyscraper motif, key pattern around rim, powder sifter and rouge compartment **140.00**
French Ivory, compact, painted red and green flowers, plastic link carrying chain, c1920
Gold, 14K yellow, fluted stippled finish, mirror, 2 × 2¹⁄₂", 67 dwt **690.00**
Goldtone, compact, heart shape, purple orchid inlaid in black plastic lid **75.00**
Illinois Watch Case Co, compact/watch combination, round, goldtone, engraved design on lid **190.00**
Kamra-Pak style, compact, brown marbleized enamel, US Navy insignia on lid, sliding lipstick, Germany . **125.00**
Lampl
    Compact, light blue enamel, five colorful three-dimensional scenes from *Alice in Wonderland* encased in plastic domes on lid **200.00**
    Compact/Cigarette Case, goldtone, rhinestones and green faux gemstones on lid, center compact flanked by cigarette compartment **140.00**
Leather, horseshoe shape, blue, one pc **50.00**
Lin-Bren, leather, green, envelope motif coin holder on lid **85.00**
Mother-of-Pearl, vanity case, black and white, attached lipstick **65.00**
Napier, SS, clamshell shape **225.00**
Nickel Silver, compact, round, red and black enamel, metal mirror, compartments for powder sifter and rouge, finger-ring carrying chain **150.00**
Petit Point, vanity case, scalloped half-moon shape, goldtone **150.00**
Rex Fifth Avenue, compact, painted, enameled, two pink flamingoes, turquoise background **90.00**
Rigaud, Mary Garden, gilt miniature, emb silhouette on slipcover lid **50.00**
Rosenfield, zippered goldtone compact, multicolor confetti sparkles and thread, Israel **40.00**

Scottie, vanity case, blue enamel, powder compartment and metal mirror open to reveal rouge compartment   **40.00**

Souvenir, silvered metal, photograph of Old Orchard Beach, ME, on lid **90.00**

Volupté

    Compact, hand shape, goldtone, lace gloved **225.00**

    Vanity Pouch, light blue collapsible leather **85.00**

CONSOLIDATED GLASS COMPANY

History: The Consolidated Lamp and Glass Company was formed as a result of the 1893 merger of the Wallace and McAfee Company, glass and lamp jobbers of Pittsburgh, and the Fostoria Shade & Lamp Company of Fostoria, Ohio. When the Fostoria, Ohio, plant burned down in 1895, Corapolis, Pennsylvania, donated a seven-acre tract of land near the center of town for a new factory. In 1911 the company was the largest lamp, globe, and shade works in the United States, employing over 400 workers.

In 1925 Reuben Haley, owner of an independent design firm, convinced John Lewis, president of Consolidated, to enter the giftware field utilizing a series of designs inspired by the 1925 Paris Exposition (l'Exposition Internationale des Arts Décoratives et Industriels Modernes) and the work of René Lalique. Initially, the glass was marketed by Howard Selden through his showroom at 225 Fifth Avenue in New York City. The first two lines were Catalonian and Martele.

Additional patterns were added in the late 1920s: Florentine (January 1927), Chintz (January 1927), Ruba Rombic (January 1928), and Line 700 (January 1929). On April 2, 1932, Consolidated closed it doors. Kenneth Harley moved about 40 molds to Phoenix. In March 1936 Consolidated reopened under new management, and the "Harley" molds were returned. During this period the famous Dancing Nymph line, based on an eight-inch salad plate in the 1926 Martele series, was introduced.

In August 1962 Consolidated was sold to Dietz Brothers. A major fire damaged the plant during a 1963 labor dispute and in 1964 the company permanently closed its doors.

References: Ann Gilbert McDonald, *Evolution of the Night Lamp*, Wallace-Homestead, 1979; Jack D. Wilson, *Phoenix & Consolidated Art Glass, 1926–1980*, Antique Publications, 1989.

Collectors' Club: Phoenix and Consolidated Glass Collectors, PO Box 81974, Chicago, IL 60681.

Ashtray, Ruba Rombic, crystal **295.00**

Basket, Catalonia, green, applied handle **45.00**

Berry Bowl, 8″ d, Criss Cross, cranberry opalescent ...   **150.00**

Box, cov, 5 × 7″, Fruit & Leaf, Martele line, scalloped edge **65.00**

Butter Dish, Cosmos, pink band **195.00**

Candlesticks, pr, Dancing Girls, French Crystal **175.00**

Celery Tray, Ruba Rombic, smoky topaz **115.00**

Cigarette Box, cov, Santa Maria, opaque white body, emb dolphins on sides, gold sailing ship on lid **135.00**

Condiment Set, Florette, blue, cased, salt and pepper shakers, cov mustard, handled stand **125.00**

Cracker Jar, Florette, light green cased body, orig SP rim, lid, and bail handle **200.00**

Creamer and Sugar, Catalonia, amethyst **50.00**

Decanter Set, Catalonia, amber, decanter and three tumblers, price for 4-pc set **125.00**

Lamp, table, Cockatoo, blue, bittersweet, tan, and white   **275.00**

Perfume Bottle, Ruba Rombic, lilac, matching stopper .   **265.00**

Pickle Castor, Cosmos insert, pink band, ornate SP frame   **495.00**

Pitcher, water, Cosmos, light dec **220.00**

Plate, 10¼″ d, Bird of Paradise, Martele line, deep amethyst stain **45.00**

Salt Shaker, Half Cone, pink cased **75.00**

Salt and Pepper Shakers, Rib & Scroll, pink cased, orig tin top, $45.00.

Sauce Dish, Criss Cross, cranberry opalescent **60.00**

Snack Set, Five Fruits, price for 8-pc set **95.00**

Spooner, Florette, pink, metal rim and handles **70.00**

Sugar Shaker, Cone, blue, orig top **125.00**

Toothpick Holder, Guttate, pink **125.00**

Tumbler, Five Fruits, green, ftd **30.00**

Umbrella Stand, Blackberry, amber **395.00**

Vase

    Katydid, 8½″ h, fan shape, white figures, frosted ground **250.00**

    Olive, pillow shape **190.00**

CONTINENTAL CHINA AND PORCELAIN (GENERAL)

History: By 1700 porcelain factories existed in large numbers throughout Europe. In the mid-18th century the German factories at Meissen and Nymphenburg were dominant. As the century ended, French potteries assumed the leadership role. The 1740s to the 1840s were the golden age of Continental china and porcelain.

Americans living in the last half of the 19th century eagerly sought the masterpieces of the European porcelain factories. In the early 20th century this style of china and porcelain was considered "blue chip" by antiques collectors.

References: Susan and Al Bagdade, *Warman's English & Continental Pottery & Porcelain*, Second Edition, Wallace-Homestead, 1991; Rachael Feild, *Macdonald Guide to Buying Antique Pottery & Porcelain*, Wallace-Homestead, 1987; Geoffrey Godden, *Godden's Guide to European Porcelain*, Random House, 1993.

Additional Listings: French—Haviland, Limoges, Old Paris, Sarreguemines, and Sevres; German—Austrian Ware, Bavarian China, Carlsbad China, Dresden/Meissen, Rosenthal, Royal Bayreuth, Royal Bonn, Royal Rudolstadt, Royal Vienna, Schlegelmilch, and Villeroy and Boch; Italian—Capo-di-Monte.

French

Chantilly
    Dish, 9¾" l, quatrefoil, Kakiemon palette, chrysanthemum, chocolate rim, c1740 .... 200.00
    Plate, 9½" d, blue and white, carnations, basket-work border, blue hunting-horn mark, c1845, price for 12-pc set 750.00
French Faience
    Milk Pitcher, floral spray dec, sgd "L. M. & Son, Creil & Montereau," price for pr 160.00
    Turkey Tureen, 15½" h, pale lavender glaze 90.00
Gallé Faience
    Compote, 9" d, scalloping rim, waisted cylindrical base, dark blue and yellow, blossom sprays, central unicorn and centaur, sgd "E Gallé Nancy," price for pr 990.00
    Figure, 13¼" h, seated brown tabby cat, green glass eyes, sgd "Gallé Nancy," minor restoration 500.00
Longwy
    Box, cov, 7½" d, circular, polychrome parrot on lid 225.00
    Plaque, 8 × 6½" oval, crane in marsh, cobalt blue field 80.00
Samson
    Basket, 10" w, allover basketweave pattern, two loop handles, male and female masks terminals, painted loose bouquets and scattered flowers, turquoise and puce chevron border, Hoechst and Samson marks 400.00

Sansom, urn, cov, rose, purple, and green floral clusters, rust diapering on body, sq base, gilt trim, late 19th C, 13" h, $495.00.

    Plate, black enameled figures in landscapes, gold vine border, price for pr 250.00
    Vase, cov, floral dec 275.00
St Cloud, cup and saucer, 2¾" d, white, plum tree branches, mid 18th C, price for pr 1,700.00
Unidentified, compote, 6½" h, 9¼" d, alternating fish scales and figures in landscape panels, mid 19th C, price for pr 815.00

German

Ansbach, coffeepot, 8" h, pear shape, dome cov with fruit finial, scrolling handle, short spout, molded female mask and feathers, loose bouquets and scattered flowers dec, c1765, blue coat of arms and "A" mark, restored finial 1,200.00
Berlin
    Ewer, 8⅞" h, scrolling handle, short spout, allover yellow and blue marbled glaze, c1720, rim chips 4,000.00
    Sweetmeat Dish, 7½" w, three molded yellow fruits and cov, white blossom finials, fixed leaf-shaped stand, branch handles, c1765, scepter mark, restored finials, minor chips 1,350.00
Frankenthal, figure, 10½" h, French General on horse-back, sgd "F. W. Wetzel" 200.00
Herend
    Dinnerware Service, green band and floral spray dec, 11 soup plates, 12 dinner plates, 9 salad plates, 5 bread plates, sauceboat with two handles, low fruit bowl, oval 14" platter 1,100.00
    Fruit Bowl, 10½" l oval, open work, hp center, pink, gold, and blue dec 250.00
Hoechst, figure, 5½" w, 5½" h, two children dancing, painted factory marks, mid 19th C 375.00
Nymphenburg
    Cup and Saucer, 3¾" d, bell-shaped bowl, Maximillian Joseph Platz, burnished gilt int. and scroll handle, c1835 .... 1,900.00
    Figure
        3¼" h, sparrow, realistically colored enamels ... 125.00
        3½" h, standing Baroque putti, blanc de chine .. 100.00
        5½" h, 18th C lady, blanc de chine 100.00
        8½" d, cow, blanc de chine 270.00
    Tea Set, black border, magenta rim, magenta floral sprays, spherical teapot, creamer, 12 teacups and saucers, cake plates, circular tray, damage to teapot 550.00

Italian

Deruta, jar, 7¼" h, majolica, scrollwork, grotesques and leaf forms, inscribed "Ghoma di Lava" 500.00
Doccia
    Cup and Saucer, flaring cylindrical cup, C-scroll handle, purple highlights, c1755, price for pr 145.00
    Dish, 9⅝" w, shell shape, central bouquet of purple flowers surrounded by floral sprays, continuous twisting branches of leaves and nuts border, purple five-pointed star mark, c1780 .... 165.00
Istoriato, charger, 16" d, majolica, underglaze blue, yellow, and red luster enamels dec, central scene of Roman legions rallying around their standards, wide scrolling grotesque border 200.00
Savona, compote, 14" d, blue and white dec, floral border, pierced, blue lighthouse mark 1,200.00

COOKIE JARS

History: Cookie jars, colorful and often whimsical, are now an established collecting category. Do not be misled by the high prices realized at the 1988 Andy Warhol auction. Many of the same cookie jars that sold for over $1,000 each can be found in the field for less than $100.

Cookie jars often were redesigned to reflect newer tastes. Hence, the same jar may be found in several different variations.

Marks: Many cookie jar shapes were manufactured by more than one company and, as a result, can be found with different marks. This often happened because of mergers or separations, e.g., Brush-McCoy which became Nelson McCoy. Molds also were traded and sold among companies.

References: Mary Jane Giacomini, *American Bisque,* Schiffer Publishing, 1994; Dana G. Morykan and Harry L. Rinker, *Warman's Country Antiques & Collectibles,* Third Edition, Wallace-Homestead, 1996; *1995 Cookie Jar Express Pricing Guide to Cookie Jars,* Paradise Publications, 1995; Fred and Joyce Roerig, *Collector's Encyclopedia of Cookie Jars,* Book I, (1991, 1993 value update), Book II (1994), Collector Books; Mark and Ellen Supnick, *The Wonderful World of Cookie Jars,* L-W Book Sales, 1995; Ermagene Westfall, *An Illustrated Value Guide to Cookie Jars,* Book I (1983, 1995 value update), Book II (1993, 1995 value update), Collector Books.

Periodicals: *Cookie Jar Collectors Express,* PO Box 221, Mayview, MO 64071; *Cookie Jarrin',* RR 2, Box 504, Walterboro, SC 29488.

Collectors' Club: The Cookie Jar Collector's Club, 595 Cross River Rd, Katonah, NY 10536.

Museum: The Cookie Jar Museum, Lemont, IL.

Abingdon
Hippo, dec	595.00
Humpty Dumpty	375.00
Jack-O'-Lantern	325.00

Advertising
Alf	150.00
Archway Van	30.00
Keebler Tree	60.00

American Bisque Co, ABC
Baby Elephant	155.00
Bear, flasher	495.00
Churn Boy	155.00
Clown, flasher	250.00
Cow Jumping over the Moon, flasher	975.00

Davy Crockett
Boy	395.00
Woodland setting	1,000.00

Dutch Boy, sailboat	60.00
French Poodle, maroon	95.00
Granny	75.00

Kitten
Beehive	65.00
Green ball of yarn	70.00

Lamb, marked "Design Patent Applied ABCo"	55.00
Paddle Boat	275.00
Pig in a Poke, yellow	90.00
Pretty Kitty, multicolored	90.00
Saddle, "Mustn't Forget" blackboard	280.00
Seal, igloo	350.00
Teddy Bear, flat hat	135.00
Brayton, Matilda	900.00

Brush
Covered Wagon	495.00
Dog, basket	345.00
Hillbilly Frog	4,200.00
Little Red Riding Hood	785.00
Cavanagh, Good Humor Truck	395.00
Gonder, sheriff, yellow	1,600.00
Hull, Barefoot Boy	400.00
Maddux of California, clown	395.00
Max, Peter	250.00

McCoy
Christmas Tree	725.00
Circus Horse	195.00
Football Boy	295.00

McCoy, mammy, $125.00.

Metlox
Bluebird on pinecone	195.00
Budweiser Wagon	325.00
Elephant	165.00
Grapes	195.00
Mammy, yellow	350.00
Mother Goose	295.00
Schoolhouse	1,100.00
Topsy, blue	550.00
Watermelon	350.00
Woodpecker on acorn	375.00

Pearl China
Chef	295.00
Mammy	900.00
Pfaltzgraff, clown with drum	475.00

Pottery Guild
Balloon Lady	115.00
Dutch Boy, brown pants	100.00
Dutch Girl, blue dress	100.00
Elsie in Barrel	385.00
Little Girl	100.00

Red Wing
Crock, large red flower	85.00
Katrina, green	295.00

Regal
Chef	475.00

Diaper-Pin Pig	425.00
Fifi Poodle	495.00
Three Bears	325.00
Shawnee	
Drum Major, gold trim	750.00
Winnie, peach collar	345.00
Sierra Vista	
Rocking Horse	325.00
Spaceship with Martians	575.00
Starnes, Barn Happy Face	295.00
Treasure Craft	
Ben Franklin	325.00
Cruisin' Dog	175.00
Stagecoach, brown, orig label	165.00
Twin Winton	
Ark	145.00
Bambi	150.00
Castle	225.00
Cookie Catcher	90.00
Cookie Tie Clock, white, black feet	165.00
Cookie Wagon	125.00
Dobbin	100.00
Dutch Girl	95.00
Poodle, at counter	90.00
Santa, black	595.00
Smokey the Bear	60.00
Vandor	
Betty Boop, top hat	145.00
Fred and Pebbles, chair	425.00
Walt Disney	
Donald on Pumpkin	395.00
Dumbo with Timothy	165.00
Mickey in car	410.00
Yona, elephant with clown	650.00

COPELAND AND SPODE

History: In 1749 Josiah Spode was apprenticed to Thomas Whieldon and in 1754 worked for William Banks in Stoke-on-Trent. In the early 1760s Spode started his own pottery, making cream-colored earthenware and blue-printed whiteware. In 1770 he returned to Banks' factory as master, purchasing it in 1776.

Spode pioneered the use of steam-powered pottery-making machinery and mastered the art of transfer printing from copper plates. Spode opened a London shop in 1778 and sent William Copeland there about 1784. A number of larger London locations followed. At the turn of the century Spode introduced bone china. In 1805 Josiah Spode II and William Copeland entered into a partnership for the London business. A series of partnerships between Josiah Spode II, Josiah Spode III, and William Taylor Copeland resulted.

In 1833 Copeland acquired Spode's London operations and seven years later the Stoke plants. William Taylor Copeland managed the business until his death in 1868. The firm remained in the hands of Copeland heirs. In 1923 the plant was electrified; other modernization followed.

In 1976 Spode merged with Worcester Royal Porcelain to become Royal Worcester Spode, Ltd.

References: Susan and Al Bagdade, *Warman's English & Continental Pottery & Porcelain,* Second Edition, Wallace-Homestead, 1991; D. Drakard & P. Holdway, *Spode Printed Wares,* Longmans, 1983; L. Whiter, *Spode: A History of the Family, Factory, and Wares, 1733–1833,* Barrie & Jenkins, 1970.

Bouillon Set, bone china, eleven cups, twelve matching saucers, polychrome and gilt floral dec, price for 21-pc set	175.00
Bowl, 8½" d, Imari type, blue, green, and range, scalloped edge, pedestal base, c1850	85.00
Bust	
8¼" h, Sir Walter Scott, parian, mounted to raised circular base, imp Copeland mark, c1875	230.00
16½" h, young Bacchante maiden, parian, after Owen Hale, dated 1881, imp Copeland marks	1,035.00
Centerpiece, 12" h, majolica, shell-form bowl surmounted by putti supporting small shell-form bowl on head, molded coral base, imp mark, c1875, rim chip repair	990.00
Charger, 13½" d, Imari style, red and blue enamels, gilt trim, floral border with scroll pattern and Chinese motif, imp "Spode New Stone China," c1810	550.00
Compote, 9½ × 2¾", white, floral dec, turquoise dots, gold trim, lattice sides	225.00
Creamer and Sugar, 3¼" h, Blue Willow, marked "Copeland's China England"	200.00
Dinnerware Service, Buttercup pattern, six dinner plates, twelve dessert plates, ten bread plates, seven cups and saucers, six bouillon cups and saucers, fruit bowl, sugar, creamer, two open vegetable dishes, 14" l platter, price for 64-pc set	55.00
Figure	
12" h, Lady of the Lake, nude figure, loosely draped cloth, seated on back, molded fish and reeds below, parian, imp marks "Marshall Fect SC, Copeland," mid 19th C	400.00
19⅛" h, Young Shrimper, holding shell, dragging net, parian, c1880, imp Copeland marks, chips	550.00
Flowerpot, 5" h, ftd base, gilt sea-serpent's-head handles and trim, hp floral panels, striped bodies, painted Spode mark, gilt rim wear, price for pr	2,185.00
Luncheon Service, pattern 1721, Kakiemon style, enameled and gilt dec, twenty-one 8½" d plates, four shrimp dishes, four 9½" oval vegetable dishes, 10¼" d oval vegetable dish, three 9" d round vegetable dishes, two 7" cov oval sauce tureens with underplates, 14" l oval compote, Spode, early 19th C, price for 40-pc set	2,875.00
Oyster Plate, hp, insects and flowers	50.00
Pitcher	
Jasper, blue, 19th C	150.00
Majolica, 7½" h, sq rim, paneled sides, enamel dec, molded lotus and lily plants, imp mark and registry code of 1877	1,495.00
Plate, 10" d, cobalt blue, raised foliate dec, early 20th C, wear, price for 13-pc set	1,725.00

Plate, impressed "Copeland/Crown," light brown transfer, 8¾" d, $8.00.

Punch Bowl, 12½" d, multicolored, Chinese garden scene, gold trim, c1810 .... **750.00**

Salt and Pepper Shakers, pr, Red Tower pattern **20.00**

Serving Dish, 12¾" w, rect, raised base, twin handles, pattern 3125, enameled floral dec black transfer, Spode, early 19th C **375.00**

Tea and Dessert Service, semi-porcelain, Black Bird pattern, red on white, teapot, cov sugar, creamer, cov warm-milk jug, eight dessert plates, seven cups and saucers, sq serving plate, minor damage, price for 31-pc set **75.00**

Tureen, cov, 7½" d, bridge scene with flowers, blue and white, matching stand, c1820 .... **125.00**

Vegetable Dish, cov, 10" l, Geisha pattern, blue **110.00**

COPPER

History: Copper objects, such as kettles, teakettles, warming pans, and measures, played an important part in the 19th-century household. Outdoors, the apple-butter kettle and still were the two principal copper items. Copper culinary objects were lined with a thin protective coating of tin to prevent poisoning. They were relined as needed.

References: Mary Frank Gaston, *Antique Brass & Copper,* Collector Books, 1992, 1994 value update; Henry J. Kauffman, *Early American Copper, Tin, and Brass: Handcrafted Metalware from Colonial Times,* Astragal Press, 1995.

Reproduction Alert: Many modern reproductions exist.

Additional Listings: Arts and Crafts Movement and Roycroft.

Notes: Collectors place great emphasis on signed pieces, especially those by American craftsmen. Since copper objects were made abroad as well, it is hard to identify unsigned examples.

Advertising Trade Sign
16" w, 14" h, coppersmith's, candle with candleholder shape, Arts and Crafts era, American **270.00**
19" h, boot mold, painted black, Minerva, NY, provenance, c1900 .... **70.00**

Ale Boot **200.00**

Apple-Butter Kettle, applied iron handle, crimped seam joining, large **75.00**

Bed Warmer, 45" l, engraved floral and bird, turned wooden handle **375.00**

Bowl
8½" d, 3½" h, hand hammered, curving rim, light patina, imp Kalo Shops mark **195.00**
15½" d, 4" h, symbol shape, rolled edge, light patina, imp Marie Zimmerman mark, No. 95 ....**1,495.00**

Box, cov, 3¼" d, 1¼" h, intricate Arts and Crafts blue, white, and purple enameling, cracked opal center, hammered finish **225.00**

Candleholder, four holders, sgd "W L Fletcher" **40.00**

Chafing Dish, 11" h, dish supported by three realistically modeled rabbits, wooden base, marked "Black, Starr & Forest" **450.00**

Coal Hod, 17" h, brass handles, 19th C **165.00**

Coffeepot, 12" l, 11" h, prospector's, orig tinning, wooden handle, c1850 .... **20.00**

Coffee Urn, 14½" h, brass fittings, label inside lid "Parkinson's Manufactury, London" **225.00**

Dipper, 80" l, orig pole with wrought-iron fittings **650.00**

Fish Cooker, 10" w, 7" h, punched-tin insert, hinged top, handles **40.00**

Hot-Water Bottle, 17½" l, oval, pewter fittings, screw cap with ring, old patina **140.00**

Jar, 11¼" d, 9" h, hammered, dovetailed seams **40.00**

Lamp, 9" h, 5¾" w, compressed sq, circular foot rim, beaded mid molding, patinated, applied silver seaweed, fish, seashells, and crab dec, orig wick holder now fitted for electricity, marked "Gorham," 1884   **3,850.00**

Measure
5" d, 3⅞" h, cylindrical, brass rim, labeled "Fairbanks & Co, US Standard New York" **300.00**
6¼" h, haystack, Continental, 19th C **75.00**

Measure, handle, 1 gal, $85.00.

Pitcher, 9¼" h, tankard shape, marked "D Bentley & Sons, N 3rd St, Phila" **75.00**

Preserving Pot, 28" d, loop wrought-iron handle, 19th C   **450.00**

Sauce Pan, 8" d, dovetailed, wrought copper handle .. **75.00**

Teakettle
    7¼" h, dovetailed, gooseneck spout **165.00**
    8" d, circular, brass knob finial, flat serving handle,
       marked "P Apple, Philadelphia," 18th/19th C .. **575.00**
    8½" d, circular, brass knob finial, flat serving handle,
       marked "C Tryon" **550.00**
Wash Boiler, canning rack **75.00**

CORALENE

History: Coralene refers to glass or china objects which have the design painted on the surface of the piece along with tiny colorless glass beads which were applied with a fixative. The piece was placed in a muffle to fix the enamel and set the beads.

Several American and English companies made glass coralene in the 1880s. Seaweed or coral were the most common design. Other motifs were Wheat Sheaf and Fleur-de-Lis. Most of the base glass was satin finished.

China and pottery coralene, made from the late 1890s until after World War II, is referred to as Japanese coralene. The beading is opaque and inserted into the soft clay. Hence, it is only one-half to three-quarters visible.

REPRODUCTION ALERT

Reproductions are on the market, some using an old glass base. The beaded decoration on new coralene has been glued and can be scraped off.

China

Bowl, 8" d, blue matte ground, purple plums, green
    leaves, c1910 .... **175.00**
Box, cov, 1½ × 2 × 3", copper matte ground, pink,
    lavender, and green thistles, marked "Kinran Pat
    16132 Japan" **120.00**
Ewer, 4" h, 3½" d, green and gold ground, pink and green
    fruit, green top and bottom trim, Japanese **200.00**
Sugar Shaker, white ground, orange coralene seaweed
    dec, orig top **175.00**
Vase, 8¼" h, cylindrical, two small handles, coralene
    beaded pink nasturtiums, trailing green leaves, brown
    ground, Japanese **425.00**

Glass

Bowl, 5½" d, blue herringbone, MOP, pink coralene
    seaweed dec, applied crimped rim **625.00**
Pitcher, 6" h, 4" d, orange, multicolored coralene water
    lilies, applied amber handle, rigaree around neck,
    patent mark on base **225.00**
Sweetmeat, 3½" d, 4¾" h, white Bristol glass base, or-
    ange coralene coral dec **325.00**
Tumbler, white satin ground, acorns and leaves dec,
    coralene outlines **45.00**
Vase
    5" h, 4" d, rose dec **65.00**
    6" h, white cased in yellow, yellow beading, ruffled
       rim **250.00**

Vase, Daisy & Leaf pattern, brown to green ground, 6⅝" h, $395.00.

6½ × 7½", blue, Diamond Quilted, satin finish ... **395.00**
7½" h, peachblow, satin finish, deep rose shading to
    pale pink, yellow crystal beads in seaweed pat-
    tern, gold trim top, white casing, polished pontil,
    c1870, marked "PATENT" **850.00**
8" h, blue ground, large pink, green, and white center
    coralene rose, Japanese **395.00**
8½" h, shades of green, green beading, gold tracery **350.00**

CORKSCREWS

History: The corkscrew is composed of three parts: handle, shaft, and worm or screw. The earliest known reference to "a Steele Worme used for drawing corks out of bottles" is 1681. Samuel Henshall, an Englishman, was granted the first patent in 1795.

Elaborate mechanisms were invented and patented from the early 1800s onward, especially in England. However, three basic types emerged: T handle (the most basic, simple form), lever, and mechanism. Variations on these three types run into the hundreds. Miniature corkscrews, employed for drawing corks from perfume and medicine bottles between 1750 and 1920, are among those most eagerly sought by collectors.

Corkscrew styles tend to reflect the preferences of specific nationalities. The English favored the helix worm and often copper-toned their steel products. By the mid-18th century English and Irish silversmiths were making handles noted for their clean lines and practicality. Most English silver handles were hallmarked.

The Germans preferred the center worm and nickel plate. The Italians used chrome plate or massive solid brass. In the early 1800s the Dutch and French developed elaborately artistic silver handles.

Americans did not begin to manufacture quality corkscrews until the late 19th century. They favored the center worm and specialized in silver-mounted tusks and carved staghorn for handles.

Reference: Fred O'Leary, *Corkscrews: 1000 Patented Ways to Open a Bottle,* Schiffer Publishing, 1996.

Collectors' Clubs: Canadian Corkscrew Collectors Club, 670 Meadow Wood Rd, Mississaugua, Ontario, L5J 2S6 Canada; Just For Openers, 3712 Sunningdale Way, Durham, NC 27707.

Pocket Type, metal holder, goes through ring to make handle, 3¼" l, $15.00.

Adv, Lemp Beer, St Louis, novelty type, brass, bullet
shape, 3" l, c1897 .... **95.00**
Bone Handle
    Mechanism type, English rack-and-pinion corkscrew,
    polished, brush and hanging ring, four plain post
    open barrel, narrow rack, long wire helix, side
    handle, sgd "Verinder" **410.00**
    T-handle, Henshall, incised button, helical worm,
    c1820 .... **125.00**
Brass Case, mechanism type, secondary wood swivel-
    jointed handle, brush, applied Royal supporters,
    marked "Thomson Patent Ne Plus Ultra" **300.00**
Bronzed Steel, lever, Heeley A1, double-lever patent,
    helical worm **65.00**
Cast Iron, clamp-on mechanism type, lacy openwork,
    emb "Phoenix," patented 1887 .... **200.00**
Celluloid, novelty type, figural mermaid, bends at waist,
    marked "Geschutz" **275.00**
Chrome, lever, zigzag design, French, 10½" l extended **65.00**
Ebony Handle, mechanism type, steel frame, foliate-
    scrolling raised arm, steel ciphered worm, marked
    "Champion, Made in USA" **110.00**
Ivory Handle, miniature, crescent shape, chromed
    turned steel shaft wire helix, c1790–1820 .... **75.00**
Palmette Handle, miniature, carved handle with MOP,
    helical worm **30.00**
Silver, novelty type, gaucho and horse, oblong platform
    handle, Archimedian screw **775.00**
Staghorn Handle, T-handle, ornate SS cap **100.00**
Wood, shaped and turned T-handle, ciphered center
    worm, bell and wire cutter, cap lifter, "Williamson"
    on shaft, marked "Pat 13 Dec 1898" **40.00**

COWAN POTTERY

History: R. Guy Cowan founded the Cowan Pottery in 1913 in
Cleveland, Ohio. The establishment remained in almost continuous operation until 1931, when financial difficulties forced closure.

Early production was redware pottery. Later a porcelainlike
finish was perfected with special emphasis placed on glazes, with
lustreware being one of the most common types. Commercial
wares marked "Lakeware" were produced from 1927 to 1931.

Marks: Early marks include an incised "Cowan Pottery" on the
redware (1913–1917), an impressed "Cowan," and an impressed
"Lakewood." The imprinted stylized semicircle, with or without
the initials "R. G.," came later.

References: Paul Evans, *Art Pottery of the United States,* Second
Edition, Feingold & Lewis Publishing Corp., 1987; Ralph and Terry
Kovel, *Kovels' American Art Pottery,* Crown Publishers, 1993; Tim
and Jamie Saloff, *The Collector's Encyclopedia of Cowan Pottery:
Identification and Values,* Collector Books, 1994.

Museums: Cowan Pottery Museum, Rocky River Public Library,
Rocky River, OH; Everson Museum of Art, Syracuse, NY.

Bookends, pr, polar bears eating fish, ivory glaze **225.00**
Bowl
    4 × 9" d, ivory glaze int., green glaze ext. **75.00**
    17" d, mint green glaze **75.00**

Bowl, orange luster, sea horse standard, 7⅞", stamped mark, $80.00.

Candleholders, pr, 3" h, ivory glaze **55.00**
Candlesticks, pr
    #681, ivory glaze **50.00**
    #782, ivory glaze **50.00**
Charger, 15½" d, low-relief mythical birds, yellow glaze,
    stamped "Cowan" **290.00**
Figure, Russian musicians and dancer, white crackled
    glaze, imp mark, some minor nicks, price for 4-pc set **3,000.00**
Flower Frog
    Nude Dancer, cream high glaze, imp logo and "66",
    11⅞" h **400.00**
    Scarf Dancer, #698, white gloss glaze **180.00**
Place-Card Holder, 3" h, cream glaze, imp mark **20.00**
Strawberry Jar, mint green glaze **75.00**
Tile, fish dec **100.00**
Vase
    7½" h, sea horse, ivory glaze **70.00**
    8½" h, 7" d, bulbous, short collar rim, emb creamy

blue squirrel, pheasant, and stork, gray-blue ground, imp mark 750.00

12" h, pillow, mythical figures, glossy royal blue crackle glaze 275.00

CRANBERRY GLASS

History: Cranberry glass is transparent and named for its color, achieved by adding powdered gold to a molten batch of amber glass and reheating at a low temperature to develop the cranberry or ruby color. The glass color first appeared in the last half of the 17th century but was not made in American glass factories until the last half of the 19th century.

Cranberry glass was blown, mold blown, or pressed. Examples often are decorated with gold or enamel. Less-expensive cranberry glass, made by substituting copper for gold, can be identified by its bluish purple tint.

Reference: William Heacock and William Gamble, *Encyclopedia of Victorian Colored Pattern Glass: Book 9, Cranberry Opalescent from A to Z,* Antique Publications, 1987.

> ## REPRODUCTION ALERT
>
> Reproductions abound. These pieces are heavier, off-color, and lack the quality of older examples.

Additional Listings: See specific categories, such as Bride's Baskets, Cruets, Jack-in-the-Pulpit Vases, etc.

Barber Bottle, Inverted Thumbprint pattern 270.00

Bottle

9¾" h, 3½" d, dainty white enameled flowers around middle, white enameled dots dec, clear teardrop stopper 175.00

10¼" h, 3¾" d, cut to clear, matching mushroom bubble stopper 250.00

Bride's Bowl, 9" sq, 3½" h, finely executed enameled apple blossom dec, fancy ornate SP orig holder marked "Middletown Silver Co," Mt Washington .. 950.00

Bowl, 5" d, Hobnail, ruffled edge, polished pontil, Hobbs Brockunier 45.00

Candlesticks, pr, 10⅝" h, heavily encrusted gold and polychrome dec 175.00

Claret Jug, 10¾" h, 4⅜" h, French emb pewter hinged top, foot, and handle 315.00

Cologne Bottle, 8⅝" h, 2⅜" d, gold scrolls, small gold flowers, matching sq cranberry bubble stopper 185.00

Creamer, rigaree feet 50.00

Cruet

6¼" h, 2¾" d, applied clear wafer foot, applied clear twisted rope handle with flower prunt at base, orig clear ribbed bubble stopper 125.00

10½" h, 3⅞" d, acid-cut herringbone double band around middle, applied clear foot, applied clear handle, clear cut faceted stopper 175.00

10¾" h, 4¾" d, applied clear wafer foot, applied spun rope handle with clear flower prunt at base, orig clear flattened bulbous ribbed bubble stopper .. 210.00

12¼" h, 4¾" d, gold scrolls and basket of flowers, applied crystal patterned foot, applied clear handle, clear bubble stopper 225.00

Cup and Saucer, 2¼" h, 3⅛" d, 5" d saucer, gold scallops at top, heavy gold flowers and foliage 245.00

Decanter, 11½" h, 3⅞" d, bulbous base, pinched-in sides, lacy gold enamel dec, dark red flowers, gold enameled centers, applied clear handle, clear cut faceted stopper 235.00

Epergne, 21" h, 16" d, center flower vase, two candleholders supported with clear glass branches, cut and etched leaf and berry design, cranberry prism drops, Victorian 575.00

Fairy Lamp, 4½" d, applied clear hand-tooled petals, clear insert marked "Clarke" 350.00

Lamp

Hall, 33" h, 10" d, ribbed ball shade, red brass frame, electrified 250.00

Peg, 20½" h, 4" d, plain cranberry font, orig brass burner, cranberry ruffled shade with emb beaded swirl design, acid-cut stippled panels, brass candlestick 345.00

Lamp Font, 5⅝" h, 3⅜" d, peg type, dainty white enameled flowers, gold dot enameled center band, orig brass burner 100.00

Mantel Lusters, pr, prisms 550.00

Mug, 4" h, 2¼" d, Baby Inverted Thumbprint pattern, applied clear handle and pedestal foot 60.00

Music Box, 12¼" h × 5¼" d decanter, emb ribs with etched leaves and stars, orig clear cut bubble stopper, not working 310.00

Night-Light, 6¼" h, 3¼" d, cranberry shade with white sanded scallops, grapes, and leaves, openwork brass top rim, gold-washed ormolu ftd frame 275.00

Pitcher

10" h, 5" d, bulbous, ice bladder, applied clear handle 235.00

11" h, 5¼" d, tankard, SP collar, hinged top, applied clear handle 275.00

Rose Bowl, Optic pattern

3¾" h, 3¾" d, worn gold rim, six-crimp top 90.00

4¼" h, 4⅜" d, six-crimp top 95.00

5⅛" h, 5¼" d 110.00

Water Bottle, blown, reverse ribbing, c1880, 6¼" h, $160.00.

Smoke Bell, 6½" d, swirled, ruffled edge 600.00
Spooner, Paneled Sprig 120.00
Sugar Bowl, cov, 6⅛" h, 4" d, applied clear wafer foot,
    applied clear ribbed bubble finial, belltone 120.00
Sugar Shaker
    Inverted Thumbprint, nine panels 145.00
    Optic Pattern, orig top 225.00
Tumbler, 4¼" h, 2¾" d, acid-cut band at top, rose sprays   65.00
Vase
    5⅞" h, 3" d, white sanded enameled scallops at top
        and base, center sanded white enameled Roman
        Key design, gold trim, ormolu feet, price for pr .. 255.00
    8" h, bud, bulbous base, flared top, white stripes ... 95.00
    9⅜" h, 3½" d, white enameled daisies and leaves,
        price for facing pr 265.00
Wine, 4½" h, etched bowl, clear stem and foot 35.00

Syrup Pitcher, melon shape, pale lemon ground, Queen's type, raised enamel dots, SP lid and handle, 3¼" d, 5½" h, $1,250.00.

CROWN MILANO

History: Crown Milano is an American art glass produced by the Mt. Washington Glass Works, New Bedford, Massachusetts. The original patent was issued in 1886 to Frederick Shirley and Albert Steffin.

Normally, it is an opaque-white satin glass finished with light-beige or ivory-colored ground embellished with fancy florals, decorations, and elaborate and thick raised gold.

Marks: Marked pieces have a purple enamel entwined "CM" with a crown on the base. Sometimes paper labels were used. Since both Mount Washington and Pairpoint supplied mountings, the silver-plated mounts often have "MW" impressed or a Pairpoint mark.

Advisors: Clarence and Betty Maier.

Atomizer, 6½" h, trumpet vine dec, swirled body 595.00
Biscuit Jar
    6" h, 7" d, pink and cream roses, raised gold outlines,
        pale green ground, marked "520," sgd 1,175.00
    9" h, 7½" d, colonial boy and girl blowing bubbles,
        flowers on reverse, gold outlines 975.00
Bowl, 10" d, 4¼" h, heavy walls, squared and crimped
    top rim, coppery and gilt enamel oak leaf and acorn
    dec, ivory satin ground, marked "300," worn gold
    rim 175.00
Ewer, 12" h, opaque white ground, freeform clusters in
    pastel enamels, raised gold swirled stripes 1,350.00
Salt and Pepper Shakers, pr, 3" h, blue and white flowers,
    coral-colored stripes, Lobe Four pattern, metal tops   225.00
Salt Shaker
    2½" h, hp hen 350.00
    4" h, blue and white daisies, ribbed 185.00
Sugar Shaker, 3" h, 4" d, pink to cream shades, blue and
    white blossoms, melon ribbed, two-part metal collar
    and lid embossed with butterfly, dragonfly, and blos-
    soms, ... 585.00
Sweetmeat Jar, cov, 5" h, ivory, deeper-colored ribs,
    worn enameled floral design, SP fittings and lid, sgd
    "M.W." 550.00

CRUETS

History: Cruets are small glass bottles used on the table and holding condiments such as oil, vinegar, and wine. The pinnacle of cruet use occurred during the Victorian era when a myriad of glass manufacturers made cruets in a wide assortment of patterns, colors, and sizes. All cruets had stoppers; most had handles.

References: Elaine Ezell and George Newhouse, *Cruets, Cruets, Cruets,* Volume I, Antique Publications, 1991; William Heacock, *Encyclopedia of Victorian Colored Pattern Glass: Book 6, Oil Cruets from A to Z,* Antique Publications, 1981.

Additional Listings: Pattern Glass and specific glass categories such as Amberina, Cranberry, and Satin.

6" h, ruby cut to clear, oval neck panels, notched cut in
    spout, 16-pointed star cut into base, orig faceted stop-
    per, clear glass handle 390.00
6¾" h, Bluerina, vivid blue neck and spout, amber body,
    Optic Thumbprint pattern, clear faceted stopper,
    ribbed handle 385.00
7" h, 3½" d, lime green, bulbous, small white enameled
    flowers, rust centers, gold leaves, applied green han-
    dle, orig green bubble stopper 120.00
7¼" h, 3⅛" d, golden amber, amber handle, amber cut
    faceted stopper 125.00
8½" h
    2¾" d, orange, lacy white enameled daisies, cream
        centers, fine optic patterning, applied clear han-
        dle, orig clear stopper 140.00
    3" d, light sapphire blue, white enameled flowers and
        foliage, yellow centers, gold grim, applied amber
        handle, amber ball stopper 175.00
8⅝" h, 3⅝" d, golden amber, emb bands, dainty white,
    green, pink, yellow, and blue enameled flowers and
    foliage, two small insects, applied amber handle,
    matching amber bubble stopper with enameled
    leaves 175.00
8¾" h, 3½" d, spatter glass, white spatter on blue ground,
    applied clear handle, clear heart-shaped stopper ... 135.00
9" h
    3½" d, lime green, small white enameled flowers,
        gold-colored centers, green leaves, applied green
        handle, orig green ball stopper 120.00
    4" d, sapphire blue, bulbous, round top, enameled
        lavender flowers, green leaves, gold trim, applied
        clear handle, clear bubble stopper 175.00

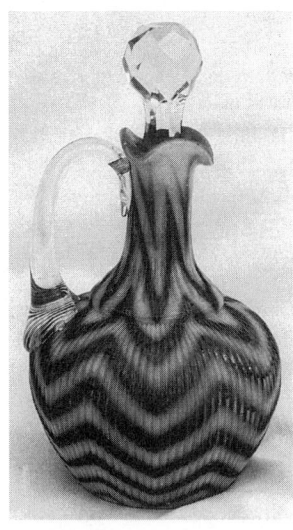

Opalescent Herringbone, cranberry, clear faceted stopper, Hobbs, Brockunier & Co, $350.00.

9½" h, 3" d, Optic pattern, Mary Gregory type white enameled young boy, three-petal top, amber applied handle, orig amber bubble stopper **250.00**

9¾" h, 3⅛" d, lime green, dainty pink enameled floral sprays, gold bird in flight, applied green handle, orig green bubble stopper **100.00**

10" h, 3¾" d, frosted pale blue, pink, white, and lavender enameled flowers, green foliage, small salmon pink branches and flowers, applied clear handle, clear cut faceted stopper **135.00**

10½" h, 4¼" d, amber, Inverted Thumbprint pattern, encased in emb French pewter frame, mask heads on side, lacy openwork, bird's head on handle, orig amber bubble stopper encased in pewter **215.00**

12" h, 5" d, amber glass, encased in emb French pewter frame, bird's head around foot, mask face on sides and ram's head, woman's head on handle, orig pewter stopper **275.00**

12¼" h, 4¾" d, cranberry, gold scrolls and basket of flowers, applied crystal patterned foot, applied crystal handle, clear bubble stopper **215.00**

CUP PLATES

History: Many early cups were handleless and came with deep saucers. The hot liquid was poured into the saucer and sipped from it. This necessitated another plate for the cup, hence the "cup plate."

The first cup plates made of pottery were of the Staffordshire variety. From the mid-1830s to 1840s, glass cup plates were favored. The Boston and Sandwich Glass Company was one of the main manufacturers of the lacy glass type.

References: Ruth Webb Lee and James H. Rose, *American Glass Cup Plates,* published by author, 1948, Charles E. Tuttle Co. reprint, 1985; Kenneth Wilson, *American Glass 1760–1930,* 2 vols., Hudson Hills Press and The Toledo Museum of Art, 1994.

Collectors' Club: Pairpoint Cup Plate Collectors of America, PO Box 890052, East Weymouth, MA 02189.

Notes: It is extremely difficult to find glass cup plates in outstanding (mint) condition. Collectors expect some signs of use, such as slight rim roughness, minor chipping (best if under the rim), and, in rarer patterns, portions of scallops missing.

The numbers used are from the Lee-Rose book in which all plates are illustrated.

Prices are based on plates in average condition.

Glass

LR 1, clear, flint, polished pontil **30.00**
LR 36, opal opaque, 17 even scallops **475.00**
LR 46, lavender, 15 even scallops **125.00**
LR 70, plain rope, Midwest origin **125.00**
LR 82, acorn and leaves, silver opaque blue, fiery opalescent **575.00**
LR 95, opal opaque, 10 sided, rope top and bottom ... **175.00**
LR 135, 24 bull's-eyes, Midwest origin **75.00**
LR 163, light green, 34 scallops, Midwest origin **65.00**
LR 179, lavender, 10 scallops, rope top and bottom, Philadelphia origin **135.00**
LR 197-E **65.00**
LR 200, 96 sawtooth scallops, Midwest orig **40.00**
LR 216-C **35.00**
LR 257 .... **35.00**
LR 271 .... **30.00**
LR 272, 43 scallops **65.00**
LR 299 .... **15.00**
LR 311 .... **15.00**
LR 323, opalescent **75.00**
LR 332-B **30.00**
LR 343-B **45.00**
LR 391 .... **15.00**
LR 395 .... **15.00**
LR 396 .... **12.50**
LR 399 .... **119.00**
LR 412, 10 sided, Sandwich origin **100.00**
LR 416 .... **20.00**
LR 439-C **40.00**
LR 440-B **35.00**
LR 455, 48 even scallops, Sandwich origin **275.00**
LR 456 .... **40.00**
LR 458-A **15.00**
LR 465-F **15.00**
LR 477 .... **15.00**
LR 479 .... **25.00**
LR 500 .... **65.00**
LR 503 .... **15.00**
LR 522, amber, flint **375.00**
LR 538 .... **15.00**
LR 547 .... **15.00**
LR 561-A, octagonal, clear, gray striations, Washington, tilted head, Midwest origin **4,000.00**
LR 565-A **30.00**
LR 575 .... **65.00**

Glass, Historical

LR 576, medium blue, Sandwich origin **95.00**
LR 605-A, octagonal, ship **95.00**

LR 619	175.00
LR 653, eagle, laurel wreath	165.00
LR 658, emerald green, Boston & Sandwich origin, two tiny scallops missing	4,250.00
LR 670	65.00
LR 676, 60 even scallops, Curling's Ft Pitt Glass Works	75.00
LR 677-A	40.00
LR 836, Geo. Peabody, Heart & Crown, 4¾" d	85.00
LR 888	25.00

Porcelain or Pottery

Leeds, raised polychrome floral dec, 3⅜" d	55.00
Ridgway	
Blind Boy pattern, scene of boy and mother seated on bench, floral border, medium blue transfer, c1830, 4¼" d	80.00
India Temple pattern, blue, emb white border, 3⅞" d	50.00
Staffordshire	
American Eagle with Shield pattern, paneled sides, medium blue and white, 3¾" d	385.00
Asian landscape scene, imp "Opaque Granite China, W. R. & Co.," light blue and white, 4" d, light stain	20.00
Basket of Flowers, imp "Adams," dark blue transfer, 4" d	155.00
Ben Franklin, boy with kite, blue and white, 3½" d	110.00
Bosphorous pattern, marked "T Mayer," c1840, light blue and white, 4" d	45.00
Boy with hoop, blue and white, 3½" d	90.00
Center fruit cluster with bird, flowers, and scroll border, c1830, dark blue transfer, 4¼" d	125.00
Cottage in woods scene, spearhead and trefoil border, marked "Clews," 3⅝" d	125.00
Parisian Chateau, marked "R. Hall & Son," 1840, black and white, 3¾" d	45.00
Recumbent sheep, floral border, Stevenson Wild Rose series, c1830, dark blue, 3¾" d	155.00
Shells, imp "Stubbs," c1830, dark blue transfer, 4" d	250.00
William Penn's Treaty, Thomas Goodwin, 1830–40, brown and white, 3¾" d	100.00
Woodlands Near Philadelphia, Joseph Stubbs and Stubbs & Kent, 1790–1831, blue and white, 3¾" d, price for pair	500.00

Porcelain, Adams, Hudson River, Fairmount, brown transfer, imp mark, 4" d, $85.00.

CUSTARD GLASS

History: Custard glass was developed in England in the early 1880s. Harry Northwood made the first American custard glass at his Indiana, Pennsylvania, factory in 1898.

From 1898 until 1915, many manufacturers produced custard glass patterns, e.g., Dugan Glass, Fenton, A. H. Heisey Glass Co., Jefferson Glass, Northwood, Tarentum Glass, and U.S. Glass. Cambridge and McKee continued the production of custard glass into the Depression.

The ivory or creamy yellow custard color is achieved by adding uranium salts to the molten hot glass. The chemical content makes the glass glow when held under a black light. The more uranium, the more luminous the color. Northwood's custard glass has the smallest amount of uranium, creating an ivory color; Heisey used more, creating a deep yellow color.

Custard glass was made in patterned tableware pieces. It also was made as souvenir items and novelty pieces. Souvenir pieces are include a place name or hand-painted decorations, e.g., flowers. Patterns of custard glass often were highlighted in gold, enameled colors, and stains.

References: Gary E. Baker et al., *Wheeling Glass 1829–1939*, Oglebay Institute, 1994, distributed by Antique Publications; William Heacock, *Encyclopedia of Victorian Colored Pattern Glass, Book IV: Custard Glass from A to Z*, Peacock Publications, 1980; William Heacock, James Measell and Berry Wiggins, *Harry Northwood: The Early Years 1881–1900,* Antique Publications, 1990.

REPRODUCTION ALERT

L. G. Wright Glass Co. has reproduced pieces in the Argonaut Shell and Grape and Cable patterns. It also introduced new patterns, such as Floral and Grape and Vintage Band. Moser reproduced toothpicks in Argonaut Shell, Chrysanthemum Sprig, and Inverted Fan & Feather.

Additional Listings: Pattern Glass.

Banana Boat, Geneva, green dec	125.00
Berry, master	
Argonaut Shell, 10½" l	145.00
Beaded Circle	185.00
Chrysanthemum Sprig	150.00
Grape and Cable, 7½" d, ruffled edge	50.00
Louis XV	115.00
Berry Set, master berry, six sauces, price for 7-pc set	
Chrysanthemum Sprig, blue	1,195.00
Everglades	750.00
Grape and Gothic Arches	475.00
Victoria	650.00
Butter Dish, cov	
Argonaut Shell	250.00
Chrysanthemum Sprig, blue	795.00
Geneva, red and green dec	150.00
Intaglio	220.00
Maple Leaf	200.00
Winged Scroll	175.00

Berry Bowl, Beaded Swag pattern, Heisey, 4³⁄₈", $50.00.

Condiment Tray, Chrysanthemum Sprig	425.00
Creamer	
Argonaut Shell, dec	145.00
Beaded Circle, 4½" h, Northwood, slight gold loss	350.00
Louis XV	75.00
Maple Leaf	125.00
Ring and Beads	35.00
Victoria, Tarentum	125.00
Winged Scroll	100.00
Cruet, orig stopper	
Argonaut Shell, gold trim	885.00
Beaded Circle, 6½" h, Northwood, slight gold loss	1,250.00
Chrysanthemum Sprig, gold trim	985.00
Wild Bouquet	525.00
Dresser Tray, Northwood Grape	225.00
Goblet	
Beaded Swag	65.00
Grape and Gothic Arches	55.00
Jelly Compote	
Geneva	100.00
Maple Leaf	375.00
Ring Band	175.00
Pitcher, water	
Beaded Circle	425.00
Cherry and Scale	350.00
Chrysanthemum Sprig	275.00
Diamond with Peg	250.00
Inverted Fan and Feather	400.00
Vermont	250.00
Salt Shaker, single	
Carnelian	225.00
Fluted Scrolls	65.00
Heart	95.00
Punty Band, souvenir	45.00
Sauce	
Argonaut Shell	65.00
Delaware, rose stain	65.00
Fan	70.00
Peacock and Urn	45.00
Spooner	
Argonaut Shell	125.00
Beaded Circle, 4¼" h, Northwood, slight gold loss	350.00
Chrysanthemum Sprig	125.00
Louis XV	65.00

Winged Scroll	100.00
Sugar, breakfast, Georgia Gem	45.00
Sugar, cov	
Beaded Circle, 6¾" h, slight gold loss	485.00
Diamond with Peg	100.00
Jefferson	150.00
Winged Scroll	165.00
Sugar, open, Chrysanthemum Sprig, blue, gold trim, script sgd	125.00
Table Set, cov butter, creamer, spooner, cov sugar	
Carnelian	850.00
Geneva	550.00
Louis XV, gold trim	500.00
Ring Band	550.00
Toothpick Holder	
Georgia Gem, souvenir	35.00
Harvard	40.00
Ivorina Verde	85.00
Washington	120.00
Wild Bouquet, blue trim, enameled dec	90.00
Tumbler	
Beaded Circle, 4", slight gold loss	300.00
Fluted Scrolls	40.00
Geneva, dec	38.00
Intaglio, green trim	40.00
Punty Band, souvenir	40.00
Vase, Grape Arbor	85.00
Whiskey, Diamond Peg, souvenir	45.00
Wine	
Punty Band	50.00
Tiny Thumbprint	50.00

CUT GLASS, AMERICAN

History: Glass is cut by grinding decorations into the glass by means of abrasive-carrying metal or stone wheels. A very ancient craft, it was revived in 1600 by Bohemians and spread through Europe to Great Britain and America.

American cut glass came of age at the Centennial Exposition in 1876 and the World Columbian Exposition in 1893. The American public recognized American cut glass to be exceptional in quality and workmanship. America's most significant output of this high-quality glass occurred from 1880 to 1917, a period now known as the Brilliant Period.

Marks: Around 1890 some companies began adding an acid-etched "signature" to their glass. This signature may be the actual company name, its logo, or a chosen symbol. Today, signed pieces command a premium over unsigned pieces since the signature clearly establishes the origin. However, signatures should be carefully verified for authenticity since objects with forged signatures have been in existence for some time. One way to check is to run a finger tip or fingernail lightly over the signature area. As a general rule, a genuine signature cannot be felt; a forged signature has a raised surface.

Many companies never used the acid-etched signature on their glass and may or may not have affixed paper labels to the items originally. Dorflinger Glass and the Meriden Glass Co. made cut glass of the highest quality, yet never used an acid-etched signature. Furthermore, cut glass made before the 1890s was not signed. Many of these wood-polished items, cut on blown blanks, were of excellent quality and often won awards at exhibitions.

References: Bill and Louis Boggess, *Identifying American Brilliant Cut Glass,* Third Edition, Schiffer Publishing, 1996; ——, *Reflections on American Brilliant Cut Glass,* Schiffer Publishing, 1995; Jo Evers, *Evers' Standard Cut Glass Value Guide,* Collector Books, 1975, 1995 value update; Bob Page and Dale Fredericksen, *A Collection of American Crystal,* Page-Fredericksen Publishing, 1995; ——, *Seneca Glass Company 1891–1983,* Page-Fredericksen Publishing, 1995; J. Michael Pearson, *Encyclopedia of American Cut & Engraved Glass,* Vols. I to III, published by author, 1975; Albert C. Revi, *American Cut & Engraved Glass,* Schiffer Publishing, 1965; Martha Louise Swan, *American Cut and Engraved Glass,* Wallace-Homestead, 1986, 1994 value update; Kenneth Wilson, *American Glass 1760–1930,* 2 vols., Hudson Hills Press and The Toledo Museum of Art, 1994.

Collectors' Club: American Cut Glass Assoc, PO Box 482, Ramona, CA 92065.

Museums: Corning Museum of Glass, Corning, NY; High Museum of Art, Atlanta, GA; Huntington Galleries, Huntington, WV; Lightner Museum, St. Augustine, FL; Toledo Museum Of Art, Toledo, OH.

REPRODUCTION ALERT

How New Is My Glass?—A Test

Reproduction glass contains up to ten times more sodium than early glass. Since sodium attracts moisture, many new reproduction glass pieces develop a film or coating resulting from airborne dust particles dissolving in the surface water of the glass. When you rub your finger across the glass, you create a greasy looking streak.

The test is not foolproof. Use it in conjunction with other testing criteria such as pattern detail, proper dimensions, correct shape, form, and decorative motif, and expected signs of wear.

Banana Bowl, Hunt's Royal **550.00**
Basket,
    5½ × 8″ h, Berlyn pattern, Quaker City Glass Co, applied twisted handle, three-step pedestal base   **375.00**
    8 × 11¾″, Panel pattern, hobstars and elongated vesicae, flaring scalloped and serrated rim, pointed overall notched handle, sgd "Hawkes" **5,000.00**
Berry Bowl, American Brilliant Period
  8″ d
    Elaborate star cutting **125.00**
    Pinwheel cut, ftd, scalloped edge **250.00**
    Three pinwheel reserves **165.00**
    8 × 3¾″ h, geometric stars, floral scalloped edge .. **80.00**
    9″ d, hobstar and fan cut, rim chip, Hawkes **210.00**
    9½″ d, well cut, sgd "Fry" **325.00**
Bowl
  8″ d
    Marseilles pattern, hobstar and star **225.00**

    Pinwheel, fan and notched prism, star-cut base, scalloped and serrated rim **125.00**
    Royal pattern, Russian pattern sides, hobstar button, pentagonal strawberry diamond lozenge and large hobstars, sgd "Hunt" **325.00**
  9″ d
    Adonis pattern, cane, fan, hobstar, and strawberry diamond, sgd "Clark" **245.00**
    Colonna pattern, hobstar, cross-cut diamond, star, and fan, sgd "Libbey" **225.00**
  9¾″ d, Myrtle pattern, Pairpoint **450.00**
  10″ d
    Iris, ftd, Hawkes **675.00**
    Jubilee pattern, Dorflinger **450.00**
Box, cov, C F Monroe, American Brilliant Period
  3¾″ d, #1 .... **410.00**
  6″ d, #2 .... **580.00**
  8″ d, #3, swivel mirror in lid **1,030.00**
Bridge Set, Whist, Huntley, price for 4-pc set **525.00**
Butter Dish, cov
  4¾″ h, dome, hobstars and rayed fluted panels, faceted knob, matching 8″ d tray, scalloped cup rim, sgd "Hawkes" **300.00**
  7½″ d underplate, hobstars and florals, domed lid .. **220.00**
Butter Tub, diamond and fan cutting, cov **225.00**
Cake Plate, 10″ d, Nassau, J Hoare, peg ftd **375.00**
Calling Card Receiver, 8½″ l, intaglio floral and leaf motifs, scalloped rim, sgd "Tuthill" **200.00**
Candlestick
  8″ h, bull's-eyes, knobbed stem, Cutting No. 126, Meriden Cut Glass **250.00**
  11″ h, amber, baluster form, hollow stem, engraved vintage pattern on stem and base **100.00**
  14″ h, blown hollow teardrop stem, star-cut bases, Hawkes trademark, price for pr **475.00**
Candy Dish, divided, 8″ d, intaglio floral, twin handles   **85.00**
Carafe
  7″ h, notched fluted neck, bulbous body, hobstars and cross-cut diamonds **115.00**
  8½″ h, 6¼″ d rayed base, Pineapple and Fan pattern, cross-cut diamond and fan, notched eight-panel neck, horizontal cutting **120.00**
Celery Tray
  10 × 5″, geometric and floral cutting **65.00**
  11 × 5″, geometric cutting **70.00**
Chalice, 12″ h, green and yellow cut to clear **2,250.00**
Champagne, Monarch pattern variant, Hoare **50.00**
Cheese Dish, cov
  5½″ h, chain of hobstars, arcadia cross hatches, notched prisms, faceted star knob, 8″ d, scalloped rim underplate **450.00**
  9″ d underplate, Harvard pattern, 24-point hobstar . **750.00**
Cigar Jar, cov, Havana pattern, Maple City, one sgd, price for matched pr **1,950.00**
Clock
  5½″ h, Colis, Pairpoint **395.00**
  7½″ h, pinwheel **375.00**
Cologne Bottle, 6½″ h, bulbous, allover cross-cut diamonds, fluted neck, flanked rim, facet-cut bulb stopper **125.00**
Compote, cranberry to clear, fan, hobstars, and diamond point cutting, price for pr **1,250.00**

Nappy, Royal pattern, Hunt Glass Co, 6″ d, 1½″ h, $125.00.

Condiment Set, two 5⅜″ h shakers with silver caps, two 6⅛″ h cruets with orig glass stoppers, two 5¼″ h cruets with orig glass stoppers, 3⅝″ open mustard, strawberry diamonds and ringed steps cutting, orig silver stand with ornate handle in form of the seal of the United States holding banner with motto ''E Pluribus Unum'' standing on round shield with 16 small stars surrounding large star, two silver shaker caps hallmarked initials ''I M,'' Pittsburgh, c1803, chips, price for 7-pc set 2,925.00

Creamer and Sugar, American Brilliant Period
    4½″ h, diamond point cutting, notched prism handles, pedestal base 325.00
    5¾″ h, hobstar, faceted knobbed pedestal base, Hawkes trademark, minor pattern roughness 550.00

Decanter
    11½″ h, Elmira Cut 33, double gooseneck, notched handle, matching stopper 895.00
    12½″ h, Kimberley, Libbey, double gooseneck, matching stopper 875.00

Dish, 8½″ l, oval, cut grapes, American Brilliant Period cut collar border, sgd ''Tuthill'' 300.00

Dresser Box, 10 × 7″, oval, Sheraton pattern, engraved medallions, triple miter-cut bands alternating with strawberry diamond bands, sgd ''Hawkes'' 225.00

Fernery, 7½″ d, pinwheels, fans, vesicae with Harvard variant, ftd 90.00

Flask, 5¾″ l, strawberry-diamond and star design, SS lid marked ''Unger Bros'' 525.00

Fruit Bowl
    10″ d, green cut to clear, pinwheel reserves, American Brilliant Period, tooth chips 1,000.00
    11½″ l, oval, scalloped rim, star and pinwheel cut, American Brilliant Period 150.00

Goblet
    Diamond, St Louis, price for 6-pc set 375.00
    Silva, price for 4-pc set 165.00

Horseradish Jar, cov, Pinwheel and Thumbprint pattern, orig stopper, American Brilliant Period 135.00

Humidor, 8½″ h, notched prisms, large hobstar lid 425.00

Ice Cream Tray, 14 x 7½″, allover Harvard, canoe shape 150.00

Ice Pail, 7″ d, fan and hobstars, American Brilliant Period, c1900, slight chips 200.00

Lamp
    Boudoir, Russian 575.00
    Table, mushroom shade, 20″ h, 11″ d, 28 prisms, Pairpoint, new wiring 3,650.00

Lemonade Pitcher, 13½″ h, wheel-cut and polished clover and fern design on body, SS spout with Art Nouveau border, Tiffany, early 20th C 1,495.00

Loving Cup, 8½″ h, hobstars, fans, and strawberry diamonds, hobstar base 3,250.00

Mayonnaise Bowl, 6¾″ d bowl, matching 7½″ d underplate, hobstars, hobnail and cross-hatches, scalloped serrated rims 350.00

Mint Tray, 6″ d, hobstars and nailhead, sawtooth and scalloped edge 120.00

Nappy, 8″ d, Iris, Hawkes 225.00

Orange Bowl, 8″ d, Rayed Points pattern 245.00

Perfume Bottle, 4″ l, curved, orig int. stopper, ornate SS top 115.00

Powder Box, cov, 4″ d, SS lid, repoussé design of maiden 150.00

Primrose Bowl, 9½″ × 4¼″, Tuthill 950.00

Punch Bowl, 14 × 13″, two part, hobstars, cane, vesicae, and fans, scalloped serrated rim and bases sgd with star in circle 1,400.00

Punch Cup, Russian pattern, hobstar foot 75.00

Rose Globe, 7½″ w, 5″ h, Cornucopia pattern, Bergen . 2,400.00

Salt, master, 3″ d, global, hobstars and crosshatches, sgd ''Hawkes'' 250.00

Smoking Set, two lidded 4″ h, cigar boxes, two ashtrays, ormolu mounts, price for set 175.00

Tankard Pitcher, 11″ h, bands of Harvard at rim and base, prism and step cuttings, fluted spout, serrated rim, double-notched handle 175.00

Tumbler, Hindoo pattern, sgd ''Hoare,'' $55.00.

Tray
    9″ d, scalloped, thumbprints, vesica, 16-pointed star 155.00
    11½″ d, octagonal, turned-up rim, chain of hobstars, center pinwheels and cane encircling hobstar, scalloped sawtooth edge 425.00

14″ l, rect, hobstars, fans, and wedges of hobnails, scalloped serrated rim, few polished teeth **165.00**

Vase

5½″ h, corset shape, Libbey, Zenobia mason mark . **475.00**

10″ h, chain of hobstars ring top and bottom, alternating columns of bull's-eyes and horizontal cut areas, Hawkes **200.00**

11½″ h, 9½″ d, SS rim, Quaker City **1,495.00**

12⅛″ h, paneled baluster body, wheel-cut floral dec, International SS top with everted rim, early 20th C **1,495.00**

16″ h, corset shape, Chain of Hobstars **875.00**

Water Pitcher, 10″ h, elaborate cutting, American Brilliant Period **160.00**

Water Set, 11″ h pitcher, four 6¼″ h, goblets, hobstar and cane cutting, American Brilliant Period, price for 5-pc set **265.00**

Wine, 6¾″ h, cranberry cut to clear, allover diamond design, tapered bowl **100.00**

CUT VELVET

History: Several glass manufacturers made cut velvet during the late Victorian era, c1870–1900. An outer layer of pastel color was applied over a white casing. The piece then was molded or cut in a high-relief ribbed or diamond shape, exposing portions of the casing. The finish had a satin velvety feel, hence the name "cut velvet."

Bottle, 8″ h, ribbed, shaded blue, white lining **175.00**

Bowl, 6″ d, 4¼″ h, shiny, pink, applied crystal rim and feet **250.00**

Celery Vase, 6½″ h, Diamond Quilted pattern body, deep blue over white, box-pleated top **725.00**

Creamer, 3½″ h, bulbous, blue, Diamond Quilted pattern, applied white satin glass handle **235.00**

Cruet, 6″ h, shiny pink, Diamond Quilted pattern body, clear faceted stopper, clear handle **685.00**

Pitcher, 8½″ h, pink, sq mouth, frosted reeded twisted handle, rosettes, and neck ring **425.00**

Tumbler, 3¾″ h, medium pink, lighter pink striping, ribbed **85.00**

Vase

4⅞″ h, 2¾″ d, stick, blue overlay, white lining, embossed ribs, lighter color between ribs **110.00**

6⅛″ h, 3⅛″ d, stick, blue overlay, white lining, prominent quilting with lighter centers to diamonds .. **125.00**

13½″ h, double gourd, long neck, pale gold, Diamond Quilted pattern **650.00**

CZECHOSLOVAKIAN ITEMS

History: Objects marked "Made in Czechoslovakia" were produced after 1918 when the country claimed its independence from the Austro-Hungarian Empire. The people became more cosmopolitan and liberated and expanded the scope of their lives. Their porcelains, pottery, and glassware reflect many influences.

Marks: A specific manufacturer's mark may include a date which precedes 1918, but this only indicates the factory existed during the years of the Bohemian or Austro-Hungarian Empire.

References: Dale and Diane Barta and Helen M. Rose, *Czechoslovakian Glass & Collectibles* (1992), Book II (1996) Collector Books; *Bohemian Glass,* n.d., distributed by Antique Publications; Ruth A. Forsythe, *Made in Czechoslovakia,* Antique Publications, 1993; Jacquelyne Y. Jones-North, *Czechoslovakian Perfume Bottles and Boudoir Accessories,* Antique Publications, 1990.

Periodical: *New Glass Review,* Bardounova 2140 149 00 Praha 4, Prague, Czech Republic.

Collectors' Club: Czechoslovakian Collectors Guild International, PO Box 901395, Kansas City, MO 64190.

Museum: Friends of the Glass Museum of Novy Bor, Kensington, MD.

Bowl, 9″ d, scalloped rim, irid gold, marked, c1925 ... **150.00**

Box, cov, 4″ h, rect, ruby red faceted glass body, brass mounts, marked "Made in Czechoslovakia," c1920 **275.00**

Candlesticks, pr, 7½″ h, red and black **55.00**

Candy Dish, multicolored spatter, black feet **45.00**

Compote, 7½″ d, 5¾″ h, art glass, bright orange cased to colorless glass, pulled black stripes, wafer, and rim rap, attributed to Michael Powolny **415.00**

Creamer, gold luster ext., black handles and trim, marked "Czechoslovakia" **15.00**

Figure, 3½″ h, girl with basket **25.00**

Gravy Boat, 10⅛″ l, 5¼″ h, silver, attached trays, Colonial Revival style, triple-ribbed rim detail, hallmarked, 800 fine, 41 troy oz, price for pr **635.00**

Jardiniere, 4½″ h, cameo, white cased to colorless, maroon and pink layers, acid-etched grape vines and clusters, partial oval mark on base "Czecho Slovakia" **260.00**

Lamp

Basket, 10½″ h, colorful faceted fruit and flower-form beads form lampshade, basket frame, electrical base imp "Made in Czechoslovakia" **525.00**

Boudoir, orange and yellow spatter shade **125.00**

Desk, two figural Scottie dogs, geometric multicolored spatter-glass globe **265.00**

Table, Art Deco lady, legs up supporting green spatter-glass globe, restored **550.00**

Lemonade Set, 10″ h pitcher, two matching tumblers, sapphire blue, green, and aubergine ground, sapphire blue threaded shoulder, blue ribbed handles, sgd, c1930, price for 3-pc set **245.00**

Plate, porcelain, white ground, floral dec, bird center, marked "Epiag," Royal, 10″ d, $25.00.

Perfume Bottle, black base, etched lady design, orig
clear stopper **95.00**
Pin Dish, Pierrot, black and white **80.00**
Pitcher, 6¾" h, hp, black trim, yellow, orange, and blue
flowers **60.00**
Plate, sq, green border, floral dec **37.50**
Scent Bottle, amber, 1" h, paneled cut glass, SS hinged
emb lid **195.00**
Vase
    5"h , white pearlescent vase hugged by angel, holly,
    berries, and star **25.00**
    10" h, black, Art Deco form **50.00**
    10½" h, applied handles, paper label, additional orig
    NY store label **225.00**
    12" h, porcelain, floral dec, gold handles **95.00**

DAVENPORT

History: John Davenport opened a pottery in Longport, Staffordshire, England, in 1793. His high-quality light-weight wares are
cream colored with a beautiful velvety texture.

The firm's output included soft-paste (Old Blue) products, lus-
ter-trimmed pieces, and pink luster wares with black transfer.
Pieces of Gaudy Dutch and Spatterware also have been found
with the Davenport mark. Later Davenport became a leading
maker of ironstone and early flow blue. His famous Cyprus pattern
in mulberry became very popular. His heirs continued the business until the factory closed in 1886.

Biscuit Jar, cov, 6½" h, Imari-style dec, SP cov and bail
handle, c1870 .... **150.00**
Bowl, red flowers, green leaves, c1840 .... **45.00**
Compote, 9" h, hp, pink flowers, gold trim, c1830 .... **90.00**
Cup and Saucer, Clifford pattern, gold trim, green wreath
mark **60.00**

Pitcher, 6" h, serpent handle, tan, transfer crack marks, $75.00.

Cup Plate, Friburg pattern **25.00**
Dessert Service, multicolored floral sprays, scroll sur-
rounds, gilt stylized foliage on green border, puce
printed mark, c1850, price for twenty-pc set **1,200.00**
Ewer, 9" h, multicolored, lower dec, c1830 .... **175.00**
Gravy Boat, blue and white flowers **85.00**
Plate, 9" d, maroon and gold border, gold medallion
center, marked "Davenport", c1850 .... **30.00**
Platter, 10 × 9", blue Oriental scene, c1820 .... **85.00**
Teapot, Imari-style design **150.00**
Urn, 6" h, white, blue and gold trim, classical figure,
handles **250.00**

DECOYS

History: During the past several years, carved wooden decoys,
used to lure ducks and geese to the hunter, have become widely
recognized as an indigenous American folk art form. Many decoys
are from the years 1880 to 1930 when commercial gunners commonly hunted using rigs of several hundred decoys. Many fine
carvers also worked through the 1930s and 1940s.

References: Joel Barber, *Wild Fowl Decoys,* Dover Publications,
n.d.; Bob and Sharon Huxford, *Collector's Guide to Decoys,* Volume II, Collector Books, 1992; Linda and Gene Kangas, *Collector's Guide to Decoys,* Wallace-Homestead, 1992; Carl F. Luckey,
*Collecting Antique Bird Decoys and Duck Calls: An Identification
& Value Guide,* Second Edition, Books Americana, 1992.

Periodicals: *Decoy Geographer,* 4532 Old Leeds Rd, Birmingham,
AL 35213; *Decoy Hunter Magazine,* 901 North 9th, Clinton, IN
47842; *Decoy Magazine,* PO Box 277, Burtonsville, MD 20866;
North America Decoys, PO Box 246, Spanish Fork, UT 84660;
Sporting Collector's Monthly, RW Publishing, PO Box 305, Camden, DE 19934; *Wildfowl Art,* Ward Foundation, 909 South Schu-
maker Dr, Salisbury, MD 21801; *Wildfowl Carving & Collecting,*
500 Vaughn St, Harrisburg, PA 17110.

Collectors' Clubs: Midwest Collectors Assoc, 1100 Bayview Dr,
Fox River Grove, IL 60021; New England Decoy Collectors Assoc,
2320 Main St, W Barnstable, MA 02668; Minnesota Decoy Collectors Assoc, PO Box 130084, St Paul, MN 55113; Ohio Decoy
Collectors & Carvers Assoc, PO Box 499, Richfield, OH 44286.

Museums: Havre de Grace Decoy Museum, Havre de Grace, MD;
Museum at Stony Brook, Stony Brook, NY; Peabody Museum of
Salem, Salem, MA; Refuge Waterfowl Museum, Chincoteague,
VA; Shelburne Museum, Inc., Shelburne, VT; Ward Museum of
Wildfowl Art, Salisbury, MD.

Reproduction Alert.

Notes: A decoy's value is based on several factors: (1) fame of the
carver, (2) quality of the carving, (3) species of wild fowl—the
most desirable are herons, swans, mergansers, and shorebirds—
and (4) condition of the original paint.

The inexperienced collector should be aware of several facts.
The age of a decoy, per se, is usually of no importance in determining value. Since very few decoys were ever signed, it is quite
difficult to attribute most decoys to known carvers. Anyone who
has not examined a known carver's work will be hard pressed to
determine if the paint on one of his decoys is indeed original.
Repainting severely decreases a decoy's value. In addition, there

are many fakes and reproductions on the market and even experienced collectors are occasionally fooled.

Decoys listed below are of average wear unless otherwise noted.

Abbreviation: o.p. = original paint.

Baird's Sandpiper, A Elmer Crowell, East Harwich, MA, sgd in ink "A. E. Crowell Cape Cod," miniature, 2¹/₁₆" h, minor paint wear 520.00
Black Brant, Dick Janson, CA 9,350.00
Black Duck
  Cobb, Nathan C, Jr., VA, hollow carved 23,100.00
  Hart, Charles, MA, carved wing tips and diamond-shaped nostrils, o.p. 400.00
  Holmes, Ben, CT, hollow carved, repainted body and bill 2,000.00
  Mason Factory, MI, premier grade, o.p. 575.00
  Unknown, hollow block, old paint, glass eyes, some paint wear and repairs, chips to tail, 19" l 95.00
Bluebill, Robert Elliston, IL, hollow carved 7,425.00
Blue-Wing Teal, mated pr, Mason Factory, MI, premier grade, o.p. 5,000.00
Brant
  Grant, Percy, o.p. 250.00
  Lincoln, Joe, MA, self bailing 1,400.00
  Mason Factory, MI, challenge grade, hollow carved, orig and old paint, worn 250.00
Bufflehead Hen, Harry C Shourds, Tuckerton, NJ, hollow carved, 1890 ....18,700.00
Canada Goose
  Chesapeake Bay area, mid 20th C
    23½" l, o.p., minor wear 200.00
    24" l, o.p., crack in neck 250.00
  Reeves, Phineas, Ontario 8,250.00
  Shourds, Harry V, Tuckerton, NJ, hollow carved
    Hen, crook neck, hissing 203,500.00
    Swimmer, minor wear 104,500.00
  Truex, Levi R, NJ 7,150.00
  Warin, George, Ontario, hollow carved hen 18,700.00
  Wheeler, Shang, Stratford, CT, c1910, sleeping, hollow carved 27,500.00
Canvasback Drake, glass eyes, old working repaint, 16½" l 95.00
Coot, wood, black repaint over worn surface, shot scars, 10¾" l 165.00
Crow, carved detail, glass eyes, old black repaint, wire legs, 18" l 330.00
Curlew
  Bruffee, Byron, carved and painted, wooden base, imp "Byron E Bruffee," 7" h 40.00
  Leeds, Daniel Lake, NJ 14,300.00
Elder Drake, unknown maker, hollow carved, head turned to right 1,350.00
Elder Hen, Pete Mitchell, ME, hollow carved, preening position, deep inlet neck 1,900.00
Fish, all wood, o.p., glass eyes, sgd "J. Ursch '86, Muskellunge," minor damage, 34½" l 165.00
Goldeneye, mated pr, unknown maker, head slightly turned, o.p., rect brand on bottom 3,000.00
Green-Wing Teal Drake
  McNair, Mark, hollow carved, sgd on bottom 595.00
  Ward Brothers, carved, standing position 1,800.00

Left to right: **Broadbill Drake, Mason Decoy Co, Detroit, standard grade, glass eye, $185.00; Canada Goose, Ward Bros, Crisfield, MD, c1930, $1,550.00; Duck, Sam Barnes, Havre de Grace, c1898, $350.00. Photograph courtesy of Freeman Fine Arts of Philadelphia.**

Least Sandpiper, A Elmer Crowell, East Harwich, MA, sgd in ink "A. E. Crowell Cape Cod", miniature, 2" h 520.00
Mallard Drake
  Mason Factory, MI, premier grade, o.p. 500.00
  Ward Brothers, raised wing tips, head turned to right 1,200.00
  Whittington, Hector, hollow body, turned head, glass eyes, old repaint, 16¾" l 200.00
Mallard Hen, old paint, glass eyes, head is loose, neck putty missing, age crack in block, chip on tail, 16" l 85.00
Merganser, red breasted
  Mason Factory, MI, Challenge grade, price for pr .11,550.00
  Parker, Lloyd, Parkertown, NJ, c1900, hollow carved, price for pr 132,000.00
  Shourds, Harry V., Tuckerton, NJ, 19th C, hollow carved 28,600.00
  Unknown, tack eyes, bolt weight, old working repaint, 15¼" l 115.00
Muskellunge, wood, o.p., glass eyes, sgd "J. Ursch '86," 34½" l 165.00
Old Squaw, NC, John Paxson 325.00
Pintail Drake
  Creve Coer, IL, hollow body, old repaint, old label, 15¾" l 110.00
  Florence, NJ, John English, later painted by John Davidson, c1920, hollow carved 143,000.00
  Knotts Island, NC 325.00
  Liverpool, IL, hollow body, old repaint, old label "Perry Wilcoxen, Liverpool, Illinois," branded "J.W.R." for Jim Rayker, Fox Lake, IL, 14½" l ... 125.00
  PA, R Frerich 7,975.00
Plover, black bellied
  Bowman, William, NY 7,150.00
  Cobb, Nathan, Cobb Island, VA, c1895 ....18,700.00
  Watson, Umbrella, VA 7,150.00
Redhead Drake
  Mason Factory, MI, challenge grade, o.p. 1,200.00
  Robert, George, NY, balsa body, head slightly turned to left 200.00
Ruddy Duck Drake, A Elmer Crowell, East Harwich, MA, circular stamp, miniature, 2¹/₁₈" h, minor paint wear 320.00
Sandpiper, unknown MA maker, sealing wax eyes, o.p., replaced bill 750.00
Scoter, John Paxson 310.00
Swan
  Mosley, William, Knotts Island, NC 285.00
  St Clair Flats, Ontario, hollow carved, repaint 16,500.00
Wiglem, Joe Lewiston, MA, bill restored 13,200.00
Willet, John Dilley, NY 10,450.00

Wood Duck, Orel LeBouef, Quebec **6,875.00**
Yellowlegs
    Holland, Mark, carved tail and wing feathers, sgd on
        base **300.00**
    Matthews, William, VA, carved wing tips and eyes,
        old paint **1,750.00**

DEDHAM POTTERY

History: Alexander W. Robertson established a pottery in Chelsea, Massachusetts, about 1866. After his brother, Hugh Cornwall Robertson, joined him in 1868 the firm was called A. W. & H. C. Robertson. Their father, James Robertson, joined his sons in 1872, and the name Chelsea Keramic Art Works Robertson and Sons was used.

Their initial products were simple flower and bean pots, but the firm quickly expanded their output to include a wide variety of artistic pottery. They produced a very fine redware body used in classical forms, some with black backgrounds imitating ancient Greek and Apulian works. They experimented with underglaze slip decoration on vases. The Chelsea Keramic Art Works Pottery also produced high-glazed vases, pitchers, and plaques with a buff clay body with either sculpted or molded applied decoration.

James Robertson died in 1880 and Alexander moved to California in 1884 leaving Hugh C. Robertson alone in Chelsea where his tireless experiments eventually yielded a stunning imitation of the prized Chinese Ming–era blood-red glaze. Hugh's vases with that glaze were marked with an impressed "CKAW." Creating these red-glazed vases was very expensive, and even though they received great critical acclaim, the company declared bankruptcy in 1889.

Recapitalized by a circle of Boston art patrons in 1891, Hugh started the Chelsea Pottery U.S., which produced gray crackle-glazed dinnerware with cobalt blue decorations, the rabbit pattern being the most popular.

The business moved to new facilities in Dedham, Massachusetts, and began production in 1896 under the name Dedham Pottery. Hugh's son and grandson operated the business until it closed in 1943, by which time between 50 and 80 patterns had been produced, some very briefly.

Marks: The following marks help determine the approximate age of items:
    "Chelsea Keramic Art Works Robertson and Sons," impressed, 1874–1880
    "CKAW," impressed, 1875–1889
    "CPUS," impressed in a cloverleaf, 1891–1895
    Foreshortened rabbit only, impressed, 1894–1896
    Conventional rabbit with "Dedham Pottery" in square blue stamped mark along with one impressed foreshortened rabbit, 1896–1928
    Blue rabbit stamped mark with "registered" beneath along with two impressed foreshortened rabbit marks, 1929–1943

References: Lloyd E. Hawes, *The Dedham Pottery and the Earlier Robertson's Chelsea Potteries,* Dedham Historical Society, 1968; Paul Evans, *Art Pottery of the United States,* Feingold & Lewis, 1974; Ralph and Terry Kovel, *Kovels' American Art Pottery,* Crown Publishers, 1993; Dana G. Morykan and Harry L. Rinker,

Warman's Country Antiques & Collectibles, Third Edition, Wallace-Homestead, 1996.

Collectors' Club: The Dedham Pottery Collectors Society, 248 Highland St, Dedham, MA 02026.

Museum: Dedham Historical Society, Dedham, MA.

REPRODUCTION ALERT

Two companies make Dedham-like reproductions primarily utilizing the rabbit pattern, but always mark their work very differently from the original.

Advisor: James D. Kaufman.

Bowl, 8½" sq
    Rabbit pattern, registered stamp **600.00**
    Rabbit pattern, registered stamp, hairline crack **275.00**
    Swan pattern, registered stamp **725.00**
Candlesticks, pr
    Elephant pattern, blue registered stamp **$525.00**
    Rabbit pattern, blue registered stamp **325.00**
Coffeepot, 8¼" h, Rabbit pattern, blue stamp **875.00**
Creamer and Sugar, 3¼" h, Rabbit pattern, type #1, blue
    stamp **550.00**

Plate, Butterfly, 9⅞", $285.00.

Demitasse Cup and Saucer, Rabbit pattern, blue stamp **320.00**
Paperweight, rabbit shape, blue registered stamp **450.00**
Pickle Dish, 10½", Rabbit pattern, blue registered stamp **650.00**
Pitcher, Rabbit pattern, blue stamp
    5" h **325.00**
    7" h **385.00**
    9" h **700.00**
Plate
    6" d
        Dolphin pattern, blue registered stamp, chipped **225.00**
        Rabbit pattern, blue stamp **145.00**
    8¼" d, Clover pattern, raised border image of alternating open and closed clovers, open clover in central field, CPUS **950.00**

Plate, central crab design, blue design, "O" rebus of Maude Davenport, extra seaweed dec, 8½" d, $875.00.

8½" d
  Central lobster design, blue stamp 575.00
  Elephant pattern, blue registered stamp 650.00
  Elephant pattern, blue registered stamp, wide irregular crackle glaze 450.00
  Magnolia pattern, blue stamp 165.00
  Rabbit pattern, blue stamp 220.00
  Snow Tree pattern, blue stamp 210.00
  Upside-down dolphin, CPUS 900.00
10" d
  Dolphin pattern, blue registered stamp 875.00
  Elephant pattern, blue registered stamp 900.00
  Turtle pattern, blue registered stamp 1,125.00
  Wolves and Owls pattern, blue stamp 4,750.00
Platter, 10 x 16", Rabbit pattern, blue registered stamp 875.00
Sherbet, Rabbit pattern, two handles, blue stamp 350.00
Tea Cup and Saucer
  Azalea pattern, registered stamp 130.00
  Butterfly pattern, registered stamp 245.00
  Duck pattern, registered stamp 170.00
  Iris pattern, registered stamp 130.00
  Rabbit pattern, registered stamp 135.00
  Turtle pattern, registered stamp 600.00
  Water Lily pattern, registered stamp 130.00

Plate, Rabbit pattern, blue stamp, "O" rebus of Maude Davenport, 8½" d, $220.00.

DELFTWARE

History: Delftware is pottery with a soft, red-clay body and tin-enamel glaze. The white, dense, opaque color came from adding tin ash to lead glaze. The first examples had blue designs on a white ground. Polychrome examples followed.

The name originally applied to pottery made in the region around Delft, Holland, beginning in the 16th century and ending in the late 18th century. The tin used came from the Cornish mines in England. By the 17th and 18th centuries English potters in London, Bristol, and Liverpool were copying the glaze and designs. Some designs unique to English potters also developed.

In Germany and France the ware is known as Faience, and in Italy as Majolica.

REPRODUCTION ALERT

Since the late 19th century much Delft-type souvenir material has been produced to appeal to the foreign traveler. Don't confuse these modern pieces with the older examples.

Bowl, 9¼" l, oval, blue and white dec, child surrounded by insects, leaves, and flowers, Dutch, late 18th/19th C, rim wear 415.00
Bust, 11¾" h, Napoleon, ceramic, artist sgd "S.B.," dated 1809 .... 500.00
Butter Pot, cov, 2⅝" h, blue and white floral sprays, English, 18th C, rim chips, hairlines, price for pr ... 230.00
Charger, 15½" d, circular, lobed curving rim, center with riffed circle, English, late 17th C 1,800.00
Dish, 10⅝" d, blue and white floral dec, Dutch, 18th C 150.00
Flask, 7" h, flattened round base, narrow short neck, round foot, blue, white, and black floral dec, windmill landscape scene of man and harp, loops for rope, sgd "AK," Holland, minor edge chips 300.00
Inkstand, 9¾" l, cov central pot, raised pen stand, blue and white landscape, floral, and insect dec, Dutch, late 18th C, glaze wear, rim chips 460.00
Jar, 8" h, blue and white, scrolled borders, central cartouches, Dutch, c1760, hairline, missing lids, price for pr 690.00
Plate
  9" d, blue floral dec, edge flakes 100.00
  9½" d, blue tin glaze, landscape and border dec, 18th C, price for pr 350.00
  10½" d, blue tin glaze, garden dec, 18th C 260.00
Posset Pot, cov, 10" h, polychrome floral dec, Dutch, c1770, glaze loss to spout rim, restorations 1,495.00
Pot, cov, 4" h, two handles, blue and white dec bird and floral designs, English, mid 18th C, rim chip to cov, glaze loss 550.00
Soup Plate, 8¾" d, blue and white floral dec, Dutch, 18th C 150.00
Tile, 5¾ × 12¼", painted blue and white, cows on coast, framed, late 19th/early 20th C 280.00
Tobacco Jar, 10" h, blue and white dec, pipe-smoking Indian seated by large cov jar, titled "St Domingo," Dutch sailing ships in distance, brass cov, Dutch, late

Figure, cow, English, 6¼" h, polychrome floral and scroll decoration, early 19th C, restored, $325.00.

18th/early 19th C, glaze wear to rim, old repair to body **575.00**
Trivet, 8½" l, triangular form, black-outlined blue and white leaves dec, circular frieze of figures in landscape, Dutch, early 19th C, slight glaze loss to rim . **100.00**
Vase
  7" h, polychrome dec, female subject within cartouche, foliate border, Dutch, late 18th/early 19th C **245.00**
  9" h, William of Orange, cut-corner rect, slender tapering sides, polychrome dec, profiles of William and Mary, Dutch, early 19th C, rim chips, price for pr **435.00**
  10" h, blue and white Oriental figural landscape, Dutch, rim damages, glaze loss **100.00**
  25" h, cov, ribbed body, floral vases in panels between scrolled floral borders, foo dog finial to cov, mark for Johannes Groen de Kloot, Dutch, late 18th/early 19th C, hairlines, carved wood base . **1,150.00**
Wall Plaque, 22½" h, tin glazed earthenware, scalloped oval, blue, yellow, green, and maganese purple Dutch landscape **850.00**

DEPRESSION GLASS

History: Depression glass was made from 1920 to 1940. It was an inexpensive machine-made glass and was produced by several companies in various patterns and colors. The number of forms made in different patterns also varied.

Depression glass was sold through variety stores, given away as premiums, or packaged with certain products. Movie houses gave it away from 1935 until well into the 1940s.

Like pattern glass, knowing the proper name of a pattern is the key to collecting. Collectors should be prepared to do research.

References: Gene Florence, *Collectible Glassware from the 40's, 50's, 60's,* Third Edition, Collector Books, 1996; ———, *Collector's Encyclopedia of Depression Glass,* Twelfth Edition, Collector Books, 1996; ———, *Elegant Glassware of the Depression Era,* Seventh Edition, Collector Books, 1996; ———, *Pocket Guide to Depression Glass & More, 1920–1960s,* Tenth Edition, Collector Books, 1996; ———, *Stemware Identification Featuring Cordials with Values, 1920s–1960s,* Collector Books, 1996; ———, *Very Rare Glassware of the Depression Era,* First Series (1988, 1991 value update), Second Series (1991), Third Series (1993), Fourth

Series (1995), Fifth Series (1996), Collector Books; Ralph and Terry Kovel, *Kovels' Depression Glass & American Dinnerware Price List,* Fifth Edition, Crown, 1995; Carl F. Luckey and Mary Burris, *An Identification & Value Guide to Depression Era Glassware,* Third Edition, Books Americana, 1994; Naomi L. Over, *Ruby Glass of the 20th Century,* Antique Publications, 1990, 1993–94 value update; Kent G. Washburn, *Price Survey,* Fourth Edition, published by author, 1994; Hazel Marie Weatherman, *Colored Glassware of the Depression Era,* Book 2, published by author 1974, available in reprint; ———, *1984 Supplement & Price Trends for Colored Glassware of the Depression Era,* Book 1, published by author, 1984.

Periodical: *The Daze,* PO Box 57, Otisville, MI 48463.

Collectors' Clubs: Canadian Depression Glass Club, PO Box 104, Mississaugua, Ontario L53 2K1 Canada; National Depression Glass Assoc, Inc, PO Box 8264, Wichita, KS 67209; 20-30-40 Society, Inc, PO Box 856, LaGrange, IL 60525.

Videotape: *Living Glass: Popular Patterns of the Depression Era,* 2 vols., Ro Cliff Communications, 1993.

REPRODUCTION ALERT

The following is a partial listing of Depression Glass patterns that have been reproduced. When available, the name of the reproduction manufacturer, shapes, and colors are given.

Adam (produced in the Far East and distributed through AA Importing of St. Louis) butter dish, pink

Avocado (Indiana Glass Company) pitcher and tumbler, in amethyst, blue, green, pink, frosted pink, red, and yellow.

Cherry Blossom (large number of manufacturers and importers) numerous forms including two-handled tray, cup and saucer, and children's set, in blue, cobalt blue, Delphite, green, iridized colors, pink, and red.

Madrid (Indiana Glass Company) goblet, grill plate, shakers, vase, and more, in crystal (clear), blue, pink, and teal.

Mayfair, cookie jars, juice pitchers, shakers, shot glasses, and more, in amethyst, blue, cobalt blue, green, pink, and red.

Miss America, covered butter dish, pitcher, shakers, and tumbler, in cobalt blue, crystal (clear), green, ice blue, pink, and red amberina.

Sharon (privately produced) covered butter in blue, cobalt blue, green (light and dark), opalescent blue, red, and umber (burnt).

Send a self-addressed stamped business envelope to *The Daze* and request a copy of their glass reproduction list. It is one of the best bargains in the antiques business.

Additional Listings: See *Warman's Americana & Collectibles* for more examples.

AMERICAN SWEETHEART, MacBeth-Evans Glass Co., 1930–36. Made in blue, Monax, pink, and red. Limited production in Cremax and color-trimmed Monax.

	Blue	Cremax	Monax	Monax color trim	Pink	Red
Berry Bowl						
3¼", flat	——	——	——	——	49.50	——
9" d, master	——	36.00	60.00	150.00	55.00	——
Cereal Bowl, 6" d	——	11.00	14.00	37.50	16.00	——
Chop Plate, 11" d	——		15.00			——
Console Bowl, 18" d 1,000.00		——	375.00	——	——	850.00
Cream Soup	——		120.00		75.00	——
Creamer	115.00	——	9.00	85.00	12.00	110.00
Cup	100.00	75.00	8.00	70.00	15.00	75.00
Lamp Shade	——	450.00	400.00	——	——	——
Pitcher						
7½" h, 60 oz	——				675.00	——
8" h, 80 oz	——				575.00	——
Plate						
6" d, bread & butter	——		4.50	13.00	5.50	——
8" d, salad	75.00	25.00	7.50	——	11.00	75.00
9" d, luncheon	——		10.00	35.00	——	——
9¾" d, dinner	——		14.00	70.00	38.00	——
10¼" d, dinner	——		24.00		38.00	——
Platter, 13" l, oval	——		75.00		55.00	——
Salt and Pepper, ftd	——		325.00		425.00	——
Salver Plate, 12" d	180.00	——	18.00		22.00	125.00
Saucer	25.00		3.00	15.00	5.75	20.00
Serving Plate, 15½" d	375.00	——	200.00	——	——	300.00
Sherbet						
3¾" h, ftd	——	——	10.50	——	22.00	——
4¼" h, ftd	——		20.00	70.00	17.00	——
Soup, flat, 9½"	——		65.00	90.00	75.00	——
Sugar lid	——		300.00			——
Sugar, open	115.00	——	7.50	85.00	11.00	100.00
Tidbit						
2 tier	250.00		95.00		——	200.00
3 tier	650.00	——	275.00	——	——	575.00
Tumbler						
3½" h, 5 oz	——	——	——	——	100.00	——
4¼" h, 9 oz	——	——	——	——	85.00	——
4¾" h, 10 oz	——	——	——	——		——
Vegetable Bowl, 11"	——	——	90.00	——	65	——

American Sweetheart, soup, 9½", flat, pink, $75.00.

ANNIVERSARY, Jeannette Glass Co., 1947–49, late 1960s to mid 1970s. Made in crystal, iridescent, and pink.

	Crystal	Iridescent	Pink
Berry Bowl, 4⅞" d	3.50	4.50	11.00
Butter Dish, cov	27.50	——	57.00
Cake Plate			
12⅜" w, square	7.00	——	16.50
12½" d, round	7.50	——	17.50
Cake Plate, metal cover	15.00	——	——
Candlesticks, pr, 4⅞" h	16.00	24.00	——
Candy Jar, cov	24.00	——	45.00
Comport			
Open, 3 legs	5.00	5.00	16.00

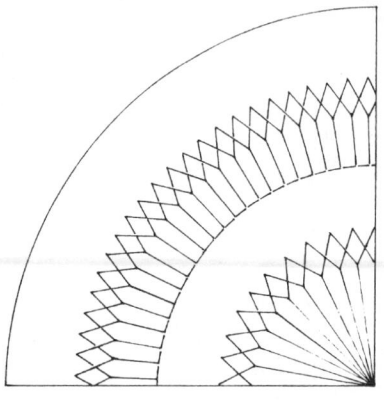

	Crystal	Irides-cent	Pink
Ruffled, 3 legs	6.50	——	——
Creamer, ftd	5.00	6.50	14.00
Cup	5.00	4.00	9.00
Fruit Bowl, 9″ d	10.00	14.00	24.00
Pickle Dish 9″ d	5.50	7.50	12.00
Plate			
6¼″ d, sherbet	2.00	3.50	4.00
9″ d, dinner	5.00	8.00	17.00
Relish Dish, 8″ d	5.60	7.50	14.00

	Crystal	Irides-cent	Pink
Sandwich Server, 12½″ d	6.50	10.00	20.00
Saucer	1.00	1.50	6.00
Sherbet, ftd	4.00	——	10.00
Soup Bowl, 7⅜″ d	7.00	7.50	17.00
Sugar, cov	10.00	8.00	18.50
Tidbit, metal handle	14.00	——	——
Vase, 6½″ h	14.00	——	28.00
Wall Pocket	15.00	——	30.00
Wine, 2½ oz	8.00	——	18.00

BOWKNOT, unknown maker, late 1920s.

	Green
Berry Bowl, 4½″ d	16.00
Cereal Bowl, 5½″ d	20.00
Cup	14.00
Plate, 7″ d, salad	12.50
Sherbet, low, ftd	24.00
Tumbler	
5″ h, 10 oz, flat	15.00
5″ h, 10 oz, ftd	15.00

Bowknot, tumbler, green, $15.00.

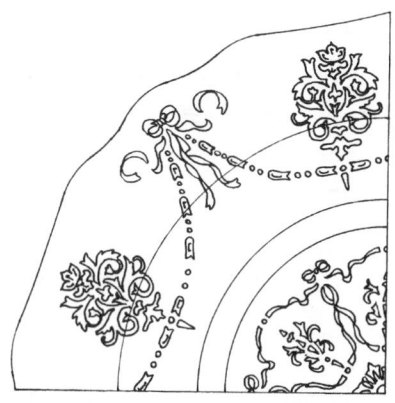

CAMEO, Ballerina, Dancing Girl, Hocking Glass Co., 1930–34. Made in crystal, green, pink, and yellow. Only the crystal has a platinum rim. Reproduced.

	Crystal	Green	Pink	Yellow
Berry Bowl				
4¼″ d	13.00	——	——	——
8¼″ d	——	——	150.00	——
Butter Dish, cov	——	220.00	——1,400.00	
Cake Plate				
10″ d, 3 legs	——	22.00	——	——
10½″ d, flat	——	95.00	150.00	——
Candlesticks, pr, 4″ h	——	85.00	——	——
Candy Jar, cov				
4″ h	——	75.00	495.00	80.00
6½″ h	——	150.00	——	——
Cereal Bowl, 5½″ d	7.50	30.00	150.00	30.00
Cocktail Shaker	500.00	——	——	——
Comport, 5″ w	——	32.00	200.00	——
Console Bowl, 3 legs, 11″ d	——	75.00	45.00	95.00

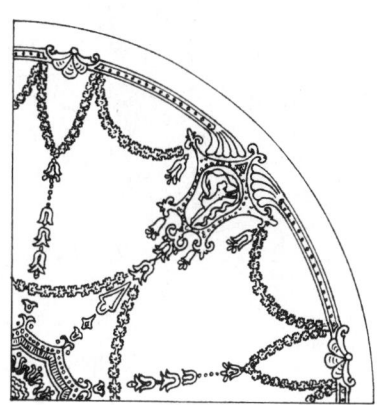

	Crystal	Green	Pink	Yellow
Cookie Jar, cov	——	60.00	——	——
Cream Soup, 4¾" d	——	175.00	——	——
Creamer				
3¼" h	——	25.00	110.00	23.00
4¼" h	——	29.00	85.00	——
Cup	10.00	15.00	——	8.00
Decanter, 10" h	200.00	175.00	——	——
Domino Tray, 7" l	125.00	135.00	250.00	——
Goblet, 6" h, water	——	52.00	165.00	——
Ice Bowl, 3" h, 5½" d	265.00	150.00	600.00	——
Jam Jar, cov, 2" h	175.00	165.00	——	——
Juice Pitcher, 6" h, 36 oz	——	60.00	——	——
Juice Tumbler				
3 oz, ftd	——	55.00	90.00	——
5 oz, 3¾" h	——	25.00	——	——
Pitcher, 8½" h, 56 oz	550.00	50.00	1,200.00	——
Plate				
6" d, sherbet	4.00	6.00	85.00	2.50
7" d, salad	12.00	——	——	——
8" d, luncheon	14.00	12.00	36.00	10.00
8½" sq	——	40.00	——	225.00
9½" d, dinner	——	18.00	75.00	9.00
10½" d, dinner, rimmed	——	90.00	145.00	——
10½" d, grill	——	10.00	55.00	6.00
Platter, 12" l	——	20.00	——	40.00
Relish, 7½" l, ftd, 3 part ...	175.00	30.00	775.00	——
Salad Bowl, 7¼" d	60.00	——	——	——
Salt and Pepper Shakers, pr, ftd	——	70.00	——	——

	Crystal	Green	Pink	Yellow
Sandwich Plate, 10" d	——	15.00	45.00	37.00
Sandwich Server, center handle	——	3,000.00	——	——
Saucer	4.00	175.00	90.00	4.50
Sherbet				
3⅛", blown	——	15.00	75.00	——
3⅛", molded	——	16.00	75.00	40.00
4⅞"	——	30.00	95.00	——
Soup Bowl, rimmed, 9" d	——	62.00	100.00	——
Sugar				
3¼" h	——	21.00	——	12.00
4¼" h	——	29.00	115.00	——
Syrup Pitcher, 5¾" h, 20 oz (or milk)	——	225.00	——	1,850.00
Tumbler				
4" h, 9 oz	16.00	30.00	80.00	——
4¾" h, 10 oz, flat	——	30.00	95.00	——
5" h, 9 oz ftd	——	29.00	115.00	14.00
5" h, 11 oz, flat	——	29.00	90.00	48.00
5¼" h, 15 oz	——	65.00	125.00	——
5¾" h, 11 oz, ftd	——	60.00	125.00	——
6⅜" h, 15 oz, ftd	——	425.00	——	——
Vase				
5¾" h	——	215.00	——	——
8" h	——	40.00	——	——
Vegetable, oval, 10" l	——	30.00	——	45.00
Wine				
3½" h	——	750.00	800.00	——
4" h	——	65.00	250.00	——

CHERRY BLOSSOM, Jeannette Glass Co., 1930–39. Made in crystal, Delphite, green, jadite, pink, and red. Production was very limited in crystal, jadite, and red. Reproduced.

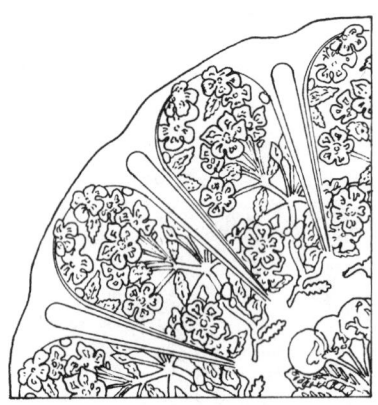

	Delphite	Green	Pink
Berry Bowl			
4¾" d	15.00	19.00	16.00
8½" d, master	50.00	48.00	42.00
Bowl, 9" d, two handles	25.00	65.00	46.00

	Delphite	Green	Pink
Butter Dish, cov	——	85.00	75.00
Cake Plate, 10¼" d, 3 legs	——	28.00	25.00
Cereal Bowl, 5¾" d	——	35.00	32.00
Coaster	——	15.00	15.00
Creamer	19.00	26.00	24.00
Cup and Saucer	24.00	30.00	27.00
Fruit Bowl, 10½" d	32.00	89.00	89.00
Mug, 7 oz	——	185.00	250.00
Pitcher			
6¾" h, AOP, 36 oz	89.00	55.00	70.00
8", PAT, 36 oz, ftd	——	55.00	55.00
8", PAT, 42 oz, flat	——	52.00	52.00
Plate			
6" d, sherbet	6.00	6.00	10.00
7" d, salad	——	21.00	17.00
9" d, dinner	18.00	26.00	22.00
9" d, grill	——	22.00	22.00
10" d, grill	——	26.00	——
Platter			
11" l, oval	40.00	48.00	35.00
13" d	——	72.00	43.00
13" divided	——	72.00	43.00
Salt and Pepper Shakers, pr, scalloped base	——	975.00	1,200.00
Sandwich Tray, 10½" d	20.00	24.00	24.00
Sherbet	15.00	18.00	17.00

	Delphite	Green	Pink
Soup, flat, 7¾" d	—	55.00	50.00
Sugar	18.00	21.00	19.00
Tumbler			
3½", 1 oz	—	18.00	15.00
3¾" h, AOP, ftd	—	20.00	20.00

	Delphite	Green	Pink
4¼" h, 9 oz	—	22.00	20.00
4½" h, 8 oz, scalloped base, AOP	—	30.00	30.00
4½" h, 9 oz	16.00	27.00	30.00
5"	20.00	70.00	72.00
Vegetable Bowl, 9" l, oval	45.00	38.00	35.00

CLOVERLEAF, Hazel Atlas Glass Co., 1930–36. Made in black, crystal, green, pink, and yellow.

	Black	Green	Pink	Yellow
Ashtray, match holder in center				
4" d	65.00	—	—	—
5¾" d	75.00	20.00	—	—
Bowl, 8" d	—	50.00	—	—
Candy Dish, cov	—	45.00	—	95.00
Cereal Bowl, 5" d	—	25.00	—	34.00
Creamer, 3⅝" h, ftd	18.00	9.00	—	18.00
Cup	16.00	8.00	7.00	10.00
Dessert Bowl, 4" d	—	18.00	15.00	25.00
Plate				
6" d, sherbet	38.00	4.50	—	7.00
8" d, luncheon	15.00	6.00	7.00	14.00
10¼" d, grill	—	20.00	—	34.00
Salad Bowl, 7" d	—	40.00	—	48.00
Salt and Pepper Shakers, pr	75.00	14.00	—	100.00
Saucer	7.00	4.00	4.00	5.00
Sherbet, 3" h, ftd	18.00	12.00	6.50	11.00
Sugar, 3⅝" h, ftd	15.00	12.00	—	20.00
Tumbler				
3¾" h, 10 oz, flat	—	35.00	22.50	—
4" h, 9 oz, flat	—	50.00	—	—
5¾" h, 10 oz, ftd	—	22.00	—	32.00

Cloverleaf, cup and saucer, pink, $11.00.

DORIC AND PANSY, Jeannette Glass Co., 1937–38. Made in ultramarine with limited production in pink and crystal.

	Crystal	Pink	Ultra-marine
Berry Bowl			
4½" d	7.50	8.00	16.00
8" d, master	—	20.00	75.00
Bowl, 9" d, handled	14.00	15.00	35.00
Butter Dish, cov	—	—	500.00
Cup and Saucer	13.00	14.00	24.00
Creamer	70.00	70.00	115.00
Plate			
6" d, sherbet	7.00	7.50	10.00
7" d, salad	—	—	35.00
9" d, dinner	7.50	8.00	30.00
Salt and Pepper Shakers, pr	—	—	400.00
Sugar, open	65.00	70.00	115.00
Tray, 10" l, handles	45.00	—	25.00
Tumbler, 4½" h, 9 oz	—	—	78.00

FLORAL AND DIAMOND BAND, U.S. Glass Co., late 1920s. Made in pink and green with limited production in black, crystal, and iridescent.

	Green	Pink
Berry Bowl		
4½" d	8.00	7.00
8" d, master	12.00	13.00
Butter Dish, cov	120.00	125.00
Comport, 5½" h	16.50	15.00
Creamer, 4¾"	20.00	17.50
Iced Tea Tumbler, 5" h	38.00	32.50
Nappy, 5¾" d, handle	12.00	11.00
Pitcher, 8" h, 42 oz	95.00	90.00
Plate, 8" d, luncheon	40.00	40.00
Sherbet	7.00	6.50
Sugar, 5¼"	15.00	14.00
Tumbler, 4" h, water	24.00	22.00

FLORENTINE NO. 1, Old Florentine, Poppy No. 1, Hazel Atlas Glass Co., 1932–35. Made in crystal, green, pink, yellow and limited production in cobalt blue. Reproduced.

	Cobalt Blue	Crystal	Green	Pink	Yellow
Ashtray, 5½" d	——	22.00	24.00	27.50	28.00
Berry Bowl					
5" d	18.00	11.00	12.00	14.00	15.00
8½" d, master	——	24.00	25.00	28.00	28.00
Butter Dish, cov	——	110.00	115.00	165.00	160.00
Cereal Bowl, 6" d	——	20.00	20.00	22.00	24.00
Coaster/ashtray, 3¾"	——	18.00	20.00	25.00	25.00
Comport, 3½" h, ruffled	60.00	25.00	25.00	15.00	——
Cream Soup, 5" d, ruffled	50.00	12.00	14.00	18.00	——
Creamer	——	8.00	8.00	25.00	18.00
Creamer, ruffled	65.00	33.00	35.00	37.00	——
Cup	85.00	8.00	8.00	9.00	10.00
Iced Tea Tumbler, 5¼" h, 12 oz, ftd	——	28.00	28.00	30.00	24.00
Juice Tumbler, 3¾" h, 5 oz, ftd ..	——	16.00	16.00	20.00	22.00
Lemonade Tumbler, 5¼" h, 9 oz	——	——	——	100.00	——
Pitcher					
6½", 36 oz, ftd	850.00	40.00	40.00	50.00	45.00
7½", 48 oz, flat, ice lip or none	——	70.00	72.00	115.00	175.00
Plate					
6" d, sherbet	——	6.50	7.00	6.50	7.00
8½" d, salad	——	7.50	8.00	12.00	12..00
10" d, dinner	——	16.00	16.00	22.00	24.00
10" d, grill	——	12.00	12.50	20.00	22.00
Platter, 11½" l, oval	——	19.00	10.00	22.00	28.00
Salt and Pepper Shakers, ftd	——	22.00	32.00	55.00	58.00
Saucer	18.00	3.50	3.50	4.00	3.00
Sherbet, 3 oz, ftd	——	7.50	7.50	10.00	16.00
Sugar, cov	——	8.00	8.50	25.00	12.00
Sugar, ruffled	55.00	30.00	30.00	35.00	——
Tumbler					
3¼" h, 4 oz, ftd	——	15.00	16.00	——	——
4" h, 9 oz, ribbed	——	14.00	14.00	22.00	——
4¾", 10 oz, ftd	——	22.00	20.00	22.00	23.00
Vegetable, cov, 9½" l, oval	——	40.00	40.00	60.00	60.00

MAYFAIR, Federal Glass Co., 1934. Made in amber, crystal, and green.

	Amber	Crystal	Green
Cereal Bowl, 6″ d	16.50	9.50	19.50
Cream Soup, 5″ d	18.00	11.00	18.00
Creamer, ftd	13.50	11.00	16.00
Cup	8.50	5.00	8.50
Plate			
6¾″ d, salad	7.00	4.50	8.50
9½″ d, dinner	14.00	10.00	14.50
9½″ d, grill	13.50	8.50	13.50
Platter, 12″ l, oval	27.50	20.00	30.00
Sauce Bowl, 5″ d	8.50	7.00	12.00
Saucer	4.50	2.50	4.50
Sugar, ftd	14.00	12.00	14.00
Tumbler, 4½″ h, 9 oz	27.50	15.00	32.00
Vegetable, 10″ l, oval	30.00	20.00	30.00

MOONSTONE, Anchor Hocking Glass Co., 1941–46. Made in crystal with opalescent hobails and limited green with opalescent hobnails.

	Crystal
Berry Bowl, 5½″ d	18.00
Bonbon, heart shape, handle	13.00
Bowl	
6½″ d, crimped, handle	20.00
7¼″ d, flat	14.00
9½″ d, crimped	20.00
Candleholder, pr	25.00
Candy Jar, cov, 6″ h	29.00
Cigarette Box, cov	25.00
Creamer	9.50
Cup	8.00
Dessert Bowl, 5½″ d, crimped	9.50
Goblet, 10 oz	24.00
Plate	
6¼″ d, sherbet	6.00
8⅜″ d, luncheon	15.00
Puff Box, cov, 4¾″ d, round	25.00
Relish, 7¼″ d, divided	12.50
Relish, cloverleaf	12.50
Sandwich Plate, 10¾″ d	28.00

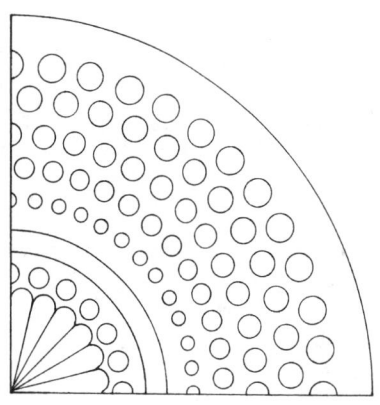

	Crystal
Saucer	6.00
Sherbet, ftd	7.00
Sugar, ftd	9.00
Vase, 5½″ h, bud	10.00

NEW CENTURY, Hazel Atlas Co., 1930–35. Made in crystal and green with limited production in amethyst, cobalt blue, and pink.

	Amethyst	Cobalt Blue	Crystal	Green	Pink
Ashtray/coaster, 5⅜″ d	—	—	27.00	28.50	—
Berry Bowl					
4½″ d	—	—	18.00	18.00	—
8″ d, master	—	—	20.00	22.00	—
Butter Dish, cov	—	—	55.00	55.00	—
Casserole, cov, 9″ d	—	—	60.00	60.00	—
Cocktail, 3¼ oz	—	—	20.00	22.00	—
Cream Soup, 4¾″ d	—	—	20.00	22.00	—
Creamer	—	—	8.50	9.50	—

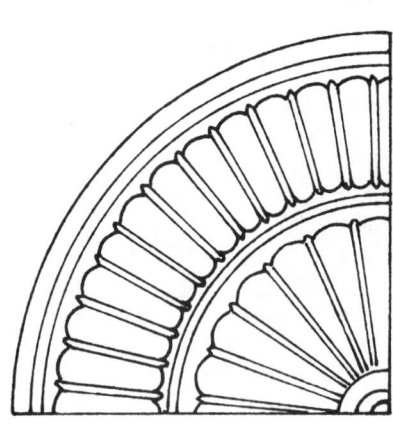

	Amethyst	Cobalt Blue	Crystal	Green	Pink
Cup	20.00	20.00	6.50	8.50	20.00
Decanter, stopper	—	—	55.00	55.00	—
Pitcher, with or without ice lip					
60 oz	35.00	35.00	37.50	37.50	30.00
80 oz	42.00	45.00	40.00	40.00	42.00
Plate					
6" d, sherbet	—	—	3.50	3.50	—
7⅛" d, breakfast	—	—	10.00	10.00	—
8½" d, salad	—	—	11.00	11.00	—
10" d, dinner	—	—	18.00	18.00	—
10" d, grill	—	—	12.00	14.00	—
Platter, 11" l, oval	—	—	18.00	20.00	—
Salt and Pepper Shakers, pr	—	—	35.00	35.00	—
Saucer	7.50	7.50	3.50	3.50	8.00
Sherbet, 3" h	—	—	9.00	9.00	—
Sugar, cov	—	—	24.00	24.00	—
Tumbler					
3½" h, 5 oz	12.00	10.00	12.00	12.00	10.00
3½" h, 8 oz	—	—	20.00	20.00	—
4" h, 5 oz, ftd	—	—	18.00	18.00	—
4¼" h, 9 oz	14.00	14.00	17.50	18.00	14.00
4⅞" h, 9 oz, ftd	—	—	20.00	20.00	—
5" h, 10 oz	16.00	16.00	17.50	17.50	16.00
5¼" h, 12 oz	25.00	25.00	25.00	25.00	20.00
Whiskey, 2½" h, 1½ oz	—	—	18.00	20.00	—
Wine, 2½ oz	—	—	25.00	25.00	—

NO. 612, Horseshoe, Indiana Glass Co., 1930–33. Made in crystal, green, pink, and yellow.

	Green	Yellow
Berry Bowl		
4½" d	25.00	20.00
9½" d, master	30.00	35.00
Butter Dish, cov	750.00	—
Candy Dish, metal holder	175.00	—

	Green	Yellow
Cereal Bowl, 6½" d	25.00	25.00
Creamer, ftd	18.00	20.00
Cup and Saucer	16.00	17.50
Pitcher, 8½" h, 64 oz	250.00	295.00
Plate		
6" d, sherbet	9.00	9.00
8⅜" d, salad	10.00	10.00
9⅜" d, luncheon	13.00	14.50
10⅜" d, grill	85.00	85.00
Platter, 10¾" l, oval	25.00	25.00
Relish, 3 part ftd	20.00	24.00
Salad Bowl, 7½" d	24.00	24.00
Sandwich Plate, 11½" d	24.00	27.50
Saucer	6.00	6.50
Sherbet	16.00	18.50
Sugar, open	15.00	15.00
Tumbler		
12 oz, ftd	140.00	150.00
4¼" h, 9 oz	150.00	—
4¾" h, 12 oz	150.00	—
9 oz, ftd	22.00	24.00
Vegetable Bowl		
8½" d	30.00	30.00
10½" d, oval	25.00	28.50

OVIDE, Hazel Atlas Glass Co., 1930–35, 1950s. Made in black, green, white Platonite with fired-on colors in the 1950s. (Illustration depicts Art Deco design.)

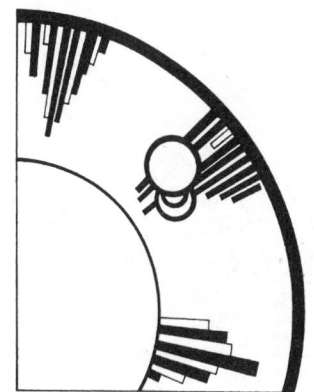

	Black	Green	Platonite
Berry Bowl			
4¾" d	——	——	7.50
8" d, master	——	——	20.00
Candy Dish, cov	45.00	24.00	35.00
Cereal Bowl, 5½" d	10.00	——	12.00
Creamer	7.00	4.50	18.00
Cup	6.50	3.50	14.00
Eggcup	——	——	22.00
Fruit Cocktail, ftd	5.00	4.50	——
Plate			
6" d, sherbet	——	2.50	6.00
8" d, luncheon	——	3.50	15.00
9" d, dinner	——	——	25.00
Platter, 11" d	——	——	24.00
Salt and Pepper Shakers, pr	28.00	28.00	25.00
Saucer	3.50	3.50	6.00
Sherbet	6.50	3.50	15.00
Sugar, open	7.00	5.00	18.00
Tumbler	15.00	——	18.00

PARROT, Sylvan, Federal Glass Co., 1931–32. Made in amber and green with limited production in blue and crystal.

	Amber	Green
Berry Bowl		
5" d	22.00	24.00
8" d, master	75.00	80.00
Butter, cov	1,150.00	375.00
Creamer, ftd	65.00	55.00
Cup	35.00	35.00
Hot Plate, 5" d		
Pointed	875.00	900.00
Round	——	950.00
Jam Dish, 7" d	35.00	——
Pitcher, 8½" h, 80 oz	——	2,500.00
Plate		
5¾" d, sherbet	24.00	35.00
7½" d, salad	——	40.00
9" d, dinner	49.00	38.00
10½" d, grill, round	32.00	
10½" d, grill, square	——	27.00
Platter, 11¼" l, oblong	50.00	55.00
Salt and Pepper Shakers, pr	——	270.00
Saucer	18.00	18.00
Sherbet, ftd, cone	27.00	24.00
Soup Bowl, 7" d	32.00	42.00
Sugar, cov	450.00	175.00

	Amber	Green
Tumbler		
4¼" h, 10 oz	100.00	130.00
5½" h, 10 oz, ftd, Madrid mold	145.00	——
5½" h, 12 oz	115.00	160.00
5¾" h, ftd, heavy	100.00	120.00
Vegetable, 10" l, oval	65.00	57.00

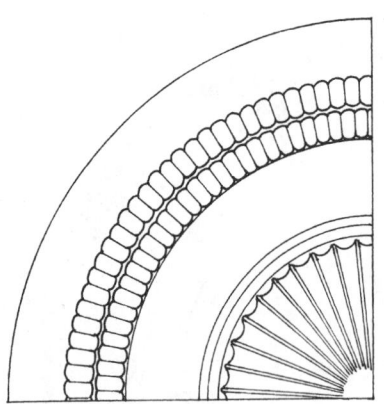

ROULETTE, Many Windows, Hocking Glass Co., 1935–39. Made in crystal, green, and pink.

	Crystal	Green	Pink
Cup	35.00	6.00	6.50
Fruit Bowl, 9″ d	10.00	15.00	15.00
Iced Tea Tumbler, 5⅛″ h, 12 oz	16.00	25.00	27.50
Juice Tumbler, 3¼″ h, 5 oz	7.50	20.00	22.00
Old Fashioned Tumbler, 3¼″ h, 7½ oz	22.00	40.00	40.00
Pitcher, 8″ h, 65 oz	30.00	35.00	35.00
Plate			
6″ d, sherbet	3.50	4.50	5.00
8½″ d, luncheon	7.00	6.00	6.00
Sandwich Plate, 12″ d	12.00	14.00	15.00
Saucer	1.50	3.00	3.00
Sherbet	7.00	6.00	6.00
Tumbler			
4⅛″ h, 9 oz	13.00	20.00	22.00
5½″ h, 10 oz, ftd	15.00	25.00	27.50
Whiskey, 2½″ h, 1½ oz	8.00	15.00	15.00

ROYAL LACE, Hazel Atlas Glass Co., 1934–41. Made in cobalt blue, crystal, green, pink, and some amethyst. Reproduced.

	Cobalt Blue	Crystal	Green	Pink
Candlesticks, pr				
Rolled edge	——	45.00	85.00	60.00
Ruffled edge	——	28.00	70.00	60.00
Straight edge	——	30.00	75.00	55.00
Cookie Jar, cov	495.00	45.00	75.00	55.00
Cream Soup Bowl, 4¾″ d	35.00	14.00	35.00	24.00
Creamer, ftd	60.00	15.00	25.00	20.00
Cup and Saucer	45.00	16.00	25.00	18.00
Nut Bowl	990.00	190.00	375.00	375.00
Pitcher				
48 oz, straight sides	150.00	40.00	110.00	85.00
64 oz, 8″ h	225.00	45.00	110.00	120.00
68 oz, 8″ h. ice lip	240.00	50.00	——	95.00
86 oz, 8″ h	——	50.00	135.00	95.00
96 oz, 9½″ h, ice lip	265.00	69.00	140.00	100.00
Plate				
6″ d, sherbet	14.00	5.00	10.00	15.00
8½″ d, luncheon	30.00	7.50	15.00	20.00
9⅞″ d, dinner	40.00	18.00	25.00	20.00
9⅞″ d, grill	35.00	15.00	23.00	20.00
Platter, 13″ l, oval	50.00	27.00	40.00	39.00
Salt and Pepper Shakers, pr	250.00	45.00	128.00	65.00
Sherbet, ftd	40.00	17.00	25.00	18.00
Sherbet, metal holder	28.00	4.00	——	——
Sugar, cov	42.00	32.00	30.00	50.00
Toddy or Cider Set	225.00	——	——	——
Tumbler				
3½″ h, 5 oz	65.00	15.00	30.00	35.00
4⅛″ h, 9 oz	45.00	16.00	30.00	20.00
4⅞″ h, 10 oz	100.00	25.00	60.00	60.00
5⅜″ h, 12 oz	125.00	25.00	50.00	55.00
Vegetable Bowl, 11″ l, oval	60.00	25.00	35.00	35.00

	Cobalt Blue	Crystal	Green	Pink
Berry Bowl				
5″ d	30.00	15.00	30.00	27.00
10″ d, master	60.00	20.00	32.00	28.00
Bowl, 10″ d, 3 legs				
Rolled edge	——	190.00	75.00	50.00
Ruffled edge	——	42.00	65.00	100.00
Straight edge	——	24.00	45.00	40.00
Butter Dish, cov	——	65.00	250.00	150.00

STRAWBERRY, U. S. Glass Co., early 1930s. Made in crystal, green, pink, and some iridescent.

	Crystal	Green	Irides-cent	Pink
Berry Bowl				
4" d	6.50	9.00	6.50	10.00
7½" d, master	16.00	20.00	16.00	20.00
Bowl, 6¼" d, 2" d	40.00	60.00	40.00	60.00
Butter Dish, cov	125.00	150.00	125.00	150.00
Comport, 5¾" d	55.00	60.00	55.00	60.00
Creamer				
Large, 4⅝" h	24.00	35.00	24.00	35.00
Small	12.00	17.50	12.00	17.50
Olive Dish, 5" l, one handle	8.50	14.00	8.50	14.00
Pickle Dish, 8¼" l, oval	8.00	14.00	8.00	14.00
Pitcher, 7¾" h	150.00	150.00	150.00	150.00
Plate				
6" d, sherbet	5.00	7.00	5.00	8.00
7½" d, salad	10.00	14.00	10.00	15.00
Salad Bowl, 6½" d	15.00	20.00	15.00	20.00
Sherbet	6.00	7.00	6.00	7.00
Sugar				
Large, cov	60.00	85.00	60.00	85.00
Small, open	12.00	32.00	12.00	32.00
Tumbler, 3⅝" h, 8 oz	20.00	30.00	20.00	30.00

SWIRL, Petal Swirl, Jeannette Glass Co., 1937–38. Made in amber, Delphite, ice blue, pink, and Ultramarine.

	Delphite	Pink	Ultra-marine
Bowl, 10" d, ftd, closed handles	—	24.00	28.00
Butter Dish, cov	—	175.00	245.00
Candleholders, pr			
Double branch	—	40.00	45.00
Single branch	115.00	—	—
Candy Dish			
Covered	—	130.00	150.00
Open, 3 legs	—	16.00	24.00
Cereal Bowl, 5¼" d	14.00	10.00	15.00
Coaster, 1 × 3¼"	—	15.00	14.00
Console Bowl, 10½" d, ftd	—	18.00	29.00
Creamer	12.00	7.50	15.00
Cup and Saucer	14.00	12.00	20.00
Plate			
6½" d, sherbet	6.50	4.50	7.50
7¼" d, luncheon	—	6.50	11.00
8" d, salad	9.00	8.50	12.00
9¼" d, dinner	12.00	13.00	19.00
10½" d, dinner	18.00	—	30.00
Platter, 12" l, oval	35.00	—	
Salad Bowl, 9" d	30.00	18.00	26.00
Salad Bowl, 9" d, rimmed	—	20.00	28.00
Salt and Pepper Shakers, pr	—	—	45.00
Sandwich Plate, 12½" d	—	20.00	27.50
Sherbet, low, ftd	—	13.00	23.00
Soup, tab handles, lug	—	25.00	35.00
Sugar, ftd	—	12.00	17.50

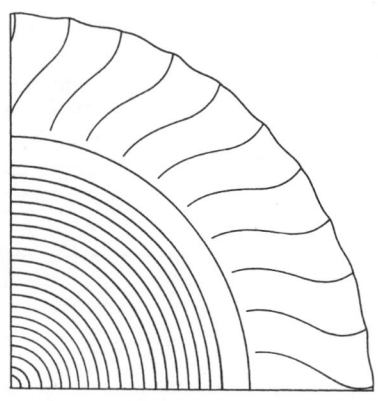

	Delphite	Pink	Ultra-marine
Tray, 10½" l, two handles	25.00	—	—
Tumbler			
4" h, 9 oz	—	18.00	42.00
4⅝" h, 9 oz	—	18.00	
5⅛" h, 13 oz	—	45.00	90.00
9 oz, ftd	—	20.00	—
Vase			
6½" d, ftd, ruffled	—	22.00	—
8½" d, ftd	—	—	30.00

WINDSOR, Windsor Diamond, Jeannette Glass Co., 1936–46. Made in crystal, green, and pink with limited production in amberina red, Delphite, and ice blue.

	Crystal	Green	Pink
Ashtray, 5¾" d	13.50	45.00	35.00
Berry Bowl			
4¾" d	4.00	11.00	9.00
8½" d, master	6.50	17.50	18.50
Bowl			
5" l, pointed edge	5.00	——	17.50
7 × 11¾", boat shape	18.00	35.00	32.00
7½" d, 3 legs	8.00	——	24.00
8" d, 2 handles	9.00	24.00	20.00
8" l, pointed edge	10.00	——	48.00
10½" l, pointed edge	25.00	——	32.00
Butter Dish	27.50	94.00	60.00
Cake Plate, 10¾" d, ftd	9.00	22.00	20.00
Candlesticks, pr, 3" h	20.00	——	85.00
Candy Jar, cov	18.00	——	——
Cereal Bowl, 5⅜" d	9.00	22.00	25.00
Chop Plate, 13⅝" d	19.00	40.00	42.00
Coaster, 3¼" d	8.50	18.00	25.00
Comport	9.00	——	——

	Crystal	Green	Pink
Cream Soup, 5" d	6.00	30.00	25.00
Creamer	5.00	15.00	19.00
Creamer, Holiday shape	7.50	——	——
Cup and Saucer	9.00	24.00	15.00
Fruit Console, 12½" d	25.00	——	95.00
Pitcher			
4½" h, 16 oz	24.00	——	115.00
6¾" h, 52 oz	15.00	55.00	33.00
Plate			
6" d, sherbet	3.75	8.00	5.00
7" d, salad	4.50	20.00	18.00
9" d, dinner	9.00	25.00	25.00
Platter, 11½", oval	7.00	25.00	22.00
Powder Jar	15.00	——	55.00
Relish Platter, 11½" l, divided	10.00	——	200.00
Salad Bowl, 10½" d	12.00	——	——
Salt and Pepper Shakers, pr	16.00	48.00	39.00
Sandwich Plate, 10" d			
Closed handle	——	——	24.00
Open handle	7.50	17.00	17.00
Sherbet, ftd	3.50	15.00	13.00
Sugar, cov	9.00	39.00	19.00
Sugar, cov, Holiday shape	12.00	——	100.00
Tray			
4" sq	5.00	12.00	10.00
4" sq, handles	6.00	——	40.00
4⅛ × 9"	5.00	16.00	10.00
4⅛ × 9", handles	9.00	——	50.00
8½ × 9¾"	7.00	35.00	25.00
8½ × 9¾", handles	14.00	45.00	85.00
Tumbler			
3¼" h, 5 oz	9.00	42.00	25.00
4" h, 9 oz	7.50	38.00	22.00
4" h, ftd	7.00	——	——
4⅝" h, 11 oz	8.00	——	——
5" h, 12 oz	11.00	55.00	30.00
5" h, ftd, 11 oz	12.00	——	——
7¼" h, ftd	19.00	——	——
Vegetable Bowl, 9½" l, oval	7.50	29.00	25.00

DISNEYANA

History: Walt Disney and the creations of the famous Disney Studios hold a place of fondness and enchantment in the hearts of people throughout the world. The 1928 release of "Steamboat Willie," featuring Mickey Mouse, heralded an entertainment empire.

Walt and his brother, Roy, were shrewd businessmen. From the beginning they licensed the reproduction of Disney characters on products ranging from wristwatches to clothing.

In 1984 Donald Duck celebrated his 50th birthday, and collectors took a renewed interest in material related to him.

References: Ted Hake, *Hake's Guide to Character Toy Premiums,* Gemstone Publishing (1966 Greenspring, Ste. 405, Timonium, MD 21093), 1996; Robert Heide and John Gilman, *Disneyana,* Hyperion, 1994; David Longest and Michael Stern, *The Collector's Encyclopedia of Disneyana,* Collector Books, 1992; Carol J. Smith, *Identification & Price Guide to Winnie the Pooh Collectibles,* Hobby House Press, 1994; Michael Stern, *Stern's Guide to Disney Collectibles,* First Series (1989, 1992 value update), Second Series (1990, 1993 value update), Third Series (1995), Collector Books; Tom Tumbusch, *Tomart's Illustrated Disneyana Catalog and Price Guide,* Vols. 1, 2, 3, and 4, Tomart Publications, 1985; ———, *Tomart's Illustrated Disneyana Catalog and Price Guide, Condensed Edition,* Wallace-Homestead, 1989.

Periodicals: *Baby Boomer Collectibles,* PO Box 437, Waupaca, WI 51; *Mouse Rap Monthly,* PO Box 1064, Ojai, CA 93024; *Storyboard Magazine for Disneyana Collectors,* 2512 Artesia Blvd, Redondo Beach, CA 90278; *Tomart's Disneyana Digest,* 3300 Encrete Ln, Dayton, OH 45439; *Tomart's Disneyana Update,* 3300 Encrete Ln, Dayton, OH 45439.

Collectors' Clubs: Imagination Guild, PO Box 907, Boulder Creek, CA 95006; Mouse Club East, PO Box 3195, Wakefield,

MA 01880; National Fantasy Fan Club for Disneyana Collectors and Enthusiasts, PO Box 19212, Irvine, CA 92713.

Archives/Museum: Walt Disney Archives, Burbank, CA 91521.

Additional Listings: See *Warman's Americana & Collectibles* for more examples.

Advisor: Ted Hake.

SPECIAL AUCTION

Hake's Americana & Collectibles
PO Box 1444, Dept 344
York, PA 17405
(717) 848-1333

Aristocats, animation cel, 12½ × 16″ acetate sheet, large 6 × 6″ cel image of Thomas O'Malley, felt-tip-pen signature of two direction animators, "Frank Thomas, Oliver Johnston," 1971 .... **500.00**

Davy Crockett
 Children's Book, *Davy Crockett Big Golden Book,* Simon & Schuster, 1955 copyright, 8½ × 11″, color hardcover, 48 pgs, color illus on every page **20.00**
 Pinback Button, 1⅜″ d, "Walt Disney's Davy Crockett Frontiersman," full color, Fess Parker in Crockett outfit, pale blue ground **35.00**

Disneyland
 Key Chain, 1½ × 2″, stiff plastic, key chain on one corner, colorful image of one of the Chipmunks, when moved his eyes and mouth open and close, reverse with paper label for owner's name and address, label includes Art Corner souvenir inscription, 1960s **12.00**
 Little Golden Book, *Disneyland on the Air,* Simon & Schuster, copyright 1955, 6¾ × 8″, first printing, 28 pgs **20.00**
 Magazine, *Disneyland Magazine,* Fawcett Publications, Issue #2, copyright 1972, 10¼ × 12½″d, colorful illus **20.00**
 Pinback Button
  1¼″ d, "Disneyland–25," silver anniversary, tiny black image of castle in center **10.00**
  2½″ d, "A.B.A. Convention Oct 21–25, 1956," black and white, Mickey in formal outfit, dollar signs decorating band of top hat **100.00**
 Playset, Marx #5995, 21 × 28 × 7″ h cardboard box with brown and yellow illus, repeated Sears logo, 1958 Walt Disney Productions, light scattered dust and minor damage to box, complete set of 6 character figures, 12 of 13 misc figures, neatly assembled Dumbo ride, orig bags and instruction sheet, other pieces with minor damage and few missing parts **725.00**

Disney World, tab, "Meet Me in the Sunshine Tree at Walt Disney World," tin litho, yellow, green, and orange Florida orange bird , orange heart inscribed "I Love You," light wear, c1970 .... **14.00**

Donald Duck
 Advertising, premium booklet

"Automotive Quiz," 5 × 7″, 8 pgs, red, white, and blue, 1941, Sunoco Oil **75.00**
 "Donald Duck/Goodyear Tires," 3½ × 6″, colorful, glossy paper, 8 pgs, prepared "By Goodyear," printed with permission of "Look Magazine Where This Material Appeared in the May 18, 1943 Issue," light cov wear **120.00**

Better Little Book, *Donald Duck and Ghost Morgan's Treasure,* Whitman #1411, 1946 copyright **75.00**

Coloring Book, Donald Duck Color Book, Whitman #670, 1936 copyright, 8¼ × 11¼″, 96 pgs of full-page art, long-billed Donald, unused **125.00**

Lamp, 9″ h, painted, glazed ceramic, three-dimensional Donald standing on 6½″ w × 6½″ d tan base, fisherman outfit, blue coat, red hat, black and yellow lantern, copyright "Underwriters Laboratories, Inc. Portable Lamp" sticker **60.00**

Original Art, 10 × 12″ sheet of animation paper, 2½ × 3¾″ lead and blue pencil image of Donald making large snowball from "Dumbbell of the Yukon," red pencil accents, from numbered sequence, numbered "71," 1946, scattered minor creases **295.00**

Pinback Button
 1¼″ d, "Donald Duck Jackets/Dry in Any Weather," bright orange and blue on white, Norwich Knitting Co, Norwich, NY, 1936, early image **600.00**
 2¼″ d, "Oregon Homecoming November 30, 1963," bright yellow and green litho, Donald in football helmet **30.00**

Bank, 9¼″ h, plastic, colored, $35.00.

Elmer the Elephant
 Children's Book, *Elmer Elephant,* David McKay Co, 1936 copyright, 6¼ × 8½″, 48 pgs, large color story art on every other page, color front cov, hardcover, minor repairs **45.00**
 Toy, roly-poly, 4½ × 4½ × 6½″ h, celluloid, three-dimensional, musical sound when moved, 1930s, marked "Japan" **425.00**

Fantasia
 Original Art, 10 × 12″ sheet of animation paper, concept drawing, 6 × 7¾″ outlined area at center

with 4½ × 7¾″ lead and orange pencil drawing of baby Pegasus sitting on large tree branch, minor pinpoint holes, scattered traces of soiling 325.00

Still, 8 × 10 glossy black and white photo, copyright 1944, slight age browning at margin edges

Bacchus and Jacchus with background 20.00

Bacchus and Jacchus without background 20.00

Centaurette and Child Nubian Centaurette, filing her nails, child filing hoofs, scene deleted before release of film 35.00

Nubian Centaurette carrying water pitcher 40.00

Ferdinand the Bull, paint book, Whitman #645, 11 × 12¾″, 1938 copyright, 32 pgs, *From the Silly Symphony Based on the Story of Ferdinand,* colorful cover on front and back 25.00

Mary Poppins

Children's Book, *Mary Poppins,* Whitman Tip Top Tales, 1964 copyright, 6½ × 7½″, 28 pgs, color story art, wraparound cov, ink name and address on title page 10.00

Lobby Card, 11 × 14″, glossy color photo, copyright 1964, six cards show both Julie Andrews and Dick Van Dyke, price for set of 8 cards 50.00

Sticker Book, *Mary Poppins Sticker Fun,* Watkins Strathmore Co, 1964 copyright, 8¼ × 11″, stiff color cov, 8 pgs with black and white illus, 4 pgs of uncut stickers, unused 20.00

Mickey Mouse

Advertising, recipe book, *Mickey Mouse Recipe Scrapbook,* 4¼ × 6¼″, 48 pgs for placement of full-color bread cards, black, white, red, yellow, and orange cov, black and white pgs, Kuss's Butter-Nut Bread, 1930s 75.00

Badge, "Tenth Pan American Games," 1½″ l, multicolor enameled full-figure Mickey next to parrot, brass lettering "Opening Ceremony Indianapolis 1987," United States Olympic Committee copyright on back 20.00

Big Little Book, *Mickey Mouse and the Sacred Jewel,* Whitman, 1935 copyright, orig owner's name .. 60.00

Children's Book, *Mickey Mouse and His Friends,* Whitman #904, 1936 copyright, 10 × 12½″, linenlike, color cover, eight pgs 100.00

Coloring Book, *A New Mickey Mouse Book to Color,* Saalfield, 1937 copyright, 10½ × 14¼″, 24 pgs, "Illustrations by the Staff of the Walt Disney Studios," minute spotting to cover 150.00

Cup, 1¾″ h, SP, stamped image of Mickey playing saxophone, black accents, International Silver Co, c1934 .... 100.00

Figure

3″ h, plaster-filled celluloid, bright red shoes and pants, gold buttons, marked "Japan," 1930s . 150.00

3¼″ h, composition, black and white, orig stood on ashtray rim, raised name and copyright on back of head 75.00

4½″ h, wood and wire, Fun-E-Flex, orig tail, cardboard ears, and chest decal 500.00

Magazine, *Mickey Mouse Magazine,* 5¼ × 7¼″, Vol 1, #3, Jan, 1934, issued by Laher's Ice Cream Co, 16 pgs, black, white, and red cov, black and white contents, reattached to spine 85.00

Watch, Ingersoll, orig band, silver stick pin mice, 1¼″ d, $225.00.

Original Artwork, 10 × 12″ sheet of animation paper, 3 × 4¾″ image in lead and red pencil, green pencil accent below, from society dog show, 1939 325.00

Pin, 1″ h, diecut, hand extended, black enamel-paint body, bright yellow enamel-paint pants, silver luster metal, early 1930s 125.00

Pinback Button

7/8″ d

"Mickey Mouse Hose," black, white, and dark red, 1930s Mickey holding paint brush ... 100.00

Wide brass rim surrounding fabric with black and white Mickey, dark gold ground, nearly full luster on brass rim 75.00

1¼″ d

"Follow My Adventures," black, white, and red, "Buy Prize Winner Bread," reverse back paper with picture of Mickey, 1930s 75.00

"Golden Wonder," full figure black, white, and red Mickey eating snack food, orange shoes, bright orange ground, red product name, Disney copyright, c1960, English .. 20.00

1⅜″ d, "Keep This Button!" black on green litho, Mickey's head about slogan, serial number to match with "Evening Herald & Express," Los Angeles newspaper, 1930s 50.00

Tab, 1⅜″ h, "Mickey Mouse Shoe," tin litho, black, cream, and orange image of Mickey, name in orange, Enterprises, Ltd. copyright, Truiff Bros shoemaker 100.00

Toothbrush Holder, 2¾ × 3 × 5″, bisque, movable right arm, curved left arm to hold toothbrush, orig tail, small paper label under base, 1930s 300.00

Mickey Mouse Club

Children's Book, *Annette and the Mystery at Smugglers' Cove,* hardcover, 5¾ × 7¾″, 212 pgs, wraparound color cov 12.00

Dixie Cup Lid, 2¾″ d, cardboard, black and red design, marked "Southern Dairies," 1930s 60.00

Paper Dolls, *Mouseketeer Annette Cut-Out Dolls,* Whitman, copyright 1958, 10½ × 12½″, stiff color cov, dolls neatly punched out, clothes neatly cut 25.00

Pinback Button

1" d, "Member/Mickey Mouse & Scrappy Club/ Tracy," paper, blue on white, 1930s, back mfg paper reads "Irvine & Jachens/California" ... **85.00**

1¼" d, "Mickey Mouse Globe Trotters–Member," black, white, and red, "I Eat Peter Pan Bread," no back paper, c1930 .... **75.00**

Minnie Mouse

Animation Cel, 10 × 12½" acetate sheet, 3¼ × 6¾" cel image of Minnie in pink and cranberry outfit, "24" of numbered sequence, 1970s **125.00**

Figure, 3¾" h, wood and wire, Fun-E-Flex, 70% of orig decal on chest, orig tail, professionally replaced ears, light paint wear **75.00**

Mug, 3" h, glazed white ceramic, red trim, Minnie as Jill, falling down, English, 1930s **160.00**

Plate, 5" d, glazed white ceramic, red trim, Minnie as Jill, falling down, marked "J & G Meakin, England," 1930s **50.00**

Miscellaneous

Children's Book

Savage Sam Big Golden Book, Simon & Schuster, copyright 1955, 8½ × 11", hardcover, 48 pgs, color illus on each page, color cov, minor wear **15.00**

Toby Tortoise and the Hare, Whitman #928, copyright 1938, 9½ × 12¼", color cover, 8 pgs **40.00**

Christmas Card, 6 × 7½", Disney Studio, stiff glossy paper, copyright 1980, 1981 calendar on back, Mickey and reindeer on white ground with snowflake designs, printed "Best Wishes Al Konetzni," overhead color photo of Main Street Railroad, orchestra, singers **40.00**

Lobby Card, 11 × 14", Alaskan Eskimo, copyright 1953, colorful illus from live-action film, price for set of four **30.00**

Original Art

9½ × 12" sheet of animation paper, 3 × 3¼" lead-pencil image of pigs from "Three Little Wolves," slightly left of center, numbered "49" and "50", 1936, price for pr **275.00**

10 × 12" sheet of animation paper, 4½ × 6½" lead- and red-pencil image of Giant from "Brave Little Tailor," holding wishing well in one hand which he is drinking, orange pencil accents, red pencil notations above head, 1938, scattered minor creases **400.00**

10½ × 15½" sheet, "Pin-Ups for Serviceman from Walt Disney Staff," textured paper, 1943, black and white front, flesh tones and red pinup illus by Fred Moore, Bill Justice, and Milt Neal, orig folded size 5 × 7¾" **85.00**

Photographic Model Sheet, Tug Boat Mickey, two 11 × 14" sheets, black and white copy of model sheet, 1939, titled "Pelican Model, 2236," different pelican characters with Mickey, scattered creases **150.00**

Postcard, 3½ × 5½", Seabees, black and white, dark blue, and orange, light blue ground, text reads "We Build and Fight With All Our Might! United States Naval Construction Battalions," ink message and 1943 postmark **20.00**

Sticker Book, *Walt Disney's Merry Menagerie Sticker*

Fun, Whitman, copyright 1953, 10½ × 12", stiff color cov, cutout circus wagons on back, 8 pgs, dot-to-dot puzzles, color pictures for stickers, unused **15.00**

War Bond Certificate, 8 × 10", issued by United States Treasury War Finance Committee, 1944, character portraits in center, typed info about orig recipient, red, white, and blue "Victory Loan" stamp, minor aging, scattered light creases **175.00**

Window Card, 14 × 22", stiff cardboard, Saludos Amigos, copyright 1942, blank area for theater printing glued to paper section, extensive dark blue staining at upper left corner, orig pink background color darkened with age to light tan **140.00**

Peter Pan, sticker book, *Sticker Fun with Peter Pan,* Whitman, copyright 1952, 10½ × 12", 8 stiff pgs, color cov, three pgs neatly completed **50.00**

Pinocchio

Children's Book, *Pinocchio Picture Book,* Grosset & Dunlap, copyright 1940, 9½ × 13", 12 stiff cardboard pgs, large color story art **35.00**

Original Art, 10 × 12" sheet of animation paper, concept drawing, center attached 4¼ × 5¾" sheet of paper, lead pencil drawing of Figaro in old shoe, front split open, looking through opening while tail hangs out back of shoe, penciled text "SC.39CU Shoe Jumps Up-Big Take," blue ink stamp "Original WDP" and emb "1939 Walt Disney Prod.," 6½" l strip of tape which has browned **350.00**

Pinback Button, 1½" d, "I've Seen Pinocchio at Hudson's," black and white, light and dark red accents on freckles, hat, and feather, red printing, Detroit department store, 1950s **60.00**

Pirates of the Caribbean, model

Fate of the Mutineers, 1972 MPC series, 7 × 9¼ × 2¾" sealed colorful box, slight damage to box still in orig shrink wrap **85.00**

Hoist High the Jolly Roger, 6 × 8¼ × 2¼" sealed colorful box **60.00**

Pluto

Ring, seated Pluto, "sterling" silver, one-piece band, 1940s **35.00**

Toy, 2 × 4 × 6" h, yellow wooden segments, black tail and nose, red collar, 10½" l green wooden base, Fisher-Price Pop-Up Kritter, red printing "Mickey Mouse's Pal Pluto," Enterprises copyright, 1930s **90.00**

Sleeping Beauty. children's book, *Sleeping Beauty,* Whitman Tell-A-Tale, copyright 1959, 5½ × 6¼", 28 pgs, large color story art **10.00**

Snow White And The Seven Dwarfs

Children's Book, *Snow White and the Seven Dwarfs,* Whitman #925, copyright 1938, 9½ × 13¼", 12 pgs, large story art, minor damage **35.00**

Pencil Sharpener, 2½" h, celluloid, raised name on base, metal sharpener insert, small copyright symbol and "Made in Japan" on back, c1938 ...... **275.00**

Swiss Family Robinson, children's book, *The Swiss Family Robinson,* Whitman, copyright 1960, 5¾ × 7¾", 212 pgs, full color cov, black and green illus **10.00**

Zorro

Children's Book, *Zorro,* Whitman, copyright 1958,

5½ × 7¾", hardcover, full-color wraparound cov, minor damage **12.00**
Comic Book, *Zorro,* Dell Publishing Co, Four Color Comic #1037, Sept–Nov 1959, color cov photo of Zorro and Annette Funicello as "Beautiful Senorita" **30.00**

DOLLHOUSES

History: Dollhouses date from the 18th century to modern times. Early dollhouses often were handmade, sometimes with only one room. The most common type was made for a young girl to fill with replicas of furniture scaled especially to fit into a dollhouse. Specially sized dolls also were made for dollhouses. All types of accessories in all types of styles were available, and dollhouses could portray any historical period.

References: Evelyn Ackerman, *The Genius of Moritz Gottschalk,* Gold House Publishing, 1994; Caroline Clifton-Mogg, *The Dollhouse Sourcebook,* Abbeville Press, 1993; Nora Earnshaw, *Collecting Dolls' Houses and Miniatures,* Pincushion Press, 1993; Flora Bill Jacobs, *Dolls' Houses in America: Historic Preservation in Miniature,* Charles Scribner's Sons, 1974; Margaret Towner, *Dollhouse Furniture,* Courage Books, 1993; Dian Zillner, *American Dollhouses and Furniture from the 20th Century,* Schiffer Publishing, 1995.

Periodicals: *Doll Castle News,* PO Box 247, Washington, NJ 07882; *International Dolls' House News,* PO Box 79, Southampton S09 7EZ England; *Miniature Collector,* 30595 Eight Mill, Livonia, MI 48152; *Miniatures Showcase,* PO Box 1612, Waukesha, WI 53187; *Nutshell News,* 21027 Crossroads Circle, PO Box 1612, Waukesha, WI 53187.

Collectors' Clubs: Dollhouse & Miniature Collectors, 9451 Lee Hwy #515, Fairfax, VA 22302; National Assoc of Miniature Enthusiasts, PO Box 69, Carmel, IN 46032; National Organization of Miniaturists and Dollers, 1300 Schroder, Normal, IL 61761.

Museums: Art Institute of Chicago, Chicago, IL; Margaret Woodbury Strong Museum, Rochester, NY; Museums at Stony Brook, Stony Brook, NY; Toy and Miniature Museum of Kansas City, Kansas City, MO; Washington Dolls' House and Toy Museum, Washington, DC.

Barn, wooden, colorful paper litho covering, horse and buggy, wear, 16" h **675.00**
Bliss, c1900, two stories, three rooms, two lower, one second story, litho paper ext., printed windows on sides and dormers, later-added wooden roof shingles, int. papered walls, some flaking, 17" h, 11½" w, 9¾" d **400.00**
Converse, wood, cottage, hinged front, two int. rooms, 12" h **300.00**
Hacker, Christian, Nuremberg, Germany, painted, front stucco facade, five rooms, two and one half story, steeple roof, two chimneys, bay window, papered int., FAO Schwarz label, 34" h **750.00**
Japanese Palace, open room with floral and bird dec, red lacquered central stairway, multi-level platform, pagoda roof, includes seven festival dolls with painted facial features and ceremonial robes, 27 × 18 × 12" **900.00**

Kiddie Grocery Store, miniature food products, Barnums Animal Crackers sample, 1930s, MIB **200.00**
McLoughlin, folding, two rooms, highly dec int., orig box, 16 × 17 × 12" **850.00**
Schoenhut, wood and fiberboard, two story, two rooms, white lace curtains at glazed windows, int. walls with orig paper, lower floor with flannel-print wall dec, repainted roof, porch floor, and two pillars, c1920, 14" h, 10½" w, 8½" d, marked "Made in U.S.A., The A. Schoenhut Company, Philadelphia, PA," wooden base, roof lists off, side wall opens **450.00**
Wood
New England, two story, pierced glazed windows, front porch with turned columns and hand rails, two hinged entrance ways, roof lifts off, c1900, 30 × 21 × 18½" **1,800.00**
Oklahoma-Style, one room, three pierced glazed windows, hinged door, clapboard sides, front porch with two columns, lift-off tiled gabled roof, c1910, 31 × 27 × 25" **650.00**
Whippany, NJ, three story, nine rooms, pierced glazed windows, hinged front door, stairs, lattice work, orig wallpaper, carpets, lace curtains, furniture and accessories, fitted with electricity and doorbell, 1901, 45 × 48 × 16" **8,500.00**

DOLLS

History: Dolls have been children's play toys for centuries. Dolls also have served other functions. From the 14th through 18th centuries, doll making was centered in Europe, mainly in Germany and France. The French dolls produced in this era were representations of adults and were dressed in the latest couturier designs. They were not children's toys.

During the mid-19th century, child and baby dolls, made in wax, cloth, bisque, and porcelain, were introduced. Facial features were hand painted; wigs were made of mohair and human hair; and the dolls were dressed in the current fashions for babies or children.

Doll making in the United States began to flourish in the 1900s with companies such as Effanbee, Madame Alexander, and Ideal.

Marks: Marks of the various manufacturers are found on the back of the head or neck or on the doll's back. These marks are very important in identifying a doll and its date of manufacture.

References: Johana Gast Anderton, *More Twentieth Century Dolls from Bisque to Vinyl,* Vols. A–H, I–Z, Revised Editions, Wallace-Homestead, 1974; John Axe, *The Encyclopedia of Celebrity Dolls,* Hobby House Press, 1983; Carol Corson, *Schoenhut Dolls,* Hobby House Press, 1993; Jan Foulke, *Insider's Guide to China Doll Collecting,* Hobby House Press, 1995;———, *Insider's Guide to Doll Buying and Selling,* Hobby House Press, 1995; ———, *Insider's Guide to Germany "Dolly" Collecting,* Hobby House Press, 1995; ———, *12th Blue Book Dolls and Values,* Hobby House Press, 1995; Polly Judd, *Cloth Dolls,* Hobby House Press, 1990; Polly and Pam Judd, *Composition Dolls,* Vol. I (1991), Volume II (1994), Hobby House Press; ———, *European Costume Dolls,* Hobby House Press, 1994; ———, *Glamour Dolls of the 1950s & 1960s,* Revised Edition, Hobby House Press, 1993; ———, *Hard Plastic Dolls,* Third Revised Edition (1993), Book II

(1994), Hobby House Press; A. Glenn Mandeville, *Alexander Dolls,* Second Edition, Hobby House Press, 1995; ———, *Ginny,* Second Revised Edition, Hobby House Press, 1994; Edward R. Pardella, *Shirley Temple Dolls and Fashion,* Schiffer Publishing, 1992; Sabine Reinelt, *Magic of Character Dolls,* Hobby House Press, 1993.

Lydia Richter, *China, Parian, and Bisque German Dolls,* Hobby House Press, 1993; Lydia and Joachim F. Richter, *Bru Dolls,* Hobby House Press, 1989; Lydia Richter and Karin Schmelcher, *Heubach Character Dolls and Figurines,* Hobby House Press, 1992; Patricia R. Smith, *Antique Collector's Dolls,* Vol. I (1975, 1991 value update), Vol. II (1976, 1991 Value update), Collector Books; ———, *Madame Alexander Collector's Dolls Price Guide #20,* Collector Books, 1995; ———, *Madame Alexander Dolls 1965–1990,* Collector Books, 1991; ———, *Modern Collector's Dolls,* Series I through VII (1973, 1975, 1976, 1979, 1984, 1994, 1995 value updates), Collector Books; ———, *Patricia Smith's Doll Values Antique to Modern,* Eleventh Series, Collector Books, 1995; ———, *Shirley Temple Dolls and Collectibles,* Vol. I (1977, 1992 value update), Vol. II (1979, 1992 value update), Collector Books; Evelyn Robson Stahlendorf, *The Charlton Standard Catalogue of Canadian Dolls,* Third Edition, Charlton Press, 1995; Carl P. Stirn, *Turn-of-the-Century Dolls, Toys and Games* (1893 catalog reprint), Dover Publications, 1990; Margaret Whitton, *The Jumeau Doll,* Dover Publications, 1981.

Periodicals: *Antique Doll World,* 225 Main St, Suite 300, Northport, NY 11768; *Cloth Doll Magazine,* PO Box 2167 Lake Oswego, OR 97035; *Costume Quarterly for Doll Collectors,* 118-01 Sutter Ave, Jamaica, NY 11420; *Doll Castle News,* PO Box 247, Washington, NJ 07882; *Doll Collector's Price Guide,* 306 East Parr Rd, Berne, IN 46711; *Doll Life,* 243 Newton-Sparta Rd, Newton, NJ 07860; *Doll Reader,* 6405 Flank Dr, Harrisburg, PA 17112; *Doll Times,* 218 W Woodin Blvd, Dallas, TX 75224; *Doll World,* 306 East Parr Rd, Berne, IN 46711; *Dollmasters,* PO Box 151, Annapolis, MD 21404; *Dolls—The Collector's Magazine,* 170 Fifth Ave, 12th Floor, New York, NY 10010; *National Doll & Teddy Bear Collector,* PO Box 4032, Portland, OR 97208.

Collectors' Clubs: Doll Collector International, PO Box 2761, Oshkosh, WI 54903; Madame Alexander Fan Club, PO Box 330, Mundeline, IL 60060; United Federation of Doll Clubs, PO Box 14146, Parkville, MO 64152.

Videotapes: *Doll Makers: Women Entrepreneurs 1865–1945,* Sirocco Productions, 1995; *Dolls of the Golden Age: 1880–n1915,* Sirocco Productions, 1993; *Extraordinary World of Doll Collecting,* Cinebar Productions, 1994.

Museums: Aunt Len's Doll House, Inc., New York, NY; Children's Museum, Detroit, MI; Doll Castle Doll Museum, Washington, NJ; Doll Museum, Newport, RI; Toy and Miniature Museum of Kansas City, Kansas City, MO; Gay Nineties Button & Doll Museum, Eureka Springs, AR; Margaret Woodbury Strong Museum, Rochester, NY; Mary Merritt Doll Museum, Douglassville, PA; Mary Miller Doll Museum, Brunswick, GA; Prairie Museum of Art & History, Colby, KS; Washington Dolls' House & Toy Museum, Washington, DC; Yesteryears Museum, Sandwich, MA.

Additional Listings: See *Warman's Americana & Collectibles* for more examples.

Alt, Beck & Gottschalck, 23" h, 784 boy, china shoulder head, painted blue eyes with red accent line, single-strike brows, closed mouth, molded blond hair, kid

body with bisque lower arms, rivet joints at hips and knees, new white wool suit and matching hat, light blue trim, blue and white crocheted socks, handmade shoes, marked "784 #9" on back of shoulder plate ... **225.00**

Bahr & Proschild

12½" h, 224 Belton, bisque socket head, flat area and three holes on top, set blue-threaded eyes, feathered brows, painted upper and lower lashes, closed mouth, accented lips, accent line and white space between lips, pierced ears, orig mohair wig, jointed wood and composition body with straight wrists, old pale blue print dress, eyelet trim, underclothing, socks, and shoes, marked "224, 5" on back of head, slight damage to body finish, neck socket loose **1,500.00**

18½" h, 585 Baby, bisque socket head, blue sleep eyes, feathered brows, painted upper and lower lashes, open mouth with accented lips, two upper teeth, mohair wig, composition bent-limb baby

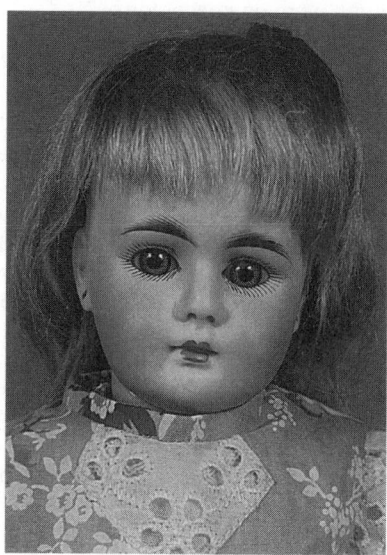

Bahr & Proschild, Belton, bisque socket head, jointed wood and composition body, orig mohair wig, set threaded blue eyes, painted facial features, redressed, marked "224,5," 12½" h, $1,500.00. Photograph courtesy of McMasters Doll Auctions.

body, long white baby dress, underclothing, antique diaper, blue booties, embroidered bonnet, marked "BP [in heart] 585, 9, Made in Germany" on back of head, replaced teeth, small filing line below right eye, lower arms repainted, right fingers repaired **350.00**

Barrois, E, 17½" h, bisque shoulder head, straight neck, pierced ears, blue painted eyes, orig brown hair wig, kid-leather fashion body, old white dotted-Swiss dress, matching hat, marked "E.B." **2,950.00**

Belton, 24" h, bisque socket head, concave area with three holes, set brown eyes, heavy feathered brows, painted upper and lower lashes, closed mouth, accent lines and white space between lips, pierced ears, human-hair wig, jointed wood and composition body with straight wrists, antique red and brown plaid dress, antique underclothing, socks, and shoes, marked "183, 15" on back of head, general wear, minor repair on elbows and knees **1,050.00**

Bergmann, C. M.

24" h, bisque socket head, set blue eyes, real and painted lashes, feathered brows, open mouth, four upper teeth, synthetic wig, jointed wood and composition body, antique blue and white dress, underclothing, new socks, and shoes, marked "C. M. Bergmann, Simon & Halbig, S & H, 3" on back of head, tiny flake on lower right lid, broken eyes set with plaster showing, unmatched legs, foot repaired **250.00**

30" h, bisque socket head, brown sleep eyes, real lashes, molded and feathered brows, painted lower lashes, open mouth, accepted lips, four upper teeth, pierced ears, human-hair wig, jointed wood and composition body, antique low-waisted dress, antique underclothing, stockings, high-button shoes, marked "C. M. Bergmann, Simon & Halbig, 13 1/2" on back of head, light rub on cheek, finish worn on front of torso **400.00**

Bru, Casimir

17" h, pressed bisque head, brown paperweight eyes, outlined open/closed mouth, cork pate, pierced ears, wood jointed body, key-wind mechanical music box, marked "Bte S.G.D.G." **6,600.00**

23" h, bisque swivel head, shoulder plate, brown paperweight eyes, highlighted lids, outlined open/closed mouth, cork pate, pierced ears, kid body, bisque lower arms, repainted wood lower legs, circle dot mark "Bru Jne 19" **1,320.00**

Bye-Lo

5" h, bisque swivel head, tiny brown sleep eyes, softly blushed brows, painted upper and lower lashes, closed mouth, all-bisque body, jointed at shoulders and hips, orig crocheted diaper with belly band, white baby dress, crocheted sweater, marked "12" on front of neck, "6-12, Copr. by Grace S. Putnam, Germany" on back, "20-32" on top of right leg **275.00**

18" h, bisque flange head, blue sleep eyes, softly blushed brows, painted upper and lower lashes, closed mouth, lightly molded and painted hair, cloth body with frog legs, celluloid hands, antique white lace-trimmed christening dress, undercloth-

ing, baby booties, embroidered bib, bonnet, marked "Copr. by Grace S. Putnam, Made in Germany" on back of head, turtle mark on celluloid hands, very fine flake at upper left eye rim, light rub to cheek **525.00**

Chase Type, 18½" h, oil-painted stockinette head, stiff neck, painted brown eyes, single-stroke brows, painted hair, applied ears, cloth body with sateen covering, oil-painted stockinette lower arms and legs, jointed at shoulders, hips and knees, pink tint on stitched fingers and toes, plain white baby dress, underclothing, old blue cotton socks, light wear, slight flaking, left ankle repaired, unmarked **550.00**

China Head

21" h, china shoulder head, light pink tint, painted brown eyes with red accent line, single-stroke brows, closed smiling mouth with white space between lips, molded and painted black hair with center part, cloth body, leather arms, individually stitched fingers, orig red print dress, black velvet ribbon trim, underclothing, socks, old handmade leather shoes, unmarked, well-repaired hairline on left side of shoulder, dark spot of kiln debris on left shoulder, fragile dress **350.00**

24" h, boy, china shoulder plate, painted blue eyes, red accent line, single-stroke brows, closed mouth, molded and painted curly hair, cloth body, leather lower arms, redressed in black and white checked two-pc suit, underclothing, black socks, marked "880 11" on back of shoulder plate **275.00**

French Fashion

16" h, bisque socket head, bisque shoulder plate, set cobalt blue eyes, multi-stroke brows, painted upper and lower lashes, closed mouth, accented lips, pierced ears, orig mohair wig, kid body with gussets at hips, individually stitched fingers, dark brown velvet suit with long train and bustle, lace trim, flowers on blue hat, handmade shoes, marked "B 3 S" on bottom of rear shoulder plate, minor repairs **1,600.00**

20" h, bisque socket head, bisque shoulder plate, high

French Fashion, bisque head, shoulder plate, arms, and hands, articulated kid body, orig wig, 17" h, $1,750.00.

forehead, pale blue paperweight eyes, multi-stroke brows, painted upper and lower lashes, closed smiling mouth, pierced ears, orig human-hair wig on cork pate, beige kid body with gussets at elbows , hips, and knees, individually stitched fingers, black silk taffeta two-pc suit trimmed in aqua and lace, underclothing, new high-button boots, back velvet hat with snood, marked "L De-pose" on bottom of back shoulder plate, 1" hair-line from crown, body may be replacement **1,100.00**

Frozen Charlie, 15" h, china, painted blue eyes, molded lids, red accent lines, single-stroke brows, closed smiling mouth, molded and painted blond hair, un-jointed body, arms held out to front, undressed, un-marked **525.00**

Gautlier, Francois

17" h, bisque poured swivel head, shoulder plate, blue-threaded glass eyes, closed mouth, blond wig, kid and silk body, marked "F. G." **995.00**

22" h, poured bisque head, blue paperweight eyes, outlined closed mouth, cork pate, pierced ears, pink silk dress, wood and composition ball-jointed repainted body, pink silk dress, marked "F.G. [within scroll] 9," body stamped "Jumeau Medal-lion d'Or Paris" **1,900.00**

Goebel, 7" h, bisque socket head, painted black sur-prised eyes, dot brows, painted upper lashes, open-closed mouth, molded and painted blond hair, five-pc composition body, molded and painted shoes and socks, marked "bee NWG,¹²⁄₀ x, Germany" on head, hand-knitted outfit **375.00**

Greiner, 28" h, papier-mâché shoulder head, painted blue eyes, single-strike brows, painted upper lashes, closed mouth, molded and painted hair with twelve vertical curls, cloth body, leather lower arms, orig black and gold plaid dress, underclothing replaced socks and shoes, white apron, marked "Greiner's Im-proved Patent Heads, Pat. march 30, '58" on label on back shoulder plate, very light touchup on face, light crazing on face, left ankle mended, water stains on orig body, lower arms discolored, orig silk dress deteriorating badly in places **450.00**

Handwerck, Heinrich, 26" h, bisque socket head, blue sleep eyes, real lashes, molded and feathered brows, open mouth, four upper teeth, pierced ears, antique human-hair wig, jointed wood and composition body, antique white eyelet dress, underclothing, socks, and shoes, marked "Germany, Heinrich Hand-werck, Simon & Halbig" on back of head, "W" on front of head at crown, worn body finish, repairs at knees and neck socket, finger missing **425.00**

Heubach, Gebruder

8½" h, Baby Stuart, bisque socket head, blue intaglio eyes, single-strike brows, closed pouty mouth, molded white bonnet trimmed with pink roses, composition bent-limb baby body, orig factory chemise with pink trim, orig dress, slip, and pants, marked "79 77 [sunburst] 4, DEP, Germany" on back of head **750.00**

10" h, character, boy, bisque shoulder head, blue intaglio eyes, molded lids, single-stroke brows, open-closed smiling mouth, molded and lightly

painted hair, cloth body, papier-mâché lower arms and legs, marked "2/0 D, Heubach [in square] Germany," redressed **275.00**

Ideal

14" h, Miss Curity, hard-plastic head, blue sleep eyes, real lashes, feathered brows, closed mouth, orig saran wig, five-pc hard-plastic body, orig tagged nurse's uniform with cape and hat, underclothing, socks, and shoes, marked "Ideal Doll, Made in USA" on back of head, "Ideal Dolls, P-90" on back, "Miss Curity" on hat, "The First Lady of First Aid, Miss Curity, The Famous Nurse Doll" on dress tag, unplayed-with condition, orig play nurse's kit, orig box **650.00**

18" h, Shirley Temple, composition head, hazel sleep eyes, painted and real lashes, feathered brows, open mouth, six upper teeth, orig mohair wig in orig set, composition five-pc child's body, orig tagged pink pleated organdy dress, blue ribbon trim, orig one-pc underwear, socks, and shoes, orig pin, marked "Shirley Temple, Corp. Ideal N & T Co.," on back of head, "Shirley Temple, 18," on back, unplayed-with condition, orig box **600.00**

21" h, Toni, hard-plastic head, blue sleep eyes with real lashes, single-stroke brows, painted lower lashes, closed mouth, orig nylon wig in orig set, five-pc hard-plastic child body, orig tagged lime green dress, pink trim, attached slip, matching panties, orig socks, and shoes, marked "P-93, Ideal Doll, Made in U.S.A." on back of head, orig wrist tag, Tony Play Wave Lotion, twelve curlers, comb, directions, shampoo, and end papers, un-played-with condition, orig box **750.00**

Jumeau, Tete

19" h, bisque socket head, bulbous brown paper-weight eyes, heavy feathered brows, long painted upper and lower lashes, closed mouth, white space between lips, pierced ears, mohair wig, jointed wood and composition body with jointed wrists, mama/papa crier, new yellow print dress, underclothing, socks, shoes, old straw bonnet, marked "Depose, Tete Jumeau, Bte S.G.D.G., 8" on back of head, Jumeau, Medaille d'Or, Paris" faint stamp on back **2,100.00**

20" h, bisque socket head, bulbous pale blue paper-weight eyes, heavy feathered brows, long painted upper and lower lashes, closed mouth with ac-cented lips, pierced ears, mohair replaced wig, jointed wood and composition body with jointed wrists, redressed, marked "Depose, Tete Jumeau, 9" stamped in red, incised "D" and "9", red and black artist marks on back of head, partial oval label on lower back **3,300.00**

Kammer & Reinhardt

6" h, child, bisque socket head, brown sleep eyes, single-stroke brows, painted upper and lower lashes, open mouth, two upper teeth, orig mohair wig, five-pc composition body, molded and painted black socks, brown two-strap shoes, orig regional costume, underclothing, and bonnet, marked "K*R" on back of head **300.00**

11" h, character, Gretchen, Mold 114, bisque head,

painted blue eyes, orig blond human-hair wig, braids rolled into buns, orig composition jointed body, jointed wrists, closed mouth, dressed in old cream crocheted dress, matching hat, socks, and shoes **2,950.00**

21" h, baby, celluloid socket head, brown sleep eyes, feathered brows, painted upper and lower lashes, open mouth, two upper teeth and tongue, orig mohair wig, jointed composition bent-limb baby body, white baby dress and underclothing, marked "K*R, 712 [turtle], 50" on back of head, celluloid yellowed, crack at eye, body finish worn, fingers repaired **180.00**

Kestner

10" h, Kewpie, bisque socket head, set brown eyes glancing to side, two-tone dot brows, painted upper lashes, closed smiling mouth, molded and painted tufts of hair, five-pc chubby composition body with starfish hands, orig two-pc blue romper, white trim, knit undershirt, blue and white socks, soft leather shoes, marked "Ges. gesch., O'Neill. J.D.K. 10" on back of head **6,400.00**

12" h, bisque socket head, blue sleep eyes, feathered brows, painted upper and lower lashes, accented nostrils, open mouth with, two upper teeth, orig mohair wig, composition bent-limb baby body, marked "F. Made in Germany 10, J.D.K., 226., Z" on back of head, white baby clothing **300.00**

J. D. Kestner, Hilda, character, $3,000.00.

17" h, bisque flange baby head, blue sleep eyes, softly blushed brows, painted upper and lower lashes, closed rosebud mouth, lightly molded and painted hair, cloth body with composition arms, jointed hips, antique white baby dress, marked "Century Doll Co., Kestner, Germany" on back of head, light specks in bisque, non-working crier, crazing on arms **550.00**

18½" h, turned-head bisque shoulder head, set brown eyes, heavy feathered brows, painted upper and lower lashes, accented nostrils, full closed mouth, replaced wig, kid body, composition lower arms

and legs, pin-jointed elbows, hips, and knees, marked "8 1/2" on back of head, beige velvet dress, antique underclothes **450.00**

Kruse, Kathe, 16"h, molded-muslin painted head, painted short brown hair, brush-stroked curls, painted blue-gray eyes, closed pouty mouth, cloth body jointed at shoulders and hips, red and white cotton dress, marked "Kathe Kruse" and numbers on sole of foot **1,750.00**

Lenci, 12" h, felt, painted facial features, blond wig, yellow dress, green coat, matching hat **675.00**

Madame Alexander, 7½" h, Dionne Quintuplets, five composition babies, painted brown eyes to the side, single-stroke brows, painted upper lashes, closed mouths, molded and painted hair, five-pc composition baby bodies with bent legs, orig tagged rompers with matching bonnets, socks, and shoes, name pins, four extra tagged organdy dresses with matching bonnets, three sets of orig underwear, extra clothing tied onto lid of orig basket with pink ribbons, orig tray with pink lace-trimmed insert, marked "Alexander" on back of head and back, "Genuine Dionne Quintuplet Dolls, All Rights Reserved, Madame Alexander-N.Y." on clothing tags, minor damage to dolls **1,600.00**

Marotte, 13" l, bisque shoulder head, set blue eyes, feathered brows, painted upper and lower lashes, open mouth with two upper teeth, orig mohair curls, head mounted on music box on stick with whistle, jester-type costume and hat, lace trim, music plays when twirled **395.00**

Marseille, Armand, 19" h, 400 character, bisque socket head, blue sleep eyes, feathered brown painted upper and lower lashes, remnants of real lashes, somber expression closed mouth, human-hair wig, jointed wood and composition body, antique maroon dress trimmed with maroon velvet, underclothing, old socks and shoes, marked "Armand Marseille, Germany, 400, A. 3. M." on back of head, "Germany, 3381" on rear torso **2,400.00**

Mascotte, 23" h, fine-quality bisque head, bulging blue paperweight glass stationary eyes, pierced ears, closed mouth, long brown curls, real French-hair wig, French composition jointed body, straight wrists, marked "M," blue satin dress with lace, matching blue hat with ostrich plume **2,900.00**

Parian, 15" h, child, untinted bisque shoulder head, painted blue eyes with red accent lines, single-strike brows, closed mouth, molded and painted blond hair with blue ribbon, kid body, bisque lower arms, new blue low-waisted dress, lace trim, underclothing, socks, and shoes, unmarked, faint rub on back of hair, replaced arms, kid repairs on both legs **525.00**

Phenix Bebe, 23" h, Star 94, French, fine-quality bisque head, brown open/closed eyes, open mouth, upper row of teeth, pierced ears, orig brown hair, good French composition body, jointed wrists, vintage clothing, socks, straw hat with flowers **1,100.00**

Schmidt, Franz, 13" h, 1295 baby, bisque socket head, blue flirty eyes, tin lids, feathered brows, painted upper and lower lashes, pierced nostrils, open mouth, two upper teeth, orig sparse mohair wig, composition bent-limb baby body, pale pink baby dress, marked

"1295, F. S. & C., Germany, 32" on back of head,³/₄"
firing line from crown, cracks in finish on torso, wear
to hands and feet **375.00**
Schoenau Hoffmeister, 19" h, 170 toddler, painted
bisque socket head, blue sleep eyes, real lashes,
feathered brows, open mouth with two upper teeth,
replaced synthetic wig, five-pc composition toddler
body, black corduroy jumper, new socks, and shoes,
marked "S PB [in star] H, 170 3 1/2" on back of head,
light wear, crazed replaced arms, torso finish cracked
and damaged, legs repainted **215.00**
Simon & Halbig
16½" h, character, deeply modeled boy's bisque
head, painted blue eyes with black liner, single-
stroke brows, accented nostrils, closed pouty
mouth, orig mohair wig, jointed wood and composition body with orig finish, orig two-pc outfit,
knit underclothing, replaced black cotton socks,
old shoes, marked "150, S & H, 0 1/2" on back
of head, "Heinrich Handwerck, Germany 01/2"
partial stamp on left hip **12,000.00**
21" h, bisque socket head, blue sleep eyes, feathered
brows, painted upper and lower lashes, open
mouth, four upper teeth, pierced ears, replaced
human-hair wig, jointed wood and composition
body, pale green organdy dress, white pinafore,
underclothing, new socks and shoes, marked "S.
H. 1079-8/2, DEP., Germany" on back of head,
red artist's mark on rim, light firing dust around
eyes and on checks, light wear to body, minor
touchup to left hip **365.00**
Societe Francaise de Bebes et Jouets
19" h, 236 toddler, bisque socket head, set dark
brown eyes, feathered brows, painted lashes,
open/closed mouth, two upper teeth, human-hair
wig, jointed wood and composition toddler body,
brown knit romper, socks, and shoes, marked
"S.F.B.J. 236, Paris, -10-" on back of head,
"S.F.B.J., 7" imp on body, repaired hairline on
back of head, minor firing line in left ear, body
finish yellowed, flaking on hands **500.00**
21" h, character, boy, fine-quality bisque head, open/
closed mouth, two upper molded teeth, blue glass
open/close eyes, dark blond orig hair, orig chunky
French toddler composition jointed body, jointed
wrists, white shirt, black and white striped shorts,
red and white striped cap, new shoes, marked
"S.F.B.J. 247 Paris" **2,750.00**
Steiner, Jules Nicholas, 24" h, bisque head, blue paperweight eyes, pierced ears, closed mouth, brown wig,
composition jointed body, marked "Steiner/Paris/Fre
A.17" **4,675.00**
Unidentified Maker
12" h, German, child, bisque socket head, brown
sleep eyes, single-strike brows, painted upper and
lower lashes, open mouth, five upper teeth, orig
mohair wig, jointed wood and composition body
with straight wrists, factory chemise, blue velvet
dress, black velvet cap, green felt hat trimmed with
mohair, orig underclothing, socks, and shoes,
marked "L.D., 3/0" on back of head, several old
repairs, slight damage **200.00**

16" h, bisque shoulder head, finely molded blond
hair, painted blue eyes, kid-leather body, pink
satin dress, black velvet and lace trim, matching
hat **550.00**
Unis France, 13½" h, bisque socket head, blue sleep
eyes, real lashes, feathered brows, open mouth, four
upper teeth, jointed composition body with jointed
wrists, orig labeled regional costume, underclothing,
socks, and shoes, orig paper label on skirt, paper wrist
tag "fabrication Jumeau Paris, Made in France,"
marked "Unis France, 71 301 149" on back of head,
"Made in France" circular stamp, pale facial coloring **475.00**
Wax, poured, 21" h, shoulder head, set pale blue eyes,
molded eyelids, single-stroke brows, closed mouth,
orig mohairs set in wax in small bunches, cloth body
with poured-wax lower arms and legs, white antique
christening dress, lace trim and tucks, pink bonnet,
and cape unmarked, attributed to Pierotti **1,300.00**

DOOR KNOCKERS

History: Before the advent of the mechanical bell or electrical
buzzer and chime, a door knocker was considered an essential
door ornament to announce the arrival of visitors. Metal was used
to cast or forge the various forms; many cast-iron examples were
painted. Collectors like to find door knockers with English registry
marks.

Brass

Cat, arched back	**50.00**
Dog, Pekinese, early 1900s	**40.00**
Federal Style, 10½" l	**240.00**
Lady, hand holds mirror	**45.00**
Sea Horse and shell	**80.00**

Bronze

Dolphin, 11" l	**275.00**
Kissing Couple, 10½" l	**50.00**

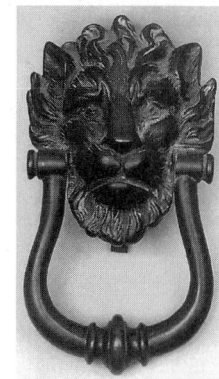

**Bronze, lion-shaped, Regency, 9½" h, c1825,
$375.00. Photograph courtesy of Morton M.
Goldberg Auction Galleries, Inc.**

Cast Iron

Basket of Roses, Hubley, 3¼ × 2¼"	**700.00**
Cardinal, bird on twigs, 5 × 3"	**305.00**
Castle, detailed casting of castle on hill, Judd Co, marked "632," 4 × 3"	**440.00**

Cherub, detailed casting of cherub with ribbon and roses, pastels, Judd Co, marked "622," 4¼ × 3" ...**1,540.00**

Cottage in the Woods, Judd Co, marked "626," 3½ × 2½" **590.00**

Flower Basket, vines and flowers, backplate also cast, Hubley, marked "205," 4 × 2½" **315.00**

Girl Knocking on Door, Grace Drayton copyright 1921, Hubley, 3½ × 2¼" **495.00**

Ivy Basket, Hubley, marked "123 Made in USA," **220.00**

Morning Glory, Judd Co, marked "608," 3¼ × 2¾" .. **275.00**

Parrot, Hubley, 4¾ × 2¾", unused, orig box **330.00**

Urn of Flowers with Bow, Hubley, pastels, blue trim, marked "124," 4 × 2¾" **150.00**

Woodpecker, Hubley, full-figured bird, tree backplate, marked "251," 3¾ × 2¾" **210.00**

DOORSTOPS

History: Doorstops became popular in the late 19th century. They are either flat or three dimensional and were made out of a variety of different materials, such as cast iron, bronze, or wood. Hubley, a leading toy manufacturer, made many examples.

References: Jeanne Bertoia, *Doorstops,* Collector Books, 1985, 1996 value update; Douglas Congdon–Martin, *Figurative Cast Iron,* Schiffer Publishing, 1994.

Collectors' Club: Doorstop Collectors of America, 2413 Madison Ave, Vineland, NJ 08630.

Videotape: *Off The Ground & Off the Wall,* Gary Roma, Iron Frog Productions.

REPRODUCTION ALERT

Reproductions are proliferating as prices on genuine doorstops continue to rise. A reproduced piece generally is slightly smaller than the original unless an original mold is used. The overall casting of reproductions is not as smooth as on the originals. Reproductions also lack the detail apparent in originals, including the appearance of the painted areas. Any bright orange rusting is strongly indicative of a new piece. Beware. If it looks too good to be true, it usually is.

Notes: Pieces described below contain at least 80 percent or more of the original paint and are in very good condition. Repainting drastically reduces price and desirability. Poor original paint is preferred over repaint.

All listings are cast-iron and flat-back castings unless otherwise noted.

Doorstops marked with an asterisk are currently being reproduced.

Ann Hathaway's Cottage, 7½ × 6⅛", three dimensional, marked "AM Greenblatt copyright 1927 #114" ...**1,155.00**

Aunt Jemima, 13¼ × 6½", Littco Products **1,155.00**

Basket of Flowers, 6½" h, 4" w, yellow, red, and blue flowers, green vase, white pedestal base, orig paint **125.00**

Bear with Honey, 15 × 6½", full figured **3,740.00**

Black Man on Cotton Bale, 6⅞ × 6⅞", full-figured pot metal figure on cast-iron bale **3,410.00**

Bloodhound, 15¼ × 4⅜", Spencer, wedge bottom ... **250.00**

Bobby Blake, 9½ × 5¼", Hubley, Grace Drayton design **330.00**

Boston Terrier, 8½" w, 10½" h, black and white, significant paint loss to body **150.00**

Butler, 11¼ × 5⅞", Bradley & Hubbard **1,100.00**

Cape Cod, 5¾ × 8¾", Eastern Specialty Mfg Co, repainted **360.00**

Cape Cod Cottage, 5½ × 7¾", Hubley, marked "444" **420.00**

Cat, 11" w, 6" h, reclining, white, green eyes, Hubley, repainted **150.00**

Cat Scratch Fever, 8¾ × 4¼", Judd Co, sgd "A Diouhy" on front and marked "cJo 1271" on back **1,760.00**

Charleston Dancers, 8⅞ × 5⅜", Hubley, Fish design, Art Deco style **2,970.00**

Cherubs, 10 × 6", partial overpaint **275.00**

Cocker Spaniel, 6¾ × 11", full figured, Hubley **690.00**

Colonial Lady, pink dress, red flower dots, white collar and cuffs, pink and black bonnet, red flowers, green leaves, orig paint **125.00**

Colonial Lawyer, 9⅝ × 5¼", orange jacket, Waverly Studios, marked "W5 Mark" **440.00**

Cornucopia of Fruit, 7½ × 7", vibrant colors **590.00**

Cottage, 5¾ × 7½", National Foundry **220.00**

Crossed Out, 7¼ × 5⅝" **880.00**

Daisy Bowl, 7½ × 5⅛", Hubley, marked "452" **200.00**

Doberman Pinscher, 8 × 8½", full figured, Hubley ... **690.00**

Dolly Dimple, 7¾ × 3¾", full figured, Hubley, Grace Drayton design **635.00**

Drum Major, 13½ × 6½", full figured **190.00**

Duck, 5 × 3¾", Hubley, wedge back **360.00**

Dutch Boy

    7½ × 6", Judd Co, marked "1275" **935.00**

    11 × 3½", full figured **420.00**

Farm House, 6 × 8", Bradley & Hubbard, orig rubber knobs **3,190.00**

Flapper, 8⅞ × 4½", slight wedge **550.00**

Flower Basket, 11 × 10¾", detailed assorted spring flowers, intricate basket base **1,265.00**

Flowered Doorway, 7⅝ × 7½" **970.00**

Footmen, Hubley, Fish design, Art Deco style

    9⅛ × 6" **1,045.00**

    12⅛ × 8¼" **1,870.00**

French Basket, 11 × 6¾", country-style basket of flowers, Hubley, marked "69" **385.00**

Fruit Basket, 11½ × 10", cherries on base, basketweave basket **1,155.00**

Geese, 8 × 8", Hubley, Fred Everett design **385.00**

Geisha, 10¼ × 3½", full figured, Hubley **860.00**

Giraffe, 12½ × 9", full figured, Hubley **4,070.00**

Goldenrods, 7⅛ × 5½", Hubley, marked "268" **360.00**

Golfer, 8⅜ × 7", putting, Hubley, marked "34" **440.00**

Grandpa Rabbit, 8⅝ × 4⅞", red jacket **1,760.00**

House, 8⅛ × 4½", Judd Co, marked "cJo 1288" **495.00**

House with Woman, 5¾ × 8½", pink house, Eastern Specialty Mfg Co, No. 50 ....**1,375.00**

Huckleberry Finn, Littco Products **585.00**

Iris, 10⅝ × 6¾", Hubley, marked "469" **470.00**

Jonquils, 7 × 6", bright colors, Hubley, marked "534" **275.00**

*Mammy, 8½ × 4½", full figured, blue dress, Hubley . **440.00**

Golfer, light blue coat and hat, red-and-green trimmed pants, 8″, $375.00.

Man with Flowers, 9 × 5¾″, vibrant paint **495.00**

Marigolds, 7½ × 8″, Hubley, pastels, marked "315 Made in USA" **215.00**

Mary Quite Contrary, 11⅜ × 9⅝″, Littco Products **587.00**

Minuet Girl, 8½ × 5″, Judd Co, marked "1278" **210.00**

Modernistic Flower, 10 × 9¾″, blue flowers, yellow and orange centers, green leaves, black base with dot dec **1,020.00**

Narcissus, 7¼ × 6¾″, Hubley, marked "266" **385.00**

Old Fashioned Lady, 7¾ × 4″, Hubley, blue dress, marked "Hubley 296" **690.00**

Oriental Man, 9 × 7¼″, full figured **275.00**

Owl, 15½ × 5″, Bradley & Hubbard **2,310.00**

Parrot, 12½ × 7½″, Albany Foundry **220.00**

Penguin, 9½ × 5¼″, sgd "No. 1, c1930, Taylor Cook," near-mint condition **3,520.00**

Persian Cat, 8½ × 6½″, full figured, Hubley **275.00**

Peter Rabbit, 9½ × 4¾″, Hubley, Grace Drayton design **330.00**

Pheasant, 9¼ × 14″, full figured **580.00**

Pirate with Sack, 11⅞ × 9⅝″, vibrant colors **1,365.00**

Popeye, 9 × 4½″, full figured, Hubley, marked "c1929 King Features Syn Made in USA" **2,310.00**

Poppies and Cornflowers, 7¼ × 6½″, Hubley, marked "265" **360.00**

Primrose, 7⅜ × 6¼″, Hubley, yellow flowers, marked "488" **195.00**

Rabbit Eating Cabbage, 8⅛ × 4⅞″ **360.00**

Reading Girls, 5 × 8⅝″, two girls with sunbonnets, seated back to back, heads bent down to read books on laps **1,595.00**

Red Riding Hood, 9½ × 5″, Hubley, Grace Drayton design **690.00**

Rooster, 13 × 8½″ **660.00**

Rose Basket, 11 × 8″, Hubley, marked "121" **590.00**

Sailor, 11⅜ × 5″, Art Deco style **825.00**

Senorita, 11¼ × 7″, holding basket of flowers in one hand at side **750.00**

Southern Belle, 6½″ h, pink and green dress, crisscross dec, holding bouquet **150.00**

Spanish Girl, 9⅞ × 5½″, green and orange dress **360.00**

Stork, 5½ × 3½″, Hubley, wedge back **385.00**

Street Singers, 6¼ × 7½″, Hubley, marked "445" **1,025.00**

Sunbonnet Sue, 9 × 5½″, orange hat, blue dress **495.00**

Tiger Lilies, 10½ × 6″, Hubley, marked "472" **250.00**

Toko, 5½ × 6¼″, full figured, Hubley **275.00**

Tropical Woman, 12 × 6¼″ h, basket of fruit on head **550.00**

Twin Cats, 7 × 5¼″, Hubley, Grace Drayton design .. **330.00**

Vase of Flowers, 11¾ × 6″, Bradley & Hubbard, orig rubber knobs **360.00**

Whistling Boy, 10 × 5½″, full figured, pot-metal black boy on cast-iron base, rubber back knobs, marked "4298" **880.00**

Whistling Jim, 14½ × 5½″, striped shirt, pants rolled up to knees, orig rubber knobs **4,290.00**

*Windmill

6¾ × 6⅞″, National Foundry **220.00**

9⅞ × 11½″, marked "AM Greenblatt Studios Boston copyright 1926" ld **1,020.00**

Wine Man, 9½ × 7″, full figured **1,045.00**

Wire-haired Terrier, orig black and white paint, minor paint chips **120.00**

Woman, 11½ × 9″, large hooped skirt **715.00**

Zinnias, 9¾ × 8½″, Hubley, marked "316" **310.00**

DRESDEN/MEISSEN

History: Augustus II, Elector of Saxony and King of Poland, founded the Royal Saxon Porcelain Manufactory in the Albrechtsburg, Meissen, in 1710. Johann Frederick Boettger, an alchemist, and Tschirnhaus, a nobleman, experimented with kaolin from the Dresden area to produce porcelain. By 1720 the factory produced a whiter hard-paste porcelain than that from the Far East. The factory experienced its golden age from the 1730s to the 1750s under the leadership of Samuel Stolzel, kiln master, and Johann Gregor Herold, enameler.

The Meissen factory was destroyed and looted by forces of Frederick the Great during the Seven Years' War (1756–1763). It was reopened, but never achieved its former greatness.

In the 19th century the factory reissued some of its earlier forms. These later wares are called "Dresden" to differentiate them from the earlier examples. Further, there were several other porcelain factories in the Dresden region and their products also are grouped under the "Dresden" designation.

Marks: Many marks were used by the Meissen factory. The first was a pseudo-Oriental mark in a square. The famous crossed swords mark was adopted in 1724. A small dot between the hilts was used from 1763 to 1774, and a star between the hilts from 1774 to 1814. Two modern marks are swords with a hammer and sickle and swords with a crown.

References: Susan and Al Bagdade, *Warman's English & Continental Pottery & Porcelain,* Second Edition, Wallace-Homestead, 1991; Robert E. Röntgen, *The Book of Meissen,* Revised Edition, Schiffer Publishing, 1996.

Dresden

Cake Tazza, floral dec, openwork border **200.00**
Candy Dish, oval, reticulated side, floral dec, price for
   pr **175.00**
Charger, 18" d, soldiers receiving provisions, flower garland border, black enamel pseudo AR cipher, 19th C **650.00**
Figure, 4½" h, peasant couple, seated on rocks, chickens
   and flowers **280.00**
Fruit Dish, circular, low front, scalloped, open wide
   sides, floral panels, floral center, price for pr **300.00**
Shrimp Server, circular, floral dec, openwork border .. **125.00**
Vase, 58" h, polychrome reserve of classical maidens
   with putti surrounded by sculpted fruit, two maidens
   at top, one holding basket, one holding basket of
   flowers, conforming base reserve surrounded by
   carve putti and maiden with basket, fully sculpted
   maiden with flower in hand, flower basket on her lap
   as finial, Carl Thieme mark, 19th C **20,700.00**

Meissen

Bowl, 6⅞" d, multicolored scattered Deutsche Blumen,
   brown rim, blue crossed-swords mark, c1740 ...... **425.00**
Bust, 9" h, child in bonnet, slight chips **950.00**
Candelabra, 19½" h, four light, flower-encrusted scroll-
   molded standard, applied seasons putti, waisted rocaille molded base, scrolled feet, blue crossed-
   swords mark, 19th C, price for pr **2,500.00**
Charger, 11" d, green ground, heavy gold overlay flowers
   and leaves, blue crossed-swords mark, c1890 ...... **225.00**
Coffeepot, cov, multicolored loose floral bouquet, fluted
   spout and handle with molded acanthus, blue
   crossed-swords and star mark **500.00**
Desk Set, 7 × 10½" tray, sander, cov inkwell, bell, gilt
   trim, framed polychrome dec harbor scenes, puce
   harbor scene medallions on border, crossed-swords
   mark, late 19th C, price for four pc set **950.00**

Plate, cobalt blue and gold, 5½", $75.00.

Dessert Plate, openwork, gilt border, two fan-shaped
   coastal-scene reserves, blue imbricated reserves, late
   19th C, price for pr **400.00**
Dinner Service, Orange Dragon pattern, service for 12
   with serving pcs **1,250.00**

Écuelle, cov, 6¼" w, two handles, gilt berry finial, un-
   derglaze blue flowers, gilding, multicolored Euro-
   pean flowers and woman seated on grassy mount,
   Hausmaierei, blue crossed-swords mark, c1750 ....**1,760.00**
Figure
   Commerce of Cupids, classical maidens inspecting
      putti in winged cart, oval molded base with gilt-
      edged leaf-chain band, 13½" h, blue crossed-
      swords mark, 19th C **6,400.00**
   Musician and lady dancing, fine attire, minor losses,
      small size, price for pr **800.00**
   Swordsman, lady, and drummer, scroll-molded base,
      9¾" h, blue crossed-swords mark, 19th C **1,775.00**
   Three putti, one leading with grapevines, one riding,
      5¾" h **1,350.00**
Plate, 8¾" d, Schmettering pattern, stylized butterfly in
   central floral spray, chocolate rims, blue crossed-
   swords mark, c1735, price for 3-pc set **1,750.00**
Tureen, cov, 9¾" d, circular, Imari pattern, blue, iron-
   red, and gilt, flower sprays in stylized lappets border,
   pinecone finial, blue crossed-swords mark, c1730 .**3,375.00**
Vase
   10" h, white ground, florals, blue crossed-swords
      mark **375.00**
   20½" h, cov, baluster, pierced body, applied scrolling
      flowering forget-me-not branches, pierced cov,
      bird finial, blue crossed-swords mark, late 19th C**1,450.00**

DUNCAN AND MILLER

History: George Duncan, Harry B. and James B., his sons, and Augustus Heisey, his son-in-law, formed George Duncan & Sons in Pittsburgh, Pennsylvania, in 1865. The factory was located just two blocks from the Monongahela River, providing easy and in-expensive access by barge for materials needed to produce glass. The men, from Pittsburgh's south side, were descendants of gen-erations of skilled glassmakers.

    The plant burned to the ground in 1892. James E. Duncan, Sr., selected a site for a new factory in Washington, Pennsylvania, where operations began on February 9, 1893. The plant pros-pered, producing fine glassware and table services for many years.

    John E. Miller, one of the stockholders, was responsible for designing many fine patterns, the most famous being Three Face. The firm incorporated and used the name The Duncan and Miller Glass Company until the plant closed in 1955. The company's slogan was "The Loveliest Glassware in America." The U.S. Glass Co. purchased the molds, equipment, and machinery in 1956.

References: Gene Florence, *Elegant Glassware of the Depression Era,* Sixth Edition, Collector Books, 1995; Naomi L. Over, *Ruby Glass of the 20th Century,* Antique Publications, 1990, 1993–94 value update.

Collectors' Club: National Duncan Glass Society, PO Box 965, Washington, PA 15301.

Additional Listings: Pattern Glass.

Ashtray, clear
   Canterbury **18.50**
   Duck, 6" **40.00**
   Tulip **30.00**
Basket, Sandwich, clear, 7" **95.00**

Bowl

Canterbury, blue, 6¼″ d	**30.00**
Caribbean, clear, 6″ d	**20.00**
Early American Hobnail, clear, flared, 12″ d	**25.00**
Language of Flowers, clear, flared, 12″ d	**37.50**

Centerpiece bowl, Sanibel, pink opalescent, 13½″ l, $40.00.

Butter, cov, Tear Drop, clear, SP lid	**27.00**
Cake Plate, King Arthur, clear, 9½″ d, skirted	**55.00**
Candlesticks, pr, Canterbury, clear, etched	**30.00**
Candy Box, cov, Canterbury, pink opalescent	**55.00**
Cheese Compote, Tear Drop, clear	**20.00**
Claret, Tear Drop, clear	**15.00**
Cocktail, Canterbury, clear, 4¼″ h, 3½″ oz	**10.00**
Condiment Set, Canterbury, clear, price for 5-pc set	**60.00**
Cup and Saucer, Caribbean, blue	**65.00**
Deviled-Egg Plate, Sandwich, clear	**50.00**
Fruit Bowl, Sandwich, clear, 11″ d, flared	**35.00**
Gardenia Bowl, Canterbury, clear	**25.00**

Goblet, water

Plaza Punties, amber	**10.00**
Tear Drop, clear	**14.00**

Iced Tea Tumbler, clear

Canterbury, 7″ h	**15.00**
Indian Tree, ftd, 6″ h	**22.00**
Jelly Compote, Caribbean, clear	**28.00**
Lemon Tray, Puritan, green, clear handle	**25.00**
Mayonnaise, Language of Flowers, clear, price for 3-pc set	**37.50**

Nappy

Indian Tree, clear, triangular, handle	**20.00**
Murano, clear, ruffled, 6″ d	**20.00**
Olive Dish, Tear Drop, clear, 2 part, 6″ l	**13.50**
Pitcher, Tear Drop, clear, 8½″ h, ice lip	**100.00**

Plate

Plaza Punties, amber, 6″ d	**5.00**

Terrace, cobalt blue

6″ d	**20.00**
7½″ d	**30.00**
8½″ d	**25.00**
Punch Bowl, Mardi Gras, clear	**150.00**

Relish Dish

Canterbury, clear, 3 part, silver overlay	**25.00**
Diamond, sienna, 2 part, oval	**18.00**
Sylvan, clear, 3 part, cobalt blue handle	**45.00**
Tear Drop, clear, 3 part, 11″, handles	**30.00**
Terrace, clear, 3 part	**35.00**
Rose Bowl, Canterbury, clear	**15.00**
Salt and Pepper Shakers, pr, Caribbean, blue, 3″ h	**75.00**

Serving Plate, Sandwich, clear, 13″ d	**40.00**
Sherbet, Tear Drop, clear, tall	**10.00**

Sugar, clear

Canterbury	**10.00**
First Love	**15.00**
Language of Flowers	**18.00**

Swan, ruby, clear neck

10″	**60.00**
12″	**95.00**
Tumbler, Plaza Punties, amber, cone shape, ftd, 10¾″ h	**10.00**

Vase

American Way, satin tone, flared, 6½″ h	**40.00**
Canterbury, blue opalescent, crimped, 5½ × 4″	**35.00**
Venetian, clear, crimped, 8″ h	**35.00**

Wine, clear

Canterbury	**12.00**
Caribbean, port type	**35.00**
Tear Drop, blown	**12.00**

DURAND

History: Victor Durand (1870–1931), born in Baccarat, France, apprenticed at the Baccarat glassworks where several generations of his family had worked. In 1884 Victor came to America to join his father at Whitall-Tatum & Co. in New Jersey. In 1897 father and son leased the Vineland Glass Manufacturing Company in Vineland, New Jersey. Products included inexpensive bottles, jars, and glass for scientific and medical purposes. By 1920 four separate companies existed.

When Quezal Art Glass and Decorating Company failed, Victor Durand recruited Martin Bach, Jr., Emil J. Larsen, William Wiedebine, and other Quezal men and opened an art-glass shop at Vineland in December 1924. Quezal-style iridescent pieces were made. New innovations included cameo and intaglio designs, geometric Art Deco shapes, Venetian Lace, and Oriental-style pieces. In 1928 crackled glass, called Moorish Crackle and Egyptian Crackle, was made.

Durand died in 1931. The Vineland Flint Glass Works was merged with Kimble Glass Company a year later, and the art glass line was discontinued.

Marks: Many Durand glass pieces are not marked. Some have a sticker with the words "Durand Art Glass," others have the name "Durand" scratched on the pontil or "Durand" inside a large V. Etched numbers may be part of the marking.

Bowl, 8″ d, 6½″ h, orange cased to opal, overall irid green leaf and vine dec, sgd in V	**1,500.00**
Candlesticks, pr, 9½″ h, baluster, amber, pulled blue feather tips, flanged rim with etched wheat and leaves	**300.00**
Compote, 8″ d, white feather dec, blue ground, pale green stem and foot	**750.00**
Lamp, 14″ h, shade with gold and green hearts and vines, irid opal ground, applied heavy gold threading, yellow int., bronze tree-form standard	**2,250.00**

Vase

6″ h, flared, tapered body, white heart and vine dec, blue ground, sgd	**1,200.00**
7½″ h, ovoid, everted lip, amber, mottled amber int., inscribed "Durand/1968-6"	**295.00**
8⅛″ h, bulbous ovoid, tapered cylindrical mouth,	

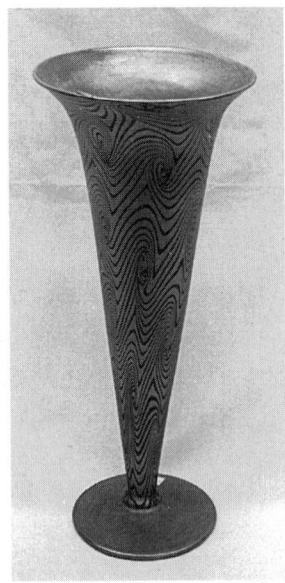

Vase, irid gold, purple, 14³/₈″, $975.00.

340023, Columbus, OH 43234; Glass Research Society of New Jersey, Wheaton Village, Glasstown Rd, Millville, NJ 08332; National Early American Glass Club, PO Box 8489, Silver Spring, MD 20907.

Museums: Bennington Museum, Bennington, VT; Chrysler Museum, Norfolk, VA; Corning Museum of Glass, Corning, NY; Glass Museum, Dunkirk, IN; Glass Museum Foundation, Redlands, CA; New Bedford Glass Museum, New Bedford, MA; Sandwich Glass Museum, Sandwich, MA; Toledo Museum of Art, Toledo, OH; Wheaton Historical Village Assoc Museum of Glass, Millville, NJ.

Additional Listings: Blown Three Mold, Cup Plates, Flasks, Sandwich Glass, and Stiegel-Type Glass.

graduated double shoulder, red irid base rim, sgd "Durand/1978" in irid silver **350.00**
9¹/₄″ h, ovoid, flared rim, transparent amber, opal and green layers of heat reactive glass, crackled, gold irid int. **550.00**

EARLY AMERICAN GLASS

History: The term "Early American glass" covers glass made in America from the colonial period through the mid-19th century. As such, it includes the early pressed glass and lacy glass made between 1827 and 1840.

Major glass-producing centers prior to 1850 were Massachusetts (New England Glass Company and the Boston and Sandwich Glass Company), South Jersey, Pennsylvania (Stiegel's Manheim factory and many Pittsburgh-area firms), and Ohio (several different companies in Kent, Mantua, and Zanesville).

Early American glass was popular with collectors from 1920 to 1950. It has now regained some of its earlier prominence. Leading auction sources for early American glass include Early Auction Company, Garth's, Glass-Works, Heckler & Company, James D. Julia, and Skinner, Inc.

References: William E. Covill, *Ink Bottles and Inkwells,* William S. Sullwold Publishing, out of print; George and Helen McKearin, *American Glass,* Crown, 1975; ———, *Two Hundred Years of American Blown Glass,* Doubleday and Company, 1950; Helen McKearin and Kenneth Wilson, *American Bottles And Flasks,* Crown, 1978; Dick Roller (comp.), *Indiana Glass Factories Notes,* Acorn Press, 1994; Jane S. Spillman, *American and European Pressed Glass,* Corning Museum of Glass, 1981; Kenneth Wilson, *American Glass 1760–1930,* 2 vols., Hudson Hills Press and The Toledo Museum of Art, 1994; ———, *New England Glass and Glassmaking,* Crowell, 1972.

Periodicals: *Antique Bottle & Glass Collector,* PO Box 187, East Greenville, PA 18041; *Glass Collector's Digest,* Antique Publications, PO Box 553, Marietta, OH 45750.

Collectors' Clubs: Early American Glass Traders, RD 5, Box 638, Milford, DE 19963; Early American Pattern Glass Society, PO Box

Apothecary Jar, blown, 16¹/₄″ h, cobalt blue, urn-shaped bowl, applied finial **1,155.00**
Bottle
Mantua, OH, 8¹/₈″ h, club shape, aqua, sixteen melon ribs, applied lip, broken lip blister **275.00**
Midwest, pattern molded, sapphire blue, club shape, 24 ribs, 7¹/₂″ h, c1815 ....**13,200.00**
Philadelphia, PA, Swaim's Panacea, green, applied sloping lip, 8″ h **310.00**
Zanesville, OH, globular, twenty-four swirled ribs
7¹/₂″ h, golden amber, minor wear **470.00**
8¹/₄″ h, amber, slight club shape **330.00**
8⁷/₈″ h, amber, some int. stain and residue **275.00**
9⁵/₈″ h, amber, light residue **525.00**
11¹/₂″ h, deep amber, unpatterned, very minor surface wear **415.00**
Bowl
3⁷/₈″ h, blown, cobalt blue, nineteen ribs, folded-rim foot **125.00**
4¹/₈″ d, 4″ h, blown, cobalt blue, ftd, minor scratches **230.00**
4³/₈″ d, blown, deep amber, Pittsburgh **90.00**
4¹/₂″ d, 2³/₄″ h, cobalt blue, blown, expanded diamond, applied foot **220.00**
9¹/₄″ d, 5¹/₄″ h aqua blue, blown, folded rim **360.00**
9³/₄″ h, cobalt blue bowl, applied colorless foot, folded rim, shallow broken int. blister in bowl, bowl slightly crooked **440.00**
9⁷/₈″ d, blown, olive green, minor chips **210.00**
14¹/₂″ d, pale pink-amber, ground pontil, folded rim **135.00**
Candlestick
7″ h, Loop and Petal pattern, canary, small chips, price for pr **360.00**
9³/₄″ h, pillar mold, colorless, flint, applied foot, hol-

low ribbed stem, applied bulbous socket, pewter insert, Pittsburgh **2,585.00**

Canister, cov, blown

9" h, colorless, two applied sapphire rings on base, one ring on matching lid with applied finial, Pittsburgh **495.00**

10¾" h, colorless, two applied cobalt blue rings, mismatched lid with applied blue ring, colorless finial, Pittsburgh, chips to finial **495.00**

15½" h, colorless, tin lid **120.00**

21¾" h, applied base, applied ring near lip, folded rim lid, cut panels and applied cut finial **660.00**

Christmas Light, 3⅛" h, cobalt blue, blown, expanded diamond, folded rim **140.00**

Cologne Bottle, 4⅝" h, canary, hexagonal, star and punty, some int. stain **250.00**

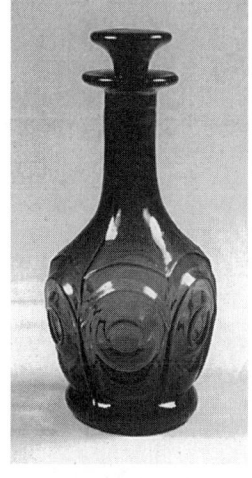

Perfume bottle, pressed glass, Bull's-Eye pattern, cobalt blue, upstate NY, 5¾" h, replaced stopper, $700.00.

Compote

5" h, 5¾" d, blown, cobalt blue **520.00**

5½" h, 7¾" d, pressed, amethyst, loop patterned bowl attached by wafer to loop-patterned base, c1850, three tiny spalls on top of base **5,500.00**

9¼" h, 11¾" d, pillar mold, colorless, applied stem and foot, slight gray/amethystine tint, Pittsburgh **660.00**

11¾" h, 8" d, blown, colorless, folded rim on bowl and lid, applied baluster stem and foot, applied finial to lid, Pittsburgh **385.00**

Creamer

3½" h, cobalt blue, blown, applied foot and handle **220.00**

3¾" h, pattern molded, pear shape, twenty-diamond design, applied solid handle, curled ending, applied solid base with rough pontil, flared mouth

Cobalt Blue **725.00**

Emerald Green, slight blue tone **2,100.00**

4¼" h, blown, colorless, nine-panel mold, applied handle **115.00**

4⅝" h, blown, sapphire blue, expanded diamond, applied foot and handle **385.00**

5" h, pattern molded, brilliant sapphire blue, twelve vertical ribs design, applied solid handle, fine curl ending, applied solid base with rough pontil, attributed to Bakewell, Pears, and Bakewell, Pittsburgh **990.00**

5¼" h, green, pear shape, applied loop handle, circular foot, broken rim, cracked **70.00**

6" h, blown, sapphire blue, spiral tooling at neck, applied handle **1,020.00**

Cream Jug, 5¼" h, blown and molded, aqua, four molded pomegranate panels, floral and diamond shoulder band, loop handle, 19th C **80.00**

Cruet, 7¼" h, blown, cobalt blue, twenty-four ribs, applied hollow handle, roughness at base of snapped handle, minor wear and stain **250.00**

Cuspidor, 5¼" d, blown, amber **85.00**

Decanter

7⅜" h, pillar mold, colorless, flint, pewter jigger cap with some damage and small hole, Pittsburgh .. **175.00**

9½" h, blown, colorless, hollow ball stopper, figure of rooster in base, 19th C **400.00**

Decanter, matching underdish, 10⅛" h, blown, flint, attributed to Thomas Caines, MA, early 19th C, band of applied chain dec on dish, minor scratches **875.00**

Hat, blown

6⅛" h, green **150.00**

6¼" h, 9" d, aqua, folded rim **160.00**

Jar, cov, 17" h, pillar mold, colorless, applied foot and stem, applied lip on bowl, folded rim and applied finial on lid **690.00**

Lamp

9½" h, pressed

Cobalt Blue, octagonal paneled font and standard, sq base, minor chips to base **920.00**

Emerald Green, octagonal paneled font and standard, sq base, minor chips, scratches **1,840.00**

11" h, blown, colorless, acanthus font, sq base, brass collar, brass fluid burner, snuffer caps missing, chips on base **220.00**

12½" h, pressed, colorless, flint, lion's-paw feet, bulbous hollow stem, conical font all jointed with wafers, brass collar, fluid burner, snuffer caps, minor chips on base **715.00**

Lantern, 17¼" h, tin, colorless pattern-molded shade, removable cylindrical colorless glass lamp insert, orig pewter collar, double burner, weighted metal base, stamped "N. E. Glass Co.," attached to carrying ring, pierced floret design at top, base pierced with series of round holes, collar of lamp rotted and loose **275.00**

Milk Bowl, 19¾" d, 5½" h, blown, colorless with slight yellow tint, folded lip, pouring spout **330.00**

Pan, Midwestern, folded rim

5¾" d, 2" h, light golden amber **385.00**

6⅜" d, 1⅝" h, golden amber **300.00**

7" d, 1¼" h, golden amber **400.00**

Roof Ornament, 4⅝" h, Gothic fleur-de-lis shape, cobalt blue, emb "Pat Dec 1, '91," chips on base **65.00**

Salt

Blown, 2 78"h, cobalt blue, twelve ribs and applied foot **250.00**

Press, molded, flint, cobalt blue **150.00**

Spill Holder, pressed

4⅜" h, grass green, minor wear, small flakes **60.00**

4¾" h, electric blue, gilding, minor wear, small flakes **75.00**

Sugar Bowl, cov

5½" h, lacy pressed, deep amethyst, Gothic Arch pattern, minor mold roughness **4,250.00**

6½" h, blown, colorless, lily-pad looping, copperwheel-engraved flowers and bird, applied foot and

handles, bird finial on cov with blue wings and
tail, one handle glued **200.00**

7" h, 4½" d, free blown, colorless, galleried rim, applied funnel-shaped base, wide folded rim, solid
pontil, domed cov with narrow folded rim, tam
finial, foil label from Richards Collection **1,870.00**

7½" h, pattern molded, brilliant sapphire blue, twelve
vertical ribs design, galleried rim, applied solid
base, domed cov with folded rim and tan finial,
attributed to Bakewell, Pears, and Bakewell, Pittsburgh, retains former Elsholz and Richards collection labels **6,150.00**

Tumbler

2⅝" h, lacy pressed, colorless, Gothic Arch pattern,
two minute spalls at base **1,045.00**

9¾" h, blown, colorless, engraved swags with star
drops at rim, applied finial and air bubble pattern
on lid **330.00**

Vase

8⅞" h, pillar mold, colorless, strawberry diamond
cutting on scalloped rim, finger-flute ribs, applied
foot with star, Pittsburgh, chips **200.00**

9¼" h, pillar mold, colorless, applied cobalt blue on
ribs and scallops, baluster stem and applied foot,
Pittsburgh, minor wear **3,740.00**

12" h, blown, baluster form, white horizontal overlay
cut to colorless, gilt floral and linear highlights,
gilt wear, price for pr **460.00**

12¼" h, canary, hexagonal Bigler variant bowl joined
by wafer to sq base, scalloped rim **1,265.00**

13⅜" h, free blown, brilliant emerald green, trumpet,
flared mouth, turned-inward folded rim, hollow
triple-knopped stem, rounded solid base, two applied bladed rings around lower portion of bowl,
polished pontil, attributed to Boston & Sandwich,
c1840 ....**2,475.00**

17½" h, blown, colorless, trumpet, applied foot and
wafer stem **495.00**

Window Pane

4 × 4", amethystine, pressed swan dec **50.00**

4 × 5"

Amethyst, pressed flowers dec **35.00**

Peacock Blue, pressed blue bells, small chip **40.00**

4⅞ × 4⅞", peacock blue, three pressed leaves and
flowers **45.00**

Wine, blown, colorless

6⅛" h, red and white spiral twist **165.00**

6⅞" h, cotton twist **175.00**

Witch Ball, 7" h, blown, colorless, opaque white looping **495.00**

ENGLISH CHINA AND PORCELAIN (GENERAL)

History: By the 19th century, more than 1,000 china and porcelain manufacturers were scattered throughout England, with the majority of the factories located in the Staffordshire district.

By the 19th century English china and porcelain had achieved a worldwide reputation for excellence. American stores imported large quantities for their customers. The special-production English pieces of the 18th and early 19th centuries held a position of great importance among early American antiques collectors.

References: Susan and Al Bagdade, *Warman's English & Continental Pottery & Porcelain,* Second Edition, Wallace-Homestead, 1991; John A. Bartlett, *British Ceramic Art: 1870–1940,* Schiffer Publishing, 1993; David Battie and Michael Turner, *19th and 20th Century British Porcelain Price Guide,* Antique Collectors' Club, 1994; Peter Bradshaw, *English Eighteenth Century Porcelain Figures, 1745–1795,* Antiques Collectors' Club, 1980; John and Margaret Cushion, *A Collector's History of British Porcelain,* Antique Collectors' Club, 1992; Rachael Feild, *Macdonald Guide to Buying Antique Pottery & Porcelain,* Wallace-Homestead, 1987; Mary J. Finegan, *Johnson Brothers Dinnerware: Pattern Directory & Price Guide,* Marfine Antiques, 1993; Geoffrey A. Godden, *Godden's Guide to Mason's China and the Ironstone Wares,* Antique Collectors' Club, 1980; ———, *Godden's Guide To English Porcelain,* Wallace-Homestead, 1992; Pat Halfpenny, *English Earthenware Figures 1740–1840,* Antique Collectors' Club, 1992; R. K. Henrywood, *Relief Molded Jugs, 1820–1900,* Antique Collectors' Club, out of print; Kathy Hughes, *A Collector's Guide to Nineteenth-Century Jugs* (Routledge Kegan Paul, 1985), Vol. II (Taylor Publishing, 1991); Llewellyn Jewitt, *The Ceramic Art of Great Britain,* Sterling Publishing, 1985 (reprint of 1883 classic); Griselda Lewis, *A Collector's History of English Pottery,* Antique Collectors' Club, 1987.

Additional Listings: Castleford, Chelsea, Coalport, Copeland and Spode, Liverpool, Royal Crown Derby, Royal Doulton, Royal Worcester, Historical Staffordshire, Romantic Staffordshire, Wedgwood, and Whieldon.

SPECIAL AUCTION

Skinner Inc.
Bolton Gallery
357 Main St
Bolton, MA 01740
(508) 779-6241

Bow

Bowl, 4¾" d, white, applied prunus branches, shaped
rim, c1755, chips **385.00**

Cream Jug, 3"h, painted birds, flowering branches, Kakiemon colors, brown rim, c1760 .... **975.00**

Dish, 8" d, leaf shape, painted fruiting vines, natural stalk
handle, c1760 .... **425.00**

Figure

5⅞" h, putto, puce-edged wings, yellow sash, lamb
in arms, bocage tree stump, pink and gold edged
mound **795.00**

7¼" h, seated woman, black hat with green bow,
green-lined lavender vest, multicolored bows on
sleeves, floral skirt, yellow apron, hurdy-gurdy on
knee, puce-lined scroll base, applied flowers, four
scroll feet, c1760, repairs **1,650.00**

Mug, 5¾" h, bell shape, white flower heads rim border,
cross-hatched ground, three panels of flowers, two
bands of cell-diaper borders, grooved strap handle,
heart-shaped terminal, c1760, base hairline crack .. **550.00**

Salt, 4½" h, modeled triangular shell, pink edge, Famille
Rose–style painted flowering branches and rocks,
modeled colored shells, coral, and seaweed, c1750,
chips **725.00**

Teabowl and Saucer, Island pattern, muted colors, open-sided pavilion flanked by trees on island surrounded by rocks, painter's numeral "3," c1755 ....   **530.00**

Brownfield

Dinner Service, partial, gilt floral dec cobalt blue border, central enamel floral dec, twelve 9⅝" d plates, four 2" h low compotes, two 4¾" h compotes, imp marks, c1865, glaze scratches, price for 18-pc set **1,610.00**

Chantilly

Basket, 10¼" d, blue painted flower sprays, pierced sides, undulating rim, hunting-horn mark, price for pr   **685.00**

Box, 4¼" d, Kakiemon-style painted fruiting pomegranate branch, reverse with clumps of bushes, crouching rabbit finial, silver mountings, red hunting-horn mark, c1835–45, cracks **1,025.00**

Chamber Pot, 4¾" h, bulbous, orange, yellow, green, lilac, and blue florals, scrolling, strap handle with trailing scroll, orange enamel hunting-horn mark, c1740–50 ....**3,000.00**

Eggcup, 3⅜" h, lobed form, fluted bowl painted with blue flower sprigs, spiral-entwined branch stem, blue accents, c1750 ....**1,250.00**

Plate, 9½" d, blue floral center, four border reserves, imbricated border, c1800, price for 7-pc set **700.00**

Potpourri, 5¾" h, applied blue, green, iron-red, and purple flowering branches, draped pavilion drapery on shoulder, c1740, crack **1,150.00**

Sweetmeat Dish, 6" h, figural seated woman, yellow bodice, puce flowering dress, shell bowl on each side with brown edges and puce ext., green and brown washed rock-work base, red hunting-horn and "L" mark, c1750 ....**1,850.00**

Derby

Cream Jug, Pattern No. 127, tapering cylindrical shape, straight spout, gilt and stylized half flower heads in arches, blue band, gilt edge and dentils, puce crown, crossed batons, and "D" mark, c1800 ....   **200.00**

Plate, 8⅞" d, multicolored center of exotic birds in landscape, stiff gilt leaves border on pale blue ground, gilt stylized flower heads on rim band, c1820, iron-red crown mark, crossed batons and "D" mark, gilder's mark attributed to John Moscrop **350.00**

Potpourri, cov, 8¾" h, deep pink enamel and gilt dec pot supported by three goat's-mask columns, hoof feet, coiled snake, red baton mark, early 19th C, rim cov nicks, snake restored, one horn repaired, gilt wear **635.00**

Vase, 12¾" h, campana-form, two handles, cobalt blue ground, white body, gilt scrolled foliage-framed panels, enamel dec floral arrangements, red baton mark, early 19th C, gilt wear, base rim chips, price for pr .**2,760.00**

Flight, Barr and Barr

Coffee Cann and Saucer, painted yellow and black, moonlight classical ruins scene, gilt scroll panel, dark blue ground, incised mark, c1807, price for pr **4,290.00**

Jug, Apostle design, Meigh, Staffordshire, blue salt glaze, c1841, applied mark, 10¾" h, $460.00.

Crocus Pot, 9" w, 4" h, D-form, molded pilasters and panels, arcaded base, pale salmon ground, gilt stylized anthemion and foliate, painted still-life panel of shells and coral, conforming top pierced panel, early 19th C **8,000.00**

Vase, 5¼" h, campana-form, painted peacock in park land, gilt-edged panel, claret ground, applied gilt caryatid handles, gilt gadrooned rim, c1820 ....**1,725.00**

Ralph Wood

Bust, 9¼" h, Handel, brown wig, green-lined puce drapery, blue coat, waisted socle, imp mark, c1790, repainted **990.00**

Figure
5⅞" h, Admiral Rodney, uniform with open coat, green enamel with manganese dots, emblems of war at feet, molded tree stump with name, sheathed sword, c1780, restored **950.00**

7¾" h, earthenware, bocage group, Birds in the Branches, two bright yellow canaries perched beneath tiny nest with three eggs, green, yellow, and brown glazes, foil and paper D. M. & P. Manheim label attributing figure to Ralph Wood, c1760, minor glaze rubs, minor restoration to one tail, tips of bocage **3,000.00**

Spill Vase, 10⅜" h, seated shepherd and shepherdess with sheep, gnarled tree with three openings, rocky-mound base, late 18th C, restored **1,000.00**

Worcester

Creamer, 3½" h, pear shape, blue Oriental dec, 18th C   **220.00**

Dish, 3¾" h, shell shape, blue and white, Two Peony Rock Bird pattern, scrolls, underglaze blue workman's mark, c1755 ....   **575.00**

Plate, 7" d, Old Japan Fan pattern, Imari palette, scalloped rim, underglaze blue pseudo character mark, c1770 ....   **390.00**

Wall Pocket, 10″ h, cornucopia shape, spiral molded, painted iron-red, purple, blue, green, yellow, and black, insects with Oriental flowering branches and scattered blossoms, pierced for hanging, c1753, price for pr **8,250.00**

ENGLISH SOFT PASTE

History: Between 1820 and 1860 a large number of potteries in England's Staffordshire district produced decorative wares with a soft earthenware (creamware) base and a plain white or yellow glazed ground.

Design or "stick" spatterware was created by a cut sponge (stamp), hand painting, or transfers. Blue was the predominant color. The earliest patterns were carefully arranged geometrics which generally covered the entire piece. Later pieces had a decorative border with a central motif, usually a tulip. In the 1850s Elsmore and Foster developed the Holly Leaf pattern.

King's Rose features a large, cabbage-type rose in red, pale red, or pink. The pink rose often is called "Queen's Rose." Secondary colors are pastels—yellow, pink, and, occasionally, green. The borders vary: a solid band, vined, lined, or sectional. The King's Rose exists in an oyster motif.

Strawberry China ware comes in three types: strawberries and strawberry leaves (often called strawberry luster), green featherlike leaves with pink flowers (often called cut-strawberry, primrose, or old strawberry), and relief decoration. The first two types are characterized by rust-red moldings. Most pieces have a cream ground. Davenport was only one of the many potteries which made this ware.

Yellow-glazed earthenware (canary luster) has a canary yellow ground, a transfer design which is usually in black, and occasional luster decoration. The earliest pieces date from the 1780s and have a fine creamware base. A few hand-painted pieces are known. Not every piece has luster decoration.

Because the base material is soft paste, the ware is subject to cracking and chipping. Enamel colors and other types of decoration do not hold well. It is not unusual to see a piece with the decoration worn off.

Marks: Marked pieces are uncommon.

Additional Listings: Adams Rose, Gaudy Dutch, Salopian Ware, Staffordshire Items.

Creamware

Basket, 11″ d, Ossier-Work, woven, applied flowers, 19th C, loss to one border loop, petals, staining **375.00**
Plate, 8⅛″ d, lattice, reticulated rim, repair **65.00**
Soup Plate, 9½″ d, red, green, and black floral dec **85.00**

Design Spatterware

Bowl, 9½″ d, serrated rim, blue, white, and black trim **300.00**
Cup and Saucer, floral, blue, green, ochre, and red ... **145.00**
Cuspidor, 7¼ × 5″, blue and white dec **95.00**
Mug, 6″ h, rosettes, blue, green bands **100.00**

Creamware, platter, alternating basketweave, scroll and lattice border, 16⅝″ × 13⅜″, $70.00.

Plate, 8¾″ d, red concentric center circles, narrow red line border, stars circled in blue **125.00**
Platter, 16″ l, purple and green **275.00**

Design spatterware, platter, Holly Leaf pattern, purple and green, Elsmore & Foster, 16″, $275.00.

King's Rose

Creamer, helmet shape, brick red rose **245.00**
Cup and Saucer, solid border **175.00**
Plate, 7½″ d, vine border **150.00**
Platter, 13″ **300.00**
Soup Plate, 9″ d **175.00**
Sugar, cov, pink rose **190.00**
Teapot, Queen Anne shape, minor chips on cov **450.00**

Pearlware

Cup, twin handles, transfer Chinoiserie scenes, cobalt blue and luster field, early 19th C **280.00**
Figure
 5¾″ h, 5¾″ w, lion, rect base, left front paw resting on yellow and black-dotted ball, black and white eyes, red mouth, brown body, chartreuse mane, green and white base with red striping, tail replaced, other restoration **900.00**
 10½″ h, Christ's Agony, kneeling figure in garden

King's Rose, plate, iron-red, 8½″ d, $295.00.

alongside plinth with kneeling angel offering food and drink, plinth reads "Father Let This Cup Pass," three branches with tiny four-petal florets bocage, white, black, green, lavender, brick-red, yellow, flesh, brown, and gray, restoration to hands, small flakes **1,600.00**
Mug, 6″ h, late 18th or early 19th C, transfer print
   Bucolic scene **275.00**
   Vignettes of musicians in grove, enameled details, rim chips, base restoration **175.00**
Platter, 20¼″ l, blue transfer Oriental dec, edge chips, wear, scratches **425.00**

Strawberry China

Bowl, 6¼″ d, pink luster, red and green enamel, wide strawberry border, c1820 .... **195.00**
Coffeepot, 1¼″ h, strawberry luster, dome cov with strawberry finial **475.00**
Creamer, 6¼″ h **195.00**
Cup and Saucer, handleless **100.00**
Plate, 8¼″ d, Cut Strawberry **195.00**
Soup Plate, 8¼″ d **175.00**
Sugar, cov, raised strawberries, strawberry finial **195.00**

Yellow Glazed

Bowl, 6⅜″ d, pink-luster floral dec, green enamel highlights, Staffordshire, c1815, restored, glaze wear ... **85.00**
Child's Mug, 2″ h, brown transfer, silver-luster rim, boys flying kite, inscribed "For a favorite" **245.00**
Cup and Saucer, handleless, brown transfer, couple at tea **300.00**
Jug
   4½″ h, Satyr, silver-luster trim and florets, enamel dec, Staffordshire, c1815, rim chips, hairline, handle repair **230.00**
   5¾″ h, black transfer print, silver-luster dec, inscribed "Accept this trifle from a friend whose love for thee shall never end," and "George Lawton, 1809" under spout **700.00**
Plate, 10″ d, pink luster and enamel floral and foliate border, Staffordshire, c1815 .... **115.00**

FAIRINGS, MATCH-STRIKERS, AND TRINKET BOXES

History: Fairings are small, charming china objects which were purchased or given away as prizes at English fairs in the 19th century. Although fairings are generally identified with England, they actually were manufactured in Germany by Conte and Boehme of Possneck.

Fairings depict an amusing scene, either of courtship and marriage, politics, war, children, or animals behaving as children. Over 400 varieties have been identified. Most fairings include a caption. Early examples, 1860–1870, were of better quality than later ones. After 1890 the colors became more garish, and gilding was introduced.

The manufacturers of fairings also made match safes and trinket boxes. Some of these were also captioned. The figures on the lids were identical to those on fairings. The market for the match safes and trinket boxes was the same as that for the fairings.

Reference: Janice and Richard Vogel, *Victorian Trinket Boxes*, published by authors (4720 S.E. Ft King St, Ocala, FL 34470), 1996.

Advisors: Barbara and Melvin Alpren.

Fairings

Baby's First Step, three children, hand in hand **200.00**
Bisque, painted, gold trim, detailed molding, marked "Conte & Boehme" **195.00**
O Do Leave Me a Drop, two cats at bowl **250.00**
Twelve Months after Marriage **200.00**

Match-Strikers

Crown and scepter, oval, applied flowers on border ... **275.00**
Tea Party, three ladies around tea table **300.00**

Trinket Boxes

Cameo, musical instruments on lid, 3¾″ d **115.00**
Chest of Drawers, bombe front, pocket watch on top . **195.00**
Girl putting on stockings, white ground, blue dec, imp marks, 3½ × 4 × 2″ **150.00**
Piano, 2⅜″ **95.00**

"Which is prettiest?," 3½ × 2 × 4″, $225.00.

FAIRY LAMPS

History: Fairy lamps, which originated in England in the 1840s, are candle-burning night lamps. They were used in nurseries, hallways, and dim corners of the home.

Two leading candle manufacturers, the Price Candle Company and the Samuel Clarke Company, promoted fairy lamps as a means to sell candles. Both contracted with glass, porcelain, and metal manufacturers to produce the needed shades and cups. For example, Clarke used Worcester Royal Porcelain Company, Stuart & Sons, and Red House Glass Works in England, plus firms in France and Germany.

Fittings were produced in a wide variety of styles. Shades ranged from pressed to cut glass, from Burmese to Nailsea. Cups are found in glass, porcelain, brass, nickel, and silver plate.

American firms selling fairy lamps included Diamond Candle Company of Brooklyn, Blue Cross Safety Candle Co., and Hobbs-Brockunier of Wheeling, West Virginia.

Two-piece (cup and shade) and three-piece (cup with matching shade and saucer) fairy lamps can be found. Married pieces are common.

Marks: Clarke's trademark was a small fairy with a wand surrounded by the words "Clarke Fairy Pyramid, Trade Mark."

References: Bob and Pat Ruf, *Fairy Lamps, Elegance in Candle Lighting,* Schiffer Publishing, 1996; John F. Solverson (comp.), *Those Fascinating Little Lamps: Miniature Lamps Value Guide,* Antique Publications, 1988.

Periodical: *Light Revival,* 35 West Elm Ave, Quincy, MA 02170.

Collectors' Club: Night Light Club, 38619 Wakefield Ct, Northville, MI 48167.

Reproduction Alert: Reproductions abound.

Burmese
> 5"h , flower and vines dec shade, clear base, marked "S Clarke/Patent/Trade Mark/Fairy" **565.00**
> 6½"h, 8" d, dome shade dec with red flowers, yellow centers, tapestry flower-bowl base with cream ground, pink flowers, aqua and gold trim, base marked "Clarke" **995.00**

Figural
> 3½" h, monkey, natural coloring, amber eyes **375.00**
> 4½" h, 3¾" d, owl's head, frosted green, red enameled eyes, clear marked Clarke base **300.00**

Goofus Glass, 7" h, rose dec, flash-fired green and red dec, three smoke holes in top, wood base **45.00**

Bisque, Austria, 4⅝", $215.00.

Nailsea, Verre Moire
> 5" h, 5½" d, white loopings, frosted cranberry body, dome-shaped shade, bowl-shaped base with ruffled edge, clear marked Clarke insert **450.00**
> 6½" h, 5¾" d, white loopings, red satin body, dome-shaped shade, bowl-shaped base with six pinched-in pleats, clear insert marked "S Clarke/Patent/Trade Mark/Fairy" **865.00**

Opalescent, 3¾ × 2⅞", blue emb rib, pyramid, clear marked Clarke base **95.00**

Peachblow, 5¼" h, clear glass candle cup, Mt Washington **250.00**

Satin Glass
> 5" h, Diamond Quilted shade, clear marked Clarke's Cricklite base **120.00**
> 6¾" h, cranberry, opaque white loopings, clear marked Clarke base **700.00**

Spatter Glass, 13¾" d, 17¾" h, double, emb ribbed overlay shades, SP Cricklite base **450.00**

FAMILLE ROSE

History: Famille Rose is Chinese export enameled porcelain on which the pink color predominates. It was made primarily in the 18th and 19th centuries. Other porcelains in the same group are Famille Jaune (yellow), Famille Noire (black), and Famille Verte (green).

Decorations include courtyard and home scenes, birds, and insects. Secondary colors are yellow, green, blue, aubergine, and black.

Rose Canton, Rose Mandarin, and Rose Medallion are mid- to late 19th-century Chinese export wares which are similar to Famille Rose.

Basin, 17" d, multicolored scene of pheasants perched on pierced rockwork, peonies and chrysanthemums, cavetto border with suspended pomegranates alternating with ruyi heads, stylized hibiscus blossoms with gilt highlights, four iron-red peony springs on underside **10,350.00**

Bowl
> 6" d, twin handles, enameled figures in pavilions dec, 19th C **200.00**
> 7¼" h, boys' festival, Qianlong seal mark, 20th C .. **225.00**
> 7¾" d, butterfly and floral motif, 20th C **150.00**

Charger, 15¾" d, courtesans panels, red enamel ground of scrolling lotus and dragons, 20th C **175.00**

Dish, 12¾" l, scrolled boat shape, waisted, raised spreading oval feet, undulating at upper rims, curled at ends, painted opaque enamels, bands of fruit and flowers, circular reserves of Chinese river landscapes, gilt details, Qianlong, price for pr **2,500.00**

Garden Stool, 18½" h, barrel shape, pierced, multicolored enamel dec, price for pr **2,400.00**

Jug, 8⅞" h, pear shape, iron-red dragonfly and two butterflies, peony branches and asters, gilt diamond and dot border, grooved strap handle, c1740 .... **3,450.00**

Plate
> 8¹³⁄₁₆" d, pink, blue, turquoise, aubergine, yellow, black, and white enamel dec, two ladies and man in pavilion garden setting, gilt highlights, cavetto

Jar, cov, botan, kika design imitating cloisonné ground surrounding fan-shaped reserves of rooster and flowers, 5½" h, $150.00.

border, pink cell-diaper ground rim, double panels
of whorls and peony blossoms, 1735–40 .... **635.00**
9³/₁₆" d, gold spotted brown stag walking on pale
green lawn, rose, gold, iron-red, turquoise, gray,
and blue fungi, green grass, gilt bamboo, butterfly
above, small chips, c1750, price for pr **690.00**
Tankard, 6" h, cylindrical, rose, iron-red, turquoise,
green, and blue, trailing branch of flowering peonies,
iron-red scalloped band, ribbed base, brown rim with
gilt blossoms and leaves, S-scroll handle, iron-red
heart shaped-terminal, c1745 .... **690.00**
Tureen, cov, 15" w, octagonal, armorial, hare's-head
handles, pomegranate finial, painted iron-red, turquoise, pale green, yellow, and blue opaque enamels, cartouche-shaped coat of arms below rampant
lion crest, c1750 ....**11,000.00**
Vase
11¾" h, baluster form, painted multicolored enamels
in continual design of women riding horseback,
floral band on neck, yellow ground, 18th C **1,150.00**
19" h, shouldered ovoid, two pierced handles on
neck, body with medallions of dragon and phoenix on yellow ground, shoulder with bands of
flower heads, butterfly, and scrolling lotus, neck
with medallions of floral arrangements, auspicious
symbols on yellow ground, early 20th C **750.00**

FANS

History: Today, people tend to think of fans as fragile, frivolous
accessories used by women; yet the origin of the fan was no doubt
highly practical. Early man may have used it to winnow his grain,
shoo flies, and cool his brow. This simple tool eventually became
a symbol of power: ancient lore maintains that Emperor Hsien
Yuan (c2697 B.C.) used fans; the tomb of Egypt's Tutankhamen
(1350 B.C.) yielded two ostrich-feather fans with gold mounts. Fans
also began to assume religious significance and were used to
whisk flies from altars. Early Christians recognized the practicality
of this device and included a flabellum, or fixed fly-whisk, in their

early services. Meanwhile, the Chinese and Japanese continued
to use fans in their courts, often incorporating precious materials
such as ivory, gold, and jade.

Until the 7th century A.D., fans were non-folding. Then, according to Japanese legend, Emperor Jen-ji noticed the logic of a
bat's folded wings and applied his insight to a new fan design.
Later, European traders returned from the East with samples of
these wonders. By the 16th century sophisticated Italian women
had appropriated the fan, use of which soon became *de rigueur*
throughout Europe. Now primarily feminine fashion accessories,
their styles changed to complement the ever-changing dress styles.
Fans' popularity led to experimentation in their production and
merchandising. They also became popular as a way for artists to
test their skills—a fan leaf's curved, folding surface offered chal-
lenges in perspective.

World War I brought about the end of the slow-paced lifestyle;
the 1920s raced at a frenetic speed. The modern woman set aside
her ubiquitous fan, freeing both hands to drive her roadster or
carry her political banner. Fans became more an advertising tool
than a fashion statement.

Some basic guidelines are:

- 19th century artisans copied 18th century styles. True Georgian figures should have gray hair; if the wigs are white, the fan is more
recent. The later fans will often have a heavier appearance, and
anachronistic costuming.
- Empire fans were also copied. The period ones have sequins made
by flattening circles of wire; a tiny line shows where the wire ends
meet. Later sequins were stamped whole out of sheet metal and have
no joining line.
- Ivory, bone, celluloid, and plastic may look somewhat alike. Ivory
often has a subtle, textureless graining pattern and may feel smooth
and buttery; bone frequently has channels. Look for mold marks in
plastic.
- Many leaves became damaged with wear and were replaced. These
"married" fans can still be delightful collectibles, but beware of
dating a fan merely based on one component.
- Loops are rarely found on fans before 1830.
- Framing a fan often causes its sticks to warp, its leaf to lose its
elasticity and ability to fold. It is also difficult to tell if a fan has been
sewn or glued to its backing, making its removal difficult.
- The number of degrees a folding fan opens is a key to dating.
- Handle fans gently, unfolding from left to right.

Fan Terminology:
Brisé—fan with no leaf, but made of rigid, overlapping sticks held
together at base by a rivet and at the other end by a ribbon.
Cockade—pleated fan opening to form complete circle.
Folding fan—fan with a flexible, pleated leaf mounted on sticks.
Fontange—shape of folding fans c1890–1935, with center of leaf
longer than guards.
Guard—the outermost sticks, usually the height of fan.
Leaf or mount—flexible, pleated material which unites the upper parts
of a folding fan's sticks.
Lithograph—printing process invented in 1797, often subsequently
hand-colored.
Loop—often U-shaped finger holder attached to rivet at base of fan;
rare before 1830.
Medallion—pictorial representation, usually circular or oval, in leaf.
Piqué-point—decorative small gold or silver points or pins set flush
with surface or sticks or guards.
Rivet—pin about which sticks of a folding fan pivot.
Sticks—rigid framework of a folding fan.

Studs—exposed end of rivet, sometimes shaped as decorative paste "gem."

Washer—small disk to prevent friction between end of rivet and fan.

References: Helene Alexander, *Fans,* Batsford, 1984; Nancy Armstrong, *The Book of Fans,* Mayflower Books, out of print; ———, *A Collector's History of Fans,* Clarkson N. Potter, 1974; ———, *Fans,* Souvenir Press, 1984; Anna Gray Bennett, *Fans In Fashion,* San Francisco Art Museum, 1981; ———, *Unfolding Beauty,* Thames and Hudson, 1988; Braintree Historical Society, *Hunt and Allen Fans,* Braintree Historical Society, 1988; Reiko Chiba, *Painted Fans of Japan,* Charles E. Tuttle, 1962; Tseng Yu-ho Ecke, *Poetry on the Wind,* Honolulu Academy of Arts, 1981; M. A. Flory, *A Book about Fans,* Macmillan, 1895; Julia Hutt and Helene Alexander, *Ogi,* Dauphin Publishing, 1992; Neville John Irons, *Fans of Imperial China,* Kaiserreich, 1981; ———, *Fans of Imperial Japan,* Kaiserreich, 1981; Susan Mayor, *Collecting Fans,* Mayflower Books, 1980; ———, *Collector's Guide to Fans,* Wellfleet Books, 1990; ———, *Fans,* Vancouver Museum, 1983; Gabriel Mourey et al., *Art Nouveau Jewellery & Fans,* Dover Publications, 1973; Mary E. G. Rhoads, *The Fan Directory,* Second Edition, Fan Collectors Press, 1993.

Collectors' Clubs: American Fan Collectors Assoc, PO Box 804, South Bend, IN 46624; Fan Circle International, Cronk-Y-Voddy, Rectory Rd, Cotishall Norwich NR12 7HF England; FANA, Fan Association of North America, 6138 Deacon Rd, Windermere, FL 34786.

Advisor: Wendy Hamilton Blue.

Note: Condition is important above all! Any tear or split in a leaf, any break in a stick, any missing part drastically reduces a fan's value, often by half or more. Most fans available on the U.S. market were produced in plentiful numbers, and many have survived in good to excellent condition.

Abbreviations:

chlth	chromolithograph
gl	guard length
op	width when opened
#/#	number of sticks/number of guards

American and European

Late 18th C, European

Satin, ivory, folding, painted satin leaf depicts 3 women and 1 man, all dressed in c1775 costume, in elegant garden, borders of leaf decorated with sequins, sticks pierced and gilt ivory, MOP washer, brass rivet,16/2, gl 11″, op 20″, 165° ... **300.00**

Silk, bone, folding, hand-colored silk, central oval etching of an opera scene, left: two men in Turkish costume sit reading at a table placed beneath a palm tree, approaching them from the middle distance two women in fashionable European dress holding parasols and sitting atop camels, approach with two men, both walking and wearing mid-Eastern dress; right: well-dressed European man, his hands bound in chains, seems to beseech equally well-garbed European woman, bone sticks, central ones painted in gold with festoons, MOP washer, brass rivet, 14/2, gl 11″, op 20½″, 165° **475.00**

c1820, horn, brisé monocular fan, small, sticks intricately pierced and clouté (inset with small cut steels),

connected by silk ribbon, pivot is set with a monocle (eye glass), rimmed in brass, 16/2, gl 6″, op 9⅝″, 160° **500.00**

Mid-19th C, satin, ivory, fire hand screens, double, cream moiré satin mounts with chenille, embroidered flowers in pastel shades, cream silk fringe atop turned ivory handles, 10½″ w mount, 18″ with fringe, overall size of each fan, including mount and handle, is 15⅞″ h, price for pr **800.00**

1860–1875, satin, carved bone, folding fan, front of double satin mount is hp, showing int. of barber shop, with one monkey shaving another, hp reverse with simple floral spray on left, MOP washer, brass nailhead rivet, 14/2, gl 10⅝″, op 20″, 170° **200.00**

c1870, tortoiseshell, brisé fan, probably Austrian, guards set with semiprecious jewels in the Art Nouveau style, brown silk tassel, 18/2, gl 9¼″, with 1″ tortoiseshell loop, op 16½″, 180° **600.00**

1880–1900, satin, wood, folding fan, probably American, deep salmon, satin double leaf, hp three robins among dogwood blossoms, plain reverse, painted and varnished in imitation of Japanese lacquer sticks painted with similar scene, guards, painted and carved with dogwood blossoms and butterflies, beveled in the style of fans from the Hunt-Allen factory in MA, MOP washer, brass loop, 14/2, gl 14⅞″, op 28″, 170° **175.00**

c1890

Gauze, wood, folding mask fan, with box, European, possibly French, translucent black silk mount, black velvet eye mask, plain sticks, upper section of the right guardstick embellished with partial figure of woman dressed as a jester, carved applied bone face and bust, rest carved from the wood stick, bone washer, brass rivet, contemporary box marked "Duvelleroy" (fan not marked), 10/2, gl 14″, op 20″, 140° **375.00**

Satin

MOP, folding fan, European, probably French, double fabric leaf front hp with trio of women, dressed in 18th C costume, feeding ducks at the edge of a pond, plain reverse, plain MOP sticks, gold-tone metal rivet, loop, 14/2, gl 12″, op 22½″, 170° **200.00**

Wood, kit folding fan, probably American, front of the blue satin, double leaf embroidered primarily in chain stitch, with a spray of flowers in cream, moss, and shades of rose, thin sticks assembled from pieces of different woods, creating the effect of marquetry, MOP washer, brass loop, 13/2, gl 13⅜″, op 25″, 160° **135.00**

1890–1910, metallic mesh, bone, Fontange fan, European, gold metallic mesh single leaf, woven roses, mounted on bone sticks incised and painted with gold roses, bone washer, nailhead rivet, brass loop, 12/2, gl 8⅝″ (leaf extends 4¼″ higher in center), op 16″, 170° **300.00**

c1900, feathers, tortoiseshell, SS, brisé fan, dyed black ostrich feathers atop tortoiseshell sticks, ornate SS guards, SS loop, 14/2, gl 10⅝″ (feathers longer), op 19″, 160° **250.00**

Advertising, cardboard brise, four heart-shaped sections, each depicts girl of the period, reverse shows C. Aultman & Co. farm equipment including thresher and straw burning engine, American, c1885, 5½" h, 3⅞" w, $300.00.

American and European Souvenir, Commemorative, and Advertising

1851, paper, wood, French, cream front, double paper leaf is printed with program of Smith's ascent of Mount Blanc, August 12–13, 1851, map and details of climb, reverse is printed with three vignettes—"The Mur de la Côte, The Grands Mulets, Coming Down," engraved by Brioude La Guerre, Rue de Fontaine 5 Paris, and published by Leroux Fan Manufacturers, 41 Street Notre Dame de Nazareth, plain wooden sticks, dark metal washer with fishscale design, brass rivet, 14/2, gl 9", op 18", 175° **650.00**

1889, linen-textured paper, wood, souvenir folding fan, French, front of the double paper leaf is a chlth, aerial view of the "Exposition Universelle 1889" Eiffel's tower center, sgd "Derosé," soft shades, primarily blues, greens, pinks, and creams, with flowers bordering the scene to the left, birds on flowering tree branches to the right, plain, cream paper reverse, back of the left guard, each of interior wooden sticks (which are painted gold) and front top of right guard are stamped in silver with representation of the Eiffel Tower and the year, tops of guards are beveled, brass loop, nailhead rivet, 14/2, gl 13½", op 25½", 175° **400.00**

1892–93, paper, wood, souvenir folding fan, two Art Nouveau–style women wearing flowing gossamer draperies stand on either side of an aerial chlth view of the exhibition area for 1893, or Pan-American, World's Fair, Chicago, print is brightly colored in greens, soft reds, yellows, and blues, reverse has a central map of fair, photo of "N Nasr, Exclusive Concessionaire of Fans Pan-American Exposition" on left, and "Hon. W. I. Buchanan, Director General Pan-American Exposition" on right, 3 photos of fair sites, with specific areas and admission prices beneath, 2 photos and similar listings to right of Buchanan, simple wood sticks

painted white, steel washer, rivet, 13/2, gl 10", op 19", 175° **175.00**

Late 19th C

Cardboard, wood, adv hand screen, American, intricately diecut to resemble a shield-shaped picture frame, the gilded, emb, and textured borders, dec cutouts, center has a chlth of beautiful young woman wearing a red bow, long, blond hair, reverse advertises a dealer of boots, shoes, and rubbers, printed by "The Best Mfg. Co. of New Haven, Ct. Cardboard," 8½" h, 6⅞" w at top, 2½" bottom, 12⅞" overall, including shaped, split-wood stick, two vertical staples **50.00**

Paper, wood, English, front double paper leaf presents seventy portraits, based on "copyright oils," of famous British stage actors of the era, "Louis Felman's Celebrity Fan" was "Printed in Photo-Mezzotype by the London Stereoscopic & Photographic Co., of 54 Cheapside E. C. & 106 & 108 Regent St. W. Principally from their copyright oils of celebrities, Patent 14948, Manufactured by Norman & Stacey, Ltd., Art Furnishers, 118, Queen Victoria Street, London, By Royal Letters Patent," plain red paper on reverse, simple wooden sticks, painted gunmetal gray, celluloid washer, brass loop, 14/2, gl 13½", op 25½", 170° **135.00**

c1900, paper, wood, folding adv, Japanese for American market, front of heavy double paper leaf touts J W Goddard & Sons's dress linings and advises the customer to "Order any Color of which the Flower-petals on this Fan are made in all Qualities of our linings. Order by Color Number," trademark manufactured by A A Vantine & Co Japan, wood sticks, split-wood guards, 6/2, gl 13", op 25¼", 175° **160.00**

1904, cardboard, wood, adv hand screen, American, diecut hand screen depicting Sunbonnet Babies, artist B L Corbett, sitting at an umbrella table and finishing their ice cream sundaes, titled "Sodalicious!," the fan printed by Brown & Bigelow, St Paul, plain white reverse adv "Wyman's Coffee and Tea," printed in black, split-wood stick, two vertical staples, 9⅝" h, 8⅜" w., overall h, including stick, 15" **70.00**

c1915, paper, wood, folding adv fan, French, cream-colored front of double paper leaf is chlth, left: mustached traffic policeman suspended from hot-air balloon, propeller extends rearward from heavy belt strapped to his waist, he signals other air traffic to stop; center background: bearded man in high hat flies plane and asks woman flying a biplane in the opposite direction, "Where you go? (sic)," she wears striped knee length pants outfit, replies, "To Louis Martin's," facade on lower left, sgd in print "Geo. Desian" center, far right, tan paper reverse dec with reddish-brown swags, laurel branches, published by "Francolin Gilet & Cie, Eventaillistes, Paris," simple wood sticks, interior ones stamped with two gold flowers each, right guard stamped with two gold putti, one rides atop a stream of champagne spurting from an opened bottle, while the other reaches overhead to pick grapes, left guard plain, etched brass loop, steel rivet, 12/2, gl 8½", 15¾", 180° **250.00**

1929, cardboard, wood, patriotic, adv hand screen, American, oval, with slightly scalloped sides, center: teenage Boy Scout salutes US naval officer in dress whites, three-masted ship sails before full moon in the dark blue background, scouting motto "Be Prepared" is on either side, which is labeled: "19009—The Great Adventure," printed by Brown & Bigelow, St Paul, MN, plain cream reverse with black print, adv PA car dealer specializing in "Durant, Chrysler and Plymouth," 9³⁄₁₆" h, 9³⁄₁₆" w at center, 14⁵⁄₁₆" h overall, including split stick **65.00**

1975, cardboard, wood, political adv, mask hand screen, American, oval, notch missing at the top, presidential candidate James Carter from just below his nose to buttons below his peanut bow tie, user fits notch under his nose to have a mask sporting famous toothy smile, red and white striped background with 2 blue stars, plain reverse, flat, tongue depressor wooden handle attached with 2 staples, 9¼" h, 8" w, 12¾" h overall, including stick **22.00**

Oriental, Pacific

c1820, ivory, folding brisé fan, Cantonese, ivory sticks are single side carved and pierced with figures in gardens and near terraced buildings and connected by silk ribbon, finials (tops of sticks) are carved with birds and foliage, central escutcheon bears owner's initials, metal rivet, washer stamped to resemble flower, 21/2, gl 8", op 14¾", 160° .. **400.00**

c1840, wood, folding brisé fan, Chinese, light wood sticks repeatedly lacquered in black, then painted in gold, central frame depicts busy life in household of member of nobility, each finial depicts a member of the household, gorge shows 5 men sitting in a garden, each guard is painted with an int. scene, bordered by butterflies and flowers, silk connecting ribbon, paste stud, SS loop, orig box, 20/2, gl 8¼", op 15", 170° **450.00**

c1870, paper, wood, folding dictionary fan, Japanese, front of delicate double paper leaf is woodblock print, center shows European woman and her Japanese counterpart, with female Japanese interpreter sitting between them, left reserve is a map of the world, while right is port scene, with masted ships in foreground, city and mountains in background, spaces between reserves and central scene carry translations of common English words, letters, and numbers, into Japanese, beneath central scene is "Japan Koto Shimomura," plain dark gray paper reverse, hollow brass rivet, bamboo sticks, 27/2, gl 10", op 18¾", 180° **360.00**

Late 19th C

Betal palm, rigid hand screen, Chinese, broad, somewhat shovel-shaped leaf is engraved with hot poker or joss sticks, resulting design is sometimes then painted and may be lacquered,

screen is slipped between the top, often rounded sections of a handle, made of another piece of betel palm, or of tortoiseshell or other rigid material, handle is both palm and wood, inscribed with the silhouette of an owl, screen 9" h, 7⁹⁄₁₆" w at top, 5¹⁄₁₂" at bottom, overall h 14" with handle **85.00**

Metal, wood, tanto fan, Japanese, resembles a simple, folded wooden brisé fan-actually the sheath of a hidden dagger, silk tassel, glass bead, no real sticks, false gl 12" **550.00**

Tulle (fine-stranded net) on horn, net leaf completely edged in needle lace, leaf is decorated with three groups of lace daffodils accented with sequins, serpentine guards with pique point decoration, 1905–10, 10¾" guard length, 21¾" w open, $400.00

c1920, paper, wood, folding fan, Japanese, leaf, painted with white peony blossoms against gold background, accented bybold, asymmetrical swerve of bright green, sgd "Yamaguchi Kayô," sticks of "Komori" or "Suychiro Ogi" (wide-ended fan), lacquered in red, the top section of guards carved in the "nekome" (cat's-eye) pattern, reverse shows Peony family mon, and inscription: "700th anniversary of a great religious leader's death" (which was officially memorialized by the royal court), 13/2, gl 11¾", op 16", 155° **300.00**

Early 20th C, bone, silk, folding fan, Japanese, single hp silk leaf, two women in kimonos right of center, one holds an opened fan and dances while other beats drum, details of fan, kimonos, and drum highlighted with both silk and metallic embroidery, sticks slightly shaped in gorge area, otherwise plain, top sections of guards simply carved with flowers, hammered nailhead rivet, steel loop, silk tassel, 18/2, gl 8⁵⁄₁₆", op 15½", 175° **75.00**

Mid-20th C, sandalwood, silk, folding fan, Japanese, narrow silk lead, 2" h, crudely painted figures of three women, stream, trees, and building in background, machine-pierced slender sticks, X's, curving lines, small sections of silk (1¼" h, 2½" w) inset into sticks to left and right of center, brass nailhead rivet, white metal, etched loop, double pink silk tassel, cardboard box covered with silver-foil paper, top inset with glass, 27/2, gl 8", op 14", 165° ... **20.00**

FENTON GLASS

History: The Fenton Art Glass Company began as a cutting shop in Martins Ferry, Ohio, in 1905. In 1906 Frank L. Fenton started to build a plant in Williamstown, West Virginia, and produced the first piece of glass there in 1907. Early production included carnival, chocolate, custard, and pressed glass, plus mold-blown opalescent glass. In the 1920s stretch glass, Fenton dolphins, jade green, ruby, and art glass were added.

In the 1930s boudoir lamps, Dancing Ladies, and slag glass in various colors were produced. The 1940s saw crests of different colors being added to each piece by hand. Hobnail, opalescent, and two-color overlay pieces were popular items. Handles were added to different shapes, making the baskets they created as popular today as then.

Through the years Fenton has beautified their glass by decorating it with hand painting, acid etching, color staining, and copper-wheel cutting

Marks: Several different paper labels have been used. In 1970 an oval raised trademark also was adopted.

References: Robert E. Eaton, Jr. (comp.), price guides for *Fenton Glass: The First Twenty-Five Years, The Second Twenty-Five Years,* and *The Third Twenty-Five Years,* Antique Publications, 1995; William Heacock, *Fenton Glass: The First Twenty-Five Years* (1978), *The Second Twenty-Five Years* (1980), *The Third Twenty-Five Years* (1989), available from Antique Publications; Alan Linn, *The Fenton Story of Glass Making,* Antique Publications, 1996; Naomi L. Over, *Ruby Glass of the 20th Century,* Antique Publications, 1990, 1993–94 value update; Ferill J. Rice (ed.), *Caught in the Butterfly Net,* Fenton Art Glass Collectors of America, Inc., 1991.

Periodical: *Butterfly Net,* 302 Pheasant Run, Kaukauna, WI 54130.

Collectors' Clubs: Fenton Art Glass Collectors Of America, Inc, PO Box 384, Williamstown, WV 26187; National Fenton Glass Society, PO Box 4008, Marietta, OH 45750; Pacific Northwest Fenton Assoc, 8225 Kilchis River Rd, Tillamook, OR 97141.

Videotape: *Glass Artistry in the Making Fenton,* Fenton Art Glass, 1992.

Museum: Fenton Art Glass Co, Williamstown, WV.

Advisor: Ferill J. Rice.

Additional Listings: Carnival Glass.

Bell, Rosaline, c1970, 7", $29.00.

Ashtray, Dogwood Flowered Hobnail, pipe, #3773 ...	**62.00**
Banana Bowl	
Hobnail, milk glass, #3720	**37.00**
Viking, crystal with crystal satin	**250.00**
Basket	
4½" h, Hobnail, topaz opal, #389	**65.00**
5" h, Coin Dot, French opal, #1924	**32.50**
5½" h, Hobnail, low, #3835	
Cranberry opal	**125.00**
Blue opal	**65.00**
French opal	**45.00**
7" h	
Black Rose, #203	**240.00**
Olde Virginia Thumbprint, #9137	**29.00**
9" h, Embossed Rose, #9235	**39.50**
11" h, aventurine green with blue, #6437	**125.00**
12" h, Coin Dot, French opal, #1353	**185.99**
Beverage Set	
Celeste blue, pitcher and six tumblers, cut, #220 ..	**350.00**
Hobnail, cranberry opal, 80 oz. #3967 pitcher, four #3947 barrel tumblers	**265.00**
Late Coin Spot, green, ice tea lip, 6 tumblers, #1352	**160.00**
Rib Optic, blue opal, six tumblers, royal blue coasters, #222	**550.00**
Bonbon	
5½" d, silver turquoise, #7225	**15.00**
6" d, tangerine stretch, crimped, sq dolphin, #1533	**85.00**
Bowl	
6" d, Basketweave, ebony	**30.00**
8" d, Grape & Cable, marigold carnival, spade ftd .	**65.00**
8½" d, Thistle, green carnival	**150.00**
9" d	
Holly, blue carnival	**85.00**
Ming, Fenton rose, 3 ftd, #249	**110.00**
10" d	
Leaf Tiers, amethyst cupped	**130.00**
Waterlily & Cattails, master berry, amethyst opal	**80.00**
11½" d, Sheffield, halo etching, #1800	**45.00**
Cake Plate, 13" d, Ebony Crest, #7213	**130.00**
Candlestick, pr	
Hobnail, topaz opal, #3974	**50.00**
Viking, crystal and crystal satin	**225.00**
Candy Dish, Hobnail, topaz, ftd, #3974	**90.00**
Candy Dish, cov	
Aquamarine, #835	**70.00**
Cameo Opal, #835	**45.00**
Hobnail, topaz opal, ftd	**130.00**
Compote	
Blue Marble Roses, #9222	**25.00**
Emerald Crest, ftd, #7228	**30.00**
Condiment Set., Hobnail, #3809, 7 pc	**37.50**
Creamer and Sugar	
Daisy and Button, blue opal, #1903	**35.00**
Hobnail, miniature, topaz opal, #389	**22.50**

Cruet, 6" h, Coin Dot, #208
    Cranberry **140.00**
    French opal **95.00**
Cup and Saucer, Emerald Crest, #7208 .... **45.00**
Decanter Set
    Blue opal, decanter and four wines, #389 .... **240.00**
    Hobnail, cranberry opal, #3761 .... **375.00**
Epergne, milk glass
    Diamond Lace, single horn **75.00**
    Hobnail, 4 pc
        #3701 .... **55.00**
        #3801 .... **45.00**
Fairy Lamp, Hobnail
    Amber, #3608, 2 pc **20.00**
    Milk glass, hp by Louise Piper, ftd, #3804, 3 pc ... **300.00**
Flowerpot, Snow Crest, green, #401 .... **30.00**
Ginger Jar, Wisteria satin etching, crystal, #893, 3 pc . **125.00**
Goblet
    Lincoln Inn, royal blue, #1700 .... **30.00**
    Plymouth, ruby, #1620 .... **20.00**
    Silver Crest, #203 .... **60.00**
Guest Set, #200, 2 pc
    Florentine Green **325.00**
    Opal Curtain Optic, topaz, blue handle **1,350.00**
Hat Vase
    8", French opal, #1922
        Coin Spot **240.00**
        Spiral Optic **75.00**
    10" h, Peach Crest, #1922 .... **125.00**
Jug/Pitcher
    Coin Spot, cream, cranberry opal, L G Wright **32.50**
    Dot Optic, French opal, black handle, #1352 ..... **120.00**
    Hobnail, 80 oz
        Blue opal, #389 .... **140.00**
        Cranberry, ice lip **275.00**
    Silver Crest, 70 oz, #1634-7467 .... **175.00**
Lamp
    Colonial, orange, oil, courting, #1790 .... **60.00**
    Melon, mulberry, cut chimney, miniature **250.00**
    Rose, #7 cutting, G-70 .... **250.00**
Lavabo, Hobnail, #3867
    Milk glass **77.00**
    Wild Rose **450.00**
Macaroon Jar, lilac, original handle and cov, #681 ... **310.00**
Mayonnaise Set, Hobnail, cranberry opal, #3903, 3 pc **145.00**
Night Set, Rib Optic, blue opal, 2 pc **250.00**
Nut Dish, Cactus, topaz opal, Levay, #3428 .... **22.50**
Plate
    7" d, Leaf, blue opal, #175 .... **22.50**
    10" d, Emerald Crest, #7210 .... **50.00**
Rose Bowl, crystal, Wisteria satin etching, crimped #894 **30.00**
Salt and Pepper Shakers
    Hobnail, cranberry opal, flat, #3806 .... **37.50**
    Rib Optic, 5" salt, 4" pepper, #1605
        Cranberry opal **95.00**
        Lime opal **85.00**
Sherbet
    Lincoln Inn, ruby, #1700 .... **20.00**
    Plymouth, Amber, #1620 .... **10.00**
Tidbit Tray, Aqua Crest, 2 tiers, #7294 .... **65.00**
Toothpick
    Daisy & Button, chocolate, 1" hat **45.00**

Hobnail, topaz opal, #3795 .... **35.00**
Tumbler
    Colonial Thumbprint, pink, juice, 4 pc **25.00**
    Hobnail Barrel, cranberry opal **35.00**
    Roses, bathroom, #9242 .... **10.00**
Vanity Set
    Diamond Optic, ruby overlay, #192 .... **100.00**
    Hobnail
        Blue opal, cov, 3 pc **125.00**
        Cranberry opal, pointed stoppers **195.00**
    Melon, blue overlay, 3 pc **135.00**
Vase
    5½" h, Fan, mandarin red, #847 .... **55.00**
    6¼" h, Crystal Crest, fan, #7357 .... **80.00**
    8", plum opal, bud, #3756 .... **32.50**

FIESTA

History: The Homer Laughlin China Company introduced Fiesta dinnerware in January 1936 at the Pottery and Glass Show in Pittsburgh, Pennsylvania. Frederick Rhead designed the pattern; Arthur Kraft and Bill Bensford molded it. Dr. A. V. Bleininger and H. W. Thiemecke developed the glazes.

The original five colors were red, dark blue, light green (with a trace of blue), brilliant yellow, and ivory. A vigorous marketing campaign took place between 1939 and 1943. In mid-1937 turquoise was added. Red was removed in 1943 because some of the chemicals used to produce it were essential to the war effort; it did not reappear until 1959. In 1951 light green, dark blue, and ivory were retired and forest green, rose, chartreuse, and gray were added to the line. Other color changes took place in the late 1950s, including the addition of a medium green.

Fiesta ware was redesigned in 1969 and discontinued about 1972. In 1986 Fiesta was reintroduced by Homer Laughlin China Company. The new china body shrinks more than the old semi-vitreous and ironstone pieces, thus making the new pieces slightly smaller than the earlier pieces. The modern colors are also different in tone or hue, e.g., the cobalt blue is darker than the old blue. Other modern colors are black, white, apricot, and rose.

References: Susan and Al Bagdade, *Warman's American Pottery and Porcelain,* Wallace-Homestead, 1994; Sharon and Bob Huxford, *The Collector's Encyclopedia of Fiesta,* Revised Seventh Edition, Collector Books, 1992; Dana G. Morykan and Harry L. Rinker, *Warman's Country Antiques & Collectibles,* Third Edition, Wallace-Homestead, 1996.

Collectors' Clubs: Fiesta Club of America, PO Box 15383, Loves Park, IL 61115; Fiesta Collectors Club, 19238 Dorchester Circle, Strongsville, OH 44136.

Reproduction Alert.

Additional Listings: See *Warman's Americana & Collectibles* for more examples.

Ashtray
    Cobalt Blue **50.00**
    Red **50.00**

Cake Server, red, Kitchen Kraft 150.00
Calendar Plate, ivory, 1954, 10″ d 40.00
Candlesticks, pr
    Bulb, yellow 35.00
    Tripod
        Light green 355.00
        Turquoise 225.00
Carafe
    Cobalt Blue, spout repaired 120.00
    Ivory 230.00
    Light Green 145.00
    Red 195.00
Casserole, cov, Medium Green, chipped handle and
    base 130.00
Casserole, French, yellow 190.00
Chop Plate
    Ivory, 13″ d 25.00
    Red, 15″ d 50.00
Coffeepot
    Light Green 195.00
    Turquoise 155.00
Compote
    Ivory, 12″ d 137.50
    Red, 12″ d 140.00
    Yellow 42.00
Creamer
    Individual, red 200.00
    Stick handle
        Light Green 30.00
        Red 65.00
Creamer and Sugar
    Ivory 60.00
    Yellow 55.00
Cup and Saucer
    Chartreuse 25.00
    Cobalt Blue 20.00
    Gray 24.00
    Ivory 20.00
    Light Green 16.50
    Medium Green 55.00
    Turquoise 20.00
    Yellow 20.00
Deep Dish Plate
    Cobalt Blue 35.75
    Ivory 27.50
    Light Green 33.00
    Medium Green 100.00
    Red 35.75
    Turquoise 20.00
    Yellow 24.75
Demitasse Cup and Saucer
    Chartreuse 260.00
    Cobalt Blue 60.00
    Ivory 55.00
    Light Green 65.00
    Red 75.00
    Turquoise 69.00
    Yellow 55.00
Demitasse Pot, cov, cobalt blue 495.00
Eggcup
    Chartreuse 115.00
    Ivory 45.00

Yellow 40.00
Gravy, turquoise 30.00
Juice Pitcher
    Cobalt Blue 45.00
    Rose 45.00
Juice Tumbler, light green 27.50
Marmalade, cobalt blue 300.00
Mixing Bowl
    #1, red 170.00
    #2
        Cobalt Blue 100.00
        Light Green 44.00
    #3
        Cobalt Blue, chip 420.00
        Ivory 77.00
    #4, ivory 77.00
    #5
        Light Green 100.00
        Red 82.50
        Turquoise 93.50
    #6
        Light Green 110.00
        Red 137.50
        Yellow 105.00
    #7, cobalt blue, rim repaired 137.50
Mug
    Cobalt Blue 55.00
    Ivory, gold letters 45.00
    Light Green 40.00
    Medium Green, chips 22.00
    Yellow 40.00
Mustard, red, chip 90.00
Nappy, 8½″ d
    Chartreuse 27.50
    Dark Green 35.00
    Medium Green 95.00
    Gray 40.00
    Red 30.00
    Rose 40.00
    Turquoise 19.25
    Yellow 7.70
Onion Soup, cov
    Ivory 360.00
    Yellow 415.00
Plate, 9″ d
    Chartreuse 14.50
    Cobalt Blue 15.00
    Ivory 6.60
    Light Green 6.60
    Medium Green 37.50
Platter, oval
    Cobalt Blue 30.00
    Gray 35.00
    Ivory 25.00
    Red 32.00
    Turquoise 27.50
    Yellow 22.00
Relish, ivory, cobalt blue center, turquoise and yellow
    side dishes 165.00
Salad Bowl, individual
    Medium Green 80.00
    Red 55.00

Pitcher, juice, ice lip, yellow, 5⅞", $32.00.

Turquoise	72.00
Salt and Pepper Shakers, pr, yellow	35.00
Sauce Boat	
Gray	50.00
Light Green	33.00
Red	55.00
Syrup	
Red	385.00
Turquoise, green top	145.00
Teapot	
Medium Green, medium size	770.00
Turquoise, large	150.00
Yellow, medium	90.00
Utility Tray	
Cobalt Blue	25.00
Red	55.00
Vase	
Bud	
Light Green	42.00
Red	88.00
8" h, cobalt blue	600.00
10" h, ivory	770.00
12" h, ivory	825.00
Water Pitcher, disc	
Chartreuse	180.00
Cobalt Blue	140.00
Dark Green	180.00
Ivory	130.00
Light Green	85.00
Medium Green, faint hairline	800.00
Red	150.00
Turquoise	90.00
Yellow	85.00

Empty figural bottles were shipped to the United States and filled upon arrival. They were then given away to customers by brothels, dance halls, hotels, liquor stores, and taverns. Some were lettered with the names and addresses of the establishment, others had paper labels. Many were used for holidays, e.g., Christmas and New Year.

Figural bottles also were made in glass and other materials. The glass bottles held perfumes, food, or beverages.

References: Ralph & Terry Kovel, *The Kovels' Bottles Price List,* Tenth Edition,, Crown Publishers, 1996; Kenneth Wilson, *American Glass 1760–1930,* 2 vols., Hudson Hills Press and The Toledo Museum of Art, 1994.

Periodical: *Antique Bottle And Glass Collector,* PO Box 187, East Greenville, PA 18041.

Collectors' Clubs: Federation of Historical Bottle Clubs, 88 Sweetbriar Branch, Longwood, FL 32750; New England Antique Bottle Club, 120 Commonwealth Rd, Lynn, MA 01904.

Museums: National Bottle Museum, Ballston Spa, NY; National Bottle Museum, Barnsley, S Yorkshire, England; Old Bottle Museum, Salem, NJ.

Bisque

Fox, 6¼" h, standing, wearing brown suit	45.00
Gentleman, 6" h, Victorian, paper label "Compliments, Holiday Greetings," orig cork stopper	150.00
Sailor, 6½" h, cartoon type, high-gloss front, white pants, blue blouse and hat, marked "Made in Germany"	115.00

Glass

Bear, 11" h, opaque white	90.00
Bunker Hill Monument, 12" h, clear, American, c1870	35.00
Elk Tooth, milk glass, orig gold paint	100.00
Moses, 10⅞" h, green, emb "Poland Spring Water"	175.00
Violin, 9" h, light electric blue, pontil scar	50.00

Porcelain

Camel, 7½" l, MOP glaze, orig stopper, German	95.00
Coachman, 10⅜" h, Bennington, Rockingham glaze, 1849 emb mark	700.00
Dog, 8" h, Majolica-type glaze, removable head	75.00
Napoleon, 10" h, 3⅜" d, orig porcelain hat stopper, gray, black, buttons, and cocked hat, flesh-tone face and hand, marked "ROBJ Paris"	345.00

FIGURAL BOTTLES

History: Porcelain figural bottles, which have an average height of three to eight inches and were made either in a glazed or bisque finish, achieved popularity in the late 1800s and remained popular into the 1930s. The majority of figural bottles were made in Germany, with Austria and Japan accounting for the balance.

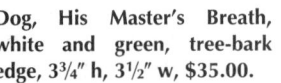

Dog, His Master's Breath, white and green, tree-bark edge, 3¾" h, 3½" w, $35.00.

Sweet Potato, 7″ l, int. glazed, Welsh, late 19th C	**75.00**
Tree, 9″ h, Indian Chief–head center, brown glaze	**95.00**
Wolf, 4⅞″ h, seated, reading book, marked "Germany" on base, late 19th C	**50.00**

Sugar Shaker, raspberry	**450.00**
Toothpick Holder	**375.00**
Water Set, water pitcher, four barrel-shaped tumblers, cream, price for 5-pc set	**2,400.00**

FINDLAY ONYX GLASS

History: Findlay onyx glass, produced by Dalzell, Gilmore & Leighton Company, Findlay, Ohio, was patented for the firm in 1889 by George W. Leighton. Due to high production costs resulting from a complex manufacturing process, the glass was made only for a short time.

Layers of glass were plated to a bulb of opalescent glass through repeated dippings into a glass pot. Each layer was cooled and reheated to develop opalescent qualities. A pattern mold then was used to produce raised decorations of flowers and leaves. A second mold gave the glass bulb its full shape and form.

A platinum luster paint, producing pieces identified as silver or platinum onyx, was applied to the raised decorations. The color was fixed in a muffle kiln. Other colors such as cinnamon, cranberry, cream, raspberry, and rose were achieved by using an outer glass plating which reacted strongly to reheating. For example, a purple or orchid color came from the addition of manganese and cobalt to the glass mixture.

References: Neila and Tom Bredenhoft, *Findlay Toothpick Holders,* Cherry Hill Publications, 1995; James Measell and Don E. Smith, *Findlay Glass: The Glass Tableware Manufacturers, 1886–1902,* Antique Publications, 1986.

Collectors' Club: Collectors of Findlay Glass, PO Box 256, Findlay, OH 45839.

Celery, cream	**450.00**
Creamer, 4½″ h, cream	**250.00**
Dresser Box, cov, 5″ d, round, cream	**675.00**
Pitcher, 7½″ h, cream, applied opalescent handle, polished rim chip	**800.00**
Spooner, 4″ h, raspberry	**800.00**
Sugar Bowl Cover	**125.00**
Sugar Bowl, with orig cover, 5½″ h, cream	**375.00**

Spooner, cinnamon ground, tulip, daisy and thistle motif, 4¼″ h, $650.00.

FINE ARTS

Notes: There is no way a listing of less than one hundred paintings can accurately represent the breadth and depth of the examples sold during the last year. To attempt to make such a list would be ludicrous.

In any calendar year, tens, if not hundreds of thousands of paintings are sold. Prices range from a few dollars to millions. Since each painting is essentially a unique creation, it is difficult to compare prices.

Since an essential purpose of *Warman's Antiques And Collectibles Price Guide* is to assist its users in finding information about a category, this Fine Arts introduction has been written primarily to identify the reference books that you will need to find out more about a painting in your possession.

Artist Dictionaries: Emmanuel Benezit, *Dictionnaire Critique et Documentaire des Peintres, Sculpteurs, Dessinateurs et Graveurs,* 10 volumes, Third Edition, Grund, 1976; Peter Hastings Falk, *Dictionary of Signatures & Monograms of American Artists,* Sound View Press, 1988; Mantle Fielding, *Dictionary of American Painters, Sculptors and Engravers,* Apollo Books, 1983; J. Johnson and A. Greutzner, *Dictionary of British Artists, 1880–1940: An Antique Collector's Club Research Project Listing 41,000 Artists,* Antique Collector's Club, 1976; Les Krantz, *American Artists,* Facts on File, 1985.

Introductory Information: Alan Bamberger, *Buy Art Smart,* Wallace-Homestead Book Company, 1990; ———, *How to Buy Fine Art You Can Afford,* Wallace-Homestead, 1994.

Price Guide References, Basic: *Art at Auction in America,* 1994 Edition, Krexpress, 1994; William T. Currier (comp.), *Currier's Price Guide to American Artists 1645–1945 at Auction,* Sixth Edition, Currier Publications, 1994; ——— (comp.), *Currier's Price Guide to European Artists 1545–1945 at Auction,* Fourth Edition, Currier Publications, 1994; Rosemary and Michael McKittrick, *The Official Price Guide to Fine Art,* Second Edition, House of Collectibles, 1993; Susan Theran, *Fine Art: Identification and Price Guide, Second Edition,* Avon Books, 1992.

Price Guide References, Advanced: R. J. Davenport, *Davenport's Art Reference & Price Guide: 1996–97,* Eighth Edition, Davenport Publishing, 1996; Peter Hastings Falk (ed.), *Art Price Index International '96,* Sound View Press, 1995; Richard Hislop (ed.), *The Annual Art Sales Index,* Weybridge, Surrey, England, Art Sales Index, since 1969; Enrique Mayer, *International Auction Record,* Paris, Editions Enrique Mayer, since 1967; Judith and Martin Miller (comps. & eds.), *Miller's Picture Price Guide,* Millers Publications, 1994; Susan Theran (ed.), *Leonard's Price Index of Art Auctions,* Auction Index, since 1980.

Museum Directories: *American Art Directory,* R. R. Bowker; American Association of Museums, *The Official Museum Directory: United States and Canada,* R. R. Bowker, updated periodically.

Collectors' Club: American Art Collectors, 610 N Delaware Ave, Roswell, NM 88201.

Fine Art, John Folett, *Sea Captain,* oil on canvas, $3,500.00.

FIREARM ACCESSORIES

History: Muzzle-loading weapons of the 18th and early 19th centuries varied in caliber and required the owner to carry a variety of equipment, including a powder horn or flask, patches, flints or percussion caps, bullets, and bullet molds. In addition, military personnel were responsible for bayonets, slings, and miscellaneous cleaning equipment and spare parts.

In the mid-19th century, cartridge weapons replaced their black-powder ancestors. Collectors seek anything associated with early ammunition—from the cartridges themselves to advertising material. Handling old ammunition can be extremely dangerous because of decomposition of compounds. Seek advice from an experienced collector before becoming involved in this area.

References: Ralf Coykendall, Jr., *Coykendall's Complete Guide to Sporting Collectibles,* Wallace-Homestead, 1996; John Delph, *Firearms and Tackle Memorabilia,* Schiffer Publishing, 1991; Jim and Vivian Karsnitz, *Sporting Collectibles,* Schiffer Publishing, 1992.

Periodical: *Military Trader,* PO Box 1050, Dubuque, IA 52004.

Reproduction Alert: There are a large number of reproduction and fake powder horns. Be very cautious!

Notes: Military-related firearm accessories generally are worth more than their civilian counterparts.

Additional Listings: Militaria.

Belt, 36" l, 2" w, thirty nickel-metal chips for holding shotshells, canvas shoulder straps, nickel-plated buckle with Savage Arms logo cast into it, nickel-plated hook **350.00**

Book

    Custom Guns, Richard Simmons, illus, 1949 .... **30.00**

    Western Ammunition Handbook, 1938, 72 pgs **35.00**

    Winchester World Standard Guns & Ammunition, 1934, 64 pgs **35.00**

Bullet Mold, 9", brass, casting six round buttons with

central raised letter "I" for infantry, one 25 mm, one 18 mm, and four 14.5 mm d, American, 18th C ... **750.00**

Canteen, 7" d, 2⅝" d, cheese-box style, dark red paint, one side painted in gold with large primitive eagle, shield breast, top of shield red with cream lettering "No. 37", other side painted in gold letters "Lt. Rufus Cook," pewter nozzle, sq nail construction, strap loops missing **1,750.00**

Cartridge Board, 30¼ × 32¼", US Cartridge Co, plaster casting of early board, displaying line of self-contained ammunition, bullets, and primers, rifle, handgun, and shotshell ammunition, laminated oak frame, refinished c1960, provenance includes display at 1892 Chicago Expo and 1904 St Louis World's Fair **1,800.00**

Cartridge Box

    3⅞ × 2 × 1", Hall & Hubbard, cal. 22, green and black label "100 No.½ 2-100/PISTOL CARTRIDGES," molted cream and black paper, empty, half green side label missing **350.00**

    3⅞ × 2⅛ × 1¼", Phoenix Metallic Cartridge Co, early green and black label, "50 CARTRIDGES/ 32-100 CALIBRE LONG," opened but full, three-quarter raised "P" head stamped cartridges **275.00**

    4 × 2⅛ × 1¼", Union Metallic Cartridge Co, cream and black label "FIFTY .32 CALIBRE/No. 2/PISTOL CARTRIDGES," engraving of Smith & Wesson 1st Model 3rd Issue, checkered covering, orange and black side labels, unopened **250.00**

Catalog, Colt Revolvers & Automatic Pistols, 1933, 40 pgs **48.00**

Display Cabinet, 56" l, 7¼" d, 33½" h, oak, glass front lift door, three drawers across bottom, rests on two Thompson carbines, back lined with red cloth, USMC logo in center, key locks at each end **500.00**

Display Case, 36 × 21½ × 10", cream-colored two-shelf metal case, plastic insert at top advertising Remington Ammunition, two sliding glass doors, applied Winchester decal on one end **250.00**

Holster, Colt Single Action Holster, tooled dec along borders on both sides, brown leather **125.00**

Powder Flask

    7¾" h, copper, pear shape, emb on both sides with group of hounds fighting with bear in woods, script initials below, brass top **100.00**

    8¼" h, brass, body emb "Rifle Horn" within a curved panel surrounded with a toothed design, orig lacquer finish, orig faded green carrying cord **170.00**

    10¼" l, iron, military, turned wooden plug for spout, body made of molded or stamped sheet iron, rolled-over seam, two steel carrying rings on each side, orig black paint, orig carrying cord, early 19th C **85.00**

Powder Horn

    9½" d, engraved, reserves on crosshatched field of ships at sea, Charleston harbor, arms of Spicer of Exeter or Wear of Devon, inscribed "South Carolina made in Charlestown Amerique 1764," minor imperfections **6,325.00**

    9½" l on outside curve, tapering from 2¾" to 1⅛" thick, dated 1684 on one side, initials "MNS" on other, carved flowers, tulip, small blossoms with leaves, cross design on edges in leaf pattern, spout

Powder horn, scrimshaw, man with pipe, dog and deer, eagle, 1858, 8½" l, $575.00.

carved in shape of duck's head with eyes and spout coming out of mouth, fitted copper band at tip, carved wooden plug, nine tiny handmade nails, leather band around duck's bill holding early hand-braided four-strand cord, small priming horn of identical design, black leather flint pouch with early brass button closure, button has over-layered "C's" surmounted by crown, greenish yellow color, dark staining near spout end, some light flaking in design area 900.00

11" l, quail, hunter with village scene, sgd "F. S. Johnson, 1818" 325.00

11½" l

Engraved, soft-wood plug, hand-wrought iron tacks, carved "WM, RDMI, 1777" and several scenes, 4" l fracture 170.00

Horn, turned and carved end plug, screw tip ... 275.00

Powder Keg, 9¼" h, 6¼" d, wood, black painted number 56, 3¼" h black and white "Oriental Powder Mills" label, 2" "Eastern Sporting FFG Gun Powder," other end with 5" "Oriental Powder Mills Boston FF Western Sporting Powder G" purple and gold label, orig wooden screw plug with slight chips 500.00

Shot Flask, 8½" l, leather, emb on both sides with Highland scene showing Scottish hunter alongside fallen stag, two hounds, brass top 75.00

Target Ball, 2¾" d, molded amber glass, overall net pattern, bottom with raised sunburst pattern, middle ½" band emb "Bogardus Glass Ball Ptd April 10, 1877," chips at neck 200.00

FIREARMS

History: The 15th-century Matchlock Harquebus was the forerunner of the modern firearm. The Germans refined the wheelock firing mechanism during the 16th and 17th centuries. English settlers arrived in America with the smoothbore musket; German settlers had rifled arms. Both used the new flintlock firing mechanism.

A major advance was achieved when Whitney introduced interchangeable parts into the manufacturing of rifles. Continued refinements in firearms continued in the 19th century. The percussion ignition system was developed by the 1840s. Minie, a French military officer, produced a viable projectile. By the end of the 19th century cartridge weapons dominated the field.

References: Robert H. Balderson, *The Official Guide to Gunmarks*, Second Edition, House of Collectibles, 1996; ———, *The*

Official Price Guide to Antique and Modern Firearms, Eighth Edition, House of Collectibles, 1996; ———, *The Official Price Guide to Collector Handguns,* Fifth Edition, House of Collectibles, 1996; Robert W. D. Ball, *Mauser Military Rifles of the World,* Krause Publications, 1996; ———, *Remington Firearms,* Krause Publications, n.d.; Ralf Coykendall, Jr., *Coykendall's Complete Guide to Sporting Collectibles,* Wallace-Homestead, 1996; Norman Flayderman, *Flayderman's Guide to Antique American Firearms And Their Values,* Sixth Edition, DBI Books, 1995; *Gun Trader's Guide,* Fifteenth Edition, Stoeger Publishing, 1992; Herbert G. Houze, *Colt Rifles and Muskets from 1847–1870,* Krause Publications, 1996; ———, *History of Winchester Repeating Arms Company,* Krause Publications, 1994; Russell and Steve Quertermous, *Modern Guns Identification & Values,* Eleventh Edition, Collector Books, 1996; Ned Schwing, *Browning Superposed,* Krause Publications, 1996; Ned Schwing and Herbert Houze, *Standard Catalog of Firearms,* Sixth Edition, Krause Publications, 1996; Jim Supica and Richard Nahas, *Standard Catalog of Smith & Wesson,* Krause Publications, 1996; Frederick Wilkinson, *Handguns,* New Burlington Books, 1993; A. B. Zhuk, *The Illustrated Encyclopedia of Handguns,* Greenhill Books, 1995.

Periodicals: *Gun List,* 700 E State St, Iola, WI 54990; *Gun Report,* PO Box 38, Aledo, IL 61231; *Historic Weapons & Relics,* 2650 Palmyra Rd, Palmyra, TN 37142; *Man at Arms,* PO Box 460, Lincoln, RI 02865; *Military Trader,* PO Box 1050, Dubuque, IA 52004; *Sporting Gun,* PO Box 301369, Escondido, CA 92030; *Wildcat Collectors Journal,* 15158 NE 6 Ave, Miami, FL 33162.

Collectors' Clubs: American Society of Military History, Los Angeles Patriotic Hall, 1816 S Figuerora, Los Angeles, CA 90015; Winchester Arms Collectors Assoc, Inc., PO Box 6754, Great Falls, MT 59406.

Museums: Battlefield Military Museum, Gettysburg, PA; National Firearms Museum, Washington, DC; Remington Gun Museum, Ilion, NY; Springfield Armory National Historic Site, Springfield, MA; Winchester Mystery House, Historic Firearms Museum, San Jose, CA.

Notes: Two factors control the pricing of firearms—condition and rarity. Variations in these factors can cause a wide range in the value of antique firearms. For instance, a Colt 1849 pocket-model revolver with a 5-inch barrel can be priced from $100 to $700 depending on whether or not all the component parts are original, whether some are missing, how much of the original finish (bluing) remains on the barrel and frame, how much silver plating remains on the brass trigger guard and back strap, and the condition and finish of the walnut grips.

Be careful to note a weapon's negative qualities. A Colt Peterson belt revolver in fair condition will command a much higher price than the Colt pocket model in very fine condition. Know the production run of a firearm before buying it.

Flintlock Pistols–Single Shot

Brown Bess, musket, third model, 39¼" barrel, bright finish, usual pitting around breech, dark patina, inspector's marks, lock stamped with crown, "G.R," and "Tower," barrel and lock also have crown and arrow marks with initials "S.G.," three short cracks around lock 990.00

English, Officer's,. cal. 64, smoothbore, 14½" l, octagonal barrel with London proofs, beveled lock with sliding half-cock safety, sgd "S. Wallis," lightly engraved steel trigger guard, plain walnut stock with shield-shaped silver wrist escutcheon, barrel rebrowned 500.00

Fowler, cherry full stock, good color, checking at wrist, simple brass hardware, diamond-shaped inlay behind breech, 40" round barrel, age cracks, restoration, top jaw missing 330.00

French, Model 1777, cal. 69, 7½" round barrel mounted on brass frame, walnut stock, frame marked "St. Etienne," French proof marks at barrel breech and on brass frame, additional proofs on stock, dated "Mars/D/1782," belt hook missing, uncleaned patina 925.00

Full stock, 40½" barrel, sgd "J. Mason" (possibly J. C. Mason, Keene, NH), cherry stock, checkered wrist, silver-wire inlay, engraved brass patch box, restoration 1,760.00

Harper's Ferry, model 1816, musket, 42" barrel secured with 3 bands, lock stamped with eagle, US, signature, and 1839, walnut stock, faint inspector's markings, bold eagle-head stamp on barrel and "1840," light gray metal, areas of light pitting, short age crack at lock bolt 1,540.00

Indian Trade, walnut full stock, engraved brass barrel, flint lock marked "Ketland Adams," 40" l 575.00

North, Simeon, Middletown, CT, Model 1816, cal. 54, smooth bore, 9¹/₁₆" round barrel, iron mounted, double-strapped front band with brass blade front sight, marks at breech "P/US/RJ," iron mounted on walnut stock, metal parts cleaned, front band retaining stud missing, main spring broken, cock, frizzen, spring, and pan are unfinished reproductions 300.00

Walker, John, KY, cal. 45, 9½" octagonal barrel, fitted with open sights, lock plate with roller frizzen spring and gooseneck hammer with some light engraved dec, sgd "John Walker/Warranted," full stock, applied trigger strips, orig heavy reddish varnish finish with brass mounts, plain fore-end cap, two faceted ramrod pipes, two engraved escutcheons for the lock plate screws, trigger guard with simple engraved pineapple finial and engraved bow, stock dec with several silver inlays 10,500.00

Waters & Co, A. H., Milbury, MA, cal. 54, smooth bore, 8½" round barrel, brass blade front sight, swivel-type ramrod, iron mounted on walnut stock, proof marks at barrel breech "U.S./JCR/P," iron furniture, all metal surfaces cleaned, medium to heavy pitting, orig flintlock butt cock, ramrod and swivel mechanism replaced 550.00

Whitney, model 1798, US contract, musket, second model, 43" barrel with areas of pitting, lock plate stamped "U. States" and "New Haven" with eagle,

walnut stock with orig finish, carved initials "A.F." and "T.C.," letters "S.C." stamped ahead of butt-plate tang, small expert repair 1,550.00

Percussion Pistols–Single Shot

Note: Conversion of flintlock pistols to percussion was common practice. Most English and U. S. military flintlock pistols listed below can be found in percussion. Values for these percussion-converted pistols are from 40 to 60% of the flintlock values as given.

Dueling, Belgian, cal. 54, rifled, 8¼" octagonal barrel, SP-brass furniture on walnut stock, Belgian proof mark on left barrel flat, engraved breech, tang, hammer, and lock plate, trigger guard with large spur, butt cap incorporates percussion cap box with hinged lid, grip carved with vertical flutes, wooden ramrod, all metal surfaces cleaned to light gray patina, minor pitting, wear to silver plating 225.00

Flintlock, pocket, 4" part round, part octagonal barrel, simple scroll engraving, raised carved leaf around tang, incised line detail around lock and side plate, restoration, 8½" 220.00

Johnson, model 1836, converted to percussion, lock has signature, town, and 1838 date, brightly finished steel, walnut stock chipped beneath lock, 14" l 335.00

Remington, cal. 50, rolling block, 8" round barrel, inspector's stamp on grip, traces of case coloring remaining on frame, wood has dents 935.00

Ruger T-512, MK-1 Bumble Bee Special, cal. 22 LR, custom pistol, modified by Bumble Bee Distributing Co, 5½" bull barrel, partridge front sight, adjustable rear sight, stag grip panels, metallic finish, bumble-bee logo (bumble bee resting on rifle) on chamber area, engraved serial number stained red, same logo medallion inlayed into right grip panel, orig red and white one-pc box, instruction booklet, papers, cardboard shipping sleeve 300.00

Williamson, made by Moore's Pt Firearms Co, cal. 41, rim fire, 2½" round barrel, engraved brass frame, walnut checkered stock, large arrow design on top of barrel 375.00

Percussion Pistol, single shot, French naval, smooth base, lock marked "Mre Rle de Chatellerault," metal ramrod on pivot, belt hook, 6" barrel, 11¾" l, $175.00.

Percussion Pistols–Multi-Shot

American Arms Co, double barrel, cal. .32, rim fire, sq butt, 3″ superimposed barrels, SP-brass frame, two-pc rosewood grips, overall light gray patina **350.00**

Bacon, Thomas K, Norwich, CT, c1852, pepperbox, cal. 31, 6 shot, 4″ ribbed barrel, barrel stamped "BACON & CO., NORWICH, CT" and "CAST STEEL," single action, under-hammer, engraved nipple shield, blued finish, walnut grips **375.00**

Browning, Hi-Power Centennial Semi-Auto, cal. 9 mm, hard chrome-plated pistol, gold-plated trigger, full checkered-medallion walnut grips, velvet-lined wooden case **500.00**

Colt, Dragoon, Second Model, cal. 44, 6 shot, 7½″ part round, part octagonal barrel, barrel stamped "ADDRESS SAML COLT NEW-YORK, COLT'S PATENT" with "U.S." cantered beneath, one-pc walnut grip, sq-back rigger guard and rect cylinder stop slots, Texas Ranger and Indian fight scene roll engraved on cylinders **4,500.00**

Remington

   Navy, 1861, cal. 36, 6 shot, 7⅜″ octagonal barrel, barrel stamped "PATENTED DEC 17, 1861/MANUFACTURED BY REMINGTON'S, ILION, N.Y.," round cylinder, walnut grips **700.00**

   Derringer, cal. 41 rim fire, one-line signature along top barrel flat, brightly finished metal, bone grip, S/N 166, 4⅞″ l **315.00**

Savage, Model 1905, semi-auto, pocket, cal. 32 ACP, 3¾″ barrel, hard-rubber Savage, Indian logo grip panels, semi-exposed hammer and word "Savage" imprinted above left grip, lanyard loop attached to lower-rear frame, small chip to right grip **200.00**

Steyr Model 1916, military, cal. 9 mm, 5″ barrel, checkered wooden grips, lanyard loop built into frame at bottom of grip, feeds from strippers through top, mismatched slide and frame **175.00**

Revolvers

Colt, officer's model, match target, cal. 38 spec, 6″ barrel, partridge ramp front sight, adjustable rear, over-size checkered Colt medallion walnut grips, 97% blue overall, thin at sides, edge wear **175.00**

H & R, Model 999 Sportsman, cal. 22, standard configuration, 6″ barrel, 2-pc medallion wood grips, Arabesque pattern covering 50%, right flat of barrel marked "One of 999," orig velvet lined wooden case, large silver-colored medallion, orig booklets, and papers **325.00**

Reid, James, knuckle-duster, 22 cal., RF, 7 shot, brass frame, SP, standard scroll engraving on side panels, marked "My Friend Patd Dec 26, 1865," 50% plating on frame and cylinder **550.00**

Remington

   Percussion, Army, new model, cal. 44, crisp signature on top flat of barrel, S/N 124304 .... **990.00**

   Single Action, model 1875, cal. 44, reblued metal surface, small putty repair in grip **880.00**

Remington-Beals, cal. 36, 7½″ octagonal barrel, grip has

carved "W" on one side, reputedly owned by Capt John Wright, 5th Regt, PA Vols, leather holster, S/N168, accompanied by copy of service record, lever latch missing **700.00**

Ruger Security Six, stainless steel, cal. 357 Mag, 6″ ribbed barrel, adjustable sights, Ruger logo checkered wood grips, leather holster, extra Pachmayr rubber grips, minor scuffing to finish **200.00**

Smith and Wesson

   Hand ejector, fourth change, cal. 32, 6″ barrel, fixed sights, S & W medallion diamond-checkered walnut grips, 95% deep blue **225.00**

   K-22 Masterpiece, cal. 22, early five-screw, 6″ barrel, partridge front, adjustable rear sights, S & W medallion diamond-checkered walnut grips, 96% deep bright blue, wear only at muzzle **325.00**

   Model 17-6 Target, cal. 22 LR, 4″ full lug barrel, partridge front sight, adjustable rear sight, smooth combat trigger and finger groove Goncalvo Alves S & W logo grips, orig one-pc blue cardboard box, cleaning kit, Gould & Goodrich right-hand belt holster **250.00**

Webley Mark-V, British military, cal. 455, 4¹⁄₁₆″ barrel, bird's-head pressed horn grips, fixed sights, dated 1914, covered all over with British proofs, broad arrows, double broad arrows **325.00**

Weston & Harrington No. 2, cal. 22 short, 7-shot fluted cylinder 2¾″ octagonal barrel, iron frame, spur trigger, bird's-head butt, nickel plated with rosewood grips, barrel marked "Wesson & Harrington, Worcester, Mass, Pat. Feb 7, June 19 '71," light flaking to nickel plating, dark bore **125.00**

Flintlock Long Arms

Kentucky, cal. 52, 45″ part round barrel, unmarked, smoothbore, thick walls at muzzle probably rifled, full stock with three brass ramrod pipes, brass trigger guard, fine raised side plate with beveled and scalloped edges, wide brass butt plate with facing at top, brass patch box, maple stock with simple carved area at wrist, simple raised carved scroll at barrel tang, late 18th C, flintlock period but not orig to piece, other minor restorations **1,850.00**

New England Flower, cal. 75, 54½″ round barrel, shallow raised rib running to the front sight and lightly engraved dec at breech and tang, lightly engraved lock plate sgd "T Earl," full cherry stock with brass mounts, cloud-shaped side plate, ornate butt plate, four ramrod pipes, orig flint, broken at wrist, poor repair **4,000.00**

U. S. Model 1808, Thomas French, Canton, MA, Contract Musket, Harper's Ferry pattern, tail of lock stamped "Canton/1810," below the pan with eagle and "US" over "French" barrel stamped "US/V" with sunken eagle and CT proof **1,500.00**

U. S. Model 1819, Hall, cal. 52, single shot, 32⅝″ round barrel, three barrel bands, breech loading, second production type, Harper's Ferry Armory, John Hall's patents, breech block deeply stamped "J. H. Hall/H. Ferry/1836" **1,250.00**

Percussion Long Arms

Note: Conversion of flintlock long arms to percussion was common practice. Most English, French, and U.S. military flintlock model long arms listed in the previous section can be found in percussion. Values for these percussion-converted long arms are from 40 to 60% of the flintlock values previously noted.

Half stock, fine curly maple stock, twelve German silver inlays, brass hardware, German silver cap box, 36″ octagon barrel stamped "Postley, Nelson & Co," top flat of barrel engraved "C.K.," carefully cleaned   ...   **750.00**

Henry, cal. 44, 24″ barrel with worn rebluing, barrel stamped "C.G.C." at breech end, brass frame marked "H.H.," walnut stock, faint inspector's mark, S/N3237, butt plate marked 3347   ....**17,050.00**

Jaeger, German, flintlock converted to percussion, checkered walnut stick, sliding wooden patch box, brass hardware with deep engraving, one ramrod pipe replaced, 26″ swamped barrel fitted with ornate rear sight, hammer spur broken off **880.00**

Kentucky, curly maple full stock attributed to Samuel Baum, PA, percussion lock marked "Rashmore & Son," incised carving with brass patch box, 48 silver inlays including fish, hearts, eagle, crescent moons, 54″ l **2,310.00**

Ohio, long, sgd "J. Legg," curly maple stock, old worn finish, 37½″ barrel, brass hardware, cast detail of dog and bird on lock, old repair at wrist and toe **635.00**

Pennsylvania, maple full stock, mellow color, two-pc brass patch box, 37½″ octagon barrel with browned finish, 3 pcs of wire inlay and end cap missing **385.00**

Springfield 1873
   Saddle ring carbine, has 1879 alterations, receiver reblued, 22″ barrel, adjustable rear sight, S/N145788   ....   **880.00**
   Trapdoor, walnut stock, 32½″ round barrel, clear markings on lock, tang, and barrel, S/N 499231   **330.00**

Whitney, 1841 U.S., cal. 54, 33″ barrel, boldly stamped signature on lock with "U.S., N. Haven" and "1851," stock has inspector's stamps **1,700.00**

Winchester, standard model, cal. 32–40, 30″ octagonal barrel, case colors remaining on receiver, minor scratches on stock, spots of surface rust, S/N54378   .**1,320.00**

Rifles

Colt, Lightning, pump action, cal. 22, 24″ octagonal barrel, half magazine, straight stock, hard-rubber butt plate, open sights, dark pitted bore, replaced forearm   **225.00**

Sharps-Borchardt, sporterized military, cal. 45–70, 29½″ tapered round barrel marked "Old Reliable," rear sight removed, wood sporterized with extremely coarse checkering, gray-brown patina overall, crack in stock, extra hole in top tang **575.00**

Smith-Corona, 1903AE National Match, cal. 30–06, barrel marked "SC/6-43," standard front sight, Redfield Olympic micrometer match sight attached to left side of receiver, orig rear sight removed, straight grip stock, solid checkered steel butt plate, bolt and handle brightly polished, orig shipping document **800.00**

U.S. Model 1844, Cadet, type 1, cal. ⁴⁵/₇₀, 29½″ round

barrel, Buffington rear sight, two-pc carbine style trigger guard, stocking swivels at top barrel band, breech block marked "U. S. Model/1774," breech markings as expected, letter "A" stamped perpendicular to breech, orig blue on receiver and trigger **675.00**

U.S. Springfield
   1903, military, bolt action, cal. 30–06, barrel dated "1-23," ³/₃₂″ wide partridge front sight, type C stock, Springfield target butt plate, 99% orig finish on wood, old refinish on metal **700.00**
   1922 M-1, bolt action, training, cal. 22 LR, 24″ tapered round barrel dated "8-26," grasping groove type B sporter stock, checkered steel butt plate, standard front sight, Lyman rear peep, 5-round magazine, wood and metal retain old refinish, drilled and tapped for target scope, two extra holes plugged in barrel **350.00**

Whitney Howard, single shot, patent action, cal. 44 RF, 24″ round barrel, integral receiver, open sights, straight stock, hard-rubber butt plate, lever action opens to sliding breech bolt on bottom of receiver to access chamber for loading and extraction, mottled blue-brown patina on metal parts, replacement stock, orig sight, good bore with sharp strong rifling **275.00**

Winchester
   Model 1886, standard-grade lever action, cal. 45–70, 26″ octagonal barrel, full magazine, straight grip stock, crescent butt, fine gray patina, some light pitting on barrel, replaced rear sight, front sight dovetail hammered and peened, two or three dings, light handling marks, bore dark and pitted with sharp rifling **850.00**
   Model 1892, lever action, cal. 32, WCF, 24″ octagonal barrel, full magazine, plain wood with straight stock, crescent steel butt plate, fine pitting on receiver, lever, hammer, and trigger, old refinish **275.00**
   Model 1894, special order, cal. 38–55, 26″ round barrel, button magazine, open sights and straight stock, crescent steel butt plate, orig 94% blue on barrel thinning over chamber and sides at muzzle, 85% dark case color on hammer, bright bore, strong rifling, minor frosting **470.00**

Shotguns

Browning, Model 12 Grade-1, pump auction, cal. 20-gauge, 26″ vent-rib modified choke barrel, deluxe checkered forearm, pistol-grip stock, Browning composition butt plate, orig shipping box **300.00**

Holland and Holland, ball and cup, 20-gauge fielding piece, side-by-side double 26″ barrels **1,150.00**

Le Fevre, DM, hammerless, 12-gauge, side-by-side 25″ barrels, patented June 20, 1880   ....**1,250.00**

Purdy, J and Son, 12-gauge, double side-by-side 29½″ barrels, engraved chamber **1,300.00**

Remington, Model 1100, semi-auto, cal. 12-guage, two barrels, one 30″ plain, full, other 28″ plain, 95% blue overall, light pitting on both barrels and receiver   ...   **275.00**

Scott, WC & Son, hammerless, 12-gauge, side-by-side 28″ barrels, engraved chambers, patented "crystal in-

dicator,'' barrels by Joseph Jakob, 1156 Passyunk Ave, Philadelphia **500.00**
Westley Richards, double barrel, engraved detail with scrollwork and dog on receiver and trigger guard, 32" damascus barrels marked ''W.R., J.P.C.'' and ''AB,'' good bore, checkered walnut stock **330.00**
Winchester
    M1911, semi-auto, cal. 12-gauge, 26" full-choke barrel, knurled cocking band, integral front sight, semi-beavertail grasping groove checkered forearm, checkered straight grip laminated stock 14¼" over a leather-faced red recoil pad, metal parts finished to high luster deep bright blue, receiver engraved with full coverage game scenes on both sides, left side with setter and pointer in field scene with two bobwhite quail, vignette surrounded by arabesque, leaves and vines, florals, Greek key, and other patterns, right side identically engraved, vignette with marsh scene, one flying and three standing mallards, sides of rounded receiver engraved with various patterns, bottom of trigger guard and front of loading port also lightly engraved, factory laminated stock, ¾" center section of slightly different-colored walnut, outside plys highly streaked and burled walnut, ¾" black diamonds inlaid on wrist on both sides, perfect bore, 96% of orig strong finish **4,500.00**
    Model 1300, Stainless Marine, pump, cal. 12-gauge, 19" stainless barrel and magazine tube, parkerized receiver, black zytel stock and pistol grip forearm **275.00**

FIREHOUSE COLLECTIBLES

History: The volunteer fire company has played a vital role in the protection and social growth of many towns and rural areas. Paid professional firemen usually are found only in large metropolitan areas. Each fire company prided itself on equipment and uniforms. Conventions and parades gave the fire companies a chance to show off their equipment. These events produced a wealth of firehouse-related memorabilia.

References: Andrew G. Gurka, *Hot Stuff! Firefighting Collectibles,* L-W Book Sales, 1994; James Piatti, *Firehouse Memorabilia: Identification and Price Guide,* Avon Books, 1994; Donald F. Wood and Wayne Sorensen, *Big City Fire Trucks, 1900–1950,* Krause Publications, 1996.

Periodical: *Fire Apparatus Journal,* PO Box 141295, Staten Island, NY 10314.

Collectors' Clubs: Antique Fire Apparatus Club of America, 5420 S Kedvale Ave, Chicago, IL 60632; Fire Collectors Club, PO Box 992, Milwaukee, WI 53201; Fire Mark Circle of the Americas, 2859 Marlin Dr, Chamblee, GA 30341; Great Lakes International Antique Fire Apparatus Assoc, 4457 285th St, Toledo, OH 43611; International Fire Buff Associates, Inc, 7509 Chesapeake Ave, Baltimore, MD 21219; International Fire Photographers Assoc, PO Box 8337, Rolling Meadows, IL 60008; Society for the Preservation & Appreciation of Motor Fire Apparatus in America, PO Box 2005, Syracuse, NY 13320.

Museums: American Museum of Fire Fighting, Corton Falls, NY; Fire Museum of Maryland, Lutherville, MD; Hall of Flame, Scotts-dale, AZ; Insurance Company of North America (INA) Museum, Philadelphia, PA; New England Fire & History Museum, Brewster, MA; New York City Fire Museum, New York, NY; Oklahoma State Fireman's Association Museum, Oklahoma City, OK; San Francisco Fire Dept Memorial Museum, San Francisco, CA.

Additional Listings: See *Warman's Americana & Collectibles* for more examples.

Alarm Box
    Gamewell Excelsior, cast iron, code-wheel and number-plate telegraph door, orig weathered paint .. **300.00**
    Hercucite, quick-acting door with glass bull's-eye, code wheel and number plate, orig paint **125.00**
    Utica Fire Alarm and Telegraph, telegraph door **500.00**
Alarm Gong
    Gamewell, Excelsior, oak case, orig finish, 6" **650.00**
    Star Electric, Binghamton, NY, fancy case with star on top, 12" **1,800.00**
    US Fire and Police Telegraph, maple ''Moses Crane'' case, fig-leaf finial, 8" **1,250.00**
Bell, apparatus style
    American La France, 700 series–type base, eagle finial, orig, 12" **550.00**
    Seagrave, bracket and clapper, orig, 12" **475.00**
Extinguisher, foam type, 2½ gal
    Ahrens Fox **215.00**
    Mack, nickel and glass **175.00**

Fire extinguisher, Auto Fyr Stop Co, Phila, PA, glass and metal, combined automatic/manual, model C-37 unit, 11" h, $35.00.

Fire Bucket, leather
    11½" h, No. 2, Goddard, 1817, leather strap off at one end **325.00**
    13" l, worn old green pint, yellow label ''S. D. Green,'' split seam **110.00**
Helmet, leather
    Charring to back brim and top, eagle's head, no badge **50.00**
    Painted badge, seams opening on back **50.00**
    Worn black paint, gilded eagle, shield missing, battered, 13" l **140.00**
Lantern
    Dewey, Mill, tin, lift cage, orig paint **60.00**
    Dietz Fire King **295.00**
    Eclipse, green-over-clear globe, marked ''American La France Fire Engine Co'' **1,000.00**

Nozzle
   8¾" l, ALFCO **60.00**
   10" l, Rookwood Water Fog, Rookwood Sprinkler Co,
      Worcester, MA, patented "Rookwood Waterfog
      2/2 SG-40" **50.00**
Print, 8 × 12¾", "The Great Fire at Boston, Nov 9th &
   10th, 1872," Currier and Ives, lithograph, typographical inscription below image, hand colored, period
   carved frame **150.00**

Print, Built by the Amoskeag Manufacturing Co, chromolitho, Charles H.
Crosby & Co, Boston, 1818–96, 24 × 31⅞", matted, minor soiling and
fox marks, $4,675.00. Photography courtesy of Skinner, Inc.

Ribbon, convention, brass scroll, 1922, San Francisco
   Fire Chiefs, hanging blue glove fire lantern **195.00**
Siren, hand crank, SS, orig mounting bracket **450.00**
Stereo Card, The Summer St Fire, Boston, Mass, Nov 9
   & 10, 1872, shows rubble of burned out buildings,
   people **25.00**
Toy, 28½" l, cast iron, hook and ladder wagon, two
   drawers, one white and two black horses, minor replacements **500.00**
Trumpet, presentation, Osborne Hose, Clinton, NY,
   1897, nickel and brass, engraved, flowers and
   steamer broadside, crossed hooks and ladders, hel-
   met-type rings for cord attachment **1,450.00**

FIREPLACE EQUIPMENT

History: In the colonial home, the fireplace was the gathering
point for heat, meals, and social interaction. It maintained its
dominant position until the introduction of central heating in the
mid-19th century.

   Because of the continued popularity of the fireplace, accessories still are manufactured, usually in an early-American motif.

References: Rupert Gentle and Rachael Feild, *Domestic Metal-
work 1640–1820,* Revised, Antique Collectors' Club, 1994; Dana
G. Morykan and Harry L. Rinker, *Warman's Country Antiques &
Collectibles,* Third Edition, Wallace-Homestead, 1996; George C.
Neumann, *Early American Antique Country Furnishings,* L-W
Book Sales, 1984, 1993 reprint.

Reproduction Alert: Modern blacksmiths are reproducing many
old iron implements.

Additional Listings: Brass and Iron.

Andirons, pr
   12¼" h, brass, baluster shaft, scroll legs, ball feet,
      c1810 .... **225.00**
   13½" h, brass, baluster shaft, scroll legs, ball feet,
      c1815 .... **175.00**
   14" h, brass, belted ball and finial, sgd " B Edmands,"
      Charleston, SC, behind log stops, c1800 ....**1,100.00**
   18½" h, brass, urn top, spurred legs, ball feet, Federal,
      early 19th C **325.00**
   19½" h, brass, lemon top, New England, c1800, im-
      perfections **865.00**
   25" h, brass, lemon top, plinth engraved with foliage
      design, American, c1800 .... **750.00**
   36" h, wrought iron, flat disc top, tapering standard
      arch, Gothic style **50.00**

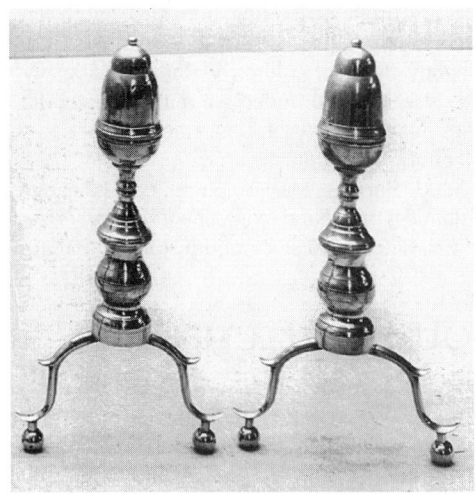

Andirons, brass, acorn top, 17" h, $250.00.

Bellows
   Papier-Mâché, spade form, enameled spray of flow-
      ers, black ground, reverse with gilt C-scrolls, dia-
      pering dec on handles, studded leather sides, Vic-
      torian, mid 19th C **225.00**
   Wood and brass, fruit and foliage dec, painted,
      16½" l **115.00**
Chenets, pr
   Empire, ormolu and patinated bronze, recumbent
      sphinx resting on ormolu plinth, applied central
      wreath and scabbard, centered by helmet flanked
      by recessed ends with lyres, lion's-paw feet **5,175.00**
   Louis XVI Style, gilt bronze, pierced bellflower guil-
      loche frieze surmounted by bellflower and acan-
      thus-cast rinceau, molded shell cast base **4,413.00**
   Victorian, bronze and gilt, urns on scroll-form bases,
      putti with outstretched arms, 22" h **2,300.00**
Chimney Cover, 12" h, oval, marked "Compliments of
   C. D. Denny Co., Kaufmann & Strauss Co., N. Y.
   1058", metal cover with picture of two little girls
   having tea party in lush spring garden, large bunny

seated at table, eight smaller bunnies on ground, doll lying under table, gold border 210.00

Clock Jack, 19" h, brass, cast-iron rotating wheel for roasting small game, replaced key, working 715.00

Coal Box, 12" w, 12" d, 13" h, copper, emb laurel wreath dec 150.00

Coal Grate, 32" w, 17" d, 38½" h, bell metal, rect basket, cast-iron back plate, dancing maidens ornament, pierced front skirt, surmounted by urns, straight tapered legs, spade feet, George III, late 18th C 315.00

Coffee Roaster, 33½" l, wrought and sheet iron, sliding lid, wooden handle, splits in end of pan 165.00

Cooking Pot, 10¼" d, 12" handle, cast brass, three feet, cast design in handle 200.00

Crane, 41" h, 39" w, wrought iron, attached kettle tilter, scrolled detail, pitted and rust damage 615.00

Fender, 44" l, brass, pierced body, paw feet, late Empire 500.00

Fire Back, 21¾" w, 27" h, cast iron, curved crest with cherubs and garlands, heat damage, crack in base . 125.00

Fire Board, 22¾" × 36¼", painted, geometric blue, yellow, green, sienna, black, and white pattern, American, 19th C 2,000.00

Fire Screen, 25" w, 42" h, carved oak scroll and floral frame, mirrored panel, English, 19th C 345.00

Log Carrier, 23" l plus tongue, wooden sled-type construction, worn red stain, sgd "...Weiss 18-8" 275.00

Peel, 16 × 32", sheet steel 140.00

Pole Screen, 54" h, hardwood, turned block and tapered post mortised frame, tripod base, snake feet, old worn dark finish, old faded needlework, wear and age cracks 660.00

Steelyard, 37" l, brass inlay, brass weight 330.00

Suite, Renaissance style, gilt bronze andirons, lion's heads, lion's-paw feet, matching stand and tools ...3,150.00

Surround, white marble, carved

Baroque Style, rect mantel over stepped leaf-carved arched opening, flanked on either side by male and female leaf-carved terminals, central putti supporting cartouche 6,325.00

Rococo Style, serpentine mantel, central carved cartouche issuing carved foliage and C-scrolls continuing to side supports, slip with urn, floral and rope carving 3,163.00

Trammel, wrought iron, sawtooth, simple tooling, "B.S. 1781," adjusts from 36" 165.00

Utensil Set, brass and wrought iron, each pc marked "F.B.S. Canton, O Pat. Jan 26, '86," (Frederick B. Smith) polished, 19" l, price for 4-pc set 385.00

Warming Oven, 28" h, tin, cast-iron paw feet, decorative handles, worn black paint with floral design, some battering and small holes, damage to door hinge ... 135.00

FISCHER CHINA

FISCHER J. BUDAPEST.

History: In 1893 Moritz Fischer founded his factory in Herend, Hungary, a center of porcelain production since the 1790s.

Confusion exists about Fischer china because of its resemblance to Meissen, Sevres, and Oriental export wares. It often was bought and sold as the product of these firms.

Fischer's Herend is hard-paste ware with luminosity and exquisite decoration. Pieces are designated by pattern names, the best known being Chantilly Fruit, Rothschild Bird, Chinese Bouquet, Victoria Butterfly, and Parsley.

Fischer also made figural birds and animal groups, Magyar figures (individually and in groups), and Herend eagles poised for flight.

Marks: Forged marks of other potteries are found on Herend pieces. The initials "MF," often joined together, is the mark of Moritz Fischer's pottery.

Ewer, 15¾" h, multicolored florals with gold trim, long spout and handle 375.00

Figure

5¼" h, rooster, multicolored, Herend, dated 1943 .. 50.00

14" h, Madonna and Child, hp, Herend mark 350.00

Plaque, 11½" h, 8¼" l, seated lady, wearing 18th-C costume, low-cut bodice, rose in one hand, table with open book and glove by side, two figures in distance in formal garden setting, script title "Mondespan C Netscher, Dresden Museum," imp "CF" for Christian Fischer, c1860–80, framed 8,500.00

Plate, 9½" d, reticulated, gold, rose, and turquoise medallions, marked "Budapest, Hungary" price for pr 350.00

Potpourri jar, reticulated multicolored floral and vine design, hexagonal, rose finial, 7" h, $295.00.

Puzzle Jug, 13" h, brown transfer of three gentlemen, polychrome and gilt accents, marked "Fischer, Budapest" 175.00

Vase, 8" h, bulbous body, pinched and crimped rim, four feet, dark blue glaze, granular cream and gilt overlay 75.00

FITZHUGH

History: Fitzhugh, one of the most-recognized Chinese Export porcelain patterns, was named for the Fitzhugh family for whom the first dinner service was made. The peak years of production were 1780 to 1850.

Fitzhugh features an oval center medallion or monogram surrounded by four groups of flowers or emblems. The border is similar to that on Nanking china. Occasional border variations are found. Butterfly and honeycomb are among the rarest.

Notes: Color is a key factor in pricing. Blue is the most common color; rarer colors are ranked in the following ascending order: orange, green, sepia, mulberry, yellow, black, and gold. Combinations of colors are scarce.

Cider Jug, cov, 11½" h, underglaze blue, 19th C **2,500.00**
Hot-Water Dish, 10⅝" d, underglaze blue, center pinecone and beast medallion, four clusters of flowers and precious objects in trellis-diaper border, spearhead and dumbbell border, blue spouts, c1840 .... **450.00**
Plate, 9" d, green, 19th C, chips, gilt wear, price for nine-pc set **1,150.00**
Platter, 14¼" l, underglaze blue pattern, professional rim repair **465.00**
Punch Bowl, 11" d, white underglaze blue, Fitzhugh border, famille rose floral sprays and shield-shaped cartouche, monogram, scalloped rim, restoration .. **500.00**
Salt, 4" l, oval, underglaze blue, center pinecone and beast medallion, four clusters of flowers and precious objects, spearhead and dumbbell border, ruffled rim, Mared pattern border, feathered edge, fluted sides, c1820, price for pr **1,450.00**
Tureen, 14" l, underglaze blue dec, braided handles, restored pineapple knop finial **1,400.00**

FLASKS

History: A flask, which usually has a narrow neck, is a container for liquids. Early American glass companies frequently formed them in molds which left a relief design on the front and/or back. Historical flasks with a portrait, building, scene, or name are the most desirable.

A chestnut is hand-blown, small, and has a flattened bulbous body. The pitkin has a blown globular body with a spiral rib overlay on vertical ribs. Teardrop flasks are generally fiddle-shaped and have a scroll or geometric design.

References: Gary Baker et al., *Wheeling Glass 1829–1939,* Oglebay Institute, 1994, distributed by Antique Publications; Ralph and Terry Kovel, *Kovels' Bottles Price* List, Tenth Edition, Crown Publishers, 1996; George L. and Helen McKearin, *American Glass,* Crown Publishers, 1941 and 1948; John Odell, *Digger Odell's Official Antique Bottle and Glass Collector Magazine Price Guide Series,* Vol. 3, published by author (1910 Shawhan Rd, Morrow, OH 45152), 1995; Michael Polak, *Bottles,* Avon Books, 1994; Kenneth Wilson, *American Glass 1760–1930,* 2 vols., Hudson Hills Press and The Toledo Museum of Art, 1994.

Periodical: *Antique Bottle & Glass Collector,* PO Box 187, East Greenville, PA 18041.

Collectors' Clubs: Federation of Historical Bottle Clubs, 88 Sweetbriar Branch, Longwood, FL 32750; The National Early American Glass Club, PO Box 8489, Silver Spring, MD 20907.

Notes: Dimensions can differ for the same flask because of variations in the molding process. Color is important in determining value—aqua and amber are the most common colors; scarcer colors demand more money. Bottles with "sickness," an opalescent scaling which eliminates clarity, are worth much less.

Chestnut, Zanesville, OH
4½" h, golden amber, 24 vertical ribs **275.00**
4⅞" h, golden amber, 24 vertical ribs, stone on one side, minor residue **220.00**
5⅛" h, golden amber, 24 vertical ribs, some light scratches, minor roughness to lip **300.00**
5½" h, golden amber, 10 diamond, good impression, some wear **935.00**
Historical
Cornucopia-Urn, Coventry Glass Works, Coventry, CT, 1820s, pt, teal green, sheared lip, pontil scar, McKearin GIII-4 .... **250.00**
Double Eagle, pt, sheared lip, pontil scar
Coventry Glass Works, Coventry, CT, c1820, olive-amber, McKearin GII-70 .... **275.00**
Kentucky Glassworks, Louisville, KY, 1850–55, sapphire blue, McKearin GII-24 ....**2,500.00**
For Pike's Peak Prospector-Eagle, pt, yellowish green, crudely applied mouth with ring, smooth base, dug, ext. roughness and stain, int. appears oil treated, McKearin GXI-35 .... **450.00**
Horse and Cart, attributed to Mt Pleasant Glass Works, Saratoga, NY, 1860–70, pt, olive green, applied round collared mouth, smooth base, manufacturer's tooling marks on neck just below collar, McKearin GV-7 .... **725.00**
Masonic-Eagle, pint
Marlboro Street Glassworks, Keene, NH, c1820, golden amber, sheared lip, pontil scar, McKearin GIV-19 .... **195.00**
New England, c1820, medium green-aqua, heavy collared lip, pontil scar, McKearin GII-7 ..... **500.00**
Monument-Sloop, Baltimore Glassworks, Baltimore, MD, c1850, half pt, medium plum amethyst, sheared mouth, pontil scar, McKearin GVI-2 .... **325.00**
Success to the Railroad, pt, golden amber, sheared lip, pontil scar, inner haze, bubbly, McKearin GII-5 .... **250.00**
Washington-Taylor, Dyottsville Glassworks, Philadelphia, PA, 1855, qt, medium blue-green, double collared lip, iron pontil, McKearin GI-51 .... **350.00**
Pictorial
Hunter-Fisherman, Whitney Glass Works, Glassboro, NJ, c1850, calabash, qt, apricot, applied sloping collared mouth, iron-pontil mark, McKearin GXIII-4 .... **475.00**

Sheaf of Grain, Baltimore Glassworks, Baltimore, MD, c1850, qt, aqua, flat collar, iron pontil, McKearin GXIII-48 .... **275.00**
Summer Tree-Winter Tree, half pt, aqua, round collar, bevel smooth base, McKearin GX-16 .... **125.00**
760–80, pint, aquamarine, applied collared mouth, smooth base, faint stain ring on int. shoulder area, McKearin GXIV-5 .... **375.00**
Will You Take/A Drink?/Will a/(duck)/ Swim?, plain reverse, c1875, half pt, aquamarine, tooled mouth, smooth base, heavy int. stain at shoulder area, McKearin GXIII-29a **475.00**
Scroll, American, c1850, qt, iron pontil mark
Brilliant blue green, double collared mouth, small crack stemming from potstone, McKearin GIX-3 **185.00**
Sapphire blue, applied mouth with ring, 1" crack on medial rib,½" deep chip on rear near base, Mc-Kearin GIX-2 .... **375.00**
Sunburst, 5¾" h, P & W, Keen, olive green, half pt, McKearin GVII1-10 .... **215.00**

FLOW BLUE

History: Flow blue, or flown blue, is the name applied to cobalt and white china whose color, when fired in a kiln, produced a flowing or blurred effect. The blue varies from dark royal cobalt to a navy or steel blue. The flow varies from very slight to a heavy blur through which the pattern cannot be easily recognized. The blue color does not permeate through the body of the china. The amount of flow on the back of a piece is determined by the position of the piece in the sagger during firing.

Credit is generally given to Josiah Wedgwood as the first to produce flow blue around 1830. He worked in the Staffordshire area of England. Many other potters followed, including Alcock, Davenport, Grindley, Johnson Brothers, Meakin, and New Wharf. The early flow blue (1830s to 1870s) was usually ironstone. The later patterns (1880s to 1900s) and modern patterns (after 1910) usually were made of the more delicate semi-porcelain. Approximately 90 percent of the flow blue was made in England, the rest was made in Germany, Holland, France, Belgium, Wales and Scotland. A few patterns were also made in the United States by Mercer, Warwick, and Wheeling Pottery companies.

References: Susan and Al Bagdade, *Warman's English & Continental Pottery & Porcelain,* Second Edition, Wallace-Homestead, 1991; Mary F. Gaston, *The Collector's Encyclopedia of Flow Blue China,* Collector Books, 1983, 1993 value update; ———, *The Collector's Encyclopedia of Flow Blue China,* Second Series, Collector Books, 1994; Ellen R. Hill, *Mulberry Ironstone: Flow Blue's Best Kept Little Secret,* published by author, 1993; Norma Jean Hoener, *Flow Blue China, Additional Patterns and New Information,* Flow Blue International Collectors' Club, Inc. (11560 W. 95th #297, Overland Park, KS 66214), 1996; Dana G. Morykan and Harry L. Rinker, *Warman's Country Antiques & Collectibles,* Third Edition, Wallace-Homestead, 1996; Jeffrey Snyder, *Historic Flow Blue,* Schiffer Publishing, 1994; Petra Williams, *Flow Blue China: An Aid to Identification,* Revised Edition, Fountain House East, 1981; ———, *Flow Blue China II, Revised Edition,* Fountain House East, 1981; ———, *Flow Blue China and Mulberry Ware: Similarity and Value Guide,* Revised Edition, Fountain House East, 1993.

Collectors' Club: Flow Blue International Collectors' Club, 11560 W 95th #297, Overland Park, KS 66214.

Museum: The Margaret Woodbury Strong Museum, Rochester, New York.

REPRODUCTION ALERT

Flow blue reproductions have been made since the mid-1950s. Many of these patterns look sloppy and blotched, with light blue allover background color. Some are plainly marked "Flo Blue" or "Romantic Flow Blue."

Advisor: Ellen G. King.

Early Patterns: c1825–1850

Berry Bowl
Amoy, Davenport, 5⅛" **150.00**
Cashmere, Morley, 5" **200.00**
Chinese, Dimmock, 5⅛" **150.00**
Oregon, Mayer, 5" **135.00**
Butter Dish, Sabraon, unknown maker, two pc **425.00**
Creamer
Canton, Maddock, 5" **495.00**
Chapoo, Wedgwood, 5¼" **850.00**
Hong Kong, Meigh, 5¼" **450.00**
Tonquin, Heath, 5" **550.00**
Wagon Wheel, brushstroke, 4⅞" **165.00**
Cup Plate
Lintin, Godwin, 4" **125.00**
Scinde, Alcock, 4" **185.00**
Cup and Saucer
Canton, Maddock, handleless cup **150.00**
Chusan, Clementson, coffee cup, paneled **475.00**
Kyber, Meir, handleless cup, paneled **225.00**
Panang, Ridgway, handleless cup **245.00**
Scinde, Alcock, handleless cup **195.00**
Footbath
Chinese, Dimmock, scalloped rim **4,200.00**
Marble, Copeland & Garrett **3,500.00**
Gravy
Arabesque, Mayer, pedestal base, no tray **450.00**
Chapoo, Wedgwood, no tray **375.00**
Scinde, Alcock, no tray **475.00**
Honey Dish, Scinde, Alcock, 5⅛" **95.00**
Mug
Seaweed & Fern, unknown maker, 4" **295.00**
Tulip & Leaf, brushstroke, 4", professional restoration **125.00**
Plate
Bamboo, Dimmock, 10½", polychrome with pink, green, and rust **225.00**
Beauties of China, M V & Co, 10½" **195.00**
Chapoo, Wedgwood, 6¼" **145.00**
Chusan, Morley, 10¼" **235.00**
Manilla, Podmore Walker, 9¾" **185.00**
Pelew, Challinor, 10" **195.00**
Scinde, Alcock, 9½", slight crazing **160.00**

Late pattern, platter, Moyune, 12 × 16″, $450.00.

Platter
Chen-Si, Meir, 10½ × 8″	425.00
Manilla, Podmore Walker, 15¾ × 12″	850.00
Scinde, Alcock, 13½ × 10¼″	450.00
Shapoo, Boote, 12½ × 9½″	395.00

Razor Box, Floral, unknown maker, polychrome with red and yellow 190.00

Relish
Amoy, Davenport, 8″	165.00
Indian, Pratt, 8¾″, mitten shape	275.00
Manilla, Podmore Walker, shell shape	395.00

Sauce Tureen
Amoy, Davenport, two-pc tureen, ladle, and tray, price for set	2,200.00
Hong Kong, Davenport, no ladle	475.00
Pekin, Dimmock, no ladle	550.00

Soap Dish, Ning Po, Hall, two pc 450.00

Soup Plate, flanged
Bamboo, Dimmock, 10⅜″, polychrome with pink, green, and rust	225.00
Hizan, unknown maker, 10½″	145.00
Sobraon, Ashworth, 10½″	150.00

Sugar
Canton, Maddock, 8″	550.00
Carlton, Alcock, 5½″	425.00
Cashmere, Morley, professional restoration to finial	775.00
Indian, Pratt, professional restoration to lid	650.00

Late pattern, soup plate, Touraine, Alcock, 10⅛″, flanged, $135.00.

Syrup Pitcher, Vine Border, unknown maker, brushstroke 165.00

Teapot
Arabesque, Mayer	1,450.00
Chapoo, Wedgwood	1,995.00
Chusan, Clementson, 9½″, gothic shape	995.00
Oregon, Mayer, 8½″, single-line shape	1,150.00
Scinde, Alcock, professional restoration	600.00

Vegetable Bowl, open
Lange Lijzen, Spode, 10″	375.00
Scinde, Walker, 12⅛″	550.00

Vegetable Tureen, cov
Gothic, Furnival, 10″	750.00
Hong Kong, Meigh, 10″	375.00
Manilla, Podmore Walker, 12½ × 9½″	1,200.00
Pelew, Challinor, 10½″	450.00

Wash Pitcher and Bowl, Scinde, Alcock, paneled, price for 2 pc 4,500.00

Waste Bowl
Chen-Si, Meir	345.00
Oregon, Mayer	475.00
Scinde, Alcock	355.00

Middle Patterns: c1850–1870

Bowl
Honc, Petrus Regout, 3″	125.00
Spinach, Jones, 8 x 6″, brushstroke	195.00

Cake Stand, Formosa, Jones, 11¾″, pedestal 425.00

Drain, Chinese Dragon & Bird, Minton, 12¼ × 9″, polychrome with rust, green, and red 450.00

Jardiniere, Lotus, Cockson & Harding, 7⅜ × 6¾″, three ftd 395.00

Pitcher
Japan, Fell, 6¼″ h, milk size	350.00
Shaghae, Furnivals, 5″ h, creamer size	375.00

Plate
Hindustan, Maddock, 10¾″	225.00
Yedo, Ashworth, 10⅜″	95.00

Platter
Coburg, Edwards, 17¾ × 13¾″	750.00
Delph, Minton, 18½ × 15¼″, well and tree	550.00
Nankin, Ashworth, 10 × 7¾″	165.00
Yedo, Ashworth, 15⅜ × 12½″	395.00

Stein, Singa, Cork, Edge & Malkin, 4⅞″ 355.00

Soup Plate
Hindustan, Maddock, 10⅝″, paneled, flanged	255.00
Shanghae, Furnivals, 9¼″, flanged	150.00

Sugar, Coburg, Edwards, 7½″, professional restoration to bottom 375.00

Vegetable Tureen, cov, Tonquin, Meir, 11″ 475.00

Waste Bowl, Hopberry, Meigh, 4¾ × 2¾″, child's 250.00

Late Patterns: c1880–1990s

Berry Bowl
Dahlia, Upper Hanley, 5½″	45.00
Daisy, Burgess & Leigh, 4¾″	35.00
Manhattan, Alcock, 5¼″	35.00
Persian Moss, Utzschneider, 5″	32.00
Roseville, Maddock, 5″	40.00
Touraine, Alcock, 5¼″	55.00

Bone Dish
    St. Louis, Johnson Bros., 6¼″ 55.00
    Vermont, Burgess & Leigh, 6½″ 48.00
    Waldorf, New Wharf, 6½″ 65.00
    Waverly, Grindley, 7¾″ 95.00
Bowl
    Lily, Adderly, 7¼″ sq, brown border trim, gold
        sponged 250.00
    Persian Spray, Doulton, 7¼ × 3¼″, oval 345.00
Butter Dish
    Iris, Wilkinson, no drainer 250.00
    Marechal Neil, Grindley, 7¾″, price for 3-pc set ... 375.00
    Touraine, Alcock, no drainer 500.00
Butter Pat
    Daisy, Burgess & Leigh, 3″ 40.00
    Eclipse, Johnson Bros., 2⅞″ 48.00
    Fairy Villas, Adams, 3⅛″ 50.00
    LaFrancais, French China Co., 3¼″ 30.00
Cake Plate, handles
    Geisha, Ford & Sons, 10″ handled serving plate, 6
        individual plates, price for 11-pc set 325.00
    Linda, Maddock, 10″ 145.00
    Madras, Doulton, 9¾″ 95.00
    Malta, Mehlem, 10″ 75.00
Cheese Dish, Delft, Minton, slant top 575.00
Creamer
    Fairy Villas, Adams, 5″ 275.00
    Kyber, Adams, 5¾″ 425.00
    Melbourne, Grindley, 3½″ 295.00
    Touraine, Alcock, 4½″ 375.00
Cup and Saucer
    Astoria, New Wharf, tea size 110.00
    Daisy, Burgess & leigh, tea size 80.00
    Gironde, Grindley, tea size 75.00
    Paris, Wood & Son, coffee size 95.00
    Touraine, Alcock, coffee size 145.00
Eggcup
    Abbey, unknown maker 110.00
    Lancaster, New Wharf 85.00
Gravy
    Florida, Grindley 145.00
    Gironde, Grindley 95.00
    Idris, Grindley, attached underplate 155.00
    Marechal Neil, Grindley 125.00
    Melbourne, Grindley, underplate 165.00
    Non Pariel, Burgess & Leigh 265.00
    Roseville, Maddock, underplate 165.00
Ladle
    Delph, Wood, 7″, sauce 165.00
    Egerton, Doulton, 13″, soup 550.00
    Poppy, unknown maker, 8″, sauce, Art Nouveau ... 235.00
    Richmond, Meakin, 8″, sauce 170.00
Muffin Dish, Chusan, Wedgwood, 10¼″, steam holes in
  cov 575.00
Oyster Plate, Messina, Cauldon, 9½″ 350.00
Pitcher
    Celtic, Grindley, 6″ h 175.00
    Chelsea, Bishop & Stonier, graduated sizes, 8¾″ h, 8″
        h, and 7¼″ h, price for 3-pc set 1,150.00
    Touraine, Stanley, 8″ h, ... 400.00
Plate
    Alaska, Grindley, 10″ 80.00

    Conway, New Wharf, 10″ 95.00
    Fairy Villas, Adams, 10½″ 135.00
    Lancaster, New Wharf, 9″ 60.00
    Marechal Neil, Grindley, 8⅞″ 50.00
    Mongolia, Johnson Bros, 10″ 125.00
    Non Pariel, Burgess & Leigh, 9⅞″ 115.00
    Oriental, Ridgway, 9″ 65.00
    Osborne, Ridgway, 9¾″ 55.00
    Vermont, Burgess & Leigh, 7″ 48.00
    Waldorf, New Wharf, 9″ 95.00
Platter
    Lorne, Grindley, 13⅞″ × 9⅞″ 195.00
    Madras, Doulton, 20 × 16″ 575.00
    Mandarin, Pountney, 18 × 13½″ 175.00
    Marechal Neil, Grindley, 12½ × 9″ 175.00
    Melbourne, Grindley, 14 × 10″ 250.00
    Normandy, Grindley, 14 ×10″ 275.00
    Vermont, Burgess & Leigh 10 × 7½″ 120.00
    Watteau, Doulton, 16 × 12½″ 425.00
Sauce Tureen, cov
    Dudley, Ford, price for 4-pc set 325.00
    Fairy Villas, no ladle, price for 3-pc set 350.00
    Madras, Upper Hanley, no ladle or underplate, price
        for 2-pc set 375.00
    Marguerite, Grindley, price for 4-pc set 425.00
Soup Plate, flanged
    Barley, Ford, 10¼″ 85.00
    Haddon, Grindley, 10″ 90.00
    Vermont, Burgess & Leigh, 10¼″ 100.00
Soap Dish, cov
    Festoon, Doulton, 5½ × 4½″, price for 2-pc set ... 325.00
    Glenwood, Crown Potter, 5¼″, inside drainer, price
        for 3-pc set 395.00
    Nankin, Burgess & Leigh, 5″, inside drainer, price for
        3-pc set 325.00
Soup Tureen
    Kyber, Adams, 1¾ qt, undertray 1,850.00
    Marie, Grindley, 3 qt, 10¾ × 6½″ 650.00
    Versailles, Furnivals, 3½ qt, ladle, 13½″ underplate,
        price for 3-pc set 995.00
Sugar
    Marechal Neil, Grindley, 6″ 235.00
    Melbourne, Grindley, 4½″ 295.00
    Normandy, Johnson Bros, 6″ 345.00
    Touraine, Alcock, 6½″ 475.00
    Watteau, Doulton, 6″ 450.00
Teapot
    Kyber, Adams, 38 oz, 7¾″ h 950.00
    Poppy, Ridgway, 32 oz 475.00
    Watteau, Doulton, 32 oz 995.00
Vegetable, cov
    Holland, Johnson Bros, 11″ 350.00
    Marechal Neil, Grindley, 11¼″ 325.00
    Marguerite, Grindley, 10″ 255.00
    Oriental, Ridgway, 11 × 8½″ 495.00
    Rose, Grindley, 11″ 225.00
    Watteau, Doulton, 8″, round 475.00
Vegetable, open
    Alaska, Grindley, 9½″ 250.00
    Fairy Villas, Adams, 10½″ 225.00
    Holland, Johnson Bros., 9″ 135.00
    LaBelle, Wheeling, 9½″, ruffled 275.00

Late Pattern, vase, Lily, Adderly, 9¼" h, brown border trim and sponged gold, $495.00.

Wash Bowl and Pitcher
Atlas, Grindley, price for 7-pc set **2,500.00**
Marguerite, Hines Bros **850.00**
Sapho, Rathbone **1,100.00**
Syria, Grindley, price for 9-pc set **2,250.00**

FOLK ART

History: Exactly what constitutes folk art is a question still being vigorously debated among collectors, dealers, museum curators, and scholars. Some want to confine folk art to non-academic, handmade objects. Others are willing to include manufactured material. In truth, the term is used to cover objects ranging from crude drawings by obviously untalented children to academically trained artists' paintings of "common" people and scenery.

References: Edwin O. Christensen, *Early American Wood Carvings*, Dover Publications, n.d.; Country Living Magazine, *Living with Folk Art*, Hearst Books, 1994; Catherine Dike, *Canes in the United States*, Cane Curiosa Press, 1995; Jean Lipman, *American Folk Art in Wood, Metal, and Stone*, Dover Publications, n.d. George H. Meyer, *American Folk Art Canes*, Sandringham Press, Museum of American Folk Art, and University of Washington Press, 1992; Dana G. Morykan and Harry L. Rinker, *Warman's Country Antiques & Collectibles*, Third Edition, Wallace-Homestead, 1996; Donald J. Petersen, *Folk Art Fish Decoys*, Schiffer Publishing, 1996.

Periodical: *Folk Art Illustrated*, PO Box 906, Marietta, OH 45750.

Museums: Abby Aldrich Rockefeller Folk Art Center, Williamsburg, VA; Daughters of the American Revolution Museum, Washington, DC; Landis Valley Farm Museum, Lancaster, PA; Museum of American Folk Art, New York, NY; Museum of Early Southern Decorative Arts, Winston-Salem, NC; Museum of International Folk Art, Sante Fe, NM.

Notes: The folk art market is subject to hype and manipulation. Neophyte collectors are encouraged to read Edie Clark's "What Really Is Folk Art?" in the December 1986 *Yankee* magazine. Clark's article provides a refreshingly honest look at the folk art market.

The folk art market is extremely trendy and fickle. What is hot today can become cool and passé tomorrow. Collecting folk art is not for the timid or the cautious investor.

Box
10½" l, walnut, cherry, and curly maple, two small drawers, inlaid polka dots, attributed to Brown County, OH, 20th C **110.00**
11" l, poplar, reddish brown stain, applied cutout and carved black dec, scalloped edge molding, stars on ends "U.V.L." on one side, two soldiers and "Co. # 23, Ky," carved inscription "Made by John Emerson at Zoar, Ohio for Mrs Atla 1901" on bottom, professional replacement lid, minor wear, edge damage **135.00**
12" l, wood, brown lacquer, old gilded trim, carved snake on lid, applied end handles **110.00**
Cane, 36½" l, carved wood, Whitsitt Hall, 19th C, elaborately carved flora and fauna, inscribed "Thomas Jefferson of VA born–April 13, 1743 was president U.S.A. 1801–1805, wrote Declaration of Independence, the Founder of University of VA, died July 4, 1826, In God We Trust. This cane was cut near Jefferson tomb," wear, minor cracks **690.00**
Carving
Eagle
18" h, carved pine, old dark finish, edge damage, several glued repairs to wings **165.00**
40" w, 20" h, holding American flag with thirteen stars, ivy leaves below, gilded and enamel dec   **350.00**
Phoenix, 32" w, painted, American, 19th C **200.00**
Picture, 8¼ × 9½", stenciled, large house by river with boats, trees, and deer, c1835, gilt frame **400.00**
Scherenschnitte, 16½" h, 13⅛" w, paper cutout and pin-prick design, birds, hearts, and flowers, old mahogany veneer beveled frame, minor stains **415.00**
Theorem
8¼" h, 11½" w, watercolor on velvet, pink, green, blue, and yellow roses and other flowers, old gilded frame **465.00**
9" h, 11" w, watercolor on paper, green, red, and yellow, cucumber, radish, and blossoms, sgd "Marion L. Fowler," old gilt frame, light stains ..   **470.00**
12¾" h, 16¾" w, watercolor on paper, yellow, red, and dark green flowers in blue vase, pen and ink inscription "Sarah Hiestand was born on 12th day of February A.D.1821 at 5.O Clock PM," matted, framed, light stains to paper ground, fold lines, minor tears **880.00**
12¾" h, 17" w, watercolor on paper, blue, green,

yellow, and red fruit and flowers, modern reeded frame, minor fading 140.00

14¾" h, 17¼" w, watercolor on paper, red, blue, green, and yellow basket of roses and other flowers, alligatored beveled frame, minor stains 550.00

18" h, 16" w, watercolor on velvet, stylized tulip with two angels, sgd "Bill Rank," sponge-painted frame 330.00

19" h, 22" watercolor on velvet, faded reds, yellow, olive, green, and blue, basket of roses and flowers, sgd under basket "Leonora L. Kellogg," old tape label on ext. reads "painted on velvet by my grandmother L. Kellogg Barrows," matted and framed 495.00

19" h, 22½" w, watercolor on velvet, still life with fruit and Canton plate, sgd "Bill Rank," sponge-painted frame 275.00

27½" h, 37¼" w, watercolor on velvet, colorful cornucopia with fruit and birds, sgd "Wm Rank," sponge-painted frame 495.00

Theorem, basket of fruit, watercolor on paper, unsigned, American, 19th C, 9¾ × 7½", light staining, small tear lower left, $2,090.00. Photograph courtesy of Skinner, Inc.

Watercolor, 11" w, 13" h, child with two cats and footstool, shade of red, blue, tan, and black, blond blue-eyed child, oval shadowbox frame 550.00

FOOD MOLDS

History: Food molds were used both commercially and in the home. Generally, pewter ice cream molds and candy molds were used commercially; pottery and copper molds were used in homes. Today, both types are collected largely for decorative purposes.

The majority of pewter ice cream molds are individual serving molds. One quart of ice cream would make eight to ten pieces. Scarcer, but still available, are banquet molds which used two to four pints of ice cream. European-made pewter molds are available.

Marks: Pewter ice cream molds were made primarily by two American companies: Eppelsheimer & Co. (molds marked "E & Co., N.Y.") and Schall & Co. (marked "S & Co."). Both companies used a numbering system for their molds. The Krauss Co. bought

out Schall & Co., removed the "S & Co." from some, but not all, of the molds, and added more designs (pieces marked "K" or "Krauss"). "CC" is a French mold mark.

Manufacturers of chocolate molds are more difficult to determine. Unlike the pewter ice cream molds, makers' marks were not always used or were covered by frames. Eppelsheimer & Co. of New York marked many of their molds, either with their name or with a design resembling a child's toy top and the words "Trade Mark" and "NY." Many chocolate molds were imported from Germany and Holland and were marked with the country of origin and, in some cases, the mold-maker's name.

Reference: Judene Divone, *Chocolate Moulds,* Oakton Hills Publications, 1987.

Museum: Wilbur's American Candy Museum, Lititz, PA.

Additional Listings: Butter Prints.

Cake, Griswold, cast iron
   Lamb 95.00
   Rabbit 175.00
Chocolate
   Alligators, Anton Reiche, 1885, price for four-pc set 125.00
   Cat, bird and rabbit, three cavities, relief-carved wood, 3⅜ × 11¾", frame type 125.00
   Clown, 9" h, numbered 15262, two-pc type 75.00
   Duck, clamp and hinge, Germany 70.00
   Heart, two cavities, 6½ × 6", frame type 75.00
   Rabbit and chicken, six rows, 11 × 17", tray type . 100.00
   Rooster, 12 × 10", single cavity, tray type 75.00
   Snowman, wearing hat, two-pc type 50.00
Ice Cream, pewter
   Black boy killing turkey, L & Co, 4" h 95.00
   Boy swinging golf club, 1900s 145.00
   Child, 5" h 45.00
   Cucumber, E & Co, #228, 4½" w, 2" h 42.00
   Drum, 2½" h 40.00
   Eagle with shield, 5" h 200.00
   Halloween witch, 5½" h 175.00
   Horse, 3" h 65.00
   Girl, golfer, 1900s 150.00
   Orange, 2½" d
      D & Co, #120 .... 32.00
      E & Co, #807 .... 35.00
   Pear, E & Co, 4" w, 2½" h 35.00
   Pears, three joined pears, L & Co, 3⅝" l 45.00
   Plum, D & Co, #121, 2½" d 32.00
   Tomato, E & Co, #239 2½" d 35.00
   Washington, George and Martha, 5½" h, price for pr 250.00
Pudding
   Basket of flowers, china, 7 × 7 × 3", Germany ... 45.00

Candy, three elephants, $70.00.

Lion, ironstone 95.00
Melon, tin, two mark, marked "Kraemer" 48.00
Shortbread, 2" floral print, chip carved, lathe turned,
English, c1840 .... 35.00

FOSTORIA GLASS   FOSTORIA

History: Fostoria Glass Co. began operations at Fostoria, Ohio, in 1887, and moved to Moundsville, West Virginia, its present location, in 1891. By 1925 Fostoria had five furnaces and a variety of special shops. In 1924 a line of colored tableware was introduced. Fostoria was purchased by Lancaster Colony in 1983 and continues to operate under the Fostoria name.

Reference: Gene Florence, *Elegant Glassware of the Depression Era*, Revised Fifth Edition, Collector Books, 1993; Ann Kerr, *Fostoria: An Identification and Value Guide of Pressed, Blown, & Hand Molded Shapes* (1994), *Etched, Carved & Cut Designs* (1996) Collector Books; Milbra Long and Emily Seate, *Fostoria Stemware,* Collector Books, 1995; Leslie Pina, *Fostoria Designer George Sakier*, Schiffer Publishing, 1996; ———, *Fostoria,* Schiffer Publishing, 1995; JoAnn Schleismann, *Price Guide to Fostoria,* Third Edition, Park Avenue Publications, n.d.; Ellen T. Schroy, *Warman's Glass,* Second Edition, Wallace-Homestead, 1995.

Periodical: *The Daze,* PO Box 57, Otisville, MI 48463.

Collectors' Clubs: Fostoria Glass Collectors, 10221 Slater Ave #103-396, Fountain Valley, CA 92708; Fostoria Glass Society of America, PO Box 826, Moundsville, WV 26041.

Museums: Fostoria Glass Museum, Moundsville, WV; Huntington Galleries, Huntington, WV.

Basket, American, reed handles 130.00
Bouillon Cup and Saucer, Versailles, blue 55.00
Bowl
  Coin, oval
    Amber, 9" l 39.50
    Olive green 30.00
  Sunray, 11" d 40.00
  Trojan, yellow, 6" d 25.00
Butter, cov, American, 1 lb 150.00
Cake Plate, Baroque, handles, Navarre etch 45.00
Candlesticks, pr, Coin, blue, 4½" 60.00
Candy Box, cov, American, 3 part 80.00
Champagne
  Meadow Rose 25.00
  Navarre, low 25.00
  Neoclassic, amethyst 15.00

Candleholder, black, 4" h, $35.00.

Versailles, blue 42.50
Cheese Compote, American 35.00
Cigar Humidor, American 500.00
Coaster, Sunray, 4" d 6.50
Cocktail, Meadow Rose 20.00
Compote, Versailles, blue 130.00
Console Bowl, Sunray, two handles 37.50
Creamer and Sugar
  Meadow Rose, ftd 36.00
  Navarre 55.00
Cruet, Raleigh, orig stopper 27.00
Cup and Saucer, Navarre 35.00
Epergne, Heirloom, French opalescent, large, two pc . 125.00
Flower Float, Heirloom, blue opalescent 24.00
Fruit Bowl, American, 13" d 60.00
Goblet
  Baroque, blue 30.00
  Buttercup 26.00
  Colony, 9 oz 15.00
  Cynthia, cut #785, 9 oz 16.00
  Laurel 14.00
  Meadow Rose, 10 oz 27.00
  Midnight Rose 35.00
  Navarre 35.00
  Neoclassic, amethyst 28.00
  Romance 24.00
  Royal, amber 15.00
Iced Tea Tumbler
  Meadow Rose 25.00
  Navarre 65.00
Lamp Chimney, 6¼" h, hanging leaves and vines with
  threading, 2" d brass top collar at base 495.00
Juice, Navarre 32.50
Mayonnaise
  Baroque, blue, 2 pc 65.00
  Colony, 3 pc 35.00
Nappy, American, 5" d 10.00
Oyster Cocktail, Meadow Rose 25.00
Pickle Dish
  Heather, 8¾" l 25.00
  Sunray, handle 30.00
Pitcher
  Hermitage 50.00
  Versailles 600.00
Plate
  7½" d
    Baroque, Chintz etch 125.00
    Bouquet 8.00
  8" d, Navarre 15.00
  9" d, Colony 20.00
  10¼" d, Versailles, blue 150.00
Punch Bowl, Sunray 115.00
Relish, 2 part
  Baroque, 6" 12.00
  Colony 16.00
  Fairfax, green 12.00
  Navarre, 3 part 65.00
Rose Bowl, American 22.00
Salt and Pepper Shakers, pr
  American, individual size, on tray 70.00
  Beverly, green 135.00
  Coin, amber 30.00

Jamestown	40.00
Salt, individual, Hermitage	4.00
Sandwich, center handle	
Colony	25.00
Vesper, green	35.00
Sauce Boat, Baroque, blue, oval, 6½" l	65.00
Sherbet, Meadow Rose	18.00
Sugar Bowl, Baroque, 3" h, individual, yellow	20.00
Sugar Pail, Oakleaf	125.00
Sweetmeat, cov, Baroque, yellow, 9½" d	295.00
Tidbit, American, 2 tier, metal handle	100.00
Tomato Icer, American	60.00
Toothpick, American	40.00
Torte Plate	
American, 13¼", oval	50.00
Century, 14" d	25.00
Tray	
American, 5 part, 12¾ × 8¾"	120.00
Fleur-de-Lis, silver hunt scene	45.00
Tumbler	
Hermitage, clear, ftd, 4¼" h	10.00
Seville, amber, 12 oz, ftd	18.00
Versailles, blue, 10 oz, ftd	50.00
Vase	
American, sweet pea	120.00
Chintz, ftd, 10" h	115.00
Colony, flared, ftd	50.00
Hermitage, green, ftd, 10" h	30.00
Wedding Bowl, cov	
American	95.00
Coin, 8¼" d, amber	55.00
Whipped Cream Pail, Versailles, blue	240.00
Wine, American, hexagonal foot	16.00

FRAKTUR

History: Fraktur, the calligraphy associated with the Pennsylvania Germans, is named for the elaborate first letter found in many of the hand-drawn examples. Throughout its history, printed, partially printed/partially hand-drawn, and fully hand-drawn works existed side by side. Frakturs often were made by schoolteachers or ministers living in rural areas of Pennsylvania, Maryland, and Virginia. Many artists are unknown.

Fraktur exists in several forms—geburts and taufschein (birth and baptismal certificates), vorschrift (writing examples, often with alphabet), haus sagen (house blessings), bookplates and bookmarks, rewards of merit, illuminated religious texts, valentines, and drawings. Although collected for decoration, the key element in fraktur is the text.

References: Dana G. Morykan and Harry L. Rinker, *Warman's Country Antiques & Collectibles,* Third Edition, Wallace-Homestead, 1996; Donald A. Shelley, *The Fraktur-Writings or Illuminated Manuscripts of the Pennsylvania Germans,* Pennsylvania German Society, 1961; Frederick S. Weiser and Howell J. Heaney (comps.), *The Pennsylvania German Fraktur of the Free Library of Philadelphia,* 2 vols., Pennsylvania German Society, 1976.

Museum: The Free Library of Philadelphia, Philadelphia, PA.

Notes: Fraktur prices rise and fall along with the American folk-art market. The key marketplaces are Pennsylvania and the Middle Atlantic states.

Hand Drawn

Birth, Geburts und Taufschein, pen and ink and watercolor

PA German, laid paper, alternating lines of red and black, red, yellow, and black border, records 1825 birth, old black beveled frame, 8½" h, 9½" w ... **440.00**

Peterman, Daniel, records birth of Catharina Trambach, 1856, central text, small flower vase in center of top with radiating floral and vine motif concluding with upside-down tulips on sides, two parrots in upper quadrants, woman flanks text on each side in bottom half, 11¾ × 14" **6,000.00**

Rudy, Durs, Thomas Weber, January 20, 1798, Lecha County, laid paper, flowers, trees, red, green, yellow, blue, black, and brown, framed, wear and tears, 8¼" h, 13⅛" w **2,475.00**

Unknown artist, wove paper, vining tulips, text square with Catharina Rusickir, June 17, 1834, orange, blue, yellow, and black, edge damage and tears, modern frame, 12¾" h, 10⅞" w **375.00**

Book Plate

Riegel, Martin, born Feb 16, 1813, black ink and pen, wove paper, stains, cross-corner chip-carved pine frame, old dark patina, 11¼" h, 9" w **330.00**

Sehaey, Daniel, Smithville, Wayne County, Ohio October 11th AD 1854, Written by JKCB, black and olive yellow, pen and ink and watercolor, pen flourishes, old beveled walnut frame, 8¾" h, 10¾" w **580.00**

Color Design, pen, ink, and watercolor, laid paper, stylized tulip, compass designs, black ink border, red, green, and yellow watercolor, stains, modern painted frame, 9¾" h, 7¾" w **660.00**

Death Notice, pen and ink and watercolor, laid paper, German, Bremen 1st Jan 1811, towers with urn finials, yellow, red, green, and black, minor stains, fold lines, framed, 14½" h, 10¼" w **385.00**

Drawing and Text, PA German, pen and ink, watercolor, laid paper

Cutout collage, verse in circle around border, red, brown, black, and blue dec, minor stains, black background, modern gilt frame, 11⅝" sq **140.00**

Design divided into sections with green grid, large tulips border with vining flowers, birds with wings spread, text and title, dated 1819, minor edge damage, small repairs and stains, center seam and paper is glued to backing, framed, 14¾" h, 17½" w **440.00**

Gottschall, Samuel, 1834, two standing women in blue-green dresses, tulips, hearts, St Sophia devices, various admonitions to youth, affixed to card, 12½ × 7⅞" **101,000.00**

Exercise Book, pen and ink, ledger paper, "David Cochran 1831 & 1832," 22 pgs with decorative title strips with watercolor designs, several include animals such as camels, moose, cow, and elephant, mathematics exercises, 12¼" h, 7½" w 330.00

Family Register, hand-colored engraving, pen and ink entries of births, deaths, etc, marriage recorded in 1859 in Branson, Branch Co, MI, eagle, flags, other dec, stains, framed, 20¼" h, 17¼" w 360.00

Hand Drawn/Printed

Birth, Geburts und Taufschein

Cetch, Marie, 1848, two shades of blue, yellow, black, and faded red, wove paper, stains, fold lines, mortised pine frame, 10¾" h, 9¾" w 500.00

Hefle, Drusylla, June 7, 1814, Somerset County, PA, German text, eagle, two angels, and fruit, wove paper, crease lines, water stains 500.00

Kaufmann, Peter, Canton, Stark County, OH, 1866 Snyder County, PA birth, good color, minor stains, paper folds, modern painted frame, 17¾" h, 15½" w 440.00

Otto, Heinrich, records birth of Jacob Thomas, 1767, parrot facing inward in upper left quadrant, geometric floral and stripe border across top, oval theme floral border across bottom 3,500.00

Simon, David, July 22, 1795, Lancaster County, PA, German calligraphy text, eagle, two angels, and fruit, wove paper, minor damage 1,600.00

Hand drawn, fish, religious text, southeastern PA, German script, 1802, 7⅞ × 6⁵⁄₁₆", $500.00.

Printed

Birth, Geburts und Taufschein

Baumann, S, Ephrata, PA, 1799 birth, red, green, yellow, and pink, some edge damage, small holes, framed, 14½" h, 16½" w 330.00

Ritter, Reading, PA

1829 Lebanon County birth, good color, stains,

tears in top edge, curly maple frame, 18¾" h, 15½" w 55.00

1843 Schuylkill County, PA, birth, faded color, stains, minor edge damage, modern painted frame, 19¼" h, 16¼" w 110.00

House Blessing, Haus Sagen

Blummer and Bush, Allentown, PA 250.00

Ritter, Reading, PA 200.00

FRANKART

History: Arthur Von Frankenberg, artist and sculptor, founded Frankart, Inc., in New York City in the mid-1920s. Frankart, Inc., mass produced practical "art objects" in the Art Deco style into the 1930s. Pieces include aquariums, ashtrays, bookends, flower vases, and lamps. Although Von Frankenberg used live female models as his subjects, his figures are characterized by their form and style rather than specific features. Nudes are the most collectible; caricatures of animals and human figures were also produced, no doubt, to increase sales.

Pieces were cast in white metal in one of the following finishes: cream—a pale iridescent white; bronzoid—oxidized copper, silver, or gold; french—medium brown with green in the crevices; gunmetal—iridescent gray; jap—very dark brown, almost black, with green in the crevices; pearl green—pale iridescent green; and verde—dull light green. Cream and bronzoid were used primarily in the 1930s.

Marks: With few exceptions, pieces were marked "Frankart, Inc.," with a patent number or "pat. appl. for."

Note: All pieces listed have totally original parts and are in very good condition unless otherwise indicated.

Ashtray

5½" d, seated honey bear, holding honey pot ashtray 135.00

9" d, ballerina dancer in center, 8" d round onyx tray 295.00

9¼" h, kneeling female nude, arms extended to left, holding green custard glass ashtray, Roman green finish 275.00

Bookends, pr

5" h, stylized circus ponies 175.00

7" h, female heads, long necks 220.00

Centerpiece Bowl, 15" d dish, 8½" h nude flower frog 275.00

Ashtray, chrome Scottie, black enamel base, marked "Frankart Inc/Pat Appld For," $125.00.

Incense Burner, 5″ h, female head on burner base, leaning back to blow smoke through mouth **195.00**
Lamp
    9″ h, two kneeling nudes, embracing 8″ d crackle glass globe **495.00**
    23″ h, two female figures wearing pajamas and wide-brimmed hats, strolling across base, silk shade .. **400.00**
Match Holder, 8″ h, burrow, pack on back **165.00**
Wall Plaque, 6″h, seated nude, floral framework **275.00**

FRANKOMA POTTERY

History: John N. Frank founded a ceramic art department at Oklahoma University in Norman and taught there for several years. In 1933 he established his own business and began making Oklahoma's first commercial pottery. Frankoma moved from Norman to Sapulpa, Oklahoma, in 1938.

A fire completely destroyed the new plant later the same year, but rebuilding began almost immediately. The company remained in Sapulpa and continued to grow. Frankoma is the only American pottery to have pieces on permanent exhibit at the International Ceramic Museum of Italy.

In September 1983 a disastrous fire struck once again, destroying 97 percent of Frankoma's facilities. The rebuilt Frankoma Pottery reopened on July 2, 1984. Production has been limited to 1983 production molds. All other molds were lost in the fire.

Prior to 1954 all Frankoma pottery was made with a honey-tan-colored clay from Ada, Oklahoma. Since 1954 Frankoma has used a brick-red clay from Sapulpa. During the early 1970s the clay became lighter and is now pink in color.

Marks: There were a number of early marks. One most eagerly sought is the leopard pacing on the "Frankoma" name. Since the 1938 fire, all pieces have carried only the name.

References: Susan and Al Bagdade, *Warman's American Pottery and Porcelain,* Wallace-Homestead, 1994; Phyllis and Tom Bess, *Frankoma and Other Oklahoma Potteries,* Schiffer Publishing, 1995; Donna Frank, *Clay in the Master's Hands,* Second Edition, Cock-A-Hoop Publishing, 1995.

Collectors' Club: Frankoma Family Collectors Assoc, PO Box 32571, Oklahoma City, OK 73122.

Ashtray, Can-Tex, green/brown glaze **18.00**
Bicentennial Plates, series **125.00**
Bowl
    Lazybones, blue **7.00**
    Wagon Wheel, prairie green **7.50**
Candleholder
    6¼″ d, Wagon Wheel, green/brown glaze, Ada clay **35.00**
    8″ d, undulating, brown or green **20.00**
Center Bowl, 12″ l, crescent shape, red bud glaze, incised "Frankoma 211" **40.00**
Christmas Plate, 1968–75, set **125.00**
Cigarette Set, interlocking cov 3¾″ l cigarette keeper and 3¾″ l ashtray, forms state of Oklahoma shape, green/brown glaze, Ada clay **50.00**
Creamer, 4″ h, Wagon Wheel, brown/gold/butterscotch glaze, Ada clay, imp mark **12.00**
Cup and Saucer
    Mayan, Aztec white **10.00**
    Westwind, yellow **12.00**

Figure
    Boots, 3¾″ h, connected by leather thong, pink clay **15.00**
    Gardener Girl, blue, Ada clay, 1942-52 .... **75.00**
Jug, 7″ h, 4″ w, Golda's Corn, reddish brown glaze, incised "Frankoma 810 1951" **35.00**
Mug
    Donkey
        1969, 1st edition **25.00**
        1975 .... **35.00**
        1977, Carter/Mondale **45.00**
        1980 .... **30.00**
    Elephant
        1968, 1st edition **75.00**
        1969, Nixon/Agnew **75.00**
        1970 .... **50.00**
        1972 .... **35.00**
        1981, Reagan/Bush **20.00**
    Mayan Aztec, 5″ h, turquoise drip glaze, Ada clay, incised "82M" and "Frankoma" **15.00**
    Uncle Sam, red, white, or blue **15.00**
Napkin Holder, Butterfly, blue **17.50**
Pitcher, 2½″ h, Thunderbird, green/brown glaze, red clay, incised "555" **15.00**
Plate
    Conestoga, 8¼″ d, 1971, gray/blue glaze, relief "Conestoga Wagon 1725–1850" and "1971 John Frank Oklahoma Association For Retarded Children, Oklahoma Jaycees 1971 State Seal," red Sapulpa clay, ink stamped #559 .... **125.00**
    Easter, 1972 .... **25.00**
    Flight to Egypt **35.00**
    Fifty Year Commemorative **25.00**
    7″ d, Wagon Wheel, prairie green **6.50**
    10″ d
        Mayan, Aztec white **10.00**
        Wagon Wheel, prairie green **7.50**
Salt and Pepper Shakers, pr, 3¼″ h, oil-derrick shape, ivory glaze, Ada clay, stamped "Frankoma" on bottom **20.00**
Vase
    6″ h, Nautilus, chambered, red-bud glaze, marked "53" **35.00**

Vase, wheel, mottled green, impressed "Frankoma 94," 6¾″ h, $12.00.

8″ h, Art Deco style, yellow/brown, Ada clay, incised
"Frankoma 43" **16.00**
Wall Mask
  Indian
    3³⁄₄″ l, mahogany glaze, Ada clay **35.00**
    5″ l, green/brown glaze, deep brown clay, incised
      mark **40.00**
  Tragedy and Comedy, white, price for pr **95.00**

FRATERNAL ORGANIZATIONS

History: Benevolent and secret societies played an important part in America from the late 18th to the mid-20th centuries. Initially, the societies were organized to aid members and their families in times of distress. They evolved from this purpose into important social clubs by the late 19th century.

In the 1950s, with the arrival of the civil rights movement, an attack occurred on the secretiveness and often discriminatory practices of these societies. Membership in fraternal organizations, with the exception of the Masonic group, dropped significantly. Many local chapters closed and sold their lodge halls. This resulted in the appearance of many fraternal items in the antiques market.

Museums: Iowa Masonic Library & Museum, Cedar Rapids, IA; Knights of Columbus Headquarters Museum, New Haven, CT; Masonic Grand Lodge Library & Museum of Texas, Waco, TX; Museum of Our National Heritage, Lexington, MA; Odd Fellows Historical Society, Caldwell, ID.

Additional Listings: See *Warman's Americana & Collectibles* for more examples.

Benevolent & Protective Order of the Elks, BPOE
  Badge, metal
    1913, Rochester **20.00**
    1939, St Louis **20.00**
    1940, Houston **20.00**
  Calling Card Case, 1¹⁄₂ × 2″, SS, inscribed and dated
    1913 .... **100.00**
  Cap, Keokuk, IA, purple and white **5.00**
  Mug, purple, elk's head and clock, silver handle and
    trim **40.00**
  Pitcher, 12″ h, china, purple-shaded elk's head and
    clock emblems, white ground, marked "National
    Art China, Trenton, NJ" **115.00**
  Program, souvenir
    1939 .... **10.00**
    1940 .... **10.00**
  Shaving Mug, gold on white, elk emblem **50.00**
Eagles, stein set, tankard, six matching steins **1,250.00**
Independent Order of Odd Fellows, IOOF
  Banner, red, white, and blue, black insignia, unfin-
    ished **45.00**
  Book, *Ceremonies for the Install. of Officers of Sub-
    ordinate Lodges...Order of Odd Fellows,* Sov.
    Lodge, 1928, 8vo, emb buckram **17.00**
  Dish, 5³⁄₄″ l, pink luster, c1840 .... **70.00**
  Letter Opener, 4³⁄₄″ l, ivory-colored celluloid, black
    1908 Denver convention inscription, bronco-rid-
    ing cowboy on reverse, officers of Indiana Chapter
    listed **35.00**

Lodge book, Solar Lodge, 171, IOOF, lists members and officers, emb color covers, 20 pgs, 2¹⁄₂ × 4¹⁄₂″, 1914, $10.00.

Shelf, 24″ h, 17″ w, walnut, relief-carved iconogra-
  phy, old varnish finish **1,815.00**
Trivet, 8¹⁄₄″ l, cast iron, insignia and heart in hand in
  laurel wreath **35.00**
Knights of Pythias
  Goblet, green, 1900 .... **50.00**
  Rug, hooked, 36″ l, 24″ w, oval with knight and
    crossed arms, red-brown border, late 19th or early
    20th C, needs rebinding **250.00**
Masonic
  Ashtray, 5¹⁄₂″ d, brass, emblem center, trowel on edge **65.00**
  Book
    The History of Freemasonry, Al Mackey, MD &
      Wm Singleton, 1898, Masonic Hist Co, NY,
      Templer ed, 6 vols, brown leather and cloth . **195.00**
    *History of Freemasonry, from the Year 1829 to the
    Present Time,* rev Geo Oliver, London, Richard
      Spencer, 1841, 1st ed, 152 pgs, orig green cloth
      cov, gilt title **65.00**
  Bowl, 10¹⁄₈″ d, Sunderland pink luster, polychromed
    enameled black transfers, farmers' farm verse
    "God Speed the Plow," sailors' farewell with
    verse, masonic emblems on ext., pink luster trim
    and berries on int. vine-work border, central fig-
    ural landscape with hp titled "Thomas & Susanna
    Gray," printed "Dixon, Austin & Co. Sunderland"
    mark, English, c1825, rim wear **635.00**
  Letter Opener, miniature trowel, Franklin Lodge,
    wooden handle **25.00**
  Loving Cup, St Paul, MN, 1907, Pittsburgh PA **65.00**
  Photograph, 10¹⁄₂ × 8¹⁄₂″, President McKinley in full
    Masonic outfit, sgd "Courtney, Canton, Ohio,"
    matted and framed **110.00**
  Plate, 8¹⁄₄″ d, Toledo, 1906, polychrome center scene,
    fraternal symbols around scalloped rim, inscribed
    "64th Annual Conclave of Toledo Commandery,
    1906," marked "Knowles, Taylor & Knowles" .. **40.00**
  Tumbler, "Landmark Lodge No. 127, Baltimore,
    1866–1916," milk glass **45.00**
Shrine
  Goblet, ruby stained, St Paul, 1908 .... **60.00**

Hat, fez, felt	**25.00**
Plate, 10½″ d, comic beat-up Shriner center, camel border, desert and palms	**65.00**
Shot Glass, cranberry, gold sheaf-of-wheat pattern, Shrine symbol, marked "Syria Temple Pittsburgh 1908, Brown, Motheral, Moore, Robinson"	**175.00**

FRUIT JARS

History: Fruit jars are canning jars used to preserve food. Thomas W. Dyott, one of Philadelphia's earliest and most innovative glass-makers, was promoting his glass canning jars in 1829. John Landis Mason patented his screw-type canning jar on November 30, 1858. This date refers to the patent date, not the age of the jar. There are thousands of different jars and a variety of colors, types of closures, sizes, and embossings.

References: Douglas M. Leybourne, Jr., *The Red Book No. 7*, published by author, 1993; Dick Roller (comp.), *Indiana Glass Factories Notes*, Acorn Press, 1994; Bill Schroeder, *1000 Fruit Jars: Priced and Illustrated*, Fifth Edition, Collector Books, 1987, 1996 value update.

Periodical: *Fruit Jar Newsletter*, 364 Gregory Ave, West Orange, NJ 07052.

Collectors' Clubs: Ball Collectors Club, 22203 Doncaster, Riverview, MI 48192; Federation of Historical Bottle Collectors, Inc, 88 Sweetbriar Branch, Longwood, FL 32750; Midwest Antique Fruit Jar & Bottle Club, PO Box 38, Flat Rock, IN 47234.

Additional Listings: See *Warman's Americana & Collectibles* for more examples.

Acheson Oildag Co Reg Aquadag US Pat Off Port Huron, MI, clear, smooth lip	**15.00**
American Fruit Jar, light green, qt, handmade, glass lid, wire bail	**100.00**
Anchor Hocking, clear, qt, machine made, glass lid, wire bail, anchor emb on side H superimposed on anchor	**5.00**
Atlas, Hazel, large HA symbol on side, clear	**5.00**

Ball

Aqua, qt, handmade, glass lid, ground top, emb script "The Ball, Pat. Apl'd For"	**40.00**
Blue, Sure Seal, smooth lip, lightning beaded neck seal	**5.00**
Blue Ribbon, clear, qt, glass lid, wire clip	**8.00**
Cadiz, aqua, ground lip	**450.00**
Clark Fruit Jar Co, blue, qt, handmade, glass lid emb "Clark Fruit Jar Cleveland"	**50.00**
Conserve, clear, qt, handmade, glass lid, wire bail	**9.00**
Dexter, aqua, ground lip, glass insert and screw band, pat Aug 8th, 1865	**35.00**
Doolittle, aqua, qt, handmade, glass lid, emb "Doolittle The Self Sealer"	**65.00**
Economy, amber, pt, metal lid, spring clip	**5.00**
Forster Jar, clear, smooth lip, glass insert and screw band	**10.00**
Good House Keepers, clear, 2 qt, machine made, zinc lid	**2.50**
Hamilton, clear, qt, handmade, glass lid, metal clip ...	**45.00**
Improved Gem, L G Co, aqua, ground lip, glass insert, screw band	**400.00**
Kerr, self-sealing trademark, patented Mason, sky blue, pt, smooth lip, 2-pc lid	**95.00**

Lafayette, aqua, script	**2.50**

Mason

Aqua, ground lip, X patent Nov 30th 1858	**15.00**
Green, qt, hand made, zinc lid, emb "S Mason's Patent 1858"	**5.00**

Whitney, Mason, pat'd 1858, clear, 1½ qt, $4.50.

Millville Atmospheric Fruit Jar, NJ, aqua, cast-iron lid fastener, aqua lid marked "Whitall's Patent," chip on lid, 9″ h	**50.00**
Ohio Quality Mason, clear, 2 qt, handmade, zinc lid .	**15.00**
Pine Deluxe Jar, clear, pt, machine made, glass lid, wire bail	**5.00**
Sure, aqua, qt, handmade, glass lid, spring wire clip ..	**225.00**
Tropical, clear, qt, machine made, zinc lid, wire clip .	**4.00**
Winslow Jar, aqua, qt, handmade, glass lid, wire clip .	**45.00**
Yeoman's Fruit Bottle, aqua, wax cork closure	**50.00**

FRY GLASS

History: The H. C. Fry Glass Co. of Rochester, Pennsylvania, began operating in 1901 and continued in business until 1933. Their first products were brilliant-period cut glass. They later produced Depression glass tablewares. In 1922 they patented heat-resisting ovenware in an opalescent color. This "Pearl Oven Glass", which was produced in a variety of pieces for oven and table, included casseroles, meat trays, and pie and cake pans.

Fry's beautiful art line, Foval, was produced only in 1926 and 1927. It is pearly opalescent, with jade green or delft blue trim. It is always evenly opalescent, never striped like Fenton's opalescent line.

Marks: Most pieces of the oven glass are marked "Fry" with model numbers and sizes.

Foval examples are rarely signed, except for occasional silver-overlay pieces marked "Rockwell."

Reference: Fry Glass Society, *Collector's Encyclopedia of Fry Glass*, Collector Books, 1989, 1990 value update.

Collectors' Club: H. C. Fry Glass Society, PO Box 41, Beaver, PA 15009.

Bouillon Cup and Saucer, Foval, two Delft-blue handles	**95.00**
Candlesticks, pr, white opalescent Foval, applied electric blue collars and threading	**375.00**
Casserole, cov, Ovenware, oval	**35.00**
Compote, 9″ d, Foval, jade stem	**375.00**
Creamer and Sugar, Foval, Delft-blue trim and handles, pedestal base	**350.00**
Cup and Saucer, Foval, jade handle	**75.00**
Demitasse Cup and Saucer, gold rim	**35.00**
Eggcup, Foval, jade base	**145.00**
Lemonade, Foval, jade handle, ftd	**85.00**
Parfait, 6½″ h, Foval, Delft-blue stem	**175.00**
Pie Plate, Ovenware	**35.00**
Pitcher, 9¼″ h, Diamond Optic, chrome green, ground pontil	**100.00**
Plate	
7½″ d, jade, SS overlay	**180.00**
8½″ d, Foval, jade trim	**95.00**
10″ d, Pearlware, banded SS floral pattern	**110.00**
Punch Cup, colorless, crackle finish, Delft-blue handle	**35.00**
Teapot, Foval, blue handle, spout, and finial	**350.00**

Hot water server, Foval, green handle and finial, 5¾″, $225.00.

Tea Set, 6½″ h cov teapot, creamer, and sugar bowl, Pearlware, white bodies, green jade opaline handles, spout, and finial, price for set	**450.00**
Trivet, Ovenware	**15.00**
Tumbler, conical, 10 oz, SS overlay, sgd "Rockland"	**110.00**
Vase, 9″ h, Foval, trumpet shape, jade base	**375.00**
Wine, 5″ h, Foval	**150.00**

FULPER POTTERY

History: The American Pottery Company of Flemington, New Jersey, made pottery jugs and housewares beginning in the early 1800s. They made Fulper Art Pottery from approximately 1910 to 1930.

Their first line of art pottery was called Vasekraft. The shapes were primarily rigid and controlled, being influenced by the Arts and Crafts Movement, or indicative of the Chinese influence. Equal concern was given to the glazes which showed an incredible diversity.

Pieces made between 1910 and 1920 were of the best quality, because less emphasis was put on production output. Almost all pieces were molded.

References: Susan and Al Bagdade, *Warman's American Pottery and Porcelain,* Wallace-Homestead, 1994; Ralph and Terry Kovel, *Kovels' American Art Pottery,* Crown Publishers, 1993.

Collectors' Club: Stangl/Fulper Collectors Club, PO Box 64-A, Changewater, NJ 07831.

Bowl	
6″ l, 2″ h, Aladdin style, scalloped edge, handles, ftd, blue	**120.00**
14″ d, 3½″ h, curved edge, Chinese Blue flambé over mustard matte, four flaring feet	**550.00**
Effigy Bowl, 7″ h, 10½″ d, three figures supporting rolled-edge bowl, mirrored back and silvery gunmetal finish, ink racetrack mark	**750.00**
Jug, 9 × 5″, cat's eye, musical, plays "How Dry I Am"	**175.00**
Pitcher, 11″ h, flagon, rose matte, #540	**200.00**
Powder Box, Art Deco lady	**225.00**
Vase	
2¾″ h, 4¾″ d, pinched opening, leopard skin and brown flambé glaze, Vasekraft label	**475.00**
5″ h, 3½″ d, bulbous, light green, yellow-green rim band, incised mark	**225.00**

Vase, dark olive matte glaze, three ftd, stamped mark, 4¾″ h, 4¾″ d, $100.00.

8″ h, 7″ w, gold and black, two handles, stamped mark **220.00**

8½″ h, trumpet fan, brown flambé to mission matte, #708 .... **250.00**

9¾″ h, 6″ d, ovoid, snake skin, green glaze, silver specks, sgd **345.00**

11½″ h, 7¼″ d, bulbous, flaring rim, Mouse Gray over Wisteria Matte flambé, raised mark, orig paper label **700.00**

11½″ h, 9¾″ d, bulbous, tapering neck, flaring rim, black-brown to Flemington Green to Elephant's Breath flambé finish, orig paper label **950.00**

15″ h, 7½″ d, classical shape, two handles, ftd, Mirrored Black to Copperdust Crystalline glaze, ink racetrack mark **1,000.00**

15¼″ h, 7½″ d, bulbous, cylindrical bulging neck, fared rim, metallic lustered Chinese Blue flambé over Flemington Green flambé, incised racetrack mark **950.00**

FURNITURE

History: Two major currents dominate the American furniture marketplace—furniture made in Great Britain and furniture made in the United States. American buyers continue to show a strong prejudice for objects manufactured in the United States. They will pay a premium for such pieces and accept them above technically superior and more aesthetically appealing English examples.

Until the last half of the 19th century, formal American styles were dictated by English examples and design books. Regional furniture, such as the Hudson River Valley (Dutch) and the Pennsylvania German styles, did develop. A less-formal furniture, often designated as "country" or vernacular style, developed throughout the 19th and early 20th centuries. These country pieces deviated from the accepted formal styles and have a charm that many collectors find irresistible.

America did contribute a number of unique decorative elements to English styles. The American Federal period is a reaction to the English Hepplewhite period. American designers created furniture which influenced, rather than reacted to, world taste in the Gothic Revival style and Arts and Crafts, Art Deco, and Modern International movements.

FURNITURE STYLES	APPROX. DATES
William and Mary	1690–1730
Queen Anne	1720–1760
Chippendale	1755–1790
Federal (Hepplewhite)	1790–1815
Sheraton	1790–1810
Empire (Classical)	1805–1830
Victorian	
French Restauration	1830–1850
Gothic Revival	1840–1860
Rococo Revival	1845–1870
Elizabethan	1850–1915
Louis XIV	1850–1914
Naturalistic	1850–1914
Renaissance Revival	1850–1880
Neó-Greek	1855–1885
Eastlake	1870–1890
Art Furniture	1880–1914
Arts and Crafts	1895–1915
Art Nouveau	1896–1914
Art Deco	1920–1945
International Movement	1940–Present

REPRODUCTION ALERT

Beware of the large number of reproductions. During the 25 years following the American Centennial of 1876, there was a great revival in copying furniture styles and manufacturing techniques of earlier eras. These centennial pieces now are over 100 years old. They confuse many dealers as well as collectors.

References: *Antique Wicker from the Heywood-Wakefield Catalog,* Schiffer Publishing, 1994; Luke Beckerdite (ed.), *American Furniture,* Chipstone Foundation, 1994; *Blackie and Son, The Victorian Cabinet-Maker's Assistant,* Dover Publications, n.d.; Joseph T. Butler, *Field Guide to American Furniture,* Facts on File Publications, 1985; Thomas Chippendale, *The Gentleman & Cabinet-Makers Director* (reprint), Dover Publications, 1966; Robert Judson Clark et al., *Design in America,* Harry N. Abrams, Detroit Institute of Arts and The Metropolitan Museum of Art, 1983; *Come-Packt Furniture Company, Illustrated Mission Furniture Catalog, 1912–1913,* Dover Publications, n.d.; Wendy Cooper, *Classical Taste in America,* Abbeville Press, 1993; Madeleine Deschamps, *Empire,* Abbeville Press, 1994; Eileen and Richard Dubrow, *American Furniture of the 19th Century,* Schiffer Publishing, 1983; ———— *Furniture, Made in America,* Schiffer Publishing, 1982, 1994 value update; Nancy Goyne Evans, *American Windsor Chairs,* Hudson Hills Press, 1996.

Fine Furniture Reproductions, Schiffer Publishing, 1996; Oscar Fitzgerald, *Four Centuries of American Furniture,* Wallace-Homestead, 1995; Benno M. Forman, *American Seating Furniture,* Winterthur Museum, W. W. Norton & Company, 1988; Don Fredgant, *American Manufactured Furniture,* Revised and Updated Edition, Schiffer Publishing, 1996; *Furniture of the Arts & Crafts Period,* L-W Book Sales, 1992, 1995 value update; Phillipe Garner, *Twentieth-Century Furniture,* Van Nostrand Reinhold, 1980; Cara Greenberg, *Mid-Century Modern,* Crown, 1995; George Hepplewhite, *The Cabinet-Maker and Upholsterer's Guide* (reprint), Dover Publications, 1969; Heywood Brothers and Wakefield Company, *Classic Wicker Furniture* (reprint of 1897 catalog), Dover Publications, 1982; Thomas Hope, *Regency Furniture and Interior Decoration,* Dover Publications, out of print; Katherine S. Howe, et al., *Herter Brothers,* Harry N. Abrams, 1994; Emyl Jenkin, *Reproduction Furniture,* Crown, 1995; Bruce Johnson, *The Pegged Joint,* Knock on Wood Publications, 1995.

Myrna Kaye, *Fake, Fraud, Or Genuine,* New York Graphic Society Book, 1987; William C. Ketchum, Jr., *American Cabinetmakers,* Crown, 1995; Russell Hawes Kettell, *The Pine Furniture of Early New England,* Dover Publications, 1929; Thomas King, *Neo-Classical Furniture Designs* (reprint of 1829 catalog), Dover Publications, n.d.; Ralph Kylloe, *A History of the Old Hickory Chair Company and the Indiana Hickory Furniture Movement,* published by author, 1995; ————, *Rustic Traditions,* Gibbs-Smith, 1993; David P. Lindquist and Caroline C. Warren, *Colonial Revival Furniture with Prices,* Wallace-Homestead, 1993; ————, *English & Continental Furniture with Prices,* Wallace-

Homestead, 1994; ———, *Victorian Furniture with Prices,* Wallace-Homestead, 1995; Robert F. McGiffin, *Furniture Care and Conservation,* Revised Third Edition, American Association for State and Local History, 1992; Edgar G. Miller, Jr., *American Antique Furniture,* 2 vols., Dover Publications, n.d.; Dana G. Morykan and Harry L. Rinker, *Warman's Country Antiques & Collectibles,* Third Edition Wallace-Homestead, 1996; Marie Purnell Musser, *Country Chairs of Central Pennsylvania,* published by author, 1990.

Milo M. Naeve, *Identifying American Furniture,* Second Edition, American Association for State and Local History, 1989; George C. Neumann, *Early American Antique Country Furnishings,* L-W Book Sales, 1984, 1993 reprint; Jacquelyn Peake, *How to Recognize and Refinish Antiques for Pleasure and Profit,* Third Edition, Globe Pequot Press (PO Box 833, Old Saybrook, CT 06475), 1995; Peter Philip, Gillian Walkling, and John Bly, *Field Guide to Antique Furniture,* Houghton Mifflin, 1992; Leslie Pina, *Fifties Furniture,* Schiffer Publishing, 1996; Ellen M. Plante, *Country Furniture,* Wallace-Homestead, 1993; Rudolf Pressler and Robin Staub, *Biedermeier Furniture,* Schiffer Publishing, 1996; Michael Regan (ed.), *American & European Furniture Price Guide,* Antique Trader Books, 1995; Steve and Roger W. Rouland, *Heywood-Wakefield Modern Furniture,* Collector Books, 1995; Rustic Hickory Furniture Co., *Porch, Lawn and Cottage Furniture* (reprint of ca. 1904 and 1926 catalogs), Dover Publications, 1990.

Albert Sack, *The New Fine Points of Furniture,* Crown, 1993; Thomas Sheraton, *The Cabinet-Maker and Upholsterer's Drawing Book* (reprint), Dover Publications, 1972; Nancy A. Smith, *Old Furniture,* Second Edition, Dover Publications, 1990; Robert W. and Harriett Swedberg, *Collector's Encyclopedia of American Furniture,* Vol. 1 (1990, 1996 value update), Vol. 2 (1992, 1996 value update), Vol. 3 (1994), Collector Books; ———, *Furniture of the Depression Era,* Collector Books, 1987, 1994 value update; ———, *Swedberg's Price Guide to Antique Oak Furniture,* First Series, Collector Books, 1994; Thonet Co., *Thonet Bentwood and Other Furniture* (1904 catalog reprint), Dover Publications, 1980; Eli Wilner, *Antique American Frames,* Avon Books, 1995; Ghenete Zelleke, Eva B. Ottillinger, and Nina Stritzler, *Against the Grain,* The Art Institute of Chicago, 1993.

There are hundreds of specialized books on individual furniture forms and styles. Two of note are: Monroe H. Fabian, *The Pennsylvania-German Decorated Chest,* Universe Books, 1978, and Charles Santore, *The Windsor Style In America,* Revised, Vols. I and II, Dover Publications, n.d.

Videotapes: BBC Enterprises Ltd., *The Story of English Furniture,* 2 vols., Home Vision, 1981; John Bivens, *Authenticating Antique Furniture,* 2 vols., Pilaster Publications, 1994.

Additional Listings: Arts and Craft Movement, Art Deco, Art Nouveau, Children's Nursery Items, Orientalia, Shaker Items, and Stickley.

Notes: Furniture is one of the types of antiques for which regional preferences are a factor in pricing. Victorian furniture is popular in New Orleans and unpopular in New England. Oak is in demand in the Northwest, not as much so in the Middle Atlantic states.

Prices vary considerably on furniture. Shop around. Furniture is plentiful unless you are after a truly rare example. Examine all pieces thoroughly—avoid buying on impulse. Turn items upside down; take them apart. Price is heavily influenced by the amount of repairs and restoration. Make certain you know if any such work has been done to a piece before buying it.

The prices listed below are "average" prices. They are only a guide. High and low prices are given to show market range.

Beds

Arts and Crafts, oak, hand-carved post corners, panels, orig side rails, 63" w, 59" h **1,035.00**

Baroque, Italian, simulated marble, high scrolling headboard dec in pastiglia with vacant cartouches and foliage, carved scrolled feet, painted, green and blue marbleized dec, losses to paint and gilt, 45¾" w, 84" h, price for pr **3,750.00**

Biedermeier, figured-mahogany veneer, octagonal posts, turned feet and finials, paneled head and footboards, orig rails, 38 × 72" mattress size, 45" h, some veneer damage, price for pair **650.00**

Chippendale, tall post, curly maple, turned posts, scrolled headboard with poplar panel, orig side rails, old mellow refinishing, minor repairs to posts, 60" w, 72" l, 80" h **3,000.00**

Chippendale Style, Drexel, mahogany, four poster, carved, 65" w, 86½" l, 67½" h **750.00**

Classical, mid-Atlantic states, c1820, tall post, red painted head posts flank scrolled headboard, spiral-carved footposts with classical acanthus leaves and beading above dies and turned feet, minor additions to orig rails, tester missing, 55⅞" w, 78¼" l, 81¾" h **2,500.00**

Country, rope

  Curly maple, turned posts and crest rails, paneled head and footboards with raised walnut panel, old varnish finish, replaced walnut side rails, 51½" w, 72" l, 42" h **550.00**

  Pine, poplar, and maple, turned posts, ball finials, orig rope pins cut flush with rails, side rails extended, old varnish finish, single size, 41" w, 76" l, 33½" h **55.00**

  Poplar, old red paint, turned posts with cannonball finials, paneled headboard with scrolled detail and turned finials, footboard posts cut down, extended orig rails, 54¾" w, 78" l, 53" h **660.00**

  Poplar, turned posts with elongated ball finials, shaped headboard, blanket roll on footboard, engraved brass plate "Made in 1842 by Matthew Patton for Unity Patton Meharry, Wingate Indiana," old dark refinishing, 53¾" w, 75" l replaced rails, 57" h **275.00**

Empire

  American

    Canopy, four poster, mahogany, carved acanthus and reeded posts, curved top headboard, 42" w, 87" h **525.00**

    High poster, birch, rope and acanthus-carved turned posts, orig rope rails, arched canopy frame, 55" w, 72" l, 66¾" h **1,500.00**

  French, c1810, mahogany, bronze-doré mounts, twin back block supports, large gilt-bronze sphere, paneled sides, front ormolu dec, block supports, classical maiden, busts, front rail with bronze-ormolu twin griffin and lion's-head mask dec, double size, 57" w, 72" l, 58" h **5,250.00**

Federal, pencil post, walnut, scalloped head and foot-

Bed, Federal, cannonball, maple, paneled headboard, turned posts with ball finials, early 19th C, 40" w, 84" d, 42" h, $1,320.00. Photograph courtesy of Leslie Hindman Auctioneers.

boards, orig rails and canopy frame, 4 6½" w, 65" l, 76½" h **4,200.00**

George III, four poster, carved walnut, brass mounted, circular tapered head posts, shaped mahogany headboard, reeded and acanthus-carved footposts, ring-turned feet, casters, 91½" h **10,000.00**

Hired Man's, pine, peaked crest, turned legs and finials, orig side rails, old dark finish over red, single size, 26" w, 73" l, 28¾" h **110.00**

Jenny Lind, poplar and hardwood, old cherry-colored finish, tall post, replaced rails, posts have been cut off and reattached, single size, 42" w, 76" l, 69½" h **110.00**

Louis XV Style, carved, enameled, and gilded, floral-and-leaf-carved and upholstered three-panel headboard, scroll feet, double size **1,050.00**

Louis XVI Style, gilded and enameled, molded and upholstered headboard and footboard, short scroll feet, double size **400.00**

Queen Anne, PA, early 19th C, low poster, turned and painted pine, head and footposts with flattened ball finials, shaped head and footboards, tapered feet, orig rope rails, orig green paint, 48½" w, 743¼" h **3,600.00**

Rococo, Portuguese, 19th C, ornately carved rosewood, headboard, footboard, and rails **1,150.00**

Sheraton, American, tester, cherry, turned posts and foot rail, shaped headboard, orig canopy **1,400.00**

Victorian
 Brass, c1900, straight top rail, curved corners, ring-shaped capitals, cast-iron side rails, 55" w, 61" h **1,200.00**
 Cottage, c1890, bamboo style, maple and bird's-eye maple **1,000.00**

Benches

Bucket, three tiered layers, refinished **285.00**
Cobbler's, American, primitive, pine, varnished, replaced leather seat, replaced case of twelve drawers, under-slung drawer missing, fourteen cobbler's tools, 49" l **600.00**

Country, cutout ends mortised through top
 Pine
  Layers of old worn repaint, 62½" l, 12¾" w, 18½" h **475.00**
  Refinished, 35½" l, 12½" w, 14" h **275.00**
  Walnut, curved front corners on seat, soft natural patina, water stains, 63" l, 13¾" d, 17¾" h **365.00**
Gothic Style, oak, carved detail, tracery, lion arms and figures on posts, made in Belgium, 19th C, old worn finish, 54" l **1,375.00**
Kneeling, Windsor, country, gray over olive green and red paint, reeded edge top, bamboo-turned legs, splayed base, 36¾" l, 6¾" d, 6" h **325.00**
Settle
 Black repaint, half-spindle back, shaped crest, scrolled arms, plank seat, turned legs, repairs, 72" l .. **225.00**
 Chippendale, Philadelphia, orig red and black graining, yellow and green striping, floral dec, turned legs, worn orig rush seat, scrolled arms, slat back, 48" l **1,200.00**
 Country, Canadian, pine, paneled construction, shaped arms, turned spindles, shaped crest, folds open into bed, old worn finish, traces of paint, 68¾" l **525.00**
 Decorated, orig gray paint, light gray seat, black and dark gray striping, stenciled and freehand flowers, and fruit, angel wing crest designs, wide plank seat, S-curved arms, half-spindle back, shaped crest, turned legs and stretchers, minor repair on one arm, 80" l **2,100.00**
Water, country, pine, old blue and green paint, cutout ends, base shelf, crest, 43" w, 18" d, 32¼" h **250.00**
Windsor, 20th C, old worn black repaint, 63" l, 18" seat, 43¾" h **1,450.00**
Window
 Arts and Crafts, Limbert, Grand Rapids, MI, 1907, No. 243, oak, canted flat sides each with four cutouts, cantering seat, leather cushion, dark color, shellac finish, branded mark, 24" w, 18" d, 24" h **4,500.00**
 Federal, c1810, mahogany, upholstered seat and rolled arms, sq tapering lefts, sq H-form stretchers, refinished, minor repair to one leg, 39½" l, 16" d, 29" h **900.00**
 George III, mid-18th C, mahogany, rect seat, scrolling arms, later velvet cov, straight legs, blind fret carved, H-form stretcher, 38" l, price for pr **4,500.00**

Bentwood

Box
 6¼" l, oval, Harvard-type construction, copper tacks, old varnish, attributed to Hersey Manufacturing, Hingham, MA **100.00**
 8" d, round, old green paint, lapped seam, iron tacks **310.00**
 8" d, 7" h, round, worn orig paint resembles wallpaper, yellow and black foliage scrolls on blue ground, some edge damage to lid **740.00**
 12" d, round, old dark finish, swivel handle, minor lid edge damage **180.00**
 14¼" d, laced seams, intricate stamped and burnt-wood designs, stylized flowers, natural patina, age

crack in lid, bottom edge damage, lacing incomplete **80.00**

14¾" l, oblong, pine, laced seams, old blue paint, edge damage **250.00**

16¼" l, oblong, pine, laced seams, orig blue paint, polychrome floral designs, full-figured man raising glass on lid, red, white, black, and yellow, wear and edge damage, lid band edge incomplete ... **935.00**

17¼" l, band, pine, orig blue paint, unusual decoupage paper scene of black man, woman, and child, foreign inscription, wear and loose bottom board **550.00**

Chair

Austrian, Vienna Secession Style, c1910, side, back splat with three circular perforations, three slender spindles, painted black, price for set of eight **5,000.00**

Thonet, arm, c1935, lacquered, pine frame, upholstered back and seat, 43" h **500.00**

Crib, Thonet **495.00**

Hat Rack **395.00**

Bentwood, cradle, mixed woods, five-spindle ends, pat 1869, replaced cushion, 37" l, 31½" h, $350.00.

Rocker, Thonet, arched twined top rail, cut-velvet fabric fitted back, armrests, and seat, elaborate scrolling frame, curved runners, 53" l **725.00**

Table, Josef Hoffman, c1905, circular top, wooden spheres dec below rim, 21¼" h **400.00**

Blanket Chests

Chippendale, American, walnut, pine and poplar secondary woods, two-board top with minor warp, dovetailed case, three dovetailed drawers, apron drop, ogee feet, wrought-iron hinges and till, old finish, replaced brasses, minor damage, some separation at seams, 50¾" l, 22½" d, 36½" h **2,900.00**

Country

Pine, PA, c1780, green and blue paint, one-board top with breadboard ends, applied lower molding, dovetailed case, strap hinges, till with molded lid, ogee feet, 45" l, 19" d, 25¼" h **1,320.00**

Poplar, dovetailed case, applied edge molding

Old worn reddish brown paint, well-shaped dovetailed bracket feet, some edge damage, rehinged lid, till lid repaired, 29" l, 14½" d, 18" h **935.00**

Refinished, bracket feet, divided int., some edge damage and repair, 18¾" l **200.00**

Walnut

Crotch-figured panels in ends and front, till with lid, hinge strip of lid restored, 43¾" l, 20¼" d, 24¾" h **425.00**

Dovetailed case, molded edge lid, till, bracket feet with exaggerated scroll detail, old worn finish, 45½" l, 14½" d, 19¾" h, one foot damaged, till lid missing, hinges reset **770.00**

Poplar secondary wood, VA, c1826, two-board top with applied molded and butt hinges, dovetailed case, base with applied molding on scalloped dovetailed bracket feet, secret drawer in till, refinished, 42" l, 20½" d, 24½" h **1,045.00**

Decorated

American, country

Cherry and poplar, orig green paint, stenciled white, yellow, and red dec, dated 1859, turned feet, base, and lid edge molding, dovetailed case, till with two drawers, spring latches, removable feet, 48¼" l, 20" d, 26½" h, minor wear, little edge damage **1,650.00**

Walnut, OH or PA, c1840–50, white pine, poplar, and chestnut secondary woods, punched tulip dec, painted dec and punched green and mustard highlights, six-board construction, dovetailed case, till with lid, single drawer, later turned feet, minor repairs, 39¾" l, 19½" d, 25¼" h **3,000.00**

Milford, CT, early 18th C, yellow pine, six board construction, vestiges of painted dec, replaced ball feet, imperfections, 42½" d, 20" d, 26½" h **920.00**

Pennsylvania

Lancaster County, pine, worn orig brown flame graining, dovetailed case and base, lid edge molding, poplar till with lid, turned feet, 44" l, 21¼" d, 27¼" h **400.00**

Perry Co, dower, c1825, poplar dovetailed case, orig lime green rag dec, marked "S. Z." on front, two bottom drawers, scalloped dovetailed bracket feet with applied wafers and black paint, reeding between drawers, grab lock, sgd "Sarah Zook Bakner" on back, 48" l, 24" d, 29" h **5,500.00**

Pine and poplar, orig brown and blue vinegar graining, reserves on front, sides, and lid, front with white heart with star flowers and name and date in red and black, "Johan Witmer 1799," black moldings and feet, dovetailed case, ogee feet, applied case, lid, and base moldings, two dovetailed overlapping drawers, bear-trap lock and wrought-iron strap hinges, till lid and secret compartment with two dovetailed drawers, minor wear, edge damage, paint wear on lid, 51¼" l, 23" d, 27" h **22,000.00**

Pennsylvania German, dower, painted, rect molded edge lift top, front with two dark panels and name "Anna Schultzin 1802," two drawers below, restored ogival bracket feet, 51½" l, 22½" d, 28¼" h **4,000.00**

Italian Renaissance Style, walnut, antique elements, 60½" l, 20" d, 21¾" h **1,955.00**

Jacobean Style, oak, rect lift lid, straight front, triple ar-

Blanket chest, Pennsylvania German, early 19th C, pine, painted, rect hinged lid with cleated ends, lidded till, bracket feet, later decoration, 44″ w, 27″ h, $1,650.00. Photograph courtesy of Butterfield & Butterfield.

chitectural frieze panels, peg feet, 19th C, 33½″ l, 15½″ d, 19″ h **500.00**

Mule, pine, thumb-molded top, two overlapping dove-tailed drawers, bracket feet, old dark finishing, int. lined with 1875 Boston newspaper, pieced repairs to feet and drawer fronts, 40″ l, 18″ d, 34¾″ h **600.00**

Sheraton, country, pine and poplar, orig red paint, molded edge top, paneled front and ends, sq corner posts, mortised and pinned frame, scalloped apron, turned feet, 44″ l, 19½″ d, 25½″ h **800.00**

William and Mary, New England, c1700, oak and yellow pine, joined, drawer base, old finish, minor imperfections, 48½″ l, 22″ d, 32¾″ h **4,315.00**

Bookcases

Arts and Crafts

Oak, golden finish, glass doors, adjustable shelves, quartersawn facade, 24½″ w, 13″ d, 55″ h **335.00**

Stickley Bros, No. 4764, double door, flush top, eight sq panes per door, three adjustable shelves, metal tag, new medium finish, 48″ w, 12″ d, 48″ h **2,600.00**

Baroque, Italian, late 19th C, walnut, upper section with adjustable shelves, reeded columns over-carved figures, lower section with double doors, built-in humidor, animal-claw feet, parts of feet missing, restorations, 43″ w, 20″ d, 96″ h, price for pr **2,600.00**

Chippendale, MD or PA, 1765–65, mahogany, three sections, upper: dentiled triangular pediment, plinth with contemporary bust of William Shakespeare, plain veneered frieze; center: bookcase with double glazed cupboard doors, astragal mullions, Chinoiserie pattern, molded base; lower: chest with short thumb-molded central drawer flanked by two similar box drawers, two graduated long box drawers, two graduated long drawers, flanked by fluted quarter columns, ogee bracket feet, 44¾″ w, 25¼″ d, 106¼″ h**16,500.00**

Chippendale Style, New England type, mahogany, broken arch pedestal over two arched paneled doors, fitted secretary int., pigeonholes, six small drawers, lower section with fall front, stepped fitted int.,

straight front, two small and two wide drawers, brass bail handle, escutcheons, lock plates, straight bracket feet, 42″ w, 24″ d, 93¾″ h **2,900.00**

Country

Cherry, step back, two pc, top: dovetailed and molded cornice, double doors each with fifteen panels of old glass; base: four paneled doors, old mellow refinishing, one end of cornice restored, 60¾ × 15¼″ cornice, 57 × 15½″ shelves, 91″ h**3,850.00**

Walnut, coved cornice, double doors, each with eight panes of glass, rounded arches in top lights, scalloped apron, cutout feet, refinished, 40¼″ w, 77″ h **1,100.00**

Edwardian, English, inlaid, stepped rect breakfront, molded cornice, applied dentils, frieze inlaid with drapery, two glazed mullioned doors, central fall front secretary drawer over three graduated drawers, flanked by two short drawers over door inlaid with foliate urns, shaped bracket feet, 88″ w, 22″ d, 86″ h**9,500.00**

Empire, American, mahogany, rect top, cushion-molded frieze, three glazed doors enclosing shelves with three-quarter columns, shaped feet, electrified, 78″ w, 17½″ d, 58½″ h **600.00**

George I, walnut, projecting molded cornice, glazed doors, int. shelf, two short and two long feather-banded drawers, bracket feet, 43¼″ w, 18¼″ d, 74½″ h **9,000.00**

Bookcase, Regency, mahogany, projecting molded cornice over two mullion glazed doors, two lower cupboard doors, int. shelves, bracket feet, 56″ w, 22″ d, 89″ h, $9,000.00. Photograph courtesy of Leslie Hindman Auctioneers.

George III Style, 19th C

 Mahogany, pair glazed doors with mullions, int. shelves, pair paneled lower doors, 48½″ w, 18¼″ d, 87″ h **3,450.00**

 Mahogany, stepped dentiled cornice, four glazed lattice doors enclosing shelves, lower section with two small over two wide cock-beaded drawers flanked by twin panel doors, ogival bracket feet, 74¾″ w, 17½″ d, 77½″ h **2,100.00**

 Pine, revolving, four circular tiers, simulated books for supports, quadruped base, 26″ d, 60″ h, price for pr **5,720.00**

Revolving, mahogany, orig finish, stenciled label "Trade Mark Danner," early 20th C, 21″ w, 20 3/4″ d, 43¼″ h **500.00**

Stacking, Globe Wernicke, Cincinnati, four-section case, and cornice, quartersawn oak, old dark finish, orig label, 34″ l, 11″ d, 59½″ h **500.00**

Victorian, walnut, two sections: upper: three glazed doors; lower: three drawers, ornate carving, 71″ w, 18″ d, 56″ h **3,355.00**

Boxes

Bible, chestnut, some curl in lid, molded edges, front panel with punched design, initials and date "L. T. 1705," int. with cov till and one drawer, wrought-iron lock, old dark patina, hasp missing, some edge damage, added pulls to drawer, 27″ l **650.00**

Book

 Poplar, old black paint, gold polychrome floral spray, red design, wear, 12″ l **360.00**

 Walnut, old varnish on cover and marbleized paper, dovetailed, minor age cracks, edge damage, 12½″ l **330.00**

Bride's, bentwood pine, orig dec of flowers on side, birds on lid, laced seams, 15¼″ l **660.00**

Candle, dovetailed

 Pine, hanging, old red repaint, two compartments, minor wear, 14″ w, 20″ h **615.00**

 Poplar, old red paint, sliding lid, 3¾″ l **330.00**

Cologne, French, c1870, marquetry walnut, serpentine case, fitted int., top inlaid with peasant scene, three gilded glass bottles, 6″ w, 3⅝″ h **460.00**

Decorated

 Beech, dome top, old worn dark blue paint, red and white floral and birds dec, iron lock, staple hinges, worm holes, some paper covering on seams missing, 25½″ l **360.00**

 Burl veneer, ebonized edge banding, painted ivy and classical foliage, minor wear, 10¾″ l **140.00**

 Pine

  Orig brown flame graining, imitation inlay striping, name "Sarah Coher" in oval in yellow paint, minor wear, int. edge break on hinged rail, 18″ l **550.00**

  Orig dark red paint, red, black, yellow and green stylized floral dec, two painted panels on front and two on lid with hearts on corners, stenciled back with freehand inscription "J. K. Hoadle, So. Woodstock, Jan. 1816," dovetailed case, molded edge lid, staple hinges, oval brass bale

and handles, int. baffle removed, some alligatoring and flaking of paint on lid, 20½″ w, 10⅝″ d, 10½″ h **2,750.00**

  Old worn white paint, polychrome tulips and flowers, dovetailed, added brass tack, bottom split, incomplete hasp, 4″ l **250.00**

  Reddish brown stain, silver stenciled pinwheels, one end with 3 drawers, brass pulls, some edge damage, 8¼″ l **220.00**

 Poplar

  Orig black paint, yellow and green striping, stenciled and freehand pineapple and foliage design on top, dome top, decoration faint, wear, age cracks, some edge damage, repaired hole in lid, lock replaced. 26″ l **110.00**

  Worn orig red paint, black striping, Roman numerals and decals of children, made to look like stack of books, floral wallpaper-lined int., secret compartment in base, keyhole hidden by sliding book, some edge damage, 9¾″ l **315.00**

  Worn red repaint, deep yellow and olive green striping, int. lined with plaid printed paper, 17″ l **110.00**

 Vinegar Grained, walnut and poplar, worn orig brown graining, wrought-iron lock, incomplete hasp, 31″ l **275.00**

Deed, orig green paint **350.00**

Desk, Queen Anne, Salem, MA, c1730, walnut, mahogany, white pine secondary wood, three-board molded top with inlaid border, central mariner's compass, very intricate int. consisting of: left side with seven pigeonholes over three dovetailed drawers; right side with doweled lid opening to reveal six small compartments in rear over two small drawers, till over three drawers, rear with four pigeonholes over two drawers, front with scalloped letter compartment, dovetailed case, engraved brass escutcheon, molded base with center drop, scalloped bracket feet, hinge repair, refinished, 21″ w, 16″ d, 8″ h **6,325.00**

Dome Top

 Country, painted yellow, red and green foliate design enclosed by black borders, monogrammed, 19th C, wear, losses, 11″ w, 6¼″ d, 6″ h **345.00**

 Hepplewhite, mahogany veneer, pine secondary wood, inlaid geometric banding on borders, two oval inlaid medallions, corner fans, one semicircular fan at keyhole, three diamonds, orig brass handle and lock, orig finish, some edge and inlay damage, 12″ l **2,970.00**

Inlaid, figured veneer, mahogany crossbanding, inlaid maple designs, stars, hearts, fitted int., dovetailed drawer, blue velvet lining, mirror on inside lid cracked, some edge and veneer damage, 11½″ l ... **330.00**

Knife

 Country, walnut, old finish, 8¾″ × 12¾″ **40.00**

 George III, inlaid mahogany, serpentine front, inlaid shell and foliage, now converted to letter box, 14¾″ l **345.00**

Letter, oblong honeycomb, wood and metal, 26 octagonal lettered slots **375.00**

Lock, pine, dovetailed, worn patina, int. dividers removed, 8″ w, 8″ d, 8″ h **55.00**

Pencil, swivel lid, carved from one pc of pine, old red
  paint, 10½" l **165.00**
Salt, oak, dovetailed, lift lid, crest, divided int., old finish,
  11½" w, 7¼" d, 9" h **100.00**
Sewing, hanging, poplar, natural and ebonized finish,
  cutout and chip-carved designs, crest with worn pincushion, two semicircular shelves for holding thread,
  hinged-lid compartment in base, 20¾" h **770.00**
Spice, dec, hanging, pine, poplar secondary wood, orig
  salmon pink paint, black, yellow, and red striping,
  polychrome paint dec on lid, edges, and front surface,
  scrolled crest, divided int., hinged lid, two nailed
  drawers with porcelain pulls, heavily alligatored over
  varnish, 13" w, 7½" d, 15½" h **19,250.00**
Trinket, CT, late 18th C, carved cherry, pinwheel dec,
  old finish, 7⅞" l **865.00**
Writing, rosewood veneer, gilded-brass trim, fitted int.,
  14" l **360.00**

Cabinets

Bar, Art Deco, walnut, sarcophagus form, two doors, sq
  top with drop-front cabinet on left, mirrored bar,
  small drawer on right between two open bays, 48" w,
  21" d, 54½" d **500.00**
Bedside, Italian, 19th C, walnut, serpentine top, conforming base, 3 drawers, 21" w, 14" d, 30" h, price
  for pr **4,025.00**
China
  Art Moderne, mahogany, double doors, floral-carved
    relief panels, int. shelves, two drawers below, 45"
    w, 17" d, 62" h **2,000.00**
  Arts and Crafts, Limbert, single door, overhanging
    top, shelves on sides supported by long corbels,
    three small panes over large pane in door, arched
    back and sides, three adjustable int. shelves, orig
    finish, branded mark, 44" w, 15½" d, 58" h **6,500.00**
  Biedermeier, highly figured and burl olive wood ve-
    neer, ebonized trim, classical-style details, archi-
    tectural cornice, single glass door, two dovetailed
    drawers, refinished, 52" w, 32" d, 58" h **950.00**
  Edwardian Style, curved glass sides, single flat glazed
    door, illuminated int., mirrored backs, 42" w, 16"
    d, 64" h, price for pr **1,610.00**
Demilune, Georgian style, painted white, shaped back-
  splash, molded-edge top, frieze drawer, two doors,
  acanthus-carved cabriole legs, claw and flattened-
  ball feet, 46"w, 23" d, 36" h **95.00**
Display
  Edwardian, c1900, paint dec satinwood, breakfront
    top, glazed doors, int. shelves, splayed legs, 42"
    w, 15" d, 48½" h **750.00**
  Edwardian Style, mahogany, inlaid dec, three glazed
    doors, adjustable shelves, mirrored back, 51" w,
    16" d, 63" h, price for pr **1,495.00**
  Rococo, South Germany, 18th C, walnut, scrolling
    heavily molded open pediment, center gilt-bronze
    cartouche plate, two arched doors of fielded pan-
    els, marquetry figures of court ladies, basal-
    molded and conforming stand, shaped apron,
    cabriole legs, 46" w, 19½" d, 71½" h **4,675.00**
Dressing, George I, c1710, gentleman's, burl walnut,

double-dome top, two inset beveled mirrored doors
  fitted with shelves and drawers, brush slide and four
  graduated feather-banded drawers in base, bracket
  feet, 42½" w, 22½" d, 79½" h **19,000.00**
Filing, American, c1910, golden oak, plain vertical
  stack, five drawers, orig brass nameplates and pulls **500.00**
Hanging, Arts and Crafts, Shop of the Crafters, Glasgow,
  Scotland, style, curving front, two milk glass leaded
  doors with floral design, two curved drawers, orig
  dark finish, paper label, 24" w, 10" d, 31½" h **950.00**
Kitchen, McDougall, Hoosier type, c1900, oak, two
  parts, three small cupboard doors with inset glass
  panels over pr of cupboard doors, white graniteware
  work surface, inset breadboard, base with three graduated drawers, cupboard door, orig hardware, bread
  drawer liner, and packing label, refinished **850.00**
Ledger, American, 19th C, walnut and mixed hard-
  woods, poplar secondary wood, dovetailed case, single paneled door, int. with divided compartments,
  later salmon paint, 15½" w, 12"d, 24" h, price for pr **500.00**

**Cabinet, Late Regency, mahogany, rect top,
pr of frieze drawers, two cupboard doors
with arched panels, plinth base, 38" w, 15½"
d, 37" h, $2,000.00. Photograph courtesy of
Leslie Hindman Auctioneers.**

Music, hardwood, cherry-colored finish, paneled door,
  applied work, crest with beveled glass, early 20th C,
  19" w, 13½" d, 49" h **55.00**
Sewing, PA, mid-19th C, step back, paint dec, red and
  black grain paint, 28¼" w, 18" d, 44" h **3,825.00**
Side, Rococo Revival, third quarter 19th C, walnut, demilune, bowed Carrara-marble top, case fitted with
  four mirrored cabinet doors, shaped base, 60" w, 19"
  d, 33½" h **1,495.00**
Spice
  Cherry, American, c1810, walnut top, single raised
    panel door, scalloped dovetailed bracket feet, int.
    with one shelf, refinished, 19" w, 8" d, 23¾" h ..**2,860.00**
  Mahogany, rect top, pencil-line inlay, leafy bronze
    bail, door conceals shelf, seven variously sized
    drawers, rear door conceals shelves, flush base,
    18th/19th C, 9¾" w, 12½" h **700.00**
  Step Back, hand crafted, nine drawers, three rows of
    differently sized drawers, four small compartments

on top, three in the middle, two larger drawers on bottom, dark brown finish, small porcelain knobs, 18" l, 12" h 900.00

Vitrine

Edwardian, c1900, mahogany and boxwood inlay, rect, Gothic-style mullioned glazed doors, sq tapering legs, spade feet, 41½" w, 14¼" d, 63¼" h 1,035.00

George III Style, late 19th/early 20th C, mahogany, rect lift top, chamfered legs, joined by shelf stretcher and fretwork, 21¼" l, 15½" d, 31¾" h . 750.00

Georgian Style, hinged beveled glass top, sq tapering legs, H-form stretcher, 27" w, 18" d, 27" h 690.00

Candle Shields

Chippendale

American, 1760–65, carved mahogany, cylindrical turned pole, adjustable cartouche-shaped screen, molded and carved frame, clustered-column pedestal with leaf-carved ball, tripod scrolled legs carved with leaves and trailing pendant vines and fruit, scrolled feet with rect molded base, 61¼" h .39,600.00

Philadelphia, c1770, attributed to Thomas Affleck, carving attributed to Bernard and Jugiez, carved mahogany, turned cylindrical pole, adjustable screen with intricately carved frame, tapering fluted shaft, acanthus-carved baluster, swirl gadroon-carved ball, acanthus-carved tripod cabriole legs overlaid with trailing husk and vines, carved hairy paw feet, 60" h 66,000.00

Georgian Style, mahogany, flame veneer frame, floral petit-point design, tapered spool-turned stem, turned base, minor veneer loss, 17¼" h 275.00

Regency, giltwood, rect panel with molded border, scrolling frame, shells and ornaments at corners with volutes, trestle base, 33" w, 48" h 1,500.00

Candlestands

Centennial, Hepplewhite, mahogany, elongated pentagonal top, tripod base, old base repairs 275.00

Chippendale

Connecticut, Litchfield, late 18th C, cherry, carved, old black paint, gilt striping, 14¾" w, 15¼" d, 25½" h 2,990.00

Connecticut River Valley, late 18th C, cherry, old refinish, minor imperfections, 17" w, 16½" d, 25½" h 16,100.00

Country, walnut, old replaced round one-board top, turned column with urn, tripod base with S-curved legs, old dark alligatored finish, top cleaned off and stained, 17¾" d, 29¼" h 330.00

New Hampshire, birch

Painted red, attributed to Lt Samuel Dunlap, old refinish, imperfections, 16½" w, 16⅛" d, 26½" h 2,875.00

Some curl in one-board scalloped edge top, turned column, tripod base, snake feet, refinished, 16¼ × 17 × 28¼" h 990.00

Philadelphia, c1750, mahogany, tilt top, circular dish top, birdcage over ring-turned vasiform standard, tripod cabriole legs, slipper feet, 21½" d, 28¼" h 8,500.00

Country, birch and hardwood, replaced one-board top

with cut corners, turned column, tripod base, snake feet, nailed repairs to base, refinished, 18¾ × 19 × 26¼" h 115.00

Decorated, poplar, round top, orig red and black graining, gilt stenciled fruit compote dec, turned column, turned tripod base, 17½" d, 28¼" h 275.00

Candlestand, Federal, American, 1st quarter 19th C, tiger maple, rounded corners on rect top, three out-curving legs, circular medial shelf, 24" w, 18" d, 28" h, $1,320.00. Photograph courtesy of Leslie Hindman Auctioneers.

Federal

Massachusetts, c1800, mahogany inlaid, molded octagonal tilt top, old refinish, 23" d, 15¾" d, 28¾" h 1,380.00

New England, c1800, cherry, dish top, old finish, minor imperfections, 15" d, 27" h 2,530.00

New Hampshire, c1810–20, maple, carved tilt top, swelled reeded post, chip-carved detail, old red varnish, minor imperfections, 20 × 15⅝" top, 29½" h 920.00

Hepplewhite

American, cherry, one-board octagonal top, turned column with chip carving, tripod base, spider legs, old refinishing, minor damage, old repair, 17¾ x 18⅛" top, 27" h 360.00

Country, birch, rect one-board tilt top, cut corners, well-turned column, spider legs, high feet, old varnish finish, dark varnish stain on base, 14½" w, 21¼" l, 28" h 750.00

Queen Anne, American, mahogany, tilt top, snake feet 1,500.00

Chairs

Arrow Back, PA, dec, orig brown paint, yellow striping, polychrome stenciled fruit and flowers on crest, 33¼" h, price for set of six 1,485.00

Art Moderne, American, designed by Lorin Jackson, c1942, Lucite, shield back, molded bunting motif, trapezoidal upholstered seat, 36¼" h 3,500.00

Arts and Crafts

Arm

Five vertical slats under V-shaped crest rail, new red leather-upholstered seat, new finish, 26" w, 21" d, 37½" h 275.00

Harden, five vertical back slats under straight crest rail, four slats under rounded arms, drop-in spring seat, through tenons, light overcoat on orig medium finish, 28½" w, 24" d, 38" h 950.00

Billiard, five vertical back slats, wooden seat, corbels, new medium finish, 27" w, 26" d, 44" h **650.00**

Morris, Shop of the Crafters, inlaid stylized peacock feathers on leg fronts, crosshatched sides, drop-in spring seat, orig dark finish, 28" w, 30" d, 41" h .**6,000.00**

Side, Stickley Bros, curved crest rail, three vertical back slats, inset tacked-on period Naugahyde seat, orig finish, marked, 18½" w, 16" d, 38" h, price for set of eight **2,750.00**

Baronial, Flemish, heavily carved backrest, acanthus and scrollwork flanked by columns and surmounted with finials **690.00**

Baroque, Spanish, mid-18th C, side, walnut, upholstered, 38" h, price for pr **575.00**

Biedermeier, dining, fruitwood and part-ebonized, black faux-leather upholstery, restorations, 36" h, price for set of four **2,300.00**

Centennial, Colonial Revival

Chippendale Style, side, carved mahogany, shaped shell-carved crest rail, pierced vasiform back splat, balloon slip seat, shell-carved apron, cabriole legs, leaf-carved knees, claw and ball feet, price for pr **800.00**

Queen Anne Style, arm, wing back, hardwood cabriole legs, turned stretcher, upholstery removed, old dark finish, 46" h **880.00**

Chippendale

American, side, walnut, shaped crest, vase splat, slip seat, square legs, H-form stretcher, refinished, some damage, replaced pins in mortise joints in base, 18" h seat, 38" h **495.00**

Massachusetts, c1780, side, mahogany, carved pierced back splat, upholstered drop-in seat, old refinish, minor imperfections, 17½" h seat, 38" h **1,150.00**

Chippendale Style, dining, splat back, floral-upholstered seat, price for pr **435.00**

Chair, Empire style, gilt bronze mounted mahogany, scrolling back continuing to flat arms supported by winged sphinxes, legs in form of winged lions, lion's-paw feet, price for matched pr, $3,300.00. Photograph courtesy of William Doyle Galleries.

Classical, New England, c1830, dining, tiger maple, wide crest rail, caned seat, old refinish, labeled "From Ryther Place in Bernardston," 17½" h seat, 43" h, price for set of six **2,185.00**

Directorie Style, early 20th C, bergère, painted cream and gray, green silk upholstery, 32½" h **690.00**

Eastlake, dining, c1870, mahogany, one armchair, six side chairs, fan-carved crest rail, reeded stiles and stretchers, block-carved front legs, minor damage, 35" h, price for set of seven **775.00**

Empire Style, arm, mahogany, rect padded back, padded arms, ormolu-mounted classical busts, bowed padded seat, sq tapering legs with brass caps, white striped fabric upholstery **825.00**

Federal

Massachusetts

Arm, inlaid mahogany, shield back with bell-flower and wheat-sheaf sprigs, pierced splat, serpentine seat, scrolled arms, sq molded tapered legs with stretcher, c1800 ....**1,350.00**

Side, inlaid mahogany, shield back, arched rail, carved foliate pendant above pierced and fluted splat, flared seat, sq molded legs, c1790 **950.00**

Mid-Atlantic states, c1800, lolling, mahogany, upholstered back and seat, sq tapered legs, H-form stretcher, restoration, imperfections, 16" h seat, 41¼" h **920.00**

Philadelphia, 1790–1810, arm, carved mahogany, molded shield-shaped and upholstered back, flanked by short shaped arms with carved rosettes over curved and molded supports, over-upholstered seat, reeded apron, sq tapering reeded legs with carved rosettes, several old repaired breaks, 35¾" h **12,100.00**

George II, provincial, c1735, corner, oak, yoke-form crest, twin baluster-form splats, pillar supports, molded seat frame, upholstered drop-in seat, deeply valanced skirt, cabriole and three turned legs **800.00**

George II Style

Arm, carved mahogany, straight crest rail, back arm pads, single cushion seat, figural Brussels tapestry, open arm, shell-carved eagle head supports and cabriole legs, claw and ball feet, 19th C **1,750.00**

Corner, mid-18th C, walnut, upholstered seat, restoration, 31" h **1,610.00**

Dining, walnut, shaped crest rail with volutes, vasiform back splat, slip seat, serpentine shell dec apron, shell-carved cabriole legs, pad feet, price for set of ten **7,500.00**

George III

Arm, c1780, mahogany, pierced ribbon back, flaring arms ending in volutes, upholstered seat, chamfered legs, box-form stretcher **500.00**

Dining, two arm chairs, two side chairs, mahogany, molded shield-form back, carved crest of wheat sheaves and bellflowers, oval parquetry panel on pierced splat, upholstered seat, serpentine front, straight tapered legs, H-form stretcher, price for set of four **3,600.00**

George III Style

Arm, mahogany, oval padded back, padded arms, bowed padded seat, molded frame, turned tapering stop fluted legs, turned feet, painted cream, ivory leather upholstery **1,200.00**

Hall, mahogany, shield-shaped back, bowed plank seat, sq tapering legs, spade feet, price for pr ... **850.00**

Wing, Gainsborough, raking sq back, padded arms, sq seat, sq legs, H-form stretcher, mushroom moquette upholstery, price for pr **3,850.00**

Hepplewhite, American, side, mahogany, shield back, rush seat **300.00**

Hitchcock, side, orig red and black graining, yellow and green striping, gilt stenciling, black painted balloon rush seat **195.00**

Jacobean Style, arm, carved frame, gold crushed velvet reupholstery, early 20th C, 50" h **770.00**

Ladder Back

Arm

Attributed to Roger Bacon, Pilgrim Century, MA, red and black grained repaint, feet ended out, slats replaced, edge damage to arm post and back post finials, very worn splint seat with wooden brace on underside, 16" h seat, 43" h **550.00**

Maple, shaped arms, four graduated arched slats, turned finials, rush seat, turned posts and legs, all wooden casters, old refinishing, 15¾" h seat, 45¼" **525.00**

Side

Hardwood, four graduated arched slats, turned finials, old rush seat, turned legs, bulbous front feet and stretcher, refinished, 42" h **770.00**

Maple and ash, painted Spanish brown over earlier red paint, early hickory splint seats, New England, late 18th C, minor imperfections, 16" h, 39½" h, price for set of four **920.00**

Louis XIV, side, gilded and carved, leaf, scroll, floral and openwork-carved high backs, hexagonal tapering trumpet legs, curved cross stretchers, price for pr .. **800.00**

Louis XV, 19th/20th C, fauteuil, gilded, floral-carved crest rail, molded frame, old verdure tapestry cov, price for pr **1,500.00**

Louis XV Style

Bergère, walnut, shaped crest rail, back arm pads, single cushion seat, celadon floral fabric cov, cabriole legs, scroll feet **250.00**

Fauteuil, late 19th/early 20th C, walnut, burgundy leather upholstery, 7½" h **4,025.00**

Louis XVI, fauteuil, gilded, oval molded backs, round tapering fluted legs, floral needlepoint, price for set of four **1,050.00**

Louis XVI Style

Bergère, high wing back, carved round tapering fluted legs, rose and floral silk brocade cov, ivory enameled, price for pr **1,750.00**

Fauteuil, walnut, leaf and ribbon-carved crest rail, oval back arm pads and seat, burgundy velvet cov, acanthus-carved arm supports, reeded tapering legs **250.00**

Moravian, side, hardwood, pierced and carved back pegged to plank seat, tapered chamfered legs, dark finish, attributed to Lebanon County, PA, age cracks in seat, 32¾" l, price for pr **385.00**

Neoclassical

Austrian, early 19th C, desk, arm, mahogany, mar-

quetry, part-ebonized, parcel-gilt, sgd "Joseph Weber, Wien," minor losses, 33" h **1,725.00**

Italian, late 18th C/early 19th C, arm

Painted blue, parcel-gilt, flaking, distressed upholstery **1,610.00**

Painted green, extensive flaking, 35" h **980.00**

Queen Anne

Arm, Philadelphia, 1740–60, walnut, shaped shell-carved crest rail, vasiform back splat, flaring open arms, terminating in knuckles and volutes, slip seat, deep shaped apron, cabriole legs, shell-carved knees, trifid feet **5,500.00**

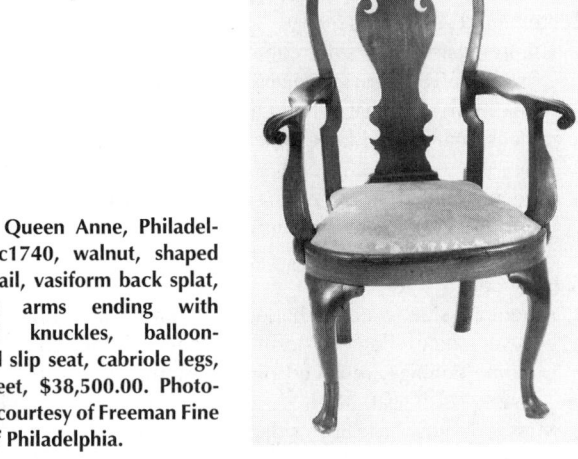

Chair, Queen Anne, Philadelphia, c1740, walnut, shaped crest rail, vasiform back splat, flaring arms ending with carved knuckles, balloon-shaped slip seat, cabriole legs, web feet, $38,500.00. Photograph courtesy of Freeman Fine Arts of Philadelphia.

Corner, RI, c1760, cherry, white pine secondary wood, pegged and rosehead nail construction, minor repairs, refinished, 28" w, 26" d, 30¾" h **5,940.00**

Side

Country

Attributed to NH, hard and soft wood, yoke crest, vase splat, paper rush seat, turned rungs, turned legs, Spanish feet, good old worn dark patina, traces of old red paint, minor scratches, repairs, 71" h **750.00**

Hard and softwood, vase splat

Shaped crest, replaced rush seat, turned legs and rungs, bulbous front stretcher, old mellow finish, feet ended out, 17" h seat, 40½" h **1,100.00**

Yoke crest, old worn rush seat, turned legs and posts, bulbous front stretcher, old dark finish, feet ended out, 38¼" h **495.00**

English, walnut, vase splat, yoke crest, balloon seat frame, slip seat, mortised stretcher, cabriole legs, slipper feet, old finish, some insect damage, old repairs, seats reupholstered in ivory damask, 42" h, price for pr **770.00**

Massachusetts, c1750

Painted, solid vasiform back splat, rush seat, Spanish foot, bulbous front stretcher, old Spanish brown paint, minor imperfections, 17¾" h seat, 41¾" h **1,955.00**

Walnut, c1750, solid vasiform back splat, crewel-upholstered seat, cabriole legs joined by turned stretchers, front frame inscribed by previous owner "Timothy Thornton Ipswich 1775," provenance included to show chairs descended in family, 17" h seat, 39¾" h, price for pr **13,800.00**

Regency, arm, carved ebony frame, green and gold floral upholstery, price for pr **1,610.00**

Regency Style, dining, bowed crest rail splat, red upholstered slip seat, ribbed saber legs, price for set of six   **650.00**

Renaissance Revival, Victorian

Dining, 19th C, four arm chairs, four side chairs, heavily carved frames surmounted by heraldic lions, center coat of arms, spiral and spool-turned supports, price for set of eight **5,980.00**

Slipper

Mahogany, c1870, carved, shaped fan-carved crest rail, ivory upholstered shield back and seat, bulbous and reeded tapering legs, casters   **200.00**

Walnut, c1875, marquetry and part-ebonized, 36" h, price for pr **2,645.00**

Rococo Revival, mid-19th C, dining, walnut, shaped back, button-upholstered seat, cabriole legs, 35½" h, price for set of six **1,150.00**

Rococo Style, Victorian, side, heavily carved fruit and floral frame, scroll legs **435.00**

Sheraton, Hitchcock type, two arm chairs, six side chairs, old red and black repaint, yellow striping, stenciled and freehand dec, replaced rush seats, 18" h seat, 33½" h, price for set of eight **2,245.00**

William and Mary

Arm, PA, 18th C, walnut, shaped crest rail, three molded vertical slats flanked by shaped arms, baluster-turned supports, solid plank seat, block-and-cylinder-turned legs, box stretcher, rear feet pierced, seat restored, 42¼" h **58,300.00**

Side

American, c1700, oak, scroll-carved crest rail flanked by turned stiles, baluster finials, three vertical molded slats, recessed plank seat, short baluster-turned and block legs, turned stretchers, 43½" h, price for pr **6,900.00**

Pennsylvania, c1710–30, walnut, shaped crest rail, three vertical molded slats flanked by rect tapering stiles, plank seat, block and ball-turned legs, paired baluster-turned front stretcher, restored seat, 40" h **60.00**

William IV, side, mahogany and red leather, restoration, 34½" h **920.00**

Windsor, mixed woods

Bamboo, side, old red repaint, white striping, floral crest, seven-spindle back, step down crest, cane seat, one seat replaced, 17½" h seat, 34½" h, price for pr **330.00**

Birdcage Back, side, seven-spindle back, early 19th C **250.00**

Bow Back

Arm, seven-spindle back

Oval-shaped seat, old black repaint, turned arm posts, shaped arms, spindle back, splayed base with bulbous turnings and H-

Chair, Windsor, New England, c1800, bow back, arm, maple, $2,500.00.

form stretcher, repaired splits in seat and arms ended out, 17½" h seat, 37½" h **650.00**

Saddle seat, splayed base with ring-turned round legs conjoined by H-form stretcher, New England, late 18th C **400.00**

Shaped seat, splayed legs with bulbous turnings, H-form stretcher, turned arm posts, shaped arms and spindle back, old dark worn finish, 14¾" h seat, 34" h **495.00**

Side, nine-spindle back, shaped seat, bamboo-turned base, old worn refinishing, 15½" h seat, 35¼" h **200.00**

Brace Back

Arm, NY, c1770–90, black paint, yellow dec, oak scrolled crest rail, hickory back posts and five spindles, maple arms, legs, and stretcher, poplar seat, 17¼" h seat, 26" w, 19½" d, 43" h ..**9,075.00**

Side, spindle back, saddle seat, splayed base with bulbous turnings, H-form stretcher, old refinishing, good color, leg turnings vary slightly, old repairs, 17¾" h seat, 37" h **660.00**

Fan Back

Arm

Old green repaint, curved crest with carved ears, spindle back, shaped arms, turned arms supports, shaped seat, splayed base, bulbous turned legs, H-form stretcher, feet ended out, 17½" h seat, 40" h **1,430.00**

Turned carved ears, turned arm posts, shaped arms, saddle seat, splayed base, bulbous turned legs, H-form stretcher, old refinishing, age cracks in seat, four plugged holes underneath, two back spindles and one arm spindle of different wood, one arm extension replaced, 18½" h seat, 44¾" h **1,450.00**

Side

Branded "E. B. Tracy" for Ebenezer Tracy, Lisbon, CT, late 18th C, old refinish, imperfections, 17" h seat, 35½" h **345.00**

Country, shaped crest, shaped seat, splayed base with H-form stretcher, old worn refinishing, faint brushed name on underside of seat, 17" h seat, 35½" h **275.00**

Hoop Back

    Arm, continuous arm, rakish turned legs, H-form stretcher, restorations, price for pr **275.00**

    Side, bamboo-turned spindle back, saddle seat

        Rakish legs, H-form stretcher, painted green, early 19th C **675.00**

        Splayed ring-turned legs, H-form stretchers, restoration, price for pr **225.00**

    Step Back, arm, seven-spindle back, turned legs and stretcher, early 19th C **200.00**

    Tall Back, New England, c1790, side, seven-spindle back, old cream paint, green highlights, 17½" h seat, 21" d, 16"d, 50¾" h **3,850.00**

    Thumb Back, New England, early 19th C, painted red, orange, and brown, metallic and green grapevine pattern stenciling, imperfections, 17" h, 33¾" h, price for set of four **1,725.00**

Chests of Drawers

Arts and Crafts, American, c1902, oak, Model No. 622, four long graduated drawers, two short drawers, panel construction sides, large red Gustav Stickley decal with "Stickley" outlined, 41" w, 22½" d, 50" h **4,750.00**

Chippendale

    Birch

        American, bowfront, beaded frame, molded edge top, four dovetailed drawers, orig oval brasses, pine secondary wood, refinished, stains in top, crack in left front foot, 39" w, 21¾" d, 36" h .**4,100.00**

        New Hampshire, early 19th C, reddish brown finish, molded cornice with relief-carved frieze, dovetailed case, six graduated drawers, detailed bracket feet, carved sunburst on center drop, replaced brasses, 36" w, 19¾" d, 62½" h**6,500.00**

    Cherry, poplar secondary wood, dovetailed case, five dovetailed drawers, molded cornice, bracket feet, refinished, replaced brasses, age cracks in top, feet with edge damage, 22¼ × 42" cornice, 39½" h, 48" h **1,760.00**

    Mahogany, Philadelphia, c1770, rect lip molded top, four graduated wide-lip molded drawers, quarter-round fluted corners, ogival bracket feet, old brass bails, 39" w **4,500.00**

    Maple

        New England, c1770–1790, rect molded edge top, conforming case, four dovetailed long drawers, molded base, straight bracket feet, orig brasses, 39½" w, 18¼" d, 32⅞" h **4,750.00**

        Pine secondary wood, dovetailed case, five overlapping dovetailed drawers, molded cornice, bracket feet, old mellow refinishing, old but not orig brasses, age cracks, shims added to two feet, 38½" × 19¼" cornice, 35⅜" w, 54½" h **4,200.00**

        Tiger Maple, projecting cornice top, six graduated drawers, bracket feet, 42" w, 19½" d, 51¾" h ...**3,500.00**

Chippendale Style, southeastern US, late 18th C, mahogany, two small drawers over three graduated drawers, bracket feet, refinished, replaced brasses, minor imperfections, 19" w, 31½" d, 31½" h **3,800.00**

Classical, coastal North Shore, MA, c1820, carved ma-

Chest of drawers, Chippendale, late 18th C, carved walnut, serpentine front, molded rect top with notched corners, five graduated drawers, cabriole legs, 33½" h, 35" w, 21¼" d, $11,000.00. Photograph courtesy of Freeman Fine Arts of Philadelphia.

hogany and mahogany veneer, bowfront, carved cornucopia and star punch dec, shaped back, conforming top without set corners, four drawers, rope-carved columns, old brasses, old refinish, imperfections, 42" w, 22½" d, 44½" h **2,100.00**

Eastlake, curly walnut, burl veneer, carved detail, scrolled crest, four dovetailed drawers, two handkerchief drawers, well-detailed molded panel fronts, refinished, 39" w, 17½" d, 46" h **550.00**

Empire

    American, c1830, mahogany, ebonized, gilt stenciled, step back fitted with swing mirror, three small drawers, lower section with single beveled drawer over two deep drawers, circular wood pulls, flanked by half-ebonized columnar sides, ring-turned legs, ball feet, 38½" d, 21½" d, 45" h **1,300.00**

    Country

        Cherry, four dovetailed drawers, turned and rope-carved pilasters, paneled ends, turned feet, refinished, small pieced repairs to back edge, 42" w, 20" d, 43" h **500.00**

        Hardwood, orig imitation rosewood graining, two step-back drawers over three dovetailed drawers, paneled ends, rope-carved edge trim, cutout feet, replaced eagle brasses, 38" w, 17" d, 40" h **660.00**

        Maine, pine, orig red and black graining, yellow and green striping, old brasses, edge damage, top poorly executed replacement, 41" w, 21¼" d, 40½" h **330.00**

Federal

    American, c1800, cherry veneer, rect top, straight front, four graduated cock-beaded drawers, oval brass bail handles, escutcheons, lock plates, shaped apron, French bracket feet, veneer loss to feet, 42½" w, 20¼" d, 39½" h **750.00**

    Massachusetts

        c1800, mahogany and mahogany veneer inlaid, bowfront, four graduated drawers, out-swept feet, refinished, replaced brasses, imperfections, 39″ w, 21½″ d, 34¾″ h **2,185.00**

c1810, cherry inlaid, four drawers, scalloped apron, old finish, replaced brasses, minor imperfections, 42¾″ w, 20″ d, 41½″ h **1,725.00**

c1815–20, mahogany and tiger maple inlay, rect top with outset corners, fluted columns surmounted by ring-turned capitals, four graduated drawers, scalloped apron, refinished, replaced brasses, imperfections, 40¾″ w, 19¾″ d, 40½″ h **2,100.00**

New England, c1790, cherry, rect top, barber-pole inlay over straight front, four graduated cock-beaded drawers, flanked by recessed pin-line inlay columns, shaped apron with center fan dec, French bracket feet, 41½″ w, 20¾″ d, 37½″ h ... **4,400.00**

Pennsylvania, western, c1815, mahogany inlaid, bowfront, contrasting crossbanded veneer surrounds, four drawers, orig brasses, minor imperfections, 23″ w, 43¼″ d, 38⅛″ h **2,000.00**

French Empire Style, bombé, gilt-bronze mountings, shaped marble top, three drawers with inlaid scroll dec, 30″ w, 16″ d, 39″ h **815.00**

George I Style, walnut, molded rect top, two crossbanded short drawers over three inlaid long drawers, later bracket feet, 37¼″ w, 20″ d, 37½″ h **1,200.00**

George III, c1770, mahogany, serpentine front, four graduated drawers, corner molding, 32¾″ w, 23¾″ d, 29¼″ h **1,725.00**

Hepplewhite

Curly Maple and Cherry, bowfront, line inlay, shaped apron, French feet, period brasses, 39½″ w, 21½″ d, 38″ h **1,100.00**

Curly Maple, poplar secondary wood, four overlapping dovetailed drawers, chamfered corners, applied top end with inlaid stringing, scalloped apron with inlay, French feet, replaced oval thistle brasses, refinished, 41½″ w, 21½″ d, 45½″ h **4,180.00**

Mahogany, inlay, five dovetailed drawers, applied edge beading, ogee feet, poplar secondary wood, replaced brasses, worn old French polish finish, pieced repairs to case, 37½″ w, 20½″ d, 35″ h ..**1,210.00**

Walnut, yellow pine secondary wood, mid-Atlantic states, four drawers, foliate and double-line inlay in each top corner, top center foliate medallion, herringbone stem and barber-pole inlay on edge with mahogany crossbanding on top edge and drawer fronts, chamfered quarter columns with vine and leaf inlay over cup with two green-colored leaves, barber-pole and herringbone inlay at base over orig French bracket feet, new brasses, refinished, partial restoration to bottom inlay, 38½″ w, 18½″ d, 38½″ h **3,395.00**

Jacobean, English, oak, old finish, quartersawn figure, elaborate facade with applied moldings and turnings, five dovetailed drawers, replaced turned bun feet, 42 × 19¼″ top, 40″ w, 47″ h **3,300.00**

Louis XV Style, lingerie, marble top, gilt-bronze mountings, six drawers, floral inlaid dec, 18″ d, 14″ d, 48″ h **980.00**

Sheraton

Cherry

American, poplar secondary wood, four dovetailed drawers, solid ends, scalloped apron, ring-turned legs, old refinishing, pieced repairs, edge damage, replaced brasses, 38″ w, 21½″ d, 44⅜″ h **800.00**

Mahatanga Valley, old yellow and brown graining over red, pine secondary wood, molded edge top, four overlapping dovetailed drawers, paneled ends, reeded stiles, turned feet, inlaid ivory escutcheons, brasses replaced with wooden knobs, 37⅝″ × 19¼″ top, 36″ w, 36½″ h **1,155.00**

Bird's-eye maple, American, c1825, four drawers, swell front, graduated wide cock-beaded drawers, half-round columnar corners, short turned feet, panel sides, 41½″ w **2,500.00**

Walnut

Ohio, c1820–30, white pine secondary wood, four graduated drawers, scratch bead and inlaid diamond escutcheon, double-line inlay on stiles and on border of top board, 41½″ w, 20″ d, 46¾″ h **1,540.00**

Poplar secondary wood, four dovetailed drawers with cock-beading, inlaid serpentine vine with flowers in an elongated panel bordered by stringing on stiles, stringing on front, paneled ends, turned feet, two inlaid escutcheons missing, hardware replaced with glass knobs, old finishing, 39½″ w, 18¼″ w, 40¾″ h **2,035.00**

Virginia, c1810, serpentine, walnut veneers, pine and poplar secondary wood, four drawers, inlaid, broken front, period brasses stamped ''H. J.,'' refinished, feet professionally restored, 38″ w, 22½″ d, 40½″ h **4,820.00**

Sheraton Style, mid-19th C, mahogany, inlaid, bowfront, four banded drawers, circular mahogany pulls, flanked by ring-turned round reeded column supports, 46″ w, 23½″ d, 40¾″ h **2,500.00**

Victorian, American, rosewood, ivory inlaid, rect top, four short and four long drawers, free standing reeded columns, inlaid base, turned feet, restoration on lower left base molding, 51½″ w, 20¼″ d, 45″ h ...**5,775.00**

William and Mary, PA, 1720–40, walnut, rect top, applied cove molding, two short drawers over three graduated long drawers, molded base, compressed ball-turned feet, 39⅝″ w, 21¾″ d, 40″ h **38,500.00**

Chests of Drawers, Other

Apothecary

Chestnut, pine side panels, top lift compartment, 7 drawers, Rockingham pulls, short turned feet, 17¼″ w, 8″ d, 27½″ h **615.00**

Pine, applied lid edge and base moldings, nine dovetail drawers with turned pulls, turned feet, worn refinishing, stains, minor repairs, 19¾″ w, 10½″ d, 23¾″ h **1,155.00**

Chest on Chest, Georgian, 18th C, mahogany, flat bonnet top, five graduated drawers over three fitted drawers, bracket feet, 45″h, 23″ d, 70″ h **2,865.00**

Chest on Frame

Chippendale, CT, curly maple, dovetailed case,

molded cornice, eight overlapping dovetailed drawers, scalloped drop and chip carving, ogee feet, old worn refinishing, replaced brasses, 40¼″ w, 20½″ d, 81″ h **15,000.00**

George I, walnut, projecting oblong molded top, conforming recessed case, two frieze and two full crossbanded drawers, molded and scalloped base, cabriole legs, pad feet, 44″ w, 20½″ d, 42″ h **4,200.00**

Chest on chest, Chippendale, maple, claw and ball feet, apron with center-carved fan pendant, 78″ h, 40½″ w, 19½″ d, $4,400.00. Photograph courtesy of William Doyle Galleries.

Queen Anne, c1760, walnut, flat molded cornice, straight front, 3 small over 5 wide graduated thumb-molded drawers, brass bail handles and lock plates, flanked by quarter-reeded columnar sides, lower section with shaped apron cabriole legs, trifid feet, 43″ w, 22½″ d, 69¾″ h **8,500.00**

William and Mary, PA, 1730–60, walnut, rect lift top, deep compartment, case with two horizontal fielded panels over two thumb-molded short drawers, inverted baluster-turned legs, ball-turned feet joined by molded box stretcher, 48⅞″ w, 24¾″ d, 40½″ h **5,500.00**

Commode

Biedermeier, figured maple veneer on poplar, galleried top, three dovetailed drawers, rounded corners, turned feet, age cracks, some veneer and edge damage, 29¼″ w, 16½″ d, 32½″ h **495.00**

Eastlake, walnut, three drawers, single door, marble top, backsplash missing, 30¼″ w, 14″ d, 27¾″ h **330.00**

French Empire, 19th C, walnut, ormolu, straight front, 4 drawers, circular bronze pulls, block feet, 49″ w, 20½″ d, 33½″ h **850.00**

Italian Rococo, mid-18th C, gilt-bronze-mounted walnut and parquetry, shaped top over four drawers, 49″ w, 23½″ d, 35½″ h **12,650.00**

Japanned, Continental, early 18th C, red lacquer, rect-shaped top, two drawers, gilt bird and blossom dec, scalloped apron, modified cabriole legs, hoof-form feet, 40″ w, 21½″ d, 35¼″ h **12,000.00**

Louis XV Style, 19th C, serpentine-lip-molded variegated marble top, bombe case, two graduated wide conforming drawers, curved legs, rich ormolu mountings and pulls, veneer losses, 48″ w **1,500.00**

Regency Style, bombe shape, parquetry kingwood, ormolu, marble top, 51″ w, 25″ d, 32½″ h **4,500.00**

Venetian, 18th/19th C, painted, rect top, molded edge, rounded corners, three incised carved wide drawers with bronze busts, shaped apron, short scroll feet, floral ivory drawer faces, raised side panels with flowers and birds, 52″ w **5,500.00**

Dresser, Welsh, oak, rect top, straight front, small drawer and single-panel door flanked by six graduated thumb-molded drawers, brass bail handles, escutcheons, and lock plates, quarter-reeded column sides, bracket feet, mid-18th C, 76½″ w, 22″ d, 36½″ h ...**4,400.00**

Étagère

Classical, New England, early 19th C, birch, orig translucent red stain, minor imperfections, 18″ w, 13¼″ d, 60½″ h **2,300.00**

Majorelle, mahogany, top with carved leaf dec over open shelf, two drawers below, single glazed panel, one panel with inlaid dec, 27″ w, 13″ d, 57″ h **6,100.00**

Highboy

Chippendale, Philadelphia, walnut, swan neck cresting with flower-head terminals, carved shell and foliate scroll, fluted quarter columns, scroll-carved apron, acanthus-carved cabriole legs, claw and ball feet, 44″ w, 95″ h **6,500.00**

Queen Anne

American, maple, flat top, six short and five long drawers, fan-carved upper and lower drawer, shaped apron, cabriole legs with duck feet, refinished, replaced hardware, 32″ w, 20¼″ d, 73½″ h **14,500.00**

Salem, MA, c1750, carved mahogany, bonnet top, swan neck pediment centering urn and spiral cartouche, center shell-carved drawers, flanked by two small drawers, four graduated wide cock-beaded drawers, brass bail handles, escutcheons, and lock plates; lower section: one wide over shell-carved center drawer, flanked by 2 small drawers, cabriole legs, pad-and-disc feet, restorations, orig hardware, 21¼″ w, 41¼″ d, 84″ h **18,000.00**

Massachusetts, c1760, maple, flat top with cornice, two small drawers over four graduated drawers over five drawer base, valanced concave carved skirt with two acorn drop pendants, cabriole legs, old refinish, replaced brasses, 37″ w, 21″ d, 73″ h **9,200.00**

New England, cherry, flat top, replaced molding on top, replaced hardware **4,000.00**

William and Mary, Philadelphia, 1715–30, stained cedar, two sections, upper: elaborate molded cornice, bolection-molded frieze drawer over case of three short drawers, three graduated long drawers, double bead-molded dividers, lower: mid-molding over short central drawer flanked by two short deep drawers, ogival arched apron, short baluster and ring-turned legs, molded arched stretcher, 42″ w, 23″ d, 67¼″ h **54,000.00**

Linen Press, Chippendale, two pc

Canadian, pine, old reddish brown flame graining, upper: molded cornice, double doors, decorative scrolled panels, lower: five dovetailed drawers, paneled ends, bracket feet, wear and edge damage, 21 × 53¼″ cornice, 49½″ w, 75¼″ h **2,750.00**

Eastern VA, late 18th C, mahogany, poplar secondary wood, upper: applied molded cornice over two paneled doors opening to reveal six graduated pullout shelves; lower: applied molded frieze over two short drawers over two long drawers with cock-beading, ogee bracket feet, orig finial and brasses, 49″ w, 19½″ d, 84″ h **11,000.00**

Low Boy

Chippendale, PA, c1765, carved and inlaid walnut, oblong quarter-veneered top, notched corners, four molded drawers, fluted quarter columns, volute and shell-carved skirt, shell-carved cabriole legs, ball and claw feet, restorations, stamped "J. Hooten" on underside of center drawer, 33¾″ w, 21¾″ d, 28″ h **17,500.00**

Chippendale Style, tiger maple and bird's-eye maple, claw and ball feet **1,100.00**

Queen Anne

American, walnut, satinwood inlay, rect molded edge top, three drawers, scalloped apron, round tapered legs, pad feet, 32″ w, 19½″ d, 28¾″ h **2,500.00**

Connecticut, cherry, thumb-molded top, three dovetailed overlapping drawers, scalloped apron, slender cabriole legs, duck feet and pads, pine secondary wood, old finish, professionally restored feet, knee returns and apron drops missing, replaced brasses, age cracks, 33½″ w, 20½″ d, 29½″ h **2,200.00**

Massachusetts, 1720–50, walnut, rect top, molded edge, three drawers with molded surrounds, shaped beaded skit hung with turned pendants, circular tapering legs, pad feet, 33¾″ w, 20½″ d, 30″ h **6,200.00**

Queen Anne Style, walnut, carved shell in skirt, drake feet **1,450.00**

Sugar Chest

Kentucky, c1830–40, cherry, poplar, and white pine secondary woods, two pc, upper: two-board top, applied molded edge; lower: one drawer, turned legs, minor repair, refinished, 29½″ w, 17¾″ d, 34″ h **3,860.00**

Missouri, walnut, dovetailed case, two boards on

each side, turned feet, two-section int., refinished, replaced feet, lid and baffle, 31½″ w, 19″ d, 30¼″ h **990.00**

Tall, Chippendale

Maryland or Virginia, late 18th C, walnut, poplar secondary wood, applied molded cornice, three over two over four graduated molded drawers, brass escutcheons, brass pulls stamped "H. J.," chamfered and fluted quarter columns, ogee feet on wafers, refinished, minor repairs, 43″ w, 21″ d, 65″ h **8,800.00**

Pennsylvania

Cherry, c1800, poplar secondary wood, applied top molding, two short over five graduated molded line-inlaid drawers, squiggle inlay across top and down stiles, chamfered and fluted quarter columns, scalloped bracket feet, orig hardware, one-board sides, two horizontal boards on back, orig finish and brasses, 41½″ w, 21″ d, 58½″ h **6,600.00**

Walnut, c1765, flat coved top, three small and five graduated wide-lip molded drawers, straight bracket feet, 39″ w, 61″ h **2,800.00**

Wardrobe

Country, variegated marble top, double curved doors, serpentine front, seven drawers, scroll feet, gilt metal mounts, 36″ w, 48″ h **325.00**

Flemish, 19th C, oak, bonnet flanked by lion's masks, single door, carved panels of fan, floral, and male masks, 47″ w, 22″ d, 81″ h **635.00**

Missouri, walnut, pine secondary wood, molded cornice, paneled door, one-board ends, flat pilasters with carved pine capitals, sq cutouts in top, 20 × 36½″ cornice, 33¼″ w, 63″ h **1,200.00**

Cradles

Chippendale, birch, canted sides, scalloped headboard, turned posts and rails, refinished, 37½″ l **400.00**

Country

Curly Maple, fiddleback, figured cherry panels, sq posts, turned finials, mortised and pinned rails, cutout designs in rails, oak rockers, 38¼″ l **300.00**

Grain Painted, New England, early 19th C, pine, yellow-ochre and burnt amber painting simulating tiger maple, 37½″ w, 19¼″ d, 25½″ h **400.00**

Poplar, old worn green paint, dovetailed, shaped rockers and scalloped ends with heart cutouts, wear and edge damage, 39″ l **350.00**

Victorian, walnut, sausage-turned spindles **350.00**

Windsor, New England, c1800, bamboo-turned spindles, worn orig finish **850.00**

Cupboards

Armoire

Dutch, 18th C, green, Chinoiserie dec, 45″ w, 24″ d, 72¼″ h **4,312.00**

French Provincial, fruitwood, flat top, incised carved rosette, two double recessed panel doors, scroll feet, 18th/19th C, 47½″ w, 67¼″ h **2,000.00**

Victorian, c1880

Rosewood, dome bonnet, applied carved scroll and shell dec, double paneled doors with applied scroll dec, two doors below, 56" w, 20" d, 101" h **2,185.00**

Walnut and ebonized, step-molded cornice, rect single mirrored door flanked by two Ionic columns, lower portion with recessed rib support on platform fitted with single drawer and molded base, 54½" w, 23" d, 91" h **2,300.00**

Chiffonier, Anglo-Indian, 19th C, rosewood, heavily carved floral and bird dec, upper section with two mirrored doors, lower section with two openwork carved doors, animal-claw feet, 46" w, 15" d, 63" h **1,380.00**

Corner

Centennial, carved walnut, concave pine int. shell, fluted pilasters, three shaped shelves over single double-arched paneled door, molded base, 19th C, 49" w, 19" d, 95" h **4,900.00**

Chippendale, Giles Co, VA, early 19th C, walnut, yellow pine and poplar secondary woods, one pc, applied dentiled cornice, two doors with three raised panels each, applied molded frieze over two raised paneled doors, canted corners, bracket feet, replaced hinges, refinished, minor repairs, 46" w, 27" d, 91" h **3,300.00**

Country

Cherry

American, c1800, molded cornice, two glazed doors each with eight panes, three drawers, two paneled cupboard doors, bracket feet, 54" w, 86½" h **1,200.00**

Molded cornice, paneled doors, scalloped apron, cutout feet, old mellow refinishing, 54½" w at cornice, 85½" h, minor edge damage, small pieced repair to cornice ... **2,750.00**

Curly Maple, one pc, coved cornice, two paneled doors, replaced bracket feet, refinished, cut down from base, 47" w, 77" h **2,900.00**

Curly Maple and Walnut, two pc, top: coved cornice, double doors each with eight panes of glass; base: paneled doors, two dovetailed drawers, cutout feet, old worn finish, minor edge damage, 47¼" w, 88¾" h **4,510.00**

Decorated, Frederick, MD, c1825, red and black grained-paint dec, poplar, two pc, upper: applied molded cornice over two arched doors with ten lights each; lower: applied molded frieze over two paneled doors, scalloped bracket feet, canted corners, later int. paint, 53" w, 23" d, 94" h **8,250.00**

Federal, cherry, two part, later swan-neck pediment, twin glazed lattice doors, three open shelves; lower: single drawer flanked by two mock drawers over twin panel doors, circular brass pulls, straight bracket feet, c1800, 52" w, 26" d, 94" h **3,800.00**

Court, Jacobean, carved oak, straight front, leaf-and-vine-carved cornice over single wide leaf-carved panel flanked by conforming twin panel doors over single wide leaf-carved drawers, ring-turned ribbed-and-block column supports, box-form stretcher, 17th C, 28" w, 20" d, 54" h **2,000.00**

Hanging, country

Cupboard, Federal, 2nd quarter 19th C, pine, projecting molded cornice, scalloped and floral carved frieze, single raised-panel cupboard door, H-form hinges, 58" w, 18½" d, 83" h, $1,210.00. Photograph courtesy of Leslie Hindman Auctioneers.

Cherry, pine secondary wood, dovetailed case, molded frame door with glass, molded cornice, 7¼ × 14¾" cornice, 13" w, 24¼" h **475.00**

Corner, pine cleaned down to old red, color enhanced with orange-red stain, applied cornice and base moldings, reeded chamfered corners, three drawers, paneled door set in beaded frame, 28½" h, 30¼" d at cornice, 46" h, moldings replaced . **1,540.00**

Decorated

Pine and poplar, old red paint, dovetailed case, molded cornice, one-board door, 11½ × 16½" cornice, 15¼" w, 24" h **495.00**

Pine

Old red grained repaint, blue int., singled glazed door with arched top, 17 × 7" cornice, 15¼" w, 21¾" h **495.00**

Old worn green sponged repaint, reddish brown trim, dovetailed case, applied moldings, one drawer, paneled door, pintle hinges, reeded diamond design in raised panel, "H.H.S. 1821" on door, 23 × 10½" cornice, 20¾" w, 30" h, drawer replaced . **425.00**

Worn dark green repaint, black and red compass star in diamond on door panel, dovetailed case, applied moldings, chamfered corners, removable door on pintle hinges, lock and key with diamond escutcheon, some edge damage, worm holes, 15¾ × 7½" cornice, 14½", 18" h   **385.00**

Pine and poplar, molded cornice, door with four panes of glass set in reeded frame, old iron thumb latch, brass knob, old finish, 34¼ × 13½" cornice, 29¾" w, 35" h   **770.00**

Walnut, cherry, and poplar, dovetailed case, paneled door, three int. shelves, molded cornice, added screen-door latch, made by William Kail, Tuscarawas County, OH, gunmaker, 27 × 11½" cornice, 25" w, 36" h   **330.00**

Hutch, Federal, pine, flat molded cornice over two open shelves, set back on rect top; lower: fitted straight-front twin drawers, circular brass pulls over twin paneled doors, straight bracket feet, 19th C, 42¼" w, 18¼" d, 76½" h   **800.00**

Jelly, country

Cherry, two drawers over two doors, raised panels, porcelain knobs, 41"w, 20½" d, 44" h   **750.00**

Walnut, dovetailed gallery, pair paneled doors, one dovetailed drawer, one-board ends, cutout feet, refinished, 40½" w, 17¾" d, 55½" h   **990.00**

Pewter

Canadian, pine, light blue and red repaint, open top with slightly bowed shelves, applied reeded molding cornice with fretwork frieze, open base with beaded frame, three drawers, 11¾ × 56¾" cornice, 51" w, 71" h, one drawer replaced, replaced bottom shelf and backboards   **2,200.00**

Primitive, walnut, step-back top, three shelves, one-board ends, paneled base doors, cutout feet, old worn finish, some repairs, age cracks, edge damage, 46" w, 16½" d, 79¼" h   **2,200.00**

Pie Safe

Hanging, late 19th C, green paint, single door, sides, and back with tin-punched Masonic symbols, 36" w, 21" d, 36" h   **1,430.00**

Ohio, c1860, poplar and white pine, light brown paint dec, two drawers over two paneled doors, two circular vents on each side, 38½" w, 15½" d, 54½" h   **365.00**

North Carolina, eastern, mid-19th C, yellow pine, red wash, three-board tongue-and-groove top, two doors with two tins each, tin motif of central compass with star in each corner, each side with two tins, some worm damage, dry scraped, 52" w, 22½" d, 65" h   **700.00**

Virginia, Wythe County, attributed to Rich Brothers shop, c1830–40, poplar, one-board top, two dovetailed drawers, two doors, punched tin panels with urn and tulip, hearts and stars, side tins with repeating motif, turned leg, 50¼" w, 18½" d, 54" h   **4,400.00**

Step Back

Decorated, Rupp family, Hanover, PA, c1850, step back, poplar and white pine, old varnish, mustard paint dec on applied upper and lower half turned columns and two drawer fronts, two doors with six glazed panes each, int. with three shelves and spoon notches, pie shelf over two paneled doors, turned feet, 52" w, 22½" d, 87" h   **9,350.00**

Country

Pine, one pc, coved cornice, dovetailed case, scalloped apron, paneled doors, double doors in top, single door in base, high pie shelf, cutout feet, old mellow refinishing, 41½ × 12½" cornice, 28¼" w, 81½" h   **2,860.00**

Walnut

Old blue paint, one pc, molded cornice, open top shelf, paneled door, some edge damage, right side boards old replacements, 25" w, 19¾" d, 75" h   **925.00**

Pennsylvania or Ohio, c1840, walnut, poplar, and hardwood secondary woods, two pc, upper: applied molded cornice, two doors with eight glazed panes each, flanked by chamfered corners with lambs tongue; lower: pie shelf, two-board top, three drawers over two paneled doors, paneled sides, turned feet, 52" w, 20" d, 93½" h   **3,850.00**

Sheraton, cherry, beveled 41 × 15¼" cornice, paneled doors, one dovetailed drawer with cock-beading, high turned feet, poplar secondary wood, refinished, 37¼" w, 89¼" h   **3,300.00**

Wall

Country

Pine, old brown graining, primitive, made from waist section of tall-case clock, 17 × 9¼" cornice, 14" w, 43½" h   **250.00**

Walnut, pine secondary wood, two pc, dovetailed cases, top: paneled doors set in beaded frames; base: two dovetailed drawers over two paneled doors with cock-beading, some edge damage, replaced hardware, old refinishing, 47½" w, 17½" d, 80½" h   **1,100.00**

Empire, married two pc, mahogany flame-grain veneer, beaded molding, scrolled feet and pilasters, six dovetailed drawers, double doors with gothic tracery, molded 44 × 14" cornice, old worn finish, some wear, veneer damage, 39½" w, 93½" h   **500.00**

Water Bench, pine, old red repaint, headboard back, open shelf, one-board ends, cutout feet, paneled doors, cast-iron thumb latches, porcelain knobs, 42" w, 16½" d, 51½" h   **1,900.00**

Wine, cellarette

Flemish, 19th C, lion, male and female masks, upper section with single glazed door, lower section with single drawer over door with carved shell dec, 34" w, 21" d, 91" h   **1,300.00**

Sheraton, American, c1825, walnut, white pine secondary wood, two-board top, applied edge, three compartments int., turned legs, old varnish finish, 17¾" w, 16½" d, 27¾" h   **3,960.00**

Desks

Arts and Crafts, American

Stickley, Gustav, Model No. 729, drop front, gallery over lid, two half drawers, three lower long drawers, paper label, int. crack, some veneer chips, 36½" w, 15" d, 45" h   **2,950.00**

Wright, Frank Lloyd and George M Niedecken, for Henry J Allen House, Wichita, KS, 1917, walnut, bank of four drawers to right, one long drawer over

Desk, lady's, New England, 1825–35, mahogany veneer, interior compartments, foldout writing surface, four drawers, turned feet, some old brass, refinished, repairs, 40¼" w, 20" d, 55½" h, $1,210.00. Photograph courtesy of Skinner, Inc.

kneehole, sq pulls, rail and stile construction on sides and back, straight legs with slightly turned-out foot, matching 36" h chair, 42" w, 24" d, 32" h **17,600.00**
Centennial, Chippendale style, carved mahogany, center single wide drawer flanked by two sets of drawers, lower ones with shell carving, quarter-reeded columnar sides, cabriole legs, claw and ball feet, 59½" h, 20½" d, 30½" h **525.00**
Chinese Export, mid-19th C, lap, black lacquer, fitted int., lidded wells, Chinese figures in pavilions and foliate borders dec, 15½" w, 12½" d **575.00**
Chippendale
  American
    Maple with some curl, pine secondary wood, dovetailed case, four overlapping drawers, hinged top with fitted int. of seven dovetailed drawers and pigeonholes with scalloped valances, bracket feet, old mellow refinishing, replaced brasses, 36" w, 19¼" d, 30½" writing height, 40½" h **5,500.00**
    Walnut, pine and poplar secondary woods, dovetailed case, four overlapping dovetailed drawers, fold-down molded-edge lid, fitted int. with twelve drawers, pigeonholes, and center door, replaced ogee feet, refinished, replaced brasses, 40" w, 21" d, 42¼" h **1,320.00**
  Connecticut River Valley, late 18th C, cherry, carved slant front, old refinish, replaced brasses, minor imperfections, 36½" w, 20" d, 46" h **9,200.00**
  Pennsylvania
    c1745, figured walnut, slant front, dovetailed case, fitted int., descended through family of James Hamilton, mayor of Philadelphia and governor of PA in 1752 ....**29,900.00**

c1779, attributed to Charles Combrooks, figured walnut, slant front, dovetailed case, fluted quarter columns, four overlapping dovetailed drawers, fitted int. with six dovetailed drawers, pigeonholes, two pullout letter files, center door conceals three int. drawers and secret compartment, ogee feet, back sgd in chalk, old repairs, replaced brasses, orig finish, 40" w, 22" d, 44" h, 32¾" writing height **4,300.00**
c1780, walnut, slant front, fitted int., straight front fitted with four graduated thumb-molded drawers, brass bail handles, escutcheons, lock plates **4,300.00**
Salem, MA, c1760, mahogany and mahogany veneer, white pine secondary wood, three fans int. with pigeonholes and drawers, four graduated cock-beaded drawers, pierced and scalloped center drop, scalloped bracket feet, orig period brasses, 40½" w, 21" d, 43¼" h **13,200.00**
Empire, early 19th C, bonheur-du-jour, mahogany, 27" w, 19½" d, 63¾" h **1,100.00**
Empire Style, second half 19th C, bonheur-du-jour, mahogany, ormolu mounts, 28¼" w, 15¾" d, 50¼" h .**1,850.00**
Federal
  Massachusetts, c1810, mahogany inlaid, tambour front, two drawers, reeded tapering legs, refinished, replaced brasses, minor imperfections, restoration, 37¾" w, 23¼" d, 41¾" h **3,680.00**
  Massachusetts or New Hampshire, c1820, mahogany, bird's-eye maple, wavy birch, setback top with center bird's-eye maple door flanked by two smaller mahogany doors over three bird's-eye drawers, foldout top, slip supports, four graduated drawers base, ring-turned feet, refinished, imperfections, 41¼" w, 20½" d, 60½" h **1,725.00**
George III
  Early 19th C, kneehole, rect top, three drawers, pedestals with three drawers each, French feet, 36¼" l, 17½" d, 31½" h **1,610.00**
  Late 18th C
    Kneehole, mahogany, restoration, 33¼" w, 20" d, 32¼" h **635.00**
    Slant front, burlwood, full fitted int., stepped drawer placement, central door, gold-tooled leather top, five drawers, bracket feet, 34" w, 20" d, 40½" h **1,000.00**
Grain Decorated, country, clerk type, pine, worn orig brown graining, slant front, two dovetailed drawers set in beaded frame, sq tapered legs, age cracks, one escutcheon missing, some edge damage, 40" w, 23¾" d, 43¼" h **625.00**
Invalid, pine, orig brown graining, cream-colored ground, slant front, mortised apron, turned legs, emb white-metal escutcheons, wear and some edge damage, 30½" w, 22½" d, 18" h **385.00**
Plantation, country, two pc, walnut, bookcase top, dovetailed case, two dovetailed drawers, double doors each with two panes of glass, molded 37¾" × 10" cornice; base: one dovetailed drawer, turned legs, old refinishing, 38" w, 21" d, 78" h **1,045.00**
Renaissance, Italian, 19th C, walnut, carved fully modeled classical figures, upper section fitted with three drawers over hinged writing surface, lower section

with two drawers over two doors, animal-paw feet, 30" w, 13" d, 64" h **5,750.00**

Rococo Style

American, John Shearer, oak, yellow pine, and walnut sapwood, slant front, three drawers, shell and quatrefoil carving, ogee, bracket feet, iron braces, tambour door, inlaid miniature portrait of King George III, slanted pulls, steep angle to fall front, int. sgd fourteen times, hidden compartment with document with reference to maker and orig owner, c1816 .... **110,000.00**

Dutch, late 19th C, lady's, mahogany and floral marquetry, slant front, five drawers, shaped legs, refinished, 27" w, 19¼" d, 37¾" h **1,495.00**

Victorian

Davenport, inlaid Pollard elm, rect top, fitted compartments above hinged slant front, two leaf-tip-carved cabriole supports backed by case fitted with four drawers opposed by four faux drawers, turned feet, wood casters, 20½" w, 21" d, 33¼" h**2,750.00**

Pedestal, mahogany, rect molded top, inset red leather writing surface, frieze fitted with three drawers over two pedestals with three graduated drawers, conforming plinth, 42½" w, 23½" d, 30" h **4,500.00**

Side by Side, oak, mirrored top, griffin supports, left side fitted with curved glass door, right side with hinged writing surface, fitted int., 3 drawers, animal-paw feet, 44" w, 15" d, 74" h **2,415.00**

Dough Troughs

Decorated, pine, one-board top, scrolled apron, splat base, turned legs, 44¾ × 25½ × 28¼" **500.00**

Maple, dovetailed, board-and-batten top, scalloped apron, rect legs, 35 × 22 × 30" **300.00**

Pine, old worn dark green repaint, one-board ends, cut-out book-jack feet, divided int., board-and-batten top, wear and edge damage, 37½" l, 16½" d, 31" h **500.00**

Poplar, old cream-colored paint, wide single-board construction, two corner chips, 30½" l **250.00**

Walnut, Louis XV, provincial, mid-18th C, oblong molded top with serpentine front, canted dough box, conforming valanced skirt carved with flowering urn, turned supports and box stretcher, 40½ × 22 × 37"**2,500.00**

Dry Sinks

Butternut, two doors, one int. shelf, orig stippling and finish, 35" w, 20" d, 42" h **650.00**

Curly Maple, rect well, work surface to right with short drawer, two poplar cupboard doors, short bracket feet, hardwood edge stripes, minor repairs, refinished, 55" w, 34½" h **2,200.00**

Grain Painted, American, mid-19th C, simulated oak graining, cupboard top with two paneled doors, hood opening over dry sink, base with four graduated drawers and two cupboard doors, cast-iron hardware, 54" w, 21½" d, 78" h **1,500.00**

Pine and Polar, old mustard yellow graining, backboard crest with vertical seam, paneled doors with orig cast-

iron latches, one dovetailed drawer, well with lift lid, turned feet, 49" w, 21½" d, 33" h **1,400.00**

Poplar, Lancaster County, PA, three paneled doors, open well and hutch top with two drawers, shelf and scalloped brackets, cutout feet, old worn orange grained repaint, replaced hardware, some edge damage, age cracks, 66" w, 19" d, 47½" h **2,585.00**

Walnut and Poplar, pr of paneled doors, one drawer, dark green paint on int. of hutch top, orig cast-iron latches with brass knobs, old finish, damage to base of feet, 52" w, 18½" d, 48" h **950.00**

Hall Benches, Hat Racks, and Hall Trees

Hall Bench, golden oak, center mirror with arched top, two pairs of four-pronged hooks, quartersawn, old finish, 35½" w, 18¾" d, 75" h **990.00**

Hall Cabinet, Italian Baroque, late 18th C, walnut, double doors, lion's-mask pulls, animal-paw feet, 31" w, 17" d, 38" h **4,025.00**

Hall Mirror, Victorian, oak, architectural-style frame, columnar sides, raised on conforming base, 40" w, 16" d, 77" h **865.00**

Hall Tree

Art Deco, French, c1925, wrought iron, rect, top set with shallow open hat shelf above octagonal mirror, shallow verde antico shelf on angled support wrought with straight bands and coils, two rect sections set with three coat hooks, outset rect umbrella stands, scrolls and imp geometric devices, 51¾" w, 75" h **12,100.00**

Cast Iron, Jack and the Beanstalk, figural, old green and gold repaint, English registry number, 33½" h **500.00**

Hat Rack, Windsor, pine, bamboo turned, six knoblike hooks, orig yellow varnish, black striping, 33¾" l .. **195.00**

Umbrella Stand, Arts and Crafts, English, oak slats, curved shell, copper repoussé insert, 22½" w, 10" d, 42½" h **865.00**

Magazine Racks

Arts and Crafts

Limbert, three tiered, overhanging top, tapering legs, two thin slats on each side, fine medium-dark orig finish, branded mark, 23" w, 14" d, 34" h **900.00**

Michigan Chair Co, c1912, paneled sides, rect top, five shelves each with six V-grooved boards, projecting pins, dark finish, 19¾" w, 11¾" d, 45½" h **700.00**

Stickley, Gustav, Toby, pedestal, sq top, applied corbels on carved flat sides, four open shelves, orig tacked leather strips, 14" w, 12¾" d, 34½" h **500.00**

George III, early 19th C, mahogany, three compartments, two graduated drawers, turned legs, casters, 20" l, 16" d, 22¼" h **1,000.00**

Regency, mahogany, five open manganese splats, ring-turned corner supports, case fitted with drawer, ring-turned tapering legs, brass caps and casters, 19¼" w, 14" d, 20" h **1,650.00**

Victorian, c1850, walnut, two handles, four compartments, pierced scrolled ends, turned supports, casters, 23" l, 19" d, 20½" h **550.00**

Lowboy, Chippendale, Delaware Valley, c1760, walnut, 33½" w, 20¾" d, 28½" h, descended in family of Richard Stockton, a signer of the Declaration of Independence, $20,900.00. Photograph courtesy of Freeman Fine Arts of Philadelphia.

Mirrors

Art Nouveau, wrought iron, octagonal, reticulated internal edge, upper part mounted by stylized fountain and floral ground, beveled edge mirror, stamped "E. Brandt" lower right corner, 43" l, 38½" w **63,500.00**

Arts and Crafts, Michigan Chair Co, Grand Rapids, MI, 1915, shaped cutouts, center rect mirror, scalloped details, orig paper label, 35½" w, 23½" h **120.00**

Chippendale

  Mahogany and gilt gesso, attributed to New England, c1790, old finish, old regilding, 17¾" w, 34" h . **460.00**

  Mahogany, scrollwork, old finish, repairs, orig glass, 17¼" h **425.00**

  Walnut, figured veneer, gilt leaves, carved floral garlands and phoenix crest, refinished, minor repairs and regilded, replaced mirror glass, backboard replaced, 24" w, 43½" h **990.00**

Chippendale Style, mahogany and gilt gesso, spread-phoenix cartouche, swan-neck pediment with rosettes, 61 × 30½" **1,050.00**

Classical, New England, c1820, over mantel, gilt gesso, center panel flanked by two smaller rect mirror plates, ring-turned swirl-carved columns, minor imperfections, 69⅜" w, 29⅜" h **1,100.00**

Eastlake, pier

  Walnut

    Burl veneer, carved detail highlighted with worn gilding, shaped marble shelf over conforming paneled base, old finish, 29¼" w, 13" d, 94" h **825.00**

    Carved detail, gilt highlights, marble shelf, carved cone-shaped legs, 32" w, 12" d, 93½" h **1,100.00**

Empire

  Architectural

    Gilt gesso on wood, acorn cornice, acanthus and floral designs with lion's head in frieze, orig eglomise reverse-glass painting of rural landscape in gold and black, blue sky, replaced mirror, sky flaking, minor touch-ups, 25" w, 46" h **425.00**

    Wood, turned pilasters, corner blocks in orig red

and white striping, black corner blocks with brass rosettes, gilt detail, reverse-glass painting of buildings and tree, minor wear, 13¾" w, 29½" h **500.00**

Shaving, bird's-eye and mahogany veneer, pine secondary wood, ogee facade, three conforming dovetailed drawers, adjustable mirror, turned feet, veneer damage, one back foot replaced, 22¼" w, 8" d, 23" h **365.00**

Two part, frame with half turnings, corner blocks with gold repaint, orig reverse-glass painting with fruit, wear and touch up, repaired corner break, 34" h, 15½" w **355.00**

Federal

  Dressing Glass, MA or NH, c1810, painted cream, red outline, gray pinstriping, top and painted foliate device in mustard brown and red, drawer with polychrome floral design, 17¾" w, 10" d, 19¼" h **1,100.00**

  Mahogany, two part

    Reeded columns, turned trim, applied foliage design in frieze, reeded cornice with acorn drops, old finish, replaced reverse-painted top glass with farmhouse scene, 16" w, 33" h **200.00**

    Rope-carved pilasters, turned and reeded detail, acorn drop cornice, orig reverse-glass painting of yellow house, wear and flaking to reverse-glass panel, 13¼" w, 21½" h **220.00**

French, pier, gilt frame, cameo-style top, draping flowers, mirror with beaded border, 43" w, 75" h **1,035.00**

George III Style, late 19th C, giltwood

  Asymmetrical frame, cresting, fox beneath fruiting arbor, sides cov with C-scrolls, vines, and columns, in the manner of John Linnell, restoration, 30" w, 55" h **2,185.00**

  Rect mirror plate surmounted by urn, scroll, and drapery, 47½" h **435.00**

  Shaped mirror plate, carved C-scrolls and foliage, 43½ × 22" **460.00**

Georgian Style, cheval, double sided, carved shell and bellflower crest flanked by finials, columnar-style supports, animal-paw feet, 38" w, 72" h **1,840.00**

Louis XVI Style, carved gilt and gesso, wall, bird, floral, torch, and arrow cartouche, 41¼" w, 68" h **825.00**

Neoclassical, Danish, late 18th/19th C, mahogany, part ebonized, parcel gilt, eglomise panel, 35¼" h **1,380.00**

Queen Anne, shaped walnut frame, solid-oak back panels, outer bands of cobalt blue beveled glass divided from main looking glass by narrow walnut frames conforming to main frame, accompanied by 1922 receipt "confirms mirrors originally formed part of the collection of the Earl of Ranfurley, Northland House, Dungannon, Ireland" 16" w, 39" h, price for matched pr **17,600.00**

Rococo Style, Italian, painted blue and cream, shaped mirror plate and frame, two candle branches, 24" h **115.00**

Sheraton, Newburyport, MA, c1808, architectural, gilt frame, reverse painting of eagle holding American shield, banner, and arrows in gold, white, and Union blue background, over mirror, minor flaking, small corner break to mirror, label reads "Barnard Cermentati," 18¼" w, 37½" h **1,100.00**

Mirror, Salem, MA, 1809–10, gilt-wood, molded cornice with outset corners, leaf molding frieze, white eglomise panel with gilt classical figures, surface imperfections, 20¼" w, 38½" h, $1,450.00. Photograph courtesy of Skinner, Inc.

Victorian
Cheval, birch, mahogany finish, cast iron and glass, ball and claw feet, turned-and-rope-carved detailed, wear to silvering on beveled glass, 78½" h ... 550.00
Hanging, comb case, towel bar, pegs, match holders, sanded match strikes, walnut, old finish, age crack in crest, mirror replaced, 24" h 220.00

Rockers

Arrow Back, orig ink graining, scrolled arms, widely splayed back 300.00
Art Deco, Louis Sognot, c1930, chromed metal, upholstered seat and back, 38" h 1,250.00
Arts and Crafts
Harden, oversized, five slats under rounded arms, drop-in spring seat, loose back seat, arched front apron, orig dark finish, old Naugahyde, 31" w, 31" d, 38" h 950.00
Limbert, five spats under flat arms, five vertical back slats, arched crest rail, drop-in spring seat, orig medium finish, 29" w, 27" d, 35" h 1,300.00
Morris, Model No. 413, oak, four horizontal slat back, poor condition, branded "L. & J. G. Stickley," 29" w, 34½" d, 36" h 975.00
Decorated, attributed to NY state, c1825, crest rail painted with red flowers, light green ground, arrow-form uprights, shaped arms and turned legs, plank seat 2,100.00
Ladder Back
Arm, country, maple, shaped arms, four slats, turned finials, turned front rung and arm posts, old refinishing, replaced woven splint seat, minor age cracks, 43" h 320.00
Half arms, four-slat back, turned finial, old soft refinishing, replaced paper rush seat, rockers worn flat, found in PA, 44¼" h 75.00
Sewing, arrow back, orig green paint, black striping, white, red, yellow, and black floral dec crest, wear, 31" h 85.00
Shaker, bar-form crest rail, triple horizontal back splat,

rush seat cylindrical supports, double box stretcher, Mt Lebanon trademark and stencil inside rocker blade 300.00
Victorian, quartersawn oak, hand-carved back, upholstered spring seat, French legs 275.00
Windsor
Bow Back, saddle seat, seven-spindle back, old finish, repairs 300.00
Comb Back, arrow slats, black repaint, gold striping, painted holly crest 295.00

Secretaries

Art Deco, Rene Drouet, c1925, parchment, fall front, oval top with inset door, leather-lined writing surface, lighted, shelved int. with two short drawers over single cupboard door, inset oval base, two ivory-mounted escutcheons, 29¼" w, 49½" h 8,500.00
Biedermeier, first quarter 19th C, sécretaire à abattant, mahogany
Closed cupboard doors over fall front over three drawers, 42" w, 19½" d, 82" h 2,300.00
Ormolu mounts, gray marble top, fall front over three drawers, 39¾" w, 19¾" d, 58¾" h 3,910.00
Chippendale, two pc
American, cherry, pine and walnut secondary woods, top: bookcase with paneled doors, adjustable shelves, molded cornice, base: slant front with fitted int. of pigeonholes and seven drawers, four dovetailed drawers with cock-beading, dovetailed bracket feet, refinished, replaced brasses, 13 × 41½" cornice, 39¾" w, 31" writing height, 80" h, pieced repairs, replaced feet 3,575.00
Massachusetts, walnut, pine secondary wood, banded inlay, dovetailed case, top: pullout candle shelves, double doors with raised arched panels, broken arch pediment with urn-and-flame finial, int. with four dovetailed drawers and shelves with pigeonholes and removable partitions, one drawer sgd in ink "Chloe Dunbar;" base: slant-front lid with fitted int. of eight dovetailed drawers, pigeonholes, two letter files with half columns, center door with one drawer and secret drawer, four dovetailed overlapping drawers, bracket feet, orig brasses, old finish, minor repairs, age cracks, finial replaced, 38" w, 21½" d, 31" writing height, 93" to top of finial 17,600.00
Country, two pc
Cherry, Zoar, OH, 1830–40, white pine secondary wood, two upper panel doors, divided compartment int., table base with single drop leaf and single dovetailed drawer, turned legs, 30¾" w, 18" d, 36½" h 1,100.00
Pine and poplar, worn blue repair on ext., int. with old brown comb graining, top doors have tree panels and oval landscape painted in style of Rufus Porter, black, green, blue, and yellow on white ground, top: molded cornice, shelves and letter files; base: slant front, fitted int. with four pigeonholes, three dovetailed drawers, scalloped bracket feet, 13½ × 35¼" cornice, 20 × 41½" desk, 85¾" h, top and base close fitting mismatch, repairs, lid and feet replaced 3,960.00

Poplar, old brownish red paint, bookcase top with double doors each with two panes of old glass, geometric fake mullions, molded cornice, lower: three overlapping dovetailed drawers, slant-front lid, fitted int. with seven dovetailed drawers, dec cutout on center drawer, cutout feet, scrolled apron, solid ends, orig hardware, 37" w, 22½" × 38" base, 14 x 41½" cornice, 81¼" h **3,520.00**

Empire, American, 1820–30

Mahogany and mahogany veneer, poplar and white pine secondary woods, two arched glazed twelve-pane doors, right door opening to reveal four drawers over four pigeonholes, left wide with shelves, front stiles carved with pineapple motif, three drawers over foldout writing surface, slide supports, three long drawers, turned feet, minor repairs, 44" w, 20" d, 69" h **1,155.00**

Mahogany, flat molded cornice over twin gothic glazed lattice doors, three open shelves and cubbyhole section over three small drawers, lower section with fall front over three drawers, brass ring pulls flanked by ring-turned columnar sides, ebonized ball feet, 47" w, 19½" d, 75¼" h **2,100.00**

Federal, American, c1800, cherry, white pine, and poplar secondary woods, two pc, upper: restored molded cornice, two paneled doors open to nine slots with three removable shelves, slant-front desk int. with four pigeonholes over two over one drawer on each side of privacy door with oval burl veneer opening to four drawers; lower: four graduated cock-beaded drawers, scalloped skirt, repaired French feet, period brasses, refinished, 39½" w, 22" d, 92" h **6,930.00**

Hepplewhite, English, two pc, mahogany, 48" w, 15" d dentiled cornice, bookcase top, double doors, geometric arrangement glass, pullout desk drawer, 8 dovetailed drawers, four pigeonholes, two letter drawers, center door in fitted int., double doors, bracket feet, old finish, some veneer repair, 45" w, 23½" d, 87" h **4,200.00**

Regency, NH, c1830, stamped "Chas Dennett" on int., cherry, mahogany veneer, white pine secondary wood, two pc, upper: doors open to two shelves, six drawers and three compartments; lower: writing surface, double lift lids, rear lid opening to reveal nine drawers, five divided compartments, two central drawers flanked by wine drawers, fully turned columns with rope twist, old finish, 38¼" w, 20½" d, 83" h **3,850.00**

Sheraton, Monroe Co, WV, c1825, walnut, yellow pine and poplar secondary woods, two pc, upper: molded cornice over pr of banded cupboard doors, dovetailed shelves, slant front, int. with central graduated drawers, four pigeonholes on each side; lower: case with slides, three graduated drawers, bracket feet, refinished, minor repairs, 37¼" w, 18" d, 85" h **2,750.00**

Victorian, walnut, figured veneer panels, upper section with two glazed doors, lower section with cylinder roll opening to two fitted-int. drawers, 47" w, 25" d, 95" h **2,875.00**

Wooton, American, 1880–84, Queen Anne pattern, walnut and maple, carved, turned, and incised three-quarter gallery, triangular carved hinged long docu-

Secretary, Victorian, burl walnut and mahogany, shaped cornice above pr of glazed cabinet doors and cylinder door enclosing writing surface over two doors, shaped base, 27" w, 22" d, 66" h, $1,000.00. Photograph courtesy of Leslie Hindman Auctioneers.

ment door, two carved and paneled bowed doors, incised carved drop front opening to fitted compartments, pigeonholes, and drawers, numerous vertical and horizontal divided compartments, four center drawers, int. of left door fitted with divided compartments, right door fitted with forty sq storage boxes, sides paneled and incised with ebonized triangles, outstretched molded, canted, and carved legs, casters, two gallery finials missing, minor damage, 42½" w, 71" h **12,000.00**

Settees

Arts and Crafts

Harden, drop-in spring seat, through-tenons

Three slats under each rounded arm, twelve slats, rounded crest rail, wear to medium finish, paper label, 80" l, 27" d, 35" h **2,900.00**

Four slats under lower, wavy arms, eleven vertical slats, straight crest rail, orig dark finish, paper label, 54" l, 24" d, 38" h **2,300.00**

Four slats under rounded arms, thirteen back slats,

straight crest rail, orig reddish brown finish, unmarked, 60" l, 23" d, 48" h **1,200.00**

Limbert, drop arm, broad vertical slats, three sq cutouts on back, one sq cutout under each arm, alternating with plain and sq cutout slats on back, webbed seat, orig dark finish, branded mark, 68" l, 26" d, 40½" h **4,250.00**

Stickley, Gustav, Model No. 208, c1905, straight rail over nine back slats, caned seat frame, 79¾" l, 31½" d, 28¾" h **9,250.00**

Chair back, Continental, early 19th C, three-lyre back, cane seat, 62" l **1,265.00**

Charles II Style, 18th C, walnut, carved and parcel gilt, shaped back with finial corners, turned shaped legs, stretcher, Flemish-tapestry upholstery, 64" l **2,500.00**

Chinese Export, early 19th C, carved hardwood, shaped crest with carved center shell, scrolled lotus-petal-carved arms, molded seat rail with acanthus-carved reserves, scrolled volute-carved and ring-turned feet, minor repairs to arms, 91" l **12,000.00**

Empire, American, carved mahogany, ivory-damask upholstery, 56" l **750.00**

Federal, North Shore, MA, 1800–15, inlaid mahogany, gently arched upholstered back, flanked by molded sloping arms, reeded baluster-turned supports, upholstered seat, turned and reeded tapering legs, headed by inlaid rect panels outlined with patterned stringing, old break with patterned stringing, old break and repair to one leg at frame junction, 71" w, 26" d, 35¼" h **16,500.00**

Settee, Louis XVI style, giltwood, 3rd quarter 19th C, acanthus carved crest, Aubusson tapestry, turned fluted legs, rosette carved knees, 51" l, $5,000.00. Photograph courtesy of Leslie Hindman Auctioneers.

Neoclassical, Italian, late 18th C, chair back, four pierced oval chair backs, carved flower heads, scrolling open arms, padded seat, carved drapery on apron, paterae on baluster-turned leaf-tip-carved legs, celadon cotton upholstery, restorations, 74" l **3,500.00**

Painted and Stenciled, American, c1825, half-spindle back, shaped crest rail, stenciled fruit, floral horizontal splat and seat, turned legs, stretchers, 71½" l . . .**1,000.00**

Sheraton, c1835, pine, half-spindle back, flat crest rail, turned legs and stretcher, 72" l **175.00**

Victorian, carved walnut frame, tufted gold floral-print upholstery, 67" l **865.00**

Windsor, mixed wood, open arm, straight crest rail, bamboo-turned spindle back, plank seat, seven shaped splayed legs, stretcher, 19th C, 73½" l **1,800.00**

Sideboards

Art Moderne, mahogany, two doors, floral-carved relief panels, center drawer, shelf below, 62" w, 22" d, 40" h **2,500.00**

Arts and Crafts, Stickley Bros No. 8507, plate rack, four rounded posts, three small drawers flanked by two paneled doors, over long linen drawer, new medium-dark finish, metal tag, 54" l, 23" d, 45" h **3,600.00**

Baroque, Italian, late 18th C, walnut, five drawers over double doors over carved panels, 57" w, 20" d, 41" h, restorations **3,175.00**

Classical, MA, c1800, mahogany and mahogany veneer, shaped top with outset corners, two long center drawers flanked by small doors over two cupboard doors flanked by two small drawers, carved capitals above fluted columns, old refinish, old brasses, imperfections, 47½" w, 22¼" d, 42" h **4,370.00**

Country

Georgia, c1820, walnut, yellow pine secondary wood, two-board top, three drawers, central raised panel door flanked by two large drawers, six sq tapered legs, 48½" l, 20"d, 43" h **7,100.00**

Kentucky

c1820, walnut, yellow pine secondary wood, two-board top, three center drawers flanked by one drawer over pair of cupboard doors, scalloped skirt, orig paper label in drawer reads " Will R Lake, Georgetown, KY," 59½" l, 21" d, 36½" h**3,850.00**

c1830, cherry, poplar secondary woods, three drawers over four doors, turned feet, orig pulls, refinished, 73" l, 20½" d, 45" h **3,100.00**

Federal

Mid-Atlantic States

c1780, mahogany and satinwood inlays, white pine secondary wood, block front, two-board top, two central drawers, lower with inlaid conch shell, flanked on each side by single large drawer, six reeded and turned tapered legs, ivory escutcheons, replaced brasses, old refinish, 72½" l, 23¾" d, 38" h **10,450.00**

c1790, mahogany and mahogany veneer, small center drawer over pr of recessed cupboard doors, flanked by pr of cupboard doors, sq tapered legs with bellflower inlay, kite-shaped escutcheons, restoration, 55⅕" w, 25½" d, 38½" h **9,775.00**

Rhode Island, c1800, mahogany and mahogany inlay, shaped top over four drawers over four cupboard doors, sq tapering legs, chalk inscription "Hilliker," old refinish, old replaced brasses, imperfections, 69" w, 26¼" d, 41" h **2,645.00**

Federal Style, mahogany, rect top, straight front, three cock-beaded drawers, oval brass bail handles, thistle dec escutcheons, flanked by two small drawers, twin panel doors, shaped apron, sq tapering legs, 66" w, 21½" d, 36½" h 425.00

Late George III, early 19th C, mahogany and inlay, rect top, case fitted with drawer and cabinet doors, square tapering legs, 56¾" w, 21" d, 54½" h, restoration, damage 2,100.00

Hepplewhite, mahogany, serpentine case, five dovetailed drawers, double doors, banded inlay around feet and top edge, stringing on legs, posts, doors, and drawers, corner fans on doors, sq legs, old replaced brasses, old finish, 67" w, 27½" d, 42¾" h, some leg banding missing, minor age cracks, veneer damage   3,850.00

Sideboard, Hepplewhite, inlaid mahogany, serpentine, American, c1800, 40" h, 75½" l, $4,500.00.

Regency, mahogany, inlaid, rect-shaped top, straight front, single drawer flanked by twin bowed deep drawers, sq tapering legs, c1800, 54" w, 24¾" d, 33¾" h 3,700.00

Renaissance Revival, walnut, upper section with carved scroll and fruit dec over mirror, lower section with marble top, three fitted drawers, double doors, carved fruit pulls, 60" w, 21" d, 54" h 3,800.00

Victorian, two parts, upper section with floral-carved top over beveled mirror flanked by single door cabinets, lower section with marble top, five fitted drawers flanked by two doors, 48" w, 23" d, 84" h 1,955.00

Sofas

Art Nouveau, Carlo Bugatti, c1900, ebonized wood, rect back and mechanical seat, slightly scrolling rect arms, parchment upholstery, painted swallows and leafy branches, hammered brass trim, four block-form feet, 66⅜" l 1,750.00

Biedermeier, fruitwood and ebonized wood, upholstered central flat top back, rounded corners, cornucopia-form scrolled ends with foliated capitals supporting broad flattened domed arm rests, cylindrical bolsters, broad seat rail above reeded flattened triangular frieze, broad sq front supports, bottle green mohair upholstery, 72" l 3,900.00

Chesterfield, English, brown leather, tufted rolled back and arms, brass nail studding, triple cushion seat, casters, 77" l 1,700.00

Chippendale Style, mahogany, camel back, rolled arms, single cushion seat, yellow damask cov, chamfered legs, stretcher, 77" l 700.00

Classical

Boston, c1825, mahogany carved and mahogany veneer, carved palmette and scrolled ends, ogee-molded frames, foliate-carved ring-turned legs, casters, old finish, imperfections, backs added, 66" l, 27" d, 26" h, price for pr 1,850.00

America, attributed to Baltimore, found in Fayetteville, NC, c1810, mahogany, marquetry and inlay cornucopias, floral, and vine patterns, 70" l, 29" d, 35" h 3,300.00

New York, c1820–25, mahogany, concave carved crest rail ending in carved eagle heads, upholstered back and seat, scroll arms extending into convex molded seat rail, carved and applied wing returns, lion's paw feet, 85" l, 37½" h 7,500.00

Classical Style, Duncan Phyfe style, mahogany, carved, yellow geometric upholstery, 82½" l 500.00

Empire, American, 1830, mahogany, scrolled back, cornucopia legs, paw feet, reupholstered, 88" l 850.00

Empire Style, mahogany, straight crest rail seat back, rolled arms and seat cov in burgundy striped and ivory floral silk, acanthus-carved arm supports, carved cornucopia, paw feet, 89" l 1,500.00

Federal, American, figured mahogany frame, crest and scrolled arms with single inlay, scrolled legs, brass paw feet, repairs to frame and front legs, old finish, new silk brocade upholstery, 71¼" l 1,200.00

George III, c1800, carved mahogany, channel-molded frame, arched back, high down-swept arms, curved seat rail, four front ring-turned tapering supports, outer supports headed by oval carved paterae below stiff leaf-carved arm supports, brass caps and casters, striped yellow satin upholstery 3,200.00

Louis XV, transitional style, giltwood, carved, rounded arms, taupe foliate silk damask upholstery, 82" l ... 1,450.00

Sheraton, mahogany frame, turned arm posts and legs, beaded frame, worn old slate blue silk damask upholstery, repairs to frame, 72" l 1,210.00

Sofa, Victorian, beechwood and parcel gilt, shaped crest above curved arms, bowed seat above shaped apron, cabriole legs, 71" l, $450.00. Photograph courtesy of Leslie Hindman Auctioneers.

Stands

Book Stand, Victorian, walnut veneer, end pieces set with pate sur pate plaques of cupids playing badminton, Bettemann's patent, retailed by Shreve Crump and Low, 16" l **650.00**

Crock Stand, country, primitive, five stepped shelves, old green repaint, late wire nail construction, 38" w, 30" d, 31" h **150.00**

Stand, book, 2nd quarter 19th C, inlaid mahogany, adjustable stand above two shelves, lower drawer on ring-turned supports, turned tapering legs ending in brass casters, 20" w, 14" d, 44" h, $1,900.00. Photograph courtesy of Leslie Hindman Auctioneers.

Dumbwaiter, George III Style, late 19th C, mahogany, two tiers, 16" d, top, 33" h **345.00**

Music, Victorian, oak and mahogany, checkered line inlaid lip, tapered reeded standard, circular platform, four stylized animal legs **1,650.00**

Plant
  Art Nouveau Style, brass, oval onyx marble insert top surrounded by alabaster flambeau finials, platform stretcher below, 19" w, 3" d, 34" h **575.00**
  Arts and Crafts, Limbert, cutout, circular overhanging top, four sided medial shelf, new dark finish, 15½" d, 26" h **1,900.00**
  Victorian
    Circular top, walnut and other wood, arched supports, ball trim, middle shelf, conforming gallery on bottom shelf, old dark worn finish, ball and claw feet, some damage, 36¼" h **190.00**
    Marble top, refinished walnut base, three cutout legs, turned column, 12½" d, 34½" h **150.00**

Reading, Georgian, mahogany, oblong tilting top, turned standard, scrolling tripod base, ball feet, 19½" w, 16" d, 25" h **1,100.00**

Sewing
  Empire, black lacquer and gilt Chinoiserie dec, case with pullout work bag, lift lid, fitted tray, turned legs, paw feet, several int. lids missing, 24¾" w, 16½" d, 29½" h **1,100.00**
  Victorian, c1870, burl walnut, lift lid, mirrored top end, bird's-eye maple int., single drawer, apron fitted with pullout yarn basket, twin arched terminal supports, shaped stretcher, caster feet, 21½" w, 15½" d, 29½" h **400.00**

Shaving, mahogany
  Folding, shelf folds, mirror slides up and down, brass candle arms with electric candles, orig casters, old finish, 19" w, 14¾" d, 49½" h **300.00**
  Swing, rect line inlaid swing mirror, turned supports, swell front base, two drawers, bun feet, 19" w, American, c1835 .... **120.00**

Side or Night
  Federal, western MA, c1800, cherry inlaid, bowfront, cock-beaded crossbanded single drawer with flanking wavy birch panels, 17¾" w, 26½" h, old refinish, replaced knob, minor imperfections **2,530.00**
  Hepplewhite, country
    Birch, one-board top, one dovetailed drawer, sq tapered legs, old worn finish, 14¾" w, 15⅛" d, 26" h, age crack in top, replaced brass pull .. **275.00**
    Walnut
      Attributed to Chillicothe, OH, two-board top, one dovetailed overlapping drawer, scalloped apron, splayed base, sq tapering legs, refinished, top loose, 16¼" w, 17¾" d, 26¼" h **1,265.00**
      Mortised and pinned apron, scalloping on four sides, sq tapered legs, old worn refinishing, replaced three-board top, 19½" w, 19½" d, 27½" h **250.00**
  Lancaster County, PA, chestnut, pine, two-board top, mortised and pinned apron, splayed base, tapered and chamfered pencil post legs, old worn dark varnish finish, 20¼" w, 21¼" d, 29¾" h **190.00**
  Sheraton, country, cherry, one dovetailed drawer
    Old black and red graining, pine secondary wood, turned legs, lock mortise pieced in wood, top old replacement, 18⅝" w, 16¾" d, 28¾" h .. **250.00**
    Two-board top, slender turned legs, refinished, edge damage and wear, 19¾" w, 19¾" d, 26¼" h **440.00**

Spool, walnut, four tiers, turned column with finials on top, one drawer, refinished, 49¼" h **295.00**

Tray on Stand, George III Style, mahogany, oval, shaped gallery, oval flower filled basket inlay, sq tapering splayed legs, X-form stretcher, 27½" w, 20½" d, 27½" h **775.00**

Urn, George III Style, mahogany, circular top, ivory baluster gallery, spiral-turned standard, acanthus-carved baluster base, down-swept tripod whorled feet, 11½" d, 47½" h **3,250.00**

Wash
  American, maple, rect top, splash back, apron drawer, turned legs, fitted shelf stretcher **300.00**
  Corner, New England, early 19th C, mahogany and bird's-eye veneer, poplar secondary wood, shaped gallery, medial shelf with drawer, refinished, minor repairs, 23" w, 16" d, 41" h **1,650.00**
  Country, walnut, galleried top, one drawer, raised paneled door, simple cutout scalloped feet, partially stripped, 26" w, 15½" d, 35¼" h **385.00**
  Decorated, Wythe Co, VA, c1840, two-board top and backsplash, red field and black squiggle dec, single walnut drawer, poplar secondary wood, four sq tapered walnut legs, lower similar paint dec shelf, 21" w, 16" d, 34" h **425.00**

Federal, Massachusetts, c1800, mahogany and mahogany veneer inlaid, top with bowl cutout, small shelf on backsplash, single drawer, tambour door, sq tapered legs, old refinish, replaced brasses, minor imperfections, 18½" w, 18¼" d, 41" h **1,495.00**

Sheraton, country, bird's-eye maple, hardwood and pine, one-board top with cutout for bowl, one dovetailed drawer, turned legs and posts, refinished, 19¾ × 20 × 29½" h **220.00**

Work

Classical, New England, c1820, cherry and mahogany veneer, rect top with outset corners, two drawers, opalescent glass pulls, ring-turned columns extend to legs, refinished, minor imperfections, 18" w, 17½" d, 29" h **1,035.00**

Sheraton

American, cherry, poplar secondary wood, one-board top, two dovetailed drawers with figured veneer fronts with applied edge beading, turned and reeded legs, clear pressed glass pulls, inlaid ivory escutcheons, refinished, age cracks, 22¾" w, 17" d, 29½" h **1,870.00**

Boston, c1800, mahogany, serpentine front, two drawers, ring-turned brass pulls flanked by spool-turned reeded tapering legs, diminutive brass casters, 17¾" w, 17¼" d, 29" h **2,500.00**

Country, cherry, two-board top, two dovetailed drawers, turned legs, old mellow refinishing, 20¾" w, 21" d, 29" h **470.00**

Steps

Bed, English, late 18th C, mahogany, emb leather applied to top of each step, top step opens to commode, 24¾ × 17¼ × 18½" **300.00**

Library

George III, late 18th C, mahogany, rect molded hinged top, eight steps, 49½" l, 53½" h extended **2,250.00**

Regency, early 19th C, mahogany, three steps, inset green leather treads, scrolling banister, sq balusters, casters, 46" w, 27" d, 56" h **23,000.00**

Stools

Broom Maker's, splayed turned legs, mid-shelf, wood and wrought-iron clamps, worn gray paint, 36" h .. **225.00**

Foot

Arts and Crafts, rect, arched rails, new leather top,

Stool, pine, five-board, 6¾" w, 9" h, 17" l, $35.00.

orig medium finish with scuffs, 18" w, 13" d, 16½" d **200.00**

Country, walnut, round, three turned legs, green velvet upholstery insert, old finish, 10" d, 8½" h ... **40.00**

Decorated, worn orig red and black graining, yellow striping, turned legs, shaped top with worn cane seat, 12½" l **115.00**

Empire, American, 1830–40, mahogany, needlepoint and burgundy velvet upholstery **150.00**

English, hardwood, turned splayed legs, old dark worn finish, 13⅜" l **135.00**

Frezian, pine, old brown patina, chip and punch carving with "Nancy" on top, 12½" l **275.00**

George I, c1740, walnut, rect, needlepoint upholstery, cabriole legs, pad feet, 20" l, 17" w, 14¾" h **1,450.00**

Jacobean Style, English, oak, rect molded top, carved frieze, baluster-turned fluted legs, block feet, box stretcher, 17 12" w, 14" d, 19½" h **550.00**

Mission, oak, rect, arched skirt, four vertical slats per side, 20¼" l, 14" d, 16" h **325.00**

Victorian, adjustable, L Postauka & Co, Cambridgeport, MA, reupholstered seat, orig label, patent date April 4, 1871 .... **395.00**

Windsor, oval, splayed base, old green repaint, 10 × 14 × 10¾" h **225.00**

Piano, adjustable, mahogany, circular seat, turned legs, worn leather upholstery, 21" h **85.00**

Side, Arts and Crafts, Limbert, arched aprons, inset leather top, some wear to orig medium finish, branded mark, 13½ × 17½" **650.00**

Tables

Altar, Chinese, 19th C, black lacquer, polychrome paint, parcel gilt, 49¾" l, 19" d, 33" h **1,035.00**

Banquet, Victorian, second half 19th C, mahogany and beechwood, 90½" l extended, 46" w, 29" h **920.00**

Book, Arts and Crafts, L & J G Stickley, Model No. 516, c1912, oak, sq overhanging top, corresponding base, each side alternating with open shelf an slat sides, sgd "The Work of L. & J. G. Stickley," minor stains, 27" sq, 29" h **3,250.00**

Breakfast

Classical, NY, c1815–20, carved mahogany and mahogany veneer, one working and one faux drawer, scalloped D-form leaves, out-swept legs with leaf carving, old refinish, 37½" w, 25" d, 28½" h **4,315.00**

George III, 18th C, mahogany, circular top, reeded edge, quadruple scrolled support, brass paw feet and casters, 47" d, 30" h **6,000.00**

Regency, mahogany, tilt-top, rect rounded corner crossbanded and line inlaid top, vasiform and reeded standard, shaped base, scrolled knees, reeded brass caster feet, 48½" w, 36" d, 27½" d .**1,650.00**

Sheraton, American, c1830, mahogany, rect top and drop leaves, shaped corners, apron drawer, rope-carved legs, ball feet **400.00**

Card

Chippendale, Philadelphia, 1760–80, carved mahogany, rect hinged top, outset rounded corners, recessed baise cov surface, corner candle pockets, conforming apron, center beaded molded short

Table, breakfast, carved burl walnut and satinwood inlaid, four-column base on downswept legs, $2,420.00. Photograph courtesy of William Doyle Galleries.

drawer, acanthus-carved cabriole legs, claw and ball feet, minor repairs and restoration, 33¾" w, 32½" d, 28¾" h **71,500.00**

Classical, PA or NY, c1815, carved mahogany and mahogany veneer, lyre-form, brass lyre strings, cast feet, old refinish, imperfections, 35¼" w, 17¾" d, 29½" h **2,100.00**

Federal

Massachusetts, western, c1800, mahogany inlaid, D-shaped hinged top, sq tapered legs, old refinish, minor imperfections, 36¼" w, 18" d, 29½" h **2,645.00**

New Hampshire, c1810

Mahogany and wavy birch inlaid, shaped hinged top, ring-turned legs, old finish, minor imperfections, 39" w, 19½" d, 29¼" h **2,300.00**

Mahogany inlaid, scalloped D-shaped hinged top, reeded legs, old refinish, imperfections, 38" w, 16" d, 30" h **3,335.00**

George I, early 18th C, walnut, foldover top, concertina, oblong top, outset corners, conforming frieze, herringbone crossbanded drawer, straight tapering legs, lappet collars, pad feet, 31½" w, 15" d, 28½" h **4,500.00**

George III, mid-18th C, mahogany, oblong foldover top, serpentine sides and front, carved blind fret edge, recessed rect frieze, concertina action with blind fret-carved straight tapered supports, 33½" w, 16" d, 28½" h **3,750.00**

Hepplewhite, mahogany, demilune, inlaid stringing on legs and apron, edge of top, banding on feet and edge of apron, sq tapering legs, swing leg support, 34⅝" w, 17" d, 28¾" h **1,210.00**

Sheraton

American, 19th C, mahogany, demilune flip top, walnut banding, two paneled supports, platform base, pin line inlay, splayed legs, brass paw caster feet, 35¾" w, 17½" d, 28¾" h **1,050.00**

North Shore, MA, c1810, mahogany, mahogany veneer, satinwood inlay, white pine secondary

wood, serpentine front, cutout corners, lift top with herringbone inlay, lower top with beveled edge, four reeded and tapered legs, repair to top, 35¼" w, 17½" d, 29½" h **4,400.00**

Center

Art Deco, French, c1925, hexagonal walnut top, ebony edge, ebonized hexagonal pedestal with relief carving of trees, vegetation, and tribesman, ivory masks mounted at midsection, three African ivory tusks with relief carving of crocodiles and birds, tapering hexagonal walnut and ebony base, 31" d, 28" h **3,850.00**

Arts and Crafts, American, oak, round top, four sq legs joined by cross stretchers, exposed tenons, pyramidal center finial, 40" d, 30" h **1,750.00**

Classic Revival Style, mahogany, gilt brass mountings, top with insert marble, base with cupid-form legs, joined by stretcher with center brass bowl, 29" w, 19" d, 28" h **1,150.00**

George III, mid-18th C, mahogany, lozenge form, galleried top, conforming frieze, straight legs pierced to form four columns, joined to frieze by spaced spandrels stepped block-form feet, 19½" w, 29¾" d, 27½" h **1,650.00**

Table, drum, c.1840, four false drawers in frieze, circular pedestal, platform base, C-scroll feet, 28" d top, 27½" h, $605.00. Photograph courtesy of Neal Auction Company.

Georgian Style, mahogany, octagonal top, two fitted drawers, six faux doors, tripod base, 31" w, 33" d, 30" h **325.00**

Louis XV Style, late 19th/early 20th C, porcelain-mounted giltwood, 30" d, 29½" h, regilded, restorations **10,925.00**

Console

Art Moderne, American, attributed to Lorin Jackson, c1942, horseshoe-shaped mahogany base and rect top, Lucite winged torch, medallion on center of mirrored back, two stylized Egyptian columns support mirrored one drawer top, applied Lucite Minoan frieze, 48″ w, 20″ d, 33½″ h **7,700.00**

Chippendale Style, mahogany, marble rect top, scroll-carved frieze, chamfered sq legs, 48½″ w, 36″ d, 27½″ h **1,500.00**

Dining

Arts and Crafts, Indiana Hickory Furniture Co, early 20th C, hickory, circular top, bentwood and log supports, branded manufacturer's mark, retailers metal tag "Paine Furniture Boston," 47½″ d, 28¾″ h **900.00**

Federal, mahogany, inlaid maple oval panel on each end, reeded baluster-form legs, plain feet, 78½″ l extended, 29″ h **3,600.00**

Federal Style, mahogany, reeded banded rect top, triple ring-turned vasiform standards, tripod reeded flaring legs, brass paw castor feet, two table boards, 48″ w, 115″ l extended, 29½″ h **6,500.00**

George III, c1800, mahogany, two pedestal **2,990.00**

Queen Anne, Connecticut River Valley, cherry and birch, painted red, minor imperfections, 40½″ w, 36″ d, 28½″ h **20,700.00**

Regency Style, mahogany, oval banded top, single vasiform standard, four splayed legs, brass capped caster feet, three table boards, 46″ w, 96″ l extended, 29″ h **475.00**

Drafting, cast-iron frame, oak drawing board, adjustments for height and tilt, pedestal with adjustable arm, oak shelf, and cubbyhole, tripod feet, old worn cream-colored paint on base with red striping, old worn and stained varnish finish, 21 × 26″ board .. **990.00**

Dressing

George I Style, walnut and inlay, rect top, three frieze drawers, cabriole legs, shell-carved knees, claw and ball feet, 31¼″ w, 19¾″ d, 27½″ h **750.00**

George II, burl walnut veneer, rect inlaid top, notched corners, straight front fitted with small single drawer flanked by twin deep drawers, brass ring pulls, shaped apron, modified cabriole legs, angular pad feet, 18th C, 33¾″ w, 20″ d, 27¾″ h ..**1,100.00**

Hepplewhite, NY state, mahogany, serpentine top, conforming apron, edge beading, sq tapering legs, minor veneer damage to apron, 42″ w, 20″ d, 30¾″ h **1,540.00**

Queen Anne, MA, c1750, mahogany, overhanging chamfered edge top, central concave carved drawer, flanked by small drawers, valanced concave carved skirt, two acorn drop pendants, four foliate-carved knees, four claw and ball feet, replaced brasses **17,250.00**

William and Mary, MA, c1720, walnut veneer, two deep drawers, small center drawer, shaped X-form stretcher with finial, replaced brasses, top re-veneered, minor imperfections, 33⅜″ w, 23″ d, 30″ h **4,000.00**

Drop Leaf

Federal, Nantucket, MA, c1820, cherry, scalloped D-shaped leaves, sq tapering legs, 23″ w, 35¾″ d, 29″ h, price for matched pr **1,000.00**

George II, mid-18th C, mahogany, 24¾″ w, 28¼″ l extended, 26¼″ h, finish distressed **865.00**

Georgian, 18th C, oak, hinged top, D-shaped leaves,

Table, drop leaf, Chippendale, RI, 18th C, mahogany, rect top, two hinged rect drop leaves, shaped frieze, six chamfered sq legs, 47¾″ w, 62″ open l, 28″ h, $2,475.00. Photograph courtesy of Butterfield & Butterfield.

circular tapering legs, pad feet, 48¼″ w, 57¾″ d, 29½″ h, damages **700.00**

Hepplewhite, cherry, one-board top and leaves, swing leg, six sq tapered legs, old finish, 47¾″ w, 17¼″ d, 29″ h, 17¾″ leaves **990.00**

Poplar top, hardwood base, attributed to Delaware Valley, PA, worn brown stain on replaced top, green repaint on base, swing leg, turned legs, duck feet, 41½″ w, 13¼″ d, 27½″ h, 13¾″ leaves, two legs replaced, age crack in top **750.00**

Queen Anne

Cherry, birch top, mortised and pinned apron, swing leg to support round top, turned legs, duck feet, 36½″ w, 11″ d, 27¼″ h, 12¼″ leaves, minor repairs **1,485.00**

Maple, round drop-leaf top, swing cabriole legs, duck feet, old mellow finish, considerable repair and restoration, 13¼″ × 40¼″ top, 26½″ h, 14½″ leaves **900.00**

Sheraton, country

Birch, curly-birch top, mortised and pinned apron, turned legs, 42″ w, 18½″ d, 28¼″ h, 11¼″ leaves, refinished **450.00**

Curly maple, one-board top and leaves, turned legs, slight warp to leaves, minor age cracks, 38″ w, 44″ l extended, 28½″ h **1,100.00**

Game

Classical

New England, c1820, carved mahogany, tiger-maple crossbanded borders, brass inlaid striping, solid lyre-form standard, out-swept carved legs, refinished, 35½″ w, 17½″ d, 28″ h **1,955.00**

New York, c1815, carved mahogany and mahogany veneer, swivel top, old refinish, minor imperfections, 36″ w, 17½″ d, 28¾″ h **7,475.00**

Empire, c1830, mahogany, lift lid, rect top

Lyre-form standard, step-molded platform base, bracket feet, 35¼″ w, 17¾″ d, 29½″ h **450.00**

Square tapering standard, platform base, cylindrical-form feet, brass casters, 37″ sq top, 30″ h . **200.00**

Federal, early 19th C, mahogany, shaped foldover top, circular reeded legs **690.00**

George III, c1800, mahogany, rect hinged top,

rounded corners, plain frieze, central drawer, reeded legs, 35½″ w, 18¾″ d, 29″ h, restored ...   **750.00**

Louis XVI, late 18th/19th C, Provincial, walnut, rect hinged top, rounded corners, leather-lined gaming surface, frieze later fitted with drawer, circular stop-fluted legs, brass caps, 32″ w, 15″ d, 28¾″ h, restoration **375.00**

Napoleon III, third quarter 19th C, ebonized and floral marquetry, shaped hinged top, plain frieze, circular tapering legs **1,265.00**

Regency, mahogany shell-and-pin-inlaid lift top, surface inset with green felt, rect stepped support, platform base, flaring banded legs, capped brass casters, c1800, 35″ w, 17½″ d, 28″ h **1,100.00**

Regency Style, mahogany, octagonal, tooled leather top, four cock-beaded fitted drawers, four mock drawers, circular brass ring pulls, ring-turned vasiform standard, reeded flaring legs, brass capped caster feet, 23¾″ w, 23¾″ d, 29″ h **650.00**

Gateleg, English, oak, oval drop-leaf base, mortised and pinned stretcher base, turned legs, old dark finish, age cracks, old repairs and restoration, 45″ w, 16″ d, 27¾″ h, 19″ leaves **385.00**

Hutch, country

Pine, three-board rect top, inset battens and cleats, wooden pins to hold top to base, one-board ends, cutout feet, hinged lid in base, old refinishing, 43 × 45½″, 28½″ h **1,320.00**

Poplar, old worn yellow repaint over gray, rect top, one-board ends, cutout feet, mortised through seat and scrubbed two-board top, minor age cracks, one orig steel barn hinge, other missing, 35½″ w, 72″ l, 30″ h **1,760.00**

Library

Arts and Crafts

Oak, quartersawn, old worn finish, two dovetailed drawers, orig wrought-copper pulls, Imperial label, 44″ l, 26″ d, 30″ h **1,100.00**

Shop of the Crafters, one-inch thick oak boards, clipped-corner top, flaring trestle legs, Maltese cross cutouts joined by wide medial stretcher, keyed through tenons, new medium finish, 51″ l, 34″ d, 29½″ h **1,100.00**

Centennial, walnut, inlay and medallions, c1876   **..7,700.00**

Low

Louis XVI Style, late 19th C, gilt-bronze-mounted tulipwood, oval top inset with black-veined marble, cabriole legs, 23″ w, 30½″ l, 20¼″ h **750.00**

Neoclassical Style, Austrian, c1800, walnut and fruitwood parquetry, later square tapering legs, 30¾″ d, 22″ h, alternations, restorations **635.00**

Occasional

Aesthetic Movement, fourth quarter 19th C, brass-mounted rosewood and mixed metal, spider-web inlay on top corner, 20″ w, 20″ d, 27″ h, minor losses **8,625.00**

Napoleon III, third quarter 19th C, ormolu-mounted ebonized wood, marble top, 19¾″ w, 14″ d, 28¼″ h **2,540.00**

Parlor

Eastlake, walnut, pink-gray marble top, black and white veins, old finish, 30″ w, 20″ d, 28½″ h **275.00**

Victorian

Marble

Oval top, walnut quadruped base, 33″ w, 25″ d, 28″ h **750.00**

Shaped top, conforming wooden pedestal base, mythical-animal-form legs, 38″ w, 28″ d, 30″ h **1,300.00**

Oak, oval top with carved border, apron fitted on each side with single drawer and faux drawer, columnar pedestal base, lion's-paw feet, 48″ w, 35″ d, 31″ h **1,100.00**

Pembroke

Federal, NY, c1810, mahogany, rect top, two shaped drop leaves, single drawer, orig pull, casters, old refinish, shaped leaves extend to 32¾″, 30″ w, 18¼″ d, 27¾″ h **1,200.00**

Hepplewhite, New England, mahogany, white pine and poplar secondary woods, inlay, shaped drop leaves, single drawer, sq tapered legs, refinished, repaired, 21″ w, 33″ d, 28″ h **1,100.00**

Sheraton, country, maple, folding apron wings, turned legs, old finish, 36¼″ w, 17¼″ d, 28″ h   **..1,250.00**

Pier

Classical, attributed to William Alexander, Sharpsburg, PA, c1840, carved mahogany and mahogany veneer, brass-inlay stringing and rosettes, acanthus-leaf and grapevine-carved frontal supports, paw feet, rect mirror flanked by turned and fluted supports, framed with black and gilt foliate design, medial shelf with inset oval marble panel, remnants of paper label, old refinish, minor imperfections, 42⅛″ w, 18⅞″ d, 40″ h **13,800.00**

Empire, Continental, last half 19th C, mahogany, ebony and gilt Egyptian-style figural front supports, gray marble top, 38½″ w, 32½″ h **1,900.00**

Regency Style, 19th C, rosewood, brass inlaid, parcel gilt, black marble top, 45″ l, 17¼″ d, 42″ h, top damaged, minor losses **2,760.00**

Serving

Arts and Crafts, Gustav Stickley, Model No. 802, c1912, oak, two short drawers, four tapering legs, arched apron, branded mark, 41¾″ w, 18″ d, 39½″ h **4,650.00**

Sheraton, American, mahogany, concave rect top, three-apron drawer, rope-carved legs, ball feet ..   **325.00**

Side

Art Moderne, American, attributed to Lorin Jackson, c1942, Lucite, oval glass top, circular skirt with applied rosettes, four tapering legs, 21¼″ d, 25¾″ h, price for pr **4,500.00**

Art Nouveau, inlaid mahogany, rounded triangular top, marquetry cock and poppies, inscribed ''Quand Le Coq Chanteaura, Mon Amour Pour Vous Finira,'' sgd ''Gallé'' in marquetry, 21¼″ w, 28½″ h **2,650.00**

Arts and Crafts, Limbert, Grand Rapids, MI, c1907, oval top, oval lower shelf, cross-member base, sq cutouts, orig dark finish, branded mark, 47½″ l, 36″ d, 29¼″ h **3,750.00**

Hepplewhite, Southern, walnut, yellow pine secondary wood, one-board top, mortised and pinned apron, fretwork corner brackets, applied molding around edge of apron, one dovetailed drawer with figured drawer front, banded inlay, orig oval brass with emb thistles, sq tapered legs, refinished, minor repairs, stains, and age cracks, 23¾" w, 19½" d, 28¼" h **1,155.00**

Italian, 19th C, floral-form top, figural griffin base, 19" d, 33" h, restorations 325.00

Majorelle, mahogany, concave sides, center inlaid floral dec, curved legs, platform stretcher, 26" w, 15" d, 30" h **1,325.00**

Neoclassical, Italian, late 18th C, walnut, oblong top with oval marquetry panel of classical figures, multiple marquetry borders, conforming recessed frieze with ornament, full end drawer, straight tapered legs, 22" w, 17" d, 27½" h **2,400.00**

Renaissance Revival, American, c1860, rosewood, gilt incised, circular black marble top, leaf-carved frieze and pedestal with geometric inlay, foliate-carved tripod base, tiger-paw feet, trefoil base on carved bun feet, losses to two feet, 19" d, 30¾" h **6,650.00**

Tavern

Chippendale, late 18th C, cherry, rect top, one wide and one small drawer, brass bail handles, escutcheons, lock plates, block and ring-turned legs, stretcher shelf 600.00

Federal, country, hardwood and pine, scrubbed finish, turned legs, mortised and pinned stretcher and apron, repaired, 38¾" l, 28" h 275.00

Hepplewhite, country, maple and pine, scrubbed pine breadboard top, sq tapered maple legs, mortised and pinned pine apron, traces of red on base, 37½" l, 26½" h 750.00

Queen Anne, American, mid-18th C, walnut, rect plank top, single drawers, circular walnut pull, shaped ring-turned round legs, box-form stretcher, ball feet **5,500.00**

Tea

Arts and Crafts, American, oak, circular top, sq sections legs joined by cross stretcher, 20" d, 26" h   900.00

Chippendale

Mid-Atlantic States, late 18th C, walnut, three-board tilt top, circular birdcage, orig iron brace with rose-head nails, early finish, 38" d, 38¾" d, 28" h **1,760.00**

New England, late 18th C, mahogany, rect tilt top, shaped corners, tripod cabriole legs, old finish, minor imperfections, 32¾" w, 33¼" d, 28¾" h **1,495.00**

Philadelphia, c1760, mahogany, rect tilt top, turned round standard, tripod cabriole legs, snake-head feet, 25" w, 16" d, 27" h 450.00

George III, mahogany, scalloped tilt top, turned and spiraled support, leaf-carved knees, ball and claw feet, 30" d, 28½" h **1,380.00**

Queen Anne, English, early 18th C, walnut, dish-shaped rect top, conforming frieze, cabriole legs, pointed pad feet, restorations, 34" w, 21¼" d, 27¼" h **3,500.00**

Work

Chippendale, country, cherry, mortised and pinned frame, two-board breadboard top, one dovetailed overlapping drawer, sq legs with molded outside corner, X-form stretcher, old finish, repaired break

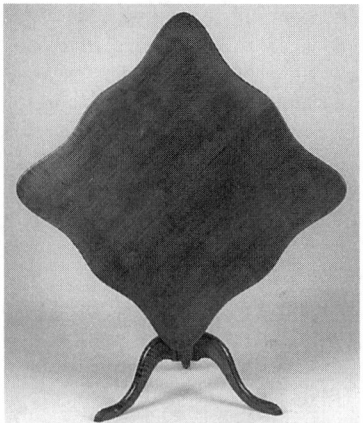

Table, tea, New England, c1800, tiger maple, tilt top, birdcage support, refinished, imperfections, 32" w, 31¾" d, 27½" h, $1,045.00. Photograph courtesy of Skinner, Inc.

in cross stretcher, old repairs and age cracks to top, 37¾" w, 25¾" d, 27" h 990.00

Country

Missouri, cherry, three-board top, one dovetailed drawer with cock-beading, orig turned wooden knobs, turned legs, old refinishing, worn surface, 34½" w, 48" d, 27½" h 275.00

Pennsylvania, second half 18th C, walnut, rect removable top, two apron drawers, turned legs with stretchers **1,900.00**

Empire, curly maple, top with mahogany cross-banded veneer edge, applied cherry edge banding, two dovetailed drawers, apron with corner posts and turned drops, turned column, four curved legs with mahogany ball feet and rosettes, replaced drawer pulls, int. dividers missing, minor repairs, mismatched turned feet, refinished, 18" w, 18" d, 28½" h **1,430.00**

Hepplewhite, country

Maple, traces of old red paint, replaced pine breadboard top, mortised and pinned apron, one overlapping dovetailed drawer, sq tapered legs, refinished, 25¼" × 46½" × 28¼" h, top set on hinges to tip 660.00

Walnut, two-board top with apron, one dovetailed drawer, long wooden pull, sq tapering legs, old refinishing, 57¾" w, 37¾" d, 30" h, old white enamel underside of top and apron 425.00

Regency, 19th C, mahogany, rect top, rounded drop leaves, drawer fitted for writing over drawer and slide, turned legs, brass caps and casters, 38½" w, 18" d, 29½" h, restored, drawer pull missing **1,265.00**

Victorian, walnut, drop leaves, single drawer over scrap bin, carved backing, 40" d, 19" d, 29" h, age cracks, veneer damage 460.00

Writing

Arts and Crafts, Grand Rapids, MI, oak, rect, two top drawers, four post legs, under-shelf stretcher, crown decal mark, 56½" l, 34" w, 29¼" h 950.00

George III, carved mahogany, tooled leather inset top,

center bowed drawer flanked by two deeper drawers, sq tapered legs, spade feet, 53½" w, 26" d, 30½" h **3,000.00**
Louis XV Style, 19th C, gilt metal mounts, marquetry dec, single drawer, pullout writing surface, 30" w, 19" d, 30" h **1,150.00**

Tea Carts

Mahogany, drop-leaf top, one drawer, old dark finish, early 20th C, 36" l, 17¼" w, 30" h, 13" leaves **115.00**
Oak, English, 19th C, trolley-table type, three-fourth gallery, carved leafy vines and acorns design, center dog's head, three open shelves, 55" w, 19" d, 59" h **1,150.00**
Oriental, black lacquer finish, raised Chinese figures in landscape, D-shaped leaves, turned legs, two wheels **350.00**
Painted, orig worn black paint, Oriental dec, glass tray, drop-leaf top, 1918 patent date, 27" l, 17" w, 29" h **75.00**
Walnut, America, early 20th C, old varnish finish, age crack in top, 17" w, 29" l, 29½" h **165.00**
Wicker, 1900–20, natural, tight-weave design, open top with utensil basket on side, bottom shelf, wooden wheels **500.00**

Wicker

Bench, photographer's, tight-weave seat, leaf-motif back, rolled arm, stick, ball and curlicue detail, natural and green, c1890 .... **650.00**
Chair
    Arm, rattan wrapped, tight weave, geometric diamond-shaped panel on back, upholstered seat .. **350.00**
    Desk, Heywood-Wakefield, c1917, reupholstered cushion **190.00**
    Side, shaped woven crest, vase-shaped ornate splat, pressed seat, 17½" w, 39" h **200.00**
Chaise Lounge, Wakefield Rattan Co, c1890, rolled arms

Wicker, rocker, Ordway Mfg Co, Bristol, TN, c1905, alternating ash splints and wicker, S-shaped arms and arched rocker base, marked with decal, 21" w, 17" d, 44½" h, $725.00. Photograph courtesy of Skinner, Inc.

with scrollwork, continuous and star caned back, wrapped legs, rolled footrest, yellow floral cushion **850.00**
Desk, attached side wastebasket, woven holder on top, Heywood-Wakefield & Lloyd Loom, c1917 .... **465.00**
Doll Carriage, tan twisted fiber, F A Whitney Co, Leominster, MA, late 1920s **275.00**
Étagère, rattan wrapped, six tiers, arch rest insert with oval mirror, scrollwork, cabriole legs, X-form stretcher, 69" h **1,100.00**
Fernery, pedestal basket, tin liner, Cape Cod–style weave, c1915 .... **150.00**
Invalid Chair, hardwood frame, wicker and cane, wire and cane wheels, labeled "C. E. Marshall Invalid Wheel Chair, Chicago," minor damage, 45" h **110.00**
Lectern, tight-weave design, round edge, shelf, diamond pattern design on front, brown, brass reading lamp, c1910 .... **300.00**
Rocker
    Child's, diamond design, c1920 .... **130.00**
    Platform, rolled edge, high back, patent date, 25" w, 47" h **500.00**
Sewing Stand, basket top, Heywood-Wakefield, Victorian, c1897 .... **229.00**
Stand, four shelf, fancy scroll, stick-ball design, c1900 **200.00**

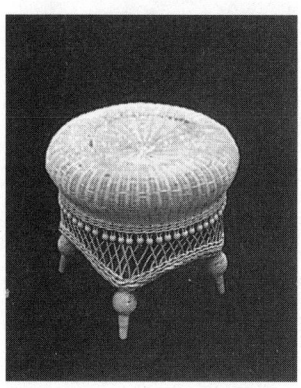

Wicker, stool, painted white, 13½" h, $150.00.

Table, sq looped edge, stick, ball, and curlicue detail, small woven tier middle, wrapped legs and stretcher, c1890 .... **395.00**
Tea Cart, brown twisted fiber, oak top with D-shaped drop leaves, orig wooden wheels and axle, c1915 . **595.00**

GAME PLATES

History: Game plates, popular between 1870 and 1915, are specially decorated plates used to serve fish and game. Sets originally included a platter, serving plates, and a sauce or gravy boat. Many sets have been divided. Today, individual plates are often used as wall hangings.

Birds

Plate
    9½" d, sgd "Max," Limoges Coronet **65.00**
    10" d, duck, white, gray, and black body, emerald green head, standing in marsh, gadrooned gilt border within traditional border, Royal Copenhagen **990.00**

10½" d, Asiatic Pheasants, R Hall	3.00
12¼" d, birds in flight, hp, gold scalloped edge, marked "Limoges"	200.00

Platter

13¾ × 9½", oval, duck, natural setting, gold handles, artist sgd, Limoges blank	225.00
18" l, pheasants, multicolored center scene, marked "R K Beck"	500.00

**Pheasant, gold edge, Z. S. & Co, Bavaria, 8¾",
$65.00.**

Set, 20½" l platter with two turkeys, twelve plates with hp designs, artist sgd, marked "Limoges, France" ..	625.00

Deer

Plate, 13¾" h, stag in woods, hp, raised enamel dec ..	200.00
Set, platter, twelve plates, deer, bear, and game birds, yellow ground, scalloped border, marked "Haviland China," artist sgd "MC Haywood"	3,000.00

Fish

Plate

9" d, bass, artist sgd "Morley," marked "Lenox" ...	75.00
10½" d, trout, cobalt blue border, marked "M Z Austria"	85.00
Platter, 16½" l, bass, water lilies, emb, artist sgd "Max," marked "Limoges"	175.00
Set, 23½" platter, twelve plates, different species on each plate, yellow border, gold trim, marked "Limoges, France"	500.00

Miscellaneous

Plate

9" d, elk, natural colors, scalloped edge	45.00
10" d, squirrel perched on tree branch, eating acorn, forest landscape background, beaded border, numbered, Royal Copenhagen	990.00
Platter, 18" l, weasel carrying red squirrel in mouth, winter scene, sky blue ground, paneled and beaded border, dentil rim, gilt and ground highlights, numbered, Royal Copenhagen	1,200.00

GAMES

History: Mass production of board games did not take place until after the Civil War. Firms like McLoughlin Brothers, Milton Bradley, and Selchow and Righter were active in the 1860s, followed by Parker Brothers, which began in 1883. Parker Brothers bought out the rights to the W. & S. B. Ives Co., which had produced some very early games in the 1840s, including the first American board game, The Mansion of Happiness. All these companies except McLoughlin Brothers are giants in the game industry today.

McLoughlin Brothers' games are a challenge to find. Not only does the company no longer exist (Milton Bradley bought them out in 1920), but the lithography on their games was the best of its era. Most board games are collected because of the bright, colorful lithography on the box covers. In addition to spectacular covers, the large McLoughlin games often had lead playing pieces and fancy block spinners, thus making them even more desirable.

References: *Board Games of the 50's, 60's & 70's with Prices,* L-W Books, 1994; Mark Cooper, *Baseball Games,* Schiffer Publishing, 1995; Lee Dennis, *Warman's Antique American Games, 1840–1940,* Wallace-Homestead, 1991; *Dexterity Games and Other Hand-Held Puzzles,* L-W Book Sales, 1995; Norman E. Martinus and Harry L. Rinker, *Warman's Paper,* Wallace-Homestead, 1994; Jack Matthews, *Toys Go to War,* Pictorial Histories Publishing, 1994; Rick Polizzi, *Baby Boomer Games,* Collector Books, 1995; Rick Polizzi and Fred Schaefer, *Spin Again,* Chronicle Books, 1991; Harry L. Rinker, *Collector's Guide to Toys, Games, and Puzzles,* Wallace-Homestead, 1991; Desi Scarpone, *Board Games,* Schiffer Publishing, 1995; Carl P. Stirn, *Turn-of-the-Century Dolls, Toys and Games* (1893 catalog reprint), Dover Publications, 1990; Bruce Whitehill, *Games: American Boxed Games and Their Makers,* Wallace-Homestead, 1992.

Periodicals: *Toy Shop,* 700 E. State St, Iola, WI 54990; *Toy Trader,* PO Box 1050, Dubuque, IA 52004.

Collectors' Clubs: American Game Collectors Assoc, 49 Brooks Ave, Lewiston, ME 04240; American Toy Collectors of America, Inc, Carter, Ledyard & Milburn, Two Wall St, 13th Floor, New York, NY 10005; Gamers Alliance, PO Box 197, East Meadow, NY 11554.

Museums: Checkers Hall of Fame, Petal, MS; Essex Institute, Salem, MA; University of Waterloo Museum & Archive of Games, Waterloo, Ontario, Canada; Washington Dolls' House and Toy Museum, Washington, D.C.

Additional Listings: See *Warman's Americana & Collectibles.*

Notes: Common games like Anagrams, Authors, Jackstraws, Lotto, Tiddledy Winks, and Peter Coddles do not command high prices, nor do the games of Flinch, Pit, and Rook, which still are being produced.

Games, with the exception of the common ones stated above, generally are rising in price. However, certain games with good graphics dealing with popular subject matter, e.g., trains, planes, baseball, and Christmas, often bring higher prices because they are also sought by collectors in those particular fields.

Condition is everything when buying. Do not buy games that have been taped or that have price-tag stickers on the face of their covers. Also, beware of games sold at outdoor flea markets where weather elements can cause fading and warping.

Aero-Chute Target Game, American Toy Works, boxed board game, 19³/₁₆ × 13³/₁₆ × 2⅝″, 8 pcs **40.00**

Auto Race, Gorham Pressed Steel Corp, c1930, 10¾ × 22″, multicolored litho metal board, five colored metal cars **185.00**

Auto Race Game, Milton Bradley, c1925, boxed board game, 16⅞ × 8¾, 8 pcs **125.00**

Bagatelle, early push-type, 1⅝ × 9¹⁵/₁₆ × 19¼″, wooden, multicolored litho pasted to face marking points, wooden stick with wooden block to push ball, one wooden and one clay ball, instructions pasted on back **135.00**

Big Trail Game, boxed board game, 13½ × 17 × 1½″, 1930 Movietone picture with John Wayne and Tyrone Power, Sr, 14 × 26″ multicolored board, wagon-train illus, instruction booklet, wooden pawns, metal figures, full-color illus box, several pawns and four figures missing **75.00**

Bradley's Toy Town Post Office, Milton Bradley, c1910, educational, 8¾ × 11″, 10 pcs **110.00**

American Boys: A Game, Milton Bradley, #4644, rules on inside of lid, red piece, six blue pieces, track game, Western tradition scouts, 11¼ × 16¼ × 1″, $70.00.

Champion Game of Baseball, Proctor Amusement, c1900, boxed board game, 9 × 12″, instructions inside cov, unused score card, litho heavy paper gameboard with baseball diamond, attached spinner, bleachers, and stands, paper markers in orig envelopes **140.00**

Charlie Chan, Whitman, 1939, boxed card game, 5 × 6 × 1″, 35 playing cards, instruction card, black, white, and red crime-fighting scenes, multicolored box **75.00**

Cinderella, Milton Bradley, c1900, card game, 6¾ × 5½″, 33 cards **20.00**

Down the Pike with Mrs. Wiggs at the St. Louis Exposition, Milton Bradley, c1904, card game, 7½ × 5½″, instructions on front of reading booklet, small cards **20.00**

Excursion to Coney Island, Milton Bradley, c1885, card game, printed cards, reading booklet **35.00**

Flap Jacks, Alderman-Fairchild, 1931, skill game, 15½ × 12½″, 30 pcs **35.00**

Game of Balloon, R Bliss Manuf, 1889, skill game, 31 × 10½″, 17 pcs, wooden stand and hoop, all-wood dovetailed and hinged box **275.00**

Game of Bang, McLoughlin, 1912, boxed board game, 15 × 8″, orig spinner, game board on box bottom, playing pcs **85.00**

Game of Old Mother Hubbard, Milton Bradley, c1890, boxed board game, 15 × 16″, 8 pcs **95.00**

Game of Parlor Baseball, McLoughlin Bros, 1897, boxed board game, 17 × 19″, vivid litho cov of early baseball players, board with playing field, two litho spinners, 18 wooden playing markers **1,600.00**

Game of Poor Jenny, Alderman-Fairchild, c1927, boxed board game, 11½ × 11½″, 9 pcs **50.00**

Honey Bee Game, Milton Bradley, c1913, boxed board game, 12¾″ sq, 26 pcs **60.00**

Jack Straws, Milton Bradley, c1900, skill, 6 × 5″, colored shaped sticks, two hooks **15.00**

Klondyke Nugget Game, c1890, boxed board game, 4 × 8 × 1″, full-color illus of mine, miner holding "Boss Nugget", multicolored game board, mine covers, gold nuggets **85.00**

Lee at Havana Game, c1898, boxed board game, 5 × 7 × 1″, Spanish-American War, set of 52 cards, instruction sheet, full-color paper label on lid **75.00**

Motor Cycle Game, Milton Bradley, c1905, boxed board game, 9″ sq, 5 pcs **40.00**

Oriental Color Game, McLoughlin Bros, 1875, 7½ × 4½″, wooden box, 54 multicolored litho cards, litho double-arrowed block spinner, instruction booklet . **85.00**

Psychology of the Hand, Baker & Bennett Co, card game, 8¾ × 12¼ × 1½″, copyright by Gertrude Ann Lindsay, five cards of hands, instruction booklet **35.00**

Raggedy Ann's Magic Pebble Game, Johnny Gruelle Co, Milton Bradley, 1941, 15½ × 8¹¹/₁₆ × 1¾″, 18 pcs **65.00**

Round the World with Nellie Bly, c1895, Statue of Liberty on board **125.00**

Strange Game of Forbidding Fruit, Parker Bros, c1900, boxed card game, 4 × 5½ ×½″, forty cards, full-color paper label on lid of three men stealing apples, charging farmyard dog **75.00**

Tally-Ho, Snow, Woodman & Co, c1880, 11¼ × 11¼″, thirty-six white wooden pegs, thirty-six black wooden pegs, lift-out board, instruction sheet, multicolored litho board with red-star center **60.00**

Toonin Radio Game, Alderman-Fairchild, separate board and pcs box, c1910, 17¾ × 17⅝″ game board, six metal speakers as tokens, six wooden cubes, instruction sheet, dice cup **75.00**

When My Ship Comes In, George S. Parker, & Co, c1888, 5½ × 4″, boxed card game, 84 cards, instruction sheet **30.00**

GAUDY DUTCH

History: Gaudy Dutch is an opaque, soft-paste ware made between 1790 and 1825 in England's Staffordshire district.

The wares first were hand decorated in an underglaze blue and fired; then additional decorations were added over the glaze. The over-glaze decoration is extensively worn on many of the antique pieces. Gaudy Dutch found a ready market in the Pennsylvania German community because it was inexpensive and extremely colorful. It had little appeal in England.

Marks: Marks of various potters, including the impressed marks of Riley and Wood, have been found on some pieces, although most are unmarked.

References: Susan and Al Bagdade, *Warman's English & Continental Pottery & Porcelain,* Second Edition, Wallace-Homestead, 1991; Eleanor and Edward Fox, *Gaudy Dutch,* published by author, 1970, out-of-print; John A. Shuman, III, *The Collector's Encyclopedia of Gaudy Dutch & Welsh,* Collector Books, 1990, 1991 value update, out-of-print.

Collectors' Club: Gaudy Collector's Society, PO Box 274, Gates Mills, OH 44040.

REPRODUCTION ALERT

Cup plates, bearing the impressed mark "CYBRIS," have been reproduced and are collectible in their own right. The Henry Ford Museum has issued pieces in the Single Rose pattern, although they are porcelain rather than soft paste.

Advisor: John D. Querry.

Butterfly
    Bowl, 11" d 3,900.00
    Coffeepot, 11" h 4,500.00
    Cup and Saucer, handleless 575.00
    Plate
        6½" d 650.00
        9¾" d 1,500.00
    Sugar 900.00
    Teapot, 5" h, squat baluster form 1,400.00
    Waste Bowl 1,275.00
Carnation
    Bowl
        5½" d 625.00
        6¼" d 750.00
    Creamer, 4¾" h 700.00
    Pitcher, 6" h 675.00
    Plate
        5¾" d 575.00
        8" d 850.00
        9¾" d 475.00
    Teabowl and Saucer 495.00
    Teapot 1,275.00
    Toddy Plate 525.00
    Waste Bowl 370.00
Dahlia
    Bowl, 6¼" d 675.00
    Plate, 8" d 1,050.00
    Teabowl and Saucer 700.00
Double Rose
    Bowl, 6¼" d 400.00

Creamer 650.00
Gravy Boat 300.00
Plate
    7" d 675.00
    10" d 750.00
Sugar, cov 775.00
Teapot 750.00
Toddy Plate, 4½" d 350.00
Waste Bowl, 6½" d, 3" h 550.00
Dove
    Creamer 675.00
    Plate, 10" d 750.00
    Waste Bowl 650.00

Dove pattern, saucer, 5⅝" d, $350.00.

Flower Basket, plate, 6½" d 185.00
Grape
    Bowl, 6½" d, lustered rim 385.00
    Plate
        6" d 450.00
        7½" d 525.00
    Sugar, cov 450.00
    Teabowl and Saucer 475.00
    Toddy Plate, 5" d 375.00
Oyster
    Bowl, 5½" d 300.00
    Coffeepot, 12" h 3,000.00
    Plate
        8¾" d 425.00
        9½" d 575.00
    Soup Plate, 8½" d 550.00
    Teabowl and Saucer 395.00
    Toddy Plate, 5½" d 425.00
Single Rose
    Bowl, 6" d 275.00
    Coffeepot, 10¾" h, double-gourd form 850.00
    Cup and Saucer 400.00
    Plate
        7" d 550.00
        8¼" d 650.00
    Quill Holder, cov 2,500.00
    Sugar, cov 675.00
    Toddy Plate, 5¼" d 250.00
Sunflower
    Bowl, 6½" d 950.00

Coffeepot, 9½″ h **6,500.00**
Creamer **850.00**
Plate, 5½″ d **650.00**
Teabowl and Saucer **775.00**
Urn
    Creamer **325.00**
    Plate, 8¼″ d **425.00**
    Sugar, cov, 6½″ h, round, tip and base restored **275.00**
War Bonnet
    Bowl, cov **210.00**
    Coffeepot **9,500.00**
    Plate
        7″ d **475.00**
        8¼″ d **775.00**
    Teapot **2,200.00**
    Toddy Plate, 4½″ d **525.00**

GAUDY IRONSTONE

History: Gaudy Ironstone was made in England around 1850. Ironstone is an opaque, heavy-bodied earthenware which contains large proportions of flint and slag. Gaudy Ironstone is decorated in patterns and colors similar to those of Gaudy Welsh.

Marks: Most pieces are impressed "Ironstone" and bear a registry mark.

Collectors' Club: Gaudy Collector's Society, PO Box 274, Gates Mills, OH 44040.

Blackberry
    Plate, 9½″ d, blue, black, yellow, red, and luster dec, imp "E. Walley," stains **195.00**
    Teapot, 10″ h, paneled, underglaze blue and black, yellow and red enamel and luster, cock's-comb handle and finial glued, chips on rim and spout **880.00**
Floral
    Cup and Saucer, handleless **75.00**
    Plate, 8½″ d, underglaze blue, polychrome and purple luster dec **100.00**
    Sugar, cov, 7¼″ h, luster trim **125.00**
    Teapot, 9½″ h, luster trim, fruit finial, marked "Walley," English registry mark **250.00**
Morning Glory
    Cup and Saucer, handleless **75.00**
    Creamer, 6½″ h, paneled, foliage handle **175.00**
    Pitcher, 8″ h, paneled, underglaze blue **250.00**
    Plate, 6¼″ d, underglaze blue, polychrome enamel and luster dec **70.00**
    Sugar, cov, 8″ h, paneled, underglaze blue, foliage handles **175.00**
Oriental, 7½″ w, 14″ l, 7½″ h, fruit compote, blue Oriental transfer, polychrome enameled gilt, Mason's **415.00**
Rose
    Cup and Saucer, handleless **75.00**
    Plate, 9½″ d, red, blue, green, and black **90.00**
Strawberry
    Cup and Saucer, handleless **75.00**
    Plate, 8¼″ d, flaked enameled berries, stains **95.00**
    Platter, 13½″ l, underglaze blue strawberries, polychrome enamel dec, purple luster **225.00**
    Sugar, cov, 8½″ h **175.00**
    Waste Bowl, 5⅜″ h **175.00**

Plate, blue with rust, green and copper luster, 8½″ d, $90.00.

Urn
    Cup and Saucer, handleless, minor flaking on saucer **115.00**
    Plate, 9½″ d **125.00**
    Toddy Plate, 4¾″ d **190.00**
Urn and Flowers
    Cup and Saucer, handleless, stains, hairline on saucer **135.00**
    Plate, 9½″ d, very worn center, wear, stains **85.00**

GAUDY WELSH

History: Gaudy Welsh is a translucent porcelain that was originally made in the Swansea area of England from 1830 to 1845. Although the designs resemble Gaudy Dutch, the body texture and weight differ. One of the characteristics is the gold luster on top of the glaze.

In 1890, Allerton made a similar ware from heavier opaque porcelain.

Marks: Allerton pieces usually bear an export mark.

References: Susan and Al Bagdade, *Warman's English & Continental Pottery & Porcelain,* Second Edition, Wallace-Homestead, 1991; John A. Shuman, III, *The Collector's Encyclopedia of Gaudy Dutch and Welsh,* Collector Books, 1990, 1991 value update, out-of-print; Howard Y. Williams, *Gaudy Welsh China,* Wallace-Homestead, out-of-print.

Collectors' Club: Gaudy Collector's Society, PO Box 274, Gates Mills, OH 44040.

Columbine
    Bowl, 10″ d, 5½″ h, ftd, underglaze blue and polychrome enamel floral dec **400.00**
    Plate, 5½″ d **65.00**
Daisy and Chain
    Creamer **175.00**
    Cup and Saucer **95.00**
    Sugar, cov **195.00**
    Teapot, cov **225.00**
Flower Basket
    Bowl, 10½″ d **190.00**
    Mug, 4″ h **90.00**
    Plate **65.00**
    Sugar, cov, luster trim **165.00**

Grape
  Bowl, 5¼" d **50.00**
  Cup and Saucer **75.00**
  Mug, 2½" h **65.00**
  Plate, 5¼" d **65.00**
Oyster
  Bowl, 6" d **80.00**
  Creamer, 3" h **100.00**
  Cup and Saucer **75.00**
  Jug, 5¾" h **85.00**
  Soup Plate, 10" d, flange rim **85.00**
Strawberry
  Creamer **90.00**
  Cup and Saucer **75.00**
  Mug, 4⅛" h **125.00**
  Plate, 8¼" d **150.00**
Tulip
  Bowl, 6¼" d **50.00**
  Cake Plate, 10" d, molded handles **120.00**
  Creamer, 5¼" h **90.00**
  Sugar, cov, 6¾" h **110.00**
  Teapot, 7¼" h **175.00**

Tulip pattern, plate, 6¼" d, $60.00.

Wagon Wheel
  Cup and Saucer **75.00**
  Mug, 2½" h **95.00**
  Pitcher, 8½" h **195.00**
  Plate, 8¾" d **85.00**

GEISHA GIRL PORCELAIN

History: Geisha Girl porcelain is a Japanese export ware whose production commenced during the last quarter of the 19th century and continued heavily until World War II. It features kimono-clad Japanese ladies and children amid Japanese gardens and temples. There are over 125 brightly colored scenes depicting the pre-modern Japanese lifestyle. Over 140 marks and almost 200 patterns and variations have been identified.

Geisha Girl ware may be totally hand painted, hand painted over a stenciled design, or occasionally decaled. The underlying stenciled design is usually red-orange, but also is found in brown, black, and green (rare).

All Geisha Girl items are bordered in a single color or a combination of blues, reds, greens, rhubarb, yellow, black, browns, and gold. The most common is red-orange. Borders may be wavy, scalloped, or banded and range from ¹⁄₁₆ to ¼ inch. The borders themselves often are further decorated with gold, white, or yellow lacing, flowers, dots, or stripes. Some examples even include interior frames of butterflies or flowers.

Geisha Girl is found in many forms including tea, cocoa, lunch, and children's sets, dresser items, vases, and serving dishes. Large plates or platters, candlesticks, miniatures, and mugs are hardest to locate. Geisha Girl advertising items add to a collection.

Reference: Elyce Litts, *The Collectors Encyclopedia of Geisha Girl Porcelain,* Collector Books, 1988.

REPRODUCTION ALERT

The popularity of Geisha Girl porcelain continued after World War II, and it is being reproduced today. To identify reproductions, look for a red-orange border, very white and smooth porcelain, and sparse coloring and detail. Reproduced items include dresser, tea and saké sets, toothpick holders, small vases, table plates, and salt and pepper shakers.

Additional Listings: See *Warman's Americana & Collectibles* for more examples.

Bowl, 10" d, Chinese Coin, ruffled, pierced handle **85.00**
Butter Pat, cherry-blossom-shaped reserve geisha, red, line int. frame, flower and butterfly backdrop **10.00**
Cracker Jar, Garden Bench E, wavy red with gold, mint green and gray geometric, gold trim **85.00**
Creamer, 4" h, Feeding the Carp, ribbed, hourglass shape **20.00**
Cup and Saucer, Garden Bench B, pedestal, lobed, scalloped saucer **25.00**
Eggcup, child reaching for butterfly **15.00**
Gravy Boat, underplate, Rice Harvesters A, leaf shape, mint green, deep green, and red, gold border **25.00**
Humidor, Battledore, blue scallop, gold line **75.00**
Nappy, Temple A, hand-fluted edge, sea-green border and handle **45.00**

Napkin Ring, River's Edge pattern, pine green border, red-orange border, marked "T" in cherry blossom and "Japan," $35.00.

Plate

6⅛" d, Flag Day, red, yellow lacing **15.00**

8½" d, children in boat, swirl, fluted, cobalt blue, gold
lacing, scalloped edge **30.00**

Relish Dish, Picnic B, red-orange, gold trim, floret edge,
reserves **25.00**

Salt and Pepper Shakers, pr, 2" h, Garden Bench F, red-
orange and gold top, cobalt blue shoulders **20.00**

Teapot, melon ribbed, red and cobalt blue **45.00**

GIRANDOLES AND MANTEL LUSTRES

History: A girandole is a very elaborate branched candleholder,
often featuring cut glass prisms surrounding the mountings. A
mantel lustre is a glass vase with attached cut glass prisms.

Girandoles and mantel lustres usually are found in pairs. It is
not uncommon for girandoles to be part of a large garniture set.
Girandoles and mantel lustres achieved their greatest popularity
in the last half of the 19th century both in the United States and
Europe.

Girandoles, pr

14" h, SP and cut glass, three tiers hung with faceted
drops, scrolled candle arms, c1900 .... **150.00**

16" h, marble base, gilt-brass stem, three arms, clear cut
prisms **220.00**

18" h, courting couple, brass relief, triple branch with
prisms, marble base **115.00**

20½" h, pierced and shaped rect frame, orig glass, damaged crest, Italian Rococo, 18th C **450.00**

21" h, gilt metal, faceted glass, three arms, Louis Phil-
lippe style **475.00**

35½" h, bronze, seven-light glass drops suspended from
pressed glass stars **600.00**

Mantel Lusters

6¼" h, 8" w, cornucopia style, opaline glass horns, emanating from gilt-bronze female hand, white marble
base, French, 19th C, price for pr **230.00**

**Mantel luster, painted pink rose on cream ground, 12¼" h,
$350.00.**

10" h, ruby, overlay with white and gilt foliage, faceted
cut glass prism, c1875 .... **425.00**

14¼" h, 9½" d urn form, onyx marble and gilt brass,
Moorish style, champleve floral dec, French, price for
pr **4,600.00**

14½" h, pink cased, enamel-painted flower swags with
gilt scrolls, scalloped bulbous bowl, two rows of clear
prisms **300.00**

20" h candelabra, cast brass, porcelain inserts, 22" h
matching porcelain French clock, price for 3-pc set **1,100.00**

GOLDSCHEIDER

History: Friedrich Goldscheider founded a porcelain and faience
factory in Vienna, Austria, in 1885. Upon his death, his widow
carried on operations. In 1920 Walter and Marcell, Friedrich's
sons, gained control. During the Art Deco period, the firm commissioned several artists to create figural statues, among which
were Pierrettes and sleek wolfhounds. During the 1930s, the company's products were mostly traditional.

In the early 1940s, the Goldscheiders fled to the United States
and re-established operations in Trenton, New Jersey. The Goldscheider Everlast Corporation was listed in Trenton City directories
between 1943 and 1950. Goldscheider Ceramics, located at 1441
Heath Avenue, Trenton, New Jersey, was listed in the *1952 Crockery and Glass Journal Directory* but was not listed in 1954.

Bust, 15¼" h, woman, stylized head, red unglazed earthenware, coiling hair, rose on collar, black-painted
wooden base, imp circular label ''Goldscheider/
Wein,'' c1925 .... **1,250.00**

**Bust, black woman, blue hair, orange highlights, sgd
''Goldschieder, Vienna, 1927'' on pedestal base,
$800.00.**

Figure

8¾" h, dancer, full yellow dress, imp and stamped
marks, inscribed ''Latour'' **450.00**

18½" h, Butterfly Girl, cape painted to resemble monarch butterfly, imp numbers, painted marks, artist sgd "Lorenzi" **2,500.00**

24" h, partially draped maiden, playing flute, leopard at feet, oval base with floral garland, sgd in base "Podola," stamped and imp marks **1,750.00**

Lamp, 32" h, figural, standing bare-breasted female, long lavender gown, holding fruit and grain garland, stepped base, column standard, printed and imp marks, matching silk beaded shade, minor restoration to base **2,500.00**

Wall Mask, 11¼" h, girl, brown curly hair, red lips, aqua scarf **195.00**

GONDER POTTERY

History: Lawton Gonder established Gonder Ceramic Arts, Inc., at Zanesville, Ohio, in 1941. He had gained experience while working for other factories in the area. Gonder experimented with glazes, including Chinese crackle, gold crackle, and flambé. Lamp bases were manufactured under the name "Eglee" at a second plant location.

The company ceased operation in 1957.

Marks: Pieces are clearly marked with the word "Gonder" in various forms.

References: Susan and Al Bagdade, *Warman's American Pottery and Porcelain,* Wallace-Homestead, 1994; Ron Hoppes, *The Collector's Guide and History of Gonder Pottery,* L-W Book Sales, 1992.

Collectors' Club: Gonder Collectors Club, PO Box 21, Crooksville, OH 43731.

Basket, 6½" h, leaf pattern, turquoise ext., pink coral int., marked "H-39 Gonder USA" **45.00**

Cornucopia, 7" l, turquoise and brown, marked "E5" .   **25.00**

Ewer, 12" h, figural, swan **35.00**

Figure, 18¼" l, panther, jade green **95.00**

Tea Set, cov teapot, creamer, and cov sugar, mottled brown **45.00**

Vase, 9" h, mottled turquoise and brown, pink int. **20.00**

GOOFUS GLASS

History: Goofus glass, also known as Mexican ware, hooligan glass, and pickle glass, is a pressed glass with relief designs that were painted either on the back or front. The designs are usually in red and green with a metallic gold ground. It was popular from 1890 to 1920 and was used as a premium at carnivals.

It was produced by several companies: Crescent Glass Company, Wellsburg, West Virginia; Imperial Glass Corporation, Bellaire, Ohio; LaBelle Glass Works, Bridgeport, Ohio; and Northwood Glass Co., Indiana, Pennsylvania, Wheeling, West Virginia, and Bridgeport, Ohio.

Goofus glass lost its popularity when people found that the paint tarnished or scaled off after repeated washings and wear. No record of its manufacture has been found after 1920.

Marks: Goofus glass made by Northwood includes one of the following marks: "N," "N" in one circle, "N" in two circles, or one or two circles without the "N."

References: Carolyn McKinley, *Goofus Glass,* Collector Books, 1984, out-of-print; Ellen T. Schroy, *Warman's Glass,* Second Edition, Wallace-Homestead, 1995.

Periodical: *Goofus Glass Gazette,* 9 Lindenwood Ct, Sterling, VA 20165.

Bowl
  Holly & Berry **55.00**
    Pinecone, Northwood, green **60.00**
Candy Dish, Grape and Cable **25.00**
Coaster, gold, red glowers, orig paint, price for 4 pc set   **40.00**
Decanter, LaBelle Rose, orig stopper **50.00**
Miniature Lamp, Cabbage Rose, 9" h **55.00**
Perfume Bottle, painted pink tulips **25.00**
Powder Jar, cov, Cabbage Rose, white rose **55.00**

Basket, leaf pattern, turquoise ext, coral pink int, marked "H-39 Gonder USA," $45.00.

Salt shaker, Grape and Leaf, 4" h, 2¼" w, $25.00.

Salt Shaker, Grape and Leaf **25.00**

Tray, Chrysanthemum, bronze and red **45.00**

Vase, Peacock, relief molded, 10½" h **85.00**

GOSS CHINA AND CRESTED WARE

History: In 1858 William H. Goss opened his Henley factory and produced terra-cotta ware. A year later he moved to Stoke-on-Trent and added Parian ware to his line. In 1883 Adolphus, William's son, expanded on his father's idea of decorating small ivory pots and vases with the coat of arms of schools, hospitals, colleges (especially Oxford and Cambridge), and other motifs to appeal to the souvenir-seeking English "day-tripper." The forms used were copied from ancient artifacts in museums.

William died in 1906, his son in 1913. Following business setbacks, the firm was sold in 1929 to Geo. Jones & Sons Ltd., which had previously acquired Arcadian, Swan, and other firms that made crested wares. As late as 1931 the Goss name was still being used. About 1936 Cauldon Potteries purchased the Goss assets. Production ceased in 1940. In 1954 Ridgway and Adderley acquired all Goss assets (molds, patterns, designs, and right to use the Goss name and trademark).

Other manufacturers of crested ware in England were Arcadian, Carlton China, Grafton China, Savoy China, Shelley, and Willow Art. Gemma in Germany also made crested wares.

Marks: Pieces made by the Goss firm between 1883 and 1931 have a printed mark comprised of "W. H. Goss" underneath the word "GOSHAWK." "England" was added on later pieces. Many early examples carry an impressed "W. H. Goss," either with or without the printed mark.

References: Sandy Andrews, *Crested China: The History of Heraldic Souvenir Ware*, Milestone Publications (England); John Galpin, *A Handbook of Goss China*, Milestone Publications; Nicholas Pine, *The 1984 Price Guide to Goss China*, Milestone Publications, 1984; Nicholas Pine and Sandy Andrews, *The 1984 Price Guide to Crested China* (including revisions to *Crested China*), Milestone Publications; Roland Ward, *The Price Guide to the Models of W. H. Goss*, Antiques Collectors' Club.

Collectors' Clubs: Crested Circle, 75 Cannon Grove, Fetcham, Leatherhead Surrey KT22 9LP England; Goss & Crested China Club, 62 Murray Rd, Horndean, Waterlooville, Hampshire PO8 9JL, England; Goss Collectors Club, 4 Khasiaberry, Walnut Tree, Milton Keynes MK7 7DP England.

Notes: Crests are of little value unless they match, e.g., Shakespeare's jug with Shakespeare's crest. Collectors tend to collect one form (e.g., vase, ewer, jug), one particular crest, or one type of object (e.g., boat, cat, dog). Price is determined not by crest, but size, condition, and mark.

Goss

Beaker, Queen Victoria's Golden Jubilee, 1887	**95.00**
Brooch, rose and lily of the valley buds, oval, colored, glazed	**125.00**
Building	
Ann Hathaway's Cottage, glazed	**120.00**
Burns' Cottage, thatched roof, unglazed	**125.00**
Lloyd George's Early Home, Criccieth, gray roof, green foliage	**190.00**
Shakespeare's House, half size, colored	**135.00**
St Nicholas Chapel, Ilfracombe, gray tiled roof, green foliage, unglazed	**200.00**
Bury Libation Vessel, cov, Bury St Edmunds, Suffolk, large	**75.00**
Bust, parian	
Beethoven, white, unglazed	**165.00**
Napoleon, St Helena	**110.00**
Scott, wearing tartan plaid, socle plinth, white, unglazed	**50.00**
Ewer	
Felixstone, Teignmouth/Devon	**30.00**
Folkestone, School of Musketry Hythe	**45.00**
Oxford, Totnes, Devon	**30.00**
Yarmouth, Africa and The East, 1909	**85.00**
Figure	
Lorna, crinoline dress and bonnet	**300.00**
Peggy, holding basket of flowers	**300.00**
Kettle, Hastings	**15.00**
Loving Cup, three handles	
Ancient Kings of Cornwall, Newquay, Cornwall ...	**18.00**
See of Lincoln, City of Lincoln, H. M. Queen Victoria	**20.00**
Menu Holder, Funchal, Madeira, tassels on each corner	**45.00**
Milk Jug, Monte Carlo	**30.00**
Pitcher, Dartmouth, Devon Oak	**18.00**
Salt Pot, Saint Malo, Stockton on Tees	**20.00**
Tray, sq, tassels in corners, brown transfer of Castle Entrance, Ruthin'	**60.00**
Urn, Hawes, Guildford	**30.00**

Other Crested-Ware Manufacturers

Arcadian	
Chess Piece	
Bishop, Bournemouth	**35.00**
Castle, Worthing	**12.00**
Knight, Nossmayo	**25.00**
Model of Highland cottage, Littlehampton	**22.50**
One Special Scotch, Cliftonville	**15.00**
St Paul's Cathedral, City of London	**25.00**
Westminister Abbey, City of London	**35.00**
Carlton	
Ball Vase, Llanberis	**5.50**
Gramaphone with Horn, His Master's Voice	**65.00**
Welsh Hat, Rhyl	**17.50**
Whelk Shell, Listen to the Sea, Milford Haven	**15.00**
Devonia Art, Drake Statue, Plymouth	**20.00**
Podmore	
Big Ben, City of London	**20.00**
Rowton Tower, Chester	**35.00**
Shelley	
German Zeppelin Bomb, Aberystwyth	**30.00**
Medal Shaped Dish, Aberystwyth	**20.00**
Rufus Stone, Lyndhurst	**15.00**
Willow Art	
Figure, walking lion, Ryhl	**30.00**
The Old Home of the Right Hon. D. Lloyd George, Esq, M.P. Llanystumdwy Near Criccieth, Aberystwyth	**60.00**

MADE IN

Zuid Holland

GOUDA POTTERY

History: Gouda and the surrounding areas of Holland have been principal Dutch pottery centers for centuries. Originally, the potteries produced a simple utilitarian tin-glazed Delft-type earthenware and the famous clay smoker's pipes.

When pipe making declined in the early 1900s, the Gouda potteries turned to art pottery. Influenced by the Art Nouveau and Art Deco movements, artists expressed themselves with free-form and stylized designs in bold colors.

Periodical: *The Dutch Potter,* 47 London Terrace, New Rochelle, NY 10804.

REPRODUCTION ALERT

With the Art Nouveau and Art Deco revivals of recent years, modern reproductions of Gouda pottery currently are on the market. They are difficult to distinguish from the originals.

Biscuit Jar, cov, 8" h, multicolored 135.00
Bowl, 5½" d, 3½" h, Damascus mark 50.00
Candlestick
   3" h, 6½" d, circular, handle, matte green, yellow,
     blue, and cream dec, marked "0139 DAM II Hol-
     land," c1885 .... 100.00
   3¾" h, green, rust, cobalt blue, ochre, marked "Can-
     dis 1137" and house mark 55.00
Charger, 12" d, multicolored flowers, rope border, black
   trim 150.00
Compote, 7⅝", black ground, geometric design, multicolored scroll int. 175.00
Ewer, 9½" h, matte finish, Anjer house mark 125.00

Vase, Windmill on obverse, lake on reverse, twig handle, extended bark neck, Springer & Co., Elfagen, Germany, c1890, imp "1208," 11½" h, $145.00.

Incense Burner, 8" h, Roba, flowers and geometric de-
   signs, green ground 110.00
Jug, 10" h, multicolored dec, black matte ground, orig
   stopper 195.00
Plate, 10½" d, matte multicolored dec 100.00
Tobacco Jar, cov, 5" h, Verona pattern 100.00
Tumbler, 4⅜" h, 3⅝" d, multicolored flowers, green
   leaves, black ground, satin finish, marked "Neri" and
   house mark 65.00
Vase, 9¼" h, painted floral dec, blue, yellow, green,
   brown, pink, and ivory high glaze, ink mark "Made
   in Holland," repaired chip at base, price for pr 210.00

GRANITEWARE

History: Graniteware is the name commonly given to enamel-coated iron or steel kitchenware.

The first graniteware was made in Germany in the 1830s. Graniteware was not produced in the United States until the 1860s. At the start of World War I, when European companies turned to manufacturing war weapons, American producers took over the market.

Gray and white were the most common graniteware colors, although each company made their own special color in shades of blue, green, brown, violet, cream, or red.

Older graniteware is heavier than the new. Pieces with cast-iron handles date between 1870 to 1890; wood handles between 1900 to 1910. Other dating clues are seams, wooden knobs, and tin lids.

References: Helen Greguire, *The Collector's Encyclopedia of Granite Ware: Colors Shapes and Values,* Book 1 (1990, 1994 value update), Book 2 (1993), Collector Books; Dana G. Morykan and Harry L. Rinker, *Warman's Country Antiques & Collectibles,* Third Edition, Wallace-Homestead, 1996.

Collectors' Club: National Graniteware Society, PO Box 10013, Cedar Rapids, IA 52410.

Reproduction Alert: Graniteware still is manufactured in many of the traditional forms and colors.

Additional Listings: See *Warman's Americana & Collectibles* for more examples.

Baking Dish, Chrysolite 145.00
Berry Bucket
   Blue Swirl
      Granite lid 315.00
      Tin lid 200.00
   Brown Swirl, granite lid 275.00
   Chrysolite, tin lid 375.00
   Cobalt Swirl, granite lid 925.00
   Dutchess Ware, tin lid 300.00
   Thistle Ware, granite lid 150.00
Biscuit Tray, Onyx 45.00
Butter Churn, gray drum, floor model 1,350.00
Candlestick, Cobalt Swirl, fluted 195.00
Canister Set, Snow on the Mountain, price for six-pc set 140.00
Clock, blue and white, 8-day movement, Dutch design 955.00
Coffee Boiler
   Chrysolite 185.00
   Columbian, 10" 215.00

Coffeepot, Savory Sterling Enameled Nickled Steel Ware, No 901, Newark, NJ, 2½ gal, 10¾" base, 13" h, $75.00.

Coffeepot
Blue Swirl	180.00
Chrysolite	275.00
Dutchess Ware, 7"	625.00
Coffeepot and Tray, tilt type, Blue Relish, pewter trim	295.00

Colander
Brown Swirl	135.00
Chrysolite	380.00
Cobalt Swirl	165.00

Cream Can
Blue Swirl, granite lid	350.00
Chrysolite, tin lid	2,500.00
Cobalt Swirl, tin lid	750.00
Columbian, tin lid	750.00
Creamer, Blue Swirl	175.00

Dipper, Windsor
Blue Swirl	140.00
Cobalt Swirl	60.00
Red Swirl	500.00
Dish Pan, Emerald Swirl	205.00

Funnel
Brown Swirl, 3" d	205.00
Cobalt Swirl, 5" d	395.00
Kettle, Emerald Swirl, small, tin lid	275.00

Lunch Box
Blue Swirl, round	275.00
Brown Swirl, oval	1,800.00
Gray, round	225.00
Measure, Parrot Gray, orig paper label	115.00
Muffin Pan, Cobalt Swirl, eight depressions	190.00
Mush Mug, Iris Swirl	150.00
Platter, 12" l, oval, deep blue and white	135.00
Roaster, Columbian	450.00

Salesman's Sample, wash basin
Blue Swirl	125.00
Chrysolite	625.00
Soap Dish, Emerald Swirl, granite insert	215.00
Spittoon, Emerald Swirl, two pc	170.00
Spooner, Brown Swirl	325.00
Sugar Bowl, cov, Cobalt Swirl	400.00

Syrup
Chrysolite	775.00
Emerald Swirl	2,200.00

Teapot, gooseneck spout
Cobalt Swirl, 10"	250.00
Columbian	950.00
Emerald Swirl, 10"	1,800.00
Lava, 7"	270.00
Tea Steeper, Chrysolite	325.00
Tray, Columbian, 10 ×18"	400.00
Tumbler, Solar Gray, orig paper label	475.00
Utensil Rack, Snow on the Mountain	195.00
Wash Bowl and Pitcher, Blue Swirl	650.00
Water Bucket, brown and white, large swirls	150.00
Water Carrier, Cobalt Swirl, granite lid	330.00

Water Pitcher
Bluebelle Ware	170.00
Chrysolite	600.00
Columbian, gallon	600.00

GREENAWAY, KATE   K.G.

History: Kate Greenaway, or "K.G." as she initialed her famous drawings, was born in 1846 in London. Her father was a prominent wood engraver. Kate's natural talent for drawing soon was evident, and she began art classes at the age of 12. In 1868 she had her first public exhibition.

Her talents were used primarily in illustrating. The cards she decorated for Marcus Ward are largely unsigned. China and pottery companies soon had her drawings of children appearing on many of their wares. By the 1880s she was one of the foremost children's book illustrators in England.

Reference: Ina Taylor, *The Art of Kate Greenaway: A Nostalgic Portrait of Childhood,* Pelican Publishing, 1991.

Collectors' Club: Kate Greenaway Society, PO Box 8, Norwood, PA 19074.

Reproduction Alert: Some Greenaway buttons have been reproduced in Europe and sold in the United States.

Almanac, 1883, published by George Routledge & Sons	100.00
Bowl, amber, Daisy and Button pattern, girl and dog on SP holder, marked "Reed & Barton"	500.00
Bust, 5" h, girl with glasses, frilly bonnet, ribbons, lace	65.00
Children's Book, *Birthday Book,* Warne, color illus	50.00
Children's Feeding Dish, nursery rhyme dec with children and dog, Haviland	100.00
Children's Play Dishes, tea set, children and dachshund pulling tablecloth, price for 7-pc set	150.00
Figure, 9½" h, children jumping rope, price for pr	600.00
Match Holder, girl helping little girl over log, place for matches and striker	100.00
Nodder, bisque, elderly couple, wearing eyeglasses, cloak, bonnet, and high hat	135.00
Plate, 9" d, children playing, oversized fruit, birds, and flowers	100.00
Print, 6 × 8", Outdoor Tea Party, fifteen girls, sgd	95.00
Sugar Shaker, boy in long coat, white ground	95.00
Thimble Holder, girl holding SS thimble	125.00
Tile, Pipe Thee High, scene with small boy and horn, Wedgwood	85.00

Trade card, 2½ × 4⅝",
$8.00.

Vase, 4" h, figural girl, holder with orig frosted dec bud
vase, sq ornate ftd base, marked "Tufts" **150.00**

GREENTOWN GLASS

History: The Indiana Tumbler and Goblet Co., Greentown, Indiana, produced its first clear, pressed glass table and bar wares in late 1894. Initial success led to a doubling of the plant size in 1895 and other subsequent expansions, one in 1897 to allow for the manufacture of colored glass. In 1899 the firm joined the combine known as the National Glass Company.

In 1900, just before arriving in Greentown, Jacob Rosenthal developed an opaque brown glass, called "chocolate," which ranged in color from a dark, rich chocolate to a lighter coffee-with-cream hue. Production of chocolate glass saved the financially pressed Indiana Tumbler and Goblet Works. The Cactus and Leaf Bracket patterns were made almost exclusively in chocolate glass. Other popular chocolate patterns include Austrian, Dewey, Shuttle, and Teardrop and Tassel. In 1902 National Glass Company bought Rosenthal's chocolate glass formula so other plants in the combine could use the color.

In 1902 Rosenthal developed the Golden Agate and Rose Agate colors. All work ceased on June 13, 1903, when a fire of suspicious origin destroyed the Indiana Tumbler and Goblet Company Works.

After the fire, other companies, e.g., McKee and Brothers, produced chocolate glass in the same pattern designs used by Greentown. Later reproductions also have been made, with Cactus among the most-heavily copied patterns.

Reference: James Measell, *Greentown Glass,* Grand Rapids Public Museum, 1979, 1992–93 value update, distributed by Antique Publications.

Collectors' Clubs: Collectors of Findlay Glass, PO Box 256, Findlay, OH 45839; National Greentown Glass Assoc, 19596 Glendale Ave, South Bend, IN 46637.

Museums: Grand Rapids Public Museum, Ruth Herrick Greentown Glass Collection, Grand Rapids, MI; Greentown Glass Museum, Greentown, IN.

Additional Listings: Holly Amber and Pattern Glass.

Reproduction Alert.

Animal Dish, cov
    Cat, hamper base, chocolate 250.00
    Dolphin, chocolate, sawtooth edge 195.00
Berry Bowl, master, Wild Rose and Berry, chocolate .. 250.00
Bowl, 8" d, Dewey, amber, ftd 35.00
Butter Dish, cov, Overall Lattice, clear 65.00
Compote, 5½" d, Cactus, chocolate 120.00
Cordial, Overall Lattice, clear 35.00
Creamer
    Cactus, chocolate 125.00
    Indian Head, Nile green 475.00
Cruet, orig stopper
    Cactus 225.00
    Chrysanthemum Leaf 850.00
Dresser Tray, Wild Rose and Bowknot, chocolate 325.00
Iced Tea Tumbler, Cactus 85.00
Mug, 4½" h, Outdoor Drinking Scene, chocolate 150.00

Mug, outdoor drinking scene,
chocolate, 4½" h, $150.00.

Paperweight, 4" d, five chocolate flowers, clear glass
    ground 55.00
Pitcher
    Cord Drapery 75.00
    Racing Deer 650.00
    Ruffled Eye, chocolate 550.00
Salt and Pepper Shakers, pr, Cactus, green opaque 40.00
Spooner
    Cupid, clear 155.00
    Water Lily and Cattails, chocolate 125.00
Syrup, Cord Drapery, chocolate, damage to handle ... 75.00
Tumbler, Teardrop and Tassel, cobalt blue 60.00
Wine, Cord Drapery 75.00

GRUEBY POTTERY

History: William Grueby was active in the ceramic industry for several years before he developed his own method of producing matte-glazed pottery and founded the Grueby Faience Company in Boston, Massachusetts, in 1897.

The art pottery was hand thrown in natural shapes, hand molded, and hand tooled. A variety of colored glazes, singly or in combinations, were produced, but green was the most popular. In 1908 the firm was divided into the Grueby Pottery Company and the Grueby Faience and Tile Co., the latter making art pottery until bankruptcy forced closure shortly after 1908.

References: Paul Evans, *Art Pottery of the United States,* Second Edition, Feingold & Lewis Publishing, 1987; Ralph and Terry Kovel, *Kovels' American Art Pottery,* Crown Publishers, 1993.

Bowl, 11" d, eleven molded leaves, cucumber-green glaze, imp mark, inscribed "RE" for artist Ruth Erickson, and "4/4" **1,400.00**
Bust, 11" h, laughing boy, unglazed terra-cotta, numbered inside **260.00**
Lamp, 22½" h, 18⅛" d shade, geometric green and yellow leaded-glass shade with swirling leaf band, marked "Tiffany Studios New York," bronze cap finial, green glazed base with imp mark, designer Ruth Erickson's monogram **17,600.00**
Paperweight, 4" l, scarab, imp mark **450.00**
Tile, 6" sq
    Knight, emb stylized caramel brown figure, blue ground, sgd "DC" on back **250.00**
    Spanish Galleon, ivory, brown, amber, and green, green ground, few edge nicks, painted "AS/GM" on back, orig price tag and paper label **1,300.00**

Tile, dark green tree, blue sky, white clouds, light green ground, 6¼ × 6¾", $400.00.

Vase
    4¾" h, compressed spherical body, cylindrical neck, heavy pale blue-green glaze, imp mark, inscribed "E. W. D." within circle **750.00**
    6" h, compressed spherical body, slightly everted rim, seven broad molded leaves, cucumber-green glaze, imp mark **850.00**
    7" h, 4½" d, bulbous, cylindrical neck, tooled and applied leaves and buds, great feathered cucumber-green matte finish, imp faience mark, small edge nick **2,000.00**
    9" h, 5¼" d, bulbous, flaring rim, tooled and applied leaves, cucumber-green matte glaze, dec by M. Seaman, imp faience mark and "MS/16," pinpoint nick at top **1,800.00**

9¼" h, 6" d, bulbous, cylindrical neck, gently flaring rim, thick, slightly feathered medium-dark-green matte glaze, imp circular mark **700.00**

HAIR ORNAMENTS

History: Hair ornaments, among the first accessories developed by primitive man, were used to remove tangles and keep hair out of one's face. Remnants of early combs have been found in many archaeological excavations.

As fashion styles evolved through the centuries, hair ornaments kept pace with changes in design and usage. Hair combs and other hair ornaments are made in a wide variety of materials, e.g., precious metals, ivory, tortoiseshell, plastics, and wood.

Combs were first made in America during the Revolution when imports from England were restricted. Early American combs were made of horn and treasured as toiletry articles.

Reference: Evelyn Haetig, *Antique Combs and Purses,* Gallery Graphics Press, 1983.

Collectors' Club: Antique Fancy Comb Collectors Club, 3291 N River Rd, Libertyville, IL 60048.

Museums: Leominster Historical Society, Field School Museum, Leominster, MA; Miller's Museum of Antique Combs, Homer, AK.

Back Comb, celluloid
    Bright teal blue pearlescent, embedded rhinestones, c1926 .... **40.00**
    Imitation ivory, hearts and flowers filigree design, row of five long teeth, c1910 .... **30.00**
    Imitation tortoiseshell, decorative wirework, prong-set rhinestones, wide row of multiple teeth, c1880 **85.00**
Barrette, 2½" d, rhinestone dec, c1950 .... **20.00**
Hair Clip, rhinestone dec, c1930, price for pr **20.00**
Hairpin
    Amber, Art Deco, c1925 .... **45.00**
    Tortoiseshell, SS filigree, English, Victorian, c1890 . **75.00**
Ornament
    Plastic, black, shaft with box-shaped dec on top, seven paste rhinestone dec on sides of box, c1960 **25.00**
    Rhinestone, elongated star shape, large paste diamond center, long silver-colored clip, c1960 ... **15.00**
Side Comb, celluloid, imitation amber, pearlescent-colored overlay, embedded rhinestones, c1926 .... **25.00**
Tiara, encircles gathered hair, hand-set rhinestones, c1940 .... **75.00**

HALL CHINA COMPANY

History: Robert Hall founded the Hall China Company in 1903 in East Liverpool, Ohio. He died in 1904 and was succeeded by his son, Robert Taggart Hall. After years of experimentation, Robert T. Hall developed a leadless glaze in 1911, opening the way for production of glazed household products.

The Hall China Company made many types of kitchenware, refrigerator sets, and dinnerware in a wide variety of patterns. Some patterns were made exclusively for a particular retailer, such as Heather Rose for Sears.

One of the most popular patterns was Autumn Leaf, a premium designed by Arden Richards in 1933 for the exclusive use of the

Jewel Tea Company. Still a Jewel Tea property, Autumn Leaf has not been listed in catalogs since 1978 but is produced on a replacement basis with the date stamped on the back.

References: Susan and Al Bagdade, *Warman's American Pottery and Porcelain,* Wallace-Homestead, 1994; Harvey Duke, *Hall China: Price Guide Update Two,* ELO Books, 1995; ———, *Official Price Guide to Pottery and Porcelain,* Eighth Edition, House of Collectibles, 1995; C. L. Miller, *Jewel Tea Company: Its History and Products,* Schiffer Publishing, 1996; ———, *Jewel Tea: Sales and Housewares Collectibles,* Schiffer Publishing, 1995; Dana G. Morykan and Harry L. Rinker, *Warman's Country Antiques & Collectibles,* Third Edition, Wallace-Homestead, 1996; Margaret and Kenn Whitmyer, *The Collector's Encyclopedia of Hall China,* Second Edition, Collector Books, 1994.

Periodicals: *The Daze,* PO Box 57, Otisville, MI 48463; *The Hall China Encore,* 317 N Pleasant St, Oberlin, OH 44074.

Collectors' Clubs: Hall Collector's Club, PO Box 360488, Cleveland, OH 44136; National Autumn Leaf Collectors Club, Route 16, Box 275, Tulsa, OK 74131.

Additional Listings: See *Warman's Americana & Collectibles* for more examples.

Patterns

Autumn Leaf
Bowl, small	15.00
Coffeepot, 8″ h	40.00
Custard Cup	5.00
Jug, ball, #3	20.00
Mixing bowl, large	25.00
Plate, 8″ d	15.00
Platter, 13½″ l	18.00
Teapot, Aladdin, 6 cup, round lid and insert	60.00

Orange Poppy
Baker, fluted	15.00
Casserole, cov, oval	30.00
Creamer and Sugar	25.00
Plate, 9″ d	8.50
Teapot	
Boston	280.00
Streamline	210.00

Red Poppy
Bowl, 5½″ d	4.25
Cereal Bowl, 6″ d	7.00
Creamer and Sugar	15.00
Cup and Saucer	6.00
Mustard, 3 pcs	45.00
Plate, 9″ d	6.00
Teapot, New York, platinum trim	60.00

Teapots
Airflow, cobalt blue, gold trim, 6 cup	165.00
Automobile, black	500.00
Basketball, Chinese Red	850.00
Birdcage, maroon, gold trim, 6 cup	200.00
Holiday, Hallcraft, Eva Zeisel, red and black, white ground	60.00
Melody, green, gold trim, 6 cup	245.00
Ohio, brown, gold trim, 6 cup	175.00
Regal, white, gold trim	90.00

Teapot, maroon, gold trim, 6 cup, gold and black marks, 6¼″ h, 10½″ w, $20.00.

Sundial, canary, gold trim	130.00
Surfside, emerald green, gold trim, 6 cup	185.00

HAMPSHIRE POTTERY

History: In 1871 James S. Taft founded the Hampshire Pottery Company in Keene, New Hampshire. Production began with redwares and stonewares, followed by majolica in 1879. A semiporcelain, with the recognizable matte glazes plus the Royal Worcester glaze, was introduced in 1883.

Until World War I the factory made an extensive line of utilitarian and art wares including souvenir items. After the war the firm resumed operations but made only hotel dinnerware and tiles. The company was dissolved in 1923.

References: Susan and Al Bagdade, *Warman's American Pottery and Porcelain,* Wallace-Homestead, 1994; Ralph and Terry Kovel, *Kovels' American Art Pottery,* Crown Publishers, 1993.

Bulb Bowl, 9⅞″ d, dark green matte glaze, yellow buds, light green leaves, glossy lime green int., unglazed bisque liner	125.00
Ewer, 6½″ h, two handles, dark green glaze, sgd ''J.S.T. & Co., Keene, NH''	115.00

Vase, dark blue, imp mark, 4¼″ h, $175.00.

Mug, 7" h, dark green glaze shading to red, relief border top and bottom **65.00**

Umbrella Stand, 17⅝" h, deep matte green, high-relief trailing ivy, textured ground **125.00**

Vase

8¼" h, bulbous, curled leaf-and-stem handle, broad leaves dec, artist's initials, imp "Hampshire Pottery" **350.00**

8½" h, swollen cylinder, wide mouth, short neck, repeating molded-tulip dec, imp Cadmon Robertson mark, c1910 .... **375.00**

11" h, cylindrical, flaring ruffled top, molded, gathered and tied at neck, matte green glaze, imp "Hampshire" **425.00**

HAND-PAINTED CHINA

History: Hand painting on china began in the Victorian era and remained popular through the 1920s. It was considered an accomplished art form for women in upper- and upper-middle-class households. It developed first in England, but spread rapidly to the Continent and America.

China factories in Europe, America, and the Orient made the blanks. Belleek, Haviland, Limoges, and Rosenthal were among the European manufacturers. American firms included A. H. Hews Co., Cambridge, Massachusetts; Willets Mfg. Co., Trenton, New Jersey; and Knowles, Taylor and Knowles, East Liverpool, Ohio. Nippon blanks from Japan were used frequently during the early 20th century.

Marks: Many pieces were signed and dated by the artist.

Collectors' Club: World Organization of China Painters, 2641 NW 10th St, Oklahoma City, OK 73107.

Museum: World Organization of China Painters, Oklahoma City, OK.

Notes: The quality and design of the blank is a key factor in pricing. Some blanks were very elaborate. Aesthetics is critical. Value is higher for a piece which has unique decorations and pleasing and unusual designs.

Bowl, 9¾" d, 4½" h, pansies, artist sgd "C. Palmer," marked "T. V. Limoges" **120.00**

Bulb Planter, 8¼" d, 4" h, daisies, blue ground, artist sgd "E. A. Matthews," rust stains on insert, marked "Theodore Haviland, Limoges" **110.00**

Bowl, Belleek blank, purple plums, green leaves, browns, gold rim, painted int, marked "LCH, Belleek, 1922," $200.00.

Candlestick, 5¾" h, pink roses, shaded yellow and blue ground, gold trim **30.00**

Cheese Dish, cov, 6¼ × 9", pink floral sprays, green leaves, pale blue shaded to white, gold trim, applied handles **100.00**

Coffeepot, 10" h, fluted pear shape, polychrome floral spray dec, C-shaped handle, gilt rim, marked "T. V. Limoges" **150.00**

Compote, 9⅞ × 5¼", multicolored flowers, romantic landscape, price for matching pr **90.00**

Dresser Tray

9¼ x 11⅝", pastel ground, pink flower and green leaves, irregular shape, French **85.00**

11" l, woman in field, thick gold-band border, framed, Limoges blank **150.00**

Jar, 6¾" h, roses, grotesque-head handles, marked "D & C France," small flakes **200.00**

Oyster Plate, four well, fish dec, cobalt blue dec, gold trim **85.00**

Pitcher, 14½" h, woman with lyre, artist sgd "E Thomas," marked "Belleek" **250.00**

Plate

11" d, scalloped gold trim border, one pastel yellow rose, green foliage, artist sgd, Haviland blank, 1901 .... **65.00**

13½" d, Hunter and His Dog, natural background, hunter and dog on one, hunter and fox on other, artist sgd, marked "Limoges," price for pr **650.00**

Punch Bowl, 14¼" d, grapes and leaves, gold rim, four gilt scroll feet, artist sgd "E.D.W.," Limoges blank . **500.00**

Shaving Mug, lady dressed in brown and white, white plumes, red hat ribbon **70.00**

Tobacco Jar, 7¼" h, multicolored Indian bust, gold trim and finial, artist sgd "Florence Weaver, 1925," initials on finial, blank marked "Favorite, Bavaria" ... **225.00**

Toothpick Holder, 2¼ × 2", shaded pink to blue, pink flowers, gold trim **35.00**

Tray, 15¾" d, polychrome vintage dec, artist sgd "E Thomas," marked "T & V Limoges" **220.00**

Vase

7½" d, bud, daffodils, Rosenthal blank **50.00**

12¾" h, roses and shepherd girl, initialed "ET" for E Thomas **200.00**

HATPINS AND HATPIN HOLDERS

History: When oversized hats were in vogue, around 1850, hatpins became popular. Designers used a variety of materials to decorate the pin ends, including china, crystal, enamel, gem stones, precious metals, and shells. Decorative subjects ranged from commemorative designs to insects.

Hatpin holders, generally placed on a dresser, are porcelain containers which were designed specifically to hold these pins. The holders were produced by major manufacturers, among which were Meissen, Nippon, R. S. Germany, R. S. Prussia, and Wedgwood.

Reference: Lillian Baker, *Hatpins & Hatpin Holders: An Illustrated Value Guide,* Collector Books, 1983, 1994 value update.

Collectors' Clubs: American Hatpin Society, 20 Monticello Dr, Palos Verdes Peninsula, CA 90274; International Club for Collectors of Hatpins and Hatpin Holders, 15237 Chanera Avenue, Gardena, CA, 90249.

Museum: Los Angeles Art Museum, Costume Dept., Los Angeles, CA.

Hatpins

Brass
    Lacy openwork, large rhinestones on dome top **35.00**
    Owl, figural **40.00**
Carnival Glass, figural, flying black bat, silver luster ... **35.00**
Celluloid
    Imitation amber, oval disc, applied brass phoenix-
      bird design, 12" l **65.00**
    Imitation ivory, fan shape, coral-colored celluloid
      beads, 10" l **25.00**
    Imitation tortoiseshell, hollow conical shape, 12" l . **18.00**
Crystal, hand cut, blown teardrop shape inside, attached
    to 10½" brass pin **125.00**
Cloisonné, Japanese, foil back, script mark **75.00**
Jet Glass, 3¼" d, cut and faceted **90.00**
Peacock Eye Glass, three-sided leaf motif, gilded brass **75.00**
Sterling Silver
    Art Nouveau design, 12" l **75.00**
    Six sided, floral dec, 7" l **60.00**

Hatpin Holders

Bisque, 5¼" h, Egyptian motif, pink and white, c1909 . **135.00**
Bronzed Metal, Art Nouveau, woman, bust, flowering
    leaves, early 1900s **90.00**
Carnival Glass, Butterfly and Berry pattern, blue, Fenton **700.00**

Hatpin holder, unknown maker, white china, red roses, green leaves, gilt circles, 4" h, $35.00.

China
    Limoges, gold emb border, cream ground **35.00**
    Nippon, 4¾" h, Bierot Airplane series, hp, lavender,
      green, and rust airplane crossing channel dec,
      beading and moriage accents **225.00**
    Royal Bayreuth, hexagonal, pearly finish, roses dec,
      gold trim, blue mark **295.00**
    Royal Doulton, 5" h, Ophelia, hp, lavender and pink,
      dark green ground and trim, seven pinholes **185.00**
    R S Prussia, 4¾" h, roses, luster finish, scalloped base **225.00**
Sterling Silver, 4" h, platform with pincushion, figural
    cherub holding ring, c1895 .... **150.00**

HAVILAND CHINA

History: In 1842, American china importer David Haviland moved to Limoges, France, where he began manufacturing and decorating china specifically for the U.S. market. Haviland is synonymous with fine, white, translucent porcelain, although early hand-painted patterns were generally larger and darker colored on heavier whiteware blanks than were later ones.

David revolutionized French china factories by both manufacturing the whiteware blank and decorating it at the same site. In addition, Haviland and Company pioneered the use of decals in decorating china.

David's sons, Charles Edward and Theodore, split the company in 1892. In 1936 Theodore opened an American division, which still operates today. In 1941 Theodore bought out Charles Edward's heirs and recombined both companies under the original name of H. and Co. The Haviland family sold the firm in 1981.

Charles Field Haviland, cousin of Charles Edward and Theodore, worked for and then, after his marriage in 1857, ran the Casseaux Works until 1882. Items continued to carry his name as decorator until 1941.

Thousands of Haviland patterns were made but were not consistently named until after 1926. The similarities in many of the patterns makes identification difficult. Numbers assigned by Arlene Schleiger and illustrated in her books have become the identification standard.

References: Susan and Al Bagdade, *Warman's American Pottery and Porcelain,* Wallace-Homestead, 1994; Mary Frank Gaston, *Haviland Collectibles & Art Objects,* Collector Books, 1984, out-of-print; Arlene Schleiger, *Two Hundred Patterns of Haviland China,* Books I–V, published by author, 1950–1977.

Collectors' Club: Haviland Collectors International Foundation, PO Box 802462, Santa Clarita, CA 91380.

Matching Services: Charles E. & Carol M. Ulrey, *Matching Services for Haviland China,* PO Box 15815, San Diego, CA 92175.

Bouillon Cup and Saucer, small green flowers and leaves **30.00**
Bowl, 5½" d, Greek Key dec, black and yellow **15.00**
Cake Plate, open handles, Schleiger #705 .... **45.00**
Coffee Service, coffeepot, creamer, and sugar, Wedding
    Anniversary pattern, marked "H & Co" **140.00**
Compote, 9" d, 2¾" h, blue and pink flowers, gold scal-
    loped edge **65.00**
Cup and Saucer, Moss Rose pattern, 1885 mark **45.00**
Dinner Service, Kenmore pattern, 165 pcs, 12 place set-
    tings, serving pcs **2,000.00**
Dresser Set, hair receiver, cov powder jar, fitted tray with
    handle, yellow florals, gilt borders **150.00**
Gravy Boat, cov, attached underplate, oval, green and
    gold geometric dec **50.00**
Oyster Plate, four wells
    Green and beige florals, gold trim, white ground,
      price for 6-pc set **375.00**
    Hand painted fish, gold trim, cobalt blue ground ... **85.00**
    Small yellow roses, brown foliage, gold edge trim,
      price for 8-pc set **595.00**
Plate
    6" d, Autumn Leaf pattern **10.00**

Gravy boat, attached underplate, conventional border, No. 278, 7" w, $50.00.

8½" d

Baltimore Rose pattern, pink, Ranson blank, marked "Haviland & Co"	25.00
Pansies, hp, pastel ground, artist sgd	25.00
Silver Anniversary pattern	25.00
10³/₁₈" d, service, gold swag and scroll design, cobalt blue border, price for 12-pc set	600.00
Platter, 11¾" l, Arbor pattern	60.00
Ramekin and Saucer, No. 24 pattern, Ranson blank	35.00
Relish, white, scattered pink flowers, scalloped edge	30.00
Soup Tureen, cov, Baltimore Rose pattern	295.00
Vegetable Dish, cov, 9½" w, octagonal, Persia pattern	200.00

HEISEY GLASS

History: The A. H. Heisey Glass Co. began producing glasswares in April 1896, in Newark, Ohio. Heisey, the firm's founder, was not a newcomer to the field, having been associated with the craft since his youth.

Many blown and molded patterns were produced in crystal, colored, milk (opalescent), and Ivorina Verde (custard) glass. Decorative techniques of cutting, etching, and silver deposit were employed. Glass figurines were introduced in 1933 and continued in production until 1957 when the factory closed. All Heisey glass is notable for its clarity.

Marks: Not all pieces have the familiar H-within-a-diamond mark.

References: Neila Bredehoft, *The Collector's Encyclopedia of Heisey Glass, 1925–1938,* Collector Books, 1986, 1993 value update; Lyle Conder, *Collector's Guide to Heisey's Glassware for Your Table,* L-W Books, 1984, 1993–94 value update; Gene Florence, *Elegant Glassware of the Depression Era,* Revised Fifth Edition, Collector Books, 1993; Ellen T. Schroy, *Warman's Glass,* Second Edition, Wallace-Homestead, 1995.

Collectors' Clubs: Bay State Heisey Collectors Club, 354 Washington St, East Walpole, MA 02032; Heisey Collectors of America, 169 W Church St, Newark, OH, 43055; National Capital Heisey Collectors, PO Box 23, Clinton, MD 20735.

Videotape: Heisey Glass Collectors of America, Inc., *A Legacy of American Craftsmanship: The National Heisey Glass Museum,* Heisey Collectors of America, Inc., 1994.

Museum: National Heisey Glass Museum, Newark, OH.

REPRODUCTION ALERT

Some Heisey molds were sold to Imperial Glass of Bellaire, Ohio, and certain items were reissued. These pieces may be mistaken for the original Heisey. Some of the reproductions were produced in colors which were never made by Heisey and have become collectible in their own right. Examples include: the Colt family in Crystal, Caramel Slag, Ultra Blue, and Horizon Blue; the mallard with wings up in Caramel Slag; Whirlpool (Provincial) in crystal and colors; and Waverly, a 7-inch, oval, footed compote in Caramel Slag.

Animal	
Goose, wings up	**125.00**
Ringneck Pheasant	**115.00**
Scottie Dog	**95.00**
Ashtray	
Cupid & Psyche, flamingo, individual size	**55.00**
Empress, Alexandrite, #1401	**295.00**
Beer Mug, Old Sandwich, Sahara	
12 oz	**245.00**
18 oz	**295.00**
Bowl	
Crystolite, 5" d	**12.00**
Orchid, 2 compartments, 6½" d	**48.00**
Cake Plate, Empress, Sahara, T handle	**105.00**
Candlesticks, pr	
Empress, clear, acid-etched dec, 7" h	**90.00**
Warwick, 2 light, Sahara, #1428	**295.00**
Candy, cov, Lariat, 5" d	**60.00**
Champagne, Rose, #5072 Rose Stem, price for pr	**40.00**
Claret	
Pied Piper, #3350 Wabash, 4 oz	**15.00**
Rose, #5072 Rose Stem, price for pr	**160.00**
Cocktail	
Arctic, Aqua Caliente, #4002	**15.00**
Fox Chase, #3405 Alibi, 3 oz	**18.00**
Sea Horse	**85.00**
Cordial, Empress, #3380 Old Dominion, flamingo, 1 oz	**150.00**
Creamer and Sugar	
Fandango	**60.00**
Orchid, #1519 Waverly, individual size	**50.00**
Ridgeleigh	**40.00**
Cup and Saucer, Empress, Sahara	**37.50**
Custard Cup, Colonial	**12.00**
Decanter, Orchid, #4036, orig stopper	**25.00**
Favor Vase, Diamond Optic, Sahara, #4229	**200.00**
Goblet	
Belvedere, etch #500, #4090 Coventry, 10 oz	**30.00**
Cassandra, #3315 Polonaise	**25.00**
Elizabeth, etch #412 Hanover, 8 oz	**25.00**
Lariat, Moonglow cut	**22.50**
Wabash, Piped Piper etch	**22.50**
Grapefruit, Chintz, #3389 Duquesne, Sahara	**45.00**
Hair Receiver, Greek Key, SP top	**80.00**
Iced Tea Tumbler, Waverly, 13 oz, ftd	**20.00**
Jelly, Crystolite, two handles, 2 part	**20.00**
Juice Tumbler, Lariat, Moonglow cut	**25.00**

Stopper, figural horse's head, crystal, orig label, $120.00.

Lemon Dish, cov, Crystolite	**75.00**
Mantel Lusters, pr, Ispwich, cobalt blue, crystal prisms, orig inserts	**990.00**
Marmalade, cov, Crystolite	**35.00**
Mayonnaise	
Orchid	**35.00**
Ridgeleigh	**30.00**
Mayonnaise and Relish Dish, cov, Rococo, Sahara, #1447	**400.00**
Mug, Fisherman, #4163 Wahley, 16 oz	**150.00**
Mustard, cov, Crystolite	**37.00**
Nappy, Crystolite, 5″ d, handle	**12.50**
Nasturtium Bowl, Empress, flamingo, 7½″ d	**300.00**
Pitcher, Pied Piper, 54 oz	**195.00**
Plate	
Landon Silhouette, #1183 Revere, 7″	**70.00**
Lariat, silver birds dec, 10″ d	**24.00**
Normandie, etch #480 Yeoman, 10½″ d, price for 6-pc set	**75.00**
Old Colony, #1401 Empress, Sahara, 7½″ d, price for 8-pc set, wear	**65.00**
Puff Box, cov, Crystolite	**60.00**
Punch Bowl, Crystolite, 12″ d	**85.00**
Punch Cup	
Crystolite	**7.00**
Greek Key	**20.00**
Relish, 3 part	
Crystolite	**28.00**
Waverly, 11 × 5″	**55.00**
Sandwich Plate, Orchid, #1509 Queen Anne, 16″ d ..	**80.00**
Sherbet	
Diana, etch #412, King Arthur	**10.00**
Frontenac, etch #440, #3350 Wabash, hawthorn, price for 6-pc set	**90.00**
Plantation Ivy, etch #516	**15.00**
Waverly, low	**7.00**
Soda Tumbler, #2401 Oakwood, 12 oz	
Fox Chase	**25.00**
Lancaster	**45.00**
Polo Player, etch #495	**32.00**
Sugar, open, Phyllis etch	**25.00**
Syrup, Sawtooth band, orig hinged lid	**95.00**
Toothpick, Sunburst #343	
Torte Plate	
Ivy, #1567 Plantation, 14″ d	**60.00**
Lariat, rolled edge, 12″ d	**24.00**

Wine	
Chintz, #3389 Duquesne, 2½ oz	**7.50**
Locket on Chain, ruby stained, gold trim	**235.00**
Minuet, #5010 Symphone, price for 7-pc set	**225.00**

HOLLY AMBER

History: Holly Amber, originally called Golden Agate, was produced by the Indiana Tumbler and Goblet Works of the National Glass Co., Greentown, Indiana. Jacob Rosenthal created the color in 1902. Holly Amber is a gold-colored glass with a marbleized onyx color on raised parts.

Holly (No. 450), a pattern created by Frank Jackson, was designed specifically for the Golden Agate color. Between January 1903 and June of that year, when the factory was destroyed by fire, more than 35 different forms were made in this pattern.

Reference: James Measell, *Greentown Glass, The Indiana Tumbler & Goblet Co.,* Grand Rapids Public Museum, 1979, 1992–93 value update, distributed by Antique Publications.

Collectors' Club: National Greentown Glass Assoc, 19596 Glendale Ave, South Bend, IN 46637.

Museums: Grand Rapids Public Museum, Ruth Herrick Greentown Glass Collection, Grand Rapids, MI; Greentown Glass Museum, Greentown, IN.

Additional Listings: Greentown Glass.

Bowl, 8½″ d	**475.00**
Butter Dish, cov, 7¼ × 6¼″	**1,200.00**
Cake Stand	**2,000.00**
Compote, cov, 7½″ h, two int. rim chips	**800.00**
Creamer, 4½″ h	**650.00**
Cruet, 6½″ h, orig stopper	**2,100.00**
Honey, cov	**750.00**
Mug, 4½″ h, two bands of amber-white, amber-white handle, small open bubble on base	**585.00**
Nappy, 4½″ d, handle	**475.00**
Parfait	**575.00**
Relish, oval	**300.00**
Salt and Pepper Shakers, pr	**500.00**
Spooner, 4″ h, 3½″ d	**500.00**
Sugar, open	**500.00**
Syrup, 5¾″ h, SP hinged lid	**2,200.00**
Toothpick Holder, 5″ h	**625.00**
Vase, 6″ h	**425.00**

HORN

History: For centuries, horns from animals have been used for various items, e.g., drinking cups, spoons, powder horns, and small dishes. Some pieces of horn have designs scratched in them. Around 1880 furniture made from the horns of Texas longhorn steers was popular in Texas and the southwestern United States.

Additional Listings: Firearm Accessories.

Beaker, 6½″ h, scratch-carved compass star	**50.00**
Box, cov, 2¾″ d, brass hinges	**35.00**
Figure, 8½″ h, courtesan, standing, carrying branch and basket, Chinese, 18th/19th C	**345.00**

Hat rack, made from three sets of different species of animal horns, mounted on rect center plaque, natural patina, $125.00.

Foot Stool, hide covering, horns form legs	**165.00**

Libation Cup
4" h, carved rhinoceros horn, lotus-blossom carving, carved hardwood stand, Chinese, minor damage **920.00**
5⅛" h, elaborately carved, cloud formation with nine writhing dragons appearing from clouds chasing pearls, dragons which reach over lip and continue inside form handle, golden honey amber brown, rhinoceros, 18th C **49,450.00**

Tumbler
2⅝" h **35.00**
5" h, engraved hunt scene **70.00**

HULL POTTERY

History: In 1905 Addis E. Hull purchased the Acme Pottery Company, Crooksville, Ohio. In 1917 the A. E. Hull Pottery Company began making art pottery, novelties, stoneware, and kitchenware, later including the famous Little Red Riding Hood line. Most items had a matte finish with shades of pink and blue or brown predominating.

After a disastrous flood and fire in 1950, J. Brandon Hull reopened the factory in 1952 as the Hull Pottery Company. New, more-modern-style pieces, mostly with glossy finish, were produced. The company currently produces wares for florists, e.g. the Regal and Floraline lines.

Marks: Hull pottery molds and patterns are easily identified. Pre-1950 vases are marked "Hull USA" or "Hull Art USA" on the bottom. Many also retain their paper labels. Post-1950 pieces are marked "Hull" in large script or "HULL" in block letters.

Each pattern has a distinctive letter or number, e.g., Wildflower has a "W" and a number; Waterlily, "L" and number; Poppy, numbers in the 600s; Orchid, in the 300s. Early stoneware pieces are marked with an "H".

References: Susan and Al Bagdade, *Warman's American Pottery and Porcelain,* Wallace-Homestead, 1994; Barbara Loveless Gick-Burke, *Collector's Guide to Hull Pottery,* Collector Books, 1993; Joan Hull, *Hull,* Fifth Edition, published by author (1376 Nevada, Huron, SD 57350), 1997; Brenda Roberts, *Collectors Encyclopedia of Hull Pottery,* Collector Books, 1980, 1995 value update.

Periodicals: *Hull Pottery News,* 466 Foreston Place, St Louis, MO 63119; *Hull Pottery Newsletter,* 11023 Tunnel Hill NE, New Lexington, OH 43764.

Collectors' Club: Hull Pottery Assoc, 4 Hilltop Rd, Council Bluff, IA 51503.

Additional Listings: See *Warman's Americana & Collectibles* for more examples.

Advisor: Joan Hull.

Pre-1950 (matte)

Bownot	
Bowl, B-18, 5¾"d	**200.00**
Teapot, B-20, 6" h	**450.00**
Vase	
B-4, 5½" h	**185.00**
B-8, 8½" h	**250.00**
Wall Planter, pitcher, B-26, 6" h	**245.00**
Calla Lily, vase, 560/33, 8" h	**300.00**
Dogwood (Wild Rose), vase, 504, 8½" h	**125.00**
Little Red Riding Hood	
Bank, 7" h	**700.00**
Cookie Jar, 13" h	**350.00**
Mustard, spoon, 5¼"	**400.00**
Pitcher, open head, 8" h	**350.00**
Mardi Gras/Granada	
Basket, 65, 8" h	**125.00**
Vase, 215, 9" h	**50.00**
Novelty	
Bank, Piggy, emb florals, 14"	**125.00**
Casserole, Cinderella, 7½" d	**40.00**
Open Rose (Camellia), pitcher, 105, 7" h	**225.00**
Orchid	
Bookends, pr, 316, 7" h	**1,200.00**
Bowl, 314, 13" d	**325.00**
Vase	
301, 4¾" h	**85.00**
304, 6" h	**135.00**
308, 4¼" h	**95.00**
309, 8½" h	**185.00**
Poppy	
Basket, 601, 9"	**650.00**
Bowl, 608, 4¾" d	**100.00**
Ewer, 610, 4¾" d	**125.00**
Vase, 612, 6½" h	**125.00**
Tulip	
Pitcher, 109-33, 13" h	**400.00**
Vase	
100-33-10, 10" h	**275.00**
104-44-6, 6½" h, bud	**110.00**
108-33, 6" h	**110.00**
110-33-6, 6" h	**125.00**
Water Lily, vase, L-16, 12½" h	**350.00**
Wildflower	
Basket, W-66, 10½"	**1,800.00**
Pitcher, W-2, 5½" h	**75.00**
Vase	
W-5, 6½" h	**75.00**
W-9, 8½" h	**140.00**
W-15-10½, 10½" h	**165.00**
W-51, 8½" h	**275.00**
W-61, 6½" h	**150.00**
Woodland	
Basket, W-9	**195.00**

Console Bowl, W-29	**295.00**
Cornucopia, W-10	**145.00**
Flowerpot, W-11, 5¾" h	**165.00**
Vase, W-8, 7½" h	**110.00**

Post-1950

Blossom Flite

Basket, T-8, 8¼" h	**125.00**
Creamer, 15	**50.00**
Cornucopia, T-6, 10½" l	**90.00**
Planter, T-12, 10½" l	**85.00**

Butterfly

Ashtray, B-3, 7" w	**55.00**
Basket, B-13, 8"	**135.00**
Bonbon, B-4, 6" d	**40.00**
Pitcher	
B-11, 8¾" h	**115.00**
Teapot, B-18	**150.00**

Capri

Leaf Dish, C-63, 10"	**85.00**
Pitcher, C-87, 12" h	**100.00**
Twin Swan, C-81	**75.00**

Ebb Tide

Basket, E-5	**100.00**
Console Bowl, E-12	**175.00**
Creamer, E-15	**50.00**
Sugar, cov, E-16	**50.00**

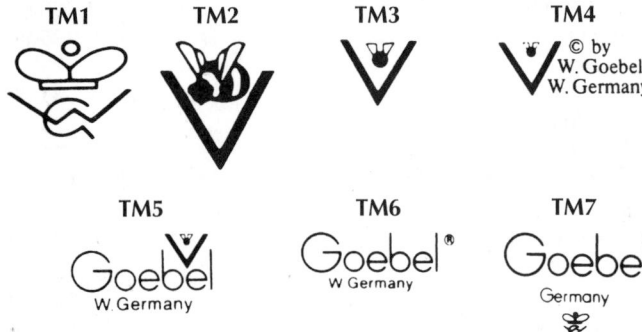

TM1 TM2 TM3 TM4
TM5 TM6 TM7

HUMMEL ITEMS

History: Hummel items are the original creations of Berta Hummel, who was born in 1909 in Massing, Bavaria, Germany. At age 18 she was enrolled in the Academy of Fine Arts in Munich to further her mastery of drawing and the palette. Berta entered the Convent of Siessen and became Sister Maria Innocentia in 1934. In this Franciscan cloister, she continued drawing and painting images of her childhood friends.

In 1935 W. Goebel Co. in Rodental, Germany, began producing Sister Maria Innocentia's sketches as three-dimensional bisque figurines. The Schmid Brothers of Randolph, Massachusetts, introduced the figurines to America and became Goebel's U.S. distributor.

In 1967 Goebel began distributing Hummel items in the U.S. A controversy developed between the two companies, the Hummel family, and the convent. Law suits and counter-suits ensued. The German courts finally effected a compromise: the convent held legal rights to all works produced by Sister Maria Innocentia

from 1934 until her death in 1946 and licensed Goebel to reproduce these works; Schmid was to deal directly with the Hummel family for permission to reproduce any pre-convent art.

Marks: All authentic Hummel pieces bear both the signature "M. I. Hummel" and a Goebel trademark. Various trademarks were used to identify the year of production:

Crown Mark (trademark 1)	1935 through 1949
Full Bee (trademark 2)	1950–1959
Stylized Bee (trademark 3)	1957–1972
Three Line Mark (trademark 4)	1964–1972
Last Bee Mark (trademark 5)	1974–1979
Missing Bee Mark (trademark 6)	1979–1990
Current Mark or New Crown Mark (trademark 7)	1991 to the present.

References: Ken Armke, *Hummel: An Illustrated History and Price Guide,* Wallace-Homestead, 1995; Carl F. Luckey, *Luckey's Hummel Figurines and Plates: A Collector's Identification and Value Guide,* Tenth Edition, Books Americana, 1994; Robert L. Miller, *The No. 1 Price Guide to M. I. Hummel: Figurines, Plates, More...,* Sixth Edition, Portfolio Press, 1995; Wolfgang Schwalto, *M. I. Hummel Collector's Handbook, Part I: Rarities and Collector Pieces,* Schwalto, GMBH, 1994; Lawrence L. Wonsch, *Hummel Copycats with Values,* Wallace-Homestead, 1987, out-of-print.

Collectors' Clubs: Hummel Collector's Club, Inc, 1261 University Dr, Yardley, PA 19067; M. I. Hummel Club, Goebel Plaza, Rte 31, PO Box 11, Pennington, NJ 08534.

Museum: The Hummel Museum, New Braunfels, TX.

Additional Listings: See *Warman's Americana & Collectibles* for more examples.

SPECIAL AUCTION

Dorothy Dous
1261 University Dr
Yardley, PA 19067-2857
(215) 321-7367

Ashtray

Joyful, #33, trademark 5	**80.00**
Let's Sing, #114, trademark 3	**125.00**
Singing Lesson, #34, trademark 6	**100.00**

Candleholder

Angel, #111/39/0, with accordion, trademark 2	**65.00**
Angel, #111/40/0, with horn, trademark 2	**65.00**
Angel, #111/38/0, with lute, trademark 3	**55.00**

Candy Dish

Chick Girl, #111/57, trademark 3, crazed, base chipped	**200.00**
Let's Sing, #111/110, trademark 3	**285.00**
Playmates, #111/58, trademark 3, 6½" h	**110.00**

Figure

Angel Serenade, #214/D, trademark 4, chip	**30.00**
Apple Tree Boy, #142/3/0, trademark 5, 4¼" h	**65.00**
Barnyard Hero, #195/1, trademark 5	**120.00**
Bird Watcher, #300, trademark 6	**135.00**
Boots, #143/0, trademark 2, 5⅜" h	**65.00**
Boy with Accordion, #390, trademark 5	**45.00**
Builder, #305, trademark 5	**155.00**

Captive, #200/1, trademark 5 .... **98.00**
Carefree, #150/2/0, trademark 5 .... **75.00**
Carnival, #328, trademark 4 .... **160.00**
Celestial Musician, #188, trademark 2, 7" h **165.00**
Chick Girl, #57/0, trademark 2 .... **95.00**
Duet, #130, trademark 3, 4⅞" h **95.00**
Feeding Time, #199, trademark 2, 5½" h **125.00**
Goose Girl, #47/0, trademark 1, "US Zone Germany," 5" h **130.00**
Happiness, #86, trademark 2, 4⅞" h **90.00**
Happy Pastime, #69, trademark 3 .... **95.00**
Joyous Christmas, #479, trademark 5 .... **30.00**
Latest News, #184, trademark 2, 5¼" h **45.00**
Little Hare, #374, trademark 5 .... **65.00**
Little Pharmacist, #322, trademark 4, 5⅝" h **45.00**
March Winds, #43, trademark 1, "US Zone Germany," 5¼" h **150.00**
Merry Wanderer, #7/1, trademark 5 .... **300.00**
Mischief Maker, #342, trademark 5 .... **120.00**
Mountaineer, #315, trademark 4, chip **30.00**
Out of Danger, #56B, trademark 5 .... **128.00**
Playmates, #58/0, trademark 2, 4" h **95.00**
Ride Into Christmas, #396, trademark 5 .... **310.00**
Shepherd's Tune, #378, trademark 5 .... **90.00**
Smart Little Sister, #346, trademark 5, 4⅜" h **65.00**
Stormy Weather, #71, trademark 5 .... **210.00**
Sunrise Shepherd, #124/0, trademark 3 .... **115.00**
Telling Her Secret, #196/0, trademark 5 .... **150.00**
Village Boy, #51, trademark 5 .... **45.00**
Waiter, #154, trademark 1, "US Zone Germany," 6¼" h **200.00**
We Congratulate, #220, trademark 2 .... **195.00**

Figure, Postman, #119, marked "Goebel, W. Germany," 5¼" h, $95.00.

Font
Angel, #22/0, sitting, trademark 2 .... **110.00**
Angel, #146, shrine, trademark 3 .... **80.00**
Lamp, To Market, #M1223, trademark 5 .... **315.00**
Plaque
Ba-Bee Ring, #30/0/B, trademark 5 .... **50.00**
Boy Standing, #168, trademark 5 .... **100.00**
Little Fiddler, #93, trademark 5 .... **115.00**
Madonna, #48/0, trademark 2 .... **175.00**
Merry Christmas, #323, trademark 5 .... **65.00**
Retreat to Safety, #126, trademark 3 .... **125.00**
Vacation Time, #125, extra picket, trademark 2 ... **245.00**

IMARI

History: Imari derives its name from a Japanese port city. Although Imari ware was manufactured in the 17th century, the pieces most commonly encountered are those made between 1770 and 1900.

Early Imari was decorated simply, quite unlike the later heavily decorated brocade pattern commonly associated with Imari. Most of the decorative patterns are an underglaze blue and overglaze "seal wax" red complimented by turquoise and yellow.

The Chinese copied Imari ware. The Japanese examples can be identified by grayer clay, thicker glaze, runny and darker blue, and deep red opaque hues.

The pattern and colors of Imari inspired many English and European potteries, such as Derby and Meissen, to adopt a similar style of decoration for their wares.

Reproduction Alert: Reproductions abound, and many manufacturers continue to produce pieces in the traditional style.

Bowl
5½" d, cov, three floral landscape reserves, iron-red, green, turquoise, and aubergine enamels, underglaze blue, age crack to one lid, price for pr **120.00**
8½" d, ten sided, The Three Friends dec, central landscape reserve **175.00**
9" d, fluted chrysanthemum form, underglaze blue and enamel, central dragon reserve, flutes dec with various patterns and flowers **275.00**
9½" d, scalloped edge, floral reserve **125.00**
15" d, floriform, naturalistic floral designs separated by scrolling floral panels, underglaze blue, iron-red, green, and gold, late 19th C **920.00**
Charger
11¾" d, floral and bird reserves **140.00**
12" d, scalloped edge, central circular reserve of flowers in basket, six border reserves **190.00**
12½" d, three reserves of women in gardens **120.00**
14¼" d, flowers, birds, and landscape reserves **240.00**
15¾" d, center fish scene surrounded by floral border, c1870 .... **425.00**
16" d, pine and flowers in basket reserve, border of chrysanthemum, peony, grasses, quail, and other flowers, 18th/19th C **1,150.00**
18½" d, underglaze blue and iron-red, green, aubergine enamels, angular reserves of dragon and foo dog, floral scrolling border **750.00**
Creamer, octagonal, underglaze dec **250.00**
Dish
9½" l, floral sprays and dragon reserves, 19th C, price for pr **525.00**
10" l, stylized fish shape, underglaze blue, enamels, gilt, ho-o bird and carp among plants, late 19th C **575.00**
Entree Dish, cov, 8" h, 13¾" l, English, pre-1837 blue Royal Arms stamped mark, chips, age cracks, price for pr **225.00**
Low Bowl, 11½" d, lobed rim, underglaze blue, red enamels, gilding, floral and garden reserves, central circular reserve of flower arrangement, 18th C, wear . **625.00**
Meat Platter, 16½ × 21½", molded drain tree and well, English, pre-1837 blue Royal Arms stamped mark .. **275.00**
Platter
10 × 12¾" d, English, pre-1837 blue Royal Arms stamped mark, price for pr **345.00**

Ginger jar, 9¼" h, $225.00.

23" d, stylized fish shape, late 19th C, small edge
  chips **460.00**
Potpourri Jar, 5¼" h, cobalt blue and orange, gilt highlights, stamped "Ironstone China Patent," English,
  19th C, price for pr **635.00**
Soup Tureen, cov, 11" l, 8½" w, English, pre-1837 blue
  Royal Arms stamped mark **345.00**
Tea Set, orange and cobalt blue, gilt highlights, English,
  19th C, teapot, creamer, cov sugar, spill, two 9¼" d
  cake plates, 6¼ × 7¾" oval tray, ten tea cups, seven
  coffee cups, 12 saucers, price for 36-pc set **920.00**

IMPERIAL GLASS

History: Imperial Glass Co., Bellaire, Ohio, was organized in
1901. Its primary product was pattern (pressed) glass. Soon other
lines were added, including carnival glass, Nuart, Nucut, and
Near Cut. In 1916 the company introduced Free-Hand, a lustered
art glass line, and Imperial Jewels, an iridescent stretch glass that
carried the Imperial cross trademark. In the 1930s the company
was reorganized into the Imperial Glass Corporation, and the firm
is still producing a great variety of wares.

Imperial recently acquired the molds and equipment of several
other glass companies—Central, Cambridge, and Heisey. Many
of the retired molds of these companies are once again in use.

Marks: The Imperial reissues are marked to distinguish them from
the originals.

References: Margaret and Douglas Archer, *Imperial Glass,* Col-
lector Books, 1978, 1993 value update; Gene Florence, *Elegant
Glassware of the Depression Era,* Sixth Edition, Collector Books,
1994; National Imperial Glass Collectors Society, *Imperial Glass
Encyclopedia: Volume I, A–Cane,* Antique Publications, 1995;
———, *Imperial Glass 1966 Catalog,* reprint, 1991 price guide,
Antique Publications; Ellen T. Schroy, *Warman's Glass,* Second
Edition, Wallace-Homestead, 1995; Mary M. Wetzel, *Candle-
wick: The Jewel of Imperial Price Guide II,* Revised Second Edi-
tion, published by author, 1993, 1995 value update.

Collectors' Clubs: National Candlewick Collector's Club, 275
Milledge Terrace, Athens, GA 30606; National Imperial Glass
Collectors Society, PO Box 534, Bellaire, OH 43906.

Videotapes: National Imperial Glass Collectors Society, *Candlewick: at Home, In Any Home, Vol. I: Imperial Beauty, Vol. II:
Virginia and Mary,* RoCliff Communications, 1993; ———, *Glass
of Yesteryears: The Renaissance of Slag Glass,* RoCliff Communications, 1994.

Additional Listings: See Carnival Glass, Pattern Glass, and *Warman's Americana & Collectibles* for more examples.

Engraved or Hand Cut

Bowl, 9½" d, three sprays of flowers, molded star base   **35.00**
Celery Vase, three side stars, cut star base **45.00**
Pitcher, 6" h, daisies, molded star base **50.00**

Jewels

Compote, 7½" d, irid teal blue **65.00**
Creamer, amethyst, pearl, and green luster **75.00**
Vase, 8" h, flared rim, irid silver dec, mulberry ground   **140.00**

Lustered, Free Hand

Bowl, 14¾" d, shallow, flared, stretched irid gold, sgd
  "Lustre Art 114," verdigris metal standard with three
  nude men **700.00**
Pitcher, spun, teal, 80 oz, ice lip **95.00**
Rose Bowl, spun, red **45.00**
Vanity Jar, 7⅝" h, spun, pink **95.00**
Vase
  8¼" h, hourglass shape, irid cobalt blue, orange
    threading **135.00**
  8½" h, white opal body, navy blue pulled-feather dec   **415.00**
  10¾" h, baluster, blue, orange trailing heart and vine
    dec **350.00**

Nucut

Berry Bowl, 7½" d **30.00**
Compote, 5½" d **30.00**

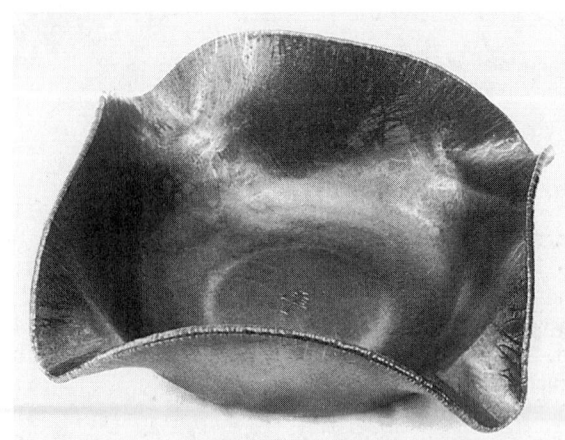

**Dish, Peacock, stretch glass, scalloped corners, 3" h, 6½" w,
$125.00.**

Creamer	**20.00**
Fern Dish, 8″ d	**40.00**
Nappy, 6″ d, heart shape	**30.00**
Tumbler	**20.00**

Pressed

Animal Dish, cov	
Hen, white milk glass	**45.00**
Lion, lacy base, purple slag	**120.00**
Rabbit, white milk glass	**50.00**
Bowl, 5¼″ w, Candlewick, heart shape	**195.00**
Cake Plate, Cape Cod, 72 candleholders	**325.00**
Candleholders, pr	
Hobnail, 4½″ h	**25.00**
Rose, white milk glass	**18.00**
Compote, Grape, white milk glass	**21.00**
Mayonnaise and Liner, Katy, blue opalescent	**120.00**
Pickle, Pillar & Flute, black, handles	**12.00**
Plate, 10″ d, Grape, white milk glass	**18.00**
Punch Cup, Grape, white milk glass	**8.00**
Salt and Pepper Shakers, pr	
Cape Cod, fern green	**75.00**
Grape, #96, white milk glass	**15.00**
Shaving Mug, red slag	**35.00**
Sherbet, Hobnail	**22.50**
Tumbler	
Grape, white milk glass, 4¼″ h	**16.00**
Hobnail	
4½″ h	**22.00**
5¼″ h	**22.00**
Vase	
6″ h, Hobnail, pedestal	**45.00**
8″ h, Hobnail	**80.00**

INDIAN ARTIFACTS, AMERICAN

History: During the historic period there were approximately 350 Indian tribes grouped into the following regions: Eskimo, Northeast and Woodland, Northwest Coast, Plains, and West and Southwest.

American Indian artifacts are quite popular. Currently, the market is stable following a rapid increase in prices during the 1970s.

References: Susan and Al Bagdade, *Warman's American Pottery and Porcelain,* Wallace-Homestead, 1994; C. J. Brafford and Laine Thom (comps.), *Dancing Colors: Paths of Native American Women,* Chronicle Books, 1992; Harold S. Colton, *Hopi Kachina Dolls,* Revised Edition, University of New Mexico Press, 1959, 1990 reprint; Gary L. Fogelman, *An Identification and Price Guide for Indian Artifacts of the Northeast,* Fogelman Publishing, 1994; Lar Hothem, *Arrowheads & Projectile Points,* Collector Books, 1983, 1995 value update; ———, *Indian Artifacts of the Midwest,* Book I (1992, 1996 value update), Book II (1995), Collector Books; ———, *North American Indian Artifacts,* Fifth Edition, Books Americana, 1994; Robert M. Overstreet *The Overstreet Indian Arrowheads Identification and Price Guide,* Fourth Edition, Avon Books, 1995; Dawn E. Reno, *Native American Collectibles,* Avon Books, 1994; Peter N. Schiffer, *Indian Jewelry on the Market,* Schiffer Publishing, 1996; John L. Stivers, *The Official Identification and Price Guide to American Indian Arrowheads,* House of Collectibles, 1994.

Periodicals: *American Indian Art Magazine,* 7314 E Osborn Dr, Scottsdale, AZ 85251; *American Indian Basketry Magazine,* PO Box 66124, Portland, OR 97266; *Indian-Artifact Magazine,* RD #1 Box 240, Turbotville, PA 17772; *Indian Trader,* PO Box 1421, Gallup, NM 87305; *Whispering Wind Magazine,* 8009 Wales St, New Orleans, LA 70126.

Collectors' Club: Indian Arts & Crafts Assoc, Suite B, 122 Laveta NE, Suite B, Albuquerque, NM 87108.

Museums: Amerind Foundation, Inc., Dragoon, AZ; The Heard Museum, Phoenix, AZ; Colorado River Indian Tribes Museum, Parker, AZ; Favell Museum of Western Art & Indian Artifacts, Klamath Falls, OR; Field Museum of Natural History, Chicago, IL; Grand Rapids Public Museum, Grand Rapids, MI; Indian Center Museum, Wichita, KS; Institute of American Indian Arts Museum, Sante Fe, NM; Maryhill Museum of Art, Goldendale, WA; Museum of Classical Antiquities & Primitive Arts, Medford, NJ; Museum of the American Indian, Heye Foundation, New York, NY; US Dept of the Interior Museum, Washington, DC; Wheelwright Museum of the American Indian, Sante Fe, NM.

Note: American Indian artifacts listed below are prehistoric or historic objects made on the North American continent.

SPECIAL AUCTIONS

W. E. Channing & Co.
53 Old Santa Fe Trail
Santa Fe, NM 87501
(505) 988-1078

Garth's Auction, Inc.
2690 Stratford Rd
PO Box 369
Delaware, OH 43015
(614) 362-4771

Eskimo

Basket, cov, 3⅜″ h, 2⅞″ d, coiled grass, faded red and green cross design	**125.00**
Cribbage Board, 16¼″ l, ivory, black pigment engravings, yellowed patina	**1,050.00**
Figure, 4″ l, walrus, carved stone, green jadite band, bottom sgd	**55.00**
Needle Case, ivory, stylized-seal form, carved, inlaid and engraved dec	**350.00**
Walrus Tusk, 10″ l, carved, detailed diorama scene	**195.00**

Northeast and Woodlands

Basket, 12 × 13″, 4″ h, split twill palmetto, attached old tag, made by Annie Tommy, Mikauski Seminole, early 20th C	**65.00**
Belt Ax, 5½″ w, 18″ l, rounded poll and eye, haft set with tacks, split rawhide, and trade-cloth dangle	**65.00**
Bow Case, 5 × 67″ plus fringe, long narrow tanned leather case, long fringe, yarn, and horsehair dec, black and white painted geometric design, stains and minor damage	**145.00**

Cuffs, pr, 7¼" l, black cotton velvet, beaded, floral motif,
silk ribbon trim, Ojibwa **250.00**

Doorpost, 16½" h, totem style, carved raven and bulldog, polychrome paint, Seneca **195.00**

Pouch, 5½" l, dark brown cotton velvet, beaded, floral
and concentric curved designs, Micmac **425.00**

Spoon, 5" l, wood, carved and incised tapered handle
mounted with perched bird, reddish-brown patina .**1,150.00**

Northwest Coast

Basket, 6¾ × 7⅞ × 4¾" h, deep slant sides, imbricated
design in cherry bark and bear grass, Thompson River
Salishan, old illegible label, five rim stitches missing **130.00**

Bowl, 8⅞" d, basketry, twined Makah polychrome, Wakashan, attached old label **115.50**

Bottle, finely woven Makah basket covered 10¾" h bottle, natural twined grass with bird whale boats, whal-
ers, colored bands, Wakashan, wear, minor damage,
small repair **240.00**

Pipe, 8¼" l, wood, carved, two opposing bears, cylindrical brass bowl, pierced stem, reddish-brown patina **225.00**

Staff, 34" l, wood, cylindrical, high-relief carved and
incised totem figures **750.00**

Trinket Box, 6½" l, 4¾" h, twined, cedar bark base,
Nootka **575.00**

Plains

Bag, 14" l, flared rect, hide, sinew sewn, beaded, banded
bar and stepped geometric design, fringe dec **600.00**

Bridle, horsehair, woven multicolored geometric designs, yellow ground, candy-striped reins, trade-glass
rosettes, Ute/Shoshone **1,150.00**

Courting Flageolet, 21" l, marked "Lakota 1870" and
"92," 20th C **220.00**

Drum, hand type

18½" d, 2½" h, one side painted blue, green, and red,
frizzy-haired man, thunderbird, and Plains cross,
other side with painted edge circle **1,760.00**

19" d, 3½" h, one side, worn skin, green, red, and
yellow, ghost dance thunderbird and symbols,
brass bell dangle, slight insect damage **1,700.00**

Leggings, pr, 32" l, hide and cloth, sinew-stitched
beaded dec **750.00**

Moccasins, pr, 9½" l, yellow ochre leather, beaded floral
designs, sinew sewn with brass button closures **475.00**

Model, 10¾" d, 12¾" l, burden basket, twill weave, conical shape, Washoe/Paiute, early 20th C, some widely
spaced rim stitches missing **250.00**

Parching Tray, 14¼ × 17⅞", twined willow, Paiute, old
tag "Pur from Lacy Markan," early 20th C, wear and
scorching **80.00**

Pipe Bag, 6 × 24", buckskin, beaded yellow, russet,
blue, pink, and red, 20th C **110.00**

Sheath and Knife, 9" l, 10" l tassels ending in tin cones,
dark and medium blue, green, yellow, and translucent red on white ground lazy-stitch beaded front,
12¼" l bone handle knife, Sioux **110.00**

Water Jar, basketry

6¾" d, 4⅜" h, martynia and willow step design, Paiute, made by Sally Rice, Carson City, NE, old label **770.00**

8" d, 11¾"h, red ochre stain, pitched, horsehair and
string handles, Paiute, late 19th C, third of rim
stitching missing **200.00**

West and Southwest

Baby Rattle, 3½" l, silver, stamped design, Navaho **95.00**

Basket

8¹/₁₆" d, 5³/₁₆" h, coiled, polychrome, Second Mesi
cloud design, Hopi **140.00**

8⅛" d, 4" h, yucca ring, plaited diamond design, Je-
mez **40.00**

10¼ × 13⅜ × 6½" h, deep oval, willow, martynia
zoomorphic figures around sides, Papago, early
20th C **360.00**

10½ × 14", oval, yucca root, martynia, and willow,
polychrome, Apache, c1910, one rim stitch missing **440.00**

21½" d, 12" h, cooking or storage type, Mono or
Yoktus, CA, rim stitches missing **4,400.00**

Bowl, basketry

6¼" d, 5" h, full- and half-twist overlay, bracken fern
and woodwardia with bear grass, Whilkut, CA,
c1890 .... **440.00**

10½" d, 3½" h, sumac, star design, loop edging, Jicarilla Apache **150.00**

12⅞" d, 3⅝" h, yucca, three female figures around
sides in martynia, Papago, several missing rim
stitches **215.00**

Bowl, pottery

4⅛" d, 3⅞" h, polished red slip, faded umber design,
Papago **30.00**

4¼" d, 2¾" h, black on blackware, sgd "Marie &
Julian," Maria Martinez, San Idelfonso, c1935,
minute wear **550.00**

5⅝" d, 4¾" h, black on blackware, Santa Clara, c1935 **330.00**

8⅝" d, 3¼" h, red ochre and umber design, creamy
orange slip, Hopi, c1930, hairline crack, small
black spots on int. **220.00**

10⅛" d, 4⅛" h, St John's polychrome, redware, white
diamond design on outside, black stylized geometric design with round center int., Anasazi,
crack and rim chips **330.00**

10⅝" d, 3⅝" h, black design, polished redware, tan
back, San Idelfonso, 19th C, wear and smudging
to rim, temper spall spot **495.00**

Burden Basket, 16¾" d, 12¾" h, red cloth and leather
bottom, red dye and martynia design, Apache, fringes
missing **935.00**

Canteen, pottery

6" d, 4" h, red ochre and umber, smoked creamy slip,
Hopu **305.00**

7½" d, 9" h, umber avian design, white slip, Acoma,
20th C, minute spalling to base **200.00**

Dough Bowl, pottery

8" d, 4" h, black on gray-buff over red, Santo Domingo, minor rim wear **105.00**

8⅞" d, 4¼" h, red ochre and umber, pale cream slip,
Laguna, c1880, wear and small rim chips **865.00**

14⅞" d, 6⅝" h, polychrome prayer stick design, bottom marked "Valencia Co, N.M.," Zuni, c1880,
heavy use wear **1,045.00**

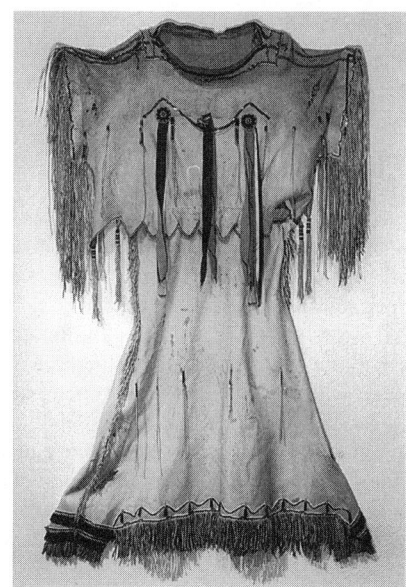

Dress, Cheyenne, hide, yoke outlined in white, blue, red, pink, and green beads, bottom outlined in red, white, and blue beads, beaded rosettes, ribbons, and sequins added later,1890s, 53" l, $2,475.00. Photograph courtesy of W. E. Channing & Co., Inc.

Effigy Jar, 7¼" d, 8½" h, pottery, yellow tattooed head broken at sides, bead collar, and red ochre design, buff body, ½" wear on glaze at front, Mojave, c1890, hairline crack at bottom, chipped spout 615.00

Figure, 7½" w, 8½" h, owl, umber and ochre, gray slip, yellow over paint beak, Zuni, c1890, tail roughness 690.00

Jar, pottery

4" h

Flaring base, cream finish, geometric line dec .. 160.00

4" d, red pottery, black dec, handle, San Idelfonso, late 19th C 165.00

4½" h, spherical, black, scalloped etched rim, sgd in pencil on bottom "Maria Julian" 150.00

5" w, 5¾" h, burnt umber and white design, orange-buff ground, Mojave, hairline, chip on one spout 165.00

6⅜" d, 6¼" h, blackware, slip on upper three fourths, concave bottom, Tewa, attributed to Nambe or San Juan, c1880–90 .... 275.00

6½" d, 6" h, polychrome heart-line deer design, Zuni, c1890, faded design, worn off on one side 275.00

7⅛" d, 6¼" h, plain micaeous clay, Taos/Picuris ... 55.00

7¾" d, 12" h, finely polished blackware, shaped molding to body and handles, Santa Clara, c1890, minor wear 1,127.50

8½" d, 7¼" h, buff water jar, polished rim, tag for "Museum of Northern Arizona Craftman Exhibition, June 24, 1958, Nia Bahongva, Hotevilla," Hopi, Third Mesa plain 30.00

9" d, 8¼" h, polychrome hatched design, red ochre and umber, cream slip, Acoma, early 20th C, minute slip flakes 580.00

10½" d, 15" h, umber design on pale slip over red ochre concave base, Acoma, 19th C, some wear to design, two red drips 1,760.00

14" d, 15¼" h, large stone-polished redware, illegible old label, Papago, 19th C, intact rim chip 935.00

Kachina Doll, Hopi

9" h, carved and painted figure, surface wear 215.00

9¾" h, simple painted figure, ruff of fiber wrapped in string, wool and feather top 115.00

Kiaha, 13½" d, model, lace coil burden basket, faded red and blue design, Papago/Pima, late 19th C 660.00

Ladle, 3¾ × 6", pottery, black on gray, numbers and "Red Lake Ariz" on back, Anasazi, handle broken, rim chips 75.00

Pitcher, 6⅛"d, 8⅞" h, pottery, polychrome red ochre and black, creamy ground, Santo Domingo, broken and repaired 110.00

Rug, Navaho

4'7" × 7'8", diamond pattern, whirling log centers, stepped border, dark red, dark brown, and natural, carded gray background, West Reservation area 850.00

4'8" × 6'10", dark brown, carded brown and natural diamond design, Toadlena area, blue and red bleeding stains, soiling, areas of crude repair ... 315.00

Sacred Corn Meal Container, 3¼" d, 2½" h, black on blackware, fine sheen, sgd "Romona," San Idelfonso, c1920 .... 330.00

Tray, basketry

7¾" d, finely woven whirling fret design, martynia and willow, Pima 440.00

12½" d, whirling fret design, martynia and willow, Pima 600.00

13⅞" d, willow and martynia star design, Apache, c1900 .... 615.00

17¾" d, 6" h, wedding or ceremonial, Hupa 330.00

19⅜" d, red yucca root, Joshua design, 28 stitches per inch, attributed to Kawaiisu or Tabatulabal, CA, 19th C, small areas of missing rim stitches 8,580.00

Tray, pottery, shallow, Hopi

9¼" d, 1⅞" h, umber avian design, orange slip, "Alva Rowena" penciled on back, minor wear to design, sticker mark 165.00

9⅜" d, 2" h, ochre and umber design, creamy slip, pierced clay tab for hanging, old paper tab on back reads "Nampeyo," c1890, glaze rim chip, slight wear to design 2,640.00

Vessel, pottery

6½" d, 7½" h, contemporary polychrome, sgd "P. Antonion, Acoma, NM," water spots on slip 275.00

9½" l, 6" h, black on gray over red banded under body, zoomorphic figures around body, stone polished slip, Tesuque, 19th C 1,100.00

Water Jar, 12" d, 11½" h, basketry, pitched inside, horsehair and rawhide attachment, Jicarilla Apache, c1890, old label "belonged to Bert C. Phillips founder of Taos Art Colony" 935.00

Water Olla, pottery, polychrome design

10" d, 7⅞" h, dark russet and umber design, white slip over buff band, dark under body with prominent puki, concave bottom, marked "111863 Zuni NM Stevenson Bur Ethnol," c1850–65, usage wear and rim chips 4,070.00

10½" d, 10" h, red ochre birds, umber geometric design, creamy white slip over concave red ochre base, Acoma, minute rim wear 1,595.00

10⅜" d, 9¾" h, red ochre and black floral design, buff slip, Santo Domingo, early 20th C, poorly repaired rim chip **1,050.00**

11" d

9" h, red ochre and umber, thin polished creamy white slip over concave red ochre base, Acoma, minor slip wear, piece broken out and glued 610.00

12¾" h, large bird and floral design, creamy buff slip over red ochre concave underbelly, Santo Domingo, early 20th C, repaired rim chip, holes for wire handle **3,100.00**

11⅛" d, 10⅝" h, black design, orange slip over red ochre concave base, Santo Domingo, 19th C, wear from use, rim chips **1,265.00**

11¼" d, 9" h, umber design, white slip, buff band with umber terrace design over dark slip under body with puki impression, concave bottom, marked "Sante Fe NM," Zuni, c1820–60, broken and glued **2,970.00**

Wedding Jar, pottery, Santa Clara

7¼" w, 10¼" h, polished orange slip, early 20th C . 100.00

9⅛" d, 12¼" h, stone polished blackware, upper three quarters slipped, minor wear 275.00

INDIAN TREE PATTERN

History: Indian Tree pattern is a popular pattern of porcelain made from the last half of the 19th century until the present. The pattern, consisting of an Oriental crooked tree branch, landscape, exotic flowers, and foliage, is found predominantly in greens, pinks, blues, and oranges on a white ground. Several English potteries, including Burgess and Leigh, Coalport, and Maddock, made wares in the Indian Tree pattern.

Bowl, 7¼" d, handles 20.00
Compote, 8" d, ftd, marked "Coalport" 60.00
Eggcup, marked "Coalport" 15.00
Fruit Bowl, 10" d, ftd, scalloped, marked "Copeland and Spode" 135.00
Pitcher, marked "Coalport" 25.00
Plate

8" d, fluted, marked "Coalport" 15.00

9½" d, marked "KPM" 17.50
Sauce Boat, matching underplate, marked "Maddock & Sons" 135.00
Soup Plate, 9" d, marked "Maddock, England" 25.00

Sugar, cov, marked "Minton" 50.00
Tea Set, teapot, creamer, sugar, six cups and saucers, six 7" d plates, marked "Coalport", price for 23-pc set   325.00

INK BOTTLES

History: Ink was sold in glass or pottery bottles in the early 1700s in England. Retailers mixed their own formula and bottled it. The commercial production of ink did not begin in England until the late 18th century and in America until the early 19th century.

Initially, ink was supplied in often poorly manufactured pint or quart bottles from which smaller bottles could be filled. By the mid-19th century, when writing implements had been improved, emphasis was placed on making an "untippable" bottle. Shapes ranging from umbrellas to turtles were tried. Since ink bottles were usually displayed, shaped or molded bottles were popular.

The advent of the fountain pen relegated the ink bottle to the back drawer. Bottles lost their decorative design and became merely functional items.

References: Ralph & Terry Kovel, *The Kovels' Bottles Price List*, Tenth Edition, Crown Publishers, 1996; John Odell, *Digger Odell's Official Antique Bottle and Glass Collector Magazine Price Guide Series*, Vol. 4, published by author (1910 Shawhan Rd, Morrow, OH 45152), 1995.

Periodical: *Antique Bottle and Glass Collector*, PO Box 187, East Greenville, PA 18041.

Additional Listings: See *Warman's Americana & Collectibles* for more examples.

Barrel Shape, clear, sq tooled lip, smooth base, emb "Pat March 1st 1870" 80.00
Carter's Permanent Blue Black Ink, 2⅛" h, six sided, cobalt blue, smooth base, c1910 .... 275.00
Davis, William A, 2½" h, 7⅛" d, Boston, aqua, emb .. 20.00
Harrison's Columbian Ink, 2" h, round, sapphire blue, rolled lip, open pontil base, c1850 .... 325.00
J. & I. E. M., 1⅝" h, igloo shape, golden amber 85.00
Mason & Co, James S., 2½" h, eight-sided umbrella, aqua, rolled lip, pontil scar, 1850–60 .... 150.00
Master, 5" l, 3" w, 6½" h, house shape, aqua, applied lip, smooth base, emb details, American, 1870–80, Covills #694 .... 650.00
Standard Brilliant Ink, 2½" h, umbrella style, aqua, rolled lip, open pontil base, c1850 .... 75.00
Umbrella Style, 2½" h, eight sided, blue-green, open pontil base, c1850 .... 135.00

Cup and saucer, Johnson Bros saucer, Madden cup, English, $25.00.

Sanford's Free Sample, amber, round, 1½" d, 3½" h, $30.00.

INKWELLS

History: Most of the commonly found inkwells were produced in the United States or Europe between the early 1800s and the 1930s. The most popular materials were glass and pottery because these substances resisted the corrosive effects of ink.

Inkwells were a sign of the office or wealth of an individual. The common man tended to dip his ink directly from the bottle. The years between 1870 and 1920 represent the golden age of inkwells when elaborate designs were produced.

References: Veldon Badders, *The Collector's Guide to Inkwells: Identification and Values,* Collector Books, 1995; William E. Covill, Jr., *Inkbottles and Inkwells,* William S. Sullwold Publishing, out of print.

Collectors' Clubs: St Louis Inkwell Collectors Society, PO Box 29396, St Louis, MO 63126; The Society of Inkwell Collectors, 5136 Thomas Ave So, Minneapolis, MN 55410.

Additional Listings: See *Warman's Americana & Collectibles* for more examples.

Bisque, figural, owl's head, glass eyes, multicolored enamel dec 225.00
Brass, 5¼" l, 9" w, Art Nouveau, hinged well, sides flaring to tray edges, etched stylized tree motifs, sgd "WD, 709" 165.00
Bronze
    5" h, 7" l, gilt, figural, three graduated-sized owls, perched on owl claw, glass well, 19th C, minor damage to glass eyes 275.00
    8½" d, figural maiden on stairs, holding parasol, carved ivory head, P Tereyzczuk 300.00

Art Nouveau, bronze and cast metal, 4¾ × 9¾", $45.00.

Cranberry glass, 2¾" h, figural, daisy, hinged pewter lid   250.00
Cut Glass, 13" l, 10½" d, 7½" h, two faceted cut glass wells, twin brass pen channels, scrolling handle, brass border, rect case with frieze drawer, engine-turned ball feet, Regency, boullé work, early 19th C **4,250.00**
Ironstone, 5⁷⁄₁₆" h, figural, human head, labeled brain areas, white, blue, and black dec, glazed, imp "By F Bridges, Phrenologist," 1850–59 ....1,450.00
Paperweight, 5½" h, glass, jumbled-cane type, broken cane mushroom-shaped stopper 140.00
Porcelain, 5" h, 2¼ × 2½", figural, cats, female in gold

dress, white cap, gold trim, male in white trousers, brick military jacket, yellow trim, black hat 300.00
Silver, sterling, 2½" h, cylindrical body, copper applied threaded cap, copper monogram dated 1895, applied copper sides, brass vines, leaves, and butterfly with mokume wings, int. glass well, marked "Tiffany & Co" 1,750.00
Staffordshire, 4⅝" h, stag and doe, salmon and gray enamel dec, gilt trim 295.00
Wedgwood, 1¾" h, basalt, vertical engraved sides, center surrounded by three small openings, imp "B" on base, 18th C 175.00
Wood
    3⅜" d, turned, worn orig brown sponging, gold stenciled dec, glass insert, paper label "S Silliman & Co, Chester, Conn" 165.00
    5½" h, carved shoe, hinged lid shaped like sock, old patina **225.50**

IRONS

History: Ironing devices have been used for many centuries, with the earliest references dating from 1100. Irons from the medieval, Renaissance, and early industrial eras can be found in Europe but are rare. Fine engraved brass irons and hand-wrought irons predominated prior to 1850. After 1850 the iron underwent a series of rapid evolutionary changes.

Between 1850 and 1910 irons were heated in four ways: 1) a hot metal slug was inserted into the body, 2) a burning solid, e.g., coal or charcoal, was placed in the body, 3) a liquid or gas, e.g., alcohol, gasoline, or natural gas, was fed from an external tank and burned in the body, or 4) conduction heat, usually drawing heat from a stove top.

Electric irons are just beginning to find favor among iron collectors.

References: Dave Irons, *Irons by Irons,* published by author (223 Covered Bridge Rd, Northampton, PA 18067), 1994; ———, *More Irons by Irons,* published by author (223 Covered Bridge Rd, Northampton, PA 18067), 1996; ———, *Pressing Iron Patents,* published by author (223 Covered Bridge Rd, Northampton, PA 18067), 1994.

Periodical: *Iron Talk,* PO Box 68, Waelder, TX 78959.

Collectors' Clubs: Club of the Friends of Ancient Smoothing Irons, PO Box 215, Carlsbad, CA 92008; Midwest Sad Iron Collectors Club, 24 Nob Hill Dr, St Louis, MO 63138.

Museums: Henry Ford Museum, Dearborn, MI; Shelburne Museum, Shelburne, VT; Sturbridge Village, Sturbridge, MA.

Additional Listings: See *Warman's Americana & Collectibles* for more examples.

Advisors: David Irons.

Charcoal
    Brass, 10" l, large box, large sole plate, Indonesian . 110.00
    Cutwork box, hinged top, 7½" l, Dutch 220.00
    Eclipse, 6¾" l, pat 1903 .... 120.00
    Junior Carbon Iron, 6" l, 1911 .... 170.00
Electric
    K & M Flat Work Ironer, 5⅞" d, round 160.00

Silver Streak, Deco Saunders

   Green 500.00

   Red 750.00

Flat

   Enterprise, lift-off handle 25.00

   P W Weida's, handle swings out to avoid heat, Philadelphia, 1870 .... 300.00

   Ober, #6, curved cast handle, pat 1912 .... 40.00

Fluters

   American Machine, Crown, machine-type, 5⅞" roll, 1877, orig paint 130.00

   Clarks, script on handle, 1879 .... 175.00

   Companion, clamp-on, 5" roll, orig paint 350.00

   Geneva, rocker, 1866 .... 80.00

   Theerie Fluter, Griswold Mfg Co, rocker 400.00

Goffering

   Clamp-on Style, 4¾" l, barrel 400.00

   Round base, S post 100.00

   Single Barrel, brass, paw ftd, turned post 425.00

Laundry Stove, holds 10 irons, Quaker 400.00

Liquid Fuel

   I Wantu Comport Gas Iron, 1910 .... 80.00

   Imperial Self Heating Iron, gasoline 120.00

   Omega, 6" l, alcohol, multiple holes in base, saw-grip handle 180.00

   The Improved Easy, gasoline 140.00

Mangle Board, 25" l, horse handle, geometric carving, Denmark, early 1800s 600.00

Slug Irons

   Brass, 7" l, square back, lift gate, English 150.00

   Oxtonque, 6½" l, saw-grip handle, hinged gate, German 160.00

   Sensible, Magic No. 1, 7½" l, top lifts off 200.00

Slug iron, Danish, brass, $100.00.

Small

   Enterprise, No. 115, holes in handle 95.00

   Sensible, No. 0, lift-off handle 120.00

   Swan, various sizes 110.00

   WP, oval Cap, French 60.00

Special Purpose

   Flower, two parts, flower design, brass parts 110.00

   French, egg on handle 90.00

   Hat, curved bottom, cast iron, McCoys 140.00

   Polisher, grid bottom, Mahony, Troy 35.00

   Round bottom, 4½" l, Carron, England 100.00

   Sleeve Iron, lift-off handle, Grand Union 40.00

IRONWARE

History: Iron, a metallic element that occurs abundantly in combined forms, has been known for centuries. Items made from iron range from the utilitarian to the decorative. Early hand-forged ironwares are of considerable interest to Americana collectors.

References: *Collectors Guide to Wagner Ware and Other Companies,* L-W Book Sales, 1994; Douglas Congdon-Martin, *Figurative Cast Iron,* Schiffer Publishing, 1994; *Griswold Cast Iron,* L-W Book Sales, 1993; Floyd, Wells & Co., *Authentic Victorian Stoves, Heaters, Ranges, Etc.,* (reprint of ca. 1898 catalog), Dover Publications, 1988; Henrie Martinie, *Art Deco Ornamental Ironwork,* Dover Publications, 1996; Kathryn McNerney, *Antique Iron Identification and Values,* Collector Books, 1984, 1995 value update; Ted Menten (comp.), *Art Nouveau Decorative Ironwork,* Dover Publications, 1981; Dana G. Morykan and Harry L. Rinker, *Warman's Country Antiques & Collectibles,* Third Edition, Wallace-Homestead, 1996; J. L. Mott Iron Works, *Mott's Illustrated Catalog of Victorian Plumbing Fixtures for Bathrooms and Kitchens* (reprint of 1888 catalog), Dover Publications, 1987; George C. Neumann, *Early American Antique Country Furnishings,* L-W Book Sales, 1984, 1993 reprint; David G. Smith and Charles Wafford, *The Book of Griswold & Wagner,* Schiffer Publishing, 1995; Diane Stoneback, *Kitchen Collectibles,* Wallace-Homestead, 1994.

Periodicals: *Cast Iron Cookware News,* 28 Angela Ave, San Anselmo, CA 94960; *Kettles 'n Cookware,* Drawer B, Perrysburg, NY 14129.

Collectors' Club: Griswold & Cast Iron Cookware Assoc, 54 Macon Ave, Asheville, NC 28801.

REPRODUCTION ALERT

Use the following checklist to determine if a metal object is a period piece or modern reproduction. This checklist applies to all cast-metal items, from mechanical banks to trivets.

Period cast-iron pieces feature well-defined details, carefully fitted pieces, and carefully finished and smooth castings. Reproductions, especially those produced by making a new mold from a period piece, often lack detail in the casting (lines not well defined, surface details blurred) and parts have gaps at the seams and a rough surface. Reproductions from period pieces tend to be slightly smaller in size than the period piece from which they were copied.

Period paint mellows, i.e., softens in tone. Colors look flat. Beware of any cast-iron object whose paint is bright and fresh. Painted period pieces should show wear. Make certain the wear is in places it is supposed to be.

Period cast-iron pieces develop a surface patina that prevents rust. When rust is encountered on a period piece, it generally has a greasy feel and is dark in color. The rust on artificially aged reproductions is flaky and orange.

Additional Listings: Banks, Boot Jacks, Doorstops, Fireplace Equipment, Food Molds, Irons, Kitchen Collectibles, Lamps, and Tools.

Andirons, pr
    20" h, cast iron, figural, Hessian, hand on hip, walking to left **225.00**
    20½" h, wrought iron, knife-blade shape, penny feet, brass urn finials **450.00**
    26½" l, wrought iron, primitive **155.00**
Anvil, 5½" d, cast iron, wood base **15.00**
Ashtray, cast iron, Griswold, No. 00, matchbook holder, logo and pattern number **65.00**
Bottle Opener, cast iron
    4⅝" l, black man, old paint **65.00**
    5" h, parrot on perch, polychrome paint **60.00**
Broiler, 11 × 12", wrought iron, sq, removable drop pan, shaped handle **220.00**
Candleholder, 12¾" h, wrought iron, primitive, hook at top for hanging on beam, curved arm with one socket **80.00**
Candlestand, 28½" h, wrought iron, tripod base, 19th C **605.00**
Candlestick, wrought iron
    5" h, hog scraper, hook, push-up lift, c1800 .... **125.00**
    6¾" h, spiral push-up, lip hanger, turned wooden base **225.00**
Cigar Lighter, 7¾" h, cast iron, sheet-metal arm, brass trim, "Gretchen Cigars, Louis Ash Co, Makers, NY" adv, "the Burnoff Mfg Co, Cinti, Oh," 1902–06 patent dates **350.00**
Cresset Lighting Device, wrought iron, primitive
    30" h, adjustable trammel post, four legs **325.00**
    33" h, twisted post and tripod base **310.00**
Door Knocker, 8" l, wrought iron, heart and scrolled detail **360.00**
Fire Mark, 7⅜ × 11½", cast iron, polychrome paint, pitted, marked "FA" **215.00**
Flue Damper, Griswold, cast iron
    5" d, New American **25.00**
    6" d, American **25.00**
Garden Figure, 10½" h, cast iron, full-bodied seated rabbit, old white repaint **190.00**
Griddle, 22" d, cast iron, fifteen sided, raised rim and spout, minor edge damage **140.00**
Hinges, pr, wrought iron
    16" l, strap, spike attachments at pins, bird's head, flattened circle **50.00**
    16½" l, scroll, Moravian type, edge damage, some scroll work missing **72.00**
    32" l, strap, bird's-head ends **110.00**
Hitching Post, 68" h, cast iron, horse's head, steel posts, price for pr **95.00**
Kettle, cast iron, gooseneck spout, wrought-iron bale handle
    8" h, swivel handle, small holes in iron **35.00**
    9" h, stationary handle **40.00**
Kettle Shelf, 10½ × 14", wrought iron **35.00**
Lock, 5 × 9¼", box type, keeper and key, sliding bolt with brass knob **220.00**
Miner's Lamp, 7½" h, cast iron, chicken finial, dent in side **140.00**
Paperweight, 5" l, cast iron, frog, worn black paint **45.00**
Peel, 42¾" l, wrought iron, ram's-horn handle **95.00**

Dough scraper, wrought iron, triangular scraper, 4¾" base, 4½" handle, $25.00.

Plate Holder, 59" h, wrought iron, triangular, seven graduated shelves **250.00**
Roasting Spit, 31" l, cast iron, wrought-iron spikes **165.00**
Rush and Splint Soaking Pan, 14½" w, 14¾" l, wrought iron, edge damage **385.00**
Shoe, 6¾" h, cast iron, high top, worn old red paint, gold buttons, price for facing pr **200.00**
Spatula, 12¾" l, wrought iron, good detail **65.00**
Stove, 14¼" w, 32" d, 19¾" h, cast iron, attributed to Ford Foundry, Concord, NH, c1870, double-arch panel door, rounded hearth, triple-arch panel sides, four cabriole legs, pad feet **635.00**
Sugar Cutter, marked "A R Timmins & Sons" **75.00**
Taper Jack, 6¼" h, wrought iron, detailed engraving .. **850.00**
Thumb Latch, 13½" l, wrought iron, orig bar, simple tooling **150.00**
Toaster
    17" l, wrought iron, scrolled detail **275.00**
    22" l, wrought iron, twisted detail, turned handle .. **110.00**
Trammel, wrought iron, sawtooth, ram's-horn finial, scrolled ratchet **225.00**
Trivet, 21½" h, wrought iron, adjustable roasting fork, wooden handle **200.00**
Waffle Iron, 27¾" l, cast and wrought iron **75.00**
Windmill Weight, 10½" l, cast iron, crescent shape, emb "Eclipse," Fairbanks, Morse & Co, Chicago **385.00**

IVORY

History: Ivory, a yellowish white organic material, comes from the teeth or tusks of animals and lends itself to carving. Many cultures have used it for centuries to make artistic and utilitarian items.

A cross section of elephant ivory will have a reticulated crisscross pattern. Hippopotamus teeth, walrus tusks, whale teeth, narwhal tusks, and boar tusks also are forms of ivory. Vegetable ivory, bone, stag horn, and plastic are ivory substitutes which often confuse collectors. For information on how to identify real ivory, see Bernard Rosett's "Is It Genuine Ivory" in Sandra Andacht's *Oriental Antiques & Art: An Identification and Value Guide* (Wallace-Homestead, 1987).

References: Edgard O. Espinoza and Mary-Jacque Mann, *Identification for Ivory and Ivory Substitutes,* Second Edition, World

Wildlife Fund, 1992; Gloria and Robert Mascarelli, *Oriental Antiques,* Wallace-Homestead, out of print.

Periodical: *Netsuke & Ivory Carving Newsletter,* 3203 Adams Way, Ambler, PA 19002.

Collectors' Club: Internation Ivory Society, 11109 Nicholas Dr, Wheaton, MD 20902.

Note: Dealers and collectors should be familiar with The Endangered Species Act of 1973, amended in 1978, which limits the importation and sale of antique ivory and tortoiseshell items.

Box, cov, 3¾" d, round
    Elaborately carved flowering iris, Japanese, base sgd, large crack to body 130.00
    Painted figures in landscape 160.00
Brush Pot, 5¾" h, inscribed with Chinese-style landscape and lengthy text, Chinese 325.00
Chop Block, 2½" h, carved elephant and attendant, Chinese, 18th C, damage and wear 120.00
Cribbage Board, 9¾" l, elongated board, lobed end, four lion's-paw feet, three carved figural reserves, scrolling foliage ground, Chinese, 19th C, made for western market 375.00
Dagger, 13½" d, carved warriors at battle, Japanese ...1,350.00

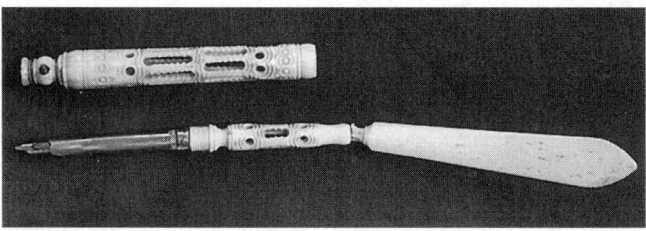

Letter opener and pen, Stanhope, map of Atlantic City, 9½" letter opener, $75.00.

Diorama, 16" w, 17½" h, carved, Roman banquet, carved wooden case designed as temple portico, 19th C 6,900.00
Dresser Box, 9" l, rect, top and sides carved with figural panels, scrolled skirt, lion's-paw and monster-mask feet, Chinese, 19th C, made for western market 400.00
Figure
    6" h, boy with fishing pole and fish, on column, Continental 600.00
    7" h, Chinese scholar and tiger, Japanese 425.00
    8½" h, immortals, polychrome dec, carved wooden stand, Japanese, 7-pc set 1,500.00
    9" l, reclining nude, lady with bound feet, flowering rose between breasts, Chinese 220.00
    10" h, archer, ceremonial armor, Chinese 625.00
    11½" h, elephant, bearing double gourd dec with symbols of eight immortals, Chinese, price for pr 350.00
    13½" l, reclining goddess, carved wooden couch, Chinese 900.00
    14" h, nobleman and woman, Chinese, price for pr 600.00
    17" h, Bodhisattva, holding stringed instrument, Japanese 750.00
    21" h, warrior, standing, armor, carrying sword, bow and arrows, red seal mark on base, carved wooden stand, Chinese, 19th C 2,300.00

Mask, 6½" h, woman with horns, sgd, Japanese 475.00
Okimono, man and girl with table and fruit, sgd, Japanese 200.00
Panel, 4½" h, curved, relief figures and dog hunting wild boar, Continental 200.00
Pen Holder, 4", cylindrical, carved, three monkeys, wooden base 125.00
Puzzle Ball, 12½" h, stand, Chinese 75.00
Snuff Bottle, 3" h, figural, polychrome, Chinese 75.00

Snuff bottle, man holding cup on obverse, five vert lines of characters on reverse, 20th C, 2¼" h, $110.00.

Table Screen Panel, 8" h, carved on one side with people in landscape, other side carved with bamboo teapot and basket of peaches, flowers, Chinese, remnants of polychrome 110.00
Tusk
    14½" l, pierced and carved figures and pavilions within landscape, Chinese 220.00
    27" h, carved lake pavilion joined to shore by causeway with ancient pine, Mt Fuji and flying geese, reverse carved with flying geese and winter grasses, silver end cap incised with shrine, sgd "Uma Hide," Japanese 1,350.00
Vase
    5" h, carved boar-hunting scene, Japanese, lacks base 425.00
    7½" h, cov, carved lotus blossom and branch lid, cranes and foliage, Japanese 200.00
    9" h, tusk form, carved farmers in landscape, Japanese, damage to wooden base 100.00

JACK-IN-THE-PULPIT VASES

History: Trumpet-shaped jack-in-the-pulpit glass vases were in vogue during the late 19th and early 20th centuries. The vases were made in a wide variety of patterns, colors, and sizes.

Additional Listings: See specific glass categories.

3½" h, bowl shape, rainbow DQ, MOP satin, repeating panels of yellow, pink, peach, and colorless stripes, turned up and down piecrust trim sgd "Patent" 1,285.00
4" h, white satin ext., emerald green int. squatty form, blossom-form opening, seven applied and frosted feet 95.00
5" h, opaline, ruffled purple top 115.00
6" h, 5" w, frosted pink and white stripes, bulbous, broad flange, Webb 375.00
6½" h, 5½" d, white ext., maroon shaded to cream overlay, flower-petal top, applied clear petal feet 110.00

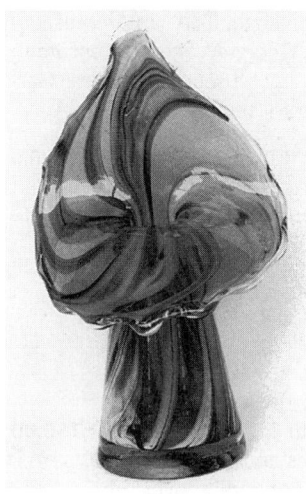

Spatter glass, predominately yellow, stripes of white, orange, green and blue, 7″ h, $50.00.

6³⁄₄″ h, pale violet blue satin ext., white int., pink ruffled
   rim **275.00**
7³⁄₈″ h, 3″ d, butterscotch rainbow MOP satin, white
   lining, clear frosted ruffled edge, brass ormolu foot . **235.00**
9¹⁄₂″ h, 5″ wide flaring piecrust rim, dec lusterless white
   ground, randomly scattered gold-outlined floral dec,
   Mt Washington **300.00**
10″ h, cranberry, applied crystal rigaree and feet **215.00**
10³⁄₄″ h, 5″ d, transparent sapphire blue, quilted, ruffled
   top, pink and white enameled flowers, green leaves,
   gold trim **200.00**
11″ h, 5″ d, deep maroon, brown, and yellow over white,
   brilliant pink int., 24 rows of pull-ups, applied clear
   edge, crimped flaring top, bulbous base, Northwood **675.00**
15¹⁄₂″ h, 6″ d, Burmese, deep salmon pink shading to
   brilliant yellow, matte finish, tightly crimped top, Mt
   Washington, 1880s **950.00**

JADE

History: Jade is the generic name for two distinct minerals: nephrite and jadeite. Nephrite, an amphibole mineral from Central Asia that was used in pre-18th-century pieces, has a waxy surface and hues that range from white to an almost-black green. Jadeite, a pyroxene mineral found in Burma and used from 1700 to the present, has a glassy appearance and comes in various shades of white, green, yellow-brown, and violet.

Jade cannot be carved because of its hardness. Shapes are achieved by sawing and grinding with wet abrasives such as quartz, crushed garnets, and carborundum.

Prior to 1800 few items were signed or dated. Stylistic considerations are used to date pieces. The Ch'ien Lung period (1736–1795) is considered the golden age of jade.

Periodical: *Bulletin of the Friends of Jade,* 5004 Ensign St, San Diego, CA 92117.

Museum: Avery Brundage Collection, de Young Museum, San Francisco, CA.

Bowl, 8¹⁄₂″ d, thinly carved as flower with radiating petals, translucent surface suffused with dark flecks ...**2,300.00**
Brush Washer, 3¹⁄₈″ h, peach born on gnarled branch
   form, slender leaves encompassing sides, gray with

dark brown, calcified to opaque buff base, Ming Dynasty **2,200.00**
Chime, 8¹⁄₂″ l, 4¹⁄₂″ h, triangular form, pierced scrolling
   borders, even white-colored stone **460.00**
Clasp, 3″ l, dragon, carved lotus button, 18th C **90.00**
Ewer, cov, 9³⁄₄″ h, baluster body, six vertical lobes,
   barbed rim encircled with key-fret border, faceted
   spout and handle carved with clouds and surmounted
   by chilong, terminating handle with tab, sage figure
   asleep amidst rocks and pine on conforming cov,
   mottled gray, Ming Dynasty **3,350.00**
Figure
   6¹⁄₈″ h, maiden, holding flute, wearing robe, topknot
     hair style, standing beside phoenix perched on
     rocks, branch sprouting peony, greenish white
     mottle **1,895.00**
   6¹⁄₂″ h, jadeite
     Crane, standing over lilies issuing from sq base,
      bird holding fish in open beak, celadon color
      stone, chestnut inclusions, carved wooden
      base, 19th C **875.00**
     Mythical dragon form carrying smaller dragon and
      pagoda with chilong finial on back, 6″ l, trans-
      lucent light green stone, dark brown inclusions **460.00**
     Phoenix, standing on rockwork base, single
      blooming flower, bird's tail tucked under body,
      head turned left, celadon-colored stone, apple
      green inclusions, pierced, carved wooden
      base, 18th/19th C **575.00**
Jewelry
   Brooch, butterfly, freshwater pearl body, red stone
     eye accents, carved wings, 14K yellow gold an-
     tennae, hallmarks **635.00**
   Ring, center oval 16.4 × 13 mm jade flanked by
     marquise diamonds, channel-set diamond ba-
     guette shoulders, platinum mount, Art Deco **4,025.00**
   Suite, bracelet with carved oval jadeite plaques with
     bead spacers, seed pearl highlights, similar ring
     with beaded foliate shoulders, 14k yg mounts,
     price for 2-pc set **520.00**
Plaque, 1³⁄₄″ l, long-tailed bird form, head turned back
   to wings, legs stretched forward, incised details on
   one side, plain on other, dark beige, Shang Dynasty **3,300.00**

Floral centerpiece, 21¹⁄₂ × 12¹⁄₂″, $325.00.

Snuff bottle, mottled brown jade, hand-carved animal design, green jade stopper, 3" h, $450.00.

Ritual Disc, 7" d, Archaic-form, three concentric bands on either side enclosing raised hooked scrolls and commas, dark green stone 865.00

Snuff Bottle, 3" h, teardrop shape, white, lapis stopper, Chinese 75.00

Tube, 6½" h, cylindrical form, translucent stone suffused with green and cream, Neolithic style 520.00

Vase, 14¼" h, quadrilobed baluster body, two figures on horseback on one side, other with twenty character inscription above two seals encircled with double-line elongated-heart border, pierced foliage scroll cascading from mouths of monster-masks handles, opaque white mottling 8,800.00

JAPANESE AND CHINESE CERAMICS

History: The Chinese pottery tradition has existed for thousands of years. By the 16th century Chinese ceramic wares were being exported to India, Persia, and Egypt. During the Ming dynasty (1368–1643), earthenwares became more highly developed. The Ch'ien Lung period (1736–1795) of the Ch'ing dynasty marked the golden age of interchange with the West.

Trade between China and the West began in the 16th century when the Portuguese established Macao. The Dutch entered the trade early in the 17th century. With the establishment of the English East India Company, all of Europe sought Chinese-made pottery and porcelain. Styles, shapes, and colors were developed to suit Western tastes, a tradition which continued until the late 19th century.

Like the Chinese, the Japanese spent centuries developing their ceramic arts. Each region established its own forms, designs, and glazes. Individual artists added their unique touches.

Japanese ceramics began to be exported to the West in the mid-19th century. Their beauty quickly made them favorites of the patrician class.

Fine Oriental ceramics continued to be made into the 20th century, and modern artists enjoy equal fame with older counterparts.

References: Christopher Dresser, *Traditional Arts and Crafts of Japan,* Dover Publications, 1994; Gloria and Robert Mascarelli, *Warman's Oriental Antiques,* Wallace-Homestead, 1992.

Periodical: *Orientalia Journal,* PO Box 94, Little Neck, NY 11363.

Collectors' Club: China Student's Club, 59 Standish Rd, Wellesley, MA 02181.

Museums: Art Institute of Chicago, Chicago, IL; Asian Art Museum of San Francisco, San Francisco, CA; George Walter Vincent Smith Art Museum, Springfield, MA; Morikami Museum & Japanese Gardens, Delray Beach, FL; Pacific Asia Museum, Pasadena, CA.

Additional Listings: Canton, Fitzhugh, Imari, Kutani, Nanking, Rose Medallion, and Satsuma.

Chinese

Bottle, 8½" h, ovoid body rising to garlic-bulb mouth, raised foot, incised single blue dragon in pursuit of flaming pearl, red floral bursts at mouth, cloud collar and key-fret border on foot, Ming dynasty, Chenghua four character mark on base, 19th C **1,150.00**

Bowl, 6¾" d, white enamel branches and trunk of blossoming prunus tree below foot, continuing over rim into int., incised details, double sq blue enameled Yongzheng character Yuzhi mark **2,700.00**

Box, cov, 6⅛" d, cushion form, blue and white, cov babao raised on lingzhi sprigs within medallion, continuous scroll on sides and box, double-line borders, Jiajing character mark **3,850.00**

Bust, 12¾" h, Lokapala, right arm raised to hold spear, left extended to side, head facing left, ferocious expression, high-collar robe splashed with green, chestnut, and cream, face and peaked helmet with traces of red and black pigment, Sanci glaze, Tang dynasty 980.00

Cache Pot, 9" h, tub form, six reserves of birds among foliage, mythical beast striding across waves, powder blue ground 300.00

Dish

7¾" d, shallow form, flared rim, overall even yellow glaze, Ming dynasty, Jiajing mark and period, rim chips, int. surface scratches 575.00

8" d, rounded sides, flared everted rim, shed edge, int. with central scene of two deer among foliage, continual scene of bird, frog, and bee amid fruiting branches border, reverse with birds perched on branches and flowers, blue and white glaze, Ming dynasty, 17th C, hairline 290.00

16" d, central dragon surrounded by two dragons, two phoenix amid peony, yellow ground, brocade border with floral cartouches, Guangxu, 1874–1907 230.00

Figure

3½" h, mythical beasts, seated on sq base, ovoid body, head with protruding eyes, open mouth, aubergine, brown, yellow, and white glazed coloring, fitted wooden base, late 19th C, price for pr 690.00

10¼" h, attendant, standing with arms by side, long court robe, traces of red and black pigments, Tang dynasty 115.00

19" h, Quan-Yin, standing, Tang style colors glaze, wooden base 125.00

Jar, cov, 17" h, ovoid, lobed famille verte enameled reserves, figures in landscapes, floral groups, powder blue ground, gilt flowers, repaired flaring lid, lotus-bud finial 225.00

Jar, open, 4¾" h, thinly potted, squat form, waisted neck, two loop handles, neck and shoulders painted in black and brown bands and crosshatching, Neolithic, Gansu Province 215.00

Ladle, 7½" l, rounded bowl, squared rim, dragon on handle, overall irid green glaze, Tang dynasty 230.00

Lotus Bowl, 15½" d, five-petal flaring form, famille verte enameled floral arrangement reserves, powder blue ground, int. with dec petals , circular central reserve **1,100.00**

Planter and Under Tray, 6⅝" h, straight sided, everted rim, enameled profusion of flowers, white ground, undertray with flower head, scrolling design, Changxu mark and period, 1874–1907 .... 520.00

Tile, 11" l, blue enamel landscapes, price for 4-pc set . 120.00

Vase

6" h, Archaic form, bluster shape, twin rabbit head handles on shoulder, six-figure Qianlong seal, one ear broken, price for pr 200.00

11" h, lantern, cylindrical, six quatrelobe openings, famille rose enamels, foliage scrolls, auspicious symbols, royal blue ground, price for pr 175.00

13¾" h, 1¾" d unglazed tapering base, ovoid slender pinched neck, flaring rim dec, four pictorial bands in famille verte enamels, bands depict various symbols and attributes, two shishi disputing ball and seal, bird among flowering branches, Kylin and phoenix, six character Kangki mark, wooden stand, some enamel retouching, crack to rim ... 475.00

Chinese Export

Figure, 5" h, naked boy standing on green glazed base, carrying single large fish on line over one shoulder, red and black highlights, white ground, early 20th C, price for pr 750.00

Fruit Bowl, 7½" d, flowers in baskets, floral sprays, 18th/19th C 200.00

Low Dish, 7½" d, painted scholar in garden, price for pr 150.00

Plate

7½" d, armorial dec, pierced rims, price for pr **1,350.00**

9" d, figures in garden dec 130.00

Platter

15" l, Thousand Butterfly dec, mid 19th C 400.00

18¾" l, Garden pattern, crest of Clerke or Clarke, motto, in memory of the Victory of King Henry VIII at Battle of Spurs, 1513, drain, c1845–63 ....**2,100.00**

Punch Bowl

9" d, elaborate floral and landscape reserves, restored 650.00

9¼" d, figural and bird reserves 400.00

Salad Bowl, 9½" w, sq, cut corners, allover landscape, polychrome festoons int. **1,800.00**

Soap Dish, 5¾" d, rect form, dish, drain, and lid 425.00

Teapot

6" h

Drum form, braided handle, strawberry finial lid, floral sprays, black enamel gilding, late 18th C 450.00

Spherical

Floral reserves, handle and spout molded in form of woody boughs, peach finial, 18th C 600.00

Two figural reserves, black diaper ground, restorations to knob and handle 260.00

7½" h, sq form, raised panels, bamboo spout and handle, allover polychrome dec with figures and landscape reserves, restoration to handle, spout, and lid **1,100.00**

Vase, 11¼" h, flat ovoid shape, twin dragon handles, reserves of figures, 18th/19th C, drilled for lamp ... 550.00

Warming Plate, 11" d, two elaborate central polychrome figural reserves, two dec borders, price for pr **2,400.00**

Japanese

Bowl, 12½" d, ext. dec with three underglaze pine boughs, int. roughened for grinding 180.00

Charger, 16" d, crane and floral dec, Yatsushiro 400.00

Dish, 12" l, boat form, stern with notch, wave ornaments on ext., floral motifs and diaper dec int., Sansei, Meiji period **1,200.00**

Ewer, 9" h, two panels with foliage and figure dec, one panel with herons on plum branches, band of stylized flower heads on neck, loop handle, underglaze blue and white, Arita, late 17th C **1,500.00**

Low Bowl, 12" d, molded ring of wrestlers, center dec in underglaze blue with raven in landscape, incised through glaze 900.00

Planter, 16" d, stenciled cobalt blue designs of landscapes in reserves, floral brocade ground 220.00

Teabowl, 4¾" d, brown and green floral dec, circular floral geometric reserves, mottled glaze, sgd 250.00

Vase

9" h, earthenware, figures in garden, cobalt blue ground, price for pr 250.00

14" h, club form, two molded fish handles on neck, one side dec with warrior and mischievous oni, reverse with four oni surrounding offering table, mounted as lamp 500.00

Japanese, vase, Sumida Gawa, two monkeys, dragon costumes, red ground, crackleglazed top, sgd cartouche, 7" h, $400.00.

Wall Pocket, 9" h, Geisha with green basket on her back, blue, red, and pink, Banko, price for matched pr ... 125.00

JASPERWARE

History: Jasperware is a hard, unglazed porcelain with a colored ground varying from the most common blues and greens to lavender, yellow, red, or black. The white designs, often classical in nature, are applied in relief. Jasperware was first produced at Wedgwood's Etruria Works in 1775. Josiah Wedgwood described it as "a fine terra-cotta of great beauty and delicacy proper for cameos."

In addition to Wedgwood, many other English potters produced jasperware. Two of the leaders were Adams and Copeland and Spode. Several Continental potters, e.g., Heubach, also produced the ware.

References: Susan and Al Bagdade, *Warman's English & Continental Pottery & Porcelain,* Second Edition, Wallace-Homestead, 1991; R. K. Henrywood, *Relief-Moulded Jugs, 1820–1900,* Antique Collectors' Club, out of print.

Reproduction Alert: Jasperware still is made today, especially by Wedgwood.

Note: This category includes jasperware pieces which were made by companies other than Wedgwood. Wedgwood jasperware is found in the Wedgwood listing.

Biscuit Jar, 6 × 6″, bulbous, dark blue ground, white relief hunting scene, SP cov, rim, and handle, marked "Adams, England" **165.00**
Bowl, 7″ d, dark blue ground, white relief classical figures **225.00**
Box, cov, 5″ l, oval, blue ground, white relief cherub and nymph, marked "Schafer & Vater, Germany" **50.00**
Chamberstick, black ground, white relief classical figures, snuffer **275.00**
Creamer, blue ground, white Kewpies, sgd **185.00**
Doorknobs, green ground, white cherubs dec, price for pr **100.00**
Hair Receiver, 3⅜ × 3½″, blue ground, white relief classical ladies and flowers, cupids on lid, marked "Germany" **90.00**
Match Box, cov, lilac dip **120.00**
Perfume Bottle, blue ground, white relief figures, hallmarked SS top **275.00**
Plaque, 6½ × 5″, green ground, white relief Indian Chief, marked "Germany" **210.00**
Salt Shaker, dark blue ground, white relief classical figures **70.00**

Pitcher, brown ground, marked "Copeland, Football/JMSD & S/1895, Reg. 180288," 5⅜″ h, $300.00.

Urn, 8″ h, cobalt blue ground, white relief hunting scene, marked "Adams, Tunstall, England" **220.00**
Vase, 8¼″ h, light blue ground, white classical figural cameos, white handles, bolted pedestal base with white scrolling vine dec **375.00**

JEWEL BOXES

History: The evolution of jewelry was paralleled by the development of boxes in which to store it. Jewel-box design followed the fashion trends dictated by furniture styles. Many jewel boxes are lined.

Bella Ware, Helmschmeid Manufacturing Co, Meriden, CT, 4½″ w, pale lavender ground, violet bunches within scroll, orig brass hardware, sgd on base **250.00**
Glass, hinged, round
3½″ h, 4¼″ d, light sapphire blue, white and cream enameled flowers on lid and sides, lacy gold leaves and vines on side **200.00**
3⅝″ h, 4⅛″ d, amethyst, white enameled leaves around sides, white enameled flowers and leaves on lid with spray of small blue enameled flowers **200.00**
3¾″ h, 4⅜″ d, cobalt blue, dainty white enameled leaf sprays around sides of box, two black, white, and blue enameled birds with flowers dec **275.00**

Amethyst glass, enameled florals and central diamond motif with child, silver rim and base, 4⅞″ h, 6″ d, $125.00.

Ivory, 8½ × 8½ x 3½″, rect, two doors including two drawers, two drawers below, stone appliqué and gilding, Oriental, losses to gilding **775.00**
Pairpoint, robin's-egg blue opal glass ground, six scalloped medallions of pink, yellow, and coral roses, green leaves, brown traceries, fancy gold wash, SP base, four ball feet, sgd and numbered **325.00**
Wood
11¾″ l, walnut, old dark alligatored finish, applied rope and bead molding, oval beveled mirror in lid, carved foliage fans, lined with old green felt, some molding missing **65.00**
14½″ l, 14″ h, carved, lift top and drawer over doors with fitted int. drawers, lower drawer, scrolled base, inlaid bone, fruits, flowers, and scroll work, Chinese **725.00**
15″ l, 11½″ d, 11″ h, coffin shaped box, pincushion lid set into projecting top supported by scrolling brackets, beaded base, four turnip turned legs, plush int., fitted insert, Renaissance Revival **140.00**

JEWELRY

History: Jewelry has been a part of every culture. It is a way of displaying wealth, power, or love of beauty. In the current antiques marketplace, it is easiest to find jewelry dating after 1830.

Jewelry items were treasured and handed down as heirlooms from generation to generation. In the United States, antique jewelry is any jewelry at least 100 years old, a definition linked to U.S. Customs law. Pieces that do not meet the antique criteria but are at least 25 years old are called "period" or "heirloom/estate" jewelry.

The names of historical periods are commonly used when describing jewelry. The following list indicates the approximate dates for each era.

Georgian	1714–1830
Victorian	1837–1901
Edwardian	1890–1920
Arts and Crafts	1890–1920
Art Nouveau	1895–1910
Art Deco	1920–1935
Retro Modern	1935–1945
Post-War Modern	1945–1965

References: Lillian Baker, *Art Nouveau & Art Deco Jewelry: An Identification & Value Guide,* Collector Books, 1981, 1994 value update; ———, *Fifty Years of Collectible Fashion Jewelry, 1925–1975,* Collector Books, 1986, 1992 value update; ———, *100 Years of Collectible Jewelry, 1850–1950,* Collector Books, 1978, 1995 value update; Howard L. Bell, Jr., *Cuff Jewelry: A Historical Account for Collectors and Antique Dealers,* published by author (PO Box 11695, Raytown, MO 64138), 1994; Jeanne Bell, *Answers to Questions about 1840–1950 Old Jewelry,* Fourth Edition, Books Americana, 1996; David Bennett and Daniela Mascetti, *Understanding Jewellery,* Revised Edition, Antique Collectors' Club, 1994; France Borel, *The Splendor of Ethnic Jewelry,* Harry N. Abrams, 1994; Shirley Bury, *Jewellery 1789–1910: The International Era,* Antique Collectors' Club, 1991; Franco Cologni and Ettore Mocchetti, *Made by Cartier: 150 Years of Tradition and Innovation,* Abbeville Press, 1993; Genevieve Cummins and Neryvalle Taunton, *Chatelaines: Utility to Glorious Extravagance,* Antique Collector's Club, 1994.

Ginny Redington Dawes and Corinne Davidov, *Victorian Jewelry: Unexplored Treasures,* Abbeville Press, 1991; F. Deboni, *Authentic Art Deco Jewelry Designs,* Dover Publications, 1983; Maurice Dufrene, *305 Authentic Art Nouveau Jewelry Designs,* Dover Publications, 1985; Alastair Duncan, *The Paris Salons 1895–1914, Jewelry,* 2 vols., Antique Collectors' Club, 1994; Lodovica Rizzoli Eleuteri, *Twentieth–Century Jewelry: Art Nouveau to Modern Design,* Electa, Abbeville, 1994; Roseann Ettinger, *Popular Jewelry, 1840–1940,* Schiffer Publishing, 1990; Joan Evans, *A History of Jewellery 1100–1870,* Dover Publications, 1989; Sibyelle Jargstorf, *Baubles, Buttons and Beads: The Heritage of Bohemia,* Schiffer Publishing, 1994; ———, *Glass Beads from Europe,* Schiffer Publishing, 1995; Susan Jonas and Marilyn Nissensor, *Cuff Links,* Harry N. Abrams, 1991; Arthur Guy Kaplan, *The Official Identification and Price Guide to Antique Jewelry,* Sixth Edition, House of Collectibles, 1990, reprinted 1994; Elyse Zorn Karlin, *Jewelry and Metalwork in the Arts and Crafts Tradition,* Schiffer Publishing, 1993; Jack and Pet Kerins, *Collecting Antique Stickpins: Identification and Value Guide,* Collector Books, 1994; George Frederick Kunz, *The Curious Lore of Precious Stones,* Dover Publications, 1970; ———, *Rings for the Finger,* Dover Publications, n.n.; George Frederick Kunz and Charles Hugh Stevenson, *The Book of the Pearl,* Dover Publications, 1973.

Patrick Mauries, *Jewelry by Chanel,* Bulfinch Press, 1993; Anna M. Miller, *Cameos Old and New,* Van Nostrand Reinhold, 1991; ———, *Illustrated Guide to Jewelry Appraising: Antique Period & Modern,* Chapman & Hall, 1990; Ginger Moro, *European Designer Jewelry,* Schiffer Publishing, 1995; Penny Chittim Morrill and Carol A. Beck, *Mexican Silver: 20th Century Handwrought Jewelry and Metalwork,* Schiffer Publishing, 1994; Gabriel Mourey et al., *Art Nouveau Jewellery & Fans,* Dover Publications, n.d.; Michael Poynder, *The Price Guide to Jewellery 3000 B.C.–1950 A.D.,* Antique Collectors' Club, 1990 reprint; Penny Proddow, Debra Healy, and Marion Fasel, *Hollywood Jewels: Movies, Jewelry, Stars,* Harry L. Abrams, 1992; Dorothy T. Rainwater, *American Jewelry Manufacturers,* Schiffer Publishing, 1988; Christie Romero, *Warman's Jewelry,* Wallace-Homestead, 1995; Nancy N. Schiffer, *Silver Jewelry Designs: Evaluating Quality,* Schiffer Publishing, 1996; ———, *Silver Jewelry Treasures,* Schiffer Publishing, 1993; Sheryl Gross Shatz, *What's It Made Of? A Jewelry Materials Identification Guide,* Third Edition, published by author (10931 Hunting Horn Dr, Santa Clara, CA 92705), 1996; Doris J. Snell, *Antique Jewelry With Prices,* Updated Edition, Wallace-Homestead, 1991; Nicholas D. Snider, *Antique Sweetheart Jewelry,* Schiffer Publishing, 1996; Ulrike von Hase-Schmundt et al., *Theodor Fahrner, Jewelry...between Avant-Garde and Tradition,* Schiffer Publishing, 1991; Janet Zapata, *The Jewelry and Enamels of Louis Comfort Tiffany,* Harry N. Abrams, 1993.

Periodicals: *Auction Market Resource for Gems & Jewelry,* PO Box 7683, Rego Park, NY 11374; *Gems & Gemology,* Gemological Institute of America, 1660 Stewart St, Santa Monica, CA 90404; *Jewelers' Circular Keystone/Heritage,* PO Box 2085, Radnor, PA 19080.

Collectors' Clubs: American Society of Jewelry Historians, Box 103, 1B Quaker Ridge Rd, New Rochelle, NY 10804; National Cuff Link Society, PO Box 346, Prospect Heights, IL 60070; Society of Antique & Estate Jewelry, Ltd, 570 Seventh Ave, Suite 1900, New York, NY 10018.

Videotapes: C. Jeanne Bell, *The Antique and Collectible Jewelry Video Series: Edwardian, Art Nouveau & Art Deco Jewelry, Circa 1887–1930's,* Volume II, Antique Images, 1994; C. Jeanne Bell, *The Antique and Collectible Jewelry Video Series: Victorian Jewelry, Circa 1837–1901,* Volume I, Antique Images, 1994; Leigh Leshner and Christie Romero, *Hidden Treasures,* Venture Entertainment (PO Box 55113, Sherman Oaks, CA 91413), 1992, includes updated printed price guide, 1995.

Advisor: Christie Romero.

Notes: The value of a piece of old jewelry is derived from several criteria, including craftsmanship, scarcity, and the current value of precious metals and gemstones. Note that antique and period pieces should be set with stones that were cut in the manner in use at the time the piece was made. Antique jewelry is not comparable to contemporary pieces set with modern-cut stones and should not be appraised with the same standards. Nor should old-mine, old-European, or rose-cut stones be replaced with modern brilliant cuts.

The pieces listed here are antique or period and represent fine jewelry (i.e., made from gemstones and/or precious metals). The list contains no new reproduction pieces. Inexpensive and mass-produced costume jewelry is covered in *Warman's Americana & Collectibles.*

SPECIAL AUCTIONS

Butterfield & Butterfield
220 San Bruno Ave
San Francisco, CA 94103
(415) 861-7500

Christie's
502 Park Ave
New York, NY 10022
(212) 546-1000

Dunning's Auction Service
755 Church Rd
Elgin, IL 60123
(847) 741-3483

Phillips Fine Art Auctions
406 E 79th St
New York, NY 10021
(212) 570-4830

Skinner, Inc.
The Heritage on the Garden
63 Park Plaza
Boston, MA 02116
(617) 350-5400

Sotheby's
1334 York Ave
New York, NY 10021
(212) 606-7000

Bracelet
  Art Deco
    Flexible, platinum
      Central marquise diamond, approx .75 ct, outlined by calibré-cut emeralds in navette-shaped diamond-set frame, flanked by tapering flexible band set with horizontal row of calibré-cut emeralds and circ-cut diamonds, approx 3.50 cts tw, seven extra links, 6½ × ⅞" 5,175.00
      Set throughout with circ-cut old European diamonds, approx 8.00 cts tw, accented at intervals with horizontal rows of calibré-cut sapphires, 6¼ × ½" 7,762.50
    Link
      Rect silver plaques, each set with large oval amazonite cabochon, alternating with sq plaques, each set with two small sq lapis cabochons, pavé-set throughout with marcasites, maker's mark for Theodor Fahrner, 7 × ¾" 1,380.00

Three rect plaques, each center set with three baguette diamonds flanked by grad row of baguettes, and set throughout with circ-cut diamonds, joined by cusped sq links set with circ-cut diamonds, approx 7.00 cts tw, platinum mount, mark for Maurice Tishman, 6¾ × ½" 7,475.00
Art Nouveau, link, yg, scrolling ribbon links, each with collet-set sapphire center, maker's mark for Sloan & Co., 7 × ½" 2,185.00
Arts and Crafts, link, silver, links of alternating grape clusters and leaves set with circ and oval lapis cabochons, maker's mark for Georg Jensen, 7 × ¾" 920.00
Georgian, link, 18K yg, central open quatrefoil with flower-head center set with oval foiled pink topaz within scrolled design set with small faceted rubies and half pearls, flanked by open C-scroll links, 7 × 1⅞" at center 1,495.00
Retro Modern
  Flexible,14K yg, brickwork mesh strap terminating in buckle clasp set with twelve square-cut sapphires and twenty-two circ-cut diamonds, 8 × ¾" 3,450.00
  Link, 18K rose and wg, beveled sq links alternating with beveled rect links, 35 dwt, 7 × 1" 920.00
Victorian
  Bangle, hinged
    14K yg, front half of bangle set with letters spelling "Mizpah," each letter set throughout with seed pearls, 2½" d, 1" w 1,150.00
    Etruscan Revival, 18K yg, front half with raised letters spelling "ROMA," each letter in circ frame, surrounded by twisted wirework and granulation, balustered finials at hinge and clasp, 2¾" d, 1¼" w 2,875.00
  Flexible, garter, 14K yg adjustable mesh strap, ½" w, surmounted by quatrefoil slide set with pearl in center of foliate motif, suspending foxtail chain tassel, completed by foxtail chain terminal, 33.0 dwt, pair 1,610.00
  Link, 14K yg, Scottish, grad circ links, three center links set with large circ-cut citrines encircled by inlaid jasper and agate, continuing to domed links inlaid with quatrefoils of agate and jasper, engraved yg mounts, fitted box, 7⅝ × 1" 2,875.00
Brooch/Pin
  Art Deco, bar pin
    18K wg, etched rock crystal bow shape bordered by small old European- and single-cut diamonds, center prong-set old European-cut diamond of approx .50 ct encircled by small diamonds, French hallmarks, sgd "Cartier London," # 6170, orig box, 2½" w, ⅜" l 7,150.00
    Center row of grad circ-cut emeralds alternating with grad sq calibré-cut emeralds in scalloped border of circ-cut diamonds, approx 2.00 cts tw, tapered platinum mount, 3½" w, ⅜" l 5,405.00
    Old European-cut diamond, approx .60 ct, flanked by row of twelve bead-set circ-cut diamonds, framed by border of calibré-cut sapphires, the ta-

pered bar set throughout with circ-cut diamonds, approx 4.25 cts tw, platinum mount, French hallmarks, 2¾" w, ¾" l at center **4,312.50**

Open circular frame set with circ-cut diamonds, bordered by inner row of calibré-cut sapphires, four evenly spaced diamond-set arcs around inner edge, diamonds approx 3.75 cts tw, 1½" d **3,910.00**

Oval carved and pierced floral and foliate motif jadeite plaque, 42.5 × 22 × 3.08 mm, prong-set in platinum frame with opposed C-scroll terminals set throughout with twenty-eight old European-cut and eight baguette diamonds, 2" w, ⅞" l **3,450.00**

Rect rock crystal quartz tablet overlaid with repeating arc pattern in silver set with coral beads and marcasites, surrounding silver frame set with border of marcasites and at compass points with row of four rect stepped-cut sapphires, maker's mark for Theodor Fahrner, Pforzheim, Germany, 1¾" w, 1½" l **1,265.00**

Art Nouveau

14K yg lotus flower and lily pads surrounded by whiplash design oval frame, blue and green plique-à-jour enamel ground, maker's mark for Riker Bros, Newark, NJ, 1" w, ¾" l **2,415.00**

Enameled pansy in shades of pink, white and green, circ-cut diamond center, set in 14K yg crescent decorated with foliate and floral repoussé design, maker's mark for Whiteside and Blank, Newark, NJ, minor enamel loss, small dent, 1⅜" w, 1" l **3,450.00**

Arts and Crafts

Bar Pin, oval turquoise cabochon set in tapering 14K yg openwork vine and leaves motif, 3½" w, ½" l **460.00**

18K yg openwork frame of engraved leaves, vines and berries set with circ-cut and sq-cut demantoid garnets, surrounding large round fire opal in matrix, engraved filigree on rev, attributed to Louis Comfort Tiffany, sgd "Tiffany & Co.," 1½" d **16,100.00**

SS, dove in circ wreath, accented with moonstones, imp "Georg Jensen," # 165, 1½" d .. **373.75**

Edwardian

Antique cushion-cut sapphire, 11.8 mm × 10.05 mm, approx 10.00 cts, set in cushion-shaped

Pin, Art Nouveau, woman with flowing hair, SS, 1½", $85.00.

openwork and pierced platinum frame set throughout with diamonds, sgd "Black, Starr & Frost," New York, NY, 1½" w, 1⅜" l **20,700.00**

Bar pin, scroll and foliate motif pierced platinum bar with spade-shaped terminals set in horizontal row of seven slightly graduated old European-cut diamonds in millegrained bezels, 3.0 cts tw, 3" w, ⅜" l **2,185.00**

Bow, pierced floral and foliate design set throughout with diamonds, approx 1.50 cts tw, platinum mount, 14K yg pin stem, 1¾" w, 1⅛" l .**3,162.50**

Dragonfly, body and pierced wings set throughout with rose-cut diamonds, the top wings edged with calibré-cut rubies, the lower wings with sapphires, the body set with larger old European-cut diamond and small rubies, ruby cabochon eyes, mounted in platinum-topped yg, several stones missing, 3½" w, 2⅛" l **8,625.00**

Retro Modern

14K yg stylized spray and scrolled ribbon motif, the center set with cluster of cabochon emeralds interspersed with small diamonds, the ribbons edged in small diamonds, 2½" w, 2¼" l **1,610.00**

18K yg butterfly perched on flowering branch set with diamonds, wings set with rows of circ-cut rubies, sapphires, and diamonds, sgd "Tiffany & Co.," 1¾" w, 2⅛" l **9,200.00**

Ballerinas of similar design, one with skirt star-cut set with diamonds and pear-shaped rose-cut diamond head, other with star-cut set rubies and diamonds, cabochon pink sapphire head, yg, 1½" w, 1¾" l, pr **6,612.00**

Tricolor gold stylized floral spray and scrolling ribbon with five circ-cut citrines prong-set at the ends of gold wires, three small single-cut diamonds set at the base of scrolled ribbon, 1½" w, 3⅛" **632.50**

Victorian

Bar pin

Micromosaic, 18K yg, the word "ROMA" in yg in center of bar flanked by disk terminals, each with micromosaic of fly, ropetwist yg borders, Italian hallmark for 18K (in use 1815–1870), minor solder, 2" w, ¾" l **632.50**

Yg, Etruscan Revival, beaded-edge bar with bead and wiretwist dec, rams' heads within circ disk terminals, 1⅞" × ½" l **522.50**

10K yg, delicate floral spray with pink, yellow and green enameled flower heads, 3 flower centers set with old mine-cut diamonds, some enamel loss, 2½" w, 1" l **220.00**

Demantoid garnet, oval faceted, approx 1.90 cts, in center of 18K yg open scrollwork design set with half pearls and 3 old mine-cut diamonds, sgd "Tiffany & Co.," 1" w, 1¼" l **7,475.00**

Enameled butterfly in shades of red, gold, and blue, old mine- and rose-cut diamonds on wings, sapphire cabochon body, silver-topped yg mount, 3⅛" w, 1½" l **4,025.00**

Japanese fan, shakudo, gilt overlay bird and foliate motifs, copper ground, 1¾" w, 1" l **316.25**

Micromosaic, oval plaque depicting Italian buildings and bridges, set in black onyx in 14K yg frame decorated with scrolled wire and flower heads, 2" w, 1½" l **805.00**

Silver-topped 10K yg, rose, head mounted en tremblant, set throughout with old mine-, European-, rose- and circ-cut diamonds, approx 5.40 cts tw, Cartier leather box, 1⅝" w, 3" l **4,600.00**

Cameo

Hardstone, oval high-relief carving of classical draped female bust set in ornate foliate and scroll rococo 18K yg frame, 2¼" w, 2" l **1,495.00**

Shell

Profile of classical warrior in 18K yg frame decorated with black enamel Greek key design, 2" w, 2¼" l **1,265.00**

Profile of woman wearing headdress, oval cameo, very good detail, bead and wirework yg frame, 1⅞" w, 3⅜" l **546.25**

Chain

Art Nouveau, 14K yg, turquoise, cable-link yg chain interspersed with scrolled foliate links alternating with oval turquoise cabochons bezel-set in scrolled foliate frames, 54" l, 25.2 dwt **1,495.00**

Edwardian, twisted bar and cable-link platinum vest chain interspersed with three spectacle-set old European-cut diamonds, 14" l, ⅛" w **275.00**

Georgian, textured circ yellow metal links, terminating in beaded clasp set with turquoise cabochon, 30" total l **1,725.00**

Victorian

14K yg, beaded split circ-link long chain terminating in swivel hook, shield-shaped slide decorated with seed pearls and taille d'épargne enamel, 53 dwt, 62" total l, slide ⅞" w, 1" l **1,955.00**

Yg, circ wirework links alternating with pearls and emerald beads (3 aventurine), 32" total l **2,875.00**

Chatelaine, Art Nouveau, SS, waist plaque of stamped and chased foliate motif suspending five appendages from cable-link chain; perfume bottle with grotesque mask, pencil, mirror, heart-shaped locket, and notebook with ivory leaves, decorated with stamped and chased foliate scrolls, cupids, maker's mark for Wm. B. Kerr, Newark, NJ, 3½" w, 8½" l **1,725.00**

Clips, pr

Art Deco, geometric stepped design set with circ-cut and baguette diamonds, approx 2.80 cts tw, platinum mount, 1" w, 1⅛" l **3,680.00**

Retro Modern, bicolor 14K gold, cylindrical stepped design, 13.9 dwt, 1" w, 1¾" l **460.00**

Cuff Links, pr

Art Deco, double linked

Matte-platinum cut-corner rectangles, one link set with diagonal row of calibré-cut emeralds, other with French-cut diamonds, sgd "Mauboussin," #93083, ⅝" × ½" **2,530.00**

Platinum ovals, one side bezel-set with circ-cut diamond, approx .75 ct tw, other side engraved cipher, ¾" × ½" **575.00**

Art Nouveau, 18K yg, fox heads with demantoid garnet eyes, joined with cable links to elliptical backs

with grape cluster motif, maker's mark for Louis Aucoc, France, ½" × ½" **2,875.00**

Victorian, 18K yg, theatrical masks, one male, one female, joined with cable links to entwined snake backs, leather box marked "Federico Fasoli, Roma," ½" × ½" **990.00**

Dress Set

Art Deco, pr of double cuff links, 4 vest studs, 3 shirt studs, diamond-set platinum square frames, black onyx centers, matching stickpin with circ-cut diamond center, cuff links ½" × ½", stickpin ⅝" × ⅝" **2,760.00**

Arts & Crafts, SS, double-sided cuff links, circ foliate design, 2 matching shirt studs, maker's mark for Georg Jensen, #9, cuff links ½" × ½" **460.00**

Earrings, pr

Art Deco, pendent

Articulated geometric surmount and triangular shaft set with old European-cut, single-cut, and baguette diamonds and geometric-cut blue sapphires, suspending bell-shaped diamond and sapphire cap and chain fringe of collet-set diamonds and pear-shaped sapphire drops, platinum mount, post findings added later, leather box, ¾" w, 2¼" l **9,200.00**

Carved and pierced jadeite plaque suspended from geometric baguette and circ-cut diamond surmount, links at top added later, platinum mount, ⅝" w, 2½" l **8,337.50**

Edwardian, pendent

Moonstone intaglio drops, diamond-set caps, suspended from articulated diamond-set shaft, bow motif at top and bottom, platinum mount, screw-back findings, ½" w, 2¼" l **4,945.00**

Platinum, inverted teardrop surmount set with circ-cut diamond, suspending knife-edge shaft and diamond drop with pear-shaped frame set with rose-cut diamonds, approx 1.75 cts tw, box marked "Leonardo Gaito," two small diamonds missing, ½" w, 1¾" total l **2,300.00**

Silver-topped yg, each pendent earring teardrop-shaped jade cabochon surmounted by diamond-set cap, suspended from vertical row of collet-set diamonds on knife-edge bar, collet-set diamond surmount, ear wires, 2" l, ¼" w **2,875.00**

Retro Modern

18K yg, multiple-looped ribbon bow set with three rect-cut topaz, sgd "Boucheron, Paris," clip backs, 1 × 1" **1,840.00**

Flower motif, 5 moonstone petals, sapphire center, 14K yg leaves, sgd "Tiffany & Co.," ¾" w, 1⅛" l **977.50**

Victorian

14K yg, cusped trefoils with chased and engraved design, cutout center suspending yg bead, cusped trefoil surmounts, ear wires, 1" w, 1½" l . **805.00**

18K yg, Etruscan Revival, round coral cabochon in circ beaded frame suspending seed-pearl-set fringe, with coral bead surmount, 2" l, ⅝" w . **690.00**

Lava cameos, carved three-dimensional classical heads, gold ear wires, ⅝" × 1" **690.00**

Micromosaic, 18K yg triangular frame suspending

triangular mosaic plaque and circ disk depicting cherub's head, fringe of tapered 14K yg drops, Italian hallmarks, 7/8" w, 2" l **1,495.00**

Rose-cut diamonds, each depicting cuffed lady's hand wearing collet-set ruby ring, 14K yg mounts, boxed, 3/4" w, 1 3/8" l **1,840.00**

Locket

Art Nouveau, circ, enameled raised die-stamped design of woman's profile, floral and foliate motifs accented with rose-cut diamonds, maker's mark for Riker Bros, Newark, NJ, 1 1/4" d **1,265.00**

Victorian, black enameled 18K yg, scrolling monogram, sgd "Tiffany & Co.," 1 1/4" w, 2" total l **690.00**

Locket & Chain

Art Nouveau, 14K yg, central raised floral and foliate motif, collet-set diamonds in flower centers, locket of lobed and scrolled outline, reeded circ-link chain, locket 1 1/4" w, 1 1/8", 14.2 dwt **1,092.50**

Victorian, yg, oval plaque pavé-set with half pearls and turquoise cabochons surmounting scalloped-edged locket, beaded bail, elongated loop-in-loop chain, 20" l, locket 1 1/4" w, 2" total l **1,150.00**

Lorgnette, Art Nouveau, 14K yg, repoussé case, laurel leaves, reeded dec, 19.87 dwt, 4 3/4" l, 1 1/4" w **770.00**

Necklace

Art Nouveau

Blue and green enameled 14K yg quatrefoil links, alternately set with demantoid garnets and old European-cut diamonds, suspending five blue and green enameled quatrefoil pendants, each set with oval opal accented with demantoid garnets and diamonds, interspersed with small cusped drops set with demantoid garnets and diamonds, four opals crazed, minor enamel loss, 17" l, 1 3/4" w at center **7,475.00**

Dog Collar, 14K yg, 4 round coral cabochons set in curvilinear foliate yg frames, connected by four rows of yg cable-link chain interspersed with coral beads, sgd "Lebolt," 12 5/8" l, 1 3/4" w **2,300.00**

Arts and Crafts, 18K yg, triangular central plaque, openwork foliate design set throughout with diamonds, joined to rect foliate links, each set with three circ-cut diamonds, alternating with sq foliate links, continuing to elongated oval-link chain, diamond-set foliate clasp, attributed to Edward Oakes, 17" total l **5,175.00**

Edwardian, dog collar, silver-topped yg, eighteen strands of seed pearls attached at intervals to five rectangular openwork silver-topped yg plaques, vertical row of four four-petaled flower heads within each frame set throughout with small rubies and rose-cut diamonds, approx 2 3/4" w, 14" l **3,850.00**

Victorian

18K yg

Etruscan Revival, fringe of alternating amphorae motifs and beveled yg beads, French hallmarks, 16" l, 1" w **12,075.00**

Row of beads interspersing fringe of dart-shaped pendants, one engraved "Jan. 12th 1869," fitted leather box stamped "Tiffany & Co.," 15" l, 1 1/8" w, approx 32 dwt **6,325.00**

Cameo, 14K yg, nine oval carved shell cameos of graduated size, depicting mythological scenes, set in plain bezels and linked with two lengths of fine chain between each cameo, fitted box, some damage, approx 15" l, 7/8" w **2,185.00**

Coral, graduated row of fancy spool-shaped carved coral beads suspending carved winged cherub's head with pendent drop, terminating in round coral beads and hidden coral clasp, approx 16" l **805.00**

Pendant

Art Nouveau, 18K yg, opals, lobed oval, foliated C-scroll design framing three collet-set oval opals and suspending collet-set pear-shaped opal drop, fleur-de-lis bail, 2 3/4" total l, 1 3/4" w **1,100.00**

Arts and Crafts, silver, turquoise, freshwater pearl, oval turquoise cabochon with matrix, framed by cast grapevine design with gold-plated leaves, suspending freshwater pearl drop, 1 5/8" w, 1 3/4" l **450.00**

Edwardian, articulated pear-shaped sapphire drop in independent rose and old mine-cut diamond wreath suspended in rose-cut diamond and calibré-cut sapphire ribbon-twist frame, platinum pendant loop, 1 1/8" d **4,600.00**

Post-War Modern, SS, open box turned 45 degrees, rect cutouts on 4 sides to hold sq labradorite cabochon in center, continuing to rect bail, Finnish hallmarks, maker's mark for Kaunis Koru, date letter for 1963, 1 1/8" w, 2 1/4" l **460.00**

Retro Modern, 14K yg, polished scroll set with emerald-cut aquamarine, 29.50 × 25 × 15.70 mm, circ-cut diamond accents on scroll and bail, 1 1/2 × 2" **2,300.00**

Pendant & Chain

Art Deco

Concentric diamond-set circles, articulated collet-set diamond in center, approx .65 ct, reverses to calibré-cut synthetic rubies, diamond-set trefoil bail, platinum and 14K yg mount, fine link 15" l platinum chain, 1" d **2,875.00**

Three-dimensional oval jadeite plaque, approx 47.0 mm × 31.0 mm, pierced and carved with asymmetrical foliate motif, suspended from black enameled and open lozenge and kite-shaped diamond-set links, attached with swivel clasp to chain of diamond-set navette-shaped platinum filigree links, 24" total l **7,150.00**

Art Nouveau, silver, enamel, freshwater pearl, inverted triangular openwork pendant with stylized foliate design accented by green and yellow plique-à-jour enamel, small rose-cut diamonds, and central oval amethyst cabochon, suspending freshwater pearl, suspended from trace-link chain, 21" l, butterfly motif maker's mark, pendant 1 7/8" w, 2 1/4" l **690.00**

Arts and Crafts

18K yg latticework cap, blue and peach enamel ground, grapevine motif border, terminating in chain and bead tassel, 14K link chain, bead and leaf finials, attributed to Edward Oakes, 32" total l **3,450.00**

Hammered silver disk, scrolled wirework in triangular cutout, round faceted citrine bezel-set in center, suspended from 16″ cable-link chain, maker's mark for Theodor Fahrner, Germany, 1⅛″ d **460.00**

Edwardian, cusped and lobed drop, center cushion-shaped blue sapphire, approx 9.20 cts, surrounded by old European-cut diamonds, band of French calibré-cut sapphires, surmounted by articulated row of collet-set diamonds, cusped triangular diamond and sapphire top, platinum chain, 15″ l, sgd "Marcus & Co.," 1″ w, 2¾″ l **23,000.00**

Pendant/Brooch, Victorian

Cross, 14K yg, trefoiled terminals, applied wiretwist and beadwork, central faceted yg dome, 1⅞ × 2¾″ **373.75**

Holbeinesque (Renaissance Revival), oval cabochon garnet center, clusters of rose-cut diamonds and pearls at compass points, red, green, blue enameled scroll and foliate gold frame, suspending emerald bead drop, some enamel loss, 1¼″ w, 2″ l **4,887.00**

Pendant/Brooch & Chain, Art Nouveau, 14K yg, openwork curvilinear circular frame with central bezel-set oval turquoise cabochon, suspending pear-shaped turquoise cabochon drop, surmounted by opposed C-scrolls and seed pearl, suspended from fine chain caught by round turquoise cabochon "knot," maker's mark for Bippart, Griscom & Osborn, Newark, NJ, pendant 1″ l, 2″ total l **517.50**

Ring

Art Deco

Cushion-shaped blue sapphire, approx 10.00 cts, within pierced scrollwork platinum mount set throughout with rose-cut diamonds (several missing), ¾″ w, ⅝″ l **7,475.00**

Stepped vertical rect, emerald-cut emerald, approx 2.35 cts, in center, four collet-set diamonds at compass points, geometric pierced platinum mount set throughout with old European- and single-cut diamonds, ⅝″ w, 1″ l ..**13,225.00**

Tapering domed mount with central collet-set old European-cut diamond, .60 ct, diamond-set crescent on top and bottom, framed by quatrefoil of twenty calibré sapphires, shoulders set with additional diamonds, pierced and engraved gallery and shank, slight nick on central diamond, 2.8 dwt **5,775.00**

Arts and Crafts, navette-shaped opal set in beaded foliate 18K yg mount, sgd "M.R." for Margaret Rogers, orig box from Society of Arts & Crafts, ¾″ w, ⅞″ l **2,645.00**

Edwardian

Openwork platinum top with center row of three old European-cut diamonds, 1.90 cts tw, octagonal mounts outlined with single-cut diamonds, center stone flanked by diamond baguettes set vertically, bent polished platinum shank, ½ × ⅞″ **1,300.00**

Pair of coiling serpents, one yg with cabochon emerald-set head, rose-cut diamond eyes, other platinum with cabochon blue sapphire-

set head and small ruby eyes, approx size 8, snake heads ½ × ⅜″, pr **6,900.00**

Pierced elongated oval top, 3 old European-cut diamonds, approx 1.40 cts tw, vertically set in platinum, accented by circ-cut diamonds, approx 2.20 cts tw, ⅞″ w, 1⅛″ l **3,162.00**

Retro Modern, 14K rose gold, ten circ-cut rubies and seven circ-cut diamonds set in scallop-edged scrolled shell motif, tapered shank, 1″ w, ¾″ l ... **633.00**

Victorian

Micromosaic oval plaque depicting swan, bezel-set in ropetwist frame flanked by foliate motifs, reeded shank, ⅝ × ½″ **747.50**

Row of 5 slightly graduated oval-cut demantoids with two small rose-cut diamonds set between each, continuing to engraved yg shank, ⅞ × ¼″ **3,450.00**

Scarf Pin/Stickpin

Art Nouveau

14K yg, depicting bearded man's head, diamond-set eyes, surmounted by freshwater pearl, American maker's mark "CS.," 2⅝″ l, ½″ w .. **517.50**

18K yg, enamel, profile head of woman with flowing hair wearing headdress set with various small colored stones, yg pin stem, European hallmark, 2¾″ l, ½″ w **575.00**

Arts and Crafts, 14K yg, mushroom shaped head with center collet-set sapphire, blue enamel, yg mount, ½ × ½″, 2½″ l **220.00**

Edwardian, platinum, rose-gold stem topped with crowned openwork old European-, rose-, and single-cut diamond-set shield, border of calibré-cut rubies mounted in yg, fitted box stamped "Cartier," 2¾ × ½″ **770.00**

Victorian

14K yg bicycle, 10K yg pin stem, 2¾ × ⅞″ w .. **402.50**

Round reverse-painted crystal intaglio of dog's head, bezel-set, yg frame, twisted wire and beaded edges, orig box, 3 × ⅞″ **770.00**

Suite

Retro Modern, earrings & ring, yg, earrings half hoop clips; ring bombé-shaped mount, each encrusted with faceted, cabochon and carved sapphires, emeralds, rubies, amethysts, citrines, earrings sgd "T & H. M." for Trabert & Hoeffer, Mauboussin, ¾″ w, 1″ l; ring 1″ w **5,750.00**

Victorian

Brooch/pin & earrings

18K yg horizontal cylindrical malachite bar, central overlaid shaped yg plaque, wirework and granulation suspending swagged chain and two large elongated malachite drops, yg caps, matching pendent earrings, single malachite drop, brooch 1½″ w, 2″, earrings ⅝″ w, 2″ **1,210.00**

Domed disk brooch with applied wirework, center cabochon garnet (carbuncle) bordered with seed pearls, suspending bell-cap coiled wirework tassel from two lengths of chain, 1⅜″ d, 2¼″ l with tassel, matching drop earrings, ⅝″ d, 1⅜″ l with tassels **990.00**

Micromosaic, brooch with central circ plaque

depicting man playing guitar in pastoral scene, within navette-shaped pierced frame decorated with mosaics, 18K yg beads and wirework, locket compartment on rev, suspending 3 detachable teardrop-shaped yg pendants, mosaic centers, 18K yg and mosaic pendent earrings with 9K yg fringe, Italian hallmarks, brooch 2½" w, 2¾" total l, earrings ¾" w, 2½" total l **6,900.00**

Necklace, brooch/pin and earrings, 18K yg, necklace of woven chain suspending fringe of alternating amphorae and spherical pendants, brooch of 3 overlapping disks surmounting oval frame, decorated with foliate motifs, granulation and wirework, suspending one amphora flanked by two spherical pendants, matching pendent earrings, Italian hallmarks, repair and restoration, fitted box, necklace approx 16" l, 1¼" w, brooch 1⅞" w, 2⅝" l, earrings ¾" w, 2¼" total length **12,650.00**

Watch Fob, Art Nouveau, 14K yg, four linked curvilinear scrolled wirework plaques with central lion's-head motif, continuing to short cable-link chain and swivel hook, 1" w, 5⅜" l, 16.20 dwts **632.50**

JUDAICA

History: Throughout history, Jews have expressed themselves artistically in both the religious and secular spheres. Most Jewish art objects were created as part of the concept of *Hiddur Mitzva,* i.e., adornment of implements used in performing rituals both in the synagogue and home.

For almost 2,000 years, since the destruction of the Jerusalem Temple in 70 A.D., Jews have lived in many lands. The widely differing environments gave traditional Jewish life and art a multifaceted character. Unlike Greek, Byzantine, or Roman art which have definite territorial and historical boundaries, Jewish art is found throughout Europe, the Middle East, North Africa, and other areas.

Ceremonial objects incorporated not only liturgical appurtenances, but also ethnographic artifacts such as amulets and ritual costumes. The style of each ceremonial object responded to the artistic and cultural milieu in which it was created. Although diverse stylistically, ceremonial objects, whether for Sabbath, holidays, or the life cycle, still possess a unity of purpose.

Reference: Penny Forstner and Lael Bower, *A Guide to Collecting Christian and Judaic Religious Artifacts,* Books Americana, 1996.

Collectors' Club: Judaica Collectors Society, PO Box 854, Van Nuys, CA 91408.

Museums: B'nai B'rith Klutznick Museum, Washington, DC; H.U.C., Skirball Museum, Los Angeles, CA; Jewish Museum, New York, NY; Yeshiva University Museum, New York, NY; Judah L. Magnes Museum, Berkeley, CA; Judaic Museum, Rockville, MD; Spertus Museum of Judaica, Chicago, IL; Morton B. Weiss Museum of Judaica, Chicago, IL; National Museum of American Jewish History, Philadelphia, PA; Plotkin Judaica Museum of Greater Phoenix, Phoenix, AZ.

Notes: Judaica has been crafted in all media, though silver is the most collectible.

SPECIAL AUCTION

Phillips Fine Art Auctions
406 E 79th St
New York, NY 10021
(212) 570-4830

Aspergillum, 11½" h, silver, cylindrical stem with three molded bands, loop handle, engraved inscription dated 1922, Maltese, 4 oz, wood and glass case ... **600.00**

Beaker, 2½" h, Russian silver, incised shtetel scenes, c1870 .... **275.00**

Etrog Container, 4 × 7" box, olive wood, octagonal, hinged lid, attached carved etrog on top, Palestine, c1940 .... **625.00**

Hanukah Lamp, 10 × 10", Polish silvered brass, Baroque foliate design on back plates, surmounted by repoussé crown, two rampant lions on either side of menorah, sgd "Warsaw," mid 19th C **1,250.00**

Kiddush Cup, 2⅛" h, Russian silver, engraved dec, hallmarks, 1888 .... **95.00**

Maté Cup, 8" h, 4" tripartite base, SS, rosewood bowl, marked with "P" on shield with crown, "LZ 925" in diamond and "84," unmarked infuser with bird and flowers dec **300.00**

Megilah, 17½"h, SS, cylinder pierced with banded design of flora and fauna, various semiprecious stones, bird finial, parchment scroll of the Book of Esther, marked "Silver 925," 20th C **900.00**

Menorah, 21½" h, SS, knopped baluster stem, six multi-scroll branches, circular wax pans, urn-form sockets, cast and engraved spread-eagle finial, double domed base with band of rose heads and foliage, four talon feet, detachable oil pitcher, Portuguese, 66.5 troy oz **9,000.00**

Rose Water Spice Container, 11½" h, Middle Eastern, silver, rounded bulbous container, incised foliage dec, long tapering top, ftd base **375.00**

Diecut, copyright by Fuld & Co., "Von stufe, zu Stufe," 3⅝" w, 2⅞" h, $10.00.

Seder Plate, 12 × 10″, ceramic, luster finish, Hebrew calligraphy in recessed compartments, Czechoslovakian, c1920 ....1,600.00

Torah Pointer, Russian, SS, sq tapered handle, two knobs and engraved dec, hand marked "84," partial assay mark of 1876, 4 troy oz 950.00

JUGTOWN POTTERY

History: In 1920 Jacques and Julianna Busbee left their cosmopolitan environs and returned to North Carolina to revive the state's dying pottery-making craft. Jugtown Pottery, a colorful and somewhat off-beat operation, was located in Moore County, miles away from any large city and accessible only "if mud permits."

Ben Owens, a talented young potter, turned the wares. Jacques Busbee did most of the designing and glazing. Julianna handled promotion.

Utilitarian and decorative items were produced. Although many colorful glazes were used, orange predominated. A Chinese blue glaze that ranged from light blue to deep turquoise was a prized glaze reserved for the very finest pieces.

Jacques Busbee died in 1947. Julianna, with the help of Owens, ran the pottery until 1958 when it was closed. After long legal battles, the pottery was reopened in 1960. It now is owned by Country Roads, Inc., a nonprofit organization. The pottery still is operating and using the old mark.

Bowl, 10⅝″ d, Chinese blue glaze, honey brown stain, imp mark **195.00**

Candlesticks, pr, 4½″ h, tapered stems, broad cups supporting candleholders, mottled blue and black high glaze, imp mark **110.00**

Jug, 8¾″ h, frogskin **250.00**

Vase
   3½″ h, thick white high glaze, imp mark **90.00**
   5½″ h
     Flared shoulder form, Chinese blue glaze, imp mark **325.00**
     Flat sloping shoulder form, gray and white high glaze, imp mark **190.00**
   10″ h
     7″ d, bulbous, four handles, collar neck, creamy white flowing satin finished glaze, imp circ mark **600.00**
     Two handled form, Chinese blue glaze, imp mark **1,200.00**

Bowl, gray glaze, cobalt blue trim, orange-peel texture, signed and imp, 3″ h, 4½″ d, $25.00.

KPM

History: The "KPM" mark has been used separately and in conjunction with other symbols by many German porcelain manufacturers, among which are the Königliche Porzellan Manufactur in Meissen, 1720s; Königliche Porzellan Manufactur in Berlin, 1832–1847; and Krister Porzellan Manufactur in Waldenburg, mid-19th century.

Collectors now use the term KPM to refer to the high-quality porcelain produced in the Berlin area in the 18th and 19th centuries.

Cup and Saucer, blue ground, continuous oak branches, yellow band, , painted black Iron Cross, dated 1914 in gilt laurel branches, figural swan's-head handle and neck, blue scepter, iron-red KPM and orb, black cross marks **250.00**

Dessert Plate, 8¾″ d, reticulated, gilt border, enamel flowers, floral garlands, price for 6-pc set **600.00**

Figure
   6½″ h, classical goddess holding fruit, polychrome enamel, gilt trim, marked "KPM" **200.00**
   8″ h, little girl with bouquet being crowned by another girl, c1925 .... **700.00**

Portrait, Renaissance lady, bronze rococo frame, 9 × 6¾″, $2,500.00.

Plaque
   8⅜ × 6⅛″, bust portrait of Christ crowned with thorns, imp marks and numerals **400.00**
   9½ × 6½″, young woman with daisies in hair and hand, sgd "Wagner" in script lower right, back marked "KPM Germany," red script "Marguerite" **6,750.00**
   10 × 7½″, Psyche, winged maiden in diaphanous drapery seated on grassy mound at edge of cliff, imp marks and numerals **5,725.00**
   10¼ x 8″, portrait of young maiden wearing locket, gilt frame **1,500.00**
   10½ x 8½″, Louis Le Brun, sgd "R Dittrich," back imp "KPM" **3,400.00**

12½ × 10¼″, monk, holding tankard, standing in front of key, painted by L Schnizel, after E Grutzner, imp marks, incised numerals **3,500.00**
Teapot, cov
5¾″ h, polychrome flowers, gilt, rose finial, damage and repair to finial **110.00**
10½″ h, floral enamels, black and aqua stripes, marked "KPM" **100.00**

KAUFFMANN, ANGELICA

History: Marie Angelique Catherine Kauffmann was a Swiss artist who lived from 1741 until 1807. Many artists who hand-decorated porcelain during the 19th century copied her paintings. The majority of the paintings are neoclassical in style.

References: Susan and Al Bagdade, *Warman's English & Continental Pottery & Porcelain,* Second Edition, Wallace-Homestead, 1991; Wendy Wassying Roworth (ed.), *Angelica Kauffmann,* Reaktion Books, 1993, distributed by University of Washington Press.

Biscuit Jar, cov, 7″ h, 5″ d, scenic panel of three ladies and gentleman, pastels, alternating gold and maroon panels, gold grim, SP rim, cov, and handle **165.00**
Bowl, 9½″ d, two maidens and child **65.00**
Condensed Milk Can Holder, cov, matching underplate, classical maiden, green ground, gold tracery **115.00**
Marmalade jar, cov, Three Graces scene **90.00**
Plate, 9⅝″ d, print dec scene of figures, 1890, price for 12-pc set **885.00**
Tobacco Jar, cov, portrait front, muted dark green, orange and yellow trim, SP rim and lid, pipe finial ... **300.00**

Tobacco jar, portrait front, muted dark green, hints of orange and yellow, SP rim and lid, pipe finial, $300.00.

KEW BLAS

History: Amory and Francis Houghton established the Union Glass Company, Somerville, Massachusetts, in 1851. The company went bankrupt in 1860, but was reorganized. Between 1870 and 1885 the Union Glass Company made pressed glass and blanks for cut glass.

Art-glass production began in 1893 under the direction of William S. Blake and Julian de Cordova. Two styles were introduced:

a Venetian style, which consisted of graceful shapes in colored glass, often flecked with gold; and an iridescent glass, called Kew Blas, made in plain and decorated forms. The pieces are similar in design and form to Quezel products but lack the subtlety of Tiffany items.

The company ceased production in 1924.

Museum: Sandwich Glass Museum, Sandwich, MA.

Candlesticks, pr, 8½″ h, twisted stem, irid gold **775.00**
Goblet, 5″ h, gold irid, inscribed "Kew-Blas," c1915 .. **115.00**
Jack-in-the-Pulpit Vase, 8¾″ h, gold irid blossom int., pulled gold and green threading, opal body, applied button pontil **550.00**
Pitcher, 5″ h, King Tut, white, green, and gold, blue handle, irid blue lining, sgd **2,000.00**
Salt, open, irid gold **275.00**
Tumbler, 5″ h, gold irid, inscribed "Kew-Blas," c1915 **95.00**

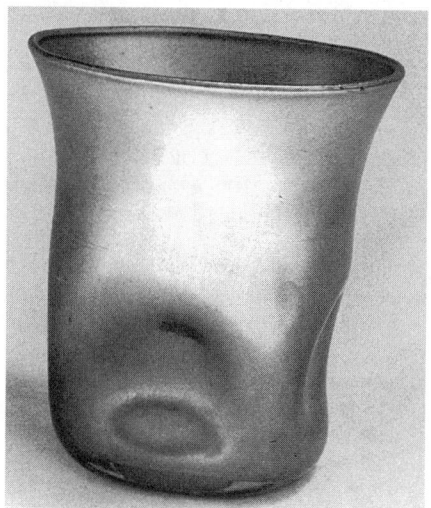

Tumbler, dimpled, gold iridescent, 3½″, $225.00.

KITCHEN COLLECTIBLES

History: The kitchen was the focal point in a family's environment until the 1960s. Many early kitchen utensils were handmade and prized by their owners. Next came a period of utilitarian products made of tin and other metals. When the housewife no longer wished to work in a sterile environment, enamel and plastic products added color, and their unique design served both aesthetic and functional purposes.

The advent of home electricity changed the type and style of kitchen products. Fads affected many items. High technology already has made inroads into the kitchen, and another revolution seems at hand.

References: Ronald S. Barlow, *Victorian Houseware,* Windmill Publishing, 1992; *Collectors Guide to Wagner Ware and Other Companies,* L-W Book Sales, 1994; Gene Florence, *Kitchen Glassware of the Depression Years,* Fifth Edition, Collector Books, 1995; Linda Campbell Franklin, *300 Years of Housekeeping Collectibles,* Books Americana, 1992; ——, *300 Hundred Years of Kitchen Collectibles,* Third Edition, Books Americana, 1991; Ambrogio Fumagalli, *Coffee Makers,* Chronicle Books, 1995; Michael J. Goldberg, *Collectible Plastic Kitchenware and Dinnerware,*

Schiffer Publishing, 1995; ———, *Groovy Kitchen Designs for Collectors,* Schiffer Publishing, 1996; *Griswold Cast Iron,* L-W Book Sales, 1993; Frances Johnson, *Kitchen Antiques,* Schiffer Publishing, 1996; Jan Lindenberger, *The 50s & 60s Kitchen,* Schiffer Publishing, 1994; ———, *Fun Kitchen Collectibles,* Schiffer Publishing, 1996.

Kathryn McNerney, *Kitchen Antiques 1790–1940,* Collector Books, 1991, 1995 value update; Gary Miller and K. M. Mitchell, *Price Guide to Collectible Kitchen Appliances,* Wallace-Homestead, 1991; Jim Moffett, *American Corn Huskers,* Off Beat Books, 1994; Dana G. Morykan and Harry L. Rinker, *Warman's Country Antiques & Collectibles,* Third Edition, Wallace-Homestead, 1996; Ellen M. Plante, *Kitchen Collectibles,* Wallace-Homestead, 1991; David G. Smith and Charles Wafford, *The Book of Griswold & Wagner,* Schiffer Publishing, 1995; Diane Stoneback, *Kitchen Collectibles,* Wallace-Homestead, 1994; Don Thornton, *Beat This: The Eggbeater Chronicles,* Off Beat Books (1345 Poplar Ave, Sunnyvale, CA 94087), 1994; *Toasters and Small Kitchen Appliances,* L-W Book Sales, 1995; Jean Williams Turner, *Collectible Aunt Jemima,* Schiffer Publishing, 1994; April M. Tvorak, *Fire-King Fever '96,* published by author, 1995.

Periodicals: *Cast Iron Cookware News,* 28 Angela Ave, San Anselmo, CA 94960; *Kettles 'n' Cookware,* PO Box B, Perrysburg, NY 14129; *Kitchen Antiques & Collectible News,* 4645 Laurel Ridge Dr, Harrisburg, PA 17110; *Piebirds Unlimited,* 14 Harmony School Rd, Flemington, NJ 08822.

Collectors' Clubs: Cookie Cutter Collectors Club, 1167 Teal Rd, SW, Dellroy, OH 44620; Glass Knife Collectors Club, 711 Kelly Dr, Lebanon, TN 37087; Griswold & Cast Iron Cookware Assoc, 54 Macon Ave, Asheville, NC 28801; International Society for Apple Parer Enthusiasts, 3911 Morgan Center Rd, Utica, OH 43080; National Reamer Collectors Assoc, 47 Midline Court, Gaithersburg, MD 20878.

Museums: Corning Glass Museum, Corning, NY; Kern County Museum, Bakersfield, CA; Landis Valley Farm Museum, Lancaster, PA.

Additional Listings: Baskets, Brass, Butter Prints, Copper, Food Molds, Fruit Jars, Graniteware, Ironware, Tinware, and Woodenware. See Warman's *Americana & Collectibles* for more examples including electrical appliances.

Apple Peeler, cast iron, Hudson Co, Leominster, MA, patent 1882	**75.00**
Bread Cutter, painted grain trough, cast-iron handle, marked "RAADVAD"	**150.00**
Bread Stick Pan, cast iron, Griswold #23	**75.00**
Broiler, 6½" d, wrought iron, wavy cross bars	**75.00**
Butter Churn, Dazey, No. 4, wooden paddles	**125.00**
Butter Paddle, 10" l, maple, curved handle, some curl, old worn patina, age crack in bowl	**55.00**
Cookie Peel, 21" l, pine, hand carved, beveled edge, rect, tapered, paddle end, patina, c1820	**85.00**
Cream and Egg Whip, Whippit, Durometal Products Co, 14" l	**25.00**
Dutch Oven, cov, cast iron	
Erie, #8	**80.00**
Griswold #8, large trademark	**100.00**
Eggbeater	
A & J, 12½" l, curly disk bottom, green knob handle, Pat Oct 9, 1923	**40.00**

Manual, "How to get the most out of your Sunbeam Mixmaster," hints and recipes, $15.00.

Cassady-Fairbank Turbine, 10½" l, Chicago, Pat Aug 20, 1912	**25.00**
Dover	
12¼" l, #8, Pat May 6, 1873, April 3, 1888, April 24, 1891 Boston USA	**55.00**
13" l, four-hole wheel standard, pat. Dec 27-98	**65.00**
Ekco Products Maid of Honor, 12" l, wooden handle, patents pending	**10.00**
Instant Whip, 11½" l, aluminum, Pat April 20, 1920	**25.00**
Ladd No. 2, 12½", Pat July 7, 1907, Oct 18, 1912, Other Pats Pending	**25.00**
Taplin	
Improved Dover Pattern	
10½" l, Pat Feb 9, 1904	**45.00**
13" l, Pat. April 14, 1903, date also on shaft	**45.00**
Light Running	
10½" l, nickel plated, Pat Nov 24, 08	**40.00**
11½" l, white wood knob handle, Pat. Nov. 24, 08	**25.00**
Fish Broiler, wrought iron, crescent shape	**75.00**
Flour Scoop, 14" l, maple, Shaker type, carved, shaped handle, finger grip	**170.00**
Food Grinder, cast iron, Griswold #4	**25.00**
Grater, 9⅝" l, tin, pine box with sliding lid and drawer, old brown varnish, wire nail construction	**95.00**
Griddle, Erie, #12, bailed	**40.00**
Kettle, cast iron, 5 qt, Wagnerware and Griswold trademarks	**80.00**
Kraut Cutter, 13 × 41", ash, cherry dovetailed hopper, refinished	**80.00**
Muffin Pan, cast iron, Griswold #10	**40.00**
Nutmeg Grater, 5¼" l, tin, wooden handle	**65.00**
Pie Crimper, 7" l, wooden handle, brass crimper	**75.00**
Rolling Pin, glass, blown	
15" l, amethyst, worn painted floral dec	**135.00**
17" l, black, wear	**115.00**
17½" l, deep amber, wear, chip on end, small broken blister	**90.00**

Pie crimper, paintbrush-style handle, bone jagging wheel, 2nd quarter 18th C, $195.00.

29" l, cobalt blue, worn painted and transfer dec,
  flowers, ships and "Think on Me When Far at Sea"   **125.00**
Scotch Bowl, cast iron, Griswold #3, large trademark .   **75.00**
Skillet, cast iron
  Griswold
    #0, heat ring, large trademark **65.00**
    #3, smooth bottom, small trademark **15.00**
    #4, smooth bottom, small trademark **15.00**
    #5, smooth bottom, small trademark **35.00**
    #6, smooth bottom, small trademark **15.00**
    #7, smooth bottom, small trademark **15.00**
    #8
      Smooth bottom, large trademark **20.00**
      Square, side handle **100.00**
    #9, hinge, small trademark **35.00**
    #10, smooth bottom, large trademark **70.00**
  Victor, #8 ....   **50.00**
  Wagnerware, #0, Randall Wagnerware paper label   **15.00**
  Wapak, #8, heat ring **100.00**
Toaster, 6 × 8¾", wire, folds over, twisted handle **75.00**
Trivet, wrought iron, heart shape **90.00**
Waffle Iron, cast iron, Griswold, American #8, high
  stand **85.00**

KUTANI

History: Kutani originated in the mid-1600s in the Kaga province of Japan. Kutani comes in a variety of color patterns, one of the most popular being Ao Kutani, a green glaze with colors such as green, yellow, and purple enclosed in a black outline. Export wares made since the 1870s are enameled in a wide variety of colors and styles.

Berry Set, master bowl, six serving bowls, multicolored
  enamel floral dec, red border, price for 7-pc set **175.00**
Bowl, 4¾" sq, polychrome, gold flowers, unglazed foot,
  sgd gold seal form **320.00**
Charger, 14" d, figural landscape, multicolored, gold
  border **225.00**
Chocolate Pot, 8½" h, red, orange, and gold, reserve
  panels of peonies and birds, people in gardens, Japanese **165.00**
Ewer, 8¼" h, duck on floral base, key-fret band, green,
  yellow, aubergine, and blue enamel **195.00**

Ginger Jar, cov, 5" h, blue, green, and carmine enamel
  dec, foo-dog finial **150.00**
Low Bowl, 13½" d, yellow, blue, green, and aubergine
  enamels, central reserve of scholar and attendant in
  pavilion, wide lappet border **650.00**
Saké Cup, 1⅞" h, floriform rim, short ring foot, enamel
  and gold dec, painted rim band, gold scrolling flower
  and trellis dec **125.00**
Umbrella Stand, 28" h, multicolored butterflies, flowers,
  foliage, and medallions **500.00**
Vase, 20" h, ovoid, twin foliage molded handles, flaring
  pierced rim, two reserves on brocade ground, one
  with patriarch among attendants, other of pigeons
  among foliage, handle repaired **325.00**

Vases, left: two men and flowers, red, 5¾" h, $125.00; right: flowers and birds, red, 7" h, $100.00.

LACE AND LINENS

History: Lace, lacy linens, embroidery, and hand-decorated textiles are different from any other antique. They are valued both as a handmade substance and as the thing the substance is made into. Thread is manipulated into stitches, stitches are assembled into lace, lace is made into handkerchiefs, edgings, tablecloths, bedspreads. Things eventually go out of style or are damaged or worn, and just as the diamonds and rubies are taken from old jewelry and placed into new settings, fine stitchery of embroidery and lace is saved and reused. Lace from a handkerchief is used to decorate a blouse, fragments of a bridal veil are made into a scarf; shreds of old lace are remounted onto fine net and used again as a veil.

At each stage in the cycle, different people become interested. Some see fragments as bits and pieces of a collage, and seek raw materials for accent pieces. Others use Victorian whites and turn-of-the-century embroidered linens to complement a life style. Collectors value and admire the stitches themselves, and when those stitches are remarkable enough, they will pay hundreds of dollars for fragments a few inches square.

Until the 1940s, lace collecting was a highly respected avocation of the wealthy. The prosperity of the New World was a magnet for insolvent European royalty, who carried suitcases of old Hapsburg, Bourbon, Stuart, and Romanov laces to suites at New York's Waldorf hotel for dealers to select from. Even Napoleon's bed hangings of handmade Alencon lace, designed for Josephine and finished for Marie Louise, found their way here. In 1932, *Fortune* magazine profiled socially prominent collectors and lace dealers. For the entire first half of this century, New York City's Needle and Bobbin Club provided a forum for showing off acquisitions.

Until 1940, upscale department stores offered antique lace and lacy linens. Dealers specializing in antique lace and lacy linens had prominent upscale shops, and offered repair, restoration, remodeling, and cleaning services along with the antique linens. In addition to collecting major pieces— intact jabots from the French Ancien Regime, Napoleonic-era Alencon, huge mid-Victorian lace shawls, Georgian bed hangings appliquéd with 17th-century needle lace—collectors assembled study collections of postcard-size samples of each known style of antique lace.

When styles changed round the 1940s and 1950s and the market for antique lace and linens crashed, some of the best collections did go to museums; others just went into hiding. With renewed interest in a gracious, romantic lifestyle, turn-of-the-century lacy cloths from the linen closets of the barons of the industrial revolution are coming out of hiding. Collectors and wise dealers know that many of the small study-pieces of irreplaceable stitchery—fragments collectors will pay ten to hundreds of dollars for— still emerge in rummage and estate sales.

Those who learn to recognize the artistry and value of old stitchery will not only enhance their lives with beauty, they may find a windfall.

References: Maryanne Dolan, *Old Lace and Linens Including Crochet,* Books Americana, 1989; Pat Earnshaw, *The Identification of Lace,* Lubrecht and Cramer, 1989; Alda Horner, *The Official Price Guide to Linens, Lace, and Other Fabrics,* House of Collectibles, 1991; Frances Johnson, *Collecting Antique Linens, Lace, and Needlework,* Wallace-Homestead, 1991; Elizabeth Kurella, *The Secrets of Real Lace,* The Lace Merchant (PO Box 222, Plainwell, MI 49080), 1994; ———, *A Pocket Guide to Valuable Old Lace and Lacy Linens,* The Lace Merchant (PO Box 222, Plainwell, MI 49080), 1996; Elizabeth Scofield and Peggy Zalamea, *Twentieth Century Linens and Lace,* Schiffer Publishing, 1995.

Periodical: *The Old Lace and Linen Merchant,* The Lace Merchant, PO Box 222, Plainwell, MI 49080.

Collectors' Club: International Old Lacers, PO Box 554, Flanders, NJ 07836.

Museums: Chicago Art Institute, Chicago, IL; Cooper Hewitt (Smithsonian), New York, NY; Metropolitan Museum of Art, New York, NY; Museum of Early Southern Decorative Arts (MESDA), Winston-Salem, NC; Museum of Fine Arts, Boston, MA; Rockwood Museum, Wilmington, DE; Shelburne, Museum, Shelburne, VT; Smithsonian Institution, Washington, DC.

Advisor: Elizabeth M. Kurella.

Bedspread
    Crochet, double size, filet crochet grid-style design, scrolling leaves design **85.00**
    Embroidered, double size, white cloth with red "turkey work" embroidery, cartoon character designs, c1930 .... **150.00**

    Princess lace (machine tapes appliquéd to machine net), scrolling flowers and leaves design **350.00**
Bridal Veil
    Oval, 65 × 48", Princess lace, machine net decorated with floral and scroll design **325.00**
    Teardrop shape, approx 7' long, edged with 12" border of Point De Gaze needle lace in rose and leaf design with scrolls and medallions **1,500.00**
Bridge Set, linen, embroidered in red and black motifs of playing-card suits, matching napkins **85.00**
Collar
    Berthe-style, Brussels mixed lace, floral and scroll-work of Duchesse bobbin lace with rose inserts of Point de Gaze, many exotic filling stitches of needle lace, 6" deep × 38" l **725.00**
    Duchesse bobbin lace, c1870, roses, daisies, and scrollwork design, 5" w at center back, 32" l **125.00**
    Point de Gaze, 19th C Belgian needle lace, roses with shaded petals and leaves design, pr of 10" l lapels, price for pr **75.00**
Curtains
    Hand-embroidered machine net, c1900, iris, roses, and filigree elaborate design, 48 × 96", price for pr **50.00**
    Machine lace, ecru, 36 × 72" **75.00**
Doily
    Crochet, roses, raised petals, 8" d round **10.00**
    Flemish bobbin lace, c1900, goldfish design in Point de Paris ground, 10" d round, 3" deep lace **75.00**
    Needle lace, rose design, 6" d round **20.00**
Dresser Scarf
    Drawnwork, Victorian, white geometric design, 28 × 48" **45.00**
    White cotton, flower basket embroidered in bright colors, white crochet edging, c1930, 24 × 38" . **10.00**
Fragments of Collector's Lace
    Gros Point de Venise, c1650, stylized scrolling floral design, motifs defined by raised and padded outlines dec with many styles of picots, 2 × 12" ... **285.00**
    Point de Neige, c1680, needle lace with minute stylized design and layers of raised picots, 10 × 18" **375.00**
    Point de Venise, design of cupid with quiver of arrows, medallions, and scrolling flowers, c1900, 12 × 16" **75.00**
    Point de Venise a Reseau, stylized floral design, Alencon mesh background, no cordonnet, 3 × 6" fragment of edging **185.00**
Handkerchief
  Linen
    Edged with colored crochet scallop design, 12" sq **2.00**
    Edged with ½" of white tatting, 12" sq **6.00**
    4" of Irish Youghal needle lace with stylized shamrocks design, background of stitched bars dec with picots, 16" sq **375.00**
    Whitework, French, 1870s, edged with embroidery, drawnwork, and needle-lace inserts **95.00**
Napkin
    Cocktail, white, edged with single scallop of needle lace, 1" sq corner inserts of needle lace worked in stylized animal design, price for 6-pc set **45.00**
    Dinner, linen with needle-lace edging, corner insert, c1900, 24" sq, price for 6-pc set **185.00**

Pillowcase
   Cotton, embroidered multicolored flower-basket design, crochet edge, c1930, price for pr **15.00**
   Linen, white, figural designs in needle-lace inserts, floral design in needle-lace edging, price for pr . **125.00**
   Madeira, white cotton, flower silhouetted in cutwork, embroidered with satin stitch, price for pr **15.00**
Pillow Cover, linen, white, dec with inserts of needle lace, scrolling floral designs embroidered in satin stitch, Cluny bobbin lace edging, 18" d round **125.00**
Pincushion, white satin, top cov with sq of white Italian drawn work in heavy linen, embroidered raised flower and tendril design, corners dec with whimsical knotted tassels, 4" sq, 1" deep **65.00**
Runner, Normandy work, patchwork of handmade Valenciennes bobbin lace and other laces, mostly handmade, central motif of French embroidered whitework with birds and flowers, oval, 24 × 18" **145.00**
Shawl
   Chantilly, flowers, ferns, and scrolls design, 4 × 8' triangle
      Handmade, bobbin lace **385.00**
      Machine, black **75.00**
   Machine-made net cov with bouquets and garlands of Brussels bobbin lace and Point de Gaze needle lace, white, c1865, 4 × 8' triangular **675.00**
Tablecloth
   Crochet, round medallions design, 48 × 68" **75.00**

Tablecloth, natural color linen, Richelieu, all handmade cutwork and embroidery, floral and scroll motif, early 20th C, 68 × 100", $575.00.

Cutwork
   Floral and scrollwork satin-stitch embroidery, needle-lace inserts, 8" deep border of filet in figural designs, Italian, c1900, 42" sq **175.00**
   Floral designs in satin-stitch embroidery, inserts of needle lace with rose designs, 68 × 140", twelve matching napkins, price for set **975.00**
   Filet, geometric design darned over knotted network, 48 × 72" **125.00**
Yardage
   Crochet, white, pinwheel design, 4" deep, per yd .. **12.00**
   Tatting, white, half-inch deep, design of round medallions with picots, per yd **5.00**

Valenciennes
   Handmade bobbin lace, strawberries and blossoms design, 4" deep, 4 yds long **850.00**
   Machine made, all cotton, floral and scrollwork design, 4" deep, per yd **10.00**

LALIQUE

History: René Lalique (1860–1945) first gained prominence as a jewelry designer. Around 1900 he began experimenting with molded-glass brooches and pendants, often embellishing them with semiprecious stones. By 1905 he was devoting himself exclusively to the manufacture of glass articles.

In 1908 Lalique began designing packaging for the French cosmetic houses. He also produced many objects, especially vases, bowls, and figurines, in the Art Nouveau and Art Deco styles. The full scope of Lalique's genius was seen at the 1925 Paris l'Exposition Internationale des Arts Décorative et Industriels Modernes.

Marks: The mark "R. LALIQUE FRANCE" in block letters is found on pressed articles, tableware, vases, paperweights, and automobile mascots. The script signature, with or without "France," is found on hand-blown objects. Occasionally, a design number is included. The word "France" in any form indicates a piece made after 1926.

The post-1945 mark is generally "Lalique France" without the "R", but there are exceptions.

References: Hugh D. Guinn (ed.), *The Glass of René Lalique at Auction,* Guindex Publications, 1992; Ellen T. Schroy, *Warman's Glass,* Second Edition Wallace-Homestead, 1995.

Collectors' Club: Lalique Collectors Society, 400 Veterans Blvd, Carlstadt, NJ 07072.

Videotape: Nicholas M. Dawes, *The World of Lalique Glass,* Award Video and Film Distributors, 1993.

REPRODUCTION ALERT

The Lalique signature has often been forged, the most common fake includes an "R" with the post-1945 mark.

Bookends, pr, 6¼" h, Chrysis, clear and frosted, kneeling Art Deco female nudes, plinth base, designed by René Lalique, c1928 .... **690.00**
Bowl
   6¼" d, shallow, frosted fish in bottom, molded bubbles **325.00**
   9¼" d, Lys, opal, four lily-pad molded feet **815.00**
   15⅜" d, Florabella, opal, sepia patina **4,025.00**
Carafe, 6⅜" h, Tokyo, clear, handle, c1930 .... **260.00**
Cigarette Lighter, 3¾" h, 3½" d, table model, lion's head **350.00**
Clock, 8" h, Rossignols, clear and frosted, Art Deco, c1931 ....**4,370.00**
Cocktail Shaker, Thomery, clear and frosted, c1928 ...**1,840.00**

Center: beverage set, frosted and clear crystal, Setubal pattern, leaf and berry design, six tumblers, 18″ tray, $770.00; left and right: luncheon service, opalescent crystal, 5¼″ bowl, 7¾″ plate, block signatures, service for six, $1,430.00. Photograph courtesy of Skinner, Inc.

Decanter Stopper, 2½″ h, 2½″ w, Caravelle, etched
   schooner **125.00**
Figure, 7½″ h, Chat Assis, clear and frosted, upright,
   designed by René Lalique, c1932 .... **520.00**
Letter Seal, 3″ h
   Pax, 2¾″ d, dove in wreath **150.00**
   Tete D'Aigle, black glass, white patina, engraved in-
     taglio monogram, c1911 .... **1,100.00**
Perfume Bottle
   Ambre, 5⅛″ h, black, made for D'Orsay, c1911 ...**1,840.00**
   Cigalia, clear and frosted, cicadas, Roger et Gallet
     Fragrances, ornamental polychromed wooden
     box, c1924 .... **3,150.00**
   L'Effleurt, clear and frosted, gray patina, Coty, c1912 **6,325.00**
Plaque, 12½″ h, Masque De Femme, clear and frosted,
   fountain-head design, orig chromed metal stand,
   back plate, 1928 .... **4,888.00**
Plate
   6¾″ d, Figurine Et Fleurs, nude woman dancing
     among spray of flowers, pale amber ground,
     molded mark, engraved "R Lalique France" sig-
     nature and pattern No. 3002, price for 6-pc set .**1,100.00**
   8½″ d, Dream Rose, 1966, second issue, orig box .. **70.00**
   14⅛″ d, Martiques, opal, fish dec, c1920 ....**3,450.00**
Powder Box, cov, Fleurs d'Amour, Roget Gallet, Paris,
   birds dec, sgd **125.00**
Tray, 4″ d, 3¼″ h, figural ram in center **150.00**
Vase
   4″ h, six butterflies, sgd "R Lalique" **330.00**
   4½″ h, 3¾″ d, raised leaf pattern, sgd **220.00**
   5¾″ h, Avalon, opal, gray patina, c1927 ....**2,185.00**
   7⅜″ h, Chevaux, charcoal gray, Art Deco, band of
     horses, c1930 .... **3,100.00**
   8½″ h
     7½″ w, Sylvania, two cuddling birds, orig glass
       flower frog insert, orig gray Lalique box **700.00**
     Plumes, emb stylistic design of overlapping feath-
       ers, satin ground, gilt shading, molded signa-
       ture **990.00**
   9⅞″ h, Ceylan, opal, blue-green patina, parakeets
     dec, c1924 .... **5,750.00**
   10¼″ h, Sauge, deep teal green, sage leaves dec,
     c1923 .... **3,740.00**
   11″ h, Sauterelles, electric blue, white patina, grass-
     hoppers and grass stalks, c1920 .... **8,100.00**

Wall Sconce, 12¾″ h, Lierre, clear and frosted, Art Deco
   ivy leaves pattern, price for pr **2,100.00**
Wine Glass, Alger, clear and frosted, c1935, price for
   10-pc set **520.00**

LAMPS AND LIGHTING

History: Lighting devices have evolved from simple stone-age oil lamps to the popular electrified models of today. Aimé Argand patented the first oil lamp in 1784. Around 1850 kerosene became a popular lamp-burning fluid, replacing whale oil and other fluids. In 1879 Thomas A. Edison invented the electric light, causing fluid lamps to lose favor and creating a new field for lamp manufacturers. Companies like Tiffany and Handel became skillful at manufacturing electric lamps, and their decorators produced beautiful bases and shades.

References: James Edward Black (ed.), *Electric Lighting of the 20s–30s* (1988, 1993 value update), *Volume 2 with Price Guide* (1990, 1993 value update), L-W Book Sales; J. W. Courter, *Aladdin Collectors Manual & Price Guide #16,* published by author (3935 Kelley Rd, Kevil, KY 42053), 1996; Arthur H. Hayward, *Colonial and Early American Lighting,* Third Edition, Dover Publications, 1962; Marjorie Hulsebus, *Miniature Victorian Lamps,* Schiffer Publishing, 1996; Nadja Maril, *American Lighting,* Schiffer Publishing, 1995; Richard Miller and John Solverson, *Student Lamps of the Victorian Era,* Antique Publications, 1992, 1992–93 value guide; Bill and Linda Montgomery, *Animated Motion Lamps 1920s to Present,* L-W Book Sales, 1991; Denys Peter Myers, *Gaslighting in America,* Dover Publications, 1990; Henry A. Pohs, *The Miner's Flame Light Book,* Hiram Press, 1995; *Quality Electric Lamps,* L-W Book Sales, 1992; Catherine M. V. Thuro, Oil Lamps, Wallace-Homestead, 1976, 1992 value update; ——, *Oil Lamps II,* Collector Books, 1983, 1994 value update; Kenneth Wilson, *American Glass 1760–1930,* 2 vols., Hudson Hills Press and The Toledo Museum of Art, 1994.

Periodical: *Light Revival,* 35 West Elm Ave, Quincy, MA 02170.

Collectors' Clubs: Aladdin Knights of the Mystic Light, 3935 Kelley Rd, Kevil, KY 42053; Coleman Collector Network, 1822 E Fernwood, Wichita, KS 67216; Historical Lighting Society of Canada, PO Box 561, Postal Station R, Toronto, Ontario M4G 4EI, Canada; Incandescent Lamp Collectors Assoc, Museum of Lighting, 717 Washington Place, Baltimore, MD 21201; Night Light, 38619 Wakefiled Ct, Northville, MI 48167; Rushlight Club, Inc., Suite 196, 1657 The Fairway, Jenkintown, PA 19046.

Museums: Kerosene Lamp Museum, Winchester Center, CT; Pairpoint Lamp Museum, River Edge, NJ.

Boudoir

Handel, 14¼″ h, circular top, sq shade with scalloped
   edge, sgd "Brown Handel 6034," riveted strapwork
   standard flaring to circular base, copper finish, imp
   "Handel" **750.00**
Pairpoint
   13¾″ h, 8″ d puffy papillon blown-out closed top sq
     glass shade, rose red blossoms, four butterflies re-
     verse painted on white ground, marked "The Pair-
     point Corp," full signed gilt metal base, marked
     "B3048" **5,750.00**

REPRODUCTION ALERT

The following is a partial list of reproduction kerosene lamps. Colors in italics indicate a period color:

Button & Swirl, 8" high—*clear,* cobalt blue, ruby

Coolidge Drake (a.k.a. Waterfall), 10" high—*clear, cobalt blue,* milk glass, ruby

Lincoln Drape, short, 8¾" high—*amber, clear,* green, and *other colors*

Lincoln Drape, tall, 9¾" high—*amber, clear, cobalt blue, moonstone,* ruby

Shield & Star, 7" high—*clear,* cobalt blue

Sweetheart (a.k.a. Beaded Heart), 10" h—*clear,* milk glass, pink, pink cased font with clear base

General clues that help identify a new lamp include parts that are glued together and hardware that is lacquered solid brass.

SPECIAL AUCTIONS

Green Valley Auctions, Inc
Rte 2, Box 434
Mt Crawford, VA 22841
(540) 434-4260

James D. Julia, Inc
PO Box 830
Fairfield, ME 04937
(207) 453-7125

16¾" h, 9" d, 11" across corners, San Remo barrel-shaped reverse-painted puffy shade with blown-out butterflies, asters, and roses, green-accented white ground, gold ext. accents, millefiore green patina metal base, under rim chip **7,900.00**

Reverse Painted

13" h, 8" d conical frosted shade, int. pink rose border, opal glass base painted brown with green highlights, marked "3114C" **500.00**

16½" h, 8" d scenic angular shade, red-roofed farm buildings, tree-lined pastoral setting, polychromed painted single socket base, imp "Made in USA 148" **345.00**

Chandeliers

Art Deco, 25" h, 34" d, silvered metal, molded and frosted shade, c1925, price for pr **2,500.00**

Arts and Crafts, 49" l, three heart-cutout lanterns, cylindrical yellow glass lanterns, hammered copper frame and fluted edge, suspended by three chains **1,750.00**

Bradley and Hubbard, 58" h, 40" d, cast iron, twelve arms, clear fonts, burners, and crimped top chimneys, ceiling fitting marked "Patent date May 26, 1868" .**1,200.00**

Queen Anne, 21" h, 27½" d, brass, six removable S-form scroll candle arms **3,100.00**

Venetian, 23½" h, eight scrolling arms, opalescent blown glass, applied colored floral dec **1,200.00**

Victorian, 47" h, gilt ormolu, eight branch, Rococo scrolls, four putti supported twin branches, frosted glass domed leaf dec shade **1,880.00**

Early American

Betty

4⅜" h, wrought iron, old hanger and pick, replaced chain **100.00**

4½" h, wrought iron, brass heart finial, hanger, stamped "1846" **375.00**

Crusie, 6½" h, wrought iron, double, ram's horn finial, hanger, pitted **325.00**

Grease, hanging

4" h, cast iron, dog and flowers edge relief design, dec hanger **95.00**

5⅜" h, wrought iron, single spout, ratched arm to adjust cant, twisted hanger with crest **120.00**

Hand, 2¾" h, pewter, marked "Wm McQuilkin, Philada" **90.00**

Lard, 7¼" h, tin, saucer base, old soldered repair **100.00**

Petticoat Peg, 4" h, tin, orig brown japanning, whale-oil burner, minor scratches, price for pr **165.00**

Rushlight Holder, 8¼" h, wrought iron, candle socket counter balance, wooden base **300.00**

Floor

Duffner and Kimberly, 66" h, 27" w diagonal, squared conical leaded glass shade, purple, lavender, rippled green, and brown glass segments arranged as broad grape leaves with clusters of bright cobalt blue grape disks plated to blue at back, conforming octagonal six-light bronze base, fine dark patina, some damage to grapes and background segments **6,750.00**

Murano Studio Glass, 65" h, 15" d conical colorless glass shade, int. sand finish over aubergine and white particles, torchere base with Lucite casing and platform **425.00**

Wilkinson Co, Brooklyn, 60" h, 22" d leaded glass domed shade of small glass segments as red roses and pink, yellow, orange blossoms, shell-shaped scrolling devices in shades of green, amber, and white, cast bronze four-light ribbed standard, foliate elements .**8,995.00**

Fluid

Adams & Co, 12" h, clear and frosted font, clear and stippled four-column base, flower display under glass in center with orig label, base can be inserted as serving bowl **900.00**

Atterbury & Co

8¼" h, Chapman pattern, clear **70.00**

9¼" h, Wave pattern, clear, paneled base, marked "October 7th 1873" **65.00**

Beaumont Glass Co, 8½" h, Optic pattern, silver stained band with frosted leaves and flowers **275.00**

Boston Silver & Glass Co, 12½" h, engraved pear-shaped font, pewter collar, marble base **550.00**

Dalzell, Gilmore & Leighton, Findlay, OH, 8" h, Queen of Hearts pattern, clear font, medium green base ... **250.00**

McKee Glass Co, 9½" h, Ribbed Tulip pattern, clear font, milk glass base **150.00**

Ripley, 12⅝" h, marriage, clear, brass collar and connector, kerosene burner, marked "D. C. Ripley & Co, Patented Sept 28, 1870" **800.00**

Unknown Maker
13½" h, 4½" d, sapphire blue, flower-patterned font, nickel-plated white metal base, matching blue patterned ruffled shade, clear chimney **425.00**

15⅛" h, patinated metal, applied band of flowers and fruits, acid-etched and wheel-cut shades, 19th C, minor chips to shades, price for pr **1,725.00**

Hanging

Adams & Westlake, 32" h, 30" w, double railway type, cast bronze and brass, orig white enameled metal shades **1,200.00**

Bradley and Hubbard, 52" h, store type, emb brass font, opaque white shade, filler cap **550.00**

Cast Iron, 32" h, 26" w, two arms, frosted and etched shades with flowers and butterflies, orig black and gold finish, c1870 .... **750.00**

Gas, brass
Single etched crystal shade
Chain and burner, 28" support tube, marked "Wellsbach 55" **75.00**
Shade holder and reflex marked "Wellsbach Co. Size No. 1," 33" support tube **110.00**
Two burners, etched crystal shades, black and copper stripes
28" support tube **175.00**
33" support tube **125.00**

Steuben, 5" h, 16" d, brass wreath edge, four suspended chain holders, four sgd white bell-shaped shades .. **975.00**

Desk, Tiffany Studios, shell-shaped shade, shaded green Favrile, stamped mark, bronze base with monogram of Tiffany Glass and Decorating Company, 13" h, $5,500.00.

Victorian, brass, hall type, deep ruby hobnail cylindrical shade, stamped brass fittings, 31" h, c1870 .... **275.00**

Student

Bridgeport Brass Co, 14¾" h, nickel-plated brass, opaque white shade, clear chimney **325.00**

Manhattan Brass Co, 20¼" h, nickel-plated brass, opaque white shade, orig kerosene burner with tubular wick, chimney ring marked **225.00**

Messenger & Son, 16¼" h, brass, dark patina, double arms, emb label "Messenger & Son, Birmingham, Manufactured for Alfred Weller, Boston," old electrification, frosted shades, price for pr **1,485.00**

Miller, 20½" h, brass, Millers Ideal, opaque white shade, clear chimney, shade frame resoldered **320.00**

Table

Arts and Crafts, 24" h, 17" d green and white slag glass paneled shades, geometric cutouts, oak base **635.00**

Bradley and Hubbard
10½" h, white metal urn-shaped lamp, gilt finish, caramel slag glass inserts, marked, price for pair ... **265.00**
21" h, 17" d bent panel shade, six fine-ribbed glass panels, painted green and brown border motif, three-socket elaborate cast-metal base, needs wiring, paint loss **675.00**

Bradley and Hubbard Type, 30" h, 24" w panel glass octagonal shade, four tiers of amber, green slag and red accent glass panels, elaborate conforming cast metal acanthus-leaf dec four-socket base **1,995.00**

Cheuret, Albert, 15" h, three carved alabaster tulip shades, slender gilt-bronze stems, sinuous leaf-form base, inscribed "Albert Cheuret, Made in France," price for pr **17,600.00**

Duffner and Kimberly, 34" h, 31½" d leaded glass shade, purple-blue glass segments to depict grape clusters among green leaves, sky blue accents, border with amber-brown vines and graduated green segments, inscribed "Duffner and Kimberly New York" on rim tag, orig Duffner cast bronze base with ribbed standard, six-light socket **21,000.00**

Genet & Michon, 20" h, 13¾" d plaffonnier-type frosted glass shade with molded Art Deco geometric blossom design, molded mark "Genet & Michon Made in France," bronzed-metal tripartite wrought shaft, reticulated base with scrolling devices **1,5000.00**

Handel
22" h, 18" d drop apron dome shade with irregular border, pink and rose-red blossoms, five-petal yellow flowers, green, blue, and brown background segments, "Handel" tag on leading, cast metal Handel bronzed base with japonesque foliate design **4,500.00**
22½" h, 18" d reverse-painted ribbed glass shade, textured interior surface painted in landscape with poplars, autumn trees, majestic purple mountains, inscribed "Handel 7111," dark gilt metal baluster turned three-socket Handel base, two flat chips on outside shade rim **4,995.00**
24" h, 18" d reverse-painted opal dome shade, tex-

Table, Handel, Chrysanthemum, reverse painted shade, $30,000.00. Photograph courtesy of James D. Julia.

tured ext. finish painted forest green with repeating foliate border elements, inscribed "Handel 6374 F," mounted on three-socket bronze-metal base imp "Handel" **3,500.00**

27" h, 15" d, Arts and Crafts, strap-work shade with yellow mica panels, copper-patinated base **395.00**

Jefferson, 23" h, 10" d hemispherical reverse-painted shade with lake scene, patinated bronze base, cast stylized dec, shade numbered and inscribed "Jefferson" **2,000.00**

Muller Freres, 18" h, frosted glass shades with stylized Art Deco molded foliate motif, adjustable gilt-metal weighted base, shades imp "Muller Freres Luneville," bases need refinishing, price for pr **600.00**

Pairpoint

15" h, 8" d hexagonal Bryn Mawr shape glass shade, reverse-painted Art Deco style sand-finished daffodils, lustered blue-purple ground, green and blue scrolls, marked "The Pairpoint Corp," copper-bronze finished sgd base **2,450.00**

20½" h, 14" d puffy Stratford angular ribbed shade, white lace wreath, torch background, multicolored pink, yellow, and white rose blossom border with hummingbirds, marked "The Pairpoint Corp" at side, full marked SP base **7,600.00**

22" h, 18" d flared Berkeley reverse-painted shade, New Bedford harbor scene, masted ships in foreground, men in small boat rowing toward town village, church spires, and village on distant shores, marked "The Pairpoint Corp," SP triple-dolphin base stamped "Pairpoint" **5,550.00**

Reverse Painted

19" h, 14" d shade, four curved panels with floral motif, yellow, green, brown, black, copper-colored cast-iron fluted base, paint loss **275.00**

23" h, 16" d Phoenix-type dome shade, double wind-

mill scene, orig gilt-metal two-socket base, split shaft needs wiring, finish corroded **750.00**

Suess Ornamental Glass Co, Chicago

24" d broad umbrella leaded glass shade, realistic yellow-centered pink shaded to white apple blossoms against various green-colored leaf and stem glass segments, cast bronze apple tree trunk base, wide platform base with grasses and plants, four-light cluster **6,750.00**

30" h, 22" d irregular rim on shaped dome leaded glass shade, red-rose peony blossoms with yellow centers, white ground with green leaves and brown stems, adjustable bronze three-light base, tripartite paw-foot shaft on platform base **6,550.00**

Van Erp, Dirk, 15½" h, 16" d copper and mica shade, bullet-form cap, four sinuous arm supports, copper melon-form base, stamped windmill mark and "Dirk Van Erp" in broken box, c1912 ....**46,200.00**

LAMP SHADES

History: Lamp shades were made to diffuse the harsh light produced by early gas lighting fixtures. These early shades were made by popular Art Nouveau manufacturers including Durand, Quezal, Steuben, and Tiffany. Many shades are not marked.

Acid Etched, 8" d, hummingbirds and leaves, clear and frosted, c1870, price for pr **175.00**

Bigelow Kennard, 18" d leaded glass dome, opal white graduated segments above and below border bands of amber and green, pine cone motif lower edge, heat cap leaded to top rim, several cracked segments ... **900.00**

Burmese, 8¾" d, birds, butterflies, and floral dec, gas style fitter ring **275.00**

Carnival Glass, marigold, swirled ribs, 10" d **200.00**

Durand, 3½" d, irid gold, candle-lamp type **150.00**

Fostoria, 5" h, gold, green leaves and vines, white luster ground **150.00**

Hobbs Bruckunier, 4½" h, 7" d, Coinspot pattern, opal and amber optic, c1880 .... **65.00**

Leaded Dome

12¼" d, 4¾" h, red, green, and opalescent white chunks of glass shards, some cracks, slightly out-of-round, European **460.00**

20" d, angular, clusters of red bead grapes among green and amber glass segments, bent glass crown, replacement two-light socket **425.00**

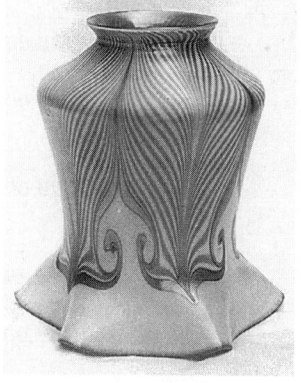

Lustre Art, blue pulled double-hooked feather, gold border on opal glass, gold iridescent int., acid-etched signature, 5" h, 2¼" fitter, $385.00.

Northwood, 8¼" d, light pink, etched flowers, frosted, ruffled **150.00**

Quezal, 5¼" h , 12" d, flared aperture on domed shade, heavy walled opal glass, opal irid coiled vertical zipper pattern, sgd on inside collet ring **1,100.00**

Steuben, 14" d, 6" h, flared bell form, rose-red dec overall with gold aurene leaf-heart and vine motif, cased to calcite white int., Carder, drilled at top ½" d with 1" slight hairline **2,995.00**

Tartan, 6" h, 1½" d, fitter ring, gaslight, white, yellow, and pink plaid of multicolored glass threads, attributed to Stourbridge, England, sgd "Tartan Rd. No. 46" **285.00**

Tiffany, 4¾" h, 2¼" fitter ring, bell-form ten-rib flared gold Favrile shade, lustrous irid inside and out, inscribed "L.C.T." inside rim, price for 8-pc matched set **5,750.00**

LANTERNS

History: A lantern is an enclosed, portable light source, hand carried or attached to a bracket or pole to illuminate an area. Many lanterns have a protected flame and can be used both indoors and outdoors. Light-producing materials used in early lanterns included candles, kerosene, whale oil, and coal oil, and, later, gasoline, natural gas, and batteries.

References: Anthony Hobson, *Lanterns that Lit Our World,* Hiram Press, reprinted 1996; Dana G. Morykan and Harry L. Rinker, *Warman's Country Antiques & Collectibles,* Third Edition, Wallace-Homestead, 1996.

Collectors' Club: Coleman Collectors Network, 1822 E Fernwood, Wichita, KS 67216.

Barn, 11½" h, wood, pine, worn red finish, hinged door, wire bail handle, age cracks, top board cracked ... **440.00**

Bicycle, 7¾" h, Majestic model, nickel plated, clear lens, faceted red and green side lights, c1900 .... **175.00**

Buggy, 9" h, E T Wright & Co, orig black paint, late 19th C **85.00**

Candle, 11¾" h, tin, pyramid top, pierced star design, old black paint, ring handle **110.00**

Dashboard, 15" h, spring clips, reflector, orig red paint, sgd brass label, Kemp Mfg Co, c1900 .... **165.00**

Inspector's, globe marked "New York Central System" and logo, pressed mark on back "Ideal Inspector Lamp," Dietz, late 19th C **75.00**

Miner, 8" h, wrought iron, chicken finial, wick pick ... **250.00**

Navy, brass, Dietz, marked "US Navy" **75.00**

Paul Revere Type, 13" h, punched tin, dented, ring handle **140.00**

Pocket, 5¾" h, folding, black and gold litho man seated on train, ruby glass panel, c1870 .... **200.00**

Post, 26" h, tin, orig glass globe, orig brass burner, marked "Dietz Tubular Globe #3," old worn green paint, light rust **220.00**

Railroad, 11⅛" h, NL Piper Railway Supply Co. Ltd., bull's-eye front lens, orig red and green side glass, corrugated reflector-lined door, Simplex burner **200.00**

Rayo, No. 60 CB **90.00**

Skater's, 7" h, brass, bail, kerosene burner, clear globe **145.00**

Tin, 12½" h, clear blown globe, pierced air vents in

Watchman's, tin, bull's-eye lens, folding handle, whale oil burner, c1850, 6" h, $65.00.

diamond design, five- and six-pointed stars, removable front, whale-oil burner, mismatched parts, wire guard missing, ring handle **215.00**

Wall, Prairie School

8" l, 5" sq, zinc and slag glass, alternating bands of cream and yellow glass, orig dark patina on metal, price for pr **400.00**

9½" h, 6" sq, four-sided brass and leaded glass, yellow, opalescent and frosted glass, orig gas fittings, price for pr **650.00**

LEEDS CHINA

History: The Leeds Pottery in Yorkshire, England, began production about 1758. Among its products was creamware that was competitive with that of Wedgwood. The original factory closed in 1820, but various subsequent owners continued until 1880. They made exceptional cream-colored wares, either plain, salt glazed, or painted with colored enamels, and glazed and unglazed redware.

Marks: Early wares are unmarked. Later pieces are marked "Leeds Pottery," sometimes followed by "Hartley-Green and Co." or the letters "LP."

Reproduction Alert: Reproductions have the same marks as the antique pieces.

Bough Pot, 9" l, D-shaped, silver-resist luster fruiting vine dec within arched panels, pierced cov, c1815 ..... **750.00**

Charger, 15½" d, five-color urn, floral spray, blue feathered edge **450.00**

Chestnut Bowl, cov, reticulated band, twisted rope handles, c1790 .... **775.00**

Creamer, 3⅜" h, brown, yellow dec **145.00**

Cup and Saucer, five color, floral and crosshatched dec **125.00**

Jug, 4½" h, baluster, transfer print, underglaze blue, iron-red, yellow, green, and brown enameled scene of hunter and two hounds, silver-resist border, blue floral garland, c1815 .... 295.00

Plate

7" d, spatterware, peafowl and green dec, green border, early 19th C 1,650.00

8" d, earthenware, molded-shell edge, green glazed rim, center dec of stylized American eagle crest, early 19th C 650.00

9⅝" d, cream, blue edge, some damage and variation to sizes, price for 5-pc set 150.00

Platter, blue border, scalloped edges, raised design, beaded bands and miniature leaves, 17½ × 14⅜", $50.00.

Sauce Tureen, cov, underplate, basketweave, green edges, floral finial, early 19th C, one handle repaired 450.00

Snuff Box, cov, 2¾" d, waisted cylinder, iron-red, puce, yellow, and green painted floral sprays, floral wreath, inscribed "When This You See, Remember Me, W. G. 1779," and "A Pinch of This Deserv's a Kiss" .. 595.00

Teapot, 7¼" h, Gaudy, blue and white floral dec, repairs to spout and lid 275.00

LEFTON CHINA

History: China, porcelain, and ceramic with that now familiar "Lefton" mark has been around since the early 1940s and is highly sought by collectors in the secondary marketplace today. The company was founded by George Zoltan Lefton, a Hungarian immigrant. In the 1930s he was a sportswear designer and manufacturer, but his hobby of collecting fine china and porcelain led him to a new business venture.

After the bombing of Pearl Harbor in 1941, Mr. Lefton aided a Japanese-American friend by helping him to protect his property from anti-Japanese groups. As a result, Lefton came in contact with and began marketing pieces from a Japanese factory owned by Kowa Toki KK.

Figurines and animals, plus many of the whimsical pieces such as the Bluebirds, Dainty Miss, Miss Priss, Cabbage Cutie, Elf Head, Mr. Toodles, and the Dutch Girl, are popular with collectors.

Marks: Until 1980, wares from the Japanese factory include a "KW" in front of the item number.

Reference: Loretta DeLozier, *Collector's Encyclopedia of Lefton China,* Vol. 1 (1995), Vol. 2 (1997), Collector Books.

Collectors' Club: National Society of Lefton Collectors, 1101 Polk St, Bedford, IA 50833.

Advisor: Loretta DeLozier.

Bank, 6½" h, owl, rhinestone eyes, No. 90195 .... 50.00

Bone Dish, Poinsettia, No. 4398 .... 18.00

Bookends, pr, birds, 5", No. 90581 .... 50.00

Bowl, 7" d, sleigh shape, white, sponged gold, pink rose, No. 321 .... 105.00

Cigarette Set, Heavenly Rose, box and ashtrays, No. 103 50.00

Coffeepot, 8-cup, Brown Heritage, fruit, No. 20591 ... 145.00

Compote, Rose Chintz, No. 650 .... 30.00

Cookie Jar

Dainty Miss, 7½" h, No. 040 .... 175.00

Honey Bee, No. 1279 .... 110.00

Miss Priss, 7½" h, No. 1502 .... 135.00

Mr. Toodles, 9" h, No. 3236 .... 200.00

Cup and Saucer, floral design, No. 911 .... 45.00

Figures, Revolutionary War soldiers, mid-1960s to early '70s, 7" h, four of a set of six, each $55.00.

Figurine

Angel, 4½" h, Kewpie of the Month, No. 130 ...... 30.00

Bird, 2" and 3" butterfly with clip, No. 80578 ...... 15.00

Boy, pink and blue, glazed, No. 3049 .... 95.00

Colonial Man and Woman, 10" h, holding musical instruments, No. 3658 .... 200.00

Deer, 5⅝" h, No. 67, pr 28.00

Gay Nineties with Shawl, 8" h, pink or white, No. 8574 .... 140.00

Girl with Shell, 6½" h, flower-filled shell, No. 693 . 50.00

Girl with Umbrella, 4" h, white and gold, No. 10531 40.00

Lady with Umbrella, 7½" h, No. 585 .... 130.00

Modern, 5¼" h, white, No. 1129, pr 50.00

Soldier, 7" h, No. 181 .... 55.00

Jam Jar, grape design, spoon, No. 299 .... 48.00

Mug, 5½" h, Robert E Lee, No. 2365 .... 40.00

Planter

Dutch Shoe, boy and girl, No. 5260, pr 60.00

Girl Pushing Cart, 4½" h, No. 50584 .... 28.00

Plate, 9¼", Blue Paisley, No. 2337 .... 28.00

Figure, Victorian woman with umbrella, early 1950s, 7½″ h, $130.00.

Salt and Pepper Shakers
    Heritage, dark green, No. 30132 .... **20.00**
    Pineapple, 2¾″ h, applied roses, No. 3053 .... **25.00**
Spoon Rest, Rustic Daisy, 7½″ l, No. 4123 .... **12.00**
Sugar and Creamer
    Americana, No. 953 .... **50.00**
    Elf's Head, 5″ h, No. 3970 .... **65.00**
Teapot
    Cabbage Cutie, No. 2123 .... **95.00**
    Dutch Girl, No. 2699 .... **145.00**
Tray, Rose Chintz, two tiers, No. 649 .... **85.00**
Vase
    6¾″ h, Mardi Gras, white bisque, pink and gold, No.
      70444 .... **60.00**
    Dainty Miss, girl's head, No. 7797 .... **110.00**
    Pink, fruit attached, No. 7365 .... **55.00**
Water Pitcher, To a Wild Rose, No. 2562 .... **95.00**

LENOX CHINA

History: In 1889 Jonathan Cox and Walter Scott Lenox established The Ceramic Art Co. at Trenton, New Jersey. By 1906 Lenox formed his own company, Lenox, Inc. Using potters lured from Belleek, Lenox began making an American version of the famous Irish ware. The firm is still in business.

Marks: Older Lenox china has one of two marks: a green wreath or a palette. The palette mark appears on blanks supplied to amateurs who hand painted china as a hobby. The Lenox company currently uses a gold stamped mark.

References: Susan and Al Bagdade, *Warman's American Pottery and Porcelain,* Wallace-Homestead, 1994; Richard E. Morin, *Lenox Collectibles,* Sixty-Ninth Street Zoo, 1993.

Additional Listings: Belleek.

Bouillon Cup, ivory ground, gold trim, SS ftd holder,
    green wreath mark, price for 10-pc set **375.00**
Box, cov, 3¾ × 4¼″, spray of flowers, green wreath
    mark **50.00**
Cake Set, Mimosa pattern, 10½″ d low pedestal plate,

    six 7½″ d plates, green wreath mark, price for 7-pc
    set **195.00**
Compote, Autumn pattern **50.00**
Creamer and Sugar, Wheat pattern **45.00**
Cup and Saucer, Castle Garden **38.00**
Decanter Set, ivory, gold trim, green wreath mark, price
    for decanter and five shot glasses **125.00**
Demitasse Cup and Saucer, made for Tiffany **18.00**
Dinner Service, Wheat pattern, service for twelve, two
    platters **275.00**
Mug, cobalt blue, SS overlay bands **75.00**
Plate, 10″ d, ivory, gold and black floral rims, marked
    "Lenox, Tiffany & Co," price for 8-pc set **175.00**
Salt, palette mark **15.00**
Shell Dish, 9½″ d, green mark **55.00**
Swan
    4½″ h, green mark **45.00**
    5″ h, green mark **32.00**
Teapot, 4¼″ h, individual, salmon color, metal lid and
    handle, made for Waldorf Astoria, 1931 .... **125.00**
Vase, 8½″ h, Acanthus Leaf pattern, green wreath mark,
    price for pr **175.00**

Vase, At the Fountain, green top and bottom bands, green wreath mark, c1915–30, 10½″ h, $225.00.

LIBBEY GLASS

History: Edward Libbey established the Libbey Glass Company in Toledo, Ohio, in 1888 after the New England Glass Works of W. L. Libbey and Son closed in East Cambridge, Massachusetts. The new Libbey company produced quality cut glass which today is considered to belong to the brilliant period.

    In 1930 Libbey's interest in art-glass production was renewed, and A. Douglas Nash was employed as a designer in 1931.

    The factory continues production today as Libbey Glass Co.

References: Bob Page and Dale Frederickson, *A Collection of American Crystal,* Page-Frederickson Publishing, 1995; Ellen T. Schroy, *Warman's Glass,* Second Edition, Wallace-Homestead, 1995; Kenneth Wilson, *American Glass 1760–1930,* 2 vols., Hudson Hills Press and The Toledo Museum of Art, 1994.

Additional Listings: Amberina Glass and Cut Glass.

Basket, 18½" h, cut, pressed, and engraved floral and geometric dec, notched rim, star-cut base stamped "Libbey" in circle 520.00

Bonbon, 7" d, 1½" h, amberina, shape #3029, six-pointed 1½" fuchsia rim, shallow pale amber bowl, sgd 595.00

Bowl, 7" d, amberina, ruffled, flared rim, sgd 350.00

Butter, cov, Maize, blue husks, custard ground 475.00

Celery Vase, Maize, colorless, amber irid kernels, blue husks 170.00

Champagne, Silhouette pattern, colorless bowl, figural squirrel stem 165.00

Claret, Silhouette pattern, colorless bowl, opalescent figural bear stem 200.00

Compote
  8" w, 6¼" h, rolled edge, flower engraving on bowl, twisted hollow oval stem, sgd 150.00
  10½" d, 4" h, clear crystal bowl with pink Nailsea-type loops, flaring top, sgd 595.00
  11" d, white opalescent elephant stem, sgd 975.00

Console Set, green and white pulled feather, sgd 825.00

Cruet, Maize pattern, milk glass, painted yellow leaves, orig stopper 875.00

Goblet, Silhouette pattern, colorless bowl, opal figural cat stem 170.00

Hair Receiver, cov, 4½" w, 2" h, two pc, amberina, deep fuchsia shading to amber, partial label 1,750.00

Pitcher, 5½" h, ribbed opal body, combed pink striping, applied cased glass handle, peppermint pink stripe, colorless foot stamped "Libbey" in circular mark .. 345.00

Salt and Pepper Shakers, pr, Maize, small size 75.00

Sherbet, Silhouette pattern, colorless bowl
  Opalescent figural rabbit stem 75.00
  Opalescent figural squirrel stem 110.00

Sugar Shaker, Maize, creamy opaque, yellow husks, gold trim, orig top 245.00

Vase
  10" h, turquoise zipper pattern, colorless ground, sgd 425.00
  11½" h, 2½" w, amberina, deep fuchsia shading to amber, slight ribbing, flaring edge, orig label,
  15" h, lily shape, amberina, sgd 850.00

LIMITED EDITION COLLECTOR PLATES

History: Bing and Grondahl made the first collector plate in 1895. Royal Copenhagen issued their first Christmas plate in 1908.

In the late 1960s and early 1970s, several potteries, glass factories, mints, and artists began issuing plates commemorating people, animals, and events. Christmas plates were supplemented by Mother's Day plates and Easter plates. Speculation swept the field, fostered in part by flamboyant ads in newspapers and flashy direct-mail promotions.

References: Susan Elliott and K. Samara, *The Official Price Guide to Limited Edition Collectibles,* House of Collectibles, 1993; Diane Carnevale Jones, *Collectors' Information Bureau's Collectibles Market Guide & Price Index,* Fourteenth Edition, Collectors' Information Bureau, 1996, distributed by Wallace-Homestead; ———, *Collectors' Information Bureau's Collectibles Price Guide*

1995, Fifth Edition, Collectors' Information Bureau, 1995, distributed by Wallace-Homestead; ———, *Collectors' Information Bureau's Directory to Limited Edition Collectible Stores,* Collectors' Information Bureau, 1993, distributed by Wallace-Homestead; ———, *Collectors' Information Bureau's Directory to Secondary Market Retailers,* Collectors' Information Bureau, 1992, distributed by Wallace-Homestead; Carl Luckey, *Luckey's Hummel Figurines & Plates,* Tenth Edition, Books Americana, 1994; Mary Sieber, *Price Guide to Limited Edition Collectibles,* Krause Publications, 1996.

Periodicals: *Collector Editions,* 170 Fifth Ave, 12th Floor, New York, NY 10010; *Collectors Mart Magazine,* 700 E State St, Iola, WI 54990; *Collectors News,* 506 Second St, PO Box 156, Grundy Center, IA 50638; *Insight on Collectibles,* 103 Lakeshore Rd, Suite 202, St Catharines, Ontario L2N 2T6 Canada; *International Collectible Showcase,* One Westminster Place, Lake Forest, IL 60045; *Plate World,* 9200 N. Maryland Ave., Niles, IL 60648; *Toybox Magazine,* 8393 East Holly Rd, Holly MI 48442.

Collectors' Clubs: Franklin Mint Collectors Society, US Route 1, Franklin Center, PA 19091; Hummel Collector's Club, Inc, PO Box 257, Yardley, PA 19067; International Plate Collectors Guild, PO Box 487, Artesia, CA 90702; M. I. Hummel Club, Goebel Plaza, Rte. 31, PO Box 11, Pennington, NJ 08534.

Museum: Bradford Museum of Collector's Plates, Niles, IL.

Additional Listings: See *Warman's Americana & Collectibles* for more examples of collector plates plus many other limited edition collectibles.

Notes: The first plate issued in a series (FE) is often favored by collectors. Condition is a critical factor, and price is increased if the original box is available.

Limited edition collector plates, more than any other object in this guide, should be collected for design and pleasure and only secondarily as an investment.

Bing and Grondahl (Denmark)

Christmas Plates, various artists, 7" d
  1895 Behind the Frozen Window 3,400.00
  1896 New Moon over Snow Covered Trees 1,975.00
  1897 Christmas Meal of the Sparrows 725.00
  1898 Christmas Roses and Christmas Star 700.00
  1899 The Crows Enjoying Christmas 900.00
  1900 Church Bells Chiming in Christmas 800.00
  1901 The Three Wise Men from the East 450.00
  1902 Interior of a Gothic Church 285.00
  1903 Happy Expectation of Children 150.00
  1904 View of Copenhagen from Frederiksberg Hill 125.00
  1905 Anxiety of the Coming Christmas Night 130.00
  1906 Sleighing to Church on Christmas Eve 95.00
  1907 The Little Match Girl 125.00
  1908 St Petri Church of Copenhagen 85.00
  1909 Happiness over the Yule Tree 100.00
  1910 The old Organist 90.00
  1911 First It Was Sung by Angels to Shepherds in the Fields 80.00
  1912 Going to Church on Christmas Eve 80.00
  1913 Bringing Home the Yule Tree 85.00
  1914 Royal Castle of Amalienborg, Copenhagen ... 75.00

Bing & Grondahl, Christmas Plate, 1930, Yule Tree in Town Hall Square of Copenhagen, $85.00.

1915 Chained Dog Getting Double Meal on Christmas Eve 120.00
1916 Christmas Prayer of the Sparrows 85.00
1917 Arrival of the Christmas Boat 75.00
1918 Fishing Boat Returning Home for Christmas .. 85.00
1919 Outside the Lighted Window 80.00
1920 Hare in the Snow 70.00
1921 Pigeons in the Castle Court 55.00
1922 Star of Bethlehem 60.00
1923 Royal Hunting Castle, The Hermitage 55.00
1924 Lighthouse in Danish Waters 65.00
1925 The Child's Christmas 70.00
1926 Churchgoers on Christmas Day 65.00
1927 Skating Couple 110.00
1928 Eskimo Looking at Village Church in Greenland 60.00
1929 Fox Outside Farm on Christmas Eve 75.00
1932 Lifeboat at Work 90.00
1934 Church Bell in Tower 75.00
1936 Royal Guard Outside Amalienborg Castle in
   Copenhagen 70.00
1938 Lighting the Candles 110.00
1940 Delivering Christmas Letters 170.00
1942 Danish Farm on Christmas Night 150.00
1944 Sorgenfri Castle 120.00
1946 Commemoration Cross in Honor of Danish Sailors Who Lost Their Lives in World War II 85.00
1948 Watchman, Sculpture of Town Hall, Copenhagen 80.00
1950 Kronborg Castle at Elsinore 150.00
1952 Old Copenhagen Canals at Wintertime with
   Thorvaldsen Museum in Background 85.00
1954 Birthplace of Hans Christian Andersen, with
   Snowman 100.00
1956 Christmas in Copenhagen 140.00
1958 Santa Claus 100.00
1960 Danish Village Chruch 180.00
1962 Winter Night 80.00
1964 The Fir Tree and Hare 50.00
1966 Home for Christmas 50.00
1968 Christmas in Church 45.00
1970 Pheasants in the Snow at Christmas 20.00

1972 Christmas in Greenland 20.00
1974 Christmas in the Village 20.00
1976 Christmas Welcome 25.00
1978 A Christmas Tale 30.00
1980 Christmas in the Woods 40.00
1982 The Christmas Tree 55.00
1984 Christmas Letter 55.00
1986 Silent Night, Holy Night 55.00
1988 In the Kings Garden 65.00
1990 Changing of the Guards 75.00
Jubilee, various artists
1915 Frozen Window 225.00
1920 Church Bells 65.00
1925 Dog Outside Window 285.00
1930 The Old Organist 225.00
1935 Little Match Girl 900.00
1940 Three Wise Men 1,950.00
1945 Amalienborg Castle 150.00
1950 Eskimos 175.00
1955 Dybbol Mill 200.00
1960 Kronborg Castle 100.00
1965 Churchgoers 40.00
1970 Amalienborg Castle 35.00
1975 Horses Enjoying Meal 50.00
1980 Yule Tree 60.00
1985 Lifeboat at Work 65.00
1990 The Royal Yacht Danneborg 95.00

Reed & Barton (United States)

Audubon Series, various artists
1970 Pine Siskin, FE 175.00
1971 Red-Shouldered Hawk 75.00
1972 Stilt Sandpiper 70.00
1974 Boreal Chickadee 60.00
1975 Yellow-Breasted Chat 60.00
1976 Bay-Breasted Warbler 60.00
1977 Purple Finch 65.00

Rosenthal (Germany)

Christmas Plates, various artists, 8½″ d
1910 Winter Peace 550.00
1911 The Three Wise Men 325.00
1912 Shooting Stars 250.00
1913 Christmas Lights 235.00
1915 Walking to Chruch 180.00
1916 Christmas during War 235.00
1918 Peace on Earth 210.00
1920 The Manger in Bethlehem 325.00
1922 Advent Branch 200.00
1924 Deer in the Woods 200.00
1926 Christmas in the Mountains 175.00
1928 Chalet Christmas 175.00
1930 Group of Deer under the Pines 225.00
1932 Christ Child 200.00
1934 Christmas Peace 200.00
1936 Nurnberg Angel 185.00
1938 Christmas in the Alps 190.00
1940 Marien Church in Danzig 250.00
1942 Marianburg Castle 300.00
1944 Wood Scape 275.00

1946 Christmas in an Alpine Valley	250.00
1948 Message to the Shepherds	875.00
1950 Christmas in the Forest	185.00
1952 Christmas in the Alps	190.00
1954 Christmas Eve	185.00
1956 Christmas in the Alps	190.00
1958 Christmas Eve	190.00
1960 Christmas in Small Village	200.00
1962 Christmas Eve	185.00
1964 Christmas Market in Nurnberg	225.00
1966 Christmas in Ulm	250.00
1968 Christmas in Bremen	195.00
1970 Christmas in Cologne	165.00
1972 Christmas Celebration in Franconia	90.00
1974 Christmas in Wurzburg	100.00

Royal Copenhagen (Denmark)

**Christmas Plates, various artists, 6" d 1908, 1909, 1910;
7" 1911 to present**

1908 Madonna and Child	1,750.00
1909 Danish Landscape	150.00
1910 The Magi	120.00
1911 Danish Landscape	135.00
1912 Elderly Couple by Christmas Tree	120.00
1913 Spire of Frederik's Church, Copenhagen	125.00
1915 Danish Landscape	150.00
1916 Shepherd in the Field on Christmas Night	85.00
1917 Tower of Our Savior's Church, Copenhagen	90.00
1918 Sheep and Shepherds	80.00
1919 In the Park	80.00
1920 Mary with the Child Jesus	75.00
1921 Aabenraa Marketplace	75.00
1922 Three Singing Angels	70.00
1923 Danish Landscape	70.00
1924 Christmas Star Over the Sea and Sailing Ship	100.00
1925 Street Scene from Christianshavn, Copenhagen	85.00
1926 View of Christmas Canal, Copenhagen	75.00
1927 Ship's Boy at the Tiller on Christmas Night	140.00
1928 Vicar's Family on Way to Church	75.00
1929 Grundtvig Church, Copenhagen	100.00
1930 Fishing Boats on the Way to the Harbor	80.00

Royal Copenhagen, Christmas plate, 1914, Sparrows in Tree at Church of the Holy Spirit, Copenhagen, $100.00.

1932 Frederiksberg Gardens with Statue of Frederik VI	90.00
1934 The Hermitage Castle	115.00
1936 Roskilde Cathedral	130.00
1938 Round Church in Osterlars on Bornholm	200.00
1940 The Good Shepherd	300.00
1942 Bell Tower of Old Church in Jutland	300.00
1944 Typical Danish Winter Scene	160.00
1946 Zealand Village Church	150.00
1948 Nodebo Church at Christmastime	150.00
1950 Boeslunde Church, Zealand	175.00
1952 Christmas in the Forest	120.00
1954 Amalienborg Palace, Copenhagen	150.00
1956 Rosenborg Castle, Copenhagen	160.00
1958 Sunshine over Greenland	140.00
1960 The Stag	140.00
1962 The Little Mermaid at Wintertime	200.00
1964 Fetching the Christmas Tree	75.00
1966 Blackbird at Christmastime	55.00
1968 The Last Umiak	40.00
1970 Christmas Rose and Cat	100.00
1972 In the Desert	85.00
1974 Winter Twilight	80.00
1976 Danish Watermill	80.00
1978 Greenland Scenery	80.00
1980 Bringing Home the Christmas Tree	60.00
1982 Waiting for Christmas	65.00
1984 Jingle Bells	55.00
1986 Christmas Vacation	55.00
1988 Christmas Eve in Copenhagen	60.00
1990 Christmas at Tivoli	75.00

Mother's Day Plates, various artists, 6¼" d

1971 American Mother	125.00
1972 Oriental Mother	60.00
1974 Greenland Mother	55.00
1976 Mermaids	50.00
1978 Mother and Child	25.00
1980 An Outing with Mother	35.00
1982 The Children's Hour	45.00

Wedgwood (Great Britain)

Christmas Series, jasper stoneware, 8" d

1969 Windsor Castle, FE	225.00
1971 Piccadilly Circus, London	40.00
1973 The Tower of London	45.00
1975 Tower Bridge	40.00
1977 Westminster Abbey	48.00
1979 Buckingham Palace	55.00
1981 Marble Arch	75.00
1983 All Souls, Langham Palace	80.00
1985 The Tate Gallery	80.00
1987 Guildhall	80.00

Mothers Series, jasper stoneware, 6½" d

1971 Sportive Love, FE	25.00
1973 The Baptism of Achilles	20.00
1975 Mother and Child	35.00
1977 Leisure Time	30.00
1979 Deer and Fawn	35.00
1981 Mare and Foal	50.00
1983 Cupid and Butterfly	55.00

1985 Cupids and Doves 55.00
1987 Tiger Lily 55.00

LIMOGES

History: Limoges porcelain has been produced in Limoges, France, for over a century by numerous factories in addition to the famed Haviland.

Marks: One of the most frequently encountered marks is "T. & V. Limoges," which is on the wares made by Tressman and Vought. Other identifiable Limoges marks are "A. L." (A. Lanternier), "J. P. L." (J. Pouyat, Limoges), "M. R." (M. Reddon), "Elite," and "Coronet."

References: Susan and Al Bagdade, *Warman's English & Continental Pottery & Porcelain,* Second Edition, Wallace-Homestead, 1991; Mary Frank Gaston, *The Collector's Encyclopedia of Limoges Porcelain,* Second Edition, Collector Books, 1992, 1996 value update.

Additional Listings: Haviland China.

Plate, carnations, orange, yellow, purple, green, gold scalloped edge, marked "T. V. France 6326" in purple, "France" in green, 8½", $30.00.

Bowl, 12" l, oval, holly dec, marked "T & V" 120.00
Box, cov
    Egg shape, multicolored flowers, brass trim 45.00
    Hexagonal, enameled Art Deco geometric dec, con-
      forming cov, Sarlandie 550.00
Cake Plate, 12" d, open handles, grapes dec, gold trim 75.00
Centerpiece Bowl, 12" d, octagon shape, base with four
    gold legs, hp colorful peaches 495.00
Chocolate Pot, 9½" h, melon ribbed, burgundy and gold
    top and handle, pink and yellow floral dec 195.00
Dessert Plate, floral dec, gilt scalloped border, price for
    10-pc set 260.00
Ewer, 6" h 8½" d, royal blue, gold dec and handle,
    marked "Jacob Petit" 225.00
Fish Service, apple green and gilt borders, fish and plant
    dec centers, set of twelve plates, platter, sauce boat,
    and tray, one plate repaired 1,600.00
Hair Receiver, hp, bluebirds, gold trim, three small feet 100.00
Humidor, shaded brown ground, gnomes smoking long
    meerschaum pipes, artist sgd "Holmes, Dec 25,
    1909," marked "GDA Limoges" 195.00
Jardiniere, 7½" h, 11" d, hp, yellow, white, and mulberry
    roses, enamel highlights, white enamel scrolled rim
    dec, marked "Limoges, France" 300.00
Nappy, 10" d, handle, maple-leaf shape, large pink roses
    dec, marked "Elite, Limoges, France" 65.00
Oyster Plate, 8½" d, five pastel colored wells, gilt scroll
    outlines, white ground, marked "Limoges," price for
    4-pc set 440.00
Pitcher, 8½" h, white, rope and anchor handle 95.00
Place Plate, gold encrusted rim, pale pink rose and leaf
    garland border, pc for 12-pc set 220.00
Plaque, 13¼ × 20¼", enameled scene of peasant by
    wall, painted by Edmond-Edouard Lavigne, after Ces-
    are Detti, c1880, giltwood frame 10,350.00
Plate, 10½" d, hanging, rococo gilt border, Victorian
    courting scene, artist sgd 150.00
Punch Bowl, 9½" d, 4½" h, three-colored grape cluster
    and foliage, pink int., pink and yellow ext., scalloped
    edge, gold trim, marked "TV" 225.00

Ramekin, white, gold trim 15.00
Ramekin and Underplate, deep pink roses, gold trim,
    price for 6-pc set 210.00
Salad Plate, gold shell, leaf and feathered edge border,
    price for 12-pc set 275.00
Salt, 4½" d, pearlized light pink to dark pink enamel,
    white swirls and gold trim edge, made for Saks Fifth
    Ave, c1920 .... 65.00
Tankard, 14¾" h, hp, gooseberries, artist sgd "Le Roy, H
    W Guerin, Limoges, France" 300.00
Tureen, cov, underplate, 14½" l, hp, gilt laurel and en-
    amel dec, factory mark and "Tiffany & Co Private
    Stock Handpainted in France," early 20th C 1,725.00
Vase, 12½" h, 9" l, hp, oval cylinder, white, yellow, and
    ruby roses, multicolored ground, two attached gold
    ring handles, four gold ball feet, artist sgd "M Perl,"
    marked "Limoges France" 550.00

LITHOPHANES

History: Lithophanes are highly translucent porcelain panels with impressed designs. The designs result from differences in the thickness of the plaque; thin parts transmit an abundance of light while thicker parts represent shadows.

Lithophanes were first made by the Royal Berlin Porcelain Works in 1828. Other factories in Germany, France, and England later produced them. The majority of lithophanes on the market today were made between 1850 and 1900.

Collectors' Club: Lithophane Collectors Club, 2030 Robinwood Ave, PO Box 4557, Toledo, OH 43620.

Museum: Blair Museum of Lithophanes and Carved Waxes, Toledo, OH.

Candle Shield, table-top type, wooden frame, movable
    rect plaque with stained glass window design 185.00
Cup and Saucer, nude, lady, moriage and dragon dec . 45.00
Fairy Lamp, 4" h, white lithophane newel post shade,
    clear marked "Clarke Cricklite" base 450.00

Lamp Shade, 13″ d, seven panes, European and American scenic views, panel of woman carrying mousetrap upstairs, copper frame **750.00**

Mug, 4¾″ h, alpine couple in landscape, blue riverscape with windmills dec, white ground, German **125.00**

Panel
 4⅛ × 5″, cupid and girl fishing, PR Sickle **175.00**
 4⅜ × 5¼″, brass-framed edge, imp scythe and PR mark, marked "Paris Lithophanie" on top brass hook
  Lady in pink dress sits by riverbank, black border **235.00**
  Maid in pink dress carrying tray, blue man hands her flower, black border **235.00**
 8 × 16″, General Zachary Taylor, holding telescope in left arm, men fighting battle in background, wreath, eagle, and two flags above, leaded frame, ruby flashed **695.00**

Plaque, classical figure in garden, smelling flower, c1860, impressed "1308/52," 5¼ × 4¼″, $125.00.

Stein, dancing couple, transfer of deer, half liter size .. **100.00**
Tea Warmer, 6 × 6″, four panels, romantic scenes, SS holder, orig burner **275.00**

LIVERPOOL CHINA

History: Liverpool is the name given to products made at several potteries in Liverpool, England, between 1750 and 1840. Seth and James Pennington and Richard Chaffers were among the early potters who made tin-enameled earthenware.

By the 1780s tin-glazed earthenware gave way to cream-colored wares decorated with cobalt blue, enameled colors, and blue or black transfers.

The Liverpool glaze is characterized by bubbles and frequent clouding under the foot rims. By 1800 about 80 potteries were working in the town producing not only creamware, but soft paste, soapstone, and bone porcelain.

Reference: Robert McCauley, *Liverpool Transfer Designs on Anglo-American Pottery,* Southworth-Anthoensen Press, out of print.

REPRODUCTION ALERT

Reproduction Liverpool pieces were documented as early as 1942. One example is a black transfer-decorated jug which was made in the 1930s. The jugs vary in height from 8½ to 11 inches. On one side is "The Shipwright's Arms"; on the other, the ship *Caroline* flying the American flag; and under the spout, a wreath with the words "James Leech."

A transfer of the *Caroline* also was used on a Sunderland bowl about 1936 and reproduction mugs were made bearing the name "James Leech" and an eagle.

The reproduction pieces have a crackled glaze and often age cracks have been artificially produced. When compared to genuine pieces, reproductions are thicker and heavier and have weaker transfers, grayish color (not as crisp and black), ecru or gray body color instead of cream, and crazing that does not spiral upward.

Bowl, 9″ d, Delft, painted yellow, blue, green, and manganese, house landscape with fence and bamboo trees, c1760 ....**1,100.00**

Jug
 6¾″ h, black and white transfer, "Success to the Farmer," twelve-line verse cartouche on opposite side, pink luster bands, pink luster "Alice Davies/ Ashton Upon/Mersey/Cheshire" under spout, minute age cracks **350.00**
 7″ h, creamware, polychrome transfer titled "East View of Liverpool Light House & Signals on Bidston Hill" over scene of lighthouse, reverse with black transfer of British sailing ship, hairlines, chips, glaze imperfections **950.00**
 7¾″ h, transfer on one side of "Arms of the United States," angel addressing seated lady amid ruins with scroll declaring date of American Independence, crack and small chips **3,750.00**
 9¾″ h, three transfers, American ship with banner "Success to Trade," couple in landscape titled "Abbas and Abra," Great Seal of the US, dated 1804, age cracks and chip on spout lip **1,500.00**

Mug, creamware
 4⅝″ h, brown transfer, eagle with shield, grasping banner in beak, laurel branch and arrow in talons, sixteen stairs, linked rings border with state names, c1800 ....**2,000.00**
 6¼″ h, black transfer, ship with American flag, "The True Blooded Yankee," chips and hairline **850.00**

Pitcher, Masonic, c1805, 7″ h, $600.00.

Pitcher, 9¾″ h, creamware, black transfer of "An Emblem of America," and "Coming into Port under An Easy Sail," first transfer with female figure holding early Federal flag while pointing out seven medallion busts mounted on a tree to two short black Indians, reverse with shipping scene with American flagged three-masted vessel under sail, title below round cartouche, two Franklin maxims enclosed in oval cartouches under spout, unseen underside base chip .. **1,900.00**

Plate, 9¾″ d, polychrome transfer, titled "Aurora of Newport John Cahoone," imp "Wilson," by Robert Wilson, c1800, restored **375.00**

Teapot, 5¼″ h, globular, emb leaf dec at spout, entwined strap handle, black transfer of British flagged three-masted vessel, "Come Box the Compass" transfer on reverse, fully rigged ship highlighted in red, blue, yellow, and green polychrome, rose finial, black transfer flowers across and around lid, good restoration to rim crack, other repairs **900.00**

LOETZ

History: Loetz is a type of iridescent art glass that was made in Austria by J. Loetz Witwe in the late 1890s. Loetz was a contemporary of L. C. Tiffany's, and he had worked in the Tiffany factory before establishing his own operation; therefore, much of the wares are similar in appearance to Tiffany products. The Loetz factory also produced items with fine cameos on cased glass.

Marks: Some pieces are signed "Loetz," "Loetz, Austria," or "Austria."

Reference: Robert and Deborah Truitt, *Collectible Bohemian Glass: 1880–1940,* R & D Glass, 1995.

Bowl, 5″ d, 3¾″ h, tricorn rim, ftd, red and yellow marbleized striations encased in colorless glass, pink slag int., gold trimmed blue leaf-forms on rim border ... **325.00**
Miniature Lamp, 6″ h, 4″ d, Loetz-type green irid shade

with irregular red threading, brass base, spider to hold shade, chimney **325.00**
Rose Bowl, alternating folded-in and folded-out rim, gold irid, sgd **395.00**
Vase
3¼″ h, 4½″ d, threaded Formosa design, scalloped and dimpled blown green body, iridized blue-gold threaded design, attributed to Edward Prochaska **600.00**
4¾″ h , crimped and flared tricorn rim, pinched green glass body, applied irid amber raised threads in continuous horizontal dec, inscribed "Loetz Austria" across pontil, attributed to Edward Prochaska **760.00**
6½″ h, flared bulbous conical form, cased pastel yellow overlaid in rose pink, double acid-etched repeating panels of stylized blossoms, vertical stem motif, notched rim, polished base, attributed to Josef Hoffman **3,220.00**
6¾″ h, shaped oval body, Papillon, gold-spotted luster, combed horizontal stripes interspersed with round irid pink elements, concave polished pontil **2,225.00**
7″ h, blue, applied vine **295.00**

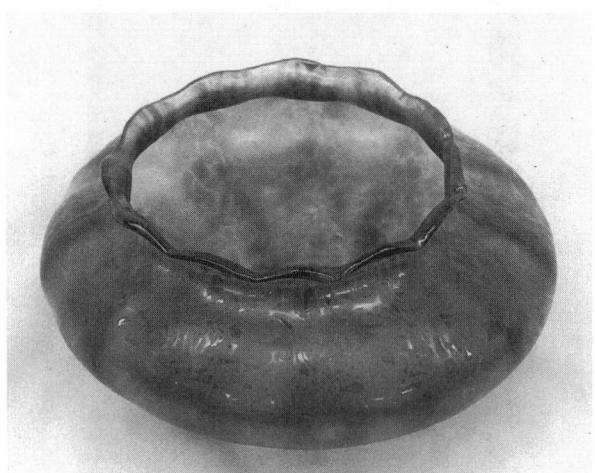

Vase, green, purple flowers, 7½″ d, 3⅝″ h, $295.00.

7½″ h
Cased oval, raised yellow rim, red-amber angled shoulder, five pinched depressions below, sparse irid spots on upper body, polished pontil marked "J. M. 1901" **950.00**
Tapering baluster, gold irid surface, base sgd "Loetz, Austria" **200.00**
8½″ h, folded tricorn rim, dimpled flared body, splotched red with horizontal combed dec, gold irid overall **500.00**
8¾″ h, striated maroon-red and green gray agate glass cased to opal white int., ruffled rim and shoulder, gilt and enameled scrollwork, Marmoriete **725.00**
10″ h, swelled oval body, four silvery-blue pulled feathers, strong irid, brilliant red int. **2,275.00**
10¼″ h, simulated tree trunk, three knothole openings, gold oil-spot coloring **1,120.00**
13¾″ h, ruffled rim, oval body, encased peach-colored int., full-length green and purple stylized stem and leaf-forms, overall irid, concave polished pontil **575.00**

LOTUS WARE CHINA

History: Knowles, Taylor and Knowles Co., East Liverpool, Ohio, made a translucent china between 1891 and 1898. It compared favorably to Belleek and was exhibited at the 1893 Columbian Exposition in Chicago. Col. John T. Taylor, company president at that time, began referring to the products as "Lotus Ware" because the body resembled the petals of the lotus blossom.

Most artist-signed pieces were made by individuals who purchased blanks and hand painted them.

Marks: Early wares were marked "K. T. & K." After 1893 the mark was changed to "Lotus Ware."

References: Susan and Al Bagdade, *Warman's American Pottery and Porcelain,* Wallace-Homestead, 1994; Mary Frank Gaston, *Collector's Encyclopedia of Knowles, Taylor & Knowles China,* Collector Books, 1996; Timothy J. Kearns, *Knowles, Taylor & Knowles: American Bone China,* Schiffer Publishing, 1994.

Bowl, 4" h, tapering globe, white, beaded netting, beaded ruffled rim, marked "Lotus Ware" **95.00**
Cream Pitcher, white enamel daisies on rim, pale green ground, green twig handle with gold trim, marked "Lotus Ware" **275.00**
Ewer, 6" h, white, emb floral rim, marked "K. T. & K" **90.00**
Pitcher, 5" h, squatty, pink and white apple blossoms, gold tied twig handle, marked "Lotus Ware" **300.00**
Shell Dish, 5" d, gold enameling and monogram **150.00**
Vase, 9" h, white, leaves forming base, gold highlights, marked "K. T. & K." **295.00**
Whiskey Jug, 7½" h, encrusted shells and glass bits, marked "K. T. & K." **800.00**

Jug, gold neck, floral dec, white ground, $325.00.

LUSTER WARE

History: Lustering on a piece of pottery creates a metallic, sometimes iridescent, appearance. Josiah Wedgwood experimented with the technique in the 1790s. Between 1805 and 1840 lustered earthenware pieces were created in England by makers such as Adams, Bailey and Batkin, Copeland and Garrett, Wedgwood, and Enoch Wood.

Luster decorations often were used in conjunction with enamels and transfers. Transfers used for luster decoration covered a wide range of public and domestic subjects. They frequently were accompanied by pious or sentimental doggerel as well phrases which reflected on the humors of everyday life.

Copper luster was created by the addition of a copper compound to the glaze. It was very popular in America during the 19th century, and collecting it became a fad from the 1920s to the 1950s. Today it has a limited market.

Pink luster was made by using a gold mixture. Silver luster pieces were first covered completely with a thin coating of a "steel luster" mixture, containing a small quantity of platinum oxide. An additional coating of platinum, worked in water, was then applied before firing.

Sunderland is a coarse type of cream-colored earthenware with a marbled or spotted pink luster decoration which shades from pink to purple. A solution of gold compound applied to the white body developed the many shades of pink.

The development of electroplating in 1840 created a sharp decline in the demands for metal-surfaced earthenware.

REPRODUCTION ALERT

The market stagnation for copper luster can be partially attributed to the large number of reproductions, especially creamers and the "polka" jug, which fool many new buyers. Reproductions are heavier in appearance and weight than the earlier pieces.

Additional Listings: English Soft Paste.

Copper
Creamer
5" h, pink and purple luster bands, 19th C **75.00**
5½" h, floral dec **85.00**
Custard Cup, 2¼" h, 3" d, band dec **35.00**
Fruit bowl, 8¼" d, circular, ftd, cobalt blue and raised figural mid band, 19th C **200.00**
Goblet, 5" h, 3⅜" d, pink luster band, orange and green enamel flowers, good copper luster **95.00**
Jug
4½" h, two transfer reserves, mythological scene ... **120.00**
6" h, central canary yellow band, three reserves, two of women and child playing shuttlecock **125.00**
Milk Pitcher, cobalt blue and figural band, 19th C **75.00**
Pitcher
6" h, white band, worn pink luster house dec, foot chips **125.00**
6½" h, couple dancing **75.00**
7" h, cream band, pink luster floral dec **175.00**
Salt and Pepper Shakers, pr, 3½" h, band and floral dec **65.00**
Waste Bowl and Pitcher, 4½" d × 3¼" h bowl, 7⅝" h pitcher, floral dec **125.00**

Pink

Bowl, 8½" d, 3¾" h, green transfer scenes, The Sailor's Farewell/Return, polychrome enamel, Staffordshire, wear and crazing **145.00**

Pink, pitcher, American naval and military heroes, 6³/₄″ h, $1,100.00.

Bust, 10½″ h, John Wesley, enamel dec, Staffordshire, c1825 ....**1,100.00**

Cup, 5″ h, mask, splash luster ground, enamel dec double faces molded to either side, Staffordshire, c1820, slight rim line, hairline **690.00**

Desk Set, stand, cov pen tray with cupid finial, three cov ink pots, gilt Greek-key borders, wigglework field on stand, Staffordshire, c1810, staining, restorations, two pots with hairlines **635.00**

Figure
  9″ h, Charity, enameled, green on top of base, yellow robe, England, c1820 ....**1,100.00**
  12½″ h, woman with children, enamel dec, Staffordshire, c1815, hairline to arm, firing line to body, retouched glaze flakes **815.00**

Furniture Rest, 3¾″ h, modeled as lion's head and front paws, Staffordshire, c1820, one with hairlines, price for pr **1,100.00**

Jug, 10″ h, figural bear, holding figure representing Napoleon, imp title "Honey," on his hat, allover mottled splash luster, enamel dec on head and honey figure, c1815, side of bear head and neck reglued, chips to paws **2,300.00**

Loving Cup, 5¼″ h, splash luster base, enamel accents, titled to one side "Nicholl Gascoine," dec on reverse with iron mongers tools, Staffordshire, c1815, rim nicks, wear to handles and rim **690.00**

Mug, 3¾″ h, House pattern, molded basketweave and fluted banding, c1820, glaze wear to rim **175.00**

Pitcher, 8¼″ h, enamel floral dec, Staffordshire, c1820   **525.00**

Plaque, 6″ l, relief, scrolled borders surrounding oval medallions of theatrical scenes, Staffordshire, c1810, rim chip repairs, scroll of one reglued, price for pr . **690.00**

Punch Bowl, 10½″ d, 6¾″ h, enameled flowers, trim and int. with pink luster and enamel floral dec, imp Thomas Fell, St Peter's Potter, Newcastle mark, c1820, rim wear **300.00**

Quintal Flower Holder, 8¾″ h, mottled enamels and leaf molded spouts, Newcastle, c1820, one imp "Sewell," damage, chips, price for pr **700.00**

Tray, 15½″ l, scalloped rim, leaf-molded handles, figural landscape by waterfall, Staffordshire, c1815, wear to rim, flaking at handles, surface scratches **460.00**

Silver

Bough Pot, 9″ l, D-shaped, raised arch silver-resist panels, one floral and berry dec, other with bird and floral dec, pierced cov, Leeds, c1815, price for pr **1,725.00**

Bust, 13½″ h, Madonna, mounted to flared circular base, Staffordshire, England, c1820 ....**1,150.00**

Cup, 3¾″, double mask, leaf dec surrounding molded and enameled faces, silver luster and silver resist, Staffordshire, c1915 .... **650.00**

Figure, 10½″ l, lion, mounted on rect base, buff body visible at relief, Staffordshire, c1820, tail repair, base chips **500.00**

Flower Font, 14¼″ h, four part, three graduated rect pots each with corner spouts, flared cov with mask finial, Staffordshire, c1820, chips **750.00**

Garniture, 5″ h, luster banding, vines, and geometric shapes, red enamel flowers, c1815, rim wear, restored chips **115.00**

Jug, sliver resist
  4½″ h, lion pattern, bird on reverse, Leeds, c1810 . **500.00**
  5″ h, commemorative, enamel dec, figure on horseback to one side titled "Marqs Wellington in the Field of Battle," satirical figural scene to other side titled "The Narrow Escape of Boney through a Window," Staffordshire, c1812, rim chip **875.00**
  5½″ h
    Bird and stag among foliage, English, first-half 19th C **180.00**
    Farmers harvesting with implements, blue trim, Staffordshire, c1815, rim line, rim glaze wear **350.00**
    Hunt Jug, black brown dec of hunters shooting at birds in landscape with dogs, Staffordshire, c1815, rim and luster wear **425.00**

Urn, 14½″ h, reticulated, mounted to graduated circular base, Leeds, c1810, damaged, price for pr **750.00**

Sunderland

Bowl, 10¼″ d, int. transfer printed and enamel dec of "The Great Eastern Steamship," marked "Moore & Co.," rim repair **375.00**

Cup and Saucer, pink trim **235.00**

Figure, 8½ to 8¾″ h, Four Seasons, allegorical, dec, pink luster trim, titled, and imp "Dixon, Austin & Co." c1825, wear, restoration, price for set **1,955.00**

Puzzle Jug, 6½″ h, house and landscape design, c1820, rim chip **750.00**

Watch Stand, 11″ h, enamel and pink luster dec, classical children flanking grandfather clock, imp "Dixon, Austin," c1825, base and finial repair **1,100.00**

LUTZ-TYPE GLASS

History: Lutz-type glass is an art glass attributed to Nicholas Lutz. He made this type of glass while at the Boston and Sandwich Glass Co. from 1869 until 1888. Since Lutz-type glass was popular, copied by many capable glassmakers, and unsigned, it is nearly impossible to distinguish genuine Lutz products.

Lutz is believed to have made two distinct types of glass: striped and threaded. The striped glass was made by using threaded glass rods in the Venetian manner, and this style is often confused with authentic Venetian glass. Threaded glass was blown and decorated with winding threads of glass.

Bowl, 3 × 3¾", white, amethyst, and yellow stripes, goldstone edges 45.00
Compote, 7" h, lavender, pink, and opal swirls, entwined serpent stem 250.00
Plate, 6¼" d, goldstone, threaded rose center shading into amber body, ruffled 95.00
Tumbler, 3" h, ftd, gold and white latticinio, threaded, six applied strawberries 90.00

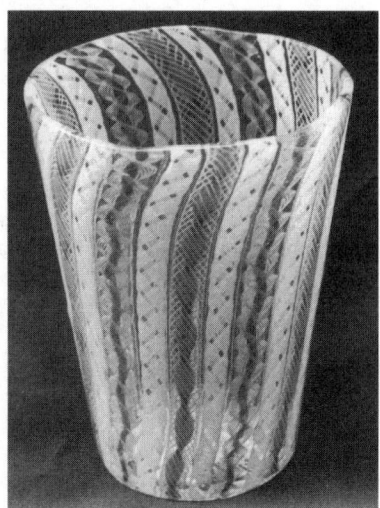

Tumbler, white, green, and orange latticinio, 3½" h, $115.00.

MAASTRICHT WARE

History: Petrus Regout founded the De Sphinx Pottery in 1836 in Maastricht, Holland. The firm specialized in transfer-printed earthenwares. Other factories also were established in the area, many employing English workmen and adopting their techniques. Maastricht china was exported to the United States in competition with English products.

Bowl, 8¼" d, gaudy floral spatter, blue, green, and yellow marked "Maastricht" 35.00
Cake Plate, 12" d, orange and blue flowers, marked "Societe Ceramic Maastricht, Made in Holland" 75.00
Cup and Saucer, Oriental pattern, dark red transfer ... 35.00
Mug, 3" h, gaudy floral spatter, polychrome dec, marked "Maastricht" 75.00
Plate
    7½" d, Castillo pattern, blue transfer, marked "Petrus Regout" 15.00
    8¾" d, ironstone, green Oriental transfer, red and yellow enamel and orange luster trim, marked "Maastricht," minor damage, price for eight-pc set   75.00

Sauce dish, marked "Society Ceramique Potiche," 5" d, $5.00.

Porringer, 3½" d, Pompeii pattern, marked "Petrus Regout" 65.00
Waste Bowl, 4³⁄₁₆" d, gaudy floral spatter, polychrome, marked "Maastricht" 20.00

MAJOLICA

History: Majolica, an opaque, tin-glazed pottery, has been produced in many countries for centuries. It was named after the Spanish Island of Majorca, where figuline (a potter's clay) is found. Today, however, the term "majolica" denotes a type of pottery which was made during the last half of the 19th century in Europe and America.

Majolica frequently depicts elements of nature: leaves, flowers, birds, and fish. Designs were painted on the soft clay body using vitreous colors and fired under a clear lead glaze to impart the rich color and brilliance characteristic of majolica.

Victorian decorative art philosophy dictated that the primary function of design was to attract the eye; usefulness was secondary. Majolica was a welcome and colorful change from the familiar blue and white wares, creamwares, and white ironstone of the day.

Marks: Wedgwood, George Jones, Holdcraft, and Minton were a few of the English majolica manufacturers who marked their wares. Most of their pieces can be identified through the English Registry mark and/or the potter-designer's mark. Sarreguemines in France and Villeroy and Boch in Baden, Germany, produced majolica that compared favorably with the finer English majolica. Most Continental pieces had an incised number on the base.

Although 600-plus American potteries produced majolica between 1850 and 1900, only a handful chose to identify their wares. Among these manufacturers were George Morely, Edwin Bennett, the Chesapeake Pottery Company, the New Milford-Wannoppee Pottery Company, and the firm of Griffen, Smith, and Hill. The others hoped their unmarked pieces would be taken for English examples.

References: Susan and Al Bagdade, *Warman's American Pottery and Porcelain,* Wallace-Homestead, 1994; ———, *Warman's English & Continental Pottery & Porcelain,* Second Edition, Wallace-Homestead, 1991; Leslie Bockol, *Victorian Majolica,* Schiffer Publishing, 1996; Mariann Katz-Marks, *The Collector's Encyclo-*

pedia of Majolica, Collector Books, 1992, 1996 value update; William C. Ketchum, Jr., *American Pottery and Porcelain,* Avon Books, 1994; Mike Schneider, *Majolica,* Schiffer Publishing, 1990, 1995 value update; Jeffrey B. Snyder and Leslie J. Bockol, *Majolica: European and American Wares, Schiffer Publishing,* 1994.

Periodical: *Majolica Market,* 2720 N 45 Rd, Manton, MI 49663.

Collectors' Club: Majolica International Society, 1275 First Ave, Ste 103, New York, NY 10021.

REPRODUCTION ALERT

Majolica-style pieces are a favorite of today's interior decorators. Many exact copies of period pieces are being manufactured. In addition, fantasy pieces incorporating late Victorian era design motifs have entered the market and confused many novice collectors.

Modern majolica reproductions differ from period pieces in these ways: (1) modern reproductions tend to be lighter in weight than their Victorian ancestors; (2) the glaze on newer pieces may not be as rich or deeply colored as on period pieces; (3) new pieces usually have a plain white bottom, period pieces almost always have colored or mottled bases; (4) a bisque finish either inside or on the bottom generally means the piece is new; and (5) if the design prevents the piece from being functional—e.g., a lip of a pitcher that does not allow proper pouring—it is a new piece made primarily for decorative purposes.

Some reproductions bear old marks. Period marks found on modern pieces include (a) "Etruscan Majolica" (the mark of Griffen, Smith and Hill) and (b) a British registry mark.

Advisor: Mary D. Harris.

Note: Prices listed below are for pieces with good color and in mint condition. For less-than-perfect pieces, decrease value proportionately according to the degree of damage or restoration.

SPECIAL AUCTION

Michael G. Strawser
200 N Main, PO Box 332
Wolcottville, IN 46795
(219) 854-2859

Asparagus Plate, teal blue ground, green and purple asparagus, Luneville **225.00**
Basket
9½ x 11", flat begonia leaf with green handles, purple, green, white and brown leaf, unattributed **375.00**

Dish, leaf-shaped, Etruscan, 7¾", $85.00.

Oval, yellow ground, pink interior, white face below each handle surrounded with pink swirled trim, unattributed **325.00**
Bread Tray, 11 x 13", pineapple pattern, brown center, green leaves, yellow pineapple, English **350.00**
Butter Pat
Cobalt ground, pink flowers, green leaves, unattributed **75.00**
Shell and waves pattern, solid green ground, unattributed **50.00**
Chamberstick, rose and rope pattern, yellow ground, cobalt band, pink rose, green leaves, English **375.00**
Compote, daisy pattern, pink interior, white ground alternating with pink and yellow daisies, Etruscan ... **375.00**
Cup and Saucer
Cauliflower design, green int., yellow and green ext. with a touch of pink, Etruscan **325.00**
Shell and seaweed pattern, cobalt ground, brown, pink, yellow and white shells, pink int., attributed to James Carr **275.00**
Cuspidor, cobalt ground, six-sided top, pink int., pink, white, brown, and yellow shells, teal seaweed, English **450.00**
Humidor
6" h, man's head with cigar, mustache, red hat with blue tassel, purple jacket, German **225.00**
Sailor with beard, smoking pipe, German **200.00**
Mug, cobalt ground, large yellow sunflower with green leaves, turquoise int., English **325.00**
Oyster Plate, 9" d, turquoise ground, green center, small shells surrounding white center well, small shells between each outside well, Minton **450.00**
Pitcher
7" h
Cobalt ground, two brown deer in green grass, pink flowers with green leaves above deer, brown handle, pink ext., unattributed **225.00**
Yellow ground, green palm trees, two running brown elephants, unattributed **300.00**
8" h, purple ground, fan, insect, and scroll design, yellow and brown fan, dark rose prunus flowers, brown-green handle, pink int., Oriental influence, Fielding, English **375.00**
Plate
6 x 6½", fan shape, raspberry ground, yellow prunus

flowers, butterfly, turquoise, yellow and brown trim, Eureka 125.00

6 x 9½″, crescent-shaped plate, mottled center, turquoise border with green spiked leaves, yellow trim, George Jones 275.00

9″ d
White ground, green maple leaves, pink and yellow trim, yellow border, Etruscan 225.00

Yellow basketweave background, large green maple leaf in center, pink trim on leaf, Etruscan 150.00

8″ d, shell and seaweed pattern, pink and blue shells, green seaweed, Etruscan 275.00

Pitcher, flying crane, green, blue, gold band, brown handle, 7½″, $125.00.

Plate and Napkin, 8″ d plate, pink morning glories on napkin, green and brown border, German 35.00

Platter
9 x 12″, acorn leaf, pink, green, and yellow, brown handle, Etruscan 250.00

9½ x 13″, rectangular, white ground, yellow corn, rose red poppies, taupe trim, Wedgwood 375.00

10½ x 15½″, oval, rose and rope pattern, turquoise ground, cobalt center, large pink wild roses, green leaves, brown trim, English 450.00

12″ d, round, white ground, green and yellow banana leaves, basketweave background, yellow border, unattributed 325.00

Salad Bowl, 8″ d, shell and seaweed pattern, pink and blue shells, green seaweed, dark pink int., Etruscan 350.00

Sardine Box, 9 x 9″, white ground, attached underplate, box and lid covered with yellow, green, blue, and rose seaweed, two lavender shells on underplate, one large and two small conch shells on lid, taupe trim, unattributed 1,600.00

Shell Bowl, 9 x 9 x 14″, cobalt ground, turquoise int., three brown conch-shell feet, English 380.00

Sugar Bowl, four sided, white ground, flying gray cranes, bamboo, butterfly, rose prunus flowers, yellow trim, Oriental influence, unattributed 250.00

Syrup Pitcher, 3″ h, white ground, turquoise and green fern-type leaves, pewter lid, unattributed 195.00

Waste Bowl, bamboo pattern, yellow ground, green and pink bamboo, brown trim, pink int., Etruscan 275.00

MAPS

History: Maps provide one of the best ways to study the growth of a country or region. From the 16th to the early 20th century, maps were both informative and decorative. Engravers provided ornamental detailing, such as ornate calligraphy and scrolling, especially on bird's-eye views and city maps. Many maps were hand colored to enhance their beauty.

Maps generally were published as plates in books. Many of the maps available today are simply single sheets from cut-apart books.

In the last quarter of the 19th century, representatives from firms in Philadelphia, Chicago, and elsewhere traveled the United States preparing county atlases, often with a sheet for each township and a sheet for each major city or town.

References: Norman E. Martinus and Harry L. Rinker, *Warman's Paper,* Wallace-Homestead, 1994; Carl Morland and David Bannister, *Antique Maps,* Phaidon Press, 1993; Dana G. Morykan and Harry L. Rinker, *Warman's Country Antiques & Collectibles,* Third Edition, Wallace-Homestead, 1996.

Periodical: *Antique Map & Print Quarterly,* PO Box 254, Simsbury, CT 06070.

Collectors' Clubs: Assoc of Map Memorabilia Collectors, 8 Amherst Rd, Pelham, MA 01002; Chicago Map Society, 60 W Walton St, Chicago, IL 60610.

Museum: Hermon Dunlap Smith Center for the History of Cartography, Newberry Library, Chicago, IL.

Notes: Although mass produced, county atlases are eagerly sought by collectors. Individual sheets sell for $25 to $75. The atlases themselves can usually be purchased in the $200 to $400 range. Individual sheets should be viewed solely as decorative and not as investment material.

SPECIAL AUCTION

Swann Galleries, Inc.
104 E 25th St
New York, NY 10010
(212) 254-4710

Africa, "Map of Tripoli and Tunis," 1816, Colburn, 10 × 16″, few minor rubs 45.00

Canada, "British American," London/New York, Tallis, 1851, engraved, outline color, 12¾ × 9½″ 85.00

Canal, "A Map of Proposed Chesapeake-Delaware Canal Routes," Philadelphia, American Philosophical society, 1771, J Smithers after W Thomas Fisher, engraving, 12⅝ × 17″ 950.00

England, southern England including Devonshire, aquatint, dated 1693, well preserved, framed, 24¼ × 38¼″ 125.00

Georgia, "A New and Accurate Map of the Province of Georgia in North America," London, J Hinton, 1779, engraving, published in "The Universal Magazine," 12¾ × 10¾″ 350.00

Jefferson County, "Map of Jefferson County from Recent Surveys with All the Changes and Improvements to the Present Time,"published and sold by Knowlton & Rice, Watertown, NY, 1849, litho by Sarony and Major, 19 × 23", wooden top hanger and roller, some staining but does not affect two-color county area 355.00

Military, "Military Map of the States of Kentucky and Tennessee, Within Eleven Miles of the 55th Parallel of Latitude or Southern Boundary of Tennessee...Commenced under the authority of the Major General Don Carols Buell by Capt N. Michler, Topog Engr USA...," Nov 1863, produced by Ehrgott, Forbriger & Co, Lithographers, Engravers & Printers, Cincinnati, O, linen backed, outline coloring, folds to 7 × 13", 88 × 48", ex-library 220.00

New York

"Catskill Forest, Map of the Catskill Forest and Adjoining Territory Compiled from Maps and Field Notes Partially Revised 1911 By..., Edward B Codwish," litho with color, orig purple cloth case, State of New York, Forest, Fish and Game Commission, 1911, three folded sections each measuring 45 × 15", broken tie 45.00

"Colton's Railroad & Township Map of...New York, with Parts of the Adjoining States & Canada, NY, G. W. & C. B. Colton & Co," 1871, hand-colored folding map, bit wrinkled in places, tears at intersection of some folds, laid into cloth covers 100.00

"Map of the Hudson between Sandy Hook & Sandy Hill with the Post Road between New York and Albany, A. T. Goodrich," drawn by Bridges, engraved by William Rollinson and published by A. T. Goodrich, 1820, cloth backed, fine silk-sewn edges, rolled and housed in crimson leather cov two-part tube with gilt stamp title and steamboat, 8' 2" × 9½", minor damage 1,400.00

Ohio, "Map of Ohio," engraving, hand colored, published in Columbus, 1822, John Kilbourne, barn-siding frame, 31 × 32" 650.00

Railroad, "Map Showing the Proposed Rail Roads from Boston to Burlington from Hale's Map of New England," Boston, JH Bufford, c1845, four alternative routes with mileage charts, 20 × 25" 65.00

Surveyor's, Hamilton County, IL, pen, ink, watercolor, and crayon on paper, modern gilt frame, 29½" h, 24¾" w 115.00

Texas, "Map of the State of Texas from the Latest Authorities," JH Young, published by Thomas, Cowperthwait, Philadelphia, c1852, multicolored, inset of Galveston City and Northern Texas, 17 × 14" 175.00

Tourist, "Newnes Motorists Touring Maps and Gazetteer," dj, 96 pgs of maps in color, 64 pgs of gazetteer, London, c1925, 8 × 10" 45.00

MARBLEHEAD POTTERY

History: This hand-thrown pottery was first made in 1905 as part of a therapeutic program introduced by Dr. J. Hall for the patients confined to a sanitarium located in Marblehead, Massachusetts.

In 1916 production was removed from the hospital to another site. The factory continued under the directorship of Arthur E. Baggs until it closed in 1936.

Most pieces found today are glazed with a smooth, porous, even finish in a single color. The most desirable pieces have a conventional design in one or more subordinate colors.

Bowl

6" d, 4" h, dark blue matte glaze, imp mark 425.00

6½" d, 3" h, olive green matte glaze, incised ribs and diagonals, imp mark 270.00

7" d, 2" w, modeled lotus leaves, blue matte 325.00

7¾" d, 3¾" h, flaring, even violet matte glaze, imp ship mark 300.00

9" d, matte green, glossy blue-green int., imp Marblehead logo 385.00

10" d, 3" h, dark blue, light blue int., imp mark 150.00

Chamberstick, 4" h, green matte glaze, imp mark, inked "1917" 250.00

Console Bowl, 12" d, light blue glaze, dark blue mottled rim and underside, imp Marblehead logo 275.00

Hanging Planter, 4" h, light purple matte glaze 190.00

Vase

3" h, light blue high glaze, pink int., imp mark 160.00

3¼" h, 3" d, ovoid, green leaves, blue grapes, speckled gray ground, Hanna Tutt, imp ship mark and "HT" 1,200.00

4" h

Broad-shouldered form, blue matte glaze, imp mark 100.00

Tapered form, purple matte glaze, imp mark 250.00

4½" h, 4" h

Cylindrical, stylized landscape, brown and green trees, mustard ground, imp ship mark, sgd "BT" in ink 3,800.00

Tapered form, blue matte glaze, imp mark 325.00

5¼" h, 4" d, pear shape, flared rim, fine even dark green matte finish, imp ship mark 475.00

6" h

Blue glaze, fan shape, emb rippled dec, imp Marblehead logo and partial paper label 385.00

Mustard matte glaze, incised ribs and diagonals, imp mark 270.00

Vase, tapered cylinder, blue matte glaze, 8" h, 4" d, $175.00.

6½" h, blue-gray matte glaze, base imp with glazed over logo 275.00

7" h, 3¾" d, corset shape, even green matte finish, imp ship mark 550.00

8¼" h, 3¾" h, cylindrical, closed rim and base, even blue matte glaze, imp ship mark 550.00

8½" h, 6" d, ovoid, medium brown pebbled matte finish, imp ship mark 1,100.00

9¼" h, 5" d, ovoid, dark blue matte glaze, imp ship mark 800.00

MARY GREGORY TYPE GLASS

History: The use of enameled decoration on glass, an inexpensive way to imitate cameo glass, developed in Bohemia in the late 19th century. The Boston and Sandwich Glass Co. copied this process in the late 1880s.

Mary Gregory (1856–1908) was employed for two years at the Boston and Sandwich Glass factory when the enameled decorated glass was being manufactured. Some collectors argue that Gregory was inspired to paint her white enamel figures on glass by the work of Kate Greenaway and a desire to imitate pate-sur-pate. However, evidence for these assertions is very weak. Further, it has never been proven that Mary Gregory even decorated glass as part of her job at Sandwich. The result is that "Mary Gregory type" is a better term to describe this glass.

Reference: R. and D. Truitt, *Mary Gregory Glassware: 1880–1990,* published by author, 1992.

Museum: Sandwich Glass Museum, Sandwich, MA.

Box, cov, dark amethyst ground, white enameled lady watering garden, floral band, 5½" d, $250.00.

REPRODUCTION ALERT

Collectors should recognize that most examples of Mary Gregory type glass seen today are either European or modern reproductions.

Atomizer, 5" h, tapering cylindrical body, cranberry, white enameled boy and girl facing each other 360.00

Biscuit Jar, cov

Clear, white enameled girl with posy basket, butterfly, IVT pattern 200.00

Emerald Green, white enameled cherub 270.00

Bottle, 9½" h, 2⅞" d, lavender stained ground, white enameled girl, champagne-colored faceted orig stopper 155.00

Box, hinged, round

2" d, 1" h, cobalt blue, white enameled little girl ... 225.00

3⅜" d, 3¼" h, amber, white enameled young boy on lid 275.00

4½" d, 3¾" h, lime green, white spray on base, white enameled detailed scene of girl standing by fence on lid 325.00

Cream Pitcher, 8" h, 3½" d, amber, sapphire blue wafer foot and applied handle, white enameled young girl 235.00

Cruet

8¾" h, 3" d, ftd spherical body, slender cylindrical neck, amber, white enameled young girl, applied amber handle, orig amber stopper 245.00

9½" h , 3" d, optic pattern, white enameled young boy, three-petal top, amber applied handle, orig amber bubble stopper 250.00

Decanter, 9½" h, 3½" d, ovoid body tapering to cylindrical neck, flat flaring rim, cushion foot, sapphire blue, white enameled young girl, orig blue bubble-shaped stopper 195.00

Dresser Box, cov, 6½" h, 3⅞" d, ovoid base, long teardrop-shaped finial, emerald green, white enameled young boy lying in grass 200.00

Ewer, 5" h, 3" d, spherical body, tall slender cylindrical neck, turquoise blue opaque, white enameled young girl, applied turquoise blue opaque handle 175.00

Lamp, kerosene

18" h, ftd urn shape, black, white enameled girl in flowing gown riding large butterfly, electrified .. 345.00

21½" h, 7" d, black base, white enameled scene of young boy, brass foot, font can and burner, orig clear ball shade and chimney 995.00

Mug, 4" h, 2½" d, barrel shape, amber, facing pair, white enameled girl on one, boy on other, applied amber handle, price for pr 130.00

Pitcher, 5" h, 3" d, green, white enameled boy holding flower, standing among lily-of-the-valleys, three-lobed rim, gold trim, applied green handle 175.00

Rose Bowl, 6½" d, 6½" h, green, white enameled boy with wings holding bird, surrounded by lattice and gold scrolls, polished pontil 225.00

Sugar, cov, 5" h, 3½" d, ftd spherical body, domed cov, knob finial, golden amber, white enameled young boy on bowl, floral trim on cov 200.00

Tumbler, 3⅜" h, 2¼" d, waisted cylindrical form, golden amber, white enameled young girl 70.00

Vase

3⅞" h, 2" d, bulbous, flaring cylindrical neck, cranberry, white enameled young girl 125.00

8" h, 3¼" d, pedestal foot, bulbous body tapering to cylindrical neck, cobalt blue, white enameled young girl 175.00

9¾" h, 4" d, ftd, cylindrical body, cupped flaring rim, dark amethyst, white enameled young girl wearing hat 210.00

10" h, 3⅝" d, sapphire blue, ruffled, white enameled young boy blowing bubbles **295.00**

11" h, 3⅜" d, slender waisted cylindrical body, lime green, white enameled young boy wearing suit . **85.00**

11½" h, 5" d, dark amethyst, white enameled young girls, one wearing hat and carrying basket of flowers, other rolling hoop with stick, price for facing pr **675.00**

13" h, 5" d, golden amber, pedestal ftd base, white enameled boy and girl blowing bubbles, price for facing pr **900.00**

MATCH HOLDERS

History: The friction match achieved popularity after 1850. The early matches were packaged and sold in sliding cardboard boxes. To facilitate storage and to eliminate the clumsiness of using the box, match holders were developed.

The first match holders were cast iron or tin, the latter often displaying advertisements. A patent for a wall-hanging match holder was issued in 1849. By 1880 match holders also were being made from glass and china. Match holders began to lose their popularity in the late 1930s with the advent of gas and electric heat and ranges.

Reference: Denis B. Alsford, *Match Holders,* Schiffer Publishing, 1994.

Advertising
Bliss Native Herbs, wall type, tin, Capitol **200.00**
Dr Shoop's Laxettes, wall type, tin **95.00**
La Confession Cuban Cigar, gentleman holding cigar, dark blue metal finish on tin, hinged lid **85.00**
Bisque, 8" h, figural, hunter with pipe, dog with bird in mouth, marked "Made in Germany," place for burnt matches, c1900 .... **115.00**
Brass, figural
Boot **35.00**
Dutch Boy, marked "England" **55.00**
Dutch Girl **55.00**
Bronze, 5½" h, guard dog beside bucket, losses **65.00**
Iron, 4½" h, traveling bear **50.00**

Noritake, desert and palm trees, purple horizon, orange sky, green mark, "M" in wreath, "Made in Japan," 3¾ × 3 × 2½", $60.00.

Glass
Clear, lady's head, striking surface, marked "Columbia" dated 1876 .... **75.00**
Custard, Winged Scroll pattern **100.00**
Silver, 1½" h, book form, metal matches on top, Gorham **75.00**
Silver-gilt, 1¾" l, rect form, transparent enameled blue over gillouchè ground, diamond set thumbpiece, marked with initials of Workmaster Henrik Wigstrom, "Fabergè" in Cyrillic and "88 standard," London 1910 import mark, St Petersburg **6,900.00**
Wood, 9½" h, hanging, chip-carved walnut, leaf shape, old alligatored finish **70.00**

MATCH SAFES

History: Match safes are small containers used to safely carry matches in one's pocket. They were first used in the 1850s. Match safes are often figural with a hinged lid and striking surface.

Reference: Audrey G. Sullivan, *A History of Match Safes in the United States,* published by author, 1978.

REPRODUCTION ALERT

Reproduction, copycat, and fantasy sterling silver match safes include:
Art Nouveau style nude with veil, rectangular case with C-scroll edges
Boot, figural
Embracing wood nymphs
Jack Daniels, 1970s fantasy item
Mermaid, with upper torso out of water, combing her hair
Owl and Moon
Many of these match safes are only marked "Sterling." Any match safe so marked requires careful inspection. Period American match safes generally are marked with the name of the manufacturer and/or a patent date. Period English match safes have the proper hallmarks. Beware of English reproduction match safes bearing the "DAB" marking.

Note: While not all match safes have a striking surface, this is one test, besides size, to distinguish a match safe from a calling card case.

Advertising, figural
Ceresota Flour, boy sitting on stool carving block of wood, feet resting on barrel of Ceresota Flour ... **250.00**
DeLaval, cream separator, two match compartments **300.00**
Number Five Cigar, brass, engraved floral pattern, lid **95.00**
Figural
Baby, in shirt **450.00**
Boy, crying, cobalt blue trim, bisque **130.00**
Bust, man **425.00**
Cat, in hat **450.00**
Elephant **650.00**
Girl, leaning on basket, pink, bisque **150.00**

Hobo	450.00
Japanese Fish	850.00
Lion	450.00
Man on pot	500.00
Pig	110.00
Rooster head	450.00
Gold, 14K yg, blue stone closure, sgd "Howard & Co," 2¼ × 1½", 19.4 dwt	345.00
Sterling Silver, Art Nouveau, floral dec, inscribed and dated 1898	125.00

Silver-plated, int. label "Compliments of G. F. Lyman/1462 Woodward Ave./Detroit, Mich.," 2½ × 1³/₁₆ × ³/₈", $30.00.

McCOY POTTERY

History: The J. W. McCoy Pottery Co. was established in Roseville, Ohio, in September 1899. The early McCoy company produced both stoneware and some art pottery lines, including Rosewood. In October 1911 three potteries merged creating the Brush-McCoy Pottery Co. This firm continued to produce the original McCoy lines and added several new art lines. Much of the early pottery is not marked.

In 1910, Nelson McCoy and his father, J. W. McCoy, founded the Nelson McCoy Sanitary Stoneware Co. In 1925 the McCoy family sold their interest in the Brush-McCoy Pottery Co. and started to expand and improve the Nelson McCoy Co. The new company produced stoneware, earthenware specialties, and artware.

Marks: Most of the pottery marked "McCoy" was made by the Nelson McCoy Co.

References: Susan and Al Bagdade, *Warman's American Pottery and Porcelain,* Wallace-Homestead, 1994; Bob Hanson, Craig Nissen and Margaret Hanson, *McCoy Pottery, Collector's Reference,* Collector Books, 1996; Sharon and Bob Huxford, *The Collectors Encyclopedia of McCoy Pottery,* Collector Books, 1980, 1995 value update; Dana G. Morykan and Harry L. Rinker, *Warman's Country Antiques & Collectibles,* Third Edition, Wallace-Homestead, 1996.

Periodicals: *NM Express,* 3081 Rock Creek Dr, Broomfield, CO 80020; *Our McCoy Matters,* PO Box 14255, Parkville, MO 64152.

Additional Listings: See *Warman's Ammericna & Collectibles* for more examples.

Basket, 9" h, leaves and red berries, high relief, glossy	75.00
Bowl, Amaryllis pattern, pastel	25.00
Cookie Jar, cov	
Hocus Pocus, gray and white	75.00
Kittens on Yarn Ball	75.00
Oaken Bucket	25.00
Cuspidor, brown	25.00
Ewer, 10" h, emb grapes and leaves, dark brown glaze, marked "Rosewood McCoy," c1905	200.00
Jardiniere, 11¾" d, 9" h, hp, tulip dec, marked "Loy-Nel-Art"	175.00
Lamp, boat, pink	35.00
Mug	
Barrel, brown	10.00
Blatz, brown	10.00
Tankard, brown	40.00
Pitcher, 7" h, water lilies on waves of water, stylized fish handle, high-glaze caramel, imp "30"	50.00
Planter	
Artisan, black glaze	12.00
Dog and cat at spinning wheel, brown and white high glaze, raised marks	45.00
Wishing Well	30.00
Punch Bowl, pedestal base, emb grapes and leaves, dark brown glaze, marked "Olympia JW McCoy"	375.00
Stein, Texas	10.00
Tea Set, green and brown high glaze, 9" w × 6" h pitcher, 6" l × 3" h creamer and sugar, repaired flake to teapot lid	100.00
Vase	
Double Tulip	55.00
Iris, yellow, tan, and brown blossoms, dark brown and green ground, Loy-Nel	140.00
Triple Tulip	65.00

Vase, turquoise ground, pink bead dec, marked "Brush-McCoy," 6" h, $85.00.

Wren house, McKee, gray body, red roof, $150.00.

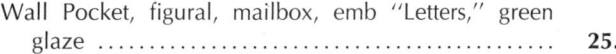

Wall Pocket, figural, mailbox, emb "Letters," green glaze 25.00

McKEE GLASS

History: The McKee Glass Co. was established in 1843 in Pittsburgh, Pennsylvania. In 1852 they opened a factory to produce pattern glass. In 1888 the factory was relocated to Jeannette, Pennsylvania, and began to produce many types of glass kitchenwares, including several patterns of Depression glass. The factory continued until 1951 when it was sold to the Thatcher Manufacturing Co.

McKee named its colors Chalaine Blue, Custard, Seville Yellow, and Skokie Green. McKee glass may also be found with painted patterns, e.g., dots and ships. A few items were decaled. Many of the canisters and shakers were lettered in black to show the purpose for which they were intended.

References: Gene Florence, *Kitchen Glassware of the Depression Years,* Sixth Edition, Collector Books, 1995; ————, *Very Rare Glassware of the Depression Years,* Third Series, (1993, 1995 value update), Fourth Series (1995), Collector Books.

Additional Listings: See *Warman's Americana & Collectibles* for more examples.

Baker, 5 × 7", oval, Skokie Green	17.50
Butter Dish, cov, rect, Seville Yellow	70.00
Clock, peacock blue, tambour shape	295.00
Decanter, pinched sides, Seville Yellow	75.00
Eggcup, Rock Crystal	15.00
Flour Shaker, Seville Yellow	25.00
Measuring Cup, Ships	25.00
Mixing Bowls, Ships, nested set of three	35.00
Reamer, Seville Yellow, grapefruit	175.00
Salt and Pepper Shakers, pr, Roman Arches, white, replaced tops	17.50
Tumbler and Coaster, Bottoms Up, Skokie Green	125.00

Wine

Rock Crystal	20.00
Sunk Buttons, blue	35.00

MEDICAL AND PHARMACEUTICAL ITEMS

History: Modern medicine and medical instruments are well documented. Some instruments are virtually unchanged since their invention; others have changed drastically.

The concept of sterilization phased out decorative handles. Handles on early instruments, which were often carved, were made of materials such as mother-of-pearl, ebony, and ivory. Today's sleek instruments are not as desirable to collectors.

Pharmaceutical items include those things commonly found in a drugstore and used to store or prepare medications.

References: A. Walker Bingham, *The Snake-Oil Syndrome: Patent Medicine Advertising,* Christopher Publishing House, 1994; Douglas Congdon-Martin, *Drugstore and Soda Fountain Antiques,* Schiffer Publishing, 1991; Patricia McDaniel, *Drugstore Collectibles,* Wallace-Homestead, 1994; Keith Wilbur, *Antique Medical Instruments: Revised Price Guide* Schiffer Publishing, 1987, 1993 value update.

Periodical: *Scientific, Medical & Mechanical Antiques,* 11824 Taneytown Pike, Taneytown, MD 21787.

Collectors' Clubs: Maryland Microscopical Society, 8621 Polk St, McLean, VA 22102; Medical Collectors Assoc, 1685A Eastchester Rd, Bronx, NY 10461.

Museums: Dittrick Museum of Medical History, Cleveland, OH; International Museum of Surgical Science & Hall of Fame, Chicago, IL; National Museum of Health & Medicine, Walter Reed Medical Center, Washington, DC; National Museum of History and Technology, Smithsonian Institution, Washington, DC; Schmidt Apothecary Shop, New England Fire & History Museum, Brewster, MA; Waring Historical Library, Medical University of South Carolina, Charleston, SC.

Advertising Trade Card, "Dr Harter's Iron Tonic, Confederate President Jefferson Davis," 1868	30.00

Apothecary Bottle

12" h, flared top, ground stopper, pontil, label, marked "PJ Gentian," c1850	325.00
15" h, deep amethyst, elongated form, bulbous stopper, labeled "R. Cincheo, Capsici," price for pr	270.00

Autograph, letter signed by Sigmund Freud, 2 pages, 3 × 5", personal correspondence card, Vienna, August

12, 1920, to nephew in German, regarding his book
Vorlesungen and mistakes in translation to English
edition **4,900.00**
Beaker, hand-blown glass, set of three graduated sizes   **195.00**
Blood Pressure Cuff, BD Manometer, cased, c1880 ...   **165.00**
Book
    Edwards, H M and P Vavasseur, *A Manual of Materia
    Medica and Pharmacy,* translated from French by
    Joseph Togno and E Durand, 5 × 7", orig speckled
    calf, 523 pgs, three fold-out tables, Carey, Lee &
    Carey, Phila, 1829, 1st ed, rubbed, both outer
    hinges broken **130.00**
    Townsend, Joseph, *Elements of Therapeutics: Or a
    Guide to Health; Being Cautions and Directions
    in the Treatment of Diseases...For the use of Stu-
    dents,* 5 × 7", orig full-calf binding, 612 pgs, Bos-
    ton, 1802 ....   **145.00**
Booklet, Dr Young's Rectal Dilator, 1920s **15.00**
Cabinet
    Mahogany facade, pine, dovetailed, forty-six draw-
    ers, wooden button knobs, four-base paneled
    doors, old finish, gilt and black labels, orig built-
    in, new plywood back, 73¼" w, 50¼" h **1,750.00**
    Pine, lift top, thirty-four bottles, int. drawer holds
    mortar and pestle, cased scales, and utensils, late
    19th C **325.00**
Catalog
    American Cabinet Co, Two Rivers, WI, 1930, 64 pgs,
    6 × 9", dental office furniture **75.00**
    Bausch & Lomb Optical Co., Rochester, NY, 1911,
    40 pages, 6½ × 9¾" h, Physicians' Laboratory
    Equipment, microscopes, blood apparatus, steril-
    izers **115.00**
    LW Cutting & H Steele, Jerseyville, IL, 1885, 24
    pages, 4¾" x 7", invalid lifters, illus of apparatus
    in use **75.00**
Display Case, Dr West's Toothbrush, counter type, glass
    front **375.00**
Doctor's Case, leather, pocket type, four 3¼" h glass vials
    with screw caps, 4¼ × 4½" **20.00**
Ear Speculum, 3 pc, silver, cased horn, American, c1860   **90.00**
Eye Cup, cobalt blue, Depression era glass **18.50**
Inhaler, Vapo-Cresolene, orig parts and box including
    bottle of medicine, c1895 ....   **325.00**
Label Cabinet, 27¾ × 15¾", wood, sixty-one rolls of
    labels **1,000.00**
Medicine Dispenser, 10 × 16", vaseline glass, cylinder
    shape, blown mold with texture, metal spigot and lid,
    emb on front "Radium Vitalizer," marked "Radium
    Assn-Chicago, Ill" **425.00**
Membership Book, *Book of General Membership of the
    Ralston Health Club,* containing doctrine, 183 pages,
    1897, Washington, DC, 6 × 9" **30.00**
Mortar, crescent-shaped cast iron, disk-shaped pestle
    with wooden handles, wooden frame, made for
    grinding herbs **1,485.00**
Quack Machine, electric shock, acid batteries, c1865 .   **165.00**
Retinascope, ivory handle, English, c1880 ....   **30.00**
Sign, carved wooden stethoscope and black bag with
    name "R. Murton MD" in gilt stencil, red and black
    lettering "Consultations, Rooms and Surgery" **750.00**
Surgeon's Kit, 3¾ × 15 × 7" refinished walnut case,

"C. Williams & Co., Baltimore, MD," three lift-out
    trays, sixty-one probes, picks, scalpels, forty-seven
    with ivory handles, few sgd "Williams,"others sgd
    "Weiss or Leiter," rest with metal handles, lock miss-
    ing, cracks to case, oval inlay replaced **1,100.00**
Veterinarian's Bleeder, blade in gun with cock, brass,
    orig box, c1850 ....   **380.00**

MEDICINE BOTTLES

History: The local apothecary and his book of formulas played a
major role in early America. In 1796 the first patent for a medicine
was issued by the U.S. Patent Office. At that time, anyone could
apply for a medicinal patent; as long as the dosage was not poisonous, the patent was granted.

Patent medicines were advertised in newspapers and magazines and sold through the general store and at "medicine" shows.
In 1907 the Pure Food and Drug Act, requiring an accurate description of contents on a medicine container's label, put an end
to the patent medicine industry. Not all medicines were patented.

Most medicines were sold in distinctive bottles, often with the
name of the medicine and location of manufacture in relief. Many
early bottles were made in the glass-manufacturing area of southern New Jersey. Later, companies in western Pennsylvania and
Ohio manufactured bottles.

References: Joseph K. Baldwin, *A Collector's Guide to Patent and
Proprietary Medicine Bottles of the Nineteenth Century,* Thomas
Nelson, 1973; Ralph and Terry Kovel, *The Kovels' Bottles Price
List,* Tenth Edition, Crown Publishers, 1996; John Odell, *Digger
Odell's Official Antique Bottle and Glass Collector Magazine
Price Guide Series,* Vol. 5, published by author (1910 Shawhan
Rd, Morrow, OH 45152), 1995.

Periodical: *Antique Bottle and Glass Collector,* PO Box 187, East
Greenville, PA 18041.

Collectors' Club: Federation of Historical Bottle Collectors, Inc,
88 Sweetbriar Branch, Longwood, FL 32750.

Alternative Syrup, Pike & Osgood, rect, olive-amber, ap-
    plied tapered lip, pontil base, Stoddard Glassworks,
    NH, c1850, 8¾" h **2,000.00**
Bennet's Magic Cure, sq, beveled edges, deep blue, ap-
    plied sq collar lip, smooth base, c1865, 5⅛" h **375.00**
Brant's Purifying Extract, rect, indented panels, aqua,
    applied double-collar lip, open-pontil base, c1850,
    10⅛" h **200.00**
Cellinian Balm, round, aqua, rolled lip, open-pontil
    base, c1850, 4⅜" h **50.00**
Dr Davis Depurative, sq, beveled edges, medium yel-
    low-green, applied tapered lip, iron-pontil base,
    c1850, 5¾" h **650.00**
Dr Leroy's Mixture, round, aqua, applied tapered lip,
    pontil base, c1850, 7½" h **165.00**
Gregory's Instant Cure, sq, indented panels, bluish aqua,
    applied tapered lip, open-pontil base, c1850, 6⅜" h   **725.00**
Howards Vegetable Cancer and Canker Syrup, rect, bev-
    eled edges, olive-yellow, applied sq collar lip, open-
    pontil base, c1850, 7⅜" h **2,500.00**
Mrs S A Allen's World's Hair Restorer, rect, indented
    panels, purplish-amethyst, sq tooled lip, c1870,
    7¼" h **125.00**

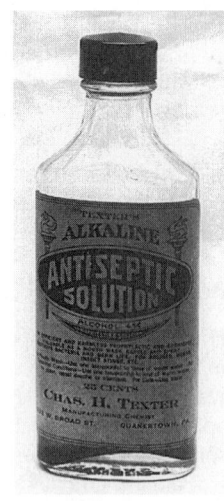

Texter's Alkaline Antiseptic Solution, 25 cents, Chas. H. Texter, manufacturing chemist, 1232 W. Broad St., Quakertown, Pa., blue letters, 5½" h, 2¼" w, $2.00.

Smith's Green Mountain Renovator, rect, beveled edges, olive-amber, applied double-ring lip, pontil base, c1850, 7" h	675.00
Swaim's Genuine Panacea, rect, beveled edges, aqua, applied tapered lip, open-pontil base, c1830, 7¾" h	250.00
True Daffy's Elixir, rect, beveled edges, yellow-green, applied ring lip, ball-pontil base, England, c1830, 4⅞" h	350.00
USA Hosp Dept, round, aqua, sq tooled lip, smooth base, c1865, 9⅛" h	250.00
Warner's Safe Cure, oval shape, golden amber, applied lip, smooth base, c1870, 9½" h	175.00

MERCURY GLASS

History: Mercury glass is a light-bodied, double-walled glass that was "silvered" by applying a solution of silver nitrate to the inside of the object through a hole in its base.

F. Hale Thomas of London patented the method in 1849. In 1855 the New England Glass Co. filed a patent for the same type of process. Other American glassmakers soon followed. The glass reached the height of its popularity in the early 20th century.

Candlesticks, pr, 11" h, enameled floral dec	125.00
Candy Dish, cov, 8¼" h, 4¼" d, clear dome cov, pedestal base	35.00
Compote	150.00
Creamer, 6¾" h, Sandwich Glass Co, etched grapevine dec, applied clear handle	125.00

Salt, individual, 3 applied clear feet, 1¾" d, 1¼" h, $32.50.

Curtain Tiebacks, pr, 2½" d	45.00
Rose Bowl, silver, ribbed ext.	95.00
Salt, 2⅞" d, 2½" h, master, silver ext., gold int., pedestal foot, initials on plug	95.00
Toothpick Holder, white enameled floral dec, gold int.	45.00
Urn, 13" h, baluster shape, marked "Harrish & Co, London"	250.00
Vase, 10½" h, cylindrical body, hp floral and leaf band around center, price for pr	115.00
Wig Stand, 10¼" h, two pieces, ball reattached to base	330.00

METTLACH

History: In 1809 Jean Francis Boch established a pottery at Mettlach in Germany's Moselle Valley. His father had started a pottery at Septfontaines in 1767. Nicholas Villeroy began his pottery career at Wallerfanger in 1789.

In 1841 these three factories merged. They pioneered underglaze printing on earthenware, using transfers from copper plates, and also were among the first companies to use coal-fired kilns. Other factories were developed at Dresden, Wadgassen, and Danischburg. Mettlach decorations include relief and etched designs, prints under the glaze, and cameos.

Marks: The castle and Mercury emblems are the two chief marks although secondary marks are known. The base of each piece also displays a shape mark and usually a decorator's mark.

References: Susan and Al Bagdade, *Warman's English & Continental Pottery & Porcelain,* Second Edition, Wallace-Homestead, 1991; Gary Kirsner, *The Mettlach Book,* Third Edition, Glentiques, 1994.

Periodical: *The Beer Stein Journal,* PO Box 8807, Coral Springs, FL 33075.

Collectors' Clubs: Stein Collectors International, 281 Shore Dr, Burr Ridge, IL 60521; Sun Steiners, PO Box 11782, Fort Lauderdale, FL 33339.

Additional Listings: Villeroy & Boch.

Note: Prices in this listing are for print-under-glaze pieces unless otherwise specified.

Advertising Mug, 4¼" h, Drink Hires Root Bear, happy child	65.00
Beaker, .25L, color	
#2327-236, man with pipe, browns	185.00
#2327-1176, Spiel-Gambling, light color transfer	115.00
#2327-1200	
Breslau	155.00
Hannover	125.00
Kohn	175.00
#2327-1299, State of Indiana	165.00
#2327-1302, American eagle with flag, small chip repair	140.00
Charger, 17¼" d, #2561, castle scene	300.00
Coaster, 4¾" d, #1032, color, dwarfs, price for pr	360.00

Flowerpot, 6½" h, early style, #237, brown, tan, and platinum, marbleized finish cov with vines, strong colors 95.00

Plaque

7½ × 8¾", oval, green ground, detailed raised white cameo of woman, pierced for hanging, castle mark   450.00

7¾" d, #2625, etched, color, cavalier, terra-cotta background 220.00

12" d, color

#1044-94, Altes Stadtthor Cochem, strong colors   250.00

#1044-196, Stolzenfelz 300.00

#1044-217, Schlosshof Heidelberg 215.00

#1044-481, Porta Nigra Trier 300.00

17" d, etched castle on the Rhine, gold border, castle mark

#1108, dated 1907 .... 920.00

#1365, dated 1909 .... 920.00

Punch Bowl, cov, under plate, blue mid band with raised cream figures, mask and branch handles 475.00

Soup Tureen, cov, under plate, #418, 14" w handle to handle, figural handles, floral relief, finial repair ... 525.00

Wine tureen, castle mark, marked "Mettlach 2234," $750.00.

Stein

Gentleman and bar maiden, pewter Indian thumb grip 425.00

#1786, one-liter size, etched dec, St Florian putting out fire, tiered steeple-shaped lid, 9¾" h 490.00

#1816, ³⁄₁₀ liter, brown, amber, blue, and cream jewel-like glaze, pewter lid with ceramic insert, marked "Mettlach #1816" 165.00

#1983, ¼ liter, multicolored floral scrolls, 5½" h .. 300.00

#2001, ½ liter, leather-bound book type, pewter hawk thumb-grip handle, 7" h 650.00

#2211, ³⁄₁₀ liter, white relief revelers, sky blue ground, 6" h, price for pr 325.00

#2784, ½ liter, painted underglaze, Man with Soft Hat, tapered cylindrical shape, brown glaze, pewter lid, 15" h 575.00

Stemware, ¼ liter, blue tin glaze garden dec, price for pr   **325.00**

Tray, 11" d, #1328, etched and glazed, repeating design   **135.00**

Urn, 10" h, #1898, three ftd, dec band and angels in relief, price for pr **550.00**

Wall Plate, 12¼" d, Caub, Rolandseck, Tellskapelle landscape, price for 3-pc set **275.00**

MILITARIA

History: Wars have occurred throughout recorded history. Until the mid-19th century soldiers often had to provide for their own needs, including supplying their own weapons. Even in the 20th century a soldier's uniform and some of his gear are viewed as his personal property, even though issued by a military agency.

Conquering armed forces made a habit of acquiring souvenirs from their vanquished foes. They also brought their own uniforms and accessories home as badges of triumph and service.

Saving militaria may be one of the oldest collecting traditions. Militaria collectors tend to have their own special shows and view themselves outside the normal antiques channels. However, they haunt small indoor shows and flea markets in hopes of finding additional materials.

References: Robert W. D. Ball, *British Army Campaign Medals,* Antique Trader Books, 1996; Thomas Berndt, *Standard Catalog of U. S. Military Vehicles,* Krause Publications, 1993; Ray A. Bows, *Vietnam Military Lore 1959–1973,* Bows & Sons, 1988; Gary R. Carpenter, *What's It Worth: A Beginner Collector's Guide to U.S. Army Patches of WW II,* published by author, 1994; W. K. Cross, *The Charlton Standard Catalogue of First World War Canadian Corps Badges,* Charlton Press, 1995; ———, *The Charlton Standard Catalogue of First World War Canadian Infantry Badges,* Second Edition, Charlton Press, 1995; Robert Fisch, *Field Equipment of the Infantry 1914–1945,* Greenberg Publications, 1989; Richard Friz, *Official Price Guide to Civil War Collectibles,* House of Collectibles, 1995; Gary Howard, *America's Finest: U.S. Airborne Uniforms, Equipment and Insignia of World War Two (ETO),* Greenhill Books, Stackpole Books, 1994.

Jon A. Maguire, *Silver Wings, Pinks & Greens: Uniforms, Wings, & Insignia of USAAF Airmen in World War II,* Schiffer Publishing, 1994; Jon A. Maguire and John P. Conway, *Art of the Flight Jacket,* Schiffer Publishing, 1995; Ron Manion, *American Military Collectibles Price Guide,* Antique Trader Books, 1995; ———, *German Military Collectibles Price Guide,* Antique Trader Books, 1995; *North South Trader's Civil War Collector's Price Guide,* Fifth Edition, North South Trader's Civil War, 1991; Harry Rinker, Jr., and Robert Heistand, *World War II Collectibles,* Running Press, Courage Books, 1993; *Schuyler, Hartley & Graham Illustrated Catalog of Civil War Military Goods* (reprint of 1864 catalog), Dover Publications, n.d.; Sydney B. Vernon, *Vernon's Collectors' Guide To Orders, Medals, and Decorations,* published by author, 1986; Ron L. Willis and Thomas Carmichael, *United States Navy Wings of Gold,* Schiffer Publishing, 1995; Richard Windrow and Tim Hawkins, *The World War II GI, U.S. Army Uniforms,* Motorbooks International, 1993.

Periodicals: *Men at Arms,* 222 W Exchange St, Providence, RI 02903; *Militaria Magazine,* PO Box 995, Southbury, CT 06488; *Military Collector Magazine,* PO Box 245, Lyon Station, PA 19536; *Military Collector News,* PO Box 702073, Tulsa, OK 74170; *Military Images,* RD1 Box 99A, Henryville, PA 18332; *Military Trader,* PO Box 1050, Dubuque, IA 52004; *North South*

Trader's Civil War, PO Drawer 631, Orange, VA 22960; *Wildcat Collectors Journal,* 15158 NE 6th Ave, Miami, FL 33162; *WWII Military Journal,* PO Box 28906, San Diego, CA 92198.

Collectors' Clubs: American Society of Military Insignia Collectors, 526 Lafayette Ave, Palmerton, PA 18071; Assoc of American Military Uniform Collectors, PO Box 1876, Elyria, OH 44036; Company of Military Historians, North Main Street, Westbrook, CT, 06498; Imperial German Military Collectors Association, 82 Atlantic St, Keyport, NJ 07735; Karabiner Collector's Network, PO Box 5773, High Point, NC 27262; Militaria Collectors Society, 137 S Almar Dr, Ft Lauderdale, FL 33334; Orders and Medals Society of America, PO Box 484, Glassboro, NJ 08028.

Reproduction Alert: Pay careful attention to Civil War and Nazi material.

Additional Listings: Firearms, Nazi, and Swords. See World War I and World War II in *Warman's Americana & Collectibles* for more examples.

SPECIAL AUCTION

Jackson's Auctioneers & Appraisers
2229 Lincoln St
Cedar Falls, IA 60613
(319) 277-2256
e-mail: jacksons@corenet.net

French and Indian War

Enlistment Document, 1-pg small oblong 8vo, Hampshire County, Massachusetts, April 6, 1759, for Ebenezer Warner who volunteered "in the present Expedition forming for the invasion of Canada" **675.00**

Powder Horn, 13¼" l, dark at nozzle, scalloped carved border, 10" l mellow light tan and faint yellow-colored engraved surface, 4⅜" long single-masted schooner fitted with three very old jibs, sides of ship with ten gun ports, three engraved fish, engraved crown over "GR," four engraved lines "Amos:Avery:His:Horn:1758/Stel:Not:This:Horn:For:Fear:/Of:Shame:For:On:It:Is:Rit/The Owners:Name," below lettering is standing shooter/hunter, two fish, decorative pattern, and big bird, slightly curved wooden plug, two very old forged nails, light yellow age patina **3,550.00**

Revolutionary War

Autograph
  Letter signed
    Adams, John, 1-pg 4to, The Hague, Oct 1, 1782, to John Jay in Paris, written while both were in Europe to negotiate peace with Great Britain **16,000.00**
    Arnold, Benedict, 2-pg folio, London, April 30, 1787, writing for assistance with business affairs, detailing travel plans from London to St John, Canada, insight into scorn and financial difficulties **6,800.00**

Note signed, back of a three-of-spades playing card, Aug 11, 1778, permit to pass through lines issued to army wagon driver **550.00**

Broadside, 1-pg small folio, Hartford, Nov 29, 1780, printed by Hudson & Goodwin, recruiting Connecticut regiment of 575 soldiers **1,200.00**

Document Signed
  Bond, 1⅓-pgs small folio, Cambridge, Massachusetts, Nov 4, 1777, to Seth Sumner to supply provisions to British brought to Boston Market, sgd by Sumner and several witnesses **1,250.00**
  Commission, 1-pg oblong small folio, Boston, July 13, 1780, to David Holbrook as Captain of 4th Regiment of Foot, sgd by James Bowdoin as President of the Mass Provincial Council, intact MA paper seal **975.00**
  Oath of Allegiance, partially printed, 6¼ × 2¾" oblong, printed in Lancaster, PA, "...voluntarily taken and subscribed by the Oak Affirmation of Allegiance and Fidelity, as directed by an Act of General Assembly of Pennsylvania, passed the 13th Day of June, A.D. 1777" **275.00**
  Pay Voucher, part printed, part manuscript, approx 6½ × 7½", sgd by "Jed[ediah] Huntington, Major General in the Continental Army," 1789 .... **55.00**

Civil War

Bond, United States Confederate, 1864, $500 face value, coupons, 34 × 22" **100.00**

Book, *Eighteen Months a Prisoner under the Rebel Flag,* SS Boggs, 1887 .... **55.00**

Broadside, "The Great Rebellion," musical performance **45.00**

Cabinet Card
  Admiral Farragut, full dress, sword, Sarony **225.00**
  Fort Marion, St Augustine, FL, oversized **45.00**

Chair, camp, folding, orig carpet seat **90.00**

Clothing, frock coat, officer's NY militia, blue piping, excelsior buttons **350.00**

Diary, pocket, Union Soldier, Elias B. Tschopp, L Co., 16th Penna Cavalry, 180-pg small 12mo, orig red leather binding, entire year of 1864, over 177 pgs of daily entries including information on troop movements, fighting, routine duties, weather, unusual occurrences, few pgs of notes and accounts for clothing **1,600.00**

Document Signed
  Arthur, Chester A, Collector in the port of New York, 1-pg oblong 8vo, March 11, 1875, witnessing oath of office for John H Davison as Customs Inspector, according to Civil War–era act of July 2, 1862, bold and dark signatures **975.00**
  Hamilton Guards to women of Hamilton County thanking them for flag which they sewed and donated **75.00**

Lance Pennant, 8' wooden shaft, silk guidon, Confederate, silk fragile and with some damage **9,500.00**

Muster Roll, Union, 28th Regiment of PA Volunteers, Company B, 1½-pg long oblong folio, Chancellorsville, VA, April 30, 1863, covers Feb 28 to April 30, lists fourteen officers, two drummers, wagoner, fifty-one privates, three men discharged, chart form, ten-line record of events, fold wear **450.00**

Stereo View
 Anthony, Rebel Artillery Soldier's, killed in trenches
  of Fort Mahone, two dead soldiers, horse **180.00**
 Taylor, Brady view of Confederate prisoners on way
  to rear guard **95.00**
Sword, presentation, 38¼" l, Ames Mfr Co, Chicopee,
 MA, mid-19th C, gilt brass hilt dec with sculptured
 eagle, military trophies, and liberty cap centering
 reeded ivory grip, engraved blade dec with scrolls,
 oak leaves, flags, eagle, and bow and quiver, marked
 on scabbard and blade, minor imperfections **1,380.00**
Tintype
 1⅞ × 2¹/₁₆", head and shoulders of young lad in
  uniform, plastic case marked "S Peck & Co. A
  Union Case Improved" **110.00**
 3⅜ × 3¾", soldier posing with unsheathed sword,
  Army tents in background, c1861, plastic case
  marked "S Peck & Co, The Crossed Cannons" .. **290.00**
Watercolor, 22¾" h, 18½" w, full-length portrait of veteran, William J Night, member of Andrews Raiders,
 wearing medal of honor, identifying information on
 back, lower right sgd "A.G. 1897," paper backed on
 stretched canvas, minor paper damage, small tear,
 inlaid frame **110.00**

World War I

Bayonet, Remington, case, 1917 .... **90.00**
Buckle, US Balloon Corps, emb hot-air balloon **30.00**
Flare Pistol, French, marked "Modele 1918" **125.00**
Map Case, leather, strap, nine orig tour maps of France **45.00**
Measure, angle, US Army Engineer's Corps, case, 1916 **45.00**
Saddle Cloth, 7th Cavalry, yellow trim, blue felt, worn **150.00**
Sheet Music
 After the War is Over, 1917 .... **4.00**
 Au Revoir, But Not Goodbye, Soldier Boy, 1917 ... **7.50**
 How 'Ya Gonna Keep 'em Down on the Farm After
  They've Seen Paree?, 1919 .... **5.00**
 Madelon, I'll Be True to the Whole Regiment, 1919 **6.00**
 Since Katy the Waitress Became An Aviatress, 1919 **8.00**
 We're All Going Calling on the Kaiser, 1918 .... **8.00**
Trench Art, fluted and hammered artillery shells, 14" h,
 price for matched pr **100.00**
Uniform
 Army, wool blouse, 4th M.G. Battalion discs, ma-
  chine gun, pin, trousers with ankle laces **225.00**
 Captain's, tunic and trousers, collar insignia, cap-
  tain's bars, 2nd division patch **295.00**
 Enlisted Man's, dress blues, tunic and trousers, no
  pockets **175.00**

World War II

Button, Royal Air Force, brass, emb wings and king's
 crown **5.00**
Flyers Goggles, Japanese, gray fur-lined cups, yellow
 lenses, boxed **15.00**
Knife, side, Imperial German, leather scabbard, well
 marked **75.00**
Medal, St Christopher, USMC **32.00**
Plate, General Marshall surrounded by Allied Nations
 flags **30.00**

World War II, blotter, U.S. Marines Women's Reserve, recruitment message, 1943, 4 × 9", $8.00.

Tunic, flight, German Luftwaffe **200.00**
Wings
 Army Air Corp, SS
  AVG, American Volunteer Group, Flying Tigers . **250.00**
  WASP, Women Army Service Pilots **265.00**
  Gunner's, 1st Model, open G **100.00**

MILK GLASS

History: Opaque white glass attained its greatest popularity at the end of the 19th century. American glass manufacturers made opaque white tablewares as a substitute for costly European china and glass. Other opaque colors, e.g., blue and green, also were made. Production of milk glass novelties came in with the Edwardian era.

The surge of popularity in milk glass subsided after World War I. However, milk glass continues to be made in the 20th century. Some modern products are reissues and reproductions of earlier forms. This presents a significant problem for collectors, although it is partially obviated by patent dates or company markings on the originals and by the telltale signs of age.

Collectors favor milk glass from the pre–World War I era, especially animal-covered dishes. The most prolific manufacturers of these animal covers were Atterbury, Challinor-Taylor, Flaccus, and McKee.

References: E. McCamley Belknap, *Milk Glass,* Crown Publishers, 1949, out-of-print; Regis F. and Mary F. Ferson, *Today's Prices for Yesterday's Milk Glass,* published by authors, 1985; ———, *Yesterday's Milk Glass Today,* published by authors, 1981; Everett Grist, *Covered Animal Dishes,* Collector Books, 1988, 1993 value update; Lorraine Kovar, *Westmoreland Glass,* 2 vols., Antique Publications, 1991; S. T. Millard, *Opaque Glass,* Fourth Edition, Wallace Homestead, 1975, out of print; Betty and Bill Newbound, *Collector's Encyclopedia of Milk Glass,* Collector Books, 1995.

Collectors' Club: National Milk Glass Collectors Society, 46 Almond Dr, Hershey, PA 17033.

Museum: Houston Antique Museum, Chattanooga, TN.

Notes: There are many so-called "McKee" animal-covered dishes. Caution must be exercised in evaluating pieces because some authentic covers were not signed. Furthermore, many factories have made, and many still are making, split-rib bases with McKee-like animal covers or with different animal covers. The prices below are for authentic McKee pieces with either the cover or base signed.

Numbers in listings prefixed with a letter refer to books listed in the references, wherein the letter identifies the first letter of the author's name.

Bottle, Statue of Liberty, 10" h, orig pewter cup cov, F-#431	235.00
Bowl, heart shape, purple flowers, Consolidated Glass Co	75.00
Compote, Jenny Lind, high standard, Atterbury, B-34	65.00
Creamer, Grape and Leaf, Northwood, multicolored dec	75.00
Cruet, Tree of Life, Challinor, green opaque	145.00

Dish, cov

American Hen, B-162a	60.00
Automobile, windshield chip, M-324b	65.00
Cruiser	70.00
Deer on Fallen Tree, Flaccus, shallow rim flakes, B-174a	250.00
Dog, 5½" l, wide rib base, blue and white, B-174b	90.00
Hand & Dove, dated with stone, B-163b	120.00
Hen, white, blue head and eyes, lacy base, 7" l, M-267a	140.00
Melon shape	135.00
Moses in Bulrushes, B-160	200.00
Pear, PV	120.00
Prairie Schooner	135.00
Quail, B-179b	45.00
Scottie Dog, blue, AA	95.00
Squirrel, blue, PV	85.00
Trunk, straps, base corner chip, B-165c	25.00
Dresser Box, cov, 4" d, horseshoe and horse's head	75.00
Inkwell, Minstrel, match holder	115.00
Jar, cov, Owl, tall, Atterbury	110.00
Lamp, oil, Log Cabin, large size	775.00

Match Holder

Chick and rabbit, hanging, M-196b	40.00
Cornucopia, paint dec, M-187d	20.00
Paneled Grape, hanging, octagonal	35.00
Paneled Rib, gilt trim, M-178b	20.00
Pipe, M-201c	20.00
Miniature Lamp, clear base	100.00
Mug, Ceres	45.00
Nappy, Oval Prism, Atterbury	22.00
Pitcher, Scroll, tall, CT	68.00
Planter, Crocus, Fostoria	55.00

Plate

Abe Lincoln	75.00
Anchor & Yacht, B-13a	30.00
Ancient Castle, B-12e	30.00
Angel & Harp, B-11c	25.00
Contrary Mule, B-12b	30.00
Cupid & Psyche, B-6b	30.00
Hand Painted, yellow and green bird, closed lattice border, 10½" d, B-31	85.00
Jefferson Davis	90.00
Niagara Falls, B-43	25.00
No Easter without Us, Rooster	60.00
Open lattice, robin dec	75.00
Serenade, B-9c	30.00
Three Owls, patent date 1901, B-10c	48.00
Woof Woof, B-13f	40.00

Salt and Pepper Shakers, pr

Acorns	70.00
Rabbit and hen, red and gold paint	62.00
Salt, flying fish, flake, M-102c	45.00
Shaving Mug, 6¼" l, busts of Pres Garfield and Mrs Lucretia Randolph Garfield, rim-point flakes	250.00
Spooner, Apple Blossom, dec	95.00
Sugar Shaker, Grape, M-187c	40.00
Toothpick Holder, Monkey	30.00

MILLEFIORI

History: Millefiori (thousand flowers) is an ornamental glass composed of bundles of colored glass rods fused together into canes. The canes were pulled to the desired length while still ductile, sliced, arranged in a pattern, and fused together again. The Egyptians developed this technique in the first century B.C. it was revived in the 1880s.

Reproduction Alert: Millefiori items, such as paperweights, cruets, and toothpicks, are being made by many modern companies.

Miniature lamp, Paneled Cosmos, white, pink trim, $220.00.

Vase, purple bands with white oval lines, white bands with red flowers with red centers, 5½" h, $140.00.

Bowl, 2" d, pink, green, and white canes, applied handles 40.00

Cruet, applied camphor handle, clear bubble stopper . 85.00

Goblet, 7½" h, deeply rounded bowl, everted rim, multicolored floral canes, hollow gilt-speckled baluster stem, circ foot, Venetian, price for 6-pc set 1,200.00

Inkwell, 4½" h, sgd "Paul Ysart" 195.00

Lamp, 12½" h, 4" d base, 6½" d dome shade, pre WWII 795.00

Rose Bowl, ruffled 155.00

Slipper, 5" l, multicolored canes, applied camphor glass ruffled and heel 100.00

Sugar, cov, 3½" h, 4" d, cobalt blue, white flowers 115.00

Vase, 5½" h, purple bands, white oval lines, white bands, red flowers with yellow centers 150.00

MINIATURE LAMPS

History: Miniature oil and kerosene lamps, often called "night lamps," are diminutive replicas of larger lamps. Simple and utilitarian in design, miniature lamps found a place in the parlor (as "courting" lamps), hallway, children's rooms, and sickrooms.

Miniature lamps are found in many glass types, from amberina to satin glass. Miniature lamps measure 2½ to 12 inches in height, with the principle parts being the base, collar, burner, chimney, and shade. In 1877 both L. J. Atwood and L. H. Olmsted patented burners for miniature lamps. Their burners made the lamps into a popular household accessory.

References: Frank R. and Ruth E. Smith, *Miniature Lamps* (1981), Book II (1982) Schiffer Publishing; John F. Solverson, *Those Fascinating Little Lamps: Miniature Lamps and Their Values,* Antique Publications, 1988, includes prices for Smith numbers.

Collectors' Club: Night Light, 38619 Wakefield Ct, Northville, MI 48167.

REPRODUCTION ALERT

Study a lamp carefully to make certain all parts are original; married pieces are common. Reproductions abound.

Note: The numbers given below refer to the figure numbers found in the Smith books.

Figure III-I, Artichoke, milk glass, white, yellow, and green fired-on paint, nutmeg burner, 7¾" h, minor flaking at top of shade 250.00

Figure XVIII-II, overshot, frosted, house scene, 5½" 750.00

#23-I, Time, clear, emb "Time and Light, Pride of America, Grand Vals Perfect Time Indicating Lam," white beehive chimney, 6⅝" h 265.00

#36-I, Little Buttercup, amethyst, applied handle, nutmeg burner, 2¾" h 100.00

#109-I, Beaded Heart, green, six-toed foot, acorn burner, 5⅜" h 315.00

#112-I, Bull's-Eye, emerald green, acorn burner, 4⅞" h 100.00

#161-II, Prism, emb Atterbury 150.00

#209-I, white milk glass, emb design and flowers, multicolored paint, nutmeg burner, 9½" h 150.00

#482, Daisy & Cube, green glass, $275.00.

#228-II, amber, 5⅞" h 125.00

#276-I, Pineapple in the Basket, white milk glass, fired-on brown paint, ruffled burner, 7⅜" h 175.00

#288-I, red satin glass, emb designs, P & A Victor burner, 11½" h 300.00

#317-I, white milk glass base and shade, green ground, pink and yellow daisy dec, nutmeg burner, 8½" h .. 375.00

#385-I, peachblow, 6⅞" h, chips on shade rim 440.00

#390-I, bright yellow, melon-ribbed shade and base, glossy finish, nutmeg burner, 7" h 525.00

#425-I, irid green, emb dec, nutmeg burner, 9¾" h ... 450.00

#458-II, white milk glass, heavily emb daisies and leaves, large white milk glass balls around base 400.00

#467-II, blue opal, applied clear feet, foreign burner, 7¾" h 325.00

#513-I, Swirl, blue opal, acorn burner, 4¾" h 165.00

#534-I, satin, canary, DQ, brass collar and burner, clear chimney, 2¾" h 165.00

MINIATURE PAINTINGS

History: Prior to the advent of the photograph, miniature portraits and silhouettes were the principal way of preserving a person's image. Miniaturists were plentiful, and they often made more than one copy of a drawing. The extras were distributed to family and friends.

Miniaturists worked in watercolors and oil and on surfaces such as paper, vellum, porcelain, and ivory. The miniature paintings were often inserted into jewelry or mounted inside or on the lids of snuff boxes. The artists often supplemented commission work by painting popular figures of the times and copying important works of art.

After careful study miniature paintings have been divided into schools, and numerous artists are now being researched. Many fine examples may be found in today's antiques marketplace.

Reference: Dale T. Johnson, *American Portrait Miniatures in the Manney Collection,* The Metropolitan Museum of Art, 1990.

Museum: Gibbes Museum of Art, Charleston, SC.

1⅜" h, oval, Admiral Sir George Rook, painted en grisaille, metal surround inscribed, back with woven hair and seed pearls, English School, 19th C 300.00

1½" h

Beautiful woman wearing tiara, ornate gilt-brass standing-type frame, ribbon bows and flowers, on ivory, Continental School, 19th C **195.00**

Elegant woman, watercolor on ivory, framed, sgd "Paulin," Continental School **245.00**

2" h, woman in plumed hat, ornate gilt-brass standing-type frame, ribbon bows and flowers, Continental School, 19th C **215.00**

2" h, 1½" w

Caleb Crane, age 4, unsigned, watercolor on ivory, giltwood frame, American School, 19th C **435.00**

Louis XV, on ivory, gilt-brass and ivory-clad frame, French School, 19th C **210.00**

2¼" h

Bare-breasted woman, blue Limoges enamel frame, French School, 19th C **400.00**

Elegant woman, watercolor on ivory, framed

After Dumas, Continental School, 19th C **250.00**

Sgd "Duistraus," Continental School **250.00**

Napoleon Bonaparte, after Isabey, French School, 19th C **800.00**

Queen Victoria, sgd "Lowe(s)" **425.00**

2½" h, young beauty, watercolor on ivory, framed, sgd "Lucas," Continental School, 19th C **300.00**

2⅝" h

George Washington, portrait on ivory, ivory frame, American School, second-half 19th C **180.00**

Madame Recamier, after Francois Gerard, unsigned, French School, 19th C **290.00**

2¾"

Circular, "The Honorable Mrs. Edward Percival," watercolor on ivory, framed, tortoiseshell and MOP backing engraved with monogram, attributed to John Smart I, British School, 1741–1811 .... **695.00**

Oval

Elegant beauty, one sgd "Hallas," French School, late 19th C, price for pr **435.00**

Emperor Franz Joseph of Austria, French School, 19th C **750.00**

Portrait of gentleman in uniform, red coat, gold-colored case with fragment of red coat fabric under back lens, on ivory, American School . **360.00**

Woman wearing plumed hat, on porcelain, ebonized wood standing-type frame **90.00**

2¼" w, Josephine, by Augustine, gilt metal and walnut frame, French Empire Revival School **475.00**

2¾" and 3" h, husband and wife, dressed in black, watercolor on ivory, framed, British School, mid-19th D, price for pr **445.00**

3" h

Watercolor on porcelain, self portrait after Vigee Le Brun, German School, late 19th C, imp mark ... **250.00**

2¼" w, Philippine Nelser and Valentine DeMilan, by T V Marussoy, Continental School, 19th C, price for pr **300.00**

2½" w, girl with coral beds, unsigned, watercolor on ivory, framed, American School, 19th C **500.00**

3¼" h, oval

Elegant young woman, watercolor on ivory, ivory frame, Continental School, late 19th C, price for pr **300.00**

Ruth, German School, late 19th C, watercolor on porcelain, imp mark **250.00**

2¼" w, elderly woman wearing lacy bonnet, on ivory, Louis XV style emb brass frame, dec with flowers and ribbons **265.00**

2½" w

Peasant girl, flowers in her hair, on vellum, ivory and wood frame **115.00**

Two beautiful women, one wearing tiara, other with plumed hat, on ivory, similar boule dec wooden frames, price for pr **460.00**

2¾" w, Elizabethan woman with jewels in her hair, on ivory, ornate Louis XV style gilt-brass filigree frame dec with bows and flowering vines **265.00**

3⅜" h, oval, Ludwig Beethoven, watercolor on ivory, gilt-metal frame, Schozzer, German School, 19th C **575.00**

3½" h, watercolor on ivory, framed

Elegant lady, Continental School, late 19th C, price for pr **550.00**

Mozart, sgd "Vogel," German School, 19th C **325.00**

Wagner, sgd "Graf," German School, 19th C **345.00**

2½" w

Napoleon Bonaparte, on ivory, artist sgd "H. Denis," ivory tortoiseshell-clad frame **230.00**

Woman wearing floral garland, on ivory, artist sgd, ornate Louis XV style gilt-brass filigree frame dec with flowers and ribbons **215.00**

2¾" w, woman seated in chair, unsigned, watercolor and ink on paper, matching carte-de-visite, American School, 19th C **195.00**

3¾" w, young nobleman, military dress, on ivory, artist sgd, ornate gilt brass Louis XV style frame . **290.00**

3¾" h

Marco Barbarizi from 1485, and Nicolo Contarini from 1629, sgd "T. V. Marussoy," watercolor on ivory, framed in gilt-tooled leather case, Continental School, third quarter 19th C, price for pr **490.00**

2¼" w, young child with coral necklace, holding toy, unsigned, attributed to Mrs Mose B Russell (Clarissa Peters, American, 1809–1854), watercolor on ivory, loss to upper cover, cracks, minor pigment loss, scratches **2,990.00**

4 × 3¾", Coronation Ride of Maria Theresa, Empress of Austria, watercolor on ivory, framed, Continental School, 19th C **550.00**

MINIATURES

History: There are three sizes of miniatures: dollhouse scale (ranging from ½ to 1 inch), sample size, and child's size. Since most early material is in museums or is extremely expensive, the most common examples in the marketplace today are from the 20th century.

Many mediums were used for miniatures: silver, copper, tin, wood, glass, and ivory. Even books were printed in miniature. Price ranges are broad, influenced by scarcity and quality of workmanship.

The collecting of miniatures dates back to the 18th century. It remains one of the world's leading hobbies.

References: George M. Beylerian, *Chairmania*, Harry N. Abrams, 1994; Caroline Clifton-Mogg, *The Dollhouse Sourcebook*, Abbeville Press, 1993; Nora Earnshaw, *Collecting Dolls' Houses and Miniatures,* Pincushion Press, 1993; Flora Gill Jacobs, *Dolls Houses in America,* Charles Scribner's Sons, 1974; ———, *History of Dolls Houses,* Charles Scribner's Sons; Constance Eileen King, *Dolls and Dolls Houses,* Hamlyn, 1989; Herbert F. Schiffer and Peter B. Schiffer, *Miniature Antique Furniture,* Schiffer Publishing, 1995; Margaret Towner, *Dollhouse Furniture,* Courage Books, Running Press, 1993.

Periodicals: *Doll Castle News,* PO Box 247, Washington, NJ 07882; *Miniature Collector,* Scott Publications, 30595 Eight Mile Rd, Livonia, MI 48152; *Nutshell News,* 21027 Crossroads Circle, PO Box 1612, Waukesha, WI 53187.

Collectors' Clubs: International Guild Miniature Artisans, PO Box 71, Bridgeport, NY 18080; Miniature Industry Assoc of America Member News, 2270 Jacquelyn Dr, Madison, WI 53711; National Assoc of Miniature Enthusiasts, PO Box 69, Carmel, IN 46032.

Museums: Margaret Woodbury Strong Museum, Rochester, NY; Mildred Mahoney Jubilee Doll House Museum, Fort Erie, Canada; Museums at Stony Brook, Stony Brook, NY; Toy and Miniature Museum of Kansas City, Kansas City, MO; Toy Museum of Atlanta, Atlanta, GA; Washington Dolls' House and Toy Museum, Washington, DC.

Additional Listings: See Dollhouse Furnishings in *Warman's Americana & Collectibles* for more examples.

Doll House Size

Armoire, oak, golden finish, 1″ scale, c1900	120.00
Bed, maple, honey finish, scalloped head and footboards, c1900, 6¼″ l	120.00
Chair, carved wood, scrolled arms and back, blue velvet seat, pr	70.00
Desk, Biedermeier, marble top, stencil dec, black ground, c1890	125.00

Doll house size, desk, slant front, Tynietoy, wood, impressed mark, c1930, 4¹³/₁₆ × 2⅛ × 3⅞″, $110.00; student lamp, brass, celluloid, green shade, c 1920, 2½″ h, $45.00.

Dining Room Suite, tin, 3½″ h oval drop-leaf table, one 2″ h armchair, five 2″ h side chairs	100.00
Dressing Table, maple, rect top, carved legs, scrolled apron, white marble top, mirrored cupboard, drawers, silver knobs, marbleized litho paper on back	150.00
Salon Set, Louis XV style, gilt metal and enamel, romantic couple dec, banquet, 4 chairs, table, price for 6-pc set	250.00
Settee, 6″ l, maple, Gothic style, carved back with three panels, curved arms, wicker seat	90.00
Table, 3½″ h, brass, tilt top	85.00

Accessories

Bath Tub, 5½″ h, tin, lavender, gold stripes and facet, tall legs, lower shelf, small matching pail, marked ''Made in Germany''	70.00
Birdcage, 2½″ h, brass, parrot	125.00
Candlesticks, pr, 4⅜″ h, brass, Queen Anne style	200.00
Chamber Pot, 2⅛″ d, yellowware, white band, applied handle	45.00
Fireplace, Regency style, Petite Princess	15.00
Kitchen Stove, Petite Princess	75.00
Lamp, 2″ h, tole ware, worn orig red paint	100.00
Mirror, 1″ h, brass, ormolu, turned columns support oval mirror, 19th C	100.00
Mortar and Pestle, brass	25.00
Sewing Machine, tin, painted, c1920	45.00
Tea Cart, Petite Princess	20.00
Towel Rack, wood, Victorian	35.00

Child Size

Box, 6″ h, 7″ w, 5″ d, fall front, fruitwood, nine small drawers, each with pictorial marquetry, Italian, 19th C	600.00
Cabinet, 16″ h, 14″ w, 7″ d, Chinese Export, gilt dec black lacquer, mid 19th C, pr of doors enclosing five drawers, bracket feet, figures and foliage dec	750.00
Chest of Drawers, 17″ h, 19½″ w, 6¼″ d, step-back type, painted, mustard, black highlights, shaped back with short backsplash, two small drawers over two larger drawers over three small drawers over two drawers, step backed to two drawers over one long drawer, 1-pc sides	1,450.00
Chair, wide crest rail, turned legs and rungs, orig dark surface, crushed red velvet upholstery, American, c1850, price for pr	310.00
Cupboard, 25¼″ h, 24½″ w, 12¼″ d, step back, wall, pine, old worn reddish brown finish, paneled doors, open top, pigeonhole int.	935.00
Herb Drying Rack, wood	90.00
Kitchen Cabinet, 50″ h, 28″ w, Hoosier type, zinc work service	770.00
Secretary, 19″ h, 9″ w, 8″ d, American, 19th C, folk carved birch and pine, carved dog finial lifts, fitted int., ornate foliate carved bookcase doors over roll-top desk, two drawers, paw feet	1,035.00
Table, 6″ h, 10″ w, 7¼″ d, inlaid mahogany, fitted drawer, sq tapered legs, top and front inlaid with checkered crossbanding, Edwardian, c1900	230.00

Doll Size

Bed, 21" l, spool, walnut, rockers, old worn finish, one
rocker replaced, one rail loose **200.00**
Chair, 13" h, ladder back, arm, splint seat, 13" h **125.00**
Chest of Drawers, 11½" h, 9¾" w, 5½" d, Empire, pine
and poplar, orig red paint, black vinegar graining,
four drawers **625.00**
Cradle, 25¼" l, poplar, dovetailed, scrolled ends, old
dark brown alligatored finish **125.00**
Dresser, 31" h, 18" w, Victorian, bamboo-turned edge
and mirror posts, two drawers, mirror, hat box **475.00**

Sample Size

Blanket Chest, walnut, sectioned int., early hand dove-
tails, replaced hardware, SE PA origin **320.00**
Butter Print, chip-carved link, heart and floral motifs .. **180.00**
Cookie Print, chip carved, double, striated heart and
relief-carved crosshatch dec **65.00**
Furnace, Mueller **425.00**
Rocker, adv for PA furniture store, painted red, gold stenciled letters, turned spindled back, plank seat, c1900 **150.00**
Spoon Rack, folk carved, remnants of orig paint **80.00**
Stand, 24" h, 15¼" w, 15⅝" d, Sheraton, stripped walnut,
applied gallery, one-board top with age cracks, single
dovetailed drawer with applied edge beading, turned
legs **450.00**

MINTON CHINA

History: In 1793 Thomas Minton joined other men to form a
partnership and build a small pottery at Stoke-on-Trent, Staffordshire, England. Production began in 1798 with blue-printed earthenware, mostly in the Willow pattern. In 1798 cream-colored
earthenware and bone china were introduced.

A wide range of styles and wares was produced. Minton introduced porcelain figures in 1826, Parian wares in 1846, encaustic
tiles in the late 1840s, and Majolica wares in 1850. Many famous
designers and artists in the English pottery industry worked for
Minton.

In 1883 the modern company was formed and called Mintons
Limited. The "s" was dropped in 1968. Minton still produces
bone-china tablewares and some ornamental pieces.

Marks: Many early pieces are unmarked or have a Sevres-type
marking. The "ermine" mark was used in the early 19th century.
Date codes can be found on tableware and majolica. The mark
used between 1873 and 1911 was a small globe with a crown on
top and the word "Minton."

References: Paul Atterbury and Maureen Batkin, *The Dictionary
of Minton,* Antique Collectors' Club; Susan and Al Bagdade, *Warman's English & Continental Pottery & Porcelain,* Second Edition,
Wallace-Homestead, 1991; Joan Jones, *Minton: The First Two
Hundred Years of Design and Production,* Swan Hill, 1993.

Museum: Minton Museum, Staffordshire, England.

Asparagus Plate, majolica, shaped rect, molded asparagus flanking well, black printed mark **95.00**
Bowl, 11" d, flower heads, leaves, and scrolls, red and
gold, green ground, c1805 ....**1,200.00**
Breakfast Set, toast rack with attached under plate, salt
and pepper shakers, Dejeuneau, green mark **195.00**
Bulb Planter, 10¾" l, majolica, emb brown fence, green
leaves, turquoise int. **165.00**
Console Set, pedestal center bowl with hp cartouche on
each side of Napoleon and Josephine, ram's-head
dec, deep aquamarine and white ground, gold trim,
pr 12" h candlesticks, sgd, price for 3-pc set **1,425.00**
Cup and Saucer, ribbon swags, rose, c1805 .... **125.00**
Ewer, 8½" h, turquoise, raised putti holding swags leading to Neptune seated under spout, mermaid handle,
c1868 .... **600.00**
Garden Seat, 14" d, 18" h, Hawthorn pattern, blue and
white, flowering vines dec, shaped feet, c1880, restorations **150.00**
Oyster Plate, emb fish, gilt rim, white ground **75.00**

**Oyster plate, five scallop shells, fish motif be-
tween scallops, white salt glaze, stamp mark
"18th Cent, Staffordshire Salt Glaze," 10⅝" d,
$75.00.**

Plate
10" d, floral center, floral garland border, price for
12-pc set **230.00**
10¼" d
Gilt foliate dec, c1884, price for 9-pc set **525.00**
Raised gilt floral border, c1911, price for 9-pc set **635.00**
Service Plate, two cobalt blue bands with wide center
gold band, one chip, price for 12-pc set **1,150.00**
Tile, 6" h, King Henry **65.00**
Vase, 11" h burnt amber, pink, and blue flowers, c1875 **175.00**

MOCHA

History: Mocha decoration usually is found on utilitarian creamware and stoneware pieces and was produced through a simple
chemical action. A color pigment of brown, blue, green, or black
was made acidic by an infusion of tobacco or hops. When the
acidic colorant was applied in blobs to an alkaline ground, it
reacted by spreading in feathery designs resembling sea plants.

This type of decoration usually was supplemented with bands of light-colored slip.

Types of decoration vary greatly, from those done in a combination of motifs, such as Cat's Eye and Earthworm, to a plain pink mug decorated with green ribbed bands. Most forms of mocha are hollow, e.g., mugs, jugs, bowls, and shakers.

English potters made the vast majority of the pieces. Collectors group the wares into three chronological periods: 1780–1820, 1820–1840, and 1840–1880.

Marks: Marked pieces are extremely rare.

References: Susan and Al Bagdade, *Warman's English & Continental Pottery & Porcelain,* Second Edition, Wallace-Homestead, 1991; Dana G. Morykan and Harry L. Rinker, *Warman's Country Antiques & Collectibles,* Third Edition, Wallace-Homestead, 1996.

Reproduction Alert.

Bowl, 9½" d, vibrant agate dec, engine-turned brown, blue, and tan border **1,650.00**
Humidor, 7" h, black, tan, and white checkerboard dec, narrow chocolate, blue, and white bands, acorn finial **2,500.00**
Measure, 6" h, gray-green band, brown and white stripes, blue molded band, black seaweed dec, applied crest with crown and "Imperial," leaf handle, stains and hairlines **150.00**
Mug
  4½" h, blue and brown horizontal sausage-linked geometric pattern **1,200.00**
  4⅞" h, blue bands, black stripe and seaweed dec, applied emb "Pint" seal **250.00**
  5½" h, bright blue, gold, and dark brown banded geometric pattern, old handwritten inside with Litchfield, NH, provenance **1,000.00**
  6" h, repeated black wave lines, black banding, pale blue ground, base with wavy bands at top and bottom **650.00**
  6¼" h, gold, brown, and blue earthworm dec, blue and brown banding **825.00**
Pepper Pot
  3½" h, pale blue, brown, and yellow scroddled pattern, white ground **550.00**

4" h, brown, black, and cream engine-turned geometric pattern **650.00**
Pitcher
  6½" h, circular brown and white dots with green incised loop band, slight discoloration, small chip **825.00**
  7" h, molded leaf handle, blue bands, green stripes, wear, crow's feet, hairline in base of handle **315.00**
  7¼" h, bright blue and brown cat's-eye and earthworm dec, blue and dark brown bands, age crack under spout **650.00**
Tavern Measure, tree pattern **265.00**
Tea Caddy, 5¼" h, marbleized brown, sienna, and white, orig lid, small nicks **1,650.00**
Teapot, 4½" h, marbleized brown, sienna, and white, green Leeds rim, minor nicks on cov and base **2,225.00**

MONART GLASS

History: Monart glass is a heavy, simply shaped art glass in which colored enamels are suspended in the glass during the glassmaking process. This technique was originally developed by the Ysart family in Spain in 1923. John Moncrief, a Scottish glassmaker, discovered the glass while vacationing in Spain, recognized the beauty and potential market, and began production in his Perth glassworks in 1924.

The name "Monart" is derived from the surnames Moncrief and Ysart. Two types of Monart were manufactured: a commercial line which incorporated colored enamels and a touch of aventurine in crystal, and the art line in which the suspended enamels formed designs such as feathers or scrolls.

Marks: Monart glass, in most instances, is not marked. The factory used paper labels.

Basket, 4" h, mottled orange and green **100.00**
Bowl, 10½" d, white, gray crackle, yellow and green flecks, oxblood red base and rim **160.00**
Candlesticks, pr, 3" h, mottled blue shading to lavender **75.00**
Vase
  6" h, green to red **395.00**
  8½" h, green rim shading to clear to brown, green pedestal **125.00**

Jug, seaweed dec, brown, ochre, and green, $400.00.

Vase, Monart, round, wide doughnut base, flaring urn body, Scottish cluthra, shading from goldstone to clear, 8½" h, $100.00.

MONT JOYE GLASS

History: Mont Joye is a type of glass produced by Saint-Hilaire, Touvier, de Varreaux & Company at their glassworks in Pantin,

France. Most pieces were lightly acid etched to give them a frosted appearance and were also decorated with enameled florals.

Note: Pieces listed below are frosted unless otherwise noted.

Bowl, 3¾" d, enameled floral dec, sgd **275.00**

Rose bowl, acid etched, enameled purple violets, gold stems, gold dec, pinched sides, 3¾" h, 4¼" d, $200.00.

Pitcher, cameo, crystal, green and gold, brass spout and
   handle, removable cov, sgd "Cristalle Rie Depantin"   **600.00**
Vase
   5½" h, Nile green, gold enameled leaves and enam-
     eled lilies of the valley dec **400.00**
   7½" h, dark green satin ground, enameled pink iris
     dec **425.00**
   9¾" h, cameo, swelled sq body, frosted amethystine
     glass, deeply etched flowering plants through pur-
     ple layer, gold enameled highlights, irid luster
     base, marked "St Danis," chip under base corner   **250.00**
   15¾" h, cameo, light green, gold encrusted band at
     neck, white, blue, yellow, and gold iris dec **850.00**

MOORCROFT

History: William Moorcroft was first employed as a potter by James Macintyre & Co., Ltd., of Burslem in 1897. He established the Moorcroft pottery in 1913.

The majority of the art pottery wares were hand thrown, resulting in a great variation among similarly styled pieces. Color and marks are keys to determining age.

Walker, William's son, continued the business upon his father's death and made wares in the same style.

Marks: The company initially used an impressed mark, "Moorcroft, Burslem"; a signature mark, "W. Moorcroft" followed. Modern pieces are marked simply "Moorcroft" with export pieces also marked "Made in England."

References: Susan and Al Bagdade, *Warman's English & Continental Pottery & Porcelain,* Second Edition, Wallace-Homestead, 1991; Frances Salmon, *Collecting Moorcroft,* Francis-Joseph Books, 1994.

Museum: Moorcroft Museum, Stoke-on-Trent, England.

Bowl, 7¾" d, blue ext., red, yellow, green orchids and
   white flowers int., sgd **425.00**
Bulb Bowl, 6½" d, 2¼" h, white and purple narcissus,
   dark blue and green ground, "Potter to the Queen"
   mark **250.00**
Candlesticks, pr, 8½" h, 4¾" d, landscape design, moonlit blue, light blue squeezebag trees, dark blue
   ground, painted "WM" in blue, imp "Moorcroft/
   Made in England," c1918–29 .... **750.00**
Jar, 22" h, floral dec, mounted as lamps, price for pr .. **850.00**
Vase
   4" h, cream ground, yellow and green flowers **200.00**
   4½" h, 6½" d, squatty bulbous, Hazledene pattern,
     celadon squeezebag trees, soft celadon ground,
     painted mark "W. Moorcroft/XII/1913" **700.00**
   6" h, 3" d, corseted, blue landscape dec, celadon
     ground, painted mark "W. Moorcroft/des," red
     mark "Made for Liberty and Co.," registry mark,
     c1903–13 .... **700.00**
   6¼" h, 3¾" d, bulbous
     Hazledene pattern, blue squeezebag trees, green
      and soft yellow ground, painted mark "W.
      Moorcroft/des," stamped "Made for Liberty
      and Co.," c1903–13 .... **950.00**
     Pomegranate pattern, red and burgundy squeeze-
      bag dec pomegranate and green leaves, ftd,
      celadon ground, painted mark "W. Moorcroft"   **500.00**
   8" h, 5¼" d, bulbous base, corseted neck, Landscape
     pattern, squeezebag puffy trees, ruby-luster finish,
     imp "Moorcroft," painted mark "W. Moorcroft,"
     post-1949 .... **475.00**

Bowl, Florian ware, blue tones, ftd, 2½" h, 7⅝" d, $575.00.

   8¼" h, 4½" d, bulbous, corseted neck, Claremont
     Toadstool pattern, red and light blue mushrooms,
     light blue glossy ground, painted mark "W. Moor-
     croft," imp "Moorcroft/Made in England," c1918–
     29 .... **1,800.00**
   10" h, 6" d, bulbous, corseted neck, black squeezebag
     peacock feathers, ruby-luster glaze, imp "Moor-
     croft," ink "WM," two orig labels **650.00**
   11½" h, 3¾" d, Florian, blue flowers, celadon leaves,
     squeezebag relief, cobalt ground, ink mark
     "Moorcroft/Des" and registry mark, pre-1913 ...**1,200.00**
   11¾" h, 4" d, Florian, yellow iris blossoms, celadon
     leaves, squeezebag relief, cobalt blue ground,
     painted mark "W. Moorcroft/Des", pre-1913 ...**2,900.00**

12" h
Floral dec, orig paper label **1,750.00**
5½" d, rounded, squeezebag and painted land-
scape dec, white trees, light blue mountains
ground, painted mark "Moorcroft" in blue,
stamped "Moorcroft/Made in England,"
c1918-29 . . . .**1,900.00**
12¼" h, 9½" d, bulbous, flaring rim, Hazledene pat-
tern, squeezebag stylized trees on rolling hills, lustered red glaze, sgd "W Moorcroft" in script,
stamped "Made for Liberty and Co." **1,800.00**
14¼" h, 8" d, Anemone pattern, large fleshy squeezebag flowers, ruby flambé finish, painted "W.
Moorcroft," imp "Moorcroft/Made in England,"
orig paper label, 1928–49 . . . .**1,900.00**

MORGANTOWN GLASS WORKS

History: The Morgantown Glass Works, Morgantown, West Virginia, was founded in 1899 and began production in 1901. Reorganized in 1903, it operated as the Economy Tumbler Company
for 20 years until, in 1923, the word "Tumbler" was dropped from
the corporate title. The firm was then known as The Economy
Glass Company until reversion to its original name, Morgantown
Glass Works, Inc., in 1929, the name it kept until its first closing
in 1937. In 1939, the factory was reopened under the aegis of a
guild of glassworkers and operated as the Morgantown Glassware
Guild from that time until its final closing. Purchased by Fostoria
in 1965, the factory operated as a subsidiary of the Moundsville-
based parent company until 1971 when Fostoria opted to termi-
nate production of glass at the Morgantown facility. Today, collectors use the generic term, "Morgantown Glass," to include all
periods of production from 1901 to 1971.

Morgantown was a 1920s leader in the manufacture of colorful
wares for table and ornamental use in American homes. The company pioneered the processes of iridization on glass as well as
gold and platinum encrustation of patterns. They enhanced Crystal
offerings with contrasting handle and foot of India Black, Spanish
Red (ruby), and Ritz Blue (cobalt blue), and other intense and
pastel colors for which they are famous. They conceived the use
of contrasting shades of fired enamel to add color to their etchings.
They were the only American company to use a chromatic silk-
screen printing process on glass, their two most famous and collectible designs being Queen Louise and Manchester Pheasant.

The company is also known for ornamental "open stems" produced during the late 1920s. Open stems separate to form an
open design midway between the bowl and foot, e.g., an open
square, a Y, or two diamond-shaped designs. Many of these open
stems were purchased and decorated by Dorothy C. Thorpe in her
California studio, and her signed open stems command high prices
from today's collectors. Morgantown also produced figural stems
for commercial clients such as Koscherak Brothers and Marks &
Rosenfeld. Chanticleer (rooster) and Mai Tai (Polynesian bis) cock-
tails are two of the most popular figurals collected today.

Morgantown is best known for the diversity of its stemware
patterns as well as for their four patented optics: Festoon, Palm,
Peacock, and Pineapple. These optics were used to embellish
stems, jugs, bowls, liquor sets, guest sets, salvers, ivy and witch
balls, vases, and smoking items.

Two well-known lines of Morgantown Glass are recognized
by most glass collectors today: #758 Sunrise Medallion and

#7643 Golf Ball Stem Line. When Economy introduced #758 in
1928, it was originally identified as Nymph. By 1931, the Morgantown front office had renamed it Sunrise Medallion. Recent
publications erred in labeling it "dancing girl." Upon careful study
of the medallion, you can see the figure is poised on one tiptoe,
musically saluting the dawn with her horn. The second well-
known line, #7643 Golf Ball, was patented in 1928; production
commenced immediately and continued until the company
closed in 1971. More Golf Ball than any other Morgantown product is found on the market today.

References: Gene Florence, *Elegant Glassware of the Depression
Era,* Sixth Edition, Collector Books, 1995; ———, *Very Rare Glassware of the Depression Years,* Fourth Series, Collector Books,
1995; Jerry Gallagher, *A Handbook of Old Morgantown Glass,*
Vol. I, published by author (420 First Ave NW, Plainview, MN
55964), 1995; ———, *Old Morgantown, Catalogue of Glassware,
1931,* Morgantown Collectors of America Research Society, n.d.;
Hazel Marie Weatherman, *Colored Glassware of the Depression
Era,* Book 2 published by author, 1974, available in reprint; ———
—, *1984 Supplement & Price Trends for Colored Glassware of the
Depression Era,* Book 1, published by author, 1984.

Periodical: *The Morgantown Newscaster,* Morgantown Collectors
of America, 420 First Ave, NW, Plainview, MN 55964.

Collectors' Clubs: Morgantown Collectors of America Research
Society, 420 First Ave, NW, Plainview, MN 55964; Old Morgantown Glass Collectors' Guild, PO Box 894, Morgantown, WV
26507.

Advisor: Jerry Gallagher.

Bowl
#12½ Woodsfield, Genova Line, 12½" d **345.00**
#17 Calypso, Spanish Red, 7¾" d **235.00**
#19 Kelsha, Danube Line, 12" d **350.00**
#22 Linwood, Topreen Line, Spiral Optic, 10" d . . . **335.00**
#26 Greer, Neubian Line, 10" d **645.00**
#35½ Elena, Old Amethyst, applied Crystal rim, 8" d **325.00**
#101 Heritage, Peacock Blue, 8" d **48.00**
#1102 Crown, Steel Blue, 9" d **50.00**
#1933 El Mexicano, console, Seaweed, 10" d **225.00**
#4355 Janice, 13" d
Crystal, #787 Maytime etch **195.00**
14K Topaz, Carlton/Madrid **135.00**
Ritz Blue **235.00**
#9937 Revere, Ruby, 6" d **55.00**
Candleholders, pr
#37 Emperor, Genova Line, 8" h **625.00**
#81 Bravo
Peacock Blue, 4½" h **48.00**
Thistle, 4½" h **120.00**
#82 Cosmopolitan, Moss Green, slant, 7" h **75.00**
#87 Hamilton, Steel Blue, 5" h **50.00**
#105 Coronet, Ebony, slant, 8¾" h **110.00**
#7620 Fontanne, Ebony filament, #781 Fontinelle
etch **485.00**
#7662 Majesty, 4" h
Randall Blue **395.00**
Spanish Red **345.00**
#7690 Monroe, Ritz Blue, 7" h, rare **750.00**
#9923 Colonial, Pineapple, 2-pc hurricane, 8½" h **120.00**

Candy Jar

#16 Rachel, Crystal, Pandora Cutting, 6″ h 345.00
#71 Jupiter, Steel Blue, 6″ h 85.00
#108 Bethann, Topreen Line, 5½″ h 485.00
#127 Yorktown, Steel Blue, 7½″ h 45.00
#1114 Jerome, Bristol Blue, 11½″ h 135.00
#1212 Michael, Spanish Red, Crystal finial, 5½″ h . 450.00
#2938 Helga, Anna Rose, Meadow Green finial, 5¼″ h 500.00
#7643-1 Alexandra, Randall Blue/Crystal Duo-Tone, 5¼″ h 625.00
#9949 Christmas Tree, Crystal, 4-part stack jar, 11″ h 140.00
#9952 Palace, Ruby, 6½″ h 50.00

Champagne

#7565 Astrid, American Beauty etch, 6 oz 37.50
#7577 Venus, Ritz Blue, Pillar Optic, 5½ oz 45.00
#7621 Ringer, Anna Rose, 6 oz 55.00
#7623 Pygon, D C Thorpe satin open stem, 5½ oz 135.00
#7630 Ballerina, #757 Elizabeth etch, 6 oz 55.00
#7640 Art Moderne, Ebony open stem, 5½ oz 65.00
#7643 Golf Ball, 5½ oz
   Ritz Blue 48.00
   Spanish Red 45.00
   Stiegel Green 40.00
#7664 Queen Anne, Azure, #758 Sunrise Medallion etch, 6½ oz 85.00
#7678 Old English, 6½ oz
   Ritz Blue 45.00
   Spanish Red 45.00
   Stiegel Green 40.00
#7705 Hopkins, Toulon gold dec, 5½ oz 125.00
#7860 Lawton, Azure, Festoon Optic, 5½ oz 48.00

Cocktail

Chanticleer, Pink Champagne bowl, 4 oz 38.00
Mai Tai, Topaz stem, 4 oz 45.00
Old Crow, 6¼″ h, 5½ oz 75.00
#7577 Venus, Venetian Green, Palm Optic, 3 oz .. 35.00
#7586 Napa, Azure, Festoon Optic, 3½ oz 48.00
#7620 Fontanne, Ebony filament, #781 Fontinelle etch, 3½ oz 85.00
#7630 Ballerina, #765 Springtime etch, 3 oz 45.00
#7643 Golf Ball, 3½ oz
   Ritz Blue 38.00
   Spanish Red 35.00
   Stiegel Green 35.00
#7654½ Legacy, Manchester Pheasant Silk Screen, 3½ oz 165.00

Compote

#201 Inverness, Meadow Green, Peacock Optic, 4½″ d, 7½″ h 145.00
#203 Marietta, Ruby, 9½″ 75.00
#206 Colette, Burgundy, 7½″ h 60.00
#7556 Helena, low w/cover, Crystal, Snowberry Cutting, 4½″ d 265.00
#7556 Toledo, high w/cover, Crystal, Forever Cutting, 4½″ d 285.00
#7620 Rarey, Spanish Red bowl, 6″ d, 6½″ h 255.00
#7654 Reverse Twist, Aquamarine, 6½″ d, 6¼″ h .. 175.00

Cordial

#788½ Roanoke, Spanish Red, 1½ oz 50.00
#7643 Golf Ball, 1½ oz

   Pastels 55.00
   Ritz Blue 60.00
   Spanish Red 55.00
   Stiegel Green 50.00
#7660½ Empress, Spanish Red, 1½ oz 75.00
#7668 Galaxy, #810 Sears' Lace Bouquet etch, 1½ oz 48.00
#7673 Lexington, Ritz Blue filament, #790 Fairwin etch, 1½ oz 135.00
#7909 Blake, Spanish Red filament, 1 oz 65.00

Goblet

#300 Festival, Gloria Blue, 8 oz 35.00
#7565 Astrid, #734 American Beauty etch, punty cut stem, 10 oz 68.00
#7568 Horizon, #735 Richmond etch, 10 oz 48.00
#7577 Venus, 9 oz
   Anna Rose, Azure foot, Tulip Optic 145.00
   #743 Bramble Rose etch 65.00
#7589 Laurette, #735 Richmond etch, 9 oz 42.00
#7614 Hampton, Anna Rose stem, Queen Louise Silk Screen, 9 oz 225.00
#7623 Pygon, D C Thorpe satin open stem, 9 oz .. 175.00
#7624 Paragon, Ebony open stem, 10 oz 165.00
#7625 Paramount, Meadow Green open stem, #765 Springtime etch, 10 oz 165.00
#7636 Square, open stem, 9 oz 225.00
#7637 Courtney, D C Thorpe satin open stem, 9 oz 195.00
#7630 Ballerina, Aquamarine/Azure, Yukon cutting, 10 oz 110.00
#7640 Art Moderne, Ritz Blue, Crystal open stem, 9 oz 125.00
#7643 Golf Ball, 9 oz
   Ritz Blue 48.00
   Spanish Red 45.00
   Stiegel Green 40.00
#7646 Sophisticate, Picardy etch, 9 oz 55.00
#7659 Cynthia, #746 Sonoma etch, 10 oz 65.00
#7664 Queen Anne, 10 oz
   Manchester Pheasant Silk Screen 210.00
   Sunrise Medallion etch 85.00
#7678 Old English, 10 oz
   Ritz Blue 55.00
   Spanish Red 55.00
   Stiegel Green 45.00

Guest Set

#23 Trudy, 6⅜″ h
   Anna Rose, Palm Optic 85.00
   Baby Blue carafe, India Black tumbler 135.00
   Jade Green 85.00
   Opaque Yellow carafe, India Black tumbler 150.00
#24 Margaret, 5⅞″ h
   Anna Rose, enamel dec 120.00
   Aquamarine/Azure, enamel dec 130.00
   Golden Iris, pulled spout, handled 375.00
   Jade Green 185.00

Jug

#6 Kaufmann, Old Bristol line, 54 oz 1,500.00
#8 Orleans, #131 Brittany cut, 54 oz 235.00
#14 Eiffel, #282 needle etch, 65 oz 195.00
#33 Martina, mint mark handle, #518 Lily of the Valley sandblast dec, 46 oz 215.00
#37 Barry, Zurich Two Tone Line, cov, 48 oz 650.00

Jug, #33, Rawsthorne, Anna Rose, Peacock Optic, reeded handle, 48 oz, $375.00.

#303 Cyrano, #203 needle etch, 54 oz **210.00**
#545 Pickford Spiral, Amber, 54 oz **125.00**
#1933 LMX Del Rey, Randall Blue non-opaque, rare, 50 oz **425.00**
#1962 Crinkle San Juan, Amethyst, tankard, 64 oz . **125.00**
#1962 Crinkle Tijuana, Peacock Blue, Juice/Martini, 34 oz **80.00**
#9844 Swirl, Burgundy, 54 oz **185.00**
Plate, #1500
   Alexandrite, #776 Nasreen etch, dessert, 7″ d **85.00**
   Anna Rose, #743 Bramble Rose etch, salad/lunch-eon, 8½″ d **40.00**
   Crystal, #734 American Beauty etch, dessert, 7″ d . **42.00**
   Platinum/Red band, Hollywood dec, torte, 14″ d ... **245.00**
   Stiegel Green, salad/luncheon, 8½″ d **38.00**
Sherbet
   #3011 Montego, Gypsy Fire, 6½ oz **35.00**
   #7620 Fontanne, #781 Fontinelle etch, 6 oz **125.00**
   #7640 Art Moderne, Ritz Blue, 5½ oz **65.00**
   #7643 Golf Ball, 5½ oz
      Ritz Blue **42.00**
      Spanish Red **38.00**
      Stiegel Green **35.00**
   #7646 Sophisticate, Picardy etch, 5½ oz **40.00**
   #7654 Lorna, Meadow Green stem, #766 Nantucket etch, 5½ oz **48.00**
   #7654½ Legacy, Manchester Pheasant Silk Screen, 6½ oz **95.00**
   #7668 Galaxy, #787 ½ Mayfair etch, 5½ oz **28.00**
Tumbler
   #1928 Ivy, Stiegel Green, ice tea, 15 oz **55.00**
   #7621 Ringer, Spanish Red, ice tea, 15 oz **50.00**
   #7622 Bracelet, Ritz Blue, ice tea, 14 oz **65.00**
   #7664 Queen Anne, Azure, #757 Elizabeth etch, ftd, 11 oz **85.00**
   #7668 Galaxy, Pink Champagne, ftd, 9 oz **22.00**
   #7703 Sextette, Old Bristol Line, ftd ice tea, 11 oz **145.00**
   #9074 Belton, Primrose (Vaseline), Pillar Optic, ftd, 9 oz **95.00**

#9051 Zenith, Venetian Green, Peacock Optic, bar, 2 oz **40.00**
Vase
   #12 Viola, Rainbow Line, Spiral Optic, 8″ d **120.00**
   #24 Roseanne, Baby Blue, Allegheny Bird Screen Print, 10″ h **350.00**
   #25 Olympic, #734 American Beauty etch, 12″ h . **345.00**
   #43 Encino, Peacock Blue, 10¼″ h **65.00**
   #53 Serenade, Yellow Opaque, 10″ h **285.00**
   #67 Grecian, Ebony, Saracenic Art Line, 6″ h **900.00**
   #73 Radio, Ritz Blue, Crystal foot, 6″ h **550.00**
   #90 Daisy, Crystal, Green and White Wash, 9½″ w **450.00**
   #91 Lalique, Crystal Satin, 8¼″ h **650.00**
   #7621 Ringer
      Bud Vase, Opaque Yellow, 10″ h, ... **275.00**
      Flip Vase, 8″ d, Aquamarine/Azure **235.00**
Wine
   #7643 Golf Ball, 3 oz
      Ritz Blue **60.00**
      Spanish Red **56.00**
      Stiegel Green **50.00**
   #7662 Majesty, Spanish Red, 3½ oz **85.00**
   #7693 Warwick, Stiegel Green, 2½ oz **48.00**

MORIAGE, JAPANESE

History: Moriage refers to applied clay (slip) relief decorations used on certain types of Japanese pottery and porcelain.

This decorating was done by one of three methods: 1) hand rolling, hand shaping, and hand application to the biscuit in one or more layers; the design and effect required determine thickness and shape, 2) tubing or slip trailing, which applied decoration from a tube, like decorating a cake, and 3) hakeme which involved reducing the slip to a liquid and decorating the object with a brush. Color was applied either before or after the process.

Bowl, 7½″ d, floral center, intricate white slip work, green ground, scalloped edge **150.00**
Demitasse Cup and Saucer, purple, burgundy, lavender, and pink flowers, gold and dotted dec **50.00**
Hatpin Holder, 4¾″ h, green beading, red flowers **65.00**
Mug, 5½″ h, pink roses, lacy slip work **85.00**
Plate, 8″ d, purple, burgundy, lavender, and pink flowers, gold and dotted dec **35.00**

Salt and pepper shakers, top with white ground and gold dec, base with green ground and blue dots, $25.00.

Sugar Shaker, pink, applied flowers 75.00
Vase, 10½" h, pink and orange on rose, floral cartouche 225.00

MOSER GLASS

Moser *Moser Karlsbad*

History: Ludwig Moser (1833–1916) founded his polishing and engraving workshop in 1857 in Karlsbad (Karlovy Vary), Czechoslovakia. He employed many famous glass designers, e.g., Johann Hoffmann, Josef Urban, and Rudolf Miller. In 1900 Moser and his sons, Rudolf and Gustav, incorporated Ludwig Moser & Söhne.

Moser art glass included clear pieces with inserted blobs of colored glass, cut colored glass with classical scenes, cameo glass, and intaglio cut items. Many inexpensive enameled pieces also were made.

In 1922 Leo and Richard Moser bought Meyr's Neffe, their biggest Bohemian art glass rival. Moser executed many pieces for the Wiener Werkstätte in the 1920s. The Moser glass factory continues to produce new items.

References: Gary Baldwin and Lee Carno, *Moser—Artistry in Glass,* Antique Publications, 1988; Mural K. Charon and John Mareska, *Ludvik Moser, King of Glass,* published by author, 1984.

Box, 4½" d, amethyst, enameled flowers and gold trim, amber applied glass salamander on lid, three salamanders form feet 650.00
Cologne, green diamond-shaped bottle, deeply engraved blossom and leaf design, conforming colorless stopper with matching motif 200.00
Cordial, 1⅜" h, cranberry bowl, clear stem, flowers, bee, and insect dec on base 65.00
Cruet, 6¾" h, five raised cabochon amber gems, burnished gold deep-cut edges, clear ground, eight alternating panels of brilliant gold squiggles and stylized leaves, orig stopper, amber overlay on neck, spout, and lower portion of stopper, applied clear handle with cutting, base sgd "4," indistinct signature on stopper 750.00
Finger Bowl, 6" d, matching 7" d under plate, gold, silver, and blue enamel arabesque dec, white petit-point dec, scalloped shaded pink and lavender ground .. 875.00
Flask, 7½" l, powder-horn shape, deep cranberry, multicolored fern enameled dec, brass spigot, fittings, and chain 775.00

Pin Tray, deep red enameled figure, gold trim 70.00
Punch Set, 13½" d, 10" h large bowl with horizontal ridged pedestal foot, 18" d integrated round under tray, six matching punch cups, enameled scrolling gold dec, price for set 500.00
Rose Bowl, 7" h, deep cameo carving, lemon yellow, sgd in cameo, artist sgd "Hoffman" 695.00
Tumbler, 3¾" h, cranberry, gold enameled flowers and bees dec 85.00
Vase
    7" h, cameo, pumpkin ground, carved green ivy leaves and vines, marked "Moser Karlsbad" 1,750.00
    11¾" h, trumpet, applied prunts, rubena verde, gilt, polychrome enamel oak leaf and acorn dec, sgd on base "Moser No. 606, D180" 2,400.00
    13½" h, intaglio cut, green to clear 250.00
    14" h, paneled, gold intaglio warriors 465.00
Wine Ewer, 9¾" h, 5" d, amber ground, multicolored enamel floral dec 200.00

MOSS ROSE PATTERN CHINA

History: Several English potteries manufactured china with a Moss Rose pattern in the mid-1800s. Knowles, Taylor and Knowles, an American firm, began production of a Moss Rose pattern in the 1880s.

The moss rose was a common garden flower grown in England. When American consumers tired of English china with Oriental themes, they purchased the Moss Rose pattern as a substitute.

Bowl, 6" d, 3½" h, ftd, marked "Haviland" 30.00
Butter Pat, sq, marked "Meakin," price for 6-pc set ... 120.00
Cake Plate, ftd, marked "Haviland" 80.00
Cup and Saucer, marked "Haviland & Co, Limoges" .. 25.00
Gravy Boat, matching under plate 75.00
Plate
    7" d, gold trim, marked "Haviland" 20.00
    8" d, marked "KTK" 30.00
Platter, 15½" × 10½", marked "CFH" 40.00
Sauce Dish, 5" d, marked "SB & Sons" 10.00
Spooner, marked "Meakin" 45.00
Sugar, cov, marked "Haviland" 40.00
Tray, 11 × 7½", marked "JM Co" 25.00
Tureen, cov, 12½" h, marked "Haviland & Co, Limoges" 90.00

Powder box, Alexandrite, Art Deco, sgd "Moser," base 3⅜ × 3⅜ × 2¾", overall height 4¾", $275.00.

Plate, 7½" d, $25.00.

MOUNT WASHINGTON GLASS COMPANY

History: In 1837 Deming Jarves, founder of the Boston and Sandwich Glass Company, established for George D. Jarves, his son, the Mount Washington Glass Company in Boston, Massachusetts. In the following years the leadership and the name of the company changed several times as George Jarves formed different associations.

In the 1860s the company was owned and operated by Timothy Howe and William L. Libbey. In 1869 Libbey bought a new factory in New Bedford, Massachusetts. The Mount Washington Glass Company began operating again there under its original name. Henry Libbey became associated with the company early in 1871. He resigned in 1874 during the general depression, and the glassworks was closed. William Libbey had resigned in 1872 when he went to work for the New England Glass Company.

The Mount Washington Glass Company opened again in the fall of 1874 under the presidency of A. H. Seabury and the management of Frederick S. Shirley. In 1894 the glassworks became a part of the Pairpoint Manufacturing Company.

Throughout its history the Mount Washington Glass Company made different types of glass including pressed, blown, art, lava, Napoli, cameo, cut, Albertine, and Verona.

References: Edward and Sheila Malakoff, *Pairpoint Lamps,* Schiffer Publishing, 1990; John A. Shuman III, *The Collector's Encyclopedia of American Art Glass,* Collector Books, 1988, 1994 value update.

Collectors Club: Mount Washington Art Glass Society, PO Box 24094, Fort Worth, TX 76124.

Museum: The New Bedford Glass Museum, New Bedford, MA.

Additional Listings: Burmese, Crown Milano, Peachblow, and Royal Flemish.

Advisor: Louis O. St. Aubin, Jr.

Box, 4½" h × 6½" l, Opal Ware, mint green ground, pink roses, red cornflowers, gold trim, blown-out flowers and ribbons, No. 3212/20 ....**1,750.00**
Bowl, Rose Amber Amberina
   1½" h, 5" l, 4½" w, oblong, slight ribs **425.00**
   4¼" h, DQ, fuschia shading to deep blue **575.00**
Celery Vase, 5" h, 3" w, MOP, Herringbone pattern, 8 melon ribs, shades of blue, white lining **325.00**
Collar and Cuff Box, collar-shaped, Opal Ware, Oriental poppies on cov, pink and orange, No. 2390/128 ... **950.00**
Fruit Bowl, 6" h, painted solid green ground, pale pink and white pond lilies ext., gold highlight traceries int., silver-plated base sgd "Pairpoint Mfg. Co. B4704" .**2,200.00**
Jewel Box, 3¼" h, 5¼" d base, Opal Ware, portrait cov, monk drinking wine, satin lining, sgd "Schindler" . **550.00**
Letter Holder, Opal Ware, white and apricot wild rose dec, blown-out flowers, gold-washed holder with cherub's head, satin lining, No. 3839/1210 .... **875.00**
Miniature Lamp, 8¾" h, sgd "Delft," ex-collection of Ruth Smith **975.00**
Perfume Bottle, 5¼" h, 3" d, Opal Ware, dark green and brown glossy ground, red and yellow nasturtiums, sprinkler top **375.00**

Pickle castor, textured insert, hp pansy dec, 9½" h, $525.00.

Pitcher, 6" h
   MOP, DQ, large loop frosted camphor shell handle **325.00**
   Verona, spider mums, leaves, and buds **425.00**
Rose Bowl, 4" h, 4½" d, Verona, clear ribbed glass, English ivy and purple flowers, gold rim **185.00**
Sugar Shaker, 4¾" h, Opal Ware, egg-shaped, pink ground, Timothy Canty dec of white and blue flowers, orig cov **425.00**

Salt shaker, Pillar Rib, hp, 4" h, $125.00.

Toothpick Holder, 2¾" h, 5" d, Mushroom, white, lusterless, enameled flowers **375.00**
Vase
   6½" h, MOP
      Bridal White, applied frosted edge, price for pr . **550.00**
      Shaded blue, bulbous, DQ, white lining **275.00**
   7¼" h, MOP, DQ, bright medium green, applied amber frosted edge, white lining **850.00**
   7¾" h, MOP, Muslin, deep gold, melon-ribbed, white lining, applied frosted edge **375.00**
   8" h, MOP, Raindrop pattern, butterscotch, crimped top, applied camphor edge **375.00**
   8¼" h, MOP, DQ, red-orange ground, ruffled top ..**1,250.00**
   8½" h, Napoli, frog sitting in bullrushes, turquoise, blue, green, and rust int., gold outlines on ext. .. **975.00**
   9" h, MOP satin glass, Raindrop pattern, crimped edge, c1880 .... **285.00**

10" h, stick, beige and gold ground, acorn and oak leaves, paper label reads "Albertine Mt. W. G. Co." **2,250.00**

11¼" h, satin glass, enameled seaweed design, gourd shape **550.00**

13½" h, white opal ground, enameled pink, gold, and brown flowers, pinched blank, marked with numbers and "P" **550.00**

MULBERRY CHINA

History: Mulberry china was made primarily in the Staffordshire district of England between 1830 and 1850. The ware often has a flowing effect like that of flow blue but the color is a dark purple, similar to that of crushed mulberries. The potters that manufactured flow blue also made mulberry china, and, in fact, frequently made some patterns in both types of wares. To date, there are no known reproductions.

References: Susan and Al Bagdade, *Warman's English & Continental Pottery & Porcelain,* Second Edition, Wallace-Homestead, 1991; Ellen R. Hill, *Mulberry Ironstone,* published by author, 1993; Petra Williams, *Flow Blue China and Mulberry Ware,* Revised Edition, Fountain House East, 1993.

Advisor: Ellen G. King.

Berry Bowl, Bryonia, Utzschneider, 4" d **35.00**
Chamber Pot, cov, Seaweed, Ridgway **250.00**
Creamer
    Flora, Walker, 5" h **195.00**
    Temple, Podmore Walker, 6" h **150.00**
Cup and Saucer
    Percy, Morley, handleless **85.00**
    Washington Vase, Podmore Walker, handleless **95.00**
Cup Plate
    Athens, Adams **60.00**
    Lady Peel, Morley, 3¾" d **65.00**

Coffeepot, Peruvian, ironstone, $135.00.

Pitcher
    Corean, Podmore Walker, 1½ qt **175.00**
    Hong, Walker, 8" h **250.00**
Plate
    Calcutta, Challinor, 10" d **125.00**
    Flora, Walker, 7½" d **55.00**
    Rhone Scenery, Mayer, 8" d **55.00**
    Vincennes, Alcock, 10½" d **70.00**
    Washington Vase, Podmore Walker, 8¾" d **60.00**

Plate, Corean, Podmore Walker, 9¾" d, $95.00.

Platter
    Pelew, Challinor, 18" l **375.00**
    Scinde, Walker, 15½" l **350.00**
    Tavoy, Walker, 15" l **275.00**
Relish, Vincennes, Alcock **180.00**
Sauce Tureen
    Bochara, Edwards, price for 3-pc set **595.00**
    Vincennes, Alcock, price for 3-pc set **295.00**
Soap Dish
    Flora, Walker, price for 3-pc set **165.00**
    Ning Po, Hall, price for 2-pc set **295.00**
Soup Tureen, Bryonia, Utzschneider, round, price for 3-pc set **185.00**
Sugar
    Cyprus, Davenport **225.00**
    Jeddo, Adams **195.00**
    Tonquin, Heath **175.00**
Teapot
    Corean, Podmore Walker **375.00**
    Pelew, Challinor, professional restoration to lid **355.00**
    Tavoy, Walker **275.00**
    Washington Vase, Podmore Walker **325.00**
Vegetable Tureen, cov
    California, Podmore Walker **225.00**
    Cyprus, Davenport **220.00**
    Pelew, Challinor **475.00**
Wash Bowl and Pitcher, Washington Vase, Podmore Walker, price for 2-pc set **625.00**
Waste Bowl
    Ning Po, Hall **225.00**
    Pelew, Challinor **175.00**

MUSICAL INSTRUMENTS

History: From the first beat of the prehistoric drum to the very latest in electronic music makers, musical instruments have been popular modes of communication and relaxation.

The most popular antique instruments are violins, flutes, oboes, and other instruments associated with the classical music period of 1650 to 1900. Many of the modern instruments, such as trumpets, guitars, and drums, have value on the "used" rather than antiques market.

The collecting of musical instruments is in its infancy. The field is growing very rapidly. Investors and speculators have played a role since the 1930s, especially in early string instruments.

References: S. P. Fjestad (ed.), *Blue Book of Guitar Values,* Second Edition, Blue Book Publications, 1994; George Gruhn and Walter Carter, *Acoustic Guitars and Other Fretted Instruments,* GPI Books, 1993; ———, *Electric Guitars and Basses,* Miller Freeman Books, GPI Books, 1994; ———, *Gruhn's Guide to Vintage Guitars,* GPI Books, 1991; Mike Longworth, *C. F. Martin & Co.,* 4 Maples Press, 1994; Paul Trynka (ed.), *The Electric Guitar,* Chronicle Books, 1993.

Periodicals: *Concertina & Squeezebox,* PO Box 6706, Ithaca, NY 14851; *Jerry's Musical Newsletter,* 4624 W Woodland Rd, Minneapolis, MN 55424; *Piano & Keyboard,* PO Box 767, San Anselmo, CA 94979; *Strings,* PO Box 767, San Anselmo, CA 94979; *Twentieth Century Guitar,* 135 Oser Ave, Hauppauge, NY 11788; *Vintage Guitar Classics,* PO Box 7301, Bismarck, ND 58507.

Collectors' Clubs: American Musical Instrument Society, RD 3, Box 205-B, Franklin, PA 16323; Automatic Musical Instrument Collectors Assoc, 919 Lantern Glow Trail, Dayton, OH 45431; Fretted Instrument Guild of America, 2344 S Oakley Ave, Chicago, IL 60608; Musical Box Society International, 887 Orange Ave E, St Paul, MN 55106; Reed Organ Society, Inc, PO Box 901, Deansboro, NY 13328.

Museums: C. F. Martin Guitar Museum, Nazareth, PA; International Piano Archives at Maryland, Neil Ratliff Music Library, College Park, MD; Miles Musical Museum, Eureka Springs, AR; Museum of the American Piano, New York, NY; Musical Museum, Deansboro, NY; Streitwieser Foundation Trumpet Museum, Pottstown, PA; University of Michigan, Stearns Collection of Musical Instruments, Ann Arbor, MI; Yale University Collection of Musical Instruments, New Haven, CT.

Accordion, Empress, Germany, c1890	75.00
Alto Saxophone, Buescher, Artistocrat	175.00
Banjo	
Bacon & Day, Senorita, nineteen fret, tenor	225.00
Gibson, five string	625.00
Vega 19, fret tenor style, orig case	325.00
Bass Clarinet, Vito Resotone	300.00
Bass Guitar, Regal Upright, small-cello size	650.00
Cello, French, Medio Fino style, cloth bag attached	275.00
Clarinet, French, wood	100.00
Coronet, Boston Musical Instrument Mfg, rotary valve	650.00
Drum, Acme, bass, 26" d, c1900	225.00
Electric Guitar	
Dan Electro	250.00
Fender	
Coronado II, semi-hollow, orig case	300.00
Stratocaster, orig case	850.00

Gibson, Hummingbird, 1965	1,000.00
Guild, F45-CE, acoustic/electric, cutaway	375.00
Hamer, Sunburst, orig case	300.00
Harmony	
Rocket, archtop	100.00
Stratotone	150.00
Ibanez, Artist	150.00
Silvertone, amplifiers	200.00
Flute, Meyer, ten key, c1900	300.00
Guitar	
Gibson, Les Paul	550.00
Martin, 1899, without bridges or turners	600.00
Harmonica, Hohner's Best, orig box	25.00
Lyre Guitar, German	800.00
Mandolin	
Gibson, A50	500.00
Martin, bowl back	150.00
Organ, Williams Organ Co, Epworth, oak case, back grill, two and three-fifths ranks of reeds and octave coupler, thirteen stops, c1890	625.00
Piano	
Fischer, New York, Ampico Model B Grand Player Piano, mahogany, matching bench and twelve music rolls	13,000.00
Kirkman & Sons, London, grand, burl maple, adjustable stool, 75" l	6,500.00
Steinway & Sons, baby grand, ebonized, late 19th C	3,750.00
Pianoforte, J Osborne, NY, Empire style, rosewood and mahogany veneer case, inlaid floral and foliate motifs, hinged rect top with projecting cylindrical cross bar, stool, c1820, 70" w, 33½" h	750.00
Tenor Saxophone, Olds & Sons	200.00
Trumpet, HN White King, Silver	300.00
Vibraharp, Deagen Model 1100	1,100.00
Vibraphone, Musser, Model 75	1,500.00
Violin, Pietro	3,000.00

Music Related

Amp Head, Peavey Century	55.00
Amplifier	
Fender	
Band Master, white vinyl	600.00
Champ	95.00

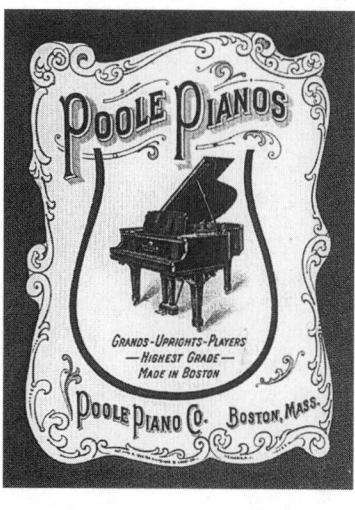

Piano, bookmark, celluloid, Poole Pianos, The Whitehead & Hoag Co., Newark, NJ, 2 × 2⅝", $12.00.

Gibson, Titan **500.00**
Standel Studio 15 .... **500.00**
Supertone Model 54C **25.00**
Twin 8 .... **100.00**
Foot Pedal, Cry Baby **55.00**
Microphone
RCA **125.00**
Shure, Model 51 .... **75.00**
Monitor Speaker, Peavey **60.00**
Music Stand, bronze, tapered neck, French, c1790 ....**3,000.00**
Piano Stool, cast iron, claw feet with glass ball **125.00**

MUSIC BOXES

History: Music boxes, invented in Switzerland around 1825, encompass a broad array of forms, from small boxes to huge circus calliopes.

A cylinder box consists of a comb with teeth which vibrate when striking a pin in the cylinder. The music these boxes produce ranges from light tunes to opera and overtures.

The first disc music box was invented by Paul Lochmann of Leipzig, Germany, in 1886. It used an interchangeable steel disc with pierced holes bent to a point which hit the star-wheel as the disc revolved, and thus produced the tune. Discs were easily stamped out of metal, allowing a single music box to play an endless variety of tunes. Disc boxes reached the height of their popularity from 1890 to 1910 when the phonograph replaced them.

Music boxes also were incorporated in many items, e.g., clocks, sewing and jewelry boxes, steins, plates, toys, perfume bottles, and furniture.

References: Gilbert Bahl, *Music Boxes,* Courage Books, Running Press, 1993; Arthur W. J. G. Ord-Hume, *The Musical Box,* Schiffer Publishing, 1995.

Collectors' Clubs: Music Box Society of Great Britain, PO Box 299, Waterbeach, Cambridge CB4 4DJ England; Musical Box Society International, 887 Orange Ave E, St Paul MN 55106.

Museums: Bellms Cars and Music of Yesterday, Sarasota, FL; Lockwood Matthews Mansion Museum, Norwalk, CT; Miles Musical Museum, Eureka Springs, AR; The Musical Museum, Deansboro, NY; The Musical Wonder House Museum, Iscasset, ME.

Additional Listings: See *Warman's Americana & Collectibles* for more examples.

Cylinder-Type

15½" l, inlaid walnut and simulated rosewood case, zither attachment, lever wind, 11" cylinder, 30 tunes, marked "1735," Swiss, c1900 .... **900.00**
17" l, 5½" h, inlaid walnut case, 6" cylinder, eight tunes, Duck Son & Pinker, c1900 .... **375.00**
18" l, Swiss, marquetry case, c1880-90 ....**1,200.00**
19¼" w, 12" d, 10¾" h, Victorian, rosewood inlay, lift lid, cylinders, bell and tympana accompaniment ...**1,300.00**
20" l, rosewood case, inlaid floral design on lid, orig tune sheet, stop/start and change repeat levers, four tunes, Mandoline, late 19th C **2,475.00**
26" l, rosewood case, fruitwood banding, orig tune sheet, side lever wind, zither attachment, stop/start and

change repeat levers, eight tunes, Bremond Sublime Harmony Piccolo, late 19th C **2,750.00**
31" l, walnut case, fruitwood banding, side lever wind, zither attachment, stop/start and change repeat levers, twelve tunes, comb plate emb "AK KI," Jaccard, late 19th C **1,200.00**

Disc-Type

9½" d, Stella Grand, table model, stained mahogany case, coffer lid, seven discs, c1900 ....**1,650.00**
14½" d disc, Polyphon, walnut case, double comb with twelve bells, sepia litho inlaid lid, crank handle, bracket feet, twelve discs, Germany, c1900, restored**5,500.00**
16¼" l, Regina, old replaced wooden case, plays 12" disks, no crank **1,240.00**
21" d disc, Olympia, table model, mahogany case, peripheral driven movement, double comb, stop/start lever, sixteen discs, c1900 ....**3,850.00**
27" d disc, Regina Orchestral, floor model, oak case, double comb, 78" h **12,750.00**

Miscellaneous

Automation, birdcage, 20½" h, brass, two feathered birds, French bellow need restoration **1,150.00**

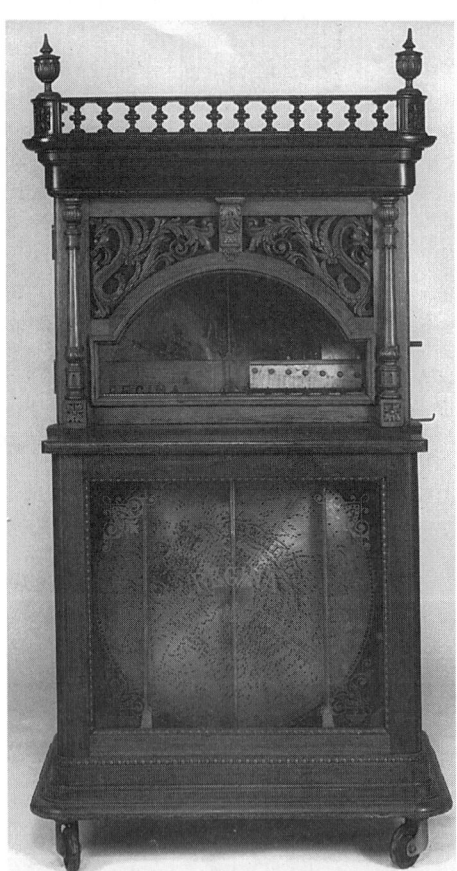

Regina, Style 8, automatic changer, coin operated, twelve 27" discs, peripheral-driven movement, double comb, spring barrel, rack, disc selector, crank wound at side, mahogany case, dragon spandrels, spooled railing, 76" h, $17,600.00.

Coin-Operated, 51½" h, Symphonion, Style 106NS, floor model, walnut case, arched fret-carved crest supporting three vasiform finials, glazed arched door with ball and baluster turnings, molded base, bun feet, duplex comb, ten 19⅛" discs, c1900 ....**3,950.00**

Organette, Mechanical Orguimette Co, five rolls, wooden floor cabinet, roll storage drawer, musical boudoir **375.00**

Roller Organ, Mascotte, walnut case, four 2½" rolls, Gately Mfg Co **250.00**

NAILSEA-TYPE GLASS

History: Nailsea-type glass is characterized by swirls and loopings, usually white, on a clear or colored ground. One of the first areas where this glass was made was Nailsea, England, 1788–1873, hence the name. Several glass houses, including American factories, made this type of glass.

Bellows Bottle, 9¼" h, clear, white loopings, applied collared mouth, pontil **90.00**

Bowl, 7⅝" d, sapphire blue, opaque white loopings, applied clear trim, feet, and handles **175.00**

Dipper, 17¾" l, clear, red loopings, white chalklike int. coating **125.00**

Fairy Lamp

5½" h, 6¾" d, ruby red and white loopings, piecrust edge on bowl, clear glass candle-cup holder, sgd "S. Clark Trade Mark Fairy U.S. Patent No. 9th 1886 No. 352296" **935.00**

6" h, cranberry and white loopings, dome-shaped shade, five clear satin wishbone feet **685.00**

6½" h, 7" w diagonally, sweeping white loopings blend into blue ground, dome-shaped shade, triangular base, three pinched-in folds, fancy ruffled edge, clear glass candle cup marked "S. Clarke Patent Trade Mark Fairy" **945.00**

Fishnet Ball, 4¾" d, white loopings, 19th C **110.00**

Flask, half pint, pale green, white loopings **195.00**

Flip, 8½" h, 6¼" d, light green, milky green loopings, plain sheared mouth, pontil **165.00**

Flask, white on clear, orig stopper, 7½" h, $150.00.

Gemel Bottle, 7⅞" l, clear, white loopings, clear applied rigaree **35.00**

Lamp Shade, 4" h, 7" d, cranberry, white pulled-ribbon pattern, ruffled edge **45.00**

Pitcher, 7" h, pear shape, ftd, white loopings **165.00**

Rolling Pin, blown

14" l, green, white loopings **200.00**

17½" l, clear, white and pink loopings **90.00**

Rose Bowl, 3" h, 4½" d, pink threaded glass over white and citron loopings, three scroll feet, berry prunt ... **385.00**

Vase, 8¼" h, flaring, white loopings **175.00**

Witch Ball, 5¼" d, clear, pink and white loopings **100.00**

NANKING

History: Nanking is a type of Chinese porcelain made in Canton, China, from the early 1800s into the 20th century. It was made for export to America and England.

Four elements help distinguish Nanking from Canton, two similar types of ware. Nanking has a spear-and-post border, as opposed to the scalloped-line style of Canton. Second, in the water's edge or Willow pattern, Canton usually has no figures; Nanking includes a standing figure with open umbrella on the bridge. In addition, the blues tend to be darker on the Nanking ware. Finally, Nanking wares often are embellished with gold, Canton is not.

Green and orange variations of Nanking survive, although they are scarce.

REPRODUCTION ALERT

Copies of Nanking ware currently are being produced in China. They are of inferior quality and are decorated in a lighter rather than in the darker blues.

Bowl, 15" l, oval, flat octagonal rim, blue and white, c1800 .... **750.00**

Chocolate Pot, 9" h, pear shape, blue and white, Buddhist-style lion finial **775.00**

Cider Jug, 7¾" h, blue and white, spearhead and lattice borders, coastal village scene, double entwined handle, molded flowers and leaves terminal, early 19th C, base rim chip **400.00**

Mug, 6⅛" h, blue and white water's-edge scene **350.00**

Platter, 17⅜ × 20", oval, blue and white, coastal-village scene, spearhead and lattice borders, minor glaze wear, early 19th C **875.00**

Sauce Tureen, cov, under plates, 8" l, blue and white, twin braided handles, floral knops, 19th C, base chips, price for pr **1,250.00**

Sugar Bowl, cov, 6½" h, cylindrical, blue and white, gilt highlights, strawberry knop finial **325.00**

Tea Caddy, 5" h, blue and white, gilt trim **750.00**

Warming Dish, 11½" l, blue and white, 19th C **180.00**

NAPKIN RINGS, FIGURAL

History: Gracious home dining during the Victorian era required a personal napkin ring for each household member. Figural napkin rings were first patented in 1869. During the remainder of the 19th century, most plating companies, including Cromwell, Eureka, Meriden, and Reed and Barton, manufactured figural rings, many copying and only slightly varying the designs of other companies.

Reference: Lillian Gottschalk and Sandra Whitson, *Figural Napkin Rings,* Collector Books, 1996.

Reproduction Alert: Quality reproductions do exist.

Additional Listings: See *Warman's Americana & Collectibles* for a listing of non-figural napkin rings.

Notes: Values are determined by the subject matter of the ring, the quality of the workmanship, and the condition.

Bird, perched on top of ring, long tail, elaborately scrolled base, Apollo Silver Plate Co	185.00
Butterfly and fan	175.00
Cap, beneath ring, horns and swords at side	335.00
Cats, two cats peeking around ring, rect base	450.00
Cherub, pulling cart, movable wheels	225.00

Figural, cherubs holding ring on backs, shaped rect base, Meriden, $245.00.

Dog, full-figure Shepherd, sitting on round base next to barrel-shaped ring, Tufts	175.00
Eagles	175.00
Fox, sitting, oval ring on back, rect base	250.00
Greenaway, Kate, boy feeding begging dog	450.00
Horse, pulling ring on wheels	450.00
Lily and Lily Pad	175.00
Monkey, standing, oval base, Derby Silver Co	295.00
Naked Boy, pushing ring, ornate base, Middletown Plate Co	395.00
Turtle Doves, spread wings support ring, Middletown Plate	195.00
Wheeled Cart, salt and pepper, ring, butter pat, figural bird atop handle	495.00

NASH GLASS

History: Nash glass is a type of art glass attributed to Arthur John Nash and his sons, Leslie H. and A. Douglas. Arthur John Nash, originally employed by Webb in Stourbridge, England, came to America and was employed in 1889 by Tiffany Furnaces at its Corona, Long Island, plant.

While managing the plant for Tiffany, Nash designed and produced iridescent glass. In 1928 A. Douglas Nash purchased the facilities of Tiffany Furnaces. The A. Douglas Nash Corporation remained in operation until 1931.

Bowl, 15½" d, Chintz pattern, amber, blue, and green opal, turned-down rim	400.00
Candlesticks, pr, 5" h, Chintz pattern, blood red, silver dec	850.00
Creamer, 4½" h, pale orchid and green design, applied clear handle	350.00
Goblet, 6½" h, Chintz pattern, blue and green	125.00
Lemon Dish, gold irid	125.00
Perfume, 7¼" h, blue and lilac rays, pale blue foot, orig pointed amber stopper, silver blue irid	750.00
Vase, 6½" h, bulbous, feathery blue strokes, bubbly lime green streaks, sgd	500.00

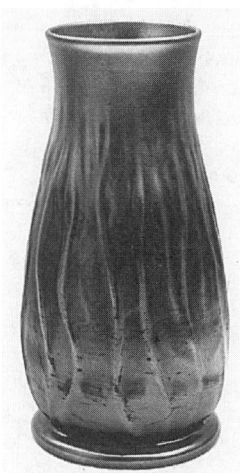

Vase, blue irid, marked "B526," 5½" h, $600.00.

NAUTICAL ITEMS

History: The seas have fascinated man since time began. The artifacts of sailors have been collected and treasured for years. Because of their environment, merchant and naval items, whether factory or handmade, must be of quality construction and long lasting. Many of these items are aesthetically appealing as well.

References: Jon Baddeley, *Nautical Antiques & Collectables,* Sotheby's Publications, 1993; Robert W. D. Ball, *Nautical Antiques,* Schiffer Publishing, 1994.

Periodicals: *Nautical Brass,* PO Box 3966, North Ft. Myers, FL 33918; *Nautical Collector,* PO Box 949, New London, CT 06320.

Collectors' Club: Nautical Research Guild, 62 Marlboro St, Newburyport, MA 01950.

Museums: Kittery Historical & Naval Museum, Kittery, ME; Lyons Maritime Museum, St Augustine, FL; Mariners' Museum, Newport News, VA; Maritime Museum of Monterey, Monterey, CA; Museum of Science and Industry, Chicago, IL; Mystic Seaport Museum, Mystic, CT; Peabody Museum of Salem, Salem, MA; Philadelphia Maritime Museum, Philadelphia, PA; San Francisco Maritime National Historical Park, San Francisco, CA; U.S. Naval Academy Museum, Naval Academy, MD.

Autograph, four-language ship's paper, 1 pg, 8 × 11",
Phila, Nov 14, 1806, for Brig *Ceres* commanded by
James A Lewis, bound for Jamaica, dark signatures of
Thomas Jefferson as President and James Madison as
Secretary of State, repairs to browned paper, dark
signatures **3,900.00**

Backstaff, wood, inlaid label "Made by William Hart in
Portsmouth, NE/for 1767," 18th C **8,000.00**

Bell, brass
    8" d, inscribed "Sunek 1958" **175.00**
    14" d, inscribed "SS Pacific Prince" **500.00**

Binnacle, 56" h, brass, mahogany base, complete **750.00**

Book
    Cram, W Bartlett, *Picture History of New England
    Passenger Vessels,* 8 × 10", dj, 414 pgs, 1980, 1st
    ed **75.00**
    Russell, Phillips, *John Paul Jones: Man of Action,* 5
    × 7", orig dec cloth, 314 pgs, illus by Leon Un-
    derwood, NY, 1927, faded spine **20.00**
    Spears, John, *Captain Nathaniel Brown Palmer, An
    Old-Time Sailor of the Sea,* 3 × 5", orig cloth,
    plates, 252 pgs, NY, 1922 .... **20.00**

Chart Chest, 48" l, pine, dovetailed, orig beckets, contains nine navigational charts, 19th C **500.00**

Chronometer, 6¼" d, brass-bound case, clock numbered
"1774," made by Charles Frodsham, London **3,500.00**

Coffeepot, 11" h, SS, engraved and cast nautical dec,
engraved "Larchmont Yacht Club, 1893," marked
"Whiting Mfg Co. NY," 37 troy oz **1,320.00**

Compass, pocket, engraved brass sundial, orig box ... **250.00**

Fog Horn, hand operated, red wooden box, side lever,
stenciled "Lothrop's Patent Fog Horn 1" **325.00**

Harpoon, 33¼" l, double flue, 19th C **250.00**

Model, ship, constructed by Charles Mitton, NJ
    27" l, 26" h, American naval coastal sloop, eight guns **475.00**
    32" l, 23" h, *Maris Stella,* Spanish Galeon **400.00**
    41" l, 30" h, English 17th C naval flag ship, 66 guns **925.00**
    44" l, 72½" h, *Ocean Queen,* wood sq rigged, three
    masts, thirteen guns, black hull **1,750.00**

Painting, framed
    8½ × 12", Winckworth Allan Gay, "Stranded Hull
    Looking Down Nantasket Beach Toward Boston
    Light and Great Brewster Island," sgd "W. A.
    Gay" lower left, identified in inscription on re-

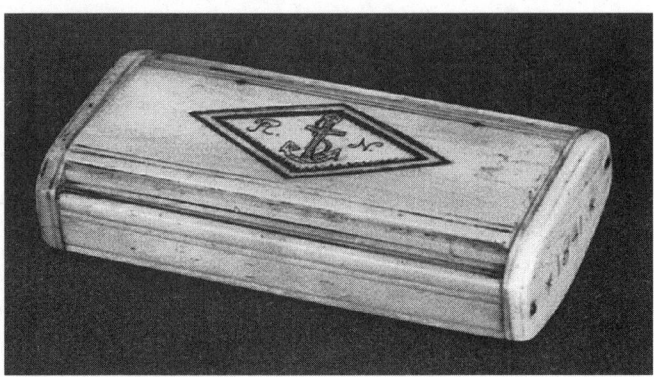

**Snuff box, oval, scrimshaw, "Capt. N. C. Norten" of Royal Navy on top,
dates of service (1831–41) on side, diamond with "R. N." and anchor on
bottom, some fluting motif, highlighted with lampblack, 3 × 1½",
$375.00.**

    verse, oil on board, curvature to support, upper
    right corner retouched **2,550.00**
    9⅜ × 20⅞", Alfred Thompson Bricher, "Coastal
    View with Lighthouse," sgd "AT Bricher" lower
    right, watercolor on paper **3,400.00**
    12 × 20½", Frank Hamilton Taylor, "Cottage, Thim-
    ble Island, CT," views presented en suite, sgd and
    dated "F. H. Taylor '78" lower right, identified on
    label from Babcock Galleries, NY, on reverse,
    gouache and graphite on paper **2,415.00**
    22 × 36", Wesley Webber, "Annisquam Point," sgd
    "W. Webber" lower right, identified and inscribed
    "Old Annisquam Light" on reverse, oil on canvas,
    minor puncture, craquelure **3,900.00**
    24 × 30", Hermann Herzog, "Sunset at Chesapeake
    Bay, Maryland," sgd "H Herzog" lower left, iden-
    tified on presentation plaque and in inscription on
    reverse, oil on canvas, lined, minor retouch, cra-
    quelure **13,800.00**
    25 × 30¼" h, Marshall Johnson, "Sailing Vessels at
    Dark," sgd "Marshall Johnson" lower left, oil on
    canvas **1,850.00**
    30¼ × 50", William Formsby Halsall, animated
    coastal view, New England, sgd and dated "Wm
    F Halsall. 78" lower left, oil on canvas **9,200.00**

Porthole, 15" d, brass, storm cov **120.00**

Print, color woodcut on paper, framed
    7½ × 8", Lemos, Pedro J, Driftwood, Oakland Ship-
    yard, sgd in pencil lower right, titled in pencil
    lower left **635.00**
    15¼ × 12½", Lindenmuth, Tod, "The Riding Light,"
    sgd in pencil lower right, titled in pencil lower left **865.00**

Quadrant, ebony, ivory inlays **550.00**

Sea Chest, 37" l, orig green and brown paint and ropework beckets, 19th C **600.00**

Sextant, 17" l, mahogany, engraved brass radial arm,
ivory nameplate engraved "H Duren, New York,"
Gregory & Wright, London, 18th C **1,200.00**

Ship's Block, 13½" l, wood, one lignium vitae, one metal
pulley **125.00**

Ship's Log, bark *Petrea,* 65-pg folio, entries from March
17 to Dec 15, 1858, voyages from Le Havre to Portsmouth, New York, and Melbourne, details activities
while in port, at sea, hourly speeds, courses, winds,
weather, including near disaster, towing to Portsmouth, repairs, trying to save mud-covered cargo,
mate with smallpox **585.00**

Stern Board, 54" w, carved mahogany, gilded eagle, P
Libbey, Maine, sgd on back **1,500.00**

Telescope, 4¾" h, brass, Swan, Hunter & Wingham Richardson Ltd, Neptune Works, dated 1840 .... **750.00**

Trail Board, 58½" l, gilded, foliate scroll carving, black
ground, 19th C **450.00**

NAZI ITEMS

History: The National Socialist German Workers Party (NSDAP)
was created on February 24, 1920, by Anton Drexler and Adolf
Hitler. Its 25-point nationalistic program was designed to revive
the depressed German economy and revitalize the government.

In 1923, after the failed Beer Hall Putsch, Hitler was sentenced to a five-year term in Landsberg Prison. He spent only a year in prison, during which time he wrote the first volume of *Mein Kampf.*

In the late 1920s and early 1930s the NSDAP developed from a regional party into a major national party. In the spring of 1933 Hitler became the Reich's chancellor. Shortly after the death of President von Hindenberg in 1934, Hitler combined the offices of president and chancellor into a single position, giving him full control over the German government as well as NSDAP. From that point until May 1945, the National Socialist German Worker's Party dominated all aspects of German life.

In the mid-1930s Hitler initiated a widespread plan—ranging from re-arming to territorial acquisition—designed to unite the German-speaking peoples of Europe into a single nation. Germany's invasion of Poland in 1939 triggered the hostilities that led to the Second World War. The war in Europe ended on VE Day, May 7, 1945.

Reference: Ron Manion, *German Military Collectibles Price Guide,* Antique Trader Publications, 1995.

Periodicals: *Der Gauleiter,* PO Box 721288, Houston, TX 77272; *Military Collector Magazine,* PO Box 245, Lyon Station, PA 19536; *Military Collectors News,* PO Box 702073, Tulsa, OK 74170; *Military History,* 602 S King St, Suite 300, Leesburg, VA 22075; *Military Trader,* PO Box 1050, Dubuque, IA 52004.

Note: The objects that appear below are associated with the NSDAP as a political party. See the Militaria listing for objects associated with the German military prior to and during World War II.

Arm Band
  Concentration-Camp Prisoner, colored triangle on white cotton
    Black, Political 55.00
    Blue, Gypsy 65.00
    Green, Criminal 55.00
    Pink, Homosexual 90.00
    Red, Communist 55.00
    Yellow, half Jewish 65.00
    Purple, Jehovah Witness 75.00
  Jewish, yellow Star of David 42.00
  Waffen SS 29.00
Autograph
  Bormann, Martin, private secretary to Adolf Hitler, letter sgd as Deputy to the Fuhrer and Chief of Staff, in German, 1 pg, 8 × 10″, on National Socialist German Labor Party letterhead, Obersalzberg, Aug 26, 1937, telling storm trooper that he has been exceeding his jurisdiction and asking him to confirm activity 850.00
  Goering, Hermann, typed letter sgd as Reichsminister for Air Travel and Commander in Chief of the Luftwaffe, in German, 1 pg, 8 × 10″, on official letterhead with emb eagle and swastika at upper left, Berlin, July 9, 1938, letter regarding sums for support of housing or studios for artists, sgd in magenta ink 1,275.00
  Keitel, Wilhelm, Hitler's chief military advisor, partially printed and typed document, sgd as General Field marshal and Chief of the High Command of the Wehrmacht, in German, 1 pg, 5 × 7″, Fuhrer

Headquarters, Jan 30, 1943, confers War Merit Cross Second Class with Swords to Willy Foll, large dark signature 700.00
Award Certificate, German, unused
  1st of October medal, 1938 .... 25.00
  Iron Cross, 2nd Class 25.00
Backpack, Army, horsehair, leather straps, maker's mark, c1936 .... 45.00
Book, *The Nazi Movement in the United States 1924–1941,* Sander A. Diamond, Cornell Univ Press, 1974, 5 × 7″, 330 pgs 20.00
Broadside, "The National Socialist Germany Greets their National Socialist Austria and the New National Socialist Regime in Honor of Unerasable Fellowship—Hiel Hitler" 42.00
Cigarettes, German Hotel, Nazi proofed pack 28.00
Dagger
  Luftwaffe, 10⅜″ unmarked blade, aluminum fittings, eagle, and Swastika handguard, yellow spiral handle with pebble-grain cast-alloy scabbard, silver sword knot attached 195.00
  SA, later scabbard 150.00
Firearm, revolver, cal. 10.75 mm, single action, 4⅝″ part octagonal/part round barrel, bag handle grip, smooth wooden panels, left side of frame marked with oval containing manufacturer's name, checkered thumb safety on left side, lanyard loop, unit marking on back strap 275.00
Flag, double sided
  Army, Regimental Battle, 84 × 144″, eagle, swastika, tricolor 75.00
  Parade, NSDAP, 45½″ l, hp black swastika on white, c1920 .... 35.00
Funeral Sash, SS, fabric and paper, silver lettering, white fringe, large silver SS Runes 125.00
Hat
  Panzer Officer, black wool, silver piping, silver eagle, two silver buttons on ear flaps, maker's mark ... 300.00
  SS, rabbit fur, quilted int., black ties at ear slaps, olive green wool body, RZM/SS, skull and eagle devices 275.00
Holster, standard issue, black clamshell holster, back marked "GXY 1942" over Nazi eagle, "WaA700" and large "P-38", spare P-38 mag in pocket, facing to brown on mag pouch, light mildew 120.00

Iron Cross, first class, with case, $65.00.

Medal, German Red Cross, 1937, black enameled eagle
and red cross, red and white ribbon **85.00**
Photo Album, 1942–43, official "Reiche-Autobahnen,"
21 photos **85.00**
Pinback button,⅝" d, "Halt Hitler," blue and white, Star
of David symbol, 1930–40 .... **20.00**
Plate, 9" d, green and white porcelain, green Luftwaffe
eagle, Unit #O-H-2 .... **20.00**
Postage Stamps, sheet of 100, Hitler portrait, WWII era **35.00**
Print, 8 × 11", Luftwaffe crew, preparing bomber for
strike, marked "Berlin, 1940" **20.00**
Sheet Music, 9 × 12", "In Anticipation of that Great
Day," black and white, caricature of Hitler on front
cov, copyright 1943, Lincoln Music Corp **25.00**

NETSUKES

History: The traditional Japanese kimono has no pockets. Daily
necessities, such as money and tobacco supplies, were carried in
leather pouches, or inros, which hung from a cord with a netsuke
toggle. The word netsuke comes from "ne"—to root—and
"tsuke"—to fasten.

Netsukes originated in the 14th century and initially were fa-
vored by the middle class. By the mid-18th century all levels of
Japanese society used them. Some of the most famous artists, e.g.,
Shuzan and Yamada Hojitsu, worked in the netsuke form.

Netsukes average from 1 to 2 inches in length and are made
from wood, ivory, bone, ceramics, metal, horn, nutshells, etc. The
subject matter is broad based, but always portrayed in a light-
hearted, humorous manner. A netsuke must have smooth edges
and balance in order to hang correctly on the sash.

Reference: Raymond Bushell, *An Introduction to Netsuke,* Charles
E. Tuttle Co., 1971.

Periodical: *Netsuke & Ivory Carving Newsletter,* 3203 Adams
Way, Ambler, PA 19002.

Collectors' Clubs: International Netsuke Society, PO Box 471686,
San Francisco, CA 94147; Netsuke Kenkyukai Society, PO Box
31595, Oakland, CA 94604.

REPRODUCTION ALERT

Recent reproductions are on the market. Many are
carved from African ivory.

Notes: Value depends on artist, region, material, and skill of craftsmanship. Western collectors favor katabori, pieces which represent an identifiable object.

Buffalo Horn, Ojime, three pc **95.00**
Elk Horn, manju shaped, incised dragon form, sgd **85.00**
Ivory
    Bird catching monkey and pig, Japanese **175.00**
    Boy with walnut, 2¼" h **50.00**
    Fishmonger with basket, 1½" h **115.00**
    Foo dog, 18th C, 1½" h **195.00**
    Frog on zori, sgd, 2" h **225.00**

Kuoto, triangle form, large Himatoshi, Baku form, Jap-
anese, 18th C, 2¾" h, age cracks bleaching **210.00**
Maiden and octopus, sgd "Kosho" **125.00**
Man, seated, 1¼" h **50.00**
Merchant, seated, ox with firewood bundles, sgd,
1½" h **400.00**
Moray eel, sgd, 2½" h **70.00**
Rat catcher with basket, sgd, 1¾" h **95.00**
Rice Cake Shape, Japanese, 18th C, 2¾" d **75.00**
Shoki subduing an Oni, Japanese, 19th C, 2¼" h ... **130.00**
Tiger, recumbent, sgd, 1¾" h **45.00**
Turtle on lily pad, sgd **75.00**
Shell, man blowing conch carved inside, ivory tip, 2¾"
l **250.00**
Stag Horn, kneeling priest presenting offering, 1½" d .. **115.00**
Tauga Nut
    Puppy, long-earred puppy peering out of pot, sgd,
    1¾" h **30.00**
    Rat atop leaves and vegetables, sgd, 2½" h **30.00**
    Rat study, 2¾" h **40.00**
Wood
    Badger, wrapped in fuki leaf **75.00**
    Japanese poet with book riding large gold fish, sgd,
    2¼" l **45.00**
    Puppy with pillow, sgd, 2" h **35.00**

NEWCOMB POTTERY

History: William and Ellsworth Woodward, two brothers, were
the founders of a series of businesses which eventually merged
into the Newcomb pottery effort. In 1885 Ellsworth Woodward, a
proponent of vocational training for women, organized a school
from which emerged the Ladies Decorative Art League. In 1886
the brothers founded the New Orleans Art Pottery Company, with
the ladies of the league serving as decorators. The first two potters
were Joseph Meyer and George Ohr. The pottery closed in 1891.

William Woodward was on the faculty at Tulane. Ellsworth
taught fine arts at the Sophie Newcomb College, a women's
school which eventually merged with Tulane. In 1895 Newcomb
College developed a pottery course with the intent of selling the
wares that were made. Some of the equipment came from the old
New Orleans Art Pottery.

Mary G. Sheerer joined the staff to teach decoration. In 1910
Paul E. Cox solved many of the technical problems connected
with making pottery in a Southern environment. Other leading
figures were Sadie Irvine, Professor Lota Lee Troy, and Kathrine
Choi. Pottery was made until the early 1950s.

Students painted quality art pottery with a distinctive high
glaze. Designs have a decidedly Southern flavor, e.g., myrtle,
jasmine, sugar cane, moss, cypress, dogwood, and magnolia motifs. Later matte-glazed pieces usually are decorated with carved-
back floral designs. Pieces depicting murky bayou scenes are most
desirable.

References: Susan and Al Bagdade, *Warman's American Pottery
and Porcelain,* Wallace-Homestead, 1994; Ralph and Terry Kovel,
Kovels' American Art Pottery, Crown Publishers, 1993; Jessie

Poesch, *Newcomb Pottery: An Enterprise for Southern Women*, Schiffer Publishing, 1984.

Collectors' Club: American Art Pottery Association, PO Box 525, Cedar Hill, MO 63016.

Museum: Newcomb College, Tulane University, New Orleans, LA.

Candlesticks, pr, corset shape, carved green, yellow and blue blossoms and leaves, shaded blue ground, Henrietta Bailey, imp "NC/HB/232/HZ52" and "HZ53" **2,500.00**
Toothpick Holder, 2¼" h, high glaze, floral, Dun, 1907 **1,600.00**
Trivet, 5" d, circular, titled "Twilight," deeply carved blue and green bayou scene, pink ground, Aurelia Arbo, 1930s, imp "NC/W90/F/AA," paper label remnant **1,300.00**
Vase
    4¼" h, 3¾" d, bulbous, carved blue trees, soft pink and light blue sky, Sadie Irvine, 1916, imp "NC/SI/JM/HW89/240/77" **2,300.00**
    5½" h
        3" d, highly glazed, modeled white clover blossoms, green leaves, medium blue ground, A F Simpson, 1909, marked "NC/AFS/JM/Q/DB91" **3,500.00**
        4¼" d, tapering, sharply carved white and light blue flowers, medium and dark blue ground, A F Simpson, 1912, imp "NC/JM/AFS/EY6/B" .. **2,200.00**
        6½" h, three-color floral design, blue ground, artist sgd "GK31AM," incised "NC/JM," mold mark 252 .... **1,800.00**
        10¼" h, 6½" d, bulbous, bayou scene, large yellow moon, deeply modeled oak trees and Spanish moss, medium blue, dark blue, and green on light blue ground, imp "NC/JM/JA45/150," paper label, 1917, invisible repair to a drill hole **4,800.00**
        11" h, 5" d, bottle shape, deeply incised white and yellow flowers, cobalt blue neck, light blue base, Sabrina Wells, 1904, imp "NC/JM/S.E. Wells/UU47/Q" **8,500.00**
        12¼" h, 5" d, ovoid, collar rim, carved pink tiger lilies and mint green leaves, soft blue ground, Henrietta Bailey, 1920, imp "NC/HB/PB16/117," paper label **3,500.00**

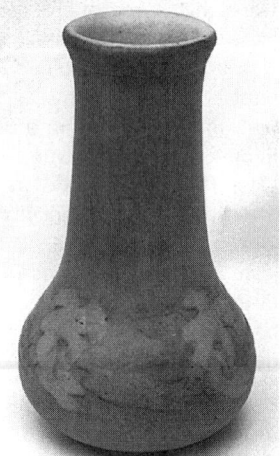

Vase, daffodils, mottled turquoise ground, sgd "Sadie Irvine," 6" h, $1,600.00.

NILOAK POTTERY, MISSION WARE

History: Niloak Pottery was made near Benton, Arkansas. Charles Dean Hyten experimented with native clay, trying to preserve its natural colors. By 1911 he perfected Mission Ware, a marbleized pottery in which the cream and brown colors predominate. The company name is the word "kaolin" spelled backwards.

After a devastating fire, the pottery was rebuilt and named Eagle Pottery. This factory included enough space to add a novelty pottery line in 1929. Mr. Hyten left the pottery in 1941, and in 1946 operations ceased.

Marks: The early pieces were marked "Niloak". Eagle Pottery products usually were marked "Hywood-Niloak" until 1934 when the "Hywood" was dropped from the mark.

References: Susan and Al Bagdade, *Warman's American Pottery and Porcelain,* Wallace-Homestead, 1994; David Edwin Gifford, *Collector's Encyclopedia of Niloak,* Collector Books, 1993.

Collectors' Club: Arkansas Pottery Collectors Society, PO Box 7617RD, Little Rock, AR 72217.

Additional Listings: See *Warman's Americana & Collectibles* for more examples, especially the novelty pieces.

Note: Prices listed below are for Mission Ware pieces.

Booklet, 1916 .... **40.00**
Candlestick, 10" h, cocoa, brown, tan, and blue swirled clay **140.00**
Chamberstick, 4" h, swirled blue, tan, light and dark brown clay **160.00**
Clock, 4" h, 5" d, semicircular, swirled clay case, orig works, die-stamped mark **600.00**

Lamp base, swirled tan, cream, and brown, $150.00.

Hatpin Holder, swirled clay **700.00**
Vase
    4" h, swirled light and dark brown clay **90.00**
    4½" h, swirled blue, light and dark brown clay **90.00**
    5" h, swirled blue, cream, light and dark brown clay, imp mark, hairline in firing **50.00**
    5¾" h, swirled blue, tan, light and dark brown clay **110.00**
    7" h, flattened form, swirling blue, tan, brown, and cream clay **200.00**

16½" h, 7½" d, bulbous, broad flaring rim, dark swirling brown, dark blue, and brick red, imp mark .. **800.00**
Wall Pocket, 6¼" l, swirled blue, light and dark brown
clay **350.00**

NIPPON CHINA, 1891–1921

History: Nippon, Japanese hand-painted porcelain, was made for export between 1891 and 1921. In 1891, when the McKinley Tariff Act proclaimed that all items of foreign manufacture be stamped with their country of origin, Japan chose to use "Nippon." In 1921 the United States decided the word "Nippon" no longer was acceptable and required all Japanese wares to be marked "Japan", ending the Nippon era.

Marks: There are over 220 recorded Nippon backstamps or marks; the three most popular are the wreath, maple leaf, and rising sun. Wares with variations of all three marks are being reproduced today. A knowledgeable collector can easily spot the reproductions by the mark variances.

The majority of the marks are found in three different colors: green, blue, or magenta. Colors indicate the quality of the porcelain used: green for first-grade porcelain, blue for second-grade, and magenta for third-grade. Marks were applied by two methods: decal stickers under glaze and imprinting directly on the porcelain.

References: Joan Van Patten, *The Collector's Encyclopedia of Nippon Porcelain,* First Series (1979, 1994 value update), Second Series (1982, 1995 value update), Third Series (1986, 1994 value update), Fourth Series, (1996), Collector Books; Kathy Wojciechowski, *The Wonderful World of Nippon Porcelain,* Schiffer Publishing, 1992.

Collectors' Clubs: ARK-LA-TEX Nippon Club, 6800 Arapaho Rd, #1057, Dallas, TX 75248; Dixieland Nippon Club, PO Box 1712, Centerville, VA 22020; International Nippon Collectors Club, 112 Oak Ave N, Owatonna, MN 55060; Lakes & Plains Nippon Collectors Society, PO Box 230, Peotone, IL 60468; Long Island Nippon Collectors Club, 145 Andover Place, W Hempstead, NY 11552; MD-PA Collectors' Club, 1016 Erwin Dr, Joppa, MD 21085; New England Nippon Collectors Club, 64 Burt Rd, Springfield, MA 01118; Sunshine State Nippon Collectors' Club, 2410 NE 84th St, Pompano Beach FL 33064; Upstate New York Nippon Collectors' Club, 122 Laurel Ave, Herkimer, NY 13350.

Additional Listings: See *Warman's Americana & Collectibles.*

Basket, 4", pale blue tiny flowers outlined in gold, gold
handle, rising sun mark **65.00**
Berry Set, large master bowl, seven matching small
bowls, large traced pink and blue flowers, green
leaves, fancy scalloped edges, Shinzo Nippon mark,
price for 8 pc set **115.00**
Biscuit Jar, cov, 8" h, hp
Floral dec, gold beading, unmarked **140.00**
Footed, green maple leaf mark **125.00**
Gold dec, blue maple leaf mark **150.00**
Bowl, hp
6½" d, sq, handles, sailboat scene, green wreath mark **45.00**
6" d, pierced handles, scenic, green M in wreath mark **25.00**
8" d, purple flowers, gold trim, fancy looped edges **75.00**

Bowl, cov, 7" d, two handles, purple floral, green lattice,
unmarked **100.00**
Butter Tub, cov, insert, two handles, hp, floral dec, TE-
OH mark **60.00**
Cake Set, master plate, four serving plates, turquoise and
flying geese **175.00**
Calling Card Tray, 7½" l, cobalt blue, pink, and red roses,
gold trim, green M in wreath mark **125.00**
Celery Set, 13½" l master celery dish, six salts, hp stalk
of celery in center, wreath mark **185.00**
Charger, 12" d, rose tapestry type **2,600.00**
Cheese Dish, cov, 8" d, hp, gold and floral dec, blue
maple leaf mark **50.00**
Condensed Milk Container, 6" h, tiny pink and white
roses, white beaded scrolling, mauve shaded ground,
RC mark **150.00**
Ewer, 13½" h, hp, unsgd **700.00**
Fernery
5½" d, ftd, sq, hp, blue enameled beading, blue maple leaf mark **140.00**
7" d, ftd, sq, hp, floral and gold dec, green maple leaf
mark **300.00**
Hair Receiver, ftd, hp, pink flowers, gold banding, rising
sun mark **35.00**
Hatpin Holder, 5" h, gold scrolled design, portrait of
young lady in oval medallion, attached underplate,
blue maple leaf mark **195.00**

Humidor, blown out, collie, green wreath mark 485.00
Inkwell, 3½ × 4½ × 2″, hp, lacy scrolls, poppies, beading, #5 rising sun mark 95.00
Loving Cup, 7″ h, two handles, hp, unsgd 90.00
Milk Pitcher, 8″ h, ftd, hp, floral dec, cobalt blue dec, unmarked 350.00
Mug, 5½″ h, moriage dragon, gray ground, artist sgd, green M in wreath mark 125.00
Mustard, cov, 5″ h, hp, matching underplate and spoon, gold dec, blue maple leaf mark 120.00
Nappy, hp, floral, moriage trim 75.00
Nut Bowl, 8″ d, hp, green wreath mark 45.00
Pin Tray, relief molded flowers, earth tones, bisque finish 50.00
Plaque
    9½″ d, moose 95.00
    10″ d
        Hand painted, Chinese boats, black and green 130.00
        Matte scenic castle overlooking river, waves crashing on shore, wide border with alternating reserves of rams' heads and flowers, gold beading 225.00

Plaque, multicolored hp trees, lake, mountains, wide gold border, raised enamel dots, gold florentine medallions, blue maple leaf mark, 9¼″, $250.00.

Plate
    6¼″ d, hp florals 45.00
    10¼″ d, large tree by lake scene, brown and cream, satin finish, moriage border, green wreath with M mark, back edge pierced for hanging 130.00
Powder Box, cov, 3¾″ d, ftd, hp, small pink flowers, blue rising sun mark 40.00
Sauce Boat, underplate, 7½″ l, floral and gold dec, blue maple leaf mark 150.00
Server, 6½″ d, hp, green wreath mark 65.00
Shaving Mug, bisque, beaded, desert scene, man with camel 225.00
Stamp Box, geometric black stripes, int. tray with two compartments, wreath mark 95.00
Sugar Shaker, 4¼″ h, cobalt blue, floral dec, blue maple leaf mark 150.00
Tankard, hp
    11″ h, red roses, gold dec 450.00
    12″ h, red roses, cobalt blue dec 275.00

Tea Bowl and Saucer, 5″ d, six panels, scalloped, ftd, hp roses, geometric dec 75.00
Tea Set
    Moriage dragon, teapot, creamer, sugar, four cups and saucers 195.00
    Wedgwood, black and gold highlights over white florals, blue ground, price for 9 pc set 675.00
Toast Rack, sections for 3 slices of toast, white ground, gold raised bunches of grapes and grape leaves, spoke mark 125.00
Tray, 5″ d, heart shape, hp, floral, gold beading, maple leaf mark 100.00
Vase
    6½″ h, two handles, hp, moriage floral and ribbon dec, blue maple leaf mark 450.00
    7½″ h, baluster, poppy dec, bold colored enameled applied handles 225.00
    8″ h, two handles, hp, Galle scene, moriage dec, blue maple leaf mark 725.00
    9″ h, two handles
        Hand-painted florals, green M in wreath mark .. 320.00
        Hand-painted florals and gold dec, blue maple leaf mark 350.00
        Moriage, blue crown mark 400.00
    9¾″ h, cobalt blue, scenic, raised beading, grapes and leaves, green M mark 375.00
    10″ h, two handles, ftd, hp
        Basketweave overlay, roses with moriage, blue maple leaf mark 500.00
        Florals, blue M in wreath mark 290.00
        Scenic, gold dec, green wreath mark 300.00
    11″ h, two handles, hp, raised enamel dec 175.00
    12″ h, two handles, hp
        Floral dec, green M in wreath mark 425.00
        Scenic cartoon, raised enameling, Imperial mark 275.00
    13″ h, two handles, hp, florals, gold dec griffins, blue M in wreath mark 700.00

NODDERS

History: Nodders are figurines with heads and/or arms attached to the body with wires to enable movement. They are made in a variety of materials—bisque, celluloid, papier-mâché, porcelain, or wood.

Most nodders date from the late 19th century, with Germany being the principal source of supply. Among the American-made nodders, those of Disney and cartoon characters are most eagerly sought.

Reference: Hilma R. Irtz, *Figural Nodders,* Collector Books, 1996.

Black Woman, seated, holding removable watermelon, gray hair, head nods, salt shaker type 75.00
Bull Dog Terrier, articulated head, papier-mâché, minor losses to paint 375.00
Cat, 5″ h, composition, black 65.00
Donkey, 3″ h, celluloid 45.00
Hobo, 3½″ h, 2¼″ w, green coat, bottle in pocket, tan pants and hat, sitting in chair, holding stick 225.00
Little Orphan Annie, bisque, marked ''Germany'' 125.00
Monkey, 6½″ h, celluloid 70.00

Seated Chinese man, blue robe, yellow and red trim, Oriental, 3¹/₄″, $110.00.

Oriental Lady, 6³/₄″ h, bisque, seated, holding fan behind
    nodding head, Continental **200.00**
Rabbit, 7″ h, papier-mâché, glass eyes **75.00**

NORITAKE CHINA

History: Morimura Brothers founded Noritake China in 1904 in
Nagoya, Japan. They made high-quality chinaware for export to
the United States and also produced a line of china blanks for
hand painting. In 1910 the company perfected a technique for the
production of high-quality dinnerware and introduced streamlined production.

During the 1920s the Larkin Company of Buffalo, New York,
was a prime distributor of Noritake China. Larkin offered Azalea,
Briarcliff, Linden, Modjeska, Savory, Sheridan, and Tree in the
Meadow patterns as part of their premium line.

The factory was heavily damaged during World War II, and
production was reduced. Between 1946 and 1948 the company
sold their china under the "Rose China" mark, since the quality
of production did not match the earlier Noritake China. Expansion
in 1948 brought about the resumption of quality production and
the use of the Noritake name once again.

Marks: There are close to 100 different marks for Noritake, the
careful study of which can determine the date of production. Most
pieces are marked "Noritake" with a wreath, "M," "N," or "Nippon." The use of the letter N was registered in 1953.

References: Aimee Neff Alden, *Collector's Encyclopedia of Early
Noritake,* Collector Books, 1995; Joan Van Patten, *Collector's En-
cyclopedia of Noritake,* First Series (1984, 1994 value update),
Second Series, (1994), Collector Books.

Collectors' Club: Noritake Collectors' Society, 1237 Federal Ave
East, Seattle, WA 98102.

Additional Listings: See *Warman's Americana & Collectibles* for
Azalea pattern prices.

Ashtray, 4³/₄″ w, tree trunk, relief-molded raccoon, green
    M in wreath mark **200.00**
Bowl, large, orange luster, scalloped, multicolored Jap-
    anese lanterns **50.00**
Bread Plate, 12″ l, ear of corn dec **50.00**
Butter Dish, cov, Tree in the Meadow pattern, orig insert **65.00**
Butter Tub, Azalea pattern **45.00**
Cake plate, Baroda pattern **25.00**

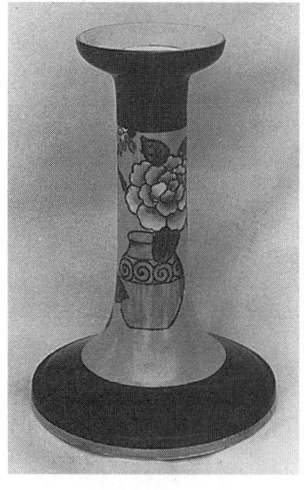

Candlestick, black bands, purple flowers, yellow ground, 6³/₈″ h, $40.00.

Candlesticks, pr, 3¹/₂″ h, 4¹/₂″ d, tan luster, blue roses,
    black handle and trim, three ftd base **75.00**
Card Holder, Art Deco style, double handles, pedestal
    base, blue and orange luster, gentleman in checkered
    cape **225.00**
Celery Tray, 12″ l, Azalea pattern **45.00**
Chocolate Pot, cov, Tree in the Meadow pattern **200.00**
Compote, blue, gold, and white, fruit dec, 2 pcs **175.00**
Condiment Set, figural, lady, pr salt and pepper shakers,
    and mustard pot, price for set **85.00**
Cracker Jar, cov, Tree in the Meadow pattern, melon
    ribbed **135.00**
Creamer and Sugar, cov, Tree in the Meadow pattern . **70.00**
Cup and Saucer, Chelsea pattern **30.00**
Dessert Set, Art Deco lady in cup, large geometric tray,
    blue luster **125.00**
Dresser Set, orange luster, figural bird final on ftd powder
    box, matching tray **250.00**
Jam Dish, gray luster, figural locust, multicolored emb
    fruits **65.00**
Lemon Dish, 5¹/₂″ d, Tree in the Meadow pattern **35.00**
Napkin Ring, Art Deco **75.00**
Plate, 8¹/₂″ d, Tree in the Meadow pattern **20.00**
Potpourri Jar, 6″ h, blue and white, pierced cov with red
    and yellow rosebud finial **85.00**
Sandwich Server, 8″ d, pearlized center, fruit dec, bird
    finial **175.00**
Teapot, cov, Tree in the Meadow pattern **100.00**
Vase
    7″ h, pink, flowers **42.00**
    10″ h, moriage dragon, two handles, green mark ... **175.00**
Wall Pocket, orange luster, figural bird peering over top **165.00**

NORTH DAKOTA SCHOOL OF MINES

History: The North Dakota School of Mines was established in
1890. Earle J. Babcock, a chemistry instructor, was impressed with
the high purity level of North Dakota potter's clay. In 1898 Babcock received funds to develop his finds. He tried to interest
commercial potteries in the North Dakota clay but had limited
success.

In 1910 Babcock persuaded the school to establish a Ceramics
Department. Margaret Cable, who studied under Charles Binns

and Frederick H. Rhead, was appointed head. She remained until her retirement in 1949.

Decorative emphasis was placed on native themes, e.g., flowers and animals. Art Nouveau, Art Deco, and fairly plain pieces were made.

Marks: The pottery is marked with a cobalt blue underglaze circle of the words "University of North Dakota/Grand Forks, N.D./Made at School of Mines/N.D. Clay". Some early pieces are marked only "U.N.D." or "U.N.D./Grand Forks, N.D." Most pieces are numbered (they can be dated from University records) and signed by both the instructor and student. Cable-signed pieces are the most desirable.

References: Susan and Al Bagdade, *Warman's American Pottery and Porcelain,* Wallace-Homestead, 1994; Ralph and Terry Kovel, *Kovels' American Art Pottery,* Crown Publishers, 1993.

Collectors' Club: North Dakota Pottery Collectors Society, PO Box 14, Beach, ND 58621.

Bowl
  7¼" d, 1¼" h, rolled edge, black and green stylized flowers, light blue ground, circ ink mark, incised decorators mark "MK" **950.00**
  12½" w, 5½" d, 1¼" h, green and brown high glaze, incised "Bunting," ink mark, flake to inside of rim on one, price for pr **100.00**
Figure, 7" h, woman with basket, tan, brown, and blue high glaze, incised "Esther Shabert, 1942" **200.00**
Lamp, 9½" h, tapered form, rich rose matte glaze, circ ink mark, incised "A.L.Mc-1928" **280.00**
Plaque, 3½" w, 5" h, high glaze, blue and gray bust of man, ink mark "18th Triennial Assembly, General Grand Council, Washington, DC, Oct 9, 10, 1933," small repair to edge **60.00**
Pot, cov, sgd **280.00**
Vase
  2" h, 4" d, squat, carved floral dec, pink blossoms, green centers, green stems and leaves, tan ground, circ blue mark, incised "Ball-Huck 1385" **180.00**
  3½" h, 3¾" d, squatty bulbous, tooled violet flowers, white ground, Huckfield, circ ink mark, incised "Huck/Jill/9/670" **450.00**

Tumbler, cylindrical, green, marked "University of North Dakota, Grand Fords, N.D., Made at School of Mines, N.D. Clay," 5¼" h, 3" d, $45.00.

4½" h, 5¾" d, prairie rose dec around shoulder, heavy raised glaze, body shading to dusty rose, artist Flora Cable Huckfield, base incised "Wolff-Huck-2837," circ ink stamp **420.00**
5" h, cylindrical, rolled rim and base, mineral colors, purple and brown tulips, dark blue ground, dec by Huckfield, tight hairline, circ ink mark "FLH8/Hucs" **850.00**
5½" h, 5" d, bulbous, carved daffodils and leaves, mustard and cream ground, Julia Mattson, circ ink mark "JM" **700.00**
5¾" h, carved and painted tulips and butterfly dec, incised "Bitney," stamped "U.N.D." in ink **450.00**
6½" h, brown drip over tan high glaze, ink mark #643-648, base chip **50.00**

WALLACE NUTTING

History: Wallace Nutting (1861–1941) was America's most famous photographer of the early 20th century. A retired minister, Nutting took more than 50,000 pictures, keeping 10,000 of his best and destroying the rest. His popular and best-selling scenes included "Exterior Scenes" (apple blossoms, country lanes, orchards, calm streams, and rural American countrysides), "Interior Scenes" (usually featuring a colonial woman working near a hearth), and "Foreign Scenes" (typically thatch-roofed cottages). Those pictures which were least popular in his day have become the rarest and most-highly collectible today and are classified as "Miscellaneous Unusual Scenes." This category encompasses such things as animals, architecturals, children, florals, men, seascapes, and snow scenes.

Nutting sold literally millions of his hand-colored platinotype pictures between 1900 and his death in 1941. Starting first in Southbury, Connecticut, and later moving his business to Framingham, Massachusetts, the peak of Wallace Nutting's picture production was 1915 to 1925. During this period Nutting employed nearly 200 people, including colorists, darkroom staff, salesmen, and assorted office personnel. Wallace Nutting pictures proved to be a huge commercial success and hardly an American household was without one by 1925.

While attempting to seek out the finest and best early-American furniture as props for his colonial Interior Scenes, Nutting became an expert in American antiques. He published nearly twenty books in his lifetime, including his ten-volume *State Beautiful* series and various other books on furniture, photography, clocks, and his autobiography. He also contributed many photographs which were published in magazines and books other than his own.

Nutting also became widely known for his reproduction furniture. His furniture shop produced literally hundreds of different furniture forms: clocks, stools, chairs, settles, settees, tables, stands, desks, mirrors, beds, chests of drawers, cabinet pieces, and treenware.

The overall synergy of the Wallace Nutting name, pictures, books, and furniture, has made anything "Wallace Nutting" quite collectible.

Marks: Wallace Nutting furniture is clearly marked with his distinctive paper label (which was glued directly onto the piece) or with a block or script signature brand (which was literally branded into his furniture).

Note: "Process Prints" are 1930s machine-produced reprints of twelve of Nutting's most popular pictures. These have minimal value and can be detected by using a magnifying glass.

References: Michael Ivankovich, *The Alphabetical & Numerical Index to Wallace Nutting Pictures,* Diamond Press, 1988; ———, *The Collector's Guide to Wallace Nutting Pictures,* Collector Books, 1997; ———, *The Guide to Wallace Nutting Furniture,* Diamond Press, 1990; ———, *The Wallace Nutting Expansible Catalog* (reprint of 1915 catalog), Diamond Press, 1987; Wallace Nutting, *Wallace Nutting: A Great American Idea* (reprint of 1922 catalog), Diamond Press, 1992; ———, *Wallace Nutting General Catalog, Supreme Edition* (reprint of 1930 catalog), Schiffer Publishing, 1977; ———, *Wallace Nutting's Windsors* (reprint of 1918 catalog), Diamond Press, 1992.

Collectors' Club: Wallace Nutting Collectors Club, PO Box 2458, Doylestown, PA 18901.

Museum: Wadsworth Athenaeum, Hartford, CT.

Advisor: Michael Ivankovich.

SPECIAL AUCTION

Michael Ivankovich Auction Co.
PO Box 2458
Doylestown, PA 18901
(215) 345-6094

Books

American Windsors, dj	100.00
Clock Book, 2nd ed	40.00
Furniture of the Pilgrim Century	100.00
Furniture Treasury	
1st ed, 3 vol	300.00
1954 ed, blue cover, vol 1 and 2	35.00
Photographic Art Secrets	125.00
State Beautiful Series	
Connecticut Beautiful, 1st ed	45.00
England Beautiful, 1st ed	55.00
Ireland Beautiful, 1st ed	50.00
Maine Beautiful, 2nd ed	35.00
Massachusetts Beautiful, 1st ed	35.00
New Hampshire Beautiful, 1st ed	40.00
New York Beautiful, 2nd ed	45.00
Pennsylvania Beautiful, 1st ed	40.00
Vermont Beautiful, 1st ed	45.00
Virginia Beautiful, 2nd ed	40.00
Wallace Nutting Biography	185.00

Furniture

Candlestand	
#17, Windsor, tripod, block brand	525.00
#21, maple screw (whirling), block brand	990.00
#22, cross-based, block brand	575.00
Candlestick, #31, curly maple	
Impressed brand	175.00
Unmarked	95.00

The Swimming Pool, 14 × 17", $150.00.

Chair	
#301, Windsor, block brand	525.00
#305, Windsor, bent-rung, bow back, bamboo turnings, block brand	800.00
#310, Windsor, slipper, paper label	550.00
#326, fan back, script brand and paper label	550.00
#377, 3-slat back, block brand	385.00
#392, 4-back ladder back, block brand	475.00
#393, pilgrim, block brand	360.00
#401, Windsor, continuous arm, block brand	925.00
#411, Brewster, arms, script brand	1,000.00
#412, Pennsylvania Windsor, comb back, arms, block brand	1,400.00
#414, Windsor, low back, paper label and block brand	525.00
#415, Windsor, comb back, arms, block brand	1,125.00
#419, Windsor, double comb back, arms, paper label	1,125.00
#421, Windsor, rocking, arms, script brand	1,100.00
#440, Windsor, writing, arms, Pennsylvania turnings with drawer, block brand	2,800.00
Mirror, #761, gold, three feathers, impressed brand	575.00
Stool	
#101, Windsor, round, block brand	300.00
#102, Windsor, oval, paper label	250.00
#164, Brewster, rushed, three legs, script brand	385.00
#166, rushed, maple, 15", block brand	300.00
#168, rushed, maple, 22", block brand	425.00
Table	
#601, oak, refractory, block brand	935.00
#616, pine, trestle, block brand	750.00
#619, maple, crane bracket, script brand	685.00
Treenware	
Pen and Pencil Tray, impressed brand	250.00
#28, salt dish, open, impressed brand	155.00

Miscellaneous

Advertising Sign	
Glass, 8 × 10"	550.00
Paper, 11 × 16"	125.00
Calendar, thin metal frame	75.00

Catalog, furniture
  Final Edition, 1937 .... 125.00
  Supreme Edition, 1930 .... 110.00
Greeting Card, Exterior Scene, 4 × 5″ 75.00
Miniature
  Exterior Scene, 4 × 5″ 65.00
  Floral Scene, 4 × 5″ 175.00
  Interior Scene, 4 × 5″ 110.00
Photograph, colorist's, 8 × 10″ 110.00
Print, pirate, swimming pool, unsigned 10.00

Pictures

Afternoon Tea, 14 × 17″ 175.00
All Sunshine, 16 × 20″, process print 25.00
A Barre Brook
  12 × 15″, process print 15.00
  13 × 16″ 125.00
A Bit of Sewing, 11 × 14″ 95.00
Colonial Days, 14 × 17″ 1,125.00
Comfort and a Cat, 14 × 17″ 325.00
The Coming Out of Rosa, 14 × 17″ 195.00
Confidences, 13 × 16″ 185.00
Decked as a Bride
  11 × 14″ 75.00
  16 × 20″, process print 20.00
An Eventful Journey 650.00
Four O'Clock, 14 × 17″ 1,275.00
A Fruit Luncheon, 16 ×20″ 295.00
A Garden of Larkspur, 13 × 16″ 85.00
Going for the Doctor, 13 × 16″ 1,100.00
Hollyhock Cottage, 13 × 16″ 135.00
Hollyhocks (Floral Scene), 8 × 10″ 525.00
LaJolla, 13 × 16″ 275.00
Larkspur, 11 × 14″ 75.00
A Listless Day, 13 ×16″ 325.00
Litchfield Minster, 11 × 14″ 165.00
Mary's Little Lamb, 13 × 16″ 250.00
The Meeting Place, 18 × 22″ 2,420.00
An Old Drawing Room, 11 × 17″ 185.00
The Pergola Amalfi, 13 × 16″ 160.00
Plymouth Curves, 11 × 17″ 145.00
Roses and Larkspur, 13 × 16″ 1,200.00
Slack Water, 11 × 17″ 150.00
A Stitch in Time, 14 × 17″ 220.00
Sunshine and Music, 13 × 16″ 225.00
The Swimming Pool, 11 × 17″ 165.00
Tea for Two, 13 × 16″ 225.00
Untitled
  Blossom and a stone wall, 7 × 9″ 175.00
  Girl by a fire, 8 × 12″ 125.00
  Girl in a garden, 7 × 9″ 65.00
  Girls having tea, 8 × 10″ 110.00
  Three-spired cathedral, 7 × 9″ 85.00
A Warm Spring Day, 11 × 17″ 275.00
The Way It Begins, 14 × 17″ 625.00

Silhouettes

Silhouette
  George and Martha Washington, price for pr 85.00
  Girl, by garden urn, 4 × 4″ 40.00

A Warm Spring Day, 15 × 22″, $375.00.

Girl, sitting at vanity, 4 × 4″ 35.00
Girl, standing by cheval mirror, 5 × 5″ 45.00
Lamb, following girl to school, 7 × 8″ 65.00

WALLACE NUTTING-LIKE PHOTOGRAPHERS

History: Although Wallace Nutting was widely recognized as the country's leading producer of hand-colored photographs during the early 20th century, he was by no means the only photographer selling this style of picture. Throughout the country literally hundreds of regional photographers were selling hand-colored photographs from their home regions or travels. The subject matter of these photographers was comparable to Nutting's, including Interior, Exterior, Foreign, And Miscellaneous Unusual scenes.

Several photographers operated large businesses, and, although not as large or well-known as Wallace Nutting, they sold a substantial volume of pictures which can still be readily found today. The vast majority of their work was photographed in their home regions and sold primarily to local residents or visiting tourists. It should come as little surprise that three of the major Wallace Nutting-like photographers—David Davidson, Fred Thompson, and the Sawyer Art Co.—each had ties to Wallace Nutting.

Hundreds of other smaller local and regional photographers attempted to market hand-colored pictures comparable to Wallace Nutting's during the period of 1900 to the 1930s. Although quite attractive, most were not as appealing to the general public as Wallace Nutting pictures. However, as the price of Wallace Nutting pictures has escalated, the work of these lesser-known Wallace Nutting-like photographers have become increasingly collectible.

A partial listing of some of these minor Wallace Nutting-like photographers includes: Babcock; J. C. Bicknell; Blair; Ralph Blood (Portland, Maine); Bragg; Brehmer; Brooks; Burrowes; Busch; Carlock; Pedro Cacciola; Croft; Currier; Depue Brothers; Derek; Dowly; Eddy; May Farini (hand-colored colonial lithographs); George Forest; Gandara; Gardner (Nantucket, Bermuda, Florida); Gibson; Gideon; Gunn; Bessie Pease Gutmann (hand-colored colonial lithographs); Edward Guy; Harris; C. Hazen;

Knoffe; Haynes (Yellowstone Park); Margaret Hennesey; Hodges; Homer; Krabel; Kattleman; La Bushe; Lake; Lamson (Portland, Maine); M. Lightstrum; Machering; Rossiler Mackinae; Merrill; Meyers; William Moehring; Moran; Murrey; Lyman Nelson; J. Robinson Neville (New England); Patterson; Own Perry; Phelps; Phinney; Reynolds; F. Robbins; Royce; Frederick Scheetz (Philadelphia, Pennsylvania); Shelton, Standley (Colorado); Stott; Summers; Esther Svenson; Florence Thompson; Thomas Thompson; M. A. Trott; Sanford Tull; Underhill; Villar; Ward; Wilmot; Edith Wilson; and Wright.

References: Carol Begley Gray, *The History of the Sawyer Pictures,* published by author, 1995 (available from Wallace Nutting Collector's Club, PO Box 2458, Doylestown, PA 18901); Michael Ivankovich, *The Guide to Wallace-Nutting Like Photographers of the Early 20th Century,* Diamond Press, 1991.

Collectors' Club: Wallace Nutting Collector's Club, PO Box 2458, Doylestown, PA 18901.

Advisor: Michael Ivankovich.

Notes: The key determinants of value include the collectibility of the particular photographer, subject matter, condition, and size. Exterior Scenes are the most common.

Keep in mind that only the rarest pictures, in the best condition, will bring top prices. Discoloration and/or damage to the picture or matting can reduce value significantly.

David Davidson

Second to Nutting in overall production, Davidson worked primarily in the Rhode and Southern Massachusetts area. While a student at Brown University around 1900, Davidson learned the art of hand-colored photography from Wallace Nutting, who happened to be the Minister at Davidson's church. After Nutting moved to Southbury in 1905, Davidson graduated from Brown and started a successful photography business in Providence, Rhode Island, which he operated until his death in 1967.

The Barefoot Boy, 9 × 16″	**195.00**
A Daughter of Sheffield, 13 ×16″	**275.00**
Diadem Aisle, 10 × 12″	**50.00**
The Dropt Stitch, 13 × 16″	**185.00**
Echo Lake, 8 × 10″	**65.00**
Her House in Order, 12 × 16″	**45.00**
Prize Pewter, 12 × 16″	**45.00**
A Puritan Lady, 12 × 16″	**75.00**
The Rambler Rose, 12 × 16″	**170.00**
The Shattered Wave, 12 × 15″	**85.00**
Sunset Point, 12 × 16″	**45.00**
The Village Maiden, 14 × 17″	**180.00**
A Welcome Guest, 9 × 15″	**155.00**
Wisteria, 13 × 16″	**95.00**
Ye Olden Tyme, 13 × 16″	**300.00**

Sawyer

A father and son team, Charles H. Sawyer and Harold B. Sawyer, operated the very successful Sawyer Art Company from 1903 until the 1970s. Beginning in Maine, the Sawyer Art Company moved to Concord, New Hampshire, in 1920 to be closer to their primary market—New Hampshire's White Mountains. Charles H. Sawyer briefly worked for Nutting from 1902 to 1903 while living in

southern Maine. Sawyer's production volume ranks third behind Wallace Nutting and David Davidson.

The Afterglow, 6 × 8″	**25.00**
Autumn Glory, 9 × 12″	**50.00**
Camel's Hump, 7 × 9″	**35.00**
Chapel, San Juan Capistrano, 13 × 16″	**155.00**
Echo Lake, Franconia Notch, 13 × 16″	**55.00**
Elephant's Head, 5 × 7″	**35.00**
Gateway to the Adirondacks, 13 × 20″	**155.00**
Joseph Lincoln's Garden, 16 × 20″	**185.00**
Lafayette Slides, 13 × 15″	**90.00**
Mt. Lafayette, 7 × 9″	**35.00**
The Old Man of the Mountains, 11 × 14″	**45.00**
Peaceful Sentinels, 11 × 14″	**60.00**
A Rock Garden, Cape Cod, 16 × 20″	**165.00**
Sunset on the Kennebec, 12 × 20″	**70.00**
Surf at Pinnacle Rock, 13 × 20″	**90.00**

Fred Thompson

Frederick H. Thompson and Frederick M. Thompson, another father and son team, operated the Thompson Art Company (TACO) from 1908 to 1923, working primarily in the Portland, Maine, area. We know that Thompson and Nutting had collaborated because Thompson widely marketed an interior scene he had taken in Nutting's Southbury home. The production volume of the Thompson Art Company ranks fourth behind Nutting, Davidson, and Sawyer.

Bridal Blossoms, 8 × 15″	**60.00**
Covered Bridge, 9 × 12″	**75.00**
Dixie Apple Blossoms, 16 × 20″	**65.00**
Fireside Fancies, 11 × 14″	**85.00**
Neath the Blossoms, 7 × 9″	**65.00**
New England Blossoms, 8 × 14″	**65.00**
Old Mill Dam, 9 × 12″	**25.00**
Pine Grove, 14 × 17″	**40.00**
Roasting Apples, 10 × 12″	**55.00**
The Roller, 8 × 14″	**85.00**
Sailing Ship, 8 × 10″	**240.00**
Sea Foam, 7 × 11″	**75.00**
Sentinels, 6 × 12″	**25.00**
Spinning Days, 14 × 17″	**95.00**
Tired of Spinning, 7 × 9″	**55.00**

Charles Higgins

Higgins worked out of Bath, Maine, and some of his finest pictures rival Nutting's best. No firm connection has been found between Higgins and Wallace Nutting.

Apple Blossom Lane, 8 × 12″	**35.00**
By the Fireplace, 11 × 14″	**125.00**
Fall Days, 8 × 14″	**35.00**
The Lane, 9 × 12″	**95.00**
Near Sugar Hill, 8 × 12″	**55.00**
The Pine Road, 8 × 10″	**30.00**
A Rocky Shore, 8 × 14″	**55.00**
Untitled exterior	**25.00**
Untitled interior, 7 × 9″	**35.00**
Untitled seascape, 7 × 11″	**65.00**

Minor Wallace Nutting-Like Photographers

Generally speaking, prices for works by minor Wallace Nutting-like photographers would break down as follows: smaller pictures (5 × 7″ to 10 × 12″), $10–$75; medium pictures (11 × 14″ to 14 × 17″), $50–$200; larger pictures (larger than 14 × 17″), $75–$200+.

OCCUPIED JAPAN

History: The Japanese economy was devastated when World War II ended. To secure necessary hard currency, the Japanese pottery industry produced thousands of figurines and other knickknacks for export. The variety of products is endless—ashtrays, dinnerware, lamps, planters, souvenir items, toys, vases, etc. Initially, the figurines attracted the largest number of collectors; today many collectors focus on other types of pieces.

Marks: From the beginning of the American occupation of Japan until April 28, 1952, objects made in that country were marked "Japan," "Made in Japan," "Occupied Japan," or "Made in Occupied Japan." Only pieces marked with the last two designations are of major interest to Occupied Japan collectors. The first two marks also were used during other time periods.

References: Florence Archambault, *Occupied Japan for Collectors,* Schiffer Publishing, 1992; Gene Florence, *Price Guide to Collector's Encyclopedia of Occupied Japan,* Collector Books, 1996 (updated prices for 5-book series *Collector's Encyclopedia of Occupied Japan*); David C. Gould and Donna Crevar-Donaldson, *Occupied Japan Toys with Prices,* L-W Book Sales, 1993; Anthony Marsella, *Toys from Occupied Japan,* Schiffer Publishing, 1995; Lynette Parmer, *Collecting Occupied Japan,* Schiffer Publishing, 1996; Carole Bess White, *Collector's Guide to Made in Japan Ceramics,* Collector Books, 1994.

Collectors' Club: The Occupied Japan Club, 29 Freeborn St, Newport, RI 02840.

Additional Listings: See *Warman's Americana & Collectibles* for more examples.

Animal-Covered Dish, hen on nest	50.00
Ashtray, 4¾″ h, metal, spring-loaded head of young black boy smoking cigar	50.00
Bowl, cov, Capo-di-Monte style, double handled, brightly colored enamel dec, winged cherubs in woodland scene, marked "Occupied Japan"	20.00
Canister Set, blue flowers and birds, set of four cov jars	75.00
Children's Dishes, tea set, Blue Willow, price for 18-pc set	375.00
Cigarette Dispenser, mechanical, inlaid wood, spring-operated sliding drawer loads cigarettes into bird's beak	55.00
Cigarette Lighter, figural, teapot, silver-colored metal, wooden handle, matching under tray, orig box	35.00
Clock, 10½″ h, bisque, double figure, colonial dancing couple, floral encrusted case	250.00
Cornucopia, 7 × 8″, chariot, rearing horse and two cherubs, multicolored beading, gold trim, unglazed bisque	80.00
Figure	
4½″ h, 5¾″ l, Chinese couple, woman playing stringed instrument, man smoking pipe	30.00

Figure, black child, green hat, white shirt, blue pants, accordion, 2¾″ h, $15.00.

5½″ h, ballerina	45.00
Finger Bowl, 5¾″ h, porcelain, winged cherub and raspberries	30.00
Flower Frog, 6″ h, figural, girl with bird on shoulder, pastel highlights, gold trim, bisque	45.00
Lamp, Colonial couple, gentleman with guitar, woman holding floral bouquet, floral emb base	25.00
Nativity Scene, bisque figures, orig box	195.00
Paperweight, bronze, marked "Captured Japanese Material" from Yokosuka Naval Air Station, USS *Webster*	60.00
Platter, 16″ l, Courtley pattern, heavy gold trim, marked "Meito Norleans China"	30.00
Salt and Pepper Shakers, pr, coffeepots, cobalt blue glass, metal tray with red Bakelite handles, orig presentation box	25.00
Tape Measure, figural, celluloid	
Kangaroo, baby in pouch, baby's head as end of tape measure, bright pink, marked "Made in Occupied Japan"	35.00
Pig, 2⅜″ l, stamped "Occupied Japan"	45.00
Toy, celluloid, windup	
Boy, riding tricycle	70.00
Couple, dancing	40.00
South Seas native, grass skirt	50.00
Vase	
6½″ h, porcelain, fluted, brightly colored, three young maidens, flowing skirts	65.00
10″ h, bisque, figural, young lady and scrolled cornucopia	65.00
Wall Pocket	
Colonial Couple, hanging out window with baskets	30.00
Flying Geese, set of one large and three smaller pockets, price for 4-pc set	25.00

OHR POTTERY

G.E. OHR, BILOXI.

History: Ohr pottery was produced by George E. Ohr in Biloxi, Mississippi. There is a discrepancy as to when he actually established his pottery; some say 1878, but Ohr's autobiography indicates 1883. In 1884 Ohr exhibited 600 pieces of his work, suggesting that he had been a potter for some time.

Ohr's techniques included twisting, crushing, folding, denting, and crinkling thin-walled clay into odd, grotesque, and, sometimes, graceful forms. His later pieces were often left unglazed.

In 1906 Ohr closed the pottery and stored over 6,000 pieces as a legacy to his family. He had hoped it would be purchased by the U.S. government, which never happened. The entire collection remained in storage until it was rediscovered in 1972.

Today Ohr is recognized as one of the leaders in the American art pottery movement. Some greedy individuals have taken the later unglazed pieces and covered them with poor-quality glazes in hopes of making them more valuable. These pieces do not have stilt marks on the bottom.

Marks: Much of Ohr's early work was signed with an impressed stamp including his name and location in block letters. His later work was often marked with the flowing script designation "G. E. Ohr."

References: Susan and Al Bagdade, *Warman's American Pottery and Porcelain,* Wallace-Homestead, 1994; Garth Clark, Robert Ellison, Jr., and Eugene Hecht, *The Mad Potter of Biloxi: The Art & Life of George Ohr,* Abbeville Press, 1989; Ralph and Terry Kovel, *Kovels' American Art Pottery,* Crown Publishers, 1993.

Bank, 8¼" l, lip shape, coin slot on top, green and pink
    mottled glaze, imp "Geo. E. Ohr Biloxi, Miss" **2,250.00**

Bank, folded clay, unglazed, imp "G.E. OHR/BILOXI, MISS.," 2¾" h, 5½" diagonal, $225.00.

Bowl
    3¼" h, pushed-down body, twisted shoulder, pinched
      and ruffled rim, gunmetal glaze, imp "G. E. Ohr,
      Biloxi, Miss" **2,250.00**
    3½" h, bulbous, boldly folded and ruffled edge,
      lavender, olive green, and blue glaze, blue and
      brown dapples, imp "Biloxi, Miss, Geo. E. Ohr"**13,200.00**
Eggcup, 2½" h, chipped edge rim and foot, Charleston
    green high glaze, stamped "Geo. E. Ohr Biloxi,
    Miss," minor glaze flakes **250.00**
Pitcher, 6" h, squatty, crumpled, folded cutout handle,
    dripping gunmetal glaze over moss green, script in-
    cised "G. E. Ohr" **3,500.00**
Vase
    3½" h, baluster, inverted rim, periwinkle blue,
      splashes of black over body, imp "G. E. Ohr, Bi-
      loxi, Miss" **750.00**
    6" h, pinched form, red and orange, incised verse on
      bottom, new glaze, repair and rim chip **500.00**
    7" h, bulbous base, two curving handles, blue and
      dark blue mottled glaze, incised "G. E. Ohr, Bi-
      loxi, Miss" **2,750.00**

9" h, 4½" w, cone shape over bulbous base, flaring
    foot, spaghetti handles, twisted neck, deep green
    spotted glaze, incised "G. E. Ohr, Biloxi, Miss,"
    restoration to neck **3,900.00**
9½" h, 3¾" d, twisted neck over broad shoulder, ta-
    pering to flared foot, deep blue glaze, incised "G.
    E. Ohr, Biloxi, Miss" **2,900.00**

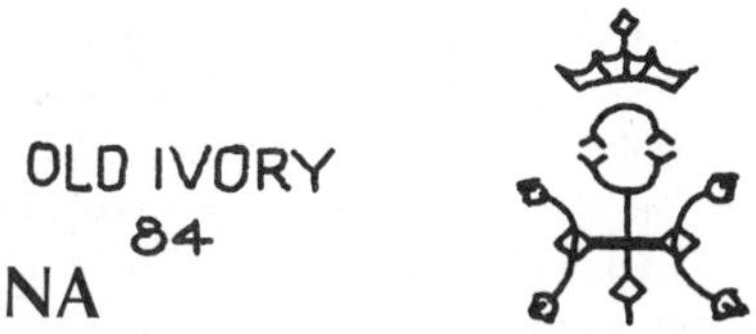

OLD IVORY
84

OLD IVORY CHINA

History: Old Ivory derives its name from the background color of the china. It was made in Silesia, Germany, during the second half of the 19th century.

Marks: Marked pieces usually have a pattern number (pattern names are not common), a crown, and the word "Silesia."

Periodical: *Old Ivory Newsletter,* PO Box 1004, Wilsonville, OR 97070.

Collectors' Club: Old Ivory Porcelain Society, PO Box 326, Osage, IA 50461.

Berry Set, master bowl and four serving bowls, 5-pc set
    #11 .... **145.00**
    #84 .... **200.00**
Biscuit Jar, cov, #15 .... **350.00**
Bowl
    #15, 9¼" d, serving type **195.00**
    #84, 6½" d **50.00**
    #200, 9¼" d, serving type **195.00**
Cake Plate, #13, 10" d, open handles, roses around bor-
    der, one in center **125.00**
Celery Bowl, #84, 11 × 5½" **150.00**
Chocolate Set, #84, chocolate pot, six cups and saucers **850.00**
Creamer, #32 .... **48.00**
Cup and Saucer, #75 .... **65.00**
Demitasse Pot, cov, #16 .... **395.00**
Ladle Holder, #84 .... **95.00**
Mustard Pot, cov, #16 .... **100.00**
Oyster Bowl, #11 .... **175.00**
Plate
    #15, 7¾" d **95.00**
    #16, 6⅛" d, bread and butter **75.00**
    #82, 8" d **85.00**
    #84, 6⅛" d, bread and butter **75.00**
Sugar, cov, #75 .... **50.00**
Teapot, cov, #15 .... **395.00**
Toothpick Holder
    #16 .... **195.00**
    #84 .... **285.00**

OLD PARIS CHINA

History: Old Paris china is fine-quality porcelain made by various French factories located in and around Paris during the 18th and 19th centuries. Some pieces were marked, but most were not. In addition to its fine quality, this type of ware is characterized by beautiful decorations and gilding. Favored colors are dark maroon, deep cobalt blue, and a dark green.

Additional Listing: Continental China and Porcelain (General).

Basket, reticulated, gold and white dec, c1825 .... **1,400.00**
Cake Stand, Honore style, green border, c1845 .... **200.00**
Dinner Service, partial, moss rose spray dec, plates and
    assorted serving pieces, c1860, price for 67-pc set . **325.00**
Figure, 18³⁄₄" h, Napoleon, standing, one arm tucked
    behind his back, other tucked into shirt, full military
    dress, gilt dec, low sq base, inscribed "Roussel-Bar-
    dell," late 19th C **650.00**
Mantel Vase, bell-like flowered handles, blue ground,
    paneled enamel portraits of lovers, gilt trim, minor
    flower damage, price for pr **325.00**
Plate, 9¹⁄₄" d, flower-basket center, gilt line and borders,
    ochre ground, c1830, price for pr **250.00**

**Plate, pale blue-gray border, multicolored center
with boy and girl, 8¹⁄₈" d, $50.00.**

Tea Set, partial, enamel dec central medallions of por-
    traits and musical instruments surrounded by gilt
    shields and spearhead border, 5³⁄₄" h cov teapot,
    creamer, compote, twelve coffee canns and saucers,
    19th C, gilt wear, minor damage, price for 15-pc set **2,875.00**
Urn, cov, 14¹⁄₂" h, painted hunting scenes, molded acan-
    thus- and palmette-scrolled double handles, gilt bor-
    der, sq plinth base, price for pr **1,200.00**
Vase, 17¹⁄₂" h, cov, ormolu mounting, mint green ground,
    enamel floral bouquet panel, center scene of children
    riding goat, molded handles and leafy garlands, gilt
    wear, late 19th C **600.00**

OLD SLEEPY EYE

History: Sleepy Eye, a Sioux Indian chief who reportedly had a droopy eye, gave his name to Sleepy Eye, Minnesota, and one of its leading flour mills. In the early 1900s Old Sleepy Eye Flour offered four Flemish-gray heavy stoneware premiums decorated in cobalt blue: a straight-sided butter crock, curved salt bowl, stein, and vase. The premiums were made by Weir Pottery Company, later to become Monmouth Pottery Company, and finally to emerge as the present-day Western Stoneware Company of Monmouth, Illinois.

Additional pottery and stoneware pieces also were issued. Forms included five sizes of pitchers (4, 5¹⁄₂, 6¹⁄₂, 8, and 9 inches), mugs, steins, sugar bowls, and tea tiles (hot plates). Most were cobalt blue on white, but other glaze hues, such as browns, golds, and greens, were used.

Old Sleepy Eye also issued many other items, including bakers' caps, lithographed barrel covers, beanies, fans, multicolored pillow tops, postcards, and trade cards. Regular production of Old Sleepy Eye stoneware ended in 1937.

In 1952 Western Stoneware Company made 22- and 40-ounce steins in chestnut brown glaze with a redesigned Indian's head. From 1961 to 1972 gift editions were made for the board of directors and others within the company. Beginning in 1973, Western Stoneware Company issued an annual limited edition stein for collectors.

Marks: The gift editions made in the 1960s and 1970s were dated and signed with a maple leaf mark. The annual limited edition steins are marked and dated.

References: Susan and Al Bagdade, *Warman's American Pottery and Porcelain,* Wallace-Homestead, 1994; Elinor Meugnoit, *Old Sleepy Eye,* published by author, 1979.

Collectors' Club: Old Sleepy Eye Collectors Club, PO Box 12, Monmouth, IL 61462.

REPRODUCTION ALERT

Blue-and-white pitchers, crazed, weighted, and often with a stamp or the word "Ironstone" are the most common reproductions. The stein and salt bowl also have been made. Many reproductions come from Taiwan.

A line of fantasy items, new items which never existed as Old Sleepy Eye originals, includes an advertising pocket mirror with miniature flour-barrel label, small glass plates, fruit jars, toothpick holders, glass and pottery miniature pitchers, and salt and pepper shakers. One mill item has been made: a sack marked as though it were old but of a size that could not possibly hold the amount of flour indicated.

Mill Items

Advertising Premium Cards, 5¹⁄₂ × 9", full-color Indian
    lore illus, text, Old Sleepy Eye Indian character trade-
    mark, price for 10-pc set 875.00
Cookbook, Sleepy Eye Milling Co, loaf of bread shape,
    portrait of chief 145.00
Demitasse Spoon, roses in bowl 145.00
Letter Opener, bronze, Indian-head handle, marked
    "Sleepy Eye Milling Co, Sleepy Eye, MN" 750.00
Pinback Button, Old Sleepy Eye for Me, bust portrait of
    chief 165.00

Pottery and Stoneware

Mug, cobalt blue on white, Indian head on handle,
    1906–37 .... 245.00

Label, egg crate, Sleepy Eye Brand, A. J. Pietrus & Sons Co., Sleepy Eye, MN, red, blue, and yellow, 9¼ × 11½", $25.00.

Pitcher
  4" h, gray ground and cobalt blue, chip on bottom . **200.00**
  8" h, cream ground and cobalt blue, minor discolor
    and crazing **350.00**
  9" h, beige ground, cobalt blue dec, c1906–37 .... **145.00**
Stein
  7¾" h, Flemish blue, gray stoneware ground, Weir
    Pottery Co, 1903 .... **525.00**
  22 oz, chestnut brown, 1952 .... **275.00**
Tile, cobalt blue and white **950.00**

ONION MEISSEN

History: The blue onion or bulb pattern is of Chinese origin and depicts peaches and pomegranates, not onions. It was first made in the 18th century by Meissen, hence the name Onion Meissen.

Factories in Europe, Japan, and elsewhere copied the pattern. Many still have the pattern in production, including the Meissen factory in Germany.

Marks: Many pieces are marked with a company's logo; after 1891 the country of origin is indicated on imported pieces.

Reference: Robert E. Röntgen, *The Book of Meissen,* Revised Edition, Schiffer Publishing, 1996.

Note: Prices given are for pieces produced between 1870 and 1930. Early Meissen examples bring a high premium.

Bowl, 8½" d, reticulated, blue crossed-swords mark,
  19th C **395.00**
Box, cov, 4½" d, round, rose finial **75.00**
Cake Stand, 13½" d, 4½" h **215.00**
Candlesticks, pr, 7" h **80.00**
Canister, marked "Prunes" **188.00**
Creamer and Sugar, gold edge, c1900 .... **175.00**
Demitasse Cup and Saucer, blue, gilt dec, underglaze
  crossed-swords mark, price for 8-pc set **295.00**
Fruit Compote, 9" h, circular, openwork bowl, five oval
  floral medallions **375.00**
Fruit Knives, price for 6-pc set **75.00**
Funnel, small **55.00**
Hot Plate, handles **125.00**

Ladle, wooden handle **115.00**
Mold, melon, handle **45.00**
Pie Crimper, wooden handle **35.00**
Plate
  8½" d **35.00**
  10" d **75.00**

Soup plate, scalloped edge, marked "Meissen" with star, late, 9¾" d, $38.00.

Platter, 12" l, oval **95.00**
Pot de Creme **65.00**
Salt and Pepper Shakers, pr **50.00**
Serving Dish, 9¼" w, 11" l, handle with floral design .. **200.00**
Tea Strainer, wood handle **25.00**
Tray, 17" l, cartouche shape, blue and white design, gilt
  edge **425.00**
Vase, 6½" d, bud **60.00**
Vegetable Dish, cov, 10" w, sq **145.00**

OPALESCENT GLASS

History: Opalescent glass, a clear or colored glass with milky white decorations, looks fiery or opalescent when held to light. This effect was achieved by applying bone ash chemicals to designated areas while a piece was still hot and then refiring it at extremely high temperatures.

There are three basic categories of opalescent glass: (1) blown (or mold blown) patterns, e.g., Daisy & Fern and Spanish Lace; (2) novelties, pressed glass patterns made in limited quantity and often in unusual shapes such as corn or a trough; and (3) traditional pattern (pressed) glass forms.

Opalescent glass was produced in England in the 1870s. Northwood began the American production in 1897 at its Indiana, Pennsylvania, plant. Jefferson, National Glass, Hobbs, and Fenton soon followed.

References: Gary Baker et al., *Wheeling Glass 1829–1939,* Oglebay Institute, 1994, distributed by Antique Publications; Bill Edwards, *The Standard Opalescent Glass,* Collector Books, 1995; William Heacock, *Encyclopedia of Victorian Colored Pattern Glass, Book II,* Second Edition, Antique Publications, 1977; William Heacock and William Gamble, *Encyclopedia of Victorian Colored Pattern Glass, Book 9,* Antique Publications, 1987; William Heacock, James Measell, and Berry Wiggins, *Dugan/Diamond,* Antique Publications, 1993; ——, *Harry Northwood*

(1990), Book 2 (1991) Antique Publications; Ellen T. Schroy, *Warman's Glass*, Second Edition, Wallace-Homestead, 1995.

Blown

Barber Bottle
    Hobnail, blue, ground pontil **145.00**
    Stripe, cranberry **195.00**
Bride's Bowl, Seaweed, 10" d, cranberry, tightly crimped
    rim **175.00**
Bowl
    Spanish Lace, 5½" d, canary **25.00**
    Stripe, 10" d, cranberry **210.00**
Butter, cov
    Reverse Swirl, canary **145.00**
    Swirl, canary **175.00**
Celery Vase
    Hobb's Hobnail, 6¼" h, cranberry, ruffled rim **135.00**
    Ribbed Opal Lattice, blue **85.00**
    Swirl, blue **115.00**
Compote, Hobb's Hobnail, cranberry, 5½ × 9" **250.00**
Creamer, Hobb's Hobnail, blue **55.00**
Decanter, Hobb's Hobnail, cranberry, orig stopper **85.00**
Jelly Compote, Coin Spot, green **30.00**
Lamp
    Daisy & Fern
        Blue, 4⅝" h, applied blue loop handle, hand type,
            base, brass collar, no burner **125.00**
        White, complete **490.00**
    Ribbed Opal Lattice, 3⅞" h, cranberry, applied col-
        orless loop handle, hand type, ribbed base, brass
        collar with patent date, wear on bottom **615.00**
Pitcher, water
    Coin Spot, 8" h, blue, ruffled rim **175.00**
    Daisy & Fern, cranberry **225.00**
    Hobb's Hobnail, cranberry **325.00**
    Seaweed, blue **500.00**
    Spanish Lace, 9½" h, blue, ruffled rim **300.00**
    Swirl, 8½" h, cranberry, sq rim, applied colorless han-
        dle **225.00**
Rose Bowl
    Daisy & Fern, cranberry **55.00**
    Spanish Lace, canary **40.00**
Salt Shaker
    Reverse Swirl, white, orig top **45.00**
Sugar Bowl, cov, Seaweed, white **115.00**
Sugar Shaker
    Coin Spot, Northwood mold, white, orig top **110.00**
    Spanish Lace, cranberry **400.00**
    Stripe, blue **225.00**
Syrup, orig metal top
    Coin Spot and Swirl, blue **200.00**
    Daisy & Fern, blue **250.00**
    Hobb's Hobnail, blue **325.00**
    Reverse Swirl, blue **195.00**
    Ring Neck Coin Spot, blue **200.00**
    Seaweed, white **130.00**
Toothpick Holder
    Reverse Swirl, canary **90.00**
    Ribbed Opal Lattice, blue **135.00**
Tumbler
    Coin Spot, cranberry **45.00**

Hobb's Hobnail, canary **95.00**
Reverse Swirl, blue **65.00**
Spanish Lace, canary **50.00**
Tumble-Up, water carafe and matching tumbler, Swirl,
    cranberry **460.00**

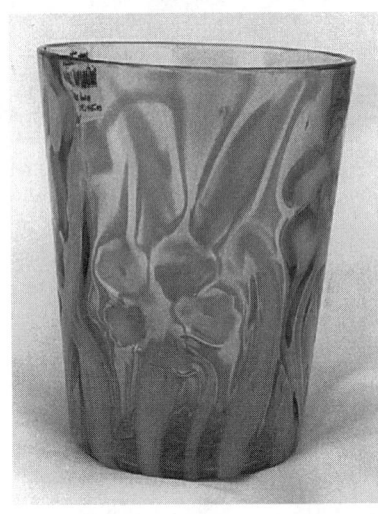

Blown, tumbler, Daffodil pattern, light green, unknown maker, c1886, $55.00.

Vase, Spanish Lace, 6" h, canary **75.00**
Water Set, pitcher and six tumblers
    Daisy & Fern, cranberry **475.00**

Novelties

Bowl
    Leaf & Diamond, white, 8½" d, three toes **30.00**
    Many Loops, green, ruffled rim **30.00**
    Palisades, blue **40.00**
    Palm & Scroll, blue, three toes **55.00**
    Pearl Flowers, blue, ftd **40.00**
    Rose Show, blue, 9" d **120.00**
    Ruffles and Rings, white, 8½" d **60.00**
    Sheherazade, blue, 8" d **55.00**
    Vintage, blue, 6½" d **40.00**
Candy Dish, Many Loops, green, triangular **45.00**
Centerpiece Bowl, 13" h, 11½" d, vaseline DQ bowl,
    heavy resilvered lady with cornucopia base, long
    flowing gown **375.00**
Compote
    Dolphin, white **200.00**
    Hilltop Vine, blue **50.00**
    Popsicle Sticks, 8" d, 4" h **40.00**
Toothpick Holder, Fluted Bars and Beads, green **40.00**
Vase
    Aurora Borealis, Jefferson Glass Co, c1903 .... **45.00**
    Beads and Bark, white, Northwood **40.00**
    Diamond & Oval Thumbprint, blue, 12" h **30.00**
    Diamond Point, blue, 11" h, ruffled rim **45.00**
    Lined Heart, 13" h, white **30.00**
    Lorna, blue **35.00**
    Twig, blue, 7" h **60.00**

Pressed

Berry Bowl, master
Everglades, blue, oblong 220.00
Flora, blue 80.00
Inverted Fan and Feather, blue, 10" d 245.00
Jewel & Flower, blue 90.00
Tokyo, blue, green 70.00

Berry Set, master bowl and six sauce dishes
Everglades, vaseline 595.00
Fluted Scrolls, canary 285.00
Jewel & Flower, blue 260.00
Regal, white 175.00
Wreath & Shell, vaseline 325.00

Bowl
Iris with Meander, blue, 9" d, ftd 35.00
Ribbed Spiral, canary, 7½" d 42.00

Butter Dish, cov
Drapery, blue 155.00
Everglades, canary 250.00
Flora, blue 260.00
Fluted Scrolls, blue 160.00
Iris and Meander, vaseline 260.00
Regal, blue 245.00
Tokyo, blue 115.00

Candy Dish, cov
Fan, green 30.00
Inverted Fan and Feather, green 285.00

Celery
Chrysanthemum Swirl, white 80.00
Fern, blue 110.00

Creamer
Circled Scroll, green 70.00
Fluted Scrolls, blue 65.00
Intaglio, blue 55.00
Inverted Fan and Feather, blue 125.00
Iris and Meander, blue 125.00
Swag with Brackets, blue 105.00
Tokyo, blue 70.00

Creamer and Sugar, cov
Hobnail, Northwood, white 50.00
Wild Bouquet, white 150.00

Cruet, orig stopper
Tokyo, blue 145.00
Wild Bouquet, blue 425.00

Dish, Argonaut Shell, vaseline, ftd 20.00

Jelly Compote
Beaded Shell, green 120.00
Everglades, blue, gold trim 95.00
Intaglio
    Blue 50.00
    White 30.00
Iris and Meander, canary 65.00
Scroll with Acanthus, blue 55.00
Swag with Brackets, blue 40.00
Tokyo, green 40.00

Mug, Diamond Spearhead, canary 55.00

Pitcher, water
Buttons and Braids, green 295.00
Everglades 275.00
Fluted Scrolls, canary 240.00
Hobnail, white 95.00

Rose Bowl
Inverted Fan and Feather, canary 45.00
Salt, open, Wreath & Shell, blue 110.00

Salt Shaker
Beatty Rib, white, no top 25.00
Fluted Scrolls, canary, orig top 65.00

Sauce Dish
Beatty Rib, white 15.00
Chrysanthemum Swirl, blue 30.00
Fan, green 30.00
Fern, blue 55.00
Fluted Scrolls, blue 35.00
Intaglio, blue 35.00
Iris and Meander, blue 25.00
Jeweled Heart, green 27.50
Reverse Swirl, blue 35.00
Ribbed Spiral, white 20.00
Wild Bouquet, white 40.00
Wreath & Shell, blue 30.00

Spooner
Diamond Spearhead, green 140.00
Flora, blue 85.00
Hobnail, white 50.00
Intaglio, blue 90.00
Inverted Fan and Feather, blue 140.00
Wreath & Shell, blue 120.00

Sugar Bowl, cov
Flora, canary 130.00
Iris and Meander, white 60.00

Sugar Shaker, orig top
Beatty Honeycomb, white 200.00

Table Set, cov butter, creamer, sugar, spooner
Diamond Spearhead, green 575.00
Drapery, blue, gold trim 450.00
Everglades, canary 515.00
Fluted Scrolls, blue 500.00
Intaglio, white 350.00
Regal, blue 500.00
Sunburst on Shield, blue 525.00
Tokyo, green 250.00
Wild Bouquet, blue 825.00
Wreath & Shell, blue 690.00

Toothpick
Beatty Honeycomb, blue 72.00
Hobnail, blue 70.00
Iris and Meander, green 85.00
Ribbed Spiral, canary 60.00
Swag with Brackets, canary 165.00
Wreath & Shell
    Vaseline 225.00
    White 150.00

Tumbler
Drapery, blue 70.00
Everglades
    Blue 70.00
    Canary, gold trim 50.00
    Vaseline 70.00
Jewel & Flower, blue 70.00
S-Repeat, blue 55.00
Swag with Brackets, canary 55.00
Wreath & Shell, canary 85.00

Vase, Diamond and Oval Thumbprint, white, 14" h ... 30.00

Water Set, pitcher and six tumblers
  Circled Scroll, blue 775.00
  Everglades, white 700.00
  Fluted Scrolls, canary 700.00

OPALINE GLASS

History: Opaline glass was a popular mid- to late 19th-century European glass. The glass has a certain amount of translucency and often is found decorated with enamel designs and trimmed in gold.

Basket, 6" h, white, gold trim, blue snake encircles handle, shiny ext., satin int. 185.00
Bowl, cov, 9" d, ftd, enameled floral dec 75.00
Box, cov, 1½" d, 1½" h, blue, gold prunus blossoms and leaves 65.00

Box, cov, pale green, gold enameling, cut dec, French, 4" d, 2½" h, $145.00.

Condiment Set, 6¾" h, 5¼" d, glossy blue, mustard with SP lid, two open salts, openwork around center, center handle, resilvered, English 235.00
Creamer, Wheat and Rushes pattern, green 45.00
Finger Bowl, matching under plate, blue 70.00
Goblet, 5" h, white 35.00
Mug, 4" h, white ground, cobalt blue trim, French 100.00
Relish, pink, Proeger Bird pattern 35.00
Ring Tree, 2½" d, round dished base, center column, blue, gold, and white trim 50.00
Soap Dish, cov, blue, hp floral dec 75.00
Vase, 12½" h, folded handkerchief shape, chain dec, blue and pink enamel flowers, green leaves, and branches, bee dec on int., price for facing pr 495.00

ORIENTALIA

History: Orientalia is a term applied to objects made in the Orient, an area which encompasses the Far East, Asia, China, and Japan. The diversity of cultures produced a variety of objects and styles.

References: Christopher Dresser, *Traditional Arts and Crafts of Japan,* Dover Publications, 1994; R. L. Hobson and A L. Hetherington, *The Art of the Chinese Potter,* Dover Publications, 1983; Duncan Macintosh, *Chinese Blue and White Porcelain,* Antique Collectors Club, 1994; Gloria and Robert Mascarelli, *Warman's Oriental Antiques,* Wallace-Homestead, 1992; Elizabeth Wilson, *A Guide to Oriental Ceramics,* Charles E. Tuttle Co., 1991.

Periodical: *Orientalia Journal,* PO Box 94, Little Neck, NY 11363.

Collectors' Club: China Student's Club, 59 Standish Rd, Wellesley, MA 02181.

Museums: Art Institute of Chicago, Chicago, IL; Asian Art Museum of San Francisco, San Francisco, CA; George Walter Vincent Smith Art Museum, Springfield, MA; Morikami Museum & Japanese Gardens, Delray Beach, FL; Pacific Asia Museum, Pasadena, CA.

Additional Listings: Canton, Celadon, Cloisonné, Fitzhugh, Nanking, Netsukes, Rose Medallion, Japanese Prints, and other related categories.

SPECIAL AUCTION

**Skinner Inc.
Bolton Gallery
357 Main St
Bolton, MA 01740
(508) 779-6241**

Arm Guard, 30" l, iron, lacquer, and silk, Japanese, Meiji Period, price for pr 450.00
Badge of Office, 14" l, embroidery, wood duck flying among symbols, Chinese 90.00
Belt, 36" l, twelve 1½" d Satsuma buttons, figures, butterflies, dragons, flowers, two 1¾" d buttons of dragons at ends 300.00
Bowl, 4½" d
  Gilt bronze and silver, rounded sides, flattened everted rim, two animal-mask and ring handles, engraved on ext. and int. with scrolling foliate design, possibly Han dynasty, ring missing, cracked, areas of encrustation 435.00
  Silver, shallow rounded sides, single crescent flange to one side, incised scrolling design, stippled ground, Song dynasty 345.00
Brush Pot, 10¼" h, bamboo, carved relief of boy lying on leaf holding peach, bat and crane flying above . 460.00
Buddha, 9½" h, bronze, standing on lotus throne, hands clasped in prayer at chest, long loose fitting robes, incised scrolling floral design, traces of gilt, red and green pigment, Ming dynasty 875.00
Ceremonial Bowl, 2¾" to 6½" d, nested set of nine, lacquer, gilt and silver dec, Japanese 850.00
Charger, 15¾" d, enameled, maidens at various pursuits in garden, elaborate scrolling floral band border, Chinese 1,300.00
Clothing
  Robe, embroidered blue silk, couched gold dragons chasing flaming pearls among clouds, red, blue, green, white, and yellow, multicolored terrestrial diagram and lishui stripe, 19th C 1,150.00
  Sur Coat, 55" l, lady's, dark blue silk, woven on front and back with eight floral, butterfly, and double-fish roundels, multicolored terrestrial diagram and lishui stripe, late 19th C 3,335.00
Cosmetic Box, 3¾" d, Blanc de Chine, circular, raised foot, molded raised floral relief on lid, 19th C 200.00

Bowl, Chinese, c1790, 5½″ d, $60.00.

Decanter Set, 7½″ w, 10″ l, 8″ h, lacquer and porcelain, lacquer case, two cylindrical and one rect bottles, blue and white wading ducks, stoppers with prunus blossoms, lids sgd "Hitakuzan Setsukowa Tgukuru," Japanese 1,250.00
Figure
    11″ h, 48½″ l, lion, Wei style, seated on haunches, head straight forward, mouth open, bearing teeth and tongue, fitted wooden base, Chinese 1,610.00
    15″ h, dignitary, horsehair mustache and beard, carved wood and gilt, lacquered, Chinese, seat missing 150.00
    17″ h, Buddha, standing in front of elaborate madorla, lacquer, Japanese 225.00
Fire Screen, 35½″ w, 42″ h, carved teak, red floral lacquered panel, applied ivory and bone, bird, blossom, and bough dec, Chinese, c1900 .... 125.00
Furniture
    Altar Table, 49″ w, 16¼″ d, 39¾″ h, teak, rect top, pierce-carved animal and key dec apron, pierce-carved twin terminal supports, Chinese 625.00
    Bench, 44″ w, 10¾″ d, 18¾″ h, elm wood, rect seat, double side stretchers attached to recessed legs, scroll spandrels, Chinese, 19th C, repairs, price for pr 800.00
    Cabinet, 31½″ w, 16¼″ d, 39″ h, rect form, sq form legs, two panels doors, single shelf containing two short drawers, red lacquered sides, back, and int., Haung Huali, 18th C, price for pr 3,105.00
    Center Table, 40½″ l, 27½″ w, 32½″ h, cypress, rect top, rounded legs, high set stretchers, 19th C ... 435.00
    Chair, arm, burgundy transparent lacquer, yoke back, scrolled crest rail, S-curve spat, out-scrolled arms, cane seat, flange brackets outline legs, braces, traces of gilt fruit design on splat, 18th C, restoration, price for pr 1,380.00
    Corner Cabinet, 31¼″ w, 16¼″ d, 39″ h, two rect doors, fitted shelf, two short drawers, short legs, Huang Huali, restorations, price for pr 805.00
    Low Cabinet, 30″ w, 19″ d, 30½″ h, hardwood, rect form, two panel drawers, two high-set short drawers int., Chinese, 19th C 500.00
    Side Table, 46″ l, 16½″ d, 31¼″ h, rect top, circ section legs, straight apron, rounded spandrels, legs

joined at each end with double braces, Tiaoan, Huang Huali 2,990.00
Gong, 19″ d, bronze, two dragons, scrolling and key-fret border, chain for hanging, Southeast Asia 125.00
Grave Attendant, 9″ h, standing male figure, Chinese, early Tang Dynasty, some restoration, price for pr .. 525.00
Hand Scroll
    Chinese, Night Banquet, color on paper, sgd "Tang Yin," comments by "Jiang Ting Xi" and "Yun Shou Ping," 19th C 3,450.00
    Korean, two birds among prunus branches, tears ... 50.00
Inkstand, 8¾ × 6½″, rect, incised dragons, fitted box with character inscriptions on lid 230.00
Koro, 16″ h, bronze, bulbous, twin beast's-head handles, two reserves of birds among foliage, tripod legs, pierced lid surmounted by mythical beast, cast seal on base, Japanese 250.00
Low Dish, 8¼″ d, enameled, central scene of figures in landscape, elaborate floral border, ext. with various Buddhist symbols, base painted with pomegranate with four character Qianlong mark, Chinese 1,250.00
Mirror, 29″ h, 39½″ l, wood, three sections within frame, carved prunus, frets, and lappets, Chinese 200.00
Paperweight, carved amethyst quartz, foo dog on rect SS base, Chinese 80.00
Pipe, 8¼″ l, silver, inlaid gold diapers, Japanese 270.00
Roof Tile, 13½″ d, earthenware, lion form, reddish body, yellow-green lead glaze, Chinese, Ming/Ching Dynasty, tail missing, some wear 350.00
Screen
    108″ l, 53½″ h, six panels, each panel depicting boys playing in palace gardens, color on silk, unsgd, Chinese, 18th/19th C 3,450.00
    192″ l, 81″ h, eight panels, each panel depicting immortals encounters, ink and color on silk, Chinese, late 18th/19th C, staining, damage to frame, price for pr 1,725.00
Sculpture, 13¾″ h, bronze, Buddha seated on open throne, Chinese, 19th C 200.00
Shrine
    14″ h, lacquer and giltwood, int. with seated Bodhisattva on lotus, Japanese 300.00

Charger, armorial, underglaze blue and famille verte, 1st quarter 18th C, arms of city of Utrecht, flowers and birds, 17″ d, $2,600.00. Photograph courtesy of William Doyle Galleries.

17½″ h, carved and lacquered, twin doors, birds, foliage, and offering on int., text on diaper ground,
int. with well-painted trompe l'oeil landscape
screen, gilt ext. trim, Chinese, minor chips 325.00

Stirrup, 7″ h, cast iron, inlaid bats and shou symbols,
Chinese or Mongolian 110.00

Table Screen, 17″ h, carved ivory panels, cricket among
vegetation, elaborately carved stand, Chinese, minor
damage 225.00

Tea Service, silver, hexagonal squat urn form, dragon,
floral, and bird panels, beaded rings, hexagonal bases, lyre form handles, 42 troy oz 800.00

Textile, embroidery panel, silk, blue five-toed dragon
with sun above, framed, Chinese, 19th C 475.00

Tsuba, 3″ d, iron, gilt-copper inlays, Mychin style, 16th
C 400.00

Vase
10″ h, sq section, blue and white, flowerings issuing
from rockwork and cranes among lotus, Chenghua
four-character mark 865.00

14½″ d, baluster, bronze, birds and foliage dec, Japanese, price for pr 260.00

17½″ d, mallet form, shaped reserves of landscapes,
floral groups, birds among foliage and antiques,
famille verte enamels, powder blue ground,
mounted as lamps, price for pr 750.00

Wall Hanging, 109″ l, 30″ h, silk, continuous village
scene, backed, Chinese, late 19th C, slight staining 800.00

ORIENTAL RUGS

History: Oriental rugs or carpets date back to 3,000 BC; but it was
in the 16th century that they became prevalent. The rugs originated in the regions of Central Asia, Iran (Persia), Caucasus, and
Anatolia. Early rugs can be classified into basic categories: Iranian,
Caucasian, Turkoman, Turkish, and Chinese. Later India, Pakistan,
and Iraq produced rugs in the Oriental style.

The pattern name is derived from the tribe which produced the
rug, e.g., Iran is the source for Hamadan, Herez, Sarouk, and
Tabriz.

References: George O'Bannon, *Oriental Rugs,* Running Press,
Courage Books, 1995; Walter A. Hawley, *Oriental Rugs, Antique
and Modern,* Dover Publications, n.d.; Charles W. Jacobsen,
Check Points on How to Buy Oriental Rugs, Charles E. Tuttle Co.,
1981; Friedrich Sarre and Hermann Trenkwald, *Oriental Carpet
Designs in Full Color,* Dover Publications, 1980; Joyce C. Ware,
Official Price Guide to Oriental Rugs, Second Edition, House of
Collectibles, 1996.

Periodicals: *HALI,* PO Box 4312, Philadelphia, PA 19118; *Oriental Rug Review,* PO Box 709, Meredith, NH 03253; *Rug News,*
34 West 37th St, New York, NY 10018.

Reproduction Alert: Beware! There are repainted rugs on the market.

Notes: When evaluating an Oriental rug, age, design, color,
weave, knots per square inch, and condition determine the final
value. Silk rugs and prayer rugs bring higher prices than other
types.

Akstafa, southeast Caucasus, second half 19th C
2′ 5″ × 1′ 9″, bagface, rosettes, palmettes, and ara-

---

besque corner motifs, sky blue, gold, rust, light
green, and dark blue-green, terra-cotta red field,
ivory border 575.00

10′ 4 × 3′ 10″, four gabled sq medallions, twin peacock motifs, red, sky blue, cochineal, gold, aubergine, and blue-green, midnight blue field, ivory
hooked sq border, even wear, small holes, crude
repairs, creases 1,850.00

Baluch, northeast Persia, early 20th C, 6′ 4″ × 3′ 6″, six
elongated rectangles and hooked diamonds, midnight and navy blue, rust, and red, diamond border
of similar coloration, good pile, moth damage to one
on back 300.00

Bessarabian Kelim, dated 1877, 14′ 4″ × 6′ 4″, three
roundels with scene of man and woman surrounded
by foliage, rose, blue, gold, tan, green, and blue-
green, dark brown field, similar colored border, small
repairs 1,495.00

Bidjar, northwest Persia, second half 19th C, 10′ 6″ ×
5′ 4″, three rows of palmettes and paired arabesque
leaves, red, rose, royal blue, gold, aubergine, and
blue-green, abrashed blue field, wide red border, areas of wear 2,100.00

Bordjalou Kazak, southwest Caucasus, last quarter 19th
C, 8′ 4″ × 4′ 3″, 2½ concentric hooked diamonds,
red, blue, and tan-gold, ivory wine-glass border,
slight moth damage, end fraying, small rewoven areas 2,100.00

Gendje, south central Caucasus, dated 1894, 9′ × 4′,
narrow zigzag stripes, hooked squares, red, navy
blue, gold, dark brown, and blue-green, ivory octagon border, good pile, brown corrosion 2,100.00

Heriz, Northwest Persia
10′ × 8′, second quarter 20th C, overall palmettes,
serrated leaves, and blossoming vines, blue, rose,
gold, ivory, and light green, terra-cotta red field,
midnight blue turtle border, small areas of minor
wear 2,645.00

12′ 4″ × 9′ 2″, second quarter 20th C, large rosette
medallion, blossoming vines, midnight blue, sky
blue, ivory, rose, gold, and blue-green, dark red
field, ivory spandrels, midnight blue border 1,150.00

Kabu, northeast Caucasus, late 19th/early 20th C, prayer,
5′ 2″ × 3′ 8″, two large flower-head medallions and
small rosettes, wine red, navy blue, red, gold, ivory,
and olive, midnight blue field, red bird motif border,
two creases, black corrosion 875.00

Karachoph Kazak, southwest Caucasus, late 19th C, 7′
6″ × 6′ 4″, large octagonal medallion, six hooked
squares, navy blue, red, and rose, blue-green field,
ivory border, areas of wear, repaired crease 1,840.00

Kashan, west central Persia, second quarter 20th C,

13′ 2″ × 10′, large double rosette medallion, multiple pendants, blossoming vines, red, rose, sky blue, ivory, gold, and blue-green, midnight blue field, red border, small areas of slight wear, small stain **6,100.00**

Kazak, southwest Caucasus

    4′ 10″ × 3′, late 19th C, five squares, each projecting two serrated leaves, navy blue, ivory, tan-gold, and blue-green, rust field, ivory S-motif border, slight moth damage, small corner gouge **1,610.00**

    9′ 2″ × 4′ 5″, early 20th C, column of five gabled rect medallions, dark red, royal blue, gold, and blue-green, navy blue field, royal blue border, slight moth damage, small repairs **2,645.00**

    9′ 6″ × 4′ 9″, early 20th C, three large diamond medallions, dark red, sky blue, apricot, ivory, and blue-green, abrashed slate blue field, sky blue meander border, good pile, slight moth damage, small creases **2,100.00**

Kerman, southeast Persia, early 20th C, 2′ 5″ × 1′ 10″, pictorial, nobleman stabbing winged lion, architectural setting, ivory, tan, gold, gold-green, and blue-green, cochineal field, midnight blue border, moth damage **460.00**

Kurd, northwest Persia, last quarter 19th C

    12′ 6″ × 3′, four elongated flowering plants and small bird, geometric motifs, midnight blue, royal blue, red, gold, and blue-green, cameo field, five narrow borders, rewoven areas **3,680.00**

    12′ 6″ × 5′ 9″, large scale Herati design, red, royal blue, gold, ivory, tan, and violet, midnight blue field, ivory spandrels, floral meander border, small areas of slight wear **1,955.00**

Ning Hsia, China, late 19th C, 2′ 3″ × 2′ 2″, mat, five sinuous dragons, midnight blue, royal blue, gold, ivory, and soft brown, deep gold field, similar colored border, good pile, one end rewoven **345.00**

Qashqai, southwest Persia

    6′ 2″ × 4′ 2″, last quarter 19th C, staggered filigree style boteh in red, sky blue, gold, rose, red-brown, and blue-green, navy blue field, ivory spandrels, red border, wear to center **2,300.00**

    8′ × 5′ 4″, second quarter 20th C, staggered hexagons, red, royal blue, gold, ivory, red-brown, and blue-green, midnight blue field, royal blue border**2,415.00**

Quchon Kurd, northeast Persia, late 19th/early 20th C, two stepped diamonds, Memling guls, midnight blue, sky blue, tan-gold, ivory, and pale blue-green, abrashed rust field, multicolored compartment border, small areas of moth damage, crease **1,150.00**

Sarouk, west Persia, early 20th C

    5′ 5″ × 3′ 4″, quatrefoil floral spray, blossoming branches, burgundy, tan-gold, dark brown, and pale blue-green, midnight blue field, burgundy border **1,725.00**

    11′ 9″ × 9′, floral sprays, midnight blue, royal blue, camel, dark red, tan-gold, and blue-green, red field, midnight blue border, gold pile, slight moth damage, small stains, and crease **2,530.00**

    13′ × 12′, floral sprays, midnight blue, navy blue, camel, tan-gold, and blue-green, deep wine red field, midnight blue palmette and vine border, good pile, slight moth damage, small crease **3,795.00**

Sarouk, ivory field woven with directional floral motif, midnight blue main border, 4′ 2″ × 6′ 4″, $725.00.

Sivas, east central Anatolia, second quarter 20th C, 5′ 9″ × 4′ 2″, prayer, hanging lamp and two columns, red field, aubergine floral spandrels, gold rosette and palmette border **575.00**

Tabriz, northwest Persia, late 19th C, 6′ × 4′ 6″, prayer, two columns, hanging lamp, midnight blue, sky blue, gold, red, tan, and light blue-green, light aubergine-rose field, ivory floral spandrels and border, areas of wear, selvage damage **1,150.00**

Ushak, west Anatolia, early 20th C, 12′ 9″ × 9′ 9″, central floral motifs, two columns, red, rust, slate blue, ice blue, gold, and green, pale green field, abrashed red-rust border, slight even wear to one end**5,175.00**

Veramin, north Persia, early 20th C, 5′ 8″ × 3′ 4″, overall Mina Khani floral lattice, midnight blue, navy blue, sky blue, red, cochineal, soft brown, light blue-green, ivory field, pale gold border, good pile, small repair and stain **2,875.00**

OVERSHOT GLASS

History: Overshot glass was developed in the mid-1800s. To produce overshot glass, a gather of molten glass was rolled over the marver upon which had been placed crushed glass. The piece then was blown into the desired shape. The finished product appeared to be frosted or iced.

Early pieces were made mainly in clear glass. As the demand for colored glass increased, color was added to the base piece and occasionally to the crushed glass.

Pieces of overshot generally are attributed to the Boston and Sandwich Glass Co. although many other companies also made it as it grew in popularity.

Museum: Sandwich Glass Museum, Sandwich, MA.

Basket, 6" d, 7½" h, octagonal, orange shaded to vaseline, emb nubs on sides, applied vaseline handle .. **225.00**
Claret Set, 12" h × 4¼" d jug, 4¾" h × 1¾" d wines, rubena overshot bowls, emb pewter bases, hinged pewter top, price for 5-pc set **500.00**
Compote, 8¾" d, 6¾" h, scalloped and ruffled, cranberry shaded to clear bowl, applied clear edging, fancy brass dome foot and pedestal base **125.00**
Jug, 9" h, applied handle, pewter lid **85.00**
Marmalade Jar, cov, matching under plate, green, gold snake entwined on cov, attributed to Boston and Sandwich **275.00**
Pitcher, 5½" h, clear, applied clear reeded handle **85.00**
Rose Bowl, 3¾" d, rubena, applied flowers and pale green leaves **150.00**
Vase, 8¼" h, fluted, pink, opal, applied clear handle .. **100.00**

Candy dish, hexagonal, amberina, 6" d, $85.00.

OWENS POTTERY

History: J. B. Owens began making pottery in 1885 near Roseville, Ohio. In 1891 he built a plant in Zanesville and in 1897 began producing art pottery. After 1907 most of the firm's production centered on tiles.

Owens Pottery, employing many of the same artists and designs as its two cross-town rivals, Roseville and Weller, can appear very similar to that of its competitors, e.g., Utopian (brown glaze), Lotus (light glaze), Aqua Verde (green glaze).

There were a few techniques used exclusively at Owens. These included Red Flame ware (slip decoration under a high red glaze)

and Mission (over-glaze, slip decorations in mineral colors) depicting Spanish Missions. Other specialties included Opalesce (semi-gloss designs in lustered gold and orange) and Coralene (small beads affixed to the surface of the decorated vases).

References: Susan and Al Bagdade, *Warman's American Pottery and Porcelain,* Wallace-Homestead, 1994; Paul Evans, *Art Pottery of the United States,* Second Edition, Feingold & Lewis Publishing, 1987; Frank Hahn, *Collector's Guide to Owens Pottery,* Green Gate Books (PO Box 934, Lima, OH 45802), 1996; Ralph and Terry Kovel, *Kovels' American Art Pottery,* Crown Publishers, 1993.

Ewer, 7" h, early standard glaze, Art Nouveau SS overlay, cluster of yellow leaves and blackberries, brown ground, incised "1773," die-stamped "O" **950.00**
Jug, 6" h, Utopian, round, hp leaves, sprig of flowers, dark brown ground, attributed to Anna Fulton Best, small glaze fleck on back **400.00**
Mug, 5" h, Utopia, orange and cream berries, orange thorned stems, broad green leaves, brown glaze, initialed "T.S." on side, imp mark **110.00**
Vase
2½" h, Utopian, high glaze, caramel, yellow, and dark brown pansies, caramel and dark brown ground, imp mark #947, rim flake **120.00**
3½" h, Utopian, broad caramel and tan leaves, brown glaze, imp mark **90.00**
4" h, Utopian, three-sided form, tan, cocoa, and dark brown blossoms, gray and tan matte ground, imp marks **50.00**
4½" h, Sudanese, pink, white, and yellow blossoms, green leaves, black high-glaze ground, imp mark #211 .... **300.00**
6½" h, 9" d, Navarre, open ribbon handles from broad base to rim, woman's head and ribbon dec, dark green and cream matte glaze, ink mark, minor surface scratches **1,500.00**
7" h, Sudanese, pale lavender and cream lily, broad light green lily pad, dark brown ground, high glaze, imp mark **350.00**
8" h, high glaze
Cream dogwood blossoms with olive centers, gray and olive branches, shaded light gray ground, imp "Owens 1253" **230.00**
White glaze, imp "Ben Owen" **425.00**
9" h
Lotus, molded broad leaves and berries, green, purple, and blue, matte glaze, imp mark **500.00**
10" d, brown glaze, brown and caramel tulips, green stems and leaves, chip and rim line **230.00**
10½" h, standard glaze, fruit and leaves dec, yellow, caramel, orange, and green, dark brown, pumpkin and tan ground, initialed by artist, imp mark #2, minute base flake **30.00**
11" h, brown glaze, tan and orange poppy blossoms and buds, green stems and leaves, imp touchmark "Owensart 1289," glaze flaws, small base chip . **70.00**
11½" h
Standard glaze, yellow, rust, dark brown, and caramel blossom atop narrow green stems, round green leaves, dark brown, caramel, and green ground, incised mark, minor surface scratches **140.00**

Vase, Utopian, matte, 13½" h, $225.00.

Wild rose dec, glossy brown int., incised "Owens 013," small glaze fleck on back 300.00
12" h, Utopian, green and yellow floral dec, brown glaze, incised "H," small base chip 100.00
14" h, Utopian, green, tan, and brown floral dec, imp mark 290.00

PAIRPOINT

History: The Pairpoint Manufacturing Co. was organized in 1880 as a silver-plating firm in New Bedford, Massachusetts. The company merged with Mount Washington Glass Co. in 1894 and became the Pairpoint Corporation. The new company produced specialty glass items often accented with metal frames.

Pairpoint Corp. was sold in 1938 and Robert Gunderson became manager. He operated it as the Gunderson Glass Works until his death in 1952. From 1952 until the plant closed in 1956, operations were maintained under the name Gunderson-Pairpoint. Robert Bryden reopened the glass manufacturing business in 1970, moving it back to the New Bedford area.

References: Edward and Sheila Malakoff, *Pairpoint Lamps,* Schiffer Publishing, 1990; John A. Shumann III, *The Collector's Encyclopedia of American Art Glass,* Collector Books, 1988, 1994 value update.

Collectors' Club: Pairpoint Cup Plate Collectors, PO Box 890052, East Weymouth, MA 02189.

Museum: Pairpoint Museum, Sagamore, MA.

Biscuit Jar, 7" h, bulbous apricot base, hp, daisy dec, sgd and numbered 300.00
Butter Dish, 5" d, silvered metal, chased ext., glass insert with cow's head, knife rest, period butter knife, monogrammed 250.00
Chalice, 12" h, sapphire blue and white pulled loop, controlled-bubble colorless stem, disk foot, Bryden Art 230.00
Chocolate Pot, 10" h, porcelain, butter yellow ground, delicate lilac blossoms, gold embellishments, molded

in swirls on body, handle, and finial, marked "Pairpoint-Limoges 2500 114" 485.00
Cologne Bottle, 7" h, green, clear foot, faceted paperweight stopper 200.00
Compote, 10½ × 11", cranberry reverse painted, peaches and gold highlights, SP handled pedestal base, sgd 1,200.00
Console Bowl, 12" d, 6¾" h, applied green, bubble ball connector, engraved Vintage pattern 175.00
Cornucopia Vase, 12½" h, border cutting, controlled bubble ball shaft, applied pedestal foot, price for pr   815.00
Creamer, opal glass, Delft blue windmill and landscape, five sailing ships on reverse, painted blue blown-out scrolls encircle base, SP handle, rim, and spout 350.00
Ice Pail, 6" d, 7½"h , clear, engraved Vintage pattern, nickel-silver rim and drain plate 195.00
Lamp
    13¾" h, 8" d shade, boudoir, blown-out closed-top sq glass shade, rose red blossoms, four butterflies, reverse painted, white ground, marked "The Pairpoint Corp," gilt metal base, fully sgd 5,750.00
    22" h, 18" d flared Berkeley glass reverse-painted shade, New Bedford harbor scene, tall-masted ships in foreground, men in small boat rowing toward town, church spires and village on distant shore, marked "The Pairpoint Corp," SP triple dolphin base stamped "Pairpoint" 4,715.00
Miniature Lamp, 16⅜" h, 9" d San Remo barrel-shapes reverse-painted puffy shade, blown-out butterflies, asters, and roses against green-accented white ground, gold ext. accents, millefiore green-patina metal base 6,900.00

Candlesticks, light blue ground, blue floral dec, gold highlights, marked "Pairpoint Mfg. Co., New Bedford, MA, Pat. Aug. 23, 93," 12½" h, price for pr, $495.00.

Smoking Stand, three opal glass bowls mounted in shield-shaped maple stand, brass trim and feet, brass cigar holder, Delft dec of windmills, houses, people, and sailing ships 650.00
Vase
    6" h, Tavern Glass, thousands of bubble inclusions, sailing galleon on wavy sea dec, c1900–38 ..... 300.00
    10" h, 3" d, cone shape, opal, floral sprigs, sgd 225.00
    14" h, porcelain, mahogany red ground, white medallion with portrait of little girl surrounded by network of interlocking gold scrolls and stylized

florals, fancy scroll work base, well worn gold dec
on reverse **835.00**

PAPER EPHEMERA

History: Maurice Rickards, author of *Collecting Paper Ephemera*, suggests that ephemera are the "minor transient documents of everyday life," material destined for the wastebasket but never quite making it. This definition is more fitting than traditional dictionary definitions that emphasize time, e.g., "lasting a very short time." A driver's license, which is used for a year or longer, is as much a piece of ephemera as is a ticket to a sporting event or music concert. The transient nature of the object is the key.

Collecting ephemera has a long and distinguished history. Among the English pioneers were John Seldon (1584–1654), Samuel Pepys (1633–1703), and John Bagford (1650–1716). Large American collections can be found at historical societies and libraries across the country, and museums, e.g., Wadsworth Athenaeum, Hartford, CT, and the Museum of the City of New York.

When used by collectors, "ephemera" usually means paper objects, e.g., billheads and letterheads, bookplates, documents, labels, stocks and bonds, tickets, and valentines. However, more and more ephemera collectors are recognizing the transient nature of some three-dimensional material, e.g., advertising tins and pinback buttons. Today's specialized paper shows include dealers selling other types of ephemera in both two- and three-dimensional form.

References: Warren R. Anderson, *Owning Western History*, Mountain Press Publishing, 1993; Patricia Fenn and Alfred P. Malpa, *Rewards of Merit*, Ephemera Society, 1994; Norman E. Martinus and Harry L. Rinker, *Warman's Paper*, Wallace-Homestead, 1994; Robert Reed, *Paper Collectibles*, Wallace-Homestead, 1995; Kenneth W. Rendell, *Forging History*, University of Oklahoma Press, 1994; Gene Utz, *Collecting Paper*, Books Americana, 1993.

Periodical: *Paper Collectors' Marketplace*, PO Box 128, Scandinavia, WI 54977.

Collectors' Clubs: Ephemera Society, 12 Fitzroy Sq, London W1P 5HQ England; Ephemera Society of America, Inc, PO Box 95, Cazenovia, NY 13035; The Ephemera Society of Canada, 36 Macauley Dr, Thornhill, Ontario L3T 5S5 Canada; National Assoc of Paper & Advertising Collectors, PO Box 500, Mount Joy, PA 17552.

Additional Listings: See Advertising Trade Cards, Catalogs, Comic Books, Photographs and Sports Cards in *Warman's Antiques and Collectibles Price Guide* for more examples. Also see Calendars, Catalogs, Magazines, Newspapers, Photographs, Postcards, and Sheet Music in *Warman's Americana & Collectibles*.

Advisor: Norman Martinus.

Blotters

Badger Soap, You Want the Best, multicolored, attached
card **15.00**
Caroid Throat Medicine, 1920s **8.50**
Dixon's Eldorado Master Drawing Pencil **5.00**
G & J Tires, 1919 .... **10.00**
Jersey Cream, 1920s, children illus, 4 × 9" **2.50**
Kellogg's Rice Krispies, multicolored **8.00**
Morton Salt **8.00**
Sundial Shoes, Bonnie Laddie, multicolored **6.50**

Booklets

Battle of Gettysburg, 1895, 56 pgs, illus **12.50**
Chrysler Building, souvenir type, emb metallic cov, 1930 **75.00**
Dennison Crepe Paper, c1922, crepe paper samples .. **35.00**
Hershey's, The Story of Chocolate and Cocoa, 32 pgs,
1926 .... **8.00**
Johnson Gasoline, c1920, girl blowing bubbles **6.00**
Kellogg's Funny Jungleland, moving pictures, 1907 ... **35.00**
Master Muskrat Methods, 1918, 43 pgs, E J Dailey author
and publisher **12.50**
Movie Program, What Price Glory? **75.00**
Pop Recording Artists, pictorial, 1953 .... **35.00**
Royal Blue Line, Boston & New England, 1926,44 pgs **7.50**

Business Cards

References: Kit Barry, *The Advertising Trade Card, Book 1*, published by author, 1981; Robert Jay, *The Trade Card in Nineteenth-Century America*, University of Missouri Press, 1987; Avery Pitzak, *Business Cards*, published by author, 1989; ———, *Business Cards*, published by author, 1992 (Editor's note: Although this book has the same title as Pitzak's previous book, it is entirely different); ———, *Make Your Business Card Incredibly Effective*, published by author, 1990.

Atlis Brewing Co, Detroit, MI, multicolored **10.00**
Commercial Hotel, Grand Rapids, MI, black and white **7.50**
Danville Female Collegiate Institute, list of teachers, tu-
ition cost, 1870s **10.00**
Fairchild & Co, Hats, Caps, and Straw Goods, New Or-
leans, red bee-shaped center **15.00**
Grubb & Richardson, Poland, China Swine **8.00**

Calling card, diecut, printed color, embossed, 1890s, 4 × 2¼", $5.00.

Milton Bradley Co, Springfield, MA, kindergarten material, school aids **15.00**

Novelties for the Holidays, Conklin, CT, blue front **5.00**

Pfeiffer Brewing Co, Detroit, MI, multicolored **15.00**

Soyer's Worlds Secret Detective Service, NY, World Wide, brown and black, logo **30.00**

Union Mills, Dusenberry & Anthony Dealers-Coffee & Spices, Troy NY, red stamped name **8.00**

Calendars

Collectors' Club: Calendar Collector Society, American Resources, 18222 Flower Hill Way #299, Gaithersburg, MD 20879.

1897, Berlin Iron Bridge Co, bridges and factory scenes, Kellogg & Bulkeley Co, 14 × 11" **80.00**

1900, Springfield Breweries Co, calendar months around oval with girl, 21 × 29" **225.00**

1910, Chinese Student Alliance, rope hanger **6.00**

1915, Magic Yeast, paper litho, barefoot boy carrying yeast and stick, Ketterlinus, Philadelphia, 18 × 10" **225.00**

1920, McCormick Machinery, top only, children illus . **275.00**

1922, Sharples Tubular Cream Separators, woman wearing hat, January pad **110.00**

1929, Compliments of H Buch, Butcher and Dealer in Fresh and Smoked Meats, color litho illus, full pad, 12 × 18¼" **30.00**

1938, Richfield, Lawson Wood Armstrong illus **60.00**

1942, Case Farm Machinery, 9½ × 17" **50.00**

1945, Double Cola, full pad **110.00**

Checks

1792, sgd by General Henry Knox **35.00**

1816, Office of Pay and Deposit of the Bank of Columbia, Washington, March 27, 1816, filled in and sgd James Madison **1,600.00**

1845, Corcoran and Ribbs Bank, sgd by Daniel Webster **28.00**

1853, Illinois Central Railroad, vignettes **30.00**

1865, P T Barnum, Oct 17, payable to S H Hurd for $500 **390.00**

1906, First National Bank of Liverpool, PA, yellow, sq photograph marked "Old Canal Boat Days, Liverpool, Pennsylvania, 1906" boats on Chesapeake and Ohio Canal, unissued **5.00**

1920, Hudson Trust Co, NY, sgd by Enrico Caruso **45.00**

1946, Pepsi-Cola, American State Bank, 10 × 3" **10.00**

Document, Government, local, tax bill, Philadelphia, PA, dated 1824, 6½ × 4", $20.00.

Labels

References: Edwin Barnes and Wayne Dunn, *The Cigar-Label Art Visual Encyclopedia with Index and Price Guide,* published by authors (PO Box 3, Lake Forest, CA 92630), 1995; Joe Davidson, *Fruit Crate Art,* Wellfleet Press, 1990; Gordon T. McClelland and Jay T. Last, *Fruit Box Labels,* Hillcrest Press (3412-G MacArthur Blvd., Santa Ana, CA 92704), 1995.

Collectors' Clubs: Cigar Label Collectors International, PO Box 66, Sharon Center, OH 44274; Citrus Label Society, 131 Miramonte Dr, Fullerton, CA 92365; Florida Citrus Label Collectors Assoc, PO Box 547636, Orlando, FL 32854; International Seal, Label & Cigar Band Society, 8915 E Bellevue St, Tucson, AZ 85715; Society of Antique Label Collectors, PO Box 24811, Tampa, FL 33623.

Bottle

  Apricot Brandy, two apricots, gilt dec, 5 × 3¼" ... **1.50**

  Old Craft Brew, four brewery workers making beer, gilt dec .... **..50**

Can

  Blue Hill, white corn, house, and river scene **3.00**

  Cocoa, Elkay Cocoa, emb, cup of cocoa, dark blue, gold, and white **10.00**

  Country Maid Evaporated Milk, milkmaid, carrying milk paint, blue and red background **2.00**

  Forest City, strawberries in glass bowl, 1920s **2.00**

  Templar Peas, knight in armor, riding horse **2.00**

  Tube City Red Alaska Salmon, fish, white, red, and blue **7.00**

Label, syrup, Red Bud Brand Strawberry Fountain Syrup, blue and red, 5 × 6", $3.00.

Cigar

  Buzzer, ornate butterfly with cigar body **4.00**

  La Boda, wedding ceremony **3.00**

  Red Tips, horse's head in horseshoe, white background **2.00**

Fruit Crate

  Airship, old four-prop commercial plane, royal blue background, Fillmore, CA, oranges **10.00**

Duckwall, wood duck standing on brick wall, pears **4.00**

Miracle, genie holding tray with three oranges, dated 1928, Placentia Oranges **4.00**

Ocean Spray, glass of lemonade, red roses in blue vase, Santa Paula Lemons **5.00**

Red Rooster Apples, crowing rooster, yellow, red, and navy background **1.00**

Letterheads and Billheads

Reference: Leslie Cabarga, *Letterheads,* Chronicle Books, 1992.

Arctic Fire Insurance Co, iceberg and sailing ship vignette **8.50**

Davis & Yonger, Horses & Mules, Oklahoma City, OK, 1919, Hommer, Wilson, Walker & Co litho, black and white, used **7.00**

Detroit Engine Works, 1914 .... **20.00**

Keystone Plow Co, New Castle, PA, 1894, blue illus, used **10.00**

Oneida Truck Mfg Co, c1910, vehicle illus, unused ... **5.00**

Standard Oil Co, New York **7.50**

United States Cigar Co, York, PA, 1933, two color **8.00**

Wright Steam Engine Works, Newburgh, NY, 1882, black and white **8.00**

Miscellaneous

Blocks, Mother Goose Nested Blocks, McLoughlin Bros, 1911, set of 7 .... **75.00**

Clipper Ship Card

Golden Fleece, Coleman's California Line, vignette of three-masted sailing ship at full sail **950.00**

Sea Serpent, Sutton & Co, vignette of coiled sea serpent holding banner in mouth, three-masted sailing ship at full sail beneath banner **1,375.00**

Invitation

Banquet, Gen Douglas MacArthur, oval portrait cov, St Anthony Hotel, TX, 11 × 7" **45.00**

Dinner, Roosevelt & Garner, victory dinner, 1937, guest of honor Eleanor Roosevelt, orig envelope **25.00**

License, entertainment, 1919, City of Providence, RI, ordering Star Spangled Banner to be played at every performance **15.00**

Newspaper, Saturday Globe, Utica, NY, 1898–1904, full-color front page litho, sewn bindings, 15 complete papers **150.00**

Program, New York Giants Football Game, Dec 19, 1943, Giants and Redskins **3.00**

Reward of Merit, 1876, Excelsior, Fifty Merits, white and blue, gold trim, used **10.00**

Ticket, Harvard Baseball Assoc, 1880s, logo on front and back, green and black **30.00**

Postcards

References: Diane Allmen, *The Official Price Guide to Postcards,* House of Collectibles, 1990; Janet Banneck, *The Antique Postcards of Rose O'Neill,* Greater Chicago Publications, 1992; J. L. Mashburn, *The Artist-Signed Postcard Price Guide,* Colonial House, 1993; ———, *Black Americana: A Century of History Preserved on Postcards,* Colonial House, 1996; ———, *Fantasy Postcards with Price Guide,* Colonial House, 1996; ———, *The*

Postcard Price Guide, Second Edition, Colonial House, 1995; ———, *The Super Rare Postcards of Harrison Fisher with Price Guide,* Colonial House, 1992; Frederic and Mary Megson, *American Exposition Postcards,* The Postcard Lovers, 1992; Ron Menchine, *A Picture Postcard History of Baseball,* Almar Press, 1992; Susan Brown Nicholson, *The Encyclopedia of Antique Postcards,* Wallace-Homestead, 1994; Cynthia Rubin and Morgan Williams, *Larger than Life: The American Tall-Tall Postcard 1905–1915,* Abbeville Press, 1990; Nouhad A. Saleh, *Guide to Artist's Signatures and Monograms on Postcards,* Minerva Press, 1993; Robert Ward, *Investment Guide to North American Real Photo Postcards,* Antique Paper Guide, 1991; Jane Wood, *The Collector's Guide to Post Cards,* L-W Book Sales, 1984, 1995 value update.

Note: An up-to-date listing of books about and featuring postcards can be obtained from Gotham Book Mart & Gallery, Inc, 41 W. 47th St., New York, NY 10036.

Periodicals: *Barr's Post Card News,* 70 S 6th St, Lansing, IA 52151; *Gloria's Corner,* PO Box 507, Denison, TX 75021; *Postcard Collector,* PO Box 1050, Dubuque, IA 52004.

Collectors' Clubs: *Barr's Post Card News* and *Postcard Collector* publish lists of over 50 regional clubs in the United States and Canada; Deltiologists of America, PO Box 8, Norwood, PA 19074; Granite State Postcard Collectors Club, PO Box 79, West Franklin, NH 03235; International Postcard Assoc Inc, PO Box 66, 1217 F S K Hwy, Keymar, MD 21757; Monumental Postcard Club, 3013 St Paul St, Baltimore, MD 21218; Postcard History Society, PO Box 1765, Manassas, VA 22110.

Artist Signed

Atwell, Mabel Lucie, comic **15.00**

Browne, Tom, advertising **15.00**

Clapsaddle, Ellen, florals **5.00**

Fisher, Harrison **25.00**

Humphrey, Maud, sgd **70.00**

Mucha, Alphonse, Art Nouveau type **125.00**

O'Neill, Rose, Kewpies **50.00**

Greetings

April Fools, American comic scene **3.00**

Christmas, Santa, German, highly emb, red suit **15.00**

Mother's Day, early **5.00**

New Year, beautiful women **15.00**

Valentines, hearts **1.00**

Puzzles

References: *Dexterity Games and Other Hand-Held Puzzles,* L-W Book Sales, 1995; Jack Matthews, *Toys Go to War,* Pictorial Histories Publishing, 1994; Harry L. Rinker, *Collector's Guide to Toys, Games and Puzzles,* Wallace-Homestead, 1991; ———, *Guide to Games and Puzzles,* Antique Trader Books, 1996; Jerry Slocum and Jack Botermans, *The Book of Ingenious & Diabolical Puzzles,* Time Books, 1994; Anne D. Williams, *Jigsaw Puzzles,* Wallace-Homestead, 1990.

Collectors' Clubs: American Game Collectors Assoc, 49 Brooks Ave, Lewiston, ME 04240; National Puzzler's League, PO Box 82289, Portland, OR 97282.

Consolidated Paper Box, Perfect Picture Puzzle, Mountain Warfare, over 375 pcs, 19½ × 15½", c1943, eight stars on box **15.00**

Janus Games, Inc., The Janus Mystery Jigsaw Puzzle, No. 1 of 4, The Case of the Snoring Skinflint, Henry Slesar, over 500 pcs, 22 × 15", story on back of cardboard box **15.00**

J Ottmann Lithography Co, Dissected Circus, sliced pcs, 18½ × 12¾" **75.00**

McLoughlin Brothers, NY

Locomotive Picture Puzzle, engine at station, 24¾ × 18", 1887 .... **225.00**

The Young Blue Jackets, set of two, United States Cruiser Columbia, 18 pcs, 10 × 6", and United States Cruiser San Francisco, 15 pcs, 9 × 6½", box lithography shows three sailors around naval gun **250.00**

Milton Bradley

Smashed-Up Locomotive, 9 × 7", wooden box **250.00**

The Dover Jig Picture Puzzle, No. 4728, The Circus, over 300 pcs, 1930s, guide picture on box, cardboard **10.00**

Oxford Specialty Co, Boston, MA, Budge: Sports, diecut cardboard, 17 × 17", cardboard box with instructions for four players **25.00**

Saalfield Publishing, No. 910, Just Kids Picture Puzzles, four-puzzle set, each puzzle approx 9¾ × 8", guide picture on front of box **40.00**

Schoenhut Co, Philadelphia, PA, Schoenhut Picture Puzzle, Let's Go, over 200 pcs, 10 × 22" box **15.00**

Stocks and Bond Certificates

Reference: Bill Yachtman, *The Stock & Bond Collectors Price Guide,* published by author, 1985, out of print.

Periodical: *Bank Note Reporter,* 700 State St, Iola, WI 54990.

Collectors' Club: Bond and Share Society, 26 Broadway at Bowling Green, Rm 200, New York, NY 10004.

Academy Motor Sales & Service, Inc. eagle vignette, unissued **12.00**

Banner Oil Co, AZ, oil-well vignette **6.00**

Hornell Airways, Inc. vignette of two women and sun rising over mountains, issued and canceled, 1920s . **75.00**

Kansas Railroad, train logo **18.50**

Missouri Railroad, train logo **18.50**

Northampton Brewery Corp, PA, orange certificate, engraved, woman, ship, and city skyline vignette, issued, 1930s **15.00**

Real Estate Assoc, Petaluma, CA, 1876, black and white, issued **25.00**

Texas Railroad, train logo **18.50**

Tuolumne County Water Co, mining methods vignette, 1854 .... **75.00**

Woolworth, F W & Co, vignette of eagle over two hemispheres, brown **3.00**

PAPERWEIGHTS

History: Although paperweights had their origin in ancient Egypt, it was in the mid-19th century that this art form reached its zenith. The finest paperweights were produced between 1834 and 1855 in France by the Clichy, Baccarat, and Saint Louis factories. Other weights made in England, Italy, and Bohemia during this period rarely match the quality of the French weights.

In the early 1850s, the New England Glass Co. in Cambridge, Massachusetts, and the Boston and Sandwich Glass Co. in Sandwich, Massachusetts, became the first American factories to make paperweights.

Popularity peaked during the classic period (1845–1855) and faded toward the end of the 19th century. Paperweight production was rediscovered nearly a century later in the mid-1900s. Contemporary weights still are made by Baccarat, Saint Louis, Perthshire, and many studio craftsmen in the U.S. and Europe.

References: Monika Flemming and Peter Pommerencke, *Paperweights of the World,* Schiffer Publishing, 1994; John D. Hawley, *The Glass Menagerie,* Paperweight Press, 1995; Sibylle Jargstorf, *Paperweights,* Schiffer Publishing, 1991; Paul Jokelson and Dena Tarshis, *Baccarat Paperweights and Related Glass,* Paperweight Press, 1990; Edith Mannoni, *Classic French Paperweights,* Paperweight Press, 1984; Bonnie Pruitt, *St. Clair Glass Collectors Guide,* published by author, 1992; Pat Reilly, *Paperweights,* Running Press, Courage Books, 1994; Lawrence H. Selman, *All About Paperweights,* Paperweight Press, 1992; ———, *The Art of the Paperweight,* Paperweight Press, 1988; ———, *The Art of the Paperweight, Perthshire,* Paperweight Press, 1983; ———, *The Art of the Paperweight, Saint Louis,* Paperweight Press, 1981 (all of the Paperweight Press books are distributed by Charles E. Tuttle Co., 1996).

Collectors' Clubs: Caithness Collectors Club, 141 Lanza Ave, Building 12, Garfield, NJ 07026; International Paperweight Society, 761 Chestnut St, Santa Cruz, CA 95060; Paperweight Collectors Assoc Inc, PO Box 1059, Easthampton, MA 01027; Paperweight Collectors Assoc of Chicago, 535 Delkir Ct, Naperville, IL 60565; Paperweight Collectors Assoc of Texas, 1631 Aguarena Springs Dr, #408, San Marcos, TX 78666.

Museums: Bergstrom-Mahler Museum, Neenah, WI; Corning Museum of Glass, Corning, NY; Degenhart Paperweight & Glass Museum, Inc, Cambridge, OH; Museum of American Glass at Wheaton Village, Millville, NJ.

Additional Listings: See *Warman's Americana & Collectibles* for examples of advertising paperweights.

Advisor: Lawrence H. Selmon.

Antique

Baccarat

2¹³⁄₁₆" d, c1920, Dupont circular garland millefiori weight, circlets of complex cog and star canes in pink, cobalt blue, pale green, orange and white, complex arrow/six-pointed star cane placed in center of each outer loop, central circlet is centered on pink, white and green stardust/bull's-eye cane **550.00**

2⁵/₁₆″ d, c1845

Faceted pompon garland weight, flower composed of numerous white recessed C-shaped petals about pale yellow stardust stamens on stalk with pair of closed white buds and emerald green leaves, arrangement floats over star-cut ground inside garland of alternating red and white stardust/bull's-eye canes, and cobalt blue, white and emerald six-pointed star/arrow canes, dome cut with allover geometric faceting **1,000.00**

Thousand-petaled rose weight, flower with numerous furled velvet red petals on stalk with emerald green leaves over star-cut ground, tiara of green leaves frames blossom which is placed in crystal dome with six and one faceting **3,500.00**

2⁹/₁₆″ d, c1845, pansy weight, flower with deep purple upper petals and black-striped purple and yellow lower petals, around stardust/bull's-eye cane on stalk with yellow and purple bud and emerald green leaves **770.00**

2³/₄″ d, c1845

Dated close packed millefiori weight, Gridel silhouettes of a rooster, a deer, a dog, love birds and a monkey, amidst six-pointed star canes, whorls, shamrocks, fortress canes, honeycomb canes, quatrefoil canes, honeycomb canes, arrow canes, stardust canes and cog canes, in orange, cobalt blue, aquamarine, coral red, cadmium green, lavender, sea green, salmon, white and pale yellow, dated with B1848 signature/date cane **2,200.00**

Signed scattered millefiori on lace weight, Gridel silhouettes of a moth, a monkey, a horse, a squirrel, a pheasant, an elephant, a goat, a rooster, a deer and a dog, complex six pointed star canes, cog canes, fortress canes, arrow canes and trefoil canes in amethyst, ruby, cadmium green, yellow, robin's-egg blue, sea green and white, on a lace ground. B1848 signature/date cane **2,500.00**

2¹¹/₁₆″ d, c1845, primrose weight, flower with six red petals, each banded with white loop, around red and white stardust/bull's eye cane on stalk with emerald green leaves on star-cut ground **1,320.00**

2⁷/₈″ d, c1845

Dated stardust carpet ground weight, coral, orange, yellow, plum, cadmium green, cobalt blue, ruby and turquoise complex canes in a sea of red and white stardust canes, Gridel silhouette canes of an elephant, two dogs, two moths, a deer, a horse, a rooster, a pheasant and a goat, also includes a millefiori flower portrait cane, dated with B1848 signature/date cane **12,000**

Garlanded butterfly on lace weight, insect, with flattened millefiori wings, marbled with shades of orange, green, blue, purple, yellow and red, attached to eggplant-purple, body with black antennae and turquoise, brown and white eyes, insect floats inside garland of alternating green and white cog canes, on a white lace ground **3,850.00**

Baccarat, strawberry on cobalt, marked "87/240," 1970, $450.00.

3″ d, c1845, close packed mushroom weight, fortress, stardust, arrow, trefoil, quatrefoil, cog, six-pointed star, whorl and honeycomb canes in cobalt blue, salmon, ruby, turquoise, cadmium green and white, three-dimensional stem extends to star-cut ground inside blue and white latticinio filigree torsade **1,550.00**

3¹/₈″ d, c1845

Blue dogrose weight, flower with white-rimmed, heart-shaped petals around red and white stardust/bull's-eye cane on stalk with emerald green leaves over star-cut diamond **1,300.00**

Macaedoine weight, pieces of twists in ruby, white, salmon, yellow, cadmium green and cobalt blue amidst white and colored lace **450.00**

Clichy, c1845

2¹/₂″ d, double clematis bouquet weight, three blossoms in pink, turquoise and auburn, on stems with three buds and emerald green leaves, each blossom contains delicate complex millefiori center, flowers tied with blue ribbon **10,000.00**

2⁷/₈″ d

Chequer weight, complex pastry mold canes, florets, cog and bull's-eye canes in pink, cherry, ruby, lilac, thalo blue, Naples yellow, royal blue, cadmium green and white. The large complex canes are divided by white lace filigree cables **1,500.00**

Robin's-egg blue and white swirl weight, alternating pinwheels emanating from emerald green and white stardust / bull's-eye cane **2,500.00**

3¹/₈″ d, c1845

Circular garlands weight with two pink and green roses, garland composed of circlets of cog, pastry mold and stardust/bull's-eye canes in pink, cadmium green, lilac, cobalt blue and white, complex cane, including two pink and green roses, placed in the center and in between each circlet, white pastry mold cane in the center of one of circlets contains third hidden pink rose, arrangement is centered around circlet of pink and cobalt blue pastry mold canes on a clear ground **1,760.00**

Close packed mushroom weight, tuft with two pink and green roses, two pink and white roses, and lilac rose amidst moss canes, pastry mold canes, bull's-eye canes, star-shaped canes, edelweiss canes and cog canes, in thalo blue, cobalt blue, pink, lilac, white, ruby and cadmium green, outer circlet of pink and white rods has been pulled down to starburst-cut ground to form stem of mushroom, five and one faceting **7,000.00**

Signed spaced millefiori color ground weight with roses, amidst pastry mold, cog, quatrefoil, star and bull's-eye canes, in lilac, cadmium green, Naples yellow, cherry, ruby, pink, thalo blue and cobalt blue on opaque turquoise ground **3,500.00**

Millville, produced at southern New Jersey glass factories such as Whitall Tatum Company/Millville during late 19th and early 20th C, 3¾″ d, 3½″ h, rose weight, fourteen full-bodied canary-yellow petals rising from three green leaves, all in clear glass sphere with circular foot **1,430.00**

New England Glass Company, c1870

2⁷⁄₁₆″ d, crown weight, twisted ribbons and latticinio filligree spokes, in red, blue, yellow, pink and white, emanating from pink, blue and white complex cog cane **1,320.00**

2¹¹⁄₁₆″ d, clematis weight, flower with six ridged blue petals around complex pale blue cog/quatrefoil cane center on stalk with opening blue bud and green leaves, flower floats on white double swirl latticinio ground inside garland of forest green, ruby and white cog/quatrefoil canes **500.00**

2¾″ d

Concentric millefiori weight with running rabbit silhouettes, complex canes and floret canes, in ruby, yellow, orange, royal blue, pink, pale green and white, over white double-swirl latticinio ground **880.00**

Scrambled weight, three canes containing eagle silhouettes, amidst whole and broken complex cog and star canes, twisted ribbon and filigree in royal blue, ruby, yellow, orange, white and green **250.00**

2⁷⁄₈″ d base, blown pear weight, three-dimensional yellow fruit displaying caramel blush, with brown stem on clear cookie base, blossom end of fruit dec with black glass stamp **1,210.00**

2⁷⁄₈″ d, fruit bouquet weight, formal arrangement with amber apples and red cherries on bed of green leaves inside white double-swirl latticinio funnel basket **900.00**

Saint Louis, c1845

2⅜″ d, miniature flat bouquet weight, four cane flowers, in raspberry, peach, white, yellow, Persian blue and powder blue, on a stalk with four spring green leaves over translucent amber ground **700.00**

2½″ d, crown weight, red and green twists alternating with white latticinio spokes emanating from central salmon, yellow and white complex bundled rod/bull's-eye cane **2500.00**

2⁷⁄₈″ d, close packed millefiori mushroom weight, tuft composed of complex cog, cross, floret and star canes, in salmon, cadmium green, Persian blue, pink, lavender and white, three-dimensional stem extends to star-cut ground inside spiral salmon and white lace filigree torsade **2,090.00**

2¹¹⁄₁₆″ d, close concentric millefiori weight, central silhouette of a camel surrounded by florets, six-

pointed star canes and crimped cog canes, in chartreuse, peach, Persian blue, powder blue, spring green and white **2,200.00**

3″ d, faceted upright bouquet weight, dimensional bouquet, containing complex star, fortress and cog canes with lampwork blossoms, in royal blue, sienna orange, sulphur yellow, powder blue and cadmium green, crowned by white clematis with yellow matched center, flowers are nestled inside bed of emerald green leaves with tapered stem that extends down to grid-cut ground, circular top facet and three rows of side facets **3,000.00**

3⅛″ d, strawberry weight, one pink and one ruby berry hanging from stem containing white blossom with yellow stamens and emerald green leaves, plant rests on a white double-swirl latticinio ground **3,000.00**

Sandwich Glass Company, c1870

3³⁄₁₆″ d, tricolor poinsettia weight, double tier of blue-striped red petals around blue and white complex cog/quatrefoil cane center on stalk with variegated green leaves **1,000.00**

3¹¹⁄₁₆″ d, cherries weight, three ruby cherries growing on stems with olive green leaves over a clear ground **1,000.00**

Modern

Ayotte, Rick

3¾″ d, 1988 American plum bouquet weight, three large ripe purple plums hanging from brown stems with three white blossoms and green leaves, signed and dated, limited edition of 50 .... **825.00**

4½″ h, 1990 Magnum Illusion upright blueberry bouquet weight, three-dimensional berries hang from stems with three large pink blossoms and pink and white wild flowers on stems with green leaves, inside amethyst halo, signed and dated **2,200.00**

Baccarat

3³⁄₁₆″ d, 1977, Gridel dancing devil patterned millefiori weight, large dancing devil silhouette cane surrounded by star-shaped arrangement of complex canes in red, pink, yellow, blue, green and white on translucent blue-over-opaque white ground, other seventeen Gridel silhouette canes are composed about edge of weight, signature/date cane, acid etched with Baccarat insignia, limited edition of 350 .... **400.00**

3¼″ d, 1990, Maltese cross millefiori weight, patterned arrangement of yellow cog canes inside double garland of pink, white and blue complex canes on opaque black ground, signature/date cane, acid etched with Baccarat insignia, limited edition of 200 .... **450.00**

Banford, Bob, ³⁄₁₆″ c, c1985, fruit bouquet weight, formal arrangement, four yellow pears with an orange blush and five ruby cherries, on bed of green leaves set on upset muslin ground inside a spiraling pink and green torsade, signature cane **700.00**

Banford, Ray, 3¹⁄₁₆″ d, c1985, ruby cabbage rose weight, tightly furled blossom grows on stalk with pair of buds and emerald green leaves over opaque cerulean blue ground, signature cane 500.00

Buzzini, Chris, 3¼" d, 1993, foxglove bouquet weight, central stalk of white foxglove surrounded by red cinquefoil, blue morning glory, lavender blue aster and yellow rosebuds, signed and dated 725.00

Grubb, Randall, 3¹/₁₆" d, 1989, violet bouquet weight, three violet blossoms encircled by cupped pink roses and pink and white bellflowers with green leaves on clear ground, signed and dated, signature cane 600.00

Held, Greg, 3¾" d, c1970, Orient and Flume magnum undersea egg weight, upright design containing yellow and black angelfish, and black and green pufferfish with two white dorsal spots, swimming through coral reef with barnacles and green seaweed, signed 300.00

Kaziun, Charles
  2⅜" d, c1960, miniature tilted millefiori color ground pedestal weight, green silhouette of four-leaf clover, encircled by complex cobalt blue and white star-shaped canes, on opaque pink ground flecked with goldstone, inside yellow and white filigree twist torsade, arrangement set on ftd crystal pedestal with 14 karat gold "K" signature on the back of dome 1,200.00
  2½" d, c1960, pink crimp rose pedestal weight, flower with furled petals cupped inside four emerald green leaves set on ftd crystal pedestal, "K" signature cane on the bottom of flower 1,200.00

Lundberg Studios, 3¹/₁₆" d, 1984, butterfly weight, five amethyst and blue butterflies fluttering beneath pair of cherry blossoms, with pink and ruby-striped ruffled petals on gray stems with green leaves, over irid gold ground, signed and dated by Daniel Salazar 300.00

Parabelle Glass
  2⁹/₁₆" d, 1992, artist's proof, spaced millefiori moss carpet ground weight, central pink and green rose encircled by eight complex pastry mold canes in ruby, cobalt blue, turquoise, aventurine green, amethyst and pink, arrangement set on moss carpet ground interspersed with prairie canes, inside spiraling ruby and white torsade, signature/date cane 660.00
  2⅞" d, 1993, nosegay piedouche weight, bouquet of lampwork flowers with millefiori centers, in ruby, lavender, turquoise, pink and white, on aventurine green stems, arrangement placed on white lace ground, encircled by a garland of pink and amethyst millefiori, in pink and white stave pedestal with spiraling torsade, limited edition of 10, signed and dated 1,210.00

Perthshire Paperweights
  2⁷/₁₆" d, 1970, dragonfly garland weigh, insect, with ruby body attached to white filigree wings, floats inside garland of fuchsia, peach, green and white complex cog canes, signed and dated, limited edition of 500 .... 250.00
  3¹/₁₆" d, 1988, ice skater weight, decal of ice skater on white lace ground inside garland composed of rings of millefiori canes and spiraling twists in green, pink, periwinkle, yellow, rust and white, circular top facet, signature/date cane 440.00

Rosenfeld, Ken, 2¹⁵/₁₆" d, 1990, rose weight, large red

rose growing on same stalk as yellow rose, red bud, yellow bud and striped green leaves, "R" signature cane, signed and dated 440.00

Saint Louis, 3" d, 1988, spiral millefiori nosegay weight, complex stardust canes, six-pointed star canes and cog canes, in ruby, white, cobalt blue and gold, arranged in spiral on turkey red ground, signature/date cane, limited edition of 400 .... 440.00

Stankard, Paul, 2⅞" d, 1978
  First Bouquet weight, meadowreath, Saint Anthony's Fire, forget-me-nots, bellflowers, chokeberry blossoms, chokeberries and foliage on clear ground, signature cane, dated, first complex lampwork bouquet Stankard created 3,000.00
  Wildrose bouquet weight, pink blossoms, with yellow filament stamens, bloom on stems with green to yellow leaves over clear ground, signature cane, signed and dated 1,750.00

Taristano, Debbie
  3⅜" d, 1984 engraved butterfly compound meadow scene weight, vine of orange and white fantasy flowers above branch of pink blossoms with brown and yellow centers, small butterfly, engraved by former Steuben master Max Erlacher, flutters near the edges of flowers, circular top facet and three rows of side facets, signed and dated by Max Erlacher, signature cane from Debbie Tarsitano 1,540.00
  4" d, c1980, Magnum Victorian fruit and flower bouquet plaque weight, three pink fantasy flowers surrounded by berries and sprays of buds, in ruby, cobalt blue, amethyst, orange and yellow, over sunburst-cut base, edges around face of plaque cut with fancy scallops, signature cane 2,500.00

Trabucco, Victor, 3⅝" d, 1984 bouquet weight, upright pink rose surrounded by three white daisies and sprays of orange buds, growing on stem with closed pink bud, opening white bud, green leaves and tendrils, signed and dated, signature cane 990.00

Ysart, Paul
  2¹³/₁₆" d, c1960, aventurine-striped pink primrose weight, gold aventurine-striped petals, around central fuchsia and white complex cog cane, on stalk with green aventurine leaves, latticinio spokes radiate from flower, arrangement set on translucent cobalt blue ground with border of seven spaced complex canes in cobalt blue, green and white, signature cane 660.00
  2¹⁵/₁₆" d, c1960, signed double clematis weight, flower with cobalt blue and pink-striped petals emanating from central complex signature cane, on stalk with green leaves floating above gold and white jasper ground, signature cane 475.00

PAPIER-MÂCHÉ

History: Papier-mâché is a mixture of wood pulp, glue, resin, and fine sand which is subjected to great pressure and then dried. The finished product is tough, durable, and heat resistant. Various finishing treatments are used, such as enameling, japanning, lacquering, mother-of-pearl inlaying, and painting.

During the Victorian era papier-mâché articles such as boxes, trays, and tables were in high fashion. Banks, candy containers, masks, toys, and other children's articles were also made of papier-mâché.

Box, 5″ w, 4½″ h, sq, MOP Chinese landscape dec, fitted
  with four glass perfume bottles, Victorian 350.00
Bread Tray, 14¼″ l, cartouche shape, blood red, floral
  spray and butterfly dec, cavetto and shaped border,
  gilt edge, black under surface, England, c1820 ..... 500.00
Candy Container, 9″ h, Santa, wearing white suit 70.00
Figure, 23″¼″ h, comic male figure, brightly colored
  polychrome paint, spot welded high-wheeled bicycle, 20th C 1,750.00

Roly Poly, left: 6½″; right: 6¼″, each $110.00.

Lap Desk, 14″ w, 11″ d, 4½″ h, painted and gilt stenciled,
  MOP inlay, lid painted with still life of fruit, bombe
  sides resting on flattened feet, foliate gilt stenciling
  throughout ext. and int., minor losses to stenciling,
  Victorian mid 19th C 865.00
Music Stand, MOP and parcel gilt dec, labeled "Chin-
  nocks Patent Screen," Victorian, second-half 19th C 700.00
Nodder
  Mother Goose, old woman in red cape riding on back
    of white goose 3,960.00
  Turkey, 3¾″ h, male and female, orig black paint,
    polychrome trim, pewter feet 120.00
Pip-Squeak, 6½″ h, rooster, spring legs, wooden bellow
  base, orig polychrome paint 75.00
Snuff Box, Dr Syntax, The Shooting Pony, round, yellow
  and brown transfer 145.00
Table, 29″ h, tilt top, Victorian, second-half 19th C ... 400.00
Tea Caddy, 5¾″ h, 7⅔″ w, MOP inlay, English 200.00
Tray, 24″ l, 19″ w, rect, polychrome and gilt rococo
  foliate dec, two handles, stamped "Jennens and Bet-
  tridge, London," c1835 .... 800.00
Wig Stand, 13″ h, figural, woman's head, white, tan, and
  brown paint, gesso, age cracks, wear 625.00

PARIAN WARE

History: Parian ware is a creamy white, translucent porcelain that resembles marble. It originated in England in 1842 and was first called "statuary porcelain." Minton and Copeland have been credited with its development; Wedgwood also made it. In Amer-

ica, parian ware objects were manufactured by Chistopher Fenton in Bennington, Vermont.

At first parian ware was used only for figures and figural groups. By the 1850s it became so popular that a vast range of items was manufactured.

References: Kathy Hughes, *A Collector's Guide to Nineteenth-Century Jugs* (1985, Routledge & Kegan Paul), Vol. II (1991, Taylor Publishing).

Bust
  14½″ h, Charles Dickens, literary except printed on
    reverse, English 345.00
  16½″ h, young Bacchante maiden, after Owen Hale,
    dated 1881, imp Copeland marks 1,035.00
  17½″ d, John Milton, folding verse-inscribed scroll,
    English, c1880 .... 300.00
Compote, 10¼″ h, low-relief grapes and vines, English 275.00
Ewer, raised scrollwork, glazed green and pink roping,
  Copeland, c1853, one handle damaged, price for pr 415.00
Figure
  10¼″ h, The Death, dog attacking stag, rocky molded
    base, horn chips 195.00
  13½″ l, Dorothea, classical female seated on rock,
    imp "Minton," cipher mark, modeler John Bell,
    1847 registry mark, chips, restoration 195.00
  14¼″ h, nude female seated on panther, rect base,
    imp "Minton," 1857 year mark 700.00
  15¼″ h, The Lion in Love, simply draped female pull-
    ing thorn from lion's paw, glazed base, imp "Min-
    ton," cipher mark 1,500.00
  16¾″ h, classic beauty drawing water from well,
    cream ground, gold and antique green highlights,
    raised pink triangle seal mark with acorn logo
    "P.P.M," stamped "1257" 520.00
  19⅛″ h, The Young Shrimper, holding shell, dragging
    net, imp Copeland marks, c1880 .... 550.00
Pitcher, 9″ h, blue and white ear of corn dec, Bennington, crow's foot in base 120.00
Posy Holder, 9½″ h, boy holding wheat sheaf, unmarked, attributed to Bennington 175.00

PATE-DE-VERRE

History: The term "pate-de-verre" can be translated simply as "glass paste." It is manufactured by grinding lead glass into a powder or crystal form, making it into a paste by adding a two- or three-percent solution of sodium silicate, molding, firing, and carving. The Egyptians discovered the process as early as 1500 B.C.

In the late 19th century the process was rediscovered by a group of French glassmakers. Almaric Walter, Henri Cros, Georges Despret, and the Daum brothers were leading manufacturers.

Contemporary sculptors are creating a second renaissance, led by the technical research of Jacques Daum.

Atomizer, 4¾″ h, cylindrical, dark orange rose blossoms
  on green vine band at top, mottled orange-splashed
  base, gilt-bronze mount imp "EFDE/Ste SOG/Made
  in France," etched " A Walter/Nancy" on side, c1900 750.00
Bowl, 4¼″ h, domed, molded central flower head, tiers
  of overlapping feathers, pink, peach, and purple,

Bowl, yellow leaves and purple vines, marked "Argy-Rousseau," 3³/₄" d, 2" h, $900.00.

scrolling wing-form handles, conical foot, molded low-relief stylized feathers, intaglio sgd "G. Argy Rousseau," c1926 ....**8,800.00**

Figure
    4" h, sparrow, honey-amber, perched on green base, Henri Berge design, base imp "A Walter Nancy," Berge mark **1,450.00**
    5" h, mermaid, rising from water, coved rect base, tinged brown hair, pale green shading to dark green body, turquoise water, intaglio sgd "A. Walter Nancy" and "JD," designed by Jean Bernard Descomps **3,250.00**
    8" h, woman, upswept hair, yellow classical robes, sitting on green and brown striated yellow plinth seat, intaglio sgd "A Walter Nancy," c1920 ....**2,750.00**

Paperweight, 4" d, grasshopper sitting in grapes, A Walter, chip 775.00

Vase
    4³/₄" h, ovoid, ftd, soft turquoise, lime green blossoms on shoulder band, sgd in mold "A Walter Nancy" and "GJ sc" **3,850.00**
    7³/₄" h, mottled green and gray, molded rim frieze of jockeys and horses, sgd in mold "Decourchemont" **14,500.00**

PATE-SUR-PATE

History: Pate-sur-pate, paste-on-paste, is a 19th-century porcelain-decorating method featuring relief designs achieved by painting layers of thin pottery paste one on top of the other.

About 1880 Marc Solon and other Sevres artists, inspired by a Chinese celadon vase in the Ceramic Museum at Sevres, experimented with this process. Solon emigrated to England at the outbreak of the Franco-Prussian War and worked at Minton, where he perfected pate-sur-pate.

Book Stand, 16" l, walnut veneer, pate-sur-pate end panels with cupids playing badminton, Bettemann's patent, sold by Shreve Crump and Low 500.00
Box, cov, triangular, blue ground, white nude seated on stream bank, gold trim, sgd "Gol" in design, base marked "F. M. Barbotine/Limoges, France" **1,500.00**
Centerpiece, 11" l, cartouches with putti, ivory and gilt reserves, brown ground, imp and printed Minton factory marks, dec by H Holls, c1872 ....**1,500.00**

Lamp Base
    11¹/₂" h vase, dark brown ground, white classical relief of female with cherub, gilt trim, Lawrence Birks, England, late 19th C **1,495.00**
    15³/₄" h vase, dark brown ground, white classical relief, sgd "F Peyrat," France, c1875 ....**1,100.00**

Plaque
    6" d, circular, Helios and his horses, white figures, celadon ground, inscribed monogram and "Limoges" 120.00
    10³/₄" d, oval, blue ground, white dec of child reaching for bunch of grapes, dec and sgd "Taxile Doat, France, 1874" **1,495.00**
    19¹/₄" d, brown and green Art Nouveau style, floral dec ground, five blue ground rect-form pate-sur-pate panels with classical genre scenes, sgd "Taxile Doat, 1901," marked "Sevres" **29,900.00**

Box, triangular, seated nude on stream bank, signed "Gol" in design, F. M. Barbotine, Limoges, France, 5¹/₂ × 5¹/₂ × 2¹/₄", $1,500.00.

Tray, 5 × 3", elegant lady, cobalt blue ground, Limoges Barbatine 75.00
Vase, 7¹/₄" h, 5³/₄" w, 2¹/₂" d, white flowers on front and back, celadon green ground, gold serpent-skin twisted handles and gold trim, attributed to Grainger, Worcester, price for pr 995.00

PATTERN GLASS

History: Pattern glass is clear or colored glass pressed into one of hundreds of patterns. Deming Jarves of the Boston and Sandwich Glass Co. invented one of the first successful pressing machines in 1828. By the 1860s glass-pressing machinery had been improved, and mass production of good-quality matched tableware sets began. The idea of a matched glassware table service (including goblets, tumblers, creamers, sugars, compotes, cruets, etc.) quickly caught on in America. Many pattern glass table services had numerous accessory pieces such as banana stands, molasses cans, and water bottles.

Early pattern glass (flint) was made with a lead formula, giving many items a ringing sound when tapped. Lead became too valuable to be used in glass manufacturing during the Civil War; and in 1864 Hobbs, Brockunier & Co., West Virginia, developed a soda lime (non-flint) formula. Pattern glass also was produced in transparent colors, milk glass, opalescent glass, slag glass, and custard glass.

The hundreds of companies that produced pattern glass experienced periods of development, expansions, personnel problems, material and supply demands, fires, and mergers. In 1899 the National Glass Co. was formed as a combine of 19 glass companies in Pennsylvania, Ohio, Indiana, West Virginia, and Maryland. U.S. Glass, another consortium, was founded in 1891. These combines resulted from attempts to save small companies by pooling talents, resources, and patterns. Because of this pooling, the same pattern often can be attributed to several companies.

Sometimes various companies produced the same patterns at different times and used different names to reflect current fashion trends. U.S. Glass created the States series by using state names for various patterns, several of which were new issues while others were former patterns renamed.

References: Gary Baker et al., *Wheeling Glass 1829–1939,* Oglebay Institute, 1994, distributed by Antique Publications; George and Linda Breeze, *Mysteries of the Moon & Star,* published by authors, 1995; William Heacock, *Encyclopedia of Victorian Colored Pattern Glass: Book 1: Toothpick Holders from A to Z,* Second Edition (1976, 1992 value update) *Book 5: U. S. Glass from A to Z (1980), Book 7: Ruby Stained Glass from A To Z (1986), Book 8: More Ruby Stained Glass (1987), Antique Publications;* ———, *Old Pattern Glass,* Antique Publications, 1981; ———, *1000 Toothpick Holders,* Antique Publications, 1977; ———, *Rare and Unlisted Toothpick Holders,* Antique Publications, 1984; Kyle Husfloen, *Collector's Guide To American Pressed Glass,* Wallace-Homestead, 1992; Bill Jenks and Jerry Luna, *Early American Pattern Glass—1850 to 1910,* Wallace-Homestead, 1990; Bill Jenks, Jerry Luna, and Darryl Reilly, *Identifying Pattern Glass Reproductions,* Wallace-Homestead, 1993; William J. Jenks and Darryl Reilly, *American Price Guide to Unitt,* Author! Author! Books (PO Box 1964, Kingston, PA 18704), 1996.

Minnie Watson Kamm, *Pattern Glass Pitchers,* Books 1 through 8, published by author, 1970, 4th printing; Ruth Webb Lee, *Early American Pressed Glass,* 36th Edition, Lee Publications, 1966; ———, *Victorian Glass,* 13th Edition, Lee Publications, 1944; Bessie M. Lindsey, *American Historical Glass,* Charles E. Tuttle, 1967; Robert Irwin Lucas, *Tarentum Pattern Glass,* privately printed, 1981; Mollie H. McCain, *The Collector's Encyclopedia of Pattern Glass,* Collector Books, 1982, 1994 value update; George P. and Helen McKearin, *American Glass,* Crown Publishers, 1941; James Measell, *Greentown Glass,* Grand Rapids Public Museum Association, 1979, 1992–93 value update, distributed by Antique Publications; Alice Hulett Metz, *Early American Pattern Glass,* published by author, 1958; ———, *Much More Early American Pattern Glass,* published by author, 1965; S. T. Millard, *Goblets I,* (1938), *Goblets II,* (1940), privately printed, reprinted Wallace-Homestead, 1975; John B. Mordock and Walter L. Adams, *Pattern Glass Mugs,* Antique Publications, 1995.

Arthur G. Peterson, *Glass Salt Shakers,* Wallace-Homestead, 1970; Ellen T. Schroy, *Warman's Glass,* Second Edition, Wallace-Homestead, 1995; ——— (ed.), *Warman's Pattern Glass,* Wallace-Homestead, 1993; Jane Shadel Spillman, *American and European Pressed Glass in the Corning Museum of Glass,* Corning Museum of Glass, 1981; ———, *The Knopf Collectors Guides to American Antiques, Glass,* Vol. 1 (1982), Vol. 2 (1983), Alfred A. Knopf; Doris and Peter Unitt, *American and Canadian Goblets,* Clock House, 1970, reprinted by The Love of Glass Publishing (Box 629, Arthur, Ontario, Canada NOG 1AO), 1996; ———, *Treasury of Canadian Glass,* Second Edition, Clock House, 1969; Peter Unitt and Anne Worrall, *Canadian Handbook, Pressed Glass Tableware,* Clock House Productions, 1983; Kenneth Wilson, *American Glass 1760–1930,* 2 vols., Hudson Hills Press and The Toledo Museum of Art, 1994.

Periodical: *Glass Collector's Digest,* The Glass Press, PO Box 553, Marietta, OH 45750.

Collectors' Clubs: Early American Pattern Glass Society, PO Box 340023, Columbus, OH 43234; The National Early American Glass Club, PO Box 8489, Silver Spring, MD 20907.

Museums: Corning Museum of Glass, Corning, NY; Jones Museum of Glass and Ceramics, Sebago, ME; National Museum of Man, Ottawa, Ontario, Canada; Sandwich Glass Museum, Sandwich, MA; Schminck Memorial Museum, Lakeview, OR.

Reproduction Alert: Pattern glass has been widely reproduced.

Additional Listings: Bread Plates, Children's Toy Dishes, Cruets, Custard Glass, Milk Glass, Sugar Shakers, Toothpicks, and specific companies.

Advisors: John and Alice Ahlfeld and Mike Anderton.

Notes: Research in pattern glass is continuing. As always, we try to use correct pattern names, histories, and forms. Reflecting the most current thinking, the listing by pattern places colored, opalescent, and clear items together, avoiding duplication.

Items in the listing marked with an * are those for which reproductions are known to exist. Care should be exercised when purchasing such pieces.

Abbreviations:

ah	applied handle
GUTDODB	Give Us This Day Our Daily Bread
hs	high standard
Ind	Individual
ls	low standard
os	original stopper

ACTRESS

Made by Adams & Company, Pittsburgh, PA, c1880. All clear 20% less. Some items, including an amethyst pickle dish, have been reproduced in clear and color by Imperial Glass Co.

	Clear and Frosted		Clear and Frosted
Bowl		Creamer	75.00
6″, ftd	45.00	Dresser Tray	60.00
7″, ftd	50.00	Goblet, Kate Claxton (2 portraits)	85.00
8″, Miss Neilson	85.00	Marmalade Jar, cov	125.00
9½″, ftd	85.00	Mug, HMS Pinafore	50.00
Bread Plate		*Pickle Dish, Love's Request Is Pickles	45.00
7 × 12″, HMS Pinafore	90.00	Pickle Relish, different actresses	
9 × 13″, Miss Neilson	72.00	4½ × 7″	35.00
Butter, cov	90.00	5 × 8″	35.00
Cake Stand, 10″	150.00	5½ × 9″	35.00
Candlesticks, pr	250.00	Pitcher	
Celery Vase		Milk, 6½″, HMS Pinafore	275.00
Actress Head	130.00	Water, 9″, Romeo & Juliet	250.00
HMS Pinafore, pedestal	145.00	Salt, master	70.00
Cheese Dish, cov, The Lone Fisherman on cov, Two Dromios on base	250.00	Salt Shaker, orig pewter top	42.50
Compote		Sauce	
Cov, hs, 12″ d	300.00	Flat	15.00
Open, hs, 10″ d	90.00	Footed	20.00
Open, hs, 12″ d	120.00	Spooner	60.00
Open, ls, 5″ d	45.00	Sugar, cov	100.00

ADONIS (Pleat and Tuck, Washboard)

Pattern made by McKee & Bros. of Pittsburgh, PA, in 1897.

	Canary	Clear	Deep Blue
Bowl, 5″, berry	15.00	10.00	20.00
Butter, cov	70.00	48.00	80.00
Cake Plate, 11″	25.00	20.00	32.00
Cake Stand, 10½″	45.00	30.00	50.00
Celery Vase	35.00	25.00	40.00
Compote			
Cov, hs	65.00	40.00	75.00
Open, hs, 8″	45.00	30.00	50.00
Open, jelly, 4½″	28.00	18.00	32.00
Creamer	28.00	22.50	32.00
Pitcher, water	55.00	35.00	60.00
Plate, 10″	25.00	18.00	32.00
Relish	18.00	15.00	20.00
Salt & Pepper, pr	40.00	35.00	45.00
Sauce, flat, 4″	10.00	8.00	12.00
Spooner	35.00	20.00	40.00
Sugar, cov	40.00	35.00	45.00
Syrup	150.00	50.00	150.00
Tumbler	20.00	16.00	20.00

ALMOND THUMBPRINT (Pointed Thumbprint, Finger Print)

An early flint glass pattern with variants in flint and non-flint. Pattern has been attributed to Bryce, Bakewell, and U. S. Glass Co. Sometimes found in milk glass.

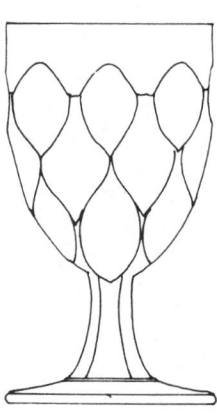

	Flint	Non-Flint		Flint	Non-Flint
Bowl, 4½" d, ftd	—	20.00	Decanter	70.00	—
Butter, cov	80.00	40.00	Eggcup	45.00	25.00
Celery Vase	50.00	25.00	Goblet	30.00	12.00
Champagne	60.00	35.00	Punch Bowl	—	75.00
Compote			Salt		
Cov, hs, 4¾", jelly	60.00	40.00	Flat, large	25.00	15.00
Cov, hs, 10"	100.00	45.00	Ftd, cov	45.00	25.00
Cov, ls, 4¾"	55.00	30.00	Ftd, open	25.00	10.00
Cov, ls, 7"	45.00	25.00	Spooner	20.00	15.00
Open, hs, 10½"	65.00	—	Sugar, cov	60.00	40.00
Cordial	40.00	30.00	Sweetmeat Jar, cov	70.00	50.00
Creamer	60.00	40.00	Tumbler	60.00	20.00
Cruet, ftd, os	55.00	—	Wine	28.00	12.00

APOLLO (Canadian Horseshoe, Shield Band)

Non-flint first made by Adams & Co., Pittsburgh, PA, c1890, and later by U. S. Glass Co. Frosted increases price 20%. Also found in ruby stained and engraved.

	Clear		Clear
Bowl		Eggcup	30.00
4"	10.00	Goblet	35.00
5"	10.00	Lamp, 10"	125.00
6"	12.00	Pickle Dish	15.00
7"	15.00	Pitcher, water	65.00
8"	20.00	Plate, 9½", sq	25.00
Butter, cov	40.00	Salt	20.00
Cake Stand		Salt Shaker	25.00
8"	35.00	Sauce	
9"	40.00	Flat	10.00
10"	50.00	Ftd, 5"	12.00
Celery Tray, rect	20.00	Spooner	30.00
Celery Vase	35.00	Sugar, cov	45.00
Compote		Sugar Shaker	45.00
Cov, hs	65.00	Syrup	110.00
Open, hs	35.00	Tray, water	45.00
Open, ls, 7"	25.00	Tumbler	30.00
Creamer	35.00	Wine	35.00
Cruet	60.00		

ARCHED GRAPE

Non-flint made by Boston and Sandwich Glass Co., Sandwich, MA, c1880.

	Non-Flint		Non-Flint
Butter, cov	45.00	Pitcher, water, ah	60.00
Celery Vase	35.00	Sauce, flat	8.00
Champagne	35.00	Spooner	30.00
Compote, cov, hs	50.00	Sugar, cov	45.00
Creamer	40.00	Wine	25.00
Goblet	25.00		

ARGUS

Flint thumbprint-type pattern made by Bakewell, Pears and Co., Pittsburgh, PA, in the early 1860s. Copiously reproduced, some by Fostoria Glass Co. with raised "H.F.M." trademark for Henry Ford Museum, Dearborn, MI. Reproduction colors include clear, red, green, and cobalt blue.

	Clear		Clear
Ale Glass	75.00	*Goblet	60.00
Bitters Bottle	60.00	Lamp, ftd	100.00
Bowl, 5½"	30.00	Mug, ah	65.00
*Butter, cov	85.00	Pitcher, water, ah	400.00
Celery Vase	90.00	Salt, master, open	30.00
Champagne	65.00	*Spooner	45.00
Compote, open, 8", scalloped	50.00	*Sugar, cov	65.00
*Creamer, ah	100.00	*Tumbler, bar	65.00
Decanter, qt	95.00	Whiskey, ah	75.00
Eggcup	30.00	*Wine	35.00

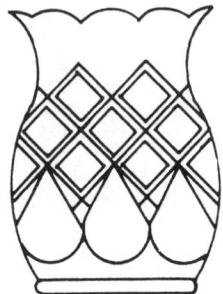

ART (Jacob's Tears, Job's Tears, Teardrop and Diamond Block)

Non-flint produced by Adams & Co., Pittsburgh, PA, in the 1880s. Reissued by U. S. Glass Co. in the early 1890s. A reproduced milk glass covered compote is known.

	Clear	Ruby Stained		Clear	Ruby Stained
Banana Stand	90.00	175.00	Cruet, os	125.00	250.00
Biscuit Jar	135.00	175.00	Goblet	60.00	—
Bowl			Pitcher		
6" d, 3¼" h, ftd	30.00	—	Milk	115.00	175.00
7", low, collar base	35.00	—	Water, 2½ qt	100.00	—
8", berry, one end pointed .	50.00	85.00	Plate, 10"	40.00	—
Butter, cov	60.00	125.00	Relish	20.00	65.00
Cake Stand			Sauce		
9"	55.00	—	Flat, round, 4"	15.00	—
10¼"	65.00	—	Pointed end	18.50	—
Celery Vase	40.00	100.00	Spooner	25.00	85.00
*Compote			Sugar, cov	45.00	125.00
Cov, hs, 7"	100.00	185.00	Tumbler	45.00	—
Open, hs, 9"	55.00	—	Vinegar Jug, 3 pt	75.00	—
Open, hs, 9½"	60.00	—			
Open, hs, 10"	65.00	—			
Creamer					
Hotel, large, round shape ..	45.00	90.00			
Regular	55.00	100.00			

ASHBURTON

A popular pattern produced by Boston and Sandwich Glass Co. and by McKee & Bros. Glass Co. from the 1850s to the late 1870s with many variations. Originally made in flint by New England Glass Co. and others and later in non-flint. Prices are for flint. Non-flint values 65% less. Also reported is an amber handled whiskey mug, flint canary celery vase ($750.00), and a scarce emerald green wine glass ($200.00). Some items known in fiery opalescent.

	Clear		Clear
Ale Glass, 5"	90.00	Cordial, 4¼" h	70.00
Bar Bottle		*Creamer, ah	210.00
Pint	55.00	Decanter, qt, cut and pressed, os .	250.00
Quart	75.00	Eggcup	
Bitters Bottle	55.00	Double	95.00
*Bowl, 6½"	75.00	Single	25.00
Carafe	175.00	Flip Glass, handled	140.00
Celery Vase, scalloped top	125.00	*Goblet	50.00
Champagne, cut	75.00	Honey Dish	15.00
*Claret, 5¼" h	50.00	*Jug, qt	90.00
*Compote, open, ls, 7½"	65.00	Lamp	75.00

	Clear			Clear
*Lemonade Glass	55.00		Water	75.00
Mug, 7″	100.00		Whiskey	60.00
*Pitcher, water	450.00		Water Bottle, tumble up	95.00
Plate, 6⅝″	75.00		Whiskey, ah	125.00
Sauce	10.00		*Wine	
*Sugar, cov	90.00		Cut	65.00
Toddy Jar, cov	375.00		Pressed	40.00
*Tumbler				
Bar	75.00			

ATLAS (Bullet, Cannon Ball, Crystal Ball)

Non-flint, occasionally ruby stained and etched, made by Adams & Co.; U. S. Glass Co. in 1891; and Bryce Bros., Mt. Pleasant, PA, in 1889.

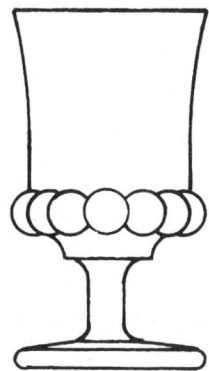

	Clear	Ruby Stained		Clear	Ruby Stained
Bowl, 9″	20.00	—	Molasses Can	65.00	—
Butter, cov, regular	45.00	75.00	Pitcher, water	65.00	—
Cake Stand			Salt		
8″	35.00	—	Master	20.00	—
9″	40.00	95.00	Individual	15.00	—
Celery Vase	28.00	—	Salt & Pepper, pr	20.00	—
Champagne, 5½″ h	35.00	55.00	Sauce		
Compote			Flat	10.00	—
Cov, hs, 8″	65.00	—	Footed	15.00	25.00
Cov, hs, 5″, jelly	50.00	80.00	Spooner	30.00	45.00
Open, ls, 7″	40.00	—	Sugar, cov	40.00	65.00
Cordial	35.00	—	Syrup	65.00	—
Creamer			Toothpick	20.00	50.00
Table, ah	30.00	55.00	Tray, water	75.00	—
Tankard	25.00	—	Tumbler	28.00	—
Goblet	45.00	65.00	Whiskey	20.00	45.00
Marmalade Jar	45.00	—	Wine	25.00	—

AUSTRIAN (Finecut Medallion)

Made by Indiana Tumbler and Goblet Co., Greentown, IN, 1897. Experimental pieces were made in cobalt blue, Nile green, and opaque colors. Some pieces were made in Chocolate glass.

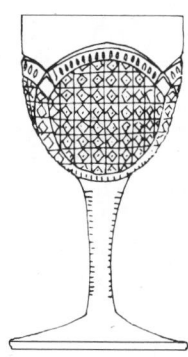

	Amber	Canary	Clear	Emerald Green
Bowl				
8″, round	—	150.00	50.00	—
8¼″, rect	—	150.00	50.00	—
Butter, cov	185.00	300.00	90.00	—
Children's table set	—	550.00	325.00	—
Compote, open, ls	—	150.00	75.00	—
Cordial	145.00	150.00	50.00	150.00
Creamer	120.00	125.00	40.00	120.00
Goblet	—	150.00	40.00	—
Mug, child's	—	—	45.00	—
Nappy, cov	—	135.00	55.00	—
Pitcher, water	—	350.00	100.00	—
Plate, 10″	—	—	40.00	—
Punch Cup	150.00	150.00	18.00	125.00
Rose Bowl	—	150.00	50.00	—
Sauce, 4⅝″ d	—	50.00	20.00	—
Spooner	—	100.00	40.00	—
Sugar, cov	—	175.00	45.00	—
Tumbler	175.00	85.00	25.00	—
Wine	175.00	150.00	30.00	150.00

BALTIMORE PEAR (Double Pear, Fig, Gipsy, Maryland Pear, Twin Pear)

Non-flint originally made by Adams & Company, Pittsburgh, PA, in 1874. Also made by U. S. Glass Company in the 1890s. Compotes were made in eighteen different sizes. Given as premiums by different manufacturers and organizations. Heavily reproduced. Reproduced in clear, cobalt blue, and pink milk glass.

	Clear		Clear
Bowl		Pickle	20.00
6"	30.00	*Pitcher	
9"	35.00	Milk	80.00
Bread Plate, 12½"	70.00	Water	95.00
*Butter, cov	75.00	*Plate	
*Cake Stand, 9"	65.00	8½"	30.00
*Celery Vase	50.00	10"	40.00
Compote		Relish	25.00
Cov, hs, 7"	80.00	*Sauce	
Cov, ls, 8½"	45.00	Flat	10.00
Open, hs	30.00	Footed	15.00
Open, jelly	25.00	Spooner	40.00
*Creamer	30.00	*Sugar, cov	50.00
*Goblet	35.00	Tray, 10½"	35.00

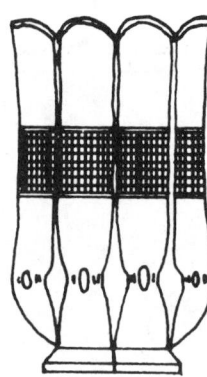

BANDED PORTLAND (Virginia #1, Maiden's Blush)

States pattern, originally named Virginia, by Portland Glass Co., Portland, ME. Painted and fired green, yellow, blue, and possibly pink; ruby stained, and rose-flashed (which Lee notes is Maiden's Blush, referring to the color rather than the pattern, as Metz lists it). Double-flashed refers to color above and below the band, single-flashed refers to color above or below the band only.

	Clear	Color-Flashed	Maiden's Blush Pink
Bowl			
4" d, open	10.00	—	20.00
6" d, cov	40.00	—	55.00
7½" d, shallow	30.00	—	55.00
8" d, cov	50.00	—	75.00
Butter, cov	50.00	195.00	85.00
Cake Stand	55.00	—	90.00
Candlesticks, pr	80.00	—	125.00
Carafe	80.00	—	90.00
Celery Tray	25.00	—	40.00
Celery Vase	35.00	—	45.00
Cologne Bottle	50.00	125.00	85.00
Compote			
Cov, hs, 7"	65.00	—	125.00
Cov, hs, 8"	75.00	—	115.00
Cov, jelly, 6"	40.00	95.00	90.00
Creamer			
Individual, oval	25.00	55.00	40.00
Regular, 6 oz.	35.00	85.00	50.00
Cruet, os	60.00	175.00	300.00
Decanter, handled	50.00	—	100.00
Dresser Tray	50.00	—	65.00
Goblet	40.00	75.00	95.00
Lamp			
Flat	45.00	—	—
Tall	50.00	—	—
Nappy, sq	15.00	55.00	65.00
Olive	18.00	25.00	35.00
Pin Tray	16.00	—	25.00
Pitcher, tankard	75.00	115.00	240.00
Pomade Jar, cov	35.00	75.00	95.00

	Clear	Color-Flashed	Maiden's Blush Pink
Punch Bowl, hs	110.00	—	300.00
Punch Cup	20.00	—	30.00
Relish			
6½″	25.00	35.00	25.00
8¼″	20.00	40.00	45.00
Ring Holder	75.00	—	125.00
Salt & Pepper, pr	45.00	95.00	75.00
Sardine Box	55.00	—	90.00
Sauce, round, flat, 4 or 4½″	10.00	—	25.00
Spooner	28.00	—	45.00
Sugar, cov	48.00	95.00	75.00
Sugar Shaker, orig top	45.00	—	85.00
Syrup	50.00	—	135.00
Toothpick	40.00	55.00	45.00
Tumbler	25.00	45.00	45.00
Vase			
6″	20.00	—	50.00
9″	35.00	—	65.00
Wine	35.00	—	85.00

BARBERRY (Berry, Olive, Pepper Berry)

Non-flint made by McKee & Bros. Glass Co. in the 1860s. The 6″ plates are found in amber, canary, pale green, and pale blue; they are considered scarce. Pattern comes in ''9-berry bunch'' and ''12-berry bunch'' varieties.

	Clear		Clear
Bowl		Cup Plate	15.00
6″, oval	20.00	Eggcup	20.00
7″, oval	25.00	Goblet	25.00
8″, oval	25.00	Pickle	10.00
8″, round, flat	25.00	Pitcher, water, ah	100.00
9″, oval	30.00	Plate, 6″	20.00
Butter		Salt, master, ftd	25.00
Cov	50.00	Sauce	
Cov, flange, pattern on edge	80.00	Flat	10.00
Cake Stand	90.00	Footed	15.00
Celery Vase	55.00	Spooner, ftd	30.00
Compote		Sugar, cov	45.00
Cov, hs, 8″, shell finial	85.00	Syrup	150.00
Cov, ls, 8″, shell finial	75.00	Tumbler, ftd	25.00
Open, hs, 8″	35.00	Wine	30.00
Creamer	30.00		

BASKETWEAVE

Non-flint, c1880. Some covered pieces have a stippled cat's-head finial.

	Amber or Canary	Apple Green	Blue	Clear	Vaseline
Bowl	20.00	—	25.00	15.00	—
Bread Plate, 11″	35.00	—	35.00	10.00	—
Butter, cov	35.00	60.00	40.00	30.00	40.00
Compote, cov, 7″	—	—	—	40.00	—
Cordial	25.00	40.00	28.00	20.00	30.00
Creamer	30.00	50.00	35.00	28.00	36.00
Cup and Saucer	35.00	60.00	35.00	30.00	38.00
Dish, oval	12.00	20.00	15.00	10.00	16.00
Eggcup	20.00	30.00	25.00	15.00	25.00

	Amber or Canary	Apple Green	Blue	Clear	Vaseline
*Goblet	28.00	50.00	35.00	20.00	30.00
Mug	25.00	40.00	25.00	15.00	30.00
Pickle	20.00	30.00	20.00	15.00	25.00
Pitcher					
Milk	40.00	60.00	45.00	35.00	50.00
*Water	60.00	75.00	80.00	45.00	85.00
Plate, 11", handled	25.00	35.00	25.00	20.00	30.00
Sauce	10.00	10.00	12.00	8.00	12.00
Spooner	30.00	36.00	30.00	20.00	30.00
Sugar, cov	35.00	60.00	35.00	30.00	40.00
Syrup	50.00	75.00	50.00	45.00	55.00
*Tray, water, scenic center	45.00	50.00	60.00	35.00	55.00
*Tumbler, ftd	18.00	30.00	20.00	15.00	20.00
Waste Bowl	20.00	35.00	25.00	18.00	25.00
Wine	30.00	50.00	30.00	20.00	30.00

BEADED GRAPE (Beaded Grape and Vine, California, Grape and Vine)

Non-flint made by U. S. Glass Co., Pittsburgh, PA, c1890. Also attributed to Burlington Glass Works, Hamilton, Ontario, and Sydenham Glass Co., Wallaceburg, Ontario, Canada, c1910. Made in clear and emerald green, sometimes with gilt trim. Reproduced in clear, milk glass, and several colors by many, including Westmoreland Glass Co.

	Clear	Emerald Green		Clear	Emerald Green
Bowl			*Goblet	35.00	50.00
5½", sq	17.50	20.00	Olive, handle	20.00	35.00
7½", sq	25.00	35.00	Pickle	20.00	30.00
8", round	28.00	35.00	Pitcher		
Bread Plate	25.00	45.00	Milk	75.00	90.00
Butter, cov	65.00	85.00	Water	85.00	120.00
Cake Stand, 9"	65.00	85.00	*Plate, 8¼", sq	28.00	40.00
Celery Tray	30.00	45.00	Salt & Pepper	45.00	65.00
Celery Vase	40.00	60.00	*Sauce, 4"	15.00	20.00
*Compote			Spooner	35.00	45.00
Cov, hs, 7"	75.00	85.00	Sugar, cov	45.00	55.00
Cov, hs, 9"	100.00	110.00	Sugar Shaker	75.00	85.00
Open, hs, 5", sq	55.00	75.00	Toothpick	40.00	65.00
Open, hs, 8"	55.00	70.00	*Tumbler	25.00	40.00
Creamer	40.00	50.00	Vase, 6" h	25.00	40.00
Cruet, os	65.00	125.00	*Wine	35.00	65.00

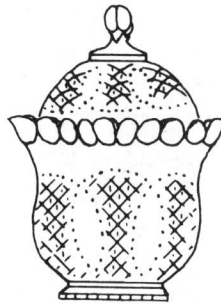

BEADED LOOP (Oregon #1)

Non-flint made by U. S. Glass Co., Pittsburgh, PA, as Pattern Line No. 15,073. After the 1891 merger, reissued as one of the States series. Rare in emerald green. Reproduced in clear and color by Imperial.

	Clear		Clear
Berry Set, master, 6 sauces	72.00	Cake Stand	
Bowl		8"	40.00
3½"	10.00	10"	55.00
6"	12.00	Carafe, water	35.00
7"	15.00	Celery Vase	30.00
Bread Plate	35.00	Compote	
Butter, cov		Cov, hs, 5", jelly	45.00
English	65.00	Cov, hs, 7"	60.00
Flanged	50.00	Open, hs, 6"	30.00
Flat	40.00	Open, hs, 8"	40.00

	Clear			**Clear**
Creamer		Sauce		
Flat	30.00	Flat, 3½ to 4"		5.00
Footed	35.00	Footed, 3½"		10.00
Cruet	50.00	Spooner		
*Goblet	35.00	Flat		24.00
Honey Dish	10.00	Footed		26.00
Mug	35.00	*Sugar, cov		
Pickle Dish, boat shape	15.00	Flat		25.00
Pitcher		Footed		30.00
Milk	40.00	Syrup		55.00
Water	60.00	Toothpick		55.00
Relish	15.00	Tumbler		25.00
Salt, master	20.00	Wine		50.00
Salt & Pepper Shakers, pr	40.00			

BIGLER

Flint made by Boston and Sandwich Glass Co., Sandwich, MA, and by other early factories. A scarce pattern in which goblets are most common and vary in height, shape and flare. Rare in color. The goblet has been reproduced as a commemorative item for Biglerville, PA.

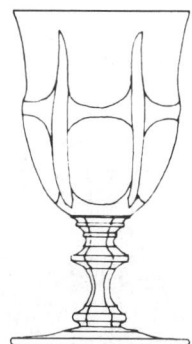

	Clear		**Clear**
Ale Glass	65.00	*Goblet	
Bar Bottle, qt	95.00	Regular	48.00
Bowl, 10" d	40.00	Short Stem	50.00
Butter, cov	125.00	Lamp, whale oil, monument base	155.00
Celery Vase	100.00	Mug, ah	60.00
Champagne	95.00	Plate, 6" d	30.00
Compote, open, 7" d	40.00	Salt, master	20.00
Cordial	65.00	Tumbler, water	65.00
Creamer	75.00	Whiskey, handled	100.00
Cup Plate	30.00	Wine	65.00
Eggcup, double	50.00		

BIRD AND STRAWBERRY (Bluebird, Flying Bird and Strawberry, Strawberry and Bird)

Non-flint, c1914. Made by Indiana Glass Co., Dunkirk, IN. Pieces occasionally highlighted by blue birds, pink strawberries, and green leaves, plus the addition of gilding.

	Clear	**Colors**		**Clear**	**Colors**
Bowl			Cup	25.00	35.00
5"	25.00	45.00	Goblet	600.00	1,000.00
9½", ftd	50.00	85.00	Nappy	40.00	65.00
10½"	55.00	95.00	Pitcher, water	235.00	350.00
Butter, cov	100.00	175.00	Plate, 12"	125.00	175.00
Cake Stand	65.00	125.00	Punch Cup	25.00	35.00
*Celery Vase	45.00	85.00	Relish	20.00	45.00
Compote			Spooner	50.00	120.00
*Cov, hs	125.00	200.00	Sugar, cov	65.00	125.00
Open, ls, ruffled	65.00	125.00	Tumbler	45.00	75.00
Jelly, cov, hs	150.00	225.00	Wine	65.00	100.00
Creamer	55.00	135.00			

BLEEDING HEART

Non-flint originally made by King Son & Co., Pittsburgh, PA, c1875, and by U. S. Glass Co. c1898. Also found in milk glass. Goblets are found in six variations. Note: A goblet with a tin lid, containing a condiment (mustard, jelly, or baking powder) was made. It is of inferior quality compared to the original goblet.

	Clear
Bowl	
7¼", oval	30.00
8"	35.00
9¼", oval, cov	65.00
Butter, cov	75.00
Cake Stand	
9"	75.00
10"	90.00
11"	100.00
Dessert slots	125.00
Compote	
Cov, hs, 8"	75.00
Cov, hs, 9"	95.00
Cov, ls, 7"	60.00
Cov, ls, 7½"	60.00
Cov, ls, 8"	75.00
Open, ls, 8½"	30.00
Creamer	
Applied Handle	60.00

	Clear
Molded Handle	30.00
Dish, cov, 7"	55.00
Eggcup	45.00
Egg Rack, cov, 3 eggs	350.00
Goblet, knob stem	35.00
Honey Dish	15.00
Mug, 3¼"	40.00
Pickle, 8¾" l, 5" w	30.00
Pitcher, water, ah	150.00
Plate	75.00
Platter, oval	65.00
Relish, oval, 5½ × 3⅝"	35.00
Salt, master, ftd	60.00
Salt, oval, flat	20.00
Sauce, flat	15.00
Spooner	25.00
Sugar, cov	60.00
Tumbler, ftd	80.00
Wine	150.00

BLOCK AND FAN (Red Block and Fan, Romeo)

Non-flint made by Richard and Hartley Glass Co., Tarentum, PA, in the late 1880s. Continued by U. S. Glass Co. after 1891.

	Clear	Ruby Stained
Biscuit Jar, cov	65.00	150.00
Bowl, 4", flat	15.00	—
Butter, cov	50.00	85.00
Cake Stand		
9"	35.00	—
10"	42.00	—
Carafe	50.00	95.00
Celery Tray	30.00	—
Celery Vase	35.00	75.00
Compote, open, hs, 8"	40.00	165.00
Condiment Set, salt, pepper & cruet on tray	75.00	—
Creamer		
Individual	—	35.00
Large	30.00	100.00
Regular	25.00	45.00
Small	35.00	75.00
Cruet, os	35.00	—
Dish, large, rect	25.00	—
Finger Bowl	55.00	—
Goblet	48.00	120.00
Ice Tub	45.00	50.00

	Clear	Ruby Stained
Orange Bowl	50.00	—
Pickle Dish	20.00	—
Pitcher		
Milk	35.00	—
Water	48.00	125.00
Plate		
6"	15.00	—
10"	18.00	—
Relish, rect	25.00	—
Rose Bowl	25.00	—
Salt & Pepper	30.00	—
Sauce		
Flat, 5"	8.00	—
Ftd, 3¾"	12.00	25.00
Spooner	25.00	—
Sugar, cov	50.00	—
Sugar Shaker	40.00	—
Syrup	75.00	95.00
Tray, ice cream, rect	75.00	—
Tumbler	30.00	40.00
Waste Bowl	30.00	—
Wine	45.00	80.00

BOW TIE (American Bow Tie)

Non-flint made by Thompson Glass Co., Uniontown, PA, c1889.

	Clear
Bowl	
8"	35.00
10¼" d, 5" h	65.00
Butter, cov	65.00
Butter Pat	25.00

	Clear
Cake Stand, large, 9" d	60.00
Compote, open	
hs, 5½"	60.00
hs, 9¼"	65.00
ls, 6½"	45.00

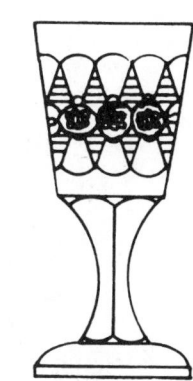

	Clear			Clear
ls, 8″	55.00	Salt		
Creamer	45.00	Individual		20.00
Goblet	60.00	Master		45.00
Honey cov	55.00	Salt Shaker		40.00
Marmalade Jar	75.00	Sauce, flat		15.00
Orange Bowl, ftd, hs, 10″	75.00	Spooner		35.00
Pitcher		Sugar		
Milk	85.00	Cov		55.00
Water	75.00	Open		40.00
Punch Bowl	100.00	Tumbler		45.00
Relish, rect	25.00			

BRIDAL ROSETTE (Checkerboard)

Made by Westmoreland Glass Co. in the early 1900s. Add 150% for ruby stained values. Reproduced since the 1950s in milk glass and, in recent years, with pink stain. The Cambridge Ribbon pattern, usually marked "Nearcut," is similar.

	Clear			Clear
Bowl, 9″, shallow	20.00	Plate		
Butter, cov	40.00	7″		15.00
Celery Tray	20.00	10″		20.00
Celery Vase	30.00	Punch Cup		5.00
Compote, open, ls, 8″	25.00	Salt & Pepper		40.00
Creamer	25.00	Sauce, flat		5.00
Cruet, os	40.00	Spooner		20.00
Cup	8.00	Sugar, cov		35.00
Goblet	28.00	Tumbler		
Honey Dish, cov, sq, pedestal	45.00	Iced Tea		25.00
Pitcher		Water		20.00
Milk	40.00	Wine		15.00
Water	35.00			

BROKEN COLUMN (Bamboo Irish Column, Notched Rib, Rattan, Ribbed Fingerprint)

Made in Findlay, OH, c1888, by Columbia Glass Co.; and later by U. S. Glass Co. Notches may be ruby stained. A cobalt blue cup is known. The square covered compote has been reproduced as have items for the Metropolitan Museum of Art and the Smithsonian Institution. Those for the Smithsonian are marked with a raised "S.I."

	Clear	Ruby Stained		Clear	Ruby Stained
Banana Stand	185.00	—	Cov, hs, 10″	110.00	350.00
Basket, ah, 12″ h, 15″ l	125.00	—	Open, hs, 8″ d	75.00	175.00
Biscuit Jar	85.00	165.00	*Creamer	42.50	125.00
Bowl			Cruet, os	85.00	150.00
4″, berry	15.00	20.00	Decanter	85.00	—
*8″	35.00	—	Finger Bowl	30.00	—
9″	40.00	—	*Goblet	55.00	100.00
Bread Plate	60.00	125.00	Marmalade Jar	85.00	—
Butter, cov	85.00	175.00	Pickle Castor, SP frame	225.00	450.00
Cake Stand, 9″ or 10″	75.00	225.00	*Pitcher, water	90.00	230.00
Carafe, water	75.00	150.00	Plate		
Celery Tray, oval	35.00	85.00	4″	25.00	40.00
Celery Vase	50.00	135.00	*7½″	40.00	95.00
Champagne	100.00	—	Punch Cup	15.00	—
Claret	75.00	—	Relish	25.00	—
Compote			Salt Shaker	45.00	65.00
Cov, hs, 5¼″ d, 10¼″ h	90.00	200.00	*Sauce, flat	10.00	20.00

	Clear	Ruby Stained			Clear	Ruby Stained
*Spooner	35.00	85.00	Toothpick	150.00	—
*Sugar, cov	70.00	135.00	Tumbler	45.00	55.00
Sugar Shaker	85.00	200.00	Vegetable, cov	90.00	—
Syrup	165.00	400.00	*Wine	80.00	125.00

BUCKLE (Early Buckle)

Flint and non-flint pattern. The original maker is unknown. Shards have been found at the sites of the following glasshouses: Boston and Sandwich Glass Co., Sandwich, MA; Union Glass Co., Somerville, MA; and Burlington Glass Works, Hamilton, Ontario, Canada. The non-flint production was made by Gillinder and Sons, Philadelphia, PA, in the late 1870s.

	Flint	Non-Flint		Flint	Non-Flint
Bowl			Goblet	40.00	25.00
8"	60.00	50.00	Pickle	40.00	15.00
10"	65.00	50.00	Pitcher, water, ah	500.00	85.00
Butter, cov	65.00	60.00	Salt		
Cake Stand, 9¾"	—	30.00	flat, oval	30.00	15.00
Champagne	60.00	—	footed	20.00	18.00
Compote			Sauce, flat	10.00	8.00
Cov, hs, 6" d	95.00	40.00	Spooner	35.00	27.50
Open, hs, 8½"	40.00	35.00	Sugar, cov	75.00	55.00
Open, ls	40.00	35.00	Tumbler	55.00	30.00
Creamer, ah	110.00	40.00	Wine	75.00	35.00
Eggcup	35.00	25.00			

BULL'S EYE

Flint made by the New England Glass Co. in the 1850s. Also found in colors and milk glass, which are worth more than double the price of clear.

	Clear		Clear
Bitters Bottle	80.00	Lamp	100.00
Butter, cov	150.00	Mug, 3½", ah	110.00
Carafe	45.00	Pitcher, water	285.00
Castor Bottle	35.00	Relish, oval	25.00
Celery Vase	85.00	Salt	
Champagne	95.00	Individual	40.00
Cologne Bottle	85.00	Master, ftd	100.00
Cordial	75.00	Spill holder	85.00
Creamer, ah	125.00	Spooner	40.00
Cruet, os	125.00	Sugar, cov	125.00
Decanter, qt, bar lip	120.00	Tumbler	85.00
Eggcup		Water Bottle, tumble up	125.00
Cov	165.00	Whiskey	70.00
Open	48.00	Wine	50.00
*Goblet	65.00		

BULL'S EYE AND DAISY

Made by U. S. Glass Co. in 1909. Also made with amethyst, blue, green, and pink stain in eyes.

	Clear	Emerald Green	Ruby Stained
Bowl	15.00	20.00	30.00
Butter, cov	25.00	45.00	90.00
Celery Vase	20.00	25.00	40.00
Creamer	25.00	35.00	50.00
Decanter	—	110.00	—

	Clear	Emerald Green	Ruby Stained
Goblet	25.00	35.00	50.00
Pitcher, water	35.00	40.00	95.00
Salt Shaker	20.00	20.00	35.00
Sauce	7.50	10.00	20.00
Spooner	20.00	25.00	40.00
Sugar	22.00	30.00	45.00
Tumbler	15.00	20.00	35.00
Wine	20.00	25.00	40.00

BULL'S EYE WITH DIAMOND POINT (Owl, Union)
Flint made by New England Glass Co. c1869.

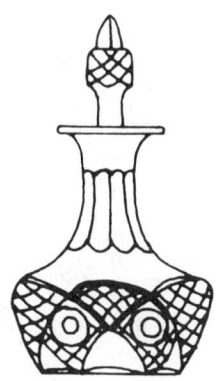

	Clear		Clear
Butter, cov	250.00	Pitcher, water, 10¼", tankard	500.00
Celery Vase	150.00	Salt, master, cov	100.00
Champagne	145.00	Sauce	20.00
Cologne Bottle, os	90.00	Spill	75.00
Creamer	200.00	Spooner	125.00
Cruet, os	225.00	Sugar, cov	175.00
Decanter, qt, os	200.00	Syrup	175.00
Eggcup	90.00	Tumbler	145.00
Goblet	120.00	Tumble-Up	165.00
Honey Dish, flat	25.00	Whiskey	150.00
Lamp, finger, ah	165.00	Wine	135.00

BUTTERFLY AND FAN (Bird in Ring, Fan, Grace, Japanese)
Non-flint made by George Duncan & Sons, Pittsburgh, PA, c1880 and by Richards and Hartley Glass Co., Pittsburgh, PA, c1888.

	Clear		Clear
Bowl	30.00	Open, hs	30.00
Bread Plate	50.00	Creamer, ftd	45.00
Butter, cov		Goblet	65.00
Flat	100.00	Marmalade Jar	75.00
Footed	75.00	Pickle Jar, SP frame and cov	80.00
Celery Vase	75.00	Pitcher, water	115.00
Compote		Sauce, ftd	15.00
Cov, hs, 8" d	95.00	Spooner	30.00
Cov, hs, 7" d	95.00	Sugar cov, ftd	50.00

CABBAGE ROSE
Non-flint made by Central Glass Co., Wheeling, WV, c1870. Reproduced in clear and colors by Mosser Glass Co., Cambridge, OH, during the early 1960s.

	Clear		Clear
Basket, handled, 12"	125.00	Celery Vase	48.00
Bitters Bottle, 6½" h	125.00	Champagne	50.00
Bowl, oval		Compote	
7½"	30.00	Cov, hs, 8½"	120.00
9½"	40.00	Cov, ls, 6"	95.00
Bowl, round		Cov, ls, 7½"	100.00
6"	25.00	Open, hs, 7½"	75.00
7½", cov	65.00	Open, hs, 9½"	100.00
Butter, cov	60.00	Creamer, 5½", ah	55.00
Cake Stand		Eggcup	45.00
11"	40.00	*Goblet	40.00
12½"	50.00	Mug	60.00

	Clear		Clear
Pickle Dish	35.00	Salt, master, ftd	25.00
Pitcher		*Sauce, 4"	10.00
Milk	150.00	Spooner	25.00
Water	125.00	Sugar, cov	55.00
Relish, 8½" l, 5" w, rose-filled horn		Tumbler	40.00
of plenty center	35.00	Wine	40.00

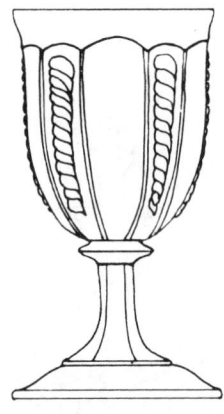

CABLE (Cable with Ring)

Flint, c1860. Made by Boston and Sandwich Glass Co. to commemorate the laying of the Atlantic Cable. Also found with amber-stained panels and in opaque colors and other colors (rare).

	Clear		Clear
Bowl		Honey Dish	15.00
8", ftd	45.00	Lamp, 8¾"	
9"	70.00	Glass Base	135.00
Butter, cov	100.00	Marble Base	100.00
Cake Stand, 9"	100.00	Miniature Lamp	500.00
Celery Vase	70.00	Pitcher, water, rare	500.00
Champagne	250.00	Plate, 6"	75.00
Compote, open		Salt, individual, flat	35.00
hs, 5½"	65.00	Salt, master	
ls, 7"	50.00	Cov	95.00
ls, 9"	35.00	Ftd	45.00
ls, 11"	75.00	Sauce, flat	15.00
Creamer	200.00	Spooner	40.00
Decanter, qt, ground stopper	295.00	Sugar, cov	120.00
Eggcup		Syrup	225.00
Cov	225.00	Tumbler, ftd	200.00
Open	60.00	Wine	175.00
*Goblet	70.00		

CANADIAN

Non-flint possibly made by Burlington Glass Works, Hamilton, Ontario, Canada, c1870.

	Clear		Clear
Bowl, 7" d, 4½" h, ftd	65.00	Goblet	45.00
Bread Plate, 10"	45.00	Mug, small	45.00
Butter, cov	85.00	Pitcher	
Cake Stand, 9¼"	85.00	Milk	90.00
Celery Vase	65.00	Water	125.00
Compote		Plate, 6", handles	30.00
Cov, hs, 6"	90.00	Sauce	
Cov, hs, 7"	100.00	Flat	15.00
Cov, hs, 8"	110.00	Footed	20.00
Cov, ls, 6"	50.00	Spooner	45.00
Cov, ls, 8"	75.00	Sugar, cov	90.00
Open, ls, 7"	35.00	Wine	45.00
Creamer	65.00		

CANE (Cane Insert, Hobnailed Diamond and Star)

Non-flint made by Gillinder and Sons Glass Co., Philadelphia, PA, and by McKee Bros. Glass Co., c1885. Goblets and toddy plates with inverted "buttons" are known.

	Amber	Apple Green	Blue	Clear	Vaseline
Butter, cov	45.00	60.00	75.00	40.00	60.00
Celery Vase	38.00	40.00	50.00	32.50	40.00
Compote, open, ls, 5¾"	28.00	30.00	35.00	25.00	35.00

	Amber	Apple Green	Blue	Clear	Vaseline
Cordial	—	—	—	25.00	—
Creamer	35.00	40.00	50.00	25.00	30.00
Finger Bowl	20.00	30.00	35.00	15.00	30.00
Goblet	25.00	40.00	35.00	20.00	40.00
Honey Dish	—	—	—	15.00	—
Match Holder, kettle	20.00	—	35.00	30.00	35.00
Pickle	25.00	20.00	25.00	15.00	20.00
Pitcher					
Milk	60.00	55.00	65.00	40.00	55.00
Water	80.00	85.00	80.00	48.00	85.00
Plate, toddy, 4½"	20.00	25.00	30.00	16.50	20.00
Relish	25.00	26.00	25.00	15.00	20.00
Salt & Pepper	60.00	50.00	80.00	30.00	70.00
Sauce, flat	—	10.00	—	7.00	—
Slipper	30.00	—	25.00	15.00	30.00
Spooner	42.00	35.00	30.00	20.00	30.00
Sugar, cov	45.00	45.00	45.00	25.00	45.00
Tray, water	35.00	40.00	50.00	30.00	45.00
Tumbler	24.00	30.00	35.00	20.00	25.00
Waste Bowl, 7½"	32.50	30.00	35.00	20.00	30.00
Wine	35.00	40.00	35.00	20.00	35.00

CAROLINA (Inverness, Mayflower)

Made by Bryce Bros., Pittsburgh, PA, c1890 and later by U. S. Glass Co., as part of the States series, c1903. Ruby-stained pieces often were made as souvenirs. Some clear pieces found with gilt or purple stain.

	Clear	Ruby Stained		Clear	Ruby Stained
Bowl, berry	15.00	—	Plate, 7½"	10.00	—
Butter, cov	35.00	—	Relish	10.00	—
Cake Stand	35.00	—	Salt Shaker	15.00	35.00
Compote			Sauce		
Open, hs, 8"	38.50	—	Flat	8.00	—
Open, hs, 9½"	20.00	—	Footed	10.00	—
Open, jelly	10.00	—	Spooner	20.00	—
Creamer	20.00	—	Sugar, cov	25.00	—
Goblet	25.00	45.00	Tumbler	10.00	—
Mug	20.00	35.00	Wine	20.00	35.00
Pitcher, milk	45.00	—			

CATHEDRAL (Orion, Waffle and Fine Cut)

Non-flint pattern made by Bryce Bros. Pittsburgh, PA, in the 1880s and by U. S. Glass Co. in 1891. Also found in ruby stained (add 50%).

	Amber	Amethyst	Blue	Clear	Vaseline
Bowl, berry, 8"	40.00	60.00	50.00	45.00	45.00
Butter, cov	60.00	110.00	40.00	45.00	60.00
Cake Stand	50.00	75.00	65.00	40.00	65.00
Celery Vase	35.00	60.00	40.00	30.00	40.00
Compote					
Cov, hs, 8"	80.00	125.00	100.00	70.00	90.00
Open, hs, 9½"	50.00	85.00	65.00	55.00	—
Open, ls, 7"	45.00	80.00	35.00	25.00	50.00
Open, jelly	—	—	—	25.00	—
Creamer					
Flat, sq	50.00	85.00	—	35.00	50.00
Tall	45.00	80.00	50.00	30.00	45.00
Cruet, os	125.00	—	—	65.00	—

	Amber	Amethyst	Blue	Clear	Vaseline
Goblet	50.00	70.00	50.00	40.00	60.00
Lamp, 12¾" h	—	—	185.00	—	—
Pitcher, water	75.00	110.00	75.00	60.00	100.00
Relish, fish shape	40.00	50.00	50.00	—	45.00
Salt, boat shape	20.00	30.00	25.00	15.00	25.00
Sauce					
Flat	15.00	30.00	20.00	15.00	20.00
Footed	15.00	35.00	20.00	15.00	20.00
Spooner	40.00	65.00	50.00	35.00	45.00
Sugar, cov	70.00	100.00	60.00	50.00	60.00
Tumbler	40.00	40.00	35.00	25.00	40.00
Wine	40.00	60.00	55.00	30.00	50.00

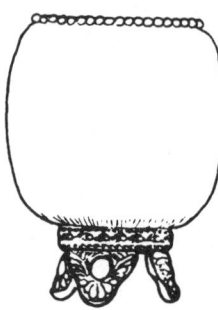

COLORADO (Lacy Medallion)

Non-flint States pattern made by U. S. Glass Co. in 1898. Made in amethyst stained, ruby stained, and opaque white with enamel floral trim, all of which are scarce. Some pieces found with ornate silver frames or feet. Purists consider these two separate patterns, with the Lacy Medallion restricted to souvenir pieces. Reproductions have been made.

	Blue	Clear	Green
Banana Stand	65.00	35.00	50.00
Bowl			
6"	35.00	25.00	30.00
7½", ftd	40.00	25.00	35.00
8½", ftd	65.00	45.00	60.00
Butter, cov	175.00	60.00	100.00
Cake Stand	70.00	55.00	65.00
Celery Vase	65.00	35.00	75.00
Compote			
Open, ls, 5"	35.00	20.00	30.00
Open, ls, 6"	45.00	20.00	40.00
Open, ls, 9¼"	85.00	35.00	65.00
Creamer			
Individual	35.00	30.00	25.00
Regular	95.00	45.00	70.00
Mug	40.00	20.00	30.00
Nappy	40.00	20.00	35.00
Pitcher			
Milk	250.00	—	100.00
Water	375.00	95.00	175.00
Plate			
6"	50.00	15.00	45.00
8"	65.00	20.00	60.00
Punch Cup	30.00	18.00	25.00
Salt Shaker	65.00	30.00	40.00
Sauce, ruffled	30.00	15.00	25.00
Sherbet	50.00	25.00	45.00
Spooner	65.00	40.00	70.00
Sugar			
Cov, regular	75.00	60.00	70.00
Open, individual	35.00	24.00	30.00
*Toothpick	55.00	30.00	35.00
Tray, calling card	45.00	25.00	35.00
Tumbler	35.00	15.00	30.00
Vase, 12"	85.00	35.00	60.00
Violet Bowl	60.00	—	—
Wine	—	25.00	40.00

COMET

Flint, possibly made by Boston and Sandwich Glass Co. in the early 1850s.

	Clear		Clear
Butter, cov	200.00	Pitcher, water	750.00
Compote, open, ls	140.00	Spooner	95.00
Creamer	175.00	Sugar, cov	175.00
Goblet	135.00	Tumbler	110.00
Mug	135.00	Whiskey, w/handle	250.00

CONNECTICUT

Non-flint, one of the States patterns made by U. S. Glass Co. c1900. Found in plain and engraved. Two varieties of ruby-stained toothpicks ($90.00) have been identified.

	Clear		Clear
Biscuit Jar	25.00	Dish, 8", oblong	20.00
Bowl		Lamp, enamel dec	85.00
4"	10.00	Lemonade, handled	20.00
8"	15.00	Pitcher, water	40.00
Butter, cov	35.00	Relish	15.00
Cake Stand	40.00	Salt & Pepper	35.00
Celery Tray	20.00	Spooner	25.00
Celery Vase	25.00	Sugar, cov	35.00
Compote		Sugar Shaker	35.00
Cov, hs	40.00	Toothpick	50.00
Open, hs, 7"	25.00	Tumbler, water	20.00
Creamer	28.00	Wine	35.00

CRYSTAL WEDDING (Collins, Crystal Anniversary)

Non-flint made by Adams Glass Co., Pittsburgh, PA, c1890 and by U. S. Glass Co. in 1891. Also found in frosted, amber stained, and cobalt blue (rare). Heavily reproduced in clear, ruby stained, and milk with enamel trim.

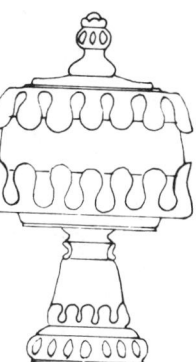

	Clear	Ruby Stained		Clear	Ruby Stained
Banana Stand	95.00	—	Milk, sq	125.00	200.00
Bowl			Water, round	110.00	210.00
4½", individual berry	15.00	—	Water, sq	165.00	225.00
7", sq, cov	75.00	85.00	Plate, 10"	25.00	40.00
8", sq, berry	50.00	85.00	Relish	20.00	40.00
8", sq, cov	60.00	95.00	Salt		
Butter, cov	75.00	125.00	Individual	25.00	40.00
Cake Plate, sq	45.00	85.00	Master	35.00	65.00
Cake Stand, 10"	65.00	—	Salt Shaker	65.00	75.00
Celery Vase	45.00	75.00	Sauce	15.00	20.00
Compote			Spooner	30.00	60.00
*Cov, hs, 7 × 13"	100.00	110.00	Sugar, cov	70.00	85.00
Open, ls, 5", sq	50.00	55.00	Syrup	150.00	200.00
Creamer	50.00	75.00	Tumbler	35.00	45.00
Cruet	125.00	200.00	Vase		
*Goblet	55.00	85.00	Footed, twisted	25.00	—
Nappy, handle	25.00	—	Swung	25.00	—
Pickle	25.00	40.00	Wine	45.00	70.00
Pitcher					
Milk, round	110.00	125.00			

DAISY AND BUTTON

Non-flint made in the 1880s by several companies in many different forms. In continuous production since inception. Original manufacturers include: Bryce Brothers, Doyle & Co., Hobbs, Brockunier & Co., George Duncan & Sons, Boston & Sandwich Glass Co., Beatty & Sons, and U.S. Glass Co. Reproductions have existed since the early 1930s in original and new colors. Reproductions, too, have been made by several companies, including L. G. Wright, Imperial Glass Co., Fenton Art Glass Co., and Degenhart Glass Co. Also found in amberina, amber stain, and ruby stained.

	Amber	Apple Green	Blue	Clear	Vaseline
Bowl, triangular	40.00	45.00	45.00	25.00	65.00
Bread Plate, 13"	35.00	60.00	35.00	20.00	40.00
*Butter, cov					
Round	70.00	90.00	70.00	65.00	95.00
Square	110.00	115.00	110.00	100.00	120.00
Butter Pat	30.00	40.00	35.00	25.00	35.00
*Canoe					
4"	12.00	24.00	15.00	10.00	24.00
8½"	30.00	35.00	30.00	25.00	35.00
12"	60.00	35.00	28.00	20.00	40.00
14"	30.00	40.00	35.00	25.00	40.00
*Castor Set					
4 bottle, glass standard	90.00	85.00	95.00	65.00	75.00
5 bottle, metal standard	100.00	100.00	110.00	100.00	95.00
Celery Vase	48.00	55.00	40.00	30.00	55.00
*Compote					
Cov, hs, 6"	35.00	50.00	45.00	25.00	50.00
Open, hs, 8"	75.00	65.00	60.00	40.00	65.00
*Creamer	35.00	40.00	40.00	18.00	35.00
*Cruet, os	100.00	80.00	75.00	45.00	80.00
Eggcup	20.00	30.00	25.00	15.00	30.00
Finger Bowl	30.00	50.00	35.00	30.00	42.00
*Goblet	40.00	50.00	40.00	25.00	40.00
*Hat, 2½"	30.00	35.00	40.00	20.00	40.00
Ice Cream Tray, 14 × 9 × 2"	75.00	50.00	55.00	35.00	55.00
Ice Tub	—	35.00	—	—	75.00
Inkwell	40.00	50.00	45.00	30.00	45.00
Parfait	25.00	35.00	30.00	20.00	35.00
Pickle Castor	125.00	90.00	150.00	75.00	150.00
*Pitcher, water					
Bulbous, reed handle	125.00	95.00	90.00	75.00	90.00
Tankard	62.00	65.00	62.00	60.00	65.00
*Plate					
5", leaf shape	20.00	24.00	12.00	12.00	25.00
6", round	10.00	22.00	15.00	6.50	24.00
7", square	25.00	35.00	25.00	15.00	35.00
Punch Bowl, stand	90.00	100.00	95.00	85.00	100.00
*Salt & Pepper	30.00	40.00	30.00	20.00	35.00
*Sauce, 4"	18.00	25.00	18.00	15.00	25.00
*Slipper					
5"	45.00	48.00	50.00	45.00	50.00
11½"	40.00	50.00	30.00	35.00	50.00
*Spooner	40.00	40.00	45.00	35.00	45.00
*Sugar, cov	45.00	50.00	45.00	35.00	50.00
Syrup	45.00	50.00	45.00	30.00	45.00
*Toothpick					
Round	40.00	55.00	25.00	40.00	45.00
Urn	25.00	30.00	25.00	15.00	30.00
*Tray	65.00	65.00	60.00	35.00	60.00
Tumbler	18.00	30.00	35.00	15.00	25.00
Vase, wall pocket	125.00	—	—	—	—
*Wine	15.00	25.00	20.00	10.00	45.00

DAISY AND BUTTON WITH CROSSBARS (Daisy and Thumbprint Crossbar, Daisy and Button with Crossbar and Thumbprint Band, Daisy with Crossbar, Mikado)

Non-flint made by Richards and Hartley, Tarentum, PA, c1885. Reissued by U.S. Glass Co. after 1891. Shards have been found at Burlington Glass Works, Hamilton, Ontario, Canada.

	Amber	Blue	Clear	Vaseline
Bowl				
6″	25.00	30.00	15.00	25.00
9″	30.00	40.00	25.00	30.00
Bread Plate	30.00	45.00	25.00	35.00
Butter, cov				
Flat	55.00	55.00	45.00	55.00
Footed	—	75.00	25.00	60.00
Celery Vase	36.00	40.00	30.00	50.00
Compote				
Cov, hs, 8″	55.00	65.00	45.00	55.00
Open, hs, 8″	45.00	50.00	30.00	45.00
Open, ls, 7″	30.00	—	20.00	45.00
Creamer				
Individual	30.00	30.00	20.00	30.00
Regular	45.00	45.00	35.00	40.00
Cruet, os	75.00	85.00	35.00	100.00
Goblet	40.00	40.00	25.00	48.00
Mug, 3″ h	15.00	18.00	12.50	20.00
Pitcher				
Milk	90.00	95.00	45.00	90.00
Water	145.00	110.00	65.00	125.00
Salt & Pepper	40.00	50.00	30.00	45.00
Sauce				
Flat	15.00	18.00	10.00	15.00
Footed	18.00	25.00	15.00	24.00
Spooner	35.00	35.00	25.00	35.00
Sugar, cov				
Individual	25.00	35.00	10.00	25.00
Regular	50.00	60.00	25.00	55.00
Syrup	125.00	125.00	65.00	125.00
Toothpick	40.00	40.00	28.00	35.00
Tumbler	20.00	25.00	18.00	25.00
Wine	30.00	35.00	25.00	30.00

DAKOTA (Baby Thumbprint, Thumbprint Band)

Non-flint made by Ripley and Co., Pittsburgh, PA, in the late 1880s and early 1890s. Later reissued by U. S. Glass Co. as one of the States patterns. Prices listed are for etched fern and berry pattern; also found with fern and no berry, and oak leaf etching, and scarcer grape etching. Other etchings known include fish, swan, peacock, bird and insect, bird and flowers, ivy and berry, stag, spider and insect in web, buzzard on dead tree, and crane catching fish. Sometimes ruby stained with or without souvenir markings. There is a four-piece table set available in a "hotel" variant, prices are about 20% higher than for the regular type.

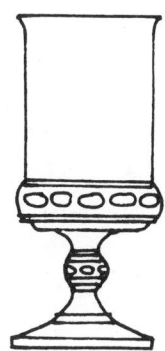

	Clear Etched	Clear Plain	Ruby Stained
Basket, 10 × 2″	205.00	175.00	300.00
Bottle, 5½″	85.00	65.00	—
Bowl, berry	45.00	35.00	—
Butter, cov	65.00	40.00	125.00
Cake Cover, 8″ d	300.00	200.00	—
Cake Stand, 10½″	65.00	45.00	—
Celery Tray	40.00	25.00	—
Celery Vase	40.00	30.00	—
Compote			
Cov, hs, 5″	60.00	50.00	—
Cov, hs, 7″	70.00	55.00	—

	Clear Etched	Clear Plain	Ruby Stained
Cov, hs, 10"	125.00	100.00	—
Open, ls, 6"	45.00	35.00	—
Open, ls, 8"	50.00	40.00	—
Open, ls, 10"	75.00	65.00	—
Condiment Tray	—	75.00	—
Creamer	55.00	30.00	60.00
Cruet	90.00	55.00	135.00
Goblet	35.00	25.00	75.00
Pitcher			
Milk	145.00	80.00	200.00
Water	125.00	75.00	190.00
Plate, 10"	85.00	75.00	—
Salt Shaker	65.00	50.00	125.00
Sauce			
Flat, 4" d	20.00	15.00	(625.00
Footed, 5" d	25.00	15.00	30.00
Spooner	30.00	25.00	65.00
Sugar, cov	65.00	55.00	85.00
Tankard	125.00	95.00	205.00
Tray			
Water, 13" d	100.00	75.00	—
Wine, 10" to 12"	125.00	90.00	—
Tumbler	35.00	30.00	55.00
Waste Bowl	65.00	50.00	75.00
Wine	30.00	20.00	55.00

DEER AND PINE TREE (Deer and Doe)

Non-flint made by Belmont Glass Co. and McKee & Bros. Glass Co. c1886. Souvenir mugs with gilt found in clear and olive green. Also made in canary (vaseline). The goblet has been reproduced since 1938. L. G. Wright Glass Co. has reproduced the goblet in clear glass using new molds.

	Amber	Apple Green	Blue	Clear
Bread Plate	90.00	100.00	100.00	65.00
Butter, cov	125.00	425.00	125.00	95.00
Cake Stand	—	—	—	75.00
Celery Vase	—	—	—	75.00
Compote				
Cov, hs, 8", sq	—	—	—	100.00
Open, hs, 7"	—	—	—	45.00
Open, hs, 9"	—	—	—	55.00
Creamer	95.00	85.00	90.00	65.00
Finger Bowl	—	—	—	55.00
*Goblet	—	—	—	55.00
Marmalade Jar	—	—	—	90.00
Mug	40.00	45.00	50.00	40.00
Pickle	—	—	—	30.00
Pitcher				
Milk	—	—	—	90.00
Water	125.00	125.00	125.00	125.00
Platter, 8 × 13"	75.00	—	80.00	60.00
Sauce				
Flat	—	—	—	20.00
Footed	—	—	—	25.00
Spooner	—	—	—	65.00
Sugar, cov	—	—	—	85.00
Tray, water	100.00	—	90.00	60.00

DELAWARE (American Beauty, Four Petal Flower)

Non-flint made by U. S. Glass Co., Pittsburgh, PA, 1899–1909. Also made by Diamond Glass Co., Montreal, Quebec, Canada, c1902. Also found in amethyst (scarce), clear with rose trim, custard, and milk glass. Prices are for pieces with perfect gold trim.

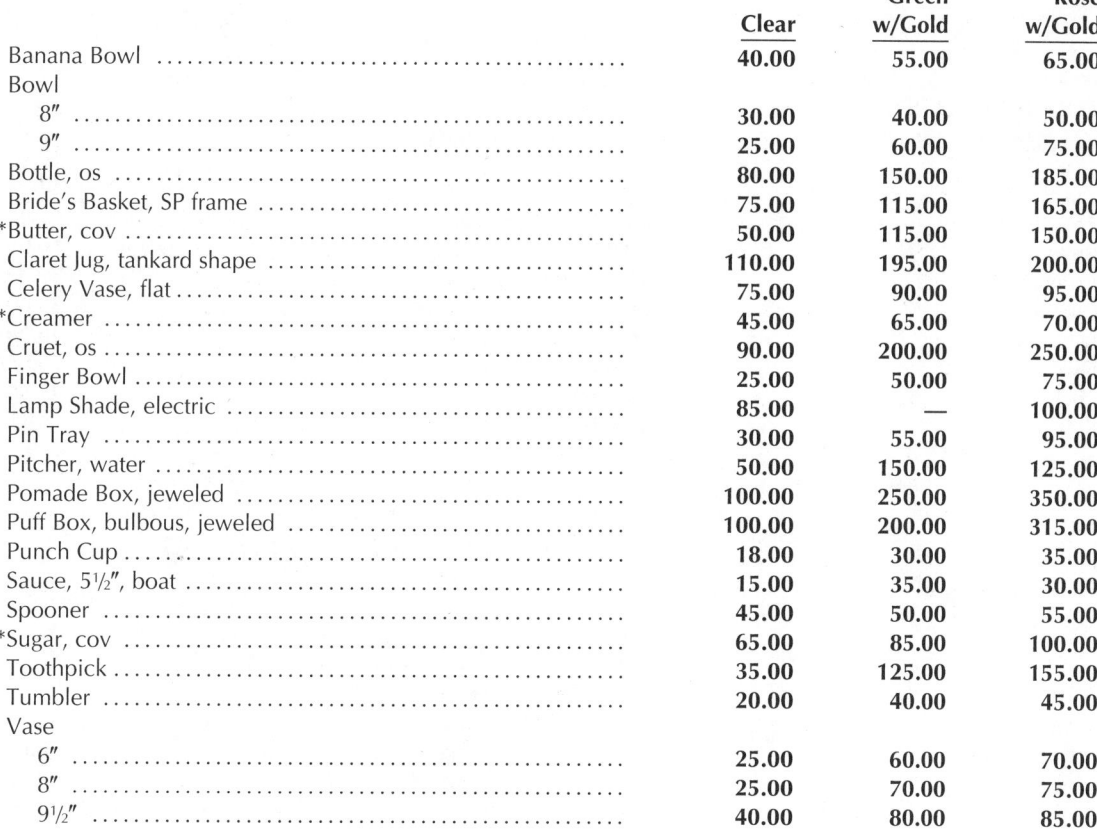

	Clear	Green w/Gold	Rose w/Gold
Banana Bowl	40.00	55.00	65.00
Bowl			
8″	30.00	40.00	50.00
9″	25.00	60.00	75.00
Bottle, os	80.00	150.00	185.00
Bride's Basket, SP frame	75.00	115.00	165.00
*Butter, cov	50.00	115.00	150.00
Claret Jug, tankard shape	110.00	195.00	200.00
Celery Vase, flat	75.00	90.00	95.00
*Creamer	45.00	65.00	70.00
Cruet, os	90.00	200.00	250.00
Finger Bowl	25.00	50.00	75.00
Lamp Shade, electric	85.00	—	100.00
Pin Tray	30.00	55.00	95.00
Pitcher, water	50.00	150.00	125.00
Pomade Box, jeweled	100.00	250.00	350.00
Puff Box, bulbous, jeweled	100.00	200.00	315.00
Punch Cup	18.00	30.00	35.00
Sauce, 5½″, boat	15.00	35.00	30.00
Spooner	45.00	50.00	55.00
*Sugar, cov	65.00	85.00	100.00
Toothpick	35.00	125.00	155.00
Tumbler	20.00	40.00	45.00
Vase			
6″	25.00	60.00	70.00
8″	25.00	70.00	75.00
9½″	40.00	80.00	85.00

DIAMOND POINT (Diamond Point with Ribs, Pineapple, Sawtooth, Stepped Diamond Point)

Flint originally made by Boston and Sandwich Glass Co. c1850 and by the New England Glass Co., East Cambridge, MA, c1860. Many other companies manufactured this pattern throughout the 19th century. Rare in color.

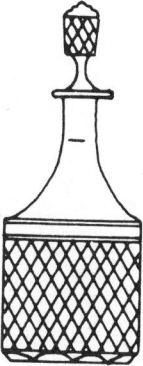

	Flint	Non-Flint		Flint	Non-Flint
Ale Glass, 6¼″ h	85.00	—	Cordial	165.00	—
Bowl			Creamer, ah	115.00	—
7″, cov	60.00	20.00	Decanter, qt, os	165.00	—
8″, cov	60.00	20.00	Eggcup		
8″, open	45.00	15.00	Cov	75.00	50.00
Butter, cov	95.00	50.00	Open	40.00	20.00
Cake Stand, 14″	185.00	—	Goblet	45.00	35.00
Candlesticks, pr	145.00	—	Honey Dish	15.00	—
Castor Bottle	25.00	15.00	Lemonade	55.00	—
Celery Vase	75.00	30.00	Mustard, cov	25.00	—
Champagne	85.00	35.00	Pitcher		
Claret	90.00	—	Pint	200.00	—
Compote			Quart	300.00	—
Cov, hs, 8″	135.00	60.00	Plate		
Open, hs 10½″, flared	100.00	—	6″	30.00	—
Open, hs, 11″, scalloped rim	110.00	—	8″	50.00	—
			Salt, master, cov	75.00	—
Open, ls, 7½″	50.00	40.00	Sauce, flat	15.00	—

	Flint	Non-Flint		Flint	Non-Flint
Spill Holder	45.00	—	Tumbler, bar	65.00	35.00
Spooner	45.00	30.00	Whiskey, ah	85.00	—
Sugar, cov	65.00	—	Wine	75.00	30.00
Syrup	150.00	—			

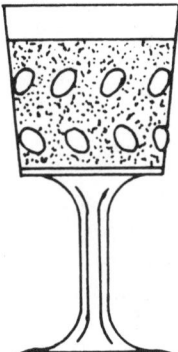

EGG IN SAND (Bean, Stippled Oval)

Non-flint, c1885. Has been reported in colors, including blue, but rare.

	Clear		Clear
Bread Plate, octagonal	25.00	Salt & Pepper	65.00
Butter, cov	40.00	Sauce	10.00
Compote, cov, jelly	45.00	Spooner, flat rim	30.00
Creamer	30.00	Sugar, cov	35.00
Dish, swan center	40.00	Tray, water	40.00
Goblet	30.00	Tumbler	30.00
Pitcher, water	45.00	Wine	35.00
Relish	15.00		

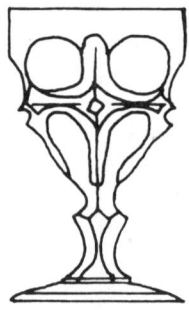

EXCELSIOR

Flint attributed to several firms, including Boston and Sandwich Glass Co., Sandwich, MA; McKee Bros., Pittsburgh, PA; and Ihmsen & Co., Pittsburgh, PA, 1850s–60s. Quality and design vary. Prices are for high-quality flint. Very rare in color.

	Clear		Clear
Ale Glass	50.00	Eggcup	
Bar Bottle	85.00	Double	45.00
Bitters Bottle	95.00	Single	40.00
Bowl, 10", open	125.00	Goblet, Maltese Cross	50.00
Butter, cov	100.00	Lamp, hand	95.00
Candlestick, 9½" h	125.00	Mug	30.00
Celery Vase, scalloped top	85.00	Pickle Jar, cov	45.00
Champagne	60.00	Pitcher, water	400.00
Claret	45.00	Salt, master	30.00
Compote		Spillholder	75.00
Cov, ls	125.00	Spooner	60.00
Open, hs	85.00	Sugar, cov	110.00
Cordial	40.00	Syrup	125.00
Creamer	85.00	Tumbler, bar	50.00
Decanter		Whiskey, Maltese Cross	65.00
Pint	85.00	Wine	45.00
Quart	85.00		

EYEWINKER (Cannon Ball, Crystal Ball, Winking Eye)

Non-flint made in Findlay, OH, in 1889. Reportedly made by Dalzell, Gilmore and Leighton Glass Co., which was organized in 1883 in West Virginia and moved to Findlay in 1888. Made only in clear glass; reproduced in color by several companies, including L. G. Wright Co. A goblet and toothpick were not originally made in this pattern.

	Clear		Clear
Banana Stand, hs	135.00	*Compote	
Bowl		Cov, hs, 6½"	85.00
6½"	25.00	Cov, hs, 9½"	150.00
9", cov	75.00	Open, 7¼", fluted	65.00
*Butter, cov	70.00	Open, 4½", jelly	45.00
Cake Stand, 8"	55.00	Creamer	65.00
Celery Vase	45.00	Cruet	65.00

	Clear			Clear
*Honey Dish	40.00		10", upturned sides	85.00
Lamp, kerosene	125.00		Salt Shaker	35.00
Nappy, folded sides, 7¼"	30.00		Sauce	15.00
*Pitcher, water	95.00		Spooner	35.00
Plate			*Sugar, cov	55.00
7"	30.00		Syrup, pewter top	125.00
9", sq, upturned sides	65.00		*Tumbler	45.00

FEATHER (Cambridge Feather, Feather and Quill, Fine Cut and Feather, Indiana Feather, Indiana Swirl, Prince's Feather, Swirl, Swirl and Feather)

Non-flint made by McKee & Bros. Glass Co., Pittsburgh, PA, 1896–1901; Beatty-Brady Glass Co., Dunkirk, IN, c1903; and Cambridge Glass Co., Cambridge, OH, c1902–03. Later the pattern was reissued with variations and quality differences. Also found in amber stain (rare).

	Clear	Emerald Green		Clear	Emerald Green
Banana Boat, ftd	75.00	175.00	Open, ls, 7"	35.00	—
Bowl, oval			Open, ls, 8"	40.00	—
7 × 9", ftd	35.00	—	Cordial	125.00	—
8½"	25.00	—	Creamer	40.00	85.00
9¼"	20.00	75.00	Cruet, os	45.00	250.00
Bowl, round			Dishes, nest of 3: 7", 8", and 9"	40.00	—
6"	20.00	—	Goblet	55.00	150.00
7"	25.00	75.00	Honey Dish	15.00	—
8"	30.00	85.00	Marmalade Jar	125.00	—
Bowl, sq			Pickle Castor	145.00	—
4½"	15.00	—	Pitcher		
8"	30.00	—	Milk	50.00	165.00
Butter, cov	55.00	150.00	Water	75.00	250.00
Cake Plate	65.00	—	Plate, 10"	50.00	75.00
Cake Stand			Relish	20.00	—
8"	45.00	125.00	Salt Shaker	35.00	70.00
9½"	50.00	125.00	Sauce	12.00	—
11"	70.00	175.00	Spooner	25.00	60.00
Celery Vase	45.00	80.00	Sugar, cov	50.00	85.00
Champagne	65.00	—	Syrup	125.00	300.00
Compote			Toothpick	85.00	165.00
Cov, hs, 8½"	125.00	250.00	Tumbler	50.00	85.00
Cov, ls, 4¼", jelly	100.00	150.00	*Wine		
Cov, ls, 8¼"	150.00	—	Scalloped border	40.00	—
Open, ls, 4"	20.00	—	Straight border	25.00	—
Open, ls, 6"	25.00	—			

FINECUT (Flower in Square)

Non-flint made by Bryce Bros., Pittsburgh, PA, c1885, and by U. S. Glass Co. in 1891.

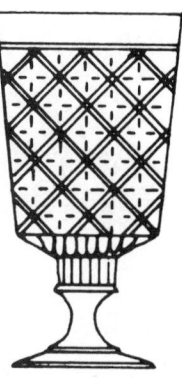

	Amber	Blue	Clear	Vaseline
Bowl, 8¼"	15.00	20.00	10.00	15.00
Bread Plate	50.00	60.00	25.00	50.00
Butter, cov	55.00	75.00	45.00	60.00
Cake Stand	—	—	35.00	—
Celery Tray	—	45.00	25.00	40.00
Celery Vase, SP holder	—	—	—	115.00
Creamer	60.00	40.00	35.00	75.00
Goblet	45.00	55.00	22.00	42.00
Pitcher, water	100.00	100.00	60.00	115.00

	Amber	Blue	Clear	Vaseline
Plate				
7"	25.00	40.00	15.00	20.00
10"	30.00	50.00	21.00	45.00
Relish	15.00	25.00	10.00	20.00
Sauce, flat	14.00	15.00	10.00	14.00
Spooner	30.00	45.00	18.00	40.00
Sugar, cov	45.00	55.00	35.00	45.00
Tray, water	50.00	55.00	25.00	50.00
Tumbler	—	—	18.00	28.00
Wine	—	—	24.00	30.00

FLAMINGO HABITAT

Non-flint, maker unknown, c1870, etched pattern.

	Clear		Clear
Bowl, 10", oval	40.00	Open, 6"	40.00
Butter, cov	65.00	Creamer	40.00
Celery Vase	45.00	Goblet	45.00
Champagne	45.00	Sauce, ftd	15.00
Cheese Dish, blown	110.00	Spooner	25.00
Compote		Sugar, cov	50.00
Cov, 4½"	75.00	Tumbler	30.00
Cov, 6½"	95.00	Wine	45.00
Open, 5", jelly	35.00		

FLORIDA (Emerald Green Herringbone, Paneled Herringbone)

Non-flint made by U. S. Glass Co., in the 1890s. One of the States patterns. Goblet reproduced in green, amber, and other colors.

	Clear	Emerald Green		Clear	Emerald Green
Berry Set	75.00	110.00	Pitcher, water	50.00	75.00
Bowl, 7¾"	10.00	15.00	Plate		
Butter, cov	50.00	85.00	7½"	12.00	18.00
Cake Stand			9¼"	15.00	25.00
Large	60.00	75.00	Relish		
Small	30.00	40.00	6", sq	10.00	15.00
Celery Vase	30.00	35.00	8½", sq	15.00	20.00
Compote, open, hs, 6½", sq ..	—	40.00	Salt Shaker	25.00	50.00
Creamer	30.00	45.00	Sauce	5.00	7.50
Cruet, os	40.00	110.00	Spooner	20.00	35.00
*Goblet, 5¾" h	25.00	40.00	Sugar, cov	35.00	50.00
Mustard Pot, attached under			Syrup	60.00	175.00
plate, cov	25.00	45.00	Tumbler	20.00	35.00
Nappy	15.00	25.00	Wine	25.00	50.00

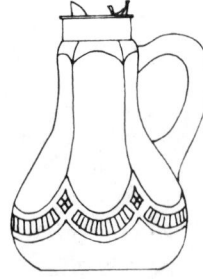

GALLOWAY (Mirror Plate, U.S. Mirror, Virginia, Woodrow)

Non-flint made by U. S. Glass Co., Pittsburgh, PA, c1904–19. Jefferson Glass Co., Toronto, Canada, produced it from 1900–25. Clear glass with and without gold trim; also known with rose stain and ruby stain. Vases known in emerald green. Toothpick reproduced in several colors.

	Clear w/ Gold	Rose Stained		Clear w/ Gold	Rose Stained
Basket, no gold	75.00	125.00	Cake Stand	70.00	95.00
Bowl			Carafe, water	55.00	85.00
6½", belled	20.00	35.00	Celery Vase	35.00	75.00
8½", oval	35.00	45.00	Champagne	60.00	175.00
8½", round	30.00	50.00	Compote		
9", rect	30.00	45.00	Cov, hs, 6"	90.00	125.00
11" d, round	45.00	65.00	Open, hs, 5½"	25.00	40.00
Butter, cov	65.00	125.00	Open, hs, 10", scalloped ..	55.00	75.00

	Clear w/ Gold	Rose Stained
Creamer	30.00	50.00
Cruet	45.00	125.00
Eggcup	40.00	60.00
Finger Bowl	40.00	65.00
Goblet	75.00	95.00
Lemonade	35.00	45.00
Mug	40.00	50.00
Nappy, tricorn	25.00	50.00
Olive, 6″	20.00	30.00
Pickle Castor, sp holder and lid	75.00	200.00
Pitcher		
Milk	60.00	80.00
Tankard	75.00	125.00
Water, ice lip	65.00	175.00
Plate, 8″, round	40.00	65.00
Punch Bowl	160.00	225.00
Punch Bowl Plate, 20″	80.00	125.00
Punch Cup	10.00	15.00

	Clear w/ Gold	Rose Stained
Relish	20.00	30.00
Rose Bowl	25.00	60.00
Salt, master	35.00	60.00
Salt & Pepper, pr	40.00	75.00
Sauce		
Flat, 4″	10.00	20.00
Footed, 4½″	10.00	20.00
Sherbet	25.00	30.00
Spooner	30.00	80.00
Sugar, cov	55.00	85.00
Sugar Shaker	40.00	100.00
Syrup	65.00	135.00
*Toothpick	30.00	55.00
Tumbler	35.00	45.00
Vase, swung	30.00	—
Waste Bowl	40.00	65.00
Water Bottle	40.00	85.00
Wine	45.00	65.00

GARFIELD DRAPE (Canadian Drape)

Non-flint issued in 1881 by Adams & Co., Pittsburgh, PA, after the assassination of President Garfield.

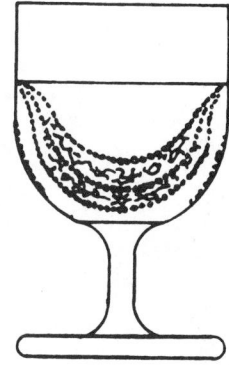

	Clear
Bread Plate	
Memorial, portrait of Garfield	65.00
"We Mourn Our Nation's Loss," portrait	75.00
Butter, cov	70.00
Cake Stand, 9½″	75.00
Celery Vase	55.00
Compote	
Cov, hs, 8″	100.00
Cov, ls, 6″	85.00
Open, hs, 8½″	40.00
Creamer	40.00
Goblet	40.00

	Clear
Honey Dish	15.00
Pitcher	
Milk	70.00
Water, ah	75.00
Water, strap handle	100.00
Relish, oval	20.00
Sauce	
Flat	8.50
Footed	12.00
Spooner	35.00
Sugar, cov	60.00
Tumbler	35.00

GEORGIA (Peacock Feather)

Non-flint made by Richards and Hartley Glass Co., Tarentum, PA, and reissued by U. S. Glass Co. in 1902 as part of the States series. Rare in blue. (Chamber lamp, pedestal base, $275.00.) No goblet known in pattern.

	Clear
Bonbon, ftd	25.00
Bowl, 8″	30.00
Butter, cov	45.00
Cake Stand, 10″	50.00
Castor Set, 2 bottles	60.00
Celery Tray, 11¾″	35.00
Children's	
Cake Stand	35.00
Creamer	35.00
Compote	
Cov, hs, 5″	35.00
Cov, hs, 6″	40.00
Cov, hs, 7″	45.00
Cov, hs, 8″	50.00
Open, hs, 5″	20.00

	Clear
Open, hs, 6″	25.00
Open, hs, 7″	30.00
Open, hs, 8″	35.00
Condiment Set, tray, oil cruet, salt & pepper	75.00
Creamer	35.00
Cruet, os	55.00
Decanter	70.00
Lamp	
Chamber, pedestal	85.00
Hand, oil, 7″	80.00
Mug	25.00
Nappy	25.00
Pitcher, water	70.00
Plate, 5¼″	15.00

	Clear			Clear
Relish	15.00	Sugar, cov		45.00
Salt Shaker	40.00	Syrup, metal lid		65.00
Sauce	10.00	Tumbler		35.00
Spooner	35.00			

HEART WITH THUMBPRINT (Bull's Eye in Heart, Columbia, Columbian, Heart and Thumbprint)

Non-flint made by Tarentum Glass Co. 1898–1906. Some clear and emerald green pieces have gold trim. Made experimentally in custard, blue custard, opaque Nile green, and cobalt.

	Clear	Emerald Green	Ruby Stain
Banana Boat	75.00	—	125.00
Barber Bottle	115.00	—	—
Bowl			
7" sq	35.00	100.00	85.00
9½" sq	35.00	125.00	90.00
10" scalloped	45.00	100.00	80.00
Butter, cov	125.00	175.00	125.00
Cake Stand, 9"	150.00	—	175.00
Carafe, water	100.00	—	150.00
Card Tray	20.00	55.00	80.00
Celery Vase	65.00	—	90.00
Compote, open, hs			
7½", scalloped	150.00	—	175.00
8½"	100.00	—	185.00
Cordial, 3" h	125.00	175.00	150.00
Creamer			
Individual	30.00	45.00	35.00
Regular	60.00	110.00	175.00
Cruet	75.00	—	—
Finger Bowl	45.00	85.00	65.00
Goblet	65.00	125.00	110.00
Hair Receiver, lid	60.00	100.00	85.00
Ice Bucket	60.00	—	—
Lamp			
Finger	95.00	150.00	—
Oil, 8"	125.00	225.00	—
Mustard, SP cov	95.00	100.00	—
Nappy, triangular	30.00	60.00	—
Pitcher, water	200.00	—	—
Plate			
6"	25.00	45.00	35.00
10"	45.00	85.00	75.00
Powder Jar, SP cov	65.00	—	—
Punch Cup	20.00	35.00	30.00
Rose Bowl			
Large	60.00	—	90.00
Small	30.00	—	75.00
Salt & Pepper, pr	95.00	—	—
Sauce, 5"	20.00	35.00	30.00
Spooner	50.00	85.00	75.00
Sugar			
Individual	25.00	35.00	35.00
Table, cov	85.00	90.00	—
Syrup	95.00	—	—
Tray, 8¼" l, 4¼" w	30.00	65.00	35.00
Tumbler	45.00	85.00	60.00
Vase			
6"	35.00	65.00	55.00
10"	65.00	100.00	85.00
Wine	55.00	150.00	125.00

HOLLY

Non-flint, possibly made by Boston and Sandwich Glass Co. in the late 1860s and early 1870s.

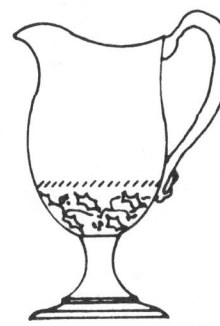

	Clear		Clear
Bowl, cov, 8″ d	150.00	Pitcher, water, ah	225.00
Butter, cov	150.00	Salt	
Cake Stand, 11″	160.00	Flat, oval	65.00
Celery Vase	110.00	Ftd	60.00
Compote, cov, hs	165.00	Sauce, flat	25.00
Creamer, ah	125.00	Spooner	60.00
Eggcup	95.00	Sugar, cov	135.00
Goblet	135.00	Tumbler	125.00
Pickle, oval	30.00	Wine	125.00

HONEYCOMB

A popular pattern made in flint and non-flint glass by numerous firms, c1850–1900, resulting in many pattern variations. Found with copper-wheel engraving. Rare in color.

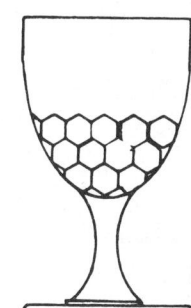

	Flint	Non-Flint		Flint	Non-Flint
Ale Glass	50.00	25.00	Honey Dish, cov	15.00	25.00
Barber Bottle	45.00	25.00	Lamp		
Bowl, cov, 7¼″ pat'd 1869,			All Glass	—	85.00
acorn finial	100.00	45.00	Marble base	—	90.00
Butter, cov	65.00	45.00	Lemonade	40.00	20.00
Cake Stand	55.00	35.00	Mug, half pint	25.00	15.00
Castor Bottle	25.00	18.00	Pitcher, water, ah	165.00	60.00
Celery Vase	45.00	20.00	Plate, 6″	—	12.50
Champagne	50.00	25.00	Pomade Jar, cov	50.00	20.00
Claret	35.00	35.00	Relish	30.00	20.00
Compote, cov, hs			Salt, master, cov, ftd	35.00	30.00
6½″ × 8½″ h	100.00	50.00	Salt Shaker, orig top	—	35.00
9¼ × 11½″ h	110.00	65.00	Sauce	12.00	7.50
Compote, open, hs			Spillholder	35.00	20.00
7 × 7″ h	60.00	40.00	Spooner	65.00	35.00
7½″, scalloped	45.00	25.00	Sugar		
8 × 6¼″ h	65.00	40.00	Frosted rosebud finial	—	50.00
Compote, open, ls,			Regular	75.00	45.00
6″ d, Saucer Bowl	35.00	25.00	Tumbler		
7½″, scalloped	40.00	25.00	Bar	35.00	—
Cordial, 3½″	35.00	25.00	Flat	40.00	12.50
Creamer, ah	35.00	20.00	Footed	45.00	15.00
Decanter			Vase		
Pint	55.00	18.50	7½″	45.00	—
Quart, os	70.00	65.00	10½″	75.00	—
Eggcup	20.00	15.00	Whiskey, handled	125.00	—
Finger Bowl	45.00	—	Wine	35.00	15.00
Goblet	25.00	15.00			

HORSESHOE (Good Luck, Prayer Rug)

Non-flint made by Adams & Co., Pittsburgh, PA, and others in the 1880s.

	Clear		Clear
Bowl, cov, oval		Butter, cov	95.00
7″	150.00	Cake Plate	40.00
8″	195.00	Cake Stand	
Bread Plate, 14 × 10″		9″	70.00
Double horseshoe handles	65.00	10″	80.00
Single horseshoe handles	40.00	Celery Vase, knob stem	40.00

	Clear
Cheese, cov, woman churning	275.00
Compote	
Cov, hs, 7", horseshoe finial ...	95.00
Cov, hs, 8 × 12¼"	125.00
Cov, hs, 11"	135.00
Creamer, 6½"	55.00
Doughnut Stand	75.00
Finger Bowl	80.00
Goblet	
Knob Stem	40.00
Plain Stem	38.00
Marmalade Jar, cov	110.00
Pitcher	
Milk	165.00
Water	135.00
Plate	
7"	45.00
10"	55.00

	Clear
Relish	
5 × 7"	20.00
8", Wheelbarrow, pewter wheels	75.00
Salt	
Individual, horseshoe shape ...	20.00
Master, horseshoe shape	100.00
Master, wheelbarrow, pewter wheels	75.00
Sauce	
Flat	10.00
Footed	15.00
Spooner	35.00
Sugar, cov	65.00
Vegetable Dish, oblong	35.00
Waste Bowl	45.00
Water Tray	125.00
Wine	150.00

ILLINOIS (Clarissa, Star of the East)

Non-flint. One of the States patterns made by U. S. Glass Co. c1897. Most forms are square. A few items are known in ruby stained, including a salt ($50.00) and a lidless straw holder with the stain on the inside ($95.00).

	Clear	Emerald Green
Basket, ah, 11½"	100.00	—
Bowl		
5", round	20.00	—
6", sq	25.00	—
8", round	25.00	—
9", sq	35.00	—
*Butter, cov	60.00	—
Candlesticks, pr	95.00	—
Celery Tray, 11"	40.00	—
Cheese, cov	75.00	—
Compote, open		
hs, 5"	40.00	—
hs, 9"	60.00	—
Creamer		
Individual	30.00	—
Table	40.00	—
Cruet	65.00	—
Finger Bowl	25.00	—
Marmalade Jar	135.00	—
Olive	18.00	—
Pitcher, milk		
Round, SP rim	175.00	—
Square	65.00	—
Pitcher, water, square	65.00	—
Plate, 7", sq	25.00	—

	Clear	Emerald Green
Relish		
7½" × 4"	18.00	40.00
8½ × 3"	18.00	—
9 × 3", canoe	40.00	—
Salt		
Individual	15.00	—
Master	25.00	—
Salt & Pepper, pr	40.00	—
Sauce	15.00	—
Spooner	35.00	—
Straw Holder, cov	275.00	400.00
Sugar		
Individual	30.00	—
Table, cov	55.00	—
Sugar Shaker	65.00	—
Syrup, pewter top	95.00	—
Tankard, SP rim	80.00	135.00
Toothpick		
Adv emb in base	45.00	—
Plain	30.00	—
Tray, 12 × 8", turned up sides	50.00	—
Tumbler	30.00	40.00
Vase, 6", sq	35.00	45.00
Vase, 9½"	—	125.00

IOWA (Paneled Zipper)

Non-flint made by U. S. Glass Co. c1902. Part of the States pattern series. Available in clear glass with gold trim (add 20%) and ruby or cranberry stained. Also found in amber (goblet, $65.00), green, canary, and blue. Add 50% to 100% for color.

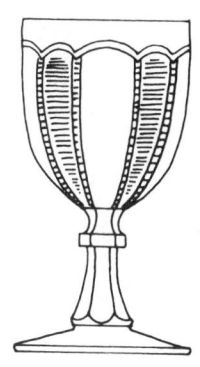

	Clear		Clear
Bowl, berry	15.00	Olive	15.00
Bread Plate, motto	80.00	Pitcher, water	50.00
Butter, cov	40.00	Punch Cup	15.00
Cake Stand	35.00	Salt Shaker, single	20.00
Carafe	35.00	Sauce, 4½"	6.50
Compote, cov, 8"	40.00	Spooner	30.00
Corn Liquor Jug, os	60.00	Sugar, cov	35.00
Creamer	30.00	Toothpick	
Cruet, os	30.00	Flat	20.00
Cup	15.00	Footed	50.00
Decanter, 1½ pts	40.00	Tumbler	25.00
Goblet	25.00	Vase, 8" h	20.00
Lamp	125.00	Wine	30.00

JACOB'S LADDER (Maltese)

Non-flint made by Bryce Bros, Pittsburgh, PA, in 1876 and by U. S. Glass Co. in 1891. A few pieces found in amber, yellow, blue, pale blue, and pale green. Bowls in variant of pattern found in flint.

	Clear		Clear
Bowl		Open, hs, 10"	40.00
6" × 8¾"	15.00	Creamer	35.00
6¾" × 9¾"	20.00	Cruet, os, ftd	85.00
7½" × 10¾"	20.00	Goblet	65.00
9", berry, ornate SP holder, ftd		Honey Dish, 3½"	10.00
(variant)	125.00	Marmalade Jar	75.00
Butter, cov	65.00	Mug	100.00
Cake Stand		Pitcher, water, ah	150.00
8" or 9"	50.00	Plate, 6¼"	20.00
11" or 12"	60.00	Relish, 9½ × 5½"	15.00
Castor Bottle	18.00	Salt, master, ftd	20.00
Castor Set, 4 bottles	100.00	Sauce	
Celery Vase	45.00	Flat, 4" or 5"	8.00
Cologne Bottle, Maltese-cross stop-		Footed, 4"	12.00
per, ftd	85.00	Spooner	35.00
Compote		Sugar, cov	80.00
Cov, hs, 6"	80.00	Syrup	
Cov, hs 7½"	100.00	Knight's Head finial	125.00
Cov, hs, 9½"	125.00	Plain top	100.00
Open, hs, 7½"	35.00	Tumbler, bar	100.00
Open, hs, 8½", scalloped	30.00	Wine	30.00
Open, hs, 9½", scalloped	38.00		

JERSEY SWIRL (Swirl)

Non-flint made by Windsor Glass Co., Pittsburgh, PA, c1887. Heavily reproduced in color by L. G. Wright Co. The clear goblet is also reproduced.

	Amber	Blue	Canary	Clear
Bowl, 9¼"	55.00	55.00	45.00	35.00
Butter, cov	55.00	55.00	50.00	40.00
Cake Stand, 9"	75.00	70.00	45.00	30.00
*Celery Vase	42.00	42.00	35.00	30.00
*Compote, hs, 8"	50.00	50.00	45.00	35.00
Creamer	45.00	45.00	40.00	30.00
Cruet, os	—	—	—	25.00
*Goblet				
Buttermilk	40.00	40.00	35.00	30.00
Water	40.00	40.00	35.00	30.00
Marmalade Jar	—	—	—	50.00

	Amber	Blue	Canary	Clear
Pickle Castor, SP frame and lid	—	—	—	125.00
Pitcher, water	50.00	50.00	45.00	35.00
Plate, round				
6"	25.00	25.00	20.00	15.00
8"	30.00	30.00	25.00	20.00
10"	38.00	38.00	35.00	30.00
*Salt, ind	20.00	20.00	18.00	15.00
Salt Shaker	30.00	30.00	25.00	20.00
Sauce, 4½", flat	20.00	20.00	15.00	10.00
Spooner	30.00	30.00	25.00	20.00
Sugar, cov	40.00	40.00	35.00	30.00
Tumbler	30.00	30.00	25.00	20.00
*Wine	50.00	50.00	40.00	15.00

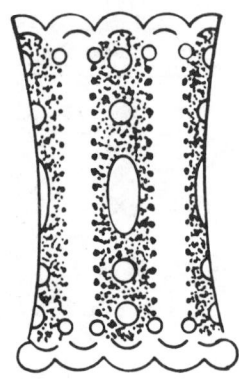

KANSAS (Jewel with Dewdrop)

Non-flint originally produced by Co-Operative Flint Glass Co., Beaver Falls, PA. Later produced as part of the States pattern series by U. S. Glass Co. in 1901 and by Jenkins Glass Co. c1915–25. Also known with jewels stained in pink or gold. Mugs (smaller and of inferior quality) have been reproduced in clear, vaseline, amber, and blue.

	Clear		Clear
Banana Stand	90.00	Creamer	40.00
Bowl		*Goblet	55.00
7", oval	35.00	*Mug	
8"	40.00	Regular	45.00
Bread Plate, ODB	45.00	Tall	25.00
Butter, cov	65.00	*Pitcher	
Cake Plate	45.00	Milk	50.00
Cake Stand		Water	60.00
7⅝"	50.00	Relish, 8½", oval	20.00
10"	85.00	Salt Shaker	50.00
Celery Vase	80.00	Sauce, flat, 4"	12.00
Compote		Sugar, cov	65.00
Cov, hs, 6"	50.00	Syrup	125.00
Cov, hs, 8"	85.00	Toothpick	65.00
Cov, ls, 5"	50.00	Tumbler	45.00
Open, hs, 6"	30.00	Whiskey	25.00
Open, hs, 8"	45.00	Wine	65.00

KENTUCKY

Non-flint made by U. S. Glass Co. c1897 as part of the States pattern series. The goblet is found in ruby stained ($50.00). A footed, square sauce ($30.00) is known in cobalt blue with gold. A toothpick holder is also known in ruby stained ($150.00).

	Clear	Emerald Green		Clear	Emerald Green
Bowl, 8" d	20.00	—	Plate, 7", sq	15.00	—
Butter, cov	50.00	—	Punch Cup	10.00	15.00
Cake Stand, 9½"	40.00	—	Salt Shaker, orig top	10.00	—
Creamer	25.00	—	Sauce, ftd, sq	10.00	15.00
Cruet, os	45.00	—	Spooner	35.00	—
Cup	10.00	20.00	Sugar, cov	30.00	—
Goblet	20.00	50.00	Toothpick, sq	35.00	85.00
Nappy	10.00	15.00	Tumbler	20.00	30.00
Olive, handle	25.00	—	Wine	28.00	38.00
Pitcher, water	55.00	—			

KING'S CROWN (Ruby Thumbprint, X.L.C.R.)

Non-flint made by Adams & Co. Pittsburgh, PA., in the 1890s and later. Known as Ruby Thumbprint when pieces are ruby stained. Made in clear and with the thumbprints stained amethyst, gold, green, and cranberry, and in clear with etching and gold trim. It became very popular after 1891 as ruby-stained souvenir ware. Approximately 87 pieces documented. Add 30% for engraved pieces. NOTE: Pattern has been copiously reproduced for the gift-trade market in milk glass, cobalt blue, and other colors. New pieces are easily distinguished: in the case of Ruby Thumbprint, the color is a very pale pinkish red.

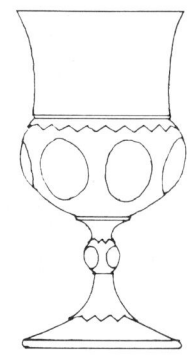

	Clear	Ruby Stained		Clear	Ruby Stained
Banana Stand, ftd	85.00	135.00	*Goblet	35.00	45.00
*Bowl			Honey Dish, cov, sq	100.00	175.00
9¼" d, pointed	35.00	90.00	*Lamp, oil, 10"	135.00	—
10" d, scalloped	45.00	95.00	Mustard, cov, 4" h	35.00	75.00
Butter, cov, 7½" d	50.00	90.00	Preserve, 10" l	35.00	50.00
*Cake Stand			*Pitcher		
9" d	68.00	125.00	Milk, tankard	75.00	100.00
10" d	75.00	125.00	Water, bulbous	95.00	225.00
Castor Set, glass stand, 4			Water, tankard	110.00	200.00
bottles	175.00	300.00	*Plate, 7"	20.00	45.00
Celery Vase	40.00	60.00	*Punch Bowl, ftd	275.00	300.00
*Champagne	25.00	35.00	*Punch Cup	15.00	30.00
*Claret	35.00	50.00	Salt		
*Compote			Ind, rect	15.00	35.00
Cov, hs, 8"	65.00	245.00	Master, sq	30.00	50.00
Cov, ls, 12"	90.00	225.00	Salt Shaker, 3⅛" h	30.00	45.00
Open, hs, 8¼"	75.00	95.00	*Sauce, 4"	15.00	20.00
Open, ls, 5¼"	30.00	45.00	Spooner, 4¼" h	45.00	50.00
*Cordial	45.00	—	*Sugar		
*Creamer, ah 3¼" h			Ind, open, 2¾" h	25.00	45.00
Ind, tankard,	25.00	35.00	Table, cov, 6¾" h	55.00	95.00
Table, 4⅞" h	50.00	65.00	Toothpick, 2¾" h	20.00	35.00
*Cup and Saucer	55.00	70.00	*Tumbler, 3¾" h	20.00	35.00
Custard Cup	15.00	25.00	*Wine, 4⅜" h	25.00	40.00

KOKOMO (Bar and Diamond, R and H Swirl Band)

Non-flint made by Richards and Hartley, Tarentum, PA, c1885. Reissued by U. S. Glass Co., c1891 and Kokomo Glass Co., Kokomo, IN, c1901. Found in ruby stained and etched. Over 50 different pieces manufactured.

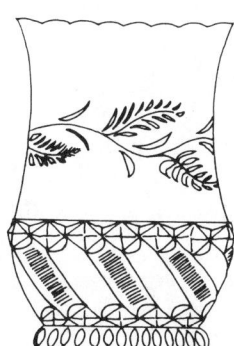

	Clear	Ruby Stained		Clear	Ruby Stained
Bowl, 8½", ftd	24.00	—	Decanter, 9¾", wine	55.00	95.00
Bread Tray	30.00	45.00	Finger Bowl	25.00	35.00
Butter, cov	35.00	—	Goblet	30.00	45.00
Cake Stand	45.00	165.00	Lamp, hand, atypical—has no		
Celery Vase	30.00	45.00	diamonds	50.00	100.00
Compote			Pitcher, tankard	55.00	100.00
Cov, hs, 7½"	35.00	165.00	Sauce, ftd, 5"	8.00	10.00
Open, hs, 6"	25.00	—	Spooner	25.00	45.00
Open, hs, 8"	35.00	—	Sugar, cov	45.00	65.00
Open, ls, 7½"	20.00	—	Sugar Shaker	35.00	75.00
Condiment Set, oblong tray,			Syrup	45.00	130.00
shakers, cruet	80.00	195.00	Tray, water	35.00	90.00
Creamer, ah	35.00	50.00	Tumbler	25.00	35.00
Cruet	35.00	—	Wine	25.00	35.00

LION (Frosted Lion)

Made by Gillinder and Sons, Philadelphia, PA, in 1876. Available in clear without frosting (20% less). Many reproductions.

	Frosted		**Frosted**
Bowl, oblong		Cordial	175.00
6½ × 4¼"	55.00	*Creamer	75.00
8 × 5"	50.00	Cup and Saucer, child size	45.00
Bread Plate, 12"	90.00	*Eggcup, 3½" h	65.00
*Butter, cov		*Goblet	70.00
Lion's-head finial	90.00	Marmalade Jar, rampant finial	90.00
Rampant finial	125.00	Pitcher	
Cake Stand	85.00	Milk	375.00
*Celery Vase	85.00	Water	300.00
Champagne	175.00	Relish, lion handles	35.00
Cheese, cov, rampant lion's-head		*Salt, master, rect lid	250.00
finial	400.00	*Sauce, 4", ftd	25.00
Children's Table Set	500.00	*Spooner	75.00
*Compote		*Sugar, cov	
Cov, hs, 7", rampant finial	150.00	Lion's-head finial	90.00
*Cov, hs, 9", rampant finial, oval,		Rampant finial	110.00
collared base	150.00	Syrup, orig top	350.00
Cov, 9", hs	185.00	Wine	200.00
Open, ls, 8"	75.00		

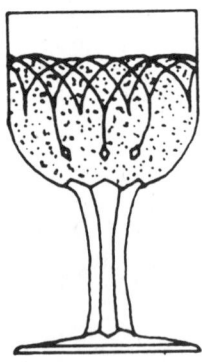

LOOP AND DART

Clear and stippled non-flint of the late 1860s and early 1870s. Made by Boston and Sandwich Glass Co., Sandwich, MA, and Richards and Hartley, Tarentum, PA. Flint add 25%.

	Clear		**Clear**
Bowl, 9", oval	30.00	Pitcher, water	75.00
Butter, cov	45.00	Plate, 6"	35.00
Cake Stand, 10"	40.00	Relish	20.00
Celery Vase	35.00	Salt, master	50.00
Compote		Sauce	5.00
Cov, hs, 8"	85.00	Spooner	25.00
Cov, ls, 8"	65.00	Sugar, cov	50.00
Creamer	35.00	Tumbler	
Cruet, os	95.00	Footed	30.00
Eggcup	25.00	Water	25.00
Goblet	25.00	Wine	35.00
Lamp, oil	85.00		

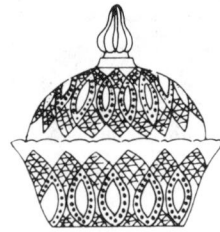

LOUISIANA (Sharp Oval and Diamond, Granby)

Made by Bryce Bros., Pittsburgh, PA, in the 1870s. Reissued by U. S. Glass Co. c1898 as one of the States patterns. Available with gold and also comes frosted.

	Clear		**Clear**
Bowl, 9", berry	20.00	Match Holder	35.00
Butter, cov	75.00	Mug, handled, gold top	25.00
Cake Stand	65.00	Nappy, 4", cov	30.00
Celery Vase	30.00	Pitcher, water	65.00
Compote		Relish	15.00
Cov, hs, 8"	75.00	Spooner	30.00
Open, hs, 5", jelly	40.00	Sugar, cov	45.00
Creamer	30.00	Tumbler	25.00
Goblet	30.00	Wine	35.00

MAINE (Paneled Stippled Flower, Stippled Primrose)

Non-flint made by U. S. Glass Co., Pittsburgh, PA, c1899. Researchers dispute if goblet was made originally. Sometimes found with enamel trim or overall turquoise stain.

	Clear	Emerald Green		Clear	Emerald Green
Bowl, 8″	30.00	40.00	Pitcher		
Bread Plate, oval, 10 × 7¾″	30.00	—	Milk	65.00	85.00
Butter, cov	48.00	—	Water	50.00	125.00
Cake Stand	40.00	60.00	Relish	15.00	—
Compote			Salt Shaker, single	30.00	—
Cov, jelly	50.00	75.00	Sauce	15.00	—
Open, hs, 7″	20.00	45.00	Sugar, cov	45.00	75.00
Open, ls, 8″	38.00	55.00	Syrup	75.00	225.00
Open, ls, 9″	30.00	65.00	Toothpick	125.00	—
Creamer	30.00	—	Tumbler	30.00	45.00
Cruet, os	80.00	—	Wine	50.00	75.00
Mug	35.00	—			

MANHATTAN

Non-flint with gold made by U. S. Glass Co. c1902. A Depression glass pattern also has the "Manhattan" name. A table-sized creamer and covered sugar are known in true ruby stained, and a goblet is known in old marigold carnival glass. Heavily reproduced by Anchor Hocking Glass Co. and Tiffin Glass Co.

	Clear	Rose Stained		Clear	Rose Stained
Biscuit Jar, cov	60.00	100.00	Bulbous, ah	70.00	—
Bowl			Tankard, ah	60.00	125.00
6″	18.00	—	Plate		
8¼″, scalloped	20.00	—	5″	10.00	—
*9½″	20.00	—	6″	10.00	30.00
10″	22.00	—	8″	15.00	—
12½″	25.00	—	10¾″	20.00	—
Butter, cov	55.00	—	Punch Bowl	125.00	—
Cake Stand, 8″	45.00	55.00	Punch Cup	10.00	—
Carafe, water	40.00	65.00	Relish, 6″	12.00	—
Celery Tray, 8″	20.00	—	Salt Shaker, single	20.00	35.00
Celery Vase	25.00	—	Sauce	14.00	20.00
Cheese, cov, 8⅜″ d	—	115.00	*Spooner	20.00	—
Compote			Straw Holder, cov	95.00	150.00
Cov, hs, 9½″	60.00	—	*Sugar		
Open, hs, 9½″	45.00	—	Individual, open	15.00	—
Open, hs, 10½″	50.00	—	Table, cov	40.00	65.00
*Creamer			Syrup	48.00	200.00
Individual	20.00	—	*Toothpick	30.00	—
Table	30.00	60.00	Tumbler		
Cruet			Iced Tea	30.00	—
Large	65.00	115.00	Water	20.00	—
Small	50.00	—	Vase, 6″	18.00	—
*Goblet	25.00	—	Violet Bowl	20.00	—
Ice Bucket	—	65.00	Water Bottle	40.00	—
Olive, Gainsborough	30.00	—	*Wine	15.00	—
Pitcher, water, ½ gal					

MARYLAND (Inverted Loop and Fan, Loop and Diamond)

Made originally by Bryce Bros., Pittsburgh, PA. Continued by U. S. Glass Co. as one of its States patterns.

	Clear w/ Gold	Ruby Stained		Clear w/ Gold	Ruby Stained
Banana Dish	35.00	85.00	Butter, cov	65.00	95.00
Bowl, berry	15.00	35.00	Cake Stand, 8″	40.00	—
Bread Plate	25.00	—	Celery Tray	20.00	35.00

	Clear w/ Gold	Ruby Stained		Clear w/ Gold	Ruby Stained
Celery Vase	30.00	65.00	Plate, 7", round	25.00	—
Compote			Relish, oval	15.00	55.00
Cov, hs	65.00	100.00	Salt Shaker, single	30.00	—
Open, jelly	25.00	45.00	Sauce, flat	10.00	15.00
Creamer	25.00	55.00	Spooner	30.00	55.00
Goblet	30.00	48.00	Sugar, cov	45.00	60.00
Olive, handled	15.00	—	Toothpick	125.00	175.00
Pitcher			Tumbler	25.00	50.00
Milk	42.50	135.00	Wine	40.00	75.00
Water	50.00	100.00			

MASCOTTE (Dominion, Etched Fern and Waffle, Minor Block)

Non-flint made by Ripley and Co., Pittsburgh, PA, in the 1880s. Reissued by U. S. Glass Co. in 1891. The butter dish shown on Plate 77 of Ruth Webb Lee's *Victorian Glass* is said to go with this pattern. It has a horseshoe finial and was named for the famous "Maude S," "Queen of the Turf" trotting horse during the 1880s. Apothecary jar and pyramid jars made by Tiffin Glass Co. in the 1950s.

	Clear	Etched		Clear	Etched
Bowl			Open, ls, 8"	30.00	45.00
Cov, 5"	—	35.00	Creamer	30.00	45.00
Cov, 7"	—	45.00	Goblet	40.00	45.00
Open 9"	35.00	40.00	Pitcher, water	55.00	65.00
Butter Pat	15.00	20.00	Plate, turned in sides	40.00	45.00
Butter, cov			Pyramid Jar, 7" d, one fits into		
"Maude S"	100.00	110.00	other and forms tall jar-type		
Regular	50.00	65.00	container with lid, three		
Cake Basket, handle	80.00	95.00	sizes with flat separators	50.00	55.00
Cake Stand	35.00	50.00	Salt Dip	25.00	—
Celery Vase	35.00	40.00	Salt Shaker, single	25.00	25.00
Cheese, cov	70.00	80.00	Sauce		
Compote			Flat	8.00	15.00
Cov, hs, 5"	35.00	40.00	Footed	12.00	15.00
Cov, hs, 7"	45.00	55.00	Spooner	30.00	35.00
Cov, hs, 8"	60.00	75.00	Sugar, cov	40.00	45.00
Cov, hs, 9"	65.00	90.00	Tray, water	40.00	55.00
Open, hs, 6"	20.00	25.00	Tumbler	20.00	35.00
Open, hs, 8"	30.00	35.00	Wine	25.00	30.00

MASSACHUSETTS (Arched Diamond Points, Cane Variant, Geneva #2, M2-131, Star and Diamonds)

Made in the 1880s, unknown maker, reissued in 1898 by U. S. Glass Co. as one of the States series. The vase ($45.00) and wine ($45.00) are known in emerald green. Some pieces reported in cobalt blue and marigold carnival glass. Reproduced in clear and colors, including cobalt blue.

	Clear		Clear
Bar Bottle, metal shot glass for cover	75.00	Creamer	28.00
Basket, 4½", ah	50.00	Cruet, os	45.00
Bowl		Goblet	45.00
6", sq	17.50	Gravy Boat	30.00
9", sq	20.00	Mug	20.00
*Butter, cov	50.00	Mustard Jar, cov	35.00
Celery Tray	30.00	Olive	8.50
Champagne	35.00	Pitcher, water	65.00
Cologne Bottle, os	37.50	Plate, 8"	32.00
Compote, open	35.00	Punch Cup	15.00
Cordial	55.00	Relish, 8½"	25.00
		Rum Jug, various sizes	90.00

	Clear		**Clear**
Salt Shaker, tall	25.00	Tumbler	30.00
Sauce, sq, 4″	15.00	Vase, trumpet	
Sherry	40.00	6½″ h	25.00
Spooner	20.00	7″ h	25.00
Sugar, cov	40.00	9″ h	35.00
Syrup	65.00	Whiskey	25.00
Toothpick	40.00	Wine	40.00

MICHIGAN (Loop and Pillar)

Non-flint made by U. S. Glass Co. c1902 as one of the States pattern series. The 10¼″ bowl ($42.00) and punch cup ($12.00) are found with yellow or blue stain. Also found with painted carnations. Other colors include "Sunrise," gold, and ruby stained.

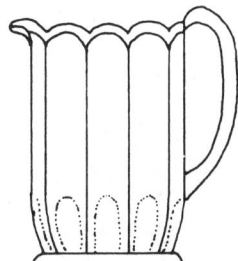

	Clear	**Rose Stained**		**Clear**	**Rose Stained**
Bowl			Olive, two handles	10.00	25.00
7½″	15.00	30.00	Pickle	12.00	20.00
9″	35.00	60.00	Pitcher		
10¼″	35.00	62.00	8″	50.00	—
Butter, cov			12″, tankard	70.00	150.00
Large	60.00	125.00	Plate, 5½″ d	15.00	—
Small	65.00	—	Punch Bowl, 8″	50.00	—
Celery Vase	40.00	85.00	Punch Cup	8.00	—
Compote			Relish	20.00	35.00
Jelly, 4½″	45.00	75.00	Salt Shaker, single, 3 types	20.00	30.00
Open, hs, 9¼″	65.00	85.00	Sauce	12.00	22.00
Creamer			Sherbet cup, handled	15.00	20.00
Ind, 6 oz, tankard	20.00	65.00	Spooner	50.00	75.00
Table	30.00	70.00	Sugar, cov	50.00	85.00
Cruet, os	60.00	225.00	Syrup	95.00	175.00
Crushed Fruit Bowl	75.00	—	*Toothpick	45.00	100.00
Custard Cup	15.00	—	Tumbler	30.00	40.00
Finger Bowl	15.00	—	Vase		
Goblet	45.00	65.00	Bud	35.00	40.00
Honey Dish	10.00	—	Ftd, large	45.00	—
Lemonade Mug	24.00	40.00	Wine	35.00	50.00
Nappy, Gainsborough handle .	35.00	—			

MINERVA (Roman Medallion)

Non-flint made by Boston and Sandwich Glass Co., Sandwich, MA, c1870 as well as other American companies. Shards have been found at Burlington Glass Works, Hamilton, Ontario, Canada.

	Clear		**Clear**
Bowl		Open, hs, 10½″, octagonal ftd .	95.00
Footed	40.00	Creamer	45.00
Rectangular		Goblet	95.00
7″	25.00	Marmalade Jar, cov	150.00
8 × 5″	30.00	Pickle	25.00
Bread Plate	65.00	Pitcher, Water	185.00
Butter, cov	75.00	Plate	
Cake Stand		8″	55.00
9 × 6½″	100.00	10″, handled	60.00
10½″	120.00	Platter, oval, 13″	65.00
13″	145.00	Sauce	
Champagne	85.00	Flat	18.50
Compote		Footed, 4″	20.00
Cov, hs, 6″	85.00	Spooner	40.00
Cov, hs, 8″	150.00	Sugar, cov	65.00
Cov, ls, 8″	125.00	Waste Bowl	50.00

MINNESOTA

Non-flint made by U. S. Glass Co. in the late 1890s as one of the States patterns.

	Clear	Ruby Stained		Clear	Ruby Stained
Banana Stand	65.00	—	Match Safe	25.00	—
Basket	65.00	—	Mug	25.00	—
Biscuit Jar, cov	55.00	150.00	Olive	15.00	25.00
Bonbon, 5″	15.00	—	Pitcher, tankard	85.00	200.00
Butter, cov	50.00	—	Plate		
Carafe	35.00	—	5″, turned up edges	25.00	—
Celery Tray, 13″	25.00	—	7⅜″ d	15.00	—
Compote			Pomade Jar, cov	35.00	—
Open, hs, 10″, flared	60.00	—	Relish	20.00	—
Open, ls, 9″, sq	55.00	—	Salt Shaker	25.00	—
Creamer			Sauce, boat shape	10.00	25.00
Individual	20.00	—	Spooner	25.00	—
Table	30.00	—	Sugar, cov	35.00	—
Cruet	35.00	—	Syrup	65.00	—
Cup	18.00	—	Toothpick, 3 handles	30.00	150.00
Goblet	35.00	50.00	Tray, 8″ l	15.00	—
Hair Receiver	30.00	—	Tumbler	20.00	—
Juice Glass	20.00	—	Wine	40.00	—

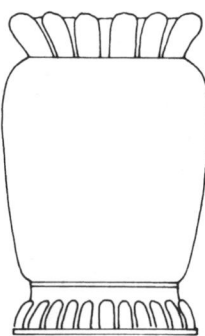

NEVADA

Non-flint made by U. S. Glass Co., Pittsburgh, PA, c1902 as a States pattern. Pieces are sometimes partly frosted and have enamel decoration. Add 20% for frosted.

	Clear		Clear
Biscuit Jar	45.00	Finger Bowl	25.00
Bowl		Jug	35.00
6″ d, cov	35.00	Pickle, oval	10.00
7″ d, open	20.00	Pitcher	
8″ d, cov	45.00	Milk, tankard	45.00
Butter, cov	70.00	Water, bulbous	50.00
Cake Stand, 10″	35.00	Water, tankard	45.00
Celery Vase	25.00	Salt	
Compote		Individual	15.00
Cov, hs, 6″	40.00	Master	20.00
Cov, hs, 7″	45.00	Salt Shaker, table	15.00
Cov, hs, 8″	55.00	Sauce, 4″ d	10.00
Open, hs, 6″	20.00	Spooner	35.00
Open, hs, 7″	30.00	Sugar, cov	35.00
Open, hs, 8″	35.00	Syrup, tin top	45.00
Creamer	30.00	Toothpick	35.00
Cruet	35.00	Tumbler	15.00
Cup, custard	12.00		

NEW HAMPSHIRE (Bent Buckle, Modiste)

Non-flint made by U. S. Glass Co., Pittsburgh, PA, c1903 in the States pattern series.

	Clear w/ Gold	Rose Stained	Ruby Stained
Biscuit Jar, cov	75.00	—	—
Bowl			
Flared, 5½″	10.00	—	25.00
Flared, 8½″	15.00	25.00	—
Round, 8½″	18.00	30.00	—
Square, 8½″	25.00	35.00	—

	Clear w/ Gold	Rose Stained	Ruby Stained
Butter, cov	45.00	70.00	—
Cake Stand, 8¼″	30.00	—	—
Carafe	60.00	—	—
Celery Vase	35.00	50.00	—
Compote			
Cov, hs, 5″	50.00	—	—
Cov, hs, 6″	60.00	—	—
Cov, hs, 7″	65.00	—	—
Open	40.00	55.00	—
Creamer			
Individual	20.00	30.00	
Table	30.00	45.00	—
Cruet	55.00	135.00	—
Goblet	35.00	45.00	—
Mug, large	20.00	45.00	50.00
Pitcher, water			
Bulbous, ah	90.00	—	—
Straight Sides, molded handle	60.00	90.00	—
Relish	18.00	—	—
Salt & Pepper, pr	35.00	—	—
Sauce	10.00	—	—
Sugar			
Cov, table	45.00	60.00	—
Individual, open	20.00	25.00	—
Syrup	75.00	150.00	50.00
Toothpick	25.00	40.00	40.00
Tumbler	20.00	35.00	40.00
Vase	35.00	50.00	—
Wine	25.00	50.00	—

NEW JERSEY (Loops and Drops)

Non-flint made by U. S. Glass Co., Pittsburgh, PA, c1900–08 in States pattern series. Items with perfect gold are worth more than those with worn gold. An emerald green 11″ vase is known (value $75.00).

	Clear w/ Gold	Ruby Stained		Clear w/ Gold	Ruby Stained
Bowl			Molasses Can	90.00	—
8″, flared	25.00	50.00	Olive	15.00	—
9″, saucer	32.50	65.00	Pickle, rect	15.00	—
10″, oval	30.00	75.00	Pitcher		
Bread Plate	30.00	—	Milk, ah	75.00	165.00
Butter, cov			Water		
Flat	75.00	100.00	Applied Handle	80.00	210.00
Footed	125.00	—	Pressed Handle	50.00	185.00
Cake Stand, 8″	65.00	—	Plate, 8″ d	30.00	45.00
Carafe	60.00	—	Salt & Pepper, pr		
Celery Tray, rect	25.00	40.00	Hotel	50.00	115.00
Compote			Small	35.00	55.00
Cov, hs, 5″, jelly	45.00	55.00	Sauce	10.00	30.00
Cov, hs, 8″	65.00	90.00	Spooner	27.00	75.00
Open, hs, 6¾″	35.00	65.00	Sugar, cov	60.00	80.00
Open, hs, 8″	60.00	75.00	Sweetmeat, 8″	70.00	90.00
Open, hs, 10½″, shallow	65.00	—	Syrup	90.00	—
Creamer	35.00	60.00	Toothpick	55.00	225.00
Cruet	50.00	—	Tumbler	30.00	50.00
Fruit bowl, hs, 12½″	55.00	110.00	Water Bottle	55.00	90.00
Goblet	40.00	65.00	Wine	45.00	60.00

ONE HUNDRED ONE (Beaded 101)

Non-flint made by Bellaire Goblet Co., Findlay, OH, in the late 1880s.

	Clear		Clear
Bread Plate, 101 border, Farm implement center, 11"	75.00	Pitcher, water, ah	125.00
Butter, cov	40.00	Plate	
Cake Stand, 9"	65.00	6"	20.00
Celery Vase	50.00	8"	30.00
Compote		Relish	15.00
Cov, hs, 7"	60.00	Sauce	
Cov, ls	60.00	Flat	10.00
Creamer	45.00	Footed	15.00
*Goblet	50.00	Spooner	25.00
Lamp, hand, oil, 10"	80.00	Sugar, cov	45.00
Pickle	20.00	Wine	60.00

PALMETTE (Hearts and Spades, Spades)

Non-flint, unknown maker, late 1870s. Shards have been found at Burlington Glass Works, Hamilton, Ontario, Canada. Syrup known in milk glass.

	Clear		Clear
Bowl		Goblet	35.00
8"	25.00	Lamp, 8½", all glass	95.00
9"	20.00	Pickle, scoop shape	20.00
Bread Plate, handled, 9"	30.00	Pitcher, bulbous, ah	
Butter Dish, cov	60.00	Milk	135.00
Butter Pat	35.00	Water	125.00
Cake Plate, tab handles	35.00	Relish	18.00
Cake Stand	100.00	Salt, master, ftd	22.00
Castor Set, 5 bottles, sp holder	125.00	Salt Shaker	55.00
Celery Vase	55.00	Sauce, flat, 6"	10.00
Champagne	75.00	Shaker, saloon, oversize	80.00
Compote		Spooner	35.00
Cov, hs, 8½"	75.00	Sugar, cov	55.00
Cov, hs, 9¾"	85.00	Syrup, ah	125.00
Open, ls, 7"	30.00	Tumbler	
Creamer, ah	65.00	Bar	75.00
Cup Plate	55.00	Water, ftd	40.00
Eggcup	40.00	Wine	110.00

PANELED FORGET-ME-NOT (Regal)

Non-flint, made by Bryce Bros., Pittsburgh, PA, c1880. Reissued by U. S. Glass Co. c1891. Shards have been found at Burlington Glass Works, Hamilton, Ontario, Canada. Made in clear, blue, and amber with limited production in amethyst and green.

	Amber	Blue	Clear
Bread Plate	35.00	45.00	30.00
Butter, cov	50.00	60.00	45.00
Cake Stand, 10"	70.00	90.00	45.00
Celery Vase	45.00	70.00	36.00
Compote			
Cov, hs, 7"	90.00	110.00	65.00
Cov, hs, 8"	80.00	100.00	68.00
Open, hs, 8½"	60.00	75.00	50.00
Open, hs, 10"	60.00	80.00	40.00
Creamer	45.00	60.00	35.00
Cruet, os	—	—	45.00
Goblet	50.00	65.00	32.00
Marmalade Jar, cov	80.00	100.00	60.00

	Amber	Blue	Clear
Pickle, boat shape	25.00	35.00	15.00
Pitcher			
Milk	90.00	110.00	50.00
Water	90.00	110.00	75.00
Relish, scoop shape	55.00	55.00	65.00
Salt & Pepper, pr	—	—	65.00
Sauce, ftd	18.00	25.00	12.00
Spooner	40.00	50.00	25.00
Sugar, cov	60.00	75.00	40.00
Wine	55.00	65.00	60.00

PENNSYLVANIA (Balder)

Non-flint issued by U. S. Glass Co. in 1898. Also known in ruby stained. A ruffled jelly compote is documented in orange carnival.

	Clear w/ Gold	Emerald Green		Clear w/ Gold	Emerald Green
Biscuit Jar, cov	75.00	125.00	Juice Tumbler	10.00	20.00
Bowl			Molasses Can	75.00	—
4"	20.00	—	Pitcher, water	60.00	—
8", berry	25.00	35.00	Punch Bowl	175.00	—
8", sq	20.00	40.00	Punch Cup	10.00	—
Butter, cov	60.00	85.00	Salt Shaker	10.00	—
Carafe	45.00	—	Sauce	7.50	—
Celery Tray	30.00	—	*Spooner	24.00	35.00
Celery Vase	45.00	—	Sugar, cov	40.00	55.00
Champagne	25.00	—	Syrup	50.00	—
Cheese Dish, cov	65.00	—	Tankard	110.00	—
Compote, hs, jelly	50.00	—	Toothpick	35.00	90.00
Creamer	25.00	50.00	Tumbler	28.00	40.00
Cruet, os	45.00	—	Whiskey	20.00	35.00
Decanter, os	100.00	—	Wine	15.00	40.00
Goblet	24.00	—			

PICKET (London, Picket Fence)

Non-flint made by the King, Son & Co., Pittsburgh, PA, c1890. Toothpick holders are known in apple green, vaseline, and purple slag.

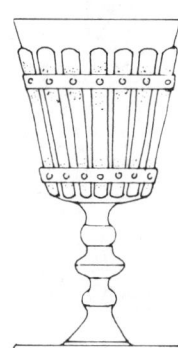

	Clear		Clear
Bowl, 9½", sq	30.00	Salt	
Bread Plate	70.00	Individual	10.00
Butter, cov	65.00	Master	35.00
Celery Vase	40.00	Sauce	
Compote		Flat	15.00
Cov, hs, 8"	85.00	Footed	20.00
Cov, ls, 8"	95.00	Spooner	30.00
Open, hs, 7", sq	35.00	Sugar, cov	50.00
Open, hs, 10", sq	70.00	Toothpick	35.00
Open, ls, 7"	50.00	Tray, water	65.00
Creamer	50.00	Waste Bowl	40.00
Goblet	50.00	Wine	85.00
Pitcher, water	75.00		

QUEEN ANNE (Bearded Man)

Non-flint made by LaBelle Glass Co., Bridgeport, OH, c1879. Finials are Maltese cross. At least 28 pieces are documented. A table set and water pitcher are known in amber.

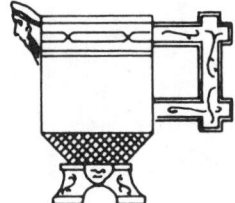

	Clear		Clear
Bowl, cov		Pitcher	
8″, oval	45.00	Milk	75.00
9″, oval	55.00	Water	85.00
Bread Plate	50.00	Salt Shaker	40.00
Butter, cov	65.00	Sauce	15.00
Celery Vase	35.00	Spooner	40.00
Compote, cov, ls, 9″	75.00	Sugar, cov	55.00
Creamer	45.00	Syrup	100.00
Eggcup	45.00		

RED BLOCK (Late Block)

Non-flint with red stain made by Doyle and Co., Pittsburgh, PA. Later made by five companies, plus U. S. Glass Co. in 1892. Prices for clear 50% less.

	Ruby Stained		Ruby Stained
Banana Boat	75.00	Mustard, cov	55.00
Bowl, 8″	75.00	Pitcher, water, 8″ h	175.00
Butter, cov	110.00	Relish Tray	25.00
Celery Vase, 6½″	85.00	Rose Bowl	75.00
Cheese Dish, cov	125.00	Salt Dip, individual	50.00
Creamer		Salt Shaker	75.00
Individual	45.00	Sauce, flat, 4½″	20.00
Table	70.00	Spooner	45.00
Decanter, 12″, os, variant	175.00	Sugar, cov	90.00
*Goblet	35.00	Tumbler	40.00
Mug	50.00	*Wine	40.00

REVERSE TORPEDO (Bull's Eye Band, Bull's Eye with Diamond Point #2, Pointed Bull's Eye)

Non-flint made by Dalzell, Gilmore and Leighton Glass Co., Findlay, OH, c1888–90. Also attributed to Canadian factories. Sometimes found with copper-wheel etching.

	Clear		Clear
Banana Stand, 9¾″	100.00	Open, hs, 8⅜″ d	45.00
Basket	175.00	Open, hs, 10½″ d, V shape bowl	90.00
Biscuit Jar, cov	135.00	Open, hs, jelly	50.00
Bowl		Open, ls, 9¼″, ruffled	85.00
8½″, shallow	30.00	Creamer	55.00
9″, fruit, piecrust rim	70.00	Doughnut Tray	90.00
10½″, piecrust rim	75.00	Goblet	85.00
Butter, cov, 7½″ d	75.00	Honey Dish, sq, cov	145.00
Cake Stand, hs	85.00	Jam Jar, cov	85.00
Celery Vase	55.00	Pitcher, tankard, 10¼″	160.00
Compote		Sauce, flat, 3¾″	10.00
Cov, hs, 6″	80.00	Spooner	30.00
Cov, hs, 7″	80.00	Sugar, cov	85.00
Cov, hs, 10″	125.00	Syrup	165.00
Open, hs, 7″	65.00	Tumbler	30.00

ROMAN ROSETTE

Non-flint made by Bryce, Walker and Co., Pittsburgh, PA, c1890. Reissued by U. S. Glass Co. in 1892 and 1898. Also seen with English registry mark and known in amber stained.

	Clear	Ruby Stained		Clear	Ruby Stained
Bowl, 8½″	15.00	50.00	Butter, cov	50.00	125.00
Bread Plate	30.00	75.00	Cake Stand, 9″	45.00	—

	Clear	Ruby Stained
Celery Vase	30.00	95.00
Compote		
Cov, hs, 4½", jelly	50.00	—
Cov, hs, 6"	65.00	—
Cordial	50.00	—
Creamer	32.00	45.00
*Goblet	40.00	—
Mug	35.00	—
Pitcher		
Milk	50.00	150.00

	Clear	Ruby Stained
Water	65.00	140.00
Plate, 7½"	35.00	65.00
Relish, oval, 9"	20.00	40.00
Salt & Pepper, glass tray	40.00	100.00
Sauce	15.00	20.00
Spooner	25.00	45.00
Sugar, cov	40.00	80.00
Syrup	85.00	125.00
Wine	45.00	65.00

ROSE-IN-SNOW (Rose)

Non-flint made by Bryce Bros., Pittsburgh, PA, in the square form c1880. Also made in the more common round form by Ohio Flint Glass Co. and after 1891 by U. S. Glass Co. Both styles reissued by Indiana Glass Co., Dunkirk, IN. Reproductions made by several companies, including Imperial Glass Co., as early as 1930 and continuing through the 1970s.

	Amber and Canary	Blue	Clear
Bowl, 8" sq	40.00	50.00	30.00
Butter, cov			
Round	65.00	125.00	45.00
Square	70.00	150.00	50.00
Cake Stand, 9"	125.00	175.00	90.00
Compote			
Cov, hs, 8"	125.00	175.00	80.00
Cov, ls, 7"	100.00	150.00	75.00
Open, ls, 5¾"	65.00	120.00	35.00
Creamer			
Round	60.00	100.00	45.00
Square	65.00	120.00	45.00
*Goblet	40.00	55.00	35.00
Marmalade Jar, cov	70.00	125.00	60.00
*Mug, "In Fond Remembrance"	65.00	125.00	35.00
*Pickle Dish			
Double, 8½" × 7"	85.00	110.00	100.00
Single, oval, handles at end	35.00	95.00	20.00
Pitcher, water, ah	175.00	200.00	125.00
Plate			
5"	40.00	40.00	35.00
6"	30.00	80.00	20.00
7"	30.00	80.00	20.00
*9"	30.00	85.00	20.00
Platter, oval	—	—	125.00
Sauce			
Flat	15.00	20.00	12.00
Footed	8.00	45.00	18.00
Spooner			
Round	30.00	80.00	25.00
Square	40.00	100.00	35.00
Sugar, cov			
Round	55.00	120.00	50.00
*Square	50.00	140.00	45.00
Sweetmeat, cov, 5¾" d	80.00	155.00	65.00
Toddy Jar, cov, under plate	150.00	155.00	125.00
Tumbler	60.00	100.00	50.00

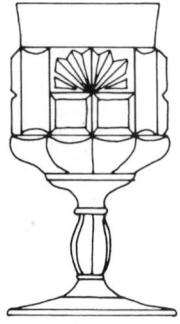

SKILTON (Early Oregon)

Made by Richards and Hartley of Tarentum, PA, in 1888 and by U. S. Glass Co. after 1891. This is not one of the U. S. Glass States pattern series and should not be confused with Beaded Loop, which is Oregon #1, named by U. S. Glass Co. It is better known as Skilton (named by Millard) to avoid confusion with Beaded Loop.

	Clear	Ruby Stained		Clear	Ruby Stained
Bowl			Olive, handled	20.00	—
5", round	15.00	—	Pickle	15.00	—
7", rect	20.00	—	Pitcher		
9", rect	30.00	—	Milk	45.00	125.00
Butter, cov	45.00	110.00	Water	50.00	125.00
Cake Stand	35.00	—	Salt & Pepper, pr	45.00	—
Celery Vase	35.00	95.00	Sauce, ftd	12.00	20.00
Compote			Spooner, flat	25.00	55.00
Cov, hs, 8"	45.00	—	Sugar, cov	35.00	85.00
Open, ls, 8"	30.00	75.00	Tray, water	45.00	—
Creamer	30.00	55.00	Tumbler	25.00	40.00
Dish, oblong, sq	25.00	—	Wine	35.00	50.00
Goblet	35.00	50.00			

SPIREA BAND (Earl, Nailhead Variant, Spirea, Squared Dot)

Non-flint made by Bryce, Higbee and Co., Pittsburgh, PA, c1885.

	Amber	Blue	Clear	Vaseline
Bowl, 8"	25.00	40.00	20.00	30.00
Butter, cov	50.00	55.00	35.00	45.00
Cake Stand, 11"	45.00	55.00	40.00	45.00
Celery Vase	40.00	50.00	25.00	40.00
Compote, cov, hs, 7"	44.00	65.00	40.00	44.00
Cordial	38.00	42.00	20.00	38.00
Creamer	32.50	44.00	35.00	35.00
Goblet	30.00	35.00	25.00	35.00
Pitcher, water	65.00	80.00	35.00	60.00
Platter, 10½"	32.00	42.00	20.00	32.00
Relish	30.00	35.00	18.00	30.00
Sauce				
Flat	10.00	12.00	5.00	10.00
Ftd	15.00	15.00	8.00	15.00
Spooner	30.00	35.00	20.00	35.00
Sugar, open	32.00	40.00	25.00	32.00
Tumbler	24.00	35.00	20.00	30.00
Wine	30.00	35.00	20.00	30.00

STATES, THE (Cane and Star Medallion)

Non-flint made by U. S. Glass Co. Pittsburgh, PA, in 1905. Also found in emerald green (add 50%). Prices given for clear with good gold trim.

	Clear		Clear
Bowl		Creamer	
7", round, 3 handles	25.00	Individual, oval	20.00
9¼", round	30.00	Regular, round	30.00
Butter, cov	65.00	Goblet	35.00
Celery Tray	20.00	Pickle Tray	15.00
Celery Vase	20.00	Pitcher, water	45.00
Cocktail	25.00	Plate, 10"	25.00
Compote		Punch Bowl, 13" d	75.00
Open, hs, 7"	30.00	Punch Cup	10.00
Open, hs, 9"	40.00	Relish, diamond shape	35.00

	Clear			Clear
Salt & Pepper	40.00		Syrup	65.00
Sauce, flat, 4", tub shape	15.00		Toothpick, flat, rectangular, curled	
Spooner	25.00		lip	45.00
Sugar			Tray, 7¼" l, 5½" w	20.00
Individual, open	15.00		Tumbler	25.00
Regular, cov	40.00		Wine	30.00

TENNESSEE (Jewel and Crescent, Jeweled Rosette)

Non-flint made by King, Son & Co., Pittsburgh, PA, and continued by U. S. Glass Co. in 1899 as part of the States series.

	Clear	Colored Jewels		Clear	Colored Jewels
Bowl			Open, ls, 7"	35.00	—
Cov, 7"	40.00	—	Creamer	30.00	—
Open, 8"	35.00	40.00	Cruet	65.00	—
Bread Plate	40.00	75.00	Goblet	40.00	—
Butter, cov	55.00	—	Mug	40.00	—
Cake Stand			Pitcher		
8"	35.00	—	Milk	55.00	—
9½"	38.00	—	Water	65.00	—
10½"	45.00	—	Relish	20.00	—
Celery Vase	35.00	—	Salt Shaker	30.00	—
Compote			Spooner	35.00	—
Cov, hs, 5"	40.00	55.00	Sugar, cov	45.00	—
Cov, hs, 7"	50.00	—	Syrup	90.00	—
Open, hs, 6"	30.00	—	Toothpick	75.00	85.00
Open, hs, 8"	40.00	—	Tumbler	35.00	—
Open, hs, 10"	65.00	—	Wine	65.00	85.00

TEXAS (Loop with Stippled Panels)

Non-flint made by U. S. Glass Co., Pittsburgh, PA, c1900, in the States pattern series. Occasionally pieces are found in ruby stained. Reproduced in solid colors, including cobalt blue, by Crystal Art Glass Co. and Boyd Glass Co., Cambridge, OH.

	Clear w/ Gold	Rose Stained		Clear w/ Gold	Rose Stained
Bowl			Pickle, 8½"	25.00	50.00
7"	20.00	40.00	Pitcher, water	125.00	400.00
9", scalloped	35.00	50.00	Plate, 9"	35.00	60.00
Butter, cov	75.00	125.00	Salt Shaker	25.00	—
Cake Stand, 9½"	65.00	125.00	Sauce		
Celery Tray	30.00	50.00	Flat	10.00	20.00
Celery Vase	40.00	85.00	Footed	20.00	25.00
Compote			Spooner	35.00	80.00
Cov, hs, 6"	60.00	125.00	Sugar		
Cov, hs, 7"	70.00	150.00	*Individual, cov	45.00	—
Cov, hs, 8"	75.00	175.00	Table, cov	75.00	125.00
Open, hs, 5"	45.00	75.00	Syrup	75.00	175.00
Creamer			Toothpick	25.00	95.00
*Individual	20.00	45.00	Tumbler	40.00	100.00
Table	45.00	85.00	Vase		
Cruet, os	75.00	165.00	6½"	25.00	—
Goblet	95.00	110.00	9"	35.00	—
Horseradish, cov	50.00	—	*Wine	75.00	140.00

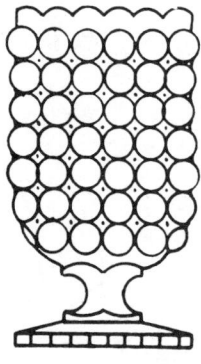

THOUSAND EYE

The original pattern was non-flint made by Adams & Co., Tarentum, PA, in 1875 and by Richards and Hartley in 1888 (pattern No. 103). It was made in two forms: Adams with a three-knob stem finial, and Richards and Hartley with a plain stem with a scalloped bottom. Several glass companies made variations of the original pattern and reproductions were made as late as 1981. Crystal Opalescent was produced by Richards and Hartley only in the original pattern. (Opalescent celery vase $70.00; open compote, 8", $115.00; 6" creamer, $85.00; ¼-gallon water pitcher, $140.00; ½-gallon water pitcher, $180.00; 4" footed sauce, $40.00; spooner, $60.00; and 5" covered sugar, $80.00.) Covered compotes are rare and would command 40% more than open compotes. A 2" mug in blue is known.

	Amber	Apple Green	Blue	Clear	Vaseline
ABC Plate, 6", clock center	60.00	70.00	60.00	50.00	60.00
Bowl, large, car-riage shape	95.00	—	95.00	—	95.00
Butter, cov					
6¼"	75.00	85.00	80.00	50.00	100.00
7½"	75.00	85.00	80.00	50.00	105.00
Cake Stand					
10"	60.00	90.00	60.00	35.00	95.00
11"	60.00	95.00	60.00	35.00	95.00
Celery, hat shape	60.00	75.00	70.00	40.00	60.00
Celery Vase, 7"	60.00	70.00	60.00	50.00	60.00
Christmas Light	35.00	50.00	40.00	30.00	45.00
Cologne Bottle	30.00	50.00	40.00	25.00	50.00
Compote, cov, ls, 8", sq	—	115.00	115.00	—	—
Compote, open					
6"	40.00	45.00	45.00	30.00	45.00
7"	50.00	60.00	50.00	40.00	50.00
8", round	45.00	60.00	50.00	40.00	60.00
8", sq, hs	45.00	60.00	60.00	45.00	60.00
9"	60.00	70.00	60.00	45.00	60.00
10"	60.00	75.00	70.00	50.00	70.00
Cordial	40.00	60.00	45.00	30.00	70.00
Creamer					
4"	40.00	45.00	45.00	30.00	45.00
6"	45.00	85.00	60.00	40.00	85.00
Creamer and Sugar Set	—	170.00	—	115.00	—
*Cruet, 6"	45.00	70.00	60.00	40.00	70.00
Eggcup	75.00	95.00	80.00	50.00	100.00
*Goblet	45.00	50.00	45.00	40.00	50.00
Honey Dish, cov,6 × 7¼"	95.00	110.00	100.00	80.00	95.00
Inkwell, 2" sq	50.00	—	85.00	40.00	90.00
Jelly Glass	30.00	35.00	30.00	20.00	30.00
Lamp, kerosene					
hs, 12"	140.00	170.00	150.00	115.00	160.00
hs, 15"	145.00	180.00	150.00	130.00	170.00
ls, handled	130.00	130.00	130.00	105.00	140.00
Mug					
2½"	30.00	35.00	30.00	25.00	40.00
3½"	30.00	35.00	30.00	25.00	40.00
Nappy					
5"	40.00	—	45.00	35.00	50.00
6"	45.00	—	50.00	40.00	60.00
8"	50.00	—	60.00	50.00	70.00
Pickle	30.00	35.00	35.00	25.00	35.00
Pitcher					
Milk, cov, 7"	95.00	130.00	130.00	85.00	120.00
Water, ¼ gal	80.00	95.00	90.00	60.00	90.00
Water, ½ gal	90.00	110.00	95.00	75.00	95.00
Water, 1 gal	100.00	115.00	110.00	95.00	115.00
*Plate, sq, folded corners					
6"	30.00	35.00	35.00	30.00	35.00

	Amber	Apple Green	Blue	Clear	Vaseline
8″	35.00	35.00	35.00	30.00	35.00
10″	40.00	60.00	45.00	30.00	40.00
Platter					
8 × 11″, oblong	45.00	60.00	50.00	45.00	50.00
11″, oval	85.00	90.00	60.00	45.00	85.00
Salt Shaker, pr					
Banded	70.00	80.00	75.00	70.00	75.00
Plain	60.00	70.00	60.00	45.00	70.00
Salt, ind	90.00	110.00	100.00	60.00	100.00
Salt, open, car- riage shape	75.00	95.00	85.00	60.00	85.00
Sauce					
Flat, 4″	15.00	25.00	20.00	10.00	20.00
Footed, 4″	20.00	25.00	20.00	15.00	25.00
Spooner	40.00	60.00	45.00	35.00	50.00
*String Holder	40.00	70.00	50.00	35.00	50.00
Sugar, cov, 5″	60.00	85.00	70.00	60.00	70.00
Syrup, pewter top	90.00	115.00	80.00	60.00	80.00
Toothpick					
Hat	45.00	70.00	80.00	40.00	60.00
Plain	40.00	60.00	60.00	30.00	45.00
Thimble	60.00	—	—	—	—
Tray, water					
12½″, round	75.00	90.00	85.00	60.00	85.00
14″, oval	75.00	90.00	85.00	70.00	85.00
*Tumbler	35.00	75.00	40.00	30.00	35.00
Waste Bowl	—	—	—	75.00	—
*Wine	40.00	60.00	45.00	25.00	45.00

THREE-FACE

Non-flint made by George A. Duncan & Son, Pittsburgh, PA, c1878. Designed by John E. Miller, a designer with Duncan, who later became a member of the firm. It has been heavily reproduced by L. G. Wright Glass Co. and other companies as early as the 1930s. Imperial Glass Co. was commissioned by the Metropolitan Museum of Art, New York, to reproduce a series of Three-Face items, each marked with the "M.M.A." monogram.

	Clear		Clear
Biscuit Jar, cov	300.00	Cov, hs, 10″	225.00
*Butter, cov	165.00	Cov, ls, 6″	160.00
*Cake Stand		Open, hs, 9″	135.00
9″	175.00	Open, ls, 6″	75.00
12½″	225.00	*Creamer	135.00
Celery Vase		*Goblet	85.00
Plain	110.00	*Lamp, oil	150.00
Scalloped	110.00	Marmalade Jar	275.00
*Champagne		Pitcher, water	425.00
Hollow stem	250.00	*Salt Dip	35.00
Saucer type	150.00	*Salt & Pepper	75.00
*Claret	110.00	*Sauce, ftd	25.00
*Compote		*Spooner	80.00
Cov, hs, 8″	175.00	*Sugar, cov	125.00
Cov, hs, 9″	190.00	*Wine	150.00

TORPEDO (Pigmy)

Non-flint made by Thompson Glass Co., Uniontown, PA, c1889. A black amethyst master salt ($150.00) is also known.

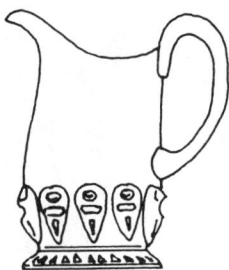

	Clear	Ruby Stained		Clear	Ruby Stained
Banana Stand	75.00	—	Marmalade Jar, cov	85.00	—
Bowl			Pickle Castor, sp holder	125.00	—
Cov, 7" d, 7¼" h	65.00	—	Pitcher		
Open, 7"	18.00	—	Milk, 8½"	75.00	150.00
Open, 9"	20.00	45.00	Water, 10½"	85.00	175.00
Butter, cov	85.00	—	Punch Cup	25.00	—
Cake Stand, 10"	85.00	—	Salt		
Celery Vase, scal-loped top ...	40.00	—	Individual	20.00	—
Compote			Master	35.00	—
Cov, hs, 4", jelly	65.00	—	Salt Shaker, single, 2 types	50.00	—
Cov, hs, 13¾"	165.00	—	Sauce, 4½", collared base	15.00	—
Creamer	50.00	—	Spooner, scalloped top	45.00	—
Cruet, os, ah	80.00	—	Sugar, cov	65.00	—
Cup and Saucer	60.00	—	Syrup	95.00	175.00
Decanter, os, 8"	85.00	—	Tray, water		
Finger Bowl	55.00	—	10", round	85.00	—
Goblet	45.00	85.00	11¾", clover shaped	75.00	—
Lamp			Tumbler	45.00	60.00
3", handled	75.00	—	Wine	90.00	—
8", plain base, pattern on bowl	85.00	—			

TRUNCATED CUBE (Thompson's #77)

Non-flint made by Thompson Glass Co., Uniontown, PA, c1894. Also found with copper-wheel engraving.

	Clear	Ruby Stained		Clear	Ruby Stained
Bowl, 8"	—	40.00	Salt Shaker, single	15.00	30.00
Butter, cov	50.00	90.00	Sauce, 4"	30.00	50.00
Celery Vase	40.00	55.00	Spooner	30.00	50.00
Creamer			Sugar, cov		
Individual	20.00	30.00	Individual	20.00	35.00
Regular	35.00	65.00	Regular	30.00	65.00
Cruet, os, ph	35.00	90.00	Syrup	40.00	100.00
Decanter, os, 12" h	60.00	150.00	Toothpick	30.00	45.00
Goblet	30.00	50.00	Tray, water	20.00	40.00
Pitcher, ah			Tumbler	22.50	35.00
Milk, 1 qt	50.00	100.00	Wine	25.00	40.00
Water, ½ gal	60.00	115.00			

U. S. COIN

Non-flint frosted, clear, and gilded pattern made by U. S. Glass Co., Pittsburgh, PA, in 1892 for three or four months. Production was stopped by the U. S. Treasury because real coins, dated as early as 1878, were used in the molds. The 1892 coin date is the most common. Lamps with coins on font and stem would be 50% more. Heavily reproduced for the gift-shop trade.

	Clear	Frosted		Clear	Frosted
Ale Glass	250.00	350.00	Cov, hs, 8", quarters and dimes	—	415.00
*Bowl			Open, hs, 7", quarters and dimes	200.00	300.00
6"	170.00	220.00	Open, hs, 7", quarters and halves	225.00	350.00
9"	215.00	325.00	Open, 8⅜" d, 6½" h	—	240.00
*Bread Plate	175.00	325.00	*Creamer	350.00	600.00
Butter, cov, dollars and halves	250.00	450.00	Cruet, os	375.00	500.00
Cake Stand, 10"	225.00	400.00	Epergne	—	1,000.00
Celery Tray	200.00	—	Goblet	300.00	450.00
Celery Vase, quarters	135.00	350.00			
Champagne	—	400.00			
*Compote					
Cov, hs, 7"	300.00	500.00			

	Clear	Frosted
Goblet, dimes	—	550.00
Lamp		
Round font	275.00	450.00
Square font	300.00	—
Mug, handled	200.00	300.00
Pickle	200.00	—
Pitcher		
Milk	600.00	600.00
Water	400.00	800.00
Sauce, ftd, 4", quarters	100.00	185.00

	Clear	Frosted
*Spooner, quarters	225.00	325.00
*Sugar, cov	225.00	400.00
Syrup, dated pewter lid	—	525.00
*Toothpick	180.00	275.00
Tray, water, 8", round	275.00	—
*Tumbler	135.00	235.00
Waste Bowl	225.00	250.00
Wine	225.00	375.00

U. S. SHERATON (Greek Key)

Made by U. S. Glass Co., Pittsburgh, PA, in 1912. This pattern was made only in clear, but can be found trimmed with gold or platinum or with a green stain. Some pieces are marked with the intertwined U. S. Glass trademark.

	Clear
Bowl	
6", ftd, sq	15.00
8", flat	12.00
Bureau Tray	30.00
Butter, cov	35.00
Celery Tray	30.00
Compote	
Open, 4", jelly	12.00
Open, 6"	14.00
Creamer	
After dinner, tall, sq ft	12.00
Berry, bulbous, sq ft	15.00
Large	18.00
Cruet, os	25.00
Finger Bowl, under plate	24.00
Goblet	18.00
Iced Tea	20.00
Lamp, miniature	50.00
Marmalade Jar	35.00
Mug	15.00
Mustard Jar, cov	30.00
Pickle	10.00
Pin Tray	12.00
Pitcher, water	
½ gal	30.00

	Clear
Squat, medium	30.00
Tankard	35.00
Plate, sq	
4½"	8.00
9"	12.00
Pomade Jar	14.00
Puff Box	14.00
Punch Bowl, cov, 14"	90.00
Ring Tree	25.00
Salt Shaker	
Squat	12.00
Tall	15.00
Salt, individual	17.00
Sardine Box	35.00
Spooner	
Handled	25.00
Tray	12.00
Sugar, cov	
Individual	15.00
Regular	20.00
Sundae Dish	10.00
Syrup, glass lid	35.00
Toothpick	35.00
Tumbler	15.00

VERMONT (Honeycomb with Flower Rim, Inverted Thumbprint with Daisy Band)

Non-flint made by U. S. Glass Co., Pittsburgh, PA, 1899–1903. Also made in custard (usually decorated), chocolate, caramel, novelty slag, milk glass, and blue. Toothpick holders have been reproduced by Crystal Art Glass Co., Mosser Glass Co., and Degenhart Glass (which marks its colored line).

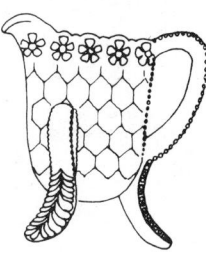

	Clear w/ Gold	Green w/ Gold
Basket, handle	30.00	45.00
Bowl, berry	25.00	45.00
Butter, cov	40.00	75.00
Card Tray	20.00	35.00
Celery Tray	30.00	35.00
Compote, hs		
Cov	55.00	125.00
Open	35.00	65.00
Creamer, 4¼"	30.00	55.00
Goblet	40.00	50.00

	Clear w/ Gold	Green w/ Gold
Pickle	20.00	30.00
Pitcher, water	50.00	125.00
Salt Shaker	20.00	35.00
Sauce	15.00	20.00
Spooner	25.00	75.00
Sugar, cov	35.00	80.00
*Toothpick	30.00	50.00
Tumbler	20.00	40.00
Vase	20.00	45.00

VIKING (Bearded Head, Bearded Prophet, Hobb's Centennial, Old Man of the Mountain)

Non-flint made by Hobbs, Brockunier, & Co., Wheeling, WV, in 1876 as its Centennial pattern. No tumbler or goblet originally made. Very rare in milk glass.

	Clear		Clear
Apothecary Jar, cov	60.00	Cup, ftd	35.00
Bowl		Eggcup	40.00
Cov, 8″, oval	55.00	Marmalade Jar	85.00
Cov, 9″, oval	65.00	Mug, ah	50.00
Bread Plate	70.00	Pickle	20.00
Butter, cov	75.00	Pitcher, water	125.00
Celery Vase	45.00	Relish	20.00
Compote		Salt, master	40.00
Cov, hs, 9″	95.00	Sauce	15.00
Cov, ls, 8″, oval	75.00	Spooner	35.00
Open, hs	60.00	Sugar, cov	65.00
Creamer, 2 types	50.00		

WAFFLE AND THUMBPRINT (Bull's Eye and Waffle, Palace, Triple Bull's Eye)

Flint made by the New England Glass Co., East Cambridge, MA, c1868 and by Curling, Robertson & Co., Pittsburgh, PA, c1856. Shards have been found at the Boston and Sandwich Glass Co., Sandwich, MA.

	Clear		Clear
Bottle, ftd	135.00	Lamp	
Bowl, 5 × 7″	30.00	9½″	115.00
Butter, cov	95.00	11″, whale oil	175.00
Celery Vase	105.00	Pitcher, water	500.00
Champagne	90.00	Salt, master	45.00
Claret	110.00	Spooner	45.00
Compote, cov, hs	150.00	Sugar, cov	125.00
Cordial	100.00	Sweetmeat, cov, hs, 6″	150.00
Creamer	125.00	Tumbler	
Decanter, os		Flip Glass	125.00
Pint	100.00	Water, ftd	75.00
Quart	145.00	Whiskey	75.00
Eggcup	45.00	Wine	70.00
Goblet, knob stem	65.00		

WESTWARD HO! (Pioneer, Tippecanoe)

Non-flint, usually frosted, made by Gillinder and Sons, Philadelphia, PA, c1879. Molds made by Jacobus, who also made Classic. Has been reproduced since the 1930s by L. G. Wright Glass Co., Westmoreland Glass Co., and several others. This pattern was originally made in milk glass (rare) and clear with acid finish as part of the design. Reproductions can be found in several colors and in clear.

	Clear		Clear
Bowl, 5″, ftd	125.00	Marmalade Jar, cov	200.00
Bread Plate	175.00	Mug	
*Butter, cov	185.00	2″	225.00
*Celery Vase	125.00	3½″	175.00
*Compote		*Pitcher, water	350.00
Cov, hs, 5″	225.00	*Sauce, ftd, 4½″	35.00
Cov, hs, 8″ d	455.00	*Spooner	95.00
Open, hs, 8″	125.00	*Sugar, cov	185.00
*Creamer	115.00	*Wine	200.00
*Goblet	120.00		

WHEAT AND BARLEY (Duquesne, Hops and Barley, Oats and Barley)

Non-flint made by Bryce Bros., Pittsburgh, PA, c1880. Later made by U. S. Glass Co., Pittsburgh PA, after 1891.

	Amber	Blue	Clear	Vaseline
Bowl, 8", cov	35.00	40.00	25.00	35.00
Butter, cov	45.00	60.00	35.00	55.00
Cake Stand				
8"	30.00	45.00	20.00	30.00
10"	40.00	50.00	30.00	40.00
Compote				
Cov, hs, 7"	45.00	55.00	40.00	45.00
Cov, hs, 8"	50.00	55.00	45.00	50.00
Open, hs, jelly	32.50	40.00	30.00	35.00
*Creamer	30.00	40.00	28.00	35.00
*Goblet	40.00	55.00	25.00	40.00
Mug	30.00	40.00	20.00	35.00
Pitcher				
Milk	70.00	85.00	40.00	95.00
Water	85.00	95.00	45.00	100.00
Plate				
7"	20.00	30.00	15.00	25.00
9", closed handles	25.00	35.00	20.00	40.00
Relish	20.00	30.00	15.00	25.00
Salt Shaker	25.00	30.00	20.00	25.00
Sauce				
Flat, handle	15.00	15.00	10.00	15.00
Footed	15.00	15.00	10.00	15.00
Spooner	30.00	40.00	24.00	30.00
Sugar, cov	40.00	50.00	35.00	40.00
Syrup	175.00	195.00	85.00	—
Tumbler	35.00	40.00	20.00	35.00

WILLOW OAK (Acorn, Acorn and Oak Leaf, Bryce's Wreath, Stippled Daisy, Thistle and Sunflower)

Non-flint made by Bryce Bros. Pittsburgh, PA, c1885 and by U. S. Glass Company in 1891.

	Amber	Blue	Canary	Clear
Bowl, 8"	45.00	40.00	50.00	20.00
Butter, cov	65.00	65.00	80.00	40.00
Cake Stand, 8½"	55.00	65.00	70.00	45.00
Celery Vase	45.00	60.00	75.00	35.00
Compote				
Cov, hs, 7½"	50.00	65.00	80.00	40.00
Open, 7"	30.00	40.00	48.00	25.00
Creamer	45.00	50.00	60.00	40.00
Goblet	40.00	50.00	60.00	30.00
Mug	35.00	45.00	54.00	30.00
Pitcher				
Milk	50.00	60.00	70.00	45.00
Water	55.00	60.00	75.00	50.00
Plate				
7"	35.00	45.00	50.00	25.00
9"	35.00	35.00	40.00	25.00
Salt Shaker	25.00	40.00	55.00	20.00
Sauce				
Flat, handle, sq	15.00	20.00	24.00	10.00
Footed, 4"	20.00	25.00	30.00	15.00
Spooner	35.00	40.00	48.00	30.00
Sugar, cov	68.50	70.00	75.00	40.00
Tray, water, 10½"	35.00	50.00	60.00	30.00
Tumbler	35.00	40.00	45.00	30.00
Waste Bowl	35.00	40.00	40.00	30.00

WISCONSIN (Beaded Dewdrop)

Non-flint made by U. S. Glass Co. in Gas City, IN, in 1903. One of the States patterns. Toothpick reproduced in colors.

	Clear		Clear
Banana Stand	75.00	Cruet, os	80.00
Bowl		Cup and Saucer	50.00
6″, oval, handled, cov	40.00	*Goblet	75.00
7″, round	42.00	Marmalade Jar, straight sides, glass	
Butter, flat flange	75.00	lid	125.00
*Cake Stand		Mug	35.00
8½″	60.00	Pitcher	
9½″	70.00	Milk	75.00
Celery Tray	40.00	Water	85.00
Celery Vase	60.00	Plate, 6¾″	25.00
Compote		Punch Cup	12.00
Cov, hs, 5″	60.00	Relish	25.00
Cov, hs, 6″	65.00	Salt Shaker	30.00
Cov, hs, 7″	75.00	Spooner	30.00
Cov, hs, 8″	90.00	Sugar, cov	60.00
Open, hs, 6″	35.00	Sugar Shaker	90.00
Open, hs, 8″	50.00	Sweetmeat, 5″, ftd, cov	40.00
Open, hs, 10″	75.00	Syrup	110.00
Condiment Set, salt & pepper, mus-		*Toothpick, kettle	55.00
tard, horseradish, tray	110.00	Tumbler	45.00
*Creamer	60.00	Wine	75.00

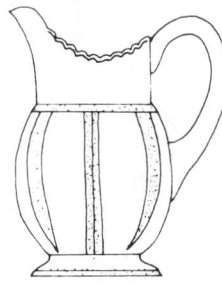

X-RAY

Non-flint made by Riverside Glass Works, Wellsburgh, WV, 1896–98. Prices are for pieces with gold trim.

	Clear	Emerald Green		Clear	Emerald Green
Bowl, berry, 8″, beaded rim	25.00	45.00	Pitcher, water	40.00	75.00
Bread Plate	30.00	50.00	Salt Shaker	10.00	15.00
Butter, cov	40.00	75.00	Sauce, flat, 4½″ d	8.00	10.00
Celery Vase	—	50.00	Spooner	25.00	40.00
Compote			Sugar		
Cov, hs	40.00	65.00	Individual, open	20.00	45.00
Jelly	—	40.00	Regular, cov	35.00	65.00
Creamer			Tumbler shape	—	75.00
Individual	20.00	50.00	Syrup	—	265.00
Regular	35.00	65.00	Toothpick	25.00	50.00
Cruet Set, 4-leaf clover tray	125.00	350.00	Tumbler	15.00	25.00
Goblet	20.00	35.00			

YALE (Crow-foot, Turkey Track)

Non-flint made by McKee & Bros. Glass Co., Jeannette, PA, patented in 1887.

	Clear		Clear
Bowl, berry, 10½″	20.00	Pitcher, water	65.00
Butter, cov	45.00	Relish, oval	10.00
Cake Stand	55.00	Salt Shaker	30.00
Celery Vase	40.00	Sauce, flat	10.00
Compote		Spooner	45.00
Cov, hs	50.00	Sugar, cov	35.00
Open, scalloped rim	25.00	Syrup	65.00
Creamer	60.00	Tumbler	25.00
Goblet	45.00		

ZIPPER (Cobb)

Non-flint made by Richards & Hartley, Tarentum, PA, c1888.

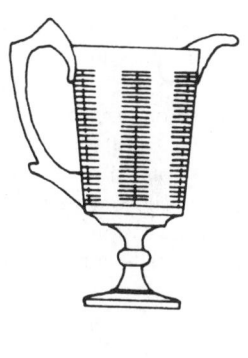

	Clear		Clear
Bowl, 7" d	15.00	Pitcher water, ½ gal	40.00
Butter, cov	45.00	Relish, 10" l	15.00
Celery Vase	25.00	Salt Dip	5.00
Cheese, cov	55.00	Sauce	
Compote, cov, ls, 8" d	40.00	Flat	7.50
Creamer	35.00	Footed	12.00
Cruet, os	45.00	Spooner	30.00
Goblet	20.00	Sugar, cov	45.00
Marmalade Jar, cov	45.00	Tumbler	20.00

S.E.G.

PAUL REVERE POTTERY

History: Paul Revere Pottery, Boston, Massachusetts, was an outgrowth of a club known as The Saturday Evening Girls. The S.E.G. was composed of young female immigrants who met on Saturday nights to read and participate in craft projects, such as ceramics.

Regular pottery production began in 1908, and the name "Paul Revere" was adopted because the pottery was located near the Old North Church. In 1915 the firm moved to Brighton, Massachusetts. Known as the "Bowl Shop," the pottery grew steadily. In spite of popular acceptance and technical advancements, the pottery required continual subsidies. It finally closed in January 1942.

Items produced range from plain and decorated vases to tablewares to illustrated tiles. Many decorated wares were incised and glazed either in an Art Nouveau matte finish or an occasional high glaze.

Marks: In addition to an impressed mark, paper "Bowl Shop" labels were used prior to 1915. Pieces also can be found with a date and "P.R.P." or "S.E.G." painted on the base.

References: Susan and Al Bagdade, *Warman's American Pottery and Porcelain,* Wallace-Homestead, 1994; Paul Evans, *Art Pottery of the United States,* Second Edition, Feingold & Lewis Publishing, 1987; Ralph and Terry Kovel, *Kovels' American Art Pottery,* Crown Publishers, 1993.

Collectors' Club: American Art Pottery Assoc, PO Box 525, Cedar Hill, MO 63016.

Bowl, 5½" d, 2¼" h, blue and white glaze, black writing "Katharine Her Bowl," marked "A.M., 4-19, S.E.G." 350.00

Chamber Stick, blue-gray glaze, single small finger hold, orig logo on paper price tag 30.00

Cup and Saucer, midnight blue glaze, sgd in glaze "P.R.P. 412-36" 35.00

Mug, 5" h, flaring cylinder, applied loop handle, incised

and painted red, yellow, blue, green, and black roosters and motto, teal ground, sgd, orig paper label, chip 650.00

Pitcher

7" h

Mottled high glaze, blue and green over tan, marked, flakes at spout 130.00

5" d, yellow semi-matte glaze, ink mark, chips at spout 260.00

Plate

7¾" d, stippled two-tone blue glaze separated by black line, imp logo and artist's initials "EV" added with brush 35.00

12¼" d, landscape scene, band of trees and hills, green, blue, and black, marked "E.G. ⁵/₁₇, S.E.G.," foot chip 520.00

Vase

6" h, 4" d, ovoid, incised and enameled landscape, green, brown, light blue, and black, dark blue matte body, sgd in black "SEG/4-17/EG," 1917. **2,900.00**

6½", wide rimmed form, teal matte glaze, ink S.E.G. mark 180.00

8½" h, swollen cylindrical, tapering towards base, wide mouth, imp mark, sgd "E 6-24" 700.00

Vase, tapered cylinder, rim band, light blue, high glaze, 5¾" h, $45.00.

PEACHBLOW

History: Peachblow, an art glass which derives its name from a fine Chinese glazed porcelain, resembles a peach or crushed strawberries in color. Three American glass manufacturers and two English firms produced peachblow glass in the late 1880s. A fourth American company resumed the process in the 1950s. The glass from each firm has its own identifying characteristics.

Hobbs, Brockunier & Co., Wheeling peachblow: Opalescent glass, plated or cased with a transparent amber glass; shading from yellow at the base to a deep red at top; glossy or satin finish.

Mt. Washington "Peach Blow": A homogeneous glass, shading from a pale gray-blue to a soft rose color; some pieces enhanced with glass appliqués, enameling, and gilding.

New England Glass Works, New England peachblow (advertised as Wild Rose, but called Peach Blow at the plant): Translucent, shading from rose to white; acid or glossy finish; some pieces enameled and gilded.

Thomas Webb & Sons and Stevens and Williams (English firms): Peachblow-style cased art glass, shading from yellow to red; some pieces with cameo-type relief designs.

Gunderson Glass Co.: Produced peachblow-type art glass to order during the 1950s; shades from an opaque faint tint of pink, which is almost white, to a deep rose.

Marks: Pieces made in England are marked "Peach Blow" or "Peach Bloom."

References: Gary E. Baker et al., *Wheeling Glass 1829–1939*, Oglebay Institute, 1994, distributed by Antique Publications; James Measell, *New Martinsville Glass*, Antique Publications, 1994; John A. Shuman III, *The Collector's Encyclopedia of American Glass*, Collector Books, 1988, 1994 value update; Kenneth Wilson, *American Glass 1760–1930*, 2 vols., Hudson Hills Press and The Toledo Museum of Art, 1994.

Gunderson

Compote, 5" h, 5½" d, 3¼" d base, acid finish, morning-glory shape, pink shading to lavender to white baluster stem **375.00**
Creamer and Sugar, 3½" h, 5¾" w, acid finish, deep pink, vertical stripes, applied reeded handles **485.00**
Decanter, 10" h, bulbous, ftd, pouring lip, deep raspberry shaded to pale pink to white, orig peachblow stopper, applied reeded shell peachblow handle ... **775.00**
Goblet, acid finish, deep raspberry, applied peachblow foot **275.00**
Toothpick Holder **150.00**
Vase, 6½" h, 3¾" d, shoulder tapering to 2½" d base, rose pink shoulder band, white rim shading **195.00**

Mt Washington

Creamer, 5¼" h, ribbon edge, applied handle, orig paper label "Patented/Peach/Mt W G Co/Blow/Dec 15 '85" **2,950.00**
Cruet, 5½" h, cylindrical ribbed body, blackberry vine dec, orig white faceted molded stopper with blue-gray tint, two small foot flakes on base **1,000.00**
Sugar, cov, orig paper label **2,950.00**

New England

Bowl, 5½" d, ruffled rim **375.00**
Celery Vase **875.00**
Creamer, 3" h, bulbous, ribbed, deep raspberry to white, white violets, leaves, and buds dec, gold trimmed handle and rim **650.00**

Hat Stand, ground pontil **140.00**
Lamp, 16" h, base with ribbed font, floral enameling, matching lift-out font, brass collar and burner **275.00**
Pitcher, 6¼" h, crimped top, applied handle **1,300.00**
Punch Cup, acid finish, deep rose shading to white, applied white handle **425.00**
Tumbler, 3¾" h, satin finish, deep raspberry red extending two-thirds down to pure white base **475.00**
Vase
    5½" h, shiny finish, deep color **485.00**
    7" h, trumpet, tricorn, deep raspberry pink shading to white base **550.00**

Webb

Bowl, 3¾" d, folded and pinched rim, stamped on bottom "Queen's Burmese Ware Patented/Thos/Webb/&/Sons" **425.00**
Scent Bottle, 2¾" d, acid finish, enameled blue, white, and yellow forget-me-nots, green leaves, creamy white lining, hallmarked SS screw-on dome top **695.00**
Vase, 8½" h, butterfly hovering near tree, gold flowers and buds, deep pink shading to white, creamy lining **795.00**

Wheeling

Cruet, 6½" h, petticoat shape, trefoil spout, cherry red shading to butter cream base, white lining **1,350.00**
Finger Bowl, 4¾" d, yellow shading to deep red, opaque white int. **400.00**
Lemonade Tumbler, 5½" h, acid finish, elongated, Hobbs Brockunier **365.00**
Pitcher
    7¼" h, bulbous, quatrefoil top, glossy, deep red shading to pale creamy green, white casing, applied amber handle, ground polished pontil, Hobbs Brockunier, c1870 .... **720.00**
    8" h, bulbous, quatrefoil top, glossy, deep coloration, white casing, applied amber handle **400.00**

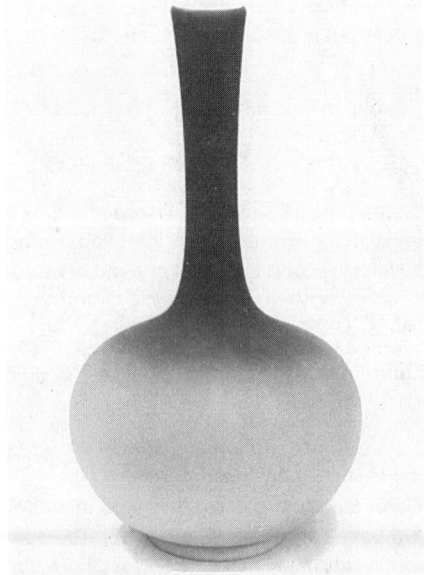

Wheeling, vase, bulbous bottom, extended neck, 10" h, $965.00.

11" h, acid finish, tankard, red to amber shading, opal glass int., applied amber reeded handle, Hobbs Brockunier **2,415.00**

Punch Cup

2¼" h, satin finish, chalk white lining, clear amber glass curled handle 575.00

2½" h, Hobbs, Brockunier 535.00

Tumbler, shiny finish 485.00

Vase

2½" h, bulbous, short collared rim, glossy, deep coloration 300.00

9¼" h, shiny finish, creamy yellow ball-shaped lower half, dark mahogany slender 5" h neck, Hobbs, Brockunier 885.00

Whimsey, 4½" h, pear, acid finish, amber, deep red blush on one side, broken pontil stem top, Hobbs Brockunier 350.00

PEKING GLASS

History: Peking glass is a type of cameo glass of Chinese origin. Its production began in the 1700s and continued well into the 19th century. The background color of Peking glass may be a delicate shade of yellow, green, or white. One style of white background is so transparent that it often is referred to as the ''snowflake'' ground. The overlay colors include a rich garnet red, deep blue, and emerald green.

Bowl

2¾" d, sq form, everted rim, white, late 19th/20th C, price for pr 90.00

5⅞" d, 2⅝" h, rounded sides, raised foot, ext. with floral branches in relief, opaque pink, 19th C, minor hairline 250.00

6½" h, deep rounded sides, gently flared rim, low foot, ruby, early 19th C 520.00

Cup and Saucer, blue overlay dragons and clouds, white ground, SS saucer 225.00

Jar, cov, 5¾" h, urn shape, cobalt blue, geometric pattern 600.00

Snuff Bottle, 19th/20th C

Ovoid

Celadon color, slender 75.00

Green and clear, fish design 95.00

Green and white 85.00

White 65.00

Spade form, clear 75.00

Vase

10" h, carved yellow scene on white, monkey in tree 95.00

Snuff bottle, pastel-colored leaves, green jade top, 2⅜" h, $185.00.

12" h, carved yellow on white, fish dec 375.00

13" h, baluster, carved crimson tropical fish and lotus dec, white ground 750.00

PELOTON

History: Wilhelm Kralik of Bohemia patented Peloton art glass in 1880. Later it was also patented in America and England.

Peloton glass is found with both transparent and opaque grounds, although opaque is more common. Opaque colored glass filaments (strings) are applied by dipping or rolling the hot glass. Generally, the filaments (threads) are pink, blue, yellow, and white (rainbow colors) or a single color. Items also may have a satin finish and enamel decorations.

Biscuit Jar, 6½" d, 7" h, white, yellow, blue, and vivid pink filaments, powder blue ground, 48 molded-in vertical ribs, SP fittings, barn swallow flying among blooming branches emb on lid 785.00

Bowl, boat shape, rainbow filaments 325.00

Pitcher, 9¾" h, colorless ground, swirled body, red, yellow, blue, and white filaments, applied colorless reeded handle 275.00

Plate, 7¾" d, colorless ground, blue filaments, enamel floral dec 115.00

Vase

4¼" h, fan shape, satin, ribbed frosted body, yellow, red, and blue filaments, frosted floral base 90.00

6" h, 4½" w, corset shape, shaded lavender to off-white opaque ground cased in colorless, vertical ribs, allover pink, white, yellow, and red filaments, tightly crimped top 500.00

9" h, baluster, sapphire blue ground, white filaments, double handles 250.00

10½" h, colorless ground, red and violet filaments . 190.00

PERFUME, COLOGNE, AND SCENT BOTTLES

History: The second half of the 19th century was the golden age for decorative bottles made to hold scents. These bottles were made in a variety of shapes and sizes.

An atomizer is a perfume bottle with a spray mechanism. Cologne bottles usually are larger and have stoppers which also may be used as applicators. A perfume bottle has a stopper that often is elongated and designed to be an applicator.

Scent bottles are small bottles used to hold a scent or smelling salts. A vinaigrette is an ornamental box or bottle that has a perforated top and is used to hold aromatic vinegar or smelling salts. Fashionable women of the late 18th and 19th centuries carried them in purses or slipped them into gloves in case of a sudden fainting spell.

References: Joanne Dubbs Ball and Dorothy Hehl Torem, *Commercial Fragrance Bottles*, Schiffer Publishing, 1993; ———, *Fragrance Bottle Masterpieces*, Schiffer Publishing, 1996; Carla Bordignon, *Perfume Bottles*, Chronicle Books, 1995; Glinda Bowman, *Miniature Perfume Bottles*, Schiffer Publishing, 1994; ———, *More Miniature Perfume Bottles*, Schiffer Publishing, 1996; Jacquelyne Jones-North, *Commercial Perfume Bottles*, Revised and Updated Edition, Schiffer Publishing, 1996; Christie

Mayer Lefkowith, *The Art of Perfume,* Thames and Hudson, 1994; Monsen and Baer, *The Beauty of Perfume,* published by authors (Box 529, Vienna, VA 22183), 1996; John Odell, *Digger Odell's Official Antique Bottle and Glass Collector Magazine Price Guide Series,* Vol. 6, published by author (1910 Shawhan Rd, Morrow, OH 45152), 1995; Jeri Lyn Ringblum, *A Collector's Handbook of Miniature Perfume Bottles,* Schiffer Publishing, 1996.

Periodical: *Perfume & Scent Bottle Quarterly,* PO Box 187, Galena, OH 43021.

Collectors' Clubs: International Perfume Bottle Assoc, PO Box 529, Vienna, VA 22180; Mini-Scents, 7 Saint John's Rd, West Hollywood, CA 90069; Parfum Plus Collections, 1590 Louis-Carrier Ste 502, Montreal Quebec H4N 2Z1 Canada.

Atomizers

Baccarat, 5″ h, 3½″ l, oval, etched crystal body, metal chrome top, marked	**115.00**
Opalescent, 5½″ h cranberry striped, orig fittings	**85.00**

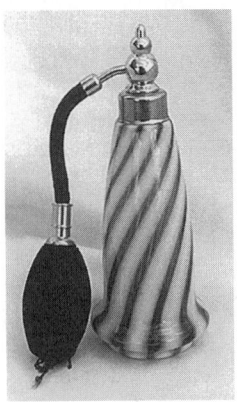

Atomizer, cranberry opalescent, 5½″ h, $85.00.

Colognes

Blown Three Mold, 6″ h, purple, tooled flared lip, pontil, ribbed	**650.00**
Bohemian Glass, 3 × 6¾″, Vintage pattern, ruby and clear, orig steeple stopper	**150.00**
Cut, 7¾″ h, turquoise blue cut to white cut to clear, matching swirled teardrop stopper	**375.00**
Opalescent, 4⅝″ h, eight tooled panels, c1860	**150.00**
Pairpoint, 7″ h, clear, elaborate floral engraving, orig open red rose in paperweight stopper, Charles Kaziun signature cane	**750.00**
Sandwich, 9″ h, opaque white, elaborate dec, satin finish, price for pr	**225.00**

Perfumes

Cameo Glass, 3¾″ h, dark brown ground cut to amber, expansive forest landscape, atomizer top, sgd "D'Argental"	**250.00**
Commercial	
Alexa, Enigma, 2″ h, dark ruby, orig dauber	**45.00**
Caron, Auit de Noel, green paper box, 3″ h	**75.00**
Schiaperelli, Shocking, purse size, dress-form bottle, pink satin-lined black-leather carrying case	**200.00**

Cranberry, 2¼ × 5¾″, sanded gold enameled leaves, white enameled flowers, clear ball stopper, gold trim	**135.00**
Cut Glass, 6″ h, green cut to clear, prism and mirror cut, cut faceted stopper	**175.00**
Czechoslovakian, 8½″ h, waisted, amber, eight-panel cut, orig conforming stopper	**150.00**
Moser, 4½″ l, lay-down type, cranberry, white overlay, gold holly leaves and thistles	**250.00**
Opaline, 8″ h, green, bell-shaped base, tulip rim, enameled gold florals and dec, orig gold enameled stopper, polished pontil, c1870	**195.00**
Staffordshire, 2¾″ h, pillow shape, hp, garlands, gold dec, corner tassels, price for pr	**250.00**

Scents

Blown Three Mold, cobalt blue, sunburst pattern	**95.00**
Northwood, 1¾″ h, pull-up design, eight horizontal bands, alternating stripes of rust, chartreuse, and white, SS cap	**390.00**
Opalescent, 3¼″ l, horizontal and vertical ribs	**85.00**
Paris, 9¾″ h, porcelain, figural, couple, slight restoration to lady, cracked to base of both	**190.00**
Rock Crystal, 2¼″ h, slightly bulbous swirled base, paneled neck with gold mouth, chased leafage at neck, domed cov with translucent enameled royal blue, moonstone thumbpiece, marked with initials of Workmaster "Henrik Wigstrom," 72 standard," incised signature of Fabergé in Cyrillic, St Petersburg, c1910	**4,888.00**

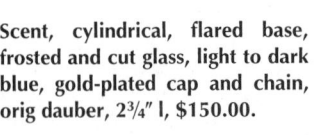

Scent, cylindrical, flared base, frosted and cut glass, light to dark blue, gold-plated cap and chain, orig dauber, 2¾″ l, $150.00.

Satin	
3¾″ h, white, MOP, Peacock Eye design, monogrammed SP lid, orig glass stopper	**435.00**
4″ d, white, MOP, 24 white vertical stripes, collar stamped "CS, FS, Std, SILr," name engraved on SS cap, several minor dents in flip top	**400.00**

Vinaigrettes

Cranberry, 2½ × 1″, rect, cut, enameled pink roses, green leaves, gold dec hinged lid, stopper, finger chain	**195.00**
German Silver, 1″ h, stein shape, enameled, marked "Gruss a Munchen"	**500.00**
Silver, rect, Victorian, engraved flowers, monogrammed "CHH," Nathaniel Mills, maker, Birmingham, 1850, suspended on neck chain	**220.00**

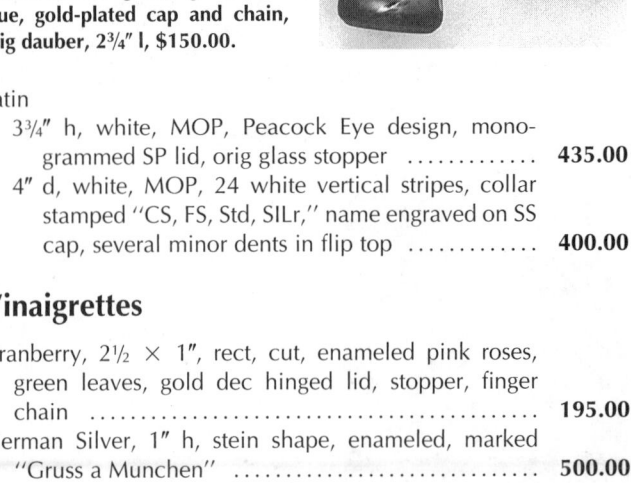

PETERS AND REED POTTERY

History: J. D. Peters and Adam Reed founded their pottery company in South Zanesville, Ohio, in 1900. Common flowerpots, jardinieres, and cooking wares comprised the majority of their early output. Occasionally art pottery was attempted, but it was not until 1912 that their Moss Aztec line was introduced and widely accepted. Other art wares include Chromal, Landsun, Montene, Pereco, and Persian.

Peters retired in 1921 and Reed changed the name of the firm to Zane Pottery Company.

Marks: Marked pieces of Peters and Reed Pottery are unknown.

Bowl, 8″ d, 3″ h, green matte glaze, raised leaf and
branch dec, unmarked **65.00**
Jug, 7½″ h, swirled form, brown glaze, portrait of Cavalier in yellow **50.00**
Mug, 5¾″ h, high glaze, floral sprigs **45.00**
Nursing Feeder, grape and leaf garland dec around
spout, glossy brown glaze **45.00**
Pitcher, 4″ h, brown glaze, yellow floral dec, unmarked,
price for pr **50.00**

Vase, Moss Aztec, designed by Frank Ferrell, 7⅞″ h, $18.00.

Vase
4⅕″ h, broad-based form, subtle raised swirls, muted
green, brown, tan, and blue matte glaze, paper
label **100.00**
6″ h, black, gunmetal glaze, ink mark **90.00**
7″ h, three-handled form, portraits of monks in yellow, dark brown shaded ground **100.00**
7½″ h, landscape dec, blue, green, and brown **350.00**
12″ h, Chromal, blue, green, and brown scenic, semi-
glaze, unmarked **325.00**

PEWTER

History: Pewter is a metal alloy consisting mostly of tin with small amounts of lead, copper, antimony, and bismuth added to make the shaping of products easier and to increase the hardness of the material. The metal can be cast, formed around a mold, spun,

easily cut, and soldered to form a wide variety of utilitarian articles.

Pewter was known to the ancient Chinese, Egyptians, and Romans. England was the primary source of pewter for the American colonies for nearly 150 years until the American Revolution ended the embargo on raw tin, allowing the small American pewter industry to flourish until the Civil War.

References: Marilyn E. Dragowick (ed.), *Metalwares Price Guide,* Antique Trader Books, 1995; Donald M. Herr, *Pewter in Pennsylvania German Churches,* Vol. XXIX, The Pennsylvania German Society, 1995; Henry J. Kauffman, *The American Pewterer,* Astragal Press, 1994.

Collectors' Club: Pewter Collectors Club of America, 504 W Lafayette St, West Chester, PA 19380.

Museum: The Currier Gallery of Art, Manchester, NH.

Note: The listings concentrate on the American and English pewter forms most often encountered by the collector.

Basin
Boardman, Thomas Danforth, faint eagle touch, 8″ d **225.00**
Ellis, Samuel, London, 18th C, 9⅛″ d **200.00**
Hamlin, Samuel, pitted, faint touch, 7¾″ d **125.00**
Rush, H N, 8″ d **650.00**
Stafford, Spencer, Albany, NY, c1820, 7¾″ d **325.00**

Basin, deep, Richard Austin, 8″ d, $450.00.

Beaker, J B Woodbury, Beverly, MA and Philadelphia,
PA, 1830–38, handle, good mark, 3″ **400.00**
Bedpan, Thomas Danforth Boardman, Hartford, CT,
c1820, triple touches, 10½″ l **400.00**
Candlestick
Calder, William, Providence, RI, 1817–56, minor pit-
ting on base, 10″ h **325.00**
Dunham, Rufus, Westbrook, ME, c1840, straight-line
touch, 6″ h, price for pr **900.00**
Gleason, Roswell, Dorchester, MA, c1840, 6½″ h .. **250.00**
Ostrander & Norris, New York City, 1848–50, saucer
base, resoldered, 4″ h **165.00**
Plumey & Felton, Philadelphia, early 19th C, flaring
around stems, circular base, 9½″ h, ... **110.00**
Smith & Co, Boston, MA, mid-19th C, curved-line
touch, 6⅛″ h **175.00**
Unmarked, attributed to Homan, Cincinnati, OH, 10″
h, price for pr **300.00**

Chamberstick, Meriden Britannia Co, 1850, saucer base, gadroon molding, 4¼" h **225.00**

Charger

Austin, Nathaniel, Charleston, MA, 13½" d **500.00**

Badger, Thomas, Boston, MA, eagle touch, 13⅜" d **650.00**

Eadem, Semper, Boston, MA, 12½" d **600.00**

King, Richard, London, England, 16½" d **375.00**

Leigh, Charles White, London, England, 14¾" d ... **325.00**

Unknown

Crowned rose touch and "P.D.B.," wear and corrosion, 14¾" d **275.00**

London, faint touch, scratches, 14¾" d **300.00**

London touch, minor scratches, 16½" d **335.00**

Coffeepot

Boardman & Hart, Hartford, CT, 1830–50, double-belly form, restored, 11½" h **230.00**

Calder, William, Providence, RI, c1839, lighthouse form, 11" h **675.00**

Gleason, Roswell, Dorchester, MA, 19th C, straight-line touch, 11" h **250.00**

Griswold, Ashbill, Meriden, CT, pyramid, 10½" l .. **250.00**

Richardson, George, Boston & Cranston, RI, 1818–45, "G. Richardson, Warranted" touch, 11" h .. **600.00**

Trash, Israel, Beverly, MA, c1830, lighthouse form, bright cut engraved band, 11" h **375.00**

Ward & Co, H B, Guilford or Wallingford, CT, c1840, lighthouse form, minor pitting and dents, 10" h . **230.00**

Communion Bowl, Hiram Yale & Co, Yalesville, CT, c1824–35, ftd, 10½" d, 5¾" h **600.00**

Communion Flagon, Eben Smith, Beverly, MA, 1814–56, lighthouse shape, heart motifs dec, 10½" h **450.00**

Communion Plate, Thomas Boardman, Hartford, CT, c1805–60, eagle touch, 13⅛" d **600.00**

Creamer, Henry Joseph, London, 1740–85, three small feet, marked "HJ" **2,500.00**

Cup, Birch & Villers, England, 1775–1820, double handles **325.00**

Deep Dish, Samuel Hamlin, Hartford, CT, late 18th C **600.00**

Flagon, Smith & Fletman, Albany, 12" h **350.00**

Food Dome, 16½" l, marked "James Dixon & Sons, Sheffield," traces of silver plating, one nut holding handle missing **125.00**

Funnel, American, unmarked, ring handle, 6⅜" l **125.00**

Ladle

Danforth, Josiah, Middletown, CT, 13¼" l **600.00**

Yates, John, Birmingham, England, c1835, minor pitting on bowl int., 13½" l **90.00**

Lamp

Gleason, Roswell, Dorchester, MA, c1830, acorn camphene font, 7¾" h **285.00**

Hopper, Henry, New York, NY, 1842–47, orig whale-oil burner, straight-line touch, 7" h, price for pr. **850.00**

Morey & Smith, petticoat, cast ear handle, fluid burner, snuff caps missing, 3⅛" h **200.00**

Ostrander & Noyes, New York, NY, 1845–50, camphene, resoldered handle, saucer base, 8½" h .. **400.00**

Porter, Freeman, Westbrook, MA, brass and tin, whale-oil burner, ring handle, 6" h **425.00**

Unmarked, cast ear handle, fluid burner, snuffer caps on chains, minor battering, wear, 6½" h **140.00**

Measure, English, 1750–1800, Channel Island Jersey type, ½ pt **375.00**

Lamp, double font, Morey and Smith, Boston, 6" h, $300.00.

Mug

Eddon, William, London, c1750, pt, tulip shape ... **175.00**

Whitmore, Jacob, Middletown, CT, c1758–90, qt, fair mark **1,750.00**

Pitcher

Dunham, Rufus, Westbrook, ME, c1845, cider type, 2 qt, 6½" h **350.00**

Homan & Co, Cincinnati, hinged lid, resoldered finial, marked, 12" h **150.00**

Unmarked, American, pigeon breasted, reverse C-handle, removable lid, 5½" h **325.00**

Plate

Austin, Nathaniel, Charlestown, MA, eagle touch, 8" d **325.00**

Badger, Thomas, Boston, MA, stamped initials on rim, 7¾" d **300.00**

Barnes, Blak(e), Philadelphia, PA, c1812, molded rim, 11¼" d **140.00**

Calder, William, Providence, RI, 1840, eagle touch, 8⅜" d **375.00**

Danford, Thomas, III, c1807, molded edge, 7¾" d . **100.00**

Danforth, William, Middletown, CT, 8" d **325.00**

Jones, Gershom, Providence, RI, 1774, single reed, 8⅜" d **550.00**

Lightner, George, Baltimore, MD, 7¾" d **225.00**

Swanson, Thomas, c1770, Ellis and Swanson marks, 7⅞" d **125.00**

Porringer

Danforth, Samuel, dolphin handle **2,540.00**

Green, Samuel, Boston, MA, cast crown handle, 5½" d **550.00**

Hamlin, Samuel, Providence, RI, c1790, flowered handle, minor int. pitting, good touch, 5½" d ... **500.00**

Unmarked, attributed to David Mellville, Newport, RI, c1780–90, flowered handle initialed "FGW," 5" d **200.00**

Salt, Boyd, Parks, Philadelphia, PA, 1795–1819, beaded rim and base, ftd **950.00**

Sugar Bowl

Boardman & Hart, NY, c1835, orig lid, little minor denting, 8" h **375.00**

Unmarked, attributed to Boyd Parks, Philadelphia, PA, c1795–1819, beaded lid, rim and foot **7,500.00**

Teapot
    Boardman, Thomas D and Samuel, Hartford, CT, cast
        acorn finial, copper bottom marked ''TD & SB,''
        8³⁄₈'' h **250.00**
    Smith, Eben, Beverly, MA, c1830, bright-cut en-
        graved band, straight-line touch, 7¹⁄₂'' h **500.00**
    Water Pitcher, cov, Thomas and Sherman Boardman,
        Hartford, CT, c1830, dents, corrosion, repair to finial,
        11'' h **345.00**

PHOENIX GLASS

History: Phoenix Glass Company, Beaver, Pennsylvania, was established in 1880. Known primarily for commercial glassware, the
firm also produced a molded, sculptured, cameo-type line from
the 1930s until the 1950s.

References: Ellen T. Schroy, *Warman's Glass,* Second Edition,
Wallace-Homestead, 1995; Jack D. Wilson, *Phoenix & Consolidated Art Glass,* Antique Publications, 1989.

Collectors' Club: Phoenix & Consolidated Glass Collectors, PO
Box 81974, Chicago, IL 60681.

Ashtray, Phlox, blue stained, large **275.00**
Bowl, Diving Girl, light pink stain **425.00**
Cigarette Box, cov, 4¹⁄₂'' d, 3¹⁄₂'' h, sculptured white flow-
    ers, blue ground **95.00**
Compote, Fish, 6'', gray **125.00**
Lamp, 22'' h overall, 11'' h body, pink dogwood high-
    lights, custard ground, metal base **150.00**
Planter, 8¹⁄₂'' l, sculptured green lion, white ground ... **75.00**
Plate, 8¹⁄₄'' d, dancing nudes, yellow **65.00**

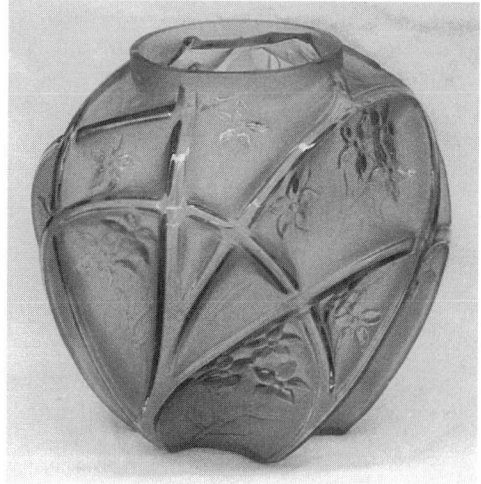

**Vase, light blue, globe, Lalique-type mold, 7'' w, 6³⁄₄''
h, $135.00.**

Vase
    Cosmos, green stain **250.00**
    Katydid, amber, 8¹⁄₄'' h **250.00**
    Nudes, white sculptured nude dancing girls, Wedg-
        wood blue ground **390.00**
    Starflower, brown stained, rim flake **90.00**

PHONOGRAPHS

History: Early phonographs were commonly called ''talking machines.'' Thomas A. Edison invented the first successful phonograph in 1877; other manufacturers followed with their variations.

References: Neil Maker, *Hand-Cranked Phonographs,* Promar
Publishing, 1993; Arnold Schwartzman, *Phono-Graphics,* Chronicle Books, 1993.

Periodicals: *The Horn Speaker,* PO Box 1193, Mabank, TX 75147;
The New Amberola Graphic, 37 Caledonia St, St. Johnsbury, VT
05819.

Collectors' Clubs: Buckeye Radio & Phonograph Club, 4572 Mark
Trail, Copley, OH 44321; California Antique Phonograph Society,
PO Box 67, Duarte, CA 91010; Hudson Valley Antique Radio &
Phonograph Society, PO Box 207, Campbell Hall, NY 10916;
Michigan Antique Phonograph Society, Inc, 2609 Devonshire,
Lansing, MI 48910; Vintage Radio & Phonograph Society, Inc, PO
Box 165345, Irving, TX 75016.

Museums: Edison National Historic Site, West Orange, NJ; Johnson's Memorial, Dover, DE; Seven Acres Antique Village & Museum, Union, IL.

American Graphophone Co, Graphophone Type Q,
    c1897 .... **275.00**
Brunswick, Parisian, collapsible cardboard horn **425.00**
Columbia, Type B Cylinder, Graphophone, Eagle, orig
    aluminum horn, Serial No. 150,716 .... **360.00**
Edison
    Amberola Model 30, table model, oak case **425.00**
    Home Cylinder Model, red morning glory horn **500.00**
    Opera, table model, walnut case, metal bail end han-
        dles, wooden horn, c1912 .... **3,500.00**
    Standard, large tin horn, orig black and red paint, gold
        label ''Thomas A Edison Triumph'' **500.00**

Edison, home, cov, brass plated, c1897–1903, $450.00.

Garrard, handcrafted snakeskin horn, 1920 .... **1,250.00**
Harmony, oak case, painted morning glory horn **425.00**
Kalamazoo Duplex **1,350.00**
Polly, portable, fold-out paper horn **375.00**
Regina Reginaphone Disc Musical Box and Phonograph,
    oak case, MOP inlay, five 15¹⁄₂'' d discs, c1904 .... **2,100.00**

Sears Roebuck & Co, Silvertone, 1914 .... **450.00**
Victor
    Model 1050, record changer **450.00**
    Model V-II, wooden horn **1,250.00**
Victrola, Model VI, table type, oak **200.00**

PHOTOGRAPHS

History: A vintage print is a positive image developed from the original negative by the photographer or under the photographer's supervision at the time the negative is made. A non-vintage print is a print made from an original negative at a later date. It is quite common for a photographer to make prints from the same negative over several decades. Changes between the original and subsequent prints usually can be identified. Limited edition prints must be clearly labeled.

References: Helmut Gernsheim, *Concise History of Photography,* Third Edition, Dover Publications, 1986; ———, *Creative Photography,* Dover Publications, 1991; Norman E. Martinus and Harry L. Rinker, *Warman's Paper,* Wallace-Homestead, 1994; Susan Theran, *Prints, Posters & Photographs,* Avon Books, 1993; Susan Theran and Katheryn Acerbo (eds.), *Leonard's Annual Price Index of Prints, Posters & Photographs,* Auction Index, published annually.

Periodicals: *CameraShopper,* 313 N Quaker Lane, PO Box 37029, W Hartford, CT 06137; *History of Photography,* 1900 Frost Rd, Suite 101, Tullytown, PA 19007; *The Photograph Collector,* Photographic Arts Center, 163 Amsterdam Ave #201, New York, NY 10023.

Collectors' Clubs: American Photographic Historical Society, Inc, 1150 Avenue of the Americas, New York, NY 10036; Assoc of International Photography Art Dealers, 1609 Connecticut Ave NW #200, Washington, DC 20009; Daguerrean Society, 625 Liberty Ave, Ste 1790, Pittsburgh, PA 15222; National Stereoscopic Assoc, PO Box 14801, Columbus, OH 43214; Photographic Historical Society, Inc, PO Box 39563, Rochester, NY 14604; Photographic Historical Society of Canada, PO Box 54620, Toronto, Ontario M5M 4N5 Canada; Photographic Historical Society of New England, PO Box 189, Boston, MA 02165; Western Photographic Collectors Assoc Inc, PO Box 4294, Whittier, CA 90607.

Museums: Center for Creative Photography, Tucson, AZ; International Center of Photography, New York, NY; International Museum of Photography at George Eastman House, Rochester, NY; International Photographic Historical Association, San Francisco, CA; National Portrait Gallery, Washington, DC.

Additional Listings: See *Warman's Americana & Collectibles* for more examples.

SPECIAL AUCTION

Swann Galleries, Inc.
104 E 25th St
New York, NY 10010
(212) 254-4710

Albumen Print, 8¾ × 7¼", Indian village near Red Cloud Agency, shows village, tepees, several Indians, and horses, label locates village near Ft Robinson, NE, 1870s **200.00**
Cabinet Card, photographic portrait
    Acrobat, Victorelli and Young Eldon, Cincinnati, OH **20.00**
    Baby, wicker baby carriage **10.00**
    Dreyfus, Captain and Mrs. Alfred Dreyfus, parlor photo, black and white, 1869 .... **15.00**
    Goodman, Ed, and Johnny Baker, mount slightly chipped at edges, paper label identifies men, Harrington, London, mount, 1890s **345.00**
    Lillie, G W, Pawnee Bill and wife, Western gear, holding shotguns, Pentz & Swords, York, PA, mount, c1880 .... **800.00**
    Lone Star Harry, frontal bust pose, wearing hat and badge, captioned in pencil beneath image "Lone Star Harry, Oklahoma Scout, Rapid Pistol Handler," c1880 .... **375.00**
    Miles, General Nelson A, ¾ length pose, full military regalia, hat and sword, Elmer Chickering, Boston, mount, c1890 .... **175.00**
    Patti, Adelina, wearing feathered hat, N Saxony, 1882 **20.00**
Carte-de-visite, photographic portrait
    Albino Girl, Charles Eisenmann Photographer, NY. **20.00**
    Burnhardt, Sarah **20.00**
    Cody, W F, bust portrait, Theatrical Photographing Co of Philadelphia mount, late 1870s **490.00**
    Greeley, Horace, Sarony, NY **15.00**
    Oakley, Annie, full length, cowgirl outfit, hat on head, shotgun in right hand, Ward of West Alexandria, OH, mount, c1885 .... **920.00**
    Sumner, Charles, Whitehurst **25.00**
Photograph
    4¼ × 3¼", sepia, Red Wolf, standing on prairie, full native attire, early inked caption on verso "No. 7 Chief Red Wolf, taken near Ft. Keogh, Montana" **70.00**
    5 × 7", int. of grocery store **20.00**
    7 × 11", Calvin Coolidge with owners of Lakeside Inn, FL **15.00**

Snapshot, Armistice Day Celebration, parade float, black and white, 1931, 8 × 10", $30.00.

9 × 11", ext. church scene, view with well-dressed men, women, and children, mounted, c1890 ...   **25.00**

9½ × 7", bride and bridesmaid, veil spread on floor, 1930 ....   **18.00**

Tintype

4 × 2¼", unknown Civil War soldier, worn **25.00**

4 × 2½", Annie Oakley, cowgirl outfit, two shotguns by her side, mount quite worn **345.00**

PICKARD CHINA

History: The Pickard China Company was founded by Wilder Pickard in Chicago, Illinois, in 1897. Originally the company imported European china blanks, principally from the Havilands at Limoges, which were then hand painted. The firm presently is located in Antioch, Illinois.

References: Susan and Al Bagdade, *Warman's American Pottery and Porcelain,* Wallace-Homestead, 1994; Alan B. Reed, *Collector's Encyclopedia of Pickard China with Additional Sections on Other Chicago China Studios,* Collector Books, 1995.

Collectors' Club: Pickard Collectors Club, 300 E Grove St, Bloomington, IL 61701.

SPECIAL AUCTION

Joy Luke Auctions
300 E Grove St
Bloomington, IL 61701
(309) 828-5533

Bowl

5½" d, raspberries and etched gold, sgd "Coufall," 1903–1905 mark **120.00**

5¾" d, Regency Water Lilies pattern, sgd "H.E.M.," 1898–1903 mark **250.00**

7¼" w, scenic panel with house, roses and floral border, two handles, 1922–1925 mark **140.00**

8¼" sq, Peaches Linear pattern, sgd "Beutlich," 1905–1910 mark **150.00**

8¾" w, poppies dec, handle, sgd "Fox," 1903–1905 mark **325.00**

10¼" w, Walled Garden, two handles, sgd "Alex," 1912–1918 mark **175.00**

11" d, Yosemite, sgd "Marker," Nippon blank **350.00**

Cake Plate, 10¾" d, two handles, scenic, trees and lake, sgd "Marker," 1912–1918 mark **225.00**

Celery Tray, 12" l, 23K gold, sgd **75.00**

Chocolate Set, cream bands, gold floral tracery, etched gold banding, chocolate pot, six cups and saucers, lidded sugar, Egerton mark, 1938–1948 mark, price for set **275.00**

Creamer and Sugar

Aura Argenta Linear pattern, sgd "Heicke," 1912–1918 mark **250.00**

Violet Border pattern, sgd "Wag," 1912–1918 mark   **150.00**

Cup and Saucer

Aura Argenta Linear pattern, sgd "Vobor," 1918–1919 mark **75.00**

Chinese Seasons pattern, sgd "Challinor," 1938–present mark **30.00**

Roses dec, sgd "Blaha," 1903–1905 mark on cup, 1898–1903 mark on saucer **225.00**

Lemonade Pitcher, 5½" h

Daisy Multiflora pattern, 1905–1910 mark **275.00**

Encrusted Linear pattern, hexagonal, 1912–1918 mark **450.00**

Milk Pitcher, 4" h, Aura Argenta Linear pattern, sgd "O.P.," 1905–1910 mark **325.00**

Mustard Pot, cov, Hessler Violets dec, sgd "R.H.," 1903–1905 mark **250.00**

Pitcher, 5¾" h, White Poppy and Daisy pattern, sgd "Gasper," 1905–1910 mark **300.00**

Plate

8½" d

Dahlia Rubra pattern, sgd "Fisher," 1910–1912 mark **220.00**

Daisy Multiflora pattern, sgd "Fisher," 1910–1912 mark **30.00**

Easter Lily Swirl pattern, sgd "Schoner," 1903–1905 mark **250.00**

Purple iris dec, sgd "F. James," 1905–1910 mark   **45.00**

8¾" d, White Poppy and Daisy pattern, sgd "Gasper," 1912–1918 mark **175.00**

Plate, scenic, blues, green, rose, back marked "Hutschenreuther/Gelb/Bavaria," gold-leaf mark, 8½" d, $265.00.

Punch Bowl

9¾" d, 10" h, Aura Argenta Linear pattern, sgd "Hess," 1905–1910 mark **1,400.00**

14¾" d, 6¾" h, int. and ext. dec with grapes and leaves, sgd "Seidel," 1903–1905 mark **1,000.00**

Tray, 15¾" l, two handled, scenic Italian Garden pattern, sgd "Gasper," 1912–1918 mark **350.00**

Vase

8¼" h, Cornflower Conventional, 1903–1905 mark   **550.00**

8¾" h, Encrusted Linear pattern, blue linear bands extend to bottom **650.00**

10¼" h

Aura Argenta Linear pattern, two handles, sgd "Heicke," 1905–1910 mark 300.00

Purple grapes, luster grapes, and leaves, sgd "Hess," 1905–1910 mark 275.00

11" h, Rose Basket, two handles, sgd "James," 1912–1918 mark 450.00

PICKLE CASTORS

History: A pickle castor is a table accessory used to serve pickles. It generally consists of a silver-plated frame fitted with a glass insert, matching silver-plated lid, and matching tongs. Pickle castors were very popular during the Victorian era. Inserts are found in pattern glass and colored art glass.

Cranberry

Bowl type insert, enameled flowers, gold stems and leaves, ornate frame, 10" h, 8" w 875.00

Vase type insert, enameled dec, SP lid and orig fork 495.00

Crown Milano, Mt Washington, bowl type insert, pastel pansies, gold tracery, white DQ ground, Pairpoint frame, lid marked "MW 520" 1,495.00

Double, clear inserts, vertical panels

Band of engraved leaves and vines, Wm Rogers frame 825.00

Unmarked resilvered frame 750.00

Florentine insert, frosted blue, enameled dec 550.00

Mt Washington

Satin, pink and frosted swirled opalescent stripes, polished pontil, SP frame, small chip under cov 350.00

Seashell and Seaweed pattern insert, cased, pink to salmon, delicate enameled flowers, leaves, scrolls, Aurora frame, 9½" h 1,150.00

Opalescent, Daisy and Fern, cranberry 450.00

Pattern

Daisy and Button, clear, Barbour Bros #117 resilvered frame 250.00

Thumbprint, cranberry insert, ornate SP holder 395.00

Pressed Glass, colorless insert

Castle-shaped insert, Warwick Castle, plated white-metal stand, 10¼" h, 6" d, price for pr 1,250.00

Engraved flowers on each of six panels, F B Rogers #435 frame, resilvered, 9" h 350.00

Satin

Blue, cased, egg shape, enameled dec, ornate holder, pickle-shaped tongs hook 700.00

Rainbow, white to pink insert, Simpson, Hall, Miller frame, 12" h 1,395.00

Vaseline, Hobstar (Imperial) pattern insert, Pairpoint frame 750.00

PIGEON BLOOD GLASS

History: Pigeon blood refers to the deep orange-red-colored glassware produced around the turn of the century. Do not confuse it with the many other red glasswares of that period. Pigeon blood has a very definite orange glow.

Berry Bowl, Open Heart 225.00

Biscuit Jar, cov

Florette 295.00

Little Shrimp 325.00

Butter Dish, cov

Coreopsis 275.00

Torquay, clear base 195.00

Carafe

Coreopsis 295.00

Open Heart 295.00

Creamer

Beaded Drape 150.00

Coreopsis 125.00

Torquay 110.00

Pickle Castor

Beaded Drape 595.00

Open Heart 375.00

Pitcher, Coreopsis, metal top 400.00

Salt Shaker, Periwinkle Variant 110.00

Syrup, Beaded Drape 595.00

Vase, 10½" h, enameled flowers 195.00

PINK SLAG

History: True pink slag is found only in the molded Inverted Fan and Feather pattern. Quality pieces shade from pink at the top to white at the bottom.

REPRODUCTION ALERT

Recently, pieces of pink slag made from molds of the now-defunct Cambridge Glass Company have been found in the Inverted Strawberry and Inverted Thistle patterns. This is not considered true pink slag and brings only a fraction of the price of the Inverted Fan and Feather pieces.

Butter Dish, cov 650.00

Creamer 475.00

Cruet, 6½" h, orig stopper 1,350.00

Marmalade Jar, cov 875.00

Punch Cup, 2¼" h 265.00

Sauce 225.00

Spooner 350.00

Tumbler 485.00

Water Pitcher 800.00

PIPES

History: Pipe making can be traced as far back as 1575. Pipes were made of almost all types of natural and manmade materials, including amber, base metals, clay, cloisonné, glass, horn, ivory, jade, meerschaum, parian, porcelain, pottery, precious metals, precious stones, semiprecious stones, and assorted woods. Some of these materials retain smoke and some do not. Chronologically, the four most popular materials and their generally accepted introduction dates are: clay, c1575; wood, c1700; porcelain, c1710; and meerschaum, c1725.

Pipe styles reflect nationalities all around the world, wherever tobacco smoking is custom or habit. Pipes represent a broad range of themes and messages, e.g., figurals, important personages, commemoration of historical events, mythological characters, erotic and pornographic subjects, the bucolic, the bizarre, the grotesque, and the graceful.

Pipe collecting began in the mid-1880s; William Bragge, F.S.A., Birmingham, England, was an early collector. Although firmly established through the efforts of freelance writers, auction houses, and museums (but not the tobacco industry), the collecting of antique pipes is an amorphous, maligned, and misunderstood hobby. It is amorphous because there are no defined collecting bounds; maligned because it is perceived as an extension of pipe smoking, and now misunderstood because smoking has become socially unacceptable (even though many pipe collectors are avid non-smokers).

References: R. Fresco-Corbu, *European Pipes,* Lutterworth Press, 1982; Benjamin Rapaport, *A Complete Guide to Collecting Antique Pipes,* Schiffer Publishing, 1979.

Periodical: *The Complete Smoker Magazine,* PO Box 7036, Evanston, IL 60204.

Collectors' Clubs: International Assoc of Pipe Smokers' Clubs, 47758 Hickory, Apt 22305, Wixom, MI 48393; New York Pipe Club, PO Box 265, Gracie Station, New York, NY 10028; North Texas Pipe Club, 1624 East Cherry St, Sherman, TX 75090; Pipe Collectors Club of America, PO Box 5179, Woodbridge, VA 22194; Sherlock Holmes Pipe Club Ltd USA, PO Box 221, Westborough, MA 01581; Society for Clay Pipe Research, PO Box 817, Bel Air, MD 21014; Southern California Pipe & Cigar Smokers' Assoc, 1532 South Bundy Dr, Apt D, Los Angeles, CA 90025.

Museums: Museum of Tobacco Art and History, Nashville, TN; National Tobacco-Textile Museum, Danville, VA; Pipe Smoker's Hall of Fame, Galveston, IN; U.S. Tobacco Museum, Greenwich, CT.

Briar, 11″ l, carved bearded man bowl, horn stem **175.00**
Clay, 4¼″ l, blue and white bowl, brown stem, Ohio. . **165.00**
Meerschaum, carved
    6¼″ l, girl with spinning wheel, cheroot holder, cracked amber stem, fitted case **550.00**
    6⅞″ l, tavern scene, maid serving hunter, cheroot holder, amber stem, fitted case **450.00**
    8″ l, laughing bearded soldier, map of France engraved on helmet and tunic, silver fitted case with turquoise **2,650.00**
    10½″ l, hunting, maidens with wolves chase stag around rose, amber stem, fitted case **1,400.00**

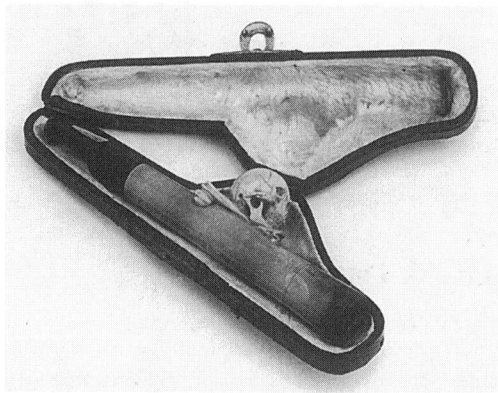

Skull, amber stem, cheroot holder, orig case, 3¹³/₁₆″, $200.00.

Porcelain, 3½″ h, Turkish gentleman bowl, bust head, jeweled and beaded turban, underglaze enamels, metal stem mount, hinged bowl cov, German, 19th C **1,500.00**
Wood
    Civil War, folk art type, highly carved and detailed, emb "Union Forever" **1,300.00**
    Hand holding bowl **85.00**

POCKET KNIVES

History: Alcas, Case, Colonial, Ka-Bar, Queen, and Schrade are the best of the modern pocket-knife manufacturers, with top positions enjoyed by Case and Ka-Bar. Knives by Remington and Winchester, firms no longer in production, are eagerly sought.

References: Jacob N. Jarrett, *Price Guide to Pocket Knives,* L-W Books, 1993, 1995 value update; Bernard Levine, *Levine's Guide to Knives and Their Values,* Third Edition DBI Books, 1993; ———, *Pocket Knives,* Apple Press, 1993; C. Houston Price, *The Official Price Guide to Collector Knives,* Eleventh Edition, House of Collectibles, 1993; Jim Sargent, *Sargent's American Premium Guide to Pocket Knives & Razors,* Fourth Edition, Books Americana, 1995; Ron Stewart and Roy Ritchie, *The Standard Knife Collector's Guide,* Second Edition, Collector Books, 1993, 1995 value update; J. Bruce Voyles, *The International Blade Collectors Association's Price Guide to Antique Knives,* Krause Publications, 1995.

Periodicals: *The Blade,* 700 E State St, Iola, WI 54990; *Knife World,* PO Box 3395, Knoxville, TN 37927.

Collectors' Clubs: American Blade Collectors, PO Box 22007, Chattanooga, TN 37422; Canadian Knife Collectors Club, Route 1, Milton, Ontario L9T 2X5 Canada; National Knife Collectors Assoc, PO Box 21070, Chattanooga, TN 37421.

Museum: National Knife Collectors Museum, Chattanooga, TN.

Additional Listings: See *Warman's Americana & Collectibles* for more examples.

Notes: Form is a critical collecting element. The most desirable forms are folding hunters (one or two blades), trappers, peanuts, Barlows, elephant toes, canoes, Texas toothpicks, Coke bottles, gun stocks, and Daddy Barlows. The decorative aspect also heavily influences prices.

Case

Case uses a numbering code for its knives. The first number (1–9) is the handle material; the second number (1–5) designates the number of blades; the third and fourth number (0–99) the knife pattern. Stag (5), pearl (8 or 9), and bone (6) are the most desirable handle materials. The most popular patterns with collectors are 5165 (folding hunters), 6185 (doctors), 6445 (scout), muskrat (marked muskrat with no number), and 6254 (trappers).

In the Case XX series, a symbol and dot code is used to designate a year.
1920–40
    5111½, blade, lock **600.00**
    5452 .... **300.00**
    6245, dog groomer **200.00**
    6261 .... **125.00**

1940–65

265	200.00
4200, melon taster, serrated blade	165.00
61093	175.00
Muskrat	90.00

1965–70, XX series

5172	150.00
5254	90.00
6143	45.00

1970–80

2137, sod buster	25.00
52131, canoe	100.00
5375, stag	75.00

Ka-Bar, Union Cutlery Co, Olean, NY

Ka-Bar knives have many stampings, including Union (inside shield); U-R Co. Tridoute (variations); Union Cutlery Co, Olean NY; Alcut, Olean, NY; Keenwell, Olean, NY; and Ka-Bar. The larger knives with a profile of a dog's head on the handle are the most desirable. Pattern numbers rarely appear on a knife prior to the 1940s.

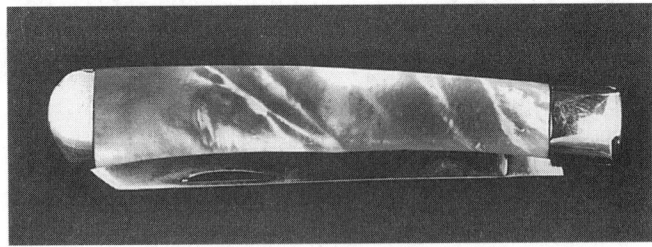

Ka-Bar, trapper, pearl handle, $40.00.

2217, rigger	75.00
6191, knife, fork, spoon	625.00
6260, KF	100.00
21107, Grizzly	2,000.00
61161, composition handle	125.00

Keen Kutter, Simons Hardware, St Louis, MO

K1771, ¾", Daddy Barlow	150.00
K1898, ¾", toothpick	100.00
K8464, ¼", Kattie	65.00

Remington, last made in 1940

3335, scout, red, white, and blue	295.00
32373, cattle	250.00
R273, Texas Jack	200.00
R1535, florist	85.00

Winchester

1701, Barlow	125.00
1920, hunter	1,000.00
2070, doctor's	95.00
3022, whittler	250.00

POISON BOTTLES

History: The design of poison bottles was meant to serve as a warning in order to prevent accidental intake or misuse of their poisonous contents. Their unique details were especially helpful in the dark. Poison bottles generally were made of colored glass, embossed with "Poison" or a skull and crossbones, and sometimes were coffin-shaped.

John H. B. Howell of Newton, New Jersey, designed the first safety closure in 1866. The idea did not become popular until the 1930s when bottle designs became simpler and the user had to read the label to identify the contents.

References: Ralph and Terry Kovel, *The Kovels' Bottles Price List,* Tenth Edition, Crown Publishers, 1996; Carlo and Dorothy Sellari, *The Standard Old Bottle Price Guide,* Collector Books, 1989.

Periodical: *Antique Bottle and Glass Collector,* PO Box 187, East Greenville, PA 18041.

Collectors' Club: Federation of Historical Bottle Collectors, Inc, 88 Sweetbriar Branch, Longwood, FL 32750.

Baker, Chester A, Boston, cobalt blue	50.00
Dicks Ant Destroyer, Finlay Dicks & Co, New Orleans	35.00
Kitner Bros, Made in England, 8¾" h, topaz, round, fluted panels, emb "POISON" on two shoulders, c1910.	90.00
Martin Poison Bottle, England, 5" h, aqua, tooled ring lip, c1902	350.00
Owl Drug Co, 4⅜" h, triangular, owl sitting on mortar and pestle, cobalt blue, tooled lip	195.00
Quilted Design, 7" h, cobalt blue, c1900, orig stopper.	85.00
Skull, 4⅛" h, figural, crossed bones on base, cobalt blue, tooled lip, smooth base, light inner haze	1,300.00
Triloids, 3½" h, emb "Poison" triangular, blue	35.00
W T & Co, 7¼" h, round, lattice and diamond pattern, cobalt blue, tooled lip, c1890	75.00

Embossed, aqua, blown, hobnail, diamond on front, rect on bank, extended neck, imp "70" on bottom, 3⁵⁄₁₆", $30.00.

POLITICAL ITEMS

History: Since 1800 the American presidency has been a contest between two or more candidates. Initially, souvenirs were issued to celebrate victories. Items issued during a campaign to show support for a candidate were actively being distributed in the William Henry Harrison election of 1840.

There is a wide variety of campaign items—buttons, bandannas, tokens, pins, etc. The only limiting factor has been the promoter's imagination. The advent of television campaigning has reduced the quantity of individual items, and modern campaigns do not seem to have the variety of materials that were issued earlier.

References: Herbert Collins, *Threads of History,* Smithsonian Institution Press, 1979; Stan Gores, *Presidential and Campaign Memorabilia With Prices,* Second Edition, Wallace-Homestead, 1988; Theodore L. Hake, *Encyclopedia of Political Buttons, United States, 1896–1972,* Americana & Collectibles Press, 1985; ———, *Political Buttons, Book II, 1920–1976,* Americana & Collectibles Press, 1977; ———, *Political Buttons, Book III, 1789–1916,* Americana & Collectibles Press, 1978; Note: Theodore L. Hake issued a revised set of prices for his three books in 1991; Ted Hake, *Hake's Guide to Presidential Campaign Collectibles,* Wallace-Homestead, 1992; Keith Melder, *Hail To The Candidate,* Smithsonian Institution Press, 1992; Edmund B. Sullivan, *American Political Badges and Medalets, 1789–1892,* Quarterman Publications, 1981; ———, *Collecting Political Americana,* Christopher Publishing House, 1991.

Periodicals: *Political Bandwagon,* PO Box 348, Leola, PA 17540; *Political Collector,* PO Box 5171, York, PA 17405.

Collectors' Clubs: American Political Items Collectors, PO Box 340339, San Antonio, TX 78234; Button Pusher, PO Box 4, Coopersburg, PA 18036; Ford Political Items Collectors, 18222 Flower Hill Way #299, Gaithersburg, MD 20879; Indiana Political Collectors Club, PO Box 11141, Indianapolis, IN 46201; NIXCO, Nixon Collectors Organization, 975 Maunawili Cr, Kailua, HI 96734; Third Party & Hopefuls, 503 Kings Canyon Blvd, Galesburg, IL 61401.

Museums: National Museum of American History, Smithsonian Institution, Washington, DC; Western Reserve Historical Society, Cleveland, OH.

REPRODUCTION ALERT

Campaign Buttons

The reproduction of campaign buttons is rampant. Many originated as promotional sets from companies such as American Oil, Art Fair/Art Forum, Crackerbarrel, Liberty Mint, Kimberly Clark, and United States Boraxo. Most reproductions began life properly marked on the curl, i.e., the turned-under surface edge.

Look for evidence of disturbance on the curl where someone might try to scratch out the modern mark. Most of the backs of these buttons were bare or had a paper label. Beware of any button with a painted back. Finally, pinback buttons were first made in 1896, and nearly all made between 1896 and 1916 were celluloid covered. Any lithographed tin button from the election of 1916 or earlier is very likely a reproduction or fantasy item.

Additional Listings: See *Warman's Americana & Collectibles* for more examples.

Advisor: Theodore L. Hake.

SPECIAL AUCTION

Hake's Americana & Collectibles
PO Box 1444, Dept 344
York, PA 17405
(717) 848-1333

Bandanna, 24″ sq, "Roosevelt Battle Flag," red and white fabric, black and white center illus of T Roosevelt, Bull Moose, 1912 .... **140.00**

Book, *Lincoln Douglas Debates,* 6 × 9″, 268 pgs, 1860, 1st ed, rebound in 1960s in black linen, hardbound, complete text of debates **150.00**

Bust, 7″ h, McKinley, white chalk, 1 × 2 × 2″ base, marked "R & L" on reverse, c1901 .... **40.00**

Cane Handle, 4″ l, Franklin Roosevelt for President '32, cast white metal, remains of white paint **40.00**

Carte de Visite
  2½ × 3¾″, sepia photo, Lincoln, beardless, dot-patterned facsimile signature "Lincoln" at bottom, artist Roberts, Rusholme studio, trimmed slightly, 1860 .... **40.00**
  2½ × 4″
    Davis, Jefferson, dressed as woman, "The Last of the Chevaliers," issued by "L Prang & Co, Boston, Mass," inscription at bottom reads "Jeff. I Thought Your Government Was More Magnanimous than to Hunt Down Women and Children," few scattered slightly brown pinpoint age dots, 1865 .... **90.00**
    Lincoln, sepia photo, with beard, Philadelphia Photographic Co, c1964 .... **55.00**

Cigar Box Label, 4 × 4½″ full color, Ulysses S Grant, titled "Our Chieftain," c1880 .... **35.00**

Clock, 4 × 10 × 14″ h, bronze-finished white metal, captioned "F. D. R. The Man of the Hour" along bottom front edge, FDR holds ship's wheel which surrounds glass cov clock face inscribed "United Electric," orig luster finish, rewired, c1936 .... **150.00**

Convention Program, 9 × 12″, Republican National Convention, 160 pgs, glossy, black and white photos, accompanying test with several full-color, full-page ads from companies like Schlitz Beer, Amco Steel, Ford, and Coca-Cola, San Francisco, 1956 .... **15.00**

Convention Ticket, 3 × 6¼″, Democratic National Convention Guest, beige ticket with stub, engraving of Woodrow Wilson on top left-hand corner, 1920 ... **20.00**

Doorstop, 8 × 10″, diecut brass, T Roosevelt on horseback, thin coat of applied matte-finished gold paint **125.00**

Horse Medallion, 3¼ × 5½″, gold bug, brass, c1896 . **100.00**

Jugate
  Bryan/Kern, black and white photos surrounded by border of two gold circles outlining light green circle in center decorated with tiny red, white, and blue stars, 1908 .... **60.00**
  McKinley/TR, 1¾″ d, black and white portraits against bright gold background, bright red, white, and blue bow **75.00**

Button, McKinley and Roosevelt, blue and gold, 1900, $25.00.

Parker/Davis, 1¼″ d, multicolor, rooster dressed as Uncle Sam with cartoon balloon by his beak inscribed "Shure Mike", vertical red stripes, back paper with instructions on how to order more "Shure Mike" buttons from "Stand Pat" button company in Detroit **300.00**

Taft/Sherman, black and white photos set in white rectangle surrounded by white stars on blue at top, red and white stripes at bottom **150.00**

Willkie/McNary, black and white litho with full names and offices printed under images **75.00**

Lapel Stud
  Cleveland, metal frame holds black and white cellophane insert with portrait, c1888 .... **45.00**
  Roosevelt, Bull Moose, diecut white metal, black finish, wording across moose's body, 1912 .... **50.00**

License Plate, 4½ × 10″, tin, Roosevelt and Garner, black and white photos, orange, black, and white illus of beer mug in center, Repeal of Prohibition .. **800.00**

Medalet, brass, Cleveland, front with name, portrait and date 1888, reverse reads "Democratic Candidate for President" **20.00**

Miniature Book, ¼″ thick, ¾″ h, 142 pages, text of Washington's Farewell Address, from 1932 series produced by Kingsport Press, TN, gold page edges, dark brown leather binding, bright gold initials "GW" with gold lines, dots, and stars **25.00**

Necktie, 26″ l, Nixon for President, burgundy acetate, white inscription, 1960, unused **15.00**

Newspaper, 11 × 15″, Democratic Star, 4 page, Vol 1, No. 1, dated June 1956, black and white photos and text extolling presidential candidacy of Averell Harriman, "A Publication of the New York Democratic State Committee" **15.00**

Pinback Button
  1¾″ d, McKinley, black and white portrait, gold background, red, white, and blue bow at top **50.00**
  3″ d, Truman, Our President, black and white, photo center **150.00**
  3½″ d
    JFK/LBJ, jugate, red, white, and blue, bluetone photo, 1960 .... **75.00**

Mamie/Pat, red, white, and blue, black and white photos, 1952 .... **15.00**

Poster, 10 × 20″, black and white, pre-1936 convention, Landon, three full vertical folds, window-type **30.00**

Ribbon
  2 × 3″, celluloid card on 2½ × 5″ red fabric ribbon for Democratic nominees Palmer and Buckner, 1896, blue text on card reads "National Democratic Party in Kings County. Election Day Nov 3d, 1896," 2″ l metal stickpin on reverse **100.00**
  2¼ × 6½″, Ladies' McKinley Club, black on light yellow linen-like fabric **60.00**
  2½ × 6″, Gen U. S. Grant, black fabric, silver type and design centered by sepia paper photo, c1885 **70.00**
  3 × 8″, Wm Lloyd Garrison Eulogy Lincoln, reads "Union League of Rhode Island. In Memory of Our Departed Brother, Abraham Lincoln, Eulogy by Wm Lloyd Garrison, June 1st, 1865," tiny fabric fraying **100.00**
  3¾ × 7½″, Blockley Clay Club, black and white ribbon, woven images of tree branches and leaves, "His Country's Friend in the Hour of Danger/ Henry Clay Price of America/People's Choice/Protector of American Industry," ⅛″ folded-over strip at top stitched, two small vertical fabric splits, c1844 .... **150.00**

Sheet Music, 10 × 13½″, Roosevelt March, copyright 1910 by McKinley Music Co, red, white, and blue cov with center bluetone photo **35.00**

Stickpin
  Harrison, brass shell, 2″ w across eagle's wing tips, center area designed as shield holding large sepia cardboard photo **150.00**
  Tilden/Hendricks 1876, jugate, ⅞″, brass luster out-

Magazine, *The Century Illustrated Monthly Magazine*, Lincoln Centennial Number, Vol. 77, No. 4, printed black-and-yellow covers, color frontispiece miniature portrait, 134 pgs, black-and-white photographs, color plates, 7 × 10″, February 1909, $25.00.

side rim holding bright green circular paper insert, crisp sepia center jugate, 1" h vertical stickpin on reverse **400.00**

Textile, printed cotton
  Harrison/Marton 1888, Protect Home Industry, 22¼" h, 24¾" w, red, blue, and brown on white, faded, some color bleeding, framed **125.00**
  McKinley/Hobart 1896 Protection, 21¾" h, 22¼" w, black on white, minor stains, framed **385.00**
Token, copper, Jackson 1837 Hard Times, front with Jackson inside chest holding saber and money bag with inscription "I Take the Responsibility," reverse with ship on the rocks with slogan "Van Buren Metallic Currency 1837," word "Government" on side of ship partially worn off **20.00**

POMONA GLASS

History: Pomona glass, produced only by the New England Glass Works and named for the Roman goddess of fruit and trees, was patented in 1885 by Joseph Locke. It is a delicate lead, blown art glass which has a pale, soft beige ground and a top one-inch band of honey amber.

There are two distinct types of backgrounds. First ground, made only from late 1884 to June 1886, was produced by making fine cuttings through a wax coating followed by an acid bath. Second ground was made by rolling the piece in acid-resisting particles and acid etching. Second ground was made in Cambridge until 1888 and until the early 1900s in Toledo, where Libbey moved the firm after purchasing New England Glass works. Both methods produced a soft frosted appearance, but fine curlicue lines are more visible on first-ground pieces. Some pieces have designs which were etched and then stained with a color. The most familiar design is blue cornflowers.

Do not confuse Pomona with Midwestern Pomona, a pressed glass with a frosted body and amber band.

References: Joseph and Jane Locke, *Locke Art Glass,* Dover Publications, 1987; Ellen T. Schroy, *Warman's Glass,* Second Edition, Wallace-Homestead, 1995; Kenneth Wilson, *American Glass 1760–1930,* 2 vols., Hudson Hills Press and The Toledo Museum of Art, 1994.

Bowl, second ground, fluted
  5" d, Rivulet pattern, blue stain **95.00**
  5¼" d, Cornflower pattern **45.00**
Celery Vase, 6½" h, 4" d, Inverted Thumbprint pattern, scalloped amber rim **125.00**
Cream Pitcher, 3¼" h, first ground, amber stain, three dainty applied feet, applied handle with heat check **245.00**
Finger Bowl, 2½" d, first ground, gold stain **75.00**
Lemonade Tumbler, Leaf pattern, first ground, ring handle **85.00**
Nappy, 5¼" d, Cornflower pattern, first ground, blue stain, applied handle **125.00**
Punch Cup, Leaf pattern, first ground, amber stain **40.00**
Spooner, 5" h, Inverted Thumbprint pattern, second ground, red-stemmed blueberry dec, crimped base . **140.00**
Toothpick Holder, applied rigaree rim **1,000.00**
Tumbler, 3¾" h, 2⅝" d, Cornflower pattern, second ground, DQ, honey amber stained top and leaves, blue stained flowers **150.00**

Mustard, Flower and Pleat, washed color, SP top, 3⅛" h, $40.00.

Vase
  4¾" h, 3" d, Inverted Thumbprint pattern, sq amber top **90.00**
  5¼" h, Cornflower pattern, first ground body, ruffled amber rim, gold and blue floral belt at waist, applied wishbone feet **375.00**

PORTRAIT WARE

History: Plates, vases, and other articles with portraits on them were popular in the second half of the 19th century. Although male subjects, such as Napoleon or Louis XVI, were used, the ware usually depicts a beautiful, and often unidentified, woman.

A large number of English and Continental china manufacturers made portrait ware. Because most was hand painted, an artist's signature often is found.

Cup and Saucer, 2½" h, cup with Marie Antoniette portrait in gilt medallion, cobalt blue ground, polychrome pastoral scene on saucer, Sevres, 18th C ... **300.00**
Dresser Tray, 12" l, two portrait medallions, four floral medallions, gold designs, white ground, marked "Nippon" **250.00**
Jewel Box, 10½ × 5", blown-out florals, ribbons on cov, center multicolored portrait of seated woman, 18th C attire, beige ground, gold highlights, marked "Mt Washington" **950.00**
Plaque
  4¼ × 6¼", rect, wrigglework to gilt ground, enameled female portrait, French, late 19th C **550.00**
  10¼ × 15¾"
    Bacchanalian revelry, maiden, cherub, and satyrs, artist sgd "H Stadler" **9,200.00**
    Samson and Dahlia, artist sgd "H Stadler," imp KPM scepter mark, further marked in blue with shield mark, "FD Vienna Austria" **9,200.00**
  14 × 11" d, Raub der Lubinerinnen, 1436, antique green and gold border with floral dec, artist sgd "F Dorfl," blue shield mark "Vienna, F & D Austria," titled on reverse **6,100.00**
Plate
  8" d, bust-length portrait of Anmuth, Vienna style, gilt scroll, diaper, and foliate pattern border, sgd "Wagner," framed **850.00**
  9½" d, George Washington, deep blue, wide garland border, Royal Doulton, c1910 .... **125.00**

Plate, woman with flowing brown hair, maroon border, gold dec, green mark "Johnson Bros, England," 8¾" d, $50.00.

9¾" d, bust-length portrait of Ariadne, Vienna style, wide gilt foliage border, metallic red ground, lobed rim, sgd "Wagner" **1,225.00**

10½" d, Rape of Sabine Woman, wide cobalt blue border, gilt floral filigree and trellis pattern, artist sgd "C Landutrut," blue Royal Vienna beehive mark **865.00**

13" d, lobed circular plate, ¾ length portrait of woman, mountainous landscape, thick gold band border surrounded by russet border, sgd "M Wantzel," Limoges **110.00**

17" d, woman, jade green border, gold trim, marked "Victoria, Austria" **225.00**

Vase, 9½" h, burgundy ground, portrait of maiden, gold framed cartouche, artist sgd, Vienna shield mark, numbered **1,275.00**

POSTERS

History: Posters were a critical and extremely effective method of mass communication, especially in the period before 1920. Enormous quantities were produced, helped in part by the propaganda role posters played in World War I.

Print runs of two million were not unknown. Posters were not meant to be saved; they usually were destroyed once they had served their purpose. The paradox of high production and low survival is one of the fascinating aspects of poster history.

The posters of the late 19th and early 20th centuries represent the pinnacle of American lithography. The advertising posters of firms such as Strobridge or Courier are true classics. Philadelphia was one center for the poster industry.

Europeans pioneered posters with high artistic and aesthetic content, and poster art still plays a key role in Europe. Many major artists of the 20th century designed posters.

References: George Theofiles, *American Posters of World War I,* Dafram House Publishers; Susan Theran, *Prints, Posters & Photographs,* Avon Books, 1993; Susan Theran and Katheryn Acerbo (eds.), *Leonard's Annual Price Index of Prints, Posters & Photographs,* Auction Index, published annually; Jon R. Warren, *Collecting Hollywood,* Third Edition, American Collector's Exchange, 1994; Bruce Lanier Wright, *Yesterday's Tomorrow,* Taylor Publishing, 1993.

Periodicals: *Afficme, The International Poster Magazine,* PO Box 75, 7940, AG Meppel, Netherlands; *Collecting Hollywood,* American Collectors Exchange, 2401 Broad St, Chattanooga, TN 37408; *Hollywood Collectibles,* 4099 McEwen Dr, Ste 350, Dallas, TX 75244; *Movie Poster Update,* American Collectors Exchange, 2401 Broad St, Chattanooga, TN 37408.

Museum: Museé de la Publicité, 107 Rue de Rivoli, Paris, France.

Additional Listings: See *Warman's Americana & Collectibles* for more examples.

Advisor: George Theofiles.

Advertising

Lady Esther Face Cream, 23 × 36", c1920, printed on board, beautiful young woman in oval vignette, "A Skin Food–An Astringent" **325.00**

Kix Cereal, 17 × 22", c1948, Lone Ranger 6-shooter ring, General Mills premium, "Only 15¢ plus Kix box top" **225.00**

Magic

Buddha and Heartstone, 14 × 26", c1914, Polish magician performing tricks, English and Polish text **100.00**

Carter the Great–A Baffling Chinese Mystery–The Elongated Maiden, 41 × 81", Otis Litho, c1920, "A pretty Chinese girl tied to a torture rack without seeming discomfort...," life-sized Chinese nobleman looking down on vignettes of complicated rack, stretched maiden, banshees, imps, devils, in color **550.00**

Friedlander Stock Magic, 14 × 19", Adolph Friedlander #6966, c1919, smiling devil holds card-like vignettes of magic acts in one hand, wand in other, yellow ground **150.00**

Kar-Mi Swallows a Loaded Gun Barrel, 42 × 28", National, 1914, "Shoots a cracker from a man's head," Kar-Mi with gun in mouth blasts away at blindfolded assistant, crowd of turbaned Indians **275.00**

Movie

African Queen, 22 × 31", c1960, French release of classic Bogart and Hepburn film, color portraits of both above steamy jungle setting **150.00**

Alias Boston Blackie, 27 × 41", Columbia Pictures, 1942, Chester Morris, full color **100.00**

Amazing Transparent Man, 27 × 41", Miller Consolidated, 1959, D Kennedy, Marguerite Chapman, sci-fi silhouette against blue **125.00**

Anatomy of a Murder, 27 × 41", Columbia, 1959, Saul Bass design **125.00**

Advertising, Arrow Shirts, litho, young couple in boat, blue water, orig frame, c1925, 22 × 28″, $450.00.

Atlantic City, 14 × 36″, Republic, 1941, Constance Moore, Jerry Colonna in drag, by James Montgomery Flagg **200.00**

Blondie in the Dough, 27 × 41″, Columbia Pictures, 1947, Penny Singleton, Chick Young's Blondie cartoon film, full color **95.00**

Buck Privates, 27 × 41″, Relart Re-Release, 1953, Bud Abbott, Lou Costello, the Andrews Sisters, full-color montage **95.00**

Dr. No, 27 × 41″, United Artist, 1962, Sean Connery, Ursula Andress **325.00**

13 Rue Madeleine, 27 × 41″, Fox, 1947, James Cagney, Annabella, Cagney coming from behind looming door, printed in US for So American market **225.00**

Farmer's Daughter, 27 × 41″, RKO, 1947, Loretta Young, Joseph Cotten, Ethel Barrymore, Cotten kneeling to pick up blond Young in maid's outfit **125.00**

Letter of Introduction, 27 × 41″, Universal, 1938, Charlie McCarthy, Edgar Bergen, Andrea Leeds, full-color dummy **300.00**

Mule Train, 27 × 41″, Columbia Pictures, 1950, Gene Autry, Champion, full-color portraits **150.00**

One-Eyed Jacks, 27 × 41″, Paramount, 1959, Marlon Brando, Karl Malden, full color **85.00**

Political and Patriotic

Bridge of Peace, 16 × 22″, Venette Willard Shearer, c1936, anti-war poster from American Friends Service Committee, National Council to Prevent War, in color, children of all nations play beneath text of song of peace **125.00**

For President Warren G Harding For Vice President Calvin Coolidge, 16 × 11″, 1920, photogravure of both **80.00**

William McKinley–Theodore Roosevelt, 28 × 20″, Edgar Marshall, 1900, election poster, black and white jugate engravings **150.00**

Theater

Bringing Up Father, 41 × 81″, McManus, c1915, "Jiggs, Maggie, Dinty Moore–George McManus's cartoon comedy with music," early newspaper cartoon characters against New York skyline **425.00**

Claudine Clérice Fr, 26 × 35″, 1910, Collette Willy opera, full color, French **275.00**

Dangers of a Great City, 21 × 28″, National Show Print, Chicago, c1900, play by Oliver North, men fighting in an office, gleaming stock ticker, "Give me the papers or I'll..." **150.00**

Key Largo, 14 × 22″, c1930, window card for play starring Paul Muni, portrait center, black and red motif **65.00**

Transportation

Motorlobene–Fano, 24 × 35″, Alfred Olsen, 1922, Danish auto race, car raising cloud of dus **1,250.00**

Royal Mail Atlantis, 25 × 38″, Padden, c1923, tourists in Royal Mail motor launch approaching harbor village, mountains in background **675.00**

SS France, 30 × 46″, Bob Peak, 1961, launching of French ocean liner, champagne and confection in front of huge, night-lit bow of ship **450.00**

SS Michelangelo and SS Raffaello, 54 × 22″, Astor, 1964, detailed cutaway of Italian ocean liners, designed for use in travel office, printed on plasticized stock, metal frame **300.00**

SS Rex, 40 × 29″, P Klodic, c1936, advertisement for Italian ocean liner, designed for use in travel office, framed **750.00**

Travel

Batumi, USSR, 24 × 39″, c1936, Intourist poster showing healthy female comrade with huge basket of oranges, panorama of bus, port, and city **350.00**

Britain in Winter, 19 × 29″, Terence Cuneo, 1948, color rendering of horseman, hunters, and tourists outside rustic inn **125.00**

Come to Ulster, 50 × 40″, Norman Wilkinson, c1935, sailboats and fishermen in front of lighthouse, full color **450.00**

Mexico, 18 × 27″, C Uruela, c1946, naive Mexican Gothic, two children **150.00**

Palace Hotel Wengen, 27 × 40″, Klara Borter, 1928, hotel in foothills of Alps **800.00**

Paris, 24 × 39″, Paul Colin, 1946, doves floating above stylized Eiffel tower and Arc de Triumph **600.00**

World War I

Call to Duty–Join the Army for Home and Country, 30 × 40″, Cammilli, 1917, recruiting image of Army bugler in front of unfurled banner **325.00**

Clear the Way!, 20 × 30″, Howard Chandler Christy, c1918, Columbia points the way for Naval gun crew **300.00**

POT LIDS

History: Pot lids are the lids from pots or small containers which originally held ointments, pomades, or soap. Although some collectors want both the pot and its lid, lids alone are more often collected. The lids frequently are decorated with multicolored underglaze transfers of rural and domestic scenes, portraits, florals, and landmarks.

The majority of the containers with lids were made between 1845 and 1920 by F. & R. Pratt, Fenton, Staffordshire, England. In 1920, F. & R. Pratt merged with Cauldon Ltd. Several lids were reissued by the firm using the original copper engraving plates. They were used for decoration and never served as actual lids. Reissues by Kirkhams Pottery, England, generally have two holes for hanging. Cauldon, Coalport, and Wedgwood were other firms making reissues.

Marks: Kirkhams Pottery reissues are often marked as such.

References: Susan and Al Bagdade, *Warman's English & Continental Pottery & Porcelain,* Second Edition, Wallace-Homestead, 1991; A. Ball, *The Price Guide to Pot-Lids and Other Underglaze Multicolor Prints on Ware,* Second Edition, Antique Collectors' Club, 1991 value update.

Note: Sizes given are for actual pot lids; size of any framing not included.

Areca Nut Tooth Paste
    Army and Navy Co-Operative Society Limited, two military men shaking hands and holding flags, black on white, 3 1/16" d, rust stains **90.00**
    Cleansing Preserving and Beautifying the Teeth/Lewis And Burrows Ltd., London, roses, black on white, 2¾" d **95.00**
Cherry Tooth Paste, Patronized by the Queen/For Beautifying and Preserving the Teeth, Prepared by John Gosnell & Co, London, profile of young Queen Victoria facing left, shades of blue, and black on white, gold band, 3³/₁₆" d **125.00**
Cold Cream, R Lemmon, Chemist, The Pharmacy Hythe, geometric border, gray on white, 2½" d **110.00**
Higgins' Cherry Tooth Paste/For Cleansing Beautifying and Preserving the Teeth & Gums/Trademark R Higgins, Chemist 235 Strand Next Temple Bar, London, street scene, black on white, 2¾" d **185.00**

The Wolf and the Lamb, 4¹/₈", $200.00.

Otto of Rose Cold Cream, SF Goss Chemist, 460 Oxford St, red rose center, green leaves, black letters, white ground, 2⁵/₈" d **115.00**
Saponaceous Shaving Compound, Prepared by X Bazin, Perfumer, Philadelphia, geometric stars border, black and white, 4³/₈" d **250.00**
Worsley Wholesale Perfumer, Philadelphia, Capitol at Washington, linear border, view of Old Capitol Building, violet on white, 3½" d **475.00**

PRATT

PRATT WARE

PRATT
PRATT
FENTON

History: The earliest Pratt earthenware was made in the late 18th century by William Pratt, Lane Delph, Staffordshire, England. From 1810 to 1818, Felix and Robert Pratt, William's sons, ran their own firm, F. & R. Pratt, in Fenton in the Staffordshire district. Potters in Yorkshire, Liverpool, Sunderland, Tyneside, and Scotland copied the products.

The wares consisted of relief-molded jugs, commercial pots and tablewares with transfer decoration, commemorative pieces, and figures and figural groups of both people and animals.

Marks: Much of the early ware is unmarked. The mid-19th century wares bear several different marks in conjunction with the name Pratt, including "& Co."

References: Susan and Al Bagdade, *Warman's English & Continental Pottery & Porcelain,* Second Edition, Wallace-Homestead, 1991; John and Griselda Lewis, *Pratt Ware 1780–1840,* Antique Collectors' Club, 1984.

Additional Listing: Pot Lids.

Bank, 5" h, house shape, coin slot in roof, open chimney, two figures, faces in windows, professional repair .. **650.00**
Creamer, 4¾" h, children at play, heart-shaped cartouche, underglaze blue, green, and brown **250.00**
Model, 4½" l, baby in cradle, underglaze yellow and blue enamels, early 19th C, nick to bonnet **350.00**
Pipe, c1800
    5" h, sailor form, stem formed as large fish swallowing male figure supporting a mask's-head bowl, restored at mouthpiece and bowl stem **890.00**
    8½" l, 4¹/₈" h, monkey form, bowl molded as bird's head, stem and bowl restored **650.00**
    9¼" l, coiled snake, bowl extending from snake's mouth, stains, hairline, and repair **400.00**
    13½" l, coil, underglaze enamels, molded figural bowl, staining **920.00**
Pitcher, 7¼" h, pearlware, molded dec of children in heart-shaped devices, titled "Mischievous Sport" and "Sportive Innocence," yellow, green, tan, blue, and brown, chips on handle and spout **535.00**
Sauce Boat, 5" h, 7" w, orange-ochre fox's head as body and spout, white with sponged brown wings swan forming handle, yellow-green acanthus leaves on white wide body base, c1790, body reglazed **850.00**
Tea Caddy, 5¼" h, applied and glazed floral dec, early 19th C **275.00**

Pitcher, molded form, green, yellow, orange, and brown enameled dec, 5⅞" h, $250.00.

Toby Jug, 9½" h, seated Mr Toby, holding jug, wearing tricorn hat, jacket, vest, knee breeches, manganese, soft green, brown ochre, yellow, and orange-ochre, 18th C, pipe bowl by chair missing, small flake on one hand **1,540.00**
Watch Stand, 10" h, tall-case clock flanked by two children wearing yellow crowns, applied sq base with mound beneath their feet, blue, orange-ochre, yellow, brown, and green, small shallow chip on base **500.00**

PRINTS

History: Prints serve many purposes. They can be a reproduction of an artist's paintings, drawings, or designs, but often are an original art form. Finally, prints can be developed for mass appeal rather than primarily for aesthetic fulfillment. Much of the production of Currier & Ives fits this latter category. Currier & Ives concentrated on genre, urban, patriotic, and nostalgic scenes.

References: William P. Carl, *Currier's Price Guide to American and European Prints at Auction,* Third Edition, Currier Publications, 1994; Clifford P. Catania, *Boudoir Art,* Schiffer Publishing, 1994; Karen Choppa and Paul Humphrey, *Maud Humphrey,* Schiffer Publishing, 1993; Erwin Flacks, *Maxfield Parrish Identification & Price Guide,* Second Edition, Collectors Press, 1994; Patricia L. Gibson, *R. Atkinson Fox & William M. Thompson Identification & Price Guide,* Collectors Press, 1994; Martin Gordon (ed.), *Gordon's 1995 Print Price Annual,* Gordon and Lawrence Art Reference, 1995; William R. Holland, Clifford P. Catania, and Nathan D. Isen, *Louis Icart,* Schiffer Publishing, 1994; William R. Holland and Douglas L. Congdon-Martin, *The Collectible Maxfield Parrish,* Schiffer Publishing, 1993; Robert Kipp, *Currier's Price Guide to Currier & Ives Prints,* Third Edition, Currier Publications, 1994; Stephanie Lane, *Maxfield Parrish,* L-W Book Sales, 1993; Coy Ludwig, *Maxfield Parrish,* Schiffer Publishing, 1973, 1993 reprint with value guide; *Maxfield Parrish,* Collectors Press, 1995; Rita C. Mortenson, *R. Atkinson Fox, His Life and Work,* Vol. 1 (1991, 1994 value update), Vol. 2 (1992), L-W Book Sales; Kent Steine and Frederick B. Taraba, *The J. C. Leyendecker Collection,* Collectors Press, 1996; Susan Theran, *Prints, Posters & Photographs,* Avon Books, 1993; Susan Theran

and Katheryn Acerbo (eds.), *Leonard's Annual Price Index of Prints, Posters & Photographs,* Auction Index, published annually.

Periodicals: *Illustrator Collector's News,* PO Box 1958, Sequim, WA 98382; *Journal of the Print World,* 1008 Winona Rd, Meredith, NH 03253; *Print Collector's Newsletter,* 119 East 79th St, New York, NY 10021.

Collectors' Clubs: American Antique Graphics Society, 5185 Windfall Rd, Medina, OH 44256; American Historical Print Collectors Society, PO Box 201, Fairfield, CT 06430; Gutmann Collector Club, PO Box 4743, Lancaster, PA 17604; Prang-Mark Society, PO Box 306, Watkins Glen, NY 14891.

Museums: American Museum of Natural History, New York, NY; Audubon Wildlife Sanctuary, Audubon, PA; John James Audubon State Park and Museum, Henderson, KY; Museum of the City of New York, NY; National Portrait Gallery, Washington, DC.

REPRODUCTION ALERT

The reproduction of Maxfield Parrish prints is a continuing process. New reproductions look new, i.e., their surfaces are shiny and the paper crisp and often pure white. The color on older prints develops a mellowing patina. The paper often develops a light brown to dark brown tone, especially if it is acid based or was placed against wooden boards in the back of a frame.

Size is one of the keys to spotting later reproductions. Learn the correct size for the earliest forms. Be alert to earlier examples that have been trimmed to fit into a frame. Check the dimensions before buying any print.

Carefully examine the edges within the print. Any fuzziness indicates a later copy. Also look at the print through a magnifying glass. If the colors separate into dots, this indicates a later version.

Apply the same principles described above for authenticating all prints, especially those attributed to Currier & Ives. Remember, many prints were copied soon after their period introduction. As a result, reproductions can have many of the same aging characteristics as period prints.

Additional Listings: See Wallace Nutting.

Note: Prints are beginning to attract a wide following. This is partially because prices have not matched the rapid rise in oil paintings and other forms of art.

Allen, James E, Plowing, litho on paper with GCM watermark, sgd "James E. Allen" in pencil lower right, stamped "Collectors of American Art, Inc., New York, N. Y." on reverse, 8¼ × 12", unmatted, unframed . **435.00**
Audubon, John James, etching, engraving, aquatint and hand-colored, wove paper with J Whatman watermark, Blue Gray Flycatcher, 1830, Havell ed, full typographical inscription, 19⅜ × 12¼", good con-

dition, taped edge tears, mount staining, scattered foxing and tape residue, creasing **450.00**

Baumann, Gustave, Morning Sun, color woodcut on cream paper, edition of 125, sgd "Gustave Baumann" in pencil with hand-in-heart chop lower right, inscribed "II 53 125" in pencil lower right, titled in pencil lower left, 10⅞ × 9¾", framed **7,475.00**

Beal, Reynolds, Cape Cod, etching, sgd and dated in pencil lower left "Reynolds Beal/1915," full margins, 7¾ × 9¾", matted and framed **250.00**

Benson, Frank Weston
Geese, 1917, drypoint on paper, fourth published state, edition of 27, sgd "Frank W. Benson" in lower left, 10¼ × 15", framed **1,840.00**
The Landing, 1915, trial proof, etching on paper, unsgd, inscribed "...Trial proof not mentioned in Paff—before removal of lightly etched float to left of man in boat..." on reverse, 7 1/2 × 11⅜", matted, unframed **2,645.00**
Portsmouth Harbor, 1916, etching on paper with Shogun watermark, published state, edition of 11, sgd "Frank W. Benson" in lower left, numbered in pencil lower right, initialed and dated in plate lower left, 7¼ × 5⅞", matted, unframed **3,220.00**
Rain Squall, 1931, etching on laid paper, published state, edition of 150, sgd "Frank W. Benson" in lower left, 6⅞ × 8¾", unmatted, unframed **1,610.00**
Second Island Outlet, 1916, etching on laid paper with indistinct watermark, published state, edition of 85, sgd "Frank W. Benson" in lower left, 8⅞ × 13⅞", matted, unframed **1,380.00**

Benton, Thomas Hart, litho on wove paper, edition of 250, published by Associated American Artists, New York, sgd "Benton" in pencil lower right and in the matrix lower left
Loading Corn, 1945, 9½ × 12¾", framed **1,150.00**
Night Firing, 1943, also identified from AAA label on reverse, 8½ × 13¼", framed **550.00**
The Race, 1942, 8⅞ × 13¼", matted, unframed ...**6,950.00**

Berry, Carroll Thayer, Petunia, color woodcut on paper, sgd "Carroll Thayer Berry" in pencil lower right, titled in pencil lower left, 8⅝ × 6½" d, framed **230.00**

Birch, William Russell, High Street from the Country Marketplace, Philadelphia-Procession of the Death of George Washington, engraving, 8¼ × 11" **250.00**

Chagall, Marc, Solomon, sgd in pencil, color litho, numbered 34/75, 1956, cream wove paper, full sheet printed to edges, 14 × 10¼" **1,500.00**

Currier & Ives
American Fruit Piece, C#161, hand-colored litho, tinted background identified in the matrix, period frame, 23" h, 30¼" w **1,265.00**
American Homestead Spring, C#170, hand-colored litho, matted and framed, tear in left margin, 13¼" h, 17½" w **165.00**
American Homestead Summer, C#171, hand-colored litho, matted and framed, 14½" d, 18½" w . **200.00**
California Scenery, Seal Rocks—Point Lobos, C#768, hand-colored litho, stains, framed, 14" h, 18½" w **360.00**
Darktown Fire Brigade—Saved!, C#1391, chromolitho, matted and framed, small damage lower right corner, 14¼" h, 17¼" w **250.00**
Darktown Fire Brigade to the Rescue!, C#1396, chromolitho, matted and framed, 14¼" h, 17¼" w ... **250.00**
Hudson River—Crow Nest, C#2978, hand-colored litho, minor stains, framed, 14" h, 18½" w **275.00**
Lieut Genl Ulysses S Grant, C#3491, hand-colored litho, stains, framed, 16½" h, 12½" w **165.00**
Midnight Race on the Mississippi, C#4117, hand-colored litho, cleaned, some recoloring, tears in margins, matted and framed, 17½" h, 21¼" w .. **250.00**
Skating Scene Moonlight, C#5546, hand-colored litho, cleaned, tear in margin, matted and framed, 12½" h, 16¾" w **470.00**
Sunnyside—On the Hudson, C#5893, hand-colored litho, minor stains, matted and framed, 14½" h, 18½" w **110.00**
Vase of Fruit, C#6364, hand-colored litho, medium folio, minor stains, matted and framed, 21¼" h, 20¼" w **385.00**

Currier, Nathaniel
Naval Heroes of the United States, C#4397, hand-colored litho, minor stains, framed, 14¼" h, 18¼" w **330.00**
Thomas W. Dore, Elected Governor of Rhode Island, hand-colored litho, period frame, 13¾ × 9½" .. **150.00**

Darley, F.O.C. and A. H. Ritchie, On the March to the Sea, hand colored, sgd in pencil by both artist and engraver, artist's proof before title, General Sherman mounted watching his troops burn, pillage, and destroy rail tracks, telegraph poles, etc, freed slaves coming in, American flag held high, bridge in distance being destroyed, 42 × 27" plus frame, publisher's description and copy of invoice for hand coloring included **1,300.00**

Durer, Albrecht, Saint Christopher, 1521, engraving on paper, later impression, monogrammed and dated 1521 within plate, 4⅝ × 2⅞", framed **1,265.00**

Hassam, Childe, The Lion Gardner House, Easthampton, 1920, etching on heavy paper, monogrammed lower right, inscribed "...Oct 8 1920, Easthampton" in the plate lower right, 10 × 14" **6,325.00**

Icart, Louis, color etching with aquatint and hand coloring on paper, sgd "Louis Icart" in pencil lower right, artist's dry stamp lower left, identified in inscription in plate upper left

Frolicking, 1920, inscribed "36" in pencil lower left, oval plate, 14¾ × 19", framed 1,100.00

Jeunesse, 1930, inscribed "40/500" in pencil lower left, 24½ × 16", framed 3,800.00

Joie de Vivre, 1929, inscribed "A 104" in ink lower left, added coloring, 24½ × 16", framed 3,565.00

L'Elan, 1928, inscribed "E107" in pencil lower left, 20¼ × 14¾", framed 3,450.00

Les Lis, 1934, 28½ × 19½", framed, glued between mats 3,565.00

Vitesse, 1928, inscribed "351" in pencil lower left, 15⅝ × 25¾", framed 3,450.00

Kellogg

Battle of Champion Hills, MS, Mar 16, 1863, litho . 125.00

Rural Sweets, litho 95.00

Kent, Rockwell, Diver, 1931, wood engraving on paper with Japan watermark, edition of 150, sgd "Rockwell Kent," 7⅞ × 5⅜", matted, unframed 980.00

Marsh, Reginald, etching on heavy paper, from the Whitney Museum edition of 100, 1969, Whitney Museum dry stamp lower right, annotated in lower margin, unmatted, unframed

Irving Place Burlesque, 1930, 9¾ × 11⅞" 230.00

Loco—Going Through Jersey City, 1930, 4⅞ × 9⅞" 230.00

Mucha, Alphonse, Emerald, 1900, color litho, sgd lower right, 38 × 15¼", framed 6,000.00

Parish, Maxfield, Daybreak, marked "The House of Art, N.Y.," 13 × 20½", framed 200.00

Patterson, Margaret Jordan, color woodcut on paper

In the High Hills, sgd "Margaret Patterson" in pencil lower right, indistinctly inscribed in pencil lower left, 11 × 8¾", framed 1,380.00

Morning Glories, edition of 100, sgd "Margaret J. Patterson" in pencil lower right and lower center, titled in pencil lower right, numbered "#4/100," 10 × 7¼", framed 1,380.00

Thayer & Co, Boston, Lithographers, View of the Grand Mass Washingtonian Convention on Boston Common,, on the 30th of May, 1844, litho, hand colored on paper, full typographical inscription below image, 8½ × 13½" image, period burl frame, minor staining and fading 200.00

Wengenroth, Stow

Barn Owl, 1971, litho on wove paper, edition of 100, sgd "Stow Wengenroth" in pencil lower right, numbered "Ed/100" in pencil lower left, identified on label from the Kennedy Galleries, NY, affixed to mat, 9½ × 15⅛", matted, unframed 435.00

Bird of Freedom, 1942, litho on paper, edition of 200, sgd "Stow Wengenroth" in pencil lower right, 15¾ × 11¾", framed 345.00

Whistler, James Abbott McNeill, The Rag Gatherers, 1858, etching on laid paper, fifth state, sgd and dated "Whistler 1858" in plate center right, 6⅛ × 3½", matted, unframed 520.00

Wilkins, Gladys Murphy, A Bouquet of Gladiolus, color woodcut on paper, edition of 50, sgd "Gladys M. Wilkins" in pencil lower right, titled and numbered "...2/50" in pencil lower left, 11¾ × 10¼", framed 320.00

Wood, Grant, litho on paper, edition of 250, published

Smith, Jessie Wilcox, "An Hour Slipped By," Child's Garden of Verses, color, $30.00.

by "Associated American Artists, New York," sgd "Grant Wood" in pencil lower right, identified from AAA label

Approaching Storm, 1940, 11⅞ × 8⅞" 4,025.00

In the Spring, 1939, 8⅞ × 11⅞" 1,610.00

PRINTS, JAPANESE

History: Buying Japanese woodblock prints requires attention to detail and abundant knowledge of the subject. The quality of the impression (good, moderate, or weak), the color, and condition are critical. Various states and strikes of the same print cause prices to fluctuate. Knowing the proper publisher and censor's seals is helpful in identifying an original print.

Most prints were copied and issued in popular versions. These represent the vast majority of the prints found in the marketplace today. These popular versions should be viewed solely as decorative since they have little monetary value.

A novice buyer should seek expert advice before buying. Talk with a specialized dealer, museum curator, or auction division head.

The following terms are used to describe sizes: chuban, 7½ × 10 inches; hosoban, 6 × 12 inches; and oban, 10 × 15 inches. Tat-e is a vertical print; yoko-e a horizontal one.

Collectors' Club: Ukiyo-E Society of America, Inc., FDR Station, PO Box 665, New York, NY 10150.

Museum: Honolulu Academy of Fine Arts, Honolulu, HI.

Note: The listings below include the large amount of detail necessary to determine value. Condition and impression are good unless indicated otherwise.

Chickanobu, two framed triptychs, one of women observing iris garden, other of a gathering of women . 200.00

Eisen, courtesan composing poetry, landscape inset printed in blue, good impression and color, framed 230.00

Harunobu, chuban of woman standing in doorway, young man kneeling on verandah, very good impression, faded, toned 400.00

Hawagawa Mitsunobu, album sheet, samizuri-e, two women entertain man with shadow puppets and music, c1730, good impression, soil 490.00

Hirosada, chuban of actor, mid 19th C, good impression and color 290.00

Hiroshi Yoshida

Ajmer Gate, Jaipur, sgd in pencil in margin, Jizuri seal, good impression and color, 14¾ × 9¾″ image size 400.00

Figures on a road, watercolor on paper, sgd lower right, "H Yoshida, 1903," 19⅜ × 26″ 3,740.00

Small Town in Chugoku, pencil sgd in margin, good color and impression 400.00

Hiroshige

Entrance gate at Enoshima from "Thirty-six Views of Fuji," 1858, very good impression and color, centerfold, some soil in margins 290.00

Night view of Sanya Canal from "One Hundred Famous Views of Edo," 1857, moderate impression, good color, backed, centerfold, torn 115.00

Night view of lake with fishermen in small boats, from series "Sixty-odd views of the Provinces," very good impression, faded, backed 320.00

Nihonbshi from "One Hundred Views of Edo," 1856, good impression, faded 375.00

Okabe from "Reisho Tokaido," oban yoko-e, c1850, very good impression and condition, slightly faded 435.00

Scene overlooking river, Fuji in background, from "Thirty-six Views of Fuji," 1858, good impression and color, full margins 290.00

Hiroshige II, townspeople from "Thirty-six Views of Fuji," 1860, very good impression and color, album backing 290.00

Hokusai, Sinsho Suwa-Ko, Lake Suma in Shiano Province, from Fugaku sanjurokkei series, "Thirty-six Views of Mt Fuji," sgd Zen Hokusai litsui hitsu, publisher's seal Eljudo, 10 × 15″ 4,250.00

Ishikawa, fisherman's village, watercolor on paper, sgd "T. Ishikawa" bottom left, toned, tear to edge, 19⅛ × 13⅛″ 2,645.00

Junichiro Sekino, II ne etat, pencil sgd lower right 53, 52/100 .... 690.00

Koryusai, chuban of two woman in an interior, c1770, good impression, some fading and soil 1,495.00

Kunimasu, hanshi-bon, actor, c1850, good impression and color 320.00

Kunisada

Fan print of Genji on shore with two women, fair impression, worn 60.00

Portrait of woman in front of mirror in an interior, c1835, good impression and color, centerfold .. 316.00

Kuniyoshi, Tuankuk print showing four drunken badgers dancing and singing, illus text passes, sgd "Ichiyusai Kuniyoski-giga," and one Nanushi and anonymous publisher's seal, fair impression and color, slightly faded 10 × 15″ 200.00

Okiie Hashimoto, girl with flowers, pencil sgd in lower margin, dated 1952, artist's seal within image, printed character to right margin, 15½ × 21½″ 805.00

Hokusai, The Aoigaka Falls in the Eastern Capitol, from the "A Journey to the Waterfalls of All the Provinces" series, sgd "Zen Hokusai litsu Hitsu," published by Eijudo, oban tate-e, $3,080.00. Photograph courtesy of Skinner, Inc.

Sadanubo, chuban yoko-e of snowy landscape, mid 19th C, good impression and color, stain to left third 145.00

Toyohiro, tiger, black and gray printed tones, very good impression, some soil 575.00

Toyokuni, portrait of Bando Mitsugoro, good impression, some wear 80.00

Toyokuni III

Ishikwa Goeman in combat, inset of temple by student of Kunisada, from "Sixty-odd Provinces," c1845 .... 145.00

Pentaptych of actors by river, 1858, very good impression, some fading, mat line, stains to edges . 435.00

Utamaro, woman on tortoise with fan, toned, faded ... 175.00

Yoshitora, triptych of goddess rising from ocean, good impression and color, general wear, framed 230.00

PURPLE SLAG (MARBLE GLASS)

History: Challinor, Taylor & Co., Tarantum, Pennsylvania, c1870s–1880s, was the largest producer of purple slag in the United States. Since the quality of pieces varies considerably, there is no doubt other American firms made it as well.

Purple slag also was made in England. English pieces are marked with British Registry marks.

Other slag colors, such as blue, green, and orange, were used, but examples are rare.

Videotape: National Imperial Glass Collectors Society, *Glass of Yesteryears, The Renaissance of Slag Glass by Imperial,* RoCliff Communications, 1994.

Additional Listings: Greentown Glass (chocolate slag) and Pink Slag.

Reproduction Alert: Purple slag has been heavily reproduced over the years and still is reproduced at present.

Bowl, 8″ d, Dart Bar	**50.00**
Butter Dish, cov, cow finial	**145.00**
Cake Stand, plain	**125.00**
Celery Vase, Jeweled Star, Challinor-Taylor, 1880s	**125.00**
Compote, Beaded Hearts	**95.00**
Match Holder, dolphin head	**75.00**
Mug, Bird in Nest, cat on base	**105.00**
Plate, 10″ d, lattice edge	**75.00**
Rose Bowl, ribbed, Northwood	**90.00**
Sauce Dish, Majestic Crown, Challinor-Taylor, 4″ d	**25.00**
Sherbet, Majestic Crown, Challinor-Taylor, 4″ d	**35.00**
Sugar, cov, Fluted	**195.00**
Toothpick, Scroll with Acanthus	**150.00**

Tumbler, purple and white swirls, paneled body, 3¼″ h, $48.00.

QUEZAL

Quezal

History: The Quezal Art Glass Decorating Company, named for the quetzal—a bird with brilliantly colored feathers—was organized in 1901 in Brooklyn, New York, by Martin Bach and Thomas Johnson, two disgruntled Tiffany workers. They soon hired Percy Britton and William Wiedebine, two more Tiffany employees.

The first products, which are unmarked, were exact Tiffany imitations. Quezal pieces differ from Tiffany pieces in that they are more defined and the decorations are more visible and brighter. No new techniques were developed by Quezal.

Johnson left in 1905. T. Conrad Vahlsing, Bach's son-in-law, joined the firm in 1918 but left with Paul Frank in 1920 to form Lustre Art Glass Company, which copied Quezal pieces. Martin Bach died in 1924 and by 1925 Quezal had ceased operations.

Marks: The "Quezal" trademark was first used in 1902 and was placed on the base of vases and bowls and on the rims of shades. The acid-etched or engraved letters vary in size and may be found in amber, black, or gold. A printed label which includes an illustration of a quetzal was used briefly in 1907.

Bowl, 12″ d, peacock blue, hammered silver base, marked "Oscar B Bach, NY"	**600.00**
Candlesticks, pr, 6½″ h, flared bobeche rim, ringed hollow baluster opal body, overall orange-green King Tut irid dec, sgd	**1,250.00**
Jack-in-the-Pulpit Vase, 11″ h, floriform, stretched irid blossom and throat, gold and white pulled feathers in stem and platform base, marked "Quezal/M/3″	**2,990.00**
Lamp Shade, 5″ h, pulled feather, gold irid int., sgd inside top fitter rim, price for 3-pc set	**600.00**
Nut Dish, triangular rim, gently rounded body, gold irid, inscribed "Quezal"	**150.00**
Vase	
4¾″ h, 6″ d, floriform, opal, gold luster lining, green and gold pulled feather dec, sgd "Quezal T457"	**575.00**

Vase, gold calcite ground, light green draping vines, heart-shaped leaves, 12″ h, $1,400.00.

8″ h, ovoid, flared rim, applied gold disk base, opal glass, gold int., broad random gold irid linear dec, sgd "Quezal"	**250.00**
8½″ h, flask form, brilliant rainbow irid, finely chased silver overlay carnation blossoms, stems, and leaves, inscribed "Quezal," Alvin Corp mark stamped on silver	**1,250.00**

QUILTS

History: Quilts have been passed down as family heirlooms for many generations. Each one is unique. The same pattern may have hundreds of variations in both color and design.

The advent of the sewing machine increased, not decreased, the number of quilts which were made. Quilts are still being sewn today.

References: Cuesta Benberry, *Always There: The African-American Presence in American Quilts,* Kentucky Quilt Project, 1992; Mary Clare Clark, *Collectible Quilts,* Running Press, Courage Books, 1994; Liz Greenbacker and Kathleen Barach, *Quilts,* Avon Books, 1992; Carter Houck, *The Quilt Encyclopedia Illustrated,* Harry N. Abrams and Museum of American Folk Art, 1991;

Jeanette Lasansky et. al., *On the Cutting Edge,* Oral Traditions Project, 1994; Dana G. Morykan and Harry L. Rinker, *Warman's Country Antiques & Collectibles,* Third Edition, Wallace-Homestead, 1996; Patsy and Myron Orlofsky, *Quilts in America,* Abbeville Press, 1992; Nancy and Donald Roan, *Lest I Shall be Forgotten,* Goschenhoppen Historians, Inc. (PO Box 476, Green Lane, PA 18054), 1993.

Periodicals: *Quilt Journal,* 635 W Main St, Louisville, KY 40202; *Quilters Newsletter,* PO Box 4101, Golden, CO 80401; *Vintage Quilt Newsletter,* 1305 Morphy St, Great Bend, KS 67530.

Collectors' Clubs: American Quilt Study Group, 660 Mission St, Ste 400, San Francisco, CA 94105; American Quilter's Society, PO Box 3290, Paducah, KY 42001; National Quilting Assoc, Inc, PO Box 393, Ellicott City, MD 21043.

Museums: Doll & Quilts Barn, Rocky Ridge, MD; Museum of the American Quilter's Society, Paducah, KY; National Museum of American History, Washington, DC; New England Quilt Museum, Lowell, MA.

Notes: The key considerations for price are age, condition, aesthetic appeal, and design. Prices are now level, although the very finest examples continue to bring record prices.

Appliqué
  Floral medallions
    Nine
      Red and green, well quilted, 70 × 70″ **350.00**
      Stylized florals, vine floral border, boldly executed date and initials, letters flanked by flowers, "1850, L. D.," deep sage green calico, solid red and yellow, pink calico, Dayton, OH area, some overall wear and soiling, 76 × 90″ **1,265.00**
    Sixteen, two shades of pink on white, border swags, well quilted, 81 × 81″ **350.00**
  Squares, twelve white squares, each square with appliquéd yellow flower, embroidered details, pale yellow grid, overall wear, machine sewn binding, 65 × 82″ **225.00**
  Sunbonnet Sue, multicolored, white ground, 1930, 62 × 76″ **300.00**
Crazy, Victorian, parlor, various scrap fabrics, deterioration to fabric
    c1885, various embroidered motifs **625.00**
    c1898, red velvet border, four embroidered corner panels, field of silk, satin, etc, scraps, initialed "JM," dated **425.00**
Pieced
  Barn Raising, satin, salmon, blue, and yellow, 1940, 80 × 80″ **450.00**
  Baskets, thirty six baskets, brown, red, and goldenrod on brown and white print squares, red and brown grid, stains, some color loss, worn whip-stitched binding, 71 × 71″ **275.00**
  Bow Tie, blue, white, and yellow, 1930, 56 × 74″ **160.00**
  Checkerboard
    Multicolored calico, white and red border stripes, minor stains, 73 × 73″ **350.00**
    White and salmon, fan of pastel prints in each salmon square, overall wear, some fading, light stains, 73 × 89″ **125.00**

Chinese Coins, multicolored, 1940, 78 × 78″ **195.00**
Diamonds, fifteen diamonds each with quilted star-flower, gold calico and white mosaic pattern ground, some overall wear, light stains, 70 x 83″ **200.00**
Dresden Plate, pastels on white, 1930, 80 × 80″ .. **495.00**
Drunkard's Path, pastel blue, pink, lavender, and yellow on white, 71 × 86″ **250.00**
Fans and stripes with embroidery, blue, deep pink, yellow, purple, and green on white, 85 × 86″ .. **350.00**
Flower Garden, yellow, pink, blue, green, and white, 1930, 76 × 82″ **495.00**
Flying geese bands, multicolored prints and solids, red calico bars, minor stains, 78 × 88″ **275.00**
Four Patch, postage stamp, multicolored, 1930, 66 × 68″ **400.00**
Honeycomb, multicolored on red, 1930, 80 × 82″ **400.00**
House pattern, sixteen houses, multicolored prints, white ground, lavender border, very worn, faded, stains, 73 × 75″ **110.00**
Irish Chain, olive and red, white ground, unusual border design, initial "CK" in one sq, some wear, light stains, 79 × 79″ **675.00**
Jacob's Ladder, blue and white, 1900, 78 × 80″ ...**1,500.00**
Joseph's Coat, multicolored, red trim, unused, 1920, 80 × 86″ **1,295.00**
Kansas Trouble, yellow and multicolored feed sacks, 1930, 60 × 76″ **225.00**
Lone Star, multicolored, white ground, 1920, 83 × 85″ **750.00**
Lovers Knot, blue and white, 1930, 74 × 76″ **650.00**
Medallions, twenty-five medallions in green and pink calico on white, wreaths and meandering border quilting, ink center inscription "Mary

Album, top, pieced and appliqued, green, red, and blue patches, white ground, sixteen square panels of flowers and foliage, swag and bow border, 19th C, 98 × 98″, $1,540.00. Photograph courtesy of Butterfield & Butterfield.

E...Presented from Mother, Nov 5," found in OH, very minor wear and stains, 106 × 107" 850.00

Nine patch, thirty six squares of pink and blue, alternating with deep yellow calico, machine-sewn binding, wear, 77 × 78" 75.00

Ocean Waves, multicolored on white, 1940, 68 × 88" 275.00

Pinwheels, pale yellow calico alternating with puffed flowers on white ground, minor stains, 80 × 92" 400.00

Snails Trails, blue and yellow, 1930, 68 × 79" 595.00

Star of Bethlehem, multicolored, shirting-type ground, 1900, 78 × 78" 575.00

Stars

Green and red stars, white ground, worn and stained, holes and damage to backing, 80 × 100" 175.00

Red and white calico, 68 × 84" 385.00

Sunshine and Shadow, pastels, 1940, 76 × 84" ... 500.00

Trip around the World, multicolored, 1930, 80 × 81" 500.00

Zigzag, red, blue, and white, 1930, 70 × 78" 275.00

Pieced and Appliquéd

Fruit appliqués in deep yellow and green, yellow and white blocks, 62 × 82" 325.00

Iris pattern, lavender, periwinkle, and light green, white ground, sawtooth and scalloped border, wear and fading, 75 × 85" 140.00

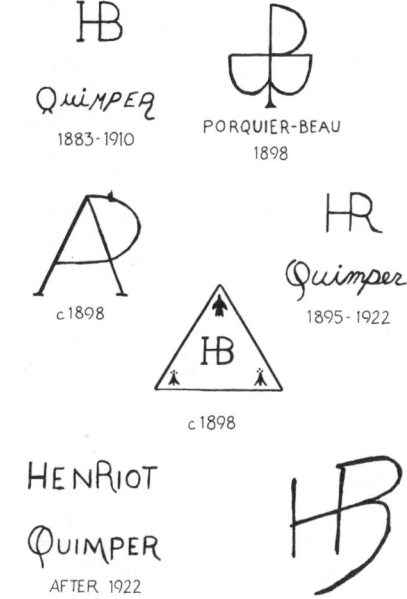

HB
QUIMPER
1883-1910

PORQUIER-BEAU
1898

AP
c1898

HB
c1898

HR
Quimper
1895-1922

HENRIOT
QUIMPER
AFTER 1922

HB

QUIMPER

History: Quimper faience, dating back to the 17th century, is named for Quimper, a French town where numerous potteries were located. Several mergers resulted in the evolution of two major houses—the Jules Henriot and Hubaudière-Bousquet factories.

The peasant design first appeared in the 1860s, and many variations exist. Florals and geometrics, equally popular, also were produced in large quantities. During the 1920s the Hubaudière-Bousquet factory introduced the Odetta line which utilized a stone body and Art Deco decorations.

The two major houses merged in 1968, the products retaining the individual characteristics and marks of the originals. The concern suffered from labor problems in the 1980s and was purchased by an American group.

Marks: The "HR" and "HR Quimper" marks are found on Henriot pieces prior to 1922. The "Henriot Quimper" mark was used after 1922. The "HB" mark covers a long time span. Numbers or dots and dashes were added for inventory purposes and are found on later pieces. Most marks are in blue or black. Pieces ordered by department stores, such as Macy's and Carson Pirie Scott, carry the store mark along with the factory mark, making them less desirable to collectors. A comprehensive list of marks is found in Bondhus's book.

References: Susan and Al Bagdade, *Warman's English & Continental Pottery & Porcelain,* Second Edition, Wallace-Homestead, 1991; Sandra V. Bondhus, *Quimper Potter,* published by author, reprinted 1985; Millicent Mali, *Quimper Faience,* Airon, 1979; Ann Marie O'Neill, *Quimper Pottery,* Schiffer Publishing, 1994; Marjatta Taburet, *La Faience de Quimper,* Editions Sous le Vent, 1979, French text.

Museums: Musee des Faiences de Quimper, Quimper, France; Victoria and Albert Museum, French Ceramic Dept, London, England.

Advisors: Susan and Al Bagdade.

Ashtray, 3¾" l, 2¾" w, clover shape, male peasant, florals, yellow ground, marked "HenRiot Quimper France" 50.00

Barometer, 7¾" h, heart shape, seated female peasant with distaff at right, male peasant at left, crest of Brittany at top in flower garland, blue flowers with leaves on edge, marked "HB" 2,000.00

Bell, 3½" h, figural female peasant, typical colors, marked "HenRiot Quimper France" 235.00

Box, 5½" l, 4" w, 3½" h, male peasant playing bagpipes, Ivoire Corbeille design, cream ground, four feet, marked "HenRiot Quimper France" 105.00

Candlesticks, pr, 8" h, figural male peasant in cobalt blue shirt, green vest, orange-yellow pants, female with green blouse, blue vest, pink apron with pink four-dot design, pot on each head, marked "HenRiot Quimper," repair to one pot 650.00

Celery Dish, 10½" l, 6¾" w, frontal view of female peasant, green blouse, blue skirt, yellow apron, holding flowers, red and green floral springs with yellow and blue forget-me-nots, blue-outlined wavy dentil rim, "Henriot Quimper Ravier" 450.00

Chamberstick, 6¼" d, 3" h, female peasant with scattered florals, yellow ground, marked "HenRiot Quimper France" 295.00

Cheese Dish, cov, 9" d, seated blond male peasant playing flute, scattered red and yellow blossoms, red crisscross and blue dot alternating panels on body and base, green and yellow serpent handle, "HenRiot Quimper 23" 275.00

Cider Jug, 8" h, male peasant on side, scattered flowers on body, blue striped side and top handle, "HenRiot Quimper France" 220.00

Coffee Pot, 10" h, female peasant on side, vertical red and green florals on body, blue sponged handle, yel-

Inkwell, heart shape, red, yellow, and blue peasant figures, band of red, yellow, blue, and green at waist, three blue starburst-outlined holes, blue outlined rim, "HB Quimper" mark, $275.00.

low and blue striped border, "HenRiot Quimper France 744 ter" **209.00**

Compote, 5½" h, 9½" d, pedestal base, frontal view of peasant woman in green blouse, purple apron, blue skirt, band on florals on int. and base, blue-outlined shaped rim, "HR Quimper" **350.00**

Crepe Server, 13" l, 6" w, young couple holding hands, girl with blue-shaded outfit and pink apron, boy with olive jacket, dark blue pants and hat, dark blue on yellow acanthus border, marked "Porquier-Beau" . **990.00**

Cup and Saucer
  Female peasant on front, scattered red and green florals, blue striped handle, yellow and blue striped rims, marked "HenRiot Quimper France" **50.00**
  Male peasant on front, scattered florals, saucer with band of florals, gray glaze, oversize, vertical ribbing, marked "HenRiot Quimper France" **110.00**

Dish, 8¼" h, oval, peasant man with hand in pocket, goose flapping wings, green decor riche border on yellow ground, shaped rim, marked "PB Quimper," c1915 .... **500.00**

Eggcup, 3⅝" h, male peasant with orange shirt, red pants, yellow stockings, red, blue, and green floral band, yellow and blue striped rim, marked "HenRiot Quimper France 272" **95.00**

Figure
  12½" h, St. Vierge, white dress with red and green sprigs and four blue dot design, yellow and red crown, Christ child in arms, marked "HR Quimper" **275.00**
  16" h, young girl holding bowl, floral shawl, yellow apron with florals, black dress, Quillivic **725.00**

Fish Platter, 24" l, male playing flute, seated female with distaff, trees and fences in background, scattered red and green florals with four dots, shaped rim, marked "HB" **1,000.00**

Gravy Boat, 9¼" l, 3⅝" h, attached undertray, curved oval shape, male peasant on side with band of red, green, and blue florals, blue and yellow striped rim, marked "HenRiot Quimper France 584" **225.00**

Jardiniere, 16¼" l, center cartouche of three children in meadow, multicolored florals, blue decor riche bor-

der, blue, yellow, and green serpent handle, marked "HenRiot Quimper France" **1,275.00**

Menu
  4¼" h, shield shape, female peasant with basket, black "Menu," blue chain border, marked "HB,"c1885 .... **350.00**
  6" h, rococo form, standing male peasant playing bagpipe, floral band and "Menu" at top, blue, green, and yellow border, marked "HR Quimper" **325.00**

Pitcher, 8½" h, melon shape, female peasant on front panel, blue cabbage rose with green, red, and blue florals on side panels, blue intertwined S panel outline, floral band on neck, blue striped handle with orange strip, marked "HenRiot Quimper France" .. **275.00**

Pitcher, male peasant on side, center band of blue, iron-red, yellow flowers with green leaves, blue and yellow banded borders, "HenRiot Quimper France" mark, 6⅛" h, $175.00.

Planter, 9" l, 8" h, figural swan, cartouche of female peasant on breast, yellow and blue sponged body feathers, blue wing feathers, yellow and gold head, marked "HenRiot Quimper France" **350.00**

Plate
  8¼" sq, clipped corners, female peasant in center with red, yellow, blue, and green stalk, blue florals outline border panels, dots and arrows at corners, marked "HenRiot Quimper France" **130.00**
  9" d, red, yellow, and blue geometric center, blue banded rim, unmarked **300.00**
  9¼" d
    Cobalt spray of cornflowers with green stems, flying insect near rim, yellow-outlined shaped rim, marked "Porquier-Beau" **650.00**
    Dancing couple in meadow, forest in background, floral panels alternating with Brittany crests on border, shaped rim, marked "HenRiot Quimper France" **350.00**
    Seated female peasant sewing, wooden fence and

Plate, red-and-blue florals, "HB Quimper" mark, 8³/₈" h, $175.00.

building in background, green decor riche border on yellow ground, Brittany crest at top, marked "Porquier-Beau" 950.00

9³/₄" d, frontal view of male peasant, flat hat, maroon shirt, blue pantaloons, yellow stockings, border with scattered florals, shaped rim, marked "HB" 275.00

10" d, relief-molded peasants with instruments, Modern Movement, brown, yellow, black, and orange, marked "HenRiot Quimper" 75.00

10" l, fish shape, frontal view of blond male peasant on one, side view of female with umbrella on other, speckled fish heads, traditional colors, both marked "HenRiot Quimper France," price for pr 475.00

10¹/₄" d, frontal view of male peasant with arms folded on one, female peasant with basket on other, blue decor riche border, Quimper crest at top, orange shaped rim, both marked "HenRiot Quimper France," price for pr 595.00

Platter, 11" l, 8" w, rect with cut corners, large red and blue open flower head, gold wheat stalks, single stroke border, fleur-de-lys in corners, blue-outlined rim, marked "HR Quimper France" 231.00

Porringer, cov, 7" handle to handle, female peasant with scattered florals, yellow ground, blue sponging, marked "HR Quimper France" 65.00

Quintal, 6" h, frontal view of female peasant holding flowers, green blouse, blue skirt, yellow apron, scattered florals, floral spray on reverse, marked "HenRiot Quimper France" 165.00

Relish Dish, 7¹/₂" l, frontal view of male peasant with arms crossed, scattered florals, molded yellow bow at top, marked "HR Quimper" on face 170.00

Snuff Bottle, 3¹/₂" h, figural fleur-de-lys, half light blue, half dark blue, cork stopper, marked "HR Quimper" 650.00

Soup Bowl, cov, 6³/₄" d, 5" h, with underplate, band of red and green florals around waist, female peasant on cov, shell knob, marked "HenRiot Quimper France" 165.00

Syrup Jug, cov, 5³/₄" h, male peasant on front, blue, red, and green vertical florals with four blue dot design, blue-outlined rims, blue striped handle with orange trim, marked "HB Quimper France" 250.00

Tea Set, 9" h pot, swirl mold, teapot with two male peasants with instruments, reverse with spray of ajone and bleeding hearts, blue acanthus borders, blue sponged handles, cov sugar with seated peasant playing flute, creamer with dancing couple, marked "HenRiot Quimper," price for set 950.00

Teapot, 6" h, hexagonal body, male and female peasants on sides, vertical florals, four blue dot and blue striped spout, blue striped and yellow-gold wishbone handle, marked "HenRiot Quimper France 95" 286.00

Trivet, 6" sq, ftd, female peasant with scattered florals, yellow ground, marked "HenRiot Quimper France" 125.00

Tulipiere, 7¹/₂" h, female peasant holding distaff, floral sprays at sides, blue dot and V-chain outline, blue and red lattice on ends and base, stylized red daisy and blue flower on reverse panel, marked "HenRiot Quimper France" 395.00

Tureen, 11" handle to handle, 10" h, female peasant on body, four blue dot design, red, yellow, blue, and green floral sprigs, male peasant on cov, blue pointed knob, blue-striped scroll handles, blue and yellow striped borders, marked "HR Quimper" on body ..1,450.00

Vase

8" h, tapered shape, Modern Movement, three walking female peasants, cream clouds in background, black, pale blue, yellow, and gold stylized borders, sgd "JE Sevellec," marked "HenRiot Quimper France" 425.00

10" h, egg shape, three figural serpent feet, dancing couple on front, blue decor riche border with yellow-outlined rim, marked "HenRiot Quimper France," c1922–25 .... 650.00

12¹/₂" h, horseshoe shape, male peasants playing instruments on sides, view of Quimper on base, blue decor riche border, figural serpent handles, yellow-outlined body, marked "HR Quimper France," c1900 ....1,350.00

15¹/₄" h, bulbous base, narrow neck, flared lip, two male peasants on face, one playing lute, other playing bagpipe, pink and yellow botanical spray on reverse, vertical blue acanthus on sides, Quimper crest on neck, marked "HenRiot Quimper" . 850.00

Wall Pocket, 7¹/₂" h, overlapped cone shape, male peasant on one, female on other, scattered florals and four dot design, blue flower head over hole, marked "HB," price for pr 425.00

Watch Safe, 8" h, seated male and female peasants at base, blue rose at top, scattered florals, blue dot border, blue sponged sides, marked "HenRiot Quimper France" 550.00

RADIOS

History: The radio was invented over 100 years ago. Marconi was the first to assemble and employ the transmission and reception instruments that permitted the sending of electric messages without the use of direct connections. Between 1905 and the end of World War I, many technical advances affected the "wireless," including the invention of the vacuum tube by DeForest. Technology continued its progress, and radios filled the entertainment needs of the average family in the 1920s.

Changes in design, style, and technology brought the radio

from the black boxes of the 1920s to the stylish furniture pieces and console models of the 1930s and 1940s, to midget models of the 1950s, and finally to the high-tech radios of the 1980s.

References: Marty and Sue Bunis, *Collector's Guide to Antique Radios,* Fourth Edition Collector Books, 1996; ———, *Collector's Guide to Transistor Radios,* Collector Books, 1994; Marty Bunis and Robert Breed, *Collector's Guide to Novelty Radios,* Collector Books, 1994; Philip Collins, *Radio Redux,* Chronicle Books, 1992; Chuck Dachis, *Radios by Hallicrafters,* Schiffer Publishing, 1996; Alan Douglas, *Radio Manufacturers of the 1920s,* Vol. 1, (1988), Vol. 2 (1989), Vol. 3 (1991), Vestal Press; Roger Handy, Maureen Erbe, and Aileen Farnan Antonier, *Made in Japan,* Chronicle Books, 1993; David Johnson, *Antique Radio Restoration Guide,* Second Edition, Wallace-Homestead, 1992; David R. and Robert A. Lane, *Transistor Radios,* Wallace-Homestead, 1994; Harry Poster, *Poster's Radio & Television Price Guide,* Second Edition, Wallace-Homestead, 1994; Ron Ramirez, *Philco Radio,* Schiffer Publishing, 1993.

Periodicals: *Antique Radio Classified,* PO Box 2, Carlisle, MA, 01741; *Horn Speaker,* PO Box 1193, Mabank, TX 75147; *Radio Age,* 636 Cambridge Road, Augusta, GA 30909; *Transistor Network,* RR1, Box 36, Bradford, NH 03221.

Collectors' Clubs: Antique Radio Club of America, 300 Washington Trails, Washington, PA 15301; Antique Wireless Assoc, 59 Main St, Bloomfield, NY 14469; New England Antique Radio Club, RR1, Box 36, Bradford, NH 03221; Vintage Radio & Phonograph Society, Inc, PO Box 165345, Irving, TX 75016.

Museums: Antique Wireless Museum, Bloomfield, NY; Caperton's Radio Museum, Louisville, KY; Muchow's Historical Radio Museum, Elgin, IL; Museum of Broadcast Communication, Chicago, IL; Museum of Wonderful Miracles, Minneapolis, MN; New England Wireless and Steam Museum, Inc., East Greenwich, RI; Voice of the Twenties, Orient, NY.

Additional Listings: See *Warman's Americana & Collectibles* for more examples.

Advisor: Lewis S. Walters.

Note: Prices of Catalin radios are dropping by about 10 to 15 percent. Collectors and dealers feel prices for these radios have reached their high side and are falling into a more realistic range.

Admiral
  Portable
    #33-35-37, c1940 .... 25.00
    #218, leatherette, 1958 .... 40.00
    #909, All World, 1960 .... 85.00
    #Y-2127, Imperial 8, 1959 .... 45.00
Air King, tombstone #1946, Art Deco, plastic, 1935 ..3,000.00
Arvin
  Character, Hoppy with lariatenna 475.00
  Table
    #444, midget, red, 1946 .... 100.00
    #522A, ivory metal, 1941 .... 60.00
  Tombstone, #617, Rhythm Maid, 1936 .... 215.00
Atwater Kent
  Breadboard
    Model 9A 550.00
    Model 10 ....1,000.00
    Model 10C 825.00
  Cathedral, #80, 1931 .... 380.00

Table, #55, Keil 225.00
Tombstone, #854, 1935 .... 155.00
Bulova, clock radio
  #100, 1957 .... 40.00
  #120, 1958 .... 40.00
Crosley
  Bandbox, #601, 1927 .... 75.00
  Gemchest, #609, 1928 .... 410.00
  Litfella, 1-N cathedral 175.00
  Pup, with box 560.00
  Sheraton cathedral, 1933 .... 290.00
  Showbox, #706, 1928 .... 100.00
  Super Buddy Boy, #122, 1930 .... 325.00
Dumont, RA-346, table, scroll work, 1956 .... 110.00
Emerson
  AU-190, Catalin, tombstone, 1938 ....1,000.00
  BT-245, Catalin, tombstone, scalloped dial, dark grill,
    1939 ....1,000.00
  #400
    Aristocrat, Catalin, 1940 .... 600.00
    Patriot, 1940 .... 750.00
  #409, Mickey Mouse, wood and metal, black and
    red 1,300.00
  #411, Mickey Mouse, pressed wood, playing instru-
    ment 1,400.00
  #570, Memento, place for pictures, 1945 .... 110.00
  #640, portable, plastic, flip-up front, battery set1950 30.00
  #888, Vanguard, transistor, portable, 1958 .... 60.00
Fada
  #43, cathedral, pressed wood 240.00
  #60W, table, plastic 75.00
  #136, table, Catalin, 1941 ....1,000.00
  #252, table, Catalin, temple, 1941 .... 575.00
Federal
  #58DX, table, 1922 .... 500.00
  #110, table, 1924 .... 425.00
General Electric
  #400, 410, 411, 414, table, all plastic 30.00
  # 515, 517, clock radio, 1950s 30.00
  K-126, console, wood, 1933 .... 150.00
  Tombstone, with stand, 1931 .... 250.00
Grebe
  CR-12, table, 1923 .... 600.00
  MU-1, table, with chain, 1925 .... 200.00
Hallicrafters
  TW-600, portable, map, whip antenna, AC/DC
    battery, 1954 .... 100.00
  TW-200, World Wide 100.00
Majestic
  Charlie McCarthy, 1938 ....1,000.00
  #92, console, 1929 .... 125.00
  #381, Treasure Chest, 1934 .... 225.00
Motorola
  Art Deco, #68X11Q 75.00
  Jet plane, #7X23E, transistor 55.00
  Jewel Box, #5J1 .... 80.00
  ''M'' logo, transistor, 1960 .... 25.00
  Pixie, transistor 45.00
  Ranger
    Portable, leatherette trim 40.00
    Ranger, #700, 1957 .... 45.00
  Table, plastic, 1950s 35.00

Olympic, radio with phonograph, lift top, wood **40.00**
Paragon
    DA-2, table, 1921 .... **450.00**
    RD-5, table, 1922 .... **600.00**
Philco
    T-7-126, transistor, plastic **65.00**
    T1000, table, clock radio **80.00**
    #17, 20, 38, cathedral **250.00**
    #37-62, table, two-tone **75.00**
    #37-602, table, Art Deco grill **90.00**
    #40-180, console, wood **130.00**
    #46-132, table **35.00**
    #49-506, Transitone **35.00**
    #52-544-I, Transitone, 1952 .... **50.00**
Radiobar, complete console, glasses, decanter **1,300.00**
Radio Corporation of America (RCA)
    LaSiesta, 1939 .... **300.00**
    Radiola
        #18 .... **55.00**
        #24 .... **160.00**
        #28, console, highboy **200.00**
        #33 .... **40.00**
        #6X7, table, plastic, 1956 .... **25.00**
        #8BT-7LE, portable, transistor, 1957 .... **35.00**
        #40X56, World's Fair, 1939 .... **975.00**

RCA Victor, Deco, $22.50.

Silvertone (Sears)
    #1, table, 1950 .... **75.00**
    #1582, cathedral, wood **225.00**
    #1955, tombstone, 1936 .... **135.00**
    #9205, transistor, plastic, 1959 .... **40.00**
Sony, transistor
    TFM-151, 1960 .... **50.00**
    TR-63, 1958 .... **140.00**
Sparton, #506, Bluebird, table, round blue or peach
    mirror **3,600.00**
Stewart-Warner, table, slant, 1938 .... **175.00**
Zenith
    Royal
        #500, transistor, owl eye, 1959 .... **75.00**
        #500D, transistor, plastic, 1959 .... **55.00**
        #750L, transistor, leather case, 1959 .... **40.00**
    Trans-Oceanic **100.00**
    #6D2615, table, boomerang dial, 1942 .... **95.00**

RAILROAD ITEMS

History: Railroad collectors have existed for decades. The merger of the rail systems and the end of passenger service made many objects available to private collectors. The Pennsylvania Railroad sold its archives at public sale.

References: Susan and Al Bagdade, *Warman's American Pottery and Porcelain,* Wallace-Homestead, 1994; Stanley L. Baker, *Railroad Collectibles,* Fourth Edition, Collector Books, 1990, 1993 value update; Richard C. Barrett, *The Illustrated Encyclopedia of Railroad Lighting,* Vol. 1, Railroad Research Publications, 1994; David Dreimiller, *The Dressel Railway Lamp & Signal Company,* Hiram Press, 1995; Joseph F. Farrell, Jr., *The Illustrated Guide to Peter Gray Railroad Hardware,* Hiram Press, 1994; Anthony Hobson, *Lanterns that Lit Our World,* Hiram Press, reprinted 1996; Richard Luckin, *Dining on Rails,* RK Publishing, 1994; Don Stewart, *Railroad Switch Keys & Padlocks,* Second Edition, Key Collectors International, 1993.

Periodicals: *Key, Lock and Lantern,* 3 Berkeley Heights Park, Bloomfield, NJ 07003; *Main Line Journal,* PO Box 121, Streamwood, IL 60107.

Collectors' Clubs: Chesapeake & Ohio Historical Society, Inc., PO Box 79, Clifton Forge, VA 24422; Illinois Central Railroad Historical Society, 14818 Clifton Park, Midlothian, IL 60445; Railroad Enthusiasts, 102 Dean Rd, Brookline, MA 02146; Railroadiana Collectors Assoc, 795 Aspen Drive, Buffalo Grove, IL 60089; Railway and Locomotive Historical Society, PO Box 1418, Westford, MA 01886; Twentieth Century Railroad Club, 329 West 18th St, Ste 902, Chicago, IL 60616.

Museums: Baltimore and Ohio Railroad, Baltimore, MD; California State Railroad Museum, Sacramento, CA; Frisco Railroad Museum, Van Buren, AR; Museum of Transportation, Brookline, MA; National Railroad Museum, Green Bay, WI; New York Museum of Transportation, West Henrietta, NY; Old Depot Railroad Museum, Dassel, MN.

Additional Listings: See *Warman's Americana & Collectibles* for more examples.

Notes: Railroad enthusiasts have organized into regional and local clubs. Join one if you're interested in this collectible field; your local hobby store can probably point you to the right person. The best pieces pass between collectors and rarely enter the general market.

Ashtray, 3½" d, Cotton Belt Route, copper, logo on bottom **25.00**
Autograph, letter, Union Pacific Railroad Co, Boston, MA, Feb 1875, 8 × 10¼", written by John M L Williams, Treas to Oakes Ames **25.00**
Baggage and Brass Check
    1¼" d, key tag, GN Ry **12.00**
    1½ × 2", SOU PAC RR, 794, strap **45.00**
Bell, locomotive, bronze, 15" **1,400.00**
Button, Erie, large silver dome, Scovill Mfg Co, Waterbury, CT **7.50**
Catalog, Pennsylvania Steel Co, Steelton, PA, 1906, 96 pgs, 4¼ × 6¾", hardcover, black, gold emb, spirals, street railway curves, formulas, tables, illus **45.00**
Check, Atlantic City & Shore Railroad Co **10.00**

China

Atchinson, Topeka & Sante Fe, gravy boat, Syracuse
China, no backstamp 165.00
Atlantic Coast Line, butter pat, 3½″ d, Flora of the
South, Buffalo China backstamp 100.00
B & O (Baltimore & Ohio)
Creamer, 4½″ h 75.00
Plate, dinner 75.00
C & O (Chesapeake & Ohio), plate, 4¾″ sq, Silhou-
ette, Martha and George Washington dancing
with hands up, Syracuse China, no backstamp .. 245.00
Delaware & Hudson, Canterbury, platter, 10¼ × 7″,
Syracuse China, no backstamp 120.00
Florida East Coast, Carolina, bowl, 5¾″ d, Buffalo
China backstamp 75.00
Mimbreno, platter, 9¼″ l, oval, deer motif 175.00
New York Central, Albany, compote, 7¼″ d, Shen-
ango China backstamp 275.00
Norfolk & Western, plate, 6¼″ d, Syracuse China, no
backstamp 80.00
UP (Union Pacific), plate, 8¼″ d, circus theme, mon-
key, clown, bareback rider 125.00
Wabash Banner, cup and saucer, logo, Syracuse
China, no backstamp 250.00

Glassware

Canadian Pacific, wine, 4″ h, etched script logo on
side, ornate facets 40.00
Lehigh Valley, highball, 4½″ h, maroon and white
train, map of northeastern US marking route 75.00
Sante Fe, cordial, 4½″ h, applied Sante Fe white script
logo 60.00
Union Pacific, goblet, 5½″ h, etched name inside
shield 20.00

Hat

Missouri Pacific, two silver bands, silver "Missouri
Pacific Lines" buttons on each side, red cap badge
with buzz-saw logo, "Missouri Pacific Lines" and
"Trainman" 165.00
Penn Central, red logo and cap badge with "Station
Master" 75.00
Hat Rack, overhead type, coach, wood and brass, six
double-sided brass hooks 200.00
Head Rest, Pennsylvania, 15 × 16″ tan linen-type fabric,
brown PRR logo and electric train 15.00
Lamp, caboose interior side, C & O, c1920, price for pr 350.00

Lantern

Great Northern Railway, Adams & Westlake, double
horizontal guard, twist-off pot and burner, 5⅜″ h
clear globe, patent date Nov 30, '97 .... 175.00
Southern Railway, red globe 150.00

Lock, brass

Boston & Maine Railroad, switch type, marked "B&M
RR LS S," made by "Sherburne & Co/Boston,
Mass" 150.00
Illinois Central Railroad, round six-lever style,
"ICRR"cast over front side 200.00
Map, Atlantic Coast Line, c1950s 150.00
Oil Can, Locomotive Oil 100.00

Playing Cards

Louisville & Nashville, engine, six scenes 50.00
Norfolk & Western, N & W in circle, blue and black 50.00
Union Pacific, river scene, two horses and riders in

foreground, c1910, 52 cards, joker, extra card,
booklet 65.00
Ruler, Soo Line, 12″ l, tin, map and logo, red letters,
white ground 10.00

Silver Flatware, top marked

Lackawanna, fruit knife, Cromwell pattern, Interna-
tional Silver 25.00
NPR (North Penn Railroad), iced tea spoon, Winthrop
pattern, Gorham 35.00
PRR (Pennsylvania Railroad), teaspoon, Kings pattern,
International Silver 30.00
Reading, fork, Kings pattern, International Silver ... 30.00
Soo Line, fork, Windsor pattern, Reed & Barton 35.00

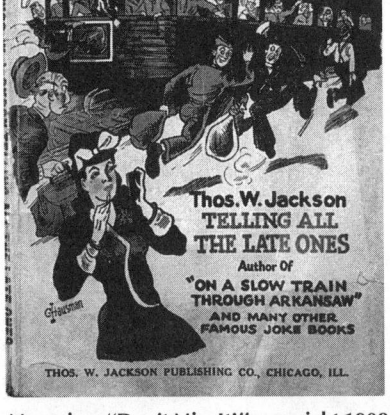

Magazine, "Don't Miss It!" copyright 1908,
revised, 1940, Thos. W. Jackson Pub. Co.,
5⅜ × 7⅞″, $10.00.

Silver Hollowware

Chesapeake & Ohio, sugar tongs, 5¼″ l, Waverly pattern, Albert Pick, top marked, no backstamp 165.00
Pennsylvania, creamer, hinged lid, raised PRR keystone logo on side, Gorham, backstamp with
name of railroad 175.00
Southern Pacific, teapot, 12 oz, Reed & Barton, backstamp reads "S.P. Lines" 145.00
Western Pacific, cheese scoop, 8¼″ l, Belmont pattern, Reed & Barton, top mark reads "W P Ry" . 125.00
Stamp Set, Atlantic Coast Line, Jacksonville, FL, freight
office, wooden drawer, seventy city stamps, c1950 150.00
Step Stool, SP Co, marked "Morton" 325.00

Stock Certificate

New York Central, vignette of engine 3404 pulling
passenger train 20.00
Western Maryland Railway, Mercury standing in front
of diesel locomotive 6.00
Western Pacific Railroad, male and female flanking
streamlined train 8.00
Time Table, Union Pacific, 1945 .... 10.00

RAZORS

History: Razors date back several thousand years. Early man used sharpened stones; the Egyptians, Greeks, and Romans had metal razors.

Razors made prior to 1800 generally were crudely stamped "Warranted" or "Cast Steel," with the maker's mark on the tang. Until 1870 razors were handmade and almost all razors for the American market were manufactured in Sheffield, England. Most blades were wedge shaped; many were etched with slogans or scenes. Handles were made of natural materials: horn, tortoiseshell, bone, ivory, stag, silver, or pearl.

After 1870 razors were machine made with hollow ground blades and synthetic handle materials. Razors of this period usually were manufactured in Germany (Solingen) or in American cutlery factories. Hundreds of molded-celluloid handle patterns were produced.

Cutlery firms produced boxed sets of two, four, and seven razors. Complete and undamaged sets are very desirable. The most-popular ones are the seven-day sets in which each razor is etched with a day of the week.

References: Ronald S. Barlow, *The Vanishing American Barber Shop,* Windmill Publishing, 1993; Jim Sargent, *Sargent's American Premium Guide to Pocket Knives & Razors,* Third Edition, Books Americana, 1992.

Periodical: *Blade Magazine,* PO Box 22007, Chattanooga, TN 37422.

Additional Listings: See *Warman's Americana & Collectibles* for more examples.

Notes: The fancier the handle or more intricately etched the blade, the higher the price. Rarest handle materials are pearl, stag, sterling silver, pressed horn, and carved ivory. Rarest blades are those with scenes etched across the entire front. Value is increased by the presence of certain manufacturers' names, e.g., H. Boker, Case, M. Price, Joseph Rogers, Simmons Hardware, Will & Finck, Winchester, and George Wostenholm.

Abbreviations:

hgb	hollow ground blade
wb	wedge blade

American Blades

American Knife Co, Plymouth Hollow, CT, wb, stamped "A Real American," rounded black horn handle, c1860 .... 85.00

Challenge Cutlery Co, Bridgeport, CT, blade etched "Rince," black peacock pattern 60.00

Henry Sears & Sons, blade etched "Genuine German Concave," imitation ivory handle, orig box with adv 25.00

Novelty Cutlery Co, Canton, OH, rounded point blade, handle with cow, horse, train, and owner's name and address, front dated "1921," German silver ends 70.00

Oscars Special, seven-day set, hgb, ivory handles, burgundy leather-cov wooden case emb "S L. McBean," slotted purple-lined int. 175.00

Union Razor Cutlery Co, Union City, GA, banded tobacco pattern handle 45.00

English Blades, Sheffield

A J Jordan, seven-day set, blades engraved with days

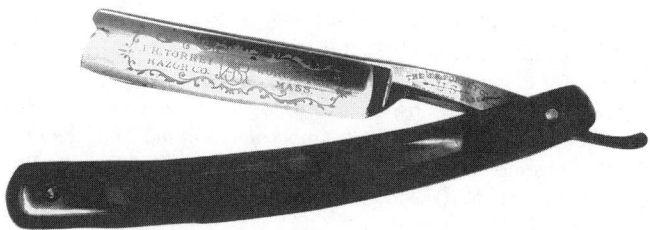

J. R. Terry & Co., Worcester, MA, fully etched blade, tortoiseshell handle, $50.00.

of week, tangs etched "Old Faithful," ivory handles with pointed ends, oak case with peeled perimeter and inlaid brass escutcheon plate, orig box with purple lining **275.00**

George Wostenholm & Sons, Celebrated I'XL Razor Washington Works, wb, etched spread American eagle and "The Congress Razor," notched point, black horn handle with five-sided pewter cap ends, c1830 .... **125.00**

Wade & Butcher, hgb, engraved and ornate escutcheon plate with two inlaid engraved star-shaped metal dec, mottled horn handle, blade etched "The Cleveland Hollow Ground Razor," c1850 **75.00**

Wm Greaves & Sons Sheaf Works, wb, sq point, mottled horn handle, engraved inlaid escutcheon plate, c1820 .... **35.00**

German Blades

Asco Cutlery Co, plain blade, burgundy and pink handle, beetle crawling on bark, oak leaves and acorns **125.00**

H & A Cutlery Co, hgb, imitation ivory handle, pearl tang **45.00**

Westfield, Mfg Co, hgb, checkered raised shield on ivory handle **60.00**

RECORDS

History: With the advent of the more sophisticated recording materials, such as 33⅓ RPM long playing records, 8-track tapes, cassettes, and compact discs, earlier phonograph records became collectors' items. Most have little value. The higher-priced items are rare (limited-production) recordings. Condition is critical.

References: Goldmine Magazine, *Goldmine's 1997 Annual,* Krause Publications, 1996; Ron Lofman, *Goldmine's Celebrity Vocals,* Krause Publications, 1994; Vito R. Marino and Anthony C. Furfero, *The Official Price Guide To Frank Sinatra Records and CDs,* House of Collectibles, 1993; William M. Miller, *How to Buy & Sell Used Record Albums,* Loran Publishing, 1994; Tim Neely, *Goldmine's Price Guide to Alternative Records,* Krause Publications, 1996; ———, *Goldmine's Price Guide to 45 RPM Records,* Krause Publications, 1996; Jerry Osborne, *The Official Price Guide to Elvis Presley Records and Memorabilia,* House of Collectibles, 1994; ———, *The Official Price Guide to Records,* Eleventh Edition, House of Collectibles, 1994; Neal Umphred, *Goldmine's Price Guide To Collectible Jazz Albums, 1949–1969,* Second Edition, Krause Publications, 1994; ———, *Goldmine's Price Guide to Collectible Record Albums,* Fifth Edition, Krause Publications, 1996; ———, *Goldmine's Rock 'n Roll 45 RPM Record Price Guide,* Third Edition, Krause Publications, 1994.

Periodicals: *Cadence,* Cadence Building, Redwood, NY 13679; *DISCoveries Magazine,* PO Box 309, Fraser, MI 48026; *Gold-mine,* 700 E State St, Iola, WI 54990; *Jazz Beat Magazine,* 1206 Decatur St, New Orleans, LA 70116; *Joslin's Jazz Journal,* PO Box 213, Parsons, KS 67357; *New Amberola Graphic,* 37 Caledonia St, St Johnsbury, VT 05819; *Record Collectors Monthly,* PO Box 75, Mendham, NJ 07945; *Record Finder,* PO Box 1047, Glen Allen, VA 23060.

Collectors' Clubs: Assoc for Recorded Sound Collections, PO Box 453, Annapolis, MD 21404; International Assoc of Jazz Record Collectors, PO Box 75155, Tampa, FL 33605.

Additional Listings: See *Warman's Americana & Collectibles* for more examples.

Note: Most records, especially popular recordings, have a value of less than $3 per disc. The records listed here are classic recordings of their type and are in demand by collectors.

Andrews, Lee & the Hearts, White Cliffs of Dover, red plastic, Rainbow 250	**95.00**
Blevins, Frank, Tar Heel Tattlers, I've Got No Honey Babe Now, Columbia	**90.00**
California Poppies, What a Wonderful Time, Sunset	**80.00**
Cannon's Jug Stompers, Wolf River Blues, Victor	**85.00**
Carlton, Bud & Orchestra, Rainy Weather Rose	**10.00**
Darby & Tarlton, Going Back to My Texas Home, Columbia	**50.00**
Down Home Serenaders, Cootie Stomp, Champion	**75.00**
Fate Morable's Society Syncopators, Frankie & Johnny, Okeh	**75.00**
Gay Notes, For Only a Moment, Drexel	**75.00**
Hornets, I Can't Believe, States	**70.00**
Jolson, Al, That Haunting Melody, Victor	**15.00**
Lombardo, Guy & His Royal Canadians, So This Is Venice, Gennett	**30.00**
Original Tuxedo Jazz Orchestra, Black Flag, Okey	**100.00**
Patton and Lee, Troubled 'Bout My Mother, Vocalion	**125.00**
Savoy Bearcats, Senegalese Stomp, Victor	**25.00**
Reeves, Jim, Teardrops of Regret, Macy	**45.00**
Taggerty, Charles Rose, Victor, 78 RPM, black label	**10.00**
Tucker, George & His Novelty Band, Doin' the New Low Down, Champion	**40.00**
Welk, Lawrence & His Orchestra, Shanghai Honeymoon, Gennett	**40.00**
Williamson, Sonny Boy, Skinny Woman, Bluebird	**25.00**
Wrens, I Won't Come to Your Wedding, Rama	**85.00**

REDWARE

History: The availability of clay, the same used to make bricks and roof tiles, accounted for the great production of red earthenware pottery in the American colonies. Redware pieces are mainly utilitarian—bowls, crocks, jugs, etc.

Lead-glazed redware retained its reddish color, but a variety of colored glazes were obtained by the addition of metals to the basic glaze. Streaks and mottled splotches in redware items resulted from impurities in the clay and/or uneven firing temperatures.

Slipware is the term used to describe redwares decorated by the application of slip, a semi-liquid paste made of clay. Slipwares were made in England, Germany, and elsewhere in Europe for decades before becoming popular in the Pennsylvania German region and other areas in colonial America.

References: Susan and Al Bagdade, *Warman's American Pottery and Porcelain,* Wallace-Homestead, 1994; William C. Ketchum, Jr., *American Pottery and Porcelain,* Avon Books, 1994; Dana G. Morykan and Harry L. Rinker, *Warman's Country Antiques & Collectibles,* Third Edition, Wallace-Homestead, 1996.

Bank	
3⅝″ h, tooled band, knob finial, unglazed, black stenciled label "Charity"	**175.00**
6½″ h, 5¾″ d, beehive shape, peg finial clear lead glaze, slight greenish int.	**225.00**
Basin, 18″ d, tin glaze	**75.00**
Basket, 3¼″ h, 6″ d, hanging type, red and white, yellow slip, green and brown glaze, notched rim, pot and saucer, three pierced holes, restored	**1,300.00**
Bottle, 11¾″ h, donut shape, amber glaze, brown flecks	**140.00**
Bowl	
12½″ d, shallow, very worn int., yellow slip bird on branch and edge design, green and brown glaze, chips	**250.00**
13½″ d, 2½″ h, shallow, coggled edge, three-line yellow slip dec, worn, center badly chipped	**400.00**
Charger, coggled edge	
11⅜″ d, four-line slip dec	**1,200.00**
13¾″ d, yellow slip combware dec	**1,350.00**
Chestnut Dish, 13½″ d, oval, slip dec, rim chips	**425.00**
Colander, 9¾″ × 7″, clear glaze, brown flecks, orange ground, rim handles, three applied feet	**350.00**
Creamer, 4″ h, incised band, four vertical lines of black irid glaze	**125.00**
Crock, 9″ h, clear glaze, brown splotches, applied handles	**190.00**
Cuspidor, 3⅞″ h, 7½″ d, red and white slip, green and brown sponged glaze under clear lead glaze, foot chips and wear	**100.00**
Custard Cup, 2⅜″ h, incised "TS Stahl, Sept 1, 1940"	**60.00**
Dish	
7⅝″ d, dark glaze, yellow slip spots, rim flake	**275.00**
8″ d, yellow slip dec, wear and chips	**200.00**
Flask, 8″ h, brown splotches, clear glaze, orange ground, New England	**275.00**
Flowerpot	
5″ h, 6⅛″ d, red and white slip, brown sponge dec, clear lead glaze ext., attached under tray imp "John Bell/Waynesboro"	**200.00**
7⅝″ h, 8⅛″ d, white slip, applied brown slip and dabbed green glaze swag design dec, double roulette rim attached ruffled under tray, imp "Solomon Bell"	**450.00**
Jar, ovoid	
6″ h	
Brown sponging, ribbed strap handle, chips	**135.00**
Light amber, brown splotches, ribbed strap handle, minor chips	**300.00**
Well-defined brown and amber glaze, minor flakes	**220.00**
6½″ h, dark ground, brown splotches, minor chips	**275.00**
9½″ h, dark green amber glaze, incised initials "SB" on side, ripped strap handle, wear, chips	**315.00**

Plate, four-slips creating waves and straight lines, crimped edges, 9½″ d, $250.00.

Whistle, figural bird, $930.00. Photo courtesy of Aston Auctioneers.

12″ h, applied shoulder handles, reddish amber glaze, chips on lip and lid **110.00**
Jug, ovoid
6½″ d, dark brown shiny glaze, ribbed strap handle, chips **145.00**
8½″ h, strap handle, incised lines at shoulder, light green glaze with amber spots, wear, glaze flaking, minor crazing **125.00**
Lamp, 23″ h overall, 9″ h jar drilled and mounted as lamp base, incised lines, applied ribbed shoulder handles and clear glaze, tan color, dark brown splotches, wear and chips, wooden base, old burlap shade **265.00**
Loaf Pan, 13″ l, rect, coggled edge, three-line yellow slip dec, worn, old chips and scratches **425.00**
Meat Roaster, 12″ l, scoop shape, applied finger-crimped rim, strap handle, end spout, greenish amber glaze **220.00**
Milk Pan, 10″ d, "1813" in yellow slip between double lines, wavy line border, black back **125.00**
Mug, 4⅜″ h, 4¼″ d, brown sponging, clear lead glaze, top and bottom thumbnail grooves, imp "John Bell" **550.00**
Pie Plate, coggled edge
9¾″ d, three-line yellow slip dec **220.00**
10″ d, three-line yellow slip dec, very worn, chips and scratches **100.00**
12¼″ d, yellow slip dec, wear and old chips **315.00**
Pitcher
5″ h, pinched spout, white slip, mottled brown glaze **95.00**
7½″ h, red and white overall slip, brown spattered dec, clear lead glaze, bold handle **325.00**
Plate
8½″ d, zigzag and parallel-lines yellow slip dec, reddish brown glaze, chips **225.00**
10¼″ d, yellow slip dec, parallel zigzag lines and commas, reddish brown glaze, rim chip and roughage **325.00**
11¼″ d, glazed face, unglazed back, applied yellow slip dec reads "Lafayette," yellow slip squiggles above and below name, coggled edge, professional restoration to 6″ l rim hairline **2,750.00**
Shaving Mug, 5¾″ h, brown-green mottled glaze, strap handle **290.00**
Turk's Head Mold, 9″ d, amber and green, dark brown ext. sponging, swirled flutes, scalloped rim **175.00**

Vase, 3⅝″ h, sgraffito, birds and flowers, tricolor, bulbous base, marked "DDR, June 5, 1828, PA" **1,750.00**

RED WING POTTERY

History: The Red Wing pottery category includes several potteries from Red Wing, Minnesota. In 1868 David Hallem started Red Wing Stoneware Co., the first pottery with stoneware as its primary product. The Minnesota Stoneware Co. started in 1883. The North Star Stoneware Co. was in business from 1892 to 1896.

The Red Wing Stoneware Co. and the Minnesota Stoneware Co. merged in 1892. The new company, the Red Wing Union Stoneware Co., made stoneware until 1920 when it introduced a pottery line which it continued until the 1940s. In 1936 the name was changed to Red Wing Potteries, Inc. During the 1930s this firm introduced several popular patterns of hand-painted dinnerware which were distributed through department stores, mail-order catalogs, and gift-stamp centers. Dinnerware production declined in the 1950s and was replaced with hotel and restaurant china in the early 1960s. The plant closed in 1967.

Marks: Red Wing Stoneware Co. was the first firm to mark pieces with a red wing stamped under the glaze. The North Star Stoneware Co. used a raised star and the words "Red Wing" as its mark.

References: Susan and Al Bagdade, *Warman's American Pottery and Porcelain,* Wallace-Homestead, 1994; Dan and Gail DePasquale and Larry Peterson, *Red Wing Collectibles,* Collector Books, 1985, 1995 value update; ———, *Red Wing Stoneware,* Collector Books, 1983, 1994 value update; B. L. Dollen, *Red Wing Art Pottery,* Collector Books, 1996; Dana G. Morykan and Harry L. Rinker, *Warman's Country Antiques & Collectibles,* Third Edition, Wallace-Homestead, 1996; Ray Reiss, *Red Wing Art Pottery Including Pottery Made for Rum Rill,* published by author (2144 N Leavitt, Chicago, IL 60647), 1996.

Collectors' Clubs: Red Wing Collectors Society, Inc, PO Box 184, Galesburg, IL 61402; RumRill Society, PO Box 2161, Hudson, OH 44236.

Additional Listings: See *Warman's Americana & Collectibles* for more examples.

Ashtray, Minnesota Twins World Series, 1965	**60.00**
Butter Crock, cov, white, blue adv, two-lb size, marked "Red Wing"	**95.00**
Casserole, cov, Saffronware	**245.00**
Cracker Jar, Saffronware	**600.00**
Crock, five-gal size, elephant-ear leaves, salt glaze	**195.00**
Custard Cup, spongeware band	**75.00**

Figure

Asian	**125.00**
Bishop	**125.00**
Flowerpot, 10" d, ribbons and berries dec	**65.00**
Jar, white, shield-shaped adv, marked	**165.00**
Jug, 5 gallon, beehive shape, white glaze	**275.00**

Pitcher

6" h, Cherry Band pattern, blue and white stoneware	**175.00**
12" h, Roundup	**250.00**
Planter, seal, blue, #941	**45.00**
Plate, 11" d, Chuckwagon	**80.00**
Relish, 13" l, chaps shape	**125.00**
Slop Jar, cov, blue stripe band, lip on front	**145.00**
Teapot, cov, stand, Bob White	**95.00**
Urn, 10" h, #762	**55.00**

Vase

7" h, trumpet, #132	**60.00**
7½" h, Cattails	**85.00**
9" h, Egyptian motif	**150.00**
10" h, Cattails	**120.00**
#188, bud	**80.00**

Vase, light blue glaze, impressed mark and "1151," 8⅛" h, $50.00.

Wall Pocket, gardenia, ivory glaze	**45.00**
Water Cooler, three gal, white, stoneware, oval "Red Wing Union Stoneware" mark	**350.00**

RELIGIOUS ITEMS

History: Objects used in worship or as expression of man's belief in a superhuman power are collected by many people for many reasons.

This category includes icons since they are religious mementos, usually paintings with a brass encasement. Collecting icons dates from the earliest period of Christianity. Most antique icons in today's market were made in the late 19th century.

Reference: Penny Forstner and Lael Bower, *Collecting Religious Artifacts (Christian and Judaic),* Books Americana, 1995.

Collectors' Club: Foundation International for Restorers of Religious Medals, PO Box 2652, Worcester, MA 01608.

Museum: American Bible Society, New York, NY.

Reproduction Alert: Icons are frequently reproduced.

Additional Listings: Russian Items.

Alms Box, 10¾" w, 16" h, oak, old brown grained repaint, Gothic style, English, wear and one incomplete scalloped bracket	**145.00**
Autograph, Joseph Smith, founder of Mormon Church, uncirculated $5 note of Kirtland Safety Society Bank, Kirtland, OH, signed by Smith as cashier and Sidney Rigdon as President, vignettes of boy standing with shovel on shoulder, another with boy in woods with dog and ax beside him, issued March 8, 1837	**795.00**
Catalog, John P. Daleiden Co, Chicago, IL, 1926, 416 pgs, 10½ × 13½", Catalog No. 98, ecclesiastical supplies, church regalia, sanctuary and sacristy supplies	**45.00**
Chalice, 10¼" h, SS, cast cherubs, portraits of saints, applied filigree, red and green jewels, marked "Benzinger Bros Maker, New York," 22 troy oz	**500.00**
Chalice and Paten, American Gothic Revival, partially gilded silver and enamel, Francis W Cooper and Richard Fisher, NY, c1855, hexafoil foot pierced with quatrefoils, dec with three panels engraved and dec with champleve opaque blue, white, and translucent red enamel depicting Crucifixion, Descent of the Holy Ghost, and Baptism of Christ, panels alternate with engraved scenes of St George slaying the dragon, St John the Evangelist, and martyrdom of a saint, all within engraved Gothic arches, openwork stem framed by free-standing spiral columns, central knop pierced with arches and quatrefoils, silver-gilt bowl with white-silver calyx chased with six angels holding emblems framing egg-shaped reserves, paten centered by champleve boss of Christ in majesty surrounded by Gothic foliage and inscription of the Eucharist within cable border, chalice marked twice on base rim "Cooper & Fisher" and "131 Amity St NY," paten similarly marked once, 44 oz gross, 9⅞" h chalice, 9½" d	**36,800.00**

Icon

8⅞ × 7", Madonna and Child, heavy foliate-dec silver riza, Lithuanian	**260.00**
12½" d, St Paraskeva, oil on round wooden panel, Russian, 19th C	**450.00**
12½ × 10½"	
Christ, heavily repoussé brass oklad, Lithuanian, late 19th/20th C	**460.00**
Vladimir Mother of God, tempera on wooden panel, overlaid silver metal riza, Russian, 19th C	**290.00**
14¾" × 10¼", Crucifixion, tempera, gold leaf on wooden panel, inset brass cross, Russian, 19th C	**600.00**
15 × 11½", Resurrection, tempera on wooden panel, central image of resurrection of Christ, surrounded	

Cross, Russian Orthodox, early 19th C, brass 3¼" h, $175.00.

by 12 great church feasts, carved, gilded klot, Russian, 19th C **800.00**
Plaque, 9¼ × 7½", Christ with crown of thorns, imp KPM marks, framed **1,265.00**
Reliquary, 20½" h, Gothic Revival, silver and gilt metal, upper section in two parts, spires and figures within niches, int. lined with amber glass, faceted and shaped stem on arched foot, 19th C **5,175.00**
Santos, 11¾" h, carved and painted wood, robed figured, stepped base, Continental, 19th/20th C **425.00**
Stele, 19½" w, 31¾" h, carved gray limestone, Buddhist Trinity, Northern Wei style, central standing robed Buddha, two standing Bodhisattvas on either side, lotus plinths being held up by animal heads, low relief-carved floral motifs on flat ground, reverse with rows of Buddhas, inscriptions, wooden stand, repairs**1,100.00**

REVERSE PAINTING ON GLASS

History: The earliest examples of reverse painting on glass were produced in 13th-century Italy. By the 17th century the technique had spread to central and eastern Europe. It spread westward as the center of the glassmaking industry moved to Germany in the late 17th century.

The Alsace and Black Forest regions developed a unique portraiture style. The half and three-quarter portraits often were titled below the portrait. Women tend to have generic names while most males are likenesses of famous men.

The English used a mezzotint, rather than free-style, method to create their reverse paintings. Landscapes and allegorical figures were popular. The Chinese began working in the medium in the 17th century, eventually favoring marine and patriotic scenes.

Most American reverse painting was done by folk artists and is unsigned. Portraits, patriotic and mourning scenes, floral compositions, landscapes, and buildings are the favorite subjects. Known American artists include Benjamin Greenleaf, A. Cranfield, and Rowley Jacobs.

In the late 19th century commercially produced reverse paintings, often decorated with mother-of-pearl, became popular. Themes included the Statue of Liberty, the capitol in Washington, D.C., and various world's fairs and expositions.

Reference: Shirley Mace, *Encyclopedia of Silhouette Collectibles on Glass,* Shadow Enterprises, 1992.

Additional Listings: Pairpoint.

Portraits

Emilie, balloon-sleeved dress, large collar, 9½ × 12" . **500.00**
Mallanderin, woman with flowers in her hair, replaced frame, 9½ × 11½" **140.00**
Oriental women, colorful costumes, 19¾" h, 13⅝" w, price for facing pr **150.00**
Sylvia, woman in red dress, blue ground, orig frame, 7¾ × 10½" **120.00**
Washington, George, oval portrait, white border, sky-blue background, mahogany veneer frame, 12¼" h, 10¼" w, paint flaking **220.00**

Cottage scene, MOP on house, green flame with gilt pilaster end pieces, 12 × 24", $75.00.

Scenes

Adoration of the Magi, later carved giltwood frame, Italian, 27 × 18½" **425.00**
Blarney Castle, forest scene, castle on right, touches of mica and abalone, 20 × 27" **150.00**
Landscape, pink, gray, white, green, and brown, Chinese Export School, 10 × 8" **175.00**
Man and woman in landscape, Chinese Export School, late 18th or early 19th C, 15¼ × 11½" **2,750.00**
Rock of Ages, gold, white, red, blue, and green, black ground, tinsel highlights, orig oak frame, 20¾" h, 17¾" w **115.00**
Summer-Winter, winter landscape with woman in velvet coat, summer landscape with young woman in straw bonnet carrying sickle, sprays of wheat, Chinese Export School, 19th C, 10 × 14½", price for facing pr **900.00**

RIDGWAY

History: Throughout the 19th century the Ridgway family, through a series of partnerships, held a position of importance in the ceramics industry in Shelton and Hanley, Staffordshire, England. The connection began with Job and George, two brothers, and Job's two sons, John and William. In 1830 John and William dissolved their partnership; John retained the Cauldon Place factory and William the Bell Works. By 1862 the porcelain division of Cauldon was carried on by Coalport China Ltd. William and his heirs continued at the Bell Works and the Church (Hanley) and Bedford (Shelton) works until the end of the 19th century.

Marks: Many early pieces are unmarked. Later marks include the initials of the many different partnerships.

References: Susan and Al Bagdade, *Warman's English & Continental Pottery & Porcelain,* Second Edition, Wallace-Homestead, 1991; G. A. Godden, *Ridgway Porcelains,* Antique Collectors' Club, 1985.

Additional Listings: Staffordshire, Historical, and Staffordshire, Romantic.

Beverage Set, 12⅜″ × 6½″ tankard, pitcher, six 4¼ × 5″ mugs, Coaching Days, caramel ground, black scene, silver-luster top bands and handles, price for 7-pc set **400.00**
Bowl
    6″ d, Shakespeare **30.00**
    8½″ w to handles, Coaching Days **35.00**
Cheese Dish, cov, light brown floral transfer **75.00**
Children's Tea Set, blue and brown flowers, gold trim, white ground, teapot, creamer, sugar, waste bowl, six cups and saucers, two plates, price for set **325.00**
Coffeepot, cov, 7½″ h, Coaching Days, silver luster ... **95.00**
Cup Plate, Marmora **45.00**
Mug
    4″ h, Shakespeare **35.00**
    4¾″ h, Coaching Days, silver luster **45.00**

Mug, silver-luster rim, black coaching scenes, caramel-mustard ground, marked "Scenes from Coaching Days, Coaching Ways by Special Permission of MacMillan & Co., Ltd.," $45.00.

Plate, 9″ d, Coaching Days **25.00**
Tea Caddy, cov, 4 × 5¾″ h, Coaching Days, scenes on all sides **175.00**
Tile, 6″ d, round, Coaching Days **115.00**
Tray, 8¼″ d, Bank of Savannah, handles **185.00**

Vase, 4⅞″ h, egg shape, Coaching Days, caramel ground, black scenes, silver-luster top band and handle **75.00**
Vegetable Bowl, cov, 12″ w, 6¼″ h, flow blue, oval, A Deak pattern **210.00**

ROCKINGHAM AND ROCKINGHAM BROWN-GLAZED WARES

History: Rockingham ware can be divided into two categories. The first consists of the fine china and porcelain pieces made between 1826 and 1842 by the Rockingham Company of Swinton, Yorkshire, England, and its predecessor firms: Swinton, Bingley, Don, Leeds, and Brameld. The Bramelds developed the cadogan, a lidless teapot. Between 1826 and 1842 a quality soft-paste product with a warm, silky feel was developed by the Bramelds. Elaborate specialty pieces were made. By 1830 the company employed 600 workers and listed 400 designs for dessert sets and 1,000 designs for tea and coffee services in their catalog. Unable to meet its payroll, the company closed in 1842.

The second category of Rockingham ware includes pieces produced in the famous Rockingham brown glaze that became an intense and vivid purple-brown when fired. It had a dark, tortoiseshell appearance. The glaze was copied by many English and American potteries. American manufacturers which used Rockingham glaze include D. & J. Henderson of Jersey City, New Jersey; United States Pottery in Bennington, Vermont; potteries in East Liverpool, Ohio; and several potteries in Indiana and Illinois.

References: Susan and Al Bagdade, *Warman's American Pottery and Porcelain,* Wallace-Homestead, 1994; Susan and Al Bagdade, *Warman's English & Continental Pottery & Porcelain,* Second Edition, Wallace-Homestead, 1991; William C. Ketchum, Jr., *American Pottery and Porcelain,* Avon Books, 1994.

Museum: The Bennington Museum, Bennington, VT.

Additional Listings: Bennington and Bennington-Type Pottery.

Bedpan, 16¾″ l **75.00**
Bowl, 14″ d, 6½″ h, emb ext. **75.00**
Figure
    6⅝″ h, 9½″ l, lion, rect base, good detail and glaze, price for pr **525.00**
    18½″ h, 36½″ w, bulldog, overall brown glaze, finely modeled, glass eyes, late 19th C, restoration to tail **2,180.00**
Food Mold, 8½″ d, Turk's head, brown glaze, green flint enamel **85.00**
Goblet, 5⅜″ h **525.00**
Inkwell, 4¾″ l, lion **185.00**
Mixing Bowl, 16½″ d, 6⅝″ h, 1849 mark **2,500.00**
Pitcher
    7¼″ h, detailed emb scenes of camel and elephant, imp mark "R Bew, Bliston" **75.00**
    7¾″ h, Paneled Grapeview pattern, brown glaze ... **1,100.00**
Teapot, 8¼″ h, emb design, portrait of lady **75.00**

Bowl, mocha and gold, 7³⁄₈" d, 3¹⁄₄" h, $65.00.

Tobacco Jar, 8" h, molded oval floral medallions, dark
    brown glaze, small rim chip **80.00**
Toby Jug, 9¹⁄₂" h, coachman, brown glaze, period pewter
    and cork pouring stopper **450.00**
Wall Pocket, toby shape, brown glaze **375.00**

ROCK 'N' ROLL

History: Rock music can be traced back to early rhythm and blues.
It progressed until it reached its golden age in the 1950s and
1960s. Most of the memorabilia issued during that period focused
on individual singers and groups. The largest quantity of collectible material is connected to Elvis Presley and The Beatles.

In the 1980s two areas—clothing and guitars—associated with
key Rock 'n' Roll personalities received special collector attention.
Sotheby's and Christie's East regularly feature Rock 'n' Roll memorabilia as part of their collectibles sales. At the moment, the
market is highly speculative and driven by nostalgia.

It is important to identify memorabilia issued during the lifetime
of an artist or performing group as opposed to material issued after
they died or disbanded. Objects of the latter type are identified as
"fantasy" items and will never achieve the same degree of collectibility as period counterparts.

References: Jeff Augsburger, Marty Eck, and Rich Rann, *The Beatles Memorabilia Price Guide,* Second Edition, Wallace-Homestead, 1993; Karen and John Lesniewski, *Kiss Collectibles,* Avon
Books, 1993; Stephen Maycock, *Miller's Rock & Pop Memorabilia,* Millers Publications, 1994; Greg Moore, *A Price Guide To
Rock & Roll Collectibles,* published by author, 1993; Jerry Osborne, *The Official Price Guide to Elvis Presley Records and Memorabilia,* House of Collectibles, 1994; ———, *The Official Price
Guide to Records,* Tenth Edition, House of Collectibles, 1993;
Michael Stern, Barbara Crawford, and Hollis Lamon, *The Beatles,*
Collector Books, 1994; Neal Umphred, *Goldmine's Price Guide
to Collectible Record Albums,* Fourth Edition, Krause Publications,
1994; ———, *Goldmine's Rock 'n' Roll 45 RPM Record Price
Guide,* Third Edition, Krause Publications, 1994.

Periodicals: Beatlefan, PO Box 33515, Decatur, GA 30033; *Good
Day Sunshine,* 397 Edgewood Ave, New Haven, CT 06511; *Instant Karma,* PO Box 256, Sault Ste. Marie, MI 49783.

Collectors' Clubs: Beatles Connection, PO Box 1066, Pinellas
Park, FL 34665; Beatles Fan Club of Great Britain, Superstore

Productions, 123 Marina St, Leonards on Sea, East Sussex, England
TN 38 0BN; Elvis Forever TCB Fan Club, PO Box 1066, Pinellas
Park, FL 34665; Graceland News Fan Club, PO Box 452, Rutherford, NJ 07070; Working Class Hero Club, 3311 Niagara St.,
Pittsburgh, PA 15213.

REPRODUCTION ALERT

Records, picture sleeves, and album jackets, especially for The Beatles, have been counterfeited.
When compared to the original, sound may be inferior, as may be the printing on labels and picture
jackets. Many pieces of memorabilia also have been
reproduced, often with some change in size, color,
and design.

Additional Listings: See The Beatles, Elvis Presley, and Rock 'n'
Roll in *Warman's Americana & Collectibles.*

Bank, Beatles, date register, 1964 .... **25.00**
Banner, Beatles, printed nylon, four Beatles in black,
    large blue print heading "The Beatles," Memphis,
    1966 ....**1,150.00**
Billfold, Beatles, red, four white signatures on one side,
    picture on other **90.00**
Concert Clothing
    James Brown, stage vest, black leather, round gold
        buttons, lined in white felt, front left wide-cut
        white leather initials "JB," white leather letters
        "Mr D" on other side **1,840.00**
    Madonna, stage shorts, low-waisted, high-cut purple
        shorts, ribbed stretch knit, legs lined in black satin,
        completely decorated with purple sequins, 1992
        Girlie Tour **1,725.00**
Concert Poster
    Bill Graham Series, marked "Six Days of Sound—
        Dec 26–New York's Eve 1967," design by Bonnie
        MacLean, includes The Doors, Chuck Berry, Big
        Brother & the Holding Co, Winterland **125.00**
    Grateful Dead, Skull in Sand, 1981 European Fall
        tour, design by Stanley Mouse, 22¹⁄₂ × 27" **85.00**
    Hells Angels Party, featuring Big Brother, God, Main
        Squeeze & Janis Joplin, May 21, 1970, design by
        Don Moses, toned, minor damage **345.00**
    Led Zeppelin, July 23–24, 1977, Oakland Stadium,
        design by Randy Tuten & William Bostedt **175.00**
    The Supremes, Trude Heller and G. Keys present—
        The Supremes—Lincoln Center, Philharmonic
        Hall, Friday, Oct 15, 1965, design by Eula, 25 ×
        38" **500.00**
Concert Program
    Michael Jackson, 1984 .... **10.00**
    Monterey Pop Festival, essays by Jan Wenner, Derek
        Taylor, Al Kooper, Bob Shelton, Leonard Bernstein, photographs, 80 pgs **220.00**
Concert Souvenir, brass ticket, Grateful Dead, Jerry Garcia illus **35.00**
Doll, Boy George, LJN, 1984, MIB **100.00**
Dress-Up Set, Michael Jackson **35.00**

Tambourine, Monkees, colored disc, white ground, copyright 1967 Raybert Productions, Inc., trademark of Screen Gems, Inc., $35.00.

Fan Club Card, Elvis Presley Fan Club, sgd in blue pen and ink by president and secretary 575.00

Guitar

  Beach Boys, Hohner MW 400N acoustic, spruce top, 20-fret rosewood fingerboard, dot inlays, pink bridge, black pick guard, sgd by Carl Wilson, Mike Love 980.00

  Black Crowes, Fender Stratocaster electric, white finish, double cutaway body, maple neck, 21-fret rosewood fingerboard with dot inlays, three pickups, three controls, selector, tremolo bridge, tail block and white pick board, sgd on body by Rich Robinson, Chris Robinson, Jeff Cease, Steve Gorman and Johnny Colt 1,500.00

Handkerchief, Elvis Presley, black silk, worn by Presley in 1962–63 movie "It Happened at the World's Fair," together with photo of Presley with the handkerchief in his breast pocket, letter of authenticity 575.00

Lyrics

  Alice Cooper, handwritten for song "Trash," composed in studio, 1989, three verses in black ink, corrections in blue ballpoint pen, two additional verses in blue ballpoint pen, written on yellow legal-size paper 300.00

  Paul McCartney, handwritten for "When I'm 64," 1967 Sgt Pepper album, lyrics and revisions ...40,250.00

Magazine, *Sixteen,* 1966, Beatles cover and article ... 15.00

Newspaper, *Memphis Press,* August 17, 1977, announcing death of Elvis Presley 30.00

Paddleball Game, Beatles 100.00

Perfume Bottle, Elvis Presley, Teddy Bear, orig box, 1957 160.00

Pin, 1½" l, Beatles Love Songs, oval, brass, brown and cream enamel design, English, c1970 .... 15.00

Pinback Button

  7/8" d, Elvis, gold record, "I Want You, I Need You, I Love You," black and white photo, gold rim, 1956 .... 20.00

  1" d, Fabian Fan Club, blue on white, litho, late 1950s 15.00

  3½" d, Monkeys, black and white photo, red and white logo, 1966 .... 25.00

  4" d, Jackson Five, black and white photo, bright red ground, copyright 1971, Motown Record Corp . 40.00

Postcard, Buddy Holly, handwritten in pencil, addressed

to his parents, sgd "Love Buddy," postmarked May 10, 1956, matted and framed with photo of Holly & The Crickets, 10½ × 18" overall 1,735.00

Radio, Elvis Presley, figural, old Elvis in suit, holding a microphone, standing atop plastic base, marked "Elvis Presley" on front, made in Hong Kong, 1977, 8" h, 1¼ × 3 × 5" base 40.00

Record, Beatles, Got to Get You into My Life, 45 rpm . 10.00

Sheet Music, Beatles, Day Tripper, 1964 .... 20.00

Sign, Pepsi-Cola, bottle cap, metal, "Drink Pepsi-Cola," sgd "Elvis Presley," and "Bellywash" in black marker, two letters of provenance, 30" d 6,100.00

Sweatshirt, Beatles, white, NEMS, 1963 .... 150.00

Tie Clip, Elvis Presley, hand-cuff design, photo of Elvis wearing tie clip and letter of authenticity 920.00

View-Master Reels, The Monkees, 4½ × 4½" envelope, color photos, complete set of three reels in single sleeve, booklet, and catalog, copyright 1967 Raybert Productions 45.00

Wristwatch, Elvis Presley, gold, automatic wind, date, and time, four-star design on face, Mathey-Tissot, letter of provenance 4,600.00

ROGERS & SIMILAR STATUARY

History: John Rogers, born in America in 1829, studied sculpture in Europe and produced his first plaster-of-paris statue, "The Checker Players," in 1859. It was followed by "The Slave Auction" in 1860.

His works were popular parlor pieces in the Victorian era. He produced at least 80 different statues, and the total number of groups made from the originals is estimated to be over 100,000.

Casper Hennecke, one of Rogers's contemporaries, operated C. Hennecke & Company from 1881 until 1896 in Milwaukee, Wisconsin. His statuary often is confused with Rogers's work since both are very similar.

References: Paul and Meta Bieier, *John Rogers' Groups of Statuary,* published by author, 1971; Betty C. Haverly, *Hennecke's Florentine Statuary,* published by author, 1972; David H. Wallace, *John Rogers,* Wesleyan University, 1976.

Periodical: *The Rogers Group,* 4932 Prince George Ave, Beltsville, MD 20705.

Museums: John Rogers Studio & Museum of the New Canaan Historical Society, New Canaan CT; Lightner Museum, Saint Augustine, FL.

Notes: It is difficult to find a statue in undamaged condition and with original paint. Use the following conversions: 10 percent off for minor flaking; 10 percent, chips; 10 to 20 percent, piece or pieces broken and reglued; 20 percent, flaking; 50 percent, repainting.

Rogers

Campfire 650.00
Challenging Union Vote 1,100.00
Courtship Sleepy Hollow 750.00
Elder's Daughter 950.00
Faust and Marguerite 800.00
Fighting Bob 1,800.00

First Love, $325.00.

First Ride	1,800.00
Ha, I Like Not That	500.00
One More Shoot	500.00
Pews	600.00
Phrenology	750.00
Politics	1,300.00
Referee	900.00
You Are a Spirit	750.00
We Boys	800.00
Why Don't You Speak	600.00
Wrestlers	1,600.00

Rogers Type

Croquet Player	200.00
Family Cares	100.00
Red Riding Hood	350.00
Welcome, alabaster	300.00

ROOKWOOD POTTERY

History: Mrs. Marie Longworth Nicholas Storer, Cincinnati, Ohio, founded Rookwood Pottery in 1880. The name of this outstanding American art pottery came from her family estate, "Rookwood," named for the rooks (crows) which inhabited the wooded grounds.

Though the Rookwood pottery filed for bankruptcy in 1941, it was soon reorganized under new management. Efforts at maintaining the pottery proved futile, and it was sold in 1956 and again in 1959. The pottery was moved to Starkville, Mississippi, in conjunction with the Herschede Clock Co. It finally ceased operating in 1967.

Rookwood wares changed with the times. The variety is endless, in part because of the creativity of the many talented artists responsible for great variations in glazes and designs.

Marks: There are five elements to the Rookwood marking system—the clay or body mark, the size mark, the decorator mark, the date mark, and the factory mark. The best way to date Rookwood art pottery is from factory marks.

From 1880 to 1882 the factory mark was the name "Rookwood" incised or painted on the base. Between 1881 and 1886 the firm name, address, and year appeared in an oval frame. Beginning in 1886, the impressed "RP" monogram appeared and a flame mark was added for each year until 1900. After 1900 a Roman numeral, indicating the last two digits of the year of production, was added at the bottom of the "RP" flame mark. This last mark is the one most often seen on Rookwood pieces in the antiques marketplace.

References: Susan and Al Bagdade, *Warman's American Pottery and Porcelain,* Wallace-Homestead, 1994; Anita J. Ellis, *Rookwood Pottery,* Rizzoli International and Cincinnati Art Museum, 1992; Ralph and Terry Kovel, *Kovels' American Art Pottery,* Crown Publishers, 1993; Herbert Peck, *The Book of Rookwood Pottery,* Crown Publishers, 1968; ———, *The Second Book of Rookwood Pottery,* published by author, 1985; *Price Guide to Rookwood,* L-W Book Sales, 1993.

Videotape: Anita Ellis, *The Collectors Series: Rookwood Pottery,* distributed by Award Video and Film Distributors, Inc, 1994.

Collectors' Club: American Art Pottery Assoc, 125 E Rose Ave, St Louis, MO 63119.

SPECIAL AUCTIONS

Cincinnati Art Galleries
635 Main St
Cincinnati, OH 45202
(513) 381-2128

Treadway Gallery, Inc.
2029 Madison Rd
Cincinnati, OH 45208
(513) 321-6742

Ashtray, 4" h, figural, pelican, glossy gunmetal glaze, bright yellow int., logo, date 1930, shape no. 6149 **350.00**

Bookends, pr

5" h, Spanish Galleons, matte green glaze, rust highlights, logo, date 1941, shape no. 2634 .... **375.00**

5⅛" h, elephants, very dark green matte glaze, logo, date 1925, shape no. 2444 D **550.00**

6¼" h, horse's heads, chocolate brown matte glaze, logo, date 1928, shape no. 6014, molded name of William McDonald, designer **600.00**

Bowl

8¼" d, Glaze Effect, Michele Blush over creamy gray over Ralphie Brown, logo, date 1932, shape no. 6313 .... **250.00**

9⅜" d, cameo glaze, apple blossom dec, painted by Harriet Wilcox, imp logo, date 1890, "W" for white clay, shape no. 431, incised artist's initials and "W" for white (cameo) glaze, very minor glaze scratches **400.00**

Demitasse Set, Blue Ship Dinnerware, cov demitasse pot, cream pitcher, cov sugar bowl, six cups and saucers, logo, shape no. M1 for cups, M2 for saucers, M11 for sugar bowl, M12 for cream pitcher, M16 for 5½" h demitasse pot, 1920s, price for set **2,100.00**

Ewer, standard glaze

7½" h, rose-hip dec, painted by Jeanette Swing, logo, late 1899, shape no. 851E, incised artist's monogram **500.00**

10½" h, grape dec, painted by Anna Valentien, logo, date 1892, shape no. 578 D, "W" for white clay, incised "L" for light standard glaze, incised artist's initials **600.00**

16¾" h, long neck, sweeping handle, lifelike yellow jonquils, bright green leaves, painted by Albert Valentien, logo, date 1890, shape no. 560 A, "W" for white clay, incised "L" for light standard glaze, incised artist's initials, minor glaze bubbles **1,400.00**

Figure, 5¼" h, cat, brown matte glaze, logo, date 1922, shape no. 1883 .... **550.00**

Flower Frog, 6⅛" h, mottled brown matte glaze, two nude kneeling women, logo, date 1921, shape no. 2338, notation "Original Model by Chester Beach," small glaze flake at base **350.00**

Medallion, 5⅝" d, designed for MacConnell & Company Engineers & Appraisers by Ruben Earl Menzel, aventurine glaze, shows Rookwood Pottery entrance gates, purchased by MacConnell in 1956, logo, date, faint imp of MacConnell company logo, Menzel's monogram, notation "Rookwood Cinti, O." **275.00**

Mug, 4¾" h, iris glaze, grape dec, dec by Ed Diers, imp logo, date 1901, shape no. 587C, incised artist's monogram, "W" for white (iris) glaze, faint line at base **700.00**

Paperweight

2¾" h, Rook, mottled brown matte glaze, logo, date 1921, shape no. 1623 .... **325.00**

3¼" h, Elephant and Clown, gunmetal glaze, designed by Wm McDonald, clown on either side of elephant's trunk, logo, date 1921, shape no. 2628, cast designer's monogram **550.00**

3⅞" h, Spanish galleon, cream-colored matte glaze, logo, date 1927, shape no. 2792, notation "S 068" painted in black slip **275.00**

Perfume Jug, 4¾" h, dull finish, carved clover dec, painted by Harriet Wenderoth, block-letter mark, date 1884, shape no. 61, "G" for ginger clay, incised artist's initials **250.00**

Tile, titled "The Lake," artist Elizabeth F. McDermott, blue-and-green pastels, artist's initials in lower right corner, 6½" × 8" image, 9½ × 13½" frame, $2,500.00.

Pin Tray, 5¼" l, peacock-feather shape, green matte glaze, blue around eye of feather, logo, date 1905, shape no. 1048 D, faint glaze crack across base ... **1175.00**

Pitcher, 7¼" h, high glaze, fanciful flowers interspersed by bizarre women's heads, dec by Jens Jensen, logo, date 1949, shape no. 6757, artist's monogram painted in brown slip **1,500.00**

Plaque

6¼ × 6¼", iris glaze, two fisherman, canoeing in shadow of snow-capped mountain, painted by Grace Young, marks on back of logo, date 1903, shape no. X499AX, incised "W" for white (iris) glaze, incised artist monogram, new frame **30,000.00**

7¾ × 4⅞", vellum glaze, dirt road running through stand of tall trees, painted by Fred Rothenbusch, artist's monogram painted in white slip on lower left hand corner, logo and date 1924 mark on back, orig paper label affixed to orig frame with notation "A Road to Town" **3,500.00**

9¼ × 14¾", vellum glaze, Venetian nocturnal scene, gondolier moving vessel past buildings, other gondolas tied to wharf, large stand of trees barely visible in upper left hand corner, painted by E T Hurley, initials incised in lower left-hand corner in front, marks on back include logo, late 1919, orig typed Rookwood label with notation "A Venetian Night E. T. Hurley" **8,000.00**

Potpourri Jar, 9¾" h, Black Opal glaze, bright green glazed inner and outer lids, small flowers dec, painted by Sara Sax, flambé-like glaze, logo, date 1923, shape no. 2451, incised artist's monogram, minor grinding of chips on base, burst bubble on outer lid **950.00**

Stein, 5⅝" h, Wiedenmann, pewter lid, eagle logo on side, imp Rookwood logo on base, date 1948, and notation "The Geo. Wiedenmann Brewing Co, Inc." **550.00**

Tea Tile, 6" d, Blue Ship, logo, shape no. M-28, 1920s **300.00**

Trivet, seagull, aventurine glaze over deep purple, logo, date 1930, shape no. 2351, fan-shaped esoteric mark **400.00**

Urn, 11½" h, Art Deco style, two loop handles, pastel stylized flowers, leaves, and fruit, three orange birds in flight, int. glazed in mottled blue over black, some allowed to drop down slightly from black slip, painted by Lorinda Epply, logo, date 1930, shape no. 6010 C, artist's monogram painted in black slip **2,200.00**

Vase

6¾" h, high glaze, bud, wisteria dec, painted by Ed Diers, logo, date 1924, shape no. 2545, incised artist's monogram **2,000.00**

6⅞" h, Glaze Effect, Randy Gray over Riley Blue over Ralphie Brown glazes, logo, date 1921, shape no. 6308 C **250.00**

7¼" h, vellum glaze, four geese flying past full moon, stand of leafy trees, painted by Sallie Coyne, logo, date 1911, shape no. 1356 E, "V" for vellum glaze body, incised artist's monogram, incised "V/G" for green vellum glaze **2,300.00**

7⅜" h, high glaze, leaping horse, fall flower, shades of gray and white, painted by Jens Jensen, imp logo, date 1946, shape no. 6325, notation "8767," artist's monogram painted on with black slip **600.00**

8¼" h, matte glaze, Art Nouveau style red poppies, painted by Kataro Shirayamadani, imp marks, logo, date 1940, shape no. 900 C, artist's cipher painted in black slip on base **3,000.00**

8⅜" h, vellum glaze, scenic, painted by ET Hurley, 1946, logo on base, logo, S (for Special shape), incised no. 5318, incised artist initials **1,900.00**

8½" h, vellum glaze, misty landscape scene, dusty rose trees and ducks, pale blue ground, painted by E T Hurley, imp mark on base, logo, date 1908, shape no. 938 C, "V" for vellum glaze, number "483" stamped twice, incised artist's initials, small glaze nick at base, two tiny glaze skips ... **800.00**

8¾" h, iris glaze, two large blue irises, yellow beards, painted by Ed Diers, logo, date 1903, shape no. 901 C, incised "W" for white (iris) glaze, tiny imp number "901", incised artist's monogram **4,000.00**

8⅞" h, iris glaze, two large night-blooming cereus flowers and stems, painted by Lenore Asbury, logo, date 1906, shape no. 900 B, incised "W", incised artist initials, nearly invisible crazing **8,750.00**

9¼" h, standard glaze, portrait of Native American wearing ceremonial garb, full headdress, painted by Grace Young, logo, date 1901, shape 829, wheel-ground X, incised notation "Umatilla P...," imp artist's monogram, slight glaze rub at rim ...**3,200.00**

9¾" h, iris glaze, finely detailed lily-of-the-valley dec, painted by Carl Schmidt, logo, date 1910, shape no. 904 CC, incised "W" for white (iris) glaze, imp artist's monogram **4,100.00**

10½" h, sea green, several sailing vessels, turbulent waters, painted by Sturgis Laurence, logo, date, shape no. 907D, incised "G" for sea green glaze, incised artist initials **5,000.00**

13⅞" h, iris glaze, nodding thistles in stages of bloom, small soft yellow buds, medium blue mature blooms, white pollen, painted by Carl Schmidt, logo, date 1907, shape no. 614B, incised "W" for white (iris) glaze, imp artist's monogram **35,000.00**

14⅞" h, vellum glaze, scenic, heavy colorful woods, small village with several buildings, castle, painted by Fred Rothenbusch, logo, date 1926, shape 614 B, incised "V" for vellum glaze, incised artist's monogram **5,500.00**

20¾" h, iris glaze, wisteria blossoms and vines, painted by Carl Schmidt, imp logo date 1908, shape 901 XX, artist's monogram, incised "W" for white (iris) glaze, small burst bubble on rim, minor scratch and glaze spot, documented as from Rookwood's own museum **30,000.00**

Whiskey Jug, 7" h, standard glaze, double gourd, hops dec, Gorham silver overlay, painted by Sallie Toohey, logo, date 1896, shape no. 674, incised artist's monogram, Gorham hallmarks and "R 2534 999/1000 FINE" on silver **1,500.00**

ROSE BOWLS

History: A rose bowl is a decorative open bowl with a crimped, pinched, or petal top which turns in but not back out again. Rose

bowls held fragrant rose petals or potpourri which served as an air freshener in the late Victorian period. Practically every glass manufacturer made rose bowls in a variety of patterns and glass types, including fine art glass.

Additional Listings: See specific glass categories.

Advisor: Johanna S. Billings.

Amberina, 3¼" h, 3¾" w, MOP satin, DQ pattern, eight crimps **485.00**

Amethyst, 3½" h, 4½" w, free blown, thirty pleated crimps, rough pontil, Blenko, c1952 .... **40.00**

Burmese
  2¼" h, prunus blossom dec, polished pontil, Webb **375.00**
  3" h, 3" w, eight crimps, semi-ground pontil, Italian, 1960s **40.00**

Cranberry, 4" h, 6½" d, collar foot, eight crimps, Fenton for L G Wright, 1960s **75.00**

Emerald Green, transparent, enameled gold-leaf iris, light green leaves, eight crimps, rough pontil **65.00**

Fenton
  Barber, Robert, 8½" h, 7¼" w, blue with white pulled-feather design, matte finish, six crimps, polished pontil, stamped "Fenton 1975," limited edition of 700 .... **125.00**

Robert Barber, blue with white pulled-feather design, matte finish, six crimps, polished pontil stamped "Fenton 1975," limited to 700, 8½" h, 7¼" w, $125.00.

Opalescent Hobnail, 2½" h, 3" h, blue, eight crimps, collar foot, c1950 .... **30.00**

Satin
  2¾" h, 3¼" w, light powder blue top shading to

Satin, pink, eight inverted ribs, eight crimps, ground pontil, enameled pale yellow and blue flowers and berries, with orange and brown stems around top and between ribs, $175.00.

creamy white bottom, enameled yellow daisies with green and brown foliage, lightly crimped rim highlighted in gold, Mt Washington 400.00

3″ h, 3″ w, cream, MOP, DQ, eight crimps, polished pontil 225.00

4½″ h
    4½″ w, blue, emb shells, eight crimps, smooth pontil 120.00
    5½″ w, yellow, eight crimps, ground pontil 50.00

4¾″ h, 5¼″ w, pink, enameled pale yellow and blue flowers, berries, orange and brown stems around top and between ribs, eight inverted ribs, eight crimps, ground pontil 175.00

7¼″ h, 8″ w, white, hp, three big yellow flowers, little blue flowers, green leaves, eight crimps with heavy gold trim, ground pontil 120.00

Spangled (Vasa Murrhina), 4½″ h, 5″ w, apricot, white int. casing, eight crimps, rough pontil 110.00

Vaseline, 4⅞″ h, 5½″ w, vertical opalescent stripes, five pink and white applied glass flowers, clear applied glass stems, eight crimps, rough pontil 125.00

ROSE CANTON, ROSE MANDARIN, AND ROSE MEDALLION

History: The pink rose color has given its name to three related groups of Chinese export porcelain: Rose Mandarin, Rose Medallion, and Rose Canton, and Rose Medallion.

Rose Mandarin, which was produced from the late 18th century to approximately 1840, derives its name from the Mandarin figure(s) found in garden scenes with women and children. The women often have gold decorations in their hair. Polychrome enamels and birds separate the scenes.

Rose Medallion, which originated in the early 19th century and was made through the early 20th century, has alternating panels of figures and birds and flowers. The elements are four in number, separated evenly around the center medallion. Peonies and foliage fill voids.

Rose Canton, which was introduced somewhat later than Rose Mandarin and was produced through the first half of the 19th century, is similar to Rose Medallion except the figural panels are replaced by flowers. People are present only if the medallion partitions are absent. Some patterns have been named, e.g., Butterfly and Cabbage and Rooster. Rose Canton actually is a catchall term for any pink enamel ware not fitting into the first two groups.

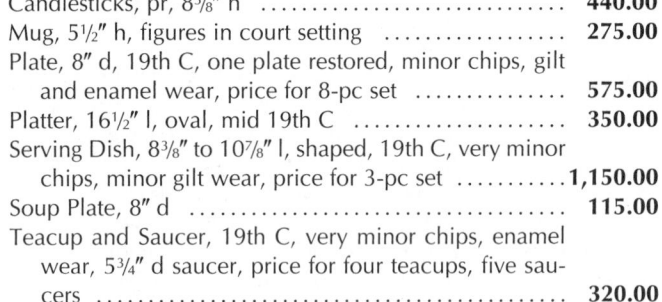

REPRODUCTION ALERT

Rose Medallion is still made although the quality does not match the earlier examples.

Rose Canton

Bowl, 10″ d, gold trim, scalloped 250.00
Box, cov, 13″ d, octagonal, dome lid, c1800 .... 265.00
Brush Pot, 4¾″ h, ladies in pavilion, reticulated, relief molded, gilt trim, c1850 .... 300.00
Creamer, 4″ h, double twisted handle, gilt trim 225.00
Plate, 8½″ d, floral, insects on border 85.00
Rice Bowl, 6¾″ d 75.00

Rose Mandarin

Box, cov, 2⅛″ h, 19th C, restoration 150.00
Brush Pot, 10″ h 225.00
Candlesticks, pr, 8⅝″ h 440.00
Mug, 5½″ h, figures in court setting 275.00
Plate, 8″ d, 19th C, one plate restored, minor chips, gilt and enamel wear, price for 8-pc set 575.00
Platter, 16½″ l, oval, mid 19th C 350.00
Serving Dish, 8⅜″ to 10⅞″ l, shaped, 19th C, very minor chips, minor gilt wear, price for 3-pc set 1,150.00
Soup Plate, 8″ d 115.00
Teacup and Saucer, 19th C, very minor chips, enamel wear, 5¾″ d saucer, price for four teacups, five saucers 320.00

Rose Mandarin, plate, 9⅞″ d, $75.00.

Rose Medallion

Bouillon Cup and Saucer 65.00
Brush Pot, 5¾″ h, cylindrical, wooden stand, carved lid, 19th C 525.00

Cache Pot, 5¾" d, 6" d underplate, hexagonal, 19th C **185.00**
Candlestick, 8" h, columnar form, flaring nozzle pan and
    base, price for 3 matched pcs, minor base chip **725.00**
Compote, 4¼" h, 9⅛" d, 19th C **230.00**
Creamer, 4" h, bulbous, late 19th C **95.00**
Dish, 14" l, lobed lozenge form, scalloped edge, ftd, 19th
    C **350.00**
Fruit Dish, 9¼" d, circular, scalloped edge, mid 19th C **130.00**
Garden Seat
    18¾" h, 19th C, repaired **475.00**
    19" h, keg design, mid 19th C **2,600.00**
Milk Jug, 6½" h, 19th C **525.00**
Plate, 8" d, center with crest of Macartney & Filgate ... **800.00**
Punch Bowl, 14½" d, 19th C, minor gilt and enamel
    wear, hairline **1,380.00**
Sauce Boat, cov, 7½" l, gold handles and finial **450.00**
Teapot and Teacup, 5¼" h teapot, orig fitted basket, early
    20th C, hairlines, gilt and enamel wear **115.00**
Vase, 10½" h, baluster, neck and shoulders with applied
    dragons and foo dogs, price for pr **700.00**
Vegetable Stand, cov, 9¼" l, rect, notched corners, gilt
    fruit handle on lid, mid 19th C **425.00**

ROSENTHAL

History: Rosenthal Porcelain Manufactory began operating at Selb, Bavaria, in 1880. Specialties were tablewares and figurines. The firm is still in operation.

Bonbon, 2½ × 5¼", Winifred pattern, pink Moss Rose
    dec, SS base **30.00**
Bowl, 10¾" d, pink, strawberries and leaves, scalloped
    gold trim, scroll handle, red glazed underside, artist
    sgd **85.00**
Cake Plate, 10" d, multicolored roses, cobalt blue and
    gold border **55.00**
Coffee Cup and Saucer, white porcelain cup, .800 silver
    holder and saucer, Art Nouveau dec, initials, price
    for 6-pc set **750.00**
Creamer and Sugar, gold trim, sgd "Donatello" **45.00**
Cup and Saucer, Maria pattern, heavy silver overlay .. **65.00**
Dessert Set, Maria pattern, teapot, creamer, cov sugar,
    six cups, saucers, and dessert plates, 1908–48, price
    for 23-pc set **350.00**
Dinner Service, Regina pattern, gold trim, price for 101-
    pc set **1,000.00**
Dresser Set, lavender flowers, gold trim, price for 3-pc
    set **75.00**
Figure
    Bird on branch, artist sgd, 6" h **135.00**
    Boy with lamb **140.00**
    Rabbit, dark brown, 3" h **65.00**
    Springer Spaniel, basket, 1932, 7½" h **195.00**
Fruit Set, 10" d bowl, six 8" d plates, blue, green, yellow,
    and pink, pink roses, gold dec, price for 7-pc set ... **395.00**

Figure, little girl holding floral bouquet in one arm, basket of flowers over other arm, 8½" h, $125.00.

Nappy, brown nuts and flowers on gold ground, ruffled
    rim **50.00**
Nut Set, master bowl, six 3½" d serving bowls, Pompa-
    dour pattern, cream ground, ornate gold scrolled rim,
    price for 7-pc set **65.00**
Place Card Holder, small multicolored floral dec **15.00**
Plate, 8" d, pastel daisies, price for 6-pc set **95.00**
Teacup and Saucer, Donatello pattern, price for 12-set **50.00**
Vase
    7" h, crackle, rust foliage, artist sgd "Stockmayer,"
    1946 .... **125.00**
    9½" h, tulip shape, hp, pastel flowers, artist sgd **95.00**
    17½" h, Studio Line, bisque ext., glazed int., cylin-
    drical, flaring neck, molded bands of figures sup-
    porting ribs of flowers, designed by Bjorn Winblad **275.00**

ROSEVILLE POTTERY

History: In the late 1880s a group of investors purchased the J. B. Owens Pottery in Roseville, Ohio, and made utilitarian stoneware items. In 1892 the firm was incorporated and joined by George F. Young who became general manager. Four generations of Youngs controlled Roseville until the early 1950s.

A series of acquisitions began: Midland Pottery of Roseville in 1898, Clark Stoneware Plant in Zanesville (formerly used by Peters and Reed), and Muskingum Stoneware (Mosaic Tile Company) in Zanesville. In 1898 the offices also moved from Roseville to Zanesville.

In 1900 Roseville introduced Rozane, an art pottery. Rozane became a trade name to cover a large series of lines. The art lines were made in limited amounts after 1919.

The success of Roseville depended on its commercial lines, first developed by John J. Herald and Frederick Rhead in the first decades of the 1900s. In 1918 Frank Ferrell became art director and developed over 80 lines of pottery. The economic depression of the 1930s brought more lines, including Pine Cone.

In the 1940s a series of high-gloss glazes were tried in an attempt to revive certain lines. In 1952 Raymor dinnerware was produced. None of these changes brought economic success and in November 1954 Roseville was bought by the Mosaic Tile Company.

References: Susan and Al Bagdade, *Warman's American Pottery and Porcelain,* Wallace-Homestead, 1994; John W. Humphries, *A Price Guide to Roseville Pottery by the Numbers,* published by author, 1993; Sharon and Bob Huxford, *The Collectors Encyclopedia of Roseville Pottery,* First Series, (1976, 1995 value update), Second Series (1980, 1993 value update), Collector Books; Ralph and Terry Kovel, *Kovels' American Art Pottery,* Crown Publishers, 1993; Randall B. Monsen, *Collector's Compendium of Roseville Pottery,* Monsen and Baer (Box 529, Vienna, VA 22183), 1995; Dana G. Morykan and Harry L. Rinker, *Warman's Country Antiques & Collectibles,* Third Edition, Wallace-Homestead, 1996; Leslie Pina, *Pottery,* Schiffer Publishing, 1994.

Collectors' Clubs: American Art Pottery Assoc, 125 E Rose Ave, St Louis, MO 63119; Roseville's of the Past, PO Box 681117, Orlando, FL 32868.

Additional Listings: See *Warman's Americana & Collectibles* for more examples.

Basket
    Fuchsia, blue, attached frog, #358, 8" h **500.00**
    Iris, 8" h, blue, #35 .... **285.00**
    Rozane, 12½" h, pink, yellow, and green flowers, white ground, unmarked, small glaze nicks **50.00**
    White Rose, 10½" h, green, marked "Roseville U.S.A. 363-10" **175.00**
Bowl
    Baneda, 7 × 3", green **300.00**
    Cherry Blossom, 6" d, 1930s **300.00**
    Snowberry, 5¼"h , two small handles, marked "Roseville U.S.A. 1RB-5" **150.00**
Candlesticks, pr
    Allover Persian floral pattern, matte green, unmarked, 14" h, 7¼" d base **600.00**
    Snowberry, blue, #1CS-2 .... **150.00**
Console Bowl, Ferella, 12" d, raspberry **600.00**
Creamer, Cream Ware, 2⅞" h, sailing ships transfer, unmarked, dark int. line and nicks on spout **50.00**
Ewer
    Clematis, blue, #18, 15" **260.00**
    Fuchsia, blue, #902, 10" h **475.00**
    Magnolia, blue, 15⅜" h, base emb with logo and shape number "15-15," blue slip-painted numbers "23" and "3" **175.00**
Frog
    Carnelian I, blue **45.00**
    Fuchsia
        Blue **275.00**
        Green **175.00**
Fruit Bowl, Snowberry, blue, #15B-10 .... **275.00**
Hanging Basket, Fuchsia, blue **600.00**
Jar, Foxglove, blue, #659, 10" **500.00**
Jardiniere
    Futura, 7" h **250.00**
    White Rose, #658, 10", hole drilled for drainage .. **290.00**
Jardiniere and Pedestal
    Florentine, ivory, 29½" h **625.00**
    Fuchsia, blue, 24" h **1,650.00**
    Sunflower, good mold and definition, unmarked, 28 × 14" **3,200.00**
Lamp, Ixia, blue **525.00**
Lamp Base, Pauleo, factory drilled, 19" h, tight hairline at drill hole **725.00**

Teapot, repeating gray, yellow, and dark blue Art Nouveau designs, white ground, clear high glaze, marked "156" on base, 8" h, small chips on inside lid **225.00**
Urn, Snowberry, blue, #1ur-8 .... **185.00**
Vase
    Baneda
        4" h, pink **325.00**
        5" h, red **300.00**
        6" h, orig paper label **325.00**
        6½" × 6", volcano, pink **550.00**
        10" h, pink **1,000.00**
        12" h, green **1,250.00**
    Blackberry, 10" **500.00**
    Cherry Blossom, 5" h, brown **300.00**
    Columbine, two handles, pink, 10¼" h, marked "Roseville U.S.A. 23-10" **200.00**
    Cosmos, two handles, imp marks and logo, shape no. 956-12, 12⅜" h **400.00**
    Della Robbia, designed by Frederick Hurten Rhead, carved and painted by artist E C, stylized Art Nouveau designs, six colors, small blue flowers with yellow centers, stylized fleur-de-lis, band of chevrons around shoulder, artist's initials carved into foot, two paper labels affixed to base, six small glaze nicks, 11¾" h, descended through family of George F Young, accompanied by unissued Roseville stock certificate and family documentation **13,000.00**
    Fuchsia
        6" h, green, 896 .... **195.00**
        8" h, blue, 898-8 .... **500.00**
        12" h, blue, 963 .... **475.00**
    Laurel, Art Deco design, orange, flowing black highlights, unmarked, 6¼" h **175.00**
    Monticello, 5" h
        557, blue **400.00**
        558 .... **300.00**
    Paneled Nude, fan, 8" h, green **400.00**
    Snowberry, blue, #1V-28 .... **175.00**
    Sunflower, 5" h, handle **425.00**
    Wisteria, 9" h, brown **525.00**

Wall Pocket, Blackberry, 8½", $375.00.

Wall Pocket

Antique matte green

11/160/3/1, 12" l 525.00

11/162/3/3 .... 475.00

Florentine, 8¾" h, marked "Roseville 1238-8," three

minor chips on back 125.00

Ivory II, double pinecone shape 295.00

ROYAL BAYREUTH

History: In 1794 the Royal Bayreuth factory was founded in Tettau, Bavaria. Royal Bayreuth introduced their figural patterns in 1885. Designs of animals, people, fruits, and vegetables decorated a wide array of tablewares and inexpensive souvenir items.

Tapestry wares, in rose and other patterns, were made in the late 19th century. The surface of the piece feels and looks like woven cloth. Tapestry ware was made by covering the porcelain with a piece of fabric tightly stretched over the surface, decorating the fabric, glazing the piece, and firing.

Royal Bayreuth still manufactures dinnerware. It has not maintained production of earlier wares, particularly the figural items. Since thorough records are unavailable, it is difficult to verify the chronology of production.

Marks: The Royal Bayreuth crest used to mark the wares varied in design and color.

References: Susan and Al Bagdade, *Warman's English & Continental Pottery & Porcelain,* Second Edition, Wallace-Homestead, 1991; Mary J. McCaslin, *Royal Bayreuth,* Antique Publications, 1994.

Collectors' Club: Royal Bayreuth Collectors Club, 926 Essex Circle, Kalamazoo, I 49008; Royal Bayreuth International Collectors' Society, PO Box 325, Orrville, OH 44667.

Devil & Cards

Candy Dish 195.00

Creamer 250.00

Cup and Saucer 175.00

Dresser Tray 250.00

Milk Pitcher 500.00

Salt, master 175.00

Grape Cluster,

Cracker Jar, cov, white pearl, blue mark 675.00

Creamer and Sugar

Purple 395.00

White pearl, blue mark 475.00

Salt and Pepper Shakers, pr, purple 165.00

Wall Pocket 500.00

Lobster, red

Ashtray 60.00

Bowl, 8" d, blue mark 375.00

Creamer 75.00

Radish Bowl, 5" d, blue mark 275.00

Miscellaneous Patterns

Bowl, Dutch children, 6" d 65.00

Candlestick, Basset, marked 600.00

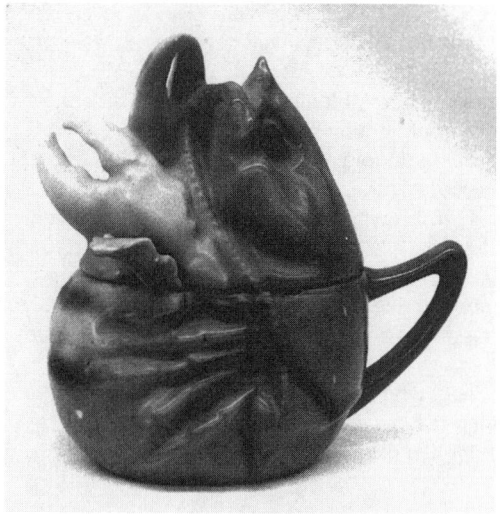

Lobster, cov mustard with leaf spoon, $125.00.

Cigarette Holder, Oak Leaf, pearl, marked 275.00

Coffeepot, 8" h, 7" w, Brittany girl with draft horse, scene of trees and meadow, blue mark, lid not orig 450.00

Creamer

Alligator, white, unmarked 550.00

Apple 250.00

Bull, red, marked 150.00

Butterfly, open wings, brown, orange, gray, and green, 3½" h, blue mark 325.00

Chick, unmarked 225.00

Cow, red 300.00

Dachshund, unmarked 145.00

Eagle, marked 450.00

Fish Head

Blue mark 250.00

Unmarked 95.00

Frog

Green, blue mark 300.00

Red, blue mark 195.00

Monkey, green, marked 575.00

Mountain Goat, marked 450.00

Oak Leaf, green luster, Depoinert 125.00

Orange, marked 175.00

Parakeet, red, unmarked 275.00

Pelican 275.00

Pig, gray, blue mark 495.00

Poodle, gray, blue mark 275.00

Robin, marked 90.00

Seal, blue mark 400.00

Shell, purple, sea-horse handle 225.00

St Bernard, unmarked 350.00

Creamer and Sugar, cov, strawberry, blue mark 450.00

Dresser Box, cov, 3 × 4½", 3 gold feet, peacock dec 250.00

Hair Receiver, cov, rose 600.00

Humidor, cov

Coachman, blue mark 795.00

Gorilla, black, blue mark 1,075.00

Match Holder

Arab on horseback, another horse beside him .. 175.00

Elk, brown 250.00

Mug, elk	550.00
String Holder, rooster, marked	500.00
Sugar, cov	
Orange, figural, blue mark	375.00
Pansy, purple, tiny rim flake	225.00
Sugar, open, double rooster, unmarked	425.00
Teapot, cov, figural, pansy, purple, blue mark	625.00
Vase, 4″ h, brown, grapes dec, cobalt blue, green, and gold	75.00

Pear

Creamer and Sugar, cov, white pearl, marked	575.00
Demitasse Cup and Saucer, pear, white pearl, marked	300.00

Poppy

Cake Plate, white pearl, open handles	225.00
Creamer, red	145.00
Match Holder, standing, red	550.00
Sugar, cov	225.00

Red Clown

Ashtray, blue mark	345.00
Candlestick, 6½ × 4½″	525.00
Creamer, blue mark	450.00
Match Holder, hanging, blue mark	425.00
Mug, unmarked	435.00

Red Devil

Ashtray, blue mark	165.00
Creamer, blue mark	550.00

Snow Babies

Cereal Set, sledding	175.00
Plate, 6″ d, babies playing	85.00
Salt Shaker	120.00
Trivet, Snow Babies, blue mark	110.00

Sunbonnet Babies

Bell, sewing, unmarked	400.00
Creamer, tall, squared mouth, worn gold trim	220.00
Creamer and Sugar, open, price for pr	475.00
Cup and Saucer, babies sewing	155.00
Hatpin Holder	250.00
Plate, 9″ d, washing clothes	245.00

Tomato

Biscuit Jar, cov	200.00
Creamer and Sugar	75.00
Cup and Saucer	115.00
Teapot, individual size, marked	225.00
Water Pitcher, marked	300.00

Rose Tapestry

Bell, pink roses	545.00
Bowl, 5″ d	450.00
Box, cov, round, dome lid, three-color roses, shape #1187	400.00
Candleholder, three-color roses, shape #1251	860.00
Chocolate Set, chocolate pot, four matching cup and saucers, three-color roses, blue mark, price for 10 pc set	2,800.00
Creamer	
Corset shape	175.00
Shape #1095, two-color roses, rose-colored ground	385.00
Cup and Saucer	400.00
Plate, 7½″ d, three-color roses, shape #1263	190.00
Shoe, pink roses, orig lace trim, blue mark	400.00
Sugar, cov, pink roses, shape #1310	220.00

Tapestry, pitcher, pastoral scene, blue mark, 5″ h, $345.00.

Sugar, matching underplate	450.00
Teapot, three-color roses	650.00

Tapestry, Miscellaneous

Creamer	
The Bathers, 3½″ h, shape #1038	285.00
Sheep	
Shape #1060	295.00
Shape #1074, 4″ h	355.00
Dresser Tray, Japanese chrysanthemum dec, leaf shape	225.00
Humidor, Bell Ringer pattern	775.00
Match Holder, sheep, wall type, shape #1059	485.00
Plate, 5½″ d, basket lady with horse, shape #949	595.00
Powder Dish, cov, 5½ × 3½″, colonial couple dancing	495.00
Vase	
The Bathers, 8¼″ h, shape #1025	435.00
Castle by the Lake, shape #1015	365.00
Cottage by Waterfall, shape #1015	365.00

ROYAL BONN

History: In 1836 Franz Anton Mehlem founded a Rhineland factory that produced earthenware and porcelain, including household, decorative, technical, and sanitary items.

The firm reproduced Hochst figures between 1887 and 1903. These figures, in both porcelain and earthenware, were made from the original molds from the defunct Prince-Electoral Mayence Manufactory in Hochst. The factory was purchased by Villeroy and Boch in 1921 and closed in 1931.

Marks: In 1890 the word "Royal" was added to the mark. All items made after 1890 include the "Royal Bonn" mark.

Biscuit Jar, 6⅝" h, 5¼" d, floral dec, beige and cream-colored ground, rose, purple, and yellow flowers, green leaves, emb scrolls	210.00
Bowl, 9½" d, cream, floral dec, metal rim, c1760	195.00
Celery Tray, floral dec	85.00
Cheese Dish, cov, pink, floral design	125.00
Cup and Saucer, blue and white, wild roses dec	45.00
Ewer, 6½" h, gold handle, floral tapestry, scene with brick fence	150.00
Mug, 4" h, blackberries and flowers, shaded green ground	65.00
Spittoon, two cartouches with Oriental scenes	150.00
Teapot, 4½ × 9½", cream, red, black, and blue florals, gold trim, marked "1755"	125.00

Vase

5½" h, Victorian boy and girl sledding, shaded fuchsia ground	150.00
7" h, globular, Boucher scenes, blue transfers, 1850	125.00
8¼" h, portrait type, artist sgd	795.00
11" h, Woman with Shawl, green ground, gold overlay base and neck, four handles, artist sgd	875.00

Vase, bulbous, floral design, light yellow-green ground, burgundy neck, gliding at top, impressed and painted marks, 9" h, $185.00.

c1889   c1923

ROYAL COPENHAGEN

History: Franz Mueller established a porcelain factory at Copenhagen in 1775. When bankruptcy threatened in 1779, the Danish king acquired ownership, appointing Mueller manager and selecting the name "Royal Copenhagen." The crown sold its interest in 1867; the company remains privately owned today.

Blue Fluted, Royal Copenhagen's most famous pattern, was created in 1780. It is of Chinese origin and comes in three styles: smooth edge, closed lace edge, and perforated lace edge (full lace). Many other factories copied it.

Flora Danica, named for a famous botanical work, was introduced in 1789 and remained exclusive to Royal Copenhagen. It is identified by its freehand illustrations of plants and its hand-cut edges and perforations.

Marks: Royal Copenhagen porcelain is marked with three wavy lines (which signify ancient waterways) and a crown (added in 1889). Stoneware does not have the crown mark.

Additional Listings: Limited Edition Collector Plates.

Bouillon Cup and Saucer, Flora Danica pattern, botanical specimen within border, pink enamel and gilding, price for 12-pc set	7,500.00
Bowl, 4½" d, orange blossoms, green leaves	95.00
Box, cov, egg shape, sea gulls on cov	195.00
Dessert Service, blue floral imbricated border, coffeepot, creamer, cov sugar, cake tray, fruit bowl, 12 cake plates, cups, and saucers	450.00

Dinner Service

Blue fluted half-lace pattern, service for 8, cups and saucers, dinner plates, bread and butter plates, teapot, sq vegetable, meat platter, serving bowl, nappy, tri-part dish, butter pats, creamer, sugar, and waste bowl, price for 43-pc set	1,600.00
Blue foliate sprays, molded basketweave borders, dinner, luncheon, bread and butter, salad plates, tea, coffee, and demitasse cups and saucers, tea set, soup bowls, 19 additional pieces, price for 175-pc set	2,645.00

Figure

Boy, sitting on rocks, whittling stick, sgd on back of rocks, #905, 7½" h	275.00
Goose Girl, #528	210.00
Mouse, seated on nut, #511, 2¾" h	45.00
Nude on Rock, #4027	150.00
Pan, sitting on column, holding flute, rabbit at base, 8½" h	375.00
Pekinese, tan and white, begging on haunches, #1776	150.00

Figure, labeled "Ole Luke Oje," Mr. Sandman from Hans Christian Anderson, triple wavy line and crown mark, 6⅞" h, $495.00.

Satyr, holding snake, sitting, #1712, 3 × 5″ **225.00**
Siamese Cat, #3281, seated, 7¾″ h **195.00**
Fruit Compote, Floridian pattern, "Potentilla Nivea L."
    inscribed underneath bowl **550.00**
Jardiniere, 13″ h, anemones dec, 1890s **275.00**
Plate, 8½″ d, outdoor winter scene **50.00**
Platter, 17¼″ l, oval, Flora Danica pattern, marked and
    numbered **450.00**
Tea Set, Fluted Lace pattern, blue and white, price for 5-
    pc set **295.00**
Tray, 6½″ d, round, rose, fish swimming **150.00**
Vase
    7″ h, mermaid on rocks, gazing into harbor **95.00**
    7¾″ h, floral and dragonfly dec, c1890 .... **150.00**
    11½″ h, Faience Moderne **140.00**

ROYAL CROWN DERBY

History: Derby Crown Porcelain Co., established in 1875 in Derby, England, had no connection with earlier Derby factories which operated in the late 18th and early 19th centuries. In 1890 the company was appointed "Manufacturers of Porcelain to Her Majesty" (Queen Victoria) and since that date has been known as "Royal Crown Derby."

Most of these porcelains, both tableware and figural, were hand decorated. A variety of printing processes were used for additional adornment. Today, Royal Crown Derby is a part of Royal Doulton Tableware, Ltd.

Marks: Derby porcelains from 1878 to 1890 carry only the standard crown printed mark. After 1891 the mark includes the "Royal Crown Derby" wording. In the 20th century "Made in England" and "English Bone China" were added to the mark.

References: Susan and Al Bagdade, *Warman's English & Continental Pottery & Porcelain,* Second Edition, Wallace-Homestead, 1991; John Twitchett, *The Dictionary of Derby Porcelain 1748–1848,* Antique Collectors' Club, out of print; John Twitchett and Betty Bailey, *Royal Crown Derby,* Antique Collectors' Club, 1988.

Bowl, Chinoiserie dec, four small feet **145.00**
Creamer and Sugar, cov, Dublin shape, Imari pattern . **300.00**
Cup and Saucer **60.00**
Demitasse Cup and Saucer **50.00**
Dish, oval, small **40.00**
Ewer, 7½″ h, raised gold dec on reticulated cobalt blue
    neck and handle, enameled flowers on gold ground **675.00**
Figure, 10¼″ h, young man, foot on lap of woman, pol-
    ychrome and gilt, edge chips on foliage **300.00**
Plate, 8¼″ d, Japan pattern, No. 2451, price for 8-pc set **115.00**
Tea Cup and Saucer, 2¼″ h cup, Japan pattern, price for
    14-pc set **115.00**
Urn, cov, 5″ h, yellow ground, leaves and butterflies,
    molded mask handles, 1887 .... **425.00**
Vase
    8″ h, 6½″ w, bottle neck, angle handle, hp flowers,
      gilt trim, cream ground, 1890–1920 .... **495.00**
    10¾″ h, ivory, polychrome floral dec, gilt trim **175.00**

Plate, Royal Crown Derby pattern 2451, 7⅛″ d, $50.00.

ROYAL
DOULTON
FLAMBE

ROYAL DOULTON

History: Doulton pottery began in 1815 under the direction of John Doulton at the Doulton & Watts pottery in Lambeth, England. Early output was limited to salt-glazed industrial stoneware. After John Watts retired in 1854, the firm became Doulton and Company, and production was expanded to include hand-decorated stoneware such as figurines, vases, dinnerware, and flasks.

In 1878, John's son, Sir Henry Doulton, purchased Pinder Bourne & Co. in Burslem. The companies became Doulton & Co., Ltd. in 1882. Decorated porcelain was added to Doulton's earthenware production in 1884.

Most Doulton figurines were produced at the Burslem plants where they were made continuously from 1890 until 1978. After a short interruption, a new line of Doulton figurines was introduced in 1979.

Dickens ware, in earthenware and porcelain, was introduced in 1908. The pieces were decorated with characters from Dickens's novels. Most of the line was withdrawn in the 1940s, except for plates which continued to be made until 1974.

Character jugs, a 20th-century revival of early Toby models, were designed by Charles J. Noke for Doulton in the 1930s. Character jugs are limited to bust portraits while Royal Doulton toby jugs are full figured. The character jugs come in four sizes and feature fictional characters from Dickens, Shakespeare and other English and American novelists, as well as historical heroes. Marks on both character and toby jugs must be carefully identified to determine dates and values.

Doulton's Rouge Flambé (Veined Sung) is a high-glazed, strong-colored ware noted primarily for the fine modeling and exquisite colorings, especially in the animal items. The process used to produce the vibrant colors is a Doulton secret.

Production of stoneware at Lambeth ceased in 1956; production of porcelain continues today at Burslem.

Marks: Beginning in 1872 the "Royal Doulton" mark was used on all types of wares produced by the company.

Beginning in 1913, an "HN" number was assigned to each new Doulton figurine design. The "HN" numbers, which referred originally to Harry Nixon, a Doulton artist, were chronological until 1940, after which blocks of numbers were assigned to each modeler. From 1928 until 1954, a small number was placed to the right of the crown mark; this number added to 1927 gives the year of manufacture.

References: Susan and Al Bagdade, *Warman's English & Continental Pottery & Porcelain,* Second Edition, Wallace-Homestead, 1991; Diana and John Callow and Marilyn and Peter Sweet, *The Charlton Price Guide to Beswick Animals,* Second Edition, Charlton Press, 1995; Jean Dale, *The Charlton Standard Catalogue of Royal Doulton Animals,* Charlton Press, 1994; ———, *The Charlton Standard Catalogue of Royal Doulton Beswick Jugs,* Charlton Press, 1995; ———, *The Charlton Standard Catalogue of Royal Doulton Beswick Storybook Figurines,* Charlton Press, 1994; ———, *The Charlton Standard Catalogue of Royal Doulton Figurines,* Fourth Edition, Charlton Press, 1994; ———, *The Charlton Standard Catalogue of Royal Doulton Jugs,* Charlton Press, 1991; Doug Pinchin, *The Doulton Figure Collectors Handbook,* Fourth Edition, Francis-Joseph Books, 1996, distributed by Wallace-Homestead.

Periodicals: *Collecting Doulton,* BBR Publishing, 2 Strattford Ave, Elsecar, Nr Barnsley, S Yorkshire, S74 8AA, England; *Doulton Divvy,* PO Box 2434, Joliet, IL 60434.

Collectors' Clubs: Heartland Doulton Collectors, PO Box 2434, Joliet, IL 60434; Mid-America Doulton Collectors, PO Box 483, McHenry, IL 60050; Royal Doulton International Collectors Club, PO Box 6705, Somerset, NJ 08873; Royal Doulton International Collectors Club, 850 Progress Ave, Scarborough Ontario M1H 3C4 Canada.

Biscuit Jar, cov, 6 × 7¾", ribbed cream ground, band of turquoise with birds and animals, SP top, rim, and handle, marked "Doulton, Burslem Pottery" 225.00
Bowl, 8⅞ × 4¼", blue, brown geometric borders, grazing cows and horses, sgd "Hannah Barlow, 1885" . 675.00
Character Jug, large
    Anne of Cleves, ears up 320.00
    Aramis 120.00
    'Arriet 280.00
    'Arry 280.00

Candlesticks, pr, tapered cylindrical standard with bulbous bottom, leaf motif on dome base and bulbous portion of standard, green, brown, and blue earth tones, sgd "Parkington," c1880–91, 5¾" d, $395.00.

Character Jugs, left: Regency Beau, D6559, $808.00; center: Punch & Judy, D6590, $465.00; right: Mikado, D6501, $462.00. Photo courtesy of Andre Ammelounx Auctions.

Athos 120.00
Auld Mac 110.00
Captain Ahab 140.00
Captain Henry Morgan 130.00
D'Artagnan 120.00
Dick Turpin 180.00
Don Quixote 140.00
Falconer, black and white striped hat 30.00
Falstaff 120.00
Farmer John 180.00
Fireman 90.00
Fortune Teller 550.00
Friar Tuck 180.00
Gardener 220.00
Gone Away 100.00
Granny 130.00
Jarge 300.00
Jockey 395.00
John Peel 220.00
Johnny Appleseed 420.00
King Henry V 280.00
Lord Nelson 380.00
Mad Hatter 175.00
Mine Host 140.00
Old Salt 120.00
Paddy 180.00
Pickwick 200.00
Porthos 120.00
Robin Hood, plain handle 180.00
Ronald Reagan 395.00
Sam Johnson 420.00
Simon the Cellarer 180.00
Simple Simon 575.00
St George & Dragon 320.00
Ugly Duchess 595.00
Uncle Tom Cobbleigh 475.00
Viking 290.00
Walrus & Carpenter 220.00
White-Haired Clown 1,500.00
Cup and Saucer, Pastoral pattern 12.00
Ewer, 9" h, Babes in Wood Series, girl with cape in woods 1,250.00
Figure
    Ann Boleyn 125.00
    Anne of Cleves 125.00
    Bell of the Ball, HN1997 .... 350.00
    Biddy Penny Farthing, HN1843, 9" h 100.00

Bo Peep, M-82 .... **500.00**
Calumet, HN2068, 6¼" h **495.00**
Carpet Seller, HN1464 .... **325.00**
Catherine of Aragon **125.00**
Farmer's Wife, HN2089 .... **470.00**
Genie, HN2989 .... **150.00**
Good King Wenceslas, HN2118 .... **400.00**
Henry VII **95.00**
Irene, HN1621, 6½" h **315.00**
J & B International
    Captain Cook **65.00**
    John Bull **95.00**
    Samurai Warrior **65.00**
    Uncle Sam **100.00**
J & B Pickwick
    Mr Pickwick **95.00**
    Mr Quaker, orig box **525.00**
    Old Mr Turveydrop **95.00**
    Sam Weller **95.00**
    Town Crier **95.00**
Julia, HN2705 .... **160.00**
Mayor, HN2280 .... **400.00**
Midnette, HN2090 .... **250.00**
New Bonnet, HN1728 .... **550.00**
Newsboy, HN2244 .... **450.00**
Owd William, HN2042 .... **210.00**
St George & Dragon, NH2051 .... **475.00**
Top o' the Hill, HN1833, 7¼" h **100.00**
Wild West, history card
    Annie Oakley **100.00**
    Buffalo Bill **100.00**
    Doc Holiday **100.00**
    Geronimo **145.00**
    Wild Bill Hickock **100.00**
    Wyatt Earp **100.00**
Flambé
Figure
    Cat, 12" h **350.00**
    Owl, 12" h **350.00**
    Rhinoceros, seated, No. 615, 9" h, 17" l **875.00**
    Vase, 7½" h, melon-shaped top, Sung, sgd "Fred
      Moore" **550.00**
Loving Cup, Three Musketeers, #216, certificate, pro-
    fessionally repaired **725.00**
Plate, bread and butter, Pastoral pattern **8.00**
Service Plate, 10½" d, apple green borders, gilded
    scrolls, printed marks, price for 12-pc set **1,100.00**
Spittoon
    European landscape, blue and white, sgd "Geneva" **275.00**
    Landscape scene, brown and green luster **160.00**
    Poppies, inner border with grapes and leaves **110.00**
Teapot, two pansy reserves and pale flowers dec, gilt
    handle, marked "Doulton Burslem," late 19th or
    early 20th C **170.00**
Toby Mug
    Capt Ahab, D6500, 6¾" h **90.00**
    Churchill, seated **75.00**
    Lord Nelson **260.00**
Toothpick Holder
    Doulton Burslem, flowers, gold trim **90.00**
    Gamp **510.00**
Vegetable Bowl, cov, Watteau pattern **315.00**

ROYAL DUX

History: Royal Dux porcelain was made in Dux, Bohemia (now the Czech Republic), by E. Eichler at the Duxer Porzellan-Manufaktur, established in 1860. Many items were exported to the United States. By the turn of the century Royal Dux figurines, vases, and accessories, especially those featuring Art Nouveau designs, were captivating consumers.

Marks: A raised triangle with an acorn and the letter "E" plus "Dux, Bohemia" was used as a mark between 1900 and 1914.

Bust, 18½" h, woman adorned with flowers, Czecho-
    slovakia, c1915 .... **460.00**
Calling Card Receiver, 4", figural, frog standing on large
    open shell, beige, matte finish, pink triangle mark .. **125.00**
Candlestick, 13" h, figural, boy wearing knickers **175.00**
Centerpiece, 11 × 4¼ × 7¾", pr of kneeling nudes,
    central flared base, creamy white, cobalt blue, and
    gold trim **450.00**
Compote, 20⅝" h, three dancing female figures, emb
    bowl and base, sgd **750.00**
Figure
    8" h, parrot, polychrome glaze, glued separation at
      wing **110.00**
    9½" h, woman, swirling cobalt blue long dress, white
      picture hat, pink triangle mark, paper label **225.00**
    10" h, Cubist woman **175.00**
    15" h, boy on donkey, pre–World War I mark **400.00**
    17" l, tiger **325.00**

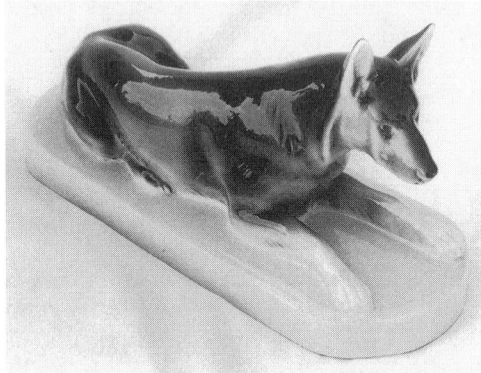

Figure, dog, pink triangle mark, stamped "Royal Dux," incised "Made in Czechoslovakia," 11¾" l, $125.00.

Pin Tray, figural, Art Nouveau maiden on wave **325.00**
Tobacco Jar, 8" h, figural, man's head, wearing nightcap,
    smoking pipe **195.00**
Vase, 16½" h, Art Nouveau, matte glaze, applied leaves,
    some losses **175.00**

ROYAL FLEMISH

History: Royal Flemish was produced by the Mount Washington Glass Co., New Bedford, Massachusetts. The process was patented by Albert Steffin in 1894.

Royal Flemish is a frosted transparent glass with heavy raised gold enamel lines. These lines form sections—often colored in russet tones—giving the appearance of stained glass windows with elaborate floral or coin medallions.

Collectors' Club: Mount Washington Art Glass Society, 60 President Ave, Providence, RI 02906.

Advisors: Clarence and Betty Maier.

Biscuit Jar, 9½″ h, 5½″ d, mythical winged gargoyle on one side, fish-like creature on other side, stylized flowers, alternating panels framed in brown **2,750.00**
Vase
   13″ h, 7½″ d, bulbous, four brownish green medallions featuring ferocious mythical creatures, three randomly placed coral-colored medallions, embellishments connected by swirling raised gold lines, pastel enamel flowers on frosted clear glass sections **2,750.00**
   14½″ h, four snow geese flying across blazing sun, rays of sun outlined in raised gold, geometric sections with raised gold borders, light blue, dark blue, tan, green and violet, attributed to Frank Guba **8,350.00**
   15″ h, ovoid, nine alternating vertical panels in dark green, light green and dark time, nine narrow dark brown stripes, raised gold embellishments on frosted clear glass fluted top, five frosted clear glass medallions featuring ferocious mythical creatures, raised gold branches, multicolored leaves **3,750.00**

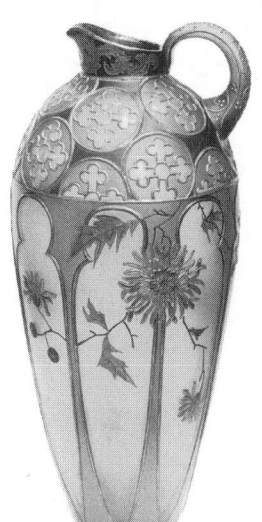

Ewer, alternating pale blue and tan lower panels surmounted by circlets of dark blue with centered light blue crosses, circlets on field of cerise, raised gold separation lines, chrysanthemum blossoms, and foliage, 11½″ h, $4,000.00.

ROYAL RUDOLSTADT

History: Johann Fredrich von Schwarzburg-Rudolstadt was the patron of a faïence factory located in Rudolstadt, Thuringen, Germany, from 1720 to c1790.

In 1854 Ernst Bohne established a factory in Rudolstadt.

The "Royal Rudolstadt" designation originated with wares which Lewis Straus and Sons (later Nathan Straus and Sons) of New York imported from the New York and Rudolstadt Pottery between 1887 and 1918. The factory manufactured several of the Rose O'Neill (Kewpie) items.

Marks: The first mark of the original pottery was a hayfork; later, crossed two-prong hayforks were used in imitation of the Meissen mark.

"EB" was the mark used by Ernst Bohne

A crown over a diamond enclosing the initials "RW" is the mark used by the New York and Rudolstadt Pottery.

Biscuit Jar, cov, 8″ h, corset shape, multicolored floral panels **165.00**
Bonbon, handle, pink roses, white ground **65.00**
Bowl, 13″ l, boat shape, hp flowers **115.00**
Cake Plate, 10¼″ d, hp, white flowers **65.00**
Celery Dish, 13″ l, handles, hp, yellow roses, gold trim, artist sgd **90.00**
Creamer and Sugar, cov, purple pansies, cream ground, gold trim **85.00**
Dresser Set, tray, hatpin holder, hair receiver, hp camellias, green leaves, pastels, gold trim, imp mark "Royal Rudolstadt Coronet B Prussia" **250.00**
Ewer, 13¼″ h, cream and light pink shell body, pebbled ground, brown worm-type handle **195.00**
Hair Receiver, hp, pastel florals **50.00**
Pitcher, 15½″ h, jeweled, inlaid gold leaves **315.00**
Plate, 8½″ d, chickens and roosters **75.00**
Sweetmeat Jar, cov, 5½ × 8″, pink florals, green and rust leaves, cream ground, SP holder, marked "Middletown" **150.00**
Urn, 25½″ h, floral dec, imp mark **595.00**
Vase, 9¼″ h, florals, gold and scroll handles, emb lip . **150.00**

Busts, polychrome bisque finish, 12½″ h, pr, $850.00.

ROYAL VIENNA

1749-1864

History: Production of hard-paste porcelain in Vienna began in 1720 with Claude Innocentius du Paquier, a runaway employee from the Meissen factory. In 1744 Empress Maria Theresa brought the factory under royal patronage; subsequently the ware became known as Royal Vienna. The firm went through many administrative changes until it closed in 1864. The quality of its workmanship always was maintained.

Marks: Several other Austrian and German firms copied the Royal Vienna products, including the use of the "Beehive" mark. Many of the pieces on today's market are from these firms.

Box, 3 × 4¾", titled "Judgment of Paris," cupid on front panel 315.00

Charger, 20½" d, titled "Columbus Triumphant Return," landing party, Indians, bountiful scene 1,500.00

Compote, 9½" d, two handles, portrait dec, cobalt blue ground, gold trim 165.00

Cup and Saucer, warriors and girl on cup, raised gold and white dec, different scenes on saucer, pink, blue, and gold 400.00

Plate, 9½" d, two girls feeding birds in garden setting, multicolored intricate raised border, beehive mark 400.00

Plate, multicolored classical scene of "Mark Anthony's Death," gold filigree on maroon border, raised gold beading on inner and outer rims, blue beehive mark, $55.00.

Portrait Plate
  Bonaparte Lady, cobalt blue and gold border, sgd "Wagner," minor chips to rim 850.00
  Dido, sitting on beach with cupid, hp, dark red and gold border, reticulated, 6" d 395.00
  Rembrandt, gold and floral border 725.00
Stein, 6" h, seated monk with stein, cobalt blue ground, gold trim, artist sgd "Wagner" 900.00
Urn, 8" h, maidens dancing, small cherub, beehive mark 175.00
Vase
  7¾" h, two handles, maroon, ornate gold bands, flowers, and leaves, portrait of woman, artist sgd "Wagner," blue underglaze beehive mark 450.00
  8" h, pillow form, red roses decal, shaded ground .. 125.00
  11½" h, cov, oval reserve of long-haired maiden, green robe, irid maroon field encrusted with gold, sgd "Wagner" 1,550.00

c1876-1891   1891

ROYAL WORCESTER

History: In 1751 the Worcester Porcelain Company, led by Dr. John Wall and William Davis, acquired the Bristol pottery of Benjamin Lund and moved it to Worcester. The first wares were painted blue under the glaze; soon thereafter decorating was accomplished by painting on the glaze in enamel colors. Among the most-famous 18th-century decorators were James Giles and Jefferys Hamet O'Neale. Transfer-print decoration was developed by the 1760s.

A series of partnerships took place after Davis's death in 1783: Flight (1783–1793); Flight & Barr (1793–1807); Barr, Flight & Barr (1807–1813); and Flight, Barr & Barr (1813–1840). In 1840 the factory was moved to Chamberlain & Co. in Diglis. Decorative wares were discontinued. In 1852 W. H. Kerr and R. W. Binns formed a new company and revived the production of ornamental wares.

In 1862 the firm became the Royal Worcester Porcelain Co. Among the key modelers of the late 19th century were James Hadley, his three sons, and George Owen, an expert with pierced clay pieces. Royal Worcester absorbed the Grainger factory in 1889 and the James Hadley factory in 1905. Modern designers include Dorothy Doughty and Doris Lindner.

References: Susan and Al Bagdade, *Warman's English & Continental Pottery & Porcelain,* Second Edition, Wallace-Homestead, 1991; John Edwards, *The Charlton Price Guide to Royal Worcester Figurines,* Charlton Press, 1996; David, John, and Henry Sandon, *The Sandon Guide to Royal Worcester Figures,* Alderman Press, 1987, out of print; Henry Sandon, *The Dictionary of Worcester Porcelain* Vol. II, Antique Collectors' Club, out of print; ———, *Flight & Barr Worcester,* Antique Collectors' Club, 1992; Henry and John Sandon, *Grainger's Worcester Porcelain,* Barrie & Jenkins, 1990; John Sandon, *The Dictionary of Worcester Porcelain* Vol. I, Antique Collectors' Club, 1993.

Museum: Charles William Dyson Perrins Museum, Worcester, England.

Biscuit Jar, cov, 6½" h, melon form, lobed sides, gilt and enamel floral dec, printed mark, c1889, gilt wear .. 225.00
Bowl, 3" d, fluted, cream, hp flowers 55.00
Cache Pot, 8" d, 7" h, circular, lug handles, Kakiemon style dec, Chamberlain, price for pr 5,995.00
Cheese Dish, 9¾" h, modeled bamboo body, brown and gilt dec, dec relief bamboo leaves, printed factory mark and "Richard Briggs Boston," c1879, slight rim nick, minor wear 635.00
Claret Jug, 8" h, gilt banded and raised prunus dec, enamel dec flowers and butterfly, printed mark, c1884, gilt rim wear, price for pr 320.00
Dessert Plate, 8½" d, fruit dec, artist "T. Lockyer," factory marks, 1923 date code 345.00
Ewer, 9½" h, enamel-dec butterflies among raised and gilt tall grass, printed mark, c1884 .... 550.00

Vegetable Dish, cov, oval, ram's-head handles, marked "Royal Worcester" in brown and "Jones McDuffee & Stratton, Boston, 4605," 6½ × 12¼ × 5¾", $95.00.

Fern Pot, 7" h, figural, boy standing by wood-simulated pot, printed mark, c1887, brim of hat restored, gilt wear 345.00

Figure

6¼" h, Elizabeth, enamel dec, imp and printed marks, c1807, gilt wear 435.00

8" h, Eastern water carriers, male and female figures holding vessels, shape 1206, printed and imp marks, c1888, one with restored neck, one with rim chip, price for pr 575.00

8½" h, girl and boy dressed in 19th C garb, each holding a basket, enamel and gilt dec, imp and printed marks, c1882, basket restored, price for pr   635.00

25¼" h, The Bather Surprised, crackle glazed body, gilt trim, colored cloth, modeled by Sir Thomas Brock, printed mark, early 20th C, firing lines, hand repair 690.00

Flowerpot, 9¼" h, frog and lotus flower, imp and printed marks, c1883, gilt wear, one base restored, price for pr 520.00

Ice Cream Set, enamel dec stylized floral and leaf designs, gilt trim, twelve sq 6¼" w plates, 14⅜" l rect tray, printed marks, c1883, glaze scratches, one plate restored, minor damage, price for 13-pc set 115.00

Ice Jug, 9¾" h, leaf-molded necks, melon shape, enamel and gilt floral sprays, printed marks, c1889, price for pr 690.00

Jardiniere

6¾" h, leaf-molded and basketweave body, scrolled handles, enamel and gilt dec, printed mark, c1897   345.00

8¼" h, enamel and gilt dec floral sprays with foliate borders, printed mark, c1891, gilt wear 460.00

Lamp, 11" d, 5½" h, 27" to top of harp, inverted funnel shape, floral, gilt, scrolled handles 165.00

Plate

8⅜" d, shell shape, gilt rim, enameled floral dec, c1889, four with restored rim chips, three with rim chips, price for 15-pc set 345.00

9" d, fruit dec, gilt border on cobalt blue ground, sgd "Albert Shuck," pattern no. W8346, printed marks, c1928, price for 18-pc set 8,100.00

Potpourri Vase, cov, 14½" h, wicker basketweave-molded bodies, raised enamel and gilt-dec water lilies, pierced borders, printed mark, c1883, finials restored, price for pr 920.00

Salad Bowl

6¾" w, sq, leaf molded, scalloped edge, pierced gal-

lery, enamel and gilt-dec floral sprays with butterflies, printed mark, c1884 .... 230.00

9" d, lobed body, gilt accented polychrome floral dec, printed mark, c1890, int. gilt wear 290.00

9¼" d, molded foliate body, enamel floral sprays, gilt trim, printed marks, c1892 .... 345.00

Tray, 14½" d, Royal Lily pattern, gilt trim, printed and imp mark, c1878 .... 190.00

Vase

3½" h, sq, white and gold frog and trim 325.00

4¾" h, Japanese style, ivory, branch-form handles, reticulated border above modeled landscape, gilt trim, printed mark, c1886, rim chip restored, price for pr 490.00

5½" h, 6" d, sack shape, applied rope, gold trim, c1886 .... 185.00

5⅝" h, elephant, gilt-trimmed body, printed mark, late 19th C 750.00

7¼" h, floral relief, enamel and gilt dec, printed mark, c1887 .... 635.00

9" h, ivory ground, polychrome floral dec, gilt trim . 175.00

9¾" h, pink and yellow roses, artist sgd "Jarman" .. 695.00

14¾" h, cov, yellow ground, polychrome floral dec, gilt trim, printed mark, c1893, finial repair, gilt wear 690.00

Wall Bracket, 8¾" l, orchid, enamel floral dec, gilt trim, printed mark, late 19th C 200.00

ROYCROFT

History: Elbert Hubbard founded the Roycrofters in East Aurora, New York, at the turn of the century. Considered a genius in his day, he was an author, lecturer, manufacturer, salesman, and philosopher.

Hubbard established a campus which included a printing plant where he published *The Philistine, The Fra,* and *The Roycrofter.* His most-famous book was *A Message to Garcia,* published in 1899. His "community" also included a furniture manufacturing plant, a metal shop, and a leather shop.

References: Kevin McConnell, *Roycroft Art Metal,* Second Edition, Schiffer Publishing, 1994; The Roycrofters, *Roycroft Furniture Catalog, 1906,* Dover, 1994; Marie Via and Marjorie B. Searl, *Head, Heart and Hand,* University of Rochester Press (34 Administration Bldg, University of Rochester, Rochester, NY 14627), 1994.

Collectors' Clubs: Foundation for the Study of Arts & Crafts Movement, Roycroft Campus, 31 S Grove St, East Aurora, NY 14052; Roycrofters-at-Large Assoc, PO Box 417, East Aurora, NY 14052.

Museum: Elbert Hubbard Library-Museum, East Aurora, NY.

Additional Listings: Arts and Crafts Movement and Copper.

Bookends, pr, hammered copper

5" h, Roycroft mark 125.00

5 × 3½", hammered stylized floral design, brass wash, good orig patina, imp orb mark 200.00

Bookends, No. 305, 1919, 5³⁄₈″ h, $200.00.

5 × 5″, Fleur-de-Lis, brass wash, heavy gauge, orb and cross mark **175.00**

5¼ × 5″, emb poppy blossoms, riveted edges, mint orig dark patina, orb and cross mark **550.00**

5¼ × 5½″, brass wash, rivets and hinged bale, orig patina, orb mark **225.00**

8¼ × 6″, rect, one open, other emb with floral design, orig dark patina, orb and cross mark **250.00**

Bowl, 7″ d, copper, polished **140.00**

Box, cov, emb stylized flower, new dark patina, orb and cross mark, 1½ × 7 × 3½″ **325.00**

Candle Sconces, pr, 8″ h, 3¼″ w, hammered copper, spade-shaped back, orig patina, orb and cross mark **425.00**

Foot Stool, leather cover, 10 × 15″, $235.00.

Furniture
Chair
#25, side, four vertical slats, Macmurdo feet, replaced leather seat, orig dark finish, minor repairs, incised orb mark, 38 × 18 × 17″ **1,800.00**

#29, straddle, long narrow oblong seat, two horizontal back slats under an elbow rest, orig dark finish, incised orb mark, 34 × 24 × 24″ **1,000.00**

Rocker, #39, mahogany, arms, corseted back slat, upholstered seat, orig dark finish, incised orb mark, 35 × 25 × 30″ **900.00**

Stand, Little Journeys, overhanging top, two shelves, trestle side, keyed through-tenons, orig medium finish, metal tag, 26 × 26 × 14″ **650.00**

Lamp, 14½ × 7½″, table, copper and mica, tapering shade rests on four-sided stem and sq base, new dark brown patina, imp orb mark **1,600.00**

Tray, 21½″ l, 9½″ w, silver over copper, oval, emb floral motif, orb and cross mark **325.00**

Vase, hammered copper
4¾ × 3½″, cylindrical, incised rim band, orig dark patina, orb and cross mark, minor pitting under lip **500.00**

7½ × 2½″, bud, lotus-shaped base holding glass tube, orig dark patina, orb and cross mark **250.00**

9½″ h, 3½″ d, cylindrical, squat base, undulating rim, tooled with bellflowers, orig patina, imp mark .. **550.00**

10″ h, 3″ d, hammered heavy-gauge copper, cylindrical, brass wash, band of stylized, diamond-shaped flowers around rim on tall stems, orig patina, orb and cross mark **1,200.00**

22½″ h, 8″ d, American Beauty, squat riveted base, tall stove-pipe neck, new dark patina, orb and cross mark **2,000.00**

RUBENA GLASS

History: Rubena crystal is a transparent blown glass which shades from clear to red. It also is found as the background for frosted and overshot glass. It was made in the late 1800s by several glass companies, including Northwood and Hobbs, Brockunier & Co. of Wheeling, West Virginia.

Rubena was used for several patterns of pattern glass including Royal Ivy and Royal Oak.

Basket, 3½ × 5½″, threaded dec, clear applied twisted handle **125.00**

Pitcher, enameled apple blossoms, applied handle, 7½″ h, $465.00.

Carafe, Aurora **150.00**

Celery Vase, Inverted Thumbprint, ruffled rim **85.00**

Compote, 8¼″ d, Honeycomb, low standard **75.00**

Creamer, Medallion Sprig, clear applied handle **165.00**
Cruet, Royal Ivy, orig stopper **465.00**
Finger Bowl, matching under plate **85.00**
Lamp Shade, 3⅞" h, applied ribbed petals, opalescent
   rim, chips at base, one petal glued **50.00**
Peg Lamp, 15¼" h, 5⅛" d, fluted top, frosted rubena
   center shades to cranberry, flowers and scrolls pat-
   terning, frosted rubena font with flowers dec, brass
   candlestick base **325.00**
Pickle Castor, Royal Oak, frosted insert, orig tongs **395.00**
Rose Bowl, 6" d, Hobnail **230.00**
Sugar Bowl, cov, Royal Oak, frosted **155.00**
Sugar Shaker, Royal Oak **325.00**
Table Set, Royal Oak, frosted **425.00**
Vase, 6" h, bud, enameled floral dec, diamond band .. **75.00**
Water Set, acid etched storks, Hobbs, price for 7-pc set **700.00**

RUBENA VERDE GLASS

History: Rubena Verde, a transparent glass that shades from red
in the upper section to yellow-green in the lower, was made by
Hobbs, Brockunier & Co., Wheeling, West Virginia, in the late
1880s. It often is found in the Inverted Thumbprint (IVT) pattern,
called "Polka Dot" by Hobbs.

Bride's Basket, 12½" d, cased, ruffled edge, dainty multicolored floral dec **375.00**
Bowl, 5½" d, opal crimped top, rigaree trim, seven shell
   feet **115.00**

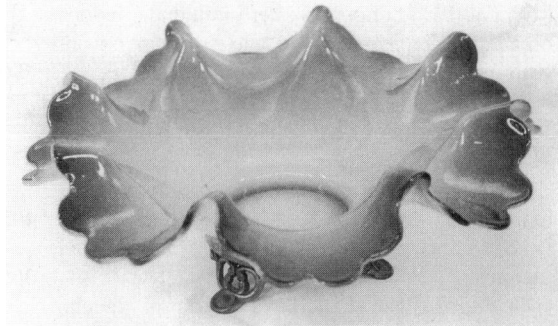

Bride's Bowl, ruffled, red rim shading to green center, cast white metal holder, 9½" d, $175.00.

Butter Dish, cov **400.00**
Epergne, 16" h, single center lily, applied rigaree, price
   for pr **500.00**
Pitcher, 8" h, bulbous, sq mouth, Hobnail, applied va-
   seline handle **295.00**
Salt Shaker, 4¼" h, pewter top, enameled floral dec ... **185.00**
Spittoon **200.00**
Syrup, IVT, applied handle, pewter lid, marked "Pat.
   March 29, '83" **345.00**
Tumbler, 4" h, Hobnail **165.00**
Vase
   6½" h, cylindrical, Hobnail **275.00**
   10" h, cylindrical, enameled florals, gold trim **195.00**

ВРАТЬЕВЪ
Baterin's factory
1812-1820

КорНИЛОВЫХЪ
Korniloff's factory
c1835

RUSSIAN ITEMS

History: During the late 19th and early 20th centuries, craftsmen
skilled in lacquer, silver, and enamel wares worked in Russia.
During the Czarist era (1880–1917), Fabergé, known for his exquisite enamel pieces, led a group of master craftsmen who were
located primarily in Moscow. Fabergé also had an establishment
in St. Petersburg and enjoyed the patronage of the Russian
Imperial family and royalty and nobility throughout Europe.

   Almost all enameling was done on silver. Pieces are signed by
the artist and the government assayer.

   The Russian Revolution in 1917 brought an abrupt end to the
century of Russian craftsmanship. The modern Soviet government
has exported some inferior enamel and lacquer work, usually
lacking in artistic merit. Modern pieces are not collectible.

References: Vladimir Guliayev, *The Fine Art of Russian Lacquered
Miniatures,* Chronicle Books, 1993; A. Kenneth Snowman, *Fabergé,* Harry N. Abrams, 1993.

Museums: Cleveland Museum of Art, Cleveland, OH; Forbes Magazine Collection, New York, NY; Hillwood, the Marjorie Merri-
weather Post Collection, Washington, DC; Virginia Museum of
Fine Arts, Lillian Thomas Pratt Collection, Richmond, VA; Walters
Art Gallery, Baltimore, MD.

Advisors: Barbara and Melvin Alpren.

Altar Cross, 9½ × 5", two-pc brass cross, engraved crucifixion image, 19th C **200.00**
Angel, 3½" h, cast and chased figural, Holy Napkin finial, pierced for suspension, spurious silver marks,
   19th C **590.00**
Baptismal Cross, cast brass, Slavonic inscription on reverse, pierced for suspension, 19th C, price for 3-pc
   set **550.00**
Beaker, 4¼" h, plique-à-jour enamel on gilded silver,
   brilliantly colored birds in garden, Ivan Khlebnikov,
   Moscow, 1900 ....**3,750.00**
Bowl
   5¼" d, sliver gilt, eight panels, enameled int. and ext.,
      colorful peacocks and foliage, gilded stippled
      ground, florals on white ground, Maria Semy-
      enova, Moscow, c1900 ....**4,500.00**

8¼" d, 3⅜" h, ceramic, red, black, and gold, Oriental dec **75.00**

Box, cov, 2⅞" l, oval, gilded silver, shaded enamel, flowers, cream ground, hinged, 6th Masters Artel, Moscow, 1910 .... **1,750.00**

Chalice, 3½" d, 5" h, two pc, gilded-silver repoussé and chasing, bowl with Deisis, base with four Evangelists, engraved and embellished, hallmarked "84, Moscow," Cyrillic maker's mark "PA" **965.00**

Charkahs, 2¼" l, Pan Slavic enameling, fitted holly wood box, clover shape, stylized bird handles, A Lubavin, Moscow, 1895, price for pr **650.00**

Cigar Box, cov, 5" l, silver, enameled tobacco-leaf domed cov, inscribed "American," paper tax band edge, engraved floral sides, presentation inscription, gilt int., 6th Artel, Moscow, c1910 .... **6,600.00**

Cigarette Case, 5¼" l, gilded silver, rect, en plain enamel scene of young girl in village by river, 11th Masters Artel, Moscow, 1900 .... **3,350.00**

Dish, 6½" l, porcelain, ram shape, ears missing **125.00**

Egg, 3" h, cased glass, enameled abbreviation for the words "Christ Has Risen," decorative brass suspension loop, 19th C **385.00**

Icon

2¼ × 6", triptych, brass, hinged panels, left with The Dormiton, central with The Resurrection, right with The Baptism of Christ, 18th C **150.00**

3 × 8", triptych, Annunciation, The Mother of God of the Sign and selected saints including John the Baptist, Nicholas, and the Three Hierarchs, hand-crafted brass case, hinged together, suspension loops, 18th C **1,870.00**

8½ × 7", tempera, gold leaf on wooden panel with kovcheg, guardian angel surrounded by saints, Floras, St Basil, St Methodist, and St Lavr, Christ blessing from above, 19th C **825.00**

8¾ × 7", tempera, gold leaf on wooden panel, 19th C

Archangel Michael, full-length image, holding fiery sword and shield **750.00**

St Panteleimon, patron saint of Doctors, holding box of medicine, reverse displays imprint stating "This icon was painted and blessed at the Russian monastery of Pantelemion on Mt Athos, Greece" **330.00**

8¾ × 7¼", The Crucifixion, tempera on wooden panel with kovcheg, borders with family saints, 19th C **965.00**

9 × 6¾", tempera on wooden panel, traditional St Nicholas delivering blessing, holding gospels, overlaid gilded-silver repoussé and chased riza, applied halo, hallmarked "84 St Petersburg," dated 1889, Chrillic maker's mark "E.G.P.," 19th C **440.00**

21 × 17", tempera, gold leaf on wooden panel, The Month of March, menelogical icon with saints and festivals commemorated during March with explanatory inscriptions, 19th C **1,265.00**

21 × 17¾", double-sided processional, tempera, gold leaf on wooden panel, raised borders, Apostle Peter and Apostle Paul, full-length images below Christ holding two crowns above them, other

Presentation goblet and tray, four hallmarks, engraved "Moskaw (small dent) 20, May 1879," 5⅜" h goblet, 8⅜" d tray, $4,250.00.

side with Holy Napkin or the "Not Made by Hands Image," 18th C **2,970.00**

28 × 21", tempera, gold leaf on wooden panel, Christ enthroned flanked by Mary and John the Baptist, flanked by Archangel Michael and Gabriel, above Apostile John, Peter, Paul, and St Nicholas, below are Northern Monastic Saints Savatly and Zosima, early 19th C **2,750.00**

30 × 11", tempera, gold leaf on wooden panel, The Mystical (Last) Supper, Western influence, haloes on all apostles except Judas who is shown in front with money bag, 19th C **3,750.00**

Icon Lamp, 19th C

15" l including chain, silver, glass insert, hallmarked "84, Moscow" **495.00**

17" l × 2⅕" including chain, silver, glass insert, hallmarked "84, Moscow" **495.00**

19 × 5" including chain, hammered brass, enamel plaques **300.00**

Kovsh, 5" l, gilded silver, shaded enamel, pastel flowers, avocado ground, hook-shaped handle, Gustav Klingert, Moscow, 1900 .... **2,750.00**

Napkin Ring, 2" d, silver and multicolored enamel, Imperial

From workshop of Alexi Nikolai Vaslievich, hallmarked "84, Moscow," c1900, price for 4-pc set **350.00**

From workshop of Zverev Nikolai Nikolaevich, hallmarked "84, Moscow," c1900, price for 4-pc set **750.00**

Pectoral Cross, 5 × 3", brass, suspension loop, inscription on reverse, 19th C **165.00**

Pendant, miniature egg, two with three blue cabochon stones, hinged lid, other with emerald and filigree overlay, indistinguishable maker's marks, Imperial, price for pr **950.00**

Snuff Box, silver, black enameled lid, dated 1873 ..... **225.00**

Spoon, 7¾" l, shaded enamel pastel flowers on gilded silver, aubergine ground, Pavel Ovchinnikov, Moscow, 1900 .... **950.00**

Wall Cross, 8¾ × 5¾", cast brass, multicolored enamel dec, 19th C 355.00

Wedding Icon Set, 8¾ × 7", oil on wooden panel, The Lord Almighty and Smolensk Mother of God, both overlaid with SP machine engraved riza, 19th C, price for pr 880.00

SABINO GLASS

History: Sabino glass, named for its creator Ernest Marius Sabino, originated in France in the 1920s and is an art glass which was produced in a wide range of decorative styles: frosted, clear, opalescent, and colored. Both blown and pressed moldings were used. Hand-sculpted wooden molds that were cast in iron were used and are still in use at the present time.

In 1960 the company introduced fiery opalescent Art Deco style pieces, including a line of one- to eight-inch high figurines. Gold was added to a batch of glass to obtain the fiery glow. These are the Sabino pieces most commonly found today.

Marks: Sabino is marked with the name in the mold, as an etched signature, or both.

Ashtray
    Butterfly 85.00
    Swallow, large 50.00
    Thistle 40.00
Berry Bowl 50.00
Bird, small
    Feeding 30.00
    Nesting 40.00
Box, Petalia 95.00
Butterfly, 2¾" l 45.00

Figure, dragonfly, 6" h, $95.00.

Elephant 75.00
Hen, 3⅝" h 40.00
Poodle 30.00
Scent Bottle, Pineapple, 5" h 175.00
Shell 60.00
Snail, 3" 75.00
Sparrow, small 50.00
Squirrel, 3" h 55.00
Statue, nude woman, long flowing hair, 6½" h 150.00
Vase, 11" h, 7" w, six lobes, Art Deco geometrics, royal blue, satin finish, polished highlights, sgd 600.00

SALOPIAN WARE   C S SALOPIAN

History: Salopian ware was made at Caughley Pot Works, Salop, Shropshire, England, in the 18th century by Thomas Turner. At one time the product was classified "Polychrome Transfer" because of the method of decoration, but the ware is better known by the more popular name "Salopian." Much of the output was sold through Turner's Salopian warehouse in London

Marks: Pieces are impressed or painted under the glaze with an "S" or the word "Salopian."

Bowl
    9¼" d, 4" h, pearlware, blue and white Oriental dec, "S" mark, wear and slightly yellowed rim repair   165.00
    11" d, Bird on Branch pattern, blue and white 415.00
Creamer and Sugar, man and woman having tea in garden, black and white transfer 450.00
Cup and Sugar, polychrome, blue, yellow, ochre, and green flowers and leaves, tiny flake on saucer foot rim 115.00
Cup Plate, 4½" d, Deer pattern, polychrome dec 450.00
Mug, 4" h, Bird on Branch pattern 250.00
Pitcher, 5½" h, Oriental scene, blue and white, c1790   425.00
Plate
    7¾" d, polychromed Creil scene of man, woman, and child, hut and church in background, black transfer with applied yellow, blue, red, and blue-green highlights 45.00
    8½" d, Double Deer, green, yellow, black, and white   225.00
    8¾" d, octagonal, Oriental scene, blue and white ..   195.00
Teapot, 4 × 8¼", boy carrying lamb, blue and white   .   465.00

Teapot, boy carrying lamb, blue, c1790, 8¼" l, 4" h, $465.00.

SALT AND PEPPER SHAKERS

History: Collecting salt and pepper shakers, whether late 19th-century glass forms or the contemporary figural and souvenir types, is becoming more and more popular. The supply and variety is practically unlimited; the price for most sets is within the budget of cost-conscious collectors. In addition, their size offers an opportunity to display a large collection in a relatively small space.

Specialty collections can be by type, form, or maker. Great

glass artisans, such as Joseph Locke and Nicholas Kopp, designed salt and pepper shakers in the normal course of their work.

References: Gideon Bosker and Lena Lencer, *Salt and Pepper Shakers,* Avon Books, 1994; Larry Carey and Sylvia Tompkins, *1002 Salt and Pepper Shakers,* Schiffer Publishing, 1995; ———, *Salt and Pepper,* Schiffer Publishing, 1994; Melva Davern, *The Collector's Encyclopedia of Salt & Pepper Shakers,* First Series (1985, 1991 value update), Second Series (1990, 1995 value update), Collector Books; Helene Guarnaccia, *Salt & Pepper Shakers,* Vol. I (1985, 1993 value update), Vol. II (1989, 1993 value update), Vol. III (1991, 1995 value update), Vol. IV (1993, 1995 value update), Collector Books; Mildred and Ralph Lechner, *The World of Salt Shakers,* Second Edition, Collector Books, 1992, 1995 value update; Arthur G. Peterson, *Glass Salt Shakers,* Wallace-Homestead, 1970, out of print; Mike Schneider, *The Complete Salt and Pepper Shaker Book,* Schiffer Publishing, 1993.

Collectors' Clubs: Antique and Art Glass Salt Shaker Collectors Society, 2832 Rapidan Trail, Maitland, FL 32751; Novelty Salt & Pepper Shakers Club, PO Box 3617, Lantana, FL 33465.

Museum: Judith Basin Museum, Stanford, MT.

Additional Listings: See *Warman's Americana & Collectibles* for more examples.

Notes: The colored sets, in both transparent and opaque glass, command the highest prices; crystal and white sets the lowest. Although some shakers, e.g., the tomato or fig, have a special patented top and need it to retain their value, it generally is not detrimental to replace the top of a shaker.

The figural and souvenir types are often looked down upon by collectors. Sentiment and whimsy are prime collecting motivations. The large variety and current low prices indicate a potential for long-term price growth.

Generally, older shakers are priced by the piece; figural and souvenir types by the set. Pricing methods are indicated in the listings. All shakers included below are assumed to have original tops unless otherwise noted. Reference numbers are from Arthur Goodwin Peterson's *Glass Salt Shakers.* Peterson made a beginning; there are hundreds, perhaps thousands, of patterns still to be cataloged.

Prices below are for individual shakers unless otherwise noted.

Art Glass

Cased

Bulging Petal, pink, pr	**45.00**
Flower Band pink	**30.00**
Peachblow, Wheeling, orig top	**325.00**
Pigeon Blood, Periwinkle variant	**110.00**
Rubena, enamel dec, pewter top	**195.00**
Spatter, vaseline and cranberry spatter, Leaf Mold, orig top	**85.00**

Figural and Sets

Billiken, white, opaque and crystal, gilt, Buddha shape, inscription on base "The God of things as they ought to be," patent 1908, tin top	**75.00**
Dogs, cast metal, 3" h, green paint, amber glass eyes, pr	**85.00**
Metal Frame, tapered panels, pr, marked "C. F. Monroe"	**205.00**

Milk Glass, ribbed base, white ground, hp floral vine, orig top, P-36V, $30.00.

Opalescent

Argonaut Shell, blue	**60.00**
Beatty Rib, white, no top	**25.00**
Fluted Scrolls, canary, orig top	**65.00**
Reverse Swirl, white, orig top	**45.00**
Windows Swirl, cranberry	**110.00**

Opaque

Bird, blue, handle	**95.00**
Bulging Petal, green, pr	**45.00**
Forget-Me-Not, pink variegated slag	**20.00**
Guttate, green	**30.00**
Inverted Fan and Feather, pink slag	**795.00**
Melonette, blue, pr	**45.00**
Rib & Swirl, blue	**45.00**
Square Scroll, pink	**25.00**

Pattern Glass

Acorn, pink, orig top	**45.00**
Banded Portland, maiden's blush	**35.00**
Feather	**20.00**
Fish	
Blue	**65.00**
Pink and white	**95.00**
Klondike, amberette, pr	**225.00**
Nestor, amethyst, dec	**55.00**
Nevada	**30.00**
Red Block	**60.00**
Thousand Eye, vaseline	**40.00**
Wheat and Barley, blue	**35.00**

SALT-GLAZED WARES

History: Salt-glazed wares have a distinctive pitted surface texture made by throwing salt into the hot kiln during the final firing process. The salt vapors produce sodium oxide and hydrochloric acid which react on the glaze.

Many Staffordshire potters produced large quantities of this type of ware during the 18th and 19th centuries. A relatively small amount was produced in the United States. Salt-glazed wares still are made today.

Batter Jug, 11" h, baluster shape, cylindrical rim, blue-slip floral dec, applied handles, imp mark and No. 2, tin lid, Cowden & Wilcox, Harrisburg, PA, 1870–80 . . . **1,750.00**

Bottle, 9¼" h, globular, applied foliage, c1755 .... **425.00**
Dish, 10" l, lobed, pierced, allover herringbone, basketweave, and diaper panels, c1860 .... **475.00**
Jar, 13¼" h, baluster shape, everted rim, two applied
handles, imp "Boston," 19th C **95.00**
Jug, 14½" h, cylindrical, sloping shoulders, blue painted
cock and bull slip dec, applied and molded handle,
imp mark, George A Satterlee and Michael Morey,
New York Stoneware Co, 1861–85 ....**1,800.00**

Jug, raised Robert Burns commemorative design, beige ground, cream portrait, mask spout, hand handle, 8½" h, $475.00.

Plate, 9½" d, polychrome, central diaper and basketweave cartouche, pierced border, c1760 .... **725.00**
Soup Plate, 9¼" d, polychrome, flowers and vase,
molded basketweave and diaper border, c1755 .... **475.00**
Teapot, cov, 7" h, trailing flowering branches, straight
spout, crabstock handle and finial **495.00**

SALTS, OPEN

History: When salt was first mined, the supply was limited and expensive. The necessity for a receptacle in which to serve the salt resulted in the first open salt, a crude, hand-carved, wooden trencher.

As time passed, salt receptacles were refined in style and materials. In the 1500s both master and individual salts existed. By the 1700s firms such as Meissen, Waterford, and Wedgwood were making glass, china, and porcelain salts. Leading glass manufacturers in the 1800s included Libbey, Mount Wasington, New England, Smith Bros., Vallerysthal, Wave Crest, and Webb. Many outstanding silversmiths in England, France, and Germany also produced this form.

Open salts were the only means of serving salt until the appearance of the shaker in the late 1800s. The ease of procuring salt from a shaker greatly reduced the use of and need for the open salts.

References: William Heacock and Patricia Johnson, *5,000 Open Salts,* Richardson Printing Corporation, 1982, 1986 value update; Allan B. and Helen B. Smith have authored and published ten books on open salts beginning with *One Thousand Individual Open Salts Illustrated* (1972) and ending with *1,334 Open Salts Illustrated: The Tenth Book* (1984). Daniel Snyder did the master salt sections in Volumes 8 and 9. In 1987 Mimi Rudnick compiled a revised price list for the ten Smith Books; Kenneth Wilson, *American Glass 1760–1930,* 2 vols., Hudson Hills Press and The Toledo Museum of Art, 1994.

Periodical: *Salty Comments,* 401 Nottingham Rd, Newark, DE 19711.

Collectors' Clubs: New England Society of Open Salt Collectors, PO Box 177, Sudbury, MA 01776; Open Salt Collectors of the Atlantic Region, 56 Northview Dr, Lancaster, PA 17601.

Note: The numbers in parentheses refer to plate numbers in the Smiths' books.

Condiment Sets with Open Salts

China, boat shape, inscribed "A Present from Cleethor-
pes" (461) **60.00**
Porcelain, light pink, gold trim, leaf-shaped holder,
marked "Made in Bavaria" (388) **135.00**
Silverplated, 3 pcs, emb pattern around bowls, Oriental
(461) **65.00**

Individuals

China, Dresden Saxony, lily dec on one side (434) **50.00**
Colored Glass
Cameo, Webb, red ground, white lacy dec around
bowl, sgd, matching spoon (137) **650.00**
Cranberry, cut back to clear (446) **85.00**
Lavender, pedestal, frosted (373) **75.00**
Ruby, blown, white lace trim (447) **95.00**
Stretch Glass, blue (485) **70.00**
Cut Glass
Eight curved sides, polished cut bottom (470) **20.00**
Pedestal, faceted base (118) **50.00**
Triangular, Star and Diamond, sgd "Hawkes" (466) **70.00**
Double Salts
China, birds, gold rims, insect on inside bottom (460) **90.00**
Glass, turquoise milk glass, sgd "Vallerystahl, Made
in France" (460) **45.00**
Majolica, flower shape, overlapping leaves, marked
"No. 35" (439) **65.00**
Metal
Copper, heavy, pedestal, deep maroon enamel (414) . **30.00**
Sterling Silver, four peacocks around outside, clear
salts, ftd, marked "Sterling" (411) **50.00**
Pattern Glass
Atlanta, frosted **40.00**
Bull's Eye **40.00**
Cable **35.00**
Liberty Bell, clear, oval, 2¼" **35.00**
Snail, ruby stained **40.00**
Thumbprint, pedestal, oval round base, wide top rim
(362) **30.00**

Washington **20.00**
Wildflower, turtle shape, amber **45.00**

Figurals

Donkey, painted, pulling colorful painted cart (458) .. **30.00**
Sleigh with Cupid driving reindeer, SS, German (352) . **425.00**

Masters

China
    Belleek, shell shape (314) **45.00**
    Leeds, boat shape, pedestal (313) **70.00**
    Minton, ftd, #57957 (314) **50.00**
Colored Glass
    Aventurine, narrow base (316) **60.00**
    Cranberry, horizontal colored ribs (316) **65.00**
    Spatter, cased, scalloped, five clear shell feet (447) . **245.00**
Cut Glass, round, diamond pattern on top, ribbed base
    (404) **35.00**

Master, fiery opalescent, flared, six panels, 2³/₄" h, $175.00.

Lacy
    Basket of Flowers, opaque blue (BF1C:324) **350.00**
    Eagle, fiery milk opalescent, American eagle on all
      four corners, shield center, Sandwich Glassworks,
      c1830, 3" l **700.00**
    Gothic Arch, clear (GA4a:410) **145.00**
    Horn of Plenty, clear (329) **75.00**
    Scrolled Heart, green (SC7:324) **275.00**
Metal
    Pewter, pedestal, cobalt blue liner (349) **65.00**
    Sterling Silver, ftd, rams' heads, Gorham (281) **85.00**
Pattern Glass
    Actress **70.00**
    Atlanta, frosted **70.00**
    Beaded Loop **20.00**
    Buckle with Star, ftd **20.00**
    Bull's Eye, ftd **100.00**
    Chandelier **30.00**
    Grape and Festoon with Stippled Leaf, ftd **25.00**
    Lily of the Valley, covered **125.00**
    Lion, covered, rect lid **250.00**
    O'Hara Diamond, ruby stained **35.00**
    Sawtooth, ftd, covered, flint **65.00**

SAMPLERS

History: Samplers served many purposes. For a young child they were a practice exercise and permanent reminder of stitches and patterns. For a young woman they were a means to demonstrate skills in a "gentle" art and a way to record family genealogy. For the mature woman they were a useful occupation and method of creating gifts or remembrances, e.g., mourning pieces.

Schools for young ladies of the early 19th century prided themselves on the needlework skills they taught. The Westtown School in Chester County, Pennsylvania, and the Young Ladies Seminary in Bethlehem, Pennsylvania, were two institutions. These schools changed their teaching as styles changed. Berlin work was introduced by the mid-19th century.

Examples of samplers date back to the 1700s. The earliest ones were long and narrow, usually done only with the alphabet and numerals. Later examples were square. At the end of the 19th century, the shape tended to be rectangular.

The same motifs were used throughout the country. The name of the person who stitched the piece is a key factor in determining the region.

References: Ethel Stanwood Bolton and Eva Johnston Coe, *American Samplers,* Dover, 1987; Glee Krueger, *A Gallery of American Samplers,* Bonanza Books, 1984 edition; Dana G. Morykan and Harry L. Rinker, *Warman's Country Antiques & Collectibles,* Third Edition, Wallace-Homestead, 1996; Betty Ring, *American Needlework Treasures,* E. P. Dutton, 1987; Anne Sebba, *Samplers,* Thames and Hudson, 1979.

Museums: Cooper-Hewitt Museum, National Museum of Design, New York, NY; Smithsonian Institution, Washington, DC.

Note: Samplers are assumed to be on linen unless otherwise indicated.

1735, Mary Heaviside, homespun, precise small stitches, prim stylized flowers, alphabets and verse in tiny letters, Lord's Prayer and Apostles' Creed, "Mary Heaviside her work aged 10 years 1735," lower right corner soiled, small holes and wear, 11 × 14½", framed **1,450.00**

1768, Rebecca Leach, New England, alphabet, pastoral landscape with alphabet, seated lady, lambs, birds, dogs, trees, and flowers, serpentine floral border, 17 × 14" **7,500.00**

1796, silk on homespun, stylized flowers, buildings, birds, stag, woman with crown standing on a stile, initials and date, faded green, brown, blue, and yellow, black and white, stains, 21½" h, 22" w, modern frame **460.00**

1799, Elizabeth Field, silk on homespun linen, flowering and geometric borders, alphabets, Ten Commandments in Verse, other verse, stylized house, trees, pots of flowers, birds, and "John Field and Dianna Field Married July 21st, Elizabeth Field, born December 25th, 1779, finished sampler at Chesterfield, October 18th, 1799," shades of green, blue, red, white, and black, stains and some missing floss, several words with missing letters, 19" h, 22½" w, framed **825.00**

1803, Dorcas Shaw, five different styles of alphabet, numerals 1 through 13, four lines of verse, softly colored landscape with house, fence, and trees, border of vine

Sampler, 1799, Elizabeth Scott Fulton, silk threads, shades of green, yellow, brown, red, and cream, linen ground, 12³/₄ × 17³/₄", $1,540.00. Photo courtesy of Skinner, Inc.

and berries, "Dorcas Shaw, Portland, AET 14 1803," 21 × 16", later oak frame **3,500.00**

1812, Ann Hootton, ship, flowers, landscape with house, trees, animals, basket of flowers, birds, etc, "Wrought by Ann Hootton Daughter of William and Hannah Hootton 1812," water stains, 19 × 17", modern frame **4,000.00**

1813, Phebe Loose, Wells School, red silk, linen homespun, alphabets, verse, birds, animals, crowns, "Phebe Loose, Wells School, Octob 6th 1813," wear, holes in line, 12¹/₂" h, 10¹/₂" w, framed **415.00**

1814, Hannah Davis, Philadelphia, PA, loosely woven linen, green, rose, yellow, blue, white, and gold silk stitches, pious verse separated by bands of stylized flowers and bunches of grapes, lower border inscribed "Hannah Davis work in the 13th year 1814," silk ribboned border, 19 × 16¹/₄", framed **5,500.00**

1821, Mary Paul, Germantown, PA, eight lines of verse entitled "Mary's Wish," flowers, birds, insects, small landscape with dog and residence in center, 25¹/₂ × 26", modern frame **5,500.00**

1822, Mary Ann Plowman, silk on linen homespun, stylized flowers, fanciful building, birds on corners, crown, deer and "Mary Ann Plowman, Aged 8 years 1822," red, pink, green, gold, white, and yellow, minor floss loss, 19³/₄" h, 18¹/₂" w, modern bird's-eye frame **650.00**

1825, Abigail F Cook, silk on linen homespun, stylized flowers, three sets of alphabets, three sections of verse, detailed border, "wrought by Abigail F. Cook, Miss Pollina Sellon's School, Hadley, Mass, AD 1825," minor losses, minor staining, toning, 16¹/₂ × 17¹/₂", framed **1,955.00**

1829, Maria Blake, six lines of verse, titled "Extract," full basket of flowers, "Work'd by Marie Blake at Eliza A. Rue's School, Pennington, NY, Anno Domini 1829," 16 × 17", gold leaf period frame **4,000.00**

1833, Lydia Whitaker, five rows of alphabets, two houses and trees, center initials, "Lydia Whitaker was born June 14 Year 1819 Age 14 Wrought This In The Year 1833," Bradford, VT, 9¹/₂ × 11³/₄" **2,200.00**

1835, Frances Emily Young, 12 years old, born Nov 1823, alphabets, 12¹/₂ × 25" **1,650.00**

1843, Pheby Ann Bush, Aged 8 years, wool on linen homespun, alphabets, stylized flowers, birds, and borders, red, blue, green, brown, and white, some wear and missing floss, bird's-eye veneer ogee frame with gilded liner, 19¹/₄" h, 20" w **365.00**

1856, MA Watkins, silk on homespun linen, geometric borders, alphabets, verse, crowns, birds, flowers and "M. A. Watkins in her 9th year 1856," blue, black, faded greens and whites, 21" h, 12¹/₄" w, new bird's-eye ogee frame **360.00**

1883, Margaret McGregor, verse and flowers, names of great authors, including Shakespeare, Cowper, Coleridge, Pope Weber Logan, Scott, initials, alphabet, numerals, vine border, 17¹/₂ × 12³/₄", framed **525.00**

Undated

Bennets, Rachael Ann, Sampler Aged 9 Years, Portage, Allegany Co, NY, silk on homespun, alphabets, flowers, verse, blue, red, salmon, green, black, and, white, minor stains, 18¹/₄" h, 19¹/₄" w, framed **650.00**

Martens, Catherine Margaret, silk on homespun linen, flowering border and strawberries, alphabets, verse, house, trees, stag and "Catherine Margaret Martens Age 9," faded red, black, blue, green, and brown, stains, very faded scene of house and deer, 18¹/₂ × 18¹/₂", framed **325.00**

Moylan, Catherine, silk with small precise stitches, alphabets, flowers, animals, crowns, houses, good color, stains, damage, and wear, 7 × 7", wicker frame **600.00**

Stader, Elizabeth Dock, silk on homespun, geometric borders, alphabets, flowers, and scene with house and dog, 9¹/₂" h, 11¹/₂" w, gilt frame **225.00**

Thompson, Mary, wool and silk, linen homespun, strawberry border, baskets of flowers, trees, house, verse titled "Virtue," many shades of red, blue, green, brown, and black, stained edges, framed, 17¹/₂" h, 16³/₄" w **825.00**

SANDWICH GLASS

History: In 1818 Deming Jarves was listed in the Boston Directory as a glass manufacturer. That same year he was appointed general manager of the newly formed New England Glass Company. In 1824 Jarves toured the glassmaking factories in Pittsburgh, left New England Glass Company, and founded a glass factory in Sandwich.

Originally called the Sandwich Manufacturing Company, it was incorporated in April 1826 as the Boston & Sandwich Glass Company. From 1826 to 1858 Jarves served as general manager. The Boston & Sandwich Glass Company produced a wide variety of wares in differing levels of quality. The factory used the free-blown, blown three mold, and pressed glass manufacturing techniques. Both clear and colored glass were used.

Competition in the American glass industry in the mid-1850s resulted in lower-quality products. Jarves left the Boston & Sandwich company in 1858, founded the Cape Cod Glass Company, and tried to duplicate the high quality of the earlier glass. Meanwhile, at the Boston & Sandwich Glass Company emphasis was placed on mass production. The development of a lime glass (non-flint) led to lower costs for pressed glass. Some free-blown and blown-and-molded pieces, mostly in color, were made. Most of this Victorian-era glass was enameled, painted, or acid etched.

By the 1880s the Boston & Sandwich Glass Company was operating at a loss. Labor difficulties finally resulted in the closing of the factory on January 1, 1888.

References: Raymond E. Barlow and Joan E. Kaiser, *The Glass Industry in Sandwich,* Vol. 1 (1993), Vol. 2 (1989), Vol. 3 (1987), and Vol. 4 (1983), distributed by Schiffer Publishing; ———, *Price Guide for The Glass Industry in Sandwich Vols. 1–4,* Schiffer Publishing, 1993; Ruth Webb Lee, *Sandwich Glass Handbook,* Charles E. Tuttle, 1966; ———, *Sandwich Glass,* Charles E. Tuttle, 1966; George S. and Helen McKearin, *American Glass,* Random House, 1979; Ellen T. Schroy, *Warman's Glass,* Second Edition, Wallace-Homestead, 1995; Catherine M. V. Thuro, *Oil Lamps II,* Collector Books, 1994 value update; Kenneth Wilson, *American Glass 1760–1930,* 2 vols., Hudson Hills Press and The Toledo Museum of Art, 1994.

Museum: Sandwich Glass Museum, Sandwich, MA.

Additional Listings: Blown Three Mold and Cup Plates.

Bowl
7¼" d, Oak Leaf, lacy, colorless **45.00**
7½" d, Tulip and Acanthus, lacy, colorless **45.00**
Candlestick, 9" h, columnar, opaque, powdery purple-blue, rough sandy finish **450.00**
Compote
6⅛" d, 7½" h, cov, Lincoln Drape, colorless **250.00**
7¼" d, Plume, lacy, colorless **175.00**
Dish, ftd, 10⅝" l, 6"h, Princess Feather, medallion and basket of flowers, canary, leaf foot, 1840–45, base of foot ground, base chips, small rim chips, annealing mark **20,700.00**
Eggcup, Horn of Plenty, flint, price for pr **95.00**
Goblet, colorless
Bull's Eye and Fleur-de-Lis **95.00**
Comet **90.00**
Lamp, whale oil
8½" h, opaque starch blue, shading to bright sapphire blue, small star and punty font attached to wafer to hexagonal stem and base, orig brass collar, c1840 .... **3,300.00**
9" h, cut faceted glass, missing burners, price for pr **300.00**
9¾" h, peacock green, pressed, short loop patterned fonts attached by wafer to octagonal bulbous stem, sq base, orig pewter collar and double burners, c1830, price for matched pr **8,250.00**
10" h
Blackberry pattern, colorless font, white base ... **145.00**
Loop pattern, cobalt blue, some chips **200.00**
Relish Dish, 6¼" l, Sandwich Star, colorless **65.00**

Salt, Christmas, yellow, green leaves, brown dec, pat Dec 15, 1877, 2¾" h, 1¾" d, $75.00.

Salt
Boat, blue opaque **1,450.00**
Crown, 2⅛" h, 3⅛" l, fiery opalescent, c1830–50, chips **260.00**
Gothic Arch and Heart, master, 3⅞" l, fiery blue opalescent **300.00**
Hexagonal, ftd, peacock blue **250.00**
Shell, pedestal base, lacy, colorless **125.00**
Sauce Dish, lacy
Peacock Eye, 4¼" d, sapphire blue, rim chips **175.00**
Sword and Cross, 4½" d, sapphire blue, rim chips .. **185.00**
Spill Holder, Sandwich Star, opaque white **300.00**
Spoon Holder, Loop, colorless **125.00**
Sugar, cov, Acanthus Leaf and Shield, lacy, colorless .. **350.00**
Vase, 9½" h, Bull's Eye and Diamond Point, colorless . **175.00**
Whiskey Taster
Flute, canary **175.00**
Lacy, colorless **195.00**

c1770

SARREGUEMINES

SARREGUEMINES CHINA

History: Sarreguemines ware is a faience porcelain, i.e., tin-glazed earthenware. The factory which made it was established in Lorraine, France, in 1770, under the supervision of Utzschneider and Fabry. The factory was regarded as one of the three most prominent manufacturers of French faience. Most of the wares found today were made in the 19th century.

Marks: Later wares are impressed "Sarreguemines" and "Germany" as a result of changes in international boundaries.

Animal Covered Dish, 5¼" l, hen and chicks, polychrome dec **175.00**
Asparagus, 9" l, majolica, naturalistic colors **90.00**
Box, cov, heart shape, floral dec, ormolu mount, c1760 **150.00**
Character Jug, 7½" h, Scotsman, red hair, blue and red hat **95.00**
Creamer, 5" h, ducks and frogs, flower border **65.00**
Ewer, 10" h, tan, gold butterflies and flowers **85.00**
Oyster Plate, price for 4-pc set **200.00**

Vases, fisheye pattern, green ground, marked and numbered "14032DT C531" under foot, 11½" h, price for pr $550.00. Photo courtesy of Leslie Hindman Auctioneers.

Plate

7¾" d, NY World's Fair, 1939	45.00
8½" d, majolica, strawberries and floral trim, aqua ground	85.00
Tea Service, florals, ornate shapes, c1840, price for 14-pc set	625.00
Tobacco Jar, cov, relief masks, brown, yellow trim	95.00
Toby Pitcher, 8¼" h, toothy grin, polychrome dec, marked "Sarreguemines, Made in Germany," stains and crazing	45.00
Vase, 8½" h, majolica, gargoyles and lizards	150.00

SARSAPARILLA BOTTLES

History: Sarsaparilla refers to the fragrant roots of a number of tropical American, spiny, woody vines of the lily family. An extract was obtained from these dried roots and used for medicinal purposes. The first containers, which date from the 1840s, were stoneware; glass bottles were used later.

Carbonated water often was added to sarsaparilla to make a soft drink or to make consuming it more pleasurable. For this reason, sarsaparilla and soda became synonymous even though they originally were two different concoctions.

References: Ralph and Terry Kovel, *The Kovels' Bottles Price List,* Tenth Edition, Crown Publishers, 1996; Carlo and Dot Sellari, *The Standard Old Bottle Price Guide,* Collector Books, 1989.

Periodical: *Antique Bottle and Glass Collector,* PO Box 187, East Greenville, PA 18041.

Additional Listings: See *Warman's Americana & Collectibles* for a list of soda bottles.

A H Bull, Hartford, 7" h	45.00
Brown's Sarsaparillia, aqua	12.00
Burr & Waters, pottery, gray salt glaze	100.00
Dalton's Sarsaparilla and Nerve Tonic, blue label	40.00

Stollo Co., Troy, NY, "The Temperance Beverage," paper label, 12 oz, $7.50.

Dr Guysott's Compound Extract of Yellow Dock and Sarsaparilla, peacock green, sloping lip, iron pontil, 9" h	1,350.00
Dr Townsend's Sarsaparilla, Albany, NY, peacock green, sloping lip, iron pontil, 9¼" h	1,150.00
Gooch's, blue	150.00
Hoods & Ayers	15.00
Merchants, green, iron pontil	150.00
Sand's Genuine, rect, qt	95.00
Sawyers Eclipse, aqua	35.00
Wetherell's, aqua	45.00

SATIN GLASS

History: Satin glass, produced in the late 19th century, is an opaque art glass with a velvety matte (satin) finish achieved through treatment with hydrofluoric acid. A large majority of the pieces were cased or had a white lining.

While working at the Phoenix Glass Company, Beaver, Pennsylvania, Joseph Webb perfected mother-of-pearl (MOP) satin glass in 1885. Similar to plain satin glass in respect to casing, MOP satin glass has a distinctive surface finish and an integral or indented design, the most well known being diamond quilted (DQ).

The most common colors are yellow, rose, or blue. Rainbow coloring is considered choice.

Additional Listings: Cruets, Fairy Lamps, Miniature Lamps, and Rose Bowls.

Reproduction Alert: Satin glass, in both the plain and MOP varieties, has been widely reproduced.

Bowl, 10¼" d, 4⅝" h, pink and white loops, ruffled rim, gold and yellow encrusted floral dec	470.00
Bride's Bowl, 9½" d, MOP, blue, moire pattern, SP holder with strawberries and leaves applied to handle, marked "Simpson, Hall, Miller Co"	375.00
Candlesticks, pr, 8¾" h, yellow, brown roses, dark painted rims and bases	170.00
Dresser Jar, cov, 3½" h, yellow, gold flowers, red leaves	185.00
Ewer	
8½" h, pink herringbone, MOP, frilly spout, applied fancy thorn handle	385.00

11¾" h, 4½" d, shaded heavenly blue, melon sections, white lining, applied frosted handles, peach-colored flowers and lacy foliage dec, price for pr   485.00

Jam Dish, 6¾" h, 5" d, shaded pink, white lining, frosted shell trim applied around top, dark berries, leaves, and bird dec, SP holder   175.00

Lamp, 19¾" h, peg, pale pink shading to deep pink, ribbed base, matching ribbed shades with ruffled rims, orig brass burners, brass base, price for pr   990.00

Miniature Lamp, pink DQ, MOP, 8½" h, $1,325.00.

Mustard, cov, 4⅛" h, melon ribs, yellow shaded to pale pink, SP fittings, SS spoon with enameled bowl   170.00

Pickle Castor, Heart Arches pattern insert, white, enameled rose-colored apple blossoms and green leaves, SP frame   395.00

Plate, 7" d, shaded rose to lighter pink, Drape MOP, marked "Patent" in glossy letters on base   200.00

Rose Bowl, 5" h, 5" d, shaded blue, pale lavender enameled sprays of leaves, eight crimp top, white lining   125.00

Salad Set, 8" × 4½" bowl, shaded gold ribbon MOP bowl, SP top rim, matching SP salad fork and spoon, gold ribbon MOP glass handles   900.00

Sweetmeat jar, 6" h, 5" d, shaded blue, DQ, MOP, white lining, white enameled flowers, brown leaves, SP top   565.00

Tumbler

3¼" h, pink herringbone, MOP   55.00

3½" h, vertical rainbow bands of vivid pink, blue, and yellow, DQ, MOP, floral dec, applied enamel branch of three white and pink single-petaled blossoms, partially opened buds, four leaves, stylized stems, gold highlights and rim   885.00

Vase

5½" h, rainbow bands of yellow, blue, white, and mahogany, encrusted gold band at ruffled rim   360.00

6½" h, 3¾" d, shaded heavenly blue, swirl, ruffled, MOP, melon sections, ormolu bases, price for pr   435.00

6¾" h

Federzeichnung, pearl satin, brown, undulating air-trap dec, marked, Rd 76057   1,350.00

3½" d, shaded blue herringbone, MOP, white lining, lavender dot flowers, thin gold leaves   235.00

9¾" h, 5" d, shaded heavenly blue, herringbone, MOP, rect closely ruffled top, white lining, frosted

applied thorny handles, three applied frosted feet, price for pr   775.00

10⅛" h, peach, gold encrusted floral dec, price for pr   235.00

SATSUMA

History: Satsuma, named for a war lord who brought skilled Korean potters to Japan in the early 1600s, is a handcrafted Japanese faience (tin-glazed) pottery. It is finely crackled, has a cream, yellow-cream, or gray-cream color, and is decorated with raised enamels in floral, geometric, and figural motifs.

Figural satsuma was made specifically for export in the 19th century. Later satsuma, referred to as satsuma-style ware, is a Japanese porcelain also hand decorated in raised enamels. From 1912 to the present, satsuma-style ware has been mass-produced. Much of the ware on today's market is of this later period.

Beaker, gold, multicolored flowers, blue ground, 20th C   190.00

Biscuit Jar, cov, 6½ × 6", orange, bamboo-type handles, diaper border   125.00

Bowl

4" d, dragon and men dec, 1890   110.00

7" d, landscape scene, seven sages, gold trim, black ext.   175.00

Brush Pot, water plants dec, Kinkozan   125.00

Button, round, peony dec, price for 4-pc set   30.00

Charger, 12⅞" d, red and black flowers and birds, white ground, gold trim   125.00

Creamer and Sugar, cov, floral pattern   350.00

Cup and Saucer, flowers and butterflies, c1900   50.00

Dish, 9⅞" h, Kannon, arhats and dragon, int. dec, scalloped, gilt ground, c1900   275.00

Incense Burner, 4" h, ovoid, three arrow-form molded flower-head reserves, cream glaze, tripod feet, reticulated cov, Meiji period   175.00

Jar, cov, 5" h, prunus branch with bird, diaper border neck band and handles   250.00

Koro, 17½" h, earthenware covered, blue field, birds and flowers dec, green foo-dog handles to lid and sides, three green foo-dog feet, 18th/19th C   425.00

Mug, 6½ × 4⅝", scenery and gold pagoda, dull black finish, sgd with Oriental characters   65.00

Pitcher, 4½" h, warrior scene, gold scrolled handle, c1920   250.00

Incense Burner, courtesans on one side, Mandarins on obv, c1875, 4" w, 3¾" h, $250.00.

Plaque, 9½" d, waterfowl and pond scene, florals, foliate, and hanging wisteria, gold and red border, gold trim, Meiji period, c1900 .... 250.00

Plate, 9" d, mother and children in garden, flowers and butterflies border, Japanese 300.00

Tea Caddy, cov, 5½" d, blooming prunus tree, bird, brocade ground, handles 195.00

Teabowl, 5" d, maple trees dec, marked "Yabu Meizan" 825.00

Teapot, Shishi motif, multicolored, cross, circle, and blue gosu, c1800 .... 700.00

Tile, 3¾ × 5½", women and children crossing bridge to crowded country inn, polychrome and gilt dec 325.00

Urn, 14" h, Geisha girl scene, bird handle, Awata Satsuma, c1920, price for pr 275.00

Vase

    4¾" h, scenic design, wooden base, orig velvet lined case, Meiji period 375.00

    6" h, Buddhist saints and bijin reserves, waisted neck, ftd 250.00

    14¾" h, four figures and dragon, gilt, dark ground . 95.00

Warming Plate, 9¾" d, hot-water compartment, polychrome, gold highlights, sgd in red underglaze 195.00

SCALES

History: Prior to 1900 the simple balance scale was commonly used for measuring weights. Since then scales have become more sophisticated in design and more accurate. There are a wide variety of styles and types, including beam, platform, postal, and pharmaceutical.

Collectors' Club: International Society of Antique Scale Collectors, Ste 1706, 176 W Adams St, Chicago, IL 60603.

Balance

    Brass, marble base, 21" h 50.00

    Fairbanks, 15½" l, 8¾" h, marked "Iz 8," 50% orig paint 65.00

    Spring Chatillons Spring Balance, hanging type, brass face, 17 × 4½" 75.00

Candy

    Anderson Computing Scale Co, 2 lb 300.00

    Enterprise Manufacturing Co, Phila, PA, tin scoop, brass slide 145.00

    National, decal, restored 350.00

Country Store, Computing Scale Co, Dayton, OH, c1905 1,250.00

Egg, 8½" × 6½" × 3", aluminum weight indicator, brass head screw, red weighing arm 50.00

Feed, red and white checkered top, blue and cream bottom, metal pan, "Purina Feed Saver and Cow Culler" adv 80.00

Grocery Store, tin, hanging, weighs to 30 lbs 50.00

Pharmacy, oak case, beveled glass and marble top, 1800s 300.00

Postal, Hanson Bros Scale Co, c1925 .... 45.00

Scale Manufacturer's Catalog

    Fairbanks & Co, St Johnsbury, VT, 1904, 24 pages, 4½ × 8", beautiful lady in yellow dress on scale on cover, scale history, halftones of many types of scales 100.00

    Troemner, Henry, Philadelphia, PA, 1908, 100 pages, 5¾ × 9¼", illus price list, many types of scales, accessories 145.00

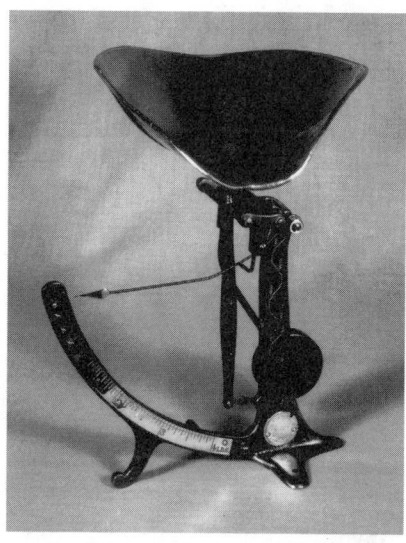

Gravity type, iron base, scoop pan, dated 1880, Fulton, Cincinnati, refinished, $125.00.

SCHLEGELMILCH PORCELAINS

History: Erdmann Schlegelmilch founded his porcelain factory in Suhl in the Thuringia region in 1861. Reinhold, his brother, established a porcelain factory at Tillowitz in Upper Silesia in 1869. In the 1860s Prussia controlled Thuringia and Upper Silesia, both rich in the natural ingredients needed for porcelain.

By the late 19th century an active export business was conducted with the United States and Canada due to a large supply of porcelain at reasonable costs achieved through industrialization and cheap labor.

The Suhl factory ceased production in 1920, unable to recover from the effects of World War I. The Tillowitz plant, located in an area of changing international boundaries, finally came under Polish socialist government control in 1956.

Marks: Both brothers marked their pieces with the "RSP" mark, a designation honoring Rudolph Schlegelmilch, their father. Over 30 mark variations have been discovered.

References: Susan and Al Bagdade, *Warman's English & Continental Pottery & Porcelain,* Second Edition, Wallace-Homestead, 1991; R. H. Capers, *Capers' Notes on the Marks of Prussia,* Alphabet Printing (667 E 6th St, El Paso, IL 61738), 1996; Mary Frank Gaston, *The Collector's Encyclopedia of R. S. Prussia and Other R. S. and E. S. Porcelain,* First Series (1982, 1993 value update), Second Series, (1986, 1994 value update), Third Series (1994), Fourth Series (1995), Collector Books.

Collectors' Club: International Assoc of R. S. Prussia Collectors Inc, 212 Wooded Falls Rd, Louisville, KY 40243.

REPRODUCTION ALERT

Many "fake" Schlegelmilch pieces are appearing on the market. These reproductions have new decal marks, transfers, or recently hand-painted animals on old, authentic R. S. Prussia pieces.

E. S. Germany

Bowl, Fox Hunt scene, green ground	225.00
Cake Plate, Monk dec, O. S. mark	145.00
Calling Card Holder, Indian Chief	75.00
Dresser Tray, lady with poppy	85.00
Plate, cobalt blue border, pink flowers	115.00
Spittoon, green and white	225.00
Vase, burgundy ground, reclining lady and cherub	275.00

R. S. Germany

Basket

Peafowls and Asian pheasants	150.00
Scallop & Fan, 5 × 3"	225.00
Candle Night-Light, 5" h, figural, owl	250.00
Creamer and Sugar, Art Deco dec	135.00

C. T. Germany, cup and saucer, purple and gilt florals, white ground, $35.00.

Demitasse Set, orange lilies	595.00
Dish, 13" l, oval, open handles, pink and yellow roses	45.00
Pitcher, 5" h, hidden images	265.00
Shaving Mug	
Stippled floral urn	185.00
Urn lily variation, mirrored	275.00
Smoke Set, blue borders, match holder and pipe	295.00
Toothpick Holder, white daisies, blue ground, gold handles and top, slight wear to gold	95.00
Tray, 15¼" l, white and green poppies, handles	250.00

R. S. Poland

Bowl, 10½" d, Heart mold, poppies, satin finish	245.00
Candlestick, 6" h, violets, lily of the valley dec, shiny finish	125.00

R. S. Poland, vases, white and yellow floral dec, cream and brown ground, 12" h, price for pr $575.00.

Hair Receiver, violets, lily of the valley dec	100.00
Powder Jar, violets, lily of the valley dec	100.00
Vase, 4½ × 8¾", cream ground, pink and white roses, gold band around top, garlands of gold roses and leaves	195.00

REPRODUCTION ALERT

Dorothy Hammond in her 1979 book *Confusing Collectibles* illustrated an R. S. Prussia decal which was available from a china-decorating supply company for $14 a sheet. This was the first of several fake R. S. Prussia reproduction marks that have caused confusion among collectors. Acquaint yourself with some of the subtle distinctions between fake and authentic marks as described in the following.

The period mark consists of a wreath that is open at the top. A five-pointed star sits in the opening. An "R" and an "S" flank a wreath twig in the center. The word "Prussia" is located beneath. In the period mark, the leg of the letter "P" extends down past the letter "r." In the reproduction mark it does not. In the period mark, the letter "i" is dotted. It is dotted in some fake marks but not in others.

The "R" and the "S" in the period mark are in a serif face and are uniform in width. One fake mark uses a lettering style that utilizes a thin/thick letter body. The period mark has a period after the word "Prussia." Some fake marks fail to include it. Several fake marks do not include the word "Prussia" at all.

The period mark has a fine center line within each leaf of the wreath. Several fake marks do not.

S & T
R S
PRUSSIA
c 1870s - 1880

R S
Prussia
c 1870s - 1914

R. S. Prussia

Berry Dish, portrait, sgd "LeBrun," Poppy mold, gold
floral edge, varied yellow and green ground **200.00**
Berry Set
    Acorn mold, pale roses in center, price for 7-pc set   **350.00**
    Blown out iris mold, roses center, price for 7-pc set **495.00**
    Leaf mold, price for 7-pc set **650.00**
Bowl
    10" d
        Iris mold, poppies, satin finish **125.00**
        Sunflower mold, satin finish **195.00**
    10¼ x 3", Water Lily & Cattail mold, petal scallops,
        cattail medallions, gold beading, roses, unmarked **250.00**

**R. S. Prussia, relish, red floral center, iris in velvet on border, pink and
lavender ground, 9½" l, 4½" w, $75.00.**

    10½ × 3½", Art Nouveau, scrolls, floral medallions,
        large roses **380.00**
    11 × 3", Fishscale mold, lilies, purple, and orange
        luster **400.00**
Cake Plate
    Carnation mold, multicolored roses, red mark **295.00**
    Leaf Wreath mold, floral dec, 11" d, unmarked **160.00**
    Spring Season, 9¾" d **1,450.00**
Celery, 12¼" l, relief daffodils, beading, flowers, gold
    trim, pierced handles, unmarked **110.00**
Children's Dishes, tea set, roses, teapot, four cups and
    saucers **595.00**
Chocolate Pot, cov
    Mold 643, green with pink roses **325.00**
    Multicolored roses, gold trim, red mark **395.00**
Cologne Bottle, Bacchus scene with figures, pan, orig
    stopper **150.00**
Compote, lilacs **135.00**
Cracker Jar, cov, 7" h, Mold 704, grape leaf dec, wreath
    mark **400.00**
Creamer and Sugar
    Art Deco swan marsh scene, raised gold, unmarked **400.00**
    Mold 601, floral dec, 4½" h, unmarked **60.00**
Cup and Saucer, sunflower mold **125.00**
Demitasse Cup and Saucer, pansy dec **75.00**

Ferner, 6¾" d, 3½" h, water lilies, pastels, piecrust rim,
    liner, tri-foot, red mark **275.00**
Fruit Bowl, 9" d, ftd, pink rose dec **180.00**
Hatpin Holder, Calla Lily **150.00**
Plate, luster, roses dec, scalloped festoon rim **95.00**
Shaving Mug, Old Star mark **175.00**
Tankard, 13¼" h, Stipple mold, large roses **625.00**

R. S. Suhl

Bowl, 10" d, sheepherder scene, cottage, red mark **500.00**
Compote, 4½" d, ftd, creamy roses, gold stencil design,
    green mark **225.00**
Pitcher, 5½" h, white ground, red roses, unmarked **115.00**
Vase, 9½" h, Gibson Girl portrait, red mark **850.00**
Spittoon, pale green, pink roses **275.00**

R. S. Suhl, bowl, yellow rose, 10" d, $75.00.

R S
TILLOWITZ
Silesia
c 1920-1930s

R. S. Tillowitz

Bowl, 10 × 6¼", oval, hp, pheasant hen and cock, blue
    mark **295.00**

**R. S. Tillowitz, bowl, roses, gold border, marked
"R & S" in green wreath and "Reinhold Schle-
gelmilch/Tillowitz/Germany," 9½" d, $45.00.**

Cheese and Cracker Dish, 8½" d, 2½" h, blue mark, "Germany" in green 65.00
Chocolate Pot, Art Nouveau dec, glossy finish 55.00
Marmalade, cov, underplate, floral dec 85.00
Plate, 7" d, stylized butterfly border, gold rim and handles, blue mark 65.00
Tray, five sided, roses dec 45.00

SCHNEIDER GLASS

History: Brothers Ernest and Charles Schneider founded a glassworks at Epiney-sur-Seine, France, in 1913. Charles, the artistic designer, previously had worked for Daum and Gallé. Robert, son of Charles, assumed art direction in 1948. Schneider moved to Loris in 1962.

Although Schneider made tablewares, stained glass, and lighting fixtures, its best-known product is art glass which exhibits simplicity of design and often has bubbles and streaking in larger pieces. Other styles include cameo-cut and hydrofluoric-acid-etched designs.

Marks: Schneider glass was signed with a variety of script and block signatures, "Le Verre Francais," or "Charder."

Bowl, 9¼" d, flattened globular shape, clear, mottled cream shading to magenta, orange and deep-purple splashes, c1925 .... 195.00
Candlestick, 5½" h, paperweight base, coral and pink double clematis dec 225.00
Compote, 8½" d, 5½" h, lavender shading to deep blue rim, wrought-iron base, clusters of glass cherries ... 250.00
Pitcher, 6¼" h, mottled pink, dark maroon handle, orig paper label, sgd 395.00
Vase
   5½" h, blue, black, and clear, cased orange int., blown into wrought-iron base, sgd, marked "France," c1925 .... 295.00
   8½" d, mottled orange, purple, cream, and yellow, sgd 310.00
   10" h, bulbous, cylindrical neck, deep lavender streaked with blue, two orange handles on neck, inscribed "Schneider/France" 450.00
   17½" h, teardrop, wide flaring lip, mottled periwinkle blue, cherry red ground, sgd, c1925 .... 975.00

SCHOENHUT TOYS

History: Albert Schoenhut, son of a toy maker, was born in Germany in 1849. In 1866 he ventured to America where he worked as a toy-piano repairman for Wanamaker's in Philadelphia, Pennsylvania. Finding the glass sounding bars inadequate, he perfected a toy piano with metal sounding bars. His piano was an instant success, and the A. Schoenhut Company had its beginning.

From that point on, toys seemed to flow out of the factory. Each of his six sons entered the business, and it prospered until 1934, when misfortune forced the company into bankruptcy. In 1935 Otto and George Schoenhut contracted to produce the Pinn Family Dolls.

The Schoenhut Manufacturing Company was formed by two other Schoenhuts. Both companies operated under a partnership agreement that eventually led to O. Schoenhut, Inc., which continues today.

Some dates of interest:
1872—toy piano invented
1903—Humpty Dumpty Circus patented
1911–1924—wooden doll production
1928–1934—composition dolls made.

References: Carol Corson, *Schoenhut Dolls,* Hobby House Press, 1993; Richard O'Brien, *Collecting Toys,* Seventh Edition, Books Americana, 1995.

Collectors' Clubs: Schoenhut Collectors Club, 1003 W Huron St, Ann Arbor, MI 48103; Schoenhut Toy Collectors, 1916 Cleveland St, Evanston, IL 60202.

Animal
   Bear, brown, glass eyes, Style III 195.00
   Buffalo, 7⅝" l, painted eyes, carved mane, leather ears and tail, very good paint 375.00
   Dromedary Camel, 8¾" l, painted eyes, leather ears, woven-cotton tail, very good paint, minor chipping and wear 250.00
   Gazelle, glass eyes, c1910 .... 500.00
   Goat, 8¼" l, painted eyes, black and white coat, leather horns and tail, leatherette ears, very good paint, minor chipping, ears damaged 175.00
   Kangaroo, painted eyes, Style II 350.00
   Leopard, 7" l, glass eyes, ball-jointed neck 350.00
   Ostrich, 9½" l, painted eyes, very good paint, minor chipping 375.00
   Rhinoceros, jointed 75.00
   Tiger, 7⅜" l, painted eyes, woven cotton tail, very good paint, minor chipping 225.00
   Zebra, 8" l, painted eyes, leather ears, woven-cotton tail, very good paint, minor chipping 225.00
Barney Google and Spark Plug, 7¾" h Barney, fabric clothing, 9" h Spark Plug, rope tail, c1922 ....1,100.00
Building Toy, Little Village Builder, orig box 85.00

Circus, tiger, painted wood, 7½" l, 5¼" h, $175.00.

Circus
   Accessories, three platforms, three ladders, four pedestals, four barrels, three white chairs, two drums, one ball, price for 20-pc set 250.00

Man, 6″ h, carved wooden head and body, oversized ears and feet, wide grin, orig cotton and felt costume **150.00**

Performers, painted eyes, 6⅜″ h lady bareback rider, 7″ h ringmaster with molded top hat, 8″ h lady bareback rider, some paint chips and fabric wear, price for 3-pc set **250.00**

Dirigible, 13″ l, orig box, c1929 .... **125.00**

Doll

14″ h, baby, bald head, decaled blue eyes, closed mouth, curved limb body, knitted outfit **300.00**

16½″ h, boy, sober face, jointed at shoulders, free-swing joint at hips for walking, mohair wig, paint scuffed, c1915 .... **350.00**

Felix the Cat, 3¾″ h, worn ears, c1920 .... **150.00**

Piano

11½″ h, 17¼″ w, 8″ d, grained wood, litho paper on wooden front panel, early 20th C, some damage **35.00**

19½ × 20 × 10″, upright, wood, stool, 18 keys, minor wear **195.00**

SCIENTIFIC INSTRUMENTS

History: Chemists, doctors, geologists, navigators, and surveyors used precision instruments as tools of their trade. Such objects were well designed and beautifully crafted. They are primarily made of brass; fancy hardwood cases also are common.

References: Florian Cajori, *A History of the Logarithmic Slide Rule and Allied Instruments,* Astragal Press, 1994; Gloria Clifton, *Directory of British Scientific Instrument Makers 1550–1851,* P. Wilson Publishers, distributed by Sotheby's, 1994.

Periodicals: *Rittenhouse,* PO Box 151, Hastings-on-Hudson, NY 10706; *Scientific, Medical & Mechanical Antiques,* PO Box 412, Taneytown, MD 21787.

Collectors' Clubs: International Calculator Collectors Club, 14561 Livingston St, Tustin, CA 92680; Maryland Microscopical Society, 8261 Polk St, McLean VA, 22102; The Oughtred Society, 2160 Middlefield Rd, Palo Alto, CA 94301; Zeiss Historical Society, PO Box 631, Clifton, NJ 07012.

Museum: National Museum of American History, Smithsonian Institution, Washington, DC.

Barograph, brass and glass, cased, sgd "Short & Mason, London, England" **500.00**

Calorimeter, 15½ × 12½ × 6¾″ dovetailed mahogany case, brass handle, labeled "S. Humble, Westminster," engraved glass beaker, balance scales, mortar and pestle, some weights **315.00**

Compass, 2″ d, convex glass lens, hand-colored engraved paper face, turned wood case **195.00**

Frictionless Propeller Conical-End Log by Edward Massey, brass instrument, orig with label, used by Captain James Woodbury **200.00**

Galvanometer, LE Knott Apparatus Co, Boston, used to test electrical currents **995.00**

Gyroscope, 10½″ h, lacquered, accessories, base sgd "T Cooke & Sons, York & London," late 19th C **650.00**

Octant, ebony and brass, ivory nameplate, ivory scale, G Heath, Erith, Kent, slight corrosion to brass **600.00**

Quadrant, ebony, brass arm, sgd "Dolland of London" **650.00**

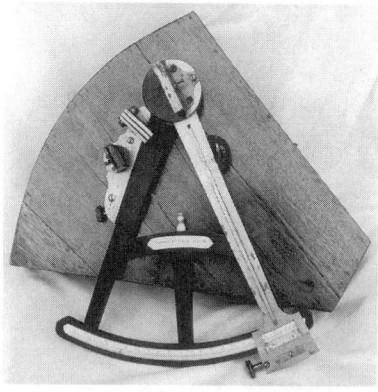

Quadrant, I. J. Messer, London, importer's label Charles Tabor & Co., New Bedford, cased, 12 × 13 × 3⅝″, $1,000.00.

Sextant, W Gerrard Liverpool, brass, orig case fitted with three lenses and extra pcs **550.00**

Slide Rule, wood and celluloid, orig case, marked "Keuffel & Esser," 1900 .... **50.00**

Specimen Case, twelve drawers, cast-iron pulls with label slot

25″ w, 64″ h, oak, pullout shelf, paneled ends, molded 28″ l, 21″ d cornice, old light natural finish **500.00**

27½″ w, 63½″ h, hardwood, paneled ends, molded 30″ l, 22″ d cornice, old light natural finish **450.00**

Surveyor's Compass, brass

14¾″ l, 6″ w dial, fitted in orig case, partial label, wood and brass tripod, sgd "G. M. Pool, Easton, Mass" **800.00**

15″ l, 6″ w dial, orig box, side sights, tripod connection, brass cover, intact level indicators, "Benj'n H. Hagger Maker, Baltimore," bezel and needle missing **275.00**

Telescope, brass, M Jaggli, Zurich, tube badly dented, oak tripod base **500.00**

Terrestrial Globe, mid to late 19th C

Carey, 12″ d, terrestrial globe corrected to 1827, celestial globe corrected to 1800, foliate carved stands, price for pr **4,140.00**

Merriam, Moore & Co, Troy, NY, c19852, 6″ h, Franklin type, scrolled wrought-iron tripod base **2,415.00**

Thury and Belnet, paper and metal, raised elevation, white marble pedestal **875.00**

SCRIMSHAW

History: Norman Flayderman defined scrimshaw as "the art of carving or otherwise fashioning useful or decorative articles as practiced primarily by whalemen, sailors, or others associated with nautical pursuits." Many collectors expand this to include the work of Eskimos and French POWs from the War of 1812.

References: Stuard M. Frank, *Dictionary of Scrimshaw Artists,* Mystic Seaport Museum, 1991; Nina Hellman and Norman Brouwer, *A Mariner's Fancy,* South Street Seaport Museum, Balsam Press, and the University of Washington Press, 1992; Martha Lawrence, *Scrimshaw,* Schiffer Publishing, 1993.

Museums: Cold Spring Whaling Harbor Museum, Cold Spring Harbor, NY; Kendall Whaling Museum, Sharon, MA; Mystic Seaport Museum, Mystic, CT; National Maritime Museum, San Francisco, CA; New Bedford Whaling Museum, New Bedford, MA; Old Dartmouth Historical Society, New Bedford, MA; Pacific Whaling Museum, Waimanalo, HI; Sag Harbor Whaling & Historical Museum, Sag Harbor, NY; San Francisco Maritime National Historical Park, San Francisco, CA; South Street Seaport Museum, New York, NY; Whaling Museum, Nantucket, MA.

REPRODUCTION ALERT

The biggest problem in the field is fakes, although there are some clues to spotting them. A very hot needle will penetrate the common plastics used in reproductions but not the authentic material. Ivory will not generate static electricity when rubbed, plastic will. Patina is not a good indicator; it has been faked by applying tea or tobacco juice, burying in raw rabbit hide, and in other ingenious ways. Usually the depth of cutting in an old design will not be consistent since the ship rocked and tools dulled; however, skilled forgers have even copied this characteristic.

Book, *Susan's Teeth and Much about Scrimshaw,* Everett
J Crosby, published Nantucket Island, limited edition,
500 copies, 1955 .... **800.00**
Buggy Whip, 82" l, whale ivory and whalebone sections,
baleen rings, two rope carvings, mid 19th C **2,000.00**
Busk
  Baleen
    13¼" h, panels of floral and geometric design,
      19th C, minor chipping to one side **200.00**
    13½" h, panels of palm trees, three-story building,
      ship, 19th C, age cracks and worming **230.00**
  Whalebone, engraved
    11½" h, whale, lighthouse, and American eagle,
      19th C **550.00**
    12½" h, heralding angel, harp, and two-story
      house, 19th C, repaired crack **230.00**
    14¼" h, panels of woman, plants, and heart, 19th
      C, in two pcs **225.00**
Butter Mold, 5⅛" h, circular, wood, carved rosette,
  whale ivory handle, early to mid-19th C **275.00**
Cane
  31⅞" h, wood and whalebone, whale ivory and ba-
    leen rings, 19th C **295.00**

37½" l, wood, whale ivory tip and knob, partially
  wound baleen and ropework, diamond-shaped
  wood inlays, 19th C **275.00**
Chest, 20¾ × 9½ × 9", walnut or mahogany and pine,
  hinged top, three inlaid abstract whalebone figures
  on front panel and initials "G. W. T." **550.00**
Cribbage Board, 18½" d, walrus tusk, 7 walruses **300.00**
Ostrich Egg, engraved sailor, sweetheart, eagle, flag,
  stars, and ship, orig ropework hanger **275.00**
Powder Horn, 9½" l, engraved reserves on crosshatched
  field of ships at sea, Charleston Harbor, arms of Spicer
  of Exeter or Weare of Devon, inscribed "South Carolina made in Charlestown Amerique 1764," minor
  imperfections **6,325.00**
Sewing Box
  6¾" l, engraved baleen, stuffed brocade pincushion
    lid, 19th C, small losses **1,100.00**
  8" sq, island wood, geometric wood inlays, inlaid
    whale ivory and abalone shell compass rose, di-
    amonds and spandrel dec, mid 19th C **650.00**
Snuff Box, 3 × 1½" l, shaped oval, top diamond inscribed "R. N.," (Royal Navy) and anchor, other side
  inscribed "Capt. N. C. Norten," dates of service,
  1831, 1841, on ends, fluting, highlighted with lampblack **450.00**
Watch Fob, whale ivory, book form, engraved colored
  Masonic symbols, mid-19th C **395.00**

Whale's Tooth, engraved on one side, eagle clutching flag and banner, "Harrison and Tyler for President" over naval battle entitled "Constitution and Guerriere," 7¼" l, 3⅞" w, $1,300.00.

Whale's Tooth, engraved
  5¼" h, vases of flowers, 19th C, price for pr **690.00**
  5¾" h, shielded American eagle, American flag
    flanked by cannons above whale boat disaster on
    one side, other side with three-masted ship flying
    American flag and whale boat, 19th C, small chip
    to tip **8,625.00**
  6¼" h, woman in formal dress, late 19th C, cracks . **375.00**
  6½" h, townscape above three-masted ship flying
    American flag on one side, other side with fash-
    ionable lady, 19th C, base chips **2,875.00**
  7¼" h, each side with three-masted ship under sail,
    19th C, age cracks, price for pr **4,900.00**
  7½" h, British ship under full sail on one side, screw
    steamer on other side, 19th C **1,265.00**

SEVRES

History: The principal patron of the French porcelain industry in early 18th-century France was Jeanne Antoinette Poisson, Marquise de Pompadour. She supported the Vincennes factory of Gilles and Robert Dubois and their successors in their attempt to make soft-paste porcelain in the 1740s. In 1753 she moved the porcelain operations to Sevres, near her home, Chateau de Bellevue.

The Sevres soft-paste formula used sand from Fontainebleau, salt, saltpeter, soda of alicante, powdered alabaster, clay, and soap. Many famous colors were developed, including a cobalt blue. The wonderful scenic designs on the ware were painted by such famous decorators as Watteau, La Tour, and Boucher. In the 18th century Sevres porcelain was the world's foremost diplomatic gift.

In 1769 kaolin was discovered in France, and a hard-paste formula was developed. The baroque gave way to rococo, a style favored by Jeanne du Barry, Louis XV's next mistress. Louis XVI took little interest in Sevres, and many factories began to turn out counterfeits. In 1876 the factory was moved to St. Cloud and was eventually nationalized.

Marks: Louis XV allowed the firm to use the "double L" in its marks.

Reproduction Alert.

Bowl, 12½" d, scrolling reserve with exotic birds, apple green ground, gilt handles, blue L mark **495.00**
Box, cov, 8" d, octagonal, amorous couple on cov, foliage on int., sgd "George Rocher," early 20th C .. **550.00**
Cache Pot, 9" h, cylindrical, reserves of elegant figures in garden landscape, pink ground, gilt scroll borders, price for pr **950.00**
Charger, 19" d, Louis XVI center portrait, Marie Antoinette above, ladies of court around edge, blue and gold, names on back **1,200.00**
Compote, 10⅝" d, center portrait medallion of Louis XVI, gilt scroll and floral border, pink ground, two gilt-lined flat handles **275.00**
Cup and Saucer, gilt and floral panels, apple green ground **75.00**

Dresser Box, cov, 5¾" l, oval, portrait medallion of lady on cov, floral side dec, gold bronze mounts **350.00**
Plate
  8" d, embracing couple, garden setting, yellow dec, scalloped gold dec rim, artist sgd, marked "Chateau St Cloud" **95.00**
  11" d, two putti, monogram, celeste blue borders, factory marks, sgd "Bruny," Louis-Philippe, 1846 **225.00**
Portrait Plate, 9½" d, Napoleon, white horse, battle scene, cobalt blue border with gold leaves, artist sgd **275.00**
Urn
  10½" h, 11" d, dark blue porcelain, gold highlights, satyr handles, ormolu mounts **850.00**
  16" h, celeste blue ground, courting couples and landscapes, gilt metal mounts, sgd "Lauque," c1880, price for pr **2,530.00**

Ewer, urn body, courting scene, French colonial dress, pastel, sgd "Le Duc," metal handles and base, dome lid, 16", $350.00.

  24¼" h, green, gold trim, oval reserves of romantic couples, mounted as lamps, price for pr **375.00**
  29⅜" h, polychrome floral enamels, scene of couple in garden, artist sgd "E. Roy," transfer marks on lid and Cincinnati retailer's label, minor chip on lid edge **3,300.00**

SEWING ITEMS

History: As recently as 50 years ago, a wide variety of sewing items were found in almost every home in America. Women of every economic and social status were skilled in sewing and dressmaking.

Iron or brass sewing birds, one of the interesting convenience items which developed, were used to hold cloth (in the bird's beak) while sewing. They could be attached to a table or shelf with a screw-type fixture. Later models included a pincushion.

References: *Advertising & Figural Tape Measures,* L-W Book Sales, 1995; Elizabeth Arbittier et al., *Collecting Figural Tape Measures,* Schiffer Publishing, 1995; Carter Bays, *The Encyclopedia of Early American Sewing Machines,* published by author, 1993; Frieda Marion, *China Half-Figures Called Pincushion Dolls,* published by author, 1974, 1994 reprint; Averil Mathias, *Antique and Collectible Thimbles and Accessories,* Collector Books, 1986, 1995 value update; Dana G. Morykan and Harry L. Rinker, *Warman's Country Antiques & Collectibles,* Third Edition, Wallace-Homestead, 1996; Wayne Muller, *Darn It!,* L-W Book Sales, 1995; Glenda Thomas, *Toy and Miniature Sewing Machines,* Collector Books, 1995; Helen Lester Thompson, *Sewing Tools & Trinkets,* Collector Books, 1996; Gertrude Whiting, *Old-Time Tools & Toys of Needlework,* Dover Publications, 1970.

Collectors' Clubs: International Sewing Machine Collectors Society, 1000 E Charleston Blvd, Las Vegas, NV 89104; Toy Stitchers, 623 Santa Florita Ave, Millbrae, CA 94030.

Museums: Fabric Hall, Historic Deerfield, Deerfield, MA; Museum of American History, Smithsonian Institution, Washington, DC; Sewing Machine Museum, Oakland, CA; Shelburne Museum, Shelburne, VT.

Additional Listings: See Thimbles and *Warman's Americana & Collectibles* for more examples.

Basket, cov, round, birch bark and quill, two bears, damaged	25.00
Bodkin, SS, engraved, floral dec, hallmarked	35.00
Catalog, King Sewing Machine Co, Buffalo, NY, 1909, 56 pgs, 6 × 9", King sewing machines, cabinets, features	25.00
Chatelaine	
Leather, three straps connect to scissors and case, thimble holder and pencil, English, c1900	215.00
Sterling Silver, ring top, chains connect to notepad, thimble and thimble case, buttonhook, English	575.00
Crochet Hooks, whale bone, carved, price for 3-pc set	245.00
Darning Ball, Nailsea, blown glass, blue, white pulled loops	115.00
Embroidery Hoop, 6¼" d, walnut and cherry, table clamp, handmade, Shaker	145.00
Hand Book, J F Ingalls, Lynn, MA, 1885, Ingall's Hand Book of Crochet & Knitted Lace with Illustrations	25.00
Hem Gauge, heart and rose, relief design	25.00
Instruction Book, Metropolitan Sewing Machine, Nyack, NY, 1910, 100 pgs, 6¼ × 9¼", care, operation, and adjustment of various Metropolitan sewing machines, illus price parts list	35.00
Magazine, *The Tailors,* E Butterick & Co, New York, NY, April, 1881, 20 pages, 7¾ ×11"	30.00
Miniature Sewing Machine, 5½ × 9¾ × 6½" h, Eagle and Casige, green metal, Germany, British Zone	125.00
Needle Cabinet, Standard Sewing Machine, dark brown, black and gilt lettering, one long compartmentalized drawer, six small drawers	1,050.00
Needle Case, ivory, book shape, fabric pages	125.00
Pincushion	
Black Girl, print fabric	40.00
Chicken, 4" h, spool base	45.00
Punch, 3⅛" l, ivory, turnings on top	40.00
Sewing Bird, 4½" h, iron, brass heart-shaped thumbscrew	125.00
Sewing Machine, Goodrich, treadle, quartersawn oak cabinet with gallery, 22½" w, 21¼" d, 30½" h	200.00
Spool Cabinet, Clark's, two drawer	450.00
Stand	
18½" w, 12" d, 27½" h, marquetry basket of flowers	

to top, foldout drawer pincushion, compartments, trestle base with flower inlay, bag drawer present but missing bag	550.00
19½" w, 14½" d, 29½" h, lift top, two false drawers, turned legs, brass castors, English	350.00
Table, drop leaf	
16½" w, 17" d, two 9 × 29" leaves, mahogany and mahogany veneers, drop leaf, flame mahogany top, two drawers, convex drawer front, reeded legs, New England	400.00
18¼" w, 18¼" d, 28¾" h, mahogany, Sheraton, molded top, three drawers, lower drawer replaced sewing bag, spiral turned legs, castor feet, refinished	900.00
Tape Measure, figural	
Baseball player, celluloid	225.00
Black man, celluloid	125.00
Cat, in boot, metal	400.00
Cello, metal	285.00
Chick, hatching from egg, celluloid	200.00
Dancing Girl, porcelain, sashed dress	185.00
Dog and puppy on cushion, celluloid	110.00
Drum, metal	300.00
Dutch Boy, porcelain	145.00
Eiffel Tower, metal	375.00
Fruit Basket, celluloid	120.00
Girl, with muff, celluloid	100.00
Golfer, celluloid	425.00
Groom, porcelain	225.00
Indian, boy, wearing headdress, celluloid	110.00
Man, with monocle, celluloid	375.00
Turtle, metal	85.00

Tape Measure, church, Westminster Abbey, celluloid, spring return, c1910–20, 1½ × 1⅝ × 1⅞", $135.00.

SHAKER

History: The Shakers, so named because of a dance they used in worship, are one of the oldest communal organizations in the United States. This religious group was founded by Mother Ann Lee who emigrated from England and established the first Shaker community near Albany, New York, in 1784. The Shakers reached their peak in 1850 when there were 6,000 members.

Shakers lived celibate and self-sufficient lives. Their philosophy stressed cleanliness, order, simplicity, and economy. Highly inventive and motivated, the Shakers created many utilitarian household forms and objects. Their furniture reflected a striving for quality and purity in design.

In the early 19th century, the Shakers produced many items for commercial purposes. Chairmaking and the packaged herb and seed business thrived. In every endeavor and enterprise, the members followed Mother Ann's advice: "Put your hands to work and give your heart to God."

References: Edward Deming Andrews and Faith Andrews, *Shaker Furniture,* Dover Publications, 1937; Michael Horsham, *The Art of the Shakers,* Apple Press, 1989; Robert F. W. Meader, *Illustrated Guide to Shaker Furniture,* Dover Publications, n.d.; Dana G. Morykan and Harry L. Rinker, *Warman's Country Antiques & Collectibles,* Third Edition, Wallace-Homestead, 1996; Charles R. Muller and Timothy D. Rieman, *The Shaker Chair,* Canal Press, 1984; June Sprigg and Jim Johnson, *Shaker Woodenware,* Berkshire House, 1991; June Sprigg and David Larkin, *Shaker Life, Work, and Art,* Stewart, Tabori & Chang, 1987; Timothy D. Rieman and Jean M. Burks, *The Complete Book of Shaker Furniture,* Harry N. Abrams, 1993.

Periodical: *The Shaker Messenger,* PO Box 1645 Holland, MI 49422.

Museums: Hancock Shaker Village, Pittsfield, MA; Shaker Historical Museum, Shaker Heights, OH; Shaker Museum and Library, Old Chatham, NY; Shaker Village of Pleasant Hill, Harrodsburg, KY 40330.

Advertisement, newspaper
  "Canterbury Shakers' World Renowned Sarsaparilla...," *The Canaan Reporter,* Sept 17, 1880, front pg adv with engraving of Shaker brother **15.00**
  "The Tall Shakers' Concert," *The Age,* ME, June 18, 1846, re traveling apostate performers **20.00**
Basket, 19¼" × 14¾", splint, four handles, 19th C, minor losses **1,495.00**
Blanket Chest, 48½" w, 23¾" d, 29½" h, pine, orig red paint, applied edge molding top, dovetailed case, dovetailed bracket feet, stenciled label on back "H. B. Bear," attributed to Ohio Community, some wear and edge damage **770.00**
Bonnet, 7¼" h, striped iridescent silk, attributed to Enfield, NH, 19th C, splits, minor tears **435.00**
Book
  Allen, Catherine, *Biographical Sketch of Daniel Fraser of the Shaker Community of Mt. Lebanon, Columbia County, NY,* Weed, Parsons & Co, Albany, 1890, 38 pgs **75.00**
  Anderson, Martha Jane, *Social Life and Vegetarianism,* Mt Lebanon, Guiding Star Printing House, Chicago, 1893, 27 pgs, small stains on cov **80.00**
  Chandler, Lloyd, *A Visit to the Shakers of East Canterbury, NH,* printed by the Shakers, 1894, 11 pgs **65.00**
  Wells, Seth Y and Calvin Green, eds., *Testimonies Concerning the Character and Ministry of Mother Ann Lee and the First Witnesses of the Gospel of Christ's Second Appearing; Given by Some of the Aged Brethren and Sisters of the United Society...,* Packard & Van Benthuysen, Albany, 1827, 178 pgs, orig blue printed wraps **200.00**
Box, bentwood
  3¾" × 3", oval, dark green, bottom of top lid reduced in one section **275.00**

5¼" × 3¾", oval, natural finish **125.00**
8" d, round, light brown finish, single-finger construction, slight reduction to top of base **155.00**
9½" d, round, old dark bluish green paint, wire bale, wooden handle, attributed to Enfield, CT, minor edge damage, bottom slightly loose **525.00**
11½" l, 4¼" h, oval, three finger construction, 19th C, staining, minor cracks and losses **260.00**
Broadside, The Shaker Museum, Founded 1931, Sabbathday Lake, Poland Spring, ME, c1970 .... **10.00**
Candlestand, 13¼" d, 22¾" h, cherry, attributed to Mt Lebanon, NY, first-half 19th C, refinished **5,750.00**
Carrier, three-finger construction
  11" l, 6½" h, painted yellow, attributed to Canterbury, NH, even wear, cracks **2,990.00**
  11¼" l, 7¼" h, painted yellow, fixed int. handle, Mt Lebanon, NY, 19th C, minor break lower edge ..**8,625.00**
Catalog
  Catalog of Fancy Goods Made at Shaker Village, Alfred, York County, Maine, Fannie Casey, Trustee and General Manager, 1908, 10 pgs **135.00**
  Catalogue of Shaker Herbs and Herbal Teas, Sabbathday, The Shaker Press, 1974, 4 pgs **20.00**
Chair, side, ladder back
  33½" h, old dark finish, Mt Lebanon, NY label on bottom slat, "3" imp on top slat, replaced woven blue and gray tape seat **470.00**
  35⅛" h, 17" h seat, red stain, two arched slats, splint seat jointed by double stretchers, tilters, early 19th C, minor imperfections **1,840.00**
  39¼" h, 16" h seat, old red paint, three-slat back, old splint seat, good turned finials, worn patina, seat missing some splint **250.00**
Clock, tall case, poplar, old red paint, base molding, overlapping door, simple bonnet, wag-on-the-wall works, painted wooden face, brass gears, wooden plates, old inscription "Repaired by Smith Mar 11, 1910 Tiffin O, Written by A. L. Norris," other unreadable notations, 78" h **5,100.00**
Dipper, 7¼" round, 8½" handle, wood, turned handle, copper tacks, good old staining, 8" horizontal crack to side **250.00**
Essay
  Blinn, Henry, "What Shall I Do To Be A Shaker?" East Canterbury, 1885, printed on both sides of single sheet **125.00**
  Hollister, Alzono, "Joyful Tiding," Mt Lebanon, 1886, 4 pgs **165.00**
Footstool, 11½ × 11¾", worn orig dark finish, Mt Lebanon, NY, label, edge wear, minor corner damage . **325.00**
Grain Sack, 37½" l, 18½" w, Enfield, NH, woven, stenciled, staining, patches **115.00**
Hymnal, *Shaker Hymnal by the Canterbury Shakers,* East Canterbury, NH, Stanhope Press, Gilson Co, Boston, 1908, 273 pgs, pencil inscription, stamped "North Family, Mt Lebanon, NY" **65.00**
Label, canned goods, Butter Beans and Fresh Tomatoes, Anna Case Trustee South Family Shakers, West Albany, Mt Lebanon, NY, chromolitho labels, matted and framed, 15" h, 20" w **315.00**
Letter
  Canterbury, NH, March 24, 1798, concerning death

of a sister, 12 × 7", splits, minor losses, toning,
staining **225.00**
New Lebanon, NY, July 15, 1849, from Sister Hannah
Treadway to her biological sister Nancy Lucks, 6
pgs **525.00**
Magazine, *The Shaker Herbalist,* No. 1, Spring, 1975 . **15.00**
Peg-Board, 38¾" l, pine and cherry, old patina, one peg
missing **50.00**
Rocker
33" h, No. 3, armless, Mt Lebanon, NY, c1900, old
finish with decal **230.00**
41" h, arms, shawl bar, worn orig dark finish, traces
of Mt Lebanon label inside of one rocker, top slat
imp "7", maroon and beige replaced tape seat . **660.00**

Rocker, Mt. Lebanon, NY, web back, new olive-and-blue taping, 20th C, 34" h, $225.00. Photo courtesy of Skinner, Inc.

Sander, 3 to 3½" h, wooden, 19th C, staining, price for
3-pc set **230.00**
Seed Box, 14¾" l, unfinished pine, black and white paper label "Shakers' Garden Seeds, Raised at New
Lebanon, NY," broken leather hinges **1,100.00**
Sewing Desk, 25" d, 28" h work surface, 40" h overall,
top with central paneled door, flanked by three lip-
molded drawers on either side, top drawers with keyhole escutcheons, mushroom-shaped walnut pulls on
lower drawers, lower portion with three large similar
drawers in front, side with paneled door above full-
length lip-molded drawers, delicate turned legs,
chestnut work surface, refinished soft wood, small
chip on one small drawer **10,000.00**
Sieve, 6⅞" l, 3⅝" h, stained wood, 19th C, minor imperfections **115.00**
Spit Box, 10" d, yellow painted, Mt Lebanon, NY, 19th
C, crack, even paint wear **1,955.00**
Stove Set, 17½" l shove, 22" l tongs, wrought iron, attributed to Canterbury, NH **495.00**
Swift, 15" h, worn orig yellow varnish, minor crack in
table clamp, attributed to Hancock, MA **220.00**
Table, work
26 × 72", 12¼" leaf, 29½" h, walnut, poplar secondary wood, one drop leaf supported by 2 swing

legs, dovetailed drawer in each end, turned tapering legs, old refinishing, attributed to Otterbein
Shaker, Lebanon, OH, age crack, repairs, replaced
hinges **2,100.00**
37½ × 48¾", 27¼" h, Hepplewhite, old red and pine
two-board top with rounded corners, old scrubbed
finish, hardwood base, sq tapered legs, mortised
and pinned apron, attributed to Enfield, NH **935.00**
Tailor's Counter, six dovetailed lip-molded drawers, top
with large swing-over work surface, orig iron supports
on side, short simple turned legs, each of drawer
fronts fitted with walnut mushroom-shaped pulls, old
mellow patina, 72" w, 40" deep when open, 38" h **21,000.00**
Teapot, 8½" h, tin, side spout **165.00**
Wood Box, 37½" w, 21" d, 31" h, pine, old mellow
finish, bin top with hinged lid with breadboard ends,
one dovetailed overlapping drawer, sq corner posts,
chamfered feet, red stain int., wear from kindling,
purchased from Shakers in Canterbury, NH, in 1940s,
old pierced repair to one end of drawer front **880.00**

c1908

SHAVING MUGS

History: Shaving mugs, which hold the soap, brush, and hot water
used to prepare a beard for shaving, come in a variety of materials
including tin, silver, glass, and pottery. One style, which has separate compartments for water and soap, is the scuttle, so called
because of its coal-scuttle shape.

Shaving mugs were popular between 1880 and 1925, a period
of great immigration to the United States. At first barber shops
used a common mug for all customers. This led to an epidemic
of a type of eczema known as barber itch.

Laws were passed requiring each individual to have his own
mug at the barber shop. Initially names and numbers were placed
on the mugs for identification purposes, but this did not work well
for those who could not read. The occupational mug developed
because illiterate workers could identify a picture of their trade or
an emblem of its tools. Fraternal emblems also were used and
were the most popular of the decorative forms. Immigrants especially liked the heraldry of the fraternal emblems since it reminded
them of Europe.

European porcelain blanks were decorated by American bar-
ber-supply houses. Prices ranged from 50¢ for a gold name mug
to $2.50 for an elaborate occupational design. Most of the art
work was done by German artists who had immigrated to America.

The invention of the safety razor by King C. Gillette, issued to
three and one-half million servicemen during World War I,
brought about changes in personal grooming—men began to
shave on their own rather than visiting the barber shop to be
shaved. As a result, the need for personalized shaving mugs declined.

References: Susan and Al Bagdade, *Warman's English & Continental Pottery & Porcelain,* Second Edition, Wallace-Homestead,
1991; Ronald S. Barlow, *The Vanishing American Barber Shop,*

Windmill Publishing, 1993; Keith E. Estep, *The Shaving Mug & Barber Bottle Book,* Schiffer Publishing, 1995.

Collectors' Club: National Shaving Mug Collectors Assoc, 320 S Glenwood St, Allentown, PA 18104.

Barber Shop: Fraternal

American Legion, emblem, star, name, gold trim	425.00
Ancient Order United Workman, anchor shield, A.O.U.W. initials	295.00
Knights of Columbus, blue wrap, gold trim, black name, red, white, and blue symbol, gold highlights, gold raised enameled flowers, green stamp mark "Germany"	95.00
Knights of Pythias, initials on shield, suit of armor, crossed halberds	125.00
Odd Fellows, name and three loops across center with gold initials "F.L.T.," marked "Royal China International"	65.00
United Mine Workers of America, flowers around rim, marked "C. T. Germany"	75.00
Woodsman of the World, blue maple leaf stump, ax, bird, logging tools	175.00

Barber Shop: Occupational

Artist, palette, brushes	250.00
Baker, putting bread in oven, dough box, workbench	395.00
Bartender, saloon scene, back bar, bottles, bartender, two customers	375.00
Baseball Player, uniformed player batting, catcher, two men in field	795.00
Butcher, skinning steer, other steer hanging on rack	475.00
Carpenter, sawing board, house frame, pile of lumber	450.00
Cigar Maker, hand holding cigar	325.00
Cyclist, man riding bike on dirt road, blue outfit, trees, grass, fence, and house	550.00
Doctor, name in gold, top and bottom bands, marked "Limoges, France"	250.00
Farmer, two horses pulling plow, farmhouse	275.00
Fireman, helmet, axes, ladder, and nozzles	400.00
Hardware Clerk, clerk showing customer saw, barrels, shelves, merchandise	475.00
Hatmaker, derby, gold trim	295.00
Musician, piano player, upright piano	375.00
Photographer, taking photo of woman in chair	1,600.00
Railroad, locomotive and coal car	150.00

Occupational, musician, trumpet, gold trim, aqua ground, multicolored flowers, $250.00.

Tinsmith, gray tools, orange highlights, numbered and marked "Vienna, Austria"	225.00
Watchmaker, gold watch and chain	295.00

Barber Shop: Other

American Eagle, perched on American shield, clutching arrows, gold trimmed banner in beak with name in black, hp, dark blue wrap, white and rouge highlights, marked "V. D. Austria"	250.00
Hunter, shooting bird, brown and white dog, sunset, marked "Koken Barbers' Supply Co. St Louis, USA"	195.00
Liberty Bell, bell with crack, date 1776 in scroll on each side	225.00
Pennsylvania, seal of "Virtue, Liberty & Independence"	225.00
Sailboats on ocean, sea gulls, rocks on shore, name in gold	135.00
Shield, compass, arms with hammer and square, emb scroll on both sides	95.00

Scuttles

Daisy dec, ivory and brown	50.00
Eagle holding arrow on flag shield	95.00
Gambling, Lucky Spots, shows spread of aces, flowers on back	150.00
Silver Plate, emb trim, ornate handle, insert, brush	95.00

SHAWNEE POTTERY

History: The Shawnee Pottery Co. was founded in 1937 in Zanesville, Ohio. The company acquired a 650,000-square-foot plant that had previously housed the American Encaustic Tiling Company. Shawnee produced as many as 100,000 pieces of pottery a day until 1961, when the plant closed.

Shawnee limited its production to kitchenware, decorative art pottery, and dinnerware. Distribution was primarily through jobbers and chain stores.

Marks: Shawnee can be marked "Shawnee," "Shawnee U.S.A.," "USA #———," "Kenwood," or with character names, e.g., "Pat. Smiley" and "Pat. Winnie."

References: Susan and Al Bagdade, *Warman's American Pottery and Porcelain,* Wallace-Homestead, 1994; Pam Curran, *Shawnee Pottery,* Schiffer Publishing, 1995; Jim and Bev Mangus, *Shawnee Pottery,* Collector Books, 1994, 1996 value update; Mark Supnick, *Collecting Shawnee Pottery,* L-W Book Sales, 1989, 1996 value update; Duane and Janice Vanderbilt, *The Collector's Guide to Shawnee Pottery,* Collector Books, 1992, 1996 value update.

Collectors' Club: Shawnee Pottery Collectors Club, PO Box 713, New Smyrna Beach, FL 32170.

Bank, Howdy Doody	395.00
Bowl, cov, Lobsterware, #907	45.00
Candlesticks, pr, 6½" h, hand dec gold trim	25.00
Casserole, cov	
Fruit, #81	60.00
King Corn	70.00
Lobsterware, 16 oz	48.00
Cookie Jar, Jill	175.00

Creamer

Elephant	**40.00**
King Corn, No. 70	**25.00**
Puss 'n' Boots, green and yellow	**82.00**

Cup and Saucer, King Corn, cup marked "90," and saucer marked "91" **45.00**

Figure

Racoon	**65.00**
Squirrel	**80.00**

Lamp, emb flowers **45.00**

Mixing bowl, King Corn

5" d	**37.00**
6¼" d	**45.00**

Pitcher

Bo Peep	**90.00**
Chanticleer, rooster, large	**125.00**
#35, tan	**25.00**

Planter

Buddha, #524	**25.00**
Dog and Jug	**24.00**
Fawn, gold trim	**20.00**
Girl at Gate	**22.00**
Ram, #515	**25.00**
Water Trough, #716	**20.00**

Plate, King Corn, 8" d **40.00**

Range Shakers, pr, Smiley, red bib **5.00**

Relish Tray, King Corn, marked "Shawnee 79" **35.00**

Salt and Pepper Shakes, pr

Chanticleer, rooster

Large	**55.00**
Small	**45.00**
Flowerpots	**25.00**
Muggsy, small	**60.00**

Sugar, cov, King Corn **42.00**

Teapot, cov, King Corn **95.00**

Teapot, Tom the Piper's Son, Pat USA, pink pig spout, light blue handle, yellow hat, 7" h, 8" w, $45.00.

Vase

#805, green	**25.00**
#827, green	**25.00**

Wall Pocket

Birdhouse	**25.00**
Grandfather Clock, #1261	**25.00**

SILHOUETTES

History: Silhouettes (shades) are shadow profiles produced by hollow cutting, mechanical tracing, or painting. They were popular in the 18th and 19th centuries.

The name came from Etienne de Silhouette, a French Minister of Finance, who cut "shades" as a pastime. In America the Peale family was well known for the silhouettes they made.

Silhouette portraiture lost popularity with the introduction of the daguerreotype prior to the Civil War. In the 1920s and 1930s a brief revival occurred when tourists to Atlantic City and Paris had their profiles cut as souvenirs.

Marks: An impressed stamp marked "PEALE" or "Peale Museum" identifies pieces made by the Peale family.

References: Shirley Mace, *Encyclopedia of Silhouette Collectibles on Glass,* Shadow Enterprises, 1992; Dana G. Morykan and Harry L. Rinker, *Warman's Country Antiques & Collectibles,* Third Edition, Wallace-Homestead, 1996.

Museums: Essex Institute, Salem, MA; National Portrait Gallery, Washington, DC.

Children

4¾" d, girl, hollow cut, turned frame, stains	**115.00**
4¾" l, 3⅝" w, boy, hollow cut, black cloth backing, discolored and stained paper, old black molded frame	**220.00**

Couple

4½ × 5¾", girl and boy, cut, titled "Agnes and Lindsey," sgd "Auguste Edouart, 1831" **450.00**

5½" h

4½" w, woman and child, hollow cut, black cloth backing, worn eglomise glass, price for pr ...	**275.00**
8¼" w, man and woman, hollow cut, one with ink detail, other with pencil detail, worn eglomise glass, both silhouettes matted in single gilt frame	**475.00**

18¾ × 15½", pen and ink, two men and women, seated on chairs, pencil room int., sgd "Aug Edouart, fecit 1840," bird's-eye maple frame ... **650.00**

Gentlemen, hollow cut

2¾ × 4", bust, inscribed "Joshua Bailey, age 37, November 20, 1835"	**495.00**
4¾" h, 3¾" w, brushed ink detail, uneven edges, paper stitched to black cloth backing, stains and tears, partial "Hubard Gallery" label on back, framed	**165.00**
5¾" h, 5⅛" w, hollow cut, young man, ink detail, eglomise glass and regilded frame, frame backing marked "J. S. Smith property"	**225.00**
7½" h, 5½" w, Henry Clay, faded black cloth backing, minor stains, tear at edge, later mat and frame ..	**95.00**

Slave, 8¼ × 6¾", praying pose, rosewood frame, 19th C **575.00**

Women

4 × 4⅜", hollow cut, young woman, black cloth backing, paper stained, gilt frame	**150.00**
4 × 4⅞", pen and ink, woman wearing lacy collar, orig black reeded frame	**295.00**
4½ × 5¼", hollow cut, old woman wearing bonnet, worn gilt detail, sgd on back "cut with scissors by E Whittre," black lacquer frame, gilt brass trim .	**150.00**

Woman, hollow cut, sgd "Elizabeth Baker, Boston, 1824," 6 × 5", $200.00.

5⅞ × 6⅝", hollow cut, young woman, paper with emb mark "Museum," (Peale Museum), black cloth backing, minor stains and creases, mahogany veneer frame **225.00**

6¼" h, 4½" w, hollow cut, black cloth ground, molded pine frame **95.00**

7" h, 6" w, hollow cut, old woman, black cloth backing, tears, stains, emb brass on wooden frame .. **115.00**

SILVER

History: The natural beauty of silver lends itself to the designs of artists and craftsmen. It has been mined and worked into an endless variety of useful and decorative items. Pure silver is too soft to be fashioned into strong, durable, and serviceable utensils. Therefore, a way was found to give silver the required degree of hardness by adding alloys of copper and nickel.

Silversmithing in America goes back to the early 17th century in Boston and New York and the early 18th century in Philadelphia. Boston artisans were influenced by the English styles, New Yorkers by the Dutch.

References: Louise Belden, *Marks of American Silversmiths in the Ineson-Bissell Collection,* University of Virginia Press, 1980; Frederick Bradbury, *Bradbury's Book of Hallmarks,* J. W. Northend, 1987; Bonita Campbell and Nan Curtis (curators), *Depression Silver,* California State University, 1995; Maryanne Dolan, *1830's–1900's American Sterling Silver Flatware,* Books Americana, 1993; Marilyn E. Dragowick (ed), *Metalwares Price Guide,* Antique Trader Books, 1995; Stephen G. C. Ensko, *American Silversmiths and Their Marks,* Dover Publications, 1983; Rachael Feild, *Macdonald Guide to Buying Antique Silver and Sheffield Plate,* Macdonald & Co., 1988; Nancy Gluck, *The Grosvenor Pattern of Silverplate,* Silver Season, 1996; Tere Hagan, *Silverplated Flatware,* Revised Fourth Edition, Collector Books, 1990, 1995 value

update; Kenneth Crisp Jones (ed.), *The Silversmiths of Birmingham and Their Marks,* N.A.G. Press, 1981, distributed by Antique Collectors Club; Henry J. Kaufman, *The Colonial Silversmith,* Astragal Press, 1995; Ralph and Terry Kovel, *Kovels' American Silver Marks,* Crown Publishers, 1989.

Joel Langford, *Silver,* Chartwell Books, 1991; Everett L. Maffett, *Silver Banquet II,* Silver Press, 1990; Meriden Britannia Company, *The Meriden Britannia Silver-Plate Treasury* (reprint of 1886 catalog), Dover Publications, n.d.; Penny C. Morrill, *Silver Masters of Mexico,* Schiffer Publishing, 1996; Penny Chittim Morrill and Carole A. Berk, *Mexican Silver 20th Century Handwrought Jewelry & Metalwork,* Schiffer Publishing, 1994; Richard Osterberg, *Silver Hollowware for Dining Elegance,* Schiffer Publishing, 1996; ———, *Sterling Silver Flatware for Dining Elegance,* Schiffer Publishing, 1994; Benton Rabinovitch, *Antique Silver Servers for the Dining Table,* Joslin Hall Publishing, 1991; Dorothy T. Rainwater, *Encyclopedia of American Silver Manufacturers,* Third Edition, Schiffer Publishing, 1986; Dorothy T. and H. Ivan Rainwater, *American Silverplate,* Schiffer Publishing, 1988; *Sterling Silver, Silverplate, and Souvenir Spoons,* Revised Edition, L-W Book Sales, 1987, 1994 value update; Charles Truman (ed.), *Sotheby's Concise Encyclopedia of Silver,* Antique Collectors' Club, 1996; Charles Venable, *Silver in America 1840–1940,* Harry Abrams, 1994; Joanna Wissinger, *Arts and Crafts Metalwork and Silver,* Chronicle Books, 1994; Seymour B. Wyler, *The Book Of Old Silver,* Crown Publishers, 1937 (available in reprint).

Periodicals: *Silver Magazine,* PO Box 9690, Rancho Santa Fe, CA 92067; *Silver News,* 1112 16th St NW, Ste 240, Washington, DC 20036; *Silver Update,* PO Box 960, Funkstown, MD 21734.

Collectors' Club: New York Silver Society, 242 E 7th St, #5, New York, NY 10009.

Museums: Bayou Bend Collection, Houston, TX; Boston Museum of Fine Arts, Boston, MA; Currier Gallery of Art, Manchester, NH; Yale University Art Gallery, New Haven, CT; Wadsworth Atheneum, Hartford, CT.

Additional Listings: See Silver Flatware in *Warman's Americana & Collectibles* for more examples.

American, 1790–1840
Mostly Coin

Coin Silver is slightly less pure than sterling silver. Coin silver has 900 parts silver to 100 parts alloy. Sterling silver has 925 parts silver. American silversmiths followed the coin standards. Coin silver is also called Pure Coin, Dollar, Standard, or Premium.

Booth, Ezra or Thomas, Philadelphia, PA, c1800, teaspoon **50.00**

Braiser, A, Philadelphia, PA, c1825, cup, 3¾" h, pear shape, thread-mold rim **275.00**

Chaudron and Roasch, c1805, tablespoon, plain fiddle handle, engraved crest of dog's head **60.00**

Crosby, S T & Co, Boston, MA, c1850, soup ladle, beaded-edge pattern, oval pierced bowl, engraved attached strainer, engraved initials, 8 troy oz **175.00**

Eoff, Garrett, New York City, c1789–1845, tea set, teapot, creamer, cov sugar, waste bowl, monogrammed "CMB," marked "Belden p157", 70 troy oz **1,725.00**

Erwin, H, soup ladle, plain fiddle handle, monogrammed "GH," US silver half dollar in bowl, first-quarter 19th C **180.00**

American, Coin, teaspoons, J. M. Mitksch, Bethlehem, PA, two from set of six, set $250.00.

Faber, W, soup ladle, plain fiddle handle, monogrammed "GWR," c1828 .... **270.00**

Fletcher & Gardiner, c1815, cup, 3" h, slight pear shape, hammered finish **220.00**

Jones, John B, Jr., Boston, c1816–37, tea and coffee set, 9" h coffeepot, teapot, creamer, cov sugar, monogrammed "MW," marked "Belden p 252," very minor dents, scratches, 79 troy oz **1,840.00**

Lang, Jeffrey, Salem, MA, 1708–58, cann, 5⅜" l, pear shape, lyre for handle, scrolled butt, circular ftd base with beaded edge, "IL" stamped twice on base, 12 troy oz **1,500.00**

Le Muir, Benjamin, Philadelphia, PA, c1790, teaspoon, oval and pointed, feathered edges, monogram **45.00**

Le Roux, Bartholomew, II, NY, c1750, cake basket, sides pierced with scrollwork and diaper, rim applied with openwork border of running grapevines, shells, and scrolls, swing handle topped by applied rococo cartouche, center engraved with contemporary arms in rococo cartouche, four paw-and-ball feet headed by lion masks, base marked "BLR" conjoined in oval twice, 71 oz, 14⅝" l, 10¾" h **112,500.00**

Lewis, Harvey, Philadelphia, PA, sugar bowl, cov, circular, acorn finial, twin scroll handles, ribbed and molded mid-bands, pedestal, circular base, monogrammed "EJ," stamped twice on base, 8¾" h, 24 troy oz **575.00**

McMullin, John, Philadelphia, c1800, cake stand, 12¾" l, oblong, extended leaf-molded handles, ribbed rim, middle reed band, reeded oblong feet, inscribed "C. Shaw,"19 troy oz **1,550.00**

Musgrave, James, Philadelphia, PA, c1795, teaspoon, oval and pointed handles, monogram **40.00**

Revere, Paul, c1805, sugar tongs, plain fiddle handles, oval grips **1,800.00**

Richardson, Joseph and Nathaniel, Philadelphia, PA, cann, pear shape, lyre-form handle, circular ftd base, monogram, 12.5 troy oz **2,200.00**

Shoemaker, Joseph, Philadelphia, PA, c1795, teaspoon, oval and pointed handles **35.00**

Watts, James, Philadelphia, PA, 1835, porringer, plain, gothic pierced handle **500.00**

Williamson, Samuel, Philadelphia, PA, c1795, teaspoon, oval handles, monograms, price for pr **50.00**

Witherber, Christian, Philadelphia, PA, c1800, dessert spoon, fiddle handle, monogram **60.00**

Woodcock, Bancroft, Wilmington, DE, 1775, coffeepot, inverted bear form, elongated swan-neck spout rising from double shells and capped by leaf, upper handle terminal cast with shell, lobed and fluted urn finial, engraved with contemporary interlaced foliate cipher "WR," base marked "B. Woodcock" in cartouche and scratch weight "37 = 11," 38 oz gross, 13¼" h **27,600.00**

Silver, American, 1840–1920
Mostly Sterling

There are two possible sources for the origin of the word sterling. The first is that it is a corruption of the name Easterling. Easterlings were German silversmiths who came to England in the Middle Ages. The second is that it is named for the starling (little star) used to mark much of the early English silver.

Sterling is 92.5 percent pure silver. Copper comprises most of the remaining alloy. American manufacturers began to switch to the sterling standard about the time of the Civil War.

Bailey & Co, mustard scoop, silver and vermeil, handle on bust of Victorian maiden **90.00**

Ball, Thomkins & Black, NY, water pitcher, 10¾" h, urn shape, scroll and leaf chased, lyre handle, 27 troy oz **1,600.00**

Black Starr & Frost
    Cocktail Set, pitcher-form shaker, twelve cups, two-handled rect 23½" tray, chased panels with shells and foliage, strapwork, borders of running leaves, 165 ozs **3,900.00**
    Tray, 30½" l, cast Chippendale scroll rim, decorative handles, marked "Black Starr & Frost Sterling," 189 troy oz **3,190.00**

Cowell & Hubbard, salver, 15½" d, cast and engraved rim, marked "Cowell & Hubbard Co. Sterling," 33 troy oz **385.00**

Dominick and Haff
    Punch Ladle, beveled border and shell design, engraved accents, Old English "R", patent date 1913, 9 troy oz **260.00**
    Salad Set, shell and thread-mold handles, monogrammed, price for 2-pc set **200.00**

Durgin Co, Wm B, Concord, NH
    Coffee and Tea Set, Colonial Revival style, paneled baluster form, chased molding, floral swag dec, coffee and teapots, creamer, open sugar, engraved monogram and date 1925 on bottom, 50 troy oz **925.00**

American, Sterling, Kerr, William, scent bottle, c1880, rococo body, fluted and ring neck, 2½", $90.00.

Platter, 19¼″ l, 13⁷⁄₁₆″ w, octagonal form, molded rim, monogrammed, 1928, 49 troy oz **345.00**

Gardener, B, NY, tea set, elaborate chased floral dec, engraved monogram and cross, marked "B. Gardener, New York," 86 troy oz **1,320.00**

Goodnow, coffee set, Federal style, paneled baluster form, bright-cut dec, engraved monogram and date 1905, 10⅝″ h coffeepot with wooden handle, creamer, cov sugar, waste bowl, 46 troy oz **825.00**

Gorham Mfg Co, Providence, RI

Basket, 12″ h, cylindrical, flared rim, reticulated and engraved dec, upright handle, 1919, 13 troy oz . **230.00**

Bell, figural, man in top hat and coat **95.00**

Centerpiece on Stand, Martelé, .9584 standard, sgd "W. C. Codman, 1909," bombé oval form on four scroll supports headed by flowers and leaves from which extend further chased sprays of flowering foliage below the undulating rim, gilt int., shaped oval stand with raised center, chased to match, all with lightly hammered ground, bases of each engraved with monogram and date "December 25, 1913," marked on bases and with codes "YRT" and "YRU," 137 oz, 17¼″ l **25,300.00**

Demitasse Coffee Set, Colonial Revival style, urn, swag, and Greek key details, 9½″ h coffeepot, creamer, open sugar, 13⅛″ l Wilcox and Wagner oval tray, 46 troy oz **1,035.00**

Fruit Bowl, 9¾″ d, six floral repoussé reserves, everted rim, three minor base dents, 9 troy oz **180.00**

Loving Cup, 6¾″ h, baluster form, lobed base, chased leaf and floral detail, scrolled handles, engraved inscription, 1896, slight dents, 41 troy oz **980.00**

Sandwich Tray, 8½″ d, circular scalloped border, reeded center, three scroll and hoofed feet, 12.5 troy oz **220.00**

Tray

14⅜″ d, round, shaped applied scroll and floral rim, engraved monogram, dents, 23 troy oz . **230.00**

18¾″ l, oval, applied Classical Revival urn and swag border, engraved monogram and date 1917 in center, 52 troy oz **490.00**

Water Pitcher, urn shape, lyre-form handle, 8¾″ h, 21 troy oz **400.00**

Hess & Culbertson, bowl, 12¼″ d, repoussé vintage rim, marked "H. W. Hess & Culbertson, Sterling," minor dents, 11 troy oz **325.00**

International

Compote, 5¹⁄₁₆″ h d, 3½″ h, LaPaglia pattern, flared bowl, openwork stem, flared base, mid-20th C, 11 troy oz, price for pr **526.00**

Julep, 3⅞″ h, engraved "B," marked "International Sterling" **85.00**

Platter, 22¾″ l, oval, marked "International Sterling," 72.8 troy oz **965.00**

Kirk, S and Son, Baltimore, MD

Bowl

9″ d, 1¾″ h, repoussé floral rim, engraved monogram, marked "S. Kirk & Son, 925," 10 troy oz **175.00**

9⅜″ d, 4″ h, ftd, engraved garlands, marked "S. Kirk & Sons Co .925," 20 troy oz **220.00**

9½″ d, 4⅜″ h, ftd, repoussé floral rim, engraved monogram, engraved presentation date 1913–

1938, marked "S. Kirk & Son Co. Sterling," 16.8 troy oz **330.00**

Compote, 9⅛″ d, 4⅜″ h, repoussé floral rim on bowl and base, marked "S. Kirk & Son Co. Sterling," 16.6 troy oz **440.00**

Water Pitcher, 7⅜″ h, repoussé, chased floral and leaf dec, engraved monogram on base, c1880, 20 troy oz **1,100.00**

Merkley Kendrick, julep, 3½″ h, marked "Merkley Kendrick Sterling," 25 troy oz, price for 5-pc set **475.00**

Redlick, bread tray, 14″ l, shaped rect form, applied pierced floral rim, engraved ribbon monogram, c1900, retailed by Gorham, 29 troy oz **635.00**

Reed & Barton, compote, 11⅝″ d, 5½″ h, repoussé floral rim, marked "Reed & Barton Francis I, Sterling," 25.7 troy oz **635.00**

Rogers, flatware service, Martha Washington, service for 12 of place fork, place knife, luncheon fork, oyster fork, salad fork, soup spoon, butter spreaders, extra teaspoons, 8 serving pieces, 131 troy oz **1,650.00**

Shreve, Crump & Low, tray, 13⅜″ d, round, wide reticulated floral and scroll border, engraved floral, scroll, and monogrammed center, late 19th C, 41 troy oz . **865.00**

Stieff

Goblet, 6½″ h, engraved "J," marked "Stieff Sterling," 32 troy oz, price for 6-pc set **220.00**

Plate, 12⅛″ d, repoussé floral rim, engraved monogram, marked "Stieff Sterling," 16.8 troy oz **385.00**

Tiffany & Co

Bowl, 9⅝″ d, 3¾″ h, scallop-sided sq, applied ribbed rim, engraved monogram, 1907–38, 25 troy oz . **490.00**

Loving Cup, presentation engraving from Manasquan River Yacht Club for 1948 and 1949, 67 troy oz total 6¾″ h **1,650.00**

Pepper Shakers, slender round reeded body, three curved legs, price for pr **230.00**

Porringer, 4⅞″ d, pierced and scrolled handle, engraved inscription on base, 1907–38, 7.5 troy oz **230.00**

Salver, circular, shell lozenge and leaf border **280.00**

Soup Ladle, Olympian pattern, 1878, 12 troy oz ... **750.00**

Vase, 10⁹⁄₁₆″ h, flared baluster form, applied relief shell and scroll band around base, 1938–47, 21 troy oz **635.00**

Towle

Flatware Service, Rambler Rose, service for 12, extra teaspoons, 7 serving pieces, 92 troy oz **600.00**

Tea Set, Louis XIV, engraved "V," marked "Sterling," 72 troy oz **1,320.00**

Unger Bros, fruit bowl, 11½″ d, round, Art Nouveau, applied bas-relief hollyhock rim, monogram, c1900, 11 troy oz **500.00**

Unknown Maker, salt, open, oval, shell rim, floral repoussé body, ram's head and hoofed feet, late 19th C, 8.5 troy oz, price for pr **275.00**

Wallace

Flatware Service, Grand Baroque, 32-pc set, service for 8, 59 troy oz **925.00**

Oyster Forks, Waverly pattern, price for set of 12 .. **190.00**

Tazza, Stradivari pattern, 10¼″ d, 14.5 troy oz **230.00**

Whiting, Frank M, tea service, oval fluted shape, urn finials, scroll and shell cased mid-bands, hot-water pot, teapot, creamer, cov sugar, waste bowl, 67 troy oz **1,350.00**

Whiting Mfg Co, NY
  Bowl
    7³/₁₆" d, round, raised and pierced scroll and floral
      dec, fluted center, 1920s, price for pr **375.00**
    8³/₈" d, hammered textured lotus blossom form,
      engraved name and 1886, 9 troy oz **345.00**
  Flagon, 10" h, dolphin handle, cast floral bands, pres-
    entation engraving Larchmont Yacht Club, 35 troy
    oz **900.00**
  Water Pitcher, 9" h, baluster form, ribbed details, re-
    tailed by C Hartdegen & Co, 22 troy oz **490.00**

Silver, Continental

   Generally, continental silver does not have a strong following
in the United States, but Danish pieces by Georg Jensen are eagerly sought. As the antiques marketplace continues to expand
globally, Continental silver has become more popular. In Canada,
Russian silver finds a strong market.

Austrian, gravy boat, attached tray, 9¹³/₁₆" l, 6⁷/₁₆" h, dou-
  ble lipped, oval bowl, oval tray, chased rococo dec,
  hallmarks, 19th C, 27 troy oz **550.00**
Belgian, creamer, helmet form, berry dec scroll handle,
  1780, 10 ozs **125.00**
Danish, Georg Jensen
  Bottle Opener, Acorn pattern **150.00**
  Cake Knife, Acorn pattern **425.00**
  Carving Set, openwork Danish floral handles **1,400.00**
  Condiment Set, mustard stand, ladle, pepper shaker,
    open circular salt, circular tray with twin scroll
    handles, blue glass liners, pineapple finials **775.00**
  Fish Set, double fish and shell pattern, six forks and
    knives, four seafood forks, four Pyramid pattern
    seafood forms, 1933–34, 25 troy oz **1,725.00**
  Pie Knife, Acorn pattern **400.00**
  Salad Set, Acorn pattern, 2 pcs **200.00**
  Tray, 13¼" l, Danish floral handles, 20 oz **2,500.00**
Dutch, candlesticks, pr, 10³/₁₆" h, tapered-column bal-
  uster form, engraved crest and floral details, remov-
  able bobeches, weighted, 19th C **550.00**
French
  Bowl, cov, 8½" d stand, lobed circular form, gadroon,
    shell and foliate borders, two handles, Charles
    Nicholas Odiot, Paris, c1840, 29 ozs **3,200.00**
  Ewer, 9⁷/₈" h, Regency style, helmet form, molded
    borders, harp-shaped handle, flat chased strap-
    work and shells, matted ground, trophy of dol-
    phins, paddles, and shells, monogrammed, Tee-
    tard Freres, Paris, c1900, 37 ozs, 10 dwts **2,500.00**
German
  Beaker, 3¼" h, tapered cylindrical form, engraved
    swag of fruit, narrow band of scrolling foliage,
    Leon Hardt Rothaer I, Hamburg, c1680, 3 ozs, 10
    dwts **3,500.00**
  Bottle, 12½" l, figural, peacock, hinged wings, re-
    movable heads, marked "800 German," 32. troy
    oz, price for pr **935.00**
  Cigarette Box, 5¼" l, repoussé classical figures, rose,
    and scroll handles **200.00**
  Tableware, simple scroll borders, knives, forks,
    spoons, sugar tongs, salad servers, serving spoons,
    price for 79 pcs **825.00**

Continental, Dutch, basket, fan-shaped handle, dec with reserves of cupids surrounded by floral motifs, 19" h, approx 31½ oz, $1,320.00. Photo courtesy of William Doyle Galleries.

  Tea Service, c1890–1900, Empire urn style, bust fin-
    ials, bird spouts, repoussé Napoleonic general re-
    serves, winged griffins, wreath dec, three animal
    legs, claw feet, Weinharnok & Schmidt **2,100.00**
Italian, vase, 9¾" h, paneled ovoid body, fluted collar
  and spreading circular base, applied leaf scroll and
  floral trophies at corners of shoulder, 800 fine silver,
  19 ozs **250.00**
Portuguese
  Ewer, 13¾" h, helmet shape, partly fluted, engraved
    with contemporary arms, applied female mask
    within strapwork, raised female caryatid handle,
    detachable calyx chased with still leaves, strap-
    work, and shells, screw-on foot, modern base, un-
    marked, c1730, 54 ozs, 10 dwts **3,000.00**
  Platter, 15½" l, highly detailed repousseé with stag,
    boar, game, handmade, 40 troy oz **915.00**
Swedish
  Cup and Saucer, c1913, 830 fine, ftd baluster form,
    bas-relief rib and floral swag dec, 4¼" h cup,
    6¹/₁₆" d saucer, 23 troy oz, price for pr **230.00**
  Punch Ladle, 17⁵/₈" l, ebonized turned wooden han-
    dle, 19th C **220.00**

Silver, English

   From the 17th century to the mid-19th century, English silversmiths set the styles which American silversmiths copied. The
work from the period exhibits the highest degree of craftsmanship.
English silver is actively collected in the American antiques marketplace.

Charles II, caudle cup, 4¾" d, slightly flared lip contained by S-form scroll cast handles with putti head
  terminals, band of chased acanthus, socle base, maker's mark "IH" over fleur-de-lis, London, c1764–65,
  approx 8 ozs **900.00**
Edward VII, seal, 4" l, I.D.A.D. maker, 1901–02, engine-
  turned column, low-relief floral bands, wax slider,
  intaglio carved man's profile carnelian seal **175.00**

English, Sheffield, silver-plated, coffee urn on stand, Neoclassical style, ring handles, shaped tray with reeded edge and bail feet, 19th C, 23″ h, $5,000.00.

George I, mug, 3¾″ h, Thomas Evesdon maker, London, 1720, cylindrical, molded base, scroll handle, engraved monogram and date, 7 troy oz **490.00**

Edwardian
  Candlestick, 10″ h, floral shell and leaf repoussé dec, Thomas Bradbury, London, 1904, price for set of four **3,200.00**
  Fruit Basket, 8¼″ d, 2¹¹⁄₁₆″ h, reticulated, round, flared rim, openwork scroll swag and floral design, CSH maker, 1904–05, 11 troy oz **230.00**
  Muffineer, 6¼″ h, inverted pear shape, spiral finial, sq plinth, marked "D & A", Birmingham, 1905 . **230.00**

George II
  Mug, 3¾″ h, William Brind maker, 1771–72, scroll handle, engraved monogram, 7 troy oz **345.00**
  Sauce Boat, 6¼″ l, 4⅛″ h, 12 troy oz, hoof feet, 1754–55 London hallmarks, engraved "H," handles have minor soldered repair, price for pr **625.00**

George III
  Creamer, ftd pear shape, floral repoussé dec, lyre handle, circular ftd base, attributed to Thomas Shields, late 18th C **230.00**
  Cruet Base, wooden bottom, London hallmarks for 1793–94, Peter and Jonathan Bateman, 6½″ d .. **250.00**
  Fish Slice, fiddle, shell, and thread handle, monogram, Paul Starr, London, 1813 .... **700.00**
  Ladle, twisted baleen handle, Peter Bateman, 1792 London hallmarks, 13″ l **330.00**
  Mayonnaise Jar, glass liner, Francis Silsberry, Jr., 1767–68 London hallmarks, 3 troy oz, 4¼″ h ... **635.00**
  Serving Spoon, 11½″ l, monogram AWC, attributed to Wm Eley, Wm Fearn, London, 1804 .... **300.00**
  Soup Ladle, Alexander Henderson, Edinburgh, 1807, engraved initials **150.00**
  Sugar Basket, 6″ l, boat shape, ftd, pierced bright-cut dec, marked "HC," attributed to Henry Cowper, London, 1788–89, slight chips to blue glass inlay **650.00**

Tablespoon, plain oval handle
  Crest, William Eles and William Fearn, London, 1799, price for 6-pc set **400.00**
  Later monogram, Hester Bateman, London 1783, price for pr **200.00**
Tea Urn, 19½″ h, vase shape, engraved coat of arms, fruit, flower, and vine handles, detachable silver base with matching coat of arms, maker Daniel Smith & Robert Sharp, 1763, London, fully hallmarked **2,750.00**
Teapot, circular squat form, ribbed edge, reeded sides, ebony reeded finial, C-form handle, Robert and Samuel Hennell, 18 troy oz **700.00**
Teaspoon, plain oval handles, attributed to Hester Bateman, London, 1789, price for pr **100.00**
Toddy Ladle, oval bowl, single lip, maker SG and RW, London, 1802 .... **160.00**
Wine Coaster, 4¾″ d, pierced leaf and flower design, armorial center, griffin, date 1793, London **450.00**

George IV
  Ladle, 13½″ l, George Angell, London, 1859–60, ram crest **200.00**
  Salver, 8¾″ d, three feet, Robert Garrard, 1825 London hallmarks, 18 troy oz **750.00**
  Stuffing Spoon, Irish, J Buckton maker, back-tipped fiddle handle, engraved monogram, 1820, 7 troy oz, price for pr **300.00**
  Tea Service, oval, scroll repoussé dec, ebony finial and handle, Sheffield, c1830 .... **550.00**
  Vegetable Dish, 10¾″ d, lobed and fluted circular form, shaped gadroon borders, conforming Sheffield cov, engraved crest and monogram, SS pepper-shaped finials, Robert Garrard & Bros, London, 1826, price for 4-pc set, 156 ozs **7,500.00**
Queen Anne, chocolate pot, 9″ h, tapering cylindrical form, stepped dome lid, scrolling spout, Henry Green, London, c1711, missing treen handle, 19 ozs **1,000.00**

Victorian
  Chamberstick, London, 1892, maker TB, shell, leaf, and gardrooned border, 2 troy oz **280.00**
  Cigar Lighter, table type, serpent, silver chased head, glass eyes, antelope body, second-half 19th C, 24¼″ l **950.00**
  Inkstand, double, ftd oval 11⅝″ l tray, 3⅞″ h, polished cut bottles, acanthus leaf with Greek key dec, London, 1878–74, EBC maker, 21 troy oz **750.00**
  Snuff Box, rect, leaf engraved back with strike catch, Hillard & Thomas, Birmingham 1878 .... **240.00**
  Vinaigrette, rect, engraved flowers and monogram, neck chain, Nathaniel Mills, Birmingham 1850 . **220.00**
  Wine Funnel, 6½″ h, 1897–98 Birmingham hallmarks, 6 troy oz **300.00**

William IV
  Hot Water Jug, 9½″ h, ribbed baluster form, lower body chased in repeating flower-head pattern, upper body chased with flowers on matted ground, shellwork foot and lip, leafy scroll handle, melon finial with marker's mark WM, Benjamin Smith III, London, 1830, 34 ozs **4,000.00**
  Soup Ladle, maker ABS, London, 1831, Queen's pattern, 4 troy oz **345.00**
  Soup Tureen, cov, 15″ l, 12″ h, ram's-head and gar-

land dec, lion's-head mask ring handles, hoofed
feet, J Charles Edington, London, 1834, 136 ozs **6,500.00**

Silver, English, Sheffield

Sheffield Silver, or Old Sheffield Plate, was a fusion method of
silver-plating that was used from the mid-18th century until the
mid-1880s when the process of electroplating silver was introduced.

Sheffield plating was discovered in 1743 when Thomas Boul-
sover of Sheffield, England, accidentally fused silver and copper.
The process consisted of sandwiching a heavy sheet of copper
between two thin sheets of silver. The result was a plated sheet of
silver which could be pressed or rolled to a desired thickness. All
Sheffield articles were worked from these plated sheets.

Most of the silver-plated items found today marked "Sheffield"
are not early Sheffield plate. They are later wares made in Sheffield, England.

Candelabra, pr
    12½" h, two low scrolled arms, higher center candle-
    holder, sq stepped base, copper shows in places **200.00**
    17¾" h, four scrolled arms, center candleholder,
    shaped sq stepped bases **495.00**
    19¼" h, two scrolled arms plus center candleholder,
    round base, copper shows in places, good detail,
    old repair **550.00**
Coffeepot, side handle, lighthouse form **250.00**
Tea Set, coffeepot, teapot, kettle on stand, creamer, cov
    sugar, waste bowl, 24" l galleried tray, price for 7-pc
    set **770.00**
Tea Tray, 29" l, oval, twin shell and leaf handles, shell
    and scroll molded border, 19th C **325.00**
Tea Urn, 12½" h, classical detail, lions' heads, silver on
    copper, soldered repair to one leg **250.00**
Tray, 24½" l, oval, serpentine, pierced gallery with ga-
    droon edge, beaded base, two cutout handles **400.00**
Tureen, 15" l, engraved dog on lid, good details **385.00**

Silver, Mexican

The popularity of Mexican Silver is quickly growing with today's collectors. Pieces tend to be well made and easily identified
by markings.

Ashtray, figural
    Scallop Shell, three ball feet, 14.5 oz, price for 18 pcs **160.00**
    Wheelbarrow, 10 oz, price for pr **100.00**
Bowl
    6" d, three ball feet, worked edges, bottom stamped
    eagle mark, "Mexican Sterling" within triangle
    mark, "Juarez 258, Plateria," and "MR" in a circle **295.00**
    17" l, 7¼" h, boat shape, ftd, marked "Sterling, Made
    in Mexico," 46.8 troy oz **275.00**
Candlesticks, 5½" w, 8" h, double, graduated stands,
    bottom marked "Sterling 925 Mexico," 1950s eagle
    stamp, 18 oz **375.00**
Cocktail Shaker, 11½" h, floral band, marked "Maciel,
    Mexico, Sterling," dents, 43.4 troy oz **200.00**
Creamer, 1¼" h, large lip, handle, bottom stamped "RR
    925 mm Hecho en Mexico DF" in square mark, "San-
    borns Mexico Sterling," and typical owl mark, 1.4 oz **95.00**

Creamer and Sugar, Aztec design, marked "Tane, Made
    in Mexico Sterling," 22 troy oz **210.00**
Creamer and Sugar on Tray, 4¼" h sugar and creamer,
    9¾ × 6" tray, stamped "sterling JR 925 Hecho en
    Mexico DF," eagle stamp, 22 oz **295.00**
Dessert Plate, 6" d, six lobes, marked "S" in upturned
    hand mark, "P Mexico Sterling 935" in triangle, 6 oz **45.00**
Julep, 3¾" h, engraved "B," marked "Sanborns, Mexico,
    925" **75.00**
Pitcher, 12⅛" h, marked "Prieto S. A. Juarez, Mexico,
    Sterling," 35.5 troy oz **225.00**
Plate, 9½" d, one sgd "Marciel," price for pr **85.00**
Salad Set, 2-pc set, plain curved and tapering round
    handles, P G Lopez, 13 oz **170.00**
Salt and Pepper Shakers, pr, 2¼" h, 1¾" d, pumpkin
    shape, twisted stem, stamped in square "Sterling
    Made in Mexico 0.925" **65.00**
Salver
    12" d, circular, serpentine, gadroon border inscribed
    as presentation, Sanborns **300.00**
    16½" d, repoussé floral rim, maker's mark "Maciel,"
    marked "900/100. Made in Mexico," 37 oz **320.00**
Serving Dish, 11¾" l, 8" w, shallow, flattened lip, bottom
    stamped "Sdela Serna Mexico 925 Sterling," 1950s
    eagle stamp on bottom, 31 oz **275.00**
Tea Set, 8" h coffeepot, teapot, creamer, sugar (lid miss-
    ing), waste bowl, marked "A. G. F. Mexico Sterling,"
    75 oz **385.00**
Tray, 11⅞" l, oval, hand hammered, chased floral rim,
    marked "Maciel, Mexico, Sterling," 15.9 troy oz .. **165.00**

Silver, Plated

Englishmen G. R. and H. Elkington are given credit for being
the first to use the electrolytic method of plating silver in 1838.

An electroplated-silver article is completely shaped and formed
from a base metal and then coated with a thin layer of silver. In
the late 19th century, the base metal was Britannia, an alloy of
tin, copper, and antimony. Other bases are copper and brass.
Today the base is nickel silver.

In 1847 the electroplating process was introduced in America
by Rogers Bros. of Hartford, Connecticut. By 1855 a number of
firms were using the method to produce silver-plated items in large
quantities.

The quality of the plating is important. Extensive polishing can
cause the base metal to show through. The prices for plated-silver
items are low, making them popular items with younger collectors.

Basket, pierced design, figural greyhound in base, Vic-
    torian **150.00**
Biscuit Stand, folding, fan form over scroll frame **350.00**
Cake Basket, fixed loop handles with bee and grasshop-
    per, copper strawberry and cherry appliqués, oblong
    dish etched with flowers and birds, gothic scroll feet,
    Meriden Silver Plate Co, 9½" h, 9½" l, 19th C **700.00**
Chafing Dish, ornate trim **265.00**
Clock, 17" h, 14" w, wall type, round dial, crest dec with
    repoussé flowers, fruit, and foliage, hour and half-
    hour chime **300.00**
Coffee Service, coffeepot, teapot, creamer, sugar, Rogers **250.00**

Plated, letter holder, Pairpoint, 5″ h, 6¼″ l, $185.00.

Cologne Bottle, bulbous, floral and flowing leaf motif, 3⅜″ h, $165.00.

Epergne, 28¾″ h, 22¾″ w, cut glass flower insert, cherubs, flowers, and vines, Eastlake style, Meridan C ..**1,250.00**

Punch Ladle, Pairpoint, cut glass handle, 15″ l, chips to handle **280.00**

Salt, clear crystal insert, Sheffield, minor wear and chips, 4″ l **80.00**

Sardine Box, handle, figural fish finial **125.00**

Table Ornament, stag beside tree, circular base, leaf scroll feet, 15½″ h, 19th C **700.00**

Tea Service,

Georgian, melon form, bright cut leaf dec, "C" form handle, ribbed base, teapot, coffeepot, kettle on warming stand, sugar, and creamer, Elkington & Co **425.00**

Spherical, overall daisy repoussé, engraved dec, tea and hot-water pot, creamer, cov sugar, and waste bowl, Wilcox **340.00**

Trophy, 5½″ h, baseball motif, 1890, Rogers Bros **125.00**

Vegetable Stand, cov, sq, ornate removable ring handle, sq floral lid band, border engraved with Confido crest **150.00**

Wash Bowl and Pitcher, 18″ d, 16″ h, swirled body, marked "Simpson Hall Miller Co Quadruple Plate" **525.00**

Water Server, 19½″ d, Tippler, Pairpoint, engraved foliate design, insulated pitcher, orig water goblet, drip tray, framework, c1880 .... **895.00**

Wine Coaster, 19″ h, double, carriage type, partial hallmark "ROB and SLA and M.P....," two wire-sided wood-based coasters with rim of flowing grapes, attached to set of dec wheels **1,000.00**

Wine Funnel, 6½″ h **125.00**

SILVER DEPOSIT GLASS

History: Silver deposit glass was popular at the turn of the century. A simple electrical process was used to deposit a thin coating of silver on glass products. After the glass and a piece of silver were placed in a solution, an electric current was introduced which caused the silver to decompose, pass through the solution, and remain on those parts of the glass on which a pattern had been outlined.

Bonbon, 7″ d, pink ground **50.00**

Bowl, 5½″ d, vines and leaves dec, scalloped edge ... **45.00**

Compote, 7″ d, floral dec **85.00**

Creamer and Sugar, cov, floral dec **90.00**

Decanter, 9″ h, emerald green, hollow stopper **75.00**

Serving Plate, 12½″ d, dark amethyst, floral dec **75.00**

Toothpick Holder, 2″ h, amber ground **50.00**

Tumbler, 4⅝″ h, flared top **25.00**

Vase, 10″ h, baluster, black ground, twin handles, parrot on branch dec **50.00**

SILVER OVERLAY

History: Silver overlay is silver applied directly to a finished glass or porcelain object. The overlay is cut and decorated, usually by engraving, prior to being molded around the object.

Glass usually is of high quality and is either crystal or colored. Lenox used silver overlay on some porcelain pieces. Most designs are from the Art Nouveau and Art Deco periods.

Reference: Lillian F. Potter, *A Re-Introduction to Silver Overlay on Glass and Ceramics,* published by author, 1992.

Bottle

6″ h, spherical, colorless glass body, chased silver floral and scroll design, orig stopper, monogrammed, price for pr **325.00**

6½″ h, colorless glass body, floral dec, matching stopper **500.00**

8″ h, pinch style, colorless glass body, men, birds, dragons, silver marked "YTK" **50.00**

10¼″ h, colorless glass body, floral overlay, heavy floral center medallion, monogrammed, matching stopper **800.00**

Claret Jug

13″ h, baluster form, colorless glass body, base cut with calyx, faceted neck with applied silver mount, hinged shell lid with spout, applied chased handle reaching down to silver-mounted base, circular dome foot, repoussé and chased floral and foliate design, unclear hallmark **1,100.00**

14″ h, tapering cylindrical form, colorless glass body, base cut with calyx, body cased with four open windows, foliate chasing around each window, applied handle, orig stopper, monogrammed ... **440.00**

Cruet

7″ h, green glass body, cornstalk pattern overlay, orig stopper **1,100.00**

8¼″ h, bulbous form, colorless glass body, base cut with calyx, chased silver floral and foliate design, applied handle, orig stopper, stamped "Black, Starr & Frost, 4000" **200.00**

Decanter

7¾" h, square, chamfered corners, colorless glass body, chased silver floral and foliate design, base with cut calyx, faceted stopper **440.00**

10½" h, bulbous, shaped base, colorless glass body, chased floral and foliate pattern, rim with tri-spout, applied handle, pinched stopper, monogrammed, unclear stamp mark **770.00**

11½" h, baluster form, colorless glass body, faceted neck, chased grape and foliate design, orig stopper, monogrammed, stamped "Thaihfimer & Frank" **715.00**

Ewer, Weller pottery base, floral dec **750.00**

Plate, 10¾" d, black glass body, elaborate Art Deco medallions, leaping gazelles, stylized foliate designs, minor skips in silver **320.00**

Vase, 9" h, pillow shape, ebony body, encrusted flowers and leaves, Cambridge **350.00**

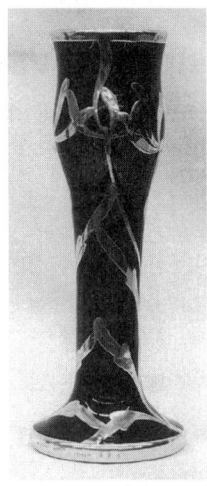

Vase, green glass, marked "Sterling Silver Deposit 196," 6" h, 2⅜" d, $225.00.

SMITH BROS. GLASS

History: After establishing a decorating department at the Mount Washington Glass Works in 1871, Alfred and Harry Smith struck out on their own in 1875. Their New Bedford, Massachusetts, firm soon became known worldwide for its fine opalescent decorated wares, similar in style to those of Mount Washington.

Marks: Smith Bros. glass often is marked on the base with a red shield enclosing a rampant lion and the word "Trademark."

References: Ellen T. Schroy, *Warman's Glass,* Second Edition, Wallace-Homestead, 1995; Kenneth Wilson, *American Glass 1760–1930,* 2 vols., Hudson Hills Press and The Toledo Museum of Art, 1994.

Reproduction Alert: Beware of examples marked "Smith Bros."

Bowl, 5½" d, 2½" h, melon ribbed, enameled daisies, red rampant-lion mark **150.00**

Box, cov, 5½" d, hinged lid, melon ribbed, opaque white ground, hp pansies **385.00**

Cracker Jar, cov, 6½" h, 6½" d, melon ribbed, peach ground, hp pansies, gold outlines, SP cov, sgd **400.00**

Creamer and Sugar, blue pansy dec, SP mountings and cov, rampant-lion mark **320.00**

Dresser Jar, cov, 5½" d, melon ribbed, multicolored pansy dec **300.00**

Ferner, 10" d, melon ribbed, glossy white, violets and leaves, orig metal insert, sgd **675.00**

Jar, cov, 4" d, melon ribbed, ivory, polychrome floral dec, gilt trim, rampant-lion mark **170.00**

Mustard Jar, 3¼" h, heron dec, SP top **85.00**

Perfume Bottle, 5" h, enameled floral dec, emb flower cap, sgd **350.00**

Rose Bowl, 5½" d, wild roses dec, jeweled stamens, autumn colored leaves, rampant-lion mark **250.00**

Salt, open, dec, price for pr **185.00**

Sugar Shaker, 6" h, 2½" d, vertical ribs, opaque white ground

Blue, pink, and gray summer blossoms, pewter top **575.00**

Snow scene **375.00**

Sweetmeat jar, cov, 5½" h, 5½" d, squatty, melon ribbed, opaque white ground, hp tiny blue flowers, SP cov, rim, and bail handle, sgd **650.00**

Toothpick Holder

2¼" h, swag of blossoms, opaque-white ribbed barrel-shaped body, blue rim dots **265.00**

2½" h, Little Lobe, single-petal rose blossoms, pale blue body, raised blue rim dots **245.00**

Vase

7¼ h, 8" w, double pilgrim style, two flattened round vases, joined at side and short cylindrical neck, creamy white ground, lavender wisteria blossoms, gold outlines, gold beading at top **1,220.00**

8¾" h, chalk white body, naturalistically shaded enameled blue wisteria blossoms and vine, green leaves, raised gold outlines, gold-dotted rim **750.00**

Vase, melon body, white ground, Royal dec, gold enamel floral dec, gold beaded rim, rampant lion in shield mark, 3¼" d, 2¼" h, $180.00.

SNOW BABIES

History: Snow babies, small bisque figurines spattered with glitter sand, were made originally in Germany and marketed in the early 1900s. There are several theories about their origin. One is that

German doll makers copied the designs from the traditional Christmas candies. Another theory, the one most accepted, is that they were made to honor Admiral Peary's daughter who was born in Greenland in 1893 and was called the "Snow Baby" by the Eskimos.

Reference: Mary Morrison, *Snow Babies, Santas, and Elves: Collecting Christmas Bisque Figures,* Schiffer Publishing, 1993.

Angel, sitting, arms outstretched, 1³⁄₄" h 195.00
Baby
    Arms outstretched, 1¹⁄₄" h 115.00
    Holding baton 115.00
    Kneeling on one knee, 1" h 85.00
    Laying on side, 1¹⁄₂" l 75.00
    Laying on tummy, 1" l 70.00
    Sitting, snow-covered cardboard box, 2¹⁄₄" h 135.00
    Skating, red suit and hat, sgd, marked "Germany," 2"
    h 130.00
    Standing, dog licking cheek, marked "Germany," 2"
    h 200.00
    Standing, wooden skis, pink cheeks, marked "Germany," 1¹⁄₂" h 115.00
Carolers, three standing in snow, lantern, marked "Germany," 2¹⁄₄" h 185.00

Baby, one on sled, one pulling sled, 1¹⁄₂" h, 2¹⁄₂" w, $95.00.

Penguin, marked "Germany," 4" h 100.00
Snow Pup, on skis, marked "Germany" 150.00
Two Babies, on yellow bisque sled, 2" h 200.00

SNUFF BOTTLES

History: Tobacco usage spread from America to Europe to China during the 17th century. Europeans and Chinese preferred to grind the dried leaves into a powder and sniff it into their nostrils. The elegant Europeans carried their snuff in boxes and took a pinch with their finger tips. The Chinese upper class, because of their lengthy fingernails, found this inconvenient and devised a bottle with a fitted stopper and attached spoon. These utilitarian objects soon became objets d'art.

Snuff bottles were fashioned from precious and semi-precious stones, glass, porcelain and pottery, wood, metals, and ivory. Glass and transparent-stone bottles often were enhanced further with delicate hand paintings, some done on the interior of the bottle.

Collectors' Club: International Chinese Snuff Bottle Society, 2601 No Charles St, Baltimore, MD 21218.

Agate, round, translucent, brown, fishing motif, c1800   750.00
Amber, round, gold, brown streaks, c1800 .... 450.00
Aquamarine, sq, stag motif, c1900 .... 575.00
Bone, figural scenes surrounding pavillion 35.00
Chalcedony, round, flat sides, pink-gray, orange streaks,
    tree and boat motif, mock handles 650.00
Cloisonné, 3" h, pear shape, blue ground, red panels of
    flowers, butterfly 95.00
Enamel, white, plants and dragonfly motif, c1800 ..... 425.00
Horn and Bone, 3¹⁄₂" h, Thousand Faces 45.00
Ivory, carved, Chinese
    2" d, flat flask shape, raised figure and mountains on
    one side, birds with bamboo shoots on other, sgd   100.00
    2¹⁄₄" h
        Flat flask shape, one side carved with two figures,
        other with bird and pine tree, green stopper,
        sgd 100.00
Jadeite
    Flattened ovoid, carved horses and goats in landscape, mottled apple green and celadon-colored stone 800.00
    2¹⁄₂" h, flattened ovoid, white ground, green carved
    leaf 4,290.00
Limestone, round, flat sides, c1800 .... 265.00
Malachite, carved front, gourds, banded, c1900 ...... 165.00
Opal, 2" h, green and pink, fish and seaweed motif ... 300.00
Porcelain, 2¹⁄₂" h, four figures in landscape, Chinese,
    19th C 990.00
Scrimshaw, 2¹⁄₂" h, horn, incised Japanese garden scenes   65.00
Taiga Nut, 3" h, eggplant form 30.00
Tiger-Eye, floral tree motif, c1800 .... 350.00
Tortoiseshell, gilt detail 450.00

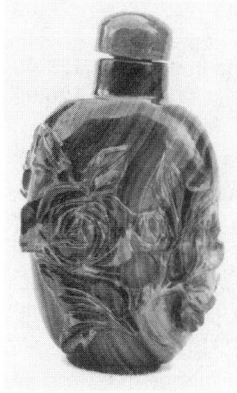

Malachite, carved roses, 2¹⁄₂" h, $265.00.

SOAPSTONE

History: The mineral steatite, known as soapstone because of its greasy feel, has been used for carving figural groups and designs by the Chinese and others. Utilitarian pieces also were made. Soapstone pieces were very popular during the Victorian era.

Reference: *Soapstone: A Price Guide,* L-W Book Sales, 1995.

Bookends, pr, elephants, c1890 .... 65.00
Box, 3 × 5", inlaid pearl dec, artist sgd 45.00

Candlesticks, pr, red tones, flowers and vases, 5⅛" h, $85.00.

Figure
5" h, pomegranate	**25.00**
7" h, two boys riding water buffalo, mottled brown and cream-colored stone, 19th C	**230.00**
16½" h, Shoulao, holding dragon-headed staff and peach, Chinese	**225.00**
Incense Burner, 8" h, black, 19th C	**350.00**
Inkwell, geometric carving on sides	**150.00**
Match Holder, elaborate carving	**70.00**
Paperweight, three carved monkeys	**75.00**

Sculpture
7" h, four chilongs and two toads carved in relief, ovoid stone, light green and chestnut-colored stone, 19th C	**460.00**
28" h, angel, Raymond Coins	**4,950.00**
Toothpick Holder, carved monkey	**70.00**
Urn, 7¼" d, 10¼" h, carved figures, buildings, florals, and trees, elephant's-head handles, wooden stand	**175.00**
Vase, 7" h, carved flowers and leaves, ftd	**120.00**

SOUVENIR AND COMMEMORATIVE CHINA AND GLASS

History: Souvenir, commemorative, and historical china and glass includes those items produced to celebrate special events, places, and people.

China plates made by Rowland and Marcellus and Wedgwood are particularly favored by collectors. Rowland and Marcellus, Staffordshire, England, made a series of blue-and-white historic plates with a wide rolled edge. Scenes from the Philadelphia Centennial in 1876 through the 1939 New York World's Fair are depicted. In 1910 Wedgwood collaborated with Jones, McDuffee and Stratton to produce a series of historic dessert-sized plates showing scenes of places throughout the United States.

Many localities issued plates, mugs, glasses, etc., for anniversary celebrations or to honor a local historical event. These items seem to have greater value when sold in the region in which they originated.

Commemorative glass includes several patterns of pressed glass which celebrate persons or events. Historical glass includes campaign and memorial items.

References: Arene Burgess, *A Collector's Guide to Souvenir Plates,* Schiffer Publishing, 1996; Bessie M. Lindsey, *American Historical Glass,* Charles E. Tuttle Company, 1967.

Periodicals: *Antique Souvenir Collectors News,* Box 562, Great Barrington, MA 01230; *The Souvenir Building Collector,* 25 Falls Rd, Roxbury, CT 06783.

Collectors' Club: Statue of Liberty Collectors' Club, 26601 Bernwood Rd, Cleveland, OH 44122.

Additional Listings: Cup Plates, Pressed Glass, Political Items, and Staffordshire, Historical. Also see *Warman's Americana & Collectibles* for more examples.

China

Cup and Saucer, Iowa State Capitol, white, gold trim	**35.00**
Demitasse Cups and Saucers, Harvard University, set of six scenic cups, Wedgwood, price for 12-pc set	**120.00**
Dresser Tray, hp, Mt Vernon, portraits of George and Martha, delicate floral borders	**110.00**
Mug, University of Pennsylvania, c1905, football player	**250.00**
Pitcher, 7½" h , Discovery of America, light blue, R & M	**275.00**

Plate
7⅛" d, Macon, MO, roses dec	**40.00**
7⅝" d, Souvenir of Salt Lake City, blue transfer, Adams	**100.00**

10" d
Alaska Yukon Pacific Expo, 1909, Seattle	**100.00**
Atlantic City, dark blue, Rowland & Marsellus	**145.00**
Denver, Rowland & Marsellus	**35.00**

10¼" d
Harvard University, blue transfer on white, c1941	**35.00**
Massachusetts Institute of Technology, scenes of different buildings, blue transfer on white, c1930, price for set of 12	**550.00**
Swarthmore College, rose transfer on white	**25.00**
University of Pennsylvania, rose transfer on white, c1940	**28.00**

Conneaut Lake Exposition Park, 1900, reticulated border, light-green tone, glass, 5½" d, $20.00.

10½" d

Dominion of Canada Coat of Arms, Wedgwood, Etruria, England

Brilliant orange border, serrated edge 210.00

Light blue border, Provinces' Coats of Arms . 150.00

Montreal Coat of Arms, brilliant orange border, serrated edge, Wedgwood, Etruria, England .. 225.00

Vancouver, British Columbia Coat of Arms, brilliant orange border, serrated edge, Wedgwood, Etruria, England 225.00

Stein, Cedar Rapids, IA, 2¾" h 65.00

Glass

Bread Tray, Three Presidents, frosted 75.00

Bust

4¾" h, frosted

Abraham Lincoln, raised name on front of base, "Centennial Exhibition" and "Gillander & Sons Inc" on back, chip on corner of base ... 425.00

Shakespeare, raised "Gillander & Sons" and "Centennial Exhibition" on base of base 275.00

5¼" h, frosted, Columbus, raised "World's Fair" and "1893" on back, minor chips 275.00

6" h

Frosted, Benjamin Harrison 250.00

Milk glass

Ulysses S Grant, raised name on front of base, "Gillander & Sons Inc" on back, small chips on bottom and rear edge of base 525.00

George Washington, raised name on front of base, "Centennial Exhibition" and "Gillander & Sons Inc" on back 450.00

6½" h, frosted glass, James A Garfield, raised name on front of base 300.00

Butter Dish, cov, 6½ × 5¾", Lancaster Fair, 1916, Button Arches pattern, ruby stained 175.00

Candlestick, 8" h, gold script "Souvenir of World's Fair" 35.00

Creamer, Liberty Bell, child size 90.00

Cup, Akron Ohio, custard, Heisey mark, 2½" h 25.00

Goblet, Knights of Pythias, 1900, green 50.00

Mug, Pacific Grove, Button Arches pattern, ruby stained 25.00

Paperweight, Plymouth Rock 65.00

Pitcher, Ocean City, NJ, 1912, King's Crown pattern, ruby stained 95.00

Plate

Niagara Falls, transfer dec 50.00

Roosevelt, Theodore, blue, rolled rim, R & M 65.00

Platter, Newark 1952 Sesquicentennial, Twist pattern, Heisey 145.00

Punch Cup, Paducah, VT, Button Arches pattern, ruby stained 35.00

Statue

Boy with dog, frosted, 1876 Expo 215.00

Woman, standing, holding child, 14½" h, raised mark of Gillander, division of United States Glass Co, 1891–1900, on back of base 850.00

Toothpick Holder, Omaha Expo, 1899, Colorado pattern 35.00

Tumbler, Scranton, PA, Mother, Button Arches pattern, ruby stained 50.00

Tray, Old State House, 12" d, blue 225.00

Whiskey, Bumper to the Flag, 3" h 100.00

SOUVENIR AND COMMEMORATIVE SPOONS

History: Souvenir and commemorative spoons have been issued for hundreds of years. Early American silversmiths engraved presentation spoons to honor historical personages or mark key events.

In 1881 Myron Kinsley patented a Niagara Falls spoon, and in 1884 Michael Gibney patented a new flatware design. M. W. Galt, Washington, D.C., issued commemorative spoons for George and Martha Washington in 1889. From these beginnings a collecting craze for souvenir and commemorative spoons developed in the late 19th and early 20th centuries.

References: George B. James, *Souvenir Spoons* (1891), reprinted with 1996 price guide by Bill Boyd (7408 Englewood Lane, Raytown, MO 64133), 1996; Dorothy T. Rainwater and Donna H. Fegler, *American Spoons,* Schiffer Publishing, 1990; ———, *Spoons from around the World,* Schiffer Publishing, 1992; *Sterling Silver, Silverplate, and Souvenir Spoons with Prices,* Revised Edition, L-W Book Sales, 1987, 1994 value update.

Collectors' Clubs: American Spoon Collectors, 7408 Englewood Lane, Raytown, MO 64133; Northeastern Spoon Collectors Guild, 52 Hillcrest Ave, Morristown, NJ 07960; The Scoop Club, 84 Oak Ave, Shelton, CT 06484.

Additional Listings: See *Warman's Americana & Collectibles* for more examples.

Arms of New York City, Tiffany 115.00

Betsy Ross, house in bowl 60.00

Boston Tea Party 40.00

Brooklyn, NY, 13th Regiment, SS 35.00

Cheyenne, Wyoming 25.00

Coney Island Skyline 60.00

Eureka, CA, courthouse, SS 30.00

Fort Ticonderoga, 1775, Ethan Allen 45.00

Golden Gate Bridge, San Francisco 35.00

Hot Springs, AK, SS 55.00

Houston, TX, SS 40.00

Jackson Monument 40.00

Kansas City, 1889, cupid handle 40.00

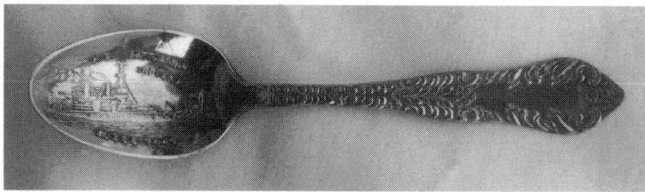

Battleship *Indiana*, SP, 4¼" l, $25.00.

Los Angeles, CA, emb palm tree in bowl, SS 40.00

Marquette, MI, Light House Point 65.00

Niagara, 1891, SS 55.00

Parry de Chein, Wisconsin, SS 28.00

Prudential Insurance Building 30.00

Santa Barbara, CA 35.00

St Augustine, FL 30.00

Texas Centennial, 1839–1936 .... 75.00

Washington's Inauguration 45.00

West Point Cadet 30.00

SPANGLED GLASS

History: Spangled glass is a blown or blown-molded variegated art glass, similar to spatter glass, with the addition of flakes of mica or metallic aventurine. Many pieces are cased with a white or clear layer of glass. Spangled glass was developed in the late 19th century and still is being manufactured.

Originally, spangled glass was attributed only to the Vasa Murrhina Art Glass Company of Hartford, Connecticut, which distributed the glass for Dr. Flower of the Cape Cod Glassworks, Sandwich, Massachusetts. However, research has shown that many companies in Europe, England, and the United States made spangled glass, and attributing a piece to a specific source is very difficult.

Basket
    5½" d, pink, crimped handle, clear reeded twisted
        thorn handle **185.00**
    7½" d, light green, ribbon-candy rim, clear briar-form
        handle **120.00**
Bowl
    3¾" d, 3⅞" h, cranberry, three clear scrolled feet,
        embossed heads, clear stars with berry centers applied around bowl, large mica flakes **165.00**
    5¾" d, 4½" h, olive green blue stripes, clear applied
        rigaree around top, clear dripping appliqué, mica flakes in bowl, clear berry prunt, applied clear feet **240.00**
    8½" d, 3" h, shaded pink overlay, clear ruffled edge,
        melon rib, white lining **175.00**
Bride's Basket, 10" h, pink shaded to white, silver flakes,
    ruffled edge, shiny finish **85.00**
Ewer, 6⅞" h, 2¾" d, blue overlay, white lining, mica
    flakes, applied clear handle, price for pr **135.00**
Fairy Lamp, 3⅝" h, 2⅞" d, embossed swirl pyramid cranberry shade with mica flakes, embedded green
    threading on clear marked "Clarke" base **155.00**
Jack-in-the-Pulpit Vase, 5¾" h, white ext., pink int., clear
    edging, mica flakes, ruffled rim **150.00**
Pitcher, 8" h, 5½" w, bulbous, six wide rib blowouts,
    silver mica flakes, rose ground, hp flowers and leaves, white lining, gold trim, patented 1883, applied clear handle, Hobbs Brockunier **500.00**
Rose Bowl, 4¼" d, white, light blue, pink, yellow, peach,

orange, and maroon spatter, silver mica flakes,
    crimped top **250.00**
Tumbler, red, silver mica flakes **95.00**
Tumble-Up, 7½" h decanter, matching tumbler, cobalt
    blue, mica flecks, white enamel and gilt dec **220.00**
Vase, 5¾" h, 4¼" d, ruffled top, deep amber, gold foil
    flakes, clear applied loop feet, three clear berry prunts **250.00**

SPATTER GLASS

History: Spatter glass is a variegated blown or blown-molded art glass. It originally was called "End-of-Day" glass, based on the assumption that it was made from batches of glass leftover at the end of the day. However, spatter glass was found to be a standard production item for many glass factories.

Spatter glass was developed at the end of the 19th century and is still being produced in the United States and Europe.

References: William Heacock, James Measell and Berry Wiggins, *Harry Northwood,* Antique Publications, 1990; Ellen T. Schroy, *Warman's Glass,* Second Edition, Wallace-Homestead, 1995.

Reproduction Alert: Many modern examples come from the area previously called Czechoslovakia.

Basket
    5 × 6½", ruffled oval top, emb swirls, peach and
        white spatter, clear applied thorn handle **165.00**
    8" h, tortoiseshell, wide handle with gold prunt and
        prunus dec **195.00**
Berry Bowl, master, Royal Ivy, cased **140.00**
Candlestick, 7½" h, flared socket, twisted hourglass
    stem, domed ribbed base, yellow, red, and white
    spatter **50.00**
Creamer, 4½" h, 2¾" d, blue and light blue opaque,
    embossed swirl, applied blue reeded handle **95.00**

Creamer, ring neck, white and pink, Northwood, 4¾" h, $42.00.

Cruet, 8¾" h, 3½" d, blue ground, white spatter, clear
    applied handle, clear heart-shaped stopper **135.00**
Darning Egg, red, yellow, and green, clear applied handle **125.00**

Tumbler, pink, white, orange, red, blue, yellow, and silver spangles, 4" h, $70.00.

Jack-in-the-Pulpit Vase, 7¼" h, green, peach, yellow,
and white spatter, green DQ body **75.00**
Jar, cov, 3¾ × 6½", maroon, white, yellow, and green,
white cased int., clear applied feet and finial **85.00**
Pitcher, 7⅞" h, bulbous, tricorn ruffled top, pink and
white, clear applied reeded handle **195.00**
Rolling Pin, 16" l, clear ground, red and blue spatter .. **200.00**
Rose Bowl, 3½" d, octagonal crimped top, rose spatter,
white cased int. **115.00**
Salt, 3¾ × 3 × 1½", maroon, yellow, and white spatter,
white lining, clear applied shell trim **50.00**
Spittoon, amber, wide rim **40.00**
Tumbler, brown and yellow spatter **35.00**
Water Set, 6 × 7⅛" pitcher, four 2¾ × 3¾" tumblers,
pink, white, maroon, green, and yellow spatter, white
int., clear reeded handle, price for 5-pc set **375.00**

SPATTERWARE

History: Spatterware generally was made of common earthenware, although occasionally creamware was used. The earliest
English examples were made about 1780. The peak period of
production was from 1810 to 1840. Firms known to have made
spatterware are Adams, Barlow, and Harvey and Cotton.

The amount of spatter decoration varies from piece to piece.
Some objects simply have decorated borders. These often were
decorated with a brush, requiring several hundred touches per
square inch to achieve the spatter effect. Other pieces have the
entire surface covered with spatter.

Marks: Marked pieces are rare.

References: Susan and Al Bagdade, *Warman's English & Continental Pottery & Porcelain,* Second Edition, Wallace-Homestead,
1991; Kevin McConnell, *Spongeware and Spatterware,* Schiffer
Publishing, 1990; Dana G. Morykan and Harry L. Rinker, *Warman's Country Antique & Collectibles,* Third Edition, Wallace-
Homestead, 1996.

REPRODUCTION ALERT

Cybis spatter is an increasingly collectible ware in
its own right. The pieces, made by the Polishman
Boleslaw Cybis in the 1940s, have an Adams-type
peafowl design. Many contemporary craftsmen also
are reproducing spatterware.

Notes: Collectors today focus on the patterns—Cannon, Castle,
Fort, Peafowl, Rainbow, Rose, Thistle, Schoolhouse, etc. The decoration on flatware is in the center of the piece; on hollow ware
it occurs on both sides.

Aesthetics and the color of spatter are key to determining value.
Blue and red are the most common colors; green, purple, and
brown are in a middle group; black and yellow are scarce.

Like any soft paste, spatterware is easily broken or chipped.
Prices in this listing are for pieces in very good to mint condition.

Bowl, 11" d, 2" h, red and green flowers, spongeware
rim, marked "Imperial Royal, Belgium" **115.00**

Creamer, Thistle, blue, rim roughness and discoloration, $300.00.

Cream Pitcher, Peafowl dec, yellow spatter, 19th C ...**1,900.00**
Cup and Saucer, handleless
Black Deer, blue spatter, cup badly damaged, chip
and hairline to saucer **330.00**
Peafowl dec
Green spatter
Red, blue, yellow, and black peafowl, very mi-
nor flakes **330.00**
Saucer imp "Stoneware B & T," early 19th C **400.00**
Pink spatter, 19th C, price for 16-pc set, one saucer
with minor chips **1,700.00**
Purple spatter **220.00**
Miniature
Cup and Saucer, handleless, stick spatter, red, green,
and yellow border, blue stripes, very minor flakes **90.00**
Sugar, cov, Fort, blue spatter **360.00**
Pepper Pot, 4¾" h, pierced dome cov, Peafowl, blue,
ochre, rose, and black peacock on branch, yellow
spatter, marked "Staffordshire," c1840 ....**1,200.00**
Plate
7" d, Peafowl, green dec and border, Leeds, early 19th
C **575.00**
8½" d, peafowl, blue spatter
Imprinted "Pearl Stoneware FW & Co" **950.00**
Imprinted "Stoneware FW & Co" **950.00**
8⅞" d, gaudy stick spatter, floral design, red border
imp "Edge Malkin & Co." **90.00**
9¼" d, gaudy stick spatter, polychrome floral dec,
black spattered rim, marked "Wm Adams Tun-
stall," wear, price for pr **165.00**
Soup Plate
9⅜" d, gaudy stick spatter, center flower, rim swags,
wear, minor damage **165.00**
9¾" d, gaudy stick spatter, blue, red, and green floral
dec, price for 6-pc set **565.00**
9⅞" d, red design spatter border, blue stripes, purple,
blue, red, green, and black thistle and lily of the
valley dec, stains, crazing, glaze wear **175.00**
Sugar Bowl, cov, blue, knop on lid, 19th C, lid chip .. **160.00**
Tea Ware, Peafowl, blue spatter, circular teapot with

chipped lid, octagonal two-handled cov sugar with repaired handles, waste bowl with blue and mauve stripes, early 19th C **1,700.00**

Teapot, 6⅛" h, Thistle, blue spatter, red and green thistle, yellowed repair at base of handle and tip of spout, small chips, mismatched lid **550.00**

Toddy, 5¾" d, red design spatter border, blue stripe, purple, green, yellow ochre, and black viola, pinpoint flakes **180.00**

Wash Bowl and Pitcher, 12" d, 10½" h, red and green rainbow spatter, both pcs cracked, foot broken off pitcher and reattached **325.00**

Cup and Saucer, handleless, purple dec, unmarked, 6" d saucer, 3⅞" d × 2¾" h cup, $125.00.

SPONGEWARE

History: Spongeware is a specific type of decoration, not a type of pottery or glaze.

Spongeware decoration is found on many kinds of pottery bodies—ironstone, redware, stoneware, yellowware, etc. It was made in both England and the United States. Pieces were marked after 1815, and production extended into the 1880s.

Decoration is varied. On some pieces the sponging is minimal with the white underglaze dominant. Other pieces appear to be solidly sponged on both sides. Pieces made between 1840 and 1860 have circular or horizontally streaked sponging.

Blue and white are the most common colors, but browns, greens, ochres, and a greenish blue also were used. The greenish blue results from blue sponging with a pale yellow overglaze. A red overglaze produces a black or navy color. Blue and red were used on English creamware and American earthenware of the 1880s. Other spongeware colors include gray, grayish green, red, dark green on stark white, dark green on mellow yellow, and purple.

References: Susan and Al Bagdade, *Warman's American Pottery and Porcelain,* Wallace-Homestead, 1994; ———, *Warman's English & Continental Pottery & Porcelain,* Second Edition, Wallace-Homestead, 1991; William C. Ketchum, Jr., *American Pottery and Porcelain,* Avon Books, 1994; Kevin McConnell, *Spongeware and Spatterware,* Schiffer Publishing, 1990.

Bowl
    8¼" h, blue, yellowware ground **100.00**
    8½" d, 4" h, blue and white, ears for wire bale handle, wear and pinpoint flakes **75.00**
    9" d, 3½" h, blue and white, molded ribs, chips to foot and several open firing blisters **85.00**
Butter Crock, 6" d, blue and white, emb label **85.00**
Cooler, blue and white
    9½" h, cov, marked "2" and "Ice Water," bung hole, no spigot, hairlines, chips to lid **110.00**
    10" h, black enameled "15," brown Albany slip int., brass spigot, surface flake **110.00**
    14¾" h, marked "5," bung hole, no spigot, chip on one handle **165.00**
    18" h, marked "8," nickel-plated spigot, minor chips on inside flange of lid **350.00**
Crock, cov, 9½" d, 6½" h, blue and white, chips **75.00**
Dish, 6" d, blue and white, molded rim **45.00**
Miniature, pitcher, blue and white
    2½" h, bulbous, porcelain **110.00**
    3½" h, paneled **115.00**

Mug, 4⅛" h, blue and white **40.00**
Mustard Pot, cov, 2¼" h, blue and white, damaged lid **55.00**
Pitcher, blue and white
    6½" h, bulbous base, labeled "UHL Pottery Co" ... **770.00**
    7½" h
        Barrel shape, small rim flakes **220.00**
        Bulbous **200.00**
    8⅜" h, rim chip, minor base flakes **220.00**
    8⅝" h, barrel shape, stripes, hairlines **315.00**
    8¾" h, large pattern, chip on table ring **470.00**
    8⅞" h
        Bulbous base, cylindrical neck, chips **220.00**
        Tankard, molded rose, minor open surface blisters **360.00**
    9" h, tankard, small rim flake **330.00**
    9⅛" h, tankard, hairline, minor flakes **330.00**
    9½" h, bulbous base **715.00**
    9¾" h, short foot hairline, minor stains **55.00**
    11¼" h, blue ext. stripes, hairlines in base **370.00**
Plate, blue and white
    7½" d, molded rim **85.00**
    9¼" d,, molded rim **115.00**
    10" d, molded rim handles **125.00**
    10¼" d, molded rim **120.00**
Platter, 15" l, blue and white **325.00**
Salt Crock, cov
    5¾" d, blue and white, molded basketweave and vintage, hairline **80.00**
    6⅜" h, blue, yellowware ground, lid missing **65.00**
Soap Dish, 3½" × 4¾", blue and white **65.00**
Sugar, cov, 7½" h, blue and white, attributed to Buford Bros, East Liverpool, OH, professional repair to lid . **165.00**
Teapot, 6½" h, bluish green and white, small chips ... **385.00**
Toothbrush Holder, 5¼" h, blue and white **45.00**
Tray, 9½" l, leaf shape, blue and white **115.00**
Umbrella Stand
    15½" h, blue stripes and sponge dec, hairlines **770.00**
    22½" h, blue stripes and sponge dec, transfer design of Dutch boy and girl in white oval with bow trim, hairlines **825.00**
Wash Bowl
    14" d, 5" h, blue and white, blue ext. stripes, hairline **75.00**
    14½" d, 12" h, blue and white, blue stripes, color and width of stripes varies **330.00**
    14¾" d, 4¼" h, blue and white **150.00**
Water Filter, 22½" h , blue and white, nickel-plated spigot, two sections and lid, slight color variations . **635.00**

SPORT CARDS

History: Baseball cards were first printed in the late 19th century. By 1900 the most common cards, known as "T" cards, were those made by tobacco companies such as American Tobacco Co. The majority of the tobacco-related cards were produced between 1909 and 1915. During the 1920s American Caramel, National Caramel, and York Caramel candy companies issued cards identified in lists as "E" cards.

During the 1930s Goudey Gum Co. of Boston (from 1933 to 1941) and Gum Inc. (in 1939) were prime producers of baseball cards. Following World War II, Bowman Gum of Philadelphia (B.G.H.L.I.), the successor to Gum, Inc., led the way. Topps, Inc., (T.C.G.) of Brooklyn, New York, followed. Topps bought Bowman in 1956 and enjoyed almost a monopoly in card production until 1981.

In 1981 Topps was challenged by Fleer of Philadelphia and Donruss of Memphis. All three companies annually produce sets numbering 600 cards or more.

Football cards have been printed since the 1890s. However, it was not until 1933 that the first bubble gum football card appeared in the Goudey Sport Kings set. In 1935 National Chickle of Cambridge, Massachusetts, produced the first full set of gum cards devoted exclusively to football.

Both Leaf Gum of Chicago and Bowman Gum of Philadelphia produced sets of football cards in 1948. Leaf discontinued production after their 1949 issue; Bowman continued until 1955.

Topps Chewing Gum entered the market in 1950 with its college-stars set. Topps became a fixture in the football card market with its 1955 All-American set. From 1956 thorough 1963 Topps printed card sets of National Football League players, combining them with the American Football League players in 1961.

Topps produced sets with only American Football League players from 1964 to 1967. The Philadelphia Gum Company made National Football League card sets during this period. Beginning in 1968 and continuing to the present, Topps has produced sets of National Football League cards, the name adopted after the merger of the two leagues.

References: *All Sports Alphabetical Price Guide,* Krause Publications, 1995; James Beckett, *The Official 1996 Price Guide to Baseball Cards,* Fifteenth Edition, House of Collectibles, 1996;———, *The Official Price Guide to Basketball Cards,* Sixth Edition, House of Collectibles, 1996; ———, *The Official Price Guide to Football Cards,* Sixteenth Edition, House of Collectibles, 1996; ———, *The Official Price Guide to Hockey Cards,* Sixth Edition, House of Collectibles, 1996; Mike Bonner, *Collecting Football Cards,* Wallace-Homestead, 1995; Tol Broome, *From Ruth to Ryan,* Krause Publications, 1994; *The Charlton Standard Catalogue of Canadian Baseball & Football Cards,* Fourth Edition, The Charlton Press, 1995; *The Charlton Standard Catalogue of Hockey Cards,* Seventh Edition, Charlton Press, 1995; Gene Florence, *Florence's Standard Baseball Card Price Guide,* Sixth Edition, Collector Books, 1995; Allan Kaye and Michael McKeever, *Baseball Card Price Guide,* Avon Books, 1996; ———, *Football Card Price Guide,* Avon Books, 1995; Troy Kirk, *Collector's Guide to Baseball Cards,* Wallace-Homestead, 1990.

Jeff Kurowski and Tony Prudom, *Sports Collectors Digest Pre-War Baseball Card Price Guide,* Krause Publications, 1993; Mark Larson, *Sports Collectors Digest Minor League Baseball Card Price Guide,* Krause Publications, 1993; Mark Larson (ed.), *The Sports Card Explosion,* Krause Publications, 1993; Bob Lemke and Sally

Grace, *Sportscard Counterfeit Detector,* Third Edition, Krause Publications, 1994; Norman E. Martinus and Harry L. Rinker, *Warman's Paper,* Wallace-Homestead, 1994; Michael McKeever, *Collecting Sports Cards,* Alliance Publishing, 1996; Alan Rosen, *True Mint,* Krause Publications, 1994; Sports Collectors Digest, *Baseball Card Price Guide,* Tenth Edition, Krause Publications, 1996; ———, *Premium Insert Sports Cards,* Krause Publications, 1995; ———, *Standard Catalog of Baseball Cards,* Sixth Edition, Krause Publications, 1996; ———, *Standard Catalog of Football, Basketball, & Hockey Cards,* Second Edition, Krause Publications, 1996.

Periodicals: *Allan Kaye's Sports Cards News & Price Guides,* 10300 Watson Rd, St Louis, MO 63127; *Baseball Update,* Suite 284, 220 Sunrise Hwy, Rockville Centre, NY 11570; *Beckett Baseball Card Monthly,* 15850 Dallas Pkwy, Dallas, TX 75248; *Beckett Football Card Magazine,* 15850 Dallas Pkwy, Dallas, TX 75248; *Canadian Sportscard Collector,* PO Box 1299, Lewiston, NY 14092; *The Old Judge,* PO Box 137, Centerbeach, NY 11720; *Sport Card Economizer,* RFD 1 Box 350, Winthrop, ME 04364; *Sports Card Price Guide Monthly,* 700 E State St, Iola, WI 54990; *Sports Cards Magazine & Price Guide,* 700 E State St, Iola, WI 54490; *Sports Card Trader,* PO Box 443, Mt Morris, IL 61054; *Sports Collectors Digest,* 700 E State St, Iola, WI 54990; *Tuff Stuff,* PO Box 1637, Glen Allen, VA 23060; *Your Season Ticket,* 106 Liberty Rd, Woodsboro, MD 21798.

Baseball

Bowman Gum Company

   1948, black and white

Common Set (48)	**1,500.00**
Common Player (1–36)	10.00
Common Player (37–48)	12.50
Common Player SP	15.00
5 Bob Feller	100.00
32 Bill Rigney	12.00

   1949

Complete Set (240)	**7,000.00**
Common Player (1–36)	7.50
Common Player (37–73)	8.50
Common Player (74–144)	6.50
Common Player (145–240)	35.00
100 Gil Hodges	80.00
214 Richie Ashburn	225.00

   1951

Complete Set (324)	**8,350.00**
Common Player (1–36)	9.50
Common Player (37–252)	6.50
Common Player (253–324)	30.00
1 Whitey Ford	310.00
122 Joe Garagiola	150.00

   1953, black and white

Complete Set (160)	**4,500.00**
Common Player (1–96)	15.50
Common Player (97–112)	16.50
Common Player (113–128)	26.00
Common Player (129–160)	18.00
59 Mickey Mantle	750.00
121 Yogi Berra	250.00

   1955, color

Complete Set (320)	**2,400.00**

SPORTS CARDS LANGUAGE

As in a dictionary, new terms and abbreviations are added to various antiques and collectibles categories. Here are some commonly used Sports Cards terms.

ACC—*American Card Catalog,* edited by Jefferson Burdick, Nostalgia Press, 1960. Lists alphabetical and numerical designations as it identifies card sets. They have devised a set of sub-abbreviations, such as F for food inserts. The one, tow, or three digit number which follows the letter prefix identifies the company and the series.

AS—All Star Card. A special card for players of the all star teams of the National League, American League, or Major League.

AU—Card with autograph.

Blank Back—refers to a card with no printing at all on the back.

Borders—white space, although sometimes colored, which surrounds the picture, used in establishing grading.

Brick—a wrapped group of cards, often of only one year.

Centering—the player should be centered on the card with even borders; an important grading factor.

Chipping—wearing away of a dark-colored border.

Combination Card—shows two or more players but not an entire team.

Common Card—ordinary player, lowest-valued card in a set.

CO—abbreviation for coach.

COR—corrected card.

CY—Cy Young award.

Ding—slight damage to the edge or corner of a card.

DP—double-quantity print run.

DR—draft choice.

ERR—error card. Card with a known mistake, misspelling, etc. When a variation card has been issued, the value of an error card goes down.

First Card—first card of a player in a national set, not necessarily a rookie card.

Foil—foil embossed stamp on card.

F/S—father and son on card.

Gloss—the amount of shine on a card, again a value determination.

Grade—condition that helps determine value.

Key Card—most important cards in a set.

Reverse Negative—common error in which picture negative is flipped so the picture comes out backward.

ROY—Rookie of the Year.

SP—single or short print, printed in lesser amounts than rest of series.

Team Card—card showing entire team.

Wrapper—paper wrapper surrounding wax packs.

YL—yellow letters, Topps, 1958.

Common Player (1–96)	3.50
Common Player (97–224)	3.25
Common Player (225–320)	14.00
184 Willie Mays	100.00
242 Ernie Banks	165.00

Topps Chewing Gum Company

1951, red backs

Complete Set (52)	350.00
Common Player (1–52)	3.10
1 Yogi Berra	45.00
38 Duke Snider	40.00

1953

Complete Set (280)	5,000.00
Common Player (1–165)	11.50
Common Player (166–220)	7.50
Common Player (221–280)	42.50
Common DP (221–280)	20.00
76 Pee Wee Reese	65.00
82 Mickey Mantle	800.00
273 Harvey Hadix	60.00

1955

Complete Set (210)	3,500.00
Common Player (1–150)	4.50
Common Player (151–160)	7.50
Common Player (161–210)	12.50
123 Sandy Koufax	400.00
164 Roberto Clemente	550.00
198 Yogi Berra	110.00

1957

Complete Set (407)	3,500.00
Common Player (1–88)	3.50
Common Player (89–176)	3.00
Common Player (177–264)	6.00
Common Player (265–352)	8.50
Common Player (353–407)	2.50
18 Don Drysdale	100.00
35 Frank Robinson	125.00

1959

Complete Set (572)	2,350.00
Common Player (1–10)	2.50
Common Player (11–198)	1.75
Common Player (199–506)	1.50
Common Player (507–572)	7.50
50 Willie Mays	70.00
380 Hank Aaron	60.00
514 Bob Gibson	185.00

Football

Bowman Gum Company

1948

Complete Set (108)	2,700.00
7 Steve Van Buren	65.00
101 Sid Luckman	85.00

1951

Complete Set (144)	1,400.00
Common Player	6.25
4 Norm Van Brocklin	80.00
20 Tom Landry	225.00

1952

Complete Set (144)	4,600.00
Common Player (1–72)	10.00

Common Player (73–144)	16.25
19 George Connor SP	40.00
72 John Schweder SP	155.00
137 Bob Waterfield	45.00

1955

Complete Set (160)	675.00
Common Player (1–64)	2.00
Common Player (65–160)	2.75
1 Doak Walker	10.00
7 Frank Gifford	60.00
62 George Blanda	45.00

Fleer Gum Company

1960

Complete Set (132)	300.00
Common Player	1.00
76 Paul Lowe	6.50
124 Jack Kemp	145.00

1961

Complete Set (220)	625.00
Common Player (1–132)	1.00
Common Player (133–220)	1.75
117 Bobby Layne	12.00
215 Don Maynard	35.00

Leaf Gum Company

1948

Complete Set (98)	2,750.00
Common Player (1–48)	7.75
Common Player (50–98)	37.50
15 Charlie Justice	25.00
54 Chuck Bednarik	115.00

1949

Complete Set (150)	650.00
Common Player	16.00
49 Charley Conerly	30.00
150 Bulldog Turner	32.00

Topps Chewing Gum Inc.

1950

Complete Set (100)	1,350.00
Common Player	12.50
20 Glen Davis	17.50
62 Leo Nomellini	45.00

Boxing, Topps, #48, Rocky Castellani, 2¹⁄₆ × 2¹⁵⁄₁₆″, very good condition, $3.00.

1951

Complete Set (75)	475.00
Common Player	6.25
2 Bill Wade	14.50
48 George Young	10.00

1955

Complete Set (100)	1,350.00
Common Player	6.50
16 Knute Rockne	115.00
37 Jim Thorpe	195.00
100 Fats Henry SP	40.00

1956

Complete Set (121)	750.00
Common Player	2.50
6 Norm Van Brocklin	12.00
53 Frank Gifford	85.00
60 Lenny Moore	40.00

1958

Complete Set (132)	600.00
Common Player	1.25
22 John Unitas	80.00
62 Jim Brown	220.00
90 Sonny Jurgensen	50.00

SPORTS COLLECTIBLES

History: People have been saving sports-related equipment since the inception of sports. Some was passed down from generation to generation for reuse; the rest was stored in dark spaces in closets, attics, and basements.

In the 1980s two key trends brought collectors' attention to sports collectibles. First, decorators began using old sports items, especially in restaurant decor. Second, card collectors began to discover the thrill of owning the "real" thing. By the beginning of the 1990s all sport categories were collectible, with baseball items paramount and golf and football running close behind.

References: Mark Allen Baker, *Sports Collectors Digest Complete Guide to Boxing Collectibles,* Krause Publications, 1995; Don Bevans and Ron Menchine, *Baseball Team Collectibles,* Wallace-Homestead, 1994; David Bushing, *Guide to Spalding Bats 1908–1938,* published by author; ———, *Sports Equipment Price Guide,* Krause Publications, 1995; Dave Bushing and Joe Phillips, *Vintage Baseball Glove Pocket Price Guide,* No. 4, published by authors (217 Homewood, Libertyville, IL 60048), 1996; ———, *Vintage Baseball Bat 1994 Pocket Price Guide,* published by authors, 1994; Bruce Chadwick and David M. Spindel authored a series of books on major-league teams published by Abbeville Press between 1992 and 1995; Duncan Chilcott, *Miller's Soccer Memorabilia,* Miller's Publications, 1994; Douglas Congdon-Martin and John Kashmanian, *Baseball Treasures,* Schiffer Publishing, 1993; Ralf Coykendall, Jr., *Coykendall's Complete Guide to Sporting Collectibles,* Wallace-Homestead, 1996.

Sarah Fabian-Baddiel, *Miller's Golf Memorabilia,* Millers Publications, 1994; Mark K. Larson, *Complete Guide to Baseball Memorabilia,* Third Edition, Krause Publications, 1996; Mark Larson, Rick Hines and David Platta (eds.), *Mickey Mantle Memorabilia,* Krause Publications, 1993; Carl Luckey, *Old Fishing Lures and Tackle,* Fourth Edition, Books Americana, 1996; Roderick A. Malloy, *Malloy's Sports Collectibles Value Guide,* Attic Books Ltd, Wallace-Homestead, 1993; Michael McKeever, *Collecting Sports*

Memorabilia, Alliance Publishing, 1966; John M. and Morton W. Olman, *Golf Antiques & Other Treasures of the Game,* Expanded Edition, Market Street Press, 1993; George Sanders, Helen Sanders, and Ralph Roberts, *The Sanders Price Guide to Sports Autographs,* 1994 Edition, Scott Publishing, 1993; Mark Wilson (ed.), *The Golf Club Identification and Price Guide III,* Ralph Maltby Enterprises, 1993.

Periodicals: *Baseball Hobby News,* 4540 Kearney Villa Rd, San Diego, CA 92123; *Beckett Focus on Future Stars,* 15850 Dallas Pkwy, Dallas, TX 75248; *Boxing Collectors Newsletter,* 59 Boston St, Revere, MA 02151; Button Pusher, PO Box 4, Coopersburg, PA 18036; *Diamond Angle,* PO Box 409, Kaunakakai, HI 97648; *Diamond Duds,* PO Box 10153, Silver Spring, MD 20904; *Fantasy Baseball,* 700 E State St, Iola, WI 54990; *Golfiana Magazine,* PO Box 688, Edwardsville, IL 62025; *Kovels on Sports Collectibles,* PO Box 22200, Beachwood, OH 44122; *Old Tyme Baseball News,* PO Box 833, Petroskey, MI 49770; *Sports Collectors Digest,* 700 E State St, Iola, WI 54990; *Tuff Stuff,* PO Box 1637, Glen Allen, VA 23060; *US Golf Classics & Heritage Hickories,* 5407 Pennock Point Rd, Jupiter, FL 33458.

Collectors' Clubs: The (Baseball) Glove Collector, 14507 Rolling Hills Lane, Dallas, TX, 75240; Boxiana & Pugilistica Collectors International, PO Box 83135, Portland, OR 97203; Golf Club Collectors Assoc, 640 E Liberty St, Girard, OH 44420; Golf Collectors Society, PO Box 491, Shawnee Mission, KS 66202; Logo Golf Ball Collector's Assoc, 4552 Barclay Fairway, Lake Worth, FL 33467; Rose Bowl Collectors, 1111 Delps Rd, Daneillsville, PA 18038; Society for American Baseball Research, PO Box 93183, Cleveland, OH 44101.

Museums: Aiken Thoroughbred Racing Hall of Fame & Museum, Aiken, SC; International Boxing Hall of Fame, Canastota, NY; Kentucky Derby Museum, Louisville, KY; Metropolitan Museum of Art, The Jefferson Burdich Collection, New York, NY; Naismith Memorial Basketball Hall of Fame, Springfield, MA; National Baseball Hall of Fame & Museum, Inc., Cooperstown, NY; National Bowling Hall of Fame & Museum, St Louis, MO; New England Sports Museum, Boston, MA; PGA/World Golf Hall of Fame, Pinehurst, NC.

Advisor: Ralf Coykendall, Jr.

SPECIAL AUCTION

Lang's
30 Hamlin Rd
Falmouth, ME 04105
(207) 797-2311

Auto Racing

Ashtray, bronze, Indianapolis Speedway, relief of race car, marked ''Clabber Girl Special, Terre Haute, IN'' **350.00**
Needle Book, multicolored racing scene, Prize Medal Needles, Germany **20.00**
Poster, 29 × 42", Auto Races—Bridgewater Grange, bright red roadster pursued by black car in background, yellow ground, c1933 .... **175.00**

Program, official, Danbury, 1930 .... **50.00**
Puzzle, 17 × 11", Crisco Racing, premium, 200 pcs .. **20.00**

Baseball

Architectural, office door, ''Boston Red Sox Information,'' from Fenway Park, c1912, honey-brown oak, brass fittings, gold lettering, red and gold sox on glass pane **5,225.00**
Bank, figural baseball, glass **40.00**
Baseball, autographed
   Durocher, Leo, 1947, Smith & Smiths ball **100.00**
   Mantle, Mickey **300.00**
Bat, Hank Aaron autograph, 1973 home run record, H & P Pro Model Bats **80.00**
Figure Set, three players, L L Rittger **275.00**
Game
   Board, Game of Base-Ball, McLoughlin Bros **1,610.00**
   Tin, Roger Maris, colorful, 1962 .... **85.00**
Magazine
   Baseball Magazine, DiMaggio, Walters, Nov 1939 . **100.00**
   Sport Life, Ted Williams, Nov 1948 .... **40.00**

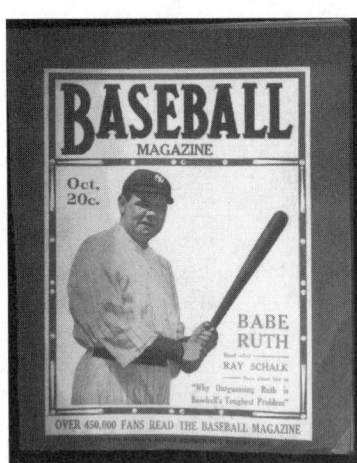

Baseball, magazine, Oct., Vol 5, No. 5, 20 cents, Babe Ruth cover, unsigned photo, $35.00.

Mug Set, baseball shape, figural handles, batter holds bat, outfielder holds glove, pottery, price for pr **120.00**
Nodder, Oakland A's, 1974, orig box, 7½" h **45.00**
Photo, rookie, Mickey Mantle, color, autographed **450.00**
Plate, dinner, Mickey Mantle **65.00**
Silhouette, boys' baseball game, framed, 1927 .... **30.00**
Trophy, Knickerbocker Trophy, match played between Gothams of NY and Knickerbocker Baseball club, 1854 .... **72,050.00**
Uniform, Joe DiMaggio's 1951 NY Yankees World Series, road flannel jersey and pants **59,690.00**

Basketball

Program, Harlem Globetrotters, 1964 .... **45.00**

Boxing

Blue Record Book, 1922 .... **60.00**
Game, Championship Fight, Frankie Goodman copy-

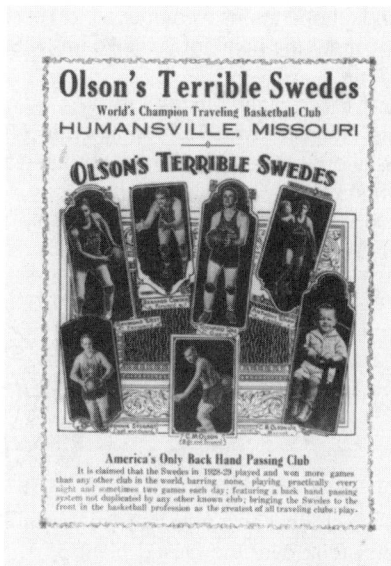

Basketball, promotional flyer, Olson's Terrible Swedes, black and white, 8 pgs, with manager's letter, 8½″ × 11″, 1929, $20.00.

right and design, US National & Intercollegiate Champion, 1940-50 .... **45.00**

Playing Cards, James J Jeffries Championship, boxer photo on each card, complete deck, 1909 copyright **100.00**

Tobacco Card, 1⅜″ × 2⅝″, Gene Tunney, Churchman Cigarettes, sepia photo, 1938 .... **25.00**

Fishing

Book
  Gingrich, Arnold, *The Well-Tempered Angler*, NY, 1965, first ed **50.00**
  Lincoln, Robert Page, *Black Bass Fishing*, Harrisburg, 1952, first ed **35.00**
Canoe Set, orig pading **935.00**
Creel, Willow, turtle trademark **2,200.00**
Decoy, trout, 12″ l brook trout, superimposed on birch back outline map of Maine, carved by Lawrence Irvine, c1970 ....**1,100.00**
Lure, Heddon Basser, #8501, orig box and tissue **165.00**
Painting, 71 × 65″, oil on canvas, Portuguese Fisherman, Clifford Ashley, 1915 ....**8,250.00**
Reel, split-cane
  6½″, Orvis, Rocky Mountain, trout, Federation of Fly Fisherman 1969 marks, orig case **600.00**
  7″, Winchester, decal, orig bag and tube **1,200.00**
  7½″, L L Bean **385.00**
  8½″, F D Devine, trout, marked "The Devine Rod, Utica, NY," revarnished **200.00**
Stickpin, small-mouth bass, celluloid, William Mills ... **85.00**

Football

Ashtray, 7½″ d, Baltimore Colts Championship, china, white, blue cartoon picture, dated Dec 29, 1958, orig box **75.00**
Figure, cast iron, player, 1900s, 5″ h **85.00**

Glass, 5¼″ h, Ohio State University Football Champions Western Conference, Appreciation Banquet, Nov 25, 1968 .... **15.00**
Nodder, 6½″ h, L A Rams, composition, 1961 .... **55.00**
Pennant, 30″ l, New York Jets, felt, white design and inscriptions, green ground, late 1960s **25.00**

Golf

Ashtray, 5½″ w, porcelain, diamond shape, golf scene, sgd "Brown," c1920 .... **150.00**
Game, Tom Thumb's Hole Golf Game, Transogram, 1954, orig box **35.00**
Golf Bag Tag, 2⅛″ l, Wolferts Roost Country Club, celluloid, black lettering, red ground, 1920–30 .... **15.00**
Ice Cream Mold, boy swinging golf club, pewter, 1900s **145.00**
Plate, All Fools Are Not Knaves But All Knaves Are Fools, showing golfers, Royal Doulton **395.00**
Tin, 7¼ × 5½″, Colonel Rubber-Cored Golf Balls, Mungo Manufacturing Co, Govan Scotland, c1909 **500.00**

Horse Racing

Cigarette lighter, Kentucky Derby, silver-colored metal, flip top, 1955 .... **125.00**
Glass, 5¼″ h, 1964 Kentucky Derby, frosted, brown horse's head, gold inscription "Kentucky Derby/ Churchill Downs," reverse with white lettering listing winners from 1875 to 1963 .... **30.00**
Nodder, 6½″ h, Shenandoah Downs jockey, composition, gold paper sticker, 1962 copyright, Japan **50.00**

Hunting

Book
  Connett, Eugene V, III, *Duck Shooting Along the Atlantic Flyway*, NY, 1947, deluxe limited edition of 149, sgd **1,000.00**
  Curtis, Paul A, *Sportsmen All*, Derrydale Press, 1938, limited edition of 950 .... **150.00**
  Gasque, Jim, *Hunting & Fishing in the Great Smokies*, Borzo/Knopf, 1948, chipped dj **50.00**
Calendar, 1891, young girl dressed for hunt surrounded by hounds, Union Metallic Cartridge Co **750.00**
Guide's License, New Brunswick, 1971 .... **40.00**
License
  New Jersey, 1938 .... **42.50**
  Wisconsin, 1930 .... **35.00**
Painting, 28 × 21″, oil on board, dead ducks, sgd "Tony Dury, 28 Church St, Liverpool," 19th C **2,415.00**
Postcard, Iver Johnson factory, full color **15.00**

Yachting

Brochure, Cruising with Safety, 1947, 76 pgs, sailboat and motorboat photos, glossy stiff covs **10.00**
Cigar Label, 5″ sq, Cutter Cigars, sailing yacht flying US flag, 1887 .... **32.00**
Game, 19⅝″ w, 10⅜″ d, 1″ h, The Newport Yacht Race, An Exciting Game, McLoughlin Bros, 1891, instructions inside cov, race course on box bottom, teetotum, two yacks, some damage to box **490.00**

Painting, 12 × 16¼", oil on canvas, Yacht Race, James
Edward Buttersworth, 1817–94 ....29,900.00

STAFFORDSHIRE, HISTORICAL

History: The Staffordshire district of England is the center of the
English pottery industry. There were 80 different potteries oper-
ating there in 1786, with the number increasing to 179 by 1802.
The district includes Burslem, Cobridge, Etruria, Fenton, Foley,
Hanley, Lane, Lane End, Longport, Shelton, Stoke, and Tunstall.
Among the many famous potters were Adams, Davenport, Spode,
Stevenson, Wedgwood, and Wood.

References: David and Linda Arman, *Historical Staffordshire*
(1974) and First Supplement (1977), published by authors, out of
print; Susan and Al Bagdade, *Warman's English & Continental
Pottery & Porcelain,* Second Edition, Wallace-Homestead, 1991;
A. W. Coysh and R. K. Henrywood, *The Dictionary of Blue and
White Printed Pottery* (1982), Vol. II (1989), Antique Collectors'
Club; Mary J. Finegan, *Johnson Brothers Dinnerware,* published
by author, 1993; Jeffrey B. Snyder, *Historical Staffordshire,* Schiffer
Publishing, 1995.

Museum: Hershey Museum, Hershey, PA.

Notes: The view is the most critical element when establishing
the value of historical Staffordshire; American collectors pay much
less for non-American views. Dark blue pieces are favored; light
views continue to remain under-priced. Among the forms, soup
tureens have shown the largest price increases.

Prices listed below are for mint examples. Reduce prices by
20 percent for a hidden chip, a faint hairline, or an invisible
professional repair; by 35 percent for knife marks through the
glaze and a visible professional repair; by 50 percent for worn
glaze and major repairs.

The numbers in parentheses refer to items in the Armans'
books, which constitute the most detailed list of American historical views and their forms.

W. ADAMS & SONS   ADAMS

Adams

The Adams family has been associated with ceramics since the
mid-17th century. In 1802 William Adams of Stoke-on-Trent produced American views. In 1819 a fourth William Adams, son of
William of Stoke, became a partner with his father and was later
joined by his three brothers. The firm became William Adams &
Sons. The father died in 1829 and William, the eldest son, became
manager.

The company operated four potteries at Stoke and one at Tunstall. Between 1830 and 1840 American views in black, light blue,
sepia, pink, and green were produced at Tunstall. William Adams

died in 1865 and all operations were moved to Tunstall. The firm
continues today under the name of Wm. Adams & Sons, Ltd.
Hudson River Series
  Fair Mount, 4" d cup plate, pink (459) **90.00**
  Fort Edwards, Hudson River, 5¼" d plate, pink (460) **65.00**
Log Cabin, medallions of Gen Harrison on border, waste
  bowl, brown (458) **265.00**
US Views, Catskill Mountain House, 10½" d soup plate,
  light blue (445) **85.00**

Clews

From sketchy historical accounts that are available, it appears
that James Clews took over the closed plant of A. Stevenson in
1819. His brother Ralph entered the business later. The firm continued until about 1836 when James Clews came to America to
enter the pottery business at Troy, Indiana. The venture was a
failure because of the lack of skilled workmen and the proper type
of clay. James Clews returned to England but did not re-enter the
pottery business.

America and Independence, States border, three-story
  building with deer on front lawn
  Plate
    6¾" d, blue and white **300.00**
    8⅜" d, dark blue, wear, pinpoints, and chips on
      back of rim **175.00**
    10⅝" d, dark blue, minor wear and scratches ... **315.00**
  Platter, 12⅞" l, dark blue transfer, wear, pinpoints,
    and chip on back rim **770.00**

Clews, plate, Christmas Eve, dark blue transfer, imp mark,
6¾" d, $175.00.

American Eagle on an Urn, salt shaker, 4½" d, h, urn
  shape, dark blue, hidden underside chip, rim flake . **500.00**
Coronation pattern, 6½" h, milk pitcher, marked "Clews
  Warranted Ironstone," rim and handle glaze chip .. **325.00**
Landing of Lafayette
  Plate
    6¾" d, blue and white **100.00**
    10" d, dark blue, wear, scratches **315.00**

10¼" d, dark blue, imp mark, minor wear **330.00**
Soup Plate, 9⅞" d, dark blue, rim chip **275.00**
Picturesque Views Series
  Hudson, Hudson River, 10½" d, soup plate, brown
    (107) **65.00**
  Near Hudson, Hudson River, 7" d plate, brown (113) **65.00**
States of American and Independence Series, dark blue
  Building, sheep on lawn, 8⅞" d plate **250.00**
  Mansion, circular drive, vegetable dish (14) **800.00**
  University Building, six chimneys, two people and
    eight sheep, 8½" d plate **265.00**

J. & J. Jackson   J&J. JACKSON

Job and John Jackson began operations at the Churchyard Works, Burslem, about 1830. The works had previously been owned by the Wedgwood family. The Jackson firm produced transfer scenes in a variety of colors, such as black, light blue, pink, sepia, green, maroon, and mulberry. Over 40 different views of Connecticut, Massachusetts, Pennsylvania, New York, and Ohio were issued. The firm is believed to have closed about 1844.

Beauties of America series
  Library, Philadelphia, 8¼" d plate, floral border, blue
    and white **200.00**

Jackson, plate, American Scenery series, Fort Conanicut, RI, 7", $80.00.

The Water Works of Philadelphia, 7½" d plate, black
  and white **110.00**
Dumb Asylum, 8½" d plate, blue and white **160.00**
Girard's Bank, Philadelphia, 6¼" d plate, one green, one
  black, two mulberry, price for 4 pcs **350.00**

Job and John Jackson, plate, View of the Canal, Little Falls, Mohawk River, black transfer, scalloped edges, c1830, 10½" d, $125.00.

The Race Bridge, Philadelphia, 9" d plate, black **100.00**
Upper Ferry Bridge, etc, Philadelphia, 9¾" l platter, red
  and white **500.00**
Water Works, Philadelphia, oak leaf and acorn border,
  10" d plate, blue and white **600.00**

Thomas Mayer

In 1829 Thomas Mayer and his brothers, John and Joshua, purchased Stubbs's Dale Hall Works of Burslem. They continued to produce a superior grade of ceramics.

Arms of States Series, dark blue
  Arms of Georgia, 11¾" l vegetable dish (500) **3,000.00**
  Arms of New York, 10" d soup plate, wear, shallow
    rim flakes, pinpoints on table ring **635.00**
  Arms of South Carolina, 4" d cup plate, unmarked . **700.00**
Lafayette at Washington's Tomb, sugar bowl, cov, dark
  blue (511) **750.00**

Rural Scenery
J&WR
JOHN & WILLIAM RIDGWAY · c1814 1830

J.W.R.
Stone China

W. RIDGWAY

J. & W. Ridgway and William Ridgway & Co.

John and William Ridgway, sons of Job Ridgway and nephews of George Ridgway who owned Bell Bank Works and Cauldon Place Works, produced the popular Beauties of America series at the Cauldon plant. The partnership between the two brothers was dissolved in 1830. John remained at Cauldon.

William managed the Bell Bank Works until 1854. Two additional series were produced based upon the etchings of Bartlett's American Scenery. The first series had various borders including narrow lace. The second series is known as Catskill Moss.

Beauties of America is dark blue. The other series are found in light transfer colors of blue, pink, brown, black, and green.

Beauties of America Series, dark blue
  Almshouse, New York, 16" l, platter (255) **625.00**
  Exchange Building, Baltimore, cup plate (254) **450.00**
  Octagon Church, Boston, 10" d soup plate (A-271) . **275.00**
  Pennsylvania Hospital, Philadelphia, 18½" octagonal
    platter **1,400.00**
  Straughton's Church, Philadelphia, 8¼" d soup plate,
    price for pr **350.00**
Catskill Moss
  Fairmount Gardens, 9" d plate, 1844 .... **90.00**
  Kosciusko's Tomb, 10" d soup plate (305) **75.00**
  Meredith, 9½" d plate (307) **65.00**

College Series

Portions of a View, 6" l gravy ladle, dark blue, repairs
to handle 325.00
Trinity Hall, Cambridge, 6¼" h, 8¼" w, gravy tureen
and cov, dark blue, underglaze mark, emb handles, floral finial 600.00

Rogers   ROGERS

John Rogers and his brother George established a pottery near
Longport in 1782. After George's death in 1815, John's son Spencer became a partner, and the firm operated under the name of
John Rogers & Sons. John died in 1916. His son continued the use
the same name until he dissolved the pottery in 1842.

Boston Harbor, dark blue (441)
Cup and Saucer 650.00
Sugar Bowl 675.00
Boston State House, dark blue (442)
Plate, 10" d 150.00
Platter, 14" l 495.00

R.S.W.

Stevenson

As early as the 17th century the name Stevenson has been
associated with the pottery industry. Andrew Stevenson of Cobridge introduced American scenes with the flower and scroll border. Ralph Stevenson, also of Cobridge, used a vine and leaf
border on his dark blue historical views and a lace border on his
series in light transfers.

The initials R. S. & W. on pieces with the acorn and leaf border
indicate that Ralph Stevenson and Williams were associated with
this design. It has been reported that Williams was Ralph's New
York agent and the wares were produced by Ralph alone.

Acorn and Oak Leaves Border, dark blue
Baltimore Exchange, 5½" d plate (348) 775.00
Harvard College, 8⅜" d plate 295.00
Park Theater, New York, 10" d plate (357) 185.00
Floral and Scroll Border, dark blue
City Hall, New York, 7" d plate (397) 1,200.00
New York from Brooklyn Heights, 10¼" d plate 995.00
Lace Border
Erie Canal at Buffalo, 10" d soup plate (386) 195.00
New Orleans, cup and saucer (387) 150.00
Vine Border
Capitol, Washington, 10" d soup plate (370) 425.00
Pennsylvania Hospital, int. with flowers and Charles-
ton Exchange, leaf-molded corners, base corners
with carved feet, 9¼" sq, 5½" h, base incorrectly
painted New York Battery, imp "Stevenson," clo-
verleaf Ralph Stevenson mark, blue and white ..7,000.00

Stubbs   STUBBS

In 1790 Stubbs established a pottery works at Burslem, England. He operated it until 1829 when he retired and sold the
pottery to the Mayer brothers. He probably produced his American views about 1825. Many of his pieces showed scenes of
Boston, New York, New Jersey, and Philadelphia.

Birds and Fruit, 9¼" h, 14" w, soup tureen, dark blue,
large shell emb scroll handles, four paw feet, replaced
floral finial, restoration to lid 1,300.00
Spread Eagle Border, dark blue
Bank of the United States, Philadelphia, plate 700.00
Fairmount Near Philadelphia
Plate, 10¼" d, medium blue 165.00
Platter, 20½" l 1,750.00
Soup Plate, 9¾" d 150.00
Mendenhall Ferry, blue and white
Plate, set of 3, 4½" d, 5¼" d, 5½" d, price for set 1,050.00
Platter, 16½" 1,000.00
Upper Ferry Bridge over the River Schuylkill
Plate, 8¾" d 160.00
Platter, 18½" l 1,350.00
Sauce Tureen, underplate, oval 275.00
Vegetable Dish, oval, open, 9⅛" l, brown and
white 575.00
Woodlands Near Philadelphia, platter, 10⅝" l 650.00

**John Stubbs, dinner plate, Fairmount Near Phil-
adelphia, blue, 10¼", $225.00.**

Unknown Makers

Boston State House/City Hall New York, 6⅞" h pitcher,
medium blue, small chips, hairlines in base 415.00
City Hall New York, 9¾" d plate, medium blue, minor
scratches 150.00

Unknown Maker, pitcher, DeWitt Clinton Eulogy and Utica inscription, dark blue, 6½" h, $1,150.00.

Dam and Waterworks, Philadelphia, 10" d plate, floral and fruit border, blue and white 575.00
Dongington Park, 4¼ × 3¼" platter, blue and white transfer, center building, flower border, hairline crack on back 125.00
Lampton Hall, Durham, 6¾" h pitcher, dark blue transfer, rim chips, hairline in base of handle 275.00
Mount Vernon, Washington's Seat, 6¾" h pitcher, dark blue, Clews-type shape, foil label from Richards Collections 1,800.00
Ship of the Line in the Downs, 9⅝" l, cov vegetable dish, mismatched cov with vintage border, transfer city scene mostly obscured by rose handle, short hairline on lid, pinpoint flakes 910.00
United Sates Hotel, Philadelphia, 10¼" d soup plate, blue and white 625.00
War of 1812, 4½" shaped pitcher, buff ground, black transfer, The United States and Macedonian/The Enterprise and Boxer, transfers marked "Bently, Wear, and Bourne Engravers & Printers, Shelton, Staffordshire," pink luster bands and highlights, pinpoint flake on tip of spout, large base spider 1,500.00

Wood

Enoch Wood, sometimes referred to as the father of English pottery, began operating a pottery at Fountain Place, Burslem, in 1783. A cousin, Ralph Wood, was associated with him. In 1790 James Caldwell became a partner and the firm was known as Wood and Caldwell. In 1819 Wood and his sons took full control.

Enoch died in 1840. His sons continued under the name of Enoch Wood & Sons. The American views were first made in the mid-1820s and production continued through the 1840s. The establishment was sold to Messrs. Pinder, Bourne & Hope in 1846.

It is reported that the pottery produced more signed historical

views than any other Staffordshire firm. Many of the views attributed to unknown makers probably came from the Woods'. Marks vary, although the name "Wood" is always included.

Catskill Mountains, Pine Orchard House, 9⅜" d soup plate, dark blue, minor wear, light scratches 525.00
Celtic China, Buffalo on Lake Erie, vegetable dish (236) 295.00
Floral Border, dark blue
   Commodore MacDonnough's Victory (154)
      Cream Pitcher, 3½" h, barrel shape 1,850.00
      Plate
         7½" d, shell border 180.00
         10¼" d, rim glaze flakes 360.00
   Dumb Asylum, 8½" d plate 95.00
   Landing of the Pilgrims, Landing of the Fathers, 10" d plate, medium blue (218), price for pr 275.00
   Marine Hospital, Louisville, Kentucky, 9¼" d plate, dark blue, wear, pinpoint flakes, rim chip on back 315.00
   Mill and Millrace, 9" d plate, blue and white 95.00
   Passaic Falls, State of New Jersey base, Hudson River cov, gravy tureen, 6⅜" h, 8" w, dark blue, underglaze mark, deep blue acanthus handles, rose finial, shallow flake 950.00
Fruit Border
   Fairmount Water Works on the Schuylkill, 9¼" d plate, black and white, price for pr 325.00
   Transylvania University, Lexington, 9½" d plate, dark blue, wear, light scratches 360.00
Highlands, Hudson River, steamboat, 12½" d platter, blue and white 1,650.00
Lafayette at the Tomb of Franklin, washstand bowl, 12" d, bottom imp "Wood" 1,250.00
Shell Border
   Pass in the Catskills, 8" w gravy tureen under tray, dark blue, underglaze mark 850.00
   Union Line, 10¼" d plate, blue and white 350.00
   View Near Philadelphia, 9¾" d plate, blue and white 310.00

Enoch Wood, teabowl and saucer, sea urchins and flowers, dark blue transfers, c1825, 3¾" h bowl, 5⅝" d saucer, $175.00.

STAFFORDSHIRE ITEMS

History: A wide variety of ornamental pottery items originated in England's Staffordshire district, beginning in the 17th century and still continuing today. The height of production took place from 1820 to 1890.

These naive pieces are considered folk art by many collectors. Most items were not made carefully; some even were made and decorated by children.

The types of objects are varied, e.g., animals, cottages, and figurines (chimney ornaments).

References: Susan and Al Bagdade, *Warman's English & Continental Pottery & Porcelain,* Second Edition, Wallace-Homestead, 1991; Pat Halfpenny, *English Earthenware Figures,* Antique Collectors' Club, 1992; P. D. Gordon Pugh, *Staffordshire Portrait Figures of the Victorian Era,* Antique Collectors' Club, 1987; Dennis G. Rice, *English Porcelain Animals of the 19th Century,* Antique Collectors' Club, 1989.

REPRODUCTION ALERT

Early Staffordshire figurines and hollowware forms were molded. Later examples were made using a slip-casting process. Slip casting leaves telltale signs that are easy to spot. Look in the interior. Hand molding created a smooth interior surface. Slip casting produces indentations that conform to the exterior design. Holes occur where handles meet the body of slip-cast pieces. There is not hole in a hand-molded piece.

A checkpoint on figurines is the firing or vent hole, which is a necessary feature on these forms. Early figurines had small holes; modern reproductions feature large holes often the size of a dime or quarter. Vent holes are found on the sides or hidden among the decoration in early Staffordshire figurines; most modern reproductions have them in the base.

These same tips can be used to spot modern reproductions of Flow Blue, Majolica, Old Sleepy Eye, Stoneware, Willow, and other ceramic pieces.

Note: The key to price is age and condition. As a general rule, the older the piece, the higher the price.

Bowl, 8½" d, 3¾" h, green transfer scenes, The Sailor's Farewell/Return, polychrome enamel, pink luster, wear and crazing **145.00**
Chimney Piece, 9" h, Rebecca at the Well, polychrome and gilt, minor flaking and crazing **175.00**
Chop Plate, 12" d, Neplus, blue-green transfer print ... **40.00**
Cup and Saucer, handleless
  Man sowing seeds, red transfer, imp "Adams," small flakes, price for 6-pc set **365.00**
  The Residence of the late Richard Jordan, New Jersey, black transfer, minor stains, pinpoint flakes **275.00**
  Vase of flowers and bird, medium blue, chips on cup rim **105.00**
Dog
  9½" h, 5" d, white, copper luster spots and chain .. **225.00**
  10" h, seated, black and white, polychrome and gilt, wear, price for married pr **440.00**

13" h, seated, white, red and polychrome dec, one is cracked, price for pr **495.00**
15" h, white, worn gilt, black and yellow enameling, price for pr **475.00**
Figure
  9½" h, mid 19th C American naval officer, leaning against pink plinth with emb relief of three white and gold American eagles, black, yellow, gold, pink, ochre, flesh, and brown, meandering hairline on side of base, unrecorded **1,200.00**
  13" h, lions, standing, two-tone brown glaze, glass eyes, price for pr **350.00**
  13" h, 9" d, Tam O'Shanter and Sooter Johnny, white jacket, gold hat and leggings, pink scarf, Johnny with white jacket, green apron, red cap, wooden keg, name in raised gold on base **565.00**
  14¼" h, Benjamin Franklin, emb title on front base, blue coat, black hat and shoes, gold buttons and buckles, flesh, red, brown on face, sprig dec waistcoat, restoration to back of stump **1,100.00**
  14½" h, George Washington, civilian dress, gold, gray, black, brown, red, and flesh-colored enamels **3,500.00**

Figure, girl and boy, green tree, blue, turquoise, rust, and white, maroon base, brown trim on base, c1820, 4¼ × 3 × 8", $695.00.

Fruit Bowl, 10" d, two views of cast-iron bridge over Wear River and two seaman's ditties, int. with five pastoral and hunt scenes, pink luster and enamel color, Morre & Co., c1796, base chips **260.00**
Hen on Nest, 6" h, 5½ × 6¾", white hen, brown basketweave oval base **245.00**
Mug, 4" h, black transfer ship, orange luster and polychrome sailor's lament, frog int., wear, crazing, hairline **165.00**
Pitcher, 5¾" to 6½" h, luster ware, raised figures of deer, hunters and horses, hounds, and dogs, John Rogers & Son, 1814–42, price for 3-pc set **750.00**
Plate, "The Residence of the late Richard Jordan, New Jersey," initials scratched on back
  10⅜" d, red transfer **250.00**
  10½" d
    Black transfer **200.00**
    Dark brown transfer **165.00**
Platter, 15½" l, Italian Lakes, brown transfer print **40.00**
Sugar, cov, 4⅞" h, red, blue, green, and black Gaudy floral dec, small flakes **115.00**
Watch Hutch, 11" h, five figures, flowers, and birds, polychrome and gilt, some crazing and hairlines ... **330.00**

STAFFORDSHIRE, ROMANTIC

History: In the 1830s two factors transformed the blue-and-white printed wares of the Staffordshire potters into what is now called "Romantic Staffordshire." Technical innovations expanded the range of transfer-printed colors to light blue, pink, purple, black, green, and brown. There was also a shift from historical to imaginary scenes with less printed detail and more white space, adding to the pastel effect.

Shapes from the 1830s are predominately rococo with rounded forms, scrolled handles, and floral finials. Over time, patterns and shapes became simpler and the earthenware bodies coarser. The late 1840s and 1850s saw angular gothic shapes and pieces with the weight and texture of ironstone.

The most dramatic post-1870 change was the impact of the craze for all things Japanese. Staffordshire designs adopted zigzag border elements and motifs such as bamboo, fans, and cranes. Brown printing dominated this style, sometimes with polychrome enamel highlights.

Marks: Wares are often marked with pattern or potter's names, but marking was inconsistent and many authentic, unmarked examples exist. The addition of "England" as a country of origin mark in 1891 helps to distinguish 20th-century wares made in the romantic style.

References: Susan and Al Bagdade, *Warman's English & Continental Pottery & Porcelain,* Second Edition, Wallace-Homestead, 1991; Petra Williams, *Staffordshire: Romantic Transfer Patterns* (1978), *Staffordshire II* (1986), Fountain House East.

Spanish Convent, Adams, platter, brown, 9⅛ × 11⅛", $55.00.

Arabesque, gray-blue, Edwards & Son
Creamer	60.00
Gravy Boat	50.00
Relish, small, oblong	35.00
Vegetable Dish, open	45.00
Waste Bowl	40.00

Balantyre, J Alcock
Bowl, 8" d	45.00
Cup Plate	55.00
Creamer	50.00
Plate, 10½" d	35.00
Teapot	195.00

Caledonia, William Adams, c1800–65
Bowl	45.00
Creamer	55.00
Cup and Saucer	45.00
Plate, 8½" d, pink	75.00
Soup Plate, red transfer, 10¾" d, imp "Adams," stains, bruise on table ring	150.00
Sugar, cov	85.00

Canna, platter, red transfer, 18" l, edge wear, minor stains ... **385.00**

Canova, vegetable, cov, red transfer, 12½" l, Mayer, stains, chips ... **225.00**

Etruscan Vase, blue and brown, Thomas, John, Joseph Mayer, c1843–55
Bowl, 7" d	45.00
Plate, 10½" d	55.00
Platter, 16 × 11½"	145.00
Relish, 5" l	45.00
Soup Plate, wide flange	65.00

Garden Scenery, pink, Mayer
Bowl, 4" d	35.00
Cup and Saucer	65.00
Cup Plate	45.00
Plate	55.00
Sauce Dish	35.00
Soup Plate	75.00
Teapot	175.00
Vegetable Bowl, open	85.00

Ivanhoe, Podmore Walker & Co, 1834–1859
Bowl	40.00
Creamer	60.00
Plate	45.00
Sugar, cov	80.00

Oriental, Ridgway, c1830–34
Creamer	75.00
Cup and Saucer, handleless	75.00
Cup Plate	60.00
Plate	85.00
Tureen, cov, octagonal	225.00

Oriental Scene of Pagoda Below Atna on the Ganges, platter, 14½" l, 11¼" w, blue and white, J Hall and Sons ... **375.00**

Priory, Edward Challinor and Co, c1853–1862
Bowl	45.00
Creamer	65.00
Cup and Saucer, handleless	45.00
Plate	55.00
Platter	95.00
Soup Plate	85.00
Toddy Plate, 5" d, light blue	45.00

Royal Cottage, sauce tureen, under plate, 8¾" l, light blue transfer, plain white ladle ... **250.00**

Undina, black and blue, J Clementson, registered Jan 7, 1852
Plate	45.00
Relish, oval, shell shape	65.00
Wash Bowl and Pitcher	295.00

STAINED AND/OR LEADED GLASS PANELS

History: American architects in the second half of the 19th century and the early 20th century used stained- and leaded-glass panels as a chief decorative element. Skilled glass craftsmen assembled the designs, the best known being Louis C. Tiffany.

The panels are held together with soft lead cames or copper wraps. When purchasing a panel, protect your investment by checking the lead and making any necessary repairs.

Periodicals: *Glass Art Magazine,* PO Box 260377, Highlands Ranch, CO 80126; *Glass Patterns Quarterly,* PO Box 131, Westport, NY 40077; *Professional Stained Glass,* PO Box 69, Brewster, NY 10509; *Stained Glass,* 6 SW 2nd St, #7, Lees Summit, MO 64063.

Collectors' Club: Stained Glass Assoc of America, PO Box 22462, Kansas City, MO 64113.

Museum: Corning Museum of Glass, Corning, NY.

Leaded Window
34 × 12", framed stylized sunrise over green landscape, with frame, some cracks to glass **200.00**
36 × 36", blue bunch of grapes, green leaves, blue
scroll, opal red ribbon, amber ground, self frame
of blue panes, orig wooden frame **550.00**
43 × 29", green, red, and blue enameled waterfall,
grassy hill, conifers and blossoming bushes, opal
blue glass sky, American, 20th C **1,200.00**
61" h, 24" w, Arts and Crafts stylized grapevines,
green, dark purple, and brown, green border, clear
ground, several cracks to background on one,
price for pr **1,500.00**
Stained Window
16½ × 14⅛", rect, mosaic, two opposing parrots, irid
colors, exotic leafage ground, c1899 ....**6,500.00**
27" sq, round stained landscape and fruit in foreground, circle border of leaded jewels with stylized leaded fans in corners **1,250.00**
29 × 20", oval, wreath and shield motif with ice-
textured clear glass, deep blue border, brass frame **350.00**

Stained, "Poseidon," Neptune's son, framed, sgd by Israeli artist Al Krotin, c1965, from Daneiger Collection, Chapel Hill, NC, 16 × 17", $225.00.

STANGL POTTERY BIRDS

History: Stangl ceramic birds were produced from 1940 until the Stangl factory closed in 1972. The birds were produced at Stangl's Trenton plant and either decorated there or shipped to their Flemington, New Jersey, outlet for hand painting.

During World War II the demand for these birds, and other types of Stangl pottery as well, was so great that 40 to 60 decorators could not keep up with the demand. Orders were contracted out to be decorated by individuals in their own homes. These orders then were returned for firing and finishing. Colors used to decorate these birds varied according to the artist.

Marks: As many as ten different trademarks were used. Almost every bird is numbered; many are artist signed. However, the signatures are used only for dating purposes and add very little to the value of the birds.

References: Susan and Al Bagdade, *Warman's American Pottery and Porcelain,* Wallace-Homestead, 1994; Harvey Duke, *The Official Identification and Price Guide to Pottery and Porcelain,* Eighth Edition, House of Collectibles, 1995; ———, *Stangl Pottery,* Wallace-Homestead, 1992; Mike Schneider, *Stangl and Pennsbury Birds,* Schiffer Publishing, 1994.

Collectors' Club: Stangl/Fulper Collectors Club, PO Box 64-A, Changewater, NJ 07831.

Additional Listings: See *Warman's Americana & Collectibles* for more examples.

Advisor: Bob Perzel.

Note: Several birds were reissued between 1972 and 1977. These reissues are dated on the bottom and are worth approximately the same as older birds if well decorated.

3250A, Standing duck **100.00**
3250C, Feeding duck, antique gold **50.00**
3273, Rooster, 5¾" **600.00**
3274, Penguin **500.00**
3275, Turkey **450.00**
3276D, pair of Bluebirds **150.00**
3285, 3286, Rooster and Hen shakers, price for pr **90.00**
3285, Rooster egg plate **100.00**
3400, Lovebird
     Revised, leaf base **60.00**
     Old, wavy base **100.00**
3402S, Oriole, 3¼" h orig tag **50.00**
3406, Kingfisher, teal **75.00**
3445, Rooster, gray **225.00**
3446, Hen, yellow **150.00**
3448, Blue-headed Viero **75.00**
3449, Parakeet **150.00**
3458, Quail **1,000.00**
3492, Cock Pheasant **225.00**
3581, Group of Chickadees **200.00**
3584, Cockatoo, large **300.00**
3592, Titmouse **60.00**
3595, Bobolink **125.00**
3596, Gray Cardinal **85.00**
3627, Rivoli Hummingbird with pink flower **150.00**
3635, Group of Goldfinches **175.00**
3715, Blue Jay with peanut **600.00**
3746, Canary with rose flower **225.00**

Cockatoo, #3580, 8⅞" h, $125.00.

3751D, pair of Red-Headed Woodpeckers, red matte .	**350.00**
3754, White-Winged Crossbill, single	**2,500.00**
3754D, pair of White-Winged Crossbills, pink glossy .	**350.00**
3757, Scissor-Tailed Flycatcher	**600.00**
3813, Evening Grosbeak	**125.00**
3848, Golden Crowned Kinglet	**100.00**
3852, Cliff Swallow	**125.00**
3923, Vermilion Flycatcher	**1,200.00**
3925, Magnolia Warbler	**2,000.00**
Stangl Bird Dealer sign	**1,000.00**

STATUES

History: Beginning with primitive cultures, man created statues in the shape of people and animals. During the Middle Ages most works were religious and symbolic in character and form. During the Renaissance the human and secular forms were preferred.

During the 18th and 19th centuries it was fashionable to have statues in the home. Many famous works were copied for use by the general public.

Reference: Lynne and Fritz Weber (eds.), *Jacobsen's Thirteenth Painting and Bronze Price Guide,* Weber Publications, 1994.

Alabaster, 18¼" h, Water Nymph, seated on rock with
mask-head fountain, sgd "G Pochini," Italian, c1880 **1,725.00**
Bronze
  13¾" h, Man Holding a Rooster, silvered, base sgd
    "Etienne Alexandre Stella" **575.00**
  16" h, woman, parcel gilt, bare breasted, standing on
    leopard skin, holding staff, mounted on revolving
    base **1,650.00**
  24⅛" h, L'Armour, rich reddish brown patina, sgd
    "Auguste Moreau Sept" **1,800.00**
  27½" h, classical woman, standing, fastening her
    drapery, brown patina **1,100.00**
  30¾" h, 12" l, Early French Soldier, verdigris high-
    lights, sgd "E. Picault" **950.00**
  31" h, owl, dark brown patina, sgd "J. Moigniez" .. **1,200.00**
  33¾" h, Aurora, Art Nouveau style, holding scarf and
    diaphanous gown, standing in chariot, cupid and
    doves, Auguste Moreau, late 19th C **2,750.00**
  36" h, Oyster Girl, medium brown and greenish pat-
    ina, sgd "E Rousseau," French, 20th C **1,265.00**

36⅛" l, Charmeuse de Pantheres, medium reddish
    brown and dark brown patina, marble pedestal
    base, Albert E Carrier-Belleuse **3,300.00**
Cast Iron, 33½" h, eagle, American, late 19th C **1,400.00**
Ceramic, 24½" h, owl, perched on oak branch, brown,
    green, and yellow polychrome dec, inscribed "Bin-
    ali," imp "Made in Italy" **200.00**
Ivory, 23" h, maiden, wearing ornate robe, holding
    flower basket in left hand, flowering branch in right,
    Chinese **1,850.00**
Limestone, 48" h, Guanyin, standing, wearing flowing
    robe, holding flower in each hand, serene features,
    tiara, Song style, mounted on detachable lotus-petal
    base **6,950.00**
Marble
  17½" h, naked woman, seated on stone wall, long
    flowing hair, vine hair wreath, two babies in lap   **800.00**

Marble, carrara, Cupid and Psyche, from Thurlow Lodge, Menlo Park, $176,500. Photo courtesy of Butterfield & Butterfield.

  35¼" h, Cupid, sgd "A. Bassetti Fec," 1876 .... **3,300.00**
  41" h, mythological Diana Being Birthed from the
    Water, unsigned, well executed, minor roughness,
    3 broken fingers **6,000.00**
Wood, 58" h, Monk, polychrome dec, Southeast Asia . **750.00**

STEIFF

History: Margarete Steiff, GmbH, established in Germany in 1880, is known for very fine-quality stuffed animals and dolls as well as other beautifully made collectible toys. It is still in business, and its products are highly respected.

The company's first products were wool-felt elephants made by Margaret Steiff. In a few years the animal line was expanded to include a donkey, horse, pig, and camel.

By 1903 the company also was producing a jointed mohair teddy bear, whose production dramatically increased to over 970,000 units in 1907. Margarete's nephews took over the company at this point.

Newly designed animals were added: Molly and Bully, the

dogs, and Fluffy, the cat. Pull toys and kites also were produced, as well as larger animals on which children could ride or play.

Marks: The bear's-head label became the symbol for the firm in about 1907, and the famous "Button in the Ear" round, metal trademark was added.

References: Margaret and Gerry Grey, *Teddy Bears,* Running Press, Courage Books, 1994; Margaret Fox Mandel, *Teddy Bears and Steiff Animals,* First Series (1984, 1993 value update), Second Series (1987, 1995 value update), Collector Books; ———, *Teddy Bears, Annalee Animals & Steiff Animals,* Third Series, Collector Books, 1990, 1996 value update; Dana G. Morykan and Harry L. Rinker, *Warman's Country Antiques & Collectibles,* Third Edition, Wallace-Homestead, 1996; Linda Mullins, *Teddy Bear & Friends Price Guide,* Fourth Edition, Hobby House Press, 1993.

Collectors' Clubs: Steiff Club USA, 225 Fifth Ave, Ste 1033, New York, NY 10010; Steiff Collectors Club, PO Box 798, Holland, OH 43528.

Additional Listings: Teddy Bears. See also Stuffed Toys in *Warman's Americana & Collectibles* for more examples.

Notes: Become familiar with genuine Steiff products before purchasing an antique stuffed animal. Plush in old Steiff animals was mohair; trimmings usually were felt or velvet. Unscrupulous individuals have attached the familiar Steiff metal button to animals that are not Steiff.

Bear, 18" l, ride-on type, tan mohair, shoe-button eyes, iron frame, c1908, mouth and fiber damage, ears missing, front wheels damaged **175.00**
Cat, 7" h, plush cotton, green glass eyes, orig red rayon bow, c1930 .... **100.00**
Dachshund, 18" l, black and brown wool, fully jointed, black shoe-button eyes, embroidered nose, mouth and claws, c1930, some fiber loss and repairs **350.00**
Elephant, 17½" l, black button eyes, pull-cord sound box, four wooden wheels, c1920 .... **295.00**
Fish, 11" l, mohair, open felt mouth, large eyes **85.00**
Fox, 10¼" l, 5½" l, mohair, fully jointed, glass eyes, embroidered nose, mouth, and claws, excelsior stuffing, c1913, ear button missing, slight moth damage **435.00**
Lamb, 12½" l, 11⅛" h, curly wool coat, ear button, felt face, ears, and legs, glass eyes, excelsior stuffing, metal frame and wheels, c1913, some moth damage **1,610.00**
Leopard, 15" l, silver button **185.00**
Mickey Mouse, 7" l, velveteen, applied leatherette eyes, painted features, red shorts, yellow gloves, ginger shoes, c1930, ear button, tag, and tail missing **1,150.00**
Monkey, 15" l, faded orange-tan mohair, felt face, hands, and feet, articulated body, button eyes, ear button, wear, moth damage to felt, holes, straw stuffing **220.00**
Owl, 5½" h, mohair, jointed head, green eyes, felt feet and wing tips **85.00**
Pigeon, 9" h, plush white felt tail and wings **100.00**
Rabbit, 5" h, velveteen, ear button, cream with rust markings, black bead eyes, 1908, some pile loss **345.00**
Squirrel, 7½" h, blond mohair, fully jointed, black steel eyes with felt backing, embroidered nose, mouth, and claws, excelsior stuffing, 1920, slight moth damage **425.00**
St Bernard, 9" l, 6" h, pewter ear button, wooden wheels **325.00**
Teddy Bear

4" h, black mohair and glass eyes, orig tags and ear button **175.00**
11" h, blond mohair, fully jointed, ear button, shoe-button eyes, embroidered features and claws, excelsior stuffing, c1906, pile and excelsior loss, pads repaired **575.00**
13" h, blond mohair, fully jointed, ear button, shoe-button eyes, embroidered features and claws, excelsior stuffing, c1906, replaced pads, some pile and stuffing loss **920.00**
15" h, blond mohair, fully jointed, ear button, shoe-button eyes, embroidered features and claws, excelsior stuffing, c1906, nose stitched over black felt, felt pads, excelsior stuffing, moth damage, fiber loss, red felt shoes bled on lower body **280.00**
Tiger, mohair, fully jointed, c1950 .... **175.00**
Wire-Haired Terrier, 21" l, 20¼" h, ride-on type, mohair plush, ear button, glass eyes, steel frame and wheels, moth and fiber loss and damage, non-functioning voice **460.00**

1892 - 1921

STEINS

History: Steins, mugs especially made to hold beer or ale, range in size from the smaller ³/₁₀ and ¼ liter to the larger 1, 1½, 2, 3, 4, and 5 liters, and in rare cases to 8 liters. (A liter is 1.05 liquid quarts.)

Master steins or pouring steins hold 3 to 5 liters and are called krugs. Most steins are fitted with a metal hinged lid with thumb lift. The earthenware character-type steins usually are German in origin.

References: Susan and Al Bagdade, *Warman's English & Continental Pottery & Porcelain,* Second Edition, Wallace-Homestead, 1991; Gary Kirsner, *German Military Steins,* Revised Edition, Glentiques (PO Box 8807, Coral Springs, FL 33075), 1995; ———, *The Mettlach Book,* Third Edition, Glentiques (PO Box 8807, Coral Springs, FL 33075), 1994.

Periodical: *Regimental Quarterly,* PO Box 793, Frederick, MD 21705.

Collectors' Clubs: Stein Collectors International, PO Box 5005, Laurel, MD 20726; Sun Steiners, PO Box 11782, Fort Lauderdale, FL 33339.

Anheuser Busch, Ceramarte, color
  Half Liter
    City series, Stuttgart **350.00**

Grant's Farm, "A" and eagle on top **115.00**
Liter, Pilique **990.00**
Brewery, stoneware, matching relief pewter lid with
brewery logo
   Half Liter, transfer and enamel dec, Joh Humbser
   Furth Bayern, in remembrance of July 31, 1912 . **345.00**
   Liter, engraved, Augustiner Brau, Munchen, lid
   slightly dented **375.00**
Capo-di-Monte, 8¼" h, painted pottery, lion finial, body
with continuous hunt scene, late 19th C **345.00**
Character, half liter
   Porcelain
      Indian, E Bohne & Sohne, inlaid lid, chips on
      feathers **340.00**
      Munich child on barrel, Schierholz, porcelain lid,
      5" h **395.00**
      Skull, E Bohne & Sohne, inlaid lid **465.00**
      Von Motlke, tan, brown, Schierholz **1,250.00**
   Pottery, black man in white striped jacket, glazed
   finish No. 138, inlaid lid **445.00**
Glass, blown, third liter, beige, enameled cavalier,
matching glass inlaid lid **215.00**
Hauber and Reuther, half liter, pottery, etched, No. 417,
Lohengrin's arrival, relief pewter lid of lady in gown
with shield, shallow chip on base **310.00**
Marzi & Remy, pottery, half liter, No. 1635, hunting
scene, etched scene, inlaid lid, c1900 .... **250.00**
Mettlach
   No. 1526, half liter, PUG, John C White successor to
   White & Krafts, Maltsters, Buffalo, NY, woman on
   one wide with factory scene on other, pewter lid **575.00**

Mettlach, #2065, 1½ L, etched, multi-colored, jeweled base, sgd "Schlitt," $1,100.00.

No. 1526-1108, half liter, PUG, H Schlitt, festive
   scene with Bock in center, relief pewter lid of bar-
   maid and target, int. stained **220.00**
No. 2028, liter, etched, Gasthaus scene, inlaid lid,
   large dwarf thumblift **615.00**
No. 2091, half liter, H Schlitt, St Florian extinguishing
   fire, orig pewter lid **640.00**
No. 2778, half liter, etched, H Slitt, carnival scene,
   inlaid lid **1,375.00**

No. 2833 B, half liter, etched, man sitting under tree,
   inlaid lid **400.00**
No. 2957, half liter, etched, bowling scene, inlaid
   lid **450.00**
No. 3135, half liter, etched, American eagle and
   flags, inlaid lid of American shield **1,155.00**
Military, half liter, stoneware, transfer and enamel dec,
8 Bavarian Infantry, Munchen, center scene, pewter
lid with relief initials on top, large lion thumb lift .. **350.00**
Musterschutz , 7" h, porcelain, pig form, German **475.00**
Occupation, half liter, porcelain, transfer and enamel
dec
   Coach Driver, named to Diermeier, large scene of
   horses pulling coach, pewter lid, pewter tear and
   repair, base chip repaired **565.00**
   Farming, named to Josef Fusseder, central scene,
   pewter lid **480.00**
   Jockey, relief pewter lid of horse jumping stone wall
   with jockey, scratches on handle, base and pewter
   strap **440.00**
Pottery, liter, transfer and enameled, Remembering the
First Year of the Pension Fund for the Munich Streetcar Drivers Oct 19, 1892, elaborate scene of horse-
drawn streetcar, pewter lid **425.00**
Regimental, half liter
   9½" h
      Porcelain, 1 Chevauleger, Nurnberg 1904–07,
      named to Chevauleger Fischer, two side
      scenes, roster, lion thumb lift, prism inlaid lid
      with scene of Chevauleger painted on under-
      side, strap repoured, base chip repaired **580.00**
      Stoneware, 15 Infantry, Neuburg 1912–14, in re-
      membrance of military bakery in Munchen
      1913/14, named to Hans Leikauf, four side
      scenes including two at bakery, roster, lion
      thumb lift, screw off lid to reveal prism, screw-
      off lid missing **810.00**
   10½" h, porcelain, 171 Infantry, Ludwigsburg, named
   to Musketier, name removed, pewter lid **200.00**
   11" h, porcelain, 22 Infantry, Zweibrucken 1902–04,
   named to Res. Conrad, two side scenes, roster,
   lion thumb lift **465.00**
   12" h, porcelain
      11 Field Artillery, Cassel 1909–11, named to Res.
      Grube, four side scenes, roster, eagle thumb lift **525.00**
      23 Infantry, Saargemund 1909–11, named to Res.
      Schwarz, two side scenes, roster, lion thumb
      lift with stanhope, wear on roster **415.00**
   12¼" h, pottery, 118 Infantry, Worms 1909–11,
   named to Res. Wolf, four side scenes, roster, lion
   thumb lift, wear on roster **320.00**
Schutzen, half liter, stoneware, transfer and enamel dec,
center scene of target with crossed weapons, male
and female with weapon and target on either side,
pewter lid **415.00**
Stoneware, liter, transfer and enameled dec
   Leib Rgt Vereinigun Muncheon 1907, presentation
   on lid to military serviceman stationed in
   Munchen **580.00**
   People walking to have steins filled, pewter lid with
   relief design around edge **375.00**
Ringer, Franz

American Soc of Mechanical Engineers, Munchen, July 7, 1913, relief pewter lid with logo **465.00**
100 Anniv Oktoberfest, Muncheon, 1810–1910, relief pewter lid of Munchen **1,510.00**
13 German Turnfes Munchen, 1923, pewter lid, old pewter tear repaired **580.00**
Wood, 1½ liter, oak, barrel shape, metal binding, wooden handle and lid **115.00**

STEUBEN GLASS

1903–32

History: Frederick Carder, an Englishman, and Thomas G. Hawkes of Corning, New York, established the Steuben Glass Works in 1904. In 1918 the Corning Glass Company purchased the Steuben company. Carder remained with the firm and designed many of the pieces bearing the Steuben mark. Probably the most widely recognized wares are Aurene, Verre De Soie, and Rosaline, but many other types were produced.

The firm is still operating, producing glass of exceptional quality.

References: Paul Gardner, *The Glass of Frederick Carder,* Crown Publishers, 1971; Paul Perrot, Paul Gardner, and James S. Plaut, *Steuben,* Praeger Publishers, 1974; Ellen T. Schroy, *Warman's Glass,* Second Edition, Wallace-Homestead, 1995; Kenneth Wilson, *American Glass 1760–1930,* 2 vols., Hudson Hills Press and The Toledo Museum of Art, 1994.

Museums: Corning Museum of Glass, Corning, NY; Rockwell Museum, Corning, NY.

Aurene

AURENE

Bowl
5½" d, 2½" h, gold Aurene calcite, wide rolled stretched rim, green and red irid **550.00**

Vase, Ivorine, flared flattened oval body, ten rib design, irid white Aurene, partial paper label on base, 9½" h, 10½" w, $500.00. Photograph courtesy of Skinner, Inc.

10" d, gold **400.00**
Candlesticks, pr, 10" h, bluish-gold, twisted stem, sgd . **950.00**
Compote, 7¼" d, 3¼" h, gold Aurene calcite, stretched rolled rim **575.00**
Lamp, 27" h, 6" d gold melon-ribbed body, ormolu mounts, black marble base **575.00**
Lemonade, 6½" h, gold, handle, circular foot **175.00**
Nut Dish, 3¼" d, gold, marked "Steuben Aurene 465" **185.00**
Perfume, melon ribbed, gold, matching stopper **225.00**
Salt, gold, #2611 .... **175.00**
Urn, 5" h, gold, sgd **375.00**
Vase
6½" h, blue, sgd **450.00**
10" h, stick, gold, blue highlights, sgd and numbered **400.00**
10¼" h, flared, ftd, blue, silver paper label **725.00**

Calcite

Bowl
6" d, 2⅝" h, wide flared rim, gold Aurene int., unmarked **220.00**
13¾" d, 3½" h, gold Aurene int., unmarked **250.00**
Parfait, gold, matching underplate **165.00**
Sherbet, gold, matching underplate **155.00**
Salt, 2⅝" d **85.00**

Grotesque

Bowl
10" d, #7535, ivorene **350.00**
12" d, #7535, ivory **260.00**
Vase, 11" h
Amethyst top shading to clear, #7090, c1920 ..... **525.00**
Ivory **300.00**

Jade

Bowl, 12" d, #3200 .... **150.00**
Compote, 6" d, 3½" h, green bowl, alabaster stem and base **125.00**
Iced Tea Glass, 6" h, translucent white handle **140.00**
Vase, 6" d, green **350.00**
Wine, 7¼" h, alabaster twist stem **110.00**

Miscellaneous

Bonbon, 2½" h, blue, amber pedestal foot, sgd **75.00**
Bowl, cov, 6½" h, colorless, ram's-head finial **250.00**
Candlestick, 14" h, teardrop vase shaft, bell-form base **275.00**
Console Bowl, 13" d, Bristol Yellow, rolled edge, optic design, crystal foot, sgd **125.00**
Console Set, 12" h candlesticks, matching bowl, applied blue rim, flower prunts, applied blue rings on bowl, Venetian style, sgd **1,800.00**
Creamer and Sugar, Celeste Blue, applied amethyst handles, pr **395.00**
Dessert Plate, 8½" d, Oriental Poppy **150.00**
Luncheon Plate, Cerise Ruby, swirled edge, sgd **50.00**
Perfume, opal, light blue stopper, #5203 .... **700.00**
Salt, 2⅜" d, clear, blue threading **85.00**
Vase
4½" h, Oriental Poppy **1,200.00**

8" h, acid cutback, green jade cut to alabaster, Matzu
   pattern 1,200.00
10" h, cylindrical, Verre de Soie 95.00

Pomona Green

Compote, 7" h, twisted hollow stem, applied glass
   prunts, price for pr 350.00
Console Bowl, 11" d, #3261 .... 50.00
Window Box, 9" rect, #6199, amber crackle glass,
   lion's-head medallions 175.00

Rosaline

Boullion Cup and Saucer, alabaster handles 150.00
Compote, 8" d, alabaster stem and foot 295.00
Cup and Saucer, alabaster handle 150.00
Goblet, 6" h, flaring rim 135.00
Sherbet, matching underplate 175.00
Vase, 6" h, trumpet, alabaster pedestal foot 195.00

STEVENGRAPHS

History: Thomas Stevens of Coventry, England, first manufactured woven silk designs in 1854. His first bookmark was produced in 1862, followed by the first Stevengraphs, perhaps in 1874, but definitely by 1879 when they were shown at the York Exhibition. The first portrait Stevengraphs (of Disraeli and Gladstone) were produced in 1886, and the first postcards incorporating the woven silk panels in 1904. Stevens offered many other items with silk panels, including valentines, fans, pincushions, and needle cases.

Stevengraphs are miniature silk pictures, matted in cardboard, and usually having a trade announcement or label affixed to the reverse. Other companies, notably W. H. Grant of Coventry, copied Stevens's technique. Their efforts should not be confused with Stevengraphs.

Collectors in the U.S. favor the Stevengraphs with American-related views, such as "Signing of the Declaration of Independence," "Columbus Leaving Spain," and "Landing of Columbus." Sports-related Stevengraphs such as "The First Innings" (baseball), and "The First Set" (tennis) are also popular, as well as portraits of Buffalo Bill, President and Mrs. Cleveland, George Washington, and President Harrison.

Postcards with very fancy embossing around the aperture in the mount almost always have Stevens's name printed on them. The two most popular embossed postcard series in the U.S. are "Ships" and "Hands across the Sea." The latter set incorporates two crossed flags and two hands shaking. Seventeen flag combinations have been found, but only seven are common. These series generally are not printed with Stevens's name. Stevens also produced silks that were used in cards made by the Alpha Publishing Co.

Stevens's bookmarks are longer than they are wide, have mitered corners at the bottom, and are finished with a tassel. Many times his silks were used as the top or bottom half of regular bookmarks.

Marks: Thomas Stevens's name appears on the mat of the early Stevengraphs, directly under the silk panel. Many of the later portraits and the larger silks (produced initially for calendars) have no identification on the front of the mat other than the phrase "woven in pure silk" and have no label on the back.

Bookmarks originally had Stevens's name woven into the foldover at the top of the silk, but soon the identification was woven into the fold-under mitered corners. Almost every Stevens' bookmark has such identification, except the ones woven at the World's Columbian Exposition in Chicago, 1892 to 1893.

References: Geoffrey A. Godden, *Stevengraphs and Other Victorian Silk Pictures,* Associated University Presses, 1971; Chris Radley, *The Woven Silk Postcard,* privately printed, 1978; Austin Sprake, *The Price Guide to Stevengraphs,* Antique Collectors' Club, 1972.

Collectors' Club: Stevengraph Collectors' Assoc, 2829 Arbutus Rd, #2103, Victoria, British Columbia, V8N 5X5, Canada.

Museums: Herbert Art Gallery and Museum, Coventry, England; Paterson Museum, Paterson, NJ.

Note: Prices are for pieces in mint or close-to-mint condition.

Bookmarks

Centennial, USA 1776–1876, General George Washington, The Father of Our Country, The First in Peace, The First in War, The First in the Hearts of Our Countrymen!, few small stains 125.00
General George Washington, The Father of Our Country, The First in Peace, The First in War, The First in the Hearts of Our Countrymen!, water damage to 1" upper piece 70.00
I Wish You a Happy New Year, small stain at bottom . 50.00
I Wish You a Merry Christmas and a Happy New Year 65.00
Jesus Behold the Man, He was despised and rejected of men; a man of sorrows, and acquainted with grief . 75.00
To My Favorite, I had a little pony his name was dapple grey. I lent him to a lady to ride a mile away. She whipped him and she slashed him, she led him through the mires. I would not lend my pony for all that lady's hire 65.00
To One I Love, Love me little, love me long is the burden of my song, Love that is too hot and strong, burneth soon to waste, Still I would not have thee cold, not too backward or too bold; Love that lasteth till this old fadeth not in haste 65.00

Stevengraph, God Speed the Plough, $250.00.

Stevengraph

Buffalo Bill, Nate Salsbury, Indian Chief, orig mat and frame, 8 × 7"	500.00
Death of Nelson	250.00
Declaration of Independence	375.00
For Life or Death, fire engine rushing to burning house, orig mat and frame	350.00
H M Stanley, famous explorer	300.00
Landing of Columbus	350.00
President Cleveland	365.00
The Water Jump	195.00

19th C

Vase, ftd, blue body, applied amber rim, rigaree and feet, sgd, 6½" w, 7½" h, $325.00.

STEVENS AND WILLIAMS

History: In 1824 Joseph Silvers and Joseph Stevens leased the Moor Lane Glass House at Briar Lea Hill (Brierley Hill), England, from the Honey-Borne family. In 1847 William Stevens and Samuel Cox Williams took over, giving the firm its present name. In 1870 the company moved to its Stourbridge plant. In the 1880s the firm employed such renowned glass artisans as Frederick C. Carder, John Northwood, other Northwood family members, James Hill, and Joshua Hodgetts.

Stevens and Williams made cameo glass. Hodgetts developed a more commercial version using thinner-walled blanks, acid etching, and the engraving wheel. Hodgetts, an amateur botanist, was noted for his brilliant floral designs.

Other glass products and designs manufactured by Stevens and Williams include intaglio ware, Peach Bloom (a form of peachblow), moss agate, threaded ware, "jewell" ware, tapestry ware, and Silveria. Stevens and Williams made glass pieces covering the full range of late Victorian fashion.

After World War I the firm concentrated on refining the production of lead crystal and achieving new glass colors. In 1932 Keith Murray came to Stevens and Williams as a designer. His work stressed the pure nature of the glass form. Murray stayed with Stevens and Williams until World War II and later followed a career in architecture.

Additional Listings: Cameo Glass.

Basket, 5" d, 9" h, creamy opaque, applied green and amber ruffled leaves, applied amber feet and handle, rose pink lining	365.00
Bowl, 7¾" d, 3¾" h, shaded gold to aqua, swirl MOP, ruffled, robin's-egg blue lining, clear leaf-shaped top	925.00
Cruet, 7¾" h, 3¾" d, Arboresque, light blue, opaque white overlay in craquelle-like effect, applied blue handle, orig blue bubble stopper	145.00
Pitcher, 10½" h, applied amber feet and rim, green handle forms green leaves and yellow flower, cranberry overlay, blue int.	650.00
Plate, 5¾" d, ruffled shell shape, swirl satin MOP, pink to green, cream underside	195.00
Rose Bowl, 2¾" h, 5" d underplate, light blue ribbon MOP, light green ribbon MOP lily pad underplate, folded edges	400.00

Sweetmeat Jar, cov, 6" h, 3½" d, cream, opaque, three applied amber and green leaves, pink lining, SP rim, lid and handle	495.00
Tumbler, 3¼" d, 3¾" h, amber, applied amber pear and apple, green leaves, amber branch	225.00
Vase	
3⅞" h, 1½" d, sq, pink overlay, white lining, intaglio cut ferns and flowers, pink opalescent scroll feet	175.00
4¼" h, 2⅛" d, ruffled top, rose pink overlay, white lining, intaglio cut flowers, leaves, and dots, opalescent wafer foot	235.00
5⅛" h, 2¾" h, narrow neck, ruffled top, rose pink overlay, white lining, intaglio cut ferns and flowers, clear wafer foot	250.00
6" h, 7¾" w at flared mouth, twisted form, Silveria, silver foil between clear glass layers, crimson, ruby red, and rosy pink top portion highlights, sky blue and turquoise blue enameled colors on lower portion, streaks and gold blotches throughout, clear green glass entwining vertical ext. lines, sgd "S & W" on pontil mark	3,950.00
7¼" h, Pompeian Swirl, MOP, powder blue body, pink air traps, two ext. flakes	545.00
9" h, 5½" d, deep rose shading to pink, applied cherries, flowers, and vines, rose, amber, yellow, and white	485.00

STICKLEYS

History: There were five Stickley brothers: Albert, Gustav, Leopold, George, and John George. Gustav often is credited with creating the Mission style, a variant of the Arts and Crafts style. Gustav headed Craftsman Furniture, a New York firm, much of whose actual production took place near Syracuse. A characteristic of Gustav's furniture is exposed tenon ends. Gustav published The Craftsman, a magazine espousing his antipathy to machines.

Originally Leopold and Gustav worked together. In 1902 Leopold and John George formed the L. and J. G. Stickley Furniture Company. This firm made Mission-style furniture and cherry and maple early-American style pieces.

George and Albert organized the Stickley Brothers Company, located in Grand Rapids, Michigan.

References: Donald A. Davidoff and Robert L. Zarrow, *Early L. & J. G. Stickley Furniture,* Dover Publications, 1992; *Furniture of the Arts & Crafts Period,* L-W Book Sales, 1992, 1995 value update; Bruce Johnson, *The Official Identification and Price Guide to Arts and Crafts,* Second Edition, House of Collectibles, 1992; *1912 and 1915 Gustav Stickley Furniture Catalogs,* Dover Publications, n.d.; Mary Ann Smith, *Gustav Stickley,* Dover Publications, 1983, 1992 reprint; *Stickley Craftsman Furniture Catalogs,* Dover Publications, n.d.

Periodical: *Arts and Crafts Quarterly,* 9 Main St, Lambertville, NJ 08530.

Collectors' Club: Foundation for the Study of Arts & Crafts Movement, Roycroft Campus, 31 S Grove St, East Aurora, NY 14052.

Museum: Craftsman Farms Foundation, Inc., Morris Plains, NJ.

Book Trough, 30½ × 26 × 12", caned panels, flaring legs, burned-in Stickley Brothers mark, replaced cane to one side, skinned finish **350.00**

Chafing Dish Stand, 26 × 24½ × 20", twelve textured matte green Grueby tiles inset on mortised top, wide medial stretcher ending in keyed through tenons, new medium finish on top and stretcher, orig dark finish on legs, paper label **15,000.00**

Charger, hammered copper, circular
   13" d, recessed center, four lobes around rim, lightened patina, imp "#14" **650.00**
   17" d, recessed center and slightly flaring rim, good orig medium-dark brown patina, die stamped "74" **650.00**

Furniture
  Bookcase
    Gustav Stickley, single door, gallery top, sixteen panes, fixed shelves, bale of pull missing, mint orig dark finish, unmarked, 56 × 36 × 13" ..**2,100.00**
    L and J G Stickley, double door, gallery top, three small panes over two on each door, one fixed and two adjustable shelves, new finish, unmarked, 54 × 48 × 12" **2,100.00**
  Chair
    #348, dining, ladder back, five side and one arm chair, three horizontal back slats, drop-in seats, skinned, orig medium-dark finish, marked, 37½ × 17 × 16", price for 6 pc set **2,100.00**
    #412, paddle arm, long corbels, open arms, loose leather cushion, framed canvas seat foundation, replaced back bar, good new medium-dark finish, remnant of L and J G Stickley "Handcraft" label, 41 × 35 × 38½" **6,250.00**
    #712, swivel office armchair, vertical back slats, corbels, black leather reupholstered spring seat, new finish, L and J G Stickley, unmarked, 39 × 27 × 21" **1,700.00**
  Desk
    Gustav, #709, five drawer, copper hardware, one bale missing, skinned finish, red decal mark, 30 × 48 × 29" **1,100.00**
    Stickley Brothers, two drawers, slatted backsplash, inlaid flowers and medallions on drawer fronts

and back slats, Macmurdo feet, early mark, 46½ × 39 × 27" **2,400.00**

Lamp Table, #544, overhanging top, legs joined by arched cross stretchers, light overcoat on orig medium finish, decal "The Work of L & J G Stickley," 29½" h, 42" d **1,500.00**

Magazine Stand
   #47, tapering sides, four shelves, arched apron, mint orig finish, L and J G Stickley "Handcraft" label, 42 × 18 × 15" **2,100.00**
   #4706, three spindles on each side, four shelves with backsplash, mint orig reddish brown finish, stenciled number and remnant of Stickley Bros paper label **1,700.00**

Morris Chair, #471, flat arm, six long slats under each arm, long corbels, drop-in spring seat, new brown leather, mint orig medium-dark finish, burnt-in "The Work of L & J G Stickley," 41 × 32 × 35" **4,000.00**

Rocker
   #319, open corbels, four horizontal back slats, new caned base, orig dark color, new finish, Gustav Stickley, unmarked, 40½ × 29¼ × 32" **700.00**
   #2603, narrow open arms ending flush with front legs, four horizontal back slats, loose cushion, rope-seat foundation, some cleaning to orig ebonized finish, red decal Gustav Stickley mark under arm, 36 × 25 × 31" **900.00**

Settle, full-sized spindles, orig seat frame, recent dark finish, minor restoration, Gustav Stickley, unmarked, 31 × 87 × 30" **14,000.00**

Sideboard, #814, plate rack, overhanging top, hammered copper strap hinges on two cabinet doors flanking three small drawers over linen drawer, new medium-dark finish, cleaned copper, burnt-in Gustav Stickley mark, 49 × 56 × 22¼" **5,000.00**

Table, #634, dining, split pedestal, four legs jointed to straight center shaft by arched stretchers, three new leaves, new finish, unmarked, attributed to Gustav Stickley, 28½" h, 54" d **3,750.00**

Sideboard, Gustav Stickley, $5,520.00. Photo courtesy of Leslie Hindman Auctioneers.

Trestle Table, scalloped shoe feet, wide medial
    stretcher fastened to legs, keyed through tenons,
    orig reddish-brown finish, gold Charles Stickley
    and Brandt decal, 29 × 48 × 30″ **1,000.00**
Vanity, five drawers, pivoting mirror, orig copper
    hardware, new medium-dark brown finish,
    branded Gustav Stickley mark, 55 × 48 × 22″ .**2,300.00**
Wing Chair, #88, wicker, flat arms, box construction,
    loose cushion seat, unmarked, 39 × 30½ × 30″**1,300.00**
Mug, 5½ × 6½″, hammered copper, rolled rim and large
    handle, lightened patina, imp "25" **225.00**
Shaving Mirror, shoe feet, tapering sides, inverted "V"
    top, orig dark finish, burnt-in Gustav Stickley mark,
    21½ × 23½ × 7″ **1,300.00**
Tray, 24 × 11″, oval, hammered copper, wrought cop-
    per riveted handles, normal wear to orig medium
    brown patina, early imp Gustav Stickley mark **1,300.00**
Vase, 7″ h, 6″ d, double gourd shape, hammered copper,
    incised branch design, small dent in body, orig pat-
    ina, Stickley Bros, imp "21" **400.00**

STIEGEL-TYPE GLASS

History: Baron Henry Stiegel founded America's first flint-glass
factory at Manheim, Pennsylvania, in the 1760s. Although clear
glass was the most common color made, amethyst, blue (cobalt),
and fiery opalescent pieces also are found. Products included
bottles, creamers, flasks, flips, perfumes, salts, tumblers, and whis-
keys. Prosperity was short-lived; Stiegel's extravagant lifestyle
forced the factory to close.

It is very difficult to identify a Stiegel-made item. As a result,
the term "Stiegel-type" is used to identify glass made during the
time period of Stiegel's firm and in the same shapes and colors as
used by that company.

Enamel-decorated ware also is attributed to Stiegel. True Stiegel pieces are rare; an overwhelming majority is of European
origin.

References: Frederick W. Hunter, *Stiegel Glass,* 1950, available
in Dover reprint; Ellen T. Schroy, *Warman's Glass,* Second Edition,
Wallace-Homestead, 1995; Kenneth Wilson, *American Glass
1760–1930,* 2 vols., Hudson Hills Press and The Toledo Museum
of Art, 1994.

Reproduction Alert: Beware of modern reproductions, especially
in enamel wares.

Enameled

Bottle
    4½″ h, rect, colorless, enameled girl and flowers ... **265.00**
    5″ h
        Oval, colorless, enameled deer, flowers, and
            verse, pewter top, dated 1770 .... **625.00**
        Rect, colorless, enameled boy **250.00**
    6¼″ h, octagonal, colorless, enameled reserve of bird
        on each side, pewter top, 18th C **925.00**
Decanter Set, painted heraldic unicorn dec, decanter
    with stopper, twelve glasses, four tumblers, each with
    different painted heraldic dec, Bavarian **1,500.00**
Flip, 3⅞″ h, clear, blown, enameled flower and running
    deer **175.00**

Bottle, red, yellow, blue, and white enameled floral design, pewter rim, 6½″
h, $325.00.

Mug, 3¾″ h, enameled "Forget Me Not," in blue dia-
    mond medallion, forget-me-nots and other flowers,
    "C" handle, ribbed base **150.00**

Etched

Flip
    5½″ h, colorless, etched and ribbed blown **160.00**
    6″ h, colorless, flaring shape, floral and leaf etch ... **170.00**
Mug, 6½″ h, colorless, floral and leaf etch, applied flat
    "C" handle **375.00**
Nursing Bottle, 3⅜″ h, blown half-post type, clear, pon-
    til, bow and leaf dec **195.00**
Tumbler, 3⅝″ h, colorless, etched and ribbed blown,
    early 19th C **130.00**

Other

Baptismal Bowl, 4¼″ h, blue, diamond mold, ftd, base
    repaired **70.00**
Bowl, 3 × 2⅛″, blown mold, Expanded DQ, deep cobalt
    blue, applied foot **1,200.00**
Creamer
    3⅝″ h, blue, diamond mold, loop handle, circular ftd
        base, 18th C **450.00**
    4″ h, blue, diamond mold, applied loop handle, cir-
        cular foot, 18th C **350.00**
Cup, 3″ h, colorless, inverted pear shape, diamond mold,
    circular base **350.00**
Finger Bowl, 4″ d, deep amethyst, diamond mold, 18th/
    19th C, price for 4-pc set **700.00**
Salt, blown mold, Expanded DQ, cobalt blue, ftd **750.00**
Scent Bottle, 2¾″ l, swirled, deep cobalt blue **195.00**
Sugar Bowl
    3¼″ h, blue, circular, rimmed base, 18th C **500.00**
    4½ × 2¾″, blue, diamond mold, ftd, 18th C **625.00**

STONEWARE

History: Made from dense kaolin and commonly salt-glazed,
stonewares were hand-thrown and high-fired to produce a simple,
bold, vitreous pottery. Stoneware crocks, jugs, and jars were made
to store products and fill other utilitarian needs. These intended

purposes dictated shape and design—solid, thick-walled forms with heavy rims, necks, and handles and with little or no embellishment. Any decorations were simple: brushed cobalt oxide, incised, slip trailed, stamped, or tooled.

Stoneware has been made for centuries. Early American settlers imported stoneware items at first. As English and European potters refined their earthenware, colonists began to produce their own wares. Two major North American traditions emerged based only on location or type of clay. North Jersey and parts of New York comprise the first area; the second was eastern Pennsylvania spreading westward and into Maryland, Virginia, and West Virginia. These two distinct geographical boundaries, style of decoration, and shape are discernible factors in classifying and dating early stoneware.

By the late 18th century stoneware was manufactured in all sections of the country. This vigorous industry flourished during the 19th century until glass fruit jars appeared and the use of refrigeration became widespread. By 1910 commercial production of salt-glazed stoneware came to an end.

References: Susan and Al Bagdade, *Warman's American Pottery and Porcelain,* Wallace-Homestead, 1994; Georgeanna H. Greer, *American Stoneware,* Revised Edition, Schiffer Publishing, 1996; William C. Ketchum, Jr., *American Pottery and Porcelain,* 1994; Jim Martin and Bette Cooper, *Monmouth-Western Stoneware,* published by authors, 1983, 1993 value update; Dana G. Morykan and Harry L. Rinker, *Warman's Country Antiques & Collectibles,* Third Edition, Wallace-Homestead, 1996; Don and Carol Raycraft, *Collector's Guide to Country Stoneware & Pottery,* First Series (1985, 1995 value update), Second Series, (1990, 1996 value update), Collector Books; ———, *Stoneware,* Wallace-Homestead, 1995; George Sullivan, *The Official Price Guide to American Stoneware,* House of Collectibles, 1993; Terry G. Taylor and Terry and Kay Lowrance, *Collector's Encyclopedia of Salt Glaze Stoneware,* Collector Books, 1996.

Collectors' Clubs: American Stoneware Assoc, 208 Crescent Ct, Mars, PA 16066; Federation of Historical Bottle Collectors, Inc, 88 Sweetbriar Branch, Longwood, FL 32750.

Museum: Museum of Ceramics at East Liverpool, East Liverpool, OH.

Apple Butter Crock, 1 gal, D Ack, Mooresburg, PA, saltglazed, freehand cobalt blue floral design, rim chip	**330.00**
Batter Jug, cobalt blue quillwork long-tailed bird, imp "4", replaced bail handle, tin lids missing, surface flakes, bottom chips, 9" h	**550.00**
Batter Pail, 1½ gal	
Cowden & Wilcox, Harrisburg, PA, saltglazed, freehand cobalt blue dec, professional repairs to ears	**925.00**
Sipe, Nicholas & Co., Williamsport, PA, saltglazed, freehand cobalt blue all around flower design, rim chips	**1,100.00**
Bowl, 11" d, 4" h, molded shells and foliage scrolls highlighted in cobalt blue, gray ground, molded lip, chips and two short rim hairlines	**85.00**
Butter Crock, cov, applied side handles, brushed cobalt blue dec, small rim flake, 11½" d	**495.00**
Canning Jar, W R F Weimer & Bro, Snydertown, PA, 2 qt, wax seal, simple cobalt blue design	**550.00**
Churn, 19½" h, ovoid, tooled neck and applied shoulder handles, brushed cobalt blue tulips, foliage, and "6," chips	**220.00**

Cooler, handled, cobalt blue rings and vining floral dec, blistered surface, 3 gal, $350.00. Photo courtesy of Arthur Auctioneering.

Cooler	
Harts, Fulton, cobalt blue quillwork, name "D. Perry," flourish, 12" h	**250.00**
Herman, P, Baltimore, saltglazed, freehand cobalt blue stylized floral dec, 2 pc, glued crack, chips	**4,400.00**
Crock, saltglazed, freehand cobalt blue dec	
1 gal	
Dilliner & Co, New Geneva, PA, stenciled design	**165.00**
Fort Edward Pottery Co, bird on branch	**440.00**
L H Yeager & Co, floral design, one handle chipped	**135.00**
Union Pottery, Newark, NJ, J Zipf Prop'r, floral design, rim chips, crack	**125.00**
Whites, Binghamton, NY, large bold floral dec, rim chips and cracks	**325.00**
1½ gal, F Schneider & Sons, Union Hill, NJ, two handles, bird on branch, 11" h, chips and cracks	**110.00**
2 gal	
F H Cowden, Harrisburg, semi-ovoid, grapes, blue at handle, rim chip, stone ping	**275.00**
Haxstun, Ottman & Co, Fort Edward, NY, bird on branch	**385.00**
3 gal	
Jacob Zipf, Union Pottery, Newark, NJ, triple flower design, slight crack	**250.00**
Savage & Rogers, Havana, NY, bold double-flower design	**550.00**
Sugar Valley, PA, stylized fern design, blue at handle, old restoration	**385.00**
T D Metcalf, Sunbury, PA, low, floral dec	**325.00**
4 gal	
A O Whittemore, Havana, NY, house, flag, and pine tree dec, tight crack, 2 rim chips	**7,700.00**
White & Wood, Binghamton, NY, bird on branch, imp label, 11¼" h, hairline, small rim chips	**380.00**
5 gal	
Haxstun, Ottman & Co, Fort Edward, NY, bird, cracked	**190.00**
Williams & Reppert, Greensboro, PA, large cobalt blue stencil and freehand design	**330.00**
6 gal	
Cowden & Wilcox, semi-ovoid, stylized leaf dec, upside-down mark	**1,045.00**
R Jones, Pittston, PA, bird on branch, glued crack	**385.00**
Whites, Utica, NY, large floral dec, cracked, mismatched lid	**250.00**

Crock, H. J. Heinz, 6¼″ d, 5¼″ h, $250.00.

Jar

A Leet, PA, 3 gal, merchant stamp, bold floral design **525.00**

Jas Hamilton & Co, Manufacturers, Greensboro, PA, saltglazed, stenciled mark **125.00**

J Swank & Co, Johnstown, PA, semi-ovoid, simple dec, some blue missing **385.00**

Whites Utica, 2 gal, imp label, cobalt blue quillwork bird on flowering branch, applied shoulder handles, 12″ h **550.00**

Jug, saltglazed, freehand cobalt blue dec

2 qt, H Door, 601 Broadway, Albany, script dec ... **235.00**

1 gal

Cowden & Wilcox, Harrisburg, PA, cluster of cherries, blue at handle, slight kiln burn **700.00**

E Norton & Co, Bennington, VT, bird on branch, spout chip **990.00**

Haidle, Union Pottery, Newark, NJ, flower **220.00**

J Fisher, Lyons, NY, name "Steele" in blue **500.00**

Johnston, Warner & Co Groceries, Wien and Spirit Merchants, 1017 Market St, Philadelphia, blue over white, coggle wheel dec **440.00**

White & Co, Binghamton, NY, large poppy design **275.00**

White & Wood, Binghamton, NY, simple floral design, spout chip **110.00**

2 gal

A J Buttler Manufacturer, New Brunswick, NJ, blue "2" and cobalt blue spots **335.00**

A K Ballard, Burlington, VT, leaf design **100.00**

A O Whittemore, Havana, NY, houseboat design, replaced handle **550.00**

Burger & Lang, Rochester, NY, strong flower design, some damage to dec **275.00**

Cowden & Wilcox, Harrisburg, PA, swan on water, blue at handle **2,860.00**

Hamilton & Jones, Greensboro, PA, simplistic freehand and stencil dec, cracked **335.00**

I Seymour, Troy, NY, polka-dot bird on branch . **800.00**

J M Pruden, Elizabeth, NJ, comb-like dec, chipped handle, some discoloration **125.00**

Julius Norton, Bennington, VT, blue wash through stamp **110.00**

Moore, Nichols & Co., Williamsport, PA, flower with two leaves **550.00**

Moyer, Harrisburg, PA, double floral design **690.00**

N Willard & Co, Wholesale & Retail Dealers In Groceries, Fruit & Provisions at the Red Store, Foot of Main St, Buffalo, ovoid, floral design, imp name **385.00**

Riedinger & Caire, Poughkeepsie, NY, stylized floral dec **235.00**

West Troy Pottery, NY, fantail bird, chipped spout **880.00**

Whites Utica, imp label, cobalt blue slip bird looking backwards, strap handle, 13¾″ h **690.00**

Wm E Warner, West Troy, chicken on table, professional repair, 13½″ h **615.00**

W W & D Weston, Ellenville, blue at handle, base chips **135.00**

3 gal

J A & C W Underwood, Fort Edward, PA, bird, chipped spout **360.00**

Unknown maker, bird on stump, blue at handle **1,650.00**

4 gal, bold triple stylized floral dec, blue at handle **1,430.00**

Milk Bowl

A Sipe & Son, Williamsport, PA, saltglazed, freehand cobalt blue floral design, blue at handles, some chips **365.00**

Unknown Maker, brushed cobalt blue commas at lip, 9″ d, edge chips **115.00**

Pitcher

Cowden & Wilcox, Harrisburg, PA, 1 gal, saltglazed, cobalt blue floral design, blue at handles, rim chip **770.00**

Preserving Jar

S Bell & Son, Strasburg, cobalt blue brushed shoulder dec, wear, glaze flaws, rim hairline, 10″ h **115.00**

Unknown Maker, cobalt blue brushed flower design, 10¼″ h **200.00**

Spittoon, EW Farrington, Elmira, NY, saltglazed, cobalt blue slip dec, cracked, chipped **125.00**

STONEWARE, BLUE AND WHITE

History: Blue-and-white stoneware refers to molded, blue saltglazed, domestic, utilitarian earthenware produced in the late 19th and early 20th centuries. Earlier stoneware was usually hand thrown and either undecorated, hand decorated in Spencerian script with flowers and other motifs, or stenciled. The stoneware of the blue-and-white period is molded and designs are impressed, embossed, stenciled, or printed.

Although known as blue-and-white, the base color is generally grayish in tone. The blue cobalt glaze may coat the entire piece, appear as a series of bands, or accent the decorative elements.

All types of household products were available in blue-and-white stoneware. Bowls, crocks, jars, pitchers, mugs, and salts are just a few examples. The ware reached its greatest popularity between 1870 and 1890. The advent of glass jars, tin containers, and chilled transportation hastened its demise. The last blue-and-white stoneware was manufactured in the 1920s.

References: M. H. Alexander, *Stoneware in the Blue and White,* Revised Edition, published by author, 1993; Kathyrn McNerney, *Blue & White Stoneware,* Collector Books, 1981, 1996 value update.

Collectors' Club: Blue & White Pottery Club, 224 12th St NW, Cedar Rapids, IA 52405.

REPRODUCTION ALERT

Many pieces of blue-and-white stoneware found in antiques shops and flea markets are unmarked reproductions from Rushville Pottery, Rushville, Ohio.

Bean Pot, cov, 7½" h, high relief of two children and "Boston Baked Beans" 330.00
Bowl, bluebirds 165.00
Bread/Cake Crock, cov, 12¼" d, 8" h, blue bands top and bottom, minor chips on edge of lid 1,100.00
Butter Crock, cov
    7" d, 4" h, molded cherries and lid, wire bale and wooden handle 250.00
    7¼" d, 4½" h, molded cows and lids, wire bale and wooden handle, minor chips on inner flange ... 500.00
Canister, cov, scroll motif
    Cereal 350.00
    Coffee 275.00
    Salt 100.00
Coffeepot, cov
    9¾"h , spiral stripes, acorn finial, tin bottom 685.00
    10½" d, spiral stripes, ball finial, tin bottom 1,320.00
Cup, blue flowers and hummingbirds, white ground .. 225.00
Jar, cov, 7½" d, stippled surface, flowers, holes for wire bale handle, old professional repair to lid 165.00
Mixing Bowl, Wedding Ring, price for nested set of three 125.00
Mug, 4⅛" h, Flying Bird, molded birds, price for set of six, hairlines in three, one with chipped lip 565.00
Pitcher
    7" h, molded cattails 200.00
    7½" h, tree bark and flowers 165.00
    7⅝" h, molded roadway lined with trees, rim chips 200.00
    7⅞" h, molded swallows flying, small edge flakes .. 525.00
    8" h, molded
        Cattle in oval, small chips and int. crazing 200.00
        Cherries, professional repairs 80.00
        Eagles and shields in ovals, minor crazing 385.00
        Leaping deer in one oval and swan in other 550.00
        Leaping stags in oval, surface flakes on spout ... 375.00
        Swans in ovals, short hairline in spout and minor surface chips 275.00
    8¼" h, molded
        Butterflies in circles, professional repair 200.00
        Indian heads in circles, small chips 415.00
    8¾" h, molded brick arches and pillars 440.00
    9" h, molded, roses, small edge flakes 440.00
    9¼" h, molded
        Teutonic royalty and German inscriptions relief designs, dolphin handle 165.00
        Vintage, star mark on bottom, small edge flakes . 180.00
Salt Cellar
    Butterflies design 95.00

Peacock design 85.00
Poppies design, cobalt blue flowers 155.00
Soap Dish
    4½" d, lion's head, small edge chips 50.00
    5" d
        Floral motif 85.00
        Roses 72.00
Spittoon, Basketweave, rose 85.00
Sugar Crock, 9¼" d, 4½" h, stripes, crow's foot in bottom 200.00
Teapot, cov, 6½" h, spiral stripes, acorn finial, wire bale and wooden handle 725.00
Wash Bowl and Pitcher, Primrose motif, overall swag . 550.00

STRETCH GLASS

History: Stretch glass was produced by many glass manufacturers in the United States between the early 1900s and the 1920s. The most prominent makers were Cambridge, Fenton (which probably manufactured more stretch glass than any of the others), Imperial, Northwood, and Steuben. Stretch glass can be identified by its iridescent, onionskin-like effect. Look for mold marks. Imported pieces are blown and show a pontil mark.

References: Ellen T. Schroy, *Warman's Glass,* Second Edition, Wallace-Homestead, 1995; Berry Wiggins, *Stretch Glass,* Antique Publications, 1972, 1987 value update.

Collectors' Club: Stretch Glass Society, PO Box 573, Hampshire, IL 60140.

Bonbon, Florentine green, dolphin handle, Fenton 65.00
Bowl
    7½" sq, orange, Imperial 60.00
    8¾" d, rolled-in edge, paneled 35.00
    9½" d, tree bark, ftd 40.00
    10" d, round, blue, sq ftd base, Northwood 50.00
Candlesticks, pr, 8½" h, vaseline 75.00
Compote, 9½" d, 5½" h, vaseline, tree-bark patterned stem, sgd "Northwood" 150.00
Dish, 6½" w, 3" h, peacock blue, scalloped at corners, Imperial, marked 150.00
Plate, 8" d, fourteen panels, amberina 45.00
Sherbet, liner, vaseline 35.00

Spittoon, 7½" top d, 5" h, $75.00.

Vase, fluted top, white irid, 5" h, $325.00.

Vase
  5" h, fluted top, white irid 325.00
  7" h, fan shape, vaseline 75.00

STRING HOLDERS

History: The string holder developed as a useful tool to assist the merchant or manufacturer who needed tangle-free string or twine to tie packages. The early holders were made of cast iron, some patents dating to the 1860s.

When the string holder moved into the household, lighter and more attractive forms developed, many made of chalkware. The string holder remained a key kitchen element until the early 1950s.

Reference: Sharon Ray Jacobs, *A Collector's Guide to Stringholders,* L-W Book Sales, 1996.

REPRODUCTION ALERT

As a result of the growing collector interest in string holders, some unscrupulous individuals are hollowing out the backs of 1950s figural-head wall plaques, drilling a hole through the mouth, and passing them off as string holders. A chef, Chinese man, Chinese woman, Indian, masked man, masked woman, and Siamese face are altered forms already found on the market.

Figural wall lamps from the 1950s and '60s also are being altered. When the lamp hardware is removed, the base can be easily altered. Two forms that have been discovered are a pineapple face and an apple face, both lamp-base conversions.

Advertising
  Buster Brown, 15" h, diecut figures, cast iron base,
    tin windmill top 550.00
  Jaxon soap, cast iron 85.00
  Red Goose Shoes, tin, hanging type 200.00
  Brass, 14" h, Victorian, small seated child atop globe
    supported by beast's head, floral dec base, marble
    plinth, c1870 .... 325.00
  Bronze, grapevine pattern, green glass, Tiffany Studios 325.00

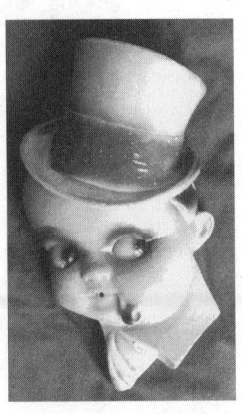

Man wearing top hat, plaster, 8³/4" h, $15.00.

Cast Iron
  6" h, 8" d base, beehive, dated "Apr 1865" 65.00
  8¹/4" h, sphere, comical woman's head with opening
    in mouth for string, ftd, old red paint 185.00
Ceramic
  Cat 25.00
  Rooster, Royal Bayreuth 225.00
Chalkware
  Apple, berries 25.00
  Cat, red ball of string 35.00
  Chef, figural, black and white 45.00
  Court Jester 45.00
  Old woman, sitting in rocking chair 35.00
Wood, teapot, chef decal 35.00

SUGAR SHAKERS

History: Sugar shakers, sugar castors, or muffineers all served the same purpose: to "sugar" muffins, scones, or toast. They are larger than salt and pepper shakers, were produced in a variety of materials, and were in vogue in the late Victorian era.

Reference: William Heacock, *Encyclopedia of Victorian Colored Pattern Glass, Book III,* Antique Publications, 1976, 1991–92 value update.

Amber, IVT, tapered 130.00
Amethyst
  Acorn, very dark, internal gold dec 395.00
  Quilted Phlox 335.00
Cranberry, Creased Optic 275.00
Emerald Green, Quilted Phlox 335.00
Milk Glass, Mellgo, dec 85.00
Mt Washington, tomato 395.00
Opalescent
  Beatty Honeycomb, cranberry 265.00
  Chrysanthemum Swirl, blue, satin finish 365.00
  Coin Dot, nine panel, blue 180.00
  Hobnail, blue, orig top, US Glass 60.00
  Reverse Swirl
    Blue 295.00
    Cranberry 495.00
    Vaseline 325.00
  Ribbed Lattice
    Blue 320.00
    Cranberry 395.00
  Spanish Lace, cranberry 495.00
  Stripe, nine panel, blue, 1940s 165.00
  Swirl
    Blue 350.00
    Cranberry 495.00
  Twist, blue, blown 335.00
  Utopia Optic, blue dec 195.00
  West Virginia Optic, tea-rose dec 85.00
Opaque
  Guttate, pink, satin 325.00
  Little Shrimp, ivory 150.00
  Pinecone, blue 125.00
Pattern Glass
  Jeweled Heart, apple green 375.00
  Keystone 295.00
  Maize, Libbey, yellow leaves 325.00

Glass, Leaf Umbrella, cased blue, Northwood at Martin's Ferry, $215.00.

Old Block	**80.00**
Rubena, Royal Ivy	**325.00**
Satin, Parian Swirl, blue	**260.00**
Silver, English	
5¼" h, blue cobalt woven wire cylinder form liner, Chester, c1906	**110.00**
6¾" h, George III, London, 1773, maker's mark "RI"	**250.00**
7" h, baluster form, allover repoussé, Birmingham, 1905, marked "J. G."	**200.00**
Spatter	
Leaf Umbrella	
Blue and white spatter	**425.00**
Cranberry and white spatter	**495.00**
Yellow and white spatter	**325.00**
Ribbed Pillar, cranberry and white spatter	**235.00**
Royal Ivy, rainbow spatter	**450.00**
Vaseline, metal elephant head	**495.00**

CAMBRIAN POTTERY
c 1783 - 1810

DILLWYN & CO.
SWANSEA
c 1811 - 1817

BEVINGTON & CO.
c 1817 - 1824

SWANSEA

History: This superb pottery and porcelain was made at Swansea (Glamorganshire, Wales) as early as the 1760s, with production continuing until 1870.

Marks: Marks on Swansea vary. The earliest marks were "Swansea" impressed under glaze and "Dillwan" under glaze after 1805. "Cambrian Pottery" was stamped in red under glaze from 1803 to 1805. Many fine examples, including the botanical series in pearlware, are not marked but may have the name of the botanical species stamped underglaze.

REPRODUCTION ALERT

Swansea porcelain has been copied for many decades in Europe and England. Marks should be studied carefully.

Note: Fine examples of Swansea often may show imperfections such as firing cracks. These pieces are considered mint because they left the factory in this condition.

Bowl, 8⅝" d, blue printed profile of George III and Queen Charlotte, inscribed "A King revered, a Queen beloved," and "Long may they live," ext. with chinoiserie scenes	**295.00**
Cup and Saucer, 3⅝" d cup, 6" d saucer, floral dec, c1815	**125.00**
Dessert Tray, 9½" l, hp, creamware, gilding, polychrome, underglaze mark, c1780	**295.00**
Dish, 11" d, botanical series, c1805	**325.00**

Dish, Botanical Series, 1805, 11½" l, $325.00.

Figure, 5½" l, two running pointers with brown markings, molded green and turquoise grass and florals, c1811	**1,825.00**
Plate, 8½" d, central floral, molded foliate scroll rim ..	**250.00**
Serving Dish, 8" sq, sweet peas, botanical, c1805	**200.00**
Tureen, cov, 6⅝" h, painted sprays of colored flowers and gilt scrollwork, plain gilt borders, double handles, gilt finial with three rams' heads, c1820	**1,550.00**

SWORDS

History: The first swords used in America came from Europe. The chief cities for sword manufacturing were Solingen in Germany, Klingenthal in France, and Hounslow and Shotley Bridge in England. Among the American importers of these foreign blades was Horstmann, whose name is found on many military weapons.

New England and Philadelphia were the early centers for American sword manufacturing. By the Franco-Prussian War, the Ames Manufacturing Company of Chicopee, Massachusetts, was exporting American swords to Europe.

Sword collectors concentrate on a variety of styles: commissioned vs. non-commissioned officers' swords, presentation swords, naval weapons, and swords from a specific military branch, such as cavalry or infantry. The type of sword helped identify a person's military rank and, depending on how he had it customized, his personality as well.

Following the invention of repeating firearms in the mid-19th century, the sword lost its functional importance as a combat weapon and became a military dress accessory.

References: *Swords and Hilt Weapons*, Barnes & Noble Books, 1993; Gerald Welond, *A Collector's Guide to Swords, Daggers & Cutlasses*, Chartwell Books, 1991.

Museum: Fort Ticonderoga Museum, Ticonderoga, NY.

Note: Condition is key to determining value.

American

Artillery, Foot, 1832, Roman-type short sword, brass eagle pommel, "Ames Mfg Co, Chicopee, MA," leather scabbard, 25" l **365.00**

Cavalry, Officer, saber, 1860, sgd "C. Roby, US, 1864," brass hilt, worn leather, missing wire, pitting **385.00**

Fraternal, blade etched on 19", obverse with profuse foliage, "Charles S. Tanner," standing knight in armor, and "Ames Sword Co,/Chicopee, Mass," gilt-brass hilt with anchor on the lancet over "HOPE," fitted with black grip with gilt cross, orig black leather scabbard with engraved gilt-brass mounts, throat engraved "IN NOC SIGNO/VINCES," with snake and cross, 29½" l **95.00**

Infantry, Officer, 1820–50, brass hilt and Indian-head pommel, MOP or ivory grip with brass wire, back etched with eagle and military motif, brass scabbard, 35" l **675.00**

Naval, cutlass, 1843, brass hilt and grip, half basket, guard, "N. P. Ames/Springfield" and "U.S.N./1843/RC," leather scabbard, 26¼" l **650.00**

English

Naval, Officer, 30" single-edged blade with rounded back, etched "PROSSER/Maker To The/Queen & Royal Family, London," naval themes, brass hilt with large gilt-brass guard, crown and naval anchor, lion's-head pommel, sharkskin over wooden grip, 35¼" l **225.00**

Officer, saber, curved single 25¼" blade, brass hilt cast in one pc with lion's-head pommel, black leather scabbard with brass mounts, 30⅜" l **200.00**

German, dress, gilt hilt, gilt trim from scabbard, engraved blade, 36" l, blade knicked **125.00**

Japanese, Samurai, 25½" l blade, bright finish, sharkskin and cloth-wrapped handle, brass guard, worn green enamel on scabbard **275.00**

American, presented to Gen. Ulysses S. Grant by Kentucky friends when he took command of the army of the North, 1864, jewel encrusted, $330,000. Photo courtesy of Butterfield & Butterfield.

Rapier, wrought-steel basket hilt, sharkskin grip, point broken off, 41" l **65.00**

TEA CADDIES

History: Tea once was a precious commodity and was stored in special boxes or caddies. These containers were made to accommodate different teas and included a special cup for blending.

Around 1700 silver caddies appeared in England. Other materials, such as Sheffield plate, tin, wood, china, and pottery, also were used. Some tea caddies are very ornate.

Burl Veneer, 9" l, dome top, dec gilded brass strapping, int. has two compartments with lids with burl veneer, knobs with brass escutcheons initialed "B" and "G," loose strapping **275.00**

Mahogany

7" h, 14" w, 7" d, George III, silver mountings, handle marked "London, 1810," int. with two lidded containers, cut glass mixing bowl **230.00**

8" h, light-wood inlay, brass feet, divided int. two lids, diamond escutcheon missing, wear to old finish, some edge damage **65.00**

12 × 6", Regency, sarcophagus shape, fitted int. with two inlaid hinged boxes, ivory ball feet, brass ring handles **450.00**

Parquetry, 7½" h, 13¼" l, 6¾" d, George III, sarcophagus shape, inlaid specimen woods, fitted int., two wells, cut glass mixing bowl, disc feet **1,725.00**

Rosewood, 14" w, 6½" d, Regency, sarcophagus, pearl-inlay medallion on top, escutcheon plate, large lion's-mask end handles on bun feet, two box inserts **350.00**

Satinwood, boxwood and hardwood garlands and flowers inlay, oval, England, c1790 ....**1,750.00**

Wood, burl walnut, brass hinges, two compartments, line and ivory key inlay, chamfered corners, 4⅜ × 7½ × 4¾", $565.00.

Silver, sterling, 5" h, applied grapevine design, monogram, Frank W Smith Silver Co, Inc, retailed by A Stowell & Co, 19th/20th C, 6 troy oz **230.00**

Tole, rect bombe shape, floral dec, black ground, ornate bronze bail, scroll feet, three-compartment int., 19th C **425.00**

Walnut, 6 × 9 × 6", Georgian, oblong molded top, bombe case, three partitioned wells, mid 18th C **650.00**

TEA LEAF IRONSTONE CHINA

History: Tea Leaf ironstone flowed into America from England in great quantities from 1860 to 1910 and graced the tables of working-class America. It traveled to California and Texas in wagons and down the Mississippi River by boat to Kentucky and Missouri. It was too plain for the rich homes; its simplicity and durability appealed to wives forced to watch pennies. Tea Leaf found its way into the kitchen of Lincoln's Springfield home; sailors ate from it aboard the *Star of India,* now moored in San Diego and still displaying Tea Leaf.

Contrary to popular belief, Tea Leaf was not manufactured exclusively by English potters in Staffordshire. Although there were more than 35 English potters producing Tea Leaf, at least 26 American potters helped satisfy the demand.

Anthony Shaw (1850–1900) is credited with introducing Tea Leaf. The most prolific Tea Leaf makers were Anthony Shaw and Alfred Meakin (1875–present), Johnson Bros. (1883–present), Henry Burgess (1864–1892), Enoch Wedgwood, and Arthur J. Wilkinson (1897–present), all of whom shipped much of their ware to America.

Although most of the English Tea Leaf is copper luster, Powell and Bishop (1868–1878) and their successors, Bishop and Stonier (1891–1936), worked primarily in gold luster. Beautiful examples of gold luster were also made by H. Burgess; Mellor, Taylor & Co. (1880–1904) used it on children's tea sets. Other English potters also were known to use gold luster, including W. & E. Corn, Thomas Elsmore, and Thomas Hughes, companies which have been recently identified as makers of this type of ware.

J. & E. Mayer, Beaver Falls, Pennsylvania, founded by English potters who immigrated to America, produced a large amount of copper luster Tea Leaf. The majority of the American potters decorated with gold luster that had no brown underglaze beneath the copper luster.

East Liverpool, Ohio, potters such as Cartwright Bros. (1864–1924), East End Pottery (1894–1909) and Knowles, Taylor & Knowles (1870–1934) decorated only in gold luster. This also is true of Trenton, New Jersey, potters, such as Glasgow Pottery, American Crockery Co., and Fell & Thropp Co. Since no underglazing was used with the gold, much of it has been washed away.

By the 1900s Tea Leaf's popularity had waned. The sturdy ironstone did not disappear; it was stored in barns and relegated to attics and basements. While the manufacture of Tea Leaf did experience a brief resurgence from the late 1950s through the 1970s, copper lustre Tea Leaf didn't recapture the hearts of the American consumer as it had a generation before.

Tea Leaf collectors recognize a number of ''variant'' decorative motifs as belonging to the Tea Leaf family: Teaberry, Morning Glory, Coral, Cinquefoil, Rose, Pre-Tea Leaf, Tobacco Leaf, Pepper Leaf, Pinwheel, Pomegranate, and Thistle & Berry, as well as white ironstone decorated with copper lustre bands and floral and geometric motifs. Once considered the stepchildren of Tea Leaf, these variants are now prized by collectors and generally bring strong prices.

Today's collectors eagerly seek out Tea Leaf and all of its variant motifs, and copper-lustre decorated white ironstone has once again become prized for its durability, beauty, simplicity, craft, and style.

References: Annise Doring Heaivilin, *Grandma's Tea Leaf Ironstone,* Wallace-Homestead, 1981, 1996 reprint distributed by L-W Book Sales; Jean Wetherbee, *White Ironstone, A Collector's Guide,* Tea Leaf Club International (324 Powderhorn Dr, Houghton Lake, MI 48629), 1996.

Collectors' Club: Tea Leaf Club International, 324 Powderhorn Dr, Houghton Lake, MI 48629.

Web Site: htpp://our world.compuserve.com/homepages/da

Museums: Lincoln Home, Springfield, IL; Ox Barn Museum, Aurora, OR; Sherman Davidson House, Newark, OH.

Advisor: Dale Abrams.

Notes: Tea Leaf values have increased steadily for the last decade, but there are some general rules of thumb for the knowledgeable collector. English Tea Leaf is still more collectible than American, except for rare pieces. The earlier the Tea Leaf production (1850s–1860s), the harder it is to find pieces and, therefore, the more expensive they are. Children's pieces are highly collectible, especially those with copper lustre decorative motifs. Hard-to-find Tea Leaf pieces include mustache cups, eggcups, covered syrup pitchers, ladles, oversized serving pieces, and pieces with significant embossing. Common pieces (plates, platters) of later production (1880–1900) need to be in excellent condition or should be priced accordingly as they are not that difficult to find.

Bone Dish
  Meakin
    Crescent shape **65.00**
    Scalloped edge **70.00**
  Shaw, scalloped edge **65.00**
Brush Vase
  Burgess, square, ridged **185.00**
  Edge Malkin, Polonaise **400.00**
  Meakin, Fishhook **175.00**
  Shaw, plain round, drain hole **195.00**
Butter Dish, cov, orig liner
  Meakin, Fishhook, price for 3 pcs **195.00**
  Shaw, hexagon, price for 3 pcs **235.00**
Butter Dish Liner **20.00**
Butter Pat, Meakin
  Round, Chelsea **14.00**
  Square **14.00**
Cake Plate
  Mayer (American), 9" sq with handles **80.00**
  Meakin, Bamboo, 8¾" with handles **75.00**
  Shaw, Cable, open handles **100.00**
Chamber Pot
  Shaw, Lily of the Valley, 2 pc **625.00**
  Wedgwood, plain, round **275.00**
Children's Dishes
  Cup and Saucer, Shaw, Lily of the Valley .. **325.00**
  Mug, Shaw **400.00**
  Tea Set
    Knowles, Taylor & Knowles (American), four cups and saucers, plates, cov teapot, creamer, and cov sugar, price for 18-pc set **800.00**
    Mellor, gold luster, six cups and saucers, plates, cov teapot, creamer, cov sugar, waste bowl, price for 24-pc set **1,550.00**
Coffeepot
  Davenport, Fig Cousin, pink luster **525.00**
  East End Pottery (American), beaded handle . **100.00**
  Johnson Bros, Acanthus **350.00**

Meakin
  Bamboo **185.00**
  Fishhook **185.00**
Shaw, Lily of the Valley **395.00**
Compote
  Meakin, apple bowl, scalloped edge **650.00**
  Mellor Taylor, 7⅞" d, 4½" h **335.00**
  Red Cliff (American), simple sq, 1950–60 .... **150.00**
  Shaw, plain, round **275.00**
  Unmarked, 8" d, 5" h, unusually deep bowl **435.00**
Creamer
  Johnson Bros, Acanthus **300.00**
  Meakin
    Bamboo **185.00**
    Pear shape **185.00**
  Shaw, Lily of the Valley **275.00**

Creamer, Burgess, 5½" h, $150.00.

Cup and Saucer
  Adams, Empress shape, 1960–70 .... **30.00**
  Meakin **65.00**
  Red Cliff (American), sq, ridged, 1950–60 .... **35.00**
  Shaw
    Basketweave **85.00**
    Niagara shape **90.00**
Eggcup
  Meakin, Boston Eggcup, 4" d, 1¾" h **350.00**
  Unmarked, 3½" h **325.00**
Gravy Boat
  Mayer (American) **90.00**
  Meakin
    Crewel **140.00**
    Fishhook **70.00**
    Wedgwood, sq **70.00**
    Wilkinson, Sunburst **95.00**
Mug
  Meakin, scroll **195.00**
  Shaw
    Basketweave **450.00**
    Chinese Shape **115.00**
    Wellsville China (American), gold luster **150.00**
Mush Bowl, Meakin **75.00**
Mustache Cup, Shaw **950.00**

Nappy
  Meakin, 4¼" sq **18.00**
  Powell & Bishop, gold luster **16.00**
  Wedgwood, sq, scalloped edge, 4¼" w **18.00**
Pitcher and Bowl Set
  Burgess, Cable **450.00**
  Meakin, Fishhook **395.00**
  Mellor Taylor, Lion's Head **425.00**
Pitcher/Jug
  Edwards, Peerless, 10" h **295.00**
  Meakin
    Chelsea **325.00**
    Fishhook **275.00**
  Shaw
    Cable shape, 7" h **225.00**
    Hanging Leaves **475.00**
Plate
  Furnival, plain, round, 8¼" d **12.00**
  Johnson Bros, acanthus, 9" d **20.00**
  Meakin, plain, round, 6¾" d **10.00**
  Shaw, plain, round, 10" d **22.00**
  Wedgwood, plain, round, 9¼" d **15.00**
Platter
  Meakin
    Chelsea, 10 × 14" oval **65.00**
    Plain, 9 × 13", rect **30.00**
  Shaw, plain, 15 × 10½" oval **40.00**
Relish Dish
  Edwards, Peerless **110.00**
  Meakin, Bamboo **45.00**
  Shaw
    Cable **85.00**
    Chinese shape **225.00**
Sauce Tureen, cov
  Adams, Empress shape, 4 pc, including ladle, 1960–
    70 .... **350.00**
  Furnival, Cable, 3 pc, no ladle **175.00**
  Meakin, Bamboo, 4 pc, including ladle **425.00**
  Red Cliff (American), 4 pc, including ladle, 1950–60 **170.00**
Serving Bowl, open, Meakin, sq, scalloped edge
  5¾" sq **45.00**
  8½" sq **45.00**
  Set of 7 nesting bowls **400.00**
Soap Dish, cov, Meakin, Bamboo, 3 pc with liner, rect **225.00**
Soup Bowl
  Meakin, plain, round
    8¾" d **25.00**
    10" d **40.00**
  Shaw, Hanging Leaves **55.00**
Soup Tureen, cov
  Meakin, Bamboo, 3 pc, without ladle **650.00**
  Shaw, Cable shape, 4 pc, with ladle **2,300.00**
Sugar Bowl, cov
  Shaw
    Bullet **125.00**
    Cable shape **145.00**
  Meakin
    Bamboo **85.00**
    Fishhook **80.00**
Vanity Box, Burgess, Pagoda, horizontal **275.00**
Vegetable, cov
  Meakin

Fishhook **125.00**
   Scroll, ftd **300.00**
Shaw
   Basketweave **225.00**
   Chinese shape **395.00**
   Wilkinson, Maidenhair Fern **165.00**
Wash Bowl, Shaw, Hanging Leaves **200.00**
Waste Bowl, unmarked, plain, round **85.00**

TEDDY BEARS

History: Originally thought of as "Teddy's Bears," in reference to President Theodore Roosevelt, these stuffed toys are believed to have originated in Germany. The first ones to be made in the United States were produced about 1902.

Most of the earliest teddy bears had humps on their backs, elongated muzzles, and jointed limbs. The fabric used was generally mohair; the eyes were either glass with pin backs or black shoe buttons. The stuffing was usually excelsior. Kapok (for softer bears) and wood-wool (for firmer bears) also were used as stuffing materials.

Quality older bears often have elongated limbs, sometimes with curved arms, oversized feet, and felt paws. Noses and mouths are black and embroidered onto the fabric.

The earliest teddy bears are believed to have been made by the original Ideal Toy Corporation in America and by a German company, Margarete Steiff, GmbH. Bears made in the early 1900s by other companies can be difficult to identify because they were all similar in appearance and most identifying tags or labels were lost during childhood play.

References: Pauline Cockrill, *Teddy Bear Encyclopedia,* Dorling Kindersley, 1993; Margaret and Gerry Grey, *Teddy Bears,* Courage Books, 1994; Pam Hebbs, *Collecting Teddy Bears,* Pincushion Press, 1992; Dee Hockenberry, *Bear Memorabilia,* Hobby House Press, 1992; ———, *The Big Bear Book,* Schiffer Publishing, 1996; Margaret Fox Mandel, *Teddy Bears and Steiff Animals,* Collector Books, 1993; Linda Mullins, *4th Teddy Bear & Friends Price Guide,* Fourth Edition, Hobby House Press, 1993; ———, *The Raikes Bear & Doll Story,* Hobby House, 1991; ———, *Teddy Bears Past & Present,* Vol. II, Hobby House Press, 1992; Cynthia Powell, *Collector's Guide to Miniature Teddy Bears,* Collector Books, 1994; Carol J. Smith, *Identification & Price Guide to Winnie the Pooh Collectibles,* Hobby House Press, 1994.

Periodicals: *Antiques & Collectables,* PO Drawer 1565, El Cajon, CA 92022; *National Doll & Teddy Bear Collector,* PO Box 4032, Portland, OR 97208; *Teddy Bear and Friends,* 6405 Flank Dr, Harrisburg, PA 17112; *Teddy Bear Review,* 170 Fifth Ave, New York, NY 10010.

Collectors' Clubs: Good Bears of the World, PO Box 13097, Toledo, OH 43613; My Favorite Bear: Collectors Club for Classic Winnie the Pooh, 468 W Alpine #10, Upland, CA 91786.

Museum: Teddy Bear Museum of Naples, Naples, FL.

Additional Listings: See Steiff.

Notes: Teddy bears are rapidly increasing as collectibles and their prices are rising proportionately. As in other fields, desirability should depend upon appeal, quality, uniqueness, and condition. One modern bear already has been firmly accepted as a valuable collectible among its antique counterparts: the Steiff teddy put out

in 1980 for the company's 100th anniversary. This is a reproduction of that company's first teddy and has a special box, signed certificate, and numbered ear tag; 11,000 of these were sold worldwide.

Bears

3″ h, brown mohair, glass eyes, pink ribbon, wear, one
   leg missing mohair **35.00**
3½″ h, Cinnamon, Schuco **145.00**
3⅞″ h, blond mohair, fully jointed, black bead eyes,
   embroidered nose and mouth, Steiff, fiber loss, head
   damaged at neck **230.00**
5″ h, gold mohair, bead eyes and articulated limbs **140.00**
7″ h, gold mohair, articulated limbs and bead eyes,
   added blue ribbon, worn mohair **170.00**
9½″ h, wool, brown, jointed limbs, swivel head, straw
   stuffed, shoe-button eyes, black sewn nose and
   mouth, felt paws, c1900 .... **185.00**
10″ h, white mohair, Twyford, English **110.00**
12″ h, gold mohair, straw stuffing, bead eyes, articulated
   limbs, paw pads repaired, worn mohair **250.00**
13″ h, blond mohair, fully jointed, steel eyes, embroidered snout and claws, felt pads, Steiff, c1904, some
   fur loss, needs restuffing, button missing **1,100.00**
15″ h, mohair
   Gold, straw stuffing, beaded eyes, articulated limbs,
     worn mohair **200.00**
   Light apricot, fully jointed, blank eye button, shoe-button eyes, embroidered nose, mouth, and claws,
     Steiff, c1903, well loved, some fur and stuffing
     loss, pads damaged **1,500.00**
   Worn red, white, and blue, straw stuffing, one eye,
     movable arms **135.00**
19″ h, curly mohair, fully jointed, shoe-button eyes, excelsior stuffing, Steiff, c1910, well loved, ears, nose,
   and pads replaced with brown corduroy, fiber and
   stuffing loss **865.00**
19½″ h, long gold mohair, fully jointed, glass eyes, embroidered nose, mouth, and claws, felt pads, straw
   stuffing, Steiff, 1950s, ear button missing, some fiber
   loss and moth damage **490.00**
27″ h, honey mohair, fully jointed, black button eyes,
   embroidered nose, mouth, and claws, excelsior stuffing, Steiff, c1906, ear button missing, moth damage,
   and fiber loss **10,350.00**

Cup and Saucer, bears golfing on saucer, soccer scene on cup, 2¼″ d × 2¼″ h cup, 4⅜″ d saucer, $115.00.

Bear-Related Items

Perfume Bottle, 3¾" h, teddy, mohair, jointed limbs, removable head, black button eyes, black sewn nose and mouth, glass bottle **200.00**

Tea Set, child's, teapot, creamer, sugar, three cups and saucers each dec with bicycling bears, marked "Bavarian China" **175.00**

Textile, 23¾" w, 20¾" h, "The Whole Bear Family," matted and framed **195.00**

TEPLITZ CHINA

History: Around 1900 there were 26 ceramic manufacturers located in Teplitz, a town in the Bohemian province of what was then known as Czechoslovakia. Other potteries were located in the nearby town of Turn. Wares from these factories were molded, cast, and hand decorated. Most are in the Art Nouveau and Art Deco styles.

Marks: The majority of pieces do not carry a specific manufacturer's mark; they are simply marked "Teplitz," "Turn-Teplitz," or "Turn."

Bowl, 5½" d, girl pulling rooster's tail, marked "Stellmacher" **75.00**

Candlestick, 5¼", figural, woman wearing flowing gown **150.00**

Compote, 6" d, Art Nouveau woman, high-relief florals, marked "Amphora-Teplitz" **400.00**

Ewer
  10" h, Art Nouveau, scrolled and gold-beaded handle, reticulated ruffled collar, goldfish lip spout, raised gold outlined flowers **425.00**
  11½" h, flower dec, ornate handle, marked "Turn Teplitz Bohemia" **225.00**

Figure, 18½" h, young woman, elaborate dress **450.00**

Loving Cup, 15" h, 9¾" w, reticulated outer wall, turquoise, amber, opal, and cobalt blue jewels, gold scalloped rim, foot, and twisted branch handles ... **350.00**

Pitcher, 9½" h, green and pink, lily pad dec, c1895 ... **225.00**

Vase
  5" h, bud, multicolored geometric dec, relief rooster head medallion, handles **95.00**
  8¼" h, gray, incised cavalier, triangular crimped rim, three rolled-under handles, marked "Stellmacher" **175.00**
  15" h, bulbous base, light and cobalt blue flowers, gold outlines, cream ground, two gold-trimmed loop handles **265.00**
  16¼" h, 8" d, barefoot maidens reaching for birds, elaborate foliage and Art Nouveau scrolls, gold trim, piercing **275.00**

Window Box, 4¾" × 5 × 14¼", yellow, purple, and lavender iris, Egyptian-form mark **225.00**

TERRA-COTTA WARE

History: Terra-cotta is ware made of hard, semi-fired ceramic. The color of the pottery ranges from a light orange-brown to a deep brownish red. It is usually unglazed, but some pieces are partially glazed and have incised, carved, or slip designs. Utilitarian objects, as well as statuettes and large architectural pieces, were made. Fine early Chinese terra-cotta pieces recently have sold for substantial prices.

Bust
  12" h, woman, orange and yellow hair **120.00**
  22" h, Court of Louis XVI, French, 18th C **1,500.00**

Figure
  5" h, boy with cap holding bundle of sticks, small vase, turquoise base, Royal Worcester, c1880 .. **435.00**
  15" h, girl, playing mandolin, c1870 .... **275.00**

Jar, cov, straight sides, disc base, enameled geometric band on shoulder and domed cov **70.00**

Vase, amphora type, base of handle sgd "G. Klint," marked "Crown Oak Ware, Teplitz/Amphora BB 3903," 15" h, $375.00.

Wall Plaque, marked "C. Conrad, Charlottenstütte, Salzburg," 8½" h, $25.00.

Match Holder, 9¼" h, figural, seated colonial man, tricorn hat, polychrome blue vest, white shirt, brown pants, holding bucket, c1800 .... **450.00**

Nodder, 3¾" h, monkey, pink vest, high glaze **160.00**

Spittoon, lady's **35.00**

Statue, 13" h, soldier, pre-Columbian type **1,700.00**

Tobacco Jar, 10" h, figural, man in long-tailed coat, white vest, skull cap **175.00**

Vase, 13" h, gourd shape, black relief dragon, two handles **95.00**

TEXTILES

History: Textiles is the generic term for cloth or fabric items, especially anything woven or knitted. Antique textiles that have survived are usually those that were considered the "best" by their original owners, since these were the objects that were used and stored carefully by the housewife.

Textiles are collected for many reasons—to study fabrics, to understand the elegance of a historical period, for decorative purposes, or to use as was originally intended. The renewed interest in antique clothing has sparked a revived interest in period textiles of all forms.

References: Gideon Bosker, Michele Mancini, John Gramstad, *Fabulous Fabrics of the 50s, and Other Terrific Textiles of the 20s, 30s, and 40s,* Chronicle Books, 1992; M. Dupont-Auberville, *Full-Color Historic Textile Designs,* Dover Publications, 1996; Dana G. Morykan and Harry L. Rinker, *Warman's Country Antiques & Collectibles,* Third Edition, Wallace-Homestead, 1996; Joy Shih, *Fun Fabrics of the 50s,* Schiffer Publishing, 1996; ———, *Funky Fabrics of the 60s,* Schiffer Publishing, 1996; Pamela Smith, *Vintage Fashion and Fabrics,* Alliance Publishing, 1995; Jessie A. Turbayne, *Hooked Rugs,* Schiffer Publishing, 1991; ———, *The Hookers' Art: Evolving Designs in Hooked Rugs,* Schiffer Publishing, 1993; Sigrid Wortmann Weltge, *Women's Work,* Chronicle Press, 1993.

Periodicals: *International Old Lacers Bulletin,* PO Box 481223, Denver, CO 80248; *The Lace Collector,* PO Box 222, Plainwell, MI 49080; *The Textile Museum Newsletter,* The Textile Museum, 2320 S St NW, Washington, DC 20008.

Collectors' Clubs: Costume Society of America, 55 Edgewater Dr, PO Box 73, Earleville, MD 21919; Stumpwork Society, PO Box 122, Bogota, NJ 07603.

Museums: Cooper-Hewitt Museum, New York, NY; Currier Gallery of Art, Manchester, NH; Ipswich Historical Society, Ipswich, MA; Lace Museum, Mountain View, CA; Museum of American Textile History, North Andover, MA; Museum of Art, Rhode Island School of Design, Providence, RI; Philadelphia College of Textiles & Science, Philadelphia, PA; Textile Museum, Washington, DC; Valentine Museum, Richmond, VA.

Additional Listings: See Clothing, Lace, Quilts, and Samplers.

Bandanna, 29¾" × 32¾", cotton, brown printed scene titled "Declaration of Independance [sic] of the United States of America 4th July 1776," after John Trumbell painting, beneath scene is key to identify above figures, blue border, small section of lower border missing **275.00**

Blanket, homespun wool, Sybil Parker, Randolph, VT, 1843, embroidered corners, one in very good condition, other worn, price for pr **425.00**

Coverlet

Jacquard, one pc, single weave

Central floral medallion with eagles in spandrels and rose border, edges labeled "Philip Allabach," red and white, minor stains and soiling, 72 × 79" **330.00**

Four rose medallions, vintage border and corners labeled "Manufactured expressly for [blank] 1858," and eagle with "Chesterfield, Ohio, 1858," navy blue and natural white, minor stains, 70 × 90" **500.00**

Jacquard, two pc

Double Weave, floral design, navy blue and white, corners dated "1853," minor wear and stains, top edge is turned and stitched, 76 × 85" **275.00**

Single Weave

Floral medallions, vintage border, corners labeled "W in Mt Vernon, Knox County, Ohio by Jacob and Machiel Ardner, 1852," navy blue and white, 70 × 79" **600.00**

Floral medallions with stars, bird border, and corners labeled "William Fasig, Richland County, Ohio, 1846," navy blue and white, seams resewn, ends turned and stitched, minor fringe loss, 66 × 88" **660.00**

Floral medallions with stars, chanticleer and bird with tree borders, corners have eagles with "F. Yearous, Loudonville, Ohio, 1850," navy, teal, red, and white, minor edge and fringe wear, 71 × 85" **550.00**

Four rose medallions, vintage border, corners labeled "Emanuel Ettinger Aronsburg 1840," navy blue, teal blue, tomato red, and natural white, some overall wear, stains, 73 × 86" **360.00**

Star medallions with chanticleer borders and corners labeled "J. Heeter, Scipio Township, Seneca County, Ohio," navy blue and white, one area with moth damage, minor fringe loss, 64 × 90" **495.00**

Embroidered Picture, 17 × 13½" d, silk, girl with basket of flowers in field in front of farm, floral vine border, "Mary Dietz, March 11, 1812," English, maple frame **425.00**

Family Register, wrought by Julia Felch born Limerick July 31 1802 aged 17 years, ground discoloration, framed, 20½ × 16½" **2,645.00**

Hooked Rug

Eagle in flight in central reserve, gray and green field, double border of stars and oak leaves, minor losses, staining, 72 × 47½" **2,415.00**

Lion in center, floral inner border, black outside border **400.00**

Pictorial, homestead with seven family members and dog, sgd in rug "Sanford Place, East Newport, Maine, BEM." [Barbara Merry], 4' 4" × 1' 11" .. **600.00**

Mattress Cover, homespun, machine sewn, minor wear

60 × 72", blue and white gingham **75.00**

68 × 70", blue and white checkered **95.00**

Memorial, wrought by Hannah Chase Nowell, Byfield Seminary under instruction of Rebecca Hasseltine Emerson, inscribed "Sacred to the memory of Prudence Nowell, Born Decr 18, 1778 obt Jany 12 1789..." silk threads needlework, watercolor background and figures, oval eglomise mat and giltwood frame, 15 × 20" **6,325.00**

Needlework Picture, framed

15¼" h, 10⅝" w, silk, linen homespun, red floral design, blue, green, gold, and white, stitched name and date in lower right "A. O. Atkinson, 1788," wear and stains, framed **385.00**

16¾ x 17", large house with trees, animals in front, floral vine border, Lydia Pittman, born Jan 25, 1810, gilt frame **1,200.00**

21 × 22", verse titled "Messiah," basket of flowers below, Rosana Highes, c1815 .... **475.00**

Needlepoint Picture, Sarah S. L. Padelford, the Balch School, Providence, RI, 1786, satin weave silk ground, blue, green, red, pink, gold, and cream silk threads, framed, paper label affixed to back with dates and provenance, $1,320.00. Photograph courtesy of Skinner, Inc.

Printed, 10½" h, 13" w, Contentment, red on white, minor stains, old gilt frame **110.00**

Show Towel, 17" w, 53" l, stylized flowers, "A.F. 1832," wear, fading, small holes **110.00**

Theorem, 13¼" h 16¼" w, basket of fruit, blues, greens, and golds, foxing to cloth, some browning **2,800.00**

THIMBLES

History: Thimbles often are thought of as common household sewing tools. Many are. However, others are miniature works of art, souvenirs of places, people, and events, or gadgets (thimbles with expanded uses such as attached threaders, cutters, or magnets).

There were many thimble manufacturers in the United States prior to 1930. Before we became a "throw-away" society, hand

sewing was a never-ending chore for the housewife. Garments were mended and altered. When they were beyond repair, pieces were salvaged to make a patchwork quilt. Thimble manufacturers continuously tried to create new thimbles to convince home sewers that "one was not enough."

By the early 1930s only one manufacturer of gold and silver thimbles remained in business in the United States—the Simons Brothers Company of Philadelphia, which was founded by George Washington Simons in 1839. Simons Brothers' thimbles from the 1904 St. Louis World's Fair and the 1893 Columbian Exposition are prized acquisitions for any collector. The thimble in the shape of the Liberty Bell is one of the most novel.

Today, the company is owned by Nelson Keyser and continues to produce silver and gold thimbles. The Simons Brothers Company designed a special thimble for Nancy Reagan as a gift for diplomats' wives who visited the White House. This thimble has a picture of the White House and the initials "N. D. R."

Thimbles have been produced in a variety of materials: gold, silver, steel, aluminum, brass, china, glass, vegetable ivory, ivory, bone, celluloid, plastics, leather, hard rubber, and silk. Common-metal thimbles usually are bought by the intended user, who makes sure the size is a comfortable fit. Precious-metal thimbles often were received as gifts. Many of these do not show signs of wear, probably because either they did not fit the recipient or were considered too elegant to use for mundane work.

During the 20th century thimbles were used as advertising giveaways. It is not unusual to find a thimble that says "You'll Never Get Stuck Using Our Product" or a political promotion stating "Sew It Up—Vote for John Doe for Senator."

References: Averil Mathis, *Antique and Collectible Thimbles and Accessories,* Collector Books, 1986, 1995 value update; Bridget McConnel, *A Collector's Guide to Thimbles, Wellfleet Press, 1990.*

Periodical: *Thimbletter,* 93 Walnut Hill Road, Newton Highlands, MA 02161.

Collectors' Clubs: Empire State Thimble Collectors, 8289 Northgate Dr, Rome, NY 13440; Thimble Collectors International, 8289 Northgate Dr, Rome, NY 13440; Thimble Guild, PO Box 381807, Duncanville, TX 75138.

REPRODUCTION ALERT

Reproductions can be the result of restrikes from an original die or can be casts from a mold made from an antique thimble. Many reproductions are sold as such and priced accordingly. Among the reproduced thimbles are a pre-revolution Russian enamel thimble and the Salem Witch thimble (the reproduction has no cap and the seam is visible).

Advisor: Estelle Zalkin.

Advertising

Aluminum, colored band, brass, advertisement or inscription **5.00**

Clark's O N T, brass **20.00**

Domestic Sewing Machine, silver, early 20th C **50.00**

Brass, ornate band, scalloped rim **75.00**
Celluloid, floral decal **5.00**
Commemorative, coronation, King George and Queen
   Mary, gold **1,200.00**
Dorcas, Daisy pattern, silver, steel lined **50.00**
Enameled, floral dec, South Staffordshire, enamel on
   brass, 19th C **2,500.00**
Gold
   American, scenic band, late 19th/early 20th C **200.00**
   Continental, band with scenic vignettes, 19th C **200.00**
   English, alternating pearls and rubies on rim, 19th C **300.00**
   Scandinavian, semiprecious stone cap **300.00**

English, Atlantic cable style, 19th C, $135.00.

Ivory, carved foliate band, 19th C **250.00**
Political
   Dewey-Brinker, plastic **75.00**
   Hoover, "Home Happiness" aluminum **60.00**
Porcelain
   American, hp floral dec, late 19th/early 20th C **50.00**
   English, bird and flowers dec, Royal Worcester, 19th
     C **350.00**
Silver, steel capped, engraved initials, 19th C **95.00**
Souvenir
   Louisiana Purchase Expo, St Louis, MO, The Golden
     Spike, gold, scenic band, 1904 ....**1,500.00**
   New Orleans, silver, applied enamel shield **20.00**
   St Peters, Rome, enamel on silver, semiprecious stone
     cap **150.00**
Steel, damascene dec band, India, 19th C **150.00**
Sterling Silver, American, 19th C **95.00**
Tortoiseshell, gold medallion, silver cap, Piercy patent **2,500.00**

THREADED GLASS

History: Threaded glass is glass decorated with applied threads of glass. Before the English invention of a glass-threading machine in 1876, threads were applied by hand. After this invention, threaded glass was produced in quantity by practically every major glass factory.

Threaded glass was revived by the art glass manufacturers such as Durand and Steuben, and it is still made today.

Atomizer, blue threads, red ground **90.00**
Basket, 3½" d, rubena, clear appl twisted handle **135.00**
Bowl, 8" d, 3¾" h, triangle, Tartan, blue, white, and pale

pink plaid, clockwise swirl on ext., reversed swirls on
   int., attributed to Wordsley Flint Glass Works, Stourbridge, small chip on one appl foot **485.00**
Cheese Dish, cov, 7½" d, light blue opal threading on
   upper half of bell-shaped dome, faceted knob **125.00**
Epergne, 9½" d, 15" h, four orange to clear threaded
   vases, petal-scalloped tops, clear branches, orange
   threaded base **675.00**
Finger Bowl, 5" d, yellow-green, scalloped rim, price for
   8-pc set **200.00**
Perfume, 5½" h, blown, machine appl threads **250.00**
Pitcher, blue rim, appl handle **65.00**

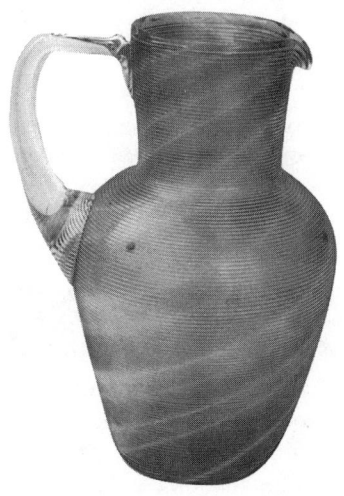

Pitcher, pink-and-yellow swirl, 6" h, $175.00.

Rose Bowl, 2¼" d, clear glass ovals, sgd "Rd 81951,"
   English
   Cranberry **275.00**
   Olive Green **275.00**
Salt, 2¾ × 1½", opaque white threads, cranberry
   ground, clear appl petal feet **75.00**
Tumbler, 4¼", aqua threads, clear ground **200.00**
Vase
   6" h, gold thread, irid blue ground **300.00**
   7¼" h, tapered, pinched top, irid satin finish, appl
     threading **110.00**

TIFFANY

History: Louis Comfort Tiffany (1849–1934) established a glass house in 1878 primarily to make stained glass windows. In 1890, in order to utilize surplus materials at the plant, Tiffany began to design and produce "small glass" such as iridescent glass lamp shades, vases, stemware, and tableware in the Art Nouveau manner. Commercial production began in 1896.

Tiffany developed a unique type of colored iridescent glass called Favrile, which differs from other art glass in that it was a composition of colored glass worked together while hot. The essential characteristic is that the ornamentation is found within the glass; Favrile was never further decorated. Different effects were achieved by varying the amount and position of colors.

Louis Tiffany and the artists in his studio also are well known for their fine work in other areas—bronzes, pottery, jewelry, silver and enamels.

Marks: Most Tiffany wares are signed with the name "L. C. Tiffany" or the initials "L.C.T." Some pieces also are marked "Favrile" along with a number. A variety of other marks can be found, e.g., "Tiffany Studios" and "Louis C. Tiffany Furnaces."

References: Victor Arwas, *Glass, Art Nouveau and Art Deco*, Rizzoli International Publications, 1977; Alastair Duncan, *Louis Comfort Tiffany*, Harry N. Abrams, 1992; Robert Koch, *Louis C. Tiffany, Rebel in Glass*, Crown Publishers, 1966; Ellen T. Schroy, *Warman's Glass*, Wallace-Homestead, 1992; John A. Shuman III, *The Collector's Encyclopedia of American Art Glass*, Collector Books, 1988, 1994 value update.

Museums: Chrysler Museum, Norfolk, VA; Corning Glass Museum, Corning, NY; University of Connecticut, The William Benton Museum of Art, Storrs, CT.

REPRODUCTION ALERT

A large number of brass belt buckles and badges bearing Tiffany markings were imported into the United States and sold at flea markets and auctions in the late 1960s. The most common marking is "Tiffany Studios, New York." Now, more than 25 years later, many of these items are resurfacing and deceiving collectors and dealers.

A partial list of belt buckles includes the Wells Fargo guard dog, Wells Fargo & Company mining stage, Coca-Cola Bottling, Southern Comfort Whiskey, Currier and Ives express train, and U.S. Mail. Beware of examples that have been enhanced through color enameling.

An Indian police shield is among the fake Tiffany badges. The badge features an intertwined "U" and "S" at the top and a bow and arrow motif separating "INDIAN" and "POLICE."

Bronze

Alarm Clock, travel type, 8 day, brown leather case ... **175.00**
Bookends, pr, 6" h, seated Buddha, gilt bronze, early
   20th C **260.00**
Candlestick, 16" h, slender shaft, double pedestal base,
   ribbed golden Favrile shade, shade sgd "L. C. T." ..**1,000.00**
Desk Set, gilt bronze, Venetian pattern, rocker blotter,
   letter rack, pen brush, match stand, pen tray, letter
   opener, memo-pad holder, cov double inkwell, four
   blotter corners **2,750.00**
Inkwell, 3¾ × 4¼", filigree bronze branch and leaf pattern, green slag glass, orig glass liner, some cleaning
   to patina, imp "Tiffany Studios/New York/CI" **400.00**

Ornament, 9¾" l, bronze framework, Favrile glass, orig bronze chains, dragonfly, wings spread, wintergreen body, red cabochon eyes, striated green and opal filigreed wings, green, amber, and opal striated ground, c1899 ....**3,500.00**

Bronze, compote, encrusted jewels and gold doré finish, stamped "Louis C. Tiffany Furnaces Inc. #504," Tiffany Art Glass Decorating Co. monogram, 7" d, 2½" h, $495.00. Photo courtesy of James D. Julia, Inc.

Stamp Box, 4½" l, gilt bronze, Favrile glass mosaic dec, rect, two amber irid scarab beetles on cov, gilt-bronze legs and center orb, azure, silvery blue irid, sea green, irid mustard, sienna, and amber brickwork pattern around int., cast with two stamp holders, imp "Tiffany Studios/New York, c1899" **16,500.00**

Glass

Bowl
   3¼" h, round tapered sides, overall gold irid, sgd "L.
     C. Tiffany Inc. Favrile" **345.00**
   6" d, ftd, butterscotch opal ground, raised DQ design,
     sgd **575.00**
   6¼" d, 2¼" h, paperweight type, wide flat bottom,
     upright sides, colorless, internally dec with bright
     emerald green heart-shaped lily pads, sgd "L. C.
     Tiffany Favrile 811 J" **1,325.00**
   6¾" d, inverted bell shape, colorless, radiating green
     feathers, sgd "L. C. T. Favrile 3987V," c1920 ... **520.00**
   8" d, ovoid, ribbed sides, overall gold irid, sgd "L. C.
     Tiffany Favrile" **700.00**
   8½" d, 3½" h, ten ribs, scalloped rim, gold Favrile,
     engraved "L. C. Tiffany Favrile," wear on bottom **525.00**
   9" d, rounded sides, irid blue, silver-gold Egyptian
     chain pattern, inscribed "D766 - L. C. T. Louis C.
     Tiffany," c1895 ....**2,300.00**
Candlesticks, pr, 12" h, bulbous socket, wide flattened
   rim, tall slender swelled and ribbed hollow stem,
   slightly domed ribbed disc foot, gold irid finish, sgd
   "LCT Favrile 1825" **1,380.00**
Center Bowl
   9" d, 4" h, five lopes, cobalt blue, irid vertical mot-
     tling, sgd "L.C.T. 0071920" **1,895.00**
   9½" d, 3¾" h, low rounded sides, lightly ribbed,
     slightly scalloped rim, orange-gold irid, sgd "L. C.
     Tiffany Favrile" **690.00**
Champagne, gold irid, very thin, long fragile stem, sgd **285.00**
Cologne, 5¾" h, mustard gold, abstract leather pattern
   on shoulder, orig stopper, sgd **650.00**

Compote

    6″ d, 3¼″ h, wide shallow bowl, short knobbed stem, wide disc foot, DQ optic design, pastel green int., opal white ext., irid stem and foot, sgd "L.C.T. Favrile" **690.00**

    6⅜″ d, 3¾″ h, gold Favrile, scalloped bowl, baluster stem, base with folded rim, engraved "LCT" **495.00**

Goblet, 9¾″ h, wide cylindrical bowl, swelled at base, raised on triple-knob stem, domed foot, disc rim, overall amber irid, sgd "L. C. Tiffany - Favrile 3976K," c1916 .... **1,100.00**

Lamp Shade, gold Favrile, sgd "L.C.T." **300.00**

Nappy, 1¼ × 5″, triangular, rolled sides, pedestal ftd, appl handle, gold irid **425.00**

Salt, master, 3¼″ d, silver/gray irid, pastel rays, sgd ... **250.00**

Shot Glass, 2″ h, gold, dimpled, sgd **165.00**

Glass, vase, conical white opaque body with white streaks, flat circular pedestal, white opaque base with blue rim, flat top with yellow stretched effect, marked "1546 L. C. Tiffany, Favrile," orig paper label, 5½″ h, 6″ top d, $1,125.00.

Vase

    2⅛″ h, Cypriote, wide low cushion body, small rolled center neck, small foot, amber, pink, and blue irid swirls, deep blue-black ground, sgd "L. C T. - Louis C. Tiffany Favrile E432," c1896 ....**4,600.00**

    4¾″ h, ovoid shouldered body tapering to cylindrical neck, 10 lightly molded ribs, small indented dimples around shoulder, cobalt blue ground, silvery blue irid, sgd "L. C. Tiffany Favrile X89" **1,100.00**

    6½″ h, paperweight type, bulbous ovoid body, closed rim, tapering to flared base, colorless ground lightly tinted pale yellow shading to turquoise blue, upper half with deep purple, puce, lavender, mustard, amber, and lime green convolvulus blossoms and trailing leaves, sgd "L. C. Tiffany Favrile 3309J" **48,875.00**

    7½″ h, Tel el Amarna, waisted ovoid, bulbous neck, cased amber irid over white, neck dec with pale green and amber chain pattern, inscribed "L. C. Tiffany-Favrile 8700G," c1912 ....**2,760.00**

    10″ h, Lava, squatty bulbous irregular base tapering to slender cylindrical irregular sides, wide cupped rim, amber ground, cobalt blue oxide, irregular gold irid spiral, sgd "L. C. Tiffany Favrile 2336C," c1908 ....**33,925.00**

    14¾″ h, floriform, tall flaring ruffled upright sides, spherical base, very tall slender slightly swelled stem, wide low domed foot, irid amber, pale violet and green pulled leaves, sgd "L. C. T. - M3057," c1900 ....**7,475.00**

Lamps

Candlestick, 17¼″ h, gilt bronze, flattened drip pan, urn form nozzle, standard cast with acanthus leaves, filigree conical shade with grapevine pattern over dusty rose glass liners, shade and base imp "Tiffany Studios/ New York," c1920 ....**2,900.00**

Chandelier, 29″ d, sharply conical shade, allover dec of full-blown blossoms and buds, mottled pastel golden yellow, dusty rose, pink, striated apricot, and multi-colored opal flowers, emerald and olive-green leaves, opal, shaded green, and sienna confetti glass ground, beaded edge, imp "Tiffany Studios/New York," c1899 ....**20,000.00**

Desk, 16″ h, lily, three gold Favrile lily shades, single standard, spreading bronze base **1,250.00**

Floor, 55″ h, hoop top, rect panel, leaded pale yellow glass circ shade, reeded bronze shaft, circ base, shade and base sgd **2,600.00**

Table, 25″ h, 18″ d Lemon Leaf shade, bronze turtle back base, sgd "Tiffany Studios, New York" **12,500.00**

Silver

Asparagus Dish, 13¾″ l, rect, undulating sides, Florence-scrolled arms, pierced cartouches topped by flower sprays, four leaf and paw feet, monogrammed, removable liner, c1891, 38 oz, 10 dwts **2,000.00**

Bowl

    9¼″ d, 3½″ h, presentation dated 1920, marked "Tiffany & Co., Sterling," 20 troy oz **440.00**

    10⅜″ d, 2″ h, shallow, short feet, marked "Tiffany & Co., Sterling," 24 troy oz **525.00**

Chafing Dish, 9¼″ d, cov, stand, chased floral circular rim, three pinecone and pine branch stag handled feet, 66 troy oz **3,100.00**

Christening Mug, dated "1/24/34," 8 oz **195.00**

Cocktail Set, Art Deco, cocktail shakers, goblets, and round tray, c1920, price for 14-pc set **9,850.00**

Cold Meat Fork, King pattern **300.00**

Flatware Service

    Gothic trellis entwined with blackberries, foliage continuing to twisted Gothic foliage monogram "MFS" on backs of bowls and tines, matte-finished gilt pieces, sixteen each dinner forks, dessert forks, plus seventeen each tablespoons, teaspoons, dessert spoons, coffee spoons, dessert forks, ice cream spoons, marked on stems and stamped "PAT. 1885," 235 oz, 151 pcs, Tiffany blond-oak fitted case with red baize lining, accompanied by photocopies of preliminary and final designs for handles, copies of patent, and manufacturing instructions, service ordered by Mary Frances Hopkins before marriage to Edward T Searles in 1887 ..**28,750.00**

King pattern, twelve tablespoons, bouillon spoons, teaspoons, luncheon forks, dinner forks, demitasse spoons, ten oyster forks, 139 troy oz **4,800.00**

Marine life dec, rect handles, twelve dinner forks, dinner knives, salad forks, soup spoons, teaspoons, flat butter spreaders, six luncheon knives, citrus fruit spoons, four tablespoons, cold meat fork **15,000.00**

Ladle, King pattern, shell bowl **525.00**

Nut Stand, oval, beaded edge, openwork sides, individual size, price for 8-pc set **400.00**

Pie Slice, King pattern **250.00**

Salad Serving Set, King pattern **425.00**

Tea and Coffee Service, Iris pattern, teapot, coffeepot, hot water jug, creamer, cov sugar bowl, waste bowl, 13″ h kettle on lamp stand, matching 32¼″ l two handled tray, bodies boldly chased in high and low relief with crossed sprays of iris buds and leaves on matted ground, acid-etched tray with matching iris blossom monogram "MVL," marked under bases and numbered "1750," 562 oz gross, c1902, price for 8-pc set **41,400.00**

TIFFIN GLASS

c1960

History: A. J. Beatty & Sons built a glass manufacturing plant in Tiffin, Ohio, in 1888. On January 1, 1892, the firm joined the U. S. Glass Co. and was known as factory R. Fine-quality Depression-era items were made at this high-production factory.

From 1923 to 1936, Tiffin produced a line of black glassware called Black Satin. The company discontinued operation in 1980.

Marks: Beginning in 1916 wares were marked with a paper label.

References: Fred Bickenheuser, *Tiffin Glassmasters,* Book I (1979), Book II (1981), Book III (1985), Glassmasters Publications; Bob Page and Dale Fredericksen, *Tiffin Is Forever,* Page-Fredericksen, 1994; Leslie Pina and Jerry Gallagher, *Tiffin Glass,* Schiffer Publishing, 1996; Ellen T. Schroy, *Warman's Glass,* Wallace-Homestead, 1992.

Collectors' Club: Tiffin Glass Collectors Club, PO Box 554, Tiffin, OH 44883.

Ashtray, Twilight, cloverleaf, 5″ d **45.00**
Basket, Twilight, 9″ h, 5½″ w **295.00**
Bowl, Twilight, wishbone ftd, 6½″ d **135.00**
Candlesticks, pr
    Cerise, double **75.00**
    Fuchsia, double **75.00**
Centerpiece, Fontaine, green, 13″ d **85.00**
Champagne
    June Night **22.50**

Twilight, optic **48.00**
Cocktail
    Flanders, pink **50.00**
    June Night **28.00**
    Persian Pheasant **22.50**
Comport, Persian Pheasant, 6″ d, blown **85.00**
Console Bowl
    Cerise **565.00**
    Flanders, pink **110.00**
Cordial
    Fuchsia **45.00**
    June Night **45.00**
Cup and Saucer, Fontaine, twilight, blown **125.00**
Flower Arranger, Twilight, 13⅝″ d
    Crystal **125.00**
    Smoke **295.00**
Flower Basket, Copen, blue and crystal, 13″ **165.00**
Garden Set, Twilight **195.00**
Goblet
    Byzantine
        Black **45.00**
        Yellow **28.00**
    Cerise **22.00**
    Classic **200.00**
    Flanders **36.00**
    June Night **38.00**
    Twilight **35.00**
Iced Tea Tumbler, Flying Nun, crystal, green base **60.00**
Juice Tumbler
    Byzantine **13.00**
    June Night, ftd **25.00**
Martini Jug, Twilight, 11½″ h **450.00**
Oyster Cocktail, Cerise **12.00**
Parfait, Byzantine, yellow **32.00**
Pitcher
    Flanders, pink **475.00**
    Flying Nun, crystal, green base, cov **450.00**
Plate
    Classic, 10½″ d, dinner **125.00**
    Flanders, 9½″ d, dinner, yellow **60.00**
    June Night, 8″ d, luncheon **16.50**
    Le Fleure, 7¼″ d, salad, yellow **15.00**
Seltzer Tumbler, Le Fleure, ftd **18.50**
Sherbet
    Cerise, low **10.00**
    Flanders, high **28.00**
Sherry, June Night, 2 oz **45.00**
Tumbler
    Classic, ftd **180.00**
    Flanders
        Pink, ftd, 12 oz **50.00**
        Yellow **22.00**
Vase
    8″ h
        Black, poppies dec, satin finish **35.00**
        Cherokee Rose, bud **45.00**
    10″ h, Cherokee Rose, bud **45.00**
    10½″ h, June Night, bud **45.00**
Wine
    Cerise **17.00**
    Flanders **75.00**
    Twilight **38.00**

c1875   c1880

c1872-1951

TILES

History: The use of decorated tiles peaked during the latter part of the 19th century. More than 100 companies in England alone were producing tiles by 1880. By 1890 companies had opened in Belgium, France, Australia, Germany, and the United States.

Tiles were not used only as fireplace adornments. Many were installed into furniture, such as washstands, hall stands, and folding screens. Since tiles were easily cleaned and, hence, hygienic, they were installed on the floors and walls of entry halls, hospitals, butcher shops, or any place where sanitation was a concern. Many public buildings and subways also employed tiles to add interest and beauty.

References: Susan and Al Bagdade, *Warman's American Pottery and Porcelain,* Wallace-Homestead, 1994; ———, *Warman's English & Continental Pottery & Porcelain,* Second Edition, Wallace-Homestead, 1991; Ralph and Terry Kovel, *Kovels' American Art Pottery,* Crown Publishers, 1993; Ralph Moore and Dinah Tanner, *Porcelain & Pottery Tea Tiles,* Antique Publications, 1994; Ronald L. Rindge et al., *Ceramic Art of the Malibu Potteries,* Malibu Lagoon Museum, 1994.

Periodical: *Flash Point,* PO Box 1850, Healdsburg, CA 95448.

Collectors' Club: Tiles & Architectural Ceramics Society, Ironbridge Gorge Museum, Ironbridge, Telford, Shropshire, England.

Notes: Condition is an important factor in determining price. A cracked, badly scuffed and scratched, or heavily chipped tile has very little value. Slight chipping around the outer edges of a tile is, at times, considered acceptable by collectors, especially if these chips can be covered by a frame.

It is not uncommon for the highly glazed surface of some tiles to have become crazed. Crazing is not considered detrimental as long as it does not detract from the overall appearance of the tile.

American Encaustic Tile Co, Zanesville, OH
   3" sq, portrait of President Wm McKinley, blue glazed
     intaglio, 1896, biography pasted on back 145.00
   4" sq, Oriental boat, pagoda in background 45.00
   6" sq, cherub and dog, small repair 35.00
   18 × 6", hunting dogs, high relief, sponged pale aqua
     and honey brown glossy glaze 250.00
Art Tile, 6" sq, seated cherubs, green gloss 160.00
Batchelder, 4" sq
   Hunter and dog in woods, bas-relief, reddish brown
     clay, high-gloss light blue rubbed into background 90.00
   Landscape of trees, water, and bridge, deeply imp,
     red clay, light chalky blue brushed into recessed
     areas 95.00

Beaver Falls, 6" sq, standing squirrel, incised and outlined in black, medium blue squirrel and border, kelly green ground, marked 65.00
California Art, 5½" sq, scenic, relief, natural colors 20.00
Claycraft, CA, 35 × 23½", 24-tile frieze, articulated scene of dirt road winding towards stone bridge, grove of fir and maple trees, Cotswold-type cottage, molded wooden frame 2,250.00
DeMorgan, William, 6" sq, hedgehog, ruby luster glaze 400.00
Dutch, 9½" × 7½", painted blue and white, man and woman in cart, sgd "O Evrelman," framed, 19th/20th C 110.00
Grueby
   4½" sq, landscape, trees, stream and mountain, green, blue, yellow, and brown, marked "Architectural" 600.00
   8" sq, mocha brown galleon, billowing white sails, choppy powder blue sea, medium blue sky, black wooden frame, sgd "EH," partial black stamp .. 850.00
Low, J & J G, Chelsea, MA
   4" sq, bearded man, laurel wreath, green gloss 165.00
   6 × 5", cupid on flying bird, olive gloss, 1883 ..... 175.00
   7 × 7½", flowers, brown shaded to amber 50.00
Marblehead, 6 × 6", scenic, house and trees, deep blue and green, imp ship mark, minor nicks 1,265.00
Minton China Works, 6" sq, transfer printed
   Adam and Eve driven out of Eden, blue cream ground 45.00

Wedgwood, Independence Hall, light brown, marked "1893 Calendar/Jones McDuffee & Stratton/Pottery Merchants Boston,/ USA," 4¹³/₁₆ × 3³/₈", $75.00.

Farmyard scene, sheep, brown on white, sgd ''W. Wise,'' 1879 .... 80.00

Hancock House, brown on white 35.00

Romeo and Juliet, sepia 35.00

Moravian Pottery & Tile Works, Doylestown, PA

4" sq, Aladdin Lamp 50.00

7¼ × 4", Knight in armor on horseback, ochre and blue 65.00

Mosaic Tile Co, Zanesville, OH

4" sq, German Shepherd dec 120.00

6" sq, Little Bo Peep, blue, tan, and cream, Walter Crane 100.00

Pardee, 4" sq, houses and trees, matte glaze, brown and green, 1910 .... 225.00

Pewabic Pottery, Detroit, MI

2¾" sq, bird of paradise, gray-taupe bird, cranberry red ground, high-luster finish 65.00

3" sq, Detroit Skyline, round, emb, brown on blue . 75.00

Richards, H, 6" sq, Art Nouveau flower, tube lined, red and green, cream ground 75.00

Robertson, 8" sq, scenic, cloisonné dec, brown road winding through green hills, fortress 1,300.00

Superior, 4 × 7", cherubs, sgd, framed 200.00

Trenton Tile Co, Trenton, NJ

4¼" sq, portrait of woman, brown glaze 65.00

6" sq, flower, tan glossy glaze 25.00

US Encaustic Tile Co

6" sq, birds, framed 75.00

18 × 6", Dawn, woman, emb green glaze 175.00

Wedgwood

6" sq, Moth from Midsummer's Night Dream, blue transfer, white ground 120.00

8" sq, hunting dog and bird, brown transfer, white ground 115.00

Wheeling, 6" sq, sailing ship 85.00

Museum: Cooper-Hewitt Museum, New York, NY.

Additional Listings: See Advertising; Kitchen Collectibles; Lanterns; Lamps and Lighting; and Tinware, Decorated.

Note: This category is a catchall for tin objects which do not fit into other categories in this book.

Battle Ax, 21 × 12", whimsey 150.00

Candle Lantern, 11¾" h, pyramid top, pierced star designs, old black paint, ring handle 110.00

Candle Tray, 9¼ × 19 × 12¾", rect, formed strap handle, holds twenty-four candles 650.00

Centerpiece, 14½" d, whimsey, tiered, traces of green paint 175.00

Churn, 21½" h, wooden dasher 200.00

Coffee Grinder, hanging, Parker 45.00

Cookie Cutter

Father Christmas, sack on back 185.00

Flower Basket 45.00

Goose, flying 45.00

Heart and hand 500.00

Horse, large 150.00

Food Grater, 14¼" l, punched, wooden frame, mortised and turned handle 95.00

Foot Warmer, 7¾ × 9", punched circle design with hearts, mortised hardwood frame, turned corner posts, old red stain 140.00

Lamp, 6¾" h, oil, saucer base, traces of gold and silver paint, Kinnear Patent 150.00

Mistletoe Ball, 6¼" d, hinged 450.00

Oyster Ladle 45.00

Quilt Pattern, 5½" l, horse, pitted and rusted 20.00

Sconce, 12½" h, elongated shield shape, minor resoldering, price for pr 770.00

Spice Canisters and Carrier, 8½ × 8½ × 5¾", crimped dec 275.00

Wedding Ball, 9½ × 3⅝", whimsey, marked patent date 125.00

TINWARE

History: Beginning in the 1700s many utilitarian household objects were made of tin. Because it is nontoxic, rust resistant, and fairly durable, tin can be used for storing food; and because it was cheap, tinware and tin-plated wares were in the price range of most people. It often was plated to iron to provide strength.

An early center of tinware manufacture in the United States was Berlin, Connecticut, but almost every small town and hamlet had its own tinsmith, tinner, or whitesmith. Tinsmiths used patterns to cut out the pieces, hammered and shaped them, and soldered the parts. If a piece was to be used with heat, a copper bottom was added because of the low melting point of tin. The industrial revolution brought about machine-made, mass-produced tinware pieces. The handmade era had ended by the late 19th century.

References: Dover Stamping Co, *1869 Illustrated Catalog,* Astragal Press, 1994 reprint; Marilyn E. Dragowick (ed), *Metalwares Price Guide,* Antique Trader Books, 1995; Dana G. Morykan and Harry L. Rinker, *Warman's Country Antiques & Collectibles,* Third Edition Wallace-Homestead, 1996; John Player, *The Origins and Craft of Antique Tin & Tole,* Norwood Publishing, 1995 (available from Christie & Christie Assoc, PO Box 392, Cookstown, Ontario, Canada L0L 1L0).

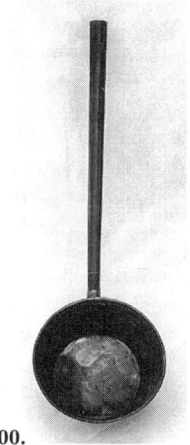

Dipper, 12½" l handle, 6" d bowl, $40.00.

TINWARE, DECORATED

History: The art of decorating sheet iron, tin, and tin-coated sheet iron dates back to the mid-18th century. The Welsh called the practice pontypool; the French, tôle peinte. In America the center for tin-decorated ware in the late 1700s was Berlin, Connecticut.

Several styles of decorating techniques were used: painting, japanning, and stenciling. Designs were done by both professionals and itinerants. English and Oriental motifs strongly influenced both form and design.

A special type of decoration was the punch work on unpainted tin practiced by the Pennsylvania tinsmiths. Forms included coffeepots, spice boxes, and grease lamps.

Reference: Marilyn E. Dragowick (ed), *Metalwares Price Guide,* Antique Trader Books, 1995.

Basket, 10½ × 9″, crimped and curled dec	**825.00**
Box, dome top, orig dark brown japanning, white band	
4¼″ l, floral dec, red and yellow stripes, wear	**115.00**
6¾″ l, floral dec, red, green, and yellow stripes, wear, one hinge loose	**115.00**
7″ l yellow, red, green, and black floral dec, hasp end broken	**125.00**
Canister, 27½″ h, country store–type, worn old black paint, red striping and gilt letters	**275.00**
Canteen, 5⅝″ h, punched star and circle dec	**95.00**
Coal Hod	
23¾″ h, old black paint, worn gilt and floral transfers, rack in back for tools, marked "GD Manf. Co." .	**225.00**
25″ h, 16″ w, 14″ d, green ground, gilt apples, lion finial, paw feet, French, c1820	**600.00**
Coffeepot, 10¾″ h, worn orig dark brown japanning, red, yellow, white, and dark green floral dec, some old touch-up repair	**715.00**
Foot Warmer, 9″ l, punched circles, hearts, and diamonds, mortised wooden frame, turned posts, worn red finish, int. pan	**225.00**
Lamp, 20½″ h, adjustable candle socket and shade, old paint, red and gold dec, brass post and finial	**615.00**
Lantern, 16″ h, old yellow japanning, hinged door, added candle socket, reflector slot	**115.00**
Nutmeg Grater, 6″ l, brown japanning, hand crank	**175.00**
Patch Box, 1½″ l, 1″ w, ½″ h, curved rect shape, ¾ hinged top, colorful flower dec	**75.00**
Pudding Mold, 4 × 6⅝ × 4¾″, punched shell and heart dec	**900.00**
Rattle, 12¼″ × 7½ × 6¼″, punched dec, inscribed "December 8, 1879 for good boys only"	**350.00**

Tea Caddy, 5¼″ h, worn orig dark brown japanning, yellow, red, and dark green floral dec, battered top and collar	**60.00**
Teapot, 8¼″ h, worn orig red paint, yellow, white, and dark green floral dec, resoldered handle	**330.00**
Tray	
16¾″ l, chromolitho scene, Cupid and Psyche, marked "Souvenir of Zoar, Ohio," very minor wear	**300.00**
18½ × 24¼″, rect, stencil and painted dec, central scene of flight from Egypt, fruit and foliate filled borders, Victorian, mid 19th C	**300.00**
24 × 17½″, cranberry red, green leaf border, early 19th C, fair condition	**125.00**
26½ × 19½″, transfer dec, wrinkled yellow ground, eight early French scenes of famous events around border, poor condition	**175.00**
30 × 23″, oval, courting couple in center, two putti, scenes of daily life around border, mustard-colored background, handles, marked on back, worn areas, 19th C	**650.00**
Urn, cov, 13″ h, black ground, acorn finial, lion's-mask handles, stenciled panel with peasants in farmyard, Neoclassical, early 19th C, price for pr	**1,500.00**

TOBACCO CUTTERS

History: Before pre-packaging, tobacco was delivered to merchants in bulk form. Tobacco cutters were used to cut the tobacco into desired sizes.

Arrow-Cupples Co	**45.00**
Battle Ax	**175.00**
Griswold, No. 3	**110.00**
Horse Head, bridle, mane, SP	**90.00**
Keen Cutter, E C Simmons	**150.00**

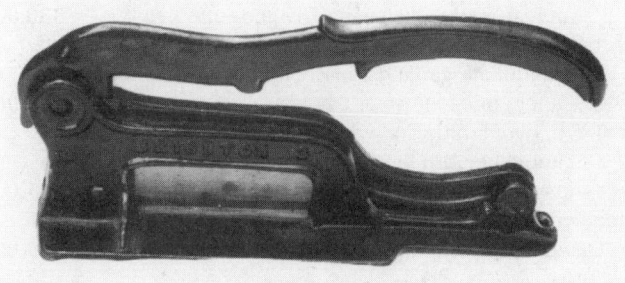

Cast Iron, Brighton 3, $30.00.

Master Workman, orig label	**115.00**
Paraflint, brass, dog, engraved sides	**225.00**
Pennsylvania Hardware Co, 1900	**50.00**
R J Reynolds Co, orig black japanned finish	**95.00**
Spear Head, ornate	**225.00**
Star Brand Tobacco, 1885	**50.00**
Wood, 10″ h, guillotine	**90.00**

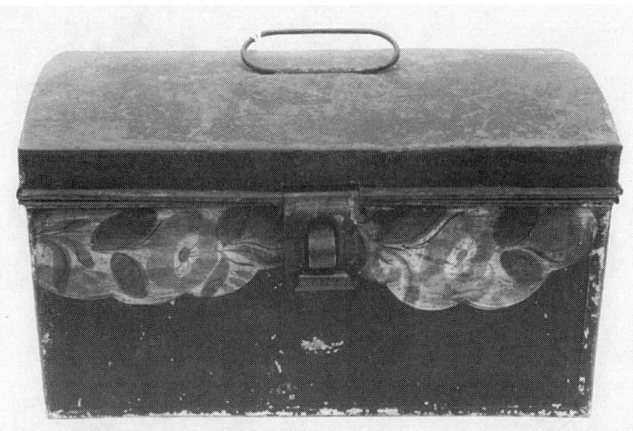

Document Box, dome lid, black ground, white band trim, red flowers, green leaves, 4 × 7¾ × 4½″, $185.00.

TOBACCO JARS

History: A tobacco jar is a container for storing tobacco. Tobacco humidors were made of various materials and in many shapes, including figurals. The earliest jars date to the early 17th century; however, most examples seen in the antiques market today were made in the late 19th or early 20th centuries.

Collectors' Club: Society of Tobacco Jar Collectors, 6370 Kirby Ridge Cove, Memphis, TN 38119.

Bisque
    Black man, wearing high-pointed collar, Germany . **225.00**
    Skull, sitting on book, wearing golfing cap **150.00**
Cut Glass, 9″ h, hobstars, strawberry diamond, fan, lid
    with cut knob **550.00**
Majolica, 4 × 5″, lady, pink turban, intaglio eyes **95.00**
Porcelain, 5½″ h, Indian, polychrome dec, set-on lid, E
    Bohne & Sohne **235.00**

Ceramic, head, student, blue cap with yellow band, light-green bow tie, high glaze, marked "6597/71", 4⅞″ h, $75.00.

Pottery
    5¼″ h, black lady, light blue headdress **115.00**
    11½″ d, blue and white scene, Indian smoking pipe
      and jar marked "Havana," Dutch **330.00**
    12″ h, ovoid, blue and white, embellished oval panel,
      blue foliate garlands, inscribed "N3," brass cap,
      Dutch, price for pr **1,250.00**
    13″ h, ovoid, blue and white, floral and foliate scroll
      cartouche, urn and stylized flower heads and
      leaves, inscribed "Rappe," brass cov, Dutch **935.00**
Stoneware, blue floral dec, gray pebbled ground, Star of
    David lid, bail handle **225.00**

TOBY JUGS

History: Toby jugs are drinking vessels that usually depict a full-figured, robust, genial drinking man. They originated in England in the late 18th century. The term "Toby" probably is related to the character Uncle Toby from *Tristram Shandy* by Laurence Sterne.

References: Susan and Al Bagdade, *Warman's English & Continental Pottery & Porcelain,* Second Edition, Wallace-Homestead, 1991; Vic Schuler, *Collecting British Toby Jugs,* Second Edition,

Kevin Francis Publishing, n.d., distributed by Wallace-Homestead.

Additional Listings: Royal Doulton.

REPRODUCTION ALERT

During the last 100 years or more, tobies have been copiously reproduced by many potteries in the United States and England.

5¼″ h, Mr Toby, seated, tricorn hat, polychrome glaze,
    luster trim **200.00**
6⅜″ h, Benjamin Franklin, seated figure, pipe, wine goblet, mottled brown Rockingham glaze, Bennington,
    1849–58 .... **550.00**
7¼″ h, Huntsman, Royal Doulton, c1910 .... **350.00**
9⅛″ h, Mr Toby, seated, holding jug, tricorn hat, jacket,
    vest, knee breeches, manganese, soft green, brown
    ochre, yellow, and orange-ochre, Prattware, 18th C,
    pipe bowl missing, slight damage **1,540.00**
9⅜″ h, seated man, blue and yellow mottled coat, yellow
    pants, brown hair, hat, and shoes, holding jug on left
    knee, pipe between legs, Leeds type, c1800 .... **850.00**
9½″ h
    Derbyshire, standing man, yellow-tan glaze, dark
      brown splashes, mid-19th C **125.00**
    Staffordshire, seated man, blue coat, yellow
      breeches, foaming jug on left knee, late 18th C . **900.00**
    Wood, Ralph, seated man, green waistcoat, gray
      jacket, dark hat, one hand raised to mouth **950.00**
10½″ h
    Napoleon, graniteware, standing, yellow waistcoat,
      blue vest, marked "Made in Trenton, NJ" **400.00**
    Sailor, seated, tricorn hat, holding jug in one hand,
      pipe in other, Staffordshire, 19th C, repairs **345.00**
10¾″ h, Napoleon, ironstone, multicolored enamel,
    marked "Napoleon Jug-patent applied for Alfred E
    Evans, Philadelphia, PA" **400.00**

Staffordshire, Lord Nelson, multicolored, c1860, 11½″ h, $350.00.

11″ h
   Chained kneeling black woman, eyes turned upward, appl green coat, gold outlines, royal blue and dark red stripes alternating with gold patterned stripes, gold belt, white shirt, gold-edged collar with gold dots, royal blue and gold bow at neck, yellow hat with blue, dark red, and yellow stripes, black painted hair, crabstock handle, slight loss to paint **6,000.00**
   Coachman, wearing tassels, Rockingham glaze, Bennington, 1849 mark **450.00**
11¼″ h, Mr Toby, seated, tricorn hat, underglaze blue, green, red, black, and brown enamel, pink flesh, orig lid, Staffordshire, repair to hat **220.00**
11½″ h, Hearty Goodfellow, full-figured man, tricorn hat, coat, waistcoat, knee breeches, carrying pitcher and ale glass, rockwork base, manganese, green, pale blue, tan, brown-ochre, olive green, Staffordshire, attributed to Ralph Wood, 18th C, professional restoration **3,575.00**

TOOLS

History: Before the advent of the assembly line and mass production, practically everything required for living was handmade at home or by a local tradesman or craftsman. The cooper, the blacksmith, the cabinet maker, and the carpenter all had their special tools.

Early examples of these hand tools are collected for their workmanship, ingenuity, place of manufacture, or design. Modern-day craftsman often search out and use old hand tools in order to authentically recreate the manufacture of an object.

References: Ronald S. Barlow, *The Antique Tool Collector's Guide to Value,* Windmill Publishing, Third Edition, 1991; Terri Clemens, *American Family Farm Antiques,* Wallace-Homestead, 1994; Kenneth L. Cope, *American Machinist's Tools,* Astragal Press, 1993; ———, *Makers of American Machinist Tools,* Astragal Press, 1994; Martin J. Donnelly, *The Catalogue of Antique Tools,* published by author (31 Rumsey St, Bath, NY 14810), 1996; Herbert P. Kean and Emil S. Pollak, *A Price Guide to Antique Tools,* Astragal Press, 1992; ———, *Collecting Antique Tools,* Astragal Press, 1990; Kathryn McNerney, *Antique Tools, Our American Heritage,* Collector Books, 1979, 1995 value update; Dana G. Morykan and Harry L. Rinker, *Warman's Country Antiques & Collectibles,* Third Edition, Wallace-Homestead, 1996; Emil and Martyl Pollak, *A Guide to American Wooden Planes and Their Makers,* Third Edition, The Astragal Press, 1994; ———, *Prices Realized on Rare Imprinted American Wood Planes, 1979–1992,* Astragal Press, 1993; *Price Guide to Keen Kutter Tools,* L-W Books, 1993; John M. Whelan, *The Wooden Plane,* Astragal Press, 1993.

Periodicals: *Fine Tool Journal,* PO Box 4001, Pittsford, VT 05763; *Plumb Line,* 10023 St Clair's Retreat, Fort Wayne, IN 46825; *Stanley Tool Collector News,* 208 Front St, PO Box 227, Marietta, OH 45750; *Tool Ads,* PO Box 33, Hamilton, MT 59840.

Collectors' Clubs: Blow Torch Collectors Club, 3328 258th Ave SE, Issaquah, WA 98027-9173; Collectors of Rare & Familiar Tools Society, 38 Colony Ct, Murray Hill, NJ 07974; Early American Industries Assoc, PO Box 2128, Empire State Plaza Station, Albany, NY 12220; Early American Industries-West, 8476 West Way Dr, La Jolla, CA 92038; Mid-West Tool Collectors Assoc, 808 Fairway Dr, Columbia, MO 65201; Missouri Valley Wrench Club, 613 N Long St, Shelbyville, IL 62565; New England Tool Collectors Assoc, 303 Fisher Rd, Fitchburg, MA 01420; Ohio Tool Collectors Assoc, PO Box 261, London, OH 43140; Pacific Northwest Tool Collectors, 2132 NE 81st St, Seattle, WA 98115; Potomac Antique Tools & Industries Assoc, 6802 Newbitt Pl, McLean, VA 22101; Rocky Mountain Tool Collectors, 2024 Owens Ct, Denver, CO 80227; Society of Workers in Early Arts & Trades, 606 Lake Lena Blvd, Auburndale, FL 33823; Southwest Tool Collectors Assoc, 7032 Oak Bluff Dr, Dallas, TX 75240; Three Rivers Tool Collectors, 39 S Rolling Hills, Irwin, PA 15642; Tool Group of Canada, 7 Tottenham Rd, Ontario MC3 2J3 Canada.

Museums: American Precision Museum Association, Windsor, VT; Mercer Museum, Doylestown, PA; Shelburne Museum, Shelburne, VT; World of Tools Museum, Waverly, TN.

SPECIAL AUCTION

Fine Tool Journal
27 Fickett Rd
Pownal, ME 04069

Beader, Stanley No. 66, full set of replacement blades, fences, 70% plating **100.00**
Bit Gauge, Stanley No. 49, orig box, early S R & L label   **22.50**
Butt Gauge, Stanley No. 95G, yellow box with reinforced corners **22.50**
Calipers, Goodell Pratt, No. 505, outside spring, 8″, faded red box **25.00**
Carving Tools, Miller Falls, No. 1, set of 6, rosewood handles, orig oak box with inside paper label **110.00**
Clapboard Maker, Stanley 88, adjustable, orig box, early S R & L label **40.00**
Dowel Jig, Stanley No. 59, 6 drill guides, orig box **40.00**
Dowel Machine, Stanley No. 77, ⅜″ cutter, blue finish, orig instructions and cardboard box **395.00**
Drill, Miller Falls type, 90% orig red detail painting, 96% japanning **110.00**
Grooving Router, Preston, adjustable, three cutters, three fences, 80% japanning **85.00**
Gouge, Ibbotson Peace & Co, graduated set of 9, cast steel **225.00**
Hammer
   Adz head, Cheney No. 777 . . . .   **65.00**
   Snowball, wrapped handle, fancy brass clip **35.00**
Level
   Goodell Pratt, 18″, cast iron, double plumb, one dry vial **15.00**
   Stratton Brothers No. 10, brass, bound 12″, rosewood, 1908 Barber quarter dollar inlaid in side **195.00**
Oat and Wheat Grinder, cast iron, orig paint, marked ''G. E. Patric Patantee, M'f'd by the Superior Drill Co, Springfield, Ohio,'' orig wooden box **400.00**
Parallel Ruler, Carrington's Patent, manufactured by William Hill, Wallingford, CT, wood, paper label **65.00**

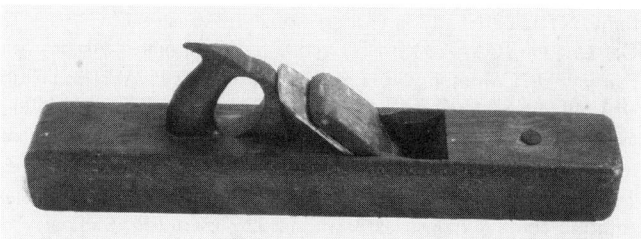

Jointer Plane, Ogontz Tool Co., pine and maple, 22" l, $30.00.

Plane
Bedrock, 604, bench, type 9, orange frog, Sweet Hart
    blade, 93% japanning **145.00**
Spiers Ayr, rosewood filled, 2⅛" iron, polished **325.00**
Stanley
    No. 47, dado, type 5, 60% japanning **395.00**
    No. 50, combination, fifteen cutters, B casting,
        70% plating **110.00**
    No. 97, chisel, 60% japanning **395.00**
    No. 278, rabbet, 85% japanning, wrong fence .. **125.00**
Ratchet Brace
    Consolidated Tool Works, Inc., No. 808, knob con-
        trolled, hardwood handles, 85% plating **45.00**
    Keystone, W A Ives Mfg Co, Wallingford, CT, lever
        controlled, hardwood handles **65.00**
Saw, Disston, right angle **30.00**
Saw Set, Stanley 42, orig box **15.00**
Screwdriver, 18½" l, Cowles Hardware Co, Warranted
    Superior, sold by T.H.E. Co., cabinetmaker's type .. **48.00**
Sharpening Stone, 13¾" l, mounted on block, carved
    designs and "James N. Rosser, 1826" **385.00**
Socket Set, PS & W Co, set of 12 in orig wood box, 9
    with applewood handles, 3 with replaced handles . **325.00**
Wrench, W & C Wynn & Co, Patent, combination
    wrench, pliers, buggy wrench, hammer, and screw-
    driver **75.00**

TOOTHPICK HOLDERS

History: Toothpick holders, indispensable table accessories of the Victorian era, are small containers made specifically to hold toothpicks.

They were made in a wide range of materials: china (bisque and porcelain), glass (art, blown, cut, opalescent, pattern, etc.), and metals, especially silver plate. Makers include both American and European firms.

By applying a decal or transfer, a toothpick holder became a souvenir item; by changing the decal or transfer, the same blank could become a memento for any number of locations.

References: William Heacock, *Encyclopedia of Victorian Colored Pattern Glass, Book I,* Second Edition, Antique Publications, 1976, 1992 value update; ———, *1,000 Toothpick Holders,* Antique Publications, 1977; ———, *Rare & Unlisted Toothpick Holders,* Antique Publications, 1984; National Toothpick Holders Collectors Society, *Toothpick* Holders, Antique Publications, 1992.

Collectors' Club: National Toothpick Holder Collectors, PO Box 246, Sawyer, MI 49221.

Additional Listings: See *Warman's Americana & Collectibles* for more examples.

Advisor: Judy Knauer.

Art Glass
Amberina, IVT, pedestal base **200.00**
Bohemian, rose with gold trim **350.00**
Cameo, Daum Nancy, NTHCS #162 .... **195.00**
Rainbow Twister **175.00**
China, Blue Rock, Shelley **25.00**
Custard Glass, Chrysanthemum Sprig **245.00**
Metal
    Egg on side, cupid and wishbone, SP, pat'd 1895,
        Derby, replated **85.00**
    Rabbit **60.00**
    This is the Rat that ate the Malt, Pairpoint **110.00**
    Yeoman of the Guard, NTHCS #837 .... **110.00**
Opalescent Glass
    Iris with Meander
        Blue **95.00**
        Green **55.00**
    Overall Hobnail, blue **45.00**
    Swan and Cattails, fiery **38.00**
Pattern Glass
    Aztec, McKee **40.00**
    Beveled Star **60.00**
    Bull's Eye & Fan, green **135.00**
    Columned Thumbprints, Westmoreland **65.00**
    Continental, Heisey **120.00**
    Elephant Toes, cranberry staining **65.00**
    Fandango, Heisey **85.00**
    Frances Ware Swirl, frosted **130.00**
    Gold Band
        Clear, gold trim **40.00**
        Vaseline, no gold **40.00**
    Hartford, Fostoria **45.00**
    Jefferson Colonial, apple green **45.00**
    Michigan, yellow stain, dec **65.00**
    Minnesota, green, gold trim **135.00**
    New Era, Ward's **35.00**
    One-O-One, blue opaque **45.00**
    Paddle Wheel and Star, clear, gold trim **25.00**
    Panelled Cane, Heisey **45.00**
    Pineapple and Fan, green, gold trim **130.00**

Silver, dog dressed as man, holding lantern, basket holder on back, marked "Meriden B #2," c1880, $185.00.

Polished Mirror
    Clear 20.00
        Heavy gold trim 30.00
    Shoesone, clear, gold trim 30.00
    Tennessee 90.00
    Vermont, green, gold trim 50.00
    X-Ray, green, gold trim 45.00
Porcelain
    Dutch children kissing 75.00
    Gamp, Royal Doulton 510.00
    Little Boy with Horn and Chick 30.00
    Tapestry, egg shape, Goose Girl, tiny nick and short
        hairline 90.00
    Two Pigs with Hat 35.00
Rubena, Bulbous Ring Neck 85.00
Ruby Stained
    Cut Block, Heisey 105.00
    The Prize 95.00
    Spearpoint Band 200.00
Spatter Glass, Royal Ivy, cased 195.00

TORTOISESHELL ITEMS

History: For many years amber and mottled tortoiseshell has been used in the manufacture of small items such as boxes, combs, dresser sets, and trinkets.

Note: Anyone dealing in the sale of tortoiseshell objects should be familiar with the Endangered Species Act and Amendment in its entirety. As of November 1978, antique tortoiseshell objects can be legally imported and sold with some restrictions.

Bowl, 7¾" d, one turned-up side, appl amber feet 115.00
Box, cov, round, small round watercolor of gentleman
    on top, early 19th C 300.00
Bracelet, 3" d, two inlaid silver animals 40.00
Dance Program Holder, 5¾ × 3⅛", rect, Continental
    silver and enamel, floral and shell engraved silver
    frame, one side with oval ¾ portrait of damsel, Vic-
    torian, mid-19th C 350.00
Hair Ornament, Art Nouveau
    Back Comb, gilt grass, turquoise glass accents 135.00
    Side, appl metallic dec, simulated gemstones 75.00
Hairpin, carved poppy blossom, heavy shell 135.00
Inkstand, 8 × 16", three cut glass bottles, brass inlay,
    shaped handles 400.00
Lorgnette, carved, black cloth trim, Victorian, price for
    pr 75.00

Pin, tortoise shape, 1½" l, $45.00.

Match Safe, pocket type, emb sides 75.00
Shaving Brush, handle with inlaid MOP dec 45.00
Tea Caddy
    5" w, 5½" h, George III, silver mounts, ivory inlay,
        late 18th C 1,375.00
    6 × 8 × 5½", William IV, oblong top, breakfront
        outline, twin canisters, conforming case resting on
        molded base, second-quarter 19th C 900.00
Vase, 8¾" h, flared top, pedestal base 165.00

TOYS

History: The first cast iron toys began to appear in America shortly after the Civil War. Leading 19th-century manufacturers include Hubley, Dent, Kenton, and Schoenhut. In the first decades of the 20th century, Arcade, Buddy L, Marx, and Tootsie Toy joined these earlier firms. Wooden toys were made by George Brown and other manufacturers who did not sign or label their work.

Nuremberg, Germany, was the European center for the toy industry from the late 18th through the mid-20th centuries. Companies such as Lehman and Marklin produced high-quality toys.

References: Linda Baker, *Modern Toys, American Toys,* Collector Books, 1985, 1993 value update; Bill Bruegman, *Toys of the Sixties,* Cap'n Penny Productions, 1991; Bertel Bruun, *Toy Soldiers Identification and Price Guide,* Avon Books, 1994; Steve Butler and Clarence Young, *Autoquotes, The Complete Reference for: Promotions, Pot Metal & Plastic with Prices,* Autohobby Publication, 1993; Jurgen and Marianne Cieslik, *Lehmann Toys,* New Cavendish Books, 1982; Don Cranmer, *Collectors Encyclopedia, Toys—Banks,* L-W Books, 1986, 1993 value update; Charles F. Donovan, Jr., *Renwal, World's Finest Toys,* published by author (11877 US Hwy 431, Ohatchee, AL 36271), 1994; Edward Force, *Lledo Toys,* Schiffer Publishing, 1996; Tom Frey, *Toy Bop: Kid Classics of the 50's & 60's,* Fuzzy Dice Productions, 1994.

Gordon Gardiner and Alistair Morris, *The Illustrated Encyclopedia of Metal Toys,* Harmony Books, 1984; Christine Gentry and Sally Gibson-Downs, *Motorcycle Toys,* Collector Books, 1994; Lillian Gottschalk, *American Toy Cars & Trucks,* Abbeville Press, 1985; David C. Gould and Donna Crevar-Donaldson, *Occupied Japan Toys with Prices,* L-W Book Sales, 1993; Morton Hirschberg, *Steam Toys,* Schiffer Publishing, 1996; Don Hultzman, *Collecting Battery Toys,* Books Americana, 1994; Ken Hutchison & Greg Johnson, *The Golden Age of Automotive Toys, 1925–1941,* Collector Books, 1996; Charles M. Jacobs, *Kenton Cast Iron Toys,* Schiffer Publishing, 1996; Dana Johnson, *Matchbox Toys 1947–1996,* Second Edition, Collector Books, 1996; Dale Kelley, *Collecting the Tin Toy Car, 1950–1970,* Schiffer Publishing, 1984; Lisa Kerr, *American Tin-Litho Toys,* Collectors Press, 1995; Constance King, *Metal Toys & Automata,* Chartwell Books, 1989.

Ernest and Ida Long, *Dictionary of Toys Sold in America,* 2 vols., published by authors; David Longest, *Antique & Collectible Toys 1870–1950,* Collector Books, 1994; ———, *Character Toys and Collectibles,* (1984, 1992 value update), Second Series (1987) Collector Books; ———, *Toys,* Collector Books, 1990, 1994 value update; Albert W. McCollough, *The New Book of Buddy L Toys,* Vol. I (1991), Vol. II (1991), Greenberg Publishing; Brian Moran, *Battery Toys,* Schiffer Publishing, 1984; Richard O'Brien, *Collecting Toy Cars & Trucks,* Books Americana, 1994; ———, *Collecting Toys,* Sixth Edition, Books Americana, 1993; ———, *The Story* of American Toys, Abbeville Press, 1990; Robert M. Overstreet, Overstreet Toy Ring Price Guide, Second Edition, Collector Books, 1996; Bob Parker, Hot Wheels, Revised Edition, Schiffer Publishing, 1996; Maxine A. Pinsky, Greenberg's Guide to Marx Toys, Vol. I (1988), Vol. II (1990), Greenberg Publishing Co; ———, Marx Toys, Schiffer Publishing, 1996.

Harry L. Rinker, Toy Price Guide, Antique Trader Books, 1996; Martyn L. Schorr, The Guide To Mechanical Toy Collecting, Performance Media, 1979; Schroeder's Collectible Toys, Third Edition, Collector Books, 1996; Carole and Richard Smith, Pails by Comparison, published by author (PO Box 2068, Huntington, NY 11743), 1996; Carl P. Stirn, Turn-of-the-Century Dolls, Toys and Games (1893 catalog reprint), Dover Publications, 1990; Jack Tempest, Post-War Tin Toys, Wallace-Homestead, 1991; Carol Turpen, Baby Boomer Toys and Collectibles, Schiffer Publishing, 1993; Gerhard G. Walter, Metal Toys from Nuremberg, Schiffer Publishing, 1992; Blair Whitton, Knopf Collector's Guide to American Antiques: Toys, Alfred A. Knopf, 1984; ———, Paper Toys of the World, Hobby House Press, 1986.

Periodicals: Antique Toy World, PO Box 34509, Chicago, IL 60634; Canadian Toy Mania, PO Box 489, Rocanville, Saskatchewan SOA 3LO Canada; Die Cast & Tin Toy Report, 559 North Park Ave, Easton, CT 06612; Model & Toy Collector Magazine, 137 Casterton Ave, Akron, OH 44303; Plane News, PO Box 845, Greenwich, CT 06836; Robot World & Price Guide, PO Box 184, Lenox Hill Station, New York, NY 10021; Toy Cannon News, PO Box 2052-N, Norcross, GA 30071; Toy Collector & Price Guide, 700 E. State St, Iola, WI 54990; Toy Collector Marketplace, 1550 Territorial Rd, Benton Harbor, MI 49022; Toy Gun Collectors of America Newsletter, 312 Starling Way, Anaheim, CA 92807; Toy Shop, 700 East State St, Iola, WI 54990; Toy Trader, PO Box 1050, Dubuque, IA 52004; Toybox Magazine, 8393 E Holly Rd, Holly, MI 48442; U.S. Toy Collector Magazine, PO Box 4244, Missoula, MT 59806; Yo-Yo Times, PO Box 1519, Herndon, VA 22070.

Collectors' Clubs: American Game Collectors Assoc, 49 Brooks Ave, Lewiston, ME 04240; Antique Engine, Tractor & Toy Club, Inc, 5731 Paradise Rd, Slatington, PA 18080; Antique Toy Collectors of America, 13th Floor, Two Wall St, New York, NY 10005; Capitol Miniature Auto Collectors Club, 10207 Greenacres Dr, Silver Spring, MD 20903; Diecast Exchange Club, PO Box 1066, Pineallas Park, FL 34665; Ertl Collectors Club, Highways 136 & 120, Dyersville, IA 52040; Farm Toy Collectors Club, PO Box 38, Boxholm, IA 50040; Majorette Diecast Toy Collectors Assoc, 13447 NW Albany Ave, Bend, OR 97701; Miniature Piano Enthusiast Club, 633 Pennsylvania Ave, Hagerstown, MD 21740; San Francisco Bay Brooklin Club, PO Box 61018, Palo Alto, CA 94306; Schoenhut Collectors Club, 45 Louis Ave, West Seneca, NY 14224; Southern California Toy Collectors Club, Ste 300, 1760 Termino, Long Beach, CA 90804;

Museums: American Museum of Automobile Miniatures, Andover, MA; Eugene Field House & Toy Museum, St Louis, MO; Evanston Historical Society, Evanston, IL 60201; Forbes Magazine Collection, New York, NY; Hobby City Doll & Toy Museum, Anaheim, CA; Margaret Woodbury Strong Museum, Rochester, NY; Matchbox & Lesney Toy Museum, Durham, CT; Matchbox Road Museum, Newfield, NJ; Museum of the City of New York, New York, NY; Smithsonian Institution, Washington, DC; Spinning Top Exploratory Museum, Burlington, WI; Toy & Miniature Museum of Kansas City, Kansas City, MO; Toy Museum of Atlanta,

Atlanta, GA; Washington Dolls' House & Toy Museum, Washington, DC; Western Reserve Historical Society, Cleveland, OH.

Additional Listings: Characters, Disneyana, Dolls, and Schoenhut. Also see Warman's Americana & Collectibles for more examples.

Notes: Every toy is collectible; the key is condition. Good working order is important when considering mechanical toys. Examples in this listing are considered to be at least in good condition, if not better, unless otherwise specified.

Arcade
Austin Roll a Plane, 7½" l, 1928 . . . . **450.00**
Blue Bird Cab, 5¼" l, black and white, good condition **625.00**

Brinks Van, 11¾" l, red, white rubber tires, rear door opens and locks, 1932, excellent condition **20,000.00**

Buick, 8½" l

Coupe, light gray, white tires, very good condition **4,000.00**

Deluxe Sedan, light gray, white rubber tires, very good condition **4,300.00**

Car and Trailer, 6½" l, red car pulls gray trailer, very good condition **110.00**

Chevy

7" l, Superior Roadster, black, spoke wheels, nickel-plated driver, 1925, near mint **2,300.00**

8" l, Sedan, single stripe, gray and black, nickel-plated driver, 1928, good condition **950.00**

9" l, Utility Stake Truck, gray and black, spoke wheels, nickel-plated driver, 1925, excellent condition **950.00**

City Ambulance, 6" l, black, white rubber tires, 1932, excellent conditon **700.00**

Cross Country Bus, 7½" l, black and white, white rubber tires, 1937, near mint condition **2,200.00**

Delivery Truck, 8⅜" l, light green, white rubber tires, excellent condition **5,500.00**

Double Decker Bus, 8" l, green, black rubber tires, nickel-plated driver, orig decal, 1929, very good condition **550.00**

Dump Truck Trailer, 20½" l, green and red, nickel-plated wheels, 1921, very good condition **1,550.00**

Express Truck, 8½" l, green, white rubber tires, nickel-plated driver, very good condition **1,650.00**

Farm Wagon, red and gray, two gray horses, separate driver, rubber tires, near mint condition **950.00**

Fire Chief Car, 5⅝" l, 1941, very good condition ... **240.00**

Fire Truck

Ladder

15¾" l, red, yellow, black tires, painted driver and fireman **1,050.00**

Doll et Cie, ferris wheel, early 1900s, painted tinplate, manually operated, 17" h, several replaced figures, $2,750.00. Photo courtesy of Sotheby's.

17¾" l, Mack, red and yellow, driver, excellent conditon **2,600.00**

Pumper, 6⅜" l, red, driver, near mint **475.00**

Monocoupe

5½" l, 1929, excellent condition **475.00**

12" wingspan, orange and black, white rubber tires, 1928, excellent condition **1,850.00**

Racer, 7¾" l, nickel-plated driver, near mint condition **750.00**

Showboat, 10⅝" l, very good condition **525.00**

Tank, 7½" l, army, crank-operated gun, rubber tires, 1937 ....**2,200.00**

Bliss

Battleship, litho on wood, 36" l, some restoration ..**4,100.00**

Boat, *Priscilla*, litho on paper **2,860.00**

Buddy L, pressed steel

Army Transport, 19½" l, end gate and canvas missing **60.00**

Oil Truck, #14, Standard Oil, red cab and truck body, black pull rod, brass spigot, c1934, 27" l, very good condition, slight scratches **4,025.00**

Pickup Truck, #210, Flivver, round decal on bottom, 1920s, 12" l, very good finish, bent windshield posts **815.00**

Steam Shovel, black, red roof, 1920s, 20" l, 13¼" h, good conditon **230.00**

Dayton, roadster, red, pressed steel, friction, late 1920s, 12½" l **320.00**

Doepke, pressed steel, 1950s

Fire Truck, American La France, extension ladder, two removable ladders, 35" l **60.00**

Sand Loader, Barber Greene, 24" l **290.00**

Unit Crane, orange, 22" l, 19" h **145.00**

Ertl, tractor, John Deere

#500, 1923 Model D, orig box **20.00**

#581, utility, orig box **25.00**

Hoge, motorcycle, litho tin windup, traffic cycle-car type, green delivery body, blue driver, rubber wheels, c1930, 10¼" l **3,220.00**

Hubley

Crash Car Motorcycle, painted cast iron, red, rubber wheels, 1930s, 4¾" l **145.00**

Racer 2330, 7¼" l, cast aluminum, #22 .... **45.00**

Road Roller, painted cast iron, green, red wheels, orig driver, c1930, 14" l, poor finish, section behind driver broken and missing **400.00**

Santa Claus, 15" l, sleigh, one reindeer, cast iron .. **500.00**

Speed Boat, painted cast iron, red, integral driver, nickel-plated wheels, 1930s, 5½" l, good finish, nicks **210.00**

Streamline Racer, 6¼" l, cast iron **30.00**

Town Car, cast iron, blue, nickel-plated grill, headlights, bumpers, running boards, and taillights, rubber wheels, late 1930s, 6¾" l, fair condition, some surface rust **290.00**

Ives and Blakeslee Co, Bridgeport, CT, horse-drawn mechanical fire pumper, painted cast iron, two figures, orig wooden box, c1890, 18¾" h, excellent condition, eagle finial missing **7,475.00**

Kelmet, pressed steel

Dump Truck, Big Boy, late 1920s, 25" l, fair condition, surface rust, tailgate missing **345.00**

Fire Truck, Big Boy, aerial truck, white rubber slip on

Gong Bell Toy Co., Keene, NY, cat and dog bell toy, $1,250.00.

Lehmann, Masuyama Family, Japanese lady holding umbrella in rickshaw, 7½" l

tires, two fire extinguishers, two operating wooden ladders, three removable wooden ladders, c1927, 29" l, very good condition, minor flaking **1,955.00**

Kenton, cast iron
  Cement Mixer, Jaeger, painted red, blue, and green, nickel-plated mixing drum, bucket, and wheels, 1930s, 6½" l **290.00**
  Overland Circus, 14" l, two horses, cage **150.00**

Keystone, pressed steel
  Ambulance, #73, Packard, khaki, canvas sides, back curtains, c1928, 27½" l, fair condition **490.00**
  Dump Truck, crank, 1920s, 26" l, repainted, tailgate missing **260.00**
  Steamroller, Ride-em, #60, black, green roof, red wheels and trim, c1931, 20" l, excellent condition **750.00**

Kingsbury, pressed steel
  Racer, Golden Arrow, windup, c1930, 19¾" l, excellent condition **920.00**
  Sedan, sky roof, windup, orange roof, nickel-plated trim, c1937, 14" l, finish fair, hood ornament and sliding celluloid sky roof missing **230.00**

Lehmann
  Balky Mule, litho tin windup, bucking mule pulling three-wheeled cart with driver, orig box, early 20th C, 7" l **490.00**

Going to the Fair, litho tin, flywheel mechanism, red fan version, orig box, c1889, 6¼" l **3,110.00**
Quack-Quack, litho tin windup, orig box, early 20th C, 7¼" l, very good condition, minor surface rust, box end flap missing **635.00**
Wild West Bronco, 6" l, 7½" h, litho tin windup, bucking bronco with rider, good condition, some chipping and wear on horse **550.00**

Lionel, boat, craft racing, painted steel, clockwork, composition figures, c1935, 18" l **520.00**

Marx
  Airplane, 6" l, 3½" h, litho tin windup, pilot wearing helmet and goggles, marked "12," good condition **75.00**
  Butterfly, 7¾" l, 2½" h, litho tin windup, brightly colored wings, rolls forward and tumbles **30.00**
  Charlie McCarthy, 8" h, litho tin windup **175.00**
  Jumpin' Jeep, 5½" l, 4¼" h, litho tin windup, driver and passenger, two small wheels in front, two large wheels at center **100.00**

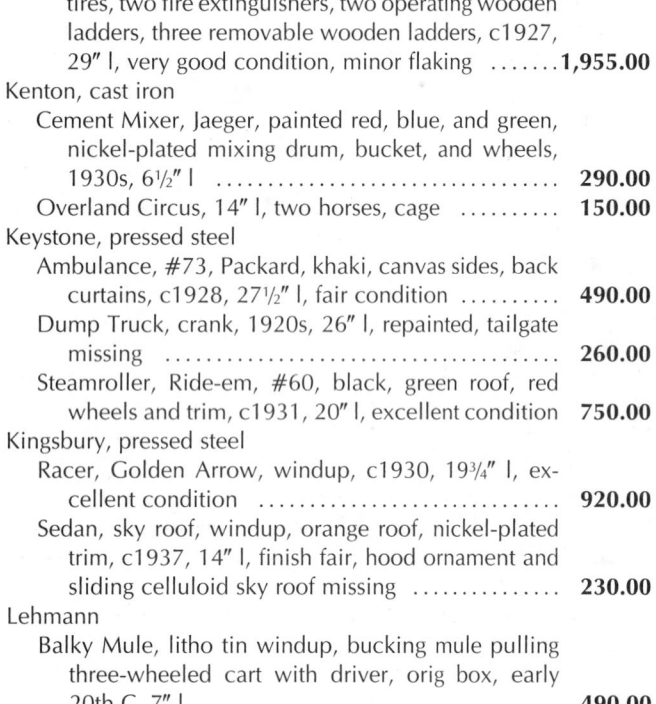

Hubley, lumber loader, plastic, red body, yellow wheels, blue loader, $15.00.

Marx, Amos 'n' Andy taxi, 8" l, $1,800.00.

Murray, pedal car, fire department ladder truck, pressed steel, 1940s, 47" l, finish good, bell and ladders missing **460.00**
Mysto, Magic Kit, c1911, orig instructions and tricks, wear to box, 19½ × 11¼" **690.00**

Neff, car, Moon Town, pressed steel, black hood and
fenders, orange body, 1920s, 12″ l, good condition   **145.00**
Pratt and Letchworth, Buffalo, NY, horse-drawn four-seat
brake, painted cast iron, four animated horses, seven
orig figures, c1890, excellent finish, one mismatched
driver, front hitch missing, drive wheels missing ..**18,400.00**
Smith Miller, truck, Bank of America Brinks, die-cast cab,
pressed-steel body, 1950s, 14″ l, good condition ...   **230.00**
Steelcraft, pressed steel
Dump Truck, Mack, red cab, khaki bed, Little Jim J C
Penney decal, 1930s, 22″ l, fair condition **320.00**
Pedal Car, Willys-Knight, yellow, black, and blue
paint, 1920s, 33″ l, orig condition **4,485.00**
Truck
Hood's Ice Cream, red, gold decal, c1930, 21¾″
l, good condition **415.00**
Wolf and Dessauer, Northern Indiana's Great
Store, maroon body, white lettering, battery-
operated headlights, 1930s, 19″ l, very good
condition, scratches to roof **690.00**
Strauss, litho tin windup
Inter-State Bus, green, yellow striping, c1930, 10¼″ l   **520.00**
Jazzbo Jim, 10″ h **300.00**
Los Angeles Zeppelin, 1930s, 10″ l, propeller missing   **345.00**
Santa and Sleigh, two reindeer, 11½″ l, 5½″ h **825.00**
Structo, pressed steel
Caterpillar Tractor, windup, iron driver, c1920, 8½″
l, very good condition **345.00**
Steam Shovel Truck, red cab, green steam shovel,
battery-operated headlights, c1930, 28″ l, good
condition **460.00**
Sturditoy, pressed steel
Army Truck, #20, c1928, khaki, orig canvas cov, 27″
l, fair to good finish, flaking, steering wheel missing **920.00**
Dump Truck, #1, c1929, green body, black fender,
red chassis and wheels, 27″ l, finish good, some
scratches, missing headlights, broken front
bumper **750.00**
Traveling Store Truck, c1926, black cab, orange
body, red frame and wheels, 26″ l, fair finish, missing back doors **750.00**
Turner, Mack two-pc ladder fire truck, pressed steel,
31½″ l, 1930s, repainted, side ladders missing **115.00**
Unknown Maker
Billiard Players, 15″ l, 6″ h, litho tin windup, pool
table, two billiards players, each holding cue
sticks **140.00**
Bird, 4¾″ h, litho tin windup, chirping, sitting on
birdhouse perch, Japan **50.00**
Cow, 5½″ l, 3¼″ h, litho tin windup, walking, cowbell
on collar, Japan **30.00**
Fire Pumper, 22″ l, cast iron, two horses, one driver   **675.00**
Squeak Toy, papier-mâché
Horse, white, black name and tail, 5″ l, late 19th
C, some wear and paint loss, paper bellows
damaged **175.00**
Panther, crouching, 3¾″ h, early 20th C, replaced
kid bellows, some repainting **115.00**
Touring Sedan, 8″ l, cast iron, driver **75.00**
Waiter, 6½″ h, litho tin windup, skating, slight rust to
right shoe, Japan **65.00**

Wyandotte
Tank Truck, pressed steel, green, wooden wheels,
1930s **115.00**
Wrecker, 14½″ l, plastic and metal, spare tires **65.00**

TRAINS, TOY

History: Railroading has always been an important part of childhood, largely because of the romance associated with the railroad
and the prominence of toy trains.

The first toy trains were cast iron and tin; wind-up motors
added movement. The golden age of toy trains was 1920 to 1955,
when electric-powered units and high-quality rolling stock were
available and names such as Ives, American Flyer, and Lionel
were household words. The advent of plastic in the late 1950s
resulted in considerably lower quality.

Toy trains are designated by a model scale or gauge. The most
popular are HO, N, O and standard. Narrow gauge was a response
to the modern capacity to miniaturize. Its popularity has decreased
in the last few years.

References: Paul V. Ambrose, *Greenberg's Guide to Lionel Trains,
1945–1969,* Vol. III, Greenberg Publishing, 1990; Paul V. Am-
brose and Joseph P. Algozzini, *Greenberg's Guide to Lionel Trains
1945–1969, Vol. IV, Uncatalogued Sets,* (1992), *Vol. V, Rare and
Unusual* (1993), Greenberg Publishing; Susan and Al Bagdade,
Collector's Guide to American Toy Trains, Wallace-Homestead,
1990; John O. Bradshaw, *Greenberg's Guide to Kusan Trains,*
Greenberg Publishing, 1987; Pierce Carlson, *Collecting Toy
Trains,* Pincushion Press, 1993; W. G. Claytor, Jr., P. Doyle, and
C. McKenney, *Greenberg's Guide to Early American Toy Trains,*
Greenberg Publishing, 1993; Joe Deger, *Greenberg's Guide to
American Flyer S Gauge* Vol. I, Fourth Edition, (1991), Vol. II
(1991), Vol. III (1992), Greenberg Publishing; Cindy Lee Floyd
(comp.), *Greenberg's Marx Train Catalogues,* Greenberg Publish-
ing, 1993; Richard Friz, *The Official Identification and Price
Guide to Toy Trains,* House of Collectibles, 1990; John Glaab,
The Brown Book of Brass Locomotives, Third Edition, Chilton,
1993.

Bruce Greenberg, *Greenberg's Guide to Ives Trains,* Vol. I
(1991), Vol. II (1992), Greenberg Publishing; ——— (edited by
Christian F. Rohlfing), *Greenberg's Guide to Lionel Trains: 1901–
1942,* Vol. 1 (1988), Vol. 2 (1988), Greenberg Publishing;
———, *Greenberg's Guide To Lionel Trains: 1945–1969,* Vol. 1,
Eighth Edition (1992), Vol. 2, Second Edition (1993), Greenberg
Publishing; *Greenberg's Lionel Catalogues,* Vol. V, Greenberg
Publishing, 1992; *Greenberg's Marx Train Catalogues,* Greenberg
Publishing, 1992; George Horan, *Greenberg's Guide to Lionel
HO,* Vol. II, Greenberg Publishing, 1993; George Horan and Vin-
cent Rosa, *Greenberg's Guide to Lionel HO,* Vol. I, Second Edi-
tion, Greenberg Publishing, 1993; John Hubbard, *The Story of
Williams Electric Trains,* Greenberg Publishing, 1987; Steven H.
Kimball, *Greenberg's Guide to American Flyer Prewar O Gauge,*
Greenberg Publishing, 1987; Roland La Voie, *Greenberg's Guide
To Lionel Trains, 1970–1991,* Vol. I (1991), Vol. II (1992) Green-
berg Publishing.

Lionel Book Committee, *Lionel Trains: Standard Of The World,
1900–1943,* Train Collectors Association, 1989; Dallas J. Maller-
ich III, *Greenberg's American Toy Trains: From 1900 with Current
Values,* Greenberg Publishing, 1990; ———, *Greenberg's Guide
to Athearn Trains,* Greenberg Publishing, 1987; Eric J. Matzke,

Greenberg's Guide to Marx Trains, Vol. I (1989), Vol. II (1990), Greenberg Publishing; Robert P. Monaghan, *Greenberg's Guide to Marklin OO/HO,* Greenberg Publishing, 1989; Richard O'Brien, *Collecting Toy Trains,* No. 3, Books Americana, 1991; John R. Ottley, *Greenberg's Guide to LGB Trains,* Greenberg Publishing, 1989; Alan R. Schuweiler, *Greenberg's Guide to American Flyer, Wide Gauge,* Greenberg Publishing, 1989; John D. Spanagel, *Greenberg's Guide to Varney Trains,* Greenberg Publishing, 1991; Robert C. Whitacre, *Greenberg's Guide to Marx Trains Sets,* Vol. III, Greenberg Publishing, 1992.

Periodicals: *Classic Toy Trains,* 21027 Crossroads Cr, PO Box 1612, Waukesha, WI 53187; *Lionel Collector Series Marketmaker,* Trainmaster, PO Box 1499, Gainesville, FL 32602.

Collectors' Clubs: American Flyer Collectors Club, PO Box 13269, Pittsburgh, PA 15234; Lionel Collectors Club of America, PO Box 479, LaSalle, IL 61301; Lionel Operating Train Society, 18 Eland Ct, Fairfield, OH 45014; Marklin Club-North America, PO Box 51559, New Berlin, WI 53151; Marklin Digital Special Interest Group, PO Box 51319, New Berlin, WI 53151; The National Model Railroad Assoc, 4121 Cromwell Road, Chattanooga, TN 37421; The Toy Train Operating Society, Inc, Suite 308, 25 West Walnut St, Pasadena, CA 91103; Train Collector's Assoc, PO Box 248, Strasburg, PA 17579.

Museum: Toy Train Museum of the Train Collectors Assoc, Strasburg, PA.

Additional Listings: See *Warman's Americana & Collectibles* for more examples.

Notes: Condition of trains is critical when establishing price. Items in fair condition and below (scratched, chipped, dented, rusted or warped) generally have little value to a collector. Accurate restoration is accepted and may enhance the price by one or two grades. Prices listed below are for trains in very good to mint condition unless otherwise noted.

SPECIAL AUCTIONS

Greenberg Auctions
7566 Main St
Sykesville, MD 21784
(410) 795-7447

Lloyd Ralston Toys
173 Post Rd
Fairfield, CT 06432
(203) 255-1233

American Flyer

Car
No. 515, coach, New York Express Chicago, orange, turquoise roof **65.00**
No. 1112, boxcar, red, type III trucks, T-slot couplers **20.00**
No. 1118, tank car, type II trucks, T-slot couplers .. **25.00**
No. 1201, coach, red, lightning strike emblems, replaced roof, price for pr **35.00**

Locomotive
Hiawatha, die-cast locomotive, steel tender, trailing wheels replaced, new pilot truck, O gauge **75.00**
Hudson, tender, No. 680, 2-6-4, O gauge **200.00**
Steam locomotive, die-cast 2-4-2, O gauge, no number plates, steel tender **75.00**

Set
Burlington Zephyr 9900, aluminum, railway express car, coach, and observation, re-wheeled motor, engine professionally serviced **400.00**
Hamiltonian, #1484, No. 4019 electric loco, #4040 baggage, America coat, Pleasantview observation, litho with red roof cars, orig box, standard gauge **375.00**
Union Pacific streamline passenger set, die-cast locomotive, three coaches, orig brown boxes, O gauge **450.00**

Ives

Car
No. 65, livestock, orange, scratched dark gray roof **55.00**
No. 66, tank car, red, green top, black frame, gold stripes, T trucks, hook-slot couplers, body badly chipped **55.00**
No. 131, baggage, wood-grain sides, dark olive, gray roof, red clerestory, type III trucks, minor rust, doors missing **50.00**

Locomotive
#66, clockwork, orig die-cast wheels, two good, two fatigued, c1930, paint good, reproduction tender **175.00**
#176, clockwork, gold rubber stamp, die-cast wheels, bottom cover plate missing, reproduction tender **45.00**

Set
No. 1117, plated cast iron steam locomotive, electric motor, reproduction tender, orange with medium-gray flaked roof C & NW 118568 boxcar, yellow with light gray roof #64388 NP boxcar, yellow with light gray roof livestock car **350.00**
No. 1122, die-cast locomotive, die-cast red tender, #141 parlor car, #142 parlor car, #141 observation car, black sides, red roofs and trucks, restored, paint flaking on engine and tender **200.00**

Lionel

Car
#219, crane car, standard gauge, yellow body, red roof, green boom **115.00**
#220, searchlight car, standard gauge **115.00**
#511, lumber car, standard gauge, dark green orig box **115.00**

Locomotive
#384, steam, tender, standard gauge, green stripe, build-a-loco motor, orig box **375.00**
#402, electric, standard gauge, mojave **260.00**
#1700E, Silver Streak, smooth sides, orange, gray frame, roof ventilator warped **225.00**

Set
#153 loco, #629 Pullman, #630 observation, dark green, orig box, track and boxed-set outfit 92, motor professionally serviced, box very faded **200.00**

Lionel, 390E steam engine and 390T tender, 1929–1933, orig box, $990.00. Photo courtesy of Bider's Antiques, Inc.

#318 electric locomotive, three #416 coal cars, #517 caboose, standard gauge, some over painting **258.00**
#408E electric locomotive, #148 parlor car, #431 dining car, #419, baggage car, #490 observation car, standard gauge, Mojave, missing one panograph **1,955.00**
#450 electric locomotive, two #610 Pullman, #612 observation cars, O gauge, orig box, minor scratches, headlights missing **2,185.00**

TRAMP ART

History: Tramp art was prevalent in the United States from 1875 to the 1930s. Items were made by itinerant artists who left no record of their identity. They used old cigar boxes and fruit and vegetable crates. The edges of the pieces were chip-carved and layered, creating the "Tramp Art" effect. Finished items usually were given an overall stain. Today they are collected primarily as folk art.

Reference: Helaine Fendelman, *Tramp Art: An Itinerant's Folk Art Guide,* E. P. Dutton & Co, 1975.

Box, 13½" l, whittled knob feet, natural patina **165.00**
Jewelry Box, 10½ × 10½ × 9", brass trim and panels, red velvet insert top, left out int. tray, hidden drawer, dated 1903 .... **175.00**
Magazine Rack, 15" w, hanging, orig dark finish, brass tacks **50.00**
Mirror, 5¾ × 7¾", chip-carved frame **85.00**
Rocker, cutout curved sides, lyre-like splat, appl chip-carved dec, alligator vanish and brown paint, two porcelain buttons in back, replaced wooden seat .. **250.00**

Box, hinged, red paper lining, alternating layers of yellow and orange pyramids, 7 × 8 × 5¼", $85.00.

Sewing Box, 9½" l, pincushion frame top, drawer, orig dark finish **50.00**
Wall Pocket, 11 × 16½" h, hanging, appl stripes **85.00**

TRANSPORTATION MEMORABILIA

History: Most of the income for the first airlines in the United States came from government mail-carrying subsidies. The first non–Post Office Department flight to carry mail was in 1926 between Detroit and Chicago. By 1930 there were 38 domestic and five international airlines operating in the United States. A typical passenger load was ten. After World War II, four-engine planes with a capacity of 100 or more passengers were introduced.

The jet age was launched in the 1950s. In 1955 Capitol Airlines used British-made turboprop airliners for domestic service. In 1958 National Airlines began domestic jet passenger service. The giant Boeing 747 went into operation in 1970 as part of the Pan American fleet. The Civil Aeronautics Board, which regulates the airline industry, ended control of routes in 1982 and fares in 1983.

Transoceanic travel falls into two distinct periods—the era of the great clipper ships and the era of the diesel-powered ocean liners. The golden age of the later craft took place between 1900 and 1940.

An ocean liner is a city unto itself. Many have their own printing rooms to produce a wealth of daily memorabilia. Companies such as Cunard, Holland-America, and others encouraged passengers to acquire souvenirs with the company logo and ship name.

Certain ships acquired a unique mystique. The *Queen Elizabeth, Queen Mary,* and *United States* became symbols of elegance and style. Today the cruise ship dominates the world of the ocean liner.

References: Lynn Johnson and Michael O'Leary, *En Route,* Chronicle Books, 1993; Karl D. Spence, *How to Identify and Price Ocean Liner Collectibles,* published by author, 1991; ———, *Oceanliner Collectibles,* published by author, 1992; Richard R. Wallin, *Commercial Aviation Collectibles: An Illustrated Price Guide,* Wallace-Homestead, 1990.

Periodical: *Airliners,* PO Box 52-1238, Miami, FL 33152.

Collectors' Clubs: Aeronautic & Air Label Collectors Club, PO Box 1239, Elgin, IL 60121; Gay Airline Club, PO Box 69A04, West Hollywood, CA 90069; National Assoc of Timetable Collectors, 125 American Inn Rd, Villa Ridge, MO 63089; Oceanic Navigation Research Society, PO Box 8005, Studio City, CA 91608-0005; Steamship Historical Society of America, Inc, Ste #4, 300 Ray Drive, Providence, RI 02906; Titanic Historical Society, PO Box 51053, Indian Orchard, MA 01151; Titanic International, PO Box 7007, Freehold, NJ 07728; Transport Ticket Society, 4 Gladridge Close, Earley, Reading Berks RG6 2DL England; World Airline Historical Society, 3381 Apple Tree Lane, Erlanger, KY 41018.

Museums: Owls Head Transportation Museum, Owls Head, ME; South Street Seaport Museum, New York, NY; University of Baltimore, Steamship Historical Society Collection, Baltimore, MD.

Additional Listings: See Automobilia and Railroad Items in *Warman's Antiques and Collectibles Price Guide* and Aviation Collectibles, Ocean Liner Collectibles, and Railroad Items in *Warman's Americana & Collectibles.*

By Air

Ashtray, Chicago & Southern Convair, chrome, figural airplane raised above circular tray **200.00**
China
    Coffee Cup, Piedmont Airline, white, bluebird logo, Hall China **12.00**
    Dish, United Airlines, rect, plastic lid with emb DC-3 designation "Mainliner," Hall China **25.00**
    Plate, Pan Am, white, dark blue band and logo, Walker China, mid-1940s **100.00**
    Salt and Pepper Shakers, pr, British Airways, white, gold trim and dec, Royal Doulton **35.00**
Map and Flight Log, United Airlines, NY to Chicago, 1931 .... **15.00**
Napkin, American Airlines, cloth, border stripes and flag logo, 1940 .... **25.00**
Painting, "Modern Progress in Transportation," Charles Sheeler, gouache on paper, 8 × 18" **54,625.00**
Playing Cards, Continental Airways, airplane illus, "The Blue Skyway" **75.00**
Stock Certificate, The Aviation Corp, eagle, shield, and US map vignettes, multicolored, 1944–47 .... **10.00**
Timetable, TWA, early 1930s **35.00**
Vase, Delta Air Lines, clear glass, gold logo, ftd **20.00**
Wine Glass, TWA, Royal Ambassador service, crystal . **20.00**

By Land

Buggy, horse drawn, Concord type, WA Patterson, Flint, folding top, side springs, wheels on rubber, shafts, restored **1,800.00**
Cart, horse drawn, tandem, Columbia Buggy Co, Detroit, MI, black and maroon, ivory wicker sides and back, drivers wedge, wheels on rubber, two sets of shafts, restored **3,100.00**
Conestoga Wagon Box, 17" w, 21" h, pine, slant top, wrought-iron strap hinges and dec hardware, traces of old paint **300.00**
Runabout, pony drawn, John Moore & Co, Warrant St, NY, wheels on rubber, shafts **550.00**
Sleigh, wooden
    Push type, boat shape, turned handle, turned spindle top, front crest pierce-carved with horn, overall paint dec with winter scenes of skaters, sleighs, buildings in landscape, Continental, dated 1723, 46½" l, 27" w, 38" h, some paint loss, front finials missing **1,200.00**
    Two seats, painted barn red, black trim, yellow pinstripes, cast-iron runners, black leather cushions, restored, small brass label with restorer's name . **800.00**

By Sea

Advertising Trade Card
    Alameda, gold lettering and border, light aqua color ground, minor water stain **190.00**
    Finance, US and Brazil Mail SS Co, red and white . **135.00**
    Guardian, red, white, and blue Comstock & Co flag, gold border, blue, green, red, and gold lettering, reverse with manuscript notation about 1867 voyage **440.00**

Ocean Liner, booklet, "1937 Cruise of the SS *Reliance* Around the World, Hamburg-American Line, North German Lloyd," printed black, blue, and gold covers, foldout map of cruise, 32 pgs, black-and-white photographs, 8½ × 11", $18.00.

    Stanford, Plymouth Rock SS Co, engraving by Lowell Co, Boston, black and white, bill of fare on reverse **190.00**
Baggage Tag, French Line, used April 21, 1954 .... **6.00**
Booklet, Cunard *Whitestar* Information for Passengers . **10.00**
Brochure, Pennsylvania Railroad Co, Steamer Richard Stockton Excursions from Jersey City to West Point and Newburgh, five-panel folder, large continuous schematic sepia map of 62 miles of Hudson River from Jersey City to Newburgh, colorful front panels, minor wear **360.00**
Builder's Model, finely detailed, twin-screw steamer *Caronia* and turbine steam *Carmania,* Cunard Steamship Co, encased in 62 × 177½" ornately carved mahogany glazed case, orig mahogany table on six tapered and reeded sq section legs **34,500.00**
Countertop Display Sign, Holland-American Line, flagship *Rotterdam,* photographic image, laminated, 11¼" w, 14" l, ... **125.00**
Mug, RMS *Mauretania,* pewter, name inscribed around base, appl handle, banner mark reads "Tudric Pewter for Liberty of London," small dents **300.00**
Passenger List
    Cunard RMS *Caronia,* July 28, 1950 .... **10.00**
    Norwegian American Line, MS *Oslofjord,* June 30, 1939, pencil notes **12.00**
    Queen Mary, May 9, 1950, including listing for Miss Elizabeth Taylor **15.00**
    Ward Line, Steamship *Havana,* Dec 24, 1921 ..... **15.00**
Timetable, Monticello Steamship Co, "On the Bay of San Francisco," 1907 .... **65.00**

TRUNKS

History: Trunks are portable containers that clasp shut and are used for the storage or transportation of personal possessions. Normally "trunk" means the ribbed flat- or domed-top models of the second half of the 19th century.

References: Martin and Maryann Labuda, *Price & Identification Guide to Antique Trunks,* published by authors, 1980; Jacquelyn Peake, *How to Recognize and Refinish Antiques for Pleasure and Profit,* Third Edition, Globe Pequot Press (PO Box 833, Old Saybrook, CT 06475), 1995.

Notes: Unrestored trunks sell for between $50 and $150. Refinished and relined, the price rises to $200 to $400, with decorators being a principal market.

Early trunks frequently were painted, stenciled, grained, or covered with wallpaper. These are collected for their folk-art qualities and, as such, demand high prices.

Dome Top
   8⅛" h, 20" l, sponge painted, red and brown spots, plain int., 19th C **195.00**
   12" l, worn dec black oilcloth and leather trim, brass tacks, lined with 1844 newspaper, hasp missing **45.00**
   12¼" w, 30" l, black and red grain paint, plain int., early 19th C **325.00**
   18" w, 16" d, 12" h, leather, alligator texture, strap-work **200.00**
   20" h, 40" l, pine, three-plank top, "Aaid 1858" painted on front, white and yellow foliate swag borders, black ground, mounted loop handles, Norwegian **625.00**
   21½" h, 41" l, pine, painted green, plain int., wrought-iron strap handles, inscribed "Adam Gates 1848 No. 1" **75.00**

Dome top, leather covered, initialed with nail heads, iron hardware and rivets, 26½ × 15 × 12½", $165.00.

   27¾" l, grain painted, pine, orig red sponging, yellow ground, wrought-iron end handles and lock, till with lid, age cracks, incomplete hasp **145.00**
   31½" l, hide bound, worn surface, incomplete leather and brass-tack trim, hasp missing **85.00**
   46" l, immigrant's, pine, old red paint, ornate dec wrought-iron strapping, tooled detail, int. with cov till, shelf along hinge rail, three dovetailed drawers, some edge damage, age cracks **160.00**
   47½" l, immigrant's, white oak, old red repaint, dovetailed, orig iron hardware, age cracks and repair in bottom **145.00**
Flat Top
   7" sq, leather cov, label "George W Tukey Portland, ME" **80.00**
   11¾" h, 18½" l, grain painted, red and brown raised molded plinth base, inscribed in red "1856, PWS" **175.00**
   27½" l, pine, dec, bowed side and lid, worn light

blue repaint int., orig brown graining, orig wrought-iron lock and hasp **200.00**
Hide Covered, 12" l, leather and brass-tack trim, orig wallpaper int., loose handle **65.00**
Leather Bound, 26" l, worn black leather, brass-tack trim, flattened seat on lid, engraved brass plaque "J. D. Warner Canandaiqua" **110.00**
Traveler's, poplar, dovetailed, dark red mahogany stain, fitted int. with doors and drawers, some repair, int. door rehinged, 24 × 13¼ × 34¾" **200.00**

TUCKER CHINA

History: William Ellis Tucker (1800–1832) was the son of a Philadelphia schoolmaster who had a small shop on Market Street, where he sold imported French china. William helped in the shop and became interested in the manufacture of china.

In 1820 kaolin, a white clay which is the prime ingredient for translucence in porcelain, was discovered on a farm in Chester County, Pennsylvania, and William earnestly began producing his own products with the plentiful supply of kaolin close at hand. The business prospered but not without many trials and financial difficulties. He had many partners, a fact reflected in the various marks found on Tucker china including "William Ellis Tucker," "Tucker and Hulme," and "Joseph Hemphill," as well as workmen's incised initials which are sometimes found.

The business operated between 1825 and 1838, when Thomas Tucker, William's brother, was forced by business conditions to close the firm. There are very few pieces available for collectors today, and almost all known pieces are in collections or museums. But you can never tell!

Museum: Pennsylvania Historical Museum, Harrisburg, PA.

Coffee Cup and Saucer, large size, floral spray, green band dec, gilt edges and handle, from set made for

Pitcher, vase shape, both sides painted in rose, iron-red, yellow, purple, blue, and green with floral cluster, gilt dec under spout, initials "JSR," neoclassical foliate motifs on spout and neck, band borders on shoulder, foot and rims, 9⅜" h, $2,400.00.

Atherton family of Chester County, PA, monogrammed "A" **1,500.00**
Creamer and Sugar, black transfer dec, landscape with
house, c1830, sugar bowl repaired, price for pr **400.00**
Fruit Dish, 11" l, oval, serpentine, gilt border, c1830 ..**1,150.00**
Perfume Vial, 1½" h, heart shape, basket of flowers and
floral bouquet dec, gilt trim **450.00**
Pitcher
8½" h, fluted urn form, rose and leaf dec, lyre handle,
gilt edges, base with impressed initial "C", c1830,
crack in handle **2,300.00**
9¼" h, urn form, peach and floral mid-band, gilt fan
and floral dec, reeded base, handle repaired **2,100.00**
Plate, luncheon, landscape, monogram **95.00**
Urn, 11¾" h, classical shape, square plinth, Blanc de
Chine glaze, twin scrolled handles, c1830, slight
damage to one, price for pr **4,750.00**

VALENTINES

History: Early cards were handmade, often containing both handwritten verses and hand-drawn pictures. Many cards also were
hand colored and contained cutwork.

Mass production of machine-made cards featuring chromoli-
thography began after 1840. In 1847 Esther Howland of Worcester, Massachusetts, established a company to make valentines
which were hand decorated with paper lace and other materials
imported from England. They had a small "H" stamped in red in
the top left corner. Howland's company eventually became the
New England Valentine Company (N.E.V. Co.).

The company George C. Whitney and his brother founded after
the Civil War dominated the market from the 1870s through the
first decades of the 20th century. They bought out several competitors, one of which was the New England Valentine Company.

Lace paper was invented in 1834. The golden age of lacy cards
took place between 1835 and 1860.

Embossed paper was used in England after 1800. Embossed
lithographs and woodcuts developed between 1825 and 1840,
and early examples were hand colored.

References: Roberta B. Etter, *Tokens of Love,* Abbeville Press,
1990; Katherine Kreider, *Valentines with Values,* Schiffer Publishing, 1996; Ruth Webb Lee, *A History of Valentines.*

Collectors' Club: National Valentine Collectors Assoc, Box 1404,
Santa Ana, CA 92702.

Advisor: Evalene Pulati.

Aquatint, 8 × 10", unrequited love series, lady and cherubs **120.00**
Cameo-Style, 5 × 7", unused sheet of lace, cherubs and
heart, embossed "Wood", London, 1840–1870s ... **22.50**
Folder
2½ × 4", Esther Howland, shiny white, gold embossed folder, added white lace, scraps, c1878 . **38.50**
3 × 4½", Whitney, lavender folder with white lace,
paste-in verse, c1868–78 .... **22.50**
3¼ × 4¼", Whitney, applied lace and scraps, paste-
in verse, 1878 .... **22.50**
6 × 6", Whitney, heart shape, child eating ice cream,
c1914 .... **10.00**

Hand-Tinted, 4½ × 7", English, woman in circle surrounded by elaborate design, c1840 .... **45.00**
Lacy Folder
2½ × 3½", American, added white lace, paste-in,
1879 .... **18.50**
4½ × 6"
Two added layers, c1890, minor soiling **12.50**
Whitney, three layers, lacy cherub overlay, 1890s **18.50**
Lacy, 5 × 7½", Mansell, scraps, embossed edge, c1850 **45.00**

Lacy Pullout, diecuts and stamped lace, decal edge, early 1900s, 4½ × 7", $35.00.

Padded Silk, 5 × 3½", fringe and hanger, forget-me-not
verse, 1885 .... **12.50**
Pulldown
5 × 8 × 3", German, 5 parts, cherub and doves,
floral background, c1914 .... **32.50**
6 × 8½ × 2¼", German, 3 parts, children, roses,
birdhouse, and doves, 1920s **27.50**
6 × 11 × 3½", German, three layers, Jewish wedding
scene with couple under pink honeycomb canopy
in rose garden, minor repair **75.00**
6½ × 8½ × 3½", Hallmark, three parts, pink, white,
and gold lacy, 1950s **8.50**
Scrap, 2½ × 3¼", German, cherub driving little car,
roses **7.50**
Sepia, 7 × 9", cherubs in front of turret, water and boats
in background, printed verse **65.00**
Stand-Up
3 × 5½", German, cardboard easel back, bulldog,
drum, 1931 .... **4.00**
4 × 4", Whitney, child's, children in front of big ship,
1930s **12.50**
4 × 5", Whitney, easel back, cardboard, added
hearts, boy, and dog **10.00**

VALLERYSTHAL GLASS

History: Vallerysthal (Lorraine), France, has been a glass-producing center for centuries. In 1872 two major factories, Vallerysthal

Vase, Vallerysthal, amberina ground, gold daffodils, 12" h, $3,500.00.

glassworks and Portieux glassworks, merged and produced art glass until 1898. Later, pressed glass animal-covered dishes were introduced. The factory continues to operate today.

Animal-Covered Dish

Dog on rug, milk glass	150.00
Frog, green, figural	90.00
Hen on nest, 1⅞ x 2⅜", opal, sgd	35.00
Robin on nest, blue milk glass	175.00

Box, cov

3½ × 4", blue milk glass	85.00
5 × 3", cameo, dark green, appl and cut dec, sgd	950.00
Butter Dish, cov, figural, radish	95.00
Candy Dish, 4⅛" d, white milk glass, basketweave, rope handles and finial	90.00
Cologne Bottle, 6¾" h, cameo, fuchsia flowers and leaves, frosted cranberry ground, gold-colored collar and screw stopper, sgd "Cristallerie Le Gantin"	495.00
Dish, cov, amber, ftd, squirrel finial	65.00
Lemon Dish, cov, figural, lemon, opaque yellow	65.00
Plate, 8" d, Thistle pattern, green	70.00
Tumbler, 4" h, cobalt blue	45.00
Vase, 9½" h, cameo, budding branches, enameled insects, frosted ground, gilt highlights, sgd, c1900	700.00

VAL ST.-LAMBERT

History: Val St.-Lambert, a 12th-century Cistercian abbey, was located during different historical periods in France, Netherlands, and Belgium (1930 to present). In 1822 Francois Kemlin and Auguste Lelievre, along with a group of financiers, bought the abbey and opened a glassworks. In 1846 Val St.-Lambert merged with the Socété Anonyme des Manufactures de Glaces, Verres à Vitre, Cristaux et Gobeletaries. The company bought many other glassworks.

Val St.-Lambert developed a reputation for technological progress in the glass industry. In 1879 Val St.-Lambert became an independent company employing 4,000 workers. The firm concentrated on the export market, making table glass, cut, engraved, etched, and molded pieces, and chandeliers. Some pieces were

finished in other countries, e.g., silver mounts were added in the United States.

Val St.-Lambert executed many special commissions for the artists of the Art Nouveau and Art Deco periods. The tradition continues. The company also made cameo-etched vases, covered boxes, and bowls. The firm celebrated its 150th anniversary in 1975.

Bottle Coaster, 6" d, cut crystal	45.00
Cordial, sgd	20.00
Decanter, 12½" h, cranberry cut to clear, sgd, orig stopper, orig paper label	175.00
Goblet, 5⅜" h, clear, brown mold, appl foot and stem	45.00
Plate, Van Dyck	75.00
Powder Jar, cov, 2½" d, clear, amber stain, sgd	65.00
Sherbet, acid cutback, blue cut to clear, scenes of children playing with animals in gold	225.00
Toothbrush Holder, clear, amber stain, sgd	65.00
Tumbler, 6" h, blue cut to clear, gilt cameo classical band	40.00
Vase, 64 beveled cuts	70.00

Vase, Val St.-Lambert pink, purple floral dec, sgd, 13¾" h, $395.00.

VAN BRIGGLE POTTERY

History: Artus Van Briggle, born in 1869, was a talented Ohio artist. He joined Rookwood in 1887 and studied in Paris under Rookwood's sponsorship from 1893 until 1896. In 1899 he moved to Colorado for his health and established his own pottery in Colorado Springs in 1901.

Van Briggle's work was heavily influenced by the Art Nouveau schools he had seen in France. He produced a great variety of matte-glazed wares in this style. Colors varied.

Artus died in 1904. Anne Van Briggle continued the pottery until 1912.

Marks: The "AA" mark, a date, and "Van Briggle" were incised on all pieces prior to 1907 and on some pieces into the 1920s. After 1920, "Colorado Springs, Colorado" or an abbreviation was added. Dated pieces are the most desirable.

References: Susan and Al Bagdade, *Warman's American Pottery and Porcelain,* Wallace-Homestead, 1994; Carol and Jim Carlton, *Colorado Pottery,* Collector Books, 1994; Ralph and Terry Kovel, *Kovels' American Art Pottery,* Crown Publishers, 1993; Richard Sasicki and Josie Fania, *Collector's Encyclopedia of Van Briggle Art Pottery,* Collector Books, 1993.

Collectors' Club: American Art Pottery Assoc, 125 E. Rose Ave, St. Louis, MO 63119.

Museum: Pioneer Museum, Colorado Springs, CO.

REPRODUCTION ALERT

Van Briggle pottery still is made today. These modern pieces often are mistaken for older examples. Among the glazes used are Moonglo (off white), Turquoise Ming, Russet, and Midnight (black).

1901–1920

Chalice, 11½" h, stylized mermaid embracing fish, velvety light green matte glaze, incised logo, name, date 1902, Roman numeral III, shape No. 1, repaired ..**14,300.00**
Dish, 5½" d, #491, circ, emb stylized black spider, dark green matte ground, incised "AA/Van Briggle/1906/Colorado Springs/491" **450.00**
Figure, dragonfly, mulberry, 6¾" h, #792, date 1920 . **200.00**
Jardiniere, 5¼" h, emb stylized tulips, mottled blue glaze, incised logo, name, Colorado Springs, shape No. 625 .... **715.00**
Lamp, owl, Sasicki plate #101 .... **425.00**
Night-Light, 5" h, grape leaf form, light crystalline mulberry glaze **150.00**
Plaque, 5¼" d, spider, green-black matte glaze, incised logo, name, date 1908, shape No. 491 .... **770.00**
Sign, 15" h, cat shape, stylized Art Deco, green, Colorado Springs **225.00**
Vase
    5 × 3¼", bulbous, tapering cylindrical neck, feathered gray-blue matte glaze, red clay exposed, mark covered by glaze, c1906–10 .... **400.00**
    5 × 5½", bulbous squat form, emb arrowhead leaves, blue matte glaze, incised "AA/Van Briggle/1904/V" **800.00**
    7 × 5", bottle shape, emb spade-shaped leaves, flowing matte blue glaze, incised "AA/Van Briggle/Colo Spgs./1-11-543" **750.00**
    8¼ × 4", #380, corseted, thistles emb under matte leathery blue-green glaze, incised "AA/Van Briggle/380/1905" **950.00**
    9" h
       Emb thistles in panels, mottled green glaze, imp logo, name, Colorado Springs, date 1906, shape No. 461, finisher's No. 8 ....**1,375.00**
       The Lorelei, emb figure of woman, long flowing gown, matte green glaze, incised logo, name, date 1905, shape No. 17, Roman numeral VX, finisher's mark No. 2 ....**6,875.00**

Vase, shades of green over tan ground, marked "86/1905/VV," $725.00.

    9½ × 4½", bulging cylinder, emb poppy pods and leaves, fine blue matte flowing glaze, red clay shows through at high spots, incised "AA/Van Briggle/1905/173/X" **1,800.00**
    10½ × 5", #228, two handles, light blue morning glories, green and dark blue leaves, soft green ground, crisp mold, incised "AA/Van Briggle/1903/III" **3,250.00**
    11" h, Lady of the Lily, nude female form, long flowing hair rests against lily-shaped vase, emb florals throughout base, fine flowing matte lime green glaze, incised logo, name, date obscured, shape No. 4 ....**11,550.00**
    12" h, 3½" d, #62, cylindrical, emb blue peacock feathers, medium green ground, incised "AA/VAN BRIGGLE/1903/III/62C," small bruise under base **1,600.00**
    14½" h, 5½" d, tall bulging cylinder, Climbing for Honey, two figural bears at opening, dark green to brown matte finish, marked "AA/1918" **5,750.00**
    17" h, 7" d, #157, tapering, emb yucca blossoms, fine matte leathery purple glaze, incised "AA/Van Briggle/157/1903/III," firing bruise on base **1,600.00**

1921–1968

Bowl
    5½" d, Yucca leaves, #747, blue, c1940 .... **60.00**
    8½" d, emb tulip dec, turquoise blue glaze, incised logo, name, Colorado Springs, No. 40, orig flower frog **40.00**
Console Set, jet black drip glaze, sgd "Anna Van Briggle, Colorado Springs" **50.00**
Figure, Hopi Maiden, blue, c1940 .... **130.00**
Vase
    3" h, #684, blue, moth, USA **60.00**
    4¾" h, #645, blue, USA, c1940 .... **65.00**
    6" h, #84, blue and aqua, USA **130.00**

VENETIAN GLASS

History: Venetian glass has been made on the island of Murano, near Venice, since the 13th century. Most of the wares are thin walled. Many types of decoration have been used: embedded gold dust, lace work, and applied fruits or flowers.

Reproduction Alert: Venetian glass continues to be made today.

Basket, 6½" d, 7½" h, flared, notched rim, purple shaded to clear, controlled bubbles, gold-flecked base	**95.00**
Berry Bowl and Under Plate, Wisteria, swirl pattern . . .	**40.00**
Bowl, 2½ × 4¼", pedestal, clear, white latticinio, ruby rim and handles, clear rigaree, price for 4-pc set . . .	**300.00**
Cologne Bottle, light green, paperweight-type stopper .	**65.00**

Compote

6" h, crystal, hollow stem	**40.00**
7½" d, blue irid bowl, fancy handles, pedestal base	**150.00**

Figure

Cockatoo, 13" h, multicolored	**95.00**
Flamenco Dancer, 7½" h, green and white	**110.00**
Harlequins, masked, male and female, 7 and 10" h, price for pr	**250.00**
Man with sack, 11½" h	**175.00**
Peasant Girl, tray of birds, 11½" h	**200.00**

Goblet

7" h, gold and clear striped bowl, gold stem and base	**95.00**
7¾" h, cranberry, clear rigaree stems, polychrome enamel dec, gilt trim, price for 6-pc set	**500.00**

Wine, colonial couple in scrolled medallions, swirled stems, c1889–90, $75.00.

Perfume Bottle, clear, gold spatter dec, orig stopper with long dauber	**375.00**
Tazza, 15" d, yellow opal glass, spiraling blue and white trails, cobalt blue trim	**250.00**
Vase, 8" h, bottle shape, frosted mauve, irid amber teardrops, amber ribbing on base, ruffled, c1895	**200.00**

VERLYS GLASS

Verlys   *A Verlys France*

History: Originally made by Verlys France (1931–1960), this Lalique-influenced art glass was produced in America by The Holophane Co. from 1935 to 1951, and select pieces by the A. H. Heisey Co. from 1955 to 1957. Holophane acquired molds and glass formulas from Verlys France and began making the art glass in 1935 at their Newark, Ohio, facility. They later leased molds

to the Heisey Co., and in 1966 finally sold all molds and rights to the Fenton Art Glass Co.

The art glass was made in crystal, topaz, amber, rose, opalescent, and Directorie Blue. Heisey added turquoise. Most pieces have etched (frosted) relief designs.

Marks: Verlys France marked the glass with mold impressed "Verlys France" and "A Verlys France." Holophane (also known as Verlys of America) marked pieces with the mold-impressed "Verlys" and a scratched-script "Verlys" signature. The A. H. Heisey Co. used only a paper label which reads "Verlys by Heisey."

Reference: Carole and Wayne McPeek, *Verlys of America Decorative Glass,* Revised Edition, published by authors, 1992.

Bowl

Chinois	**80.00**
Cupid	**125.00**
Cuspidon	**90.00**
Orchid	**175.00**

Pinecone

Blue	**175.00**
Opal	**175.00**
Poppies	**200.00**
Tassels	**150.00**
Thistle, topaz	**250.00**

Tripartite design, frosted

6¼" d, pinecones and needles	**135.00**
8¾" d, thistle design	**75.00**
Water Lily, dusty rose	**500.00**
Wild Duck	**175.00**

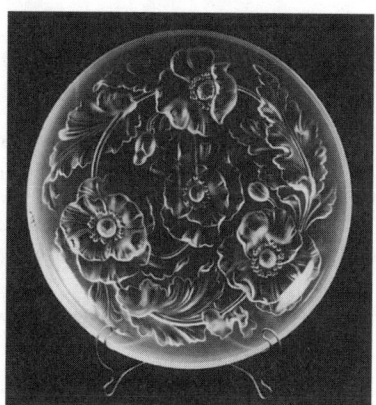

Salad Bowl, Poppy pattern, Heisey, Norwalk, OH, script sgd, 13½" h, $125.00.

Box, cov, band of flowers	**75.00**
Candleholders, pr, Eagle	**500.00**
Charger, dragonfly	**135.00**
Dish, cov, 8" d, 1½" lid, three moths and glass knob . .	**225.00**
Vase, 10" h, mermaids, dolphins, crystal and frosted . .	**750.00**

Vase

Alpine Thistle, topaz	**400.00**
Eglantine, opal, base chips	**250.00**
Gems	**200.00**
Grasshopper, base chips	**125.00**
Lovebirds	**150.00**
Mandarian	**500.00**

Mermaids, topaz, straight top **1,200.00**
Oriental figures 350.00
Seasons 450.00

VILLEROY & BOCH

History: Pierre Joseph Boch established a pottery near Luxembourg, Germany, in 1767. Jean Francis, his son, introduced the first coal-fired kiln in Europe and perfected a water-power-driven potter's wheel. Pierre's grandson, Eugene Boch, managed a pottery at Mettlach; Nicholas Villeroy also had a pottery nearby.

In 1841 the three potteries merged into the firm of Villeroy & Boch. Early production included a hard-paste earthenware comparable to English ironstone. The factory continues to use this hard-paste formula for its modern tablewares.

References: Susan and Al Bagdade, *Warman's English & Continental Pottery & Porcelain,* Second Edition, Wallace-Homestead, 1991; Gary Kirsner, *The Mettlach Book,* Third Edition, Glentiques, 1994.

Additional Listings: Mettlach.

Bowl, 10½" d, blue floral dec, handles 175.00
Cruet, 8½" h, blue and white, orig stopper 85.00
Demitasse Cup and Saucer, Patermo 25.00
Mug, 3½" h, tan, leaf and twig dec, twig handle 65.00
Pitcher, 10⅝" h, six sided, dark gray raised scrolls, leaves, pods, and birds, gray ground, white int., beige crest mark 275.00

Punch Bowl, etched, multicolored, 15" h, $300.00.

Plaque, 12" h, reticulated lilies of the valley dec 225.00
Plate, 12½" d, Chintz pattern, marked "Villeroy & Boch," price for 8-pc set 120.00
Stein, 6½" h, half liter, #171, five white figures, blue ground, Mercury mark 225.00
Teapot, 6¼" d, blue and white 135.00
Tray, 11 × 16", cavalier, PUG 165.00
Vase, 7" h, white floral relief dec, yellow ground 115.00

WARWICK

History: Warwick China Manufacturing Co., Wheeling, West Virginia, was incorporated in 1887 and remained in business until 1951. The company was one of the first manufacturers of vitreous glazed wares in the United States. Production was extensive and included tableware, garden ornaments, and decorative and utilitarian items.

Pieces were hand painted or decorated with decals. Collectors seek portrait items and fraternal pieces from groups such as the Elks, Eagles, and Knights of Pythias.

Some experimental, eggshell-type porcelain was made before 1887. A few examples are found in the antiques market.

Ale Set, tankard pitcher, seven matching mugs, BPOE emblem and elk dec, shaded brown ground 325.00
Bone Dish, flow blue scenic dec 45.00
Chocolate Pot, cov, 10½" h, Pansy pattern, flow blue dec, c1893–98 .... 300.00
Creamer, speckled blue and white, gold trim, raised leaves around rim, marked "Warwick China" 40.00
Humidor, cov, portrait of woman, brown ground, marked "IOGA" 215.00
Lemonade Pitcher, portrait dec, brown glaze 175.00

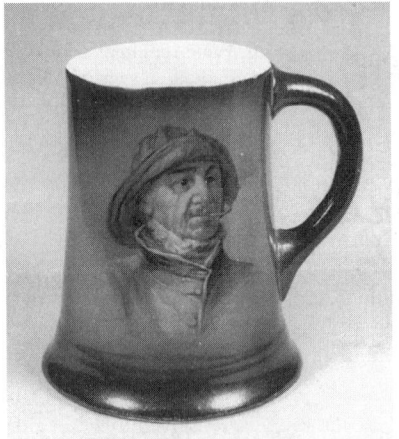

Mug, Seaman, brown glaze, white int., marked "IOGA, Warwick," 5" h, $80.00.

Portrait Plate, 10" d, Indian, yellow shading to brown ground 75.00
Spittoon, beige ground, red roses 140.00

Tankard, 13″ h, portrait of monk and mug of ale **250.00**
Vase

  8″ d, ftd, portrait of woman, large hat with peacock feathers, holding rose to her lips, shaded brown to cream ground, marked "IOGA" **125.00**

  10″ h, amaryllis dec, orange blossoms, brown ground, marked "IOGA" **95.00**

  11½″ h, ring handles, marked "IOGA Madam Le Brun" **285.00**

  12″ h, brown, hibiscus, marked "IOGA" **130.00**

WATCHES, POCKET

History: Pocket watches can be found in many places—from flea markets to the specialized jewelry auctions. Condition of movement is the first priority; design and detailing of the case is second.

Descriptions of pocket watches may include the size (16/0 to 20), number of jewels in the movement, whether the face is open or closed (hunter), and the composition (gold, gold filled, or some other metal). The movement is the critical element since cases often were switched. However, an elaborate case, especially if gold, adds significantly to value.

Pocket watches designed to railroad specifications are desirable. They are between 16 and 18 in size, have a minimum of 17 jewels, adjust to at least five positions, and conform to many other specifications. All are open faced.

Study the field thoroughly before buying. There is a vast amount of literature, including books and newsletters from clubs and collectors.

References: James M. Dowling and Jeffrey P. Hess, *Rolex Wristwatches,* Schiffer Publishing, 1996; The Ehrhardts, *European Pocket Watches, Book 2,* Heart of America Press, 1993; Roy Ehrhardt and Joe Demsey, *Cartier Wrist & Pocket Watches, Clocks,* Heart of America Press, 1992; ———, *Patek Phillipe,* Heart of America Press, 1992; ———, *American Pocket Watch Serial Number Grade Book,* Heart of America Press, 1993; Edward Faber and Stewart Unger, *American Wristwatches,* Revised Edition, Schiffer Publishing, 1996 Anton Kreuzer, *Omega Wristwatches,* Schiffer Publishing, 1996; Cooksey Shugart and Richard E. Gilbert, *Complete Price Guide to Watches,* Thirteenth Edition, Cooksey Shugart Publications, 1993; Fritz von Osterhausen, *The Movado History,* Schiffer Publishing, 1996.

Periodical: *Watch & Clock Review,* 2403 Champa St, Denver, CO 80205.

Collectors' Clubs: American Watchmakers Institute Chapter 102, 3 Washington Sq, Apt 3C, Larchmont, NY 10538; Early American Watch Club Chapter 149, PO Box 5499, Beverly Hills, CA 90210; National Assoc of Watch & Clock Collectors, 514 Poplar Street, Columbia, PA 17512.

Museums: American Clock & Watch Museum, Bristol, CT; Hoffman Clock Museum, Newark, NY; National Association of Watch and Clock Collectors Museum, Columbia, PA; The Time Museum, Rockford, IL.

Abbreviations:

gf	gold filled
j	jewels
S	size
yg	yellow gold

A Goley Fil & Stahl, Geneva, 18K yg, open face, brushed-metal dial, Arabic numerals, subsidiary seconds dial, serial no. 26660, stem missing **320.00**

A Goley-Leresche & Fils, 18K yg, demi-hunter, white enamel dial, Roman numerals, crystal missing **550.00**

Bailey, Banks & Biddle Co, 14K yg, hunter case, 17j, white enamel dial, black Arabic numerals, subsidiary dial for seconds, engraved dust covers, movement marked "Royal A.W.W. Co. for Waltham Watch Company" **490.00**

Bigelow & Kennard, Boston, 18K yg, hunter case, porcelain enamel dial, Arabic numerals, subsidiary seconds dial **750.00**

Brooch, Pery, 14K yg, violin shape, chased scrolling design highlighted by seed pearls, circular brushed dial with goldtone markers **635.00**

Columbus Watch Co, Columbus, OH, 14K yg, open face, porcelain enameled dial, Roman numerals, subsidiary seconds dial, serial no. 79965, recased **520.00**

Elgin National Watch Co

  Gold filled, watch fob with $2 gold piece **220.00**

  10K, 2³⁄₁₆″ d, clear crystal front and back **165.00**

  14K

    Hunter case, porcelain dial, Arabic numerals, serial no. 1644509 .... **550.00**

    Open face, porcelain enamel dial, Roman numerals, subsidiary seconds dial, serial no. 1466466 **375.00**

Freres, Mermod, 18K yg, polychrome enamel of woman and child, white dial, Roman numerals, case stamped "E #4277," suspended from enamel link chain with key, orig box, missing crystal, dial cracked, minor enamel loss **635.00**

Hamilton, open face

  14K yg

    19j **225.00**

    21j **250.00**

  Gold-plated case, 17j **115.00**

  White gold, 19j **110.00**

Harvey-London, H, 18K yg, Verge, tricolor gold engine turn dial, key-wind movement, open face, price for pr **490.00**

Howard, E, Watch Co, open face

  14K yg, brushed metal dial, Arabic numerals **175.00**

  Gold plated, 17j, porcelain enamel dial, Arabic numerals **100.00**

Hunter Case

18K yg

Engraved stars and foliate design, enhanced with black enamel tracery, white dial, Roman numerals, subsidiary dial for seconds, case stamped "LD 5281," boxed 290.00

Retailed by Tiffany & Co, NY, porcelain enameled dial, Arabic numerals, subsidiary seconds dial 635.00

Niello, quatrefoil pattern, white enamel dial, black Arabic numerals, subsidiary dial for seconds, European hallmarks, minor wear 230.00

Illinois

14K tricolor gold, hunter case, deer in naturalistic setting, white enamel dial, black Arabic numerals, subsidiary dial for seconds, fob and plated watch chain 1,610.00

14K yg, engraved monogram, 1⅞" d 150.00

International Watch Co, Schaffhausen, 14K yg, open face, brushed metal dial, Arabic numerals, subsidiary seconds dial 415.00

Longines, 14K yg, open face, 17j movement, brushed metal dial, Arabic numerals, price for pr 375.00

National Watch Co, 2¼" d, engraved 18K yg case 990.00

Oliver, John, 18K yg, hunter case with engraved design and black enamel tracery, white porcelain dial, black Roman numerals, subsidiary dial for seconds, start-stop mechanism, gold-filled watch chain, hairline crack to dial 575.00

Patek Philippe and Co, 18K yg, open face, case sgd and #253138, repeater, made for Shreve Crump & Low, triple sgd, movement #147035, cover 1,495.00

Pendant, Edwardian, guilloche blue enamel, 18k yg, Black Starr & Frost, suspended from baton enamel and 14K yg link chain, 19" l, minor enamel loss ... 865.00

Patek Philippe, Geneve, 18K gold, open face, minute repeating, split second chronograph, perpetual calendar, moon phases, register, and central alarm, c1920, $600,600.00. Photo courtesy of Sotheby's.

Pickard, James, Geneva, 18K yg, hunter case, glass dust cov, porcelain enameled dial, Roman numerals, subsidiary seconds dial 815.00

Railroad, 2¾" d, silver case, tooled locomotive in laurel wreath, sgd "F Hauser," white enameled face with red and black, crystal and hands missing 55.00

Swiss, 20K yg, open face, porcelain enameled dial, Arabic numerals, subsidiary seconds dial, armorial device enameled on back case, retailed by Bigelow, Kennard & Co, Boston, c1884 .... 920.00

Tracy & Co, Waltham, MA, open face, Appleton, porcelain enamel dial, Roman numerals, subsidiary seconds dial, serial no. 2110282, cracked 230.00

Waltham Watch Co

Hunter case

14K yg

Porcelain enamel dial, Arabic numerals, subsidiary seconds dial, 17j, serial no. 13032049 .... 230.00

Porcelain enamel dial, Roman numerals, full backplate, serial no. 3890786, hand missing 490.00

White enamel dial, black Arabic numerals, subsidiary dial for seconds, chased case, suspended from 10K ropetwist chain with turquoise slide 500.00

18K yg, Riverside, 23j, porcelain enamel dial, Arabic numerals, subsidiary seconds dial, serial no. 10552668 .... 1,150.00

Lapel, fleur-de-lis pin set with tiny pearls 230.00

Lapel, 14K yg

Embossed floral back, porcelain enameled dial, suspended from griffin set with small diamond and green eye 865.00

Floral engraved case, initials "G.R.," 1⅝" d 110.00

Open Face, porcelain dial, Arabic numerals, subsidiary seconds dial

American Waltham Watch Co

14K yg, 17j, serial no. 65661194 .... 345.00

14K yg, 21j, adjusted five positions, serial no. 18010984 .... 375.00

18K yg, serial no. 6500163 .... 1,150.00

Hillside, 14K yg, serial no. 2581679 .... 175.00

Riverside, 14K yg

Serial no. 6010436, cracked seconds dial ... 490.00

Serial no. 6527109 .... 775.00

Royal, 14K yg, 17j 125.00

Warwick, 14K yg, serial no. 5999324 .... 425.00

WATCHES, WRIST

History: The definition of a wristwatch is simply "a small watch that is attached to a bracelet or strap and is worn around the wrist." However, a watch on a bracelet is not necessarily a wristwatch. The key is the ability to read the time. A true wristwatch allows you to read the time at a glance, without making any other motions. Early watches on an arm bracelet had the axis of their dials, from 6 to 12, perpendicular to the band. Reading them required some extensive arm movements.

The first true wristwatch appeared about 1850. However, the key date is 1880 when the stylish, decorative wristwatch appeared and almost universal acceptance occurred. The technology to create the wristwatch existed in the early 19th century with Brequet's shock-absorbing "Parachute System" for automatic watches and Ardien Philipe's winding stem.

The wristwatch was a response to the needs of the entrepreneurial age with its emphasis on punctuality and planned free time. Sometime around 1930 the sales of wristwatches surpassed that of pocket watches. Swiss and German manufacturers were quickly joined by American makers.

The wristwatch has undergone many technical advances during the 20th century including self-winding (automatic), shock-resistance, and electric movements.

References: Hy Brown and Nancy Thomas, *Comic Character Timepieces,* Schiffer Publishing, 1992; Gisbert L. Brunner and Christian Pfeiffer-Belli, *Wristwatches,* Schiffer Publishing, 1993; Roy Ehrhardt and Joe Demsey, *Cartier Wrist & Pocket Watches, Clocks,* Heart of America Press, 1992; ———, *Patek Phillipe,* Heart of America Press, 1992; ———, *Rolex Identification and Price Guide,* Heart of America Press, 1993; Sherry and Roy Ehrhardt and Joe Demsey, *Vintage American & European Wrist Watch Price Guide,* Book 6, Heart of America Press, 1993; Heinz Hampel, *Automatic Wristwatches from Switzerland,* Schiffer Publishing, 1994; Gerd J. Lang and Reinhard Meis, *Chronograph Wristwatches,* Schiffer Publishing, 1993; Isabella de Lisle Selby, *Wrist Watches,* Courage Books, 1994; Cooksey Shugart and Richard E. Gilbert, *Complete Price Guide to Watches,* Thirteenth Edition, Cooksey Shugart Publications, 1993.

Periodical: *International Wrist Watch,* 242 West Ave, Darien, CT 06820.

Collectors' Clubs: International Wrist Watch Collectors Chapter 146, 5901C Westheimer, Houston, TX 77057; National Assoc of Watch & Clock Collectors, 514 Poplar Street, Columbia, PA 17512; The Swatch Collectors Club, PO Box 7400, Melville, NY 11747.

Museums: American Clock & Watch Museum, Bristol, CT; Hoffman Clock Museum, Newark, NY; National Association of Watch and Clock Collectors Museum, Columbia, PA; The Time Museum, Rockford, IL.

Bulgari, Costa Mesa, gentleman's
  Black face and bezel engraved "Bulgari," automatic, date display, back crystal to reveal works, Bulgari strap, orig box **1,725.00**
  18K yg, SQ27GI, black square dial with goldtone chapters, wide bezel engraved "Bulgari" on side, black leather band and Bulgari buckle **2,300.00**
Cartier
  Gentleman's, 18K yg and steel, Santos, manual wind, white dial, black Roman numerals, date display and second-hand sweep, steel band with gold screws **1,380.00**
  Lady's, Art Deco, platinum and diamond, European watch and clock movement #35074, 18j, two positions, curved lozenge-shaped case edged in diamonds, rose-cut diamond crown, collet-set lugs and black cord band, set with diamond slides, diamond clasp, 18K yg black with monogram, sgd "Cartier," French hallmarks, c1913 .... **17,250.00**
Corum, 18K yg
  #3843, gentleman's, fifteen-gram gold bar from Bank of Switzerland, black crocodile band **950.00**

#5512, lady's, five-gram gold bar from Bank of Switzerland, brown lizard strap **747.00**
European, lady's, Retro, yellow gold and ruby, square dial and scrolling lugs set with square-cut rubies and round diamond accents, double snake chain bracelet, European hallmarks **575.00**
Gotham, stainless steel, white dial, subsidiary seconds dial, day and month display, sweep second hand, flexible band with blue and coral eagle motif inlaid in silver **115.00**
Gubelin, E, Lucerne #32202, 18K yg, chronograph, split second minute chapter, white porcelain dial, monogram, orig box **6,325.00**
Hamilton, Art Deco, platinum and diamond, 17j set with two rows of diamonds, caliber-cut sapphires, approx 1.50 ct, two sapphires missing **2,200.00**
International Schaffhausen, 18K yg, abstract markers, leather band, c1970 .... **550.00**
Jurgensen, Jules, 18K yg, abstract markers, thin model, leather band **175.00**
LaFemme, 14K white gold, framed by domed lozenge form with star-set diamonds, approx .54 ct, mounted on two pierced square-link bypass chains **690.00**
Marchak, lady's, Retro, set with oval citrines ranging in color from pale yellow to deep red-brown, five channel-set diamonds, 18K yg mount, sgd "Marchak, France," French hallmarks **2,875.00**
Movado, stainless steel, chronograph, 17j, three registers, lizard strap **635.00**
Omega, gentleman's
  Gold and stainless, Constellation, date, leather band, c1970 .... **175.00**
  14K yg, automatic, engine-turned striped dial, applied markers, subsidiary dial for seconds, leather band, 14K yg Omega buckle, c1950 .... **175.00**
  18K yg, Constellation, automatic chronometer, woven gold bracelet with deployant buckle **920.00**
  Stainless steel, Speedmaster Moonwatch **635.00**
Patek Philippe, gentleman's
  18K white gold, matte dial, abstract chapters, woven flexible band, 1960s **2,300.00**
  18K yg
    Blue dial, abstract chapters, date window, integral 18K yg Philippe band, c1960 .... **5,175.00**
    Round dial, abstract chapters, flexible gold band with deployant buckle, inscribed with owner's name in appreciation of his 25th anniversary with Max Factor **4,830.00**
    Round dial, gold band with deployant buckle, c1953 .... **5,750.00**
    Silver dial, abstract chapters, subsidiary dial for seconds, one chapter repaired, leather strap, c1950 .... **4,025.00**
    White dial, abstract markers, leather strap, retailed by Gubelin, c1960 .... **2,415.00**
Piaget, 18K yg
  Gentleman's, brushed gold dial, Roman numerals, ultra-thin case, leather strap with 18K yg Piaget buckle, c1970, slight discoloration on dial **490.00**
  Lady's, pavé set diamond face with diamond bezel 72 single-cut diamonds, red leather band, 18K yg buckle **650.00**

Textured 18K yg bracelet, buckle clasp, approx
1.50 ct **4,255.00**
Piquet, Audemars, gentleman's
18K yg, brushed dial, thin model, leather strap, c1970   **750.00**
21K yg, chronograph, automatic central motor, water
resistant, crocodile band, deployant bucket, orig
box **6,612.00**
Rolex, gentleman's
Brushed stainless steel, oyster bracelet, steel deployant clasp **130.00**
Oyster Datejust, 18K yg and stainless, automatic
winding, black dial, appl markers, sweep second-
hand, magnifying glass on date aperture, jubilee
bracelet **1,150.00**
Oyster Perpetual
14K yg and stainless, date, luminescent accents
on chapters, leather band, c1960 .... **1,265.00**
14K yg and stainless, metal dial, leather band,
c1960 .... **980.00**
18K yg, date, fluted bezel, leather band, c1960 . **2,990.00**
Two-tone, date window and deployant buckle .. **1,840.00**
Universal, Geneva, 18K yg, Golden Shadow, automatic,
silver-tone dial, black Roman numerals, crocodile
strap **230.00**
Vacheron and Constantin, 18K yg
Circular white dial, gold chapters and hands, 18K yg
Florentine frame with 14K yg integral brick-link
bracelet **1,150.00**
Diamond dial, textured gold bracelet, approx total
.75 ct **1,840.00**

WATERFORD

History: Waterford crystal is high-quality flint glass commonly
decorated with cuttings. The original factory was established at
Waterford, Ireland, in 1729. Glass made before 1830 is darker
than the brilliantly clear glass of later production. The factory
closed in 1852. One hundred years later it reopened and continues in production today.

Brandy Snifter, Lismore pattern **45.00**
Butter Dish, cov, mushroom finial **250.00**
Candlesticks, pr, 7″ h, pear shape, hollow center, hori-
zontal oval cuts on wafers between fluted top and
rayed base, looped cross cuttings in two sizes, down-
ward spray with star cut **175.00**
Centerpiece Bowl, 10″ d, ftd, master cutter, Archive Col-
lection **1,395.00**
Champagne, saucer
Alana pattern **48.00**
Lismore pattern **45.00**
Cocktail, Kylemore pattern **35.00**
Compote, ftd
Colleen, large, #3821371200 .... **100.00**
Glandore, 5¼″ h, #3814341200 .... **90.00**
Cordial
Ashling pattern **30.00**

Pitcher, ribbed, applied handle,
10½″ h, $215.00.

Clare pattern	34.00
Kinsale pattern	28.00
Kylemore pattern	28.00
Lismore pattern	31.00
Creamer and Sugar, Powerscort pattern	115.00
Decanter	
Alana pattern	195.00
Kenmare pattern	195.00
Lismore pattern, captain's type	195.00
Powerscort pattern	335.00
Goblet	
Boyne pattern	35.00
Lismore pattern	35.00
Ice Bucket, Powerscort pattern	195.00
Martini, Lismore pattern	37.00
Pitcher, water, Powerscort pattern	195.00
Tumbler	
Boyne pattern	32.00
Clare pattern	50.00
Vase, master cutter, Noah, limited edition, no. 21 of 250, sgd ''T. Cooke,'' 1973	1,800.00
Wine	
Kildare pattern	35.00
Kylemore pattern	40.00
Lismore pattern	32.00

**WAVE CREST
WARE**

WAVE CREST

c1892

History: The C. F. Monroe Company of Meriden, Connecticut,
produced the opal glassware known as Wave Crest from 1898
until World War I. The company bought the opaque, blown-
molded glass blanks from the Pairpoint Manufacturing Co. of New
Bedford, Massachusetts, and other glassmakers, including European factories. The Monroe company then decorated the blanks,
usually with floral patterns. Trade names used were ''Wave Crest
Ware,'' ''Kelva,'' and ''Nakara.''

References: Wilfred R. Cohen, *Wave Crest: The Glass of C. F.
Monroe,* Collector Books, out-of-print; Elsa H. Grimmer, *Wave
Crest Ware,* Wallace-Homestead, out-of-print.

Ash Receiver

    3¼″ sq, Egg-Crate mold, enameled floral dec **180.00**

    4″ d, ormolu handles, enameled floral dec, sgd, black mark **110.00**

Biscuit Jar, 5¼″ h, blue and white, Delft dec **550.00**

Bonbon, cov, 8″ d, bail handle, rococo mold, sgd **925.00**

Box, cov

    3″ d, Double Shell mold, tiny blue and yellow flowers, green leaves, opaque white ground, hinged lid **200.00**

    4″ d, charcoal dec, ftd, Kelva **625.00**

    4½″ d, 2¾″ h, spray of single-petaled roses, rococo border, raised white beads, mottled olive green ground, sgd ''Kelva Trade Mark,'' two white beads missing **400.00**

    5½″ d

        3½″ h, wide spiral alternating green and pink panels on base and edge of hinged lid, center large oval reserve of dancing storks, dainty florals, scrolls, gilt metal fittings, unsgd **1,150.00**

        Oval, emb scrolling on top and sides, roses, blue ground, hinged lid **510.00**

    5¾″ d, Petticoat and Mushroom mold, light blue ... **675.00**

    6″ d, 6″ h, Egg-Crate mold, two classical women dec, hinged lid **800.00**

    7¼″ d, Baroque Shell mold, pink daisies, sky blue border, lavender outlines, hinged lid **765.00**

    8″ d, Helmschmied Swirl mold, hp florals, hinged lid **500.00**

Calling Card Holder, upright rect form, emb frame design, gilt-metal rim, cloth lining, hp blue flowers, pink border **360.00**

Cigar Humidor, 8¾″ h, blue ground, single-petaled pink rose dec, pink ''Cigar'' signature, pewter collar, bail, and lid fittings, flame-shaped finial, sgd ''Kelva'' ... **685.00**

Collars & Cuff Box, Rococo mold, blue **1,550.00**

Cookie Jar, cov, 8″ h, 5¾″ d, emb cream designs, white satin ground, rose, blue, and yellow pansies, SP top, rim, and handle, unmarked **300.00**

Cracker Jar, cov, smooth tapering cylindrical body, large white and purple iris, green leaves, cream ground, pale tan scrolled borders, metal lid, rim, and twisted bail handle, unmarked **375.00**

Creamer and Sugar, 3¼″ h, blown-out swirls, enameled floral dec **330.00**

Dish

    5½″ d, cobalt blue, blown out dec **475.00**

    6″ d, green, open handle, sgd ''Kelva'' **575.00**

Salt and Pepper Shakers, pr, Erie Twist, satin, hp floral dec, two-pc pewter top, C. F. Monroe Co., $84.00.

Ferner, 7″ sq

    Blown out, beaded twist, enameled, floral dec, sgd, banner mark **220.00**

    Egg-Crate mold, yellow wild roses, metal twisted-rope rim **650.00**

Hair Receiver, cov, 5½″ d, gold trim, marked ''Nakara'' **685.00**

Humidor, cov, 7½″ h, 5½″ d, pink emb designs, white satin ground, yellow floral dec, SP dome lift-off lid, unmarked **365.00**

Jardiniere, 8″ h, bulbous body, short cylindrical rim, hp mums and foliate, gold lacy rim trim **550.00**

Jewel Tray, 6″ l, 2¾″ h, oval, ftd, Rococo mold, sgd, banner mark, two handles **275.00**

Paperweight **595.00**

Photo Receiver, 6½″ w, 4″ h, Rococo mold, enameled floral dec, sgd, banner mark **360.00**

Pin Tray, 4″ d, blown-out swirl, enameled floral dec .. **85.00**

Salt and Pepper Shakers, pr, 4″ h, pink ground, blue forget-me-nots and scroll work **395.00**

Salt Shaker, 2½″ h, Erie Twist, hp flowers **185.00**

Spittoon, silver top **200.00**

Spooner, cylindrical paneled-rib shape, floral transfer, SP rim and loop handles **285.00**

Sugar Shaker, 3″ h, 3″ d, Helmschmied Swirl, caladium leaves, purple centers, white enamel dots, green and brown borders, tiny fuchsia flower blossom sprays, swirling mottled blue and white ground, orig metal lid dented **685.00**

Tobacco Jar

    4½″ h, 5¼″ sq, polychrome blooming clover dec, ivory ground, gilded fittings, broken int. blister .. **550.00**

    5″ h, 4″ d, Rococo mold, enameled floral dec, sgd, banner mark **495.00**

Tray, 4½″ d, mirrored **550.00**

Vase

    3½″ h, bud, enameled floral dec, sgd, black mark .. **360.00**

    12½″ h, Opal Ware, stylized blue and white iris blossoms on bright blue band, gold accent lines and borders, ormolu mounts **2,450.00**

WEATHER VANES

History: A weather vane indicates wind direction. The earliest known examples were found on late 17th-century structures in the Boston area. The vanes were handcrafted of wood, copper, or tin. By the last half of the 19th century, weather vanes adorned farms and houses throughout the nation. Mass-produced vanes of cast iron, copper, and sheet metal were sold through mail-order catalogs or at country stores.

    The champion vane is the rooster—in fact, the name weathercock is synonymous with weather vane—but the styles and patterns are endless. Weathering can affect the same vane differently; for this reason, patina is a critical element in collectible vanes.

    Whirligigs are a variation of the weather vane. Constructed of wood and metal, often by the unskilled, whirligigs indicate the direction of the wind and its velocity. Watching their unique movements also provides entertainment.

References: Robert Bishop and Patricia Coblentz, *A Gallery of American Weathervanes and Whirligigs*, E. P. Dutton, 1981; Ken Fitzgerald, *Weathervanes and Whirligigs*, Clarkson N. Potter,

1967; Dana G. Morykan and Harry L. Rinker, *Warman's Country Antiques & Collectibles,* Third Edition, Wallace-Homestead, 1996; A. B. & W. T. Westervelt, *American Antique Weathervanes* (1883 catalog reprint), Dover Publications, 1982.

Reproduction Alert: Reproductions of early models exist, are being aged, and then sold as originals.

Angel, 35" l, wood, tin trumpet, brown and yellow paint **2,500.00**
Cockerel, 31 × 31½", sheet metal, cast iron, and zinc,
   red tin tail, Rochester Ironwork **1,500.00**
Cow, 24" l, copper, solid metal head, horn cracked ... **600.00**
Fire Chief, silhouette, folk art type **935.00**
Horse
   21" h, 30" l, running, tin, iron base, stamped "J Harris
     & Son, Boston," early 19th C, minor repairs **1,980.00**
   26" l, 22" h, stallion, full round, sgd "Westervelt" on
     bar, by AB and WT Westervelt, Church, NY, 1883 **6,000.00**
   27" l, running, hollow copper body, cast-zinc head,
     old dark patina **825.00**
   31" l, running, copper body, lead ears, small cracks **1,350.00**
Horse and Jockey, 34" l, copper **5,100.00**
Horse and Rider, 27" h, attributed to A L Jewell & Co,
   Waltham, MA, third-quarter 19th C, traces of gilt,
   imperfections including repaired bullet holes **7,475.00**
Horse and Sulky, 38" l, copper, full bodied, mustard
   paint **9,200.00**

Horse and Sulky, molded, parcel gilt and painted, full-bodied running horse, 19th C, 48" l, 20" h, minor repairs to horse, $4,400.00. Photo courtesy of Butterfield & Butterfield.

Rooster
   14" h, wood, silhouette, crowing, old weathered
     white repaint, red and black dec, attributed to
     Amish **200.00**
   20½" h, 20" l, copper body, cast-metal feet mounted
     on board, overall patina **1,300.00**
   21" h, copper, gilt, and verdigris surface, trace of old
     dark red paint, c19th C **1,955.00**
Schooner, 25¼" l, 18" h, old black and white paint ... **395.00**
Whirligig, painted wood
   17½" h, soldier, red tunic, late 19th/early 20th C,
     repairs, repainted **865.00**
   21" l, two figures with mule **110.00**
   32" l, Santa, reindeer, some repairs and restoration . **175.00**

WEBB, THOMAS & SONS

History: Thomas Webb & Sons was established in 1837 in Stourbridge, England. The company probably is best known for its very beautiful English cameo glass. However, many other types of colored art glass were produced, including enameled, iridescent, heavily ornamented, and cased.

References: Charles R. Hajdamach, *British Glass, 1800–1914,* Antique Collectors' Club, 1991; Ellen T. Schroy, *Warman's Glass,* Wallace-Homestead, 1992.

Additional Listings: Burmese, Cameo, and Peachblow.

Bowl
   7½" d, 4⅞" h, glossy peachblow, cream lining, gold
     prunus and bird dec, three appl reeded feet **850.00**
   12½ × 5⅞ × 7" oval, shaded blue, overlay, green
     and tan enamel leaves, yellow flowers, ruffled .. **350.00**
Bride's Bowl, 12" d, enameled florals, pink shaded to
   strawberry red ground, sgd **275.00**
Cologne Bottle, cameo, carved white florals, amber
   ground, SS top and mounting **1,450.00**
Compote, 5" d, 1⅝" h, Alexandrite, Optic Honeycomb
   pattern, pale amber int., 1" w fuchsia band, honey-
   colored wafer base **975.00**
Goblet, 8½" h, Alexandrite, circular wafer-thin base,
   twisted stem, four textured leaves appl to base of
   bowl, amber tulip-shaped bowl shading to fuchsia .**1,850.00**
Perfume Bottle, 5½" l, teardrop shape, lay-down type,
   MOP shaded blue, DQ **575.00**
Pitcher, 5½" h, scalloped top, gold shaded to white, appl
   frosted handle, sgd **265.00**
Rose Bowl, 3¼" h, prunus blossom dec, yellow body, sq
   top **345.00**
Scent Bottle, 2½" d, 3½" h, Burmese, acid finish, gold
   leaves and berries dec, hallmarked SS screw-on dome
   cap **750.00**
Vase
   3" h, 4½" d, yellow satin, heavy gold prunus blos-
     soms, gold butterfly on side, bold band on top and
     bottom, cream int. **325.00**
   4" h, 3¾" d, square, dimples on each side, shaded
     blue, gold prunus blossoms and branches, cream
     lining **245.00**

Vase, cameo, four layer, elongated bottle form, crystal cased to bright red, yellow over white layers, cameo cut repeating Oriental pattern of stylized scrolling geometric and floral devices, stamped "Thomas Webb & Sons Gem Cameo," 7⅛" h, $8,250.00. Photograph courtesy of Skinner, Inc.

5¼" h, simulated ivory cameo, brown stain shading
to ivory, flowers, leaves, and panel of three birds,
scalloped top, sgd 875.00
6" h, gourd shape, gold flowers and insects, shaded
brown ground 200.00
9" h, deep coral red overlay, white lining, heavy gold
branch and flowers dec 385.00
9⅜" h, 5⅛" d, flattened oval, glossy peachblow, gold
and silver dec, propeller mark 695.00

WEDGWOOD

History: In 1754 Josiah Wedgwood and Thomas Whieldon of
Fenton Vivian, Staffordshire, England, became partners in a pottery enterprise. Their products included marbled, agate, tortoiseshell, green glaze, and Egyptian black wares. In 1759 Wedgwood
opened his own pottery at the Ivy House works, Burslem. In 1764
he moved to the Brick House (Bell Works) at Burslem. The pottery
concentrated on utilitarian pieces.

Between 1766 and 1769 Wedgwood built the famous works
at Etruria. Among the most-renowned products of this plant were
the Empress Catherina of Russia dinner service (1774) and the
Portland Vase (1790s). The firm also made caneware, unglazed
earthenwares (drabwares), piecrust wares, variegated and marbled
wares, black basalt (developed in 1768), Queen's or creamware,
and Jasperware (perfected in 1774).

Bone china was produced under the direction of Josiah Wedgwood II between 1812 and 1822 and revived in 1878. Moonlight
luster was made from 1805 to 1815. Fairyland luster began in
1920. All luster production ended in 1932.

A museum was established at the Etruria pottery in 1906. When
Wedgwood moved to its modern plant at Barlaston, North Staffordshire, the museum was expanded.

References: Susan and Al Bagdade, *Warman's English & Continental Pottery & Porcelain,* Second Edition, Wallace-Homestead,
1991; Diana Edwards, *Black Basalt,* Antique Collectors Club,
1994; Robin Reilly, *Wedgwood,* Antique Collectors Club, 1994;
Peter Williams, *Wedgwood,* Wallace-Homestead, 1992.

Periodical: *ARS Ceramica,* 5 Dogwood Court, Glen Head, NY
11545.

Collectors' Clubs: Wedgwood Collectors Society, PO Box 14013,
Newark, NJ 07198; The Wedgwood Society, The Roman Villa,
Rockbourne, Fordingbridge, Hants, SP6 3PG, England.

Museums: Art Institute of Chicago, Chicago, IL; Birmingham Mu-
seum of Art, Birmingham, AL; Cincinnati Museum of Art, Cincin-
nati, OH; Cleveland Museum of Art, Cleveland, OH; Henry E.
Huntington Library and Art Gallery, San Marino, CA; Nassau
County Museum System, Long Island, NY; Nelson-Atkins Museum
of Art, Kansas City, MO; Potsdam Public Museum, Potsdam, NY;
Rose Museum, Brandeis University, Waltham, MA; Wadsworth
Atheneum, Hartford, CT.

Basalt

Bowl, 4¼" d, black, engine-turned body, hp floral sprigs,
imp mark, 19th C 345.00
Cassolette, 9¼" h, black, drapery and foliate reliefs, imp
Wedgwood & Bentley marks, 18th C, chips to sconce
rim, restored foot 1,610.00
Club Jug, 7½" h, black, enamel dec floral sprays, imp
marks, c1870, body hairlines 230.00
Figure, black
12¼" h, Apollo, nude standing with cloth draped over
arm, imp mark, 19th C, chip to lyre 1,035.00
16" h, Shakespeare, full figure standing at podium,
marked "W.W.," c1850 .... 1,200.00
Jar, cov, 4½" h, classical figures, marked "Wedgwood,
Made in England" 110.00
Lamp, 8¼" h, oval shape, bronzed and gilt black, carved
fluting over appl acanthus and bellflower relief, handle formed as female figure seated at one end with
book in hand, imp mark, c1875, gilt retouched, finial
reglued, socle rim chip 1,320.00

**Basalt, box, cov, ribbed body,
figural finial, imp mark, 4½" h,
$295.00.**

Model, black,
3½" h, cat, c1913 .... 550.00
4¼" l, reclining baby, after Della Robbia, imp mark,
mid-19th C, foot rim chip 435.00
Portrait, 3⅜ × 4¼" oval, black, Sir Isaac Newton, self
framed, imp mark, 18th C 230.00
Tea Caddy, cov 5¾" h, engine-turned border below classical children in relief, imp marks, late 18th C, rim
nicks 1,035.00
Tea Set, engine-turned black bodies, 6" h cov teapot with
widow finial, 3¾" h creamer, 5" d waste bowl, imp
marks, 19th C, price for set 490.00
Vase
10⅜" h, Encaustic dec, white and black accented

iron-red figural design to one side, Greek-key gadroon and stiff leaf bands, imp marks, c1840 ...**2,300.00**
10½" h, cov, putti-head handles, body with relief
cupid figures supporting wreath, fruiting grapevine
border, engine-turned to cov, neck and foot, imp
circular stamp Wedgwood & Bentley marks, restoration, price for pr **6,325.00**

Caneware

Game Pie Dish, cov, 9½" l, oval, molded hare finial,
fruiting grapevines, game on body, stained liner, imp
mark, mid-19th C **490.00**
Inkwell, 2¼" h, black basalt relief, imp mark, c1800,
handles restored **375.00**
Potpourri, cov, 11½" l, pierced lid, rosso antico fruiting
grapevine relief, imp mark, early 19th c, rim chips to
married lid, insert missing **410.00**
Teapot, cov, 5" h, arabesque molded and spaniel finial,
imp mark, c1820, chip to spout and cov collar int. . **230.00**
Vase, 5¾" h, engine-turned borders on either side of
rosso antico leafy vine work, imp mark, early 19th C,
repair to relief, no cov **115.00**

Creamware

Dish, 12¼" d, polychrome Masonic dec, imp mark, late
18th/19th C **320.00**
Soup Tureen, cov, and Platter, 12¼" l tureen, 21½" l
platter, iron-red trim, black and green enamel crests,
early 19th C, hairline on tureen, wear to platter, price
for matching pr **415.00**
Soup Tureen, cov, stand, 13½" d stand, imp mark,
c1800, hairline to cov, foot rim and chip under tureen, price for 3-pc set **980.00**

Diceware

Cup and Saucer, 5⅜" d saucer, white running laurel
borders, appl yellow quatrefoils, green dip ground,
imp mark, late 19th/early 20th C **1,610.00**
Tea Set, 5½" h cov teapot, 3¼" h creamer, 4" h cov sugar,
white running laurel borders, appl yellow quatrefoils,
green dip ground, imp mark, late 19th/early 20th C **3,335.00**
Vase, 8¾" h, black jasper ground, central frieze of dancing hours in white relief, lower dice-patterned band
with yellow quatrefoils, imp mark, mid-19th C, restored base chips, manufactured cov **1,495.00**

Drabware

Teapot, cov, 4½" h, appl blue classical relief, imp mark,
19th C **435.00**
Tea Set, 7½" h cov teapot with widow finial, 3⅛" h
creamer, 4" h cov sugar, appl white fruit and floral
banding, imp marks, 19th C **425.00**

Jasperware

Bell Pull, 2½" h, white relief of Poor Maria, Lady Templeton design, solid pale blue, late 18th C **345.00**
Biscuit Jar, cov, 7½" d, sage green, appl white bust me-

dallions of Washington, Franklin, and Lafayette,
acorn finial, minor rim chip **360.00**
Button, 1⅜" d, white classical relief dec, blue ground,
multifaceted cut-steel mountings attributed to Matthew Boulton, late 19th C, price for 12-pc set **5,750.00**
Cache Pot, blue ground, white grape and leaf garlands,
classical theatrical figures, early 20th C **110.00**
Chess Set, 4¼" h maximum, 16 pc each side, blue-dip
and lilac-dip base, designed by John Flaxman, Jr, imp
marks, late 18th C, minor damage and restoration,
price for 32-pc set **17,825.00**
Clock Garniture, 13" h clock, 9" h pr candlesticks, 12" h
pr cov urns, appl black classical medallions between
floral swags separated by ram's heads and trophies,
yellow-dip ground, imp "Etruria" marks, early 20th
C, non-operational Bailey, Banks & Biddle, Philadelphia, clock, minor damage and restoration, price for
5-pc set **2,300.00**
Coffee Cann and Saucer, 5⅜" d, 2½" h, white running
laurel border, green appl quatrefoils, lilac ground,
imp marks, mid-19th C **1,610.00**
Cracker Jar, cov
6" h, 5" d, barrel shape, white relief classical figures,
dark blue ground, SP rim, cov and bail handle,
marked "Wedgwood" **200.00**
6¼" h, bulbous ovoid body, white relief classical figures, dark blue ground, flat SP rim, cov, and
twisted bail handle, marked "Wedgwood" **220.00**
7" h, cylindrical, white relief classical figures, blue
ground, flat SP cov, lid, bail handle, and base ring,
ball feet, marked "Wedgwood, England" **165.00**
Creamer and Sugar, cov, blue, marked "Wedgwood,
England," price for pr **145.00**
Dish, 4½" h, heart shape, white relief classical figures,
red ground, marked "Wedgwood, England," c1920 **395.00**
Jardiniere
4½" h, copper plated, classical relief, imp mark, late
19th C **320.00**
5¼" h, black classical relief, yellow dip, imp mark,
20th C, chip to acanthus relief **375.00**
9" h, white classical relief, crimson dip, imp mark,
c1920 ....**1,265.00**
Match Striker/Candleholder, cov, 3¾" h, 2⅜" d, cylindrical body, finial to hold candle, white relief classical figures, blue ground, marked "Wedgwood,
England" **225.00**
Medallion, oval
2⅝" × 3¼", white relief of children after Lady
Templeton design, dark blue dip, modeled for a
buckle, polished edge, imp mark, 18th C **320.00**
3⅛" l, white classical relief, lilac, green, yellow to
dark blue ground, imp mark, early 19th C **1,150.00**
Mug
4¼" h, white classical relief, crimson dip, imp mark **1,035.00**
5" h, 3¾" d, cylindrical, rope twist handle, silver
top rim, white relief classical ladies and cupids
on sides, small white medallion at front showing
two soldiers, dark blue ground, marked "Wedgwood" **125.00**
Pin Tray, 2⅜" w, 5⅞" l, white relief classical figures,
bleeding green ground, marked "Wedgwood, England" **50.00**

Pitcher

    3″ h, 2″ d, tankard shape, raised white classical women, grapes and leaves border, lavender ground, marked "Wedgwood England" **85.00**

    3½″ h, white classical relief, crimson dip, imp mark, c1920 .... **750.00**

    3¾″ h, 3⅞″ d, cylindrical, white scrolls and heads of Franklin and Washington, dark green ground, C-scroll handle, marked "Wedgwood, England" .. **325.00**

    6⅜″ h, 3¾″ d, tankard, cylindrical, white relief classical ladies and cupids, border of relief grapes, sage green ground, marked "Wedgwood, England" **155.00**

Plaque

    6½ × 23¼″, rect, white relief Bacchanalian boys after design by Lady Diana Beauclerk, solid light blue, imp mark, 19th C, crazing to relief, plaque restored **1,610.00**

    8¾ × 18¾″, rect, white classical relief, pale blue ground, imp mark, late 18th/19th C, giltwood frame **920.00**

Portrait Medallion, 45½″ l, oval, white relief of Prince and Princess of Wales, solid blue jasper ground, inscribed titles, imp marks, 19th C, price for pr **520.00**

Potpourri Vase, cov, 8″ handle to handle, white classical relief, dark blue ground, pierced cov with appl florets, imp mark, mid-19th C, foot rim chips **635.00**

Sugar, cov, 4″ h, 4⅜″ d, white raised mythological figures, light blue ground, marked "Wedgwood" **120.00**

Tea Caddy Spoon, 2⅛″ l, solid blue, shell-form bowl, imp mark, early 19th C **435.00**

Tea Canister, cov, 5¼″ h, white classical relief, crimson dip, imp mark, c1920, ball finial missing **920.00**

Teapot, cov, 4½″ h, black dip, white classical and foliate relief, imp mark, late 19th C **980.00**

Urn, cov, 9¼″ h, campana form, tall flaring body, loop handles, ringed pedestal, sq foot, stepped and domed cov, knob finial, white relief classical figures and leaf bands, lavender ground, marked "Wedgwood" **1,200.00**

Vase

    4⅞″ h, Portland, white relief classical figures, dark blue ground, c1840 .... **185.00**

Jasper, vase, cov, white cameos of Pegasus card for by Nymphs, Bellerophon watering Pegasus at the Sacred Spring, Ulysseus staying the Chariot of Victory, and Aurora in her Chariot, green ground, diceware on blue ground, base and cov, early 19th C, $1,520.00.

    5″ h

        Green and lilac classical and foliate relief, white ground, imp mark, mid-19th C **920.00**

        White relief classical figures, dark blue ground, two handles, marked "Wedgwood, England" **425.00**

    5½″ h, Portland, white relief classical figures, dark blue ground, c1840 .... **250.00**

    6½″ h, 3″ d, angled baluster, handles at shoulder, white relief classical figures, dark blue ground, marked "Wedgwood, England" **225.00**

    7¾″ h, Portland, white relief classical figures, dark blue ground, c1840 .... **395.00**

Wine Ewer, 16¼″ h, black dip, white satyr seated on shoulders, ram's head below spout, inscribed under base "J. Sidebotham, July 6, 1882," imp factory mark, c1882, restorations **865.00**

Lustres

Bronze, bowl, 6½″ d, multicolored fruit ext., MOP lustre int. with fruit, pattern Z5458, printed mark, c1928 . **230.00**

Dragon, vase, 23¼″ h, shape #2413, Oriental motif, mottled blue ground, printed mark, c1920, hairline to foot rim, gilt rim wear **750.00**

Fairyland

    Punch Bowl, 11¼″ d, black poplar trees ext., woodland bridge int., pattern Z4968, printed mark, c1925, hairlines, rim chip restored, gilt wear ...**1,380.00**

    Vase

        7¼″ h, Castle on a Road, daylight coloring, shape #2442, pattern Z4968, printed mark, c1920 .**3,335.00**

        9½″ h, Firbolgs, trumpet shape, ruby ground, MOP int., fish border, printed mark, c1920, restored **260.00**

        15¾″ h, Ghostly Wood, cov, shape #2046, pattern Z4968, printed marks, c1920, rim restoration **8,625.00**

Fish

    Bowl, K'ang Hsi, 7¼″ d, mixed blue ext., satin glazed MOP int., pattern Z4920, printed mark, c1920 .. **920.00**

    Plate, 8¾″ d, green ground, sponged brown, red and blue, reverse with similar sponging to MOP ground, pattern Z6, printed mark, c1920 .... **345.00**

Hummingbird, vase, 6″ h, mottled blue ext., orange int., flying geese border, pattern Z5294, printed mark, c1920, price for pr **750.00**

Moonlight

    Caudle Cup and Saucer, 3¾″ h, imp marks, c1815 . **320.00**

    Cup and Saucer, 5½″ d, saucer, imp marks, c1810, glaze wear **230.00**

    Dish, 11⅜″ h, oval shell shape, imp mark, c1810, price for pr **635.00**

Majolica

Compote, 11⅛″ d, multicolored glazes, leaves surrounding central blue medallion, imp mark, c1875 ...... **345.00**

Creamer, cov, 5½″ h, cauliflower, molded body, green glazed leaves below cream glazed florets, late 18th C **1,265.00**

Plate, seashell shape, pr **250.00**

Salt, 1½″ d, scrolled tripod base supporting bowl, rams'

heads between drapery, imp marks, c1868, int. glaze, nick to one head **345.00**

Tile, 8" sq, polychrome dec of bird in flight within water and floral landscape, imp mark, c1877, restored chip **375.00**

Vase, 10¼" h, glazed brown stoneware, imp mark, c1877 .... **230.00**

Miscellaneous

Bowl, 10¼" h, Liberty Bowl, black transfer dec, sold J E Caldwell & Co **230.00**

Bust, parian

 3½" h, Raleigh, inscribed "trial no. 2," imp mark and title, mid-19th C **410.00**

 14½" h, 8½" d, Milton, by E W Wyon, marked "Wedgwood" **900.00**

Candlestick, 9¾" h, blue glaze, molded shell relief surrounding rect base, imp mark and date letters, 1870, chip, glaze flaking, staining, wear **260.00**

Cassolette, 9⅝" h, variegated agate, mounted to stepped basalt plinth, gilding to handles and finial, imp wafer Wedgwood and Bentley wafer mark, gilt wear, rim chips **2,645.00**

Chestnut Compote, 8¾" d, blue, red, and gilt floral dec, late 19th C, price for pr **230.00**

Figure

 7" h, Fallow Deer, cream glaze, imp "J. Skeaping," factory mark, c1927 .... **200.00**

 14½" h, Taurus the Bull, modeled and designed by Arnold Machin, black glaze, allover gold printed zodiac symbols, imp mark, c1945 .... **415.00**

Garden Seat, 17½" h, transfer printed, foliate terra-cotta-colored enamel, cream ground, imp and printed marks, c1891, slight int. glaze line **635.00**

Plaque, 4½ × 5⅜" oval, white terra-cotta, depicting Pan and Syrinx in relief, imp Wedgwood and Bentley mark, c1775 .... **1,495.00**

Plate

 7" d, Appledore pattern **22.00**

 10" d, Ivanhoe series, Black Knight Exchanges with Friar, blue **65.00**

Serving Dish, 11¾" l, oval, three part, armorial crest, blue enamel and gilt trim, colored crests, imp mark, late 18th/early 19th C **425.00**

Teabowl and Saucer, 3½" d saucer, yellow glazed earthenware, green enamel banded bodies, circular black medallions, imp mark, early 19th C **345.00**

Pearlware

Figure, 7¼" h, boy, enamel dec, classical costume, feeding spaniel, imp mark, 19th C, slight foot rim nicks, hand and nose restored, glaze flake **635.00**

Pitcher, 7⁹⁄₁₆" h, jug shape, transfer-printed black on one side of ship, yellow hull, red, white, and blue American flag and pennant above green sea, black enameled inscription "The Amazon, A. H. Burrows, Commander," reverse with oval scene of ship in distress on stormy sea, red and blue figurehead, under spout dec of eagle beneath thirteen stars, banderole inscribed "E Pluribus Unum," worn gilt edge, imp "Wedgwood," c1810, small spout chip **2,300.00**

Potpourri Vase, cov, 7½" h, slip dec, central drapery swags within band flanked by engine-turned fluting, imp mark, c1800, vase rim and pierced lid restored **490.00**

Weights, 1 to 4", graduated from 1 oz to 7 lb, printed weight and "W. & T Avery Birmingham" on each, imp mark, c1872, minor damage and restoration, price for 8-pc set **1,100.00**

Queen's Ware

Centennial Jug, caneware glazed with brown transfers of Independence and Memorial Halls, molded body with star band to rim, ribbed band with thirteen orig states in relief, imp marks, c1874, slight rim line ... **200.00**

Compote, 6¾" h, Japonica pattern, triangular base modeled with three dolphins, gilt and enamel dec, imp mark, c1872 .... **345.00**

Slop Pail, cov, 11" d, enamel oak-leaf border, imp mark, c1886, rim chip repair **435.00**

Vase, cov, 8½" h, engine-turned body, swag drapery banding, bacchus-head handles, acorn finial, imp mark, mid-19th C **375.00**

Rosso Antico

Club Jug, 4⅞" h, floral sprays, imp mark, mid-19th C, rim chip and repair **250.00**

Club Pitcher, 4¾" h, floral dec, imp mark, mid-19th C **460.00**

Creamer, 5" l, basalt creamware trim, hieroglyphics and meander banding, imp mark, early 19th C **575.00**

Cup and Saucer, black-outlined turquoise enamel and gilt dec, elves scene, cup titled "Get up, silly" and "Hello," 5⅜" d saucer titled "Look out froggie," imp mark, late 19th C **920.00**

Figure, 4⅝" l, boy sleeping, after model of one of the "Five Boys of Fiammingo," imp mark, 19th C **575.00**

Plaque, 2¼ × 3½" oval, caneware relief, Marriage of Cupid and Psyche, imp mark, early 19th C, mounted in giltwood frame **520.00**

Vase, 6½" h, basalt classical relief, two handles, mounted atop drum base, imp mark, early 19th C, base nicks, chips, socle restored, no cov **345.00**

Stoneware

Mortar and Pestle, 6½" d mortar, 8¼" l wooden-handled pestle imp #3, 19th C **290.00**

Sugar, cov, 3" h, tricolor glaze, appl green acanthus and lilac bellflowers, imp mark, mid-19th C **460.00**

Vase, 4½" h, white, Portland, painted black ground, classical relief with half-length figure wearing Phrygian cap under base, imp Etruria mark, mid-19th C **635.00**

Wine Cask Label, 5¾" l, labeled Maderia, Port, Moselle, and Sherry, imp mark, 19th C, price for 4-pc set ... **500.00**

Victoria Ware

Plaque

 5⅜ × 7", white classical relief, deep teal ground, design by Charles Toft, giltwood frame, imp mark, c1880 .... **490.00**

 7¾ × 10⅞" oval, white relief of War & Peace, olive green ground, designed by Charles Toft for 1878

Exhibition, imp mark, c1878, glaze wear and relief repair **690.00**
Vase
5" h, portrait, white relief, pale blue ground, iron red ground medallions, black borders, imp mark, c1880 .... **815.00**
7¼" h, cov, white dancing hours and foliate relief, deep teal and iron-red ground, gilt bacchus-head handles and trim, imp mark, c1875, cov and socle rim restored **865.00**
7½" h, cov, white classical and foliate relief, dark blue and burnt red ground, gilt trim, mounted on drum base, imp mark, c1880 ....**1,265.00**

WELLER POTTERY

History: In 1872 Samuel A. Weller opened a small factory in Fultonham, near Zanesville, Ohio. There he produced utilitarian stoneware, such as milk pans and sewer tile. In 1882 he moved his facilities to Zanesville. Then in 1890 Weller built a new plant in the Putnam section of Zanesville along the tracks of the Cincinnati and Muskingum Railway. Additions followed in 1892 and 1894.

In 1894 Weller entered into an agreement with William A. Long to purchase the Lonhuda Faience Company, which had developed an art pottery line under the guidance of Laura A. Fry, formerly of Rookwood. Long left in 1895, but Weller continued to produce Lonhuda under the new name "Louwelsa." Replacing Long as art director was Charles Babcock Upjohn. He, along with Jacques Sicard, Frederick Hurten Rhead, and Gazo Fudji, developed Weller's art pottery lines.

At the end of World War I, many prestige lines were discontinued and Weller concentrated on commercial wares. Rudolph Lorber joined the staff and designed lines such as Roma, Forest, and Knifewood. In 1920 Weller purchased the plant of the Zanesville Art Pottery and claimed to produce more pottery than anyone else in the country.

Art pottery enjoyed a revival when the Hudson Line was introduced in the early 1920s. The 1930s saw Coppertone and Graystone Garden ware added. However, the Depression forced the closing of the Putnam plant and one on Marietta Street in Zanesville. After World War II inexpensive Japanese imports took over Weller's market. In 1947 Essex Wire Company of Detroit bought the controlling stock, but early in 1948 operations ceased.

References: Susan and Al Bagdade, *Warman's American Pottery and Porcelain,* Wallace-Homestead, 1994; Sharon and Bob Huxford, *The Collectors Encyclopedia of Weller Pottery,* Collector Books, 1979, 1994 value update; Ralph and Terry Kovel, *Kovels' American Art Pottery,* Crown Publishers, 1993.

Collectors' Club: American Art Pottery Assoc, 125 E. Rose Ave, St. Louis, MO 63119.

Additional Listings: See *Warman's Americana & Collectibles* for more examples.

Bowl, Sabrinian, 6½" d **275.00**
Candlestick
Silvertone, price for pr **200.00**
Woodcraft, 8" w, 13½" h, double, molded as owl perched in top of apple tree, c1917 .... **360.00**
Cigarette Holder, figural, frog, Coppertone **200.00**
Console Bowl, Silvertone, 12" l, flower frog, c1928 ... **325.00**
Cream Pitcher, two appl slip trailing trees, white leaves, green trunk, blue ground, clear high glaze, chrome-plated brass lid, unmarked, 4" h **300.00**
Ewer, 5" h, 3¼" d, spherical, molded lizard around sides, cylindrical neck, pinched spout, long angled handle, mottled matte green-blue glaze, die-stamped "Weller" **600.00**
Figure, Muskota, fishing boy, seated on rockwork, 6½" h, c1915 .... **225.00**
Frog, figural
Coppertone, lily pads, 14" h **375.00**
Muskota, c1915
4¼" h, small nude boy kneeling on large green rock base, unmarked **275.00**
4½" h, frog, half immersed in water lily **225.00**
9" h, kingfisher **375.00**
Garden Ornament, frog playing banjo, sitting on white water lily, name incised in script on lily pad base, 12⅛" h, well-done repair to banjo **8,000.00**
Jardiniere
6 × 7", two handles, Glasgow roses and foliage, die-stamped mark **400.00**
7¼" h, bulbous ovoid, wide molded mouth flanked by four small ribbon handles, shoulder molded with stylized flowers, matte green, c1904, unmarked **525.00**
8" h, matte green, embossed hosta leaves dec, c1904 **250.00**
8¼" h, 11" d, wide cylindrical body, molded rim flanked by four small loop handles, four wide ribs, rounded bottom edge, emb wide center herringbone band, unmarked **360.00**
9½" h, Woodcraft, slightly tapering cylindrical tree-trunk form, molded branch, acorns, and leaves, figural squirrel and woodpecker, c1917 .... **675.00**
10" h, Silvertone, c1928 .... **350.00**
12½" h, 14½" d, Sicardo, wide bulbous body, short arcade feet, sides emb with large Moorish ara-

Vase, Hudson, white ground, imp mark, 6¾" h, $475.00.

besques, wide short flaring scalloped neck, irid purple, gold and green glaze, painted "Weller Sicard" on side **1,650.00**
Jug, Louwelsa, small **140.00**
Lamp Base
  14" h, 7" d, matte green, Art Nouveau design, slender swelled cylindrical body, flaring base, four wide strap handles, band of molded flowers around top, brass mount, c1904 .... **935.00**
  14½" h, 8½" d, matte green, wide bulbous multilobed gourd-shaped body tapering sharply to slender cylindrical neck, molded rim, emb grotesque devils' heads, raised narrow flaring base, four knob feet, smooth matte green glaze, orig gas fittings, complete, c1904, unmarked **440.00**
Lawn Ornament, 11¾" h, 11½" w, Woodcraft, c1917, figural, large seated squirrel, holding acorn, mottled green and brown, stamped "Weller Pottery," restoration **2,530.00**
Pitcher, Coppertone, fish handle, semicircular ink stamp logo, notations "12, T" painted in black slip, orig "Weller Coppertone Ware" paper label, two small glaze flakes off fish's dorsal fin **700.00**
Planter, Woodcraft, cats on fence, flowerpots **795.00**
Plate, Zona, 7" d, Juvenile line, rolled edge, ducks dec **85.00**
Powder Jar, cov, 7½" h, 5" d, Muskota, Southern Belle, wide hoop skirt, red roses, blue bows, glossy yellow ground, c1915, marked "27" **310.00**
Sand Jar, Forest, 13" h, large block-letters mark, several base chips **550.00**
Tumbler, 4¾" h, white, yellow, green, and brown low-relief flower, gray-brown ground, wear, crazing and edge flakes **60.00**
Umbrella Stand, Zona, 20" h, 10" d, cylindrical, women in purple dresses, long red floral garlands, grapevines, white ground, c1920 .... **715.00**
Urn, Birdimal, moonlit scene repeated on each side, small block-letter mark, 8⅜" h **250.00**
Vase
  3¼" h, 5¾" d, Sicardo, ftd, cushion shape, short widely flaring trefoil neck, bright satin dec of gold arabesques, lustered green and burgundy ground, sgd on side **715.00**
  4⅜" h, Jap Birdimal, slip floral dec, bubble-blowing fish, slip-train sea, three small feet, one with incised artist initials "V.M.H.," also imp "F, 589" **750.00**
  5" h, Sicardo, baluster, multicolored irid glaze, mistletoe branches dec, sgd **440.00**
  5" h, 5" w, bulbous, emb burgundy morning glories and green leaves, feathered matte glaze, incised "Weller" **400.00**
  5½" h, 3" d, Sicardo, cylindrical, Art Nouveau style, swirled arabesques, green and purple irid glaze, script marks on body "Weller" and "Sicard," imp "7" on base **500.00**
  6½" h, 4¼" d, Sicardo, tapering ovoid, bulbous compressed and closed neck, small loop handles, irid gold flowers, deep purple ground, unmarked ...**1,100.00**
  7" h
    Hudson, autumn scene, vividly colored trees and grasses, very heavy slip, artist's name "Mae Timberlake" painted in black slip on side, base

marked with semicircular ink stamp logo, tight 3" line descends from rim **900.00**
    Sicardo, three lobes, undulating upright body, floral designs on sides, irid green and gold glaze**1,150.00**
  7⅞" h, Rhead Faience, slip dec of geisha playing stringed instrument, standing in wooded area, incised "Weller Rhead Faience," imp "X" and "O" **750.00**
  8½" h, Silvertone, c1928, ftd, bulbous, heavy loop handles, short neck, ruffled rim, molded pink and yellow flowers, green leaves, brown branches .. **425.00**
  12" h
    Hudson, multicolored hibiscus flowers, buds, and leaves, black outlines, another pink and white floral spray on back, artist Hester Pillsbury's last name in black slip on side, semicircular ink stamp mark **1,600.00**
    Silvertone, c1928, poppies and butterflies, professional chip repairs **395.00**
  12½" h, 5" h, two heavily emb Art Nouveau women, flowing diaphanous gowns, richly textured green matte glaze **2,800.00**
  13⅛" h, Hudson, blue and white dec, two birds perched in flowering tree, flying insect, imp "Weller" in large block letters **1,800.00**
  13½" h, Woodcraft, 1917, double bud, tall slender tree trunks, flanking apple blossom branch with small owl **500.00**
  14⅝" h, Jap Birdimal, Rhead Faience, detailed geisha standing in grove of Rhead-like trees, slip trailing and slip painting, side sgd "CMM," incised shape no. 570 and "Rhead," minor glaze abrasions, small drill hole professionally repaired **1,000.00**
  15" h, Silvertone, c1928, molded calla lilies **500.00**
  15¼" h, 7" d, Woodcraft, 1917, cylindrical tree-trunk form, pierced, large hole on one side, figural owl on other, cluster of apples and leaves, polychrome matte glaze, die-stamped "Weller" **1,100.00**
  19½" h, 13" d, Sicardo, Art Nouveau style, ovoid body, scroll molded feet, sides tapering to bulbous pierced rim, molded whiplash swirls above large pendent blossoms, relief-molded figures of two swirling Art Nouveau maidens flanked by long scrolls, gold, green, blue, and purple irid glaze, sgd "Weller Sicard" **7,700.00**
Wall Pocket
  Glendale, right curve **325.00**
  Roma **195.00**
  Sabrinian **475.00**
  Souevo **195.00**
  Sydonia, blue **225.00**
  Woodcraft
    9" h, tree trunk form, molded leaves, purple plus **400.00**
    10" h, conical, molded owl's head in trunk opening **300.00**

WHALING

History: Whaling items are a specialized part of nautical collecting. Provenance is of prime importance since collectors want assurances that their pieces are from a whaling voyage. Since ship's equipment seldom carries the ship's identification, some individuals have falsely attributed a whaling provenance to general nautical items. Know the dealer, auction house, or collector from whom you buy.

Special tools, e.g., knives, harpoons, lances, and spades, do not overlap the general nautical line. Makers' marks and condition determine value for these items.

References: Nina Hellman and Norman Brouwer, *A Mariner's Fancy,* South Street Seaport Museum, Balsam Press, and University of Washington Press, 1992; Martha Lawrence, *Scrimshaw,* Schiffer Publishing, 1993.

Museums: Cold Spring Harbor Whaling Museum, Cold Spring Harbor, NY; Kendall Whaling Museum, Sharon, MA; Mystic Seaport Museum, Mystic, CT; National Maritime Museum Library, San Francisco, CA; New Bedford Whaling Museum, New Bedford, MA; Pacific Whaling Museum, Waimanalo, HI; Sag Harbor Whaling & Historical Museum, Sag Harbor, NY; South Street Seaport Museum, New York, NY.

Additional Listings: Nautical Items and Scrimshaw.

Bill of Sale, bark *Mars,* dated Nov 25, 1882, New Bedford artist Charles H Gifford appears as part owner .   **175.00**

Cane
  36″ l, wood shaft, turned whale-ivory knob, American, mid-19th C **195.00**
  36⅝″ l, inlaid ivory, wood, and baleen rings, faceted knob, 19th C **250.00**

Captain's Speaking Trumpet, metal, Captain Nathaniel Mathews, *Alarm,* Boston, 1860s **1,045.00**

Crew List, whaleboat *Montpelier,* Sept 6, 1853, names, position, number of shares in voyages to be received   **125.00**

Flag, whaleboat *William S Henry,* 139½ × 76½″, 37 stars, marked "DB Greene" **650.00**

Game Box, 18½″ sq, wood, abalone shell and whalebone inlays, chess ext., backgammon board int., mid-19th C **1,650.00**

Hand Pulls, 24 and 16½″ l, used on gangways and hatchways, orig white paint, price for two pr **175.00**

Hat Rack, 27⅞″ l, oak board, mounted with five whale's teeth, 19th C **450.00**

Hourglass, 5″ d, 8¾″ h, ebony, whale-ivory feet and blocking, late 18th C **850.00**

Jagging Wheel, 6″ l, with crimper fork, whale ivory, 19th C **635.00**

Knitting Needles, pr, 14½″ l, coconut wood, whale-ivory tips, whale-ivory finial dec with alternating exotic wood and whale ivory, 19th C **695.00**

Pointer, 32⅝″ l, whalebone, baleen separator, carved faceted whale-ivory knob **195.00**

Print, South Sea Whale Fishery, Thomas Sutherland, 1825, identified within plate, etching and aquatint, hand coloring on paper, 19¾ × 25½″, framed **320.00**

Quarter Board, 84″ l, *Edith Nute,* orig gold lettering, old black paint traces, worn, 19th C **250.00**

Registration Certificate, brig *Gold Hunter,* Edgartown, MA, issued to Joseph Mayhew, dated Aug 31, 1837, framed **395.00**

Ship's Log, 17½″ l, brass, orig box, marked "T Walker and Sons, Patent" **550.00**

Swift, 18½″ h, whale bone and ivory, turned wood base with ivory feet, 19th C, repairs to ribs **1,850.00**

Wheel, 36″ d, ship *Aria,* brass, made and sgd "Edison Mfg Co, Boston, Mass," dated 1903 ....**1,950.00**

WHIELDON   WHIELDON

History: Thomas Whieldon, a Staffordshire potter, established his shop in 1740. He is best known for his mottled ware, molded in the shapes of vegetables, fruits, and leaves. Josiah Spode and Josiah Wedgwood, in different capacities, had connections with Whieldon.

Whieldon ware is a generic term. His wares were never marked, and other potters made similar items. Whieldon ware is agate-tortoiseshell earthenware, in limited shades of green, brown, blue and yellow. Most pieces are utilitarian items, e.g., dinnerware and plates, but figurines and other decorative pieces also were made.

Figure, 3¼″ h, seated pug dog, ochre, brown, and gray glaze **450.00**

Plate, 9¼″ d, emb scalloped rim, brown, gray, green, and ochre tortoiseshell glaze, brown and cream speckled back **295.00**

Porringer, 4¾ × 2¾″, creamware, sponged manganese, green, and ochre brushed glaze, c1770 ....   **650.00**

Stirrup Cup, 4¹⁵⁄₁₆″, stag's head, creamware head, brown and green stripes highlighted with brown and ochre dots, brown ears, incised eyelashes, dimpled nose, ochre whorl-molded crest, c1780, minor repairs ...**4,250.00**

Branding Iron, cast and wrought iron, E. S. Mitchell, Dartmouth, c1850, 32¾″ l, $65.00.

Teapot, tortoiseshell glaze, bird finial, c1760, 5¼″ h, $2,300.00.

Sugar, cov, 4¼″ h, Pineapple Ware, translucent green
  and yellow glazes, c1765, restored **925.00**
Tea Canister, 3⅝″ h, oval, Cauliflower Ware, molded
  lower body with green glazed leaves below cream
  glazed florets, rim chips and repair **230.00**
Teapot, 4½″ h, Cauliflower Ware, molded lower body
  and handle with green glazed leaves below cream
  glazed florets, spout repair **805.00**
Wall Pocket, 8½″ h, cornucopia, cartouche with goddess, brown, ochre, and green glaze **1,500.00**

Witch Ball, decanter vase with wafer-type foot,
white Nailsea loopings, $665.00.

WHIMSIES, GLASS

History: During lunch or after completing their regular work
schedule, glassworkers occasionally spent time creating unusual
glass objects known as whimsies, e.g. candy-striped canes, darn-
ers, hats, paperweights, pipes, and witch balls. Whimsies were
taken home and given as gifts to family and friends.

Because of their uniqueness and infinite variety, whimsies can
rarely be attributed to a specific glass house or glassworker.
Whimsies were created wherever glass was made, from New Jersey to Ohio and westward. Some have suggested that style and
color can be used to pinpoint region or factory, but no one has
yet developed an identification key that is adequate.

Glass canes are among the most collectible types of whimsies.
These range in length from very short (under one foot) to ten feet
or more. They come in both hollow and solid form. Hollow canes
can have a bulb-type handle or the rarer C- or L-shaped handle.
Canes are found in many fascinating colors, with the candy striped
being a regular favorite with collectors. Many canes are also filled
with various colored powders, gold and white being the most
common and silver being harder to find. Sometimes they were
even used as candy containers.

References: Gary Baker et al., *Wheeling Glass 1829–1939,* Og-
lebay Institute, 1994, distributed by Antique Publications; Joyce
E. Blake, *Glasshouse Whimsies,* published by author, 1984; Joyce
E. Blake and Dale Murschell, *Glasshouse Whimsies: An Enhanced
Reference,* published by authors, 1989.

Collectors' Club: The Whimsey Club, 20 William St, Dansville,
NY 14437.

Advisors: Joyce E. Blake and Lon Knickerbocker.

Bellows Bottle, 10½″ l, unusual candy striping, some
  threading missing **225.00**
Darning Egg, white
  Amethyst Nailsea loop dec **125.00**
  Multicolored splotches **80.00**
Mallet Style Hammer, 8″ l, clear, red and blue splotches
  on head, c1920 .... **75.00**
Pipe, 7″ h, standing on three legs, spatter style dec **95.00**
Powder Horn, 12″ l, clear, white Nailsea looping, rasp-
  berry-colored drape-type striping, early Pittsburgh,
  c1830–50 .... **350.00**
Rolling Pin
  Clear
    Pink and white Nailsea looping, c1860, 15½″ l . **285.00**
    White powder lining, red and blue splotches, Eng-
      lish, c1860 .... **195.00**

Stocking Darner, 7½″ l
  Spatter glass, pink, green, blue, and yellow splotches,
    c1920 .... **175.00**
  White, red Nailsea looping **250.00**
Wedding Bell, two-pc handle attached to bell base with
  plaster of Paris
  10½″ h, dark green base, clear handle with intricate
    red and blue int. threading, English, c1850 ..... **285.00**
  11″ h, cranberry base, clear handle with white thread-
    ing **295.00**
Witch Ball
  4″ d, cobalt blue, early Pittsburgh, c1840 .... **110.00**
  4½″ d, white ground, red and blue Nailsea loop dec,
    c1870 .... **450.00**

WHISKEY BOTTLES, EARLY

History: The earliest American whiskey bottles were generic in
shape and were blown by pioneer glass makers in the 18th century. The Biningers (1820–1880s) were the first bottles specifically
designed for whiskey. After the 1860s distillers favored the cylindrical "fifth" design.

The first embossed brand-name bottle was the amber E. G.
Booz Old Cabin Whiskey bottle which was issued in 1860. Many
stories have been told about this classic bottle; unfortunately, most
are not true. Research has proven that "booze" was a corruption
of the words "bouse" and "boosy" from the 16th and 17th centuries. It was only a coincidence that the Philadelphia distributor
also was named "Booz." This bottle has been reproduced extensively.

Prohibition (1920–1933) brought the legal whiskey industry to
a standstill. Whiskey was marked "medicinal purposes only" and
distributed by private distillers in unmarked or paper-labeled bottles.

The size and shape of whiskey bottles are standard. Colors are
limited to amber, amethyst, clear, green, and cobalt blue (rare).
Corks were the common closure in the early period, with the
inside screw top being used between 1880 and 1910.

Bottles made prior to 1880 are the most desirable. When purchasing a bottle with a label, condition of that label is a critical
factor. In the 1950s distillers began to issue collectors' special-
edition bottles to help increase sales.

References: Ralph & Terry Kovel, *The Kovels' Bottles Price List,*
Tenth Edition, Crown Publishers, 1996; John Odell, *Digger
Odell's Official Antique Bottle and Glass Collector Magazine*

Price Guide Series, Vol. 8, published by author (1910 Shawhan Rd, Morrow, OH 45152), 1995 Carlo and Dorothy Sellari, *The Standard Old Bottle Price Guide,* Collector Books, 1989.

Periodicals: *Antique Bottle and Glass Collector,* PO Box 187, East Greenville, PA 18041; *Bottles & Extras,* PO Box 154, Happy Camp, CA 96039.

Museum: The Seagram Museum, Waterloo, Ontario, Canada.

Additional Listing: See *Warman's Americana & Collectibles* for a listing of Collectors' Special Editions Whiskey Bottles.

Bear Creek, amber, cork stopper, dated 1868	35.00
Belle of Anderson, milk glass, tooled mouth	30.00
Casper's Whiskey, Made by Honset, North Carolina People, cobalt blue, 1870–90	225.00
E. G. Booz's Old Cabin, Philadelphia, amber, 1840 ...	65.00
Ginter Co, Importers, deep yellow-green, 1860–90	65.00
Hayner, clear, label, qt, 1916	10.00
Jesse Moore, dark red amber	50.00
Nathans Bros 1863, Philadelphia, amber, emb	125.00
Oxford Rye Whiskey, label, 1880s	25.00
Phoenix Old Bourbon, honey amber, bird and coffin, pt	125.00
Sour Mash 1867, amber, barrel shape	35.00
Topper Rye Whiskey, clear, white lettering	210.00
Turner Brothers, sq, olive green, 1860–90	75.00
Wormser Bros, San Francisco, amber, double ring, bubbles	95.00

Troyka Vodka, Siberian Vodka Co., San Francisco, CA, ⅘ qt, 12″ h, $15.00.

WHITE-PATTERNED IRONSTONE

History: White-patterned ironstone is a heavy earthenware, first patented under the name "Patent Ironstone China" in 1813 by Charles Mason, Staffordshire, England. Other English potters soon began copying this opaque, feldspathic, white china.

All-white ironstone dishes first became available in the American market in the early 1840s. The first patterns had simple Gothic lines similar to the shapes used in transfer wares. Pattern shapes, such as New York, Union, and Atlantic, were designed to appeal to the American housewife. Motifs, such as wheat, corn,

oats, and poppies, were embossed on the pieces as the American prairie influenced design. Eventually, over 200 shapes and patterns, with variations on finials and handles, were made.

White-patterned ironstone is identified by shape names and pattern names. Many potters only identified the shape in their catalogs. Pattern names usually refer to the decorative motif.

References: Dana G. Morykan and Harry L. Rinker, *Warman's Country Antiques & Collectibles,* Third Edition, Wallace-Homestead, 1996; Jean Wetherbee, *White Ironstone,* Antique Trader Books, 1996.

Collectors' Clubs: Mason's Ironstone Collectors' Club, 542 Seskeyon Blvd, Ashland, OR 97520; White Ironstone China Assoc, RD #1, Box 23, Howes Cave, NY 12092.

Bowl, cov, 7⅞″ d, Leaf Fan, Alcock	115.00
Butter Pat, emb scrolled rim, price for 6-pc set	45.00
Cake Plate, 12″ d, Cable and Ring, reticulated handles, Anthony Shaw and Son, England	50.00
Coffeepot, Wheat and Blackberry, Clementson Bros ...	195.00

Coffeepot, Wheat and Clover, melon ribbed sides, 10½″ h, $125.00.

Compote, Pearl Syndenham, ftd, Mason	195.00
Creamer	
Basketweave, rect, marked "Opaque Stone China, Anthony Stone and Son, England"	45.00
Wheat and Clover, Turner & Tomkinson	65.00
Cup and Saucer	
Acorn and Tiny Oak, Parkhurst	45.00
President, handleless, Edwards	50.00
Gravy Boat, 5″ l, Ceres	65.00
Nappy, Prairie Flowers, Livesley Powell	35.00
Pancake Server, octagonal, Boote, 1851	50.00
Pitcher	
Ceres, Elsmore & Forster	150.00
Wheat, ribbed	135.00
Plate	
7″ d, Wheat and Clover, Turner & Tomkinson	25.00
8¾″ d, Corn and Oats, Wedgwood, 1863	25.00
9″ d, Ceres Wheat, Elsmore & Forster	25.00
Platter, 14½″ l, Lily of the Valley, Alfred Meakin	65.00
Relish Dish, Parish shape, Alcock	35.00

Sauce Tureen, matching under tray, Fluted Pearl,
J Wedgwood 120.00
Soup Tureen, cov, ladle, oval, Hyacinth 250.00
Sugar, cov
    Ceres, Elsmore & Forster 85.00
    Fuchsia, Meakin 75.00
Teapot, Laurel Wreath, luster trim 225.00
Toothbrush Holder, cov, Hyacinth, Wedgwood 75.00
Vegetable, cov, Ceres 150.00
Waste Bowl, Morning Glory, Elsmore & Forster 95.00

WILLOW PATTERN CHINA

History: Josiah Spode developed the first "traditional" willow pattern in 1810. The components, all motifs taken from Chinese export china, are a willow tree, "apple" tree, two pagodas, fence, two birds, and three figures crossing a bridge. The legend, in its many versions, is an English invention based on this scenic design.

By 1830 there were over 200 makers of willow pattern china in England. The pattern has remained in continuous production. Some of the English firms that still produce it are Burleigh, Johnson Bros. (Wedgwood Group), Royal Doulton (continuing production of the Booths' pattern), and Wedgwood.

By the end of the 19th century, production of this pattern spread to France, Germany, Holland, Ireland, Sweden, and the United States. Buffalo Pottery made the first willow pattern in the United States beginning in 1902. Many other companies followed, developing willow variants using rubber-stamp simplified patterns as well as overglaze decals. The largest American manufacturers of the traditional willow pattern were Royal China and Homer Laughlin, usually preferred because it is dated. Shenango pieces are the most desirable among restaurant-quality wares.

Japan began producing large quantities of willow pattern china in the early 20th century. Noritake began about 1902. Most Japanese pieces are porous earthenware with a dark blue pattern using the traditional willow design, usually with no inner border. Noritake did put the pattern on china bodies. Unusual forms include salt and pepper shakers, one-quarter pound butter dishes, and canisters. The most desirable Japanese willow is the fine quality NKT Co. ironstone with a copy of the old Booths pattern. Recent Japanese willow is a paler shade of blue on a porcelain body.

The most common dinnerware color is blue. However, pieces can also be found in black (with clear glaze or mustard-colored glaze by Royal Doulton), brown, green, mulberry, pink (red), and polychrome.

The popularity of the willow design has resulted in a large variety of willow-decorated products: candles, fabric, glass, graniteware, linens, needlepoint, plastic, tinware, stationery, watches, and wall coverings. All this material has collectible value.

Marks: Early pieces of Noritake have a Nippon "Royal Sometuke" mark. "Occupied Japan" may add a small percentage to the value of common table wares. Pieces marked "Maruta" or "Moriyama" are especially valued.

References: Robert Copeland, *Spode's Willow Pattern and Other Designs after the Chinese,* Studio Vista, 1980, 1990 reprint; Mary Frank Gaston, *Blue Willow,* Revised Second Edition, Collector Books, 1990, 1994 value update.

Periodicals: *American Willow Report,* PO Box 900, Oakridge, OR 97463; *The Willow Word,* PO Box 13382, Arlington, TX 76094.

Collectors' Clubs: International Willow Collectors, 2903 Blackbird Rd, Petroskey, MI 49770; Willow Society, 39 Medhurst Rd, Toronto Ontario M4B 1B2 Canada.

REPRODUCTION ALERT

The Scio Pottery, Scio, Ohio, currently manufactures a willow pattern set sold in variety stores. The pieces have no marks or backstamps, and the transfer is of poor quality. The plates are flatter in shape than those of other manufacturers.

Note: Although colors other than blue are hard to find, there is less demand; thus, prices may not necessarily be higher priced.

Bowl, 9" d, marked "Royal" 15.00
Butter Dish, cov, marked "Japan" 55.00
Cake Plate, pierced sides 65.00
Children's Dishes
    Dinner Service, four plates, cups and saucers, creamer, cov sugar, cov teapot, platter, cov casserole, gravy boat, marked "Japan" 295.00
    Tea Set, marked "Occupied Japan," price for 18-pc set 375.00
Creamer, 2⅜" h, handle, pitcher style, marked "Shenango" 20.00
Cup and Saucer, marked "Adams" 25.00
Eggcup, 2¼" h, border on base, marked "England" ... 20.00
Gravy Boat and Under Plate, light blue, marked "Copeland" 65.00
Pitcher, 8½" h, marked "Willow England" 140.00
Plate
    8½" d, ivory ground, scalloped edge, light brown daisy border, blue allover willow pattern, gold bands on edge and base of border 65.00
    9" d, pink, marked "Allerton" 10.00

Left: bowl, ext. with border on rim, pattern beneath, int. border on rim only, marked "Allertons/Made in/England," 6⅛" d, 3¼" h, $35.00; right: vegetable bowl, scalloped edge, double border, pattern in center, Allerton crown mark, 8¹/₁₆" d, 2⅛" h, $30.00.

Platter
  14" l, English **175.00**
  20" l, English **200.00**
Sauceboat with Under Plate, 14" l **115.00**
Soup Plate, flanged, marked "Allerton" **25.00**
Teapot, cov, pink, marked "Royal" **45.00**
Toothpick Holder, 1¾" h, border at top, English **45.00**

WOODENWARE

History: Many utilitarian household objects and farm implements were made of wood. Although they were subjected to heavy use, these implements were made of the strongest woods and were well cared for by their owners.

References: Dana G. Morykan and Harry L. Rinker, *Warman's Country Antiques & Collectibles,* Third Edition, Wallace-Homestead, 1996; George C. Neumann, *Early American Antique Country Furnishing,* L-W Book Sales, 1984, 1993 reprint.

Additional Listings: See *Warman's Americana & Collectibles* for more examples.

Note: This category serves as a catchall for wooden objects which do not fit into other categories.

Bowl
  8" d, turned poplar, matching cov, old dark varnish
    finish **250.00**
  13½" d, 3½" h, burl, good figure, dark patina, minor
    rim damage, short tight age crack, drilled hanging
    hole **715.00**
Box, 16½" d, dovetailed, chip to front lid **300.00**
Bucket, cov, 13" d, lid and central section bound with
  interlocking wooden splint, 19th C **60.00**
Butter Churn, 19½" h, stave constructed, old red paint **195.00**
Butter Paddle, 10" l, burl, crook end, old varnish finish **220.00**
Candle Drying Rack, 39" h, eight rotating arms, each
  with rack which holds 32 candle wicks, hardwood,
  old green paint **775.00**
Candle Mold, 21" l, 16" h, pine frame, 30 pewter tubes,
  old worn patina, edge use damage **770.00**
Candlesticks, pr, 23" h, turned, tin sockets, painted black **125.00**

Candle Mold, 24 redware tubes, PA, mid-19th C, $1,900.00. Photo courtesy of Aston Auctioneers.

Canteen, 7" d, stave construction, scratch-carved initials,
  damage to bung hole **165.00**
Cookie Board
  5" w, 17¼" d, carved chestnut, primitive relief carving
    of couple and large cat, slight age crack **220.00**
  6" w, 9¾" h, carved birch, man on horseback with
    flag, reverse with rooster and hen, initialed "F. E.,"
    old varnish finish, age cracks, few worm holes .. **470.00**
Cranberry Scoop, 32" l, curved and bentwood handles,
  orig red paint, branded label "Cranberry Co" **250.00**
Drying Rack, 27 × 42", accordion folded **55.00**
Goblet, turned, dark patina **15.00**
Grain Shovel, 36½" l, painted scene of Niagara Falls on
  bowl, ivy on handle, wear **60.00**
Herb Grinder, 5¾" h mortar with table clamp, pestle,
  hardwood, old varnish finish, worm holes in mortar **325.00**
Jar, cov
  4" h, orig sponged green paint, red trim, German
    inscription, foot damaged **100.00**
  4¼" h, treen, poplar, worn orig red sponged fans,
    yellow ground, age crack **525.00**
  8¼" h, Pease, turned, wire bale handle, old worn
    finish, age crack in base, replacement lid **250.00**
Keg, 6¾" l, worn red paint, scratch-carved initials and
  date "J. G. 1809," minor age cracks **140.00**

Eggcup, Lehneware, hp leafy stem and border, appl rose decals, pink ground, 3½" h, $200.00.

Knife Box, walnut, 8¾" × 12¾", old finish **40.00**
Lemon Squeezer, carved, turned, two pcs **45.00**
Nutmeg Grater, 2½" l, bottle shape, rasp end handle .. **275.00**
Panel, 8 × 27", relief-carved gargoyles, oak, old soft
  finish, some edge damage **150.00**
Pantry Box, 9½" d, wire bail, wooden handle, butter
  carrier **185.00**
Pump, stenciled "Stows Pump, Patd 1875, Manufac-
  tured by ASA Williams & Co, Everett, PA" **525.00**
Shelf Sorter, 14 × 14½" base, 46" h, canted sides, old
  dark varnish stain finish **165.00**
Shelves, 31" h, 25" w, worn olive green repaint, rounded
  tops on sides, three shelves **330.00**
Skimmer, 4½ × 6½", pierced holes, tab handle, hole for
  hanging **275.00**
Smoothing Board, 27½" l, chip carved and stamped,
  heart and circle design **175.00**
Snuff Box, 3¾" d, walnut, inlaid cherry circle, ink inscription "William Adolphus Donninton Smith
  1859" **185.00**

Spice Box, 10½" w, 7" d, 14¼" h, hanging, poplar, old red paint, dovetailed drawer, divided six-part int., lift lid with two-part int., crest, repaired break in lid at hinge rail **550.00**

Spoon, 7" l, carved, smooth knob hook handle, 18th C   **150.00**

Sugar Bucket, 12" h, staved construction, old dark finish   **145.00**

Utensil Rack, 31" l, pine, scalloped crest, chip-carved vertical bands, nine wrought-iron holes **75.00**

Wall Pocket, 26¾" h, 15¼" w, figured walnut, old finish, carved foliage detail **250.00**

Yarn Reel, 53" h, chestnut and pine, dark patina, cross chamfered base, adjustable top reel **65.00**

WORLD'S FAIRS AND EXPOSITIONS

History: The Great Exhibition of 1851 in London marked the beginning of the World's Fair and Exposition movement. The fairs generally featured exhibitions from nations around the world displaying the best of their industrial and scientific achievements.

Many important technological advances have been introduced at world's fairs, including the airplane, telephone, and electric lights. Ice cream cones, hot dogs, and iced tea were first sold by vendors at fairs. Art movements often were closely connected to fairs, with the Paris Exhibition of 1900 generally considered to have assembled the best of the works of the Art Nouveau artists.

References: *Crystal Palace Exhibition Illustrated Catalgoue (London, 1851),* Dover Publications, n.d.; Robert L. Hendershott, *1904 St Louis World's Fair Mementos and Memorabilia,* Kurt R. Krueger Publishing (160 N Washington, Iola, WI 54945), 1994; Frederick and Mary Megson, *American Exposition Postcards,* The Postcard Lovers, 1992.

Collectors' Clubs: 1904 World's Fair Society, 529 Barcia Dr, St Louis, MO 63119; World's Fair Collectors' Society, Inc, PO Box 20806, Sarasota, FL 34276.

Museums: Buffalo & Erie County Historical Society, Buffalo, NY; California State University, Madden Library, Fresno, CA; 1893 Chicago World's Fair Columbian Exposition Museum, Columbus, WI; Museum of Science & Industry, Chicago, IL; Presidio Army Museum, San Francisco, CA; The Queens Museum, Flushing, NY.

Advisor: Herbert Rolfes.

1851, London Crystal Palace
  Book, The Great Exposition, by Tally **100.00**
  Cup, porcelain, white ground, blue picture of Crystal Palace **125.00**
  Pipe, white clay, picture of Crystal Palace on bowl   **175.00**
1853, New York Crystal Palace
  Coin, so-called dollar, 1⅞", obv Liberty seated, rev picture of Crystal Palace **300.00**
  Print, "Burning of the Crystal Palace," Currier & Ives   **300.00**
1876, Philadelphia Centennial
  Book, history of the centennial, 6 × 9", 874 pgs ...   **75.00**
  Shoe, frosted glass, Gillinder **40.00**
  Stevengraph, 1½ × 9¾"
    Lincoln **125.00**
    Washington **125.00**
  Textile, Memorial Hall, eagle on top, star border 18½ × 24½" **75.00**
  Ticket, 2¼ × 4", "Admit One" **10.00**

1889, Paris
  Clock, Eiffel Tower shape, 19" h, cast iron, alarm ..   **400.00**
  Guide Book **40.00**
  Textile, 22 × 22", bird's-eye view of fair **65.00**
1893, Chicago Columbian Exposition
  Barber Bottle, 4½" d, 10½" h, bulbous, gold-imprinted Columbus medal **150.00**
  Cane, pull-out map of World's Columbian Exposition   **350.00**
  Doll Furniture, chairs, sofas, soft lead, price for each piece **35.00**
  Guide Book **35.00**
  Medallion, 1¾" d, ferris wheel, aluminum **35.00**
  Periodical, The Youth's Companion **30.00**
  Pop-Up, 12⅛ × 10¼", Electrical Building, Hall of Mines, Wisconsin State Building **150.00**
  Toothpick Holder, 2½" d, 2¾ h", ruby glass, thumbprint **85.00**

Chicago, Columbian Exposition, 1893, eggs, salt and pepper shakers, orig pewter tops, Mount Washington, left: matte finish, blue letters, $75.00; right: glossy finish, orange letters, blue numbers, $65.00.

1898, Omaha Trans-Mississippi
  Pin, 2" d, Nebraska Day, Oct 19, 1898 ....   **60.00**
  View Book, 5 × 6¾" **25.00**
1901, Buffalo, Pan-American Exposition
  Frying Pan, 4" l, aluminum **25.00**
  Mug, 5" h, beer, stoneware **225.00**
  Poster, 25 × 48", Maid of the Mist **1,200.00**
  Souvenir Book **25.00**
  Vase, 6" h, Indian Congress **175.00**
1904, St. Louis, Louisiana Purchase Exposition
  Book, Universal Exposition, 9½ × 12", 81 pgs **30.00**
  Clock, 10" h, shaped like Festival Hall **1,800.00**
  Handkerchief, 10 × 10", various prints embroidered on one corner **35.00**
  Match Safe, Jefferson and Napoleon, SP **85.00**
  Pitcher, 6" h, ruby glass **200.00**
  Pocket Knife, Cascade Gardens **125.00**
  Toy, egg, 2" h, tin, multicolored picture of ferris wheel   **75.00**
  Tumbler, 5" h, milk glass **30.00**
1915, San Francisco, Panama-Pacific International Exposition
  Book, Art of the Exposition, 6 × 9" **25.00**
  Buttons, two coat, two sleeve, price for four-pc set .   **20.00**
  Medals, 1¾" d, opening day and closing day, ribbons, colorful, price for pr **125.00**

1926, Philadelphia Sesquicentennial
   Book, Sesqui-Centennial, 6½ × 9¼", 500+ pgs ...   **35.00**
   Compact, 2½" d, Liberty Bell in center **50.00**
   Lamp, 8" h, 4" w, glass Liberty Bell shade **60.00**

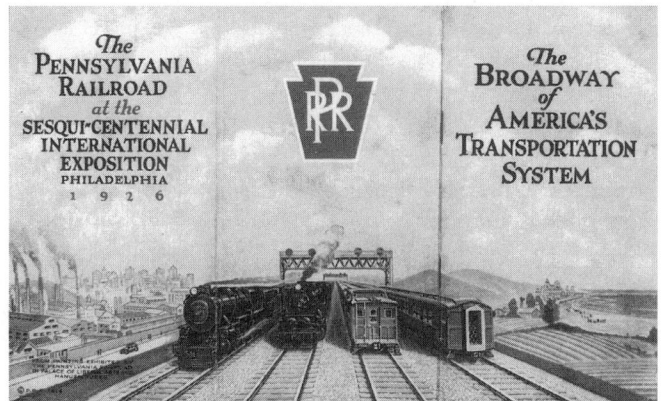

Sesquicentennial, 1926, Philadelphia, booklet, "The Broadway of America's Transportation System," PA Railroad giveaway, four-part foldout photo of general view of exhibit, 20 pgs, 3½ × 6", $15.00.

1933, Chicago, Century of Progress
   Cigarette Case, 3¼ × 6½", Art Deco, red and black   **125.00**
   Coffee Cup, Stewart's Private Blend, marked "Made
      in Bavaria" **75.00**
   Crumb Set, engraved with World's Fair pavilions,
      white metal **25.00**
   Medallion, 2⅝", bronze, Emil Zettler sculpture, MIB   **75.00**
   Photograph, 10 × 60", panoramic view **75.00**
   Plate, 8¼" d, pictures Carillon Tower, marked "Pick-
      ard" **35.00**
   Playing Cards, each card has different view, sealed
      deck **40.00**
   Purse, 3¼ × 4", beaded, green and white, marked
      "Century of Progress 1934" **100.00**
   Ring, comet, marked "World's Fair" **20.00**
   Tip Tray, 4" d, Federal Building picture, yellow rim,
      marked "Century of Progress" **12.00**
   Toy, Greyhound bus, 11½" l, tandem, blue and white,
      Arcade **400.00**
1939, New York, New York World's Fair
   Booklet, Futurama, General Motors pavilion, 7 ×
      8¼" **25.00**
   Coaster, 5 × 9⅞", cardboard, punch-out of trylon
      and perisphere **25.00**
   Magazine, Popular Science, parachute jump on cover   **30.00**
   Map, 11¼" sq, multicolored, Tony Sarg **50.00**
   Peep Show, 5 × 6½", opens to approximately 20" .   **100.00**
   Plate, white painted trylon and perisphere, Syroco-
      wood **30.00**
   Playing Cards, Tiffany, deck **85.00**
   Sheet Music, "Dawn for a New Day," George and
      Ira Gershwin **35.00**
   Snow Dome, trylon and perisphere inside **100.00**
   Spoon, Rogers Brothers, SP **6.00**
   Stick Pin, three-leaf clover shape, multicolored,
      Bakelite **45.00**
1939, San Francisco, Golden Gate International Expo-
   sition

Guide Book **25.00**
Matchbook, 2 × 3", unused **30.00**
1958, Brussels, model, 4 × 4 × 4", Atomium, metal .   **40.00**
1962, Seattle
   Candy Dish, 7" d, Space Needle, silver overlay **50.00**
   Salt and Pepper Shakers, Space Needle shape, plastic   **20.00**
1965–65, New York
   Figure, 2 × 3 × 3", Pieta, plaster **25.00**
   Glass, 6" h, Shaefer beer **25.00**
   Magazine, Life, May 1, 1964, opening day **20.00**

YARD-LONG PRINTS

History: In the early 1900s many yard-long prints could be had for a few cents postage and a given number of wrappers or box tops. Others were premiums for renewing a subscription to a magazine or newspaper. A large number were advertising items created for a store or company and had calendars on the front or back. Many people believe that the only true yard-long print is 36 inches long and titled "A Yard of Kittens," etc. But lately collectors feel that any long and narrow print, horizontal or vertical, can be included in this category. It is a matter of personal opinion.

Values are listed for full-length prints in near-mint condition, nicely framed, and with original glass.

References: C. G. and J. M. Rhoden and W. D. and M. J. Keagy, *Those Wonderful Yard-Long Prints and More* (1989), Book 2 (1992), Book 3 (1995), published by authors (605 No. Main, Georgetown, IL 61846).

Reproduction Alert: Some prints are being reproduced. Know your dealer.

Advisors: Charles G. and Joan M. Rhoden, W. D. and M. J. Keagy.

Note: Numbers in parentheses below indicate the Rhoden and Keagy book number and page on which the item is illustrated, e.g. (3-52) refers to Book 3, page 52.

Calendar
   1905, Swift's Premium, by W H McEntee, four ladies
      of the era with three-months calendar beside them
      (3-112) **350.00**
   1906, Pabst Extract Indian, Hiawatha's Wooing poem
      with picture of Minnehaha on back of print, metal
      hanger at top, cardboard roll at bottom (2-101) .   **450.00**
   1907, Metropolitan Life Insurance Co, showing the
      four stages of life (3-111) **400.00**
   1909, In Grandmother's Garden, Charles C Curran
      (3-81) **350.00**
   1912, National Stockman and Farmer Magazine, The
      Stockman Bride, beautiful bride in full wedding
      attire, magazine adv on back (1-12) **450.00**
   1914, A Walk-Over Girl, C Everett Johnson, lady sit-
      ting in twig chair with Chinese lanterns behind her
      (3-77) **400.00**
   1918, Selz Good Shoes, lovely lady in black dress,
      holding red rose at her side (2-83) **350.00**
   1930, Butterick pattern lady, adv for Butterick trans-
      fers, etc, lady sitting on railing, dressed in pink
      skirt, reddish sleeveless sweater over white long-
      sleeve blouse (3-42) **450.00**

Snowballs and Roses, $200.00.

Print

At the Gate, lovely lady in pink dress, standing beside iron gate (3-82)	350.00
At the North Pole, copyright 1904 by Jos Hoover & Son, Philadelphia (2-29)	350.00
Beatrice, copyright 1911 by J Baumgarth Co, Chicago, adv for Belle of Drexel, Chicago's Best 5 cent cigar (3-41)	450.00
Home, Sweet Home, Paul DeLongpre, dated 1901 (2-36)	250.00
Pigs in Clover, ten pigs, one with foot resting on rim of trough (3-25)	500.00
Yard of Cherries, by Guy Bedford, copyright 1906 by James Lee Co, Chicago (2-69)	200.00
Yard of Violets (3-37)	200.00

Pompeian by Forbes, 1916–1917, signed "Sincerely Mary Pickford," $350.00.

YELLOWWARE

History: Yellowware is a heavy earthenware which varies in color from a rich pumpkin to lighter shades, which are more tan than yellow. The weight and strength varies from piece to piece. Although plates, nappies, and custard cups are found, kitchen bowls and other cooking utensils are most prevalent.

The first American yellowware was produced at Bennington, Vermont. English yellowware has additional ingredients which make its body much harder. Derbyshire and Sharp's were foremost among the English manufacturers.

References: Susan and Al Bagdade, *Warman's American Pottery and Porcelain,* Wallace-Homestead, 1994; William C. Ketchum, Jr., *American Pottery and Porcelain,* Avon Books, 1994; Joan Leibowitz, *Yellow Ware,* Schiffer Publishing, 1985, 1993 value update; Lisa S. McAllister, *Collector's Guide to Yellow Ware,* Collector Books, 1996; Lisa S. McAllister and John L. Michael, *Collecting Yellow Ware,* Collector Books, 1993; Dana G. Morykan and Harry L. Rinker, *Warman's Country Antiques & Collectibles,* Third Edition, Wallace-Homestead, 1996.

Bowl

5¾" d, white band, brown stripes	65.00
8¼" d, 3⅝" h, emb ext., plume-like foliage, green and brown sponging	95.00
Butter Crock, round, emb ribs	95.00
Colander, yellow bands, white int., round	195.00
Foot Warmer, wedge shape, yellow, cork plug	175.00
Mixing Bowl, 11⅝" d, 4¾" h, pouring spout, emb dec	95.00

Mixing Bowls, nesting set of six, continuous molded design, girl watering flowers outside window, price for set $350.00.

Mug, brown and white stripes	195.00

Pitcher

8" h, blue stripes	175.00
9" h, emb hunt scene, hanging game and "Miss Miria B Handy, Marion, Mass," brown sponging, blue, green, yellow, and ochre highlights, white slip int. with frog	250.00
Rolling Pin, wooden handles	175.00
Vase, 9" h, baluster, light sponge dec, emb ribs	40.00
Wash Bowl, 12" d, plain, 1865	95.00
Washboard, blue mottled glaze, pine frame, c1880	475.00

ZANESVILLE POTTERY   LA MORO

History: Zanesville Art Pottery, one of several potteries located in Zanesville, Ohio, began production in 1900. At first, a line of utilitarian products was made; art pottery was introduced shortly thereafter. The major line was La Moro, which was hand painted and decorated under glaze. The firm was bought by S. A. Weller in 1920 and became known as Weller Plant No. 3.

Marks: The impressed block-print mark "La Moro" appears on the high-glazed and matte-glazed decorated ware.

References: Louise and Evan Purviance and Norris F. Schneider, *Zanesville Art Pottery in Color*, Mid-America Book Company, 1968; Evan and Louise Purviance, *Zanesville Art Tile in Color*, Wallace-Homestead, 1972, out-of-print.

Bowl, 6½″ d, mottled blue, fluted edge 50.00
Flower Frog
    5″ w, 2½″ h, frog shape, mottled light blue and tan matte glaze, base flakes 30.00
    6″ w, mushroom shape, blue matte glaze 75.00
Jardiniere, 9″ h, brown and gold glaze 165.00
Paperweight, A E Tiling Co, Ltd, 1890, calendar on back 40.00
Tile, 24″ sq, sixteen tiles, elk, resembles needlepoint, "Mosaic" in oval and round circle mark 125.00
Vase
    9″ h, classic form
        Green and black drip, high glaze 90.00
        Yellow, green, and black, dark blue ground 80.00
    21″ h, 15″ d, floor type, lion and ring dec, mottled light green over pink, matte glaze, imp mark, large chips and repair to base 170.00

Figure, irid green-gold, marked "Made in Hungary, Zsolnay" and castle mark, 6¼″ h, $125.00.

ZSOLNAY POTTERY

History: Vilmos Zsolnay (1828–1900) assumed control of his brother's factory in Pécs, Hungary, in the mid-19th century. In 1899 Miklos, Vilmos's son, became manager. The firm still produces ceramic ware.

The early wares are highly ornamental, glazed, and have a cream-colored ground. Eosin glaze, a deep rich play of colors reminiscent of Tiffany's iridescent wares, received a gold medal at the 1900 Paris exhibition. Zsolnay Art Nouveau pieces show great creativity.

Marks: Originally, no trademark was used; but in 1878 the company began to use a blue mark depicting the five towers of the cathedral at Pécs. The initials "TJM" represent the names of Miklos's three children.

Note: Zsolnay's recent series of iridescent glazed figurines, which initially were inexpensive, now are being sought by collectors and are steadily increasing in value.

Bowl, 7½″ h, 5″ h, fully reticulated, flower and leaf dec, steel blue, rust, yellow, and pink, four ftd 260.00
Cache Pot
    4½″ h, 5″ d, shape no. 5897, metallic eosin glaze, high-style Secession design, round raised trademark, minor glaze flakes, c1900 .... 950.00
    6¾″ h, multicolored courting couple in landscape scene, incised "ZW Pecs," hp blue steeple mark, c1880, Armin Klein artist 1,650.00

Ewer, 10″ h, reticulated, Persian shape, crescent finial, minor chips to lid 190.00
Figure
    Deer, irid green-blue 65.00
    Nude, irid 95.00
    Polar Bear, two, irid green 345.00
    Turtle, irid green-blue 70.00
Jar, cov, 7″ h, blue and cream snowflake design, coral ground, painted millennium mark, c1894 .... 1,650.00
Pitcher
    5½″ h, metallic cream dec, purple-blue metallic ground, millennium mark, c1865 .... 1,250.00
    18″ h, stylized crowing cock, green highly metallic eosin glaze, c1905, round raised mark, minor restoration to beak 4,000.00
    Woman dec, irid green-blue 135.00
Vase
    7¾″ h, Egyptian style, gilded white metal, mottled purple, gold, blue and green Labrador glaze, mount sgd Osiris, c1905 .... 2,250.00
    8″ h, shape no. 5743, green eosin glaze, midnight blue glaze, round raised trademark, c1898, minor wear and restoration 2,750.00
    8″ l, earthenware, elongated melon shape, pierced collar, scrolling flowers dec 110.00
    8¼″ h, 7″ w, reticulated ext. resembling Arabic scrollwork 275.00
    8½″ h, shape no. 6011, landscape dec with trees, highly lustrous eosin leaves, high-style dec, Nabis school of design, c1906 .... 6,500.00
    9¼″ h, double-gourd shape, highly metallic luster surface, blue, green, and silver Labrador glaze, millennium mark, c1896 .... 1,350.00
    10½″ h, shape no. 3939, red and putty dec, white glaze, Iznik design 2,750.00
    11¾″ h, shape no. 7804, metallic gold and blue painted dec, deep burgundy ground, flower and leaf dec, high-style Secession design elements, round raised steeple mark, lip repair 1,750.00
    13″ h, completely reticulated, double walled 1,500.00
Wine Flask, 16½″ h, metallic blue eosin glaze, stylized Secession flowers raised and attached with plastic, orig stopper, designed by Lajos Mach, round raised steeple mark, minor edge flakes 7,500.00

INDEX

See *Warman's Americana & Collectibles, 7th Edition* (1995)
for expanded listings of categories preceded by †.